# Tolley's Corporate Governance Handbook

## Second Edition

Andrew Chambers
Management Audit Ltd

**Members of the LexisNexis Group worldwide**

| | |
|---|---|
| United Kingdom | LexisNexis Butterworths Tolley, a Division of Reed Elsevier (UK) Ltd, 2 Addiscombe Road, CROYDON CR9 5AF |
| Argentina | LexisNexis Argentina, BUENOS AIRES |
| Australia | LexisNexis Butterworths, CHATSWOOD, New South Wales |
| Austria | LexisNexis Verlag ARD Orac GmbH & Co KG, VIENNA |
| Canada | LexisNexis Butterworths Canada Ltd, MARKHAM, Ontario |
| Chile | LexisNexis Chile Ltda, SANTIAGO DE CHILE |
| Czech Republic | Nakladatelství Orac sro, PRAGUE |
| France | Editions du Juris-Classeur SA, PARIS |
| Germany | LexisNexis Deutschland GmbH, FRANKFURT, MUNSTER |
| Hong Kong | LexisNexis Butterworths, HONG KONG |
| Hungary | Hvg-Orac, BUDAPEST |
| India - | LexisNexis Butterworths, NEW DELHI |
| Ireland | LexisNexis, DUBLIN |
| Italy | Giuffré Editore, MILAN |
| Malaysia | Malayan Law Journal Sdn Bhd, KUALA LUMPUR |
| New Zealand | LexisNexis Butterworths, WELLINGTON |
| Poland | Wydawnictwo Prawnicze LexisNexis, WARSAW |
| Singapore | LexisNexis Butterworths, SINGAPORE |
| South Africa | LexisNexis Butterworths, DURBAN |
| Switzerland | Stämpfli Verlag AG, BERNE |
| USA | LexisNexis, DAYTON, Ohio |

A CIP Catalogue record for this book is available from the British Library.

ISBN 0 7545 2411 6

Typeset by Columns Design Ltd, Reading, England
Printed and bound in Great Britain by Clays Ltd, St Ives plc

**Visit LexisNexis UK at www.lexisnexis.co.uk**

# Preface

As many readers are likely to need a convenient way to consult the new 'Combined Code on Corporate Governance – July 2003' we have made it Part 1 of this handbook. When the Financial Reporting Council published this new Combined Code they included within the publication not only the revised Code itself but also the Turnbull and Smith Reports and much the Higgs Report as well. This gives us the opportunity to show in one place (Part 1 of this handbook) all of the current, relevant UK corporate governance pronouncements. We continue to show in this 2004 edition the superseded Cadbury (1992) and Greenbury (1995) codes as well as the superseded first version of the Combined Code (1998), being aware that some still have reason to refer to these earlier counsels.

The new 'Combined Code on Corporate Governance – July 2003' has transferred the original Combined Code provision D.2.2 from the 'Internal control' section of the 1998 Code to the 'Audit Committee and Auditors' part of the new Code – as C.3.5. Furthermore, the 1998 Combined Code principle D.2 and the associated provision D.2.1 (on directors' responsibilities for internal control) are also renumbered in the new Code – as C.2 and C.2.1 respectively. However, the new publication 'Combined Code on Corporate Governance – July 2003', while renumbering these elements of the Code, has retained the original numbering in their reproduction of the Turnbull Report. So, except for our reproduction of the Turnbull Report in Part 1 of this handbook, we have throughout the handbook renumbered the principles and provisions to correspond to the numbering now accorded to them in the new, revised Combined Code.

I am particularly grateful to Cliff Weight for strengthening this handbook by providing the authoritative content on remuneration packages to supersede much of what we carried in the first edition, and to deal with it in appropriately greater depth. Cliff is a Director of Independent Remuneration Solutions, who provide advice on executive directors' remuneration packages, annual and long term incentives and non-executive directors' fees. He can be contacted at IRS at 9 Savoy Street, London WC2R 0BA Phone 020 7836 5831 or cliffweight@msn.com.

The general approach we have taken is to regard the board as being at the node of corporate governance, in that corporate governance is to do both with the accountability of the board to stakeholders and their exercise of *external* control, and also with the oversight by the board of the *internal* arrangements within the enterprise, including the formulation of policies and monitoring their implementation. In addition to interpreting corporate governance in this holistic way, we have attempted to develop a handbook which is appropriate for those who focus on the governance of companies, of entities within the public sector and of 'not-for-profit' entities.

Much of the practical content of this handbook has been suggested by our experiences of working on corporate governance projects for a wide variety of clients over the past eleven years, and from involvement on boards of listed and unlisted companies and of public sector entities.

While it is invidious to single out anyone, I have to thank my friend Trevor Smith for somehow finding the time to write the Foreword.

As a source of reference I am mindful more of its omissions than of any inaccuracies – though there are likely to be some of these too. Tolley's intention is that this handbook in future is to be updated annually as a new edition.

It will not take long for those who use this handbook to realise how dependent I have been on the contributions of others. Certainly, there is a vast amount of talent working currently on these issues. I am deeply grateful for the contributions of individual specialists and also, of course, for the opportunity to include the authoritative pronouncements which are an essential part of a work of this kind. Institutional investors, and those who work on their behalf, have been particularly generous in their assistance. If I have failed to seek permission to use any quoted material, I offer my sincere apologies – and will be pleased to rectify the position in future editions of this handbook.

For me it was an exciting experience to develop the first edition of the Tolley's Corporate Governance Handbook and then to work on the extensive revisions required for this second edition. I am grateful to everyone at Tolley for putting a fascinating opportunity my way, and for their impressive work on the production side of this volume. Katie Twells at Management Audit has been of sterling assistance too – not least by coping with my preoccupation with this project.

I would like to hear from those who use this handbook, with comments and suggestions.

Andrew Chambers
November 2003

Management Audit Limited
6 Market Street
Sleaford
Lincolnshire
NG34 7SF

E-mail: achambers@management-audit.com
Website: http://www.management-audit.com
Telephone: +44 (0) 1529 413344
Fax: +44 (0) 1529 413355

## About the author

Andrew Chambers has eleven years' listed company board experience and four years on the board of an NHS acute hospital trust, belonging to and chairing both audit and remuneration committees. Andrew was Dean of City University Business School, London. He is director of Management Audit, who advise on corporate governance (www.management-audit.com).

# Foreword

To say that this publication is timely would be a huge understatement in view of the series of major corporate scandals that continue to hit the headlines. In recent decades governments have endeavoured to tackle the problems of commercial malfeasance but to little avail. The greater the efforts by governments, the greater the crises seem to become: indeed, as the case of Enron (the largest bankruptcy to date) vividly illustrates, the situation is in danger of spiralling out of control. There are likely to be two main responses.

The first is predictable enough. Governments will seek to tighten still further the regulatory frameworks within which business should be conducted. The public will demand more positive and stronger action and governments will feel obliged to respond. That this will happen there can be little doubt. However, in the light of the failure of previous attempts to reduce or contain corrupt practices, the question to be posed is whether more draconian legislation will be any more successful in stemming the epidemic? (Perhaps it should be accepted that contemporary capitalism has become completely detached from whatever ethics, Protestant or otherwise, to which it may once have had some sort of connection.) This, however, would be a philosophy of despair.

Secondly, valiant attempts will be made to refurbish the concept of self-regulation by professional associations, trade associations and the like. As one crisis of corporate misbehaviour has been overtaken by another of yet more serious proportions, so self-regulation increasingly risks becoming forfeit. Time has almost run out on the seemingly endless re-writing of voluntary codes of practice as a credible response to an ever-worsening situation, but, however difficult the task of restoring faith in self-policing, the attempt must be made. One of the advantages claimed for the earlier separation of ownership from control in large-scale enterprise was that the red in tooth and claw avarice of the old-style owner-manager, intent on profit maximisation at almost any cost, had given way to a new-style manager whose professional integrity would give the modern enterprise a public interest perspective. The 'managerial revolution', as this transformation was termed, would ensure that other, more social and civic criteria would be added to the pursuit of profit, and thus Original Sin, at least in trade and industry, would be tamed.

The 'managerial revolution' more or less coincided, in Britain at least, with the development of the Beveridgian welfare state and its concomitant the Keynesian economy. All three came together and constituted the conventional wisdom of the age for the middle years of the twentieth-century. Somewhat ruthlessly, it was succeeded by a very different prevailing paradigm that has largely influenced the policies of the governments of James Callaghan, Margaret Thatcher, John Major and Tony Blair. It is an admixture of monetarist economics and a related conviction that privatisation should replace the nationalisation of virtually all public utilities and even many public services. In many ways it embodied a return to the nineteenth-century with its emphasis on robust entrepreneurialism, unbridled capitalism, individual responsibility and charitable works. The aim was to stimulate economic growth and prosperity, even if it meant a growing disparity of income levels between the 'haves' and the 'have nots'.

Another unintended, though possibly predictable, consequence was that this renewed stress on entrepreneurialism would give rise, as it increasingly has, to a buccaneering culture in some boardrooms. Having put a premium on results, or 'outcomes' as they were termed, it was inevitable that corners would be cut, protocols bent, and blind eyes turned to sharp practices. Accountants and too many non-executive directors colluded in sustaining this unhealthy state of affairs.

A reaction is already underway – and not before time. It is clear there will be much more rigorous legislation; this will likely involve strict separation between auditing and consultancy for so-called 'chinese walls' have proved to be flimsier in commerce than they are in reality. For their part, both the professions and boardrooms will be making serious efforts to ensure commercial probity and good corporate governance. This book provides an essential work of reference for those engaged in that vital task.

Trevor Smith

# Contents

*Contents*

*Contents*

Contents

*Contents*

# The 2003 Combined Code

## The Combined Code on Corporate Governance  A1.1

**Preamble**

1.  This Code supersedes and replaces the Combined Code issued by the Hampel Committee on Corporate Governance in June 1998. It derives from a review of the role and effectiveness of non-executive directors by Derek Higgs[1] and a review of audit committees[2] by a group led by Sir Robert Smith.

2.  The Financial Services Authority has said that it will replace the 1998 Code that is annexed to the Listing Rules with the revised Code and will seek to make consequential Rule changes. There will be consultation on the necessary Rule changes but not further consultation on the Code provisions themselves.

3.  It is intended that the new Code will apply for reporting years beginning on or after 1 November 2003.

4.  The Code contains main and supporting principles and provisions. The existing Listing Rules require listed companies to make a disclosure statement in two parts in relation to the Code. In the first part of the statement, the company has to report on how it applies the principles in the Code. In future this will need to cover both main and supporting principles. The form and content of this part of the statement are not prescribed, the intention being that companies should have a free hand to explain their governance policies in the light of the principles, including any special circumstances applying to them which have led to a particular approach. In the second part of the statement the company has either to confirm that it complies with the Code's provisions or – where it does not – to provide an explanation. This 'comply or explain' approach has been in operation for over ten years and the flexibility it offers has been widely welcomed both by company boards and by investors. It is for shareholders and others to evaluate the company's statement.

5.  While it is expected that listed companies will comply with the Code's provisions most of the time, it is recognised that departure from the provisions of the Code may be justified in particular circumstances. Every company must review each provision carefully and give a considered explanation if it departs from the Code provisions.

6.  Smaller listed companies, in particular those new to listing, may judge that some of the provisions are disproportionate or less relevant in their case. Some of the provisions do not apply to companies below FTSE 350.

Such companies may nonetheless consider that it would be appropriate to adopt the approach in the Code and they are encouraged to consider this. Investment companies typically have a different board structure, which may affect the relevance of particular provisions.

7.  Whilst recognising that directors are appointed by shareholders who are the owners of companies, it is important that those concerned with the evaluation of governance should do so with common sense in order to promote partnership and trust, based on mutual understanding. They should pay due regard to companies' individual circumstances and bear in mind in particular the size and complexity of the company and the nature of the risks and challenges it faces. Whilst shareholders have every right to challenge companies' explanations if they are unconvincing, they should not be evaluated in a mechanistic way and departures from the Code should not be automatically treated as breaches. Institutional shareholders and their agents should be careful to respond to the statements from companies in a manner that supports the 'comply or explain' principle. As the principles in Section 2 make clear, institutional shareholders should carefully consider explanations given for departure from the Code and make reasoned judgements in each case. They should put their views to the company and be prepared to enter a dialogue if they do not accept the company's position. Institutional shareholders should be prepared to put such views in writing where appropriate.

8.  Nothing in this Code should be taken to override the general requirements of law to treat shareholders equally in access to information.

9.  This publication includes guidance on how to comply with particular parts of the Code: first, "Internal Control: Guidance for Directors on the Combined Code",[3] produced by the Turnbull Committee, which relates to Code provisions on internal control (C.2 and part of C.3 in the Code); and, second, "Audit Committees: Combined Code Guidance", produced by the Smith Group, which relates to the provisions on audit committees and auditors (C.3 of the Code). In both cases, the guidance suggests ways of applying the relevant Code principles and of complying with the relevant Code provisions.

10. In addition, this volume also includes suggestions for good practice from the Higgs report.

11. The revised Code does not include material in the previous Code on the disclosure of directors' remuneration. This is because "The Directors' Remuneration Report Regulations 2002"[4] are now in force and supersede the earlier Code provisions. These require the directors of a company to prepare a remuneration report. It is important that this report is clear, transparent and understandable to shareholders.

**Code of best practice**

| | |
|---|---|
| **SECTION 1** | **COMPANIES** |
| **A** | **DIRECTORS** |
| **A.1** | **The Board** |
| **Main Principle** | **Every company should be headed by an effective board, which is collectively responsible for the success of the company.** |
| **Supporting Principles** | The board's role is to provide entrepreneurial leadership of the company within a framework of prudent and effective controls which enables risk to be assessed and managed. The board should set the company's strategic aims, ensure that the necessary financial and human resources are in place for the company to meet its objectives and review management performance. The board should set the company's values and standards and ensure that its obligations to its shareholders and others are understood and met. |

All directors must take decisions objectively in the interests of the company.

As part of their role as members of a unitary board, non-executive directors should constructively challenge and help develop proposals on strategy. Non-executive directors should scrutinise the performance of management in meeting agreed goals and objectives and monitor the reporting of performance. They should satisfy themselves on the integrity of financial information and that financial controls and systems of risk management are robust and defensible. They are responsible for determining appropriate levels of remuneration of executive directors and have a prime role in appointing, and where necessary removing, executive directors, and in succession planning.

**Code Provisions**

A.1.1    The board should meet sufficiently regularly to discharge its duties effectively. There should be a formal schedule of matters specifically reserved for its decision. The annual report should include a statement of how the board operates, including a high level statement of which types of decisions are to be taken by the board and which are to be delegated to management.

A.1.2    The annual report should identify the chairman, the deputy chairman (where there is one), the chief executive, the senior independent director and the chairmen and members of the nomination, audit and remuneration committees. It should also set out the number of meetings of the board and those committees and individual attendance by directors.

A.1.3   The chairman should hold meetings with the non-executive directors without the executives present. Led by the senior independent director, the non-executive directors should meet without the chairman present at least annually to appraise the chairman's performance (as described in A.6.1) and on such other occasions as are deemed appropriate.

A.1.4   Where directors have concerns which cannot be resolved about the running of the company or a proposed action, they should ensure that their concerns are recorded in the board minutes. On resignation, a non-executive director should provide a written statement to the chairman, for circulation to the board, if they have any such concerns.

A.1.5   The company should arrange appropriate insurance cover in respect of legal action against its directors.

**A.2**   **Chairman and chief executive**

**Main Principle**   **There should be a clear division of responsibilities at the head of the company between the running of the board and the executive responsibility for the running of the company's business. No one individual should have unfettered powers of decision.**

**Supporting Principle**   The chairman is responsible for leadership of the board, ensuring its effectiveness on all aspects of its role and setting its agenda. The chairman is also responsible for ensuring that the directors receive accurate, timely and clear information. The chairman should ensure effective communication with shareholders. The chairman should also facilitate the effective contribution of non-executive directors in particular and ensure constructive relations between executive and non-executive directors.

**Code Provisions**

A.2.1   The roles of chairman and chief executive should not be exercised by the same individual. The division of responsibilities between the chairman and chief executive should be clearly established, set out in writing and agreed by the board.

A.2.2[5]   The chairman should on appointment meet the independence criteria set out in A.3.1 below. A chief executive should not go on to be chairman of the same company. If exceptionally a board decides that a chief executive should become chairman, the board should consult major shareholders in advance and should set out its reasons to shareholders at the time of the appointment and in the next annual report.

**A.3**

**Board balance and independence**

**Main Principle**

**The board should include a balance of executive and non-executive directors (and in particular independent non-executive directors) such that no individual or small group of individuals can dominate the board's decision taking.**

**Supporting Principles**

The board should not be so large as to be unwieldy. The board should be of sufficient size that the balance of skills and experience is appropriate for the requirements of the business and that changes to the board's composition can be managed without undue disruption.

To ensure that power and information are not concentrated in one or two individuals, there should be a strong presence on the board of both executive and non-executive directors.

The value of ensuring that committee membership is refreshed and that undue reliance is not placed on particular individuals should be taken into account in deciding chairmanship and membership of committees.

No one other than the committee chairman and members is entitled to be present at a meeting of the nomination, audit or remuneration committee, but others may attend at the invitation of the committee.

**Code provisions**

A.3.1

The board should identify in the annual report each non-executive director it considers to be independent[6]. The board should determine whether the director is independent in character and judgement and whether there are relationships or circumstances which are likely to affect, or could appear to affect, the director's judgement. The board should state its reasons if it determines that a director is independent notwithstanding the existence of relationships or circumstances which may appear relevant to its determination, including if the director:

● has been an employee of the company or group within the last five years;

● has, or has had within the last three years, a material business relationship with the company either directly, or as a partner, shareholder, director or

5

senior employee of a body that has such a relationship with the company;

- has received or receives additional remuneration from the company apart from a director's fee, participates in the company's share option or a performance-related pay scheme, or is a member of the company's pension scheme;
- has close family ties with any of the company's advisers, directors or senior employees;
- holds cross-directorships or has significant links with other directors through involvement in other companies or bodies;
- represents a significant shareholder; or
- has served on the board for more than nine years from the date of their first election.

A.3.2

Except for smaller companies[7], at least half the board, excluding the chairman, should comprise non-executive directors determined by the board to be independent. A smaller company should have at least two independent non-executive directors.

A.3.3

The board should appoint one of the independent non-executive directors to be the senior independent director. The senior independent director should be available to shareholders if they have concerns which contact through the normal channels of chairman, chief executive or finance director has failed to resolve or for which such contact is inappropriate.

**A.4**

**Appointments to the board**

**Main Principle**

**There should be a formal, rigorous and transparent procedure for the appointment of new directors to the board.**

**Supporting Principles**

Appointments to the board should be made on merit and against objective criteria. Care should be taken to ensure that appointees have enough time available to devote to the job. This is particularly important in the case of chairmanships.

The board should satisfy itself that plans are in place for orderly succession for appointments to the board and to senior management, so as to maintain an appropriate balance of skills and experience within the company and on the board.

**Code Provisions**

A.4.1

There should be a nomination committee which should lead the process for board appointments and make recommendations to the board. A majority of members of the nomination committee should be independent non-executive directors. The chairman or an independent non-executive director should chair the committee, but the chairman should not chair the nomination committee when it is dealing with the appointment of a successor to the chairmanship. The nomination committee should make available[8] its terms of reference, explaining its role and the authority delegated to it by the board.

A.4.2      The nomination committee should evaluate the balance of skills, knowledge and experience on the board and, in the light of this evaluation, prepare a description of the role and capabilities required for a particular appointment.

A.4.3      For the appointment of a chairman, the nomination committee should prepare a job specification, including an assessment of the time commitment expected, recognising the need for availability in the event of crises. A chairman's other significant commitments should be disclosed to the board before appointment and included in the annual report. Changes to such commitments should be reported to the board as they arise, and included in the next annual report. No individual should be appointed to a second chairmanship of a FTSE 100 company[9]

A.4.4      The terms and conditions of appointment of non-executive directors should be made available for inspection[10]. The letter of appointment should set out the expected time commitment. Non-executive directors should undertake that they will have sufficient time to meet what is expected of them. Their other significant commitments should be disclosed to the board before appointment, with a broad indication of the time involved and the board should be informed of subsequent changes.

A.4.5      The board should not agree to a full time executive director taking on more than one non-executive directorship in a FTSE 100 company nor the chairmanship of such a company.

A.4.6      A separate section of the annual report should describe the work of the nomination committee, including the process it has used in relation to board appointments. An explanation should be given if neither an external search consultancy nor open advertising has been used in the appointment of a chairman or a non-executive director.

**A.5**      **Information and professional development**

**Main Principle**      **The board should be supplied in a timely manner with information in a form and of a quality appropriate to**

**enable it to discharge its duties. All directors should receive induction on joining the board and should regularly update and refresh their skills and knowledge.**

**Supporting Principles**

The chairman is responsible for ensuring that the directors receive accurate, timely and clear information. Management has an obligation to provide such information but directors should seek clarification or amplification where necessary.

The chairman should ensure that the directors continually update their skills and the knowledge and familiarity with the company required to fulfil their role both on the board and on board committees. The company should provide the necessary resources for developing and updating its directors' knowledge and capabilities.

Under the direction of the chairman, the company secretary's responsibilities include ensuring good information flows within the board and its committees and between senior management and non-executive directors, as well as facilitating induction and assisting with professional development as required.

The company secretary should be responsible for advising the board through the chairman on all governance matters.

**Code Provisions**

A.5.1

The chairman should ensure that new directors receive a full, formal and tailored induction on joining the board. As part of this, the company should offer to major shareholders the opportunity to meet a new non-executive director.

A.5.2

The board should ensure that directors, especially non-executive directors, have access to independent professional advice at the company's expense where they judge it necessary to discharge their responsibilities as directors. Committees should be provided with sufficient resources to undertake their duties.

A.5.3

All directors should have access to the advice and services of the company secretary, who is responsible to the board for ensuring that board procedures are complied with. Both the appointment and removal of the company secretary should be a matter for the board as a whole.

**A.6**          Performance evaluation

**Main Principle**    **The board should undertake a formal and rigorous annual evaluation of its own performance and that of its committees and individual directors.**

**Supporting Principles**    Individual evaluation should aim to show whether each director continues to contribute effectively and to demonstrate commitment to the role (including commitment of time for board and committee meetings and any other duties). The chairman should act on the results of the performance evaluation by recognising the strengths and addressing the weaknesses of the board and, where appropriate, proposing new members be appointed to the board or seeking the resignation of directors.

**Code Provision**

A.6.1          The board should state in the annual report how performance evaluation of the board, its committees and its individual directors has been conducted. The non-executive directors, led by the senior independent director, should be responsible for performance evaluation of the chairman, taking into account the views of executive directors.

**A.7**          Re-election

**Main Principle**    **All directors should be submitted for re-election at regular intervals, subject to continued satisfactory performance. The board should ensure planned and progressive refreshing of the board.**

**Code Provisions**

A.7.1          All directors should be subject to election by shareholders at the first annual general meeting after their appointment, and to re-election thereafter at intervals of no more than three years. The names of directors submitted for election or re-election should be accompanied by sufficient biographical details and any other relevant information to enable shareholders to take an informed decision on their election.

A.7.2          Non-executive directors should be appointed for specified terms subject to re-election and to Companies Acts provisions relating to the removal of a director. The board should set out to shareholders in the papers accompanying a resolution to elect a non-executive director why they believe an individual should be elected. The chairman should confirm to shareholders when proposing re-election that, following formal performance evaluation, the individual's performance continues to be effective and to demonstrate commitment to the role. Any term beyond six years (e.g. two three-year terms) for a non-executive director should be subject to particularly rigorous review, and should take into account the need for progressive refreshing of the board. Non-executive directors may serve longer than nine years (e.g. three three-year terms), subject to annual re-election. Serving more than nine years could be relevant to the determination of a non-executive director's independence (as set out in provision A.3.1).

| | |
|---|---|
| **B** | **REMUNERATION** |
| **B.1** | **The Level and Make-up of Remuneration[11]** |

**Main Principles**   **Levels of remuneration should be sufficient to attract, retain and motivate directors of the quality required to run the company successfully, but a company should avoid paying more than is necessary for this purpose. A significant proportion of executive directors' remuneration should be structured so as to link rewards to corporate and individual performance.**

**Supporting Principle**   The remuneration committee should judge where to position their company relative to other companies. But they should use such comparisons with caution, in view of the risk of an upward ratchet of remuneration levels with no corresponding improvement in performance. They should also be sensitive to pay and employment conditions elsewhere in the group, especially when determining annual salary increases.

**Code Provisions**

**Remuneration policy**

B.1.1   The performance-related elements of remuneration should form a significant proportion of the total remuneration package of executive directors and should be designed to align their interests with those of shareholders and to give these directors keen incentives to perform at the highest levels. In designing schemes of performance-related remuneration, the remuneration committee should follow the provisions in Schedule A to this Code.

B.1.2   Executive share options should not be offered at a discount save as permitted by the relevant provisions of the Listing Rules.

B.1.3 Levels of remuneration for non-executive directors should reflect the time commitment and responsibilities of the role. Remuneration for non-executive directors should not include share options. If, exceptionally, options are granted, shareholder approval should be sought in advance and any shares acquired by exercise of the options should be held until at least one year after the non-executive director leaves the board. Holding of share options could be relevant to the determination of a non-executive director's independence (as set out in provision A.3.1).

B.1.4 Where a company releases an executive director to serve as a non-executive director elsewhere, the remuneration report[12] should include a statement as to whether or not the director will retain such earnings and, if so, what the remuneration is.

**Service Contracts and Compensation**

B.1.5 The remuneration committee should carefully consider what compensation commitments (including pension contributions and all other elements) their directors' terms of appointment would entail in the event of early termination. The aim should be to avoid rewarding poor performance. They should take a robust line on reducing compensation to reflect departing directors' obligations to mitigate loss.

B.1.6 Notice or contract periods should be set at one year or less. If it is necessary to offer longer notice or contract periods to new directors recruited from outside, such periods should reduce to one year or less after the initial period.

**B.2** **Procedure**

**Main Principle** **There should be a formal and transparent procedure for developing policy on executive remuneration and for fixing the remuneration packages of individual directors. No director should be involved in deciding his or her own remuneration.**

**Supporting Principles** The remuneration committee should consult the chairman and/or chief executive about their proposals relating to the remuneration of other executive directors. The remuneration committee should also be responsible for appointing any consultants in respect of executive director remuneration. Where executive directors or senior management are involved in advising or supporting the remuneration committee, care should be taken to recognise and avoid conflicts of interest.

The chairman of the board should ensure that the company maintains contact as required with its principal shareholders about remuneration in the same way as for other matters.

**Code Provisions**

B.2.1

The board should establish a remuneration committee of at least three, or in the case of smaller companies[13] two, members, who should all be independent non-executive directors. The remuneration committee should make available[14] its terms of reference, explaining its role and the authority delegated to it by the board. Where remuneration consultants are appointed, a statement should be made available[15] of whether they have any other connection with the company.

B.2.2

The remuneration committee should have delegated responsibility for setting remuneration for all executive directors and the chairman, including pension rights and any compensation payments. The committee should also recommend and monitor the level and structure of remuneration for senior management. The definition of 'senior management' for this purpose should be determined by the board but should normally include the first layer of management below board level.

B.2.3

The board itself or, where required by the Articles of Association, the shareholders should determine the remuneration of the non-executive directors within the limits set in the Articles of Association. Where permitted by the Articles, the board may however delegate this responsibility to a committee, which might include the chief executive.

B.2.4

Shareholders should be invited specifically to approve all new long-term incentive schemes (as defined in the Listing Rules) and significant changes to existing schemes, save in the circumstances permitted by the Listing Rules.

C

**ACCOUNTABILITY AND AUDIT**

C.1

**Financial Reporting**

**Main Principle**

**The board should present a balanced and understandable assessment of the company's position and prospects.**

**Supporting Principles**

The board's responsibility to present a balanced and understandable assessment extends to interim and other price-sensitive public reports and reports to regulators as well as to information required to be presented by statutory requirements.

**Code Provisions**

C.1.1      The directors should explain in the annual report their responsibility for preparing the accounts and there should be a statement by the auditors about their reporting responsibilities.

C.1.2      The directors should report that the business is a going concern, with supporting assumptions or qualifications as necessary.

**C.2**      **Internal Control[16]**

**Main Principle**      **The board should maintain a sound system of internal control to safeguard shareholders' investment and the company's assets.**

**Code Provision**

C.2.1      The board should, at least annually, conduct a review of the effectiveness of the group's system of internal controls and should report to shareholders that they have done so. The review should cover all material controls, including financial, operational and compliance controls and risk management systems.

**C.3**      **Audit Committee and Auditors[17]**

**Main Principle**      **The board should establish formal and transparent arrangements for considering how they should apply the financial reporting and internal control principles and for maintaining an appropriate relationship with the company's auditors.**

**Code provisions**

C.3.1      The board should establish an audit committee of at least three, or in the case of smaller companies[18] two, members, who should all be independent non-executive directors. The board should satisfy itself that at least one member of the audit committee has recent and relevant financial experience.

C.3.2      The main role and responsibilities of the audit committee should be set out in written terms of reference and should include:

- to monitor the integrity of the financial statements of the company, and any formal announcements relating to the company's financial performance, reviewing significant financial reporting judgements contained in them;

- to review the company's internal financial controls and, unless expressly addressed by a separate board

> risk committee composed of independent directors, or by the board itself, to review the company's internal control and risk management systems;
>
> - to monitor and review the effectiveness of the company's internal audit function;
>
> - to make recommendations to the board, for it to put to the shareholders for their approval in general meeting, in relation to the appointment, re-appointment and removal of the external auditor and to approve the remuneration and terms of engagement of the external auditor;
>
> - to review and monitor the external auditor's independence and objectivity and the effectiveness of the audit process, taking into consideration relevant UK professional and regulatory requirements;
>
> - to develop and implement policy on the engagement of the external auditor to supply non-audit services, taking into account relevant ethical guidance regarding the provision of non-audit services by the external audit firm; and to report to the board, identifying any matters in respect of which it considers that action or improvement is needed and making recommendations as to the steps to be taken.

C.3.3   The terms of reference of the audit committee, including its role and the authority delegated to it by the board, should be made available[19]. A separate section of the annual report should describe the work of the committee in discharging those responsibilities.

C.3.4   The audit committee should review arrangements by which staff of the company may, in confidence, raise concerns about possible improprieties in matters of financial reporting or other matters. The audit committee's objective should be to ensure that arrangements are in place for the proportionate and independent investigation of such matters and for appropriate follow-up action.

C.3.5   The audit committee should monitor and review the effectiveness of the internal audit activities. Where there is no internal audit function, the audit committee should consider annually whether there is a need for an internal audit function and make a recommendation to the board, and the reasons for the absence of such a function should be explained in the relevant section of the annual report.

| | |
|---|---|
| C.3.6 | The audit committee should have primary responsibility for making a recommendation on the appointment, reappointment and removal of the external auditors. If the board does not accept the audit committee's recommendation, it should include in the annual report, and in any papers recommending appointment or re-appointment, a statement from the audit committee explaining the recommendation and should set out reasons why the board has taken a different position. |
| C.3.7 | The annual report should explain to shareholders how, if the auditor provides non-audit services, auditor objectivity and independence is safeguarded. |

**D**     **RELATIONS WITH SHAREHOLDERS**

**D.1**     **Dialogue with Institutional Shareholders**

**Main Principle**     **There should be a dialogue with shareholders based on the mutual understanding of objectives. The board as a whole has responsibility for ensuring that a satisfactory dialogue with shareholders takes place.**[20]

**Supporting Principles**     Whilst recognising that most shareholder contact is with the chief executive and finance director, the chairman (and the senior independent director and other directors as appropriate) should maintain sufficient contact with major shareholders to understand their issues and concerns.

The board should keep in touch with shareholder opinion in whatever ways are most practical and efficient.

**Code Provisions**

| | |
|---|---|
| D.1.1 | The chairman should ensure that the views of shareholders are communicated to the board as a whole. The chairman should discuss governance and strategy with major shareholders. Non-executive directors should be offered the opportunity to attend meetings with major shareholders and should expect to attend them if requested by major shareholders. The senior independent director should attend sufficient meetings with a range of major shareholders to listen to their views in order to help develop a balanced understanding of the issues and concerns of major shareholders. |
| D.1.2 | The board should state in the annual report the steps they have taken to ensure that the members of the board, and in particular the non-executive directors, develop an understanding of the views of major shareholders about their company, for example through direct face-to-face contact, analysts' or brokers' briefings and surveys of shareholder opinion. |

15

**D.2**                        **Constructive Use of the AGM**

**Main Principle**      **The board should use the AGM to communicate with investors and to encourage their participation.**

**Code Provisions**

D.2.1                      The company should count all proxy votes and, except where a poll is called, should indicate the level of proxies lodged on each resolution, and the balance for and against the resolution and the number of abstentions, after it has been dealt with on a show of hands. The company should ensure that votes cast are properly received and recorded.

D.2.2                      The company should propose a separate resolution at the AGM on each substantially separate issue and should in particular propose a resolution at the AGM relating to the report and accounts.

D.2.3                      The chairman should arrange for the chairmen of the audit, remuneration and nomination committees to be available to answer questions at the AGM and for all directors to attend.

D.2.4                      The company should arrange for the Notice of the AGM and related papers to be sent to shareholders at least 20 working days before the meeting.

**SECTION 2**          **INSTITUTIONAL SHAREHOLDERS**

**E**                            **INSTITUTIONAL SHAREHOLDERS**[21]

**E.1**                         **Dialogue with companies**

**Main Principle**      **Institutional shareholders should enter into a dialogue with companies based on the mutual understanding of objectives.**

**Supporting Principles**         Institutional shareholders should apply the principles set out in the Institutional Shareholders' Committee's "The Responsibilities of Institutional Shareholders and Agents – Statement of Principles"[22], which should be reflected in fund manager contracts.

**E.2**                         **Evaluation of Governance Disclosures**

**Main Principle**      **When evaluating companies' governance arrangements, particularly those relating to board structure and composition, institutional shareholders should give due weight to all relevant factors drawn to their attention.**

**Supporting Principles**         Institutional shareholders should consider carefully explanations given for departure from this Code and make reasoned judgements in each case. They should give an explanation to the company, in writing where appropriate, and be prepared to enter a dialogue if they do not accept the company's position. They should avoid a box-ticking approach to assessing a company's corporate governance. They should bear in mind in particular the size and complexity of the company and the nature of the risks and challenges it faces.

**E.3**   **Shareholder Voting**

**Main Principle**   **Institutional shareholders have a responsibility to make considered use of their votes.**

**Supporting Principles**   Institutional shareholders should take steps to ensure their voting intentions are being translated into practice.

Institutional shareholders should, on request, make available to their clients information on the proportion of resolutions on which votes were cast and non-discretionary proxies lodged.

Major shareholders should attend AGMs where appropriate and practicable. Companies and registrars should facilitate this.

**Schedule A: Provisions on the design of performance related remuneration**

1.  The remuneration committee should consider whether the directors should be eligible for annual bonuses. If so, performance conditions should be relevant, stretching and designed to enhance shareholder value. Upper limits should be set and disclosed. There may be a case for part payment in shares to be held for a significant period.

2.  The remuneration committee should consider whether the directors should be eligible for benefits under long-term incentive schemes. Traditional share option schemes should be weighed against other kinds of long-term incentive scheme. In normal circumstances, shares granted or other forms of deferred remuneration should not vest, and options should not be exercisable, in less than three years. Directors should be encouraged to hold their shares for a further period after vesting or exercise, subject to the need to finance any costs of acquisition and associated tax liabilities.

3.  Any new long-term incentive schemes which are proposed should be approved by shareholders and should preferably replace any existing schemes or at least form part of a well considered overall plan, incorporating existing schemes. The total rewards potentially available should not be excessive.

4.  Payouts or grants under all incentive schemes, including new grants under existing share option schemes, should be subject to challenging

performance criteria reflecting the company's objectives. Consideration should be given to criteria which reflect the company's performance relative to a group of comparator companies in some key variables such as total shareholder return.

5.  Grants under executive share option and other long-term incentive schemes should normally be phased rather than awarded in one large block.

6.  In general, only basic salary should be pensionable.

7.  The remuneration committee should consider the pension consequences and associated costs to the company of basic salary increases and any other changes in pensionable remuneration, especially for directors close to retirement.

**Schedule B: Guidance on liability of non-executive directors: care, skill and diligence**

1.  Although non-executive directors and executive directors have as board members the same legal duties and objectives, the time devoted to the company's affairs is likely to be significantly less for a non-executive director than for an executive director and the detailed knowledge and experience of a company's affairs that could reasonably be expected of a non-executive director will generally be less than for an executive director. These matters may be relevant in assessing the knowledge, skill and experience which may reasonably be expected of a non-executive director and therefore the care, skill and diligence that a non-executive director may be expected to exercise.

2.  In this context, the following elements of the Code may also be particularly relevant.

    (i)   In order to enable directors to fulfil their duties, the Code states that:

    - The letter of appointment of the director should set out the expected time commitment (Code provision A.4.4); and

    - The board should be supplied in a timely manner with information in a form and of a quality appropriate to enable it to discharge its duties. The chairman is responsible for ensuring that the directors are provided by management with accurate, timely and clear information. (Code principles A.5).

    (ii)  Non-executive directors should themselves:

    - Undertake appropriate induction and regularly update and refresh their skills, knowledge and familiarity with the company (Code principle A.5 and provision A.5.1).

    - Seek appropriate clarification or amplification of information and, where necessary, take and follow appropriate professional advice (Code principle A.5 and provision A.5.2).

- Where they have concerns about the running of the company or a proposed action, ensure that these are addressed by the board and, to the extent that they are not resolved, ensure that they are recorded in the board minutes (Code provision A.1.4).

- Give a statement to the board if they have such unresolved concerns on resignation (Code provision A.1.4).

3.  It is up to each non-executive director to reach a view as to what is necessary in particular circumstances to comply with the duty of care, skill and diligence they owe as a director to the company. In considering whether or not a person is in breach of that duty, a court would take into account all relevant circumstances. These may include having regard to the above where relevant to the issue of liability of a non-executive director.

### Schedule C: Disclosure of corporate governance arrangements

The Listing Rules require a statement to be included in the annual report relating to compliance with the Code, as described in the preamble.

For ease of reference, the specific requirements in the Code for disclosure are set out below:

The annual report should record:

- a statement of how the board operates, including a high level statement of which types of decisions are to be taken by the board and which are to be delegated to management (A.1.1);

- the names of the chairman, the deputy chairman (where there is one), the chief executive, the senior independent director and the chairmen and members of the nomination, audit and remuneration committees (A.1.2);

- the number of meetings of the board and those committees and individual attendance by directors (A.1.2);

- the names of the non-executive directors whom the board determines to be independent, with reasons where necessary (A.3.1);

- the other significant commitments of the chairman and any changes to them during the year (A.4.3);

- how performance evaluation of the board, its committees and its directors has been conducted (A.6.1);

- the steps the board has taken to ensure that members of the board, and in particular the non-executive directors, develop an understanding of the views of major shareholders about their company (D.1.2).

The report should also include:

- a separate section describing the work of the nomination committee, including the process it has used in relation to board appointments and an explanation if neither external search consultancy nor open advertising has been used in the appointment of a chairman or a non-executive director (A.4.6);

- a description of the work of the remuneration committee as required under the Directors' Remuneration Reporting Regulations 2002, and including, where an executive director serves as a non-executive director elsewhere, whether or not the director will retain such earnings and, if so, what the remuneration is (B.1.4);

- an explanation from the directors of their responsibility for preparing the accounts and a statement by the auditors about their reporting responsibilities (C.1.1);

- a statement from the directors that the business is a going concern, with supporting assumptions or qualifications as necessary (C.1.2);

- a report that the board has conducted a review of the effectiveness of the group's system of internal controls (C.2.1);

- a separate section describing the work of the audit committee in discharging its responsibilities (C.3.3);

- where there is no internal audit function, the reasons for the absence of such a function (C.3.5);

- where the board does not accept the audit committee's recommendation on the appointment, reappointment or removal of an external auditor, a statement from the audit committee explaining the recommendation and the reasons why the board has taken a different position (C.3.6); and

- an explanation of how, if the auditor provides non-audit services, auditor objectivity and independence is safeguarded (C.3.7).

**The following information should be made available (which may be met by making it available on request and placing the information available on the company's website):**

- the terms of reference of the nomination, remuneration and audit committees, explaining their role and the authority delegated to them by the board (A.4.1, B.2.1 and C.3.3);

- the terms and conditions of appointment of non-executive directors (A.4.4) (see footnote 10 on page 9); and

- where remuneration consultants are appointed, a statement of whether they have any other connection with the company (B.2.1).

**The board should set out to shareholders in the papers accompanying a resolution to elect or re-elect:**

- sufficient biographical details to enable shareholders to take an informed decision on their election or re-election (A.7.1).

- why they believe an individual should be elected to a non-executive role (A.7.2).

- on re-election of a non-executive director, confirmation from the chairman that, following formal performance evaluation, the individual's performance continues to be effective and to demonstrate commitment to the role, including commitment of time for board and committee meetings and any other duties (A.7.2).

**The board should set out to shareholders in the papers recommending appointment or reappointment of an external auditor:**

- if the board does not accept the audit committee's recommendation, a statement from the audit committee explaining the recommendation and from the board setting out reasons why they have taken a different position (C.3.6).

**Notes**

1. 'Review of the role and effectiveness of non-executive directors', published January 2003.
2. 'Audit Committees Combined Code Guidance', published January 2003.
3. 'Internal Control: Guidance for Directors on the Combined Code', published by the Institute of Chartered Accountants in England and Wales in September 1999.
4. The *Directors' Remuneration Report Regulations 2002, SI 2002/1986.*
5. Compliance or otherwise with this provision need only be reported for the year in which the appointment is made.
6. A.2.2 states that the chairman should, on appointment, meet the independence criteria set out in this provision, but thereafter the test of independence is not appropriate in relation to the chairman.
7. A smaller company is one that is below the FTSE 350 throughout the year immediately prior to the reporting year.
8. The requirement to make the information available would be met by making it available on request and by including the information on the company's website.
9. Compliance or otherwise with this provision need only be reported for the year in which the appointment is made.
10. The terms and conditions of appointment of non-executive directors should be made available for inspection by any person at the company's registered office during normal business hours and at the AGM (for 15 minutes prior to the meeting and during the meeting).
11. Views have been sought by the Department of Trade and Industry by 30 September 2003 on whether, and if so how, further measures are required to enable shareholders to ensure that compensation reflects performance when directors' contracts are terminated: See "Rewards for Failure": Directors' Remuneration – Contracts, performance and severance, June 2003.
12. As required under the *Directors' Remuneration Report Regulations.*
13. See footnote 7
14. See footnote 8
15. See footnote 8
16. The Turnbull guidance suggests means of applying this part of the Code.
17. The Smith guidance suggests means of applying this part of the Code.
18. See footnote 7
19. See footnote 8.
20. Nothing in these principles or provisions should be taken to override the general requirements of law to treat shareholders equally in access to information.
21. Agents such as investment managers, or voting services, are frequently appointed by institutional shareholders to act on their behalf and these principles should

accordingly be read as applying where appropriate to the agents of institutional shareholders.

22. Available at website: www.investmentuk.org.uk/press/2002/20021021–01.pdf

# Guidance on Internal Control (The Turnbull Guidance) A1.2

## Contents

Note: Principle D.2, provision D.2.1 and provision D.2.2 of the old (1998) Code appear in the new (2003) Code as principle C.2, provisions C.2.1 and (in an amended form) provision C.3.5. The Code references in the guidance on internal control should be read accordingly.

# Introduction

## Internal control requirements of the Combined Code

1.   When the Combined Code of the Committee on Corporate Governance (the Code) was published, the Institute of Chartered Accountants in

England & Wales agreed with the London Stock Exchange that it would provide guidance to assist listed companies to implement the requirements in the Code relating to internal control.

2.  Principle D.2 of the Code states that 'The board should maintain a sound system of internal control to safeguard shareholders' investment and the company's assets'.

3.  Provision D.2.1 states that 'The directors should, at least annually, conduct a review of the effectiveness of the group's system of internal control and should report to shareholders that they have done so. The review should cover all controls, including financial, operational and compliance controls and risk management'.

4.  Provision D.2.2 states that 'Companies which do not have an internal audit function should from time to time review the need for one'.

5.  Paragraph 12.43A of the London Stock Exchange Listing Rules states that 'in the case of a company incorporated in the United Kingdom, the following additional items must be included in its annual report and accounts:

    (a)  a narrative statement of how it has applied the Principles set out in Section 1 of the Combined Code, providing explanation which enables its shareholders to evaluate how the Principles have been applied;

    (b)  a statement as to whether or not it has complied throughout the accounting period with the Code Provisions set out in Section 1 of the Combined Code. A company that has not complied with the Code Provisions, or complied with only some of the Code Provisions or (in the case of Provisions whose requirements are of a continuing nature) complied for only part of an accounting period, must specify the Code Provisions with which it has not complied, and (where relevant) for what part of the period such non-compliance continued, and give reasons for any non-compliance'.

6.  The Preamble to the Code, which is appended to the Listing Rules, makes it clear that there is no prescribed form or content for the statement setting out how the various Principles in the Code have been applied. The intention is that companies should have a free hand to explain their governance policies in the light of the Principles, including any special circumstances which have led to them adopting a particular approach.

7.  The guidance in this document should be followed by boards of listed companies in:

    •  assessing how the company has applied Code principle D.2;

    •  implementing the requirements of Code Provisions D.2.1 and D.2.2; and

    •  reporting on these matters to shareholders in the annual report and accounts.

## Objectives of the guidance

8.   This guidance is intended to:

  - reflect sound business practice whereby internal control is embedded in the business processes by which a company pursues its objectives;

  - remain relevant over time in the continually evolving business environment; and

  - enable each company to apply it in a manner which takes account of its particular circumstances.

The guidance requires directors to exercise judgement in reviewing how the company has implemented the requirements of the Code relating to internal control and reporting to shareholders thereon.

9.   The guidance is based on the adoption by a company's board of a risk-based approach to establishing a sound system of internal control and reviewing its effectiveness. This should be incorporated by the company within its normal management and governance processes. It should not be treated as a separate exercise undertaken to meet regulatory requirements.

## The importance of internal control and risk management

10.   A company's system of internal control has a key role in the management of risks that are significant to the fulfilment of its business objectives. A sound system of internal control contributes to safeguarding the shareholders' investment and the company's assets.

11.   Internal control (as referred to in para 20) facilitates the effectiveness and efficiency of operations, helps ensure the reliability of internal and external reporting and assists compliance with laws and regulations.

12.   Effective financial controls, including the maintenance of proper accounting records, are an important element of internal control. They help ensure that the company is not unnecessarily exposed to avoidable financial risks and that financial information used within the business and for publication is reliable. They also contribute to the safeguarding of assets, including the prevention and detection of fraud.

13.   A company's objectives, its internal organisation and the environment in which it operates are continually evolving and, as a result, the risks it faces are continually changing. A sound system of internal control therefore depends on a thorough and regular evaluation of the nature and extent of the risks to which the company is exposed. Since profits are, in part, the reward for successful risk-taking in business, the purpose of internal control is to help manage and control risk appropriately rather than to eliminate it.

## Groups of companies

14. Throughout this guidance, where reference is made to 'company' it should be taken, where applicable, as referring to the group of which the reporting company is the parent company. For groups of companies, the review of effectiveness of internal control and the report to the shareholders should be from the perspective of the group as a whole.

## The Appendix

15. The Appendix to this document contains questions which boards may wish to consider in applying this guidance.

# Maintaining a sound system of internal control

## Responsibilities

16. The board of directors is responsible for the company's system of internal control. It should set appropriate policies on internal control and seek regular assurance that will enable it to satisfy itself that the system is functioning effectively. The board must further ensure that the system of internal control is effective in managing risks in the manner which it has approved.

17. In determining its policies with regard to internal control, and thereby assessing what constitutes a sound system of internal control in the particular circumstances of the company, the board's deliberations should include consideration of the following factors:

   • the extent and categories of risk which it regards as acceptable for the company to bear;

   • the likelihood of the risks concerned materialising;

   • the company's ability to reduce the incidence and impact on the business of risks that do materialise; and

   • the costs of operating particular controls relative to the benefit thereby obtained in managing the related risks.

18. It is the role of management to implement board policies on risk and control. In fulfilling its responsibilities, management should identify and evaluate the risks faced by the company for consideration by the board and design, operate and monitor a suitable system of internal control which implements the policies adopted by the board.

19. All employees have some responsibility for internal control as part of their accountability for achieving objectives. They, collectively, should have the necessary knowledge, skills, information and authority to establish, operate and monitor the system of internal control. This will require an understanding of the company, its objectives, the industries and markets in which it operates, and the risks it faces.

## Elements of a sound system of internal control

20. An internal control system encompasses the policies, processes, tasks, behaviours and other aspects of a company that, taken together:

    - facilitate its effective and efficient operation by enabling it to respond appropriately to significant business, operational, financial, compliance and other risks to achieving the company's objectives. This includes the safeguarding of assets from inappropriate use or from loss and fraud, and ensuring that liabilities are identified and managed;

    - help ensure the quality of internal and external reporting. This requires the maintenance of proper records and processes that generate a flow of timely, relevant and reliable information from within and outside the organisation;

    - help ensure compliance with applicable laws and regulations, and also with internal policies with respect to the conduct of business.

21. A company's system of internal control will reflect its control environment which encompasses its organisational structure. The system will include:

    - control activities;

    - information and communications processes; and

    - processes for monitoring the continuing effectiveness of the system of internal control.

22. The system of internal control should:

    - be embedded in the operations of the company and form part of its culture;

    - be capable of responding quickly to evolving risks to the business arising from factors within the company and to changes in the business environment; and

    - include procedures for reporting immediately to appropriate levels of management any significant control failings or weaknesses that are identified together with details of corrective action being undertaken.

23. A sound system of internal control reduces, but cannot eliminate, the possibility of poor judgement in decision-making; human error; control processes being deliberately circumvented by employees and others; management overriding controls; and the occurrence of unforeseeable circumstances.

24. A sound system of internal control therefore provides reasonable, but not absolute, assurance that a company will not be hindered in achieving its business objectives, or in the orderly and legitimate conduct of its business, by circumstances which may reasonably be foreseen. A system of internal control cannot, however, provide protection with certainty

against a company failing to meet its business objectives or all material errors, losses, fraud, or breaches of laws or regulations.

## Reviewing the effectiveness of internal control

### Responsibilities

25. Reviewing the effectiveness of internal control is an essential part of the board's responsibilities. The board will need to form its own view on effectiveness after due and careful enquiry based on the information and assurances provided to it. Management is accountable to the board for monitoring the system of internal control and for providing assurance to the board that it has done so.

26. The role of board committees in the review process, including that of the audit committee, is for the board to decide and will depend upon factors such as the size and composition of the board; the scale, diversity and complexity of the company's operations; and the nature of the significant risks that the company faces. To the extent that designated board committees carry out, on behalf of the board, tasks that are attributed in this guidance document to the board, the results of the relevant committees' work should be reported to, and considered by, the board. The board takes responsibility for the disclosures on internal control in the annual report and accounts.

### The process for reviewing effectiveness

27. Effective monitoring on a continuous basis is an essential component of a sound system of internal control. The board cannot, however, rely solely on the embedded monitoring processes within the company to discharge its responsibilities. It should regularly receive and review reports on internal control. In addition, the board should undertake an annual assessment for the purposes of making its public statement on internal control to ensure that it has considered all significant aspects of internal control for the company for the year under review and up to the date of approval of the annual report and accounts.

28. The reference to 'all controls' in Code Provision D.2.1 should not be taken to mean that the effectiveness of every internal control (including controls designed to manage immaterial risks) should be subject to review by the board. Rather it means that, for the purposes of this guidance, internal controls considered by the board should include all types of controls including those of an operational and compliance nature, as well as internal financial controls.

29. The board should define the process to be adopted for its review of the effectiveness of internal control. This should encompass both the scope and frequency of the reports it receives and reviews during the year, and also the process for its annual assessment, such that it will be provided with sound, appropriately documented, support for its statement on internal control in the company's annual report and accounts.

30.  The reports from management to the board should, in relation to the areas covered by them, provide a balanced assessment of the significant risks and the effectiveness of the system of internal control in managing those risks. Any significant control failings or weaknesses identified should be discussed in the reports, including the impact that they have had, could have had, or may have, on the company and the actions being taken to rectify them. It is essential that there be openness of communication by management with the board on matters relating to risk and control.

31.  When reviewing reports during the year, the board should:

- consider what are the significant risks and assess how they have been identified, evaluated and managed;

- assess the effectiveness of the related system of internal control in managing the significant risks, having regard, in particular, to any significant failings or weaknesses in internal control that have been reported;

- consider whether necessary actions are being taken promptly to remedy any significant failings or weaknesses; and

- consider whether the findings indicate a need for more extensive monitoring of the system of internal control.

32.  Additionally, the board should undertake an annual assessment for the purpose of making its public statement on internal control. The assessment should consider issues dealt with in reports reviewed by it during the year together with any additional information necessary to ensure that the board has taken account of all significant aspects of internal control for the company for the year under review and up to the date of approval of the annual report and accounts.

33.  The board's annual assessment should, in particular, consider:

- the changes since the last annual assessment in the nature and extent of significant risks, and the company's ability to respond to changes in its business and the external environment;

- the scope and quality of management's ongoing monitoring of risks and of the system of internal control, and, where applicable, the work of its internal audit function and other providers of assurance;

- the extent and frequency of the communication of the results of the monitoring to the board (or board committee(s)) which enables it to build up a cumulative assessment of the state of control in the company and the effectiveness with which risk is being managed;

- the incidence of significant control failings or weaknesses that have been identified at any time during the period and the extent to which they have resulted in unforeseen outcomes or contingencies that have had, could have had, or may in the future have, a material impact on the company's financial performance or condition; and

- the effectiveness of the company's public reporting processes.

34.  Should the board become aware at any time of a significant failing or weakness in internal control, it should determine how the failing or weakness arose and re-assess the effectiveness of management's ongoing processes for designing, operating and monitoring the system of internal control.

## The board's statement on internal control

35.  In its narrative statement of how the company has applied Code Principle D.2, the board should, as a minimum, disclose that there is an ongoing process for identifying, evaluating and managing the significant risks faced by the company, that it has been in place for the year under review and up to the date of approval of the annual report and accounts, that it is regularly reviewed by the board and accords with the guidance in this document.

36.  The board may wish to provide additional information in the annual report and accounts to assist understanding of the company's risk management processes and system of internal control.

37.  The disclosures relating to the application of Principle D. 2 should include an acknowledgement by the board that it is responsible for the company's system of internal control and for reviewing its effectiveness. It should also explain that such a system is designed to manage rather than eliminate the risk of failure to achieve business objectives, and can only provide reasonable and not absolute assurance against material misstatement or loss.

38.  In relation to Code Provision D.2.1, the board should summarise the process it (where applicable, through its committees) has applied in reviewing the effectiveness of the system of internal control. It should also disclose the process it has applied to deal with material internal control aspects of any significant problems disclosed in the annual report and accounts.

39.  Where a board cannot make one or more of the disclosures in paragraphs 35 and 38, it should state this fact and provide an explanation. The Listing Rules require the board to disclose if it has failed to conduct a review of the effectiveness of the company's system of internal control.

40.  The board should ensure that its disclosures provide meaningful, high-level information and do not give a misleading impression.

41.  Where material joint ventures and associates have not been dealt with as part of the group for the purposes of applying this guidance, this should be disclosed.

## Internal audit

42.  Provision D.2.2 of the Code states that companies which do not have an internal audit function should from time to time review the need for one.

43.  The need for an internal audit function will vary depending on company-specific factors including the scale, diversity and complexity of the company's activities and the number of employees, as well as cost/benefit considerations. Senior management and the board may desire objective assurance and advice on risk and control. An adequately resourced internal audit function (or its equivalent where, for example, a third party is contracted to perform some or all of the work concerned) may provide such assurance and advice. There may be other functions within the company that also provide assurance and advice covering specialist areas such as health and safety, regulatory and legal compliance and environmental issues.

44.  In the absence of an internal audit function, management needs to apply other monitoring processes in order to assure itself and the board that the system of internal control is functioning as intended. In these circumstances, the board will need to assess whether such processes provide sufficient and objective assurance.

45.  When undertaking its assessment of the need for an internal audit function, the board should also consider whether there are any trends or current factors relevant to the company's activities, markets or other aspects of its external environment, that have increased, or are expected to increase, the risks faced by the company. Such an increase in risk may also arise from internal factors such as organisational restructuring or from changes in reporting processes or underlying information systems. Other matters to be taken into account may include adverse trends evident from the monitoring of internal control systems or an increased incidence of unexpected occurrences.

46.  The board of a company that does not have an internal audit function should assess the need for such a function annually having regard to the factors referred to in paragraphs 43 and 45 above. Where there is an internal audit function, the board should annually review its scope of work, authority and resources, again having regard to those factors.

47.  If the company does not have an internal audit function and the board has not reviewed the need for one, the Listing Rules require the board to disclose these facts.

# Appendix

## Assessing the effectiveness of the company's risk and control processes

Some questions which the board may wish to consider and discuss with management when regularly reviewing reports on internal control and carrying out its annual assessment are set out below. The questions are not intended to be exhaustive and will need to be tailored to the particular circumstances of the company.

This Appendix should be read in conjunction with the guidance set out in this document.

1.  *Risk assessment*

    *   Does the company have clear objectives and have they been communicated so as to provide effective direction to employees on risk assessment and control issues? For example, do objectives and related plans include measurable performance targets and indicators?

    *   Are the significant internal and external operational, financial, compliance and other risks identified and assessed on an ongoing basis? (Significant risks may, for example, include those related to market, credit, liquidity, technological, legal, health, safety and environmental, reputation, and business probity issues. )

    *   Is there a clear understanding by management and others within the company of what risks are acceptable to the board?

2.  *Control environment and control activities*

    *   Does the board have clear strategies for dealing with the significant risks that have been identified? Is there a policy on how to manage these risks?

    *   Do the company's culture, code of conduct, human resource policies and performance reward systems support the business objectives and risk management and internal control system?

    *   Does senior management demonstrate, through its actions as well as its policies, the necessary commitment to competence, integrity and fostering a climate of trust within the company?

    *   Are authority, responsibility and accountability defined clearly such that decisions are made and actions taken by the appropriate people? Are the decisions and actions of different parts of the company appropriately co-ordinated?

    *   Does the company communicate to its employees what is expected of them and the scope of their freedom to act? This may apply to areas such as customer relations; service levels for both internal and outsourced activities; health, safety and environmental protection; security of tangible and intangible assets; business continuity issues; expenditure matters; accounting; and financial and other reporting.

    *   Do people in the company (and in its providers of outsourced services) have the knowledge, skills and tools to support the achievement of the company's objectives and to manage effectively risks to their achievement?

    *   How are processes/controls adjusted to reflect new or changing risks, or operational deficiencies?

3. *Information and communication*

- Do management and the board receive timely, relevant and reliable reports on progress against business objectives and the related risks that provide them with the information, from inside and outside the company, needed for decision-making and management review purposes? This could include performance reports and indicators of change, together with qualitative information such as on customer satisfaction, employee attitudes etc.

- Are information needs and related information systems reassessed as objectives and related risks change or as reporting deficiencies are identified?

- Are periodic reporting procedures, including half-yearly and annual reporting, effective in communicating a balanced and understandable account of the company's position and prospects?

- Are there established channels of communication for individuals to report suspected breaches of laws or regulations or other improprieties?

4. *Monitoring*

- Are there ongoing processes embedded within the company's overall business operations, and addressed by senior management, which monitor the effective application of the policies, processes and activities related to internal control and risk management? (Such processes may include control self-assessment, confirmation by personnel of compliance with policies and codes of conduct, internal audit reviews or other management reviews).

- Do these processes monitor the company's ability to re-evaluate risks and adjust controls effectively in response to changes in its objectives, its business, and its external environment?

- Are there effective follow-up procedures to ensure that appropriate change or action occurs in response to changes in risk and control assessments?

- Is there appropriate communication to the board (or board committees) on the effectiveness of the ongoing monitoring processes on risk and control matters? This should include reporting any significant failings or weaknesses on a timely basis.

- Are there specific arrangements for management monitoring and reporting to the board on risk and control matters of particular importance? These could include, for example, actual or suspected fraud and other illegal or irregular acts, or matters that could adversely affect the company's reputation or financial position?

# Guidance on Audit Committees (The Smith Guidance)        **A1.3**

## Contents

Note: The following guidance is closely based on Sir Robert Smith's proposed guidance published in January 2003 (see footnote 2, page 1), modified for consistency with the final revised Code.

# Audit Committees – Combined Code Guidance

## 1. Introduction

1.1. This guidance is designed to assist company boards in making suitable arrangements for their audit committees, and to assist directors serving on audit committees in carrying out their role.

1.2. The paragraphs in bold are taken from the Combined Code (Section C3). Listed companies that do not comply with those provisions should include an explanation as to why they have not complied in the statement required by the Listing Rules.

1.3. Best practice requires that every board should consider in detail what arrangements for its audit committee are best suited for its particular circumstances. Audit committee arrangements need to be proportionate to the task, and will vary according to the size, complexity and risk profile of the company.

1.4.  While all directors have a duty to act in the interests of the company the audit committee has a particular role, acting independently from the executive, to ensure that the interests of shareholders are properly protected in relation to financial reporting and internal control.

1.5.  Nothing in the guidance should be interpreted as a departure from the principle of the unitary board. All directors remain equally responsible for the company's affairs as a matter of law. The audit committee, like other committees to which particular responsibilities are delegated (such as the remuneration committee), remains a committee of the board. Any disagreement within the board, including disagreement between the audit committee's members and the rest of the board, should be resolved at board level.

1.6.  The Code provides that a separate section of the annual report should describe the work of the committee. This deliberately puts the spotlight on the audit committee and gives it an authority that it might otherwise lack. This is not incompatible with the principle of the unitary board.

1.7.  The guidance contains recommendations about the conduct of the audit committee's relationship with the board, with the executive management and with internal and external auditors. However, the most important features of this relationship cannot be drafted as guidance or put into a code of practice: a frank, open working relationship and a high level of mutual respect are essential, particularly between the audit committee chairman and the board chairman, the chief executive and the finance director. The audit committee must be prepared to take a robust stand, and all parties must be prepared to make information freely available to the audit committee, to listen to their views and to talk through the issues openly.

1.8.  In particular, the management is under an obligation to ensure the audit committee is kept properly informed, and should take the initiative in supplying information rather than waiting to be asked. The board should make it clear to all directors and staff that they must cooperate with the audit committee and provide it with any information it requires. In addition, executive board members will have regard to their common law duty to provide all directors, including those on the audit committee, with all the information they need to discharge their responsibilities as directors of the company.

1.9.  Many of the core functions of audit committees set out in this guidance are expressed in terms of 'oversight', 'assessment' and 'review' of a particular function. It is not the duty of audit committees to carry out functions that properly belong to others, such as the company's management in the preparation of the financial statements or the auditors in the planning or conducting of audits. To do so could undermine the responsibility of management and auditors. Audit committees should, for example, satisfy themselves that there is a proper system and allocation of responsibilities for the day-to-day monitoring of financial controls but they should not seek to do the monitoring themselves.

1.10. However, the high-level oversight function may lead to detailed work. The audit committee must intervene if there are signs that something may be seriously amiss. For example, if the audit committee is uneasy about the explanations of management and auditors about a particular financial reporting policy decision, there may be no alternative but to grapple with the detail and perhaps to seek independent advice.

1.11. Under this guidance, audit committees have wide-ranging, time-consuming and sometimes intensive work to do. Companies need to make the necessary resources available. This includes suitable payment for the members of audit committees themselves. They – and particularly the audit committee chairman – bear a significant responsibility and they need to commit a significant extra amount of time to the job. Companies also need to make provision for induction and training for new audit committee members and continuing training as may be required.

1.12. This guidance applies to all companies to which the Code applies – i.e. UK listed companies. For groups, it will usually be necessary for the audit committee of the parent company to review issues that relate to particular subsidiaries or activities carried on by the group. Consequently, the board of a UK-listed parent company should ensure that there is adequate cooperation within the group (and with internal and external auditors of individual companies within the group) to enable the parent company audit committee to discharge its responsibilities effectively.

## 2 Establishment and role of the audit committee; membership, procedures and resources

**Establishment and role**

**2.1** **The board should establish an audit committee of at least three, or in the case of smaller companies two, members.**

**2.2** **The main role and responsibilities of the audit committee should be set out in written terms of reference and should include:**

- **to monitor the integrity of the financial statements of the company and any formal announcements relating to the company's financial performance, reviewing significant financial reporting judgements contained in them;**

- **to review the company's internal financial controls and, unless expressly addressed by a separate board risk committee composed of independent directors or by the board itself, the company's internal control and risk management systems;**

- **to monitor and review the effectiveness of the company's internal audit function;**

- **to make recommendations to the board, for it to put to the shareholders for their approval in general meeting, in relation to** the appointment of the external auditor and to approve the remuneration and terms of engagement of the external auditor;

- to review and monitor the external auditor's independence and objectivity and the effectiveness of the audit process, taking into consideration relevant UK professional and regulatory requirements;

- to develop and implement policy on the engagement of the external auditor to supply non-audit services, taking into account relevant ethical guidance regarding the provision of non-audit services by the external audit firm;

and to report to the Board, identifying any matters in respect of which it considers that action or improvement is needed, and making recommendations as to the steps to be taken.

### Membership and appointment

**2.3   All members of the committee should be independent non-executive directors. The board should satisfy itself that at least one member of the audit committee has recent and relevant financial experience.**

2.4   The chairman of the company should not be an audit committee member.

2.5   Appointments to the audit committee should be made by the board on the recommendation of the nomination committee (where there is one), in consultation with the audit committee chairman.

2.6   Appointments should be for a period of up to three years, extendable by no more than two additional three-year periods, so long as members continue to be independent.

### Meetings of the audit committee

2.7   It is for the audit committee chairman, in consultation with the company secretary, to decide the frequency and timing of its meetings. There should be as many meetings as the audit committee's role and responsibilities require. It is recommended there should be not fewer than three meetings during the year, held to coincide with key dates within the financial reporting and audit cycle[1]. However, most audit committee chairmen will wish to call more frequent meetings.

2.8   No one other than the audit committee's chairman and members is entitled to be present at a meeting of the audit committee. It is for the audit committee to decide if non-members should attend for a particular meeting or a particular agenda item. It is to be expected that the external audit lead partner will be invited regularly to attend meetings as well as the finance director. Others may be invited to attend.

2.9   Sufficient time should be allowed to enable the audit committee to undertake as full a discussion as may be required. A sufficient interval should be allowed between audit committee meetings and main board meetings to allow any work arising from the audit committee meeting to be carried out and reported to the board as appropriate.

2.10 The audit committee should, at least annually, meet the external and internal auditors, without management, to discuss matters relating to its remit and any issues arising from the audit.

2.11 Formal meetings of the audit committee are the heart of its work. However, they will rarely be sufficient. It is expected that the audit committee chairman, and to a lesser extent the other members, will wish to keep in touch on a continuing basis with the key people involved in the company's governance, including the board chairman, the chief executive, the finance director, the external audit lead partner and the head of internal audit.

## Resources

2.12 The audit committee should be provided with sufficient resources to undertake its duties.

2.13 The audit committee should have access to the services of the company secretariat on all audit committee matters including: assisting the chairman in planning the audit committee's work, drawing up meeting agendas, maintenance of minutes, drafting of material about its activities for the annual report, collection and distribution of information and provision of any necessary practical support.

2.14 The company secretary should ensure that the audit committee receives information and papers in a timely manner to enable full and proper consideration to be given to the issues.

2.15 The board should make funds available to the audit committee to enable it to take independent legal, accounting or other advice when the audit committee reasonably believes it necessary to do so.

## Remuneration

2.16 In addition to the remuneration paid to all non-executive directors, each company should consider the further remuneration that should be paid to members of the audit committee to recompense them for the additional responsibilities of membership. Consideration should be given to the time members are required to give to audit committee business, the skills they bring to bear and the onerous duties they take on, as well as the value of their work to the company. The level of remuneration paid to the members of the audit committee should take into account the level of fees paid to other members of the board. The chairman's responsibilities and time demands will generally be heavier than the other members of the audit committee and this should be reflected in his or her remuneration.

## Skills, experience and training

2.17 It is desirable that the committee member whom the board considers to have recent and relevant financial experience should have a professional qualification from one of the professional accountancy bodies. The need for a degree of financial literacy among the other members will vary according to the nature of the company, but experience of corporate financial matters will normally be required. The availability of appropriate financial expertise will be particularly important where the company's activities involve specialised financial activities.

2.18 The company should provide an induction programme for new audit committee members. This should cover the role of the audit committee, including its terms of reference and expected time commitment by members; and an overview of the company's business, identifying the main business and financial dynamics and risks. It could also include meeting some of the company staff.

2.19 Training should also be provided to members of the audit committee on an ongoing and timely basis and should include an understanding of the principles of and developments in financial reporting and related company law. In appropriate cases, it may also include, for example, understanding financial statements, applicable accounting standards and recommended practice; the regulatory framework for the company's business; the role of internal and external auditing and risk management.

2.20 The induction programme and ongoing training may take various forms, including attendance at formal courses and conferences, internal company talks and seminars, and briefings by external advisers.

# 3 Relationship with the board

3.1 The role of the audit committee is for the board to decide and to the extent that the audit committee undertakes tasks on behalf of the board, the results should be reported to, and considered by, the board. In doing so it should identify any matters in respect of which it considers that action or improvement is needed, and make recommendations as to the steps to be taken.

3.2 The terms of reference should be tailored to the particular circumstances of the company.

3.3 The audit committee should review annually its terms of reference and its own effectiveness and recommend any necessary changes to the board.

3.4 The board should review the audit committee's effectiveness annually.

3.5 Where there is disagreement between the audit committee and the board, adequate time should be made available for discussion of the issue with a view to resolving the disagreement. Where any such disagreements cannot be resolved, the audit committee should have the right to report the issue to the shareholders as part of the report on its activities in the annual report.

# 4    Role and responsibilities

## Financial reporting

4.1    The audit committee should review the significant financial reporting issues and judgements made in connection with the preparation of the company's financial statements, interim reports, preliminary announcements and related formal statements.

4.2    It is management's, not the audit committee's, responsibility to prepare complete and accurate financial statements and disclosures in accordance with financial reporting standards and applicable rules and regulations. However the audit committee should consider significant accounting policies, any changes to them and any significant estimates and judgements. The management should inform the audit committee of the methods used to account for significant or unusual transactions where the accounting treatment is open to different approaches. Taking into account the external auditor's view, the audit committee should consider whether the company has adopted appropriate accounting policies and, where necessary, made appropriate estimates and judgements. The audit committee should review the clarity and completeness of disclosures in the financial statements and consider whether the disclosures made are set properly in context.

4.3    Where, following its review, the audit committee is not satisfied with any aspect of the proposed financial reporting by the company, it shall report its views to the board.

4.4    The audit committee should review related information presented with the financial statements, including the operating and financial review, and corporate governance statements relating to the audit and to risk management. Similarly, where board approval is required for other statements containing financial information (for example, summary financial statements, significant financial returns to regulators and release of price sensitive information), whenever practicable (without being inconsistent with any requirement for prompt reporting under the Listing Rules) the audit committee should review such statements first.

## Internal controls and risk management systems

4.5    The audit committee should review the company's internal financial controls (that is, the systems established to identify, assess, manage and monitor financial risks); and unless expressly addressed by a separate board risk committee comprised of independent directors or by the board itself, the company's internal control and risk management systems.

4.6    The company's management is responsible for the identification, assessment, management and monitoring of risk, for developing, operating and monitoring the system of internal control and for providing assurance to the board that it has done so. Except where the board or a risk committee is expressly responsible for reviewing the effectiveness of the internal control and risk management systems, the audit committee should receive reports from management on the effectiveness of the systems they have established and the conclusions of any testing carried out by internal and external auditors.

4.7 Except to the extent that this is expressly dealt with by the board or risk committee, the audit committee should review and approve the statements included in the annual report in relation to internal control and the management of risk.

**Whistleblowing**

**4.8 The audit committee should review arrangements by which staff of the company may, in confidence, raise concerns about possible improprieties in matters of financial reporting or other matters. The audit committee's objective should be to ensure that arrangements are in place for the proportionate and independent investigation of such matters and for appropriate follow-up action. The internal audit process**

**4.9 The audit committee should monitor and review the effectiveness of the company's internal audit function. Where there is no internal audit function, the audit committee should consider annually whether there is a need for an internal audit function and make a recommendation to the board, and the reasons for the absence of such a function should be explained in the relevant section of the annual report.**

4.10 The audit committee should review and approve the internal audit function's remit, having regard to the complementary roles of the internal and external audit functions. The audit committee should ensure that the function has the necessary resources and access to information to enable it to fulfil its mandate, and is equipped to perform in accordance with appropriate professional standards for internal auditors[2].

4.11 The audit committee should approve the appointment or termination of appointment of the head of internal audit.

4.12 In its review of the work of the internal audit function, the audit committee should, inter alia:

- ensure that the internal auditor has direct access to the board chairman and to the audit committee and is accountable to the audit committee;

- review and assess the annual internal audit work plan;

- receive a report on the results of the internal auditors' work on a periodic basis;

- review and monitor management's responsiveness to the internal auditor's findings and recommendations;

- meet with the head of internal audit at least once a year without the presence of management; and

- monitor and assess the role and effectiveness of the internal audit function in the overall context of the company's risk management system.

## The external audit process

4.13 The audit committee is the body responsible for overseeing the company's relations with the external auditor.

*Appointment*

**4.14 The audit committee should have primary responsibility for making a recommendation on the appointment, reappointment and removal of the external auditors. If the board does not accept the audit committee's recommendation, it should include in the annual report, and in any papers recommending appointment or reappointment, a statement from the audit committee explaining its recommendation and should set out reasons why the board has taken a different position.**

4.15 The audit committee's recommendation to the board should be based on the assessments referred to below. If the audit committee recommends considering the selection of possible new appointees as external auditors, it should oversee the selection process.

4.16 The audit committee should assess annually the qualification, expertise and resources, and independence (see below) of the external auditors and the effectiveness of the audit process. The assessment should cover all aspects of the audit service provided by the audit firm, and include obtaining a report on the audit firm's own internal quality control procedures.

4.17 If the external auditor resigns, the audit committee should investigate the issues giving rise to such resignation and consider whether any action is required.

*Terms and Remuneration*

4.18 The audit committee should approve the terms of engagement and the remuneration to be paid to the external auditor in respect of audit services provided.

4.19 The audit committee should review and agree the engagement letter issued by the external auditor at the start of each audit, ensuring that it has been updated to reflect changes in circumstances arising since the previous year. The scope of the external audit should be reviewed by the audit committee with the auditor. If the audit committee is not satisfied as to its adequacy it should arrange for additional work to be undertaken.

4.20 The audit committee should satisfy itself that the level of fee payable in respect of the audit services provided is appropriate and that an effective audit can be conducted for such a fee.

*Independence, including the provision of non-audit services*

4.21 The audit committee should have procedures to ensure the independence and objectivity of the external auditor annually, taking into consideration relevant UK professional and regulatory requirements. This assessment should involve a consideration of all relationships between the company and the audit firm (including the provision of non-audit services). The audit committee should consider whether, taken as a whole and having regard to the views, as appropriate, of the external auditor, management and internal audit, those relationships appear to impair the auditor's judgement or independence.

4.22 The audit committee should seek reassurance that the auditors and their staff have no family, financial, employment, investment or business relationship with the company (other than in the normal course of business). The audit committee should seek from the audit firm, on an annual basis, information about policies and processes for maintaining independence and monitoring compliance with relevant requirements, including current requirements regarding the rotation of audit partners and staff.

4.23 The audit committee should agree with the board the company's policy for the employment of former employees of the external auditor, paying particular attention to the policy regarding former employees of the audit firm who were part of the audit team and moved directly to the company. This should be drafted taking into account the relevant ethical guidelines governing the accounting profession. The audit committee should monitor application of the policy, including the number of former employees of the external auditor currently employed in senior positions in the company, and consider whether in the light of this there has been any impairment, or appearance of impairment, of the auditor's judgement or independence in respect of the audit.

4.24 The audit committee should monitor the external audit firm's compliance with applicable United Kingdom ethical guidance relating to the rotation of audit partners, the level of fees that the company pays in proportion to the overall fee income of the firm, office and partner, and other related regulatory requirements.

4.25 The audit committee should develop and recommend to the board the company's policy in relation to the provision of non-audit services by the auditor. The audit committee's objective should be to ensure that the provision of such services does not impair the external auditor's independence or objectivity. In this context, the audit committee should consider:

- whether the skills and experience of the audit firm make it a suitable supplier of the non audit service;

- whether there are safeguards in place to ensure that there is no threat to objectivity and independence in the conduct of the audit resulting from the provision of such services by the external auditor;

- the nature of the non-audit services, the related fee levels and the fee levels individually and in aggregate relative to the audit fee; and

- the criteria which govern the compensation of the individuals performing the audit.

4.26 The audit committee should set and apply a formal policy specifying the types of non-audit work:

- from which the external auditors are excluded;

- for which the external auditors can be engaged without referral to the audit committee; and

- for which a case-by-case decision is necessary.

In addition, the policy may set fee limits generally or for particular classes of work.

4.27 In the third category, if it is not practicable to give approval to individual items in advance, it may be appropriate to give a general pre-approval for certain classes for work, subject to a fee limit determined by the audit committee and ratified by the board. The subsequent provision of any service by the auditor should be ratified at the next meeting of the audit committee.

4.28 In determining the policy, the audit committee should take into account relevant ethical guidance regarding the provision of non-audit services by the external audit firm, and in principle should not agree to the auditor providing a service if, having regard to the ethical guidance, the result is that:

- the external auditor audits its own firm's work;

- the external auditor makes management decisions for the company;

- a mutuality of interest is created; or

- the external auditor is put in the role of advocate for the company.

The audit committee should satisfy itself that any safeguards required by ethical guidance are implemented.

**4.29 The annual report should explain to shareholders how, if the auditor provides non-audit services, auditor objectivity and independence is safeguarded.**

*Annual audit cycle*

4.30 At the start of each annual audit cycle, the audit committee should ensure that appropriate plans are in place for the audit.

4.31 The audit committee should consider whether the auditor's overall work plan, including planned levels of materiality, and proposed resources to execute the audit plan appears consistent with the scope of the audit engagement, having regard also to the seniority, expertise and experience of the audit team.

4.32 The audit committee should review, with the external auditors, the findings of their work. In the course of its review, the audit committee should:

- discuss with the external auditor major issues that arose during the course of the audit and have subsequently been resolved and those issues that have been left unresolved;

- review key accounting and audit judgements; and

- review levels of errors identified during the audit, obtaining explanations from management and, where necessary the external auditors, as to why certain errors might remain unadjusted.

4.33 The audit committee should also review the audit representation letters before signature by management and give particular consideration to matters where representation has been requested that relate to non-standard issues[3]. The audit committee should consider whether the information provided is complete and appropriate based on its own knowledge.

4.34 As part of the ongoing monitoring process, the audit committee should review the management letter (or equivalent). The audit committee should review and monitor management's responsiveness to the external auditor's findings and recommendations.

4.35 At the end of the annual audit cycle, the audit committee should assess the effectiveness of the audit process. In the course of doing so, the audit committee should:

- review whether the auditor has met the agreed audit plan and understand the reasons for any changes, including changes in perceived audit risks and the work undertaken by the external auditors to address those risks;

- consider the robustness and perceptiveness of the auditors in their handling of the key accounting and audit judgements identified and in responding to questions from the audit committees, and in their commentary where appropriate on the systems of internal control;

- obtain feedback about the conduct of the audit from key people involved, e.g. the finance director and the head of internal audit; and

- review and monitor the content of the external auditor's management letter, in order to assess whether it is based on a good understanding of the company's business and establish whether recommendations have been acted upon and, if not, the reasons why they have not been acted upon.

# 5   Communication with shareholders

5.1   The terms of reference of the audit committee, including its role and the authority delegated to it by the board, should be made available. A separate section in the annual report should describe the work of the committee in discharging those responsibilities.

5.2   The audit committee section should include, inter alia:

- a summary of the role of the audit committee;

- the names and qualifications of all members of the audit committee during the period;

- the number of audit committee meetings;

- a report on the way the audit committee has discharged its responsibilities; and

- the explanation provided for in paragraph 4.29 above.

5.3   The chairman of the audit committee should be present at the AGM to answer questions, through the chairman of the board, on the report on the audit committee's activities and matters within the scope of audit committee's responsibilities.

**Notes**
1.   For example, when the audit plans (internal and external) are available for review and when interim statements, preliminary announcements and the full annual report are near completion.
2.   Further guidance can be found in the Institute of Internal Auditors' Code of Ethics and the International Standards for the Professional Practice of Internal Auditing Standards.
3.   Further guidance can be found in the Auditing Practices Board's Statement of Auditing Standard 440 'Management Representations'.

# Suggestions For Good Practice From The Higgs Report   A1.4

## Contents

Guidance for the chairman
Guidance for non-executive directors
Summary of the principal duties of the remuneration committee
Summary of the principal duties of the nomination committee
Pre-appointment due diligence checklist for new board members
Sample letter of non-executive director appointment
Induction checklist
Performance evaluation checklist

## Guidance On The Role Of The Chairman

The chairman is pivotal in creating the conditions for overall board and individual director effectiveness, both inside and outside the boardroom. Specifically, it is the responsibility of the chairman to:

- run the board and set its agenda. The agenda should take full account of the issues and the concerns of all board members. Agendas should be forward looking and concentrate on strategic matters rather than formulaic approvals of proposals which can be the subject of appropriate delegated powers to management;

- ensure that the members of the board receive accurate, timely and clear information, in particular about the company's performance, to enable the board to take sound decisions, monitor effectively and provide advice to promote the success of the company;

- ensure effective communication with shareholders and ensure that the members of the board develop an understanding of the views of the major investors;

- manage the board to ensure that sufficient time is allowed for discussion of complex or contentious issues, where appropriate arranging for informal meetings beforehand to enable thorough preparation for the board discussion. It is particularly important that non-executive directors have sufficient time to consider critical issues and are not faced with unrealistic deadlines for decision-making;

- take the lead in providing a properly constructed induction programme for new directors that is comprehensive, formal and tailored, facilitated by the company secretary;

- take the lead in identifying and meeting the development needs of individual directors, with the company secretary having a key role in facilitating provision. It is the responsibility of the chairman to address the development needs of the board as a whole with a view to enhancing its overall effectiveness as a team;

- ensure that the performance of individuals and of the board as a whole and its committees is evaluated at least once a year; and

- encourage active engagement by all the members of the board.

## The effective chairman

- upholds the highest standards of integrity and probity;

- sets the agenda, style and tone of board discussions to promote effective decision-making and constructive debate;

- promotes effective relationships and open communication, both inside and outside the boardroom, between non-executive directors and executive team;

- builds an effective and complementary board, initiating change and planning succession in board appointments, subject to board and shareholders' approval;

- promotes the highest standards of corporate governance and seeks compliance with the provisions of the Code wherever possible;

- ensures clear structure for and the effective running of board committees;

- ensures effective implementation of board decisions;

- establishes a close relationship of trust with the chief executive, providing support and advice while respecting executive responsibility; and

- provides coherent leadership of the company, including representing the company and understanding the views of shareholders.

## Guidance On The Role Of The Non-Executive Director

As members of the unitary board, all directors are required to:

- Provide entrepreneurial leadership of the company within a framework of prudent and effective controls which enable risk to be assessed and managed;

- Set the company's strategic aims, ensure that the necessary financial and human resources are in place for the company to meet its objectives, and review management performance; and

- Set the company's values and standards and ensure that its obligations to its shareholders and others are understood and met.

In addition to these requirements for all directors, the role of the non-executive director has the following key elements:

- **Strategy.** Non-executive directors should constructively challenge and help develop proposals on strategy.

- **Performance.** Non-executive directors should scrutinise the performance of management in meeting agreed goals and objectives and monitor the reporting of performance.

- **Risk.** Non-executive directors should satisfy themselves on the integrity of financial information and that financial controls and systems of risk management are robust and defensible.

- **People.** Non-executive directors are responsible for determining appropriate levels of remuneration of executive directors, and have a prime role in appointing, and where necessary removing, executive directors and in succession planning.

Non-executive directors should constantly seek to establish and maintain confidence in the conduct of the company. They should be independent in judgement and have an enquiring mind. To be effective, non-executive directors need to build a recognition by executives of their contribution in order to promote openness and trust.

To be effective, non-executive directors need to be well-informed about the company and the external environment in which it operates, with a strong command of issues relevant to the business. A non-executive director should insist on a comprehensive, formal and tailored induction. An effective induction need not be restricted to the boardroom, so consideration should be given to visiting sites and meeting senior and middle management. Once in post, an effective non-executive director should seek continually to develop and refresh their knowledge and skills to ensure that their contribution to the board remains informed and relevant.

Best practice dictates that an effective non-executive director will ensure that information is provided sufficiently in advance of meetings to enable thorough consideration of the issues facing the board. The non-executive should insist that information is sufficient, accurate, clear and timely.

An element of the role of the non-executive director is to understand the views of major investors both directly and through the chairman and the senior independent director.

## The effective non-executive director

- upholds the highest ethical standards of integrity and probity;

- supports executives in their leadership of the business while monitoring their conduct;

- questions intelligently, debates constructively, challenges rigorously and decides dispassionately;

- listens sensitively to the views of others, inside and outside the board;

- gains the trust and respect of other board members; and

- promotes the highest standards of corporate governance and seeks compliance with the provisions of the Code wherever possible.

# Summary Of The Principal Duties Of The Remuneration Committee

The Code provides that the remuneration committee should consist exclusively of independent non-executive directors and should comprise at least three or, in the case of smaller companies[1], two such directors.

## Duties

The committee should:

- determine and agree with the board the framework or broad policy for the remuneration of the chief executive, the chairman of the company and such other members of the executive management as it is designated to consider[2]. At a minimum, the committee should have delegated responsibility for setting remuneration for all executive directors, the chairman and, to maintain and assure their independence, the company secretary. The remuneration of non-executive directors shall be a matter for the chairman and executive members of the board. No director or manager should be involved in any decisions as to their own remuneration;

- determine targets for any performance-related pay schemes operated by the company;

- determine the policy for and scope of pension arrangements for each executive director;

- ensure that contractual terms on termination, and any payments made, are fair to the individual and the company, that failure is not rewarded and that the duty to mitigate loss is fully recognised[3];

- within the terms of the agreed policy, determine the total individual remuneration package of each executive director including, where appropriate, bonuses, incentive payments and share options;

- in determining such packages and arrangements, give due regard to the contents of the Code as well as the UK Listing Authority's Listing Rules and associated guidance;

- be aware of and advise on any major changes in employee benefit structures throughout the company or group;

- agree the policy for authorising claims for expenses from the chief executive and chairman;

- ensure that provisions regarding disclosure of remuneration, including pensions, as set out in the Directors' Remuneration Report Regulations 2002 and the Code, are fulfilled;

- be exclusively responsible for establishing the selection criteria, selecting, appointing and setting the terms of reference for any remuneration consultants who advise the committee;

- report the frequency of, and attendance by members at, remuneration committee meetings in the annual reports; and make available the committee's terms of reference. These should set out the committee's delegated responsibilities and be reviewed and, where necessary, updated annually.

This guidance has been compiled with the assistance of ICSA who have kindly agreed to produce updated guidance on their website www.icsa.org.uk in the future.

# Summary Of The Principal Duties Of The Nomination Committee

There should be a nomination committee which should lead the process for board appointments and make recommendations to the board.

A majority of members of the committee should be independent non-executive directors. The chairman or an independent non-executive director should chair the committee, but the chairman should not chair the nomination committee when it is dealing with the appointment of a successor to the chairmanship.

## Duties

The committee should:

- be responsible for identifying and nominating for the approval of the board, candidates to fill board vacancies as and when they arise;

- before making an appointment, evaluate the balance of skills, knowledge and experience on the board and, in the light of this evaluation, prepare a description of the role and capabilities required for a particular appointment;

- review annually the time required from a non-executive director. Performance evaluation should be used to assess whether the non-executive director is spending enough time to fulfil their duties;

- consider candidates from a wide range of backgrounds and look beyond the "usual suspects";

- give full consideration to succession planning in the course of its work, taking into account the challenges and opportunities facing the company and what skills and expertise are therefore needed on the board in the future;

- regularly review the structure, size and composition (including the skills, knowledge and experience) of the board and make recommendations to the board with regard to any changes;

- keep under review the leadership needs of the organisation, both executive and non-executive, with a view to ensuring the continued ability of the organisation to compete effectively in the marketplace;

- make a statement in the annual report about its activities; the process used for appointments and explain if external advice or open advertising has not been used; the membership of the committee, number of committee meetings and attendance over the course of the year;

- make available its terms of reference explaining clearly its role and the authority delegated to it by the board; and

- ensure that on appointment to the board, non-executive directors receive a formal letter of appointment setting out clearly what is expected of them in terms of time commitment, committee service and involvement outside board meetings.

The committee should make recommendations to the board:

- as regards plans for succession for both executive and non-executive directors;

- as regards the re-appointment of any non-executive director at the conclusion of their specified term of office;

- concerning the re-election by shareholders of any director under the retirement by rotation provisions in the company's articles of association;

- concerning any matters relating to the continuation in office of any director at any time; and

- concerning the appointment of any director to executive or other office other than to the positions of chairman and chief executive, the recommendation for which would be considered at a meeting of the board.

This guidance has been compiled with the assistance of ICSA who have kindly agreed to produce updated guidance on their website www.icsa.org.uk in the future.

# Pre-Appointment Due Diligence Checklist For New Board Members

## Why?

Before accepting an appointment a prospective non-executive director should undertake their own thorough examination of the company to satisfy themselves that it is an organisation in which they can have faith and in which they will be well suited to working.

The following questions are not intended to be exhaustive, but are intended to be a helpful basis of the pre-appointment due diligence process that all non-executive directors should undertake.

## Questions to ask

What is the company's current financial position and what has its financial track record been over the last three years?

What are the key dependencies (e.g. regulatory approvals, key licences, etc)?

What record does the company have on corporate governance issues?

If the company is not performing particularly well is there potential to turn it round and do I have the time, desire and capability to make a positive impact?

What are the exact nature and extent of the company's business activities?

Who are the current executive and non-executive directors, what is their background and their record and how long have they served on the board?

What is the size and structure of the board and board committees and what are the relationships between the chairman and the board, the chief executive and the management team?

Who owns the company i.e. who are the company's main shareholders and how has the profile changed over recent years? What is the company's attitude towards, and relationship with, its shareholders?

Is any material litigation presently being undertaken or threatened, either by the company or against it?

Is the company clear and specific about the qualities, knowledge, skills and experience that it needs to complement the existing board?

What insurance cover is available to directors and what is the company's policy on indemnifying directors?

Do I have the necessary knowledge, skills, experience and time to make a positive contribution to the board of this company?

How closely do I match the job specification and how well will I fulfil the board's expectations?

Is there anything about the nature and extent of the company's business activities that would cause me concern both in terms of risk and any personal ethical considerations?

Am I satisfied that the internal regulation of the company is sound and that I can operate effectively within its stated corporate governance framework?

Am I satisfied that the size, structure and make-up of the board will enable me to make an effective contribution?

Would accepting the non-executive directorship put me in a position of having a conflict of interest?

## Sources of information

- Company report and accounts, and/or any listing prospectus, for the recent years.
- Analyst reports.
- Press reports
- Company web site
- Any Corporate Social Responsibility or Environmental Report issued by the company.

- Rating agency reports

- Voting services reports

- Published material is unlikely to reveal wrong-doing, however a lack of transparency may be a reason to proceed with caution.

This guidance has been compiled with the assistance of ICSA who have kindly agreed to produce updated guidance on their website www.icsa.org.uk in the future.

# Sample Letter Of Non-Executive Director Appointment

On [date], upon the recommendation of the nomination committee, the board of [company] ('the Company') has appointed you as non-executive director. I am writing to set out the terms of your appointment. It is agreed that this is a contract for services and is not a contract of employment.

## Appointment

Your appointment will be for an initial term of three years commencing on [date], unless otherwise terminated earlier by and at the discretion of either party upon [one month's] written notice. Continuation of your contract of appointment is contingent on satisfactory performance and re-election at forthcoming AGM's.

Non-executive directors are typically expected to serve two three-year terms, although the board may invite you to serve an additional period.

## Time commitment

Overall we anticipate a time commitment of [number] days per month after the induction phase. This will include attendance at [monthly] board meetings, the AGM, [one] annual board away day, and [at least one] site visit per year. In addition, you will be expected to devote appropriate preparation time ahead of each meeting.

By accepting this appointment, you have confirmed that you are able to allocate sufficient time to meet the expectations of your role. The agreement of the chairman should be sought before accepting additional commitments that might impact on the time you are able to devote to your role as a non-executive director of the company.

## Role

Non-executive directors have the same general legal responsibilities to the company as any other director. The board as a whole is collectively responsible for the success of the company. The board:

- Provides entrepreneurial leadership of the company within a framework of prudent and effective controls which enable risk to be assessed and managed;

- Sets the company's strategic aims, ensures that the necessary financial and human resources are in place for the company to meet its objectives, and reviews management performance; and

- Sets the company's values and standards and ensure that its obligations to its shareholders and others are understood and met.

All directors must take decisions objectively in the interests of the company.

In addition to these requirements of all directors, the role of the non-executive director has the following key elements:

- **Strategy.** Non-executive directors should constructively challenge and help develop proposals on strategy;

- **Performance.** Non-executive directors should scrutinise the performance of management in meeting agreed goals and objectives and monitor the reporting of performance;

- **Risk.** Non-executive directors should satisfy themselves on the integrity of financial information and that financial controls and systems of risk management are robust and defensible; and

- **People.** Non-executive directors are responsible for determining appropriate levels of remuneration of executive directors and have a prime role in appointing, and where necessary removing, executive directors and in succession planning.

## Fees

You will be paid a fee of £[amount] gross per annum which will be paid monthly in arrears, [plus [number] ordinary shares of the company per annum, both of] which will be subject to an annual review by the board. The company will reimburse you for all reasonable and properly documented expenses you incur in performing the duties of your office.

## Outside interests

It is accepted and acknowledged that you have business interests other than those of the company and have declared any conflicts that are apparent at present. In the event that you become aware of any potential conflicts of interest, these should be disclosed to the chairman and company secretary as soon as apparent.

[The board of the Company have determined you to be independent according to provision A.3.1 of the Code.]

## Confidentiality

All information acquired during your appointment is confidential to the Company and should not be released, either during your appointment or following termination (by whatever means), to third parties without prior clearance from the chairman.

Your attention is also drawn to the requirements under both legislation and regulation as to the disclosure of price sensitive information. Consequently you should avoid making any statements that might risk a breach of these requirements without prior clearance from the chairman or company secretary.

## Induction

Immediately after appointment, the Company will provide a comprehensive, formal and tailored induction. This will include the information pack recommended by the Institute of Chartered Secretaries and Administrators (ICSA), available at www.icsa.org.uk. We will also arrange for site visits and meetings with senior and middle management and the Company's auditors. We will also offer to major shareholders the opportunity to meet you.

## Review process

The performance of individual directors and the whole board and its committees is evaluated annually. If, in the interim, there are any matters which cause you concern about your role you should discuss them with the chairman as soon as is appropriate.

## Insurance

The Company has directors' and officers' liability insurance and it is intended to maintain such cover for the full term of your appointment. The current indemnity limit is £ [amount]; a copy of the policy document is attached.

## Independent professional advice

Occasions may arise when you consider that you need professional advice in the furtherance of your duties as a director. Circumstances may occur when it will be appropriate for you to seek advice from independent advisors at the company's expense. A copy of the board's agreed procedure under which directors may obtain such independent advice is attached. The Company will reimburse the full cost of expenditure incurred in accordance with the attached policy.

## Committees

This letter refers to your appointment as a non-executive director of the Company. In the event that you are also asked to serve on one or more of the board committees this will be covered in a separate communication setting out the committee(s)'s terms of reference, any specific responsibilities and any additional fees that may be involved.

This sample appointment letter has been complied with the assistance of ICSA who have kindly agreed to produce updated guidance on their website www.icsa.org.uk in the future.

# Induction Checklist

## Guidance on Induction

Every company should develop its own comprehensive, formal induction programme that is tailored to the needs of the company and individual non-executive directors. The following guidelines might form the core of an induction programme.

As a general rule, a combination of selected written information together with presentations and activities such as meetings and site visits will help to give a new appointee a balanced and real-life overview of the company. Care should be taken not to overload the new director with too much information. The new non-executive director should be provided with a list of all the induction information that is being made available to them so that they may call up items if required before otherwise provided.

The induction process should:

1.   Build an understanding of the **nature of the company, its business and the markets in which it operates**. For example, induction should cover:

   - the company's products or services;

   - group structure / subsidiaries /joint ventures;

   - the company's constitution, board procedures and matters reserved for the board;

   - summary details of the company's principal assets, liabilities, significant contracts and major competitors;

   - the company's major risks and risk management strategy;

   - key performance indicators; and

   - regulatory constraints.

2.   Build a link with the **company's people** including;

   - meetings with senior management;

   - visits to company sites other than the headquarters, to learn about production or services and meet employees in an informal setting. It is important, not only for the board to get to know the new non-executive director, but also for the non-executive director to build a profile with employees below board level; and

   - participating in board strategy development. 'Awaydays' enable a new non-executive director to begin to build working relationships away from the formal setting of the boardroom.

3.   Build an understanding of the **company's main relationships** including meeting with the auditors and developing a knowledge of in particular:

- who are the major customers;
- who are the major suppliers; and
- who are the major shareholders and what is the shareholder relations policy – participation in meetings with shareholders can help give a first hand feel as well as letting shareholders know who the non-executive directors are.

## The induction pack

On appointment, or during the weeks immediately following, a new non-executive director should be provided with certain basic information to help ensure their early effective contribution to the company. ICSA has produced, and undertaken to maintain, on their website www.icsa.org a guidance note detailing a full list of such material.

# Performance Evaluation Guidance

## Guidance on performance evaluation

The Code provides that the board should undertake a formal and rigorous annual evaluation of its own performance and that of its committees and individual directors. Individual evaluation should aim to show whether each director continues to contribute effectively and to demonstrate commitment to the role (including commitment of time for board and committee meetings and any other duties). The chairman should act on the results of the performance evaluation by recognising the strengths and addressing the weaknesses of the board and, where appropriate, proposing new members be appointed to the board or seeking the resignation of directors. The board should state in the annual report how such performance evaluation has been conducted.

It is the responsibility of the chairman to select an effective process and to act on its outcome. The use of an external third party to conduct the evaluation will bring objectivity to the process.

The non-executive directors, led by the senior independent director, should be responsible for performance evaluation of the chairman, taking into account the views of executive directors.

The evaluation process will be used constructively as a mechanism to improve board effectiveness, maximise strengths and tackle weaknesses. The results of board evaluation should be shared with the board as a whole while the results of individual assessments should remain confidential between the chairman and the non-executive director concerned.

The following are some of the questions that should be considered in a performance evaluation. They are, however, by no means definitive or exhaustive and companies will wish to tailor the questions to suit their own needs and circumstances.

The responses to these questions and others should enable boards to assess how they are performing and to identify how certain elements of their performance areas might be improved.

## Performance evaluation of the board

How well has the board performed against any performance objectives that have been set?

What has been the board's contribution to the testing and development of strategy?

What has been the board's contribution to ensuring robust and effective risk management?

Is the composition of the board and its committees appropriate, with the right mix of knowledge and skills to maximise performance in the light of future strategy? Are inside and outside the board relationships working effectively?

How has the board responded to any problems or crises that have emerged and could or should these have been foreseen?

Are the matters specifically reserved for the board the right ones?

How well does the board communicate with the management team, company employees and others? How effectively does it use mechanisms such as the AGM and the annual report?

Is the board as a whole up to date with latest developments in the regulatory environment and the market?

How effective are the board's committees? [Specific questions on the performance of each committee should be included such as, for example, their role, their composition and their interaction with the board.]

The processes that help underpin the board's effectiveness should also be evaluated e.g.:

- Is appropriate, timely information of the right length and quality provided to the board and is management responsive to requests for clarification or amplification? Does the board provide helpful feedback to management on its requirements?

- Are sufficient board and committee meetings of appropriate length held to enable proper consideration of issues? Is time used effectively?

- Are board procedures conducive to effective performance and flexible enough to deal with all eventualities?

In addition, there are some specific issues relating to the chairman which should be included as part of an evaluation of the board's performance e.g.:

- Is the chairman demonstrating effective leadership of the board?

- Are relationships and communications with shareholders well managed?

- Are relationships and communications within the board constructive?

- Are the processes for setting the agenda working? Do they enable board members to raise issues and concerns?

- Is the company secretary being used appropriately and to maximum value?

## Performance evaluation of the non-executive director

The chairman and other board members should consider the following issues and the individual concerned should also be asked to assess themselves. For each non-executive director:

- How well prepared and informed are they for board meetings and is their meeting attendance satisfactory?

- Do they demonstrate a willingness to devote time and effort to understand the company and its business and a readiness to participate in events outside the boardroom such as site visits?

- What has been the quality and value of their contributions at board meetings?

- What has been their contribution to development of strategy and to risk management?

- How successfully have they brought their knowledge and experience to bear in the consideration of strategy?

- How effectively have they probed to test information and assumptions? Where necessary, how resolute are they in maintaining their own views and resisting pressure from others?

- How effectively and proactively have they followed up their areas of concern?

- How effective and successful are their relationships with fellow board members, the company secretary and senior management?

- Does their performance and behaviour engender mutual trust and respect within the board?

- How actively and successfully do they refresh their knowledge and skills and are they up to date with:

  o the latest developments in areas such as corporate governance framework and financial reporting ?

  o the industry and market conditions?

- How well do they communicate with fellow board members, senior management and others, for example shareholders? Are they able to present their views convincingly yet diplomatically and do they listen and take on board the views of others?

**Notes**
1.  A smaller company is one that is below the FTSE 350 throughout the year immediately prior to the reporting year.
2.  Some companies require the remuneration committee to consider the packages of all executives at or above a specified level such as those reporting to a main board director whilst others require the committee to deal with all packages above a certain figure.
3.  Remuneration committees should consider reviewing and agreeing a standard form of contract for their executive directors, and ensuring that new appointees are offered and accept terms within the previously agreed level.

*Reproduced by kind permission of the copyright holder, the Financial Reporting Council. For more information on the Combined Code please call the Financial Reporting Council on 020 7611 9700.*

# Understanding the 2003 Combined Code

## Introduction                                                              A2.1

This Code was published by the Financial Reporting Council on 23 July 2003. The publication makes it clear that there will be no further consultation on the Code provisions themselves (we assume this also includes the Code's 'main principles' and the new 'supporting principles', not just the 'provisions' ) but that there is to be consultation on the consequential Listing Rules changes.

## Transitional arrangements                                                 A2.2

It is likely that the consultation on the rule changes may introduce transitional arrangements for implementing this revised Code, but the intention of the FRC is that it will apply to companies reporting for years beginning on or after 1 November 2003. So there is only a short lead-in period. Without transitional arrangements this may be inadequate time for companies to put in place changes to bring their practices in alignment with the 2003 Code in time for their reports for the year ended 31 December 2004 – particularly in those cases where the arrangements must have been in place for the whole of the year being reported. The new 2003 Combined Code publication does not discuss which parts of the new Combined Code must be observed for the whole of the year being reported. One case in point is the Code's provision A.3.2 that FTSE 350 company boards should, excluding the chairman, comprise at least 50% independent directors while smaller companies should have at least two independent directors. The lead time for some companies to come in line with this provision will undoubtedly be long. It is this provision in part which has led to suggestions that it will be necessary to widen the gene pool from which independent directors are recruited and resulted in the DTI commissioning the Tyson report[1], which has just been published.

## Background to the new Combined Code                                       A2.3

This new version replaces the original Combined Code which was published in June 1998. The original Combined Code was so-called because it combined the Cadbury (1992) and Greenbury (1995) Codes with the modifications and additions that the Hampel Committee had decided upon, all of which the Stock Exchange then adopted. The 2003 Combined Code carries forward the 1998 Combined Code and makes amendments to reflect the Higgs[2] (January 2003) and Smith[3] (January 2003) recommended code changes – as adjusted by the Financial Reporting Council (FRC) after consultation. The FRC now has oversight of the Code, although not of its enforcement. To the extent that there is any regulatory enforcement of the Code, it is the responsibility of the Financial Services Authority (FSA). However, it is not clear that there is any regulatory enforcement either of the principles and supporting principles (both of which are expressed in the listing rules in a way which suggests they are mandatory) nor of the provisions (which the listing rules apply to companies on a 'comply or explain' basis. We give the listing rule below.

The 23 July 2003 publication has some rough edges. For instance the Turnbull Report, which is part of it, still uses the reference numbering which applied to the listing of principles and provisions within the 1998 Combined Code. We presume this will be ironed out in time.

# Fundamental changes in the 2003 Combined Code

**A2.4**

Apart from the considerable significance of some of the changes and additions to the principles and provisions (which we identify and discuss at **A2.7** below), there are three notable departures in style from the original Combined Code.

First, the scale of the 2003 Code is much greater. The 19 'comply or explain' provisions in the 1992 Cadbury Code had grown to 17 principles and 47 provisions in the 1998 Combined Code and have now reached the level of 43 principles (including supporting principles) and 48 provisions in the 2003 Code. Indeed, this is an underestimate of the growing burden as it excludes:

(a)  the seven Schedule A Provisions on the design of performance related remuneration which were part of the Combined Code and continue in the revised Combined Code; and

(b)  the seven Schedule B Provisions on what should be included in the Remuneration Report, which were part of the Combined Code but are not included in the revised Combined Code as there are now separate regulations in force (the *Directors' Remuneration Report Regulations 2002 (SI 2002/1986)*) which supersede the earlier Code provisions.

(See also **B2.1** SHORT HISTORY OF CORPORATE GOVERNANCE DEVELOPMENTS and Table B at **B2.8**.)

Secondly, there is the introduction for the first time of 'supporting principles' nesting between 'main principles' and 'provisions'. The 2003 publication tells us that the part of the listing rule which applies to 'principles' (ie '(a)' below) is to apply to both main and supporting principles, and that '(b)' (below) continues to apply to 'provisions' viz:

'12.43A In the case of a company incorporated in the United Kingdom, the following additional items must be included in its annual report and accounts:

(a)  'A narrative statement of how it has applied the principles set out in Section 1 of the Combined Code, providing sufficient explanation which enables its shareholders to evaluate how the principles have been applied;

(b) 'a statement as to whether or not it has complied throughout the accounting period with the provisions set out in Section 1 of the Combined Code. A company that has not complied with the Code provisions, or complied with only some of the Code provisions or (in the case of provisions whose requirements are of a continuing nature) complied for only part of an accounting period, must specify the provisions with which it has not complied, and (where relevant) for what part of the period such non-compliance continued, and give reasons for any non-compliance; ... '

There is thus no difference in the nature of the obligation of UK listed companies to observe the new category of supporting principles and their obligation with respect to the main principles. Notwithstanding that 'supporting principles' have been given the same status as 'main principles', presentationally at least they tend to assist in making the 2003 Code appear less onerous than might otherwise be the case. It is the case that since 1998 boards have been challenged much more over non-compliance with provisions than for failing to apply principles: it has proved easier for institutional investors to box-tick company compliance with provisions than to box-tick whether the principles are being applied. So, classifying some aspects of the new Code as 'supporting principles' rather than as 'provisions' takes some pressure off boards, notwithstanding the apparent more compulsory character of principles, per the listing rule – whether main or supporting.

Thirdly, the publication now not only includes the Code itself but also the two reports which provide guidance on implementing certain aspects of the Code (the Turnbull and Smith Reports) as well as some of the useful annexes from the Higgs Report. Curiously the guidance on complying with the going concern provision, published at about the same time as the Turnbull report, is not part of the publication – whether by intent or, we suspect, oversight. The useful appendices of the Smith report are also not included.

# Status of the Turnbull and Smith reports    A2.5

Since publication of the Turnbull Report compliance in full with all of the guidance therein has been a prerequisite if compliance with the associated parts of the Code is to be claimed.[4] If that is still the case, then the content of the Turnbull report could be regarded as comprising 'supporting principles' and/or 'supporting provisions'. However, the latter phrase is never used, and neither does the FRC refer to the Turnbull report as containing 'supporting principles'. The status of the Turnbull guidance is now ambiguous. The Stock Exchange's 1998 foreword to the original Turnbull Report had said:

'We consider that compliance with the guidance will constitute compliance with Combined Code provisions D.2.1 and D.2.2 and provide appropriate narrative disclosure of how Code principle D.2 has been applied.'

and paragraph 7 of the preamble to the Turnbull Report has always said (and continues to do so in the 2003 Combined Code version):

'The guidance in this document should be followed by boards of listed companies in:

- assessing how the company has applied Code principle D.2;
- implementing the requirements of Code provisions D.2.1 and D.2.2; and
- reporting on these matters to shareholders in the annual report and accounts.'

[the numbering of the provisions in the above quotation is the numbering which applied in the 1998 Code.]

The version of the Smith Report which appears within the 2003 Combined Code publication has been watered down in the sense that none of its guidance is expressed as being guidance which 'should' be followed. In the original Smith Report those parts which the Smith Committee regarded should be obligatory for compliance with the Code to be claimed had been printed in bold, with the following explanation to convey their status:

'This guidance includes certain essential requirements that every audit committee should meet. These requirements are presented in **bold** in the text. Compliance with these is necessary for compliance with the Code. Listed companies that do not comply with these requirements should include an explanation as to why they have not complied with these requirements in the statement required by the Listing Rules.'[5]

The bolding has been removed, as has the above quotation, from, the version of the Smith Report contained in the 2003 Combined Code publication. Some but not all of this bold text has been promoted by the FRC so that it is now in the 2003 Code itself. One example where this is not so is the Smith intention that:

'The chairman of the company should not be an audit committee member.'[6]

As an example of placating concerned chairmen of companies (a theme running through the FRC's editing), the nearest the new Code gets to concurring with this sentiment is an A.3 supporting principle which reads:

'The value of ensuring that committee membership is refreshed and that undue reliance is not placed on particular individuals should be taken into account in deciding chairmanship and membership of committees.'

As an aside, this example does also illustrate the importance of taking the Code as a whole. Principles and provisions relevant to, for instance, audit committees are not repeated within the audit committees section of the Code if they have already been stated elsewhere in the Code.

Except where now in the new 2003 Code, the implication must be that the FRC regards those parts of the Smith report previously in bold to be discretionary with regard to compliance with the associated provisions in the Combined Code.

So, we are left with the conundrum of discerning whether the Turnbull guidance has a different and higher status than the Smith guidance, or whether the former should now be regarded as having the lesser status of the latter. In support of the latter interpretation, the preamble to the 2003 Combined Code merely states that:

> 'In both cases [Turnbull and Smith] the guidance suggests ways of applying the relevant Code principles and of complying with the relevant Code provisions.' [7]

# FRC addresses opposition to the Higgs report    A2.6

The opposition to Higgs' proposals, and to a lesser extent those of Smith as well, had three main thrusts:

- Although technically the provisions have a 'comply or explain' status, the over-simplistic perception of outside parties (especially institutional investors) that non-compliance means poor corporate governance, has meant that there has been excessive and often counter-productive pressure upon companies to comply. The Hampel Committee's intention of building flexibility into the Code so that one Code could be used by companies in all circumstances and of all sizes has thus been compromised.

- The proposed strengthening of the Code in relation to avoiding excessive concentration of power at the top of the business, had the effect of making it harder for the chairman of a company to run the board.

- The remorseless growth in size of the Code threatened to deflect the focus of boards from responsibilities other than corporate governance.

The preamble to the revised Code attempts to address the first two of these concerns, stressing that while it is expected that listed companies will comply with the Code's provisions most of the time, it is recognised that departure from the provisions may be justified in particular circumstances, and that smaller companies, and in particular those new to listing, may judge that some of the provisions are disproportionate or less relevant in their case. It is helpful that the FRC stresses that companies making an IPO should not necessarily be expected to have in place all the aspects of the Combined Code. Indeed the Code itself in places applies different standards to companies of different sizes, for instance:

- small companies comply with the Code if they have two independent directors, rather than 50% of the board excluding the chairman (A.3.2);

- an executive director may have only one FTSE 100 non-executive directorship and should not chair a FTSE 100 board;

- small companies comply if their remuneration and audit committees have at least two, not three, members (B.2.1 and C.3.1 respectively).

The Preamble states that every company must review each provision carefully and give a considered explanation if it departs from any Code provisions.

The corollary of this is that shareholders, particularly institutional investors evaluate a company's governance …

> 'with common sense in order to promote partnership and trust, based on mutual understanding [and not] in a mechanistic way and departures from the Code should not be automatically treated as breaches. … Institutional shareholders and their agents should be careful to respond to the statements from companies in a manner that supports the 'comply or explain' principle … They should put their views to the company and be prepared to enter a dialogue if they do not accept the company's position. Institutional shareholders should be prepared to put such views in writing where appropriate.'[8]

In essence, what is good for the goose is good for the gander. Boards are responsible for good governance and must account for how they are discharging their responsibility. But by the same token, institutional investors are responsible for the judgements they come to about companies and should also be held accountable. Responsibility without accountability tends to engender irresponsibility – whether by companies, institutional investors or by pressure groups.

The preamble to the 2003 Code sounds a note of warning that:

> 'Nothing in this Code should be taken to override the general requirements of law to treat shareholders equally in access to information.' [9]

Higgs has said that he believes that his report's the principal contribution to good governance is likely to be the effect it has on evaluating board, board committee and individual director performance. Perhaps the next significant development in governance which is needed is to iron out the potential conflicts which exist in terms of access to information. Company briefings of analysts and major shareholders almost inevitably put those parties in pole position to act ahead of small shareholders who do not have that access. When major shareholders (whether family or financial institutions) or providers of debt capital have their nominees of the board, again there are challenges. Is it acceptable for a nominee director to consult the party who nominated him or her with respect to how to vote at the board? A supporting principle in the 2003 Combined Code states:

> 'All directors must take decisions objectively in the interests of the company.'[10]

Is it acceptable for the nominee director to feed back information about the company to the party who nominated him or her? If so, how does this square with treating shareholders equally in access to information?

# Changes within the 2003 Combined Code compared to the 1998 Code A2.7

We have already discussed the modification of the Code's structure to include not only main 'principles' and 'provisions' but also 'supporting principles', allowing companies greater flexibility in how they implement the Code. KPMG has complained about this, on the grounds that it is likely to result in huge swathes of disclosure in company accounts:

> 'One has to question whether it will provide a meaningful insight into how each organisation is governed, if investors will read it, and whether it will influence company behaviour?'

Apart from that, the two most profound effects of the 2003 Code are likely to be the clarification the role of the chairman vis à vis the board as a whole and the non-executive directors in particular; and secondly the effect of the new Code on introducing more formal evaluations of board, board committee and individual director performance. In the rest of this chapter we highlight some of the main developments in the new 2003 Code, and focus on adjustments made by the FRC to Higgs' original proposals.

## Duties of directors A2.8

The Code now has a supporting principle (A.1) that all directors must take decisions objectively in the interests of the company. Higgs had proposed this as a provision.[11] While this does nothing to alter the duties of directors, it is helpful that the Code now refers to this. The interests of the company may not always equate to the interest of maximizing share value, nor to the interests of majority shareholders, nor the executive interests of particular directors.

Another duty of a director is covered where the new Code includes (as D.2.3) the 1998 provision C.2.3 that the chairman of the board should arrange for the chairmen of the audit, remuneration and nomination committees to be available to answer questions at the AGM. Whereas Higgs had proposed, perhaps by oversight, that this be extended to include that the chairman should arrange for all non-executive directors to attend the AGM, the final wording rightly broadens this to 'all directors'. Since it has been the provisions rather than the principles that have caused most of the problems in the past, it is significant that we now have this additional provision that the chairman will arrange for the directors to attend the AGM. While, as previously, the chairs of these three committees are to be available to answer questions at the AGM, we believe it remains the case that questions are asked at the AGM of the chairman of the board who then determines whether to answer them personally or to divert them to someone else of his/her choosing to be answered – notwithstanding the questioner's intention perhaps that the question should be answered by a particular director who chairs a board committee. The 1998 Hampel Report had this to say:

> 'Cadbury recommended that the chairman of the audit committee should be available to answer questions about its work at the AGM (report,

Appendix 4, paragraph 6(f)), and Greenbury made a similar recommendation relating to the chairman of the remuneration committee (code, A8). It was suggested to us that the chairman of the nomination committee should make himself available in the same way. We believe that it should be for the chairman of the meeting to decide which questions to answer himself and which to refer to a colleague; but in general we would expect the chairman of the three committees to be available to answer questions at the AGM.' [12]

Higgs has proposed[13] that:

'Where they have concerns about the way in which a company is being run or about a course of action being proposed by the board, directors should ensure that their concerns are recorded in the board minutes if they cannot be resolved. A written statement should be provided to the chairman, for circulation to the board, setting out the reasons where a non-executive director resigns'

and the final Code adds the words (2003 Code provision A.1.4):

'if they have any such concerns'

## Clarification of the role of the chairman vis-à-vis the non-executive directors                                                    A2.9

Much of the debate over the Higgs proposals centred on the respective responsibilities of the chairman and the other directors. Some chairmen were concerned that the Higgs proposals would, if implemented, undermine their authority and make it more difficult for them to discharge their responsibilities to run the board. (The new Code stipulation that the chairman arranges for all directors to attend the AGM is, however, an example of enhancing the chairman's authority over the board.)

Notwithstanding the much publicised concerns of many company chairmen, most of Higgs' proposals in this area have survived into the new Code. In the debate it was largely overlooked that the 1992 Cadbury Code had already established the role of the 'senior non-executive director' when the posts of chairman and chief executive were combined, and that the 1998 Code had specified the senior non-executive director position as appropriate even when these two roles were separated.[14]

The objections to Higgs in this area were largely to do with Higgs proposals that:

● the chairman of the company should not chair the nominations committee;

● the senior non-executive director should convene regular meetings with the other non-executive directors without the chairman of the board being present;

● the senior non-executive director should communicate the views of institutional investors to the other non-executive directors.

## The senior and other non-executive directors and institutional investors A2.10

'Hermes' guide for shareholders and independent outside directors' (see **B10.79**) has some useful advice on the role of the senior independent director.

There is still a requirement that the senior independent director should be identified in the annual report (provision A.1.1) and the substance of Higgs' further proposal has survived in provision A.3.3 which includes the words:

'The senior independent director should be available to shareholders if they have concerns which contact through the normal channels of chairman, chief executive or finance director has failed to resolve or for which such contact is inappropriate'.

The FRC had added 'finance director' to Higgs' draft.

Provision D.1.1 of the 2003 has been toned down to include the words:

'The senior independent director should attend sufficient regular meetings of management with a range of major shareholders to develop a balanced understanding of the themes, issues and concerns of shareholders'.

Higgs' proposal that:

'the senior independent director should communicate these views to the non-executive directors and, as appropriate, to the board as a whole'

has been removed and it is now the chairman who ...

'should ensure that the views of shareholders are communicated to the board as a whole.'

Higgs' proposed provision wording has survived in regard that ...

'non-executive directors should be able to attend regular meetings with major investors and should expect to attend them if requested by major shareholders.'

A supporting principle of the new Code (D.1) now reads:

'The board should keep in touch with shareholder opinion in whatever ways are most practical and efficient.'

and the related main principle on 'Dialogue with institutional investors' includes the words:

'The board as a whole has responsibility for ensuring that a satisfactory dialogue with shareholders takes place'

and provision D.1.2 now reads (with the bold words added by the FRC to Higgs' original proposal):

'Boards should state in the annual report the steps they have taken to ensure that the members of the board, and in particular the non-executive directors, develop an understanding of the views of major investors, **for example through direct face-to-face contact, analysts' or brokers' briefings and surveys of shareholder opinion.**'

Higgs' proposed provision C.1.3, which read:

'On appointment, non-executive directors should meet major investors, as part of the induction process.'

Has been changed to read, as part of provision A.5.1:

' ... the company should offer to major shareholders the opportunity to meet a new non-executive director.'

'Hermes' guide for shareholders and independent outside directors' (**B10.79**) has some useful advice on induction meetings and meetings subsequent to induction.

**Interfacing the chairman and the non-executive directors**　　　**A2.11**

Higgs suggested in provision B.2.5 that the remuneration committee should consult the chairman and/or chief executive about their proposals relating to the remuneration of other executive directors has survived but as a supporting principle (B.2). Whereas the Higgs proposal had been that:

'The non-executive directors should meet regularly as a group and at least once a year without the chairman present'[15]

new provision A.1.3 now reads:

'The chairman should hold meetings with the non-executive directors without the executives present. Led by the senior non-executive director, the non-executive directors should meet without the chairman being present at least annually to appraise the chairman's performance (as described in A.6.1) and on such other occasions as are deemed appropriate'

and there is a requirement that there should be a statement in the annual report on whether the non-executive directors have met without the chairman or executives present.

**Nomination committee**　　　**A2.12**

Whereas Higgs has allowed that the nomination committee might include the chairman of the board, Higgs' proposed provision would have meant that it would be chaired by an independent non-executive director (other than the chairman). The final 2003 Code has backed down from this, allowing only that (provision A.4.1):

'The chairman or an independent director should chair the committee but the chairman should not chair the nomination committee when it is dealing with the appointment of a successor to the chairmanship.'

Higgs' proposal that the terms of reference of the nomination committee should be made publicly available has been clarified by the addition of the words

'on request and by including the information on the company's website'

– wording used elsewhere in the 2003 Code – for instance with respect to terms and conditions of appointment of non-executive directors. Similarly, the remuneration committee should make publicly available its terms of reference (by request and on website), explaining its role and the authority delegated to it by the board. It is assumed that the word 'and' is intentional and that it is therefore intended that this information should always be available on a company's website.

Whereas Higgs proposed that the nomination committee should set out in the letter of appointment the time and responsibility (including in relation to chairmanship or membership of board committees or as the senior independent director) envisaged in the appointment of a non-executive director, the words 'and responsibility' have not survived. The Higgs' suggestion that a new non-executive director's other commitments should be disclosed to the company has been tightened to require that the disclosure is to the board itself.

The Higgs' intended requirement that the nomination committee explain in the annual report if external advice or open advertising has not been used has been restricted in the final 2003 Code to the appointment of a chairman or a non-executive director.

## Chief executives may exceptionally go on to become chairmen                                                     A2.13

The final 2003 Code has persevered with Higgs' proposal that a chief executive should not go on to become chairman of the same company, but has qualified this by adding the words:

> 'If exceptionally a board decides that a chief executive should become chairman, the board should consult major shareholders in advance and should set out its reasons to shareholders at the time of the appointment and in the next annual report.'

The 2003 Code (in provision A.2.2) has adopted Higgs' proposal that on appointment, the chairman should meet the independence criteria set by Higgs and incorporated into his suggested Code, and no changes have been made to those independence criteria which are within the 2003 Code.

## Smaller companies                                                     A2.14

The 2003 Code defines 'smaller listed companies' as those below the FTSE 350 and relaxes the rule on the number of independent non-executives to 'at least two' instead of 'at least 50% excluding the chairman'. Smaller companies also meet the 2003 Code requirements if they have two rather than three members of their remuneration and audit committees. Whereas the 1998 Combined Code allowed that the majority of members of the audit committee should be independent, now they all should be (as was previously the case, and continues to be the case, for remuneration committees; and as has been the case for some time in the US). Also following US practice, audit committees must now have at least one member with significant, recent and relevant financial experience. A supporting principle to A.3 states that only committee members are entitled to attend board committees but others may attend at the invitation of the committee.

## Remuneration of non-executive directors                          A2.15

Higgs intended the Code to state simply that remuneration for non-executive directors in The form of share options should be avoided, but the final Code has added (2003 Code provision B.1.3):

> 'If, exceptionally, options are granted, shareholder approval should be sought in advance and any shares acquired by exercise of the options should be held until at least one year after the non-executive director leaves the board. Holding of share options could be relevant to the determination of a director's independence.'

## Particularly rigorous review rather than special explanation when non-executive directors are re-elected beyond six years                                     A2.16

Higgs' intention with respect to the length of time that a non-executive director might serve, especially those whom the board relies upon to be independent, have survived largely intact. The wording is now (2003 Code provision A.7.2):

> 'Non-executive directors should be appointed for specified terms subject to re-election and to Companies Acts provisions relating to the removal of a director. The board should set out to shareholders in the papers accompanying a resolution to elect a non-executive director why they believe an individual should be elected. The chairman should confirm to shareholders when proposing re-election that, following formal performance evaluation, the individual's performance continues to be effective and to demonstrate commitment to the role. Any term beyond six years (e.g. two three-year terms) for a non-executive director should be subject to particularly rigorous review, and should take into account the need for progressive refreshing of the board. Non-executive directors may serve longer than nine years (e.g. three three-year terms), subject to annual re-election. Serving more than nine years could be relevant to the determination of a non-executive director's independence (as set out in provision A.3.1).'

## Changes to audit committee, internal control and internal audit aspects                                          A2.17

There is much more in the 2003 Code on audit committees than there was in the 1998 Code, reflecting to some extent the recommendations of the Smith Committee (which Higgs had incorporated into his proposed revised Code), and the US developing requirements under the *Sarbanes-Oxley Act 2002* and the draft NYSE corporate governance standards (see **B26** INTERNATIONAL DIMENSIONS). The wording of the principle on internal control remains unchanged from the 1998 Code, except for the addition of the word 'systems' to the end of the old Code provision D.2.1 on the directors' internal control review – so that it now reads 'risk management systems' rather than merely 'risk management'.

The other provision in the 1998 Code which was filed within the internal control part of that Code has now been moved to the audit committees part of the new Code, as provision C.3.5 which reads:

> 'The audit committee should monitor and review the effectiveness of the internal audit activities. Where there is no internal audit function, the audit committee should consider annually whether there is a need for an internal audit function and make a recommendation to the board, and the reasons for the absence of such a function should be explained in the relevant section of the annual report.'

The 1998 Code had no requirement for the board to publicly explain the reasons for not having an internal audit function, which idea first surfaced in the Smith Report.

The audit committee's responsibilities are stated as including:

- to review the company's internal financial control system;

- unless expressly addressed by a separate risk committee (the FRC has added in the final 2003 Code 'composed of independent directors' to Higgs' proposal on this) or by the board itself, to review the company's internal control and risk management systems (the FRC added in the final 2003 Code 'internal control' to Higgs' proposal);

- to monitor and review the effectiveness of the company's internal audit function;

- to make recommendations to the board in relation to the appointment of the external auditor and to approve the remuneration and terms of engagement of the external auditor (note the final 2003 Code wording is enhanced by the addition of the word 'removal' and the addition to the Code of provision C.3.6 which reads:

  > 'The audit committee should have primary responsibility for making a recommendation on the appointment and removal of the external auditors. If the board does not accept the audit committee's recommendation, it should include in the annual report, and in any papers recommending appointment or re-appointment, a statement from the audit committee explaining the recommendation and should set out reasons why the board has taken a different position.'

- to monitor and review the external auditor's independence, objectivity and effectiveness, taking into consideration relevant UK professional and regulatory requirements;

- to develop and implement policy on the engagement of the external auditor to supply non-audit services, taking into account relevant ethical guidance regarding the provision of non-audit services by the external audit firm. The following wording has been added by the FRC beyond what appeared in Higgs' proposed code:

  'and to report to the board, identifying any matters in respect of which it considers action or improvement is needed and making recommendations as to the steps to be taken.'

Although not in the audit committees section of the 2003 Code, provision A.5.2 states that the audit committee should be provided with sufficient resources to undertake its duties. Similarly provision C.3.3 now carries the requirement that the annual report should contain a separate section that describes the role and responsibilities of the committee and the actions taken by the committee to discharge those responsibilities and also states that the committee's terms of reference should be made available.

As we mentioned earlier, the 2003 Code includes, as provision D.2.3, that the chairman of the board should arrange for the chairman of the audit committee to be present at the AGM to answer questions.

## More formal evaluations of board, board committee and individual director performance                                          A2.18

Derek Higgs has volunteered that he considers the new material within the 2003 Code on performance evaluation could represent the single largest contribution to corporate governance best practice to be made by the new Code. Performance evaluation is expressed in the new Code as a requisite to be applied to the board as a whole, to its committees and to individual directors. The main principle reads:

'The board should undertake a formal and rigorous annual evaluation of its own performance and that of its committees and individual directors'

and the supporting principle:

'Individual evaluation should aim to show whether each director continues to contribute effectively and to demonstrate commitment to the role (including commitment of time for board and committee meetings and any other duties). The chairman should act on the results of the performance evaluation by recognising the strengths and addressing the weaknesses of the board and, where appropriate, proposing new members be appointed to the board or seeking the resignation of directors.'

2003 Code Provision A.6.1 reads:

'The board should state in the annual report how performance evaluation of the board, its committees and its individual directors has been conducted. The non-executive directors, led by the senior independent director, should be responsible for performance evaluation of the chairman, taking into account the views of executive directors.'

The FRC has added to the 2003 Code that no director should be re-elected unless continuing to perform satisfactorily, and that ...

'the chairman should confirm to shareholders when proposing re-election that, following formal performance evaluation, the individual's performance continues to be effective and to demonstrate commitment to the role. Any term of appointment beyond six years (e.g. two three-year terms) for a non-executive director should be subject to particularly rigorous review.'

1.  The Tyson Report on the Recruitment and Development of Non-Executive Directors, (June 2003), A report commissioned by the Department of Trade & Industry following the publication of the Higgs Review of the Role and Effectiveness of Non-Executive Directors in January 2003. Laura Tyson is Dean of London Business School. Information on the Higgs Review and the Tyson Report can be accessed at www.dti.gov.uk/cld/non_exec_review and www.london.edu
2.  'Review of the Role and Effectiveness of Non-executive Directors'. The report as well as full details of the research conducted, can be downloaded from www.dti.gov.uk/cld/non_exec_review
3.  Audit Committees Combined Code Guidance – a report and proposed guidance by an FRC-appointed committee chaired by Sir. Robert Smith. The report (modified slightly for consistency with the final revised Combined Code) is now part of the expanded Combined Code publication which is reproduced as Part 1 of this Handbook. The original version of The Smith report can be downloaded from www.frs.org.uk/publications/content/ACReport.pdf
4.  Old Principle D.2 and old Provisions D.2.1 and D.2.2 (now new Principle C.2 and Provisions C.2.1 and C.3.5. Both these provisions have been amended in the new Code, in the latter case extended, but the Turnbull guidance continues unchanged.
5.  Section 1.2 of the original Smith report (not in the version which is incorporated into the 2003 Combined Code publication.).
6.  Section 3.2 on p6 of the Smith report.
7.  Preamble, section 9.
8.  Preamble, section 7.
9.  Preamble, section 8.
10.  Under main principle A.1
11.  Higgs, provision A.3.3
12.  Committee On Corporate Governance – The Hampel Committee (January 1998), Final Report, chaired by Sir Ronald Hampel (Gee Publishing, London), ISBN 1 86089 034 2, para. 5.19.
13.  Higgs provision A.1.6
14.  Code Provision A.2.1 of the 1998 Code had read:
15.  'A decision to combine the posts of chairman and chief executive officer in one person should be publicly justified. Whether the posts are held by different people or the same person, there should be a strong and independent non-executive element on the board, with a recognised senior member other than the chairman to whom concerns can be conveyed. The chairman, chief executive and senior independent director should be identified in the annual report.'
16.  Higgs proposed provision A.1.5

# Introduction

## Introduction B1.1

'The proper governance of companies will become as crucial to the world economies as the proper governing of countries.'
*(James D. Wolfensohn, President of the World Bank, c. 1999)*

'There is one and only one social responsibility of business – to use its resources and engage in activities designed to increase its profits so long as it stays within the rules of the game ... '
*(Milton Friedman)*

Even Milton Friedman, the arch-advocate of companies concentrating solely on maximising the return to their shareholders, makes the important qualification that they should stay within the rules of the game – a qualification often omitted when Friedman is quoted. He explains in the same article that, by the rules of the game, he means

'the basic rules of society, both those embodied in law and those embodied in ethical custom'.

It is more straightforward to show that failures of corporate governance are associated with adverse outcomes than to demonstrate that higher standards of corporate governance contribute significantly to corporate success.

It is invariably possible to point the finger at shortcomings in the corporate governance of an entity which has got itself into difficulties – not least because it is axiomatic in such a case that the system of corporate governance has not succeeded in delivering success. Corporate governance is now so broadly defined as to make it unlikely that deficiencies in corporate governance would not be involved when entities decline or collapse – and this will appear so particularly with the wisdom of hindsight.

## Spectacular collapses B1.2

It is significant that the contemporary focus on corporate governance in the UK had its genesis in the spectacular collapses of listed companies – for instance London & Commonwealth, Poly Peck, BCCI and Maxwell – the last two being mentioned by name in the Preface to the Cadbury Report[1]. The US Treadway Report[2], which came five years earlier than the Cadbury Report, was commissioned through concern about the fraudulent financial reporting of Wall Street listed companies. The common ground behind Cadbury and Treadway was, therefore, in the main, deceitful, untrustworthy, unreliable top managements and boards, or as Cadbury put it more diplomatically:

'It is, however, the continuing concern about standards of financial reporting and accountability, heightened by BCCI, Maxwell and the controversy over directors' pay, which has kept corporate governance in the public eye.'

*(Cadbury Report, Preface, p9)*

It is arguable that the UK's focus for more than a decade on better corporate governance has assisted the UK to weather the economic storms of the current economic downturn more effectively than did the UK in the late 1980s/early 1990s. With the new version of the Combined Code released by the Financial Reporting Council on 23 July 2003, the UK now has its 'Mark III' Code, whereas the US, in the wake of Enron etc, now has its first version of corporate governance standards – though only in draft form.

| UK | Mark I | Cadbury (1 December 1992) and Greenbury (17 July 1995) |
|----|--------|---|
| | Mark II | Combined Code (June 1998) |
| | Mark III | Combined Code (revised by FRC) (23 July 2003) and The Turnbull Report (September 1999) |

| US | Mark I | NYSE Corporate Governance rule proposals to SEC (16 August 2002); amended proposals published 4 April 2003 (www.nyse.com) and still not adopted by October 2003.(SEC rules implementing parts of the Sarbanes-Oxley Act (2002) also address particular aspects of corporate governance) |
|----|--------|---|

It is tempting to speculate that the recent avoidance by the UK of spectacular corporate collapses like Enron, WorldCom and Tyco is attributable to a quite long term, more balanced, mature approach to corporate governance within the UK. Against this needs to be set the obvious scope for more spectacular corporate debacles in the US where the size of businesses tends to be much greater. Neither can it be claimed that the UK has emerged entirely unscathed. Marconi is a case in point. But, if it is possible to make the distinction, Marconi was more a failure of the board with respect to *strategy* whereas the US failures have been a repeat of the old fashioned (1980s and 1990s) failures of *internal control* allowing rampant fraudulent financial reporting by deceitful top management teams to go unchecked for long periods of time. However, recently in the UK, lesser entities such as Independent Insurance and Claims Direct have failed through fundamental weaknesses in internal control.

## Good governance as a driver of corporate success B1.3

When corporations succeed brilliantly there is not the same incentive to attribute the success to exemplary corporate governance. Indeed, in such cases, protective corporate governance mechanisms, such as the assertiveness of the outside directors, will most probably not have been needed to be activated so obviously. There will have been other causes of success, apart from what we usually regard as 'good corporate governance' – such as technological innovation, changes in the environment, effective strategy, world class management, and so on. But the positioning of the entity to develop and exploit these competitive advantages is to do with good corporate governance.

There is also the conundrum that a successful company is better placed to invest in high standards of corporate governance. It is often only when its circumstances change and the company finds it has its back to the wall that these quality corporate governance mechanisms will be tested. A failing company may feel it has neither the time nor the energy, nor the resources to devote to improving its corporate governance processes – as it focuses single-mindedly on turning the company round. It is this conundrum which has led some to claim that audit committees work best in well-run companies which need them least, and are less likely to work well in the poorly-run companies who need them most. A less extreme view is that it is best to set up an audit committee before the bad times arrive, so that the committee is well-placed to ensure that the company does not sail close to the wind when it is later tempted to do so. The same prudent approach should be applied to other aspects of corporate governance best practice; it is wise to establish effective mechanisms of corporate governance during the good times – not merely to encourage excellence and to avoid mistakes, but so that the bulwarks are in place in anticipation of the possibility that the business may enter harder times when it could be tempted into disreputable decisions and practices in order to paper over the cracks rather than to correct the fundamentals. So good corporate governance is a means of more effectively achieving corporate objectives and a safeguard against future corporate malaise.

The efficacy of corporate governance has been suggested by studies which compare the market capitalisation of companies with similar fundamentals operating in economies with differing standards of corporate governance. It has been shown that market capitalisation is likely to be many times greater for companies in economies noted for high standards of corporate governance – not least for the greater confidence this gives to investors. But again, is it the better corporate governance that results in the higher market capitalisation, or is it the lower cost of capital which provides the opportunities for entities to invest in better corporate governance? In economies where corporate governance is a jungle, higher standards of corporate governance in one company might not contribute to corporate survival when pitted against the less impressive business practices of the local competition.

## Correlating corporate performance with corporate conformance B1.4

Dulewicz and Herbert[3] found scant support for the more prominent theories of the board with respect to better corporate governance contributing to better corporate performance. They found no relationship between company financial performance[4] and the proportion of NEDs, the tenure of NEDs or the existence of audit and remuneration committees. Sales turnover tended to grow more slowly when there were more NEDs both as a proportion of the board and in absolute numbers. However they found that companies with a non-executive chairman separate from the CEO tended to perform better, as did companies with more executive directors and companies whose directors owned more shares.

These results support the UK corporate governance best practice of separating the chairman's role (which role they characterise as being 'pivotal') from that of the chief executive and ensuring that the chairman is non-executive. But, at least in terms of company performance, the results question the perceived 'best practice' of perhaps half the board being non-executive and for their tenure as well as their personal shareholdings to be limited.

Dulewicz and Herbert acknowledge that some corporate governance best practice may have an 'accountability' rather than a 'performance' purpose. We would say that, for instance, audit and remuneration committees are justified, in part at least, as tools of accountability. But in principle, better accountability should reduce the costs of capital (as investors have more confidence to invest capital). Lower costs of capital in turn should contribute to better financial performance, but there is nothing in Dulwicz and Herbert's study to show that this occurs. However, we should not overlook that all of their sample were UK companies: differences in accountability practices are more stark between countries than between companies within one country.

While Dulewicz and Herbert showed that several accepted criteria of good corporate governance had not contributed to corporate performance in their sample UK companies, we consider it is possible that these criteria may nevertheless have been a bulwark against corporate corruption and demise in some companies and had thus contributed to performance in that way. Dulewicz and Herbert's study was based on what happened to 86 of 134 companies originally studied by Dulewicz and Herbert in 1997. The remaining 48 companies 'had gone into liquidation, been taken over, merged with another company, or broken up'. If it had been possible to factor in those 'failed' companies into Dulewicz and Herbert's 2003 study, it is perhaps possible that a correlation between good corporate governance and company performance might have emerged.

At the end of this Introductory chapter we reproduce Hermes thoughtful publication on 'The Value of Corporate Governance'(see **B1.44**).

## Is corporate governance a dangerous distraction?     B1.5

As more formalised approaches to corporate governance emerged in the UK over the last years of the previous millennium, concerns were expressed as to whether these truly contributed to, or detracted from, building up great companies. Might it have been that an excessive board focus on corporate governance was distracting boards from building business prosperity? Alternatively, or additionally, might it have been that the emergence of codes of best practice for corporate governance merely encouraged a superficial 'box ticking' mentality?

The Hampel Report[5] commenced with the words:

'The importance of corporate governance lies in its contribution both to business prosperity and to accountability'.

The draft Hampel Report[6] had gone on to say that:

'In the UK the latter has preoccupied much public debate over the past few years **to the detriment of the former**'.

The bolding is ours. The words in bold were dropped from the final Hampel Report which did however continue to say, as in the draft:

'We would wish to see the balance corrected'.

For our part we see this as a false dichotomy. Much of the present debate continues to be about improving the quality of accountability by boards to stakeholders – especially so that shareholders can make better investment decisions which are themselves essential prerequisites for building prosperous businesses. Likewise, we see more effective internal control as contributing to, rather than being a drain upon, the bottom line. Indeed, so did Hampel, for instance in his wording of the Combined Code's Principle on Internal Control:

'The board should maintain a sound system of internal control to safeguard shareholders' investment and the company's assets'.

*(2003 Combined Code, Principle C.2)*

## Entities of all sorts and types                                B1.6

We also believe the contention of superficial 'box ticking' has been overstated, and that the focus on corporate governance has immeasurably strengthened corporate entities in the UK. Nevertheless, the Hampel Committee set out to address the challenge of perceived 'box ticking' by distilling mandatory principles from the list of more detailed provisions within the Combined Code, and making adherence to the principles mandatory for listed companies while allowing the provisions to be discretionary. In this way, Hampel ensured that one code could be regarded as applicable for all listed companies whatever their size and characteristics, and likely to be broadly applicable to other types of entity, such as private companies, mutual societies or government agencies.

The principles of best practice for corporate governance should be regarded as having much wider applicability that just for listed companies. Most public companies are not listed, and many have not offered securities to the public.

'In the UK, of the 11,600 or so plcs on the register at 31 March 2000, only some 2,500 were listed, with a further 400 quoted on AIM and about 50 quoted only on an overseas market'.

*(Consultation Document, November 2000, Volume 8, p53)*

# Defining 'corporate governance' and 'the board'   B1.7

'Corporate governance is concerned with holding the balance between economic and social goals and between individual and communal goals. The governance framework is there to encourage the efficient use of resources and equally to require accountability for the stewardship of those resources. The aim is to align as nearly as possible the interests of individuals, corporations, and society.'[7]

The Oxford New English Dictionary on Historical Principles (1901) (OED) described governance as 'the action or manner of governing', or 'controlling, directing, or regulating influence; control, sway or mastery', or 'the manner in which something is governed or regulated; method of management, system of regulations.' It appears from the OED that the term 'governance' was initially applied in a divine context before being used in a slightly more temporal, ecclesiastical way. It was only a matter of time before these early auspicious uses[8] were to be joined by associating the word, quite recently, with systems of national regulation and now with corporate direction and control. Perhaps this journey reflects the changing preoccupations of the contemporary time when, by some methods of measurement, more than half the largest economies of the world can now be said to be corporations, and suggests the gravity with which we should approach the challenges of corporate governance.

According to the United Nations Conference on Trade and Development, measured on the basis of value-added – the yardstick used to calculate countries' gross domestic product – the activities of the largest 100 companies accounted for 4.3 per cent of world GDP in 2000, up from 3.5 per cent in 1999. On that basis 29 of the world's biggest economic entities were then companies. Exxon, with an estimated value-added of £40 billion at that time was larger than all but 44 national economies and the same size as Pakistan. Ford, DaimlerChrysler, General Electric and Toyota were comparable in size with Nigeria. Value-added can be construed as corresponding most closely to the GDP calculation.[9]

Further related discussion can be found at **B26.1**.

## Coining the phrase 'corporate governance'   B1.8

We have not found very visible use of the term 'corporate governance' before 1984 when it appeared as the title of a book[10] written by Tricker who, in echoes of Henri Fayol (often regarded as the 'father of management theory'), deserves the accolade 'father of corporate governance'. As far back as 1976, the year that Harold Wilson's 'The Governance of Britain' appeared, Tricker had used the expression 'corporate governance' in a book titled 'The Independent Director'[11] and he was to continue to be prolific on corporate governance until the new millennium. In 1993 he had been the founder editor of what has become a leading journal on corporate governance, handing over this mantle in 2001.

'Corporate governance … is concerned with the way corporate entities are governed, as distinct from the way businesses within those companies are managed. Corporate governance addresses the issues facing boards of directors, such as the interaction with top management, and relationships with the owners and others interested in the affairs of the company … '.

In this handbook, we take the perspective of the Cadbury Report that, in essence, corporate governance is to do with the processes by which a corporate entity is directed and controlled:

'Corporate governance is the system by which companies are directed and controlled. Boards of directors are responsible for the governance of their companies. The shareholders' role in governance is to appoint the directors and the auditors and to satisfy themselves that an appropriate governance structure is in place. The responsibilities of the board include setting the company's strategic aims, providing the leadership to put them into effect, supervising the management of the business and reporting to shareholders on their stewardship. The board's actions are subject to laws, regulations and the shareholders in general meeting.

While this is a balanced definition, much of the emphasis within the Cadbury Report was on the control side of things – the monitoring of, and accounting for, the implementation of sound board policy – rather than on the formulation of policy and the development of strategy which are the starting points of good corporate governance. Indeed, some inappropriately consider that corporate governance is *only* to do with the control side. Take, for instance, the Treasury's control-oriented definition of corporate governance in the public sector as being:

'the system by which Accounting Officers carry out their responsibility for ensuring that effective management systems, including financial monitoring and control systems have been put in place.'

In this handbook we adopt the perspective that the board is at the pivotal point of corporate governance, looking outwards especially to the stakeholders of the entity who need to exercise external control, and looking inwards to oversee the execution of board policy. The draft Cadbury Report's definition of corporate governance expressed this better than did the final Report (quoted above):

'Corporate governance is the system by which companies are run. At the centre of the system is the board of directors whose actions are subject to laws, regulations and the shareholders in general meeting. The shareholders in turn are responsible for appointing the directors and the auditors and it is to them that the board reports on its stewardship at the Annual General meeting.

'The link between the board and the shareholders is the reporting system through which the board accounts to them for the activities and progress of the company. The role of the auditors is to provide the shareholders with an external and objective check on the directors' financial statements which form the basis of that reporting system. Although the reports of the directors are addressed to the shareholders, they are important to a wider audience, not least to employees whose interests boards have a statutory duty to take into account.'

*(Draft Report issued for public comment, 27 May 1992, The Committee on The Financial Aspects of Corporate Governance, pp7–8, paras 2.5, 2.6)*

Tricker (1984) had a closely similar view in superimposing governance on management (see his diagram below), and describing the process of corporate governance as having four principal activities:

*'Direction:*         Formulating the strategic direction for the future of the enterprise in the long term;

*Executive action:*   Involvement in crucial executive decisions;

*Supervision:*        Monitoring and oversight of management performance; and

*Accountability:*     Recognising responsibilities to those making legitimate demand for accountability.' (Tricker, Robert I., 1984, Corporate Governance, op cit, p7)

*The activities of governance and management compared (Tricker's 1984 diagram)*

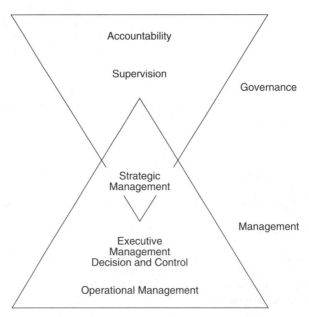

The OECD has achieved a good balance in its recent definition of corporate governance[12]:

'a set of relationships between a company's management, its board, its shareholders and other stakeholders. Corporate governance ... provides the structure through which the objectives of the company are set, and the means of attaining those objectives and monitoring performance … Good corporate governance should provide proper incentives for the board and management to pursue objectives that are in the interests of the company and shareholders and should facilitate effective monitoring, thereby encouraging firms to use resources more efficiently.'

## Relevant theories                                                        B1.9

In an important though brief article in July 2003[13] Sumantra Ghoshal, professor of strategy and international management at London Business School, challenged the frenzied development of new and redesigned courses on corporate social responsibility as business schools' responses to Enron and Tyco. Rather he laid the blame for corporate scandals business schools' focus on agency theory, transaction cost economics and strategy theory[14] – as well as their general tendency to treat business as a science:

> 'The problem is that, unlike theories in the physical sciences, theories in the social sciences tend to be self-fulfilling. … A management theory, if it gains enough currency, changes the behaviour of managers. Whether right or wrong to begin with, the theory becomes "true" as the world comes to conform to its doctrine.

> That is why it is nonsense to pretend that management theories can be completely objective and value-free. … By incorporating negative and highly pessimistic assumptions about people and institutions, pseudo-scientific theories of management have done much to reinforce, if not create, pathological behaviour on the part of managers and companies. It is time the academics who propose these theories and the business schools and universities that employ them acknowledged the consequences.'

### Douglas McGregor's Theory X and Theory Y                               B1.10

> 'Theories X and Y are not strategies of managing: they are assumptions about the nature of people which influence the adoption of a strategy for managing' [15]

*Theory X and Theory Y Assumptions* [16]

| | Traditional view:<br>Theory X | | The more innovative view:<br>Theory Y |
|---|---|---|---|
| 1 | *A proposition common in Theories X and Y*: Management is responsible for organising elements of productive enterprise – money, materials, equipment, people – in the interest of economic ends. | | |
| 2 | With respect to people, this is a process of directing their actions, modifying their behaviour to fit the needs of the organisation. | 2 | People are not by nature passive, or resistant to organisational needs., They have become so as a result of experience in organisations. |

| | Traditional view: Theory X | | The more innovative view: Theory Y |
|---|---|---|---|
| 3 | Without this active intervention by management, people would be passive – even resistant – to organisational needs. They must therefore be persuaded, rewarded, punished, controlled – their activities must be directed. This is management's task. We often sum it up by saying that management consists of getting things done through people. | 3 | The motivation, the potential for development, the capacity for assuming responsibility, the readiness to direct behaviour toward organisational goals are all present in people. Management does not put them there. It is a responsibility of management to make it possible for people to recognise and develop these human characteristics for themselves. |
| 4 | The average person is by nature indolent – he or she works as little as possible. | 4 | The essential task of management is to arrange organisational conditions and methods of operation so that people can achieve their own goals *best* by directing *their own* efforts toward organisational objectives. |
| 5 | He or she lacks ambition, dislikes responsibility, prefers to be led. | | |
| 6 | He or she is inherently self-centred, indifferent to organisational needs. | | |
| 7 | He or she is by nature resistant to change. | | |
| 8 | He or she is gullible, not very bright, the ready dupe of the charlatan and the demagogue. | | |

## Herzberg's theory of motivators and hygiene factors                 B1.11

'Job attitude data suggests that after the glow of the initial year on the job, job satisfaction plummets to its lowest level in the work life of individuals. From a life time of diverse learning, successive accomplishment through the various academic stages, and periodic reinforcement of efforts, the entrant to our modern companies finds that, rather than work providing an expanding psychological existence, the opposite occurs; and successive amputations of his or her self-conceptions, aspirations, learning and talent are the consequence of earning a living.'[17]

Herzberg considered attributes, all of which relate closely to the job itself, to be *motivators* (that is, *satisfiers*) whereas other attributes which relate more to the surroundings of the job (such as working conditions, salary, supervision, company policy and administration) he designated *hygiene factors* (that is, *dissatisfiers*). Herzberg's view was that no amount of attention to the hygiene factors would positively motivate an employee although unsatisfactory hygiene factors would be a source of discontent. His was thus a two-factor hypothesis:

'Factors involved in producing job satisfaction were separate and distinct from the factors that led to dissatisfaction.'[18]

Hygiene factors also have a much shorter *half life* than motivators: for instance, the favourable impact of a salary increase wears off very quickly (implying that a little and often is more effective) whereas the impact of achievement, recognition of achievement, or advancement last much longer.

## Stewardship theory                                                    B1.12

'The original corporate concept enshrined a philosophical assumption about the nature of man, one that has been reflected in subsequent developments of company law – a view that man is essentially trustworthy, able to act in good faith in the interests of others with integrity and honesty. This is implicit in the fiduciary relationship required of directors. This perspective has been termed 'stewardship theory'.[19,20]

Stewardship theory is consistent with McGregor's 'Theory Y'. Stewardship theory takes the view that people *can* be trusted to act in the public good in general and in the interests of the shareholders in particular.

Donaldson and Davis undertook an empirical study[21] which came up with conclusions that would seem to us counterintuitive ten years later:

'Stewardship theory stresses the beneficial consequences on shareholder returns of facilitative authority structures which unify command by having roles of CEO and chair held by the same person. The empirical evidence is that the ROE returns to shareholders are improved by combining, rather than separating, the role-holders of the chair and CEO positions. Thus the results fail to support agency theory and lends some support to stewardship theory. The safeguarding of returns to shareholders may be along the track, not of placing management under greater control, by owners, but of empowering managers to take autonomous executive action.'

A useful source is Muth, M. and Donaldson, L., 1998, 'Stewardship Theory and Board Structure – A Contingency Approach', Corporate Governance, [Blackwells, Vol 6, No 1, pp 5–28].

## Agency theory                                                        B1.13

Michael Jenson, who taught at Harvard, was the creator of agency theory. Under this theory, shareholders are seen as *principals* and management are their *agents*.

'Agency theory argues that agents will act with rational self-interest, not with the virtuous, wise and just behaviour assumed in the stewardship model.'[22]

Agency theory takes the view that people *cannot* be trusted to act in the public good in general and in the interests of the shareholders in particular. So, 'managers could not be trusted to do their job – which of course is to maximise shareholder value'.[23] They need to be monitored and controlled to ensure compliance and this results in *agency costs* which, the theory goes, should be incurred to the point at which the reduction of the loss from non-compliance equals the increase in enforcement costs.[24]

In the context of corporate governance, agency theory emphasises the need to ...

'... control managerial 'opportunism' by having a board chair independent of the CEO and using incentives to bind CEO interests to those of shareholders.' [25]

Agency costs are the sum of[26]:

1.    the monitoring expenditures of the principal (ie owner/shareholders);

2.    the boding expenditures by the agent (eg the cost of transparent reporting to the principal by the agent);

3.    the residual loss (ie 'the key feature'):

'residual loss is the reduction in the value of the firm that obtains when the entrepreneur dilutes his ownership. This shift out of profits and into managerial discretion induced by the dilution of ownership is responsible for this loss. Monitoring expenditures and bonding expenditures can help restore performance toward pre-dilution levels. The irreducible agency cost is the minimum of the sum of these three factors.' [27]

The 'agency problem' is a result of separation of management and ownership in large public companies. Consequently the interests of owners and managers are likely to diverge.

1.    Inside directors (ie corporate employees) tend to be self-serving by maximising its utility at the expense of non-management shareholders, through

●    monetary compensation;

●    job stability;

●    on-the-job prerequisites.

2.    Inside directors are not likely to aggressively oversee the CEO. (But perhaps outside directors may be even less critical of management?)

The shareholder relationship is one of agency:

> ' ... a contract under which one or more persons (the principals) engage another person (the agent) to perform some service on their behalf which involves delegating some decision making authority to the agent. If both parties to the relationship are utility maximizers there is good reason to believe the agent will not always act in the best interests of the principal ...'[28]

## The theory of market for corporate control  B1.14

'Questions of control are framed as a struggle between management and shareholders with the board of directors serving as the platform for the struggle. On the one side are those who argue that management makes its decisions in its own self-interest and needs only to appease shareholders. [29] The board of directors is a buffer that serves management interests and deflects shareholder demands. Since private property rights for shareholders are attached only to their certificates and since ownership is so widely dispersed, management use of corporate assets is influenced little by shareholders. On the other side of the debate are those who argue that shareholders maintain control over the use of corporate assets through their behavior in financial markets. [30] The buying and selling of stock as a reflection of shareholder control, it is argued, should not be minimised. Management that makes decisions contrary to shareholder interests is penalized, through the market, and thus, risks its position in management. Boards of directors that ignore shareholder interests are similarly subject to the penalties of the market.' [31]

## The theory of transaction cost economics  B1.15

Developed by Oliver Williamson and taught at Berkeley and Stanford, this theory emphasises that managers should be strongly incentivised to ensure that staff are tightly controlled so that they do what they do what is expected of them.

## Theory of competitive strategy  B1.16

Exemplified by Michael Porter[32], this theory emphasises that companies need to compete effectively not just with their competitors but with other stakeholders such as employees, suppliers and regulators. In essence, profits are made by the company that succeeds in restricting competition.

## External and internal control  B1.17

A fundamental purpose of corporate governance is to minimise the risk associated with the separation of 'ownership' from 'management'. So, corporate governance includes the control exercised by the legitimate stakeholders over their respective stakes in the entity; and the mechanisms (such as the accountability of the directors) that facilitate this external control. In part it is also internal control which comprises the oversight of management by the board of directors together with the internal control mechanisms which management implement and apply (including management's accountability to the board) in order that the board has reasonable assurance of the achievement of the entity's objectives.

There is a distinction, too often blurred, between the responsibilities of the board and the responsibilities of management. It is understandable that the distinction between the responsibilities of the board and those of management is the more blurred in the case of the Anglo-Saxon unitary board which may be balanced in its membership between executives and non-executives. Nevertheless an executive who is a board director is not acting in a managerial capacity when he or she participates in decision making at the board. He or she is acting in a managerial capacity when reporting to the board on the operation(s) for which he or she has executive responsibility.

## Unitary and two-tier boards                                   B1.18

The distinction between the responsibilities of the board and the responsibilities of management is potentially clearer in the case of two-tier boards. For instance, in 2000, Deutsche Telecom had a 20 member supervisory board, made up of ten shareholder representatives and ten representatives of the workforce. Under Germany's two-tier system, the supervisory board appoints members of the management board and supervises their actions. The management board runs the company's day-to-day business.[33]

The board is overall responsible for what happens within the entity and must therefore hold to itself the determination of overall policy and the oversight of its implementation. With respect to the latter, the board needs to put itself in the position of being reasonably certain that it knows 'where the company is at'. This includes the board forming a well-informed view about the effectiveness of internal control – since it should be a policy of the board that the entity should have effective internal control. Effective internal control provides reasonable assurance of the achievement of corporate objectives.

Late in June 1999, having received inputs from both member and non-member countries as well as from the World Bank and the International Monetary Fund, the Organisation for Economic Co-operation and Development (OECD) published their 'Principles of Corporate Governance'.[34] The OECD had not been in a position to advocate a particular board structure, and indeed even the term 'board' was a bit of a challenge to them in view of the existence of both unitary and two-tier board structures in different countries. OECD resolved this challenge by applying the term 'board' to the 'supervisory board' in a typical two-tier system, and the phrase 'key executives' to the 'management board' in a two-tier system. They added:

> 'In systems where a unitary board is overseen by an internal auditor's board, the term "board" [as used in this OECD publication] includes both.'

In times of convergence towards globally accepted principles of corporate governance it is interesting to see some convergence between the unitary and two-tier board structures. Many, probably most, UK and US companies now have an executive board under the main board; and the main board is tending towards greater in dependence from management. Many German companies are accepting that a supervisory board, comprising 'the great and the good' and representative of key stakeholder groups, may not be an effective overseer of management. One indication of this is the creation of more and more audit committees in German companies where previously often it had been considered that the existence of supervisory boards obviated the need for audit committees.

The Cadbury (and now the Combined) Code provision that listed companies should have audit committees comprising at least three non-executive directors the majority of whom should be *independent* non-executive directors, has often had the indirect effect of bolstering the independent element on UK unitary boards – an element already taken care of in the case of two-tier board structures. But this is not to say that companies with two-tier boards have no need for audit committees. The need is largely the same as for unitary boards – financial statements which are to be published, risk management and internal control, as well as external and internal audit, need a degree of detailed scrutiny on behalf of the supervisory board which that board is unlikely to be able to do for itself.

# Internal control **B1.19**

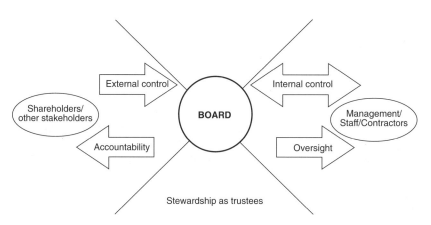

As we have indicated, our view is that corporate governance is to do with external as well as internal control – as illustrated in the diagram. It comprises the processes of accountability to, and oversight by, stakeholders – which provide the means by which external control can be exercised. And it comprises the processes of accountability to and oversight by the board – which are necessary if risk management and internal control are to be effective so that corporate objectives can be achieved.

The Hampel Committee's 1998 Combined Code's Principle on Internal Control first stated:

'The board should maintain a sound system of internal control to safeguard shareholders' investment and the company's assets.'
*(This wording is continued in the 2003 Combined Code, Principle C.2)*

While this is a non-standard statement as to the objectives of internal control, and gives the *board* a 'maintenance' responsibility which we would prefer to attribute to *management,* nevertheless it makes the point that internal control is central to the responsibilities of the board.

The Turnbull Report[35] expressed much better than the Hampel Committee the respective responsibilities for internal control of the board, management and other personnel, *viz*:

'The board of directors is responsible for the company's system of internal control. It should set appropriate policies on internal control and seek regular assurance that will enable it to satisfy itself that the system is functioning effectively. The board must further ensure that the system of internal control is effective in managing risks in the manner which it has approved'

*(Turnbull Report, para 16)*

and

'It is the role of management to implement board policies on risk and control. In fulfilling its responsibilities, management should identify and evaluate the risks faced by the company for consideration by the board, and design, operate and monitor a suitable system of internal control which implements the policies adopted by the board'.

*(Turnbull Report, para 18)*

and

'All employees have some responsibility for internal control … '

*(Turnbull Report, para 19)*

The Turnbull Report has now been included by the Financial Reporting Council as part of the 2003 Combined Code, and we reproduce it in PART A.

So the board is at the pivotal point of corporate governance. Internal control is an essential part of corporate governance and thus internal auditors are important players in corporate governance. Internal auditors, in their assessment of risk management and internal control, largely focus on the internal dimensions of corporate governance – but not exclusively so.

## Internal audit                                                B1.20

On 9 April 2001 The Wall Street Journal Europe said, in its leading front page article entitled 'European Companies Shy Away From Issuing Profit Warnings':

'Faced with a sudden cooling of the economy, North American companies have been churning out profit warnings. In Europe, however, only a few companies have admitted they won't live up to analysts' expectations.

Why the ominous silence in Europe? The short answer is denial. Many companies seem to be hoping to avoid the global slowdown. Others appear unwilling to show their hands before regularly scheduled releases of results.

Investors aren't waiting. These days, they dump shares on the mere suspicion that a profit warning is due, reasoning that if US competitors are issuing them, the Europeans must be sharing their pain. "It often seems that companies should have known their problems much earlier," grumbles Markus Straub of SdK, a shareholder-rights group in Germany. **"At best, you can say they need to improve their internal auditing; at worst it could be criminal.'"**

(The emphasis is ours.) An interesting point here is that at least one corporate governance pressure group considers that internal auditors have a role to influence the reliability of disclosures to the market, and to prevent fraudulent financial reporting. A more cautious view would be that internal audit plays in a particular position on the corporate governance pitch – reserving itself to that part of corporate governance which takes place *within* the entity.

There are, however, indications that internal audit is moving across the divide between 'internal' and 'external' corporate governance, even though to date there is no general obligation for internal audit itself to report publicly within the annual report of the company. Examples are:

- assisting the board in formulating their published reports on internal control;

- contributing to the reliability of financial statements;

- involvement in environmental audit and reporting;

- assurances to the board on other operational analyses which are published, especially those not subject to other independent attestation;

- advising the audit committee on external audit; and

- in some companies, providing secretariat and other services to the audit committee.[36]

An interesting example of how internal audit may affect share price was reported in August 2003.[37] The giant Australian insurer AMP was in talks with the Financial Services Authority to safeguard UK policyholders' interests amid worries that its plans to pull out of Britain might leave more than 2 million savers high and dry. The company, which also had around 60,000 small shareholders in the UK, wanted to float its British operation in London. Doubts surfaced about the demerger, and AMP's share price plunged, after it was learnt that a draft internal audit report had warned about shortcomings in its risk controls at one part of its UK operations – notwithstanding that AMP said the draft contained 'some inaccuracies'.

**Definitions of 'corporate governance'** **B1.21**

|   | Date | Source | Definition |
|---|------|--------|------------|
| 1. | 1992 | Cadbury Report | Corporate governance is the system by which companies are directed and controlled. |
| 2. | 1994 | Tricker | Corporate governance … is concerned with the way corporate entities are governed, as distinct from the way businesses within those companies are managed. Corporate governance addresses the issues facing boards of directors, such as the interaction with top management, and relationships with the owners and others interested in the affairs of the company … |
| 3. | 1999 | OECD | A set of relationships between a company's management, its board, its shareholders and other stakeholders. Corporate governance … provides the structure through which the objectives of the company are set, and the means of attaining those objectives and monitoring performance … Good corporate governance should provide proper incentives for the board and management to pursue objectives that are in the interests of the company and shareholders and should facilitate effective monitoring, thereby encouraging firms to use resources more efficiently. |
| 3. | About 2000 | | HM Treasury (UK) The system by which Accounting Officers carry out their responsibility for ensuring that effective management systems, including financial monitoring and control systems have been put in place. |
| 3. | 2001 | IIA (Institute of Internal Auditors) *Standards* Glossary definition | **Governance Process** – The procedures utilised by the representatives of the organisation's stakeholders (e.g., shareholders, etc.) to provide oversight of risk and control processes administered by management. |

**Definitions of 'the board'** **B1.22**

|   | Date | Source | Definition |
|---|------|--------|------------|
| 1. | 1992 | Cadbury Report | Boards of directors are responsible for the governance of their companies … The responsibilities of the board include setting the company's strategic aims, providing the leadership to put them into effect, supervising the management of the business and reporting to shareholders on their stewardship. |
| 2. | 2001 | IIA (Institute of Internal Auditors) *Standards* Glossary definition | **Board** – A board of directors, audit committee of such boards, head of an agency or legislative body to whom internal auditors report, board of governors or trustees of a non-profit organisation, or any other designated governing bodies of organisations. |

# Grand themes in corporate governance – the ten 'principia' B1.23

The challenge for boards is to direct entities in circumstances where the future is always uncertain, in circumstances where the future is at the beck and call of governments, of speculators and of almost chance happenings. The iron law of business is that the only certainty about the future is that the future is uncertain. It sometimes seems that almost without exception businesses plan for the future on the misguided assumption that current trends will continue, when the truth is that current trends will always terminate. Future dislocation, or future shock, is the backcloth against which corporate plans should be developed. Business developments must be planned so that survival, even success, is feasible when the traffic lights change from green to amber or even to red.

'The problem is not simply that we plan too little; we also plan too poorly'.[38]

Boards have twin responsibilities – for policy and overall strategy, and for corporate governance. These two responsibilities are not mutually exclusive: entities need policies and strategies to improve their corporate governance; and good corporate governance reduces the risk of damaging decisions being made in medium to long term plans.

Here we seek highlight some fundamentals of good corporate governance practice that can be a bulwark against future shock.

So what are the ground rules for effective corporate governance? Here we offer a ten point programme. Of course, it is the principles behind the prescription which are most important. It is the principles which should be achieved – the method is secondary. With some interpretation, we believe this prescription is broadly applicable to entities within both private and public sectors.

## The ten principia of good corporate governance            B1.24

These are the ten 'principia' of effective corporate governance.[39]

1. Stakeholder control of the business.

2. Maximum and reliable public reporting.

3. Avoidance of excessive power at the top of the business.

4. A balanced board composition.

5. A strong, involved board of directors.

6. A strong, independent element on the board.

7. Effective monitoring of management by the board.

8. Competence and commitment.

9. Risk assessment and control.

10. A strong audit process.

## Stakeholder control of the business            B1.25

First and foremost, the stakeholders must be in control of the entity. This is at least as vital, though harder to achieve, in cases where only a small percentage of the capital of a company has been floated. Outside investors should be particularly vigilant of the corporate governance arrangements of companies where a majority of shares are in a few hands – especially when those shareholders are members of the board and perhaps members of a single family.

Here we are addressing *external* control – which is the control of the stakeholders over their stakes in the business. Whether one conceives of the stakeholder constituency extending beyond the shareholding or other proprietors of the business is very much a matter of personal and corporate philosophy. Joseph Johnston, an American corporate lawyer, and the American Bar Association's expert on corporate governance, in a pamphlet published by the UK Social Affairs Unit, an independent think-tank, argued that

> '[a broad view of] stakeholding is part of the European corporatist tradition but is alien to Anglo-American ideas of corporate governance.'[40]

Johnston concluded that directors should obey the law, but that their ethical obligation is to act in the exclusive interest of the shareholders, the people who risk their capital:

> 'every time company directors bow to stakeholder demands, they betray their duty to company shareholders'.

**Safeguards in a free market**                                      **B1.26**

If this approach to accountability is to work for the greater good of society it is reliant upon:

- legislation rather than corporate conscience dictating the social and environmental responsibility of firms;

- shareholder pressure for social and environmental responsibility perhaps in the form of ethical investment funds; and

- a long term corporate perspective which perceives the enlightened self-interest of the corporation partly in terms of its social and environmental responsibility.

A prerequisite of effective shareholder or broader stakeholder control is an informed shareholder/stakeholder body. This requires maximum, reliable reporting by the board to them.

**Appointment of directors**                                         **B1.27**

Of equal importance is effective control by the shareholders over the composition of the board of directors. It should be realistically feasible for the members of the company to remove one or more directors at any time by exercising their powers to ensure that meetings of the shareholders are convened and to ensure that the appointment and reappointment of directors is voted upon by the shareholders at the annual general meeting, with perhaps one third of directors coming up for reappointment at each annual general meeting. The relevant requirements and powers for this will be laid down in the constitutional documents, such as the articles, of the company. The chairman and the managing director are sometimes excluded from this requirement of re-election by rotation. Reappointment should not be automatic but should be on the basis of an assessment of the needs of the company and the anticipated contribution that the individual appointee will make in the future.

Likewise, with respect to both executive and non-executive directors, the remuneration and other elements of compensation of directors, which should be fully disclosed, should be subject to approval by the shareholders in general meeting.

A change in UK law (effective 2003) now requires the remuneration report of a company with respect to its directors to be put to the vote at the company's AGM. It quickly led, in 2003, to GlaxoSmithKline's shareholders rejecting proposed severance pay arrangements for its chief executive (where concern was largely about the perception of 'rewarding failure'); to Tesco coming under renewed pressure to change directors' contracts (where the concern was their perceived excessive length beyond the acceptable twelve month term); and to Cable and Wireless suffering a sizeable revolt in protest at a share incentive scheme for five non-executive directors (where the concern was that non-executive directors, being involved in setting share performance targets for executive directors, should not have their independence compromised in this way). With respect to this last example, participation by NEDs in schemes where directors are incentivised through the opportunity to acquire shares on special terms, is acceptable in the US; best UK practice is that non-executive directors should only receive a fee for their non-executive directorship responsibilities though part of that fee may be paid in shares acquired in the usual way in market at the price prevailing at the time). In the US, under the NYSE draft corporate governance standards (August 2002) shareholders are to vote on ESOP schemes.

**Directors' contracts**                                                **B1.28**

While directors should come up for reappointment perhaps once every three years, their contracts with the company generally should not exceed twelve months, though this twelve months may be on a rolling basis; very rarely indeed need they exceed twelve months for non-executive directors. This avoids the risk of directorship posts becoming too secure to encourage the continuance of committed performance. It also significantly reduces the risk of excessive severance payments being required under the terms of the directors' contracts – a situation which can appear to reward, and therefore encourage, failure rather than success.

Directors' contracts of appointment should not be secret. Their full terms should be brought to the board and approved by the board in each case. *Section 318* of the *Companies Act 1985* requires, with only incidental exceptions, a copy of each director's service contract to be available for inspection by members at the company's registered office; or if there is no such written contract, for a written memorandum of its terms to be kept and to be available for inspection. Since directors' contracts are available for scrutiny by members, it follows that there can be no objection, indeed the opposite, to each director being privy to the terms within the service contracts of all the other directors.

The fees of non-executive directors should relate to their contribution to the business and the time they devote to it. The compensation packages of executive directors should not exceed market rates.

Where possible there should be a planned, orderly turnover of directors so that the board is not denuded of too much experience at one moment in time. Non-executive directors should be chosen largely for the contribution they will be able to make and should generally not serve on the board for much more than seven to ten years so as to preserve the independence of judgement which the non-executive directors are able to bring to bear.

**Retirement of directors**                                             **B1.29**

The retirement age for directors should be set out in the constitutional documents of the company, and should not be excessive. Beyond the age of 70, directors should come up for re-election annually, rather than once every three years.

There is a view that non-executive directors over the age of 70 may have reduced independence in view of the probability that they must know that the chances are not good of them being invited to join other boards. It is however risky to generalise, and if this is a potential impediment to effective independence, it is often more that counterbalanced by the extra willingness of people of advanced years to take independent positions on issues.

**Appointment and oversight of auditors**   **B1.30**

Different legislations vary as to whether the shareholders always have regular opportunity to vote on the appointment and reappointment of the auditors of the business, and on their fee. In the UK, the board recommends to the shareholders the appointment of the auditors, and the shareholders vote to confirm their appointment. Having this opportunity increases the control of the shareholders over the business. The published financial statements of the company are the statements of the directors, and it is reasonable that those to whom they are addressed should have a very significant part in determining who, as auditors, shall report to them, the shareholders.

# Maximum and reliable public reporting   B1.31

In the case of a public company the market capitalisation (ie today's quoted share price times the number of issued shares) should be capable of being rationally based on investors' informed judgements of the performance and prospects of the company. In the medium to long term, market capitalisation and therefore the cost to the company of capital, are maximised by a policy of full, timely and reliable disclosure. The market will rightly become nervous of a company which is opaque, tardy, unreliable or surprising in its reporting. At the time of the crisis of the 'tiger economies' in the late 1990s Singapore's Deputy Prime Minster Lee Hsien Loong pointed out to Singapore's Parliament that lack of disclosure by local banks had led people to fear the worst even though the institutions were sound:

> 'The problem is we have not put out as much as we could have done, and as a result, even though the banks are sound, people fear the worst, which is not really justified.'[41]

Already public companies are carrying their annual reports on the worldwide web – though at present generally in summary form only, without much of the narrative content which is so informative. Modern IT will make it possible for companies to report in real-time, continuously updating their reports even on a daily basis. We can expect those companies to become the favoured stocks of investors. Clearly, real-time reporting will have implications for the approach which will be required of auditors.

The proprietors of private companies and other entities also need full, reliable information as a basis for rational investment decisions.

Non-standard and creative accounting policies are to be avoided. With the emergence of more multinational companies and international investment funds, published accounts really should accord with international accounting standards, even when there is a need for a second set to be produced to satisfy local legislative requirements. However, there should be only one set of books and no 'off balance sheet' transactions, assets or accounts.

**Disclosing directors' remuneration**                                                          **B1.32**

The annual report and accounts should make full disclosure of all elements of the compensation packages of the directors. Shareholders have a right and need for this information which should be held up to the light of day and justified. Total board costs need to be monitored carefully, compared with those of other similar enterprises and justified fully. Excessively large boards are both unnecessarily costly and also less likely to be effective. Six to ten directors is likely to be adequate in most cases though, of course, there may be a conclusive case for larger or smaller boards in particular instances. Sleeping directors should be avoided.

It is an aspect of transparency and accountability that the chair of the board and of its remuneration and audit committees, as well as the partner in charge of the external audit, should be available at general meetings of the members to answer questions put by shareholders. It is good practice that other directors should also be available at general meetings for this purpose.

# Avoidance of excessive power at the top of the business   B1.33

The choice of new board members should be a recommendation of the full board subject to the approval of the shareholders. Reliance should be placed upon a nominations committee of the board which should be responsible for succession planning as well as for recommending to the board who should be appointed to the board. The board should not be presented with a virtual *fait accompli* by the chairman, the chief executive or any other party. If this occurs it is likely that there is excessive concentration at the top of the business. Where a seat, or seats, on the board are to be nominated by a particular party or body[42], it is still desirable that the board should concur in the appointment.

*Prima facie* there is likely to be excessive concentration of power at the top of the business if the roles of chairman and chief executive are combined.

There is a rather similar problem if the chairman is an *executive* chairman. This is not a matter of how the chairman's post is designated in terms of 'job title', but rather a matter of the reality. If the chairman is virtually full time, has an office adjacent to the managing director, shares secretariat support with the executive directors and has duties of an executive nature – then such a chairman is an executive chairman regardless of designation.

**When the roles of 'chairman' and 'chief executive' are combined**   **B1.34**

There may be justification for combining the posts of chairman and chief executive. This may be so when particularly strong leadership is needed quickly at a time of crisis. Generally it should be regarded as a temporary expedient to be rectified as quickly as practical. Where these two posts are combined it is good practice for the board, on the advice of the non-executive directors, to formally designate one of the non-executive directors to be the senior non-executive director. Companies in compliance with one of the provisions of the UK's Combined Code will have designated one of the non-executive board members as the 'senior non-executive director' – *whether or not* the posts of chairman and chief executive are combined; the equivalent Cadbury Code provision had made this a requirement only when these two posts had been combined. This director has a special monitoring role with respect to the executive and is a focal point for investors and non-executive directors to express their concerns.

It is good practice for all the non-executive directors of any board to meet from time to time informally without executive directors present. This should be additional to the meetings of the remuneration and audit committees – which may not involve all non-executive directors.

## A balanced board composition                                    B1.35

Balance is needed principally between:

- executive and non-executive directors;

- the functional areas and technical skills represented on the board;

- age, gender, ethnic and other balance – as appropriate in particular cases.

A healthy board is likely to need an approximately even balance of executive and non-executive directors. This is a matter of balancing the number of these and also the strength of personality and the technical skills they possess.

Some boards apply the practice, formally or informally, of nominating a non-executive director to 'shadow' a particular executive director.

## A strong, involved board of directors                           B1.36

It is an absolute essential that the board and its individual members set the highest ethical standards. Their example will be noticed and emulated. Considerable emphasis should be placed by the nominations committee upon confirming the past record of probity of those the committee recommends for appointment to the board.

The board is responsible for ensuring that the business has an effective control environment. In part this includes the ethical example set by board members in their own conduct. It also includes promulgating appropriate, clear ethical principles throughout the business.

Consistency is an important characteristic of a board. Not only must the personal example of directors be appropriate and consistent, the board collectively and its members individually must also be consistent in their application of ethical and other principles to others. If not, staff and business partners will not know where they stand. The board should monitor that management too is consistent in the application of ethical standards and rules of business conduct.

Ethical principles and rules of conduct must be observed by board members themselves whose example is crucial if these are to be observed by other staff. A clear, unambiguous signal needs to be given at all times. The Cadbury Committee's Report gave some emphasis to the part that internal rules should play in corporate governance, *viz*:

> 'It is important that all employees should know what standards are expected of them. We regard it as good practice for boards of directors to draw up codes of ethics or statements of business practice and to publish them both internally and externally'.

## A strong, independent element on the board                              B1.37

Independence is hard to define but important to achieve. In essence, it means freedom from impediments to the exercise and expression of objective judgement. The 1998 Combined Code was no more prescriptive than to say that independence meant:

> 'independent of management and free from any business or other relationship which could materially interfere with the exercise of their independent judgement'[43]

but others have interpreted this general guidance in much more prescriptive ways. Indeed, because of the development of a number of different lists of criteria to define director independence, the Higgs Committee recommended at a standard list should be incorporated into the 2003 Combined Code, where provision A.3.1 now reads:

> 'The board should identify in the annual report each non-executive director it considers to be independent[44]. The board should determine whether the director is independent in character and judgement and whether there are relationships or circumstances which are likely to affect, or could appear to affect, the director's judgement. The board should state its reasons if it determines that a director is independent notwithstanding the existence of relationships or circumstances which may appear relevant to its determination, including if the director:
>
> • has been an employee of the company or group within the last five years;
>
> • has, or has had within the last three years, a material business relationship with the company either directly, or as a partner, shareholder, director or senior employee of a body that has such a relationship with the company;
>
> • has received or receives additional remuneration from the company apart from a director's fee, participates in the company's share option or a performance-related pay scheme, or is a member of the company's pension scheme;

- has close family ties with any of the company's advisers, directors or senior employees;

- holds cross-directorships or has significant links with other directors through involvement in other companies or bodies;

- represents a significant shareholder; or

- has served on the board for more than nine years from the date of their first election.'

Non-executive directors may bring the essential quality of independence to the board, but not all non-executive directors can be regarded as independent. Every board will benefit from a strong, independent element, and every public company or public sector enterprise should have this element of independence.

Because independence is so difficult to define in individual cases, the board should decide in each case whether a director is an independent director. It is good practice for the board to report publicly which directors it considers to be independent, as will be the case with companies in compliance with provision A.3.1 of the 2003 Combined Code.

Being the spouse or close relative of an executive director or having previously been an executive in the business are, for instance, two attributes which should always be regarded as disqualifying the director concerned from being regarded as 'independent'.

## Effective monitoring of management by the board          B1.38

There is a crucial need for board members to be provided with adequate information, and for this information to be made available to them in time to influence decisions. In particular it is likely that the non-executive directors will be inadequately informed, but this can also apply to the board as a whole. Executive directors may not be in a strong position to protest about this if it is the chief executive who is being selective in feeding information to the board. The confidence of board members can be irretrievably lost if suspicions develop amongst them that the board is not being kept properly informed.

In extreme cases, individual directors may become worried about whether the company is a going concern if they consider there are risks that the board is not being kept fully informed. Of particular concern is the risk of liabilities, contingent or actual, being kept from the board. For instance, the executive may know that there is a potential claim from a customer for non-delivery under the terms of a contract, but this may be kept from the board. Or the financial circumstances of the company might have led to failure to pay a tax liability, but the board has not been informed. When suggestions of the withholding of information from the board become fixed in non-executive directors' minds, it can be almost impossible to restore their confidence. Of particular importance here is the degree of confidence that the board has in its finance director and that this confidence is well placed. Related to this is the confidence that the board has in the oversight by the chief executive of the finance director.

It is increasingly common for audit committees to formally consider as an important agenda item at least once a year, the quality of information that the board receives.

Allied to these issues is the nature of the arrangements for the meetings of the board and its committees.

**Directors' handbook**                                                           **B1.39**

A major challenge for most boards is for their members to be able to recall readily all past resolutions of the board. Usually these were originally resolved upon for good reason and after careful consideration: not only should they be regarded as binding upon the board until rescinded but they are likely to represent prudent practice. Of equal difficulty is for the board to be sure that they are fully aware of all material contract terms which the entity has entered into and which, if breached, would place the company and the board in default of their duties – either by virtue of the breach or by failure to disclose the breach to the other parties. An example would be a clause in a financing agreement which requires any 'material adverse change' to be drawn to the attention of the other party(ies). Another, sometimes related, example would be a clause in a contract which makes it an automatic breach of the terms of the contract if an accommodation is made with a party to another contract, or if a disclosure is made to a party to another contract of a material adverse change.

It is sound practice for each director to have an up-to-date directors' handbook giving them ready access to documents and information of continuing importance to the board. The handbook will be maintained by the company secretariat function.

**Reserving matters to the board**                                        **B1.40**

There should be no ambiguity as to the matters which are reserved to the board. What these matters are should be the subject of a formal board resolution.

Many boards will have required and endorsed more elaborate guidelines on the delegation of authority which will specify the levels of management authorised to make decisions up to certain authority limits and the required manner in which the decisions are to be arrived at[45].

# Competence and commitment                                          **B1.41**

Directors, executive and non-executive, must know their general and specific responsibilities and it is wise that this is stated in writing rather than agreed verbally and then likely to be overlooked.

Directors should be chosen in part for the special expertise they can bring to the board. The board will require particular technical expertise in many cases.

Beyond that, it will be necessary for directors to commit sufficient time to their directorship responsibilities so as to act on behalf of the business, to prepare thoroughly for meetings and to attend reliably and participate in meetings.

It is a good practice for directors' attendance records at board and board committee meetings to be kept and for a summary to be an agenda paper at a board meeting once a year. It is up to the chairman to ensure that board members attendance is satisfactory. The chairman is responsible for the effective performance of the board. Excessive absence should require resignation.

## Risk assessment and control                              B1.42

Risk assessment is now understood to be an essential component of an effective system of internal control. It is for the board to ensure that management has in place an effective system of internal control. One part of this is for the board to ensure that the business has in place effective ways of assessing and managing risk. Many businesses have a committee of the board responsible for monitoring risk and reporting to the board. Where there is no such committee, the board must undertake more of the detail for itself. The risks associated with proposed major capital commitments need to be assessed before commitment and thereafter revisited and reassessed. Likewise with other forms of major financial exposure.

It is important to recognise that the board is responsible for monitoring *all* types of risk. It is not just a matter of financial risk. Operational risks are at least as important. Thus, for instance, the board of a hospital is responsible for financial risk and control, but is also responsible for clinical risk and control.

An essential aspect of risk to be assessed by businesses is the risk factors associated with national economic and other policies.

Forward projections on the basis of present trends continuing uninterrupted are always inadequate. Particular emphasis should be placed on the business consequences of possible future change, and of course great care should be taken to identify the possible future changes which have the potential to impact significantly upon the business.

Single point estimates of future outcomes are too simplistic to be a basis for decision making. The future impacts of different possible scenarios need to be assessed, and probabilities associated with each.

## A strong audit process                                    B1.43

Financial reporting concerns have been close to the centre of the developing corporate governance debate. This means that independent audit issues are not merely peripheral to the corporate governance debate. So it was disappointing that the issues within the Cadbury Code closest to the accounting and statutory auditing professions were the issues that caused the most trouble. Indeed, it was only those two provisions within the Cadbury Code which were closest to the accounting profession (that directors should report on going concern and that directors should report on the effectiveness of internal control) the implementation of which had to be delayed pending the development of guidance first for directors and then for auditors.

The audit firm should be chosen for its ability to thoroughly and effectively audit the affairs of the business. In general there are grounds for concern if a large business is audited by a small firm. Even where there is no legal requirement for an audit, or for a full audit, it is good corporate governance practice for a full annual audit to be conducted.

Internal audit plays a vital role in the corporate governance of the modern business. The review of risk management and internal control are themselves essential components of effective risk management and internal control; and this is the mission of the modern internal audit function. Line management and staff may neither have the time, inclination nor competence to undertake all of this monitoring. Internal audit does what management would do if management had the time and knew how.

Primarily internal audit is a service *for* management, but to an extent internal audit also is an audit *of* management when it reports to the audit committee of the board. Since as far back as 1978 the Worldwide Standards for Internal Auditing have referred to internal audit as 'serving the organisation', not just serving management and certainly not just serving the accounting and finance functions.

The terms of reference, or 'charter' of the internal audit function should give internal audit unlimited scope and unrestricted access to information and staff at all times. The terms of reference of the audit committee of the board should require the committee to monitor the adequacy of internal audit, and should stipulate that the head of internal audit should not be appointed or removed without the prior concurrence of the audit committee.

The head of the internal audit function should have unrestricted access to the chair of the audit committee and to the committee itself at all times; the audit committee should meet with the head of internal audit from time to time, and upon his or her request, without executive management being present. Similarly the audit committee should meet with the external auditors without any member of the executive being in attendance.

The principal responsibilities of the audit committee, on behalf of the board, are to satisfy itself as to:

(*a*)   the reliability of financial reports for publication; and

(*b*)   the effectiveness of risk management and internal control.

Arising from these responsibilities are the committee's responsibilities to monitor:

(*c*)   the quality of the external audit;

(*d*)   the quality of internal audit.

The audit committee is a *sine qua non* of the modern enterprise. The best model for an audit committee is one which is entirely non-executive, with at least a majority of its members also being independent.

# The Value of Corporate Governance                 B1.44

This brief review of the evidence for a link between corporate governance and investment performance was written by Colin Melvin, Hermes' Director of Corporate Governance in July 2003. Further corporate governance guidance can be obtained from the Hermes website: http://www.hermes.co.uk/corporate-governance. This Handbook carries certain Hermes guidance and discussion as follows.

- 'Hermes on Auditor Independence' (see **B6.6**).

- 'Hermes: Statement on UK Corporate Governance and Voting Policy' (2001) (see **B7.7**).

- 'Hermes' Guide For Shareholders and Independent Outside Directors' (see **B10.79**).

- 'Not Badly Paid, But Paid Badly' (see **B15.15**).

- 'Value Drivers: Paying a Fair Price for Non-executive Directors' (see **B15.16**).

- 'Hermes International Corporate Governance Principles' (see **B26.8**).

## Introduction

The term 'corporate governance' has come to mean many things, from a description of the quality of companies' internal management to the processes by which they are directed and controlled. For the investor it refers both to the encouragement of companies' compliance with codes and an investment technique based on active ownership.

It follows that the nature and success of any attempt to link corporate governance and investment performance will depend in part on the definitions used.

In this paper we discuss research which supports the proposition that 'good corporate governance enhances value' and we review some evidence to the contrary[i]. Although our review is not comprehensive, we consider that the studies described here provide sufficient grounds to justify pursuing corporate governance as part of a process for the management of long-term investments.

We have selected studies that follow three basic approaches[ii]. These can be categorised as:

- opinion-based;
- governance ranking;
- focus list.

We also consider the performance of funds set up specifically to use active ownership to add value.

## Opinion-based research

The most widely quoted recent study on the link between corporate governance and company value could also be considered the least empirical. In its 'Global Investor Opinion Survey' of over 200 institutional investors first undertaken in 2000 and updated in 2002, McKinsey found that 80% of the respondents would pay a premium for well governed companies[iii]. The size of the premium varied by market, from 11% for Canadian companies to around 40% for companies where the regulatory backdrop was least certain (those in Morocco, Egypt and Russia[iv]) . Although McKinsey provided no evidence that the investors it surveyed actually acted on their opinions, we believe that this result reflects a growing perception amongst market participants that companies which are demonstrably well managed and structured to look after the interests of investors benefit from a lower cost of capital.

Two further opinion-based studies, which also have features in common with the governance ranking research discussed below, have sought to link broad perceptions of the quality of companies to superior share price performance. In a study of five year cumulative returns of Fortune Magazine's survey of 'most admired firms', Antunovich et al found that those 'most admired' had an average return of 125%, whilst the 'least admired' firms returned 80%[v]. In a separate study Business Week enlisted institutional investors and 'experts' to assist in differentiating between boards with good and bad governance and found that companies with the highest rankings had the highest financial returns[vi]. These studies support McKinsey's finding that investors appear to favour companies that they perceive to have relatively high quality of management. However, all three studies fail to describe a practical approach to using corporate governance to make better investment decisions.

## Governance ranking research

Most of the research into the connection between corporate governance and investment performance seeks to link an objective and relative measure of the quality of a company's governance to movements in its share price. This approach has had varying degrees of success, with some researchers claiming either no link or a negative one.

However, these 'negative' studies generally focus on a single governance feature in isolation, such as board independence[vii]. For example, in a recent paper Bagahat and Black found that companies with more independent boards

108

do not perform better than other companies[viii]. This confirmed their findings in an earlier study, that board composition was an unreliable predictor of company performance[ix]

The most celebrated governance ranking study supporting a positive link was published by Gompers et al in 2001. Using a universe of 1500 US companies, Gompers found that if a fund had taken long positions in companies scoring in the top decile of their governance ranking and short positions in companies in the bottom decile it would have outperformed the market by 8.5% per year throughout the 1990s[x]. The impact of this research was due to its suggestion for an active investment strategy based on corporate governance structure and rankings. However, we note that the hypothesis was tested with historical data and that no investment was undertaken.

Following on from Gompers' study, Drobetz *et al* found that if a fund had taken long positions in companies highly ranked for corporate governance and short positions in those lowly ranked for governance it would have outperformed the DAX100 index by 12% per year between 1998 and 2000xi. Using data collected by Deminor Rating, Bauer and Guenster have also successfully replicated Gompers' findings in Europe, concluding that portfolios of companies with high corporate governance standards have better performance than those poor standards[xii].

Similar evidence, without a suggested investment strategy, had previously been described by Millstein and MacAvoy who found that over five years, well-governed companies (identified according to CalPERS ratings) outperformed by 7%, which represented over a quarter of their overall performance[xiii].

Further support has been provided in a recent CLSA research paper. Gill found that although the average US$ return over three years for the 100 largest emerging markets companies was 127%, that from those in the top quartile by corporate governance was 267%. The same analysis over five years produced figures of 388% and 930% respectively[xiv].

Lastly, a related study undertaken by the Institute of Business Ethics found that larger UK companies with codes of ethics outperformed those who claimed not to have such codes[xv].

Much of the governance ranking research provides encouragement for investors to consider corporate governance in their assessments of companies. However, we would note that studies of this type are based on companies' compliance with standards of governance, which are variable and market-specific. Moreover, although it is generally more limited in scope, the presence of contradictory evidence suggests that the extent of compliance is only part of the story. What is missing is an analysis of the effect on companies' value of the actions taken by investors to improve the quality of their governance.

## Focus list research

Focus lists are issued in various forms by some investors and investor groups. They are an attempt to publicise the failings of those companies listed in the hope that this will induce their management to take remedial action. They may also represent a statement of the intent of the investor issuing the list to engage with the listed companies to encourage improvements. In the case of the most established and successful lists, the fact of listing can promote a positive market reaction.

Although still linked to the perceived quality of quality of corporate governance, research into the effects of focus lists suggests that a key driver of corporate performance is investor pressure and oversight. We consider that this research provides the most convincing evidence for a causal link between corporate governance and company performance. Moreover, unlike the opinion-based and ranking research, it is relevant to markets with different governance structures.

First described in 1994 and updated in 1995 and 1997, 'the CalPERS effect' continues to represent the most influential research in this area. Based on the last update in 1997, CalPERS focus list companies outperformed by 23% in five years after focus listing, compared to 89% underperformance in five years before[xvi].

However, the CalPERS effect has been replicated elsewhere with only limited success[xvii]. In a recent paper, Caton et al hypothesised that this was because most focus list studies fail to distinguish between those companies that have potential to respond to investor pressure and those that do not. They found no statistically-significant performance differential on an overall sample of CII focus list companies, but once the sample was ranked using Tobin's Q, there was a striking result. The target companies with Tobin's Q>1 showed a 7% outperformance in the 90-day period following the announcement of the focus list[xviii].

It follows that the most significant factor linking corporate governance and company performance is likely to be the process of active ownership, rather than the fact of companies' compliance with extant codes.

## Active ownership funds

There are a small number of funds that invest in poorly performing companies with the specific intention of using the fact of their part-ownership and the rights attached to their shares to encourage improvements that they consider will lead to an increase in the value of their investment.

Hermes' Focus Funds take such an approach, investing in companies whose businesses are fundamentally strong, but where concerns about the company's direction or governance mean that its shares are underperforming. The Funds' representatives then meet with the companies' executive and non-executive directors and with other shareholders and use their influence as owners to help resolve these concerns.

The first Focus Fund was established in October 1998. Hermes' parent BT Pension Scheme was an initial investor and has seen impressive performance, with a 28.6% return to 30 June 2003, which was 33.2% above its benchmark (FTSE AllShare total return index) over the same period.

## Conclusion

The opinion based and governance ranking studies discussed in this paper point towards a link between the way in which a company is governed and its performance. This is perhaps unsurprising, as a fundamental feature of active investment in equities is an assessment of the quality of corporate management. The difficulty with these studies is their reliance on circumstantial or historical data and their reference to supposed good corporate governance structures, which are market dependent.

More convincing are the focus list studies, which suggest a link between active ownership and improved performance of companies that have potential to improve. Significantly, this also suggests that the corporate governance structure itself is less important than the extent to which ownership oversight is exercised[xx]. It is the exercise of active ownership that is behind Hermes engagement programmes both in relation to its core investments and Focus Funds.

Hermes corporate governance activities are based on the premise that, other things being equal, companies with active, interested and involved shareholders will tend to outperform. In undertaking engagement on its core index-tracking holdings and Focus Fund investments, Hermes seeks to identify underperforming companies that will respond to investor pressure. The focus list studies described in this paper provide significant support to this approach, suggesting that it is not the absolute 'quality' of governance that is important in terms of compliance with codes but rather the process of active ownership and oversight of management. This is demonstrated most clearly in the approach taken by Hermes Focus Funds and in the Funds' success.

*References*

Antunovich, Laster, Mitnick (Jan 2000), 'Are High Quality Firms also High Quality Investments?', Current Issues in Econ & Finance.

Bhagat and Black (2002), 'The Non-correlation Between Board Independence and Long-Term Firm Performance', Journal of Corporate Law.

Bhagat and Black (1999), 'The Uncertain Relationship between Board Composition and Firm Performance', Business Lawyer.

Bhagat, Carey and Elson (2000), 'Director Ownership, Corporate Performance and Management Turnover'.

Bauer and Guenster (2003), 'Good Corporate Governance Pays Off!'

BusinessWeek (1997, 2000) 'Best and Worst Boards Survey'.

Carleton, Nelson and Weisbach (1998), 'Influence of Institutions on Corporate Governance through Private Negotiations', Journal of Finance.

Caton, Goh and Donaldson (2001), 'The Effectiveness of Institutional Activism', Financial Analysts Journal

Coombes & Watson (McKinsey) (2000, 2002, 'Global Investor Opinion Survey'.

Dalton, Daily, Ellstrand and Johnson (1998), 'Meta-Analytic Reviews of Board Composition, Leadership Structure, and Financial Performance', Strategic Management Journal.

Demsetz and Villalonga (2001), 'Ownership Structure and Corporate Performance', University of California.

Drobetz, Schillhofer and Zimmermann (2003), 'Corporate Governance and Expected Stock Returns: Evidence from Germany', WWZ/Department of Finance Basel University Working Paper No. 2/03.

Gill (2001), 'Corporate Governance in Emerging Markets – Saints & Sinners: Who's Got Religion?', CLSA Emerging Markets Research Paper.

Gompers, Ishii, Metrick (2001), 'Corporate Governance and Equity Prices', National Bureau of Economic Research Working Paper 8449 and Quarterly Journal of Economics (forthcoming).

Millstein and MacAvoy (1998), 'The Active Board of Directors and Performance of the Large Publicly Traded Corporation', Columbia Law Review.

Nesbitt (1997), 'The CalPERS Effect', Wilshire Associates.

Opler and Sokobin (1997), 'Does Co-ordinated Institutional Activism Work?'.

Webley and More (2003), 'Does Business Ethics Pay: Ethics and Financial Performance', the Institute of Business Ethics.

*Notes*

i.  Such studies tend to be of the 'governance ranking' variety and suggest either no link between single corporate governance features (generally board independence) and company performance or a correlation with underperformance. Examples are:

  ● Bhagat and Black (2002), 'The Non-correlation Between Board Independence and Long-Term Firm Performance', Journal of Corporate Law.

- Bhagat and Black (1999), 'The Uncertain Relationship between Board Composition and Firm Performance', Business Lawyer.

- Dalton, Daily, Ellstrand and Johnson (1998), 'Meta Analytic Reviews of Board Composition, Leadership Structure, and Financial Performance', Strategic Management Journal

- Demsetz and Villalonga (2001), 'Ownership Structure and Corporate Performance', University of California

ii.  We have elected not to discuss a fourth approach, 'event studies', most of which track the outcome of shareholder resolutions. As these are generally dependent on the outcome of specific and unique situations, we considered them less instructive for a discussion of the value of corporate governance-related investment processes.

iii. Coombes & Watson (McKinsey) (2000, 2002), 'Global Investor Opinion Survey'.

iv.  The UK and US scored 12% and 14% respectively.

v.  Antunovich, Laster, Mitnick (Jan 2000), 'Are High Quality Firms also High Quality Investments?', Current Issues in Econ & Finance.

vi.  (1997, 2000) 'Best and Worst Boards Survey', BusinessWeek

vii. See note (i). A study providing evidence that a single measure can be linked to performance is Bhagat, Carey and Elson (2000), 'Director Ownership, Corporate Performance and Management Turnover'. Bhagat et al found that firms where the outside directors have significant personal shareholdings tend to outperform. Moreover, such companies are also more likely to replace CEOs in the context of underperformance.

viii. Bhagat and Black (2002), 'The Non-correlation Between Board Independence and Long-Term Firm Performance', Journal of Corporate Law.

ix.  Bhagat and Black (1999), 'The Uncertain Relationship between Board Composition and Firm Performance', Business Lawyer.

x.  Gompers, Ishii, Metrick (2001), 'Corporate Governance and Equity Prices' National Bureau of Economic Research Working Paper 8449 and Quarterly Journal of Economics (forthcoming). This study also identifies a positive correlation between governance and Tobin's Q, which we discuss further under 'focus list research'.

xi.  Drobetz, Schillhofer and Zimmermann (2003), 'Corporate Governance and Expected Stock Returns: Evidence from Germany', WWZ/Department of Finance Basel University Working Paper No. 2/03. This study also suggested that companies with better corporate governance have a lower cost of capital, as evidenced by lower dividend yields and higher PE ratios.

xii. Bauer and Guenster (2003), 'Good Corporate Governance Pays Off!' The authors conclude, 'The encouraging results ... of this study should convince institutional investors to account for corporate governance standards in their investment process.'

xiii. Millstein and MacAvoy (1998), 'The Active Board of Directors and Performance of the Large Publicly Traded Corporation', Columbia Law Review

xiv. Gill (2001), 'Corporate Governance in Emerging Markets – Saints & Sinners: Who's Got Religion?', CLSA Emerging Markets Research Paper

xv. Webley and More (2003), 'Does Business Ethics Pay: Ethics and Financial Performance', the Institute of Business Ethics. The authors found that companies with a code of ethics generated significantly more 'economic value added' and 'market value added' than those without codes. Companies with codes also had less volatile P/E ratios and generated more profits.

xvi. Nesbitt (1997), 'The CalPERS Effect', Wilshire Associates.

xvii. A successful attempt on the Council of Institutional Investors focus list was achieved by Opler and Sokobin, who demonstrated that focus list companies outperformed the market over the following two years and improve operating profitability. [Opler and Sokobin (1997), 'Does Co-ordinated Institutional Activism Work?'] Less successful were Carleton et al, who examined 62 TIAA-Cref targets between 1992 and 1996 and mixed valuation impacts from engagements on different issues. [Carleton, Nelson and Weisbach (1998), 'Influence of Institutions on Corporate Governance through Private Negotiations', Journal of Finance.]

xviii. Caton, Goh and Donaldson (2001), 'The Effectiveness of Institutional Activism', Financial Analysts Journal. Tobin's Q is a ratio which compares the company's share price to the replacement value of its assets.

xix. As at 31 December 2002, HFAM had around £550m invested in its UK Focus Funds on behalf of 25 institutional clients, including four of the largest seven UK pension funds. Because of the size of the UK Focus Funds, they tend to invest in FTSE 350 companies. In March 2002, HFAM launched a new UK Small Companies Focus Fund to specifically target those quoted companies outside the FTSE 350. This fund has a similar philosophy and approach to the main UK fund, but is managed by a team with specialist small companies' experience.

xx. This suggest in turn that the relative merits, for example, of two-tier and unitary board structures may be less important that the nature of ownership and that continental European ownership models could provide more effective oversight of company management than the disparate ownership typical of the UK and the US. As the data becomes available, we would consider that a comparison of the effects of active ownership in different markets would be a useful area for future research.

1   Report of the Committee on the Financial Aspects of Corporate Governance ('The Cadbury Report'), (1 December 1992), published by Gee Publishing, London; Report only; ISBN 0 85258 913 1; Report with Code of Best Practice: ISBN 0 85258 915 8, 91 A5 pages; Code of Best Practice: ISBN 0 85258 914 X.

2   Committee of Sponsoring Organizations Of The Treadway Commission (September 1992): Internal Control – Integrated Framework, (AICPA, New York).

3   Dulewicz, Victor and Peter Herbert, (2003), 'Does the Composition and Practice of UK Boards Bear Any Relationship to the Performance of Listed Companies?', Henley Management College (Greenlands, Henley-on-Thames, Oxon, RG9 3AU), Working Paper Series, HWP 0304; ISBN 1 86181 158 6.

4   Based on cash flow return on total assets (CFROTA) and sales turnover.

5   Committee on Corporate Governance: Final Report, (January 1998), chaired by Sir Ronald Hampel; Gee Publishing Limited, 100 Avenue Road, Swiss Cottage, London, NW3 3PG. Tel: 0345 573113. Fax: 0207 393 7463. ISBN 1 86089 034 2, 66 pages. (This report does not include The Combined Code).

6   Committee on Corporate Governance: Preliminary Report, (August 1997), chaired by Sir Ronald Hampel; Committee Secretary: John Healey. Tel.: +44 (0)171 797 4575. Final Report was published in January 1998. £10 from Gee Publishing Ltd, 100 Avenue Road, Swiss Cottage, London, NW3 3PG. Tel: +44 (0)345 573113. Fax: +44 (0)207 393 7463. ISBN 1 86089 034 2.

7   Foreword by Sir Adrian Cadbury to Magdi R. Iskander and Nadereh Chamlou's Corporate Governance: A Framework for Implementation, World Bank Group, 1999.

8   Wyclif, c1380; Chaucer, 1391.

9   Guy Jonquières, (13 August 2002), 'Companies Bigger Than Many Nations', Financial Times, p7; see also www.unctad.org.

10  Tricker, Robert I. (1984), Corporate Governance – Practices, Procedures and Powers in British Companies and Their Boards of Directors, UK, Gower, ISBN 0–566–00749–5, 319 pages.

11  Tricker, Robert I. (1976), 'The Independent Director – A Study of the Non-executive Director and of the Audit Committee', Croydon, UK, Tolley Publishing, ISBN 0 510 49378–5, 104 pages. Vide: p68.

12  Our present models of management, the way we distinguish and typify corporate governance, are inadequate.

13  Organisation for Economic Co-Operation and Development, (June 1999). The publication can be downloaded in HTML or PDF format from their website: www.oecd.org/daf/governance/principles.htm or /principles.pdf

14  Ghoshal, Sumantra (18 July 2003), 'Business schools share the blame for Enron', The Financial Times, p19.

15  Vide, eg. Michael Porter of Harvard's work.

16  Robert Albanese (1978), Managing toward Accountability and Performance, [Richard D. Irwin, Illinois, ISBN 0–256–02039–6], p281

17  Adapted from Robert Albanese, (1978); source Douglas McGregor (1960), The Human Side of Management, New York, McGraw-Hill.

18  Herzberg, F. (1966), 'Work and the Nature of Man', Cleveland, Ohio, World.

19  Herzberg, F. (1959) 'The Motivation to Work', John Wiley & Sons, New York.

20  Donaldson, Lex and James H. Davis (1988), 'CEO Governance and Shareholder Returns: Agency Theory or Stewardship Theory', Academy of Management Meetings and offered to Australian Journal of Management in early 1990s (uncertain whether published).

21  Tricker, Robert I. (1994) International Corporate Governance, Prentice Hall, Singapore, ISBN 0–13–475070–5; pbk: 0–13–475054–3, p102.

22  Donaldson, L. and J. H. Davis, op cit.

23 Tricker, Robert I., op cit, p4.
24 Ghoshal, Sumantra (18 July 2003), 'Business schools share the blame for Enron', The Financial Times, p19. Sumantra Ghoshal is professor of strategy and international management at London Business school.
25 Jensen, M.C. and W.H. Meckling (1986), 'Theory of the firm – managerial behaviour, agency costs and ownership structure', Journal of Financial Economics, No. 3, pp305–60.
26 Donaldson, L. and J. H. Davis, op cit.
27 Jensen, M.C. and W.H. Meckling, op cit.
28 Williamson, Oliver E. (July 1988), 'Corporate finance and corporate governance', Journal of Finance, Vol. XLII/3.
29 Jensen, M.C. and W.H. Meckling (1976).
30 Eg Nader, Green and Seligman (1976).
31 Eg Baysinger and Butler (1985).
32 Cochran, Philip L. and Steven L. Wartick (1988), 'Corporate Governance – A Review of the Literature', Financial Executives Research Foundation, New York.
33 Eg Porter, Michael (1985), 'Competitive Advantage: Creating and Sustaining Superior Performance', [The Free Press and Macmillan, London and New York, ISBN 0–02–925090–0]; see also his Competitive Strategy: Techniques for Analysing Industries and Competitors, [The Free Press, 1980].
34 The Wall Street Journal Europe, 12 April 2001.
35 The publication can be downloaded in HTML or PDF format from their website: www.oecd.org/daf/governance/principles.htm or /principles.pdf.
36 'Internal Control – Guidance to Directors on the Combined Code' is published by The Institute of Chartered Accountants in England & Wales, ISBN 1 84152 010 1. It is available from Accountancy Books, PO Box 21375, London, WC1N 1QP. Tel. +44 (0)20 7920 8991; fax.: +44 (0)20 7920 8992; www.accountancybooks.co.uk. Currently the guidance can be downloaded from ICAEW's website: www.icaew.co.uk/internal control.
37 As proposed in The Institute of Internal Auditors' Practice Advisory 2060–2, released in December 2002, on 'Relationship with the audit committee' to be found at http://www.theiia.org/ecm/printfriendly.cfm?doc_id=4044.
38 Daily Mail, London, 12 August 2003, p 6.
39 Alvin Toffler, Future Shock
40 Chambers, A.D. (March 1998), 'A failure of governance?', Corporate Governance, ISSN: 0219–1040, (newsletter for the Far East of FTMS Consultants (S) Pte Ltd, Tel.: (65) 735 0003).
41 Nils Pratley: 'Directors must look exclusively to shareholders', (review of pamphlet published by Social Affairs Unit, 26 January 1998) in the UK Daily Telegraph 26 January 1998, p25.
42 Reported in The Straits Times, 15 January 1998.
43 As with, for instance, the composition of boards of subsidiary companies, of joint venture entities or of public bodies.
44 The Combined Code – Provision A.3.2.
45 A.2.2 states that the chairman should, on appointment, meet the independence criteria set out in this provision, but thereafter the test of independence is not appropriate in relation to the chairman.
46 Eg originated by 'a', approved by 'b', after consultation with 'c' and 'd'.

# The Corporate Governance Framework

## Short history of corporate governance developments                    B2.1

For the UK, the Thatcher years were tumultuous. Radical themes ran through those years and shaped policy both for the UK and elsewhere. Under the panoply of a free market philosophy, state subsidies and 'the nanny state' were spurned, while the monopoly privileges of the professions were questioned. Too much government and too much red tape were identified as curses to be exorcised: determined attempts were made to roll back the frontiers of the state with the intention of liberating the entrepreneurial spirit and leading to the creation of more wealth. Self regulation was seen as better than state control. The market should regulate itself – government should just provide a level playing field.

Competition was perceived as not only good but essential. On the global stage, there was seen to be no place for businesses which were internationally uncompetitive – in the UK they went to the wall in droves during the Thatcher years. Unemployment mushroomed – but not, the protagonists argued, through the loss of 'real jobs'. 'If it wasn't hurting it wasn't working', one UK government minister memorably pronounced. The interventionist approaches of the corporate state were replaced by a self-interested individualism symbolised by Margaret Thatcher's protestation that 'there is no such thing as society'. Personal ambition and self-fulfilment reigned supreme. Some would say that the UK saw the development of a more selfish society and a more distinct underclass. The unthinkable maxim that 'greed is good' came to be given a sort of legitimacy and arguably contributed to the current perception of excessive levels of reward for top executives blighting the corporate governance scene today.

There is now a debate as to whether this level playing field should extend beyond the UK to the whole of the European Community or even beyond. For instance, is it legitimate for EU countries to compete through their differences in labour and taxation laws, not to mention corporate governance approaches?

## The UK chronology                                                        B2.2

### The Committee on the Financial Aspects of Corporate Governance ('The Cadbury Committee')                                 B2.3

It was the harsh economic climate of the late 1980s and early 1990s which had exposed company reports and accounts to unusually close scrutiny, together with continuing concern about standards of financial reporting and accountability, heightened by BCCI, Maxwell and the controversy in the UK over directors' pay. All these had brought corporate governance into the public eye. It was for these reasons that the Cadbury Committee was set up in May 1991 by the Financial Reporting Council, the London Stock Exchange, and the accountancy profession to address the financial aspects of corporate governance. The Committee issued a draft report for public comment on 27 May 1992. Its final report, taking account of submissions made during the consultation period and incorporating a Code of Best Practice was published on 1 December 1992.

The Committee's central recommendation was that the boards of all listed companies registered in the United Kingdom should comply with the Code. The Committee also encouraged as many other companies as possible to aim to meet its requirements. After all, the proprietors of private companies and other entities also need full, reliable information as a basis for, for instance, rational investment decisions.

The formal scope of the Cadbury Committee's report was on the *financial* aspects of corporate governance. Some held this restriction against the Committee. For instance, some suggested that the Cadbury Code provision that directors should report publicly on the effectiveness of internal control must have meant internal financial control in view of the intended scope of the Cadbury Committee's remit. But it was transparently clear that Cadbury meant *all* aspects on internal control since the world 'financial' had been removed by the Cadbury Committee from their final report wherever internal control was referred to (including within the Cadbury Code itself) whereas the word 'financial' had always been present in the exposure draft of the Cadbury Report. There were good reasons why Cadbury meant that directors should report publicly on internal control 'in the round'. Internal financial control cannot be neatly differentiated from the other aspects of internal control; organisations achieve their objectives not through having effective internal financial control alone – arguably operational control is more crucial to the achievement of objectives. Furthermore, the readers of published results already have some inkling about the effectiveness of internal financial control in view of the presence of audited financial statements; but to learn about the effectiveness of operational and legal and regulatory compliance control is to tell the readers something extra – so long as it is, and can be, reliably reported. As we have said, maximising reliable disclosure is an underlying theme of contemporary developments in corporate governance best practice.

**The Greenbury Committee**                                                    **B2.4**

In the UK, following the seminal Cadbury Code of Best Practice came the Greenbury Report[1] on directors' remuneration with its own Code on executive remuneration (reproduced in **B3 CORPORATE GOVERNANCE PRONOUNCEMENTS – UK** at **B3.10**). Some would argue that the Greenbury Committee would not have been convened had it not been for the excesses of individual greed evidenced in particular in the 'fat cat remuneration' of senior executives within newly privatised utilities – beneficiaries of Thatcherite privatisation policies. Certainly, Greenbury had not been anticipated at the time of the Cadbury Report.

**The Hampel Committee**                                            **B2.5**

The Cadbury Committee had recommended that its sponsors, convened by the Financial Reporting Council, should appoint a new Committee by the end of June 1995 to examine how far compliance with the Code had by then progressed, how far its other recommendations had been implemented, and whether the Code needed updating; and that until then the existing Cadbury Committee would remain responsible for reviewing the implementation of its proposals. The Hampel Committee was in fact set up in November 1995[2], and the Cadbury Committee remained convened for a while so that it could indeed, in the meantime, review the implementation of their Code, publishing a research study thereon in May 1995[3].

More recently we have had the Hampel Report[4] which consolidated, amended and added to the Cadbury and Greenbury Codes in the form of the 1998 Combined Code – so called because it combines the Cadbury and Greenbury Codes with Hampel's own additions and changes (original version reproduced in **B3 CORPORATE GOVERNANCE PRONOUNCEMENTS – UK** at **B3.11**). So, in the event, the Hampel Committee had been asked to roll into its review not only the functioning of the Cadbury Code, but the Greenbury Code as well. This Combined Code has applied to companies listed in the UK reporting for years ending on or after 31 December 1998 until the new revised Combined Code came into effect for reporting years beginning on or after 1 November 2003 (new Combined Code reproduced in Part A of this handbook). There were transitional adoption arrangements and the Code Principle D.2 together with its associated Provision D.2.1 and D.2.2 were deferred from being implemented, pending the development and roll-out of guidance which came in the form of the Turnbull Report.

The Hampel Committee did not give us their proposed wording of the original Combined Code within their draft or final reports. Instead they gave indications of the sort of changes they were minded to make. This undoubtedly had the effect of making it easier to get general 'buy-in' to the proposed changes – but arguably because there was less appreciation of what they would be. After the Hampel Report was accepted, the Hampel Committee quickly drew up the wording of the original Combined Code which was exposed only briefly before being adopted. In contrast, Higgs gave us in his report the suggested wording of a revised Combined Code with the result that it was easier to dispute it; consequently the wording was revised before adoption by the Financial Reporting Council in 2003.

# UK corporate governance listing requirements   B2.6

Since the adoption of the first version of the Combined Code by the London Stock Exchange, the Financial Services Authority has taken over from the London Stock Exchange the regulation of UK listed companies. The Listing Rules, which used to be referred to as 'The Yellow Book' have now become 'The Purple Book'.[5]

The 1998 Combined Code was appended to the Listing Rules, as had been the Cadbury and Greenbury Codes previously. The Combined Code did not form part of the Listing Rules themselves[6] and neither does the new revised Combined Code. The 'Definitions' section (May 2000) towards the start of the Listing Rules attributes the following status to the 1998 Combined Code:

> 'Combined Code: the principles of good governance and code of best practice prepared by the Committee on Corporate Governance, chaired by Sir Ronald Hampel, published in June 1998 and appended but not forming part of, the Listing Rules.'

So, as with the Cadbury Code, it is not be a listing requirement for a listed company to comply with the Combined Code. Chapter 12: Financial Information (May 2000) of the Listing Rules, the section on 'Corporate Governance and Directors' Remuneration' includes obligations only requiring a company to include in its annual report two statements, *viz*:

> '12.43A In the case of a company incorporated in the United Kingdom, the following additional items must be included in its annual report and accounts:
>
> (a) A narrative statement of how it has applied the principles set out in Section 1 of the Combined Code, providing sufficient explanation which enables its shareholders to evaluate how the principles have been applied;
>
> (b) a statement as to whether or not it has complied throughout the accounting period with the provisions set out in Section 1 of the Combined Code. A company that has not complied with the Code provisions, or complied with only some of the Code provisions or (in the case of provisions whose requirements are of a continuing nature) complied for only part of an accounting period, must specify the provisions with which it has not complied, and (where relevant) for what part of the period such non-compliance continued, and give reasons for any non-compliance; ... '

Certain provisions of the 1998 Combined Code had already been explicitly required by the Listing Rules as they were already requirements at the time of the introduction of the 1998 Combined Code, as follows, and a broadly similar situation pertains with respect to the 2003 Code.

## Steadily increasing burden of compliance          B2.7

The following table summarises the extent to which adherence to UK corporate governance codes of best practice has become a more demanding business over the last decade or so.

|  |  | **Cadbury Code 1992** | **Greenbury Code 1995** | **Combined Code 1998** | **Revised Combined Code 2003** |
|---|---|---|---|---|---|
| **Main principles** | General | – | – | – | 14 |
|  | Addressed to institutional investors | – | – | – | 3 |
|  | Total | 0 | 0 | 0 | 17 |
| **Supporting principles** | General | – | – | – | 21 |
|  | Addressed to institutional investors | – | – | – | 5 |
|  | Total | 0 | 0 | 0 | 26 |
| **Principles** | General | – | – | 14 | 35 |
|  | Addressed to institutional investors | – | – | 3 | 8 |
|  | Total | 0 | 0 | 17 | 43 |
| **Provisions** | General | 19 | 39 | 44* | 48* |
|  | Addressed to institutional investors | 0 | 0 | 3 | 0 |
|  | Total | 19 | 39 | 47* | 48* |

* Excluding (a) the seven Schedule A Provisions on the design of performance related remuneration which were part of the Combined Code and continue in the revised Combined Code, and (b) the seven Schedule B Provisions on what should be included in the Remuneration Report which were part of the Combined Code but are not included in the revised Combined Code as there are now separate regulations in force (the *Directors' Remuneration Report Regulations 2002/1986*, available www.hmso.gov.uk/so2002/20021986.htm and www.hmso.gov.uk/so2002/2001780.htm) which supersede the earlier Code provisions. Note that in the past the additional guidance within the Turnbull Report has to be followed if adherence to the internal control and internal audit aspects of the Combined Code was claimed, though whether this is strictly still

the case is not entirely clear. The FRC has abandoned the Smith Committee's intention that some of the guidance within the Smith Report should also be followed if adherence with the audit committee aspects of the revised Combined Code is being claimed; however the FRC has promoted some of this guidance by placing it in the new Code itself (see **A1** THE **2003** COMBINED CODE).

# The corporate governance framework – laws, regulations, codes of best practice, etc      B2.8

With many of the world's largest entities being corporations, not nation states, their effective governance, and in particular their accountability, become key imperatives. Sir Adrian Cadbury has described the corporate governance framework in these terms[8].

> 'Corporations work within a governance framework which is set first by the law and then by regulations emanating from the regulatory bodies to which they are subject. In addition, publicly quoted companies are subject to their shareholders in general meeting and all companies to the forces of public opinion. The influence of public opinion should not be underestimated; it compelled Shell to change its plans for the disposal of the Brent Star platform. Not only is public opinion a governance force, but it is one whose impact cannot be precisely foreseen in the same way as that of the law and regulations; it is not fixed in form as they are, but responds to the mood of the moment. The views of investors and public opinion reflect their current thinking, and boards of directors and members of professional bodies need to respond by being continually alert to the changing expectations of those whom they serve.

> 'Clearly the balance between these governance forces varies between countries. Where the opinions of shareholders and of the public cannot make themselves sufficiently felt, the gap needs to be filled by the law and appropriate regulations. This is why each country has to devise its own governance framework. But how effective is this framework of governance? The legal rules are clear-cut and carry known penalties if boards of directors contravene them. Regulations are equally straightforward; if quoted companies do not abide by the rules of the London Stock Exchange, they risk de-listing.'

The Cadbury Committee's report also gave some emphasis to the part that internal rules should play in corporate governance, *viz.*

> 'It is important that all employees should know what standards are expected of them. We regard it as good practice for boards of directors to draw up Codes of ethics or statements of business practice and to publish them both internally and externally'.

## The importance of disclosure  B2.9

Sir Adrian Cadbury said of the Cadbury Code of Best Practice that its foundation, and the foundation of its equivalents elsewhere, is based on disclosure[9].

> 'Disclosure is the lifeblood of governance. Provided those with interests in, or responsibilities towards, companies know how they are directed and controlled, they can influence their boards constructively. A leading bank responded to the Code by including a section in its Annual Report headed 'How our business is run'. This covered the role of the board, the work of its committees and the responsibilities of directors; information which had never previously been accessible. Investors, lenders, employees and the public can only play their governance roles provided they have the information they need in order to do so. Transparency is the aim. This requires clear reporting of the state of the business, of the way it is directed and controlled and of its place in the community. Openness by companies is the basis of public confidence in the corporate system. It also enables external governance forces to function as they should. Institutional investors, in particular, have the means and the incentive to use Codes to promote board effectiveness. As to whether Codes work, the degree to which the majority of quoted companies responded to the Code of Best Practice is evidence that Codes can give a lead which will be followed, provided they genuinely represent best practice and thus are going with the grain of investor and corporate opinion.'

Important, related aspects of governance are accountability and disclosure.

> 'Without audit, no accountability; without accountability, no control; and if there is no control, where is the seat of power? ... great issues often come to light only because of scrupulous verification of details.'[10]

## Substance, not form  B2.10

Sir Adrian Cadbury emphasised that the focus has to be, not on the form of governance, but on its quality, for which legal tests would be difficult to devise. He has pointed out that the Cadbury Code of Best Practice, for example, referred to the need for boards to include non-executive directors of sufficient calibre for their views to carry significant weight in the boards' decisions.[11]

> 'A word like 'calibre' may have no legal standing, but it can certainly be recognised by investors and financial commentators. When a major UK company appointed its first batch of non-executive directors, they were seen as not measuring up to this requirement of the Code. Investor pressure and press comment resulted in the appointment of a further non-executive director of sufficient bottom.'

To take another example, the Cadbury Committee said in its report that, in principle, the chairman and chief executive should not be the same person. Being non-prescriptive, however, the Code did not make separation of the top two corporate posts a requirement for companies observing the Code.[12]

'If separation were to be a legal requirement, boards could circumvent it by giving two of their members different titles, while in reality power remained in one pair of hands. If shareholders queried the balance of power on such a board, the board could reply that they complied with the law and that there was no more to be said.'

The Cadbury Code, however, required that:

'There should be a clearly accepted division of responsibilities at the head of a company ... such that no one person has unfettered powers of decision.

Shareholders can demand to know precisely how powers are divided, and continue probing until they are satisfied. In that sense, a Code recommendation can prove a sterner test in practice of a true separation of powers than a law to the same effect.

A further reason for backing statutory regulation with market regulation is that Codes can reflect changing circumstances or new governance issues as they arise, whereas the law by its nature takes time to catch up with new situations. In the same way the law sets a floor to corporate or professional behaviour, whereas Codes can promote best practice beyond lawful practice. The law is limited to the letter, while Codes can put substance above form.'

## Compliance                                                    B2.11

As Sir Adrian Cadbury has said, an important concern is that legislators may enact laws and regulators may introduce rules, but at the end of the day what matters is that these are observed, breaches are identified and tough sanctions are consistently applied. Where there is doubt, as for instance in Indonesia, about the diligence or even-handedness of the authorities or the independence of the judiciary, then there will always be doubt about standards of corporate governance – however impressive might be the company law or the stock exchange regulations.

In the UK there has been concern about flouting of aspects of the Combined Code[13], – especially the provisions on directors' appointments and remuneration[14]. Pensions and Investment Research Consultants (PIRC)[15], who led a survey which highlighted these concerns, and also other bodies which represent institutional investors, have overlaid the Provisions of the Combined Code with their own more demanding interpretations and prescriptions which are not to be found in the Combined Code and do not therefore have the authority of the listing rules.[16] (The Listing Rules require listed companies to explain how they are adhering to the 'Principles' of the Combined Code, and to draw attention to which of the 'Provisions' they are not adhering to, giving reasons. So it is not a Listing Rule that a listed company should necessarily comply with *any* of the Provisions; and certainly not a Listing Rule that companies should comply with the more onerous extensions promulgated in the policies of bodies which represent institutional investors.) It is however entirely appropriate that institutional (and other) investors should seek to exercise effective external control over the way companies, in which they invest, are governed; and so, to the extent that the policies of bodies representing institutional investors are followed by the institutional investors themselves, these policies assume an authority of their own. Perhaps we should point out that these representative bodies are less inclined to draw attention to those companies that go *much further* than the Combined Code provisions require. It has also been pointed out that the corporate governance arrangements of many institutional investors themselves fall far short of the best practice being commended by the Combined Code, let alone the more demanding requirements of the bodies which represent these institutional investors.

The research by PIRC, referred to above[17], which covered 468 companies in the FTSE All Share index, found that just 9 – less than 2 per cent – put critical remuneration committee reports to the vote of shareholders at the annual general meetings. Almost half the companies had still not imposed one-year contracts on executive directors, or adopted a policy of reducing contracts to this.[18] (This recommendation dates back to the 1995 Greenbury Code on executive remuneration.) Only 77 per cent staffed their remuneration committees with non-executives they believed to be independent.

PIRC found 27 per cent of companies were happy to disclose that they had considered putting pay committee reports to an AGM vote, but most companies gave no indication either way. Stuart Bell, PIRC research director, said:

'If they are not disclosing the information, shareholders can have little confidence that they are following the Code. [It was] disappointing that compliance on pay issues is relatively low'.

Just 51 per cent of companies reported that their practice or policy was one year, rolling contacts for all directors. Bell said that the Code

'represents a base-line standard'.

He expected the best companies:

'to go beyond it in providing better information to investors and improving their governance structure. This was important because it 'will contribute to competitiveness in the long term.'[19]

Study of the wording of the Combined Code does however show that PIRC is taking a much more stringent line than the Code intended with respect to most of these matters. For instance, to take just one example, a reasonable interpretation of the Code on 'independence' allows that it is for the board to decide whether a past or even a present relationship (with management, the business or with anyone or anything else) is an impediment to the exercise of independent judgement. In defence of PIRC, the Hampel Committee was at pains to assert that it is the spirit of the Principles contained within the Combined Code that it is mandatory for companies to adhere to, and of course it becomes a matter of judgement as to how such adherence can be achieved.

# Status of the Combined Code in the UK       B2.12

There are options as to the regulatory framework to be followed in order to ensure that organisations observe satisfactory standards of corporate governance. It is hard to avoid the conclusion that the route we have chosen to follow within the UK is typically British. The Code of Best Practice for Corporate Governance has not been enshrined in statute. There has been no legal requirement for listed companies to comply with the provisions of the Code. Instead, the Code is an appendix to the Purple Book.[20] We should not run away with the impression that compliance with the provisions within the Code of Best Practice has ever been a regulatory requirement, previously of the Stock Exchange or now of the FSA. The Listing Rules themselves just require that a listed company should state within its annual report whether it complies with the provisions of the Code and, if not, with which provisions does it not comply and the reasons for non-compliance. That has been enough for most listed companies, most of the time, to endeavour to apply with most or all of the provisions within the Code – few companies would wish, for instance, to have to draw attention to the absence of an audit committee and then have to try to explain why the company does not have an audit committee; or to the absence of a report on internal control and then to try to explain that away. It is easier to comply.

The Combined Code has been appended to the Listing Rules, but does not form part of the Listing Rules themselves. So, as with the Cadbury Code, it is not a listing requirement for a listed company to comply with the provisions within the Combined Code. Excluding quite detailed disclosure requirements on directors' remuneration[21], the listing requirements only require a company to include in its annual report two statements, *viz*:

> 'A narrative statement of how it has applied the principles set out in section 1 of the Combined Code providing explanation which enables its shareholders to evaluate how the principles have been applied.'[22]

and:

> 'A statement as to whether or not it has complied throughout the accounting period with the Code provisions set out in Section 1 of the Combined Code. A company that has not complied with the Code provisions, or complied with only some of the Code provisions or (in the case of provisions whose requirements are of a continuing nature) complied for only part of an accounting period, must specify the Code provisions with which it has not complied, and (where relevant) for what part of the period such non-compliance continued, and give reasons for any non-compliance.'[23]

# Principles, provisions – and 'box ticking'       B2.13

This raises the question as to the extent to which compliance has been nominal and superficial. Hampel referred disparagingly to this as 'box ticking' – which his committee felt was all too prevalent. This has not been the experience of the author. It could be that a listed company might have established an audit committee only because of the Cadbury Code – not because it believed in it nor even because it had any intention that it would be effective. But, over time, the committee would tend to develop a life of its own. Its non-executive members would not be willing to be mere ciphers for a possibly corrupt executive. The written terms of reference would start to give teeth to the committee. Setting up the committee in the good times would mean it was already in place when bad times came along and the company was then tempted to sail closer to the wind.

The striking change, following the Hampel Report and the introduction of the new Combined Code, is that *above* the level of the Code Provisions we now have higher level Code 'Principles'. It is interesting to observe how the Hampel Committee has forged overarching 'Principles' from the lower level Code 'Provisions'. The first new listing rule quoted above indicates that companies are expected to comply with the 'Principles' though not necessarily with the 'Provisions' – companies must therefore include a statement showing *how* they have complied with the 'Principles', not (as with the Code 'Provisions') *whether*, and not *if not* – *why not*. Strictly, there is also no requirement to explain *how* a 'Provision' has been complied with: *how* applies to Principles – *whether* applies to Provisions.

Although the Code 'Provisions' are therefore, in a sense, optional – so were those within the earlier Cadbury Code which nevertheless came to be followed in most respects by the vast majority of UK listed companies. Having to draw attention to ways in which they were not being complied with, and to give reasons for non-compliance, was enough to encourage companies to ensure compliance. This same approach has usually been adopted for the new Code 'Provisions'.

## Adoption beyond listed companies                            B2.14

Clearly there is more public concern about the governance of public companies than of other companies. Yet the Cadbury Committee expressed the view that their Code of Best Practice had a much broader applicability than just to the listed company sector. Indeed, it became the yardstick against which to measure the governance of other companies, enterprises incorporated not under company law and also public sector entities.

The public sector in the UK has become one of the keenest advocates of the Code, with the encouragement in particular of HM Treasury. In the UK, just as the public sector attempts to adopt emerging accounting and auditing standards, so now this sector is keen to adopt the corporate governance Code.

While the major concerns which had led to the Cadbury Committee being set up were concerns within the listed company sector, and the Code was directed primarily to the boards of directors of quoted companies, the Committee said in its report that it ...

> 'would encourage as many other companies as possible to aim at meeting its requirements.'

127

Indeed there has been a very widespread adoption of the Code outside of the listed sector, and not least by public sector bodies. There tends to be a two year (or so) time lag before the public sector adopts newly specified best practices and it is only recently that most of the public sector has, for instance, got round to providing directors' reports on internal control – often much more impressive ones than the private sector provides. Now, in some respects, the public sector has been left high and dry as the private sector has moved away from Cadbury to Hampel, and from Rutteman to Turnbull; so there is now another catching up process under way within the public sector. Of course, separately, the public sector has not been idle in developing its own tailor-made Codes – especially those contained within the Nolan Report (paragraphs 9.1–9.3).

While there is more public concern about the governance of public companies than of other companies, this indicates how dated is the content of these corporate governance Codes. The general concern about environmental responsibility, sustainability and the social responsibility of corporations is a concern which is especially, but not exclusively, directed towards public, listed companies. But contemporary corporate governance codes, at least in the UK, are silent on those issues.[24] They focus on the concerns of only one stakeholder – the shareholder. Their focus on disclosure is largely on disclosures which are of value to shareholders alone.

# Postscript                                                                  B2.15

Perhaps the last word should be with Sir Adrian Cadbury. In 1998 he said:

'The Committee considered that companies as a whole would see it as in their interest to comply (with the Code of Best Practice for Corporate Governance). Compliance would publicly confirm that they met the standards expected of well-run businesses. The Code was literally based on best practice, on the way in which successful companies were directed and controlled. Meeting best practice has to be a logical aim for boards and we expect investors, especially the institutions, to encourage the companies in which they held shares to comply. In effect, the Committee was looking to market regulation, rather than strictly self-regulation, to win board acceptance for its recommendations. Provided investors, analysts and lenders valued compliance with the Code, it would confer a market advantage on companies which complied, possibly assisting their credit rating and lowering their costs of capital. In addition, good corporate governance is increasingly being linked to good corporate performance and so complying with the Code could be expected to add to a company's competitive edge. Indeed, my continuing involvement with corporate governance is founded on the positive contribution which I am convinced it can make to board effectiveness.

Similar codes around the world have equally relied on companies seeing it as in their best interest to comply. None is mandatory and most are backed by the appropriate Stock Exchange. In sum, I believe that such codes are effective, both in assisting boards to direct their companies well and in providing some insurance against fraud and failure, provided that they are based firmly on best practice, not on what best practice in the abstract might be thought to be, and that they have some market discipline behind them. Thus Codes can usefully fill a layer below the law and regulations and help to clarify the rules of the game. But why not make compliance compulsory, on the argument that well-intentioned companies will no doubt follow the best practice lead in any case, but it is precisely the less well-intentioned who most need to be brought within the rules? There is clearly force in that argument. However, an important reason why I believe that there is a place for Codes in establishing the rules of the game is that it is hard to frame legislation which will raise governance standards.'[25]

Sir Adrian Cadbury's full speech is reproduced at **B2.25** below.

# Developing and implementing codes of best practice for corporate governance **B2.16**

In developing codes of best practice for corporate governance, it is clearly important to arrive at a set of sentiments which have widespread support – otherwise they will fail to be implemented satisfactorily and will become discredited. Singapore has found this, and has had to backtrack. It is not easy to get agreement to anything. One or two exposure drafts will be necessary, as has been the case in the UK. This consultative process needs to be taken seriously, with the committee willing to make changes during the consultation phase.

## Exposure drafts **B2.17**

Nevertheless, there is a risk associated with changes at the exposure draft stage – others will not be consulted on whether they concur with the changes. In the UK we have had instances of changes slipping in between the exposure draft and the final report which would not have had a wide consensus had they been exposed first. Thus, for instance, between the exposure draft and final versions of the Cadbury Report and Code of Best Practice, the committee removed the world *financial* from the phrase internal *financial* control – wherever it appeared in the Report and in the Code. This had the effect of broadening the scope of the directors' public reports on internal control to cover *all* aspects of internal control, not just internal *financial* control. While this was clearly Cadbury's intention (and the change was probably made due to persuasive lobbying by The Institute of Internal Auditors at the exposure draft stage), it did not have widespread support and was reversed by the Rutteman Committee when that committee developed guidance for directors in the matter. Later, the Hampel Committee was to revert to the Cadbury intention.

## Implementing codes **B2.18**

Implementing a national corporate governance code has to be managed by the regulators with care. Of course, one expedient can be to defer the implementation of particular parts of the Code pending the development of guidance – as was the case for the 'going concern' and 'internal control' parts of the Cadbury Code, and then later for the revised 'internal control' parts of the Combined Code – or for some other reason.

In the UK, where implementation of parts of the Code has been deferred, during this deferral period, companies have been allowed to claim full compliance with the Code regardless of their practices with respect to the deferred parts of the Code. Where a revision to part of the Code is made some years later but its implementation is deferred pending the development and adoption of guidance, the original requirement (as contained within the original wording of that part of the Code) can continue to apply until the revision is adopted. This was the case with respect to the revised internal control reporting requirements within the UK's 1998 Combined Code.

In general, for companies to indicate compliance with most or all of the Provisions in the Code will only be permissible if the appropriate measures have been in place and have been followed for the whole of the year that is being reported. This means that the first annual report of a company which will be required to disclose code compliance will most likely have to be significantly more than twelve months after the publication of the Code in its final form and after its adoption as a regulatory requirement – as companies will need at least a modicum of notice to introduce the requisite measures by the commencement of that financial year. In the case of the 2003 Combined Code's internal control reporting Provision D.2.1 (see **B3.11**), compliance is also required for the period between the year end date and the date that the financial statements are signed (the 'subsequent events' period).

An alternative is a particular transitional approach which allows a company to claim complete compliance with the Code in its *first* annual report after the Code has been adopted by the regulatory authorities – so long as the company had put in place the requisite measures by the end of the year being reported; but for *all* of the following year the company must have followed the requisite measures that they had put in place towards the end of the previous year if it is to claim compliance. This was the approach recommended by Turnbull for those parts of the Combined Code covered by the Turnbull guidance, and was subsequently broadly endorsed by the Stock Exchange.

The choice of the specific calendar date for implementation of the Code may be significant. In the UK companies are allowed to vary their year end date by up to one week without obtaining shareholder approval for this. Consequently, accounting standards are often introduced with an operative date of 23 December so that companies are not readily able to defer compliance by a full year simply by varying their usual December 31 year end date by a few days. For the first time, this device was used outside of the arena of accounting standards when Turnbull set 23 December as the operative date. So, for the initial transitional period, companies with year ends on or after December 23, 1999 were able to claim compliance with the aspects of the Combined Code covered by the Turnbull Committee if they had in place the requisite measures before the end of that financial year. Twelve months later, that is for companies reporting for their first year ending on or after December 23, 2000, compliance required that the requisite measures had been in place and applied for all of that year which is being reported (as well as the 'subsequent events' period).

The dates set for implementation of a code of corporate governance, or parts of it, may need to be sympathetic to the external audit dimension. For instance, where external auditors are required to review and perhaps report on directors' compliance with aspects of the Code, allowance may need to be made for the time it will take for guidance to be developed by the auditing profession on how the auditors should undertake that review and how they should report. It will probably not be practical to develop that guidance until after such guidance as may be needed has been developed for directors with regard to what compliance means for them. This was the case with respect to both the 'going concern' and 'internal control' provisions within the Cadbury Code.

## Impact of subsequent guidance                                    B2.19

When guidance is developed following the publication and/or adoption of a code of best practice for corporate governance, the guidance may have the effect of watering down the intention of a provision in the code. This happened with the Rutteman guidance on directors reporting on the effectiveness of internal control – they were relieved of the obligation to disclose their opinion, if any, of effectiveness, and were permitted to restrict the scope of their report just to internal *financial* control (see **B4.15**). On the other hand, guidance may have the effect of strengthening and extending the requirements of a provision. For instance, the Turnbull guidance on the Code provision that cohas interpreted this to mean, in effect, that:

(a)   the *board* itself should undertake this review;

(b)   the review should be done at least annually; and

(c)   the review should be undertaken even when there is an already existing internal audit function, so as to determine its appropriateness,

and from 2003 the Smith guidance has further strengthened this Code provision by requiring explanation of a decision not to have an internal audit function.

## Significant revisions to codes of best practice for corporate governance                                    B2.20

It was always intended that Cadbury would be revisited after a few years to review how well it was working and to consider whether any changes were needed. In the event, as we have indicated, the review was delayed a few months and Cadbury himself declined to lead it, expressing the view that the review needed a more impartial approach. As with love and independence, there is probably no such thing as pure 100 per cent impartiality. It was probably inevitable that the new committee, chaired by Sir Ronnie Hampel, would have been influenced by those who had been most vociferous in their opposition to aspects of the Cadbury Code, or to the whole idea of a code: those who were content with the workings of the Cadbury Code were perhaps less likely to have expressed their views strongly to the Hampel Committee.

Hampel approached the challenge of getting consensus to his exposure draft by not revealing the wording of his intended Combined Code – even in the Committee's final report. While the intended Combined Code was exposed very briefly by the Stock Exchange later, criticism had been effectively stifled as it had not been very practical to challenge Hampel's sentiments within his committee's final report when the precise wording of the intended Code had not been revealed.

## Drafting carelessness                                           B2.21

A further challenge in developing codes of best practice for corporate governance is to avoid carelessness or rashness. Here we give a few examples from the UK experience, in the area of internal control:

First, in the initial printing of the 1998 Combined Code Provision D.2.1 (now, with a slight amendment, 2003 Combined Code Provision C.2.1), the omission of a comma between 'financial' and 'operational' suggested to some a different meaning from that intended, *viz*:

> 'The directors should, at least annually, conduct a review of the effectiveness of the group's system of internal controls and should report to shareholders that they have done so. The review should cover all controls, including financial operational and compliance controls and risk management.'

Secondly, the draft Rutteman Report did not keep entirely to the COSO framework for internal control, although comments at the exposure draft stage largely rectified this by the time the final Rutteman Report was published. Even so, there were definitions of internal control and internal financial control which differed somewhat from the generally accepted COSO definitions (see table at **B8.25**) More recently, the Turnbull Report (see PART A) has moved further away from the COSO framework, by (a) suggesting that there are only four, not five, components of internal control and (b) giving us a new definition of internal control. It is to be questioned whether a working party with one particular brief should take upon itself to redefine key concepts already defined by another working party which had the specific brief to do so. The effect is that we are in danger of moving away from generally accepted paradigms, originally developed with great care and at risk of being overturned casually and superficially.

Thirdly, the draft Hampel Report suggested that Rutteman 'encouraged' directors to disclose their opinion on internal control 'effectiveness' but this was not so. Rutteman merely said that they might, and reserved 'encouragement' to extending the scope of their report to cover all aspects of internal control.

Fourthly, although the Hampel Report and the resulting Combined Code recommend that remuneration committees should be empowered to take outside advice, a similar recommendation for audit committees (which had been made by Cadbury) is absent, presumably inadvertently, from both the Hampel Report and also from the Combined Code.

## The copyright issue                                      B2.22

To encourage its dissemination, which can only be described as having been very successful, copyright restrictions were waived with respect to unrestricted reproduction of the original Cadbury Code. So we think it rather surprising that the London Stock Exchange negotiated to Gee & Co, the London-based publishers, the right to license reproduction in publications of the new Combined Code. We intend no criticism of Gee who took an opportunity here, but we query the appropriateness of a body such as the Stock Exchange putting an obstacle in the way of wide and open circulation of this admirable new Combined Code.

### Further information                                     B2.23

1.   Gee charged a flat fee of £500 for reproduction of all or part of the Combined Code. Now that the Stock Exchange has transferred responsibility for the regulation of UK listed companies to the FSA (and the Combined Code is now an appendix within the FSA's 'Purple Book' ('the Listing Rules'), we understand that the £500 payment to Gee may no longer apply and that requests for permission to reprint the Combined Code should be addressed direct to the FSA, but we advise that enquirers should check out carefully with Gee and FSA before reprinting.

# The future for governance: the rules of the game         B2.24

*This is the text of Sir Adrian Cadbury's 1998 lecture to Gresham College in London, delivered at Mansion House, London. Sir Adrian's insights into the background to modern developments as well as of the principles which underpin effective governance are profound and practical, stimulating and persuasive.*

*(Readers may also wish to refer to the text of another more recent, indeed last, speech on corporate governance by Sir Adrian which we also reprint in this handbook at* **B2.26** THE CORPORATE GOVERNANCE SAGA.*)*

*Sir Adrian chaired the committee that produced the Report of the Committee on the Financial Aspects of Corporate Governance. From 1970 to 1994 he was a director of the Bank of England, and from 1975–89 he was chairman of Cadbury Schweppes. He wrote the book 'The Company Chairman', 1990, published by Director Books in association with the Institute of Directors.*

*Of course, since Sir Adrian gave this address, the London Stock Exchange has published an updated code –the Combined Code in June 1998 (***B3.11***), and in 2003 the Financial Reporting Council published its amended Combined Code (reproduced in* PART A*).*

*Gresham College is an independent institution in the City of London, established long before London University in 1597 by Sir Thomas Gresham.*

*Part of his legacy to the development of economics is 'Gresham's Law' that 'bad money tends to drive out good'. Readers can find out more about Gresham College by consulting the book 'A Brief History of Gresham College 1597 – 1997', by Richard Chartres and David Vermont.*

> 'There is one and only one social responsibility of business – to use its resources and engage in activities designed to increase its profits so long as it stays within the rules of the game ... '
>
> *Milton Friedman*

I was honoured to be asked to give this lecture and I am grateful to Gresham College for the opportunity to reflect on what I have learnt from my involvement in corporate governance since 1991, when I was asked to chair a committee on the subject. We delivered our Report and Code of Best Practice at the end of the following year and imagined that this would be the end of the matter and that we could retire to cultivating our gardens. This, however, was not to be, because by then corporate governance, which we had defined as the system by which companies are directed and controlled, had become a matter of considerable public interest worldwide. We disbanded as a committee in May 1995 after publishing an assessment of compliance with our Code of Best Practice. Since then I have continued to be involved through taking part in debates and conferences on corporate governance around the world. I aim to end this governance odyssey with my forthcoming visits to Spain and Chile, which is why this is an appropriate time for reflection.

## Background

Governance is a word used by Chaucer, but not often heard until Harold Wilson took it up in reference to the governance of the country – a field from which I have managed to steer clear! It means either the action or manner of governing, or the method of management, and it is in that second sense that it is applied to companies or corporations. In Chaucer's time the word carried with it the connotation 'wise and responsible', which fits well with the theme of my talk.

Governance's Latin root means 'to steer' and an apt quotation from classical times is

> 'He that governs sits quietly at the stern and scarce is seen to stir'.

The analogy of the quiet steersman sums up what I see as the right approach to governance – a light hand on the tiller, thanks to looking ahead and identifying in good time when a change of course is needed. But how does the steersman know what course to set and who it is that we expect to respond to his guidance?

Our Committee's Code of Best Practice was directed primarily to the boards of directors of quoted companies, although we said in our Report that we

> 'would encourage as many other companies as possible to aim at meeting its requirements.'

It was an addition to the complex set of forces which regulate corporate behaviour and less directly the conduct of those belonging to professional bodies. It is those forces which I propose to discuss in the light of the international debate on corporate governance in which I have taken part. I chose the title 'The Rules of the Game' because that is the issue. What are the rules, who sets them and do they matter?

I take as my text the quotation from an article by Professor Milton Friedman which heads this lecture. Milton Friedman is the arch-advocate of companies concentrating solely on maximising the return to their shareholders, but the important qualification which he puts on that aim, staying within the rules of the game, is too often omitted. He explains in the same article that, by the rules of the game, he means:

> 'while conforming to the basic rules of the society, both those embodied in law and those embodied in ethical custom'.

What are these rules embodied in law and in ethical custom to which corporate officials should conform?

## The governance framework

A useful distinction is between externally imposed rules and internally imposed ones. Internal rules in turn break down into those which companies or professions set for themselves and those which we as individuals set for ourselves, our personal ethical values, or the rules by which we live.

Corporations work within a governance framework which is set first by the law and then by regulations emanating from the regulatory bodies to which they are subject. In addition, publicly quoted companies are subject to their shareholders in general meeting and all companies to the forces of public opinion. The influence of public opinion should not be underestimated; it compelled Shell to change its plans for the disposal of the Brent Star platform. Not only is public opinion a governance force, but it is one whose impact cannot be precisely foreseen in the same way as that of the law and regulations; it is not fixed in form as they are, but responds to the mood of the moment. The views of investors and public opinion reflect their current thinking, and boards of directors and members of professional bodies need to respond by being continually alert to the changing expectations of those whom they serve.

Clearly the balance between these governance forces varies between countries. Where the opinions of shareholders and of the public cannot make themselves sufficiently felt, the gap needs to be filled by the law and appropriate regulations. This is why each country has to devise its own governance framework. But how effective is this framework of governance? The legal rules are clear-cut and carry known penalties if boards of directors contravene them. Regulations are equally straightforward; if quoted companies do not abide by the rules of the London Stock Exchange, they risk de-listing.

When it comes to codes, such as the one drawn up by our Committee, there is not the same degree of external discipline. The recommendations of the Code of Best Practice were neither mandatory nor prescriptive. Boards were required to state in their annual report how far they complied with the Code and to give reasons for areas of non-compliance. Boards had to make a *compliance statement.* Compliance itself was left as a matter between boards and their shareholders. What made that requirement effective was that it had the authority of the London Stock Exchange behind it. Publication of a compliance statement became a condition of listing on the Stock Exchange and that backing was all-important.

The Committee considered that companies as a whole would see it as in their interest to comply. Compliance would publicly confirm that they met the standards expected of well-run businesses. The Code was literally based on best practice, on the way in which successful companies were directed and controlled. Meeting best practice has to be a logical aim for boards and we expect investors, especially the institutions, to encourage the companies in which they held shares to comply. In effect, the Committee was looking to market regulation, rather than strictly self-regulation, to win board acceptance for its recommendations. Provided investors, analysts and lenders valued compliance with the Code, it would confer a market advantage on companies which complied, possibly assisting their credit rating and lowering their costs of capital. In addition, good corporate governance is increasingly being linked to good corporate performance and so complying with the Code could be expected to add to a company's competitive edge. Indeed, my continuing involvement with corporate governance is founded on the positive contribution which I am convinced it can make to board effectiveness.

Similar codes around the world have equally relied on companies seeing it as in their best interest to comply. None is mandatory and most are backed by the appropriate Stock Exchange. In sum, I believe that such codes are effective, both in assisting boards to direct their companies well and in providing some insurance against fraud and failure, provided that they are based firmly on best practice, not on what best practice in the abstract might be thought to be, and that they have some market discipline behind them. Thus codes can usefully fill a layer below the law and regulations and help to clarify the rules of the game. But why not make compliance compulsory, on the argument that well-intentioned companies will no doubt follow the best practice lead in any case, but it is precisely the less well-intentioned who most need to be brought within the rules? There is clearly force in that argument. However, an important reason why I believe that there is a place for codes in establishing the rules of the game is that it is hard to frame legislation which will raise governance standards.

## Regulatory form

First, the focus has to be, not on the form of governance, but on its quality, for which legal tests are difficult to devise. The Code of Best Practice, for example, refers to the need for boards to include non-executive directors of sufficient calibre for their views to carry significant weight in the boards' decisions. A word like 'calibre' may have no legal standing, but it can certainly be recognised by investors and financial commentators. When a major UK company appointed its first batch of non-executive directors, they were seen as not measuring up to this requirement of the Code. Investor pressure and press comment resulted in the appointment of a further non-executive director of sufficient bottom.

To take another example, the Committee said in its report that in principle the chairman and chief executive should not be the same person. Being non-prescriptive, however, the Code did not make separation of the top two corporate posts a recommendation. If separation were to be a legal requirement, boards could circumvent it by giving two of their members different titles, while in reality power remained in one pair of hands. If shareholders queried the balance of power on such a board, the board could reply that they complied with the law and that there was no more to be said. The Code, however, requires that:

'There should be a clearly accepted division of responsibilities at the head of a company ... such that no one person has unfettered powers of decision'.

Shareholders can demand to know precisely how powers are divided, and continue probing until they are satisfied. In that sense, a code recommendation can prove a sterner test in practice of a true separation of powers than a law to the same effect.

A further reason for backing statutory regulation with market regulation is that codes can reflect changing circumstances or new governance issues as they arise, whereas the law by its nature takes time to catch up with new situations. In the same way the law sets a floor to corporate or professional behaviour, whereas codes can promote best practice beyond lawful practice. The law is limited to the letter, while codes can put substance above form.

## Disclosure

The foundation on which the Code of Best Practice and its equivalents elsewhere are based is that of disclosure. Disclosure is the lifeblood of governance. Provided those with interests in, or responsibilities towards, companies know how they are directed and controlled, they can influence their boards constructively. A leading bank responded to the Code by including a section in its annual report headed 'How our business is run'. This covered the role of the board, the work of its committees and the responsibilities of directors; information which had never previously been accessible. Investors, lenders, employees and the public can only play their governance roles provided they have the information they need in order to do so. Transparency is the aim. This requires clear reporting of the state of the business, of the way it is directed and controlled and of its place in the community. Openness by companies is the basis of public confidence in the corporate system. It also enables external governance forces to function as they should. Institutional investors, in particular, have the means and the incentive to use codes to promote board effectiveness. As to whether codes work, the degree to which the majority of quoted companies responded to the Code of Best Practice is evidence that codes can give a lead which will be followed, provided they genuinely represent best practice and thus are going with the grain of investor and corporate opinion.

## City rules

If the law, regulations, codes of best practice and the shareholders in general meeting (where appropriate) form the external rules of the game, what about the rules which companies and professionals draw up for themselves? Most professions, for example, have rules to which qualified entrants subscribe. On the corporate side, the natural example to take, given where we stand, is that offered by what might loosely be called 'The City', that is to say the financial services centred on London.

Looking back over the last century, the internal rules which the City set for itself could be said to be based on those of a London Club. They relied on peer pressure for their effectiveness. There was a generally accepted code of conduct, and those who transgressed it could find themselves expelled from the Club and debarred from taking further part in City activities. There are advantages to such Club rules. They carry no top-hamper of bureaucracy, the incentive to conform is strong and the penalties for flouting the rules are swift and condign. The growth of the City over the years is a tribute to their efficacy.

The danger with the Club rule approach to governance is that the members may come to put their own interests ahead of those who ultimately provide them with their livelihood. Clubs, whether of financiers or of members of professional bodies, have a tendency to close ranks against the outside world to protect their interests. The Steam Loop case is a fascinating example of how Club rules can fall behind Milton Friedman's basic rules of society.

## The Steam Loop

The Steam Loop, in the words of its promoters, was a process 'designed to secure to steam users economy of fuel, water and power', and in 1890 a company was formed to exploit it. Slaughter and May were solicitors both to the company and to one of the promoters. To ensure a successful launch, the promoters rigged the market by creating an artificial premium on the opening transactions in Steam Loop shares. A dispute over the transfer of shares led to a lawsuit and brought the rigging of the market to the attention of a judge. Such activities were apparently accepted practice in the City at the time, as one of the defendants declared: 'You have only to ask anyone about new companies if it [that is, creating a false premium] is not a necessity'.

The judge, however, took a very different view in his commentary:

> ' ... I do say that if persons, for their own purposes of speculation, create an artificial price in the market by transactions which are not real, but are made at a nominal premium merely for the purpose of inducing the public to take shares, they are guilty of as gross a fraud as has ever been committed ... '

Slaughter and May appealed, reckoning that the judge was simply out of touch with the ways of the City. But his judgement was upheld by their Lordships. William May touchingly referred to the case to the end of his life as 'a magnificent miscarriage of justice'.

The case is interesting in many ways. The argument that 'everybody does it' is as readily used to excuse today's scandals as it was in the nineteenth century. The City Club reasoning was that the advantages of an efficient capital market outweighed the disadvantage that some public subscribers for shares were fleeced. The interests of Club members took precedence over those of outsiders to, what turned out to be, an unacceptable extent. The balance between the two sets of interests was wrongly struck. The fundamental problem, at that stage, was that the Club had lost touch with the world outside. In the clash between internal and external rules, the law ruled that fraud was fraud, however much it might be thought to assist the working of the market for new issues. Club members, like William May, had insulated themselves from outside opinion and were no doubt genuinely unaware that the standards expected of business behaviour had changed. Market rigging might have continued but for this chance lawsuit. However, once the fraud involved in company flotations came to light, the practice was clearly illegal and without the rules. It was disclosure which led to the reform of the capital market and to Club rules giving way to the rule of law. This underlines the importance of a governance framework which includes an appropriate mix of external and internal rules.

Nevertheless, the City rules were on the whole effective in maintaining the position of London as a financial centre, although the rules on activities like insider trading were designed not to stop the practice but to keep it under control. The authorities no doubt took as their text:

> 'Thou shalt not muzzle the ox when he treadeth out the corn'
>
> *(Deuteronomy 25.4)*

Those working in City firms were likely at times to be privy to market sensitive information and it was accepted that they would use it for their own gain. The rules were aimed at not allowing such self-serving to get out of hand. The rules of the insider trading game were house rules within the overall City rules. Most City houses in the past were partnerships and the house rules and tone of the firm were set by the partners. They gave the lead and ensured that those entering their firms knew what conduct was acceptable and what was not. The reputation of their firms were valuable assets and a close eye was kept on the conduct of those in their employ.

## The breakdown of the City rules

The Club approach to governance in the City gave way when the cohesion of its members was broken. The efficacy of the Club rules was rooted in the self-interest of the membership in maintaining the reputation of the City and of their own firms within it. It was based on a community of interest and on the personal links between those involved. Those links were broken by a series of momentous changes. One was the sudden expansion of London's financial services sector in the 1980s. Individual firms grew rapidly in size and the rules could no longer be based on personal contact with those at their head. At the same time, the old boundaries between different types of financial activity with their differing rules were swept away. Many of the new entrants to the City did not share the values of what they saw as the past and did not see their futures as lying with a single firm; thus the significance of reputation carried less weight with them. A further change was the influx of foreign firms, as the City became a truly international financial centre. These firms brought their own methods of working with them and were more used to the rules of the game being set statutorily, rather than by conventions of conduct.

The gap in the framework of rules which arose in the much enlarged City was that nothing was put in place of the personal links with the heads of firms. There was no consistent means of passing on business values to newcomers and ensuring that they were adhered to. The rules based on personal example of the earlier City needed to be replaced by more formal rules of conduct. These could no longer be within a framework of City rules, since those had gone. It was up to individual City firms to establish their own codes of conduct. Before, however, discussing such company codes, it is worth pointing out in the context of the internationalisation of the City that the concept of voluntary regulation is a very British one. It is neither well understood nor well accepted elsewhere in Europe.

The Advertising Standards Authority does not have its equivalent on the Continent, nor does the Takeover Panel. The latter is a particularly significant self-regulating body. It rules in a field where the pluses of a non-statutory authority, such as speed of decision, a swift response to new issues as they arise and avoidance of the costs of the legal system, are particularly valuable. Statutory regulation, however, inevitably drives out self-regulation – a kind of inverse Gresham's Law! The Takeover Panel will no longer be able to rule as it does if the EU legislates on takeovers and mergers. Its authority depends on the acceptance by city practitioners of its rulings. The ability to appeal to a court over a Panel ruling would destroy that authority.

## Independence

There is, however, an important governance principle exemplified by the Takeover Panel and which applies to the disciplinary bodies set up by the professions.

The principle is that of including an independent element on these bodies, alongside representatives of the practitioners. This helps to ensure that the interests of those whose conduct they regulate are balanced against the interests of those they serve. It was because their councils lacked that outside view that the City lost touch with external moral standards at the time of the Steam Loop.

In the same way, the Committee's Code of Best Practice recommended that the majority of non-executive directors on a board should be independent, and independence was defined as being:

'independent of management and free from any business or other relationship which could materially interfere with the exercise of their independent judgement'.

The presence of independent members of boards does not imply that they have inherently higher standards of morality than their executive colleagues. It is simply that it is easier for them to take an objective view of whatever matters are under review. They stand further back from the action, they bring outside standards to bear on the issues and their interests are less directly at stake. The argument for independent members of professional disciplinary bodies rests on the same grounds.

## Company codes

I said earlier that the house rules of City firms were originally conveyed to the members of those firms orally and by example. In today's more turbulent times, when those personal links are weaker, the argument for putting company codes of conduct in writing becomes stronger. Our Committee's Report said:

> 'It is important that all employees should know what standards are expected of them. We regard it as good practice for boards of directors to draw up codes of ethics or statements of business practice and to publish them both internally and externally'.

The aim is to assist those working in a company to know what standards of conduct are expected of them and how to deal with the kind of problems which they may come across in the course of their duties. An early example of such a code were the Rules for the Conduct of Life which have been given to Freemen of the City of London since the eighteenth century. It opens with:

> Rule 1 – Whatever you at any time intend to do, consider the end which you therein propose to yourself and be sure that it be always really good, or at least innocent. He who does anything, and knows not why or wherefore, acts foolishly: and he who aims at an unlawful end acts wickedly, which is the worst sort of folly. If you are careful always to observe this fundamental rule, you will therefore avoid many sins which would disturb your conscience, and also many trifling actions which would tend to your discredit, or trouble your repose.

This remains excellent advice, if not quite in the form that codes of conduct take today. From a company's point of view, codes of conduct provide a safeguard for their reputation. They strengthen what are otherwise unwritten rules of behaviour, picked up by observing the way things are done in a given working environment. In drawing up a company code, the starting point is, therefore, what is and what is not accepted practice within a company. The code may aim to change the way things are done within the company and raise standards of conduct, but the base from which those standards are to be raised has to be existing practice. This underlines the importance in drafting codes of involving those to whom they are to apply. If they are to be expected to abide by codes, they need to have played a part in framing them.

Quite apart from the scepticism with which a code handed down from the board on high, without consultation, will understandably be received, boards are not usually well placed to know how things are done within the enterprises which they direct. I believe that, to be effective, company codes should build on existing standards and embody the best of the existing values of the organisation concerned. They should not be taken off the shelf, so to speak, but should reflect matters that are relevant and important to everyone within a particular company. If they are drawn up in good faith, and provided, crucially, they are backed by example from the top, they have two important attributes.

First, they act as a practical guide to individual employees faced with uncertainty about the courses of action which they should take. Second, they give those whose decisions are questioned, or who question the decisions of others – normally their superiors – a firm basis on which to stand their ground. I, therefore, have no doubt as to the value of company codes in clarifying the rules of the game at company level and in encouraging high standards of conduct.

A company code, however, which is cynically introduced as a facade is likely to have the effect of debasing standards, because it will be seen to reflect the motives of those who drew it up. The same result is likely if there is uncertainty about whether a code truly means what it says. That situation is well illustrated in a price-fixing case brought against General Electric in the US in the 1950s. An account of the case includes the following passage:

> Some of those who signed 20.5 (the company rule against price-fixing) did not believe it was to be taken seriously. They assumed that 20.5 was mere window dressing, that it was on the books solely to provide legal protection for the company and for the higher-ups; that meeting illegally with competitors was recognised and accepted as standard practice within the company, and that often when a ranking executive ordered a subordinate executive to comply with 20.5, he was actually ordering him to violate it.

It all, apparently, turned on whether the order was given with a wink or not. The outcome of this confusion over whether the code meant what it said, or the precise opposite, landed some of the higher-ups in gaol. Clearly those who drew up the GE code did not involve those to whom it applied and they seem to have been unaware of the existing standards and practices within their company.

## Code interpretation

Misunderstandings over the meaning of codes raises the issue of the words used in their preparation. An important use of codes is to provide guidance to individuals with uncertainty over the right course of conduct. When attempting to give such guidance in my former company, I had in mind managers out on their own in countries like Nigeria and Indonesia. To have a code of conduct which says magisterially, 'Thou shalt neither offer nor accept bribes', is not particularly helpful to managers on the spot. It begs the question of definition –

what is a bribe – and takes no account of local custom. I, therefore, set down two practical rules of thumb which seemed to make sense to those who had met this kind of situation. They were to test whether a payment made, or gift received was acceptable from the company's point of view.

For payments, the rule was that they had to be on the face of the invoice; that is to say, they had to go through the books of account. Some bizarre payments came to notice as a result, in developed as well as not so developed countries. However, they met the rule; they were accounted for and audited and, as far as I know, backhand payments in cash or kind were avoided. Accounting for payments may not be sufficient as an ethical test, but payments which are outside the company's system and control will almost certainly be corrupt and corrupting.

On gifts the rule was, 'Would you be happy for your acceptance of a gift to be written up in the company newspaper?' A gift becomes a bribe when it puts the recipient under an obligation to the giver, which could override their duty to the company. There is no set tariff which can measure this degree of obligation and thus determine, by reading off a scale, when the acceptable limit has been passed. However, those who receive gifts and their colleagues can recognise those limits unerringly. If the knowledge that you have accepted something as a gift would be an embarrassment, that limit has been reached. We are back to disclosure. The logic behind both these rules of conduct is that openness and ethics go together and that actions are unethical if they will not stand scrutiny.

## The character of the company

As chairman of Cadbury Schweppes, I drafted a brief statement of what I felt the company stood for, entitled 'The Character of the Company'. This was circulated around the company, at home and abroad, and formed the basis of discussions with groups of employees when I visited company sites around the world. As a result of those discussions, the final wording reflected the views of as wide a sample as possible of the workforce worldwide. In this way a sense of ownership of the statement was gained throughout the enterprise and it dealt with matters which were relevant to those who read it. In addition, the discussions gave me the opportunity to answer questions about the way in which I thought we in the company should handle difficult issues. The aim was to achieve as wide a degree of agreement as possible on how best to resolve the kind of problems which confront those in business in balancing their duties to people, to the community and to their company. It also meant that individuals faced with decisions, but with no-one on hand to consult, would have a lead as to the course they might take, whether or not in the event they chose to take it.

When I first suggested attempting to set down what the company stood for and then getting agreement to it, some board members were sceptical of its usefulness and said it would simply end up in a filing cabinet. In the event, the degree to which the statement was valued and called on seemed to be a function of distance from the perceived centre of authority. It was the smaller business units and those furthest from the head office in the UK which particularly felt that it filled a need, and it was those lowest down in the hierarchy who turned to it most often.

Although 'The Character of the Company' was not a code as such, it was a statement of values. Values are important both in their own right as aspects of the ethical custom to which Milton Friedman referred and because they are the glue which holds an organisation together in an increasingly fragmented world. Drafting a code is a difficult task, even though there are guides to doing so provided by bodies like the Institute of Business Ethics. The point to keep in mind is that what may seem platitudinous to the drafter can prove invaluable to those down the line who look to the code for a lead in times of uncertainty.

I believe, therefore, that a governance framework of external rules, embodied in the law, regulations and national codes of best practice, supplemented by internal rules, such as those set by company codes, make up the corporate rules of the game. That still leaves one piece missing from the framework, the rules which we set for ourselves as individuals, the rules by which we live. It is the personal standards of those involved in company affairs which ultimately determine how the rules of the game are applied in practice. In a game of football, it is the player who has the ball at his feet who decides the course of the match, not the referee; the players choose whether to keep the ball in play and whether to abide by the rules or to set them aside.

## Personal responsibility

The same is true of corporate governance. The prime responsibility for business standards lies with boards of directors; however, shareholders, professional advisers to companies, those who comment on business affairs and the wider public, all have a part to play in defining the boundaries of acceptable conduct, in determining the rules of the game. To take a specific example, a Board of Trade enquiry found that Robert Maxwell, 'could not be relied upon to exercise proper stewardship of a publicly quoted company'. The enquiry could not have established his breaches of the rules of the game more plainly. Yet after those findings were published, there were still directors prepared to join his boards, there were shareholders ready to invest in his enterprises and banks eager to lend him money. They could have played to the rules of the game, but they brushed them aside in the hope of gain. Only Maxwell's employees had little opportunity to blow the whistle at his contempt for the rules, since there was no internal code of conduct to which they could appeal.

The Guinness affair provides another instance of a similar kind. There the DTI inspectors said that three findings stood out:

Firstly, the cynical disregard of laws and regulations; secondly, the cavalier misuse of company monies; thirdly a contempt for truth and common honesty; all these in a part of the City which was thought respectable.

The rules of the game can be set externally and internally, but the degree to which they are honoured and are therefore effective is the responsibility of everyone involved in the game, in whatever capacity. Rules of the game have to be established in the corporate world and they need reviewing and updating from time to time in response to the changing scene. They can guide and inspire, but the spirit to which they are played is collectively our responsibility. The bedrock of good governance remains Milton Friedman's ethical custom. We should not lay a greater burden on the law and regulation than they can carry.

The risk in relying too much on statutory rules in corporate affairs is that business and personal morality could come to be seen as distinct and separate. If standards of business conduct are thought of as being primarily set by the law, then compliance with the law could become all that was required, even though keeping on the right side of the law would normally count as a minimum requirement, setting the floor to acceptable conduct. If business standards are to rise, in response to the expectations which society has of business, then personal morality has to give the lead to business morality; the two should not be divorced. If the two were to be seen as separate, then an increase in statutory intervention could lower standards of business ethics, as regulatory standards took the place of personal standards.

## Do ethical standards matter?

The final issue is how far do the ethical customs which are embodied in the rules of the game really matter in an internationally competitive world? They clearly matter to society. Trust has always played a vital part in business, as the authors of the 'Rules for the Conduct of Life' recognised. Trust is in many ways more important today than it was even in the eighteenth century, given the scale and speed of the transactions now carried out through the ether, across national boundaries and impersonally, rather than face to face. In contrast, distrust is a barrier to the flow of trade and of information. If all business had to be based on contract, the pace of trade would be unimaginably slow. Equally, regulation is costly, to an extent that those who ultimately pay for it are usually unaware.

Ethical standards and abiding by the rules matter to companies. If unethical practices are ignored or condoned in a business, there is no means of knowing where the line between acceptable and unacceptable behaviour is to be drawn. The danger is that this uncertainty will result in a downwards slide in standards, which may become cumulative and end in disaster. A further consideration for companies is their need to attract able recruits. A business whose ethical standards are seen to be uncertain has to be at a disadvantage in recruitment, against companies with higher reputations and against other occupations which may be ranked more highly on the ethical scale. Thus business standards matter to individual companies and to the company sector in aggregate.

To conclude: the rules of the corporate game need to be understood and to be backed by all those who are in a position to influence the way in which companies are run. Those at the head of companies should ensure that everyone in their enterprises knows what is expected of them and that their reward system gives credit to those who play to the rules. The rules, from the law downwards, set the framework within which companies carry on their business. The manner in which the rules are applied is the responsibility of individuals within companies. The standards of a company reflect the standards of those who make it up. In the end business morality is personal morality writ large. As Henry David Thoreau observed:

> 'It is true enough said that a corporation has no conscience. But a corporation of conscientious men is a corporation with a conscience'.

It is to that end that the rules of the game are framed.

© Sir Adrian Cadbury

# The future for boards – professionalisation or incarceration?                                      B2.25

*This article was written in August 2002 by Bob Garratt. It is reprinted by kind permission of the author and the European Business Forum (www.ebfonline.com), a quarterly publication which provides a European perspective on global management issues. It was the winning essay in the third PricewaterhouseCoopers Annual European Shareholder Value Award held in partnership with EBF and Financial News. Bob Garratt is chairman of two companies and a visiting Professor at Imperial College, London. He can be contacted at garratts@btconnect.com.*

## Context

Is the sudden international interest in effective 'corporate governance', combined with flat or falling markets, beginning to deflect both our corporate and national interests from developing wise, robust and implementable business policies and strategies?

Yes – but only if you have a simple, binary view of business life. In the world of true business direction-giving, as distinct from being an operational 'executive', the stated dilemma is false. Both horns are the two sides of the same coin. One cannot pursue a purely compliance-based stance on corporate governance – the 'board conformance' approach – without ending up with lots of ticked boxes and little overall picture of the business or its strategy. Yet neither can one focus only on developing the world's most imaginative strategy – the 'board performance approach' – without due regard for the law, sound accounting practices, assessment of the organisational capability to deliver the strategy, and the efficient control of the day-to-day operations. An effective board must balance both continuously.

This essay is set in the context of UK, US and Commonwealth law. It argues that, to ensure the future development of effective strategies, and to add shareholder value, it is necessary to treat directing as a competence-based profession; and to train and appraise it as such.

The art of direction-giving, of being an effective board member, is to balance continuously the dilemma of driving the enterprise forward to add shareholder value whilst simultaneously keeping it under prudent control. Sustaining this dynamic, changing, balance is the essence of effective corporate governance. This requires two radical, and unusual, assumptions in today's business world. First, that being a board director is a professional job, quite distinct from management. Second, that boards and individual directors need training, development, and regular appraisal for them to do the job *competently*. In future, investors, staff and customers will demand proof of directoral competence from their boards. Post-Enron they demand assessment of the directoral prudent control mechanisms through overseeing the output of the short-term executive tools of budgets, efficient project management, management ratios and trendlines, and healthy profit and loss accounts. But in addition they demand clarity that 'shareholder value' is added by the board, via the regular and transparent disclosure of the board's judgement in policy-formulation, strategic thinking, risk-assessment, decision-taking and strategy implementation. This is achieved through assessing their wisdom in investments in people, projects and asset acquisition – the value they add for shareholders.

## Adding shareholder value

What is 'shareholder value'? The most helpful definition I know is:

'Shareholder Value is the surplus of economic value added after satisfying all reasonable short-term stakeholder expectations, taking into account the cost of capital, and after providing for the long-term health and security of the business'.

This spans succinctly both 'board conformance' and 'board performance' aspects. It does not make the mistake made by many current Chief Executives of assuming that a short-term rise in share price is the same as adding long-term shareholder value. Importantly, it addresses also the wider issue that increasing shareholder value is not simply a matter of the board taking an internal focus only. It assumes that a business exists in its society and must, therefore, be acceptable to those 'stakeholders' who have direct, or indirect, sanctions on whether it retains a 'licence to operate' in that community. With the sudden vapourisation of Andersens and Marconi, it is not surprising that many shareholders are as concerned with the maintenance of their business's long-term reputation as with its immediate profit performance. If these two are not linked positively in the public's mind, then any thought of increasing shareholder value disappears.

## Three directoral myths which block adding shareholder value

How have we reached a point where even many directors are confused about the very notion of adding shareholder value? My experience is that the problems come not from a lack of economic understanding, but rather lacunae of their directoral roles and tasks and, hence, their over-concentration on the immediate executive roles at the long-term expense of the business.

## B2.25   *The future for boards – professionalisation or incarceration?*

There are three directoral myths which have wide, and alarming, currency at present:

- that the primary duty of a board director is to the shareholders;

- that the Chief Executive is the leader of the board; and

- that there are two types of directors – 'executive directors' and 'non-executive' directors.

None of these is legally correct, but common practice has many believing that they must be.

Let us look at their pernicious effects on the shareholder value concept. First, that the primary duty of the board director is to the shareholders. Legally this cannot be so, as at the very moment of their appointment by the shareholders, the primary duty and loyalty of a director moves to the company itself as a separate legal entity. This is rarely understood by directors or shareholders, so it is not surprising that short-term shareholder demands which may risk the long term health of the company are often conceded by directors. Ignorance is the enemy of a director's 'fiduciary duty'; and is leading the general public into distrusting directors' abilities to add long term shareholder value.

Second, the myth that the Chief Executive is the leader of the board. This is common on many boards. But the illegal, sometimes criminal, behaviour of some US CEOs has thrown into sharp relief the urgency to re-establish the supremacy of the board as the critical review mechanism of executive actions. The Chairman is 'the boss of the board'. The Managing Director is the 'boss of the Operations of the business'. These are quite different roles and need be treated as such. The habit of combining both roles has been broken in the UK. Here now less than twenty percent of listed company boards do this. However, it is alarmingly common in the US where most listed company Chief Executive Officers (legally not board members) insist on having also the Chairman of the Board role and, thereby, capture all corporate power. This causes long-term subtracted shareholder value in many cases as the personal, and 'achievement', greed of the CEO loses their focus on their primary duties.

Third, the myth that there are such roles as 'executive' and 'non-executive' directors. This is particularly debilitating. At law there is only the term 'director'; and as much of the description of directors' accountabilities comes from the Insolvency Acts as from the Companies Acts. The problem of adding shareholder value comes from two aspects of bad practice: behaving as though there are two types of director; and giving 'executive directors' priority over others. To counter these it is wise to emphasise the legal position that *all* directors are equal around the boardroom table and must, therefore, be paid the same director's fee. In the case of 'executive directors' this will be separate from any executive pay package. The board must accept that all directors are legally collegial, part-time, and under the neutral leadership of the Chairman. This focuses all directors' minds on the fact that they are paid to give 'direction' and must, therefore, budget time and build competence to do the job effectively.

# Future board roles

When all three myths combine, the chances of the board adding significant shareholder value fall dramatically. There are unlikely to be sufficient variety of experience and intellectual capacity around the boardroom to undertake the onerus complex roles needed. To expand this point I will review briefly recent UK corporate governance history. Bob Tricker's original book 'Corporate Governance' was published before the Maxwell, Guinness and Polly Peck scandals and so attracted little public attention. However, those scandals led to political action – the Cadbury Report on the Financial Aspects of Corporate Governance in 1992. This focused on the directoral need to review critically and regularly the executive's actions. It raised, amongst other questions, the advisability of splitting the Chairman and Managing Director's roles, the independence of outside directors, the crucial role of the Audit Committee, and the need for external legal advice for independent directors. Cadbury begat the Greenbury Report of 1995 on board remuneration and benefits. This was less successful in influencing attitudes and behaviours. Greenbury begat the Hampel Report of 1998 which expanded the Cadbury proposals. All three reports were consolidated in 1998 into the Combined Codes of the London Stock Exchange which became an international benchmark for effective corporate governance.

# From board conformance to board performance

However, these reports focus only on the conformance/compliance aspects of corporate governance. They are necessary, but not sufficient, for the delivery of shareholder value. Sufficiency comes from the 'board performance' aspects – and these are much harder to put into any 'tick box' form. They concern directors' 'experience' – their knowledge, skills, values and behaviours – areas in which it is difficult to legislate without causing unintended consequences. 'Board conformance' deals with the legal and regulatory frameworks within which a business must work. 'Board performance' demands a board *learning* system that refines continuously those board competences which give superior added shareholder value. This fits into a historical progression.

The Turnbull Report of 1999 marks a significant shift in corporate governance thinking. By insisting on an annual declaration to the owners of the boards risk-assessment and decision-making processes, or explaining why these do not exist, the quality of the corporate governance game is raised. When combined with the 'Myners Report' of 2001 which insists that pension fund *trustees* should be trained to competence, and obliged to intervene in the boards of their under-performing investments, a major change in governance mind-set is seen. And it is weighted firmly to protecting and improving shareholder value.

The argument is that a board should be selected, trained, developed and appraised on their directoral abilities to:

- formulate policy and so give foresight;
- think strategically;
- collect accurate external and internal data;

149

- generate imaginative ideas;

- be capable of open questioning and critical review;

- be rigorous in risk assessments;

- be collegial in strategic decision-making;

- learn systematically from their directoral strengths and weaknesses;

- ensure organisational capabilities for successful strategic implementation;

- ensure rapid feedback for honest information on the implementation of the strategy.

These are still beyond the comprehension of many directors. Yet this list may well become the future specification for selecting and evaluating effective boards – or the ones that add consciously shareholder value.

## Creating the conditions for developing board performance

Whilst these statements may shock many existing directors and executives the techniques for developing and assessing directoral competence are long-established. Until now these have usually been considered an optional extra, an indulgence, which can only be considered seriously if the board chooses the luxury of time and money to spend on themselves. Suddenly, however, the ignorance and arrogance of untrained chairmen, boards, and CEOs have been thrown into stark public relief internationally by the media spotlight on Enron and Andersens. Many 'Celebrity CEOs' are seen to have run businesses for their own, rather than shareholder, needs. Many boards allowed them to do this, provided that the share price rose – even though this often fed only the CEO's share options. This has undermined the very foundations of investors' trust and mutual risk-sharing – the very basis of Western capitalism since the seventeenth century. The last decade has set back the slow movement towards the 'civil society' to which many people from Adam Smith and Rousseau onwards aspired.

We have bred a generation of executives, investment bankers, analysts, lawyers, accountants and even auditors who seem conscienceless, and lacking in personal integrity. They have lost the concept of professionalism – of putting one's client's need in front of your own, even if there is short-term loss. We have lived through a time of moral torpor. Gordon Gecko's 'greed is good' speech from the film *Wall Street,* and Alan Greenspan's concerned comments initially on the 'irrational exuberance of the markets', and later on 'the infelicitous greed' and 'outsized increase in the opportunities for avarice', typify this emotional climate – or did so until the 'dotcoms' became the dotbombs. And then came Enron. Suddenly we are into *mea culpa*, the beating of City and Wall Street breasts, and the sudden return by some to religion as a penance. It is remarkably similar to the emotional cycle described in *On the Madness of Crowds* relating to the South Sea Bubble and the Dutch Tulip Mania – both of which also destroyed long term shareholder value.

Whilst much of the public focus, and political and regulatory response, has been on corporate corruption and bribery, a lot less has been said about the non-competence, under-performance, and lack of fiduciary duty of the boards themselves. It is as much from the development of new directoral attitudes and competences, as through legislation, that improvement will come.

## Back to basics: the ten directoral duties

How can one make a significant contribution to righting matters? I suggest that all directors, present and aspiring, study and behave according to the draft of the 'Ten Directoral Duties' proposed by the Commonwealth Association for Corporate Governance (CACG). This has the beauty of being drafted by practitioners across the fifty four Commonwealth countries: and is built on the English language, and well-tested common law principles. With China interested in these, and the US and India already on board, it is likely to become by sheer volume alone the world benchmark for inducting and developing directoral competence.

The CACG Ten Directoral Duties are founded on the long-established corporate governance values of:

- accountability;
- probity;
- transparency.

and distil the essence of company law over the last three centuries. The duties for all boards and individual directors are:

| | | |
|---|---|---|
| 1. | Duty of Legitimacy | (operating within the law) |
| 2. | Duty of Upholding the Director's Primary Loyalty | (to the company) |
| 3. | Duty of Upholding the Director's Primary Role | (to drive the enterprise forward whilst keeping it under prudent control) |
| 4. | Duty of Holding the Company in Trust | (fiduciary duty) |
| 5. | Duty of Ensuring Critical Review of Proposals To The Board | |
| 6. | Duty of Ensuring Directoral Care | (in decision-taking) |
| 7. | Duty of Upholding the Three Values of Corporate Governance | |
| 8. | Duty of Upholding the Rights of Minority Owners | |
| 9. | Duty of Ensuring Corporate Social Responsibility | |
| 10. | Duty of Ensuring Board Learning, Development and Communication | |

Adherence in attitude and behaviour by each director to these ten long-tested concepts means that a board will be more firmly focused to deliver shareholder value. These would also do much to rebalance unwise political initiatives, and restore public trust, on both sides of the Atlantic.

## Political over-reactions

Politicians have swung dangerously in favour of using the criminal law first for corporate issues. The current nonsensical US regulation that CEOs and CFOs must sign their *quarterly* accounts as accurate, or risk a maximum of twenty year's jail, betrays the politician's knee-jerk reaction to rush to the opposite extreme when under public pressure. The likely consequence is the not-thought-through abreaction – that Law of Unintended Consequences – usually delivering the opposite of what was intended.

Who can say ever that necessarily hastily prepared quarterly accounts will be entirely accurate? And who would now want to be a CEO or a Chief Financial Officer? Taking logic to absurdity, it would now be more time-efficient for a CEO to murder their CFO as they are likely to get only twelve years incarceration, rather than the twenty for getting their quarterly accounts wrong. Stopping those who can create wealth from so doing seems a perverse way of creating shareholder value. One unintended consequence is that directors and officers' liability insurance rates are rising to unprecedented levels.

Adam Smith recognised that to create wealth was not a criminal activity in itself. He valued the creation of the limited liability company with a separate legal personality (whilst warning of its four main long-term dangers); yet he understood also that the wealth generated had to be distributed thoughtfully across society. Indeed, he was the first holder of a chair in Political Economy having written a book on 'Moral Sentiment' before his opus. Nearly half of 'The Wealth Of Nations' concerns moral sentiment. It is not just about 'the invisible hand of the markets', or pin manufacture, as some mechanical and inhumane process. He understood that the creation of shareholder value was a subtle blend of optimising short-term gains whilst ensuring long-term, fiduciary, duty through giving back to the society in which the enterprise lives.

The present political and legislative over-reaction is understandable but not forgivable. Examples of the current offenders in destroying shareholder value fall into two camps. In one camp are, for example, Enron, WorldCom, Adelphia, HIH in Australia, Elan in Ireland, and many Japanese banks, where there seemed intent to deceive the shareholders whilst rewarding the executives and advisers. In the other camp are those who made strategically bad decisions, in many cases 'betting the company' on a single strategy with no contingency plan. Examples are Marconi, Vodafone, Equitable Life, Vivendi and Kirch.

These erode public confidence in business, in the markets and, unbalance, as George Orwell stressed, the stabilising forces of the 'democratic bourgeoisie'. Once these see shareholder value eroded, then you are in a growing crisis well beyond the wildest dreams of any mixture of Marxist, terrorists, anti-capitalist, or eco-warrior groups. When a July headline of the *New York Times* asks 'Are capitalists destroying capitalism?' then you have a serious societal problem.

## Professionalising board directors

If laws are now being put in place, and the accounting and corporate governance systems strengthened internationally, why is it that the general public, and particularly the shareholders, do not feel these measures sufficient to restore trust in business leaders? I argue that it will not be until directing a board is treated as an *accredited* profession that order will be restored. No longer will it be OK to recruit to your board a mixture of golf club friends, executives from other companies on whose board you sit, or that dreadful, chilling phrase so commonly used of US listed companies – 'ten friends of the Chief Executive, a woman and a black'.

## Developing effective boards

I am arguing that sustained improvement in shareholder value will come when directors are selected, trained, developed, appraised, and sacked, in an open and systematic way. None of these techniques are new. Most businesses use them until they reach board level. At this point something curious happens. Those who select direction-givers (a crucial role in any organisation) assume that those selected become omniscient at the moment of their appointment. Suddenly, people who have been functional or professional specialists all of their working lives, are deemed capable of knowing everything that is happening inside and outside their organisation; and can instantly generate imaginative business policies and strategies, debate courageously, and make wise risk assessments which lead to sound decision-taking focused on adding shareholder value. This is patent nonsense. It is odd to me that the time and money budgets found in the rest of the organisation for training and development stop below board level. We leave the crucial job of ensuring shareholder value creation in the hands of people who are not assessed or developed for that job. This is just perverse.

What can be done? First, budget time and money for director selection, induction, training and continuing development. The basis of such directoral training and appraisal is often the *Learning Board* model whose four quadrants cover the activities of:

* policy formulation and foresight;
* strategic thinking;
* supervising management;
* accountability.

Note that the first two concern 'board performance' and the latter two 'board conformance'.

Second, set up an annual director appraisal system under the chairman. Legally, it is the chairman's job to ensure board competence. This can be designed as a '360 degree' appraisal with a mixture of peer reviews, direct report reviews (where appropriate), and a chairman's review. As the managing director is simply a member of the board they are part of this process. Handled sensitively, and with all directors being treated as equal, this can transform significantly the effectiveness of any board. But who then appraises the chairman? Ideally, one follows the same 360 degree process for 270 degrees but as 'the chairman reports only to God' the last 90 degrees can be tricky. I tend to use a small sample of key shareholders and key customers to complete the cycle.

Third, ensure the collective development of the board as an effective working group so that during the few times they are together they may *learn* collegially to play to their strengths as a Learning Board.

The world standard for systematic director development processes is currently held by the UK whose Chartered Director initiative has created a robust and rigorous system of a written examination, an oral examination of a minimum five years of full (not specialist) directoral experience, the signing of a code of conduct, and a monitored system of continuing professional development. This has created great international interest, except in Europe, and has been installed by the Japanese Management Association.

Where does the European Union stand? It has maintained a very low profile, possibly because corporate governance issues highlight some of the EU's structural weaknesses. With two major systems of law – case law and the Code Napoleon – in apparent conflict, with a complex tangle of long established national laws and politics, with no central fiscal powers, and with a maze of different financial rules and practices; the EU cannot respond rapidly to the present global crisis.

Does it see the need to? The political worry is that such reforms suggested above may benefit the shareholder value creation, but at the expense of the long-standing cross-shareholdings, and alliances between businesses and major political parties, which have become enshrined in the 'social market' model. The European Commission's early attempts to suggest a standard – two-tier – board structure for EU member country boards received short shrift. This was not because the structure itself was flawed but because current European practice has a high potential for bribery and corruption – as Helmut Kohl, Jacques Chirac, and Silvio Berlusconi have found. The main problem is that the Supervisory Board element tends to comprise of 'representatives' from groups such as the workers, lenders, and shareholders. This is shown frequently to be flawed as few act as though the company's, or shareholders', interests are paramount. In the name of 'social balance' political deals have been done of which any self-respecting board would be ashamed.

The European Commission is slow at learning – so far. This is shown in their latest proposal, in August 2002, to homogenise the listings rules of all the EU's stock exchanges – a key to their plan of building a single securities market by 2003. However, at a time of global corporate governance crisis, these proposals will significantly *decrease* UK investor protections. Sir Howard Davies, Chairman of the Financial Services Authority, says 'This is a very curious time to choose to dismantle a well-functioning feature of our regulation of corporate governance.'. As an example of masterly understatement this is hard to beat. The EU should not seek the lowest common denominator, but strive for international best practice, even if it breaks the comfy politics of the last five decades. This way shareholder value lays.

It will only be when such best practices are established and monitored internationally, that we can say with any certainty that most boards will add shareholder value. Perhaps then the politicians will cease to use their 'one club' regulation of corporate governance through focusing only on board conformance? But I doubt it.

# The corporate governance saga      B2.26

*This is the text of Sir Adrian Cadbury's final speech on corporate governance to the Hermes sponsored Stewardship and Performance seminar, held at the Chartered Accountants' Hall, Moorgate Place, London on 20 October 2000. Readers may also wish to refer to the text of another speech by Sir Adrian (see* **B2.24** THE FUTURE FOR GOVERNANCE: THE RULES OF THE GAME*). In our introduction to that speech we provide a short background on Sir Adrian.*

I am grateful for this opportunity to make a positively last appearance on the governance stage in the Hall where my involvement started nearly ten years ago and to do so among friends. What is astonishing about the corporate governance saga is that in that time it has moved from an arcane technical term to figuring on the agenda of the G8 Summit. What has been its impact and what has driven it to these heights? My object is not to add a footnote to history, but to attempt to understand what has been happening in this field to help foresee what course governance might take in the future.

The development of the concept of corporate governance has had its impact mainly on boards of directors and on shareholders, with a knock-on effect on the supporting professions of accountancy and law. The move by the SEC to separate the auditing and consulting functions of accounting firms is an example of the impact which governance continues to have on the professions. Nevertheless, my focus is on boards and shareholders and the ways in which corporate governance doctrines have changed their worlds and will continue to do so.

What has driven the changes that have taken place? Key is the concentration of share ownership, from individuals to institutions, which has provided the engine for change. With it goes a change in investor attitudes which has led to a more interventionist approach. Other drivers have been the need to attract international investment and the need by companies to tap world capital markets. Then there has been the worldwide move towards privatisation, shifting assets and the control of those assets from the state sector to the market economy, alongside an acceptance that good governance is a useful indicator of good performance in the marketplace. Finally comes the changing expectations that society has of the purpose of companies and of investment, a force which is changing, and will continue to change, the nature of your businesses and whose potency must not be underestimated.

All these forces have their impact against the background of a world that is being transformed by globalisation and information technology; which in turn act as accelerators of change. To a great extent the changes that have taken place, and will continue to do so, reflect shifts in the balance of power between the key players. Codes of governance practice are in the main expressions of these forces rather than causes of them.

## Boards and shareholders

I start with boards and shareholders. In the US the first shift in the balance of power was triggered by the collapse of Penn Central, then the sixth largest US corporation. The SEC enquiry into the collapse concluded, 'the somnolent Penn Central board ... was typical of most giant corporations' boards in the post-war period. 'Such boards were not doing their job and were ineffective. Neither boards nor shareholders had the information they needed to exercise proper control and power lay with the executive managers of these corporations. The answer from the shareholders' viewpoint was to free up the market in the control of assets. Let more aggressive managers bid for control of under-performing corporations and take them over. The takeover wake-up call had the plus of putting all businesses which could conceivably be bid for on notice, but it also led to managers entrenching their position in order to counter the shift in power.

As US share ownership became more concentrated in institutional hands, the institutions began to use their muscle to ginger up under-performing boards. This process culminated in the changes that were brought about in the leadership of companies such as GM, IBM and Eastman Kodak. It involved investors bringing pressure to bear on the outside directors of those corporations to the point where they took action. Shareholders were now exercising their power over boards and directors were having to do their job, thereby taking back some power from executive managers.

This country had its share of somnolent boards and more than its share of complacent ones. Boards were not on the whole in the driving seat and were satisfied with modest results. The outside directors on boards were drawn from a narrow interconnected group, were often ornamental (if that) and reflected the British amateur tradition that the less you knew about a subject the more objective and therefore valuable would be your opinions. This club-like board world began to come under pressure from shareholders, as competition became more international and this country's competitive position declined.

Some boards responded to the pressure to meet higher shareholder expectations by requiring their finance directors to produce results which would match analysts' forecasts. Competitive auditing and lax accounting standards led to what was known as 'creative accounting', a euphemism for varying degrees of fudge to fraud. Shareholders were handicapped in countering this, because disclosure was limited and unreliable.

## Corporate governance committee

This was where our Committee came in. The Stock Exchange, the Financial Reporting Council and the main accounting firms became concerned about their reputations and the reputation of London as a financial centre. Polly Peck for example went from a market value of £1.75 billion to a deficit of nearly £400 million in four weeks. What reliance could be put on reports and accounts and their audit statements if that could happen? We were asked to focus on the financial aspects of corporate governance but had hardly begun our work before the BCCI Bank went down, Maxwell drowned and the disquiet over directors' pay became a political issue. We found ourselves therefore dealing with corporate governance as a whole, but with pensions and pay hived off to committees of their own.

As a result of being set up by the financial sector, but addressing our Code to boards of directors, many of whom were not happy about our remit, we had a potential problem. We did our best to overcome this by testing how far we had support for our approach by issuing a draft for discussion before completing our report. The draft was well received and that gave us the mandate we needed. It was surprising and encouraging how quickly the larger quoted companies complied with the Code. This was because, I believe, they were aware that action was called for and were looking for a lead.

## The UK Code

The aim of the Code was to raise the level of corporate performance by making boards more accountable to their shareholders and clarifying what they were there for. I firmly believe that compliance with Code Principles assists boards to do their job more effectively. If I did not believe that I would not have spent the time I have on governance issues. What the Code established was:

- the need for boards to be crystal clear over their responsibilities;

- the need for checks and balances in the governance structure especially at board level;

- the extent of the board's responsibilities for financial reporting and financial controls;

- the need for independent-minded outside directors of calibre and for committees of the board largely made up of outside directors;

- above all the need for openness about company performance and governance; disclosure is the fundamental plank on which the Code rests.

The Code was to provide a checklist for boards and an agenda for shareholders. The listing obligation required boards to disclose how far they complied with the Code. Compliance itself was left to boards and their shareholders. We wrote:

'The widespread adoption of our recommendations will turn in large measure on the support which all shareholders give to them. The obligation on companies to state how far they comply with the Code provides institutional and individual shareholders with a ready-made agenda for their representations to boards. It is up to them to put it to good use. The Committee is looking to such primarily market-based regulation to turn its proposals into action.'

It was not for the Committee to judge whether the response of boards to the Code in the light of their individual circumstances was adequate; it was for their shareholders. We also made recommendations to investors. We recommended that institutional investors should make use of their votes and declare their policies on the use of their voting rights. There was no response at the time to this recommendation. Institutional disclosure was not forthcoming. What then encouraged greater use of votes by institutions and greater openness about their policies?

Clearly some institutions accepted that governance principles had a certain universality and became more open about their policies and actions in- line with boards of directors. Others moved in response to various pressures most of which reflected recognition of their position of power. Institutional investors own around 80 per cent of the shares of British companies and pension funds alone around one-third. This concentration of ownership had two consequences. First, the institutions collectively were locked in. This meant that the use of voting strength to improve performance had advantages over trying to sell out of an underperforming company. Second, social pressures began to make themselves felt. Members of pension funds may be primarily concerned with financial performance, but many are also concerned with the state of the society into which they are retiring and with the quality of their lives as pensioners. This is a point to which I will return.

In the meantime, boards had changed in line with investor opinion and competition. In this country they had on average become smaller with a higher proportion of outside directors, who were being selected more professionally for the value they could add. Board committees were largely proving their worth, although there were concerns about the ability of remuneration committees to ensure that directors' pay was truly earned. The contribution of independent-minded outside directors to the direction and control of companies was becoming increasingly accepted. Boards in general had greater control over their enterprises and accounting standards were being tightened. The role of directors was perceived as being more responsible and demanding than it had been in the past. Boards needed to make these changes to compete effectively in what were now global markets.

## Investors and society

The shareholding picture was changing too. International investment was rising fast. In 1997 the assets of institutional investors in the US, UK, Germany, France and Japan totalled $23,000 billion. Not only had funds under management grown but they had become more concentrated. Of the $400 billion of international equities held by US institutions, two-thirds is in the hands of 25 pension funds. It is precisely those funds who take corporate governance seriously as an aid to performance and in many cases, like Hermes, have drawn up their own governance codes (the Hermes Codes are reproduced at **B7.7** and **B26.8**). With power comes responsibility. There are a range of reasons why society in a broad sense now expects the investing institutions to play a greater role socially than they did in the past.

One is a consequence of the decline of the state sector worldwide and the corresponding growth of the market sector. The state as a shareholder was seen as able and willing to be a guardian of social and community interests. The expectations which society had of state enterprises has to an extent been transferred to their private sector successors. Companies are perceived as the most powerful force in society today and because in a global world large corporations do not fall under any single national jurisdiction, investors are seen as the only countervailing balance to their use of their power. Citizens look to an extent to today's major investors to take account of the interests of society in the way the state sector was thought to do in the past.

The stakeholder debate reflects the view that companies should take a wider view of their responsibilities and equally that those who own their shares should see that they do. Again the emergence of this concept of the social role of companies has been remarkably rapid. I would not have expected to see a report like Shell's 'Profits and Principles – Does There Have To Be A Choice?' even five years ago. Individual shareholders are raising issues of human rights, fair trading, child labour and the environment at AGMs and are supported by some institutions.

In July 2000, trustees of UK occupational pension schemes were required to disclose their policy on socially responsible investment. A survey has just been published which shows that 59 per cent of the funds that responded are incorporating SRI principles – the recognition of that shorthand is itself indicative of the acceptance of the concept. The survey concludes, 'The survey demonstrates clearly that the UK's major pension funds are concerned about the implications of social, ethical and environmental issues. A large proportion want their fund managers to understand them and take them into account. The challenge is now for the fund management industry to respond.'

Against that background of changing social expectations of companies and investors, we have to take account of the impact of communications technology. It was significant that those protesting against Shell's Brent Spar decision marshalled their forces more speedily than the company via the internet. There are now far more sources of news, news is more instant and there are news sites specialising in every type of interest. The economic world has become far more open and this has its impact on investors. The appetite for disclosure is gargantuan.

# Convergence?

Before summing-up what the future may hold, I will turn to a point on which I was asked to comment – how far are corporate governance principles and approaches likely to converge internationally? There are two forces for convergence and both reflect that the markets for investment and capital are global. First, any country that wishes to attract international investment has to meet the requirements of the leading institutional investors. They require the same standards of corporate governance as they enjoy in their home countries. Second, any company that needs to raise funds from other than domestic sources has to meet the governance standards set by world capital markets.

These market forces for convergence have been backed by the work of the OECD Task Force (paragraph 21.26). It has developed a set of non-binding core principles which countries can then adapt to meet their particular needs and values. These are:

- protection of shareholder rights;

- equitable treatment of all shareholders, including foreign and minority shareholders;

- a corporate governance framework which would recognise the rights of stakeholders as established by law and encourage active co-operation between companies and stakeholders in creating wealth, jobs and sustainable enterprises;

- the framework should ensure disclosure of timely and accurate information on the financial situation, performance, ownership and governance of the company;

- the framework should ensure strategic guidance and effective monitoring by boards and board accountability to the company and to shareholders.

The wording related to stakeholders was the outcome of a considerable debate between the proponents of the US/UK and of the Continental concepts of the nature and purpose of companies. It is further evidence of convergence. That convergence will be of governance principles not of structures and processes. Structures are important, their precise nature in my view is not. The last and vital step in the convergence process will be agreement on an international set of accounting principles.

## Conclusion

Now to sum up, starting with boards of directors. I would expect the movement towards more committed and better trained directors to continue with a growing proportion of independent outside members of boards. They will increasingly have to grapple with the difficult task of how best to assess their own performance as a board, which I see as a major issue for them. IT advances will lead to more direct contacts between shareholders, analysts and commentators and boards. More disclosure will be demanded and faster. I hope there will be more questioning of directors up for election. Shareholders should be asking what value individual nominees will be adding to the board. Ideally, shareholders should be able to interview candidates via their TV sets, and ask them to make a brief presentation of the qualities they will bring to the board if elected. I hope that the UK will at least adopt the US practice of providing comprehensive backgrounds to prospective directors, so that shareholders can make informed choices.

There are two aspects of the future to which I believe investors should give serious thought. The first is the rise of employee share ownership. Figures from the US suggest that ESOP participants alone number 9 million and control on average 10–15 per cent of their companies' stock. Their interests may at times be in conflict with those of less involved investors. They are likely to be well organised, vocal and to grow in power. More generally, the spread of share options will have a significant effect on share ownership and one that is difficult to map, given the unwillingness of companies to accept that options are not costless and should be reported on in the accounts. There is a contingent liability here from the investors' point of view, which is at present concealed.

The second aspect of the future which I suggest will need addressing is the accountability of the investing institutions to those who have entrusted their funds to them. Institutional investors are perceived to hold considerable power. They may, for example, decide whether one company takes over another. They are increasingly expected to be guardians of society's interests. Their power derives from those who put their money with them and it is they who will increasingly demand that their views on how that power should be exercised should be taken into account.

Of course, the majority of, say, pension fund members will be content to leave everything to those running their fund. A minority will want to register their views on policies and decisions with those who vote on their behalf and will expect to be able to engage in direct discussions with their vote-holders. In the past this would have been impractical. With modern technology that is no longer so. Holding the balance between the claims of a variety of single interest activists and the interests of a less vocal majority will call for judgmental and communication skills of the highest order!

I remain amazed at the pace of change and see no evidence of it slowing down. Performance and accountability will continue to be the watchwords underwritten by disclosure. Watch the balance of power and bear in mind what is known as the Iron Law of Responsibility, 'In the long run those who do not use power in a manner which society considers responsible will tend to lose it.'

**Notes**
1. Confederation of British Industry – The Greenbury Committee (July 1995), Directors' Remuneration – Report of a Study Group, chaired by Sir Richard Greenbury.
2. Committee On Corporate Governance – Preliminary Report (August 1997), chaired by Sir Ronald Hampel, see Foreword.

3. Compliance With The Code Of Best Practice (24 May 1995), Report of the Committee on the Financial Aspects of Corporate Governance, Gee Publishing, London, ISBN 1 86089 006 7.

4. Committee On Corporate Governance – The Hampel Committee (January 1998), Final Report, chaired by Sir Ronald Hampel, Gee Publishing, London, ISBN 1 86089 034 2.

5. UK Listing Authority, a division of the Financial Services Authority, 25 The North Colonnade, Canary Wharf, London, E14 5HS. Tel: +44 (0)20 7676 1000. http://www.fsa.gov.uk

6. The 'Definitions' section (May 2000) towards the start of the Listing Rules, attributes (within the definition) a status to the Combined Code, as follows:
   'Combined Code: the principles of good governance and code of best practice prepared by the Committee on Corporate Governance, chaired by Sir Ronald Hampel, published in June 1998 and appended to, but not forming part of, the listing rules.'

7. Consultation issues, para 12.

8. Cadbury, Sir Adrian, (1998): 'The future of governance: the rules of the game', Corporate Governance, Volume 1, No. 8, September, ISSN: 0219–1040, [newsletter of FTMS Consultants (S) Pte Ltd, tel.: (65) 735 0003]; originally delivered to a public lecture at Gresham College, London. The full paper is reproduced in the 'Contributed articles' section of this Handbook.

9. Cadbury, Sir Adrian, (1998), op cit.

10. Professor W.J.M. Mackenzie in the foreword to The Accountability and Audit of Governments by E.L. Normanton, Manchester University press (1966), p. vii. Also published by Frederick A. Prager, New York (1966). The book was based on Normanton's M.Phil thesis from the University of Manchester.

11. Cadbury, Sir Adrian, (1998), ibidem.

12. Cadbury, Sir Adrian, (1998), ibidem.

13. Committee on Corporate Governance – The Combined Code, June 1998, Gee Publishing, London, fax: +44 (0)171 722 4762, ISBN 1 86089 036 9.

14. Dec 1999 PIRC survey. PIRC, 4th Floor, Cityside, 40 Adler Street, London, E1 1EE. Tel.: +44 (0)207 247 2323. Fax: +44 (0)207 247 2457. E-mail: Info@pirc.co.uk; website:www.pirc.co.uk

15. Research by PIRC, reported in the London Evening Standard (26 January 1998, p34).

16. The Listing Rules require listed companies to explain how they are adhering to the 'Principles' of the Combined Code, and to draw attention to which of the 'Provisions' they are not adhering to, giving reasons. So, it is not a Listing Rule that a listed company should necessarily comply with any of the Provisions; and certainly not a Listing Rule that companies should comply with the more onerous extensions promulgated in the policies of bodies which represent institutional investors.

17. See 15 above.

18. This recommendation dates back to the 1995 Greenbury Code on executive remuneration.

19. Target, Simon (20 December 1999), 'Most companies flout Code on corporate governance', The Financial Times, p2; article on PIRC survey.

20. Previously known as 'The Yellow Book' when the London Stock Exchange, rather than the FSA regulated listed companies.

21. FSA Listing Rule 12.43A (c).

22. FSA, Listing Rule 12.43A (a).

23. London Stock Exchange, now FSA, Listing Rule 12.43A (b).

24. The second King Report from S. Africa (2001), while not formally adopted as a corporate governance Code, does not have the same defect of neglecting the social and environmental 'triple bottom line' issues.

25. Cadbury, Sir Adrian, (1998), ibidem.

# Early Corporate Governance Pronouncements – UK

## UK corporate governance listing requirements     B3.1

Since the adoption of the Combined Code by the London Stock Exchange, the Financial Services Authority has taken over from the London Stock Exchange the regulation of UK listed companies. The Listing Rules, which used to be referred to as 'The Yellow Book', have now become 'The Purple Book'[1]. The UK Listing Authority is a division of the Financial Services Authority, 25 The North Colonnade, Canary Wharf, London E14 5HS. Tel: +44 (0)20 7676 1000. Website: www.fsa.gov.uk.

The 1998 Combined Code is appended to the Listing Rules, as were the Cadbury and Greenbury Codes. As with these earlier codes, the Combined Code does not form part of the Listing Rules themselves[2]. The 'Definitions' section (May 2000) towards the start of the Listing Rules, attributes (within the definition) a status to the Combined Code, as follows:

'Combined Code:    the principles of good governance and code of best practice prepared by the Committee on Corporate Governance, chaired by Sir Ronald Hampel, published in June 1998 and appended to, but not forming part of, the listing rules.')

So, as with the Cadbury Code, it is not a listing requirement for a listed company to comply with the Combined Code. Chapter 12: Financial Information (May 2000) of the Listing Rules, in the section on 'Corporate Governance and Directors' Remuneration' includes two continuing obligations (rules) which only require a company to include in its annual report two statements, *viz*:

'12.43A In the case of a company incorporated in the United Kingdom, the following additional items must be included in its annual report and accounts:

(a) 'A narrative statement of how it has applied the principles set out in Section 1 of the Combined Code, providing sufficient explanation which enables its shareholders to evaluate how the principles have been applied;

(b) 'a statement as to whether or not it has complied throughout the accounting period with the provisions set out in Section 1 of the Combined Code. A company that has not complied with the Code provisions, or complied with only some of the Code provisions or (in the case of provisions whose requirements are of a continuing nature) complied for only part of an accounting period, must specify the provisions with which it has not complied, and (where relevant) for what part of the period such non-compliance continued, and give reasons for any non-compliance; … '

Certain provisions of the Combined Code were already explicitly required by the Listing Rules, as they were already requirements at the time of the introduction of the Combined Code, as follows[3].

## Code Provisions                                                        B3.2

**A.9**   (Last sentence) Identification of independent non-executive directors, which is required by paragraph 12.43(I) of the Listing Rules.

**B.17**  The report to shareholders on remuneration, currently required by paragraph 12.43(I) of the Listing Rules.

**B.18**  The setting out of the company's policy on executive directors' remuneration currently required by paragraph 12.43(x)(I) of the Listing Rules.

**B.19**  The requirement for the remuneration report to follow Schedule B of the Combined Code – all the provisions of which are required by the Listing Rules (except paragraph 3 of Schedule B) (see paragraphs 12.43(x)(iii), (iv), (v), (vi) and (vii) of the Listing Rules.

**D.4**   the going concern statement, which is required by paragraph 12.43(v) of the Listing Rules.

The London Stock Exchange had said:

'In the Exchange's opinion, compliance with the relevant Listing Rules will automatically constitute compliance in full with the equivalent Code provision (with the exception of paragraph 3 of Schedule B). The Exchange is not, however, proposing to "carve out" these Code provisions from the disclosure statement (as is done in the current Cadbury compliance statement contained in paragraph 12.43(j)) believing that an unduly complex listing rule would result.'[4]

# The 1992 'Cadbury Code'                                                 B3.3

Note that this Code was superseded by some of the contents of the 1998 Combined Code. The Combined Code was amended in 2003 to reflect the Higgs and Smith Reports which are being adopted by the Financial Reporting Council (FRC) (see PART A).

# Report of the Committee on the Financial Aspects of Corporate Governance (The 'Cadbury Committee')

## The Code of Best Practice

### Introduction

1.   The Committee was set up in May 1991 by the Financial Reporting Council, the London Stock Exchange, and the accountancy profession to address the financial aspects of corporate governance.

2.   The Committee issued a draft report for public comment on 27 May 1992. Its final report, taking account of submissions made during the consultation period and incorporating a Code of Best Practice, was published on 1 December 1992. This extract from the report sets out the text of the Code. It also sets out, as Notes, a number of further recommendations on good practice drawn from the body of the report.

3.   The Committee's central recommendation is that the board of all listed companies registered in the United Kingdom should comply with the Code. The Committee encourages as many other companies as possible to aim at meeting its requirements.

4.   The Committee also recommends:

(a)   that listed companies reporting in respect of years ending after 30 June 1993 should make a statement in their report and accounts about their compliance with the Code and identify and give reasons for any areas of non-compliance;

(b)   that companies' statements of compliance should be reviewed by the auditors before publication. The review by the auditors should cover only those parts of the compliance statement which relate to provisions of the Code where compliance can be objectively verified (see Note 14).

5.   The publication of a statement of compliance, reviewed by the auditors, is to be made a continuing obligation of listing by the London Stock Exchange.

6.   The Committee recommends that its sponsors, convened by the Financial Reporting Council, should appoint a new Committee by the end of June 1995 to examine how far compliance with the Code has progressed, how far its other recommendations have been implemented, and whether the Code needs updating. In the meantime the present Committee will remain responsible for reviewing the implementation of its proposals.

7.   The Committee has made clear that the Code is to be followed by individuals and boards in the light of their own particular circumstances. They are responsible for ensuring that their actions meet the spirit of the Code and in interpreting it they should give precedence to substance over form.

8.    The Committee recognises that smaller listed companies may initially have difficulty in complying with some aspects of the Code. The boards of smaller listed companies who cannot, for the time being, comply with parts of the Code should note that they may instead give their reasons for non-compliance. The Committee believes, however, that full compliance will bring benefits to the boards of such companies and that it should be their objective to ensure that the benefits are achieved. In particular, the appointment of appropriate non-executive directors should make a positive contribution to the development of their businesses.

# The Code of Best Practice (The 'Cadbury Code')

## 1.    The board of directors

1.1    The board should meet regularly, retain full and effective control over the company and monitor the executive management.

1.2    There should be a clearly accepted division of responsibilities at the head of a company, which will ensure a balance of power and authority, such that no one individual has unfettered powers of decision. Where the chairman is also the chief executive, it is essential that there should be a strong and independent element on the board, with a recognised senior member.

1.3    The board should include non-executive directors of sufficient calibre and number for their views to carry significant weight in the board's decisions. (Note 1.)

1.4    The board should have a formal schedule of matters specifically reserved to it for decision to ensure that the direction and control of the company is firmly in its hands. (Note 2.)

1.5    There should be an agreed procedure for directors in the furtherance of their duties to take independent professional advice if necessary, at the company's expense. (Note 3.)

1.6    All directors should have access to the advice and services of the company secretary, who is responsible to the board for ensuring that board procedures are followed and that applicable rules and regulations are complied with. Any question of the removal of the company secretary should be a matter for the board as a whole.

## 2.    Non-executive directors

2.1    Non-executive directors should bring an independent judgement to bear on issues of strategy, performance, resources, including key appointments, and standards of conduct.

2.2    The majority should be independent of management and free from any business or other relationship which could materially interfere with the exercise of their independent judgement, apart from their fees and shareholding. Their fees should reflect the time which they commit to the company. (Notes 4 and 5.)

2.3   Non-executive directors should be appointed for specified terms and reappointment should not be automatic. (Note 6.)

2.4   Non-executive directors should be selected through a formal process and both this process and their appointment should be a matter for the board as a whole. (Note 7.)

**3.   Executive directors**

3.1   Directors' service contracts should not exceed three years without shareholders' approval. (Note 8.)

3.2   There should be full and clear disclosure of directors' total emoluments and those of the chairman and highest-paid UK director, including pension contributions and stock options. Separate figures should be given for salary and performance-related elements and the basis on which performance is measured should be explained.

3.3   Executive directors' pay should be subject to the recommendations of a remuneration committee made up wholly or mainly of non-executive directors. (Note 9.)

**4.   Reporting and controls**

4.1   It is the board's duty to present a balanced and understandable assessment of the company's position. (Note 10.)

4.2   The board should ensure that an objective and professional relationship is maintained with the auditors.

4.3   The board should establish an audit committee of at least 3 non-executive directors with written terms of reference which deal clearly with its authority and duties. (Note 11.)

4.4   The directors should explain their responsibility for preparing the accounts next to a statement by the auditors about their reporting responsibilities. (Note 12.)

4.5   The directors should report on the effectiveness of the company's system of internal control. (Note 13.)

4.6   The directors should report that the business is a going concern, with supporting assumptions or qualifications as necessary. (Note 13.)

# Notes

**These notes include further recommendations on good practice. They do not form part of the Code**.

1.   To meet the Committee's recommendations on the composition of sub-committees of the board, boards will require a minimum of three non-executive directors, one of whom may be the chairman of the company provided he or she is not also its executive head. Additionally, two of the three non-executive directors should be independent in the terms set out in paragraph 2.2 of the Code.

2.  A schedule of matters specifically reserved for decision by the full board should be given to directors on appointment and should be kept up to date. The Committee envisages that the schedule would at least include:

    (a) acquisition and disposal of assets of the company or its subsidiaries that are material to the company;

    (b) investments, capital projects, authority levels, treasury policies and risk management policies.

    The board should lay down rules to determine materiality for any transaction, and should establish clearly which transactions require multiple board signatures. The board should also agree the procedures to be followed when, exceptionally, decisions are required between board meetings.

3.  The agreed procedure should be laid down formally, for example in a Board Resolution, in the Articles, or in the Letter of Appointment.

4.  It is for the board to decide in particular cases whether this definition of independence is met. Information about the relevant interest of directors should be disclosed in the Directors' Report.

5.  The Committee regards it as good practice for non-executive directors not to participate in share option schemes and for their service as non-executive directors not to be pensionable by the company, in order to safeguard their independent position.

6.  The Letter of Appointment for non-executive directors should set out their duties, term of office, remuneration and its review.

7.  The Committee regards it as good practice for a nomination committee to carry out the selection process and to make proposals to the board. A nomination committee should have a majority of non-executive directors on it and be chaired either by the chairman or a non-executive director.

8.  The Committee does not intend that this provision should apply to existing contracts before they become due for renewal.

9.  Membership of the remuneration committee should be set out in the Directors' Report and its chairman should be available to answer questions on remuneration principles and practice at the Annual General Meeting. Best practice is set out in PRO NED's Remuneration Committee guidelines, published in 1992. (Available at the price of £5 from PRO NED, 1 Kingsway, London WC2B 6XF, telephone 071 240 8305).

10. The report and accounts should contain a coherent narrative, supported by the figures, of the company's performance and prospects. Balance requires that setbacks should be dealt with as well as successes. The need for the report to be readily understood emphasises that words are as important as figures.

11. The Committee's recommendations on audit committees are as follows:

(a) They should be formally constituted as sub-committees of the main board to whom they are answerable and to whom they should report regularly; they should be given written terms of reference which deal adequately with their membership, authority and duties; and they should normally meet at least twice a year.

(b) There should be a minimum of three members. Membership should be confined to the non-executive directors of the company and a majority of the non-executives serving on the committee should be independent of the company, as defined in paragraph 2.2 of the Code.

(c) The external auditor and, where an internal audit function exists, the head of internal audit should normally attend committee meetings, as should the finance director. Other board members should also have the right to attend.

(d) The audit committee should have a discussion with the auditors at least once a year, without executive board members present, to ensure that there are no unresolved issues of concern.

(e) The audit committee should have explicit authority to investigate any matters within its terms of reference, the resources which it needs to do so, and full access to information. The committee should be able to obtain outside professional advice and if necessary to invite outsiders with relevant experience to attend meetings.

(f) Membership of the committee should be disclosed in the annual report and the chairman of the committee should be available to answer questions about its work at the Annual General Meeting.

Specimen terms of reference for an audit committee, including a list of the most commonly performed duties, are set out in the Committee's full report.

12. The statement of directors' responsibilities should cover the following points:

● the legal requirement for directors to prepare financial statements for each financial year which give a true and fair view of the state of affairs of the company (or group) as at the end of the financial year and of the profit and loss for that period;

● the responsibility of the directors for maintaining adequate accounting records, for safeguarding the assets of the company (or group), and for preventing and detecting fraud and other irregularities;

● confirmation that suitable accounting policies, consistently applied and supported by reasonable and prudent judgements and estimates, have been used in the preparation of the financial statements;

● confirmation that applicable accounting standards have been followed, subject to any material departures disclosed and explained in the notes to the accounts. (This does not obviate the need for a formal statement in the notes to the accounts disclosing whether the accounts have been prepared in accordance with applicable accounting standards.)

The statement should be placed immediately before the auditors' report which in future will include a separate statement (currently being developed by the Auditing Practices Board) on the responsibility of the auditors for expressing an opinion on the accounts.

13. The Committee notes that companies will not be able to comply with paragraphs 4.5 and 4.6 of the Code until the necessary guidance for companies has been developed as recommended in the Committee's report.

14. The company's statement of compliance should be reviewed by the auditors in so far as it relates to paragraphs 1.4, 1.5, 2.3, 2.4, 3.1 to 3.3 and 4.3 to 4.6 of the Code.

© 1992 The Committee on the Financial Aspects of Corporate Governance and Gee and Co Ltd.

Reproduction of this publication is unrestricted. Separate restrictions apply to the reproduction of the full report of the Committee on the Financial Aspects of Corporate Governance.

# The 1995 'Greenbury Code'                                        B3.4

Note that this Code was superseded by some of the contents of the Combined Code (see **B3.5**). The Code printed here incorporates the two late corrections made after the Greenbury Report was printed, which had been shown on a loose erratum slip in the first printing of the Report. Code references to paragraphs relate to the Greenbury Report itself.

# Directors' remuneration

## Report of a study group chaired by Sir Richard Greenbury

17 July 1995

### The Code

#### A   The remuneration committee

A1   To avoid potential conflicts of interest, Boards of Directors should set up remuneration committees of Non-Executive Directors to determine on their behalf, and on behalf of the shareholders, within agreed terms of reference, the company's policy on executive remuneration and specific remuneration packages for each of the Executive Directors, including pension rights and any compensation payments (paragraphs 4.3–4.7).

A2 Remuneration committee Chairmen should account directly to the shareholders through the means specified in this Code for the decisions their committees reach (paragraph 4.1).

A3 Where necessary, companies' Articles of Association should be amended to enable remuneration committees to discharge these functions on behalf of the Board (paragraph 4.3).

A4 Remuneration committees should consist exclusively of Non-Executive Directors with no personal financial interest other than as shareholders in the matters to be decided, no potential conflicts of interest arising from cross-directorships and no day-to-day involvement in running the business (paragraphs 4.8 and 4.11).

A5 The members of the remuneration committee should be listed each year in the committee's report to shareholders (B1 below). When they stand for re-election, the proxy cards should indicate their membership of the committee (paragraphs 4.12 and 5.25).

A6 The Board itself should determine the remuneration of the Non-Executive Directors, including members of the remuneration committee, within the limits set in the Articles of Association (paragraph 4.13).

A7 Remuneration committees should consult the company Chairman and/or Chief Executive about their proposals and have access to professional advice inside and outside the company (paragraphs 4.14–4.17).

A8 The remuneration committee Chairman should attend the company's Annual General Meeting (AGM) to answer share-holders' questions about Directors' remuneration and should ensure that the company maintains contact as required with its principal shareholders about remuneration in the same way as for other matters (paragraph 5.27).

A9 The committee's annual report to shareholders (B1 below) should not be a standard item of agenda for AGMs. But the committee should consider each year whether the circumstances are such that the AGM should be invited to approve the policy set out in their report and should minute their conclusions (paragraphs 5.28–5.32).

## B    Disclosure and approval provisions

B1 The remuneration committee should make a report each year to the shareholders on behalf of the Board. The report should form part of, or be annexed to, the company's Annual Report and Accounts. It should be the main vehicle through which the company accounts to shareholders for Directors' remuneration (paragraph 5.4).

B2 The report should set out the Company's policy on executive Directors' remuneration, including levels, comparator groups of companies, individual components, performance criteria and measurement, pension provision, contracts of service and compensation commitments on early termination (paragraphs 5.5–5.7).

B3   The report should state that, in framing its remuneration policy, the committee has given full consideration to the best practice provisions set out in sections C and D below (paragraph 5.25).

B4   The report should also include full details of all elements in the remuneration package of each individual Director by name, such as basic salary, benefits in kind, annual bonuses and long-term incentive schemes including share options (paragraphs 5.8–5.12).

B5   Information on share options, including SAYE options, should be given for each Director in accordance with the recommendations of the Accounting Standards Board's Urgent Issues Task Force Abstract 10 and its successors (paragraphs 5.13–5.16).

B6   If grants under executive share option or other long-term incentive schemes are awarded in one large block rather than phased, the report should explain and justify (paragraph 6.29).

B7   Also included in the report should be pension entitlement earned by each individual Director during the year, calculated on a basis to be recommended by the Faculty of Actuaries and the Institute of Actuaries (paragraphs 5.17–5.23).

B8   If annual bonuses or benefits in kind are pensionable the report should explain and justify (paragraph 6.44).

B9   The amounts received by, and commitments made to each Director under B4, B5 and B7 should he subject to audit (paragraph 5.4).

B10  Any service contracts which provide for, or imply, notice periods in excess of one year (or any provisions for predetermined compensation on termination which exceed one year's salary and benefits) should be disclosed and the reasons for the longer notice periods explained (paragraph 7.13).

B11  Shareholdings and other relevant business interests and activities of the Directors should continue to be disclosed as required in the Companies Acts and London Stock Exchange Listing Rules (paragraph 5.24).

B12  Shareholders should be invited specifically to approve all new long-term incentive schemes (including share option schemes) whether payable in cash or shares in which Directors and senior executives will participate which potentially commit shareholders' funds over more than one year or dilute the equity (paragraph 5.33).

**C   Remuneration policy**

C1   Remuneration committees must provide the packages needed to attract, retain and motivate Directors of the quality required but should avoid paying more than is necessary for this purpose (paragraphs 6.5–6.7).

C2   Remuneration committees should judge where to position their company relative to other companies. They should be aware what other comparable companies are paying and should take account of relative performance (paragraphs 6.11–6.12).

C3 Remuneration committees should be sensitive to the wider scene, including pay and employment conditions elsewhere in the company, especially when determining annual salary increases (paragraph 6.13).

C4 The performance-related elements of remuneration should be designed to align the interests of Directors and shareholders and to give Directors keen incentives to perform at the highest levels (paragraph 6.16).

C5 Remuneration committees should consider whether their Directors should be eligible for annual bonuses. If so, performance conditions should be relevant, stretching and designed to enhance the business. Upper limits should always be considered. There may he a case for part-payment in shares to be held for a significant period (paragraphs 6.19–6.22).

C6 Remuneration committees should consider whether their Directors should be eligible for benefits under long-term incentive schemes. Traditional share option schemes should be weighed against other kinds of long-term incentive scheme. In normal circumstances, shares granted should not vest, and options should not be exercisable, in under three years. Directors should be encouraged to hold their shares for a further period after vesting or exercise subject to the need to finance any costs of acquisition and associated tax liability (paragraphs 6.23–6.34).

C7 Any new long-term incentive schemes which are proposed should preferably replace existing schemes or at least form part of a well-considered overall plan, incorporating existing schemes, which should be approved as a whole by shareholders. The total rewards potentially available should not be excessive (paragraph 6.35). (See also B12.)

C8 Grants under all incentive schemes, including new grants under existing share option schemes, should he subject to challenging performance criteria reflecting the company's objectives. Consideration should be given to criteria which reflect the company's performance relative to a group of comparator companies in some key variables such as total shareholder return (paragraphs 6.38–6.40).

C9 Grants under executive share option and other long-term incentive schemes should normally be phased rather than awarded in one large block (paragraph 6.29). (See B6.)

C10 Executive share options should never he issued at a discount (paragraph 6.29).

C11 Remuneration committees should consider the pension consequences and associated costs to the company of basic salary increases, especially for Directors close to retirement (paragraphs 6.42–6.45).

C12 In general, neither annual bonuses nor benefits in kind should be pensionable (paragraph 6.44). (See B8.)

**D   Service contracts and compensation**

D1 Remuneration committees should consider what compensation commitments their Directors' contracts of service, if any, would entail in the event of early termination, particularly for unsatisfactory performance (paragraph 7.10).

D2    There is a strong case for setting notice or contract periods at, or reducing them to, one year or less (see B10). Remuneration committees should, however, he sensitive and flexible, especially over timing. In some cases notice or contract periods of up to two years may he acceptable. Longer periods should be avoided wherever possible (paragraphs 7.11–7.15).

D3    If it is necessary to offer longer notice or contract periods, such as three years, to new Directors recruited from outside, such Periods should reduce after the initial period (paragraph 7.16).

D4    Within the legal constraints, remuneration committees should tailor their approach in individual early termination cases to the wide variety of circumstances. The broad aim should be to avoid rewarding poor performance while dealing fairly with cases where departure is not due to poor performance (paragraphs 7.17 – 7.18).

D5    Remuneration committees should take a robust line on payment of compensation where performance has been unsatisfactory and on reducing compensation to reflect departing Directors' obligations to mitigate damages by earning money elsewhere (paragraphs 7.19–7.20).

D6    Where appropriate, and in particular where notice or contract periods exceed one year, companies should consider paying all or part of compensation in instalments rather than one lump sum and reducing or stopping payment when the former Director takes on new employment (paragraph 7.20).

# The 1998 Combined Code                                      B3.5

(Note that the 1998 Combined Code has been superseded by the 2003 version reproduced in **PART A.**)

## The 1998 Combined Code

### Part 1: Principles of Good Governance

*Section 1: Companies*

*A. Directors*

### The Board

1.    Every listed company should be headed by an effective board which should lead and control the company.

### Chairman and CEO

2.    There are two key tasks at the top of every public company – the running of the board and the executive responsibility for the running of

the company's business. There should be a clear division of responsibilities at the head of the company which will ensure a balance of power and authority, such that no one individual has unfettered powers of decision.

**Board Balance**

**3.** The board should include a balance of executive and non-executive directors (including independent non-executives) such that no individual or small group of individuals can dominate the board's decision taking.

**Supply of Information**

**4.** The board should be supplied in a timely manner with information in a form and of a quality appropriate to enable it to discharge its duties.

**Appointments to the Board**

**5.** There should be a formal and transparent procedure for the appointment of new directors to the board.

**Re-election**

**6.** All directors should be required to submit themselves for re-election at regular intervals and at least every three years.

*B. Directors' Remuneration*

**The Level and Make-up of Remuneration**

**1.** Levels of remuneration should be sufficient to attract and retain the directors needed to run the company successfully, but companies should avoid paving more than necessary for this purpose. A proportion of executive directors' remuneration should be structured so as to link rewards to corporate and individual performance.

**Procedure**

**2.** Companies should establish a formal and transparent procedure for developing policy on executive remuneration and for fixing the remuneration packages of individual directors. No director should be involved in deciding his or her own remuneration.

**Disclosure**

**3.** The company's annual report should contain a statement of remuneration policy and details of the remuneration of each director.

*C. Relations with Shareholders*

**Dialogue with Institutional Shareholders**

**1.** Companies should be ready, where practicable, to enter into a dialogue with institutional shareholders based on the mutual understanding of objectives.

## Constructive Use of the AGM

**2.** Boards should use the AGM to communicate with private investors and encourage their participation.

*D. Accountability and Audit*

### Financial Reporting

**1.** The board should present a balanced and understandable assessment of the company's position and prospects.

### Internal Control

**2.** The board should maintain a sound system of internal control to safeguard shareholders' investment and the company's assets.

### Audit Committee and Auditors

**3.** The board should establish formal and transparent arrangements for considering how they should apply the financial reporting and internal control principles and for maintaining an appropriate relationship with the company's auditors.

*Section 2: Institutional Investors*

*E.   Institutional Investors*

### Shareholder Voting

**1.** Institutional shareholders have a responsibility to make considered use of their votes.

### Dialogue with Companies

**2.** Institutional shareholders should be ready, where practicable, to enter into a dialogue with companies based on the mutual understanding of objectives.

### Evaluation of Governance Disclosures

**3.** When evaluating companies' governance arrangements, particularly those relating to board structure and composition, institutional investors should give due weight to all relevant factors drawn to their attention.

**Part 2: Code of Best Practice**

*Section 1: Companies*

*A. Directors*

**A.1  The Board**

**Principle   Every listed company should be headed by an effective board which should lead and control the company.**

## Code Provisions

**A.1.1**   The board should meet regularly.

**A.1.2**   The board should have a formal schedule of matters specifically reserved to it for decision.

**A.1.3**   There should be a procedure agreed by the board for directors in the furtherance of their duties to take independent professional advice if necessary at the company's expense.

**A.l.4**   All directors should have access to the advice and services of the company secretary, who is responsible to the board for ensuring that board procedures are followed and that applicable rules and regulations are complied with. Any question of the removal of the company secretary should be a matter for the board as a whole.

**A.1.5**   All directors should bring an independent judgement to bear on issues of strategy performance, resources (including key appointments) and standards of conduct.

**A.1.6**   Every director should receive appropriate training on the first occasion that he or she is appointed to the board of a listed company, and subsequently as necessary.

### A.2  Chairman and CEO

**Principle**   **There are two key tasks at the top of every public company – the running of the board and the executive responsibility for the running of the company business. There should be a clear division of responsibilities at the head of the company which will ensure a balance of power and authority, such that no one individual has unfettered powers of decision.**

#### Code Provision

**A.2.1**   A decision to combine the posts of chairman and chief executive officer in one person should be publicly justified. Whether the posts are held by different people or the same person, there should be a strong and independent non-executive element on the board, with a recognised senior member other than the chairman to whom concerns can be conveyed. The chairman, chief executive and senior independent director should be identified in the annual report.

### A.3  Board Balance

**Principle**   **The board should include a balance of executive and non-executive directors (including independent non-executives) such that no individual or small group of individuals can dominate the board's decision taking.**

## Code Provisions

**A.3.1**   The board should include non-executive directors of sufficient calibre and number for their views to carry significant weight in the board's decisions. Non-executive directors should comprise not less than one third of the board.

**A.3.2**   The majority of non-executive directors should be independent of management and free from any business or other relationship which could materially interfere with the exercise of their independent judgement. Non-executive directors considered by the board to be independent in this sense should be identified in the annual report.

## A.4   Supply of Information

**Principle**   **The board should be supplied in a timely manner with information in a form and of a quality appropriate to enable it to discharge its duties.**

## Code Provision

**A.4.1**   Management has an obligation to provide the board with appropriate and timely information, but information volunteered by management is unlikely to be enough in all circumstances and directors should make further enquiries where necessary. The chairman should ensure that all directors are properly briefed on issues arising at board meetings.

## A.5   Appointments to the Board

**Principle**   **There should be a formal and transparent procedure for the appointment of new directors to the board.**

## Code Provision

**A.5.1**   Unless the board is small, a nomination committee should be established to make recommendations to the board on all new board appointments. A majority of the members of this committee should be non-executive directors and the chairman should be either the chairman of the board or a non-executive director. The chairman and members of the nomination committee should be identified in the annual report.

## A.6   Re-election

**Principle**   **All directors should be required to submit themselves for re-election at regular intervals and at least every three years.**

## Code Provisions

**A.6.1**   Non-executive directors should be appointed for specified terms subject to re-election and to Companies Act provisions relating to the removal of a director, and reappointment should not be automatic.

**A.6.2**   All directors should be subject to election by shareholders at the first opportunity after their appointment, and to re-election thereafter at intervals of no more than three years. The names of directors submitted for election or re-election should be accompanied by sufficient biographical details to enable shareholders to take an informed decision on their election.

*B. Directors' remuneration*

**B.1    The Level and Make-up of Remuneration**

**Principle    Levels of remuneration should he sufficient to attract and retain the directors needed to run the company successfully, but companies should avoid paying more than is necessary for this purpose. A proportion of executive directors' remuneration should be structured so as to link rewards to corporate and individual performance.**

**Code Provisions**

*Remuneration Policy*

**B.1.1**   The remuneration committee should provide the packages needed to attract, retain and motivate executive directors of the quality required but should avoid paying more than is necessary for this purpose.

**B.1.2**   Remuneration committees should judge where to position their company relative to other companies. They should be aware what comparable companies are paying and should take account of relative performance. But they should use such comparisons with caution, in view of the risk that they can result in an upward ratchet of remuneration levels with no corresponding improvement in performance.

**B.1.3**   Remuneration committees should be sensitive to the wider scene, including pay and employment conditions elsewhere in the group, especially when determining annual salary increases.

**B.1.4**   The performance-related elements of remuneration should form a significant proportion of the total remuneration package of executive directors and should be designed to align their interests with those of shareholders and to give these directors keen incentives to perform at the highest levels.

**B.1.5**   Executive share options should not be offered at a discount save as permitted by paragraphs 13.30 and 13.31 of the Listing Rules.

**B.1.6**   In designing schemes of performance-related remuneration, remuneration committees should follow the provisions in Schedule A to this Code.

*Service Contracts and Compensation*

**B.1.7**   There is a strong case for setting notice or contract periods at, or reducing them to, one year or less. Boards should set this as an objective, but they should recognise that it may not be possible to achieve it immediately.

**B.1.8**   If it is necessary to offer longer notice or contract periods to new directors recruited from outside, such periods should reduce after the initial period.

**B.1.9**   Remuneration committees should consider what compensation commitments (including pension contributions) their directors' contracts of service, if any, would entail in the event of early termination. They should, in particular, consider the advantages of providing explicitly in the initial contract for such compensation commitments except in the case of removal for misconduct

**B.1.10**   Where the initial contract does not explicitly provide for compensation commitments, remuneration committees should, within legal constraints, tailor their approach in individual early termination cases to the wide variety of circumstances. The broad aim should be to avoid rewarding poor performance while dealing fairly with cases where departure is not due to poor performance and to take a robust line on reducing compensation to reflect departing directors' obligations to mitigate loss.

**B.2      Procedure**

**Principle**   **Companies should establish a formal and transparent procedure for developing policy on executive remuneration and for fixing the remuneration packages of individual directors. No director should be involved in deciding his or her own remuneration.**

**Code Provisions**

**B.2.1**   To avoid potential conflicts of interest, boards of directors should set up remuneration committees of independent non-executive directors to make recommendations to the board, within agreed terms of reference, on the company's framework of executive remuneration and its cost: and to determine on their behalf specific remuneration packages for each of the executive directors, including pension rights and any compensation payments.

**B.2.2**   Remuneration committees should consist exclusively of non-executive directors who are independent of management and free from any business or other relationship which could materially interfere with the exercise of their independent judgement.

**B.2.3**   The members of the remuneration committee should be listed each year in the board's remuneration report to shareholders (B.3.1 below).

**B.2.4**   The board itself or, where required by the Articles of Association, the shareholders should determine the remuneration of the non-executive directors, including members of the remuneration committee, within the limits set in the Articles of Association. Where permitted by the Articles, the board may however delegate this responsibility to a small sub-committee, which might include the chief executive officer.

**B.2.5** Remuneration committees should consult the chairman and/or chief executive officer about their proposals relating to the remuneration of other executive directors and have access to professional advice inside and outside the company.

**B.2.6** The chairman of the board should ensure that the company maintains contact as required with its principal shareholders about remuneration in the same way as for other matters.

**B.3 Disclosure**

**Principle** **The company's annual report should contain a statement of remuneration policy and details of the remuneration of each director.**

**Code Provisions**

**B.3.1** The board should report to the shareholders each year on remuneration. The report should form part of, or be annexed to, the company's annual report and accounts. It should be the main vehicle through which the company reports to shareholders on directors' remuneration.

**B.3.2** The report should set out the company's policy on executive directors' remuneration. It should draw attention to factors specific to the company.

**B.3.3** In preparing the remuneration report, the board should follow the provisions in Schedule B to this Code.

**B.3.4** Shareholders should be invited specifically to approve all new long-term incentive schemes (as defined in the Listing Rules) save in the circumstances permitted by paragraph 13.13A of the Listing Rules.

**B.3.5** The hoard's annual remuneration report to shareholders need not be a standard item of agenda for AGMs. But the board should consider each year whether the circumstances are such that the AGM should be invited to approve the policy set out in the report and should minute their conclusions.

*C. Relations with Shareholders*

**C.1 Dialogue with Institutional Shareholders**

**Principle** **Companies should be ready, where practicable, to enter into a dialogue with institutional shareholders based on the mutual understanding of objectives.**

**C.2 Constructive Use of the AGM**

**Principle** **Boards should use tile AGM to communicate with private investors and encourage their participation.**

**Code Provisions**

**C.2.1** Companies should count all proxy votes and, except where a poll is called, should indicate the level of proxies lodged on each resolution, and the balance for and against the resolution, after it has been dealt with on a show of hands.

**C.2.2** Companies should propose a separate resolution at the AGM on each substantially separate issue and should in particular propose a resolution at the AGM relating to the report and accounts.

**C.2.3** The chairman of the board should arrange for the chairmen of the audit, remuneration and nomination committees to be available to answer questions at the AGM.

**C.2.4** Companies should arrange for the Notice of the AGM and related papers to be sent to shareholders at least 20 working days before the meeting.

*D. Accountability and Audit*

**D.1    Financial Reporting**

**Principle    The board should present a balanced and understandable assessment of the company's position and prospects.**

**Code Provisions**

**D.1.1** The directors should explain their responsibility for preparing the accounts and there should be a statement by the auditors about their reporting responsibilities.

**D.1.2** The board's responsibility to present a balanced and understandable assessment extends to interim and other price-sensitive public reports and reports to regulators as well as to information required to be presented by statutory requirements.

**D.1.3** The directors should report that the business is a going concern, with supporting assumptions or qualifications as necessary.

**D.2    Internal Control**

**Principle    The board should maintain a sound system of internal control to safeguard shareholders investment and the company's assets.**

**Code Provisions**

**D.2.1** The directors should, at least annually, conduct a review of the effectiveness of the group's system of internal controls and should report to shareholders that they have done so. The review should cover all controls, including financial, operational and compliance controls and risk management

**D.2.2** Companies which do not have an internal audit function should from time to time review the need for one.

**D.3    Audit Committee and Auditors**

**Principle    The board should establish formal and transparent arrangements for considering how they should apply the**

financial reporting and internal control principles and for maintaining an appropriate relationship with the company's auditors.

**Code Provisions**

**D.3.1** The board should establish an audit committee of at least three directors, all non-executive, with written terms of reference which deal clearly with its authority and duties. The members of the committee, a majority of whom should be independent non-executive directors, should be named in the report and accounts.

**D.3.2** The duties of the audit committee should include keeping under review the scope and results of the audit and its cost effectiveness and the independence and objectivity of the auditors. Where the auditors also supply a substantial volume of non-audit services to the company, the committee should keep the nature and extent of such services under review, seeking to balance the maintenance of objectivity and value for money.

*Section 2: Institutional Shareholders*

*E. Institutional Investors*

**E.1  Shareholder Voting**

**Principle**  **Institutional shareholders have a responsibility to make considered use of their votes.**

**Code Provisions**

**E.1.1** Institutional shareholders should endeavour to eliminate unnecessary variations in the criteria which each applies to the corporate governance arrangements and performance of the companies in which they invest.

**E.1.2** Institutional shareholders should, on request, make available to their clients information on the proportion resolutions on which votes were cast and non-discretionary proxies lodged.

**E.1.3** Institutional shareholders should take steps to ensure that their voting intentions are being translated into practice.

**E.2  Dialogue with Companies**

**Principle**  **Institutional shareholders should be ready, where practicable, to enter into a dialogue with companies based on the mutual understanding of objectives.**

**E.3  Evaluation of Governance Disclosures**

**Principle**  **When evaluating companies' governance arrangements, particularly those relating to board structure and composition, institutional investors should give due weight to all relevant factors drawn to their attention.**

### Schedule A: Provisions on the Design of Performance-related Remuneration

1.   Remuneration committees should consider whether the directors should be eligible for annual bonuses. If so, performance conditions should he relevant, stretching and designed to enhance the business. Upper limits should always be considered. There may be a case for part payment in shares to be held for a significant period.

2.   Remuneration committees should consider whether the directors should be eligible for benefits under long-term incentive schemes. Traditional share option schemes should be weighed against other kinds of long-term incentive schemes. In normal circumstances, shares granted or other forms of deferred remuneration should not vest, and options should not be exercisable, in under three years. Directors should be encouraged to hold their shares for a further period after vesting or exercise, subject to the need to finance any costs of acquisition and associated tax liability.

3.   Any new long-term incentive schemes which are proposed should be approved by shareholders and should preferably replace existing schemes or at least form part of a well considered overall plan, incorporating existing schemes. The total rewards potentially available should not be excessive.

4.   Payouts or grants under all incentive schemes, including new grants under existing share option schemes, should be subject to challenging performance criteria reflecting the company's objectives. Consideration should be given to criteria which reflect the company's performance relative to a group of comparator companies in some key variables such as total shareholder return.

5.   Grants under executive share option and other long-term incentive schemes should normally be phased rather than awarded in one large block.

6.   Remuneration committees should consider the pension consequences and associated costs to the company of basic salary increases and other changes in remuneration, especially for directors close to retirement.

7.   In general, neither annual bonuses nor benefits in kind should be pensionable.

### Schedule B: Provisions on what should be included in the Remuneration Report

1.   The report should include full details of all elements in the remuneration package of each individual director by name, such as basic salary, benefits in kind, annual bonuses and long-term incentive schemes including share options.

2.   Information on share options, including SAYE options, should be given for each director in accordance with the recommendations of the Accounting Standards Boards Urgent Issues Task Force Abstract 10 and its successors.

**3.**   If grants under executive share option or other long-term incentive schemes are awarded in one large block rather than phased, the report should explain and justify.

**4.**   Also included in the report should be pension entitlements earned by each individual director during the year, disclosed on one of the alternative bases recommended by the Faculty of Actuaries and the Institute of Actuaries and included in the Stock Exchange Listing Rules. Companies may wish to make clear that the transfer value represents a liability of the company, not a sum paid or due to the individual.

**5.**   If annual bonuses or benefits in kind are pensionable the report should explain and justify.

**6.**   The amounts received by, and commitments made to, each director under 1, 2 and 4 above should be subject to audit.

**7.**   Any service contracts which provide for, or imply, notice periods in excess of one year (or any provisions for predetermined compensation on termination which exceed one year's salary and benefits) should be disclosed and the reasons for the longer notice periods explained.

**Notes**

[1.]   UK Listing Authority, a division of the Financial Services Authority, 25 The North Colonnade, Canary Wharf, London, E14 5HS. Tel.: +44 (0)20 7676 1000; http://www.fsa.gov.uk

[2.]   The 'Definitions' section (May 2000) towards the start of the Listing Rules, attributes (within the definition) a status to the Combined Code, as follows:
'Combined Code: the principles of good governance and code of best practice prepared by the Committee on Corporate Governance, chaired by Sir Ronald Hampel, published in June 1998 and appended to, but not forming part of, the listing rules.'

[3]   Proposed changes to the Listing Rules – Corporate Governance (Principles of Good Governance and Code of Best Practice – Consultation Draft, (March 1998), the London Stock Exchange, London, EC2N 1HP, [Tel.: 0171 797 1000], Introduction, para 11.

[4.]   Consultation issues, para 12.

# Reporting On Internal Control And The Turnbull Report

## Turnbull: 'Internal Control – Guidance to Directors on the Combined Code'                                    B4.1

We reproduce the Turnbull guidance[1] in PART A of this handbook. It was published just before the end of September 1999, and was quickly adopted by the London Stock Exchange as describing what is required of companies claiming to be adhering to the 1998 Combined Code Principle D.2 (renumbered C.2 in the 2003 Combined Code, also to be found in PART A) and complying with the associated Provisions D.2.1 and D.2.2 (renumbered C.2.1 and C.3.5 in the 2003 Combined Code). The original 1998 Combined Code is reproduced at **B3.11**. So the 1998 Combined Code provision on internal audit has now been reclassified in the part of the new 2003 Code which has to do with audit committees and auditors. In this chapter we show the old 1998 as well as the new 2003 Code numbering since the Turnbull Report continues to use the numbering as well as the wording of the 1998 Code.

## Scope of the Turnbull Report                                                      B4.2

The Turnbull Committee was tasked with developing guidance for directors on the internal control Principle and Provisions within the 1998 Combined Code[2] (see **B3.11**) and on reporting on these matters to shareholders in the annual report annual report and accounts, *viz.*

### 'D.2 (now C.2) Internal Control

**Principle**     **The board should maintain a sound system of internal control to safeguard shareholders investment and the company's assets.**

**Code Provisions**

**D.2.1 (now C.2.1)**     The directors should, at least annually, conduct a review of the effectiveness of the group's system of internal controls and should report to shareholders that they have done so. The review should cover all controls, including financial operational and compliance controls and risk management.

**D.2.2 (now C.3.5)**     Companies which do not have an internal audit function should from time to time review the need for one.'

**C.3.5 (2003)**     The audit committee should monitor and review the effectiveness of the internal audit activities. Where there is no internal audit function, the audit committee should consider annually whether there is a need for an internal audit function and make a recommendation to the board, and the reasons for the absence of such a function should be explained in the relevant section of the annual report.'

Note that the 2003 Code has added the word 'material' to C.2.1 and uses the phrase 'risk management systems' rather than merely 'risk management'.

## Scope required within the company for compliance        B4.3

The final Turnbull guidance was consistent with the Committee's earlier consultation draft in that a UK incorporated listed company adhering to and complying with the above Principle and Provisions was required to have put in place the Turnbull approach by the time of its first financial year-end on or after 23 December 1999, or provide an explanation of when they expected to have those procedures in place and, *pro temps*, to have continued to have followed the old Rutteman guidance. Thereafter, for the first year-end on or after 23 December 2000, and for subsequent year-ends, the company is to be able to assert that it has been in full compliance with the Turnbull approach (a) over the entire year being reported and also (b) over the period between the year-end and the date of the finalisation of the accounts, and (c) this to apply to all of the parts of the business consolidated into the annual financial results of the listed company.

In view of paragraph 12.43A of the Listing Rules (see **B3.1** and **B4.4**), for this compliance to have been over the whole of the year being reported, the Turnbull guidance (para 35 – see **B4.27**) states that it is necessary that compliance 'has been in place for the year under review and up to the date of approval of the annual report and accounts'.

## Status of Turnbull in the Listing Rules        B4.4

In the original Foreword to the Turnbull Report, Paul Geradine, Head of Listing at the London Stock Exchange pointed out that the Stock Exchange considered compliance with the Turnbull guidance is consistent with the related Listing Rules' disclosure requirements and to constitute compliance with 1998 Combined Code Provisions D.2.1 and D.2.2. and provide appropriate narrative disclosure of how the Code Principle D.2 has been applied.

The relevant references in the Listing Rules are in the July 1998 amendment (para 12.43A) to the Stock Exchange Listing Rules, specifying listed companies' obligations with respect to the Combined Code.

'In the case of a company incorporated in the United Kingdom, the following additional items must be included in its annual report and accounts:

(a) a narrative statement of how it has applied the principles set out in Section 1 of the Combined Code, providing explanation which enables its shareholders to evaluate how the principles have been applied;

(b)   a statement as to whether or not it has complied throughout the accounting period with the Code provisions set out in Section 1 of the Combined Code. A company that has not complied with the Code provisions, or complied with only some of the Code provisions or (in the case of provisions whose requirements are of a continuing nature) complied for only part of an accounting period, must specify the Code provisions with which it has not complied, and (where relevant) for what part of the period such non-compliance continued, and give reasons for any non-compliance … '

## Turnbull reporting is mainly on risk management and internal control process   B4.5

The Turnbull guidance means that the focus of the internal control statement which directors publish is now much more on disclosures affirming compliance with a process followed than on disclosures which either itemise or conclude on the results of the process followed or are phrased in any particular words. The process that a company must follow to give effect to the Turnbull guidance can be summed up as requiring each of the following.

1.   There must be embedded monitoring processes for the review of internal control on a continuous basis.

2.   The board should regularly receive and review reports on internal control. When doing this:

   'the board should:

   consider what are the significant risks and assess how they have been identified, evaluated and managed;

   assess the effectiveness of the related system of internal control in managing the significant risks, having regard, in particular, to any significant failings or weaknesses in internal control that have been reported;

   consider whether necessary actions are being taken promptly to remedy any significant failings or weaknesses; and

   consider whether the findings indicate a need for more extensive monitoring of the system of internal control.' (para 31).

3.   The board should undertake an annual assessment for the purposes of making its public statement on internal control, so as to ensure that it has considered all significant aspects of internal control for the company for the year under review and up to the date of approval of the annual report and accounts.

   'The board's annual assessment should, in particular, consider:

   ●   the changes since the last annual assessment in the nature and extent of significant risks, and the company's ability to respond to changes in its business and the external environment;

- the scope and quality of management's ongoing monitoring of risks and of the system of internal control, and where applicable, the work of its internal audit function and other providers of assurance;

- the extent and frequency of the communication of the results of the monitoring to the board (or board committee(s)) which enables it to build up a cumulative assessment of the state of control in the company and the effectiveness with which risk is being managed;

- the incidence of significant control failings or weaknesses that have been identified at any time during the period and the extent to which they have resulted in unforeseen outcomes or contingencies that have had, could have had, or may in the future have, a material impact on the company's financial performance or condition; and

- the effectiveness of the company's public reporting process' (para 33).

4.   The board should define the process to be adopted for this review by the board, covering the scope and frequency of the reports it receives and reviews during the year (see 2 above) and also the process of its annual assessment (see 3 above).

5.   The board (a) takes responsibility for the disclosures on internal control in the annual report and accounts; and the board itself must therefore (b) consider the results of any relevant board committee's (such as the audit committee's) reviews of internal control which give effect to aspects of the Turnbull guidance; and (c) the board must form its own view on internal control effectiveness after due and careful enquiry.

Turnbull avoids prescriptive, 'boilerplate' wording for the content of reports on these matters to shareholders and one of the best aspects of the internal control statements which have been published by listed companies is the freedom of expression and variety of content that has appeared, though sadly more uniform wording is being adopted over time. The intention is that the guidance (a) reflects sound business practice whereby internal control is embedded in the business processes by which the company pursues its objectives, (b) will remain relevant over time in the continually evolving business environment, and (c) will enable each company to apply the guidance in a manner which takes account of its particular circumstances.

Giving effect to some of the wording in the 1998 Combined Code's Provision D.2.1 (C.2.1) above, the Turnbull guidance is based on the adoption by a company's board of a risk-based approach to establishing a sound system of internal control and reviewing its effectiveness. The Turnbull Committee stated that this should be incorporated by a company within its normal management and governance processes and should not be treated as a separate exercise undertaken to meet regulatory requirements.

# Significant Turnbull changes from Rutteman                    B4.6

A significant change to the old Rutteman guidance is that companies are no longer required to publish a 'description of the key procedures that the directors have established and which are designed to provide effective internal [financial] control'[3]. The intention to make this change had been apparent in the Turnbull consultation draft. Under the old Rutteman guidance the scope of this could be restricted to internal financial control at the discretion of the company. However, Turnbull (para 36) allows that in the board's published statement on internal control ...

> 'The board may wish to provide additional information ... to assist understanding of the company's risk management processes and system of internal control.'

Significant changes between the Turnbull consultation draft and the final Turnbull guidance were as follows.

- The final guidance does not allow for a comprehensive specific review (perhaps by outside consultants) of the system of internal control to be carried out as an alternative to an embedded monitoring process within the business, as was allowed in the consultation draft. The final guidance states:

  > 'effective monitoring on a continuous basis is an essential component of a sound system of internal control'.

- The consultation draft had extended the Rutteman requirement that directors should refer in their published statement on internal control to any material losses which were a consequence of a breakdown of internal financial control. The extension required that any significant losses which were due largely to a breakdown of any aspect of internal control (not just internal financial control) should be referred to in the directors' statement; as with Rutteman, directors were to explain what action the directors had taken or why the directors considered no action was necessary. The test of 'significance' was to have been whether the event or events (financial or otherwise) which had occurred, and had resulted in significant losses, was caused mainly by a breakdown in internal control and was an event(s) the consequences of which had been referred to elsewhere within the annual report and accounts.

Strictly speaking, the final Turnbull Report has dropped all this: directors no longer need to refer to particular significant internal control breakdowns, whether financial or not, in their internal control statement. In this regard, all that the final Turnbull guidance requires to be contained within the directors' internal control statement is a disclosure of ...

> 'the process it [the board] has applied to deal with material internal control aspects of any significant problems disclosed in the annual report and accounts'.

Even so, scrutiny of post-Turnbull annual reports shows that most companies continue to refer in their internal control statement to significant breakdowns in internal control (now covering financial, operational and compliance breakdowns) and then explain the measures they are taking to deal with the matter(s) and prevent recurrence – just as they were required to do under the Rutteman guidance with respect to significant internal financial control breakdowns. The advice given by the 'Big Four' audit firms encourages this approach, and we should remember that Code Provision D.2.1 is one of the seven Provisions that external auditors are required to review and report on if they disagree with what the directors are reporting (see the table at the end of **B5.5**).

The Turnbull guidance does require management to report to the board any significant control failings or weaknesses identified, including the impact that they have had, or could have had, or may have, on the company and the actions being taken to rectify them (para 30).

## Internal audit                                                    B4.7

**'D.2.2 (now C.3.5)**   Companies which do not have an internal audit function should from time to time review the need for one.

**C.3.5 (2003)**   The audit committee should monitor and review the effectiveness of the internal audit activities. Where there is no internal audit function, the audit committee should consider annually whether there is a need for an internal audit function and make a recommendation to the board, and the reasons for the absence of such a function should be explained in the relevant section of the annual report.'

The Turnbull guidance also covers this Provision D.2.2 (now C.3.5). In addition to the guidance that companies who do not have an internal audit function should assess the need for one annually, having regard to criteria that Turnbull gives, Turnbull also guides that where there is an internal audit function the board should annually review its scope of work, authority and resources, having regard to the same criteria. Those criteria can be summarised as (see para 45):

● trends or current factors relevant to the company's activities, markets or other aspects of its external environment, that have increased, or are expected to increase, the risks faced by the company;

● an increase in risk from internal factors such as organisational restructuring or from changes in reporting processes or underlying information systems; and

● adverse trends evident from monitoring of internal control systems or the increased incidence of unexpected occurrences etc.

If the company does not have an internal audit function and the board has not reviewed the need for one, the Listing Rules require the board to disclose those facts (para 47). The new 2003 Combined Code incorporates into C.3.5 the Smith Committee addition that where a board decides not to have an internal audit function, it should publicly justify its decision

So Turnbull has made the impact of this Provision more demanding in three ways.

- The review must be at least once a year.

- The review must be done even when there already is an internal audit function.

- It is the board, not merely 'the company' that must do this review. Clearly, the hard graft of this review can be delegated by the board, but the results of the review should come through to the board for consideration and approval.

- Public defence of a decision not to have an internal audit function.

## Other matters of interest                                    B4.8

There are other points of note in the Turnbull guidance. At last we have a clear acknowledgement of the distinctions between management's and the board's responsibilities as well as those of other staff – all so conspicuously missing from the Hampel Report, *viz.* (from the Turnbull guidance):

'The board of directors is responsible for the company's system of internal control. It should set appropriate policies on internal control and seek regular assurance that will enable it to satisfy itself that the system is functioning effectively. The board must further ensure that the system of internal control is effective in managing risks in the manner which it has approved' (para 16).

and (also from the Turnbull guidance):

'It is the role of management to implement board policies on risk and control. In fulfilling its responsibilities, management should identify and evaluate the risks faced by the company for consideration by the board and design, operate and monitor a suitable system of internal control which implements the policies adopted by the board' (para 18).

and (also from the Turnbull guidance):

'All employees have some responsibility for internal control … ' (para 19).

We were impressed by the presentation in checklist form of nineteen major questions to be addressed as criteria for assessing the effectiveness of the company's risk and control processes (Appendix to the Turnbull Report).

We were not so impressed by the downgrading of 'the control environment' component of internal control. Turnbull has combined into a single component of internal control two of the COSO/Rutteman components – 'control environment' and 'control activities' (Appendix to the Turnbull Report). The Turnbull Committee omitted both the 'control environment' and also the 'assessment of risks' from what they refer to as being included within a system of internal control. Turnbull implied that 'the control environment' is just, or at least mainly, about organisational structures whereas it is much more than that covering, for instance, policies on business conduct and ethics, and the example set by the board.

Finally, we should not overlook the provision by Turnbull of a modified definition of internal control. Its notable features are the incorporation of a business risk dimension into the definition and the classification under *operational* control of the control objective of 'safeguarding assets from inappropriate use ... '. This latter is consistent with COSO but was abandoned by Rutteman who desired that directors should report on this aspect of internal control even if they restricted the scope of their internal control report to just internal financial control. Rutteman was therefore obliged to classify this aspect of internal control rather inelegantly under 'internal financial control'. Now that the Combined Code/Turnbull guidance requires the directors' internal control report to cover all aspects of internal control, this pragmatic approach of Rutteman is no longer necessary.

## Turnbull's modified definition of internal control                B4.9

'An internal control system encompasses the policies, processes, tasks, behaviours and other aspects of a company that, taken together:

- facilitate its effective and efficient operation by enabling it to respond appropriately to significant business, operational, financial, compliance and other risks to achieving the company's objectives. This includes the safeguarding of assets from inappropriate use or from loss and fraud, and ensuring that liabilities are identified and managed;

- help ensure the quality of internal and external reporting. This requires the maintenance of proper records and processes that generate a flow of timely, relevant and reliable information within and outside the organisation;

- help ensure compliance with applicable laws and regulations, and also with internal policies with respect to the conduct of business.'

It is disappointing that in amending the standard COSO definition of internal control the Turnbull Committee did not take the opportunity to indicate within the definition that an enterprise's internal control very often happens within the businesses of service providers – all the more so now that so much is outsourced (see **B8.29** and **B8.31–B8.34**). Now that COSO (www.coso.org) has an exposure draft of their new enterprise risk management framework, we can expect that this will gradually supersede in practice the concept of an internal control framework. This is likely to be so particularly in the UK where the directors' review and report since 1998 has had to embrace internal control and enterprise risk management (systems).

# Turnbull buries Cadbury's intention to report on the effectiveness of internal control B4.10

The word 'reporting' is not in the title of the final Turnbull guidance, as it was in Rutteman guida

nce which it replaced. Many will breathe a sigh of relief; others will see it as an opportunity finally lost.

If we applied the drift of the new Turnbull guidance on control to the financial statements themselves, then financial results would no longer be reported! There would just be opaque disclosures about processes followed to arrive at undisclosed financial results.

The 1992 Cadbury Code provision had been:

'Directors should report on the effectiveness of the company's systems of internal control'.

'Effectiveness' is about results – the achievement of objectives.

## Resistance to disclosing an opinion on 'effectiveness' B4.11

Hardly had the ink dried on the Cadbury Code than a war of attrition was waged by many external auditors and finance directors to undermine that Cadbury requirement. Should we entrust to those parties the determination of what should be reported? In Turnbull we have the final dénouement.

This was the only part of the Cadbury Code to be watered down in its (deferred) 1995 implementation. The Rutteman working party watered it down by allowing directors not to disclose opinions on control effectiveness and to restrict their reports to financial control. Cadbury had not intended either: the phrase 'internal financial control' in the draft Cadbury Report had been replaced by 'internal control' in the final Cadbury Report. The device of allowing directors to report that they had 'reviewed' the effectiveness of control without disclosing the results of that review was an unsubtle way round the core Cadbury intention. In a brave foreword to Rutteman, the Cadbury Committee could only welcome Rutteman as a step 'towards full implementation of this section of the Code'. Now we have taken several steps backwards.

At least Rutteman had required directors to describe publicly the key procedures they had established which were designed to provide effective internal financial control. Where weaknesses in internal financial control had resulted in material losses, Rutteman required directors to describe what corrective action had been taken or was intended, or to explain why changes were unnecessary.

Then, along came Hampel – encouragingly disagreeing that directors should restrict their scope to just internal financial control, and requiring that operational and compliance controls and risk management should also be covered (1998 Code Provisions D.2.1 of the Combined Code – see **B3.11**). The sting in the tail was that Hampel ratified the Rutteman guidance that directors need not report on 'effectiveness'.

## Turnbull's further back stepping on reporting about internal control 'effectiveness'                                                  B4.12

Hampel's part in unravelling Cadbury may have given heart to Turnbull to go further. Following Turnbull, reporting on internal control effectiveness has now well and truly disappeared from corporate radar screens. The Turnbull Committee's main task was to develop guidance for directors on the Combined Code Provision resulting from Hampel and replacing Cadbury:

> 'The directors should, at least annually, conduct a review of the effectiveness of the group's system of internal controls and should report to shareholders that they have done so. The review should cover all controls, including financial operational and compliance controls and risk management.'
>
> *('Risk Management Systems' in C.2.1 of 2003 Combined Code)*

While Rutteman had required the 'principle mechanisms' of control to be disclosed, Turnbull dropped this at the consultation stage. At that point Turnbull had retained the disclosure requirements which required implications of material control breakdowns to be disclosed publicly and indeed had extended them to cover all aspects of internal control, not just internal financial control. They were dropped entirely from the final Turnbull Report, and there was no consultation on this significant change from the consultation draft.

## Impact on the public sector                                            B4.13

Swathes of the public sector, having adopted enthusiastically the corporate governance codes of the private sector, are now left washed up high and dry. The public sector had not displayed the same degree of reluctance to report on 'effectiveness' (even if sometimes they described it as 'appropriateness') and had developed their own guidance on how to approach this. For instance, directors of NHS authorities and trusts now make public disclosure of the control mechanisms they have in place, and express an opinion on internal control 'appropriateness'. Because of the approximately two-year time delay in converting governance codes to be applicable to the public sector, it was only when listed companies were finally burying the idea of reporting on the concept of 'effectiveness' that this was in the process of being implemented in many parts of the public sector. In future we can expect more public sector caution over adopting 'best practice' developed mainly with the private sector in mind.

## Reporting on 'process' alone is not very informative        B4.14

Open systems have inputs, processes and outputs. Disclosures about inputs and outputs are the essence of informative reports. Detail on 'process' is largely of interest to the readers of annual reports only if it throws light upon the basis on which the disclosed results were prepared – for instance if sales were credited only when despatch takes place. If results are not reported, then information on process throws little light on anything. By analogy, there would be little point in publishing a statement of accounting policies without also publishing a set of financial statements prepared consistent with those policies. Likewise, there is little point in reporting on the process of internal control unless one also reports on the results of that process, including the board's opinion as to whether internal control has been effective. Financial statements are published in the name of the board, indicating the opinion of each director as to their reliability. The internal control statement would be greatly improved if it included the directors' opinion as to the effectiveness of internal control. Not only is no opinion required to be published, but there is no clear requirement for the directors to arrive at such an opinion even for internal use only – they are just required to review the effectiveness of internal control and report that they have done so.

What now is reported by directors on internal control is about process – and in very general, uninformative terms. Boards report they have an ongoing process, regularly reviewed by the board, to identify, evaluate and manage significant risks – but they need not describe what that process is. As before under Rutteman, there is an acknowledgement of the board's responsibility for internal control and a 'disclaimer' to the effect that it can only provide reasonable assurance against material misstatement or loss. The board describes, in summary, the process it has applied to review the effectiveness of internal control but not the results of that review. And the board need now only describe the general process it has applied to deal with material breakdowns in control, but not whether there have been such breakdowns, nor what they were.

It is true that Turnbull allows that the board 'may wish to provide additional information' and should in any case 'ensure its disclosures provide meaningful, high-level information' – but is this more than whistling in the wind?

Arguments for and against reporting on internal control effectiveness are summarised in **B4.15** below.

# Arguments for and against directors publicly disclosing their opinion on internal control effectiveness
**B4.15**

## Rutteman's adjustment of Cadbury
**B4.16**

The Rutteman Working Party's report, 'Guidance to Directors on Reporting on Internal Control', watered down the Cadbury Committee's intention in Provision 4.5 of the Cadbury Code (see **B3.4**) which had read:

'The directors should report on the effectiveness of the company's system of internal control.'

Rutteman allowed that directors should not be required to disclose in the company's annual report their opinion as to the effectiveness of internal control, though Rutteman said that directors might do so if they wished, without encouraging them to do so.[4]

There was strong resistance to making disclosure of the effectiveness of internal control a requirement for claiming full compliance with Cadbury Code Provision 4.5. Directors and others were uncertain as to how 'effectiveness' could be assessed; they were even unclear as to the meaning of 'effectiveness' and of 'internal control'. Nor, in view of the litigation risk[5], were they keen to publicly commit themselves to a position as to the effectiveness of internal control – in case they appeared foolish retrospectively.

## Hampel's reconsideration  B4.17

In view of the emasculation by the Rutteman working party of Cadbury's intention in Provision 4.5, it was inevitable that the Hampel Committee, convened to review the Cadbury and Greenbury Codes, would look very carefully at the wording and requirement of Provision 4.5. Hampel declined to endorse the narrowed scope to just internal financial control, which Rutteman had allowed.

On the other hand, the final position in the Combined Code was that no disclosure of 'effectiveness' was to be required – endorsing the position that the Rutteman guidance had taken.

It is illuminating that the draft 1998 Combined Code passed to, and recommended to, the London Stock Exchange by the Hampel Committee, had replaced the wording of the Cadbury Code Provision 4.5 with this wording:

> 'The directors should review the effectiveness of the company's system of internal control and should report to shareholders. This report should cover all controls, including financial, operational and compliance controls and risk management.'

Yet the same Provision (Provision D.2.1) published shortly thereafter in the final version of the 1998 Combined Code, which was adopted by the Stock Exchange, had been amended to read:

> 'The directors should, at least annually, conduct a review of the effectiveness of the group's system of internal controls and should report to shareholders that they have done so. The review should cover all controls, including financial operational and compliance controls and risk management.'
>
> *(2003: 'Risk Management Systems')*

So, the obligation for entities complying with this Provision became simply to report that they had conducted the review, but not to report on what was revealed by that review; nor necessarily to refer to all controls (financial, operational and compliance) nor to risk management. The Hampel Report itself (paras 6.10–6.13), although slightly opaque, implies that the committee had intended that the report would be informative on what was revealed by the review rather than being merely a report that the review had been conducted. While the subsequent Turnbull Report, whose guidance was adopted by the Stock Exchange for entities intending to comply with this Provision, did not adopt such a minimalist position in every respect, it remains the case that the emphasis of the directors' report is to report that they have conducted the review rather than to report on the results of their review. The original intentions of Cadbury had been sadly laid to rest.

(**B2.17** DEVELOPING AND IMPLEMENTING CODES OF BEST PRACTICE FOR CORPORATE GOVERNANCE explores related aspects of the development of corporate governance guidance on internal control.) (**B4.10** TURNBULL BURIES CADBURY INTENTION TO REPORT ON THE EFFECTIVENESS OF INTERNAL CONTROL is also relevant.) The Auditing Practices Board's 'Providing Assurance on the effectiveness of internal control' ((July 2001), The Auditing Practices Board, £5.50 each, post-free from ABG Professional Information, PO Box 21375. London, WC1N 1QP, tel: +44 (0)20 7920 8991; fax: +44 (0)20 7920 8992; e-mail: info@abgpublications.co.uk) also clearly draws attention to the considerable challenges associated with formulating reliable opinions about internal control effectiveness and how one can set about doing so[6]. This handbook also carries an article by Steven Leonard elaborating upon the APB's briefing paper (**B4.20** PROVIDING ASSURANCE ON THE EFFECTIVENESS OF INTERNAL CONTROL).

## 1. Arguments for directors publicly disclosing their opinion on internal control effectiveness.

- Maximum disclosure, if not misleading, is generally regarded as a desirable feature of efficient markets.

- A thorough, careful, responsible process can be followed by directors in arriving at their opinion as to internal control effectiveness. It can be thoroughly minuted. If the conclusions are consistent with what is revealed during the process, then it would be difficult to pin a charge of recklessness or negligence upon the board of directors or upon any member of the board.

- Careful wording, going beyond standard phrases such as 'reasonable assurance', can be used to avoid giving a false degree of reassurance about the effectiveness of internal control.

- Although the directors' opinion as to internal control effectiveness will always include a large degree of judgement, there is significant judgement behind many of the statements contained in companies' annual reports. Indeed it can be argued that those statements which are entirely verifiable in an objective way are often less valuable to the readers of annual reports, as, for instance, with the historical cost of a freehold building. On the other hand those statements which involve a large degree of subjective judgement are often more valuable, as for instance, with respect to the chairman's report on future prospects. The external audit opinion itself is highly judgmental.

**2. Arguments against directors publicly disclosing their opinion on internal control effectiveness:**

- If they have established a practice of disclosing that their systems of internal control are, in their view, effective it would become difficult to disguise the occasion when they do not believe that such is the case.

- Making such a statement may raise the due standard of skill and care which common law expects directors to exercise, and give extra ammunition in any action alleging breach of this duty.

- Under *section 214* of the *Insolvency Act 1986* relating to wrongful trading, a court may require a director to contribute to a company's assets if he or she had not taken every reasonable step to minimise the loss to creditors as soon as the company had become terminally ill. A positive statement about internal control effectiveness made about a reported year during which the point of no return was passed could be construed as negligent, or that the director should have known better, or that the director may have known better – and thus make it more likely that a court order might be made. Compensation for damages might be due from a director or directors to the company itself or to the shareholders as a body if the annual report contained any negligent misstatements.

- *Section 47(1)* of the *Financial Services Act 1986* makes it a criminal offence in this sector to knowingly or recklessly make a statement which is misleading, false or deceptive if it might influence someone to enter into an investment agreement – which might include the purchase of shares.

- Why disclose when there is no obligation to do so?

**Further information**                                              **B4.18**

1. Rutteman reserved 'encouragement' to reporting on all aspects of internal control (financial, operational and compliance), rather than restricting the scope of the public report to just 'financial' control – which limited scope Rutteman allowed as being all the scope that was required to claim to be in full compliance with the Cadbury Code provision 4.5 (see **B3.4**).

2. In particular it was considered there was a litigation risk if readers of their public report on internal control could claim they were damaged by relying upon the directors' assertions regarding internal control effectiveness.

# Is public reporting on internal control an important part of governance?                                              B4.19

*Dr Curtis C Verschoor, CIA, CPA, CMA, CFE contributed this article which carefully explains the development and characteristics of the US position on control reporting, comparing it with the UK. Curt is Ledger & Quill Research Professor, School of Accountancy, DePaul University, Chicago, IL 60604 USA.*

He can be contacted at cverscho@condor.depaul.edu. Tel: +00 847 381 8115. Fax: +00 847 381 2310.

The concept of internal control has been an important aspect of accounting literature for more than fifty years. One of the ten 'generally accepted' professional standards for external auditors has always required a review and evaluation of a client's internal control system. However, there has been much less agreement on what governance benefits result from a public report on internal controls. It is interesting to note that all corporations listed in the UK and complying with the relevant provisions in the Combined Code must publish an annual risk-based evaluation of internal controls that must be reviewed by the company's auditing firm.

In the US since 1993 and the bank/savings institution debacle, a public report on internal control has been mandated by statute for large insured institutions. Yet even prior to that time, a large majority of very large publicly held US corporations have voluntarily included a report on internal control in their annual shareholder report. Controversy over what is the appropriate definition of internal control has clouded the issue of whether to report and its value. Now, under the 2002 Sarbanes-Oxley Act there is a requirement to report on internal financial control.

## Legal mandate for proper internal control

Under provisions of The Foreign Corrupt Practices Act (FCPA), publicly held US corporations of all sizes must maintain an adequate system of internal control. Con

gress enacted this law in 1977 as an amendment to the Securities Exchange Act of 1934[7]. The law adopted the four-part definition of internal accounting control distinguishing those controls for which external auditors were responsible that was contained in auditing literature at the time. This stated that internal control comprised the plan of organisation and the procedures and records concerned with the safeguarding of assets and the reliability of financial records and consequently are designed to provide reasonable assurance that:

- transactions are executed in accordance with management's general or specific authorisation;

- transactions are recorded as necessary to (1) permit preparation of financial statements in accordance with generally accepted accounting principles and (2) to maintain accountability for assets;

- access to assets is permitted only in accordance with management's authorisation; and

- the recorded accountability for assets is compared with the existing assets at reasonable intervals and appropriate action is taken with respect to any differences.

The need under law for all publicly held corporations to formally evaluate the effectiveness of their internal control systems triggered much wider utilisation of internal auditing in large US corporations. In recognition of the increased stature and prominence of internal auditing, The Institute of Internal Auditors in 1978 issued *Professional Standards for the Practice of Internal Auditing*. This document included a much broader definition of internal control than that utilised by external auditors. Revisions and enhancements have been made subsequent to the initial publication to reflect changes in the business environment. A total revision of the Standards was issued in 2000 (see **B23.3–B23.4**). This document broadly suggests the internal audit activity should evaluate the adequacy and effectiveness of controls encompassing:

'the organization's governance, operations, and information systems. This should include:

- Reliability and integrity of financial and operational information.

- Effectiveness and efficiency of operations.

- Safeguarding of assets.

- Compliance with laws, regulations, and contracts.'[8]

## The Treadway Commission recommendation for internal control reporting

Additional public and investor interest in reliable financial reporting led to the formation in 1985 of the National Commission on Fraudulent Financial Reporting. This commission was also called the Treadway Commission after its chairperson, James C Treadway, Jr, a former SEC commissioner. The final report issued in October 1987 contained many recommendations to audit committees, corporations, and others. They suggested corporations implement sound ethical policies and strong internal controls, appoint 'an informed, vigilant, and effective audit committee' who would oversee ethics and internal control matters, and form an independent internal auditing function.[9]

One of the specific Treadway recommendations for implementation by public corporations was that audit committees should issue an annual report on their activities and results in the corporation's annual report to shareholders. Treadway also recommended that management issue a periodic report on internal controls, also in the annual report to shareholders. The recommendation states:

'All public companies should be required by SEC rule to include in their annual reports to stockholders management reports signed by the chief executive officer and the chief accounting officer and /or the chief financial officer. The management report should acknowledge management's responsibilities for the financial statements and internal control, discuss how these responsibilities were fulfilled, and provide management's assessment of the effectiveness of the company's internal controls.'[10]

As to the appropriate scope of the recommended management report on internal control, Treadway believed that a broad definition of internal control would provide the most benefit to shareholders and others. The Treadway recommendation stated:

> 'Management's opinion should encompass the entire system of internal control, a broader concept than the FCPA's internal accounting control.'[11]

No attestation by external auditors was contemplated.

## The COSO study of internal control

The most complete and insightful definition of internal control resulted from the work of the Treadway Commission's Committee of Sponsoring Organizations or COSO. Pursuant to a specific recommendation, a working committee was formed by the five sponsoring accounting organisations. These were: American Accounting Association, American Institute of CPAs, Financial Executives Institute, Institute of Internal Auditors, and Institute of Management Accountants. The group embarked in 1990 on a formal study of internal control concepts. A common definition was considered important in view of the divergent concepts in use by auditors, corporations, regulators, legislators, investors, and the general public. COSO believed new guidance would also provide a standard against which all organisations, large or small, business or not-for-profit, could judge the effectiveness of their internal control and determine how to improve it.

The four-volume report published by COSO in September 1992, 'Internal Control: Integrated Framework' defines internal control as follows:

> 'Internal control is broadly defined as a process, effected by an entity's board of directors, management and other personnel, designed to provide reasonable assurance regarding the achievement of objectives in the following categories:
>
> - Effectiveness and efficiency of operations
>
> - Reliability of financial reporting
>
> - Compliance with applicable laws and regulations.'[12]

The COSO definition has several key emphases. As a process, internal control should be viewed as a means to an end rather than an end in itself. People at every level of the organisation must appropriately implement internal control for it to be effective. A well-designed system that is poorly operated cannot be effective. Internal control must be 'built into' an entity's operating structures and not 'added on' for its own sake. As a process, internal control must be effective during a period of time, not just at a particular point in time.

Although not part of the formal definition, the COSO report declares that internal control consists of five interrelated components. These are the control environment, risk assessment, control activities, information and communication, and monitoring. These components are part of an effectiveness criterion for any internal control system. All five of the components must be present and functioning effectively in an organisation to conclude that internal control is effective.

Although all five internal control components must be satisfied before an internal control system can be judged as effective, COSO emphasises that the control environment is the foundation for all the other components. It provides discipline and structure. Factors such as the integrity, ethical values and competence of an entity's people have a pervasive influence on how well the other components function. The effectiveness of internal controls cannot rise above the integrity and ethical values of the people who create, administer and monitor them. This emphasis on integrity and ethical values is one of COSO's greatest contributions to management literature.

Whether and how entities should report their internal control effectiveness to external parties was perhaps the most contentious issue faced by COSO. The final framework volume took no position on the form or desirability of such reports. However, another of the four COSO volumes gave guidance to those who wished to report publicly on only the internal controls over preparation of published financial statements. No other reporting was considered appropriate. The reporting volume was considered supplementary since public reporting was neither a component of nor a criterion for effective internal control.

Several commentators including the US General Accounting Office (GAO) have stated that a public report by management on the effectiveness of just the internal controls over historical financial reporting has little if any value.[13] Because of pressure brought to bear by the GAO to include an internal control objective of safeguarding assets within the context of financial reporting, COSO in May 1994 issued an 'addendum' to the reporting volume.[14] This brief statement allows for inclusion of the internal controls over safeguarding assets in a public report, but only if they are limited to those involving unauthorised acquisition or disposal of assets.

There has been considerable discussion over the years about how to reconcile the broad COSO framework of internal controls with very narrow and limited public reporting. Users of financial information logically place reliance on the assurance provided by external auditors as to the proper presentation of financial statements themselves, rather than the quality of the internal controls used in their preparation. For example, logic supports the view that the auditors' opinion on the quality of the financial statements themselves is the important report upon which the public relies for credibility, not reports on internal controls over the methods used in their preparation, which may or may not be relied upon by the auditor. A committee of the American Bar Association has expressed a similar view.[15]

## FDIC Improvement Act requirements

As an aftermath of the banking and savings institution crisis of the 1980s, Congress passed and President Bush signed in December 1991 the FDIC Improvement Act (FDICIA)[16]. This statute set in motion a dramatic overhaul of the regulatory processes for insured banking and savings institutions. Many new regulations became effective in 1993, especially for the nearly 1,000 institutions with assets over $500 million. Because analysis of losses from failed banks showed them to be concentrated in institutions having poor internal control, Congress followed recommendations of the General Accounting Office (GAO) and instituted strict measures in the Act prescribing that institutions maintain strong internal controls over operations and that regulators focus on assuring adequate internal controls are always in place.

FDICIA also mandates periodic public reporting on just the internal controls over financial reporting and on compliance with designated laws and regulations[17]. The management of banks and savings institutions having more than $500 million in assets must prepare an annual public statement of certain specific responsibilities. These include preparation of financial statements, maintenance of an adequate internal control structure and procedures for financial reporting, and compliance with designated laws and regulations relating to the institution's safety and soundness. This annual public report must contain management's assertion that a bank's internal controls over financial reporting are effective and that the institution has complied with several designated laws and regulations. FDICIA also provides for attestation by the institution's external auditor as to the reliability of both of management's assertions. It is paradoxical that FDICIA allows assertions to be made as to internal controls as of year-end, whereas the need for such controls from an operating perspective is present throughout the year. At the time of their enactment, there was criticism that these requirements added considerable costs to the banking industry[18]. Many observers also questioned whether these additional costs provided any real benefits.[19]

The recent failure of an FDIC insured institution illustrates the premise set forth in the early 1990s that controls over financial reporting will not prevent granting of poor loans. In July 2001, the federally insured savings and loan, Superior Bank of Oakbrook Terrace, IL was closed and the FDIC appointed as receiver. The failure is expected to cost the federal insurance fund an estimated $500 million, making it one of the costliest failures ever of a United States financial institution. The regulators found that Superior had lost nearly all its assets and had engaged in poor lending practices, inadequate supervision of employees and poor record keeping[20]. In other words, the limited internal control assertions required by FDICIA, together with an attestation as to their propriety by Superior's external auditor, Ernst & Young, were not sufficient to prevent this significant loss.

# GAO involvement in internal control reporting

GAO's revision of Government Auditing Standards in 1994[21] continued its emphasis on the importance of internal controls in audits of government agencies as well as audits of organisations like universities who receive substantial government funds. For financial statement audits, the report should include irregularities, illegal acts, other material non-compliance with laws and regulations and any reportable conditions in internal controls. For performance audits, the report should include all significant instances of both non-compliance and abuse, plus any significant weaknesses found in management controls.

As part of its oversight on behalf of Congress, the GAO also reiterated in September 1996 its previous recommendations on the subject of public reporting on internal control by publicly held companies. The GAO's very comprehensive report to Congress (139 pages plus a 174 page appendix volume) summarises the status of recommendations made to the accounting profession over a 20-year period by major study groups. In this volume, GAO states:

> 'In the long run, GAO expects that audits will be expanded to include internal control reporting, either because of market demand or some systemic crisis.'[22]

## Recommendations about internal control reporting by other bodies

In March 1993, the Public Oversight Board (POB) of the AICPA SEC Practice Section recommended (in V-12) that the SEC should require a report by management on the effectiveness of an entity's internal control structure relating to financial reporting.[23]

In 1999 at the request of the SEC, the POB appointed a Panel on Audit Effectiveness. The Panel's report was issued in August 2000[24] and included several suggestions regarding reporting about internal control. It recommended that audit committees should

> '[O]btain a written report from management on the effectiveness of internal control over financial reporting.'[25]

Another recommendation was that audit committees

> '[R]equest management to report on the control environment within the entity.'[26]

Research is known to be underway as to what proportion of audit committees disclose any oversight activities relating to internal controls in their charters.

The former Chief Accountant of the SEC emphasised in August 2001 the need for public reporting on internal controls. He stated in a speech to a committee of the American Accounting Association:

> 'I believe we need to require that management report to investors on their internal accounting controls. These controls are critical to quality financial reporting and investors have a right to understand whether management thinks those controls are working effectively or not. If management is nervous about having to make such disclosures, then I suggest investors may be just as nervous about the numbers they are getting.'[27]

## Many large corporations do report on internal control

For several years, this researcher has studied the internal control reports made by US corporations in their annual reports to shareholders. As noted earlier, in spite of the many recommendations for their adoption, such reports continue to be voluntary as there is no legislative mandate, except in the banking industry. As a consequence, companies generally do not follow any rigid format for their reports, and there is little evidence of 'boiler-plate' language. Once initiated, reports stay the same from year to year.

Results of studying the largest companies are set forth in the following paragraphs for 1999 with available comparisons for 1995 and 1992. The industries represented in the study are as follows:

|  | 1999 | 1995 | 1992 |
|---|---|---|---|
|  | N=471 | N=500 | N=262 |
| **Manufacturing** | 52.0% | 57.0% |  |
| **Financial** | 14.2 | 14.6 |  |
| **Service** | 33.8 | 28.4 |  |
| **Total** | 100% | 100% | 100% |

It is interesting to note there were very substantial changes in the names of the US public companies included in the 'largest' list in just the last four years. Although the total number of companies represented in many industries did not vary significantly, only 61.4 per cent of the specific companies in the 1995 group still remain in the 1999 analysis. Minor name changes (like Citicorp becoming Citigroup) were not considered a cause for counting as a new entity in spite of the fact that a minor name change there masks a significant change in the company.

Each of the annual shareholder reports in each industry was examined to determine whether it did or did not contain a voluntary report by management on internal control. Results of this analysis showed a large majority of company annual reports do contain a management report on internal control:

|  | 1999 | 1995 | 1992 |
|---|---|---|---|
| **Manufacturing** | 65.7% | 72.3% |  |
| **Financial** | 57.6 | 75.3 |  |
| **Service** | 60.3 | 79.6 |  |
| **Total** | 62.7% | 74.8% | 80.2% |

One of the major causes of the decline over time in the number of reports being made is the trend toward issuance of condensed annual reports that do not allow space for a management report or an auditor's opinion. In the 1999 sample, 5.5 per cent of the total number of companies issued condensed annual reports.

Additionally, increasing numbers of companies have decided to issue an annual report that consists of a few pages wrapped around their Form 10-K. Since there is no requirement for a management report in the Form 10-K, many companies have chosen to omit it. The reduction in management reports in financial institutions is believed to be due largely to the fact that insured institutions apparently consider one public report on internal controls, the one given to the FDIC, to be sufficient. As regulated organisations, banks seem to be following a philosophy of providing only required information.

A further analysis was performed of the content of each management report to ascertain whether it did or did not contain management's conclusion as to the adequacy of the internal control system. Very few companies state a formal 'opinion,' but many conclude that the design and operation of their system does provide reasonable assurance that one or more objectives of internal control are being achieved. Very few attestations by auditing firms were noted. The proportion of management reports that did state a conclusion is as follows:

|  | **1999** | **1995** | **1992** |
|---|---|---|---|
| **Manufacturing** | 44.0% | 52.0% |  |
| **Financial** | 48.4 | 52.8 |  |
| **Service** | 58.3 | 58.3 |  |
| **Total** | 49.4% | 54.0% | 31.9% |

Although the analysis was not designed to determine the factors motivating management to include a voluntary report on internal control, it appears that large majorities of public corporations believe that their shareholders and the general public assign value to such reports. For the internal control reports that did not contain an explicit effectiveness assertion, a strong case can be made that they did contain an implicit assertion of effectiveness. Virtually all management reports included a description of the techniques designed by management and being used to assure that strong internal controls were in fact in place. These include a program of internal auditing, audit committee oversight, external auditor testing as part of the annual audit, personnel selection and training, and management awareness and follow-up on any weaknesses. A smaller number note that their code of conduct is an important strategy for assuring effective internal control. No company advised that their internal control system was weak or inadequate in any way.

Some of the value of public reporting on internal control is undoubtedly the hoped-for projection of a favourable image that the corporation is well managed. The frequency that corporate codes of conduct and ethics are mentioned may be an indication of management's desire to characterise their company as one utilising ethical business practices as a good corporate citizen.

## Internal control reporting in the UK

Pursuant to findings of the Cadbury Committee in 1992, considerable efforts have been expended toward implementing its recommendation that

'the directors should make a statement in the [annual] report and accounts on the effectiveness of their system of internal control and that the auditors should report thereon.'[28]

Beginning in 1998, the rules of the UK Listing Authority require companies to comply with the principles within what has become known as the Combined Code. The Institute of Chartered Accountants of England and Wales (ICAEW) issued guidance on the internal control part of the Code known as the Turnbull Report after its chairperson. The Code requires the directors' annual review of the effectiveness of internal control to

'cover all controls, including financial, operational, and compliance controls and risk management.'[29]

The Turnbull guidance contains the premise that a company's board should bring about a risk-based approach to establishing a sound system of internal control whereby internal control and the monitoring of its effectiveness are embedded within its operating processes by which an entity pursues its objectives and is not be treated as a separate exercise.

A Briefing Paper (BP) issued in 2001 by the UK Auditing Practices Board[24] is designed to assist directors regulators and others as well as practitioners in understanding how to express assurance on the reliability of systems of internal control. The extent of such required assurance is limited to only a review and not a full opinion. Further, the BP suggests that the judgmental issues of the internal control process, such as risk identification, risk assessment and internal control system design are likely to lead to a lengthy narrative report rather than a stylized short-form report. The BP thus concludes that internal control reports not be published.

## Conclusions

It is noteworthy that a majority of large US corporations do voluntarily choose to present a public management report covering internal control responsibilities and how they are being carried out. It is also striking that such a significant proportion of these voluntary management reports do contain an explicit assertion as to the quality of the internal control system. Most of the assertions are not in the form of an 'opinion,' but rather a statement that the system does achieve specific internal control objectives that are noted. Further, a case can be made that the remainder of the reports contain an implicit assertion of quality in view of the fact that almost all reports describe the measures the entity has used to assure the system is of high quality and none state that their system is deficient in any way.

Although voluntary, it can certainly be argued that management reporting on internal control was undertaken originally to avoid the probability of more onerous legally mandated requirements. The fact that management in industry at large chooses to use formats that vary in many cases from that prescribed by law for one industry is also of interest. The voluntary nature of the reporting preserves management's prerogative to communicate about internal control in language free of regulatory influences. The fact that there are very few attestations by external accountants in the voluntary reports may be a contributing factor to their popularity and a major reason stereotyped language and uninformative report content has been avoided.

The recent experience of Superior Bank demonstrates that a narrow preoccupation with only the internal controls over financial reporting may not address the important objective of safeguarding the assets of an insured bank or savings institution. Asset safeguarding through proper controls over loan origination was the principal purpose for enactment of the internal control reporting requirement in the FDICIA statute. Contemporary criticism in 1993 and 1994 of what was called a limited focus in the law has unfortunately been proven correct by the severity of the losses at Superior Bank in 2001. Finger pointing as to the blame will undoubtedly involve Superior's directors and audit committee, its external auditors, Ernst & Young, and the regulatory agencies involved, the Office of Thrift Supervision and Federal Deposit Insurance Corp.

The determination of what function internal controls should play in the governance of US public corporations is still evolving. Also, whether a requirement for public reporting on the quality of some or all aspects of an organisation's internal control structure motivates an organisation to improve its internal controls is also an open question in the US. This occurs despite developments in the UK that appear to successfully integrate an annual risk assessment and corresponding control effectiveness evaluation with director responsibilities and external auditor attestation. It does appear likely, however, that US reporting on the internal controls over financial reporting may not favourably affect the quality of other controls. Undoubtedly, the specific needs of investors, creditors, regulators, or the general public about various aspects of internal controls have been inadequately considered in the debate. The continuing parade of large public US corporations revealing serious adverse outcomes that directly result from ineffective internal controls also ensures that greater emphasis in the future will be placed on the design and implementation of internal control and the place of mandated public reporting and external attestation on them.

# Providing assurance on the effectiveness of internal control B4.20

*This article is contributed by Steven Leonard who is a Project Director at the Auditing Practices Board. Any views expressed are his own. In this article he explains why the Auditing Practices Board hopes that its Briefing Paper 'Providing assurance on the effectiveness of internal control', published in July 2001 will contribute to developing a model of how auditors might report on the reliability of internal control.*

*The Briefing Paper will be of particular interest to those who may be required to report on the effectiveness of internal control to an audit committee or to a regulator. From reading the Briefing Paper practitioners may gain some insight into why the 1992 proposal of the Cadbury Committee, quoted at the beginning of this article, has not been as straightforward to implement as many hoped at the time.*

*'Providing assurance on the effectiveness of internal control', (July 2001), The Auditing Practices Board, £5.50 each, post-free from ABG Professional Information, PO Box 21375. London, WC1N 1QP (tel: +44 (0)20 7920 8991; fax: +44 (0)20 7920 8992; e-mail: info@abgpublications.co.uk).*

*Steven can be contacted at The Auditing Practices Board, 117 Houndsditch, London, EC3A 7BT. E-mail: leonard-apb@accountancyfoundation.com*

Since the publication of the report of the Cadbury Committee in 1992 considerable efforts have been made to put into effect what might have seemed to be a fairly straightforward proposition:

> 'Since an effective internal control system is a key aspect of the efficient management of a company, we recommend that the directors should make a statement in the report and accounts on the effectiveness of their system of internal control and that the auditors should report thereon.'[31]

This recommendation was made because Cadbury had identified the absence of a clear framework for ensuring that directors kept under review the controls in their business, as an important factor in the perceived low level of confidence in financial reporting.

Initial guidance for directors[32], published in 1994, focused on internal financial control. However, the Combined Code required the directors' annual review of the effectiveness of internal control to ...

> 'cover all controls, including financial, operational and compliance controls and risk management'.[33]

With the publication of the Turnbull Report[34] in 1999, guidance for directors was broadened and explicitly based on the presumption that a company's board should adopt a risk-based approach to establishing a sound system of internal control whereby internal control and the monitoring of its effectiveness are embedded in the business processes by which an entity pursues its objectives.

Under the FSA Listing Rules and the associated Auditing Practices Board (APB) guidance[35] a company's external auditors review whether the company's published summary of the process it has adopted in reviewing the effectiveness of its system of internal control is both supported by the documentation prepared by, or for, the directors and appropriately reflects that process. The auditors are not required to provide assurance on the effectiveness of the company's internal control and the standard audit report for listed companies has been amended to explicitly state that the auditors ...

'are not required to … form an opinion on the effectiveness of the company's corporate governance procedures or its risk and control procedures.'[36]

Why are auditors reluctant to publicly express opinions on the effectiveness of internal control? The APB has explored this subject in two discussion papers[37] that were published in the 1990s. These papers explained the issues associated with providing assurance on internal control, especially in reports that are made public, and explored a number of possible approaches. Responses to these papers indicate that there is still some way to go before a consensus is reached on how practitioners should perform such engagements and in particular how conclusions should be reported.

The 1998 paper set out a number of possible reports for a range of hypothetical engagements. These reports were criticised by many commentators who saw them as being unhelpful because they were:

- overly formalised (boiler plate); and

- unnecessarily defensive and 'caveated'.

Many of these commentators whilst suggesting that reports on internal control should be narrative, rather than presented in a standardised short-form style, acknowledged the difficulties that could arise from publishing such discursive reports.

The 1998 paper also emphasised the need for 'suitable evaluation criteria', and suggested that, before being in a position to express an opinion on the effectiveness of internal control, the practitioner would need generally accepted criteria or a detailed list of control objectives. Commentators were concerned, because such criteria are typically not available to practitioners, that detailed control objectives would need to be provided before an engagement could be undertaken. This was interpreted by some commentators as reducing the role of the practitioner to 'certificate provider' rather than 'useful adviser'. Many commentators, including regulators, considered this unhelpful and expressed the view that the value they were seeking from practitioners would likely involve them in contributing to the identification and assessment of risks or providing advice on the design of the system of internal control.

Companies and their internal control needs differ by industry, size, culture and management philosophy. When designing a system of internal control there are many options as to the nature and extent of controls that may be implemented. Controls, for example, may be preventive or detective in nature and may be performed by people or by information technology systems. There is a balance to be achieved between the cost of implementation of controls and the benefits derived from the controls. Consequently, one company's internal control system may be very different from another's in relation to similar business processes.

In the absence, therefore, of generally accepted criteria, commentators recognised that the practitioner's report would itself need to provide sufficient information to allow users to put the practitioner's judgments into an appropriate context. This seemed to provide further support for narrative rather than standardised short-form reporting.

In considering the comments received on the 1998 paper and in light of subsequent developments such as Turnbull, the APB has developed its thinking regarding the interrelationship between business objectives, risk identification, risk assessment, internal control design and the operation of internal controls.

This has led the APB to publish a Briefing Paper entitled 'Providing assurance on the effectiveness of internal control'. The APB hopes it will contribute to developing a model of how practitioners might be able to express assurance on the reliability of systems of internal control. APB Briefing Papers are intended to deal with issues that require continuing debate and development and as a consequence do not set out mandatory requirements.

The Briefing Paper is also intended to assist directors, regulators and others who might engage practitioners to perform engagements to provide assurance on internal control, to better appreciate the considerable challenges involved and in particular the advantages of providing assurance through a narrative report.

The Briefing Paper sets out a framework for forming an opinion on the effectiveness of internal control. The framework describes the key considerations relating to the following distinct processes undertaken by management:

● risk identification;

● risk assessment;

● designing internal controls; and

● operating internal controls in accordance with the design.

The Briefing Paper discusses the complex judgements involved in evaluating each of the processes and why practitioners may be able to provide only a moderate, rather than a high, level of assurance with respect to the more judgmental of the processes such as risk identification, risk assessment and internal control design.

Following the concepts described in the Briefing Paper will, almost invariably, give rise to a lengthy narrative report. Such a report is necessary in order to communicate effectively the various judgments made by the practitioners, the reasoning underpinning those judgments, and the context in which the opinion is given. Owing to the lack of generally accepted suitable criteria available to practitioners in carrying out such engagements, and the difficulties of communicating conclusions relating to internal control, a standardised short-form report to the effect that internal control is 'effective' or 'adequate' is likely to lead to misunderstandings and unfulfilled user expectations.

**B4.20** *Providing assurance on the effectiveness of internal control*

An important element of the Briefing Paper is an illustration (which runs to nine pages) of a narrative report based on an imaginary engagement to provide assurance on the effectiveness of a newspaper publishing company's system of internal control over the recording of advertising revenue. It is clearly impractical to circulate widely reports of such length and, therefore, it seems most likely that reports on internal control effectiveness will be provided by practitioners to those who have instructed them, and not be published.

**Notes**

1. Internal Control – Guidance to Directors on the Combined Code is published by The Institute of Chartered Accountants in England & Wales, ISBN 1 84152 010 1. It is available from Accountancy Books, PO Box 21375, London, WC1N 1QP, tel. +44 (0)20 7920 8991; fax.: +44 (0)20 7920 8992; www.accountancybooks.co.uk. Currently the guidance can be downloaded from ICAEW's website: www.icaew.co.uk/internal control.

2. The Combined Code, originally an appendix to The Stock Exchange Listing Rules ('the Yellow Book') and available from Gee Publishing Limited, 100 Avenue Road, Swiss Cottage, London, NW3 3PG, England [Tel.: +44 (0)171 393 7400; fax.: +44 (0)171 722 4762]. Now an appendix to the SFA's 'Purple Book'.

3. Under the old Rutteman guidance the scope of this could be restricted in scope to internal financial control at the discretion of the company.

4. Rutteman reserved 'encouragement' to reporting on all aspects of internal control (financial, operational and compliance), rather than restricting the scope of the public report to just 'financial' control – which limited scope Rutteman allowed as being all the scope that was required to claim to be in full compliance with the Cadbury Code provision 4.5.

5. In particular it was considered there was a litigation risk if readers of their public report on internal control could claim they were damaged by relying upon the directors' assertions regarding internal control effectiveness.

6. Providing assurance on the effectiveness of internal control (July 2001), The Auditing Practices Board, £5.50 each, post-free from ABG Professional Information, PO Box 21375. London, WC1N 1QP (Tel.: +44 (0)20 7920 8991; fax.: +44 (0)20 7920 8992; e-mail: info@abgpublications.co.uk.

7. American Bar Association (ABA), Committee on Corporate Law and Accounting (CCLA), "A Guide to the New Section 13(b)(2) Accounting Requirements of the Securities Exchange Act of 1934", 34 Business Lawyer, 1978

8. IIA, Standards for the Professional Practice of Internal Auditing, Altamonte Springs, FL: IIA, 2000.

9. Treadway, James C., Chm, Report of the National Commission on Fraudulent Financial Reporting, Washington, DC: National Commission on Fraudulent Financial Reporting, 1987

10. Treadway Report, page 44

11. Treadway Report, page 46

12. Committee of Sponsoring Organizations of the Treadway Commission (COSO), Internal Control: Integrated Framework, New York: COSO, 1992

13. Verschoor, Curtis C., "FDICIA Besets Bankers With Unwarranted Costs," Accounting Today, October 24, 1994

14. COSO, Addendum to AReporting to External Parties@, New York: COSO, 1994

15. ABA, CCLawA, "'Management' Reports on Internal Control: A Legal Perspective", 49 Business Lawyer, February 1994

16. Federal Deposit Insurance Corporation Improvement Act of 1991, 12 U.S. Code #1831m

17. Verschoor, Curtis C., "Internal Control Reporting: It's Here and Now," 49 The Internal Auditor, June 1992

18. Verschoor, Curtis C., "Internal Control Requirements Cost Banks $100 Million Last Year," American Banker, October 6, 1994
19. Verschoor, Curtis C., "FDICIA's Section 112: Compliance Costs High, Benefits Questionable," 70 Bank Management, September/October 1994
20. "Regulators Close An S & L. in Illinois," New York Times, July 28, 2001, page C14
21. United States General Accounting Office (GAO), Government Auditing Standards, 1994 Revision, Washington, DC: GAO, 1994
22. GAO Report to the Ranking Minority Member, Committee on Commerce, House of Representatives, The Accounting Profession Major Issues: Progress and Concerns, GAO/AIMD 96 98, Washington, DC: GAO, 1996
23. AICPA SEC Practice Section Public Oversight Board, In the Public Interest, New York: AICPA, 1993
24. AICPA SEC Practice Section Public Oversight Board, The Panel on Audit Effectiveness, Report and Recommendations, New York: AICPA, 2000
25. Panel on Audit Effectiveness Report, page 33
26. Panel on Audit Effectiveness Report, page 95
27. Lynn E. Turner, "We're Good, But We Can Be Better," Speech August 12, 2001 to the Public Interest Section of the American Accounting Association, Washington, DC: SEC, 2001
28. Report of the Committee on the Financial Aspects of Corporate Governance, London: Gee Publishing Co., 1992
29. Internal Control: Guidance for Directors on the Combined Code, London: ICAEW, 1999
30. APB, Providing Assurance on the Effectiveness of Internal Control, London, APB, 2001
31. Report of the Committee on the Financial Aspects of Corporate Governance, Gee, 1992, para. 4.32.
32. Internal Control and Financial Reporting: Guidance for directors of listed companies registered in the UK, ICAEW, 1994.
33. Code Provision D.2.1. of the Combined Code
34. Internal Control: Guidance for Directors on the Combined Code, ICAEW, 1999.
35. APB Bulletin 1999/5 The Combined Code: Requirements of Auditors under the Listing Rules of the London Stock Exchange, Accountancy Books, 1999.
36. See Appendix 1 in APB Bulletin 2001/2, Revisions to the Wording of Auditors' Reports on Financial Statements and the Interim Review Report, Accountancy Books, 2001.
37. Internal financial control effectiveness, APB, 1995, and Providing assurance on internal control, APB, 1998.

# External Control

## Introduction                                                          B5.1

In **B1.23–B1.43** GRAND THEMES IN CORPORATE GOVERNANCE we touched on the issue of 'stakeholder control of the business'. Here we focus more on trends in the provision of independent assurance on reports to stakeholders.

'Control' divides into *external* control by the stakeholders of an entity (such as the shareholders, debenture holders, creditors) and internal control by the board, management and other personnel. (See **B8** RISK MANAGEMENT AND INTERNAL CONTROL for a consideration of internal control.)

External control is facilitated in part by shareholder election of directors to (a) oversee the management of their interests and (b) to render an account to them:

> 'Without audit, no accountability; without accountability, no control; and if there is no control, where is the seat of power? ... great issues often come to light only because of scrupulous verification of details.'
>
> *(Professor W J M Mackenzie, foreword to The Accountability and Audit of Governments)*[1]

This well known quotation came from the foreword to a book written by an auditor of the European Court of Auditors, the external auditors of the European Commission. It crystallises the idea that the audit is a necessary, independent attestation of the accountability to the stakeholders by the stewards (that is, the board of directors) of the enterprise. Where the stakeholders and the stewards are the same, arguably the need for the audit is less.

'Without accountability, no control' – the control being referred to here is *external* control by the stakeholders, often the shareholders, over their stake in the business. For this, a necessary prerequisite is for the shareholders to receive an account from those they have chosen to direct the business on their behalf. Today the shareholders are more inquisitive, better informed, better organised, more assertive and more prepared to exercise this external control as they are intent upon squeezing the last ounce of value out of their investments. Other stakeholders are flexing their muscles too.

External auditors make a distinction between what they 'read' (all of the annual report), what they 'review' (a few of the directors' corporate governance assertions) and what they 'audit' (the financial statements).[2]

## External reporting on internal control                              B5.2

But if there is external control then there is also a need for internal control. If external control is control by the stakeholders, then internal control is control by the board, management and staff. The board is at the pivotal point between these two controls and the audit committee[3] pays attention to both. (For more discussion on this, refer to **B1.7** DEFINING 'CORPORATE GOVERNANCE' AND 'THE BOARD'). Indeed there are myriad overlaps between external and internal control.

There is a whole raft of emerging requirements for external assurances on internal control and services are emerging to fill this need. Recently we had the WebTrust seal of approval[4]. The WebTrust service was designed in the US by the American Institute of Certified Public Accountants and launched there and in Canada (the latter by The Canadian Institute of Chartered Accountants) in 1997. WebTrust is a 'Seal of Approval' applied to individual websites which meet strict conditions of good business practice. The service was designed to provide consumers with the confidence that using approved websites for transacting business on the internet was as safe as doing business in the high street. In doing so it is expected the volume of e-commerce business undertaken will increase and benefit all those wishing to develop e-commerce activities as website operators, suppliers, service providers or consumers. We now have finalised Auditing Practices Board guidance on providing assurance on internal control[5]. We believe there are no current examples of external reporting on internal control by internal audit, but it has happened before, for instance throughout most of the 1970s by Anglian Water, now one of the UK FTSE 100 listed companies (see **B23.14–B23.20** PUBLISHED REPORTS ON INTERNAL CONTROL BY INTERNAL AUDIT).

A significant change is the development of public reports progressively further and further beyond the bounds of financial statements alone, with parallel demands for attestation services to cover these extensions. A key issue is whether the auditing profession is well placed to inherit this future – or whether this future belongs to quality auditors, environmental auditors, ethics auditors, sustainability auditors and even to internal auditors. We should not overlook the Scottish Chartered Accountants' research report 'Auditing Into The Twenty-first Century'[6] which floated the idea of the 'total audit' with the audit committee of the board (as it matures) becoming, in effect, the conductor of the orchestra, and today's external auditor becoming the 'assessor' of this total audit process.

On the whole these other audits (quality, environmental and so on) have not become straitjacketed into boilerplate wordings for their audit reports, as have auditors of financial statements; and we must recognise that longer form, discursive commentary, rather than boilerplate wording is likely to be called for more often in the future.

## The future of the audit                                        B5.3

Downwards fee pressures have threatened to turn the statutory audit of the financial statements into a commodity service, no longer attracting the levels of fees to which large external audit firms had become accustomed. Using the audit as a loss leader has become an attractive option but there are concerns about independence and objectivity if the external auditor has significant additional non-audit responsibilities within audit client businesses: the 1998 Combined Code addressed this (see especially 1998 Code Provision D.3.2; the 2003 Code develops this further).

### 1998: D.3    Audit Committee and Auditors

**Principle**  **The board should establish formal and transparent arrangements for considering how they should apply the financial reporting and internal control principles and for maintaining an appropriate relationship with the company's auditors.**

### 1998 Code Provisions

**D.3.1**  The board should establish an audit committee of at least three directors, all non-executive, with written terms of reference which deal clearly with its authority and duties. The members of the committee, a majority of whom should be independent non-executive directors, should be named in the report and accounts.

**D.3.2**  The duties of the audit committee should include keeping under review the scope and results of the audit and its cost effectiveness and the independence and objectivity of the auditors. Where the auditors also supply a substantial volume of non-audit services to the company, the committee should keep the nature and extent of such services under review, seeking to balance the maintenance of objectivity and value for money.

The US Sarbanes-Oxley Act is now much more demanding.

Many would say, for instance, that there is a conflict if internal auditing is outsourced to the external auditor. From 2001, the SEC's so-called '50 per cent rule' ruled against a client obtaining more than 50 per cent of its internal auditing from the accounting firm that undertakes the external audit; but there is argument as to whether the 50 per cent should apply to the internal auditing of operational and other matters as well as to the internal auditing of accounting aspects. Now Sarbanes-Oxley outlaws internal auditing by an external auditor.

In the longer term, liberalisation of trade across national frontiers can be expected to break the statutory monopoly in the provision of financial auditing services in the UK and elsewhere, leading to further fee pressures and perhaps to the relocation of the major audit practices to low cost countries – as we have previously seen with respect to manufacturing industry. Online auditing, and the use of audit software embedded into client systems will make this entirely feasible.

At the outset we mentioned that, today, shareholders are more inquisitive and better informed. Rational markets require reliable and complete information. Companies already place their annual reports on their websites and it will not be long before companies that report in real time are rewarded with a premium on their P/E ratios. Real time reporting will require real time auditing – a continuous, very automated audit approach with a recharged emphasis upon confirming the reliability of the system of internal financial control.

The audit expectations gap continues and one aspect of this is the consumer's expectation that the auditor should be effective at detecting fraud.

## Conclusion                                                                    B5.4

We certainly live in an audit society. Not so long ago we called it the affluent society. Downsizing and re-engineering is intended to eliminate superfluous and inessential activities. Just as the outsourcing decision is made on unavoidable 'value for money' grounds, so the future of control and audit will essentially be determined on similar grounds. Audit needs to provide cost-effective added value. The audit itself cannot survive by offering peripheral added value extras, such as management letters, to honey the core audit. The audit has to survive on its own merit.

# External audit review of corporate governance assertions                                                                    B5.5

After representations made to the Hampel Committee by external auditors, the committee backed away from requiring external auditors to produce a report to shareholders on the results of their review of the board's adherence to any aspects of the Combined Code. Professional rules require external auditors to indicate within their Comprehensive Statement of Responsibilities (which is now printed within the annual report and accounts of listed companies) the Provisions within the Combined Code with respect to which they are reviewing directors' compliance (see the table at **B5.5**). Only if the external auditor notes that there is non-compliance (which is not clearly acknowledged by the board themselves within their corporate governance statement which is published) will the external auditor report on this non-compliance, the report of which is now incorporated into the main audit report.

Although the 1998 Combined Code was much more extensive than the Cadbury Code (17 Principles and 53 Provisions in the Combined Code as compared with just 19 Provisions in the Cadbury Code[7]) (the Combined Code did however also absorb the 29 Provisions in the Greenbury Code on executive remuneration)), the requirement for the auditors to review the directors' assertions of compliance with the Provisions has not been extended beyond the 7 Provisions identified for this purpose within the Cadbury Report (see Note 14 at the end of **B3.4**). This was a victory for the external auditing profession who, in present circumstances, are reluctant to become involved in this.

However, in one respect the scope of the external auditor's review was extended. They have been reviewing all of the 1998 Code Provision D.2.1 which, post Hampel, now covers all of internal control (not just internal financial control) and risk management:

'The directors should, at least annually, conduct a review of the effectiveness of the group's system of internal controls and should report to shareholders that they have done so. The review should cover all controls, including financial, operational and compliance controls and risk management.'

*(2003 Code: 'Risk Management Systems')*

The Hampel Committee's preamble to the 1998 Combined Code[8] stated:

'We have not included in the Combined Code principle D.IV in Chapter 2 of our final report, which reads as follows:

"External Auditors: The external auditors should independently report to shareholders in accordance with statutory and professional requirements and independently assure the board on the discharge of its responsibilities under D.I and D.II above in accordance with professional guidance."

We say in paragraph 6.7 of the report that we recommend neither any additional prescribed requirements nor the removal of any existing requirements for auditors in relation to governance or publicly reported information, some of which derive from the Listing Rules. This recommendation is accepted by the London Stock Exchange. But the existing requirements for auditors will be kept under review, as a matter of course, by the responsible organisations.'

Paragraph 12.43A of the Listing Rules ends with the following (at the time of going to print, the Code numbering was still as per the 1998 Code).

**'Requirements of auditors**

'A company's statement under 12.43A(b) must be reviewed by the auditors before publication only insofar as it relates to Code provisions A.1.2, A.1.3, A.6.1, A.6.2, D.1.1, D.2.1 and D.3.1 of the Combined Code. The scope of the auditors' report on the financial statements must cover the disclosures made pursuant to paragraph 12.43A9(c)(ii), (iii), (iv), (ix) and (x) above. The auditors must state in their report if in their opinion the company has not complied with any of the requirements of paragraph 12.43A (c)(ii), (iii), (iv), (ix) and (x) of the listing rules and, in such a case, must include in their report, so far as they are reasonably able to do so, a statement giving the required particulars.'

12.43A (c)(ii), (iii), (iv), (ix) and (x) are to do with aspects of directors' remuneration, as follows:

(ii) the amount of each element in the remuneration package for the period under review of each director by name, including, but not restricted to, basic salary and fees, the estimated money value of benefits in kind, annual bonuses, deferred bonuses, compensation for loss of office and payments for breach of contract or other termination payments, together with the total for each director for the period under review and for the corresponding prior period, and any significant payments made to former directors during the period under review; such details to be presented in tabular form, unless inappropriate, together with explanatory notes as necessary.

(iii) information on share options, including SAYE options, for each director by name in accordance with the recommendations of the Accounting Standards Board's Urgent Issues Task Force Abstract 10: such information to be presented in tabular form together with explanatory notes as necessary.

(iv) Details of any long-term incentive schemes, other than share option details of which have been disclosed under (iii) above, including the interests of each director by name in the long-term incentive schemes at the start of the period under review; entitlements or awards granted and commitments made to each director under such schemes during the period, showing which crystallise either in the same year or subsequent years; the money value and number of shares, cash payments or other benefits received by each director under such schemes during the p[period; and the interests of each director in the long-term incentive schemes at the end of the period;

(ix) for defined benefit schemes (as in *Part 1* of *Schedule 6* to the *Companies Act 1985*):

(a) details of the amount of the increase during the period under review (excluding inflation) and of the accumulated total amount at the end of the period in respect of the accrued benefit to which each director would be entitled on leaving service or is entitled having left service during the period under review;

(b) and either:

(i) the transfer value (less director's contributions) of the relevant increase in accrued benefit (to be calculated in accordance with Actuarial Guidance Note GN11 but making no deduction for any underfunding) as at the end of the period: or

(ii) so much of the following information as is necessary to make a reasonable assessment of the transfer value in respect of each director:

(a) current age;

(b) normal retirement age;

(c) the amount of any contributions paid or payable by the director under the terms of the scheme during the period under review;

(d) details of spouse's and dependents' benefits;

(e) early retirement rights and options, expectations of pension increases after retirement (whether guaranteed or discretionary); and

(f) discretionary benefits for which allowance is made in transfer values on leaving and any other relevant information which will significantly affect the value of the benefits.'

Voluntary contributions and benefits should not be disclosed; and

(x) for money purchase schemes (as in *Part 1* of *Schedule 6* to the *Companies Act 1985*) details of the contribution or allowance payable or made by the company in respect of each director during the period under review.'

The table below summarises the relevant Combined Code Provisions which auditors are required to review. In the table we use the wording from the 1998 Combined Code. At the time of going to print, no decisions had been made as to whether the scope of external auditors' reviews would be amended in view of the 2003 changes to the 1998 wording of these provisions. There is a weak precedent here in that external auditors did revise the scope of their review of directors' internal control assertions to reflect the way the 1998 Code (Provisions D.2.1; see **B3.11**) amended the wording of the equivalent provisions in the earlier Cadbury Code (Cadbury Code provision 4.5; see **B3.4**).

| Combined Code Provision reference | 2003 Combined Code Provision reference (Part A) | Wording (as in the 1998 Combined Code) |
|---|---|---|
| A.1.2 | A.1.1 | The board should have a formal schedule of matters specifically reserved to it for decision. |
| A.1.3 | A.5.2 | There should be a procedure agreed by the board of directors in the furtherance of their duties to take independent advice if necessary, at the company's expense. |
| A.6.1 | A.7.2 | Non-executive directors should be appointed for specified terms subject to re-election and to Companies Act provisions relating to the removal of a director, and re-appointment should not be automatic. |
| A.6.2 | A.7.1 | All directors should be subject to election by shareholders at the first opportunity after their appointment, and to re-election thereafter at intervals of no more than three years. The names of directors submitted for election or re-election should be accompanied by sufficient biographical details to enable shareholders to take an informed decision on their election. |

| Combined Code Provision reference | 2003 Combined Code Provision reference (Part A) | Wording (as in the 1998 Combined Code) |
|---|---|---|
| D.1.1 | C.1.1 | The directors should explain their responsibility for preparing the accounts and there should be a statement by the auditors about their reporting responsibilities. |
| D.2.1 | C.2.1 | The directors should, at least annually, conduct a review of the effectiveness of the group's system of internal controls and should report to shareholders that they have done so. The review should cover all controls, including financial, operational and compliance controls and risk management. |
| D.3.1 | C.3.1 | The board should establish an audit committee of at least three directors, all non-executive, with written terms of reference which deal clearly with its authority and duties. The members of the committee, a majority of whom should be independent non-executive directors, should be named in the report and accounts. |

## Internal control in the Combined Code                B5.6

So, the annual report of a listed company now contains a narrative statement of how the company has applied the Combined Code Principle C.2 (2003), *viz.*

### C.2      Internal Control

**Principle   The board should maintain a sound system of internal control to safeguard shareholders investment and the company's assets.'**

This narrative statement, as a minimum, is expected to disclose that there is an ongoing process for identifying, evaluating and managing the significant risks faced by the company, and that it is regularly reviewed by the board. The Turnbull guidance also states that the board may wish to provide additional information to assist understanding of the company's risk management processes and system of internal control. The content of such narrative statements is likely, therefore, to vary widely from company to company – as indeed a review of subsequent published annual reports shows that it does: a standard sort of boilerplate wording is gratifyingly absent.

There are requirements under Auditing Standards for auditors to read the narrative statement and to seek to resolve any apparent misstatements or material inconsistencies with the audited financial statements[9].

Although the Turnbull guidance addresses all the internal control requirements of the Combined Code, paragraph 12.43A of the Listing Rules requires the auditors to review only the disclosures made with respect to 1998 Code Provision D.2.1 (2003, C.2.1) which reads:

'The directors should, at least annually, conduct a review of the effectiveness of the group's system of internal controls and should report to shareholders that they have done so. The review should cover all controls, including financial, operational and compliance controls and risk management.'[10]

The Turnbull guidance defined 'all controls' (per Provision D.2.1 above) in this way:

'The reference to 'all controls' in Code provision D.2.1 (now, in the 2003 Code, C.2.1) should not be taken to mean that the effectiveness of every internal control (including controls designed to manage immaterial risks) should be subject to review by the board. Rather it means that, for the purposes of this guidance, internal controls considered by the board should include all types of controls including those of an operational and compliance nature, as well as internal financial controls.' (The Turnbull Report, paragraph 28)

The formal scope of the Cadbury Committee's report was on the financial aspects of corporate governance. Some held this restriction against the committee. For instance, some suggested that the Cadbury Code provision that directors should report publicly on the effectiveness of internal control must have meant internal financial control in view of the intended scope of the Cadbury Committee's remit. But it was transparently clear that Cadbury meant all aspects on internal control since the word 'financial' had been removed by the Cadbury Committee from their final report wherever internal control was referred to (including within the Cadbury Code itself) whereas the word 'financial' had always been present in the exposure draft of the Cadbury Report. There were good reasons why Cadbury meant that directors should report publicly on internal control 'in the round'. Internal financial control cannot be neatly differentiated from the other aspects of internal control; organisations achieve their objectives not through having effective internal financial control alone – arguably operational control is more crucial to the achievement of objectives. Furthermore, the readers of published results already have some inkling about the effectiveness of internal financial control in view of the presence of audited financial statements; but to learn about the effectiveness of operational and legal and regulatory compliance control is to tell the readers something extra – so long as it is, and can be, reliably reported. Directors have oversight responsibility for all aspects of internal control – financial, operational and compliance. Maximising reliable disclosure is an underlying theme of contemporary developments in corporate governance best practice.

**Notes**
[1.] Also published by Frederick A. Prager, New York (1966). The book was based on Normanton's M.Phil thesis from the University of Manchester.

2. Auditors' responsibility statements and auditors' reports on corporate governance, (July 1998), The Auditing Practices Board of The Consultative Committee of Accounting Bodies, Copies are available free from the Auditing Practices Board, 8th Floor, Chartered Accountants' Hall, PO Box 433, Moorgate Place, London, EC2P 2BJ (Fax: +44 (0)20 7638 6009).

3. See Communication between external auditors and audit committees, Audit Briefing Paper, The Auditing Practices Board, June 1998, 18 pps, £5, Accountancy Books, PO Box 620, Central Milton Keynes, MK9 2JX (Tel: + 44 (0)1908 248000.

4. The WebTrust service was designed in the US by the American Institute of Certified Public Accountants and launched there and in Canada (the latter by The Canadian Institute of Chartered Accountants) in 1997. It has quickly been accepted by the business community as a leader in its field and although not unique provides the greatest breadth of review available to date. It is now available in the UK and Ireland and will soon be available in Australia, New Zealand and mainland Europe: all countries adopt the same approach to provide an international solution to a global issue. WebTrust is a 'Seal of Approval' applied to individual web sites which meet strict conditions of good business practice. The service was designed to provide consumers with the confidence that using approved web sites for transacting business on the Internet was as safe as doing business in the High Street. In doing so it is expected the volume of e-commerce business undertaken will increase and benefit all those wishing to develop e-commerce activities as web site operators, suppliers, service providers or consumers.

5. 'Providing assurance on the effectiveness of internal control', (July 2001), The Auditing Practices Board, £5.50 each, post-free from ABG Professional Information, PO Box 21375. London, WC1N 1QP (Tel.: +44 (0)20 7920 8991; fax.: +44 (0)20 7920 8992; e-mail: info@abgpublications.co.uk].

6. 'Auditing into the twenty-first century', (1993), [The Institute of Chartered Accountants of Scotland, ISBN 1 871250 27 7], 63 pps.

7. The Combined Code did however also absorb the 29 Provisions in the Greenbury Code on executive remuneration.

8. June 1998, reproduced in an Appendix to the Listing Rules (May 2000)

9. 'Other information in documents containing audited financial statements', (SAS 160, revised), paragraphs 22–23.

10. The Turnbull Report, paragraph 28.

# External Audit

## The impact of external auditors on corporate governance, and vice versa                         B6.1

The position adopted by the UK auditing profession during the development and adoption of Codes of best practice for corporate governance has been fascinating to observe. It has been notable how reluctant the auditing profession has been to take on new responsibilities. It is hard to think of any other occupational group that would adopt such an apparently negative posture to a proffered enhancement of its role. The main key to this negativity must surely be the legalised monopoly rights enjoyed by just a few professional accounting bodies with respect to the provision of statutory audit services in the UK.

## Audit exemption                                                            B6.2

The auditor must be an approved member of one of a small number of recognised professional accounting bodies. With the exception of companies for whom 'audit exemption' applies, all UK companies must have an annual statutory audit of their financial statements. Many companies for whom audit exemption applies will elect to continue to have an annual audit on account of the credibility this brings to their financial statements – in particular in the eyes of creditors and banks. Companies entitled to take advantage of audit exemption are still required to obtain an approved independent accountant's complication certificate confirming that the financial statements have been complied in accordance with the underlying accounting records, but not giving any opinion as to whether or not those underlying accounting records were sound. In practice, for very small companies, a compilation certificate may be almost as expensive to obtain as a full audit report.

Audit exemption was introduced in the 1990s for companies with a turnover of less than £350,000. When introduced it was announced that it was intended to raise this limit. The bar is now set at £1million and a threshold of 250 employees. The White Paper proposals on Company Law Reform (16 July 2002) proposed raising the limit to £4.8million and since then the Department of Trade and Industry has floated a higher possible figure (£5.6million) with the apparent general intention of achieving and maintaining approximate parity with European Union requirements. The threshold of 250 employees does however mean that many companies with small turnovers will be unable to 'benefit' from any raising of the turnover for audit exemption. Whether it is indeed a 'benefit' is controversial: not having an audit can all too easily lead to the underlying accounting records getting out of control, and may also lead to a company becoming relatively cut off from the advice that their auditors have traditionally been able to give on related matters during the year. In the case of small, closely held companies as distinct from large public companies it is not really a valid argument to suggest that the reliability of the audit is compromised if the auditors provide other services to the same client (as is now effectively banned for US listed companies caught by the *Sarbanes-Oxley Act 2002*, for instance).

## Internationalisation of audit                                    B6.3

We must look forward to the time when national barriers to the provision of professional services are removed – so that appropriately qualified auditors based in India or elsewhere will be permitted to audit the financial statements of UK companies. Free trade in professional services is as important, or more so, for efficient markets in the emerging global economy as is free trade in commodities or manufacturing. Perhaps we can conceive of the Big Four accounting firms locating their main audit practices in low-cost countries from whence they will audit their multi-national client base. Online, real-time auditing of companies who are reporting online in real-time are likely to be characteristics of this brave new world.

Already public companies are carrying their annual reports on the worldwide web – although at present generally in summary form only, without much of the narrative content which is so informative. Modern IT will make it possible for companies to report in real-time – continuously updating their reports even on a daily or minute-by-minute basis. We can expect those companies who do so to become the favoured stocks of investors. Clearly, real-time reporting will have implications for rules on disclosure and on the approach which will be required of auditors.

## External audit review of corporate governance assertions                                                        B6.4

We should not forget that concerns about the quality of financial reporting have been key drivers of developments in corporate governance. This means that independent audit issues are not merely peripheral to the corporate governance debate. So it is disappointing that the issues within the Cadbury Code closest to the accounting and statutory auditing professions were the issues that caused the most trouble. Indeed, it was only those two Provisions within the Cadbury Code which were closest to the accounting profession (that directors should report on 'going concern' and that directors should report on the effectiveness of 'internal control'), the implementation of which had to be delayed pending the development of guidance first for directors and then for external auditors.

Guidance was needed for auditors as Cadbury had identified certain Provisions within the Cadbury Code which the committee considered were objectively verifiable and therefore should be reviewed by the statutory auditors during their annual audit. This was a burden (or an opportunity) which the audit profession took to with exceedingly great reluctance.

A reason for the negativity of the auditing profession to becoming involved in reviewing directors' corporate governance assertions has been the risk of litigation damages in an environment of unlimited auditor liability. Another reason has been the auditor's canny realisation that extended auditor responsibilities in the area of corporate governance attestation are unlikely to extract commensurately enhanced audit fees from reluctant clients.

As we have indicated, Cadbury had identified a number of Code Provisions which the committee considered were objectively verifiable and they recommended that a company's compliance with these should be reviewed by the company's external auditors. The Cadbury Report, most probably as an oversight, omitted to specify that the external auditors should report on the results of their review of these matters. This allowed the external auditors the discretion to address their report on their review to the directors and not to the shareholders. Most companies nevertheless chose to print this report from the auditors, addressed to the directors, in the annual report. Addressing the report to the directors gave an indication of the preference that external auditors have that their comments on corporate governance matters should preferably, they consider, be made privately to management and the board – along the lines of the external auditor's traditional management letter on internal control and other matters.

One of the areas of directors' code compliance that Cadbury recommended the external auditors review was the directors' report on the effectiveness of internal control. The external auditors led the fight to water down this requirement. It became the only provision in the Cadbury Code which was watered down before it was implemented. Together with one other Code requirement close to the accounting profession (that directors should report on 'going concern'), implementation was also deferred. The Rutteman Working Party, who developed the watered down guidance, was convened by main professional auditing body in the UK – the Institute of Chartered Accountants in England and Wales, and chaired by a senior audit partner from Ernst & Young. Later, the Turnbull Working Party which provided the replacement guidance was also to be a working party of ICAEW though it was to be chaired by a finance director not by an external auditor (the Turnbull working party's deputy chairman was Roger Davies, head of professional affairs at PriceWaterhouseCoopers who is said to have played an active part in its work); arguably also not sufficiently independent of the issues at stake, but nevertheless obliged to work within the strictures of the Hampel Committee's Report which reversed some of the watering down.

A key responsibility of the Hampel Committee was to review the functioning of the Cadbury Code. Since Rutteman had watered down the Code provision on internal control, this was clearly a provision at which the Committee would look closely. The Hampel Committee condoned the watering down which allowed directors not to disclose their opinion on the effectiveness or otherwise of internal control, but reversed the watering down which allowed the scope of the directors' internal control report to be restricted to internal financial control, insisting that it should cover the other aspects of internal control (operational and legal and regulatory compliance control) and risk management. Hampel's judgement on these matters has been carried forward into the 2003 Combined Code.

The external auditors' report on some of the directors' corporate governance assertions has been, since Cadbury, a rather sorry and embarrassing affair. For instance, with respect to the directors' internal control report, it has been a negative assurance report. Within the report the auditors have been at pains to state that they had not done the extra work which would have been necessary for them to positively affirm that the directors' internal control assertions were justified, but only that during the course of their audit work they had stumbled across nothing which indicated to the auditors that the directors' assertions were not justified. Where the directors had gone further than the minimum watered down requirements of Rutteman (by covering more aspects of internal control than just internal financial control, or by expressing an opinion on effectiveness, or both), the external auditors in their report were at pains to point out that they were not reporting on any aspect of this extended scope of the directors' report.

With respect to compliance with the other Code Provisions that the auditors were required to review, the auditors restricted themselves to a high level confirmation of fact, without investigating the quality of compliance. For instance, the auditors were required to review whether there was a schedule of matters reserved to the board, or whether there was an audit committee which met at least twice a year and which had written terms of reference. If this appeared to be factually correct, then the auditors regarded their review of these items as completed.

Following publication of the final Turnbull Report, the Auditing Practices Board has now published its guidance to external auditors on their review of directors' corporate governance assertions within the annual report[1]. The guidance resolves the uncertainty as to whether the auditors will restrict their review of the directors' internal control assertions to just internal financial control, or broaden it to all controls in view of the broader scope of the Combined Code's 'Provision' compared to the Rutteman interpretation of the older provision in the Cadbury Code. In fact, the auditors will cover all controls in their review.

It is also interesting that the guidance suggests that the external auditors should attend meetings of the board of directors (if there is no audit committee of the board) at which the annual report and accounts, including the statement of compliance, are considered and approved for submission to the board of directors.

It is hard to escape the conclusion that this new guidance for external auditors entails additional audit work beyond what would be needed if there were no requirement for the external auditors to review certain of the directors' corporate governance assertions, though most of this additional work will have already been incorporated into external audit work plans since the implementation of Cadbury. In the US, the requirement for external auditors to attest to the CEO's and CFO's certification of internal control over financial reporting means that there is now a much more significant extra burden upon US external auditors than upon UK auditors.

The objective of the UK auditors' review is to assess whether the company's summary of the process the board (and where applicable its committees) has adopted in reviewing the effectiveness of the system of internal control, is both supported by the documentation prepared by or for the directors and appropriately reflects that process.

To achieve this objective the auditors:

(a)   through enquiry of the directors obtain an understanding of the process defined by the board for its review of the effectiveness of internal control and compare their understanding to the statement made by the board in the annual report and accounts;

(b)   review the documentation prepared by or for the directors to support their statement made in connection with the Code provision on internal control and assess whether or not it provides sound support for that statement; and

(c)   relate the statement made by the directors to the auditors' knowledge of the company obtained during the audit of the financial statements. The scope of the directors' review will be considerably broader in its scope than the knowledge the auditors can be expected to have based on their audit.

(a) to (c) (above) are in addition to the general evidence that the auditors must obtain to support each of the seven corporate governance disclosures which are within the scope of the auditors' review. That general evidence is as follows:

(a)   reviewing the minutes of the meetings of the board of directors, and of relevant board committees;

(b)   reviewing relevant supporting documents re (a) (above);

(c)   making enquiries of certain directors and the company secretary regarding procedure and its implementation, to satisfy the auditors; and

(d)   attending meetings of the audit committee (or the full board if there is no audit committee) at which the annual report and accounts, including the statement of compliance, are considered and approved for submission to the board of directors.

When the Cadbury Code came up for review by Hampel, the external auditing profession made a pitch to be excluded from any requirement to review any of the directors' corporate governance assertions. But the Hampel Committee recommended no change and the Stock Exchange agreed. That left an ambiguity as one of these directors' corporate governance assertions had itself changed in scope – the one on internal control and for a while it was not clear whether 'no change' meant that the auditors review continued to be based on the old more limited scope or should cover the new more extended scope.

Having lost the battle to move altogether out of reviewing any of the directors' corporate governance assertions, the external audit profession, through the

Auditing Practices Board did some delicate, quick footwork. Here again, we are left wondering whether was appropriate for the Auditing Practices Board which at that time set auditing standards, to be in effect the agent of the auditing profession – and indeed this has now been addressed in a move to make the replacement of APB more independent of the auditing profession. The position taken by APB was that auditors are required to 'read' everything that is to appear in the annual report and accounts, to 'review' certain items (including these seven directors' corporate governance assertions) and to 'audit' the financial statements.

APB has introduced a comprehensive auditors' responsibility statement which now appears in every audited annual report. Within this auditors' responsibility statement is a specification of those corporate governance assertions that the auditors are required to review. There is no longer a specific report from the auditors on the results of their review of these assertions. Only if the auditors disagree about the correctness of an assertion by the directors will the audit report itself draw attention to this disagreement. As before, it will be disagreement of a factual rather than a qualitative kind which would lead to such a dissenting reference in the auditors' report.

# Internal control in the Combined Code    B6.5

The annual report of a listed company now carries a narrative statement of how the company has applied the 2003 Combined Code Principle C.2 (Principle D.2 in the 1998 Code), *viz.*

**D.2    Internal Control**

**Principle    The board should maintain a sound system of internal control to safeguard shareholders investment and the company's assets.**

This narrative statement, as a minimum, is expected to disclose that there is an ongoing process for identifying, evaluating and managing the significant risks faced by the company, and that it is regularly reviewed by the board. The Turnbull guidance also states that the board may wish to provide additional information to assist understanding of the company's risk management processes and system of internal control. The content of such narrative statements is likely, therefore, to vary widely from company to company.

The Listing Rules do not require the auditors to review the narrative statement, but there are requirements under Auditing Standards for auditors to read the narrative statement and to seek to resolve any apparent misstatements or material inconsistencies with the audited financial statements. (Other information in documents containing audited financial statements, (SAS 160, revised), paragraphs 22–23.)

Although the Turnbull guidance addresses all the internal control requirements of the Combined Code, Listing Rule 12.43A requires the auditors to review only the disclosures made with respect to Code Provision C.2.1 (Provision D.2.1 in the 1998 Code), which reads:

'The directors should, at least annually, conduct a review of the effectiveness of the group's system of internal controls and should report to shareholders that they have done so. The review should cover all controls, including financial, operational and compliance controls and risk management systems.'

So, the other Provision which had been classified in the 1998 Code within the Internal Control section (Provision D.2.2, now C.3.5 (2003)) does not need to be reviewed by the auditors under Listing Rule 12.43A. This other Provision now reads:

'The audit committee should monitor and review the effectiveness of the internal audit activities. Where there is no internal audit function, the audit committee should consider annually whether there is a need for an internal audit function and make a recommendation to the board, and the reasons for the absence of such a function should be explained in the relevant section of the annual report.'

Prior to 2003 it had read:

'Companies which do not have an internal audit function should from time to time review the need for one.'

The Turnbull guidance defined 'all controls' (per the above Provision) in this way:

'The reference to 'all controls' in Code provision D.2.1 should not be taken to mean that the effectiveness of every internal control (including controls designed to manage immaterial risks) should be subject to review by the board. Rather it means that, for the purposes of this guidance, internal controls considered by the board should include all types of controls including those of an operational and compliance nature, as well as internal financial controls.' (The Turnbull Report, para 28.)

## Auditor independence                                                  B6.6

This document is aimed at promoting and ensuring auditor independence that has been developed by members of the Global Institutional Governance Network (GIGN), an informal international group of investment institutions which seek to promote good corporate governance at those companies in which they invest.

The document is intended as a minimum best practice standard. Some GIGN members are keen to establish higher standards in their home jurisdictions, but are content to set this as the minimum level internationally.

The following members of the GIGN have agreed to back the document publicly:

- ABP, the Netherlands
- Alecta Investment Management, Sweden
- California Public Employees' Retirement System (CalPERS), US
- Hermes Investment Management Ltd, UK
- Morley Fund Management, UK
- Ontario Teachers' Pension Plan, Canada
- PGGM, the Netherlands
- SPF Beheer, the Netherlands
- Standard Life Investment Management, UK
- TIAA-Cref, US

GIGN members hope that the companies in which they invest on their own behalf or for clients will regard this as a useful contribution to the debate, and as helpful in laying out the expectations of their major international investors.

### Auditor independence – a global best practice outline from institutional investors                                              B6.7

We, as large institutional investors, regard the independence of auditors, both in reality and perception, as of paramount importance to maintaining both the confidence of shareholders, who rely on audited financial statements, and the stability of global financial markets.

In this regard, we expect the corporations in whose securities we invest, or might invest, to give careful consideration to the following guidelines.

- Corporations should have effective audit committees, which are genuinely independent of both management and auditors. Such committees should:
  - ○ annually conduct a meaningful evaluation of the audit services and the relationship between the auditor and the corporation's directors and officers;
  - ○ ensure they establish and maintain independent channels of communication with the auditors, including other members of the audit team in addition to the engagement partner when appropriate;
  - ○ have a clear policy, supported by effective processes, to ensure the provision of non-audit services by the auditor and its affiliates does not affect the auditors' independence, perceived or real;
  - ○ annually consider the re-appointment of the auditors, and make an appropriate recommendation to the Board and or to the shareholders as appropriate;
  - ○ consider the benefits of seeking tenders for the audit at regular and appropriate intervals. In evaluating such tenders we expect audit

committees to pay particular regard to the quality of the audit and not just its cost;

○ have access to independent sources of advice, including but not limited to technical accounting advice. This advice should be sought and obtained when the audit committee deems it necessary; and

○ approve employment policies designed to prevent conflicts of interest arising from the interchange of personnel between the audit team and corporation's audit related staff.

● Corporations should, subject to constraints of commercial confidentiality, disclose:

○ the nature and quantum of audit and non-audit services provided by the auditor, analysed in sufficient detail to enable shareholders to make an informed decision in respect of the resolution to re-elect the auditors;

○ a summary of the audit committee's charter; and

○ a commentary on the audit committee's composition and activities, up to and including the date of the audit report. This could include

  □ the number of meetings held;

  □ the factors that influenced the balance of the committee and the selection of its members; and

  □ a summary of the process used to control the provision of non-audit services by the auditor and its affiliates.

● Corporations should promptly inform investors when there has been a change of auditors, and explain why the change was made.

● Corporations should have processes designed to ensure the competence of their audit committee and its members and when appropriate, they should provide independent training to ensure that competence is maintained.

● When appointing new auditors, regard should be had to any conflicts of interest arising from pre-existing relationships between the corporation and the proposed new firm of auditors.

At our discretion, we will use best endeavours to communicate to corporations when we have concerns about the independence of the auditors. We may reinforce our concerns, especially if such concerns have not been addressed to our satisfaction.

# Reviewing the performance of the external auditor
B6.8

The external audit should not be viewed as a commodity to be purchased at lowest cost with splendid disregard for its quality. Still less should companies welcome external audits which are superficial. A high quality audit is an essential part of effective corporate governance – for which the board of directors is responsible. It is an essential control in the process of disclosure to stakeholders.

Opaqueness of disclosure was blamed for much of the loss of investor confidence in Far Eastern companies during the late 1990s. Concerns were expressed about perceived variations in the quality of the main external audit brands with the suggestion that at times the rigor of an external audit conducted by a 'Big Five' firm of public accountants in the Far East may not have corresponded to a similar audit conducted in the western world – even disregarding local variations in laws, regulations and standards. In the US and the UK concerns are frequently expressed about the quality of external audits – by no means always justifiably and usually retrospectively by damaged parties.

Practice in different countries of the world, as well as within different sectors of their respective economies, varies as to whether the external auditors are appointed by the board, by the shareholders or even by government or regulators. But in every case it should be regarded as the responsibility of top management and the board to monitor the quality of the external audit to ensure that the best quality audit is obtained commensurate with acceptable cost. It will usually fall to the audit committee of the board to undertake this on behalf of the board.

Just as the audit committee might reasonably ask the external auditors for their views on the quality of the accounting and internal audit processes within the business, so the audit committee is likely to call for reports on the quality of external audit from the accounting and internal audit functions of the business. At one meeting of the committee, the audit committee will consider the external auditor's plan for their audit and at the later meeting which considers the year-end financial statements will receive a report from the auditors on their completed audit.

One matter to be considered by the audit committee is the external auditor's concept of materiality which, under external auditing standards, is required to be presented to be explained to the audit committee, and this will be done at the meeting which considers the plan for the audit. Here we give an example.

**External auditor's statement to audit committee on audit materiality**

The materiality guideline is used as a gauge of the significance of adjustments and other findings of our audit and is set out below for the Group.

|  | £'000 |
|---|---|
| Forecast profit before tax for the Group | 35,200 |
| Effective tax rate – 30% | (10,560) |
| Profit after tax | 24,640 |
|  | 7.5% |
| Materiality guideline | 1,848 |

The above materiality level is set using annualised profits before tax based on the Management accounts up to the end of October 2000 and is subject to change based on actual results for the year ended 31 December 2000.

Our audit will be designed to identify errors of a lower amount than the materiality level in order to ensure that any undetected errors do not exceed the materiality level.

Each individual subsidiary will have a materiality level based on a sliding scale of turnover, which will not exceed the group materiality level.

It would be advisable for the audit committee to review the management of the information flow from management to the external auditor, because late disclosure of information by management towards the end of the audit can mean it is effectively too late for the external auditor to deal with the information.. Cynics have claimed that that 'audit materiality is 3x the audit fee divided by the number of days left to complete the audit'!

(Readers are also referred to **B20.11** THE AUDIT COMMITTEE'S OVERSIGHT RESPONSIBILITY FOR EXTERNAL AUDIT).

The company should regularly consider whether a change should be made in the provider of external audit services. One view is that the external audit firm should be changed perhaps once every five years in order to maintain adequate auditor independence. In the end, it is said, the external auditor will 'go native' – just as the independent director might after, say, eight to ten years on the board. It is however rare for there to be mandatory requirements for the external audit firm to be changed regularly, though it is more common that the partner in charge of the audit may be required, by professional rules, to be changed from time to time.

Whether or not there is an imposed obligation to change the external audit firm periodically (there is no such requirement for companies in the UK, listed or not listed), the company should certainly regularly consider the matter. An important point to make here is that the initial consideration should be made at an early stage – otherwise it will be too late to make any change before the next annual audit has to be underway. For this reason, many companies each year fail to address this issue. It will fall to the audit committee to consider the audit bids made by rival accounting firms and to recommend to the board the decision to be taken.

Very commonly, the existing audit firm will be invited to bid to continue in that role, but should not be asked to do so if there is no chance of that firm being reselected. Preparing and presenting a bid is a costly process which should not be asked of the incumbent auditors unless there is a prospect of their reappointment.

In the UK, the Combined Code for corporate governance enjoins that the duties of the audit committee should include reviewing and monitoring the external auditor's independence and objectivity and the effectiveness of the audit process. 2003 Code Provision D.3.2 says that where the auditors also supply a substantial volume of non-audit services to the company, the committee should develop and implement policy on the engagement of the external auditor to supply non-audit services – a much less onerous 'requirement' than the US position post the Sarbanes-Oxley Act (see **B26 INTERNATIONAL DIMENSIONS**). The Principles (in this case D.3) are not intended to be optional – indeed companies must include within their annual report a statement explaining how (not whether) they have followed the Principles. On the other hand, the Provisions are in a sense optional – companies need to explain in their annual report why they have not complied with any Provision.

### C.3  Audit Committee and Auditors[2]

**Main Principle**   **The board should establish formal and transparent arrangements for considering how they should apply the financial reporting and internal control principles and for maintaining an appropriate relationship with the company's auditors.**

**Code Provisions**

C.3.2   The main role and responsibilities of the audit committee should be set out in written terms of reference and should include:

- to make recommendations to the board, for it to put to the shareholders for their approval in general meeting, in relation to the appointment, re-appointment and removal of the external auditor and to approve the remuneration and terms of engagement of the external auditor;

- to review and monitor the external auditor's independence and objectivity and the effectiveness of the audit process, taking into consideration relevant UK professional and regulatory requirements;

- to develop and implement policy on the engagement of the external auditor to supply non-audit services, taking into account relevant ethical guidance regarding the provision of non-audit services by the external audit firm; and to report to the board, identifying any matters in respect of which it considers that action or improvement is needed and making recommendations as to the steps to be taken.

C.3.6   The audit committee should have primary responsibility for making a recommendation on the appointment, reappointment and removal of the external auditors. If the board does not accept the audit committee's recommendation, it should include in the annual report, and in any papers recommending appointment or re-appointment, a statement from the audit committee explaining the recommendation and should set out reasons why the board has taken a different position.

C.3.7   The annual report should explain to shareholders how, if the auditor provides non-audit services, auditor objectivity and independence is safeguarded.'

Later in this chapter we reproduce as an excellent guide, 'Appraising The Auditors', developed by The Institute of Chartered Accountants of Scotland. It primary intention is to establish best practice guidance on the involvement of non-executive directors, and in particular audit committees, in the process of appointing auditors of listed companies and it offers a framework to apply to the appointment of a new audit firm. The guide makes the point that the performance of the auditors and their relationship with the company are important issues and shows how listed companies should monitor these matters on a positive, constructive basis, and thus implement an environment of continuous improvement in the audit.

**Checklist for the Annual Audit Review**                                        **B6.9**

**1.   Audit approach**

1.1   Is the external auditor's general approach satisfactory?

1.2   Does the timing of external audit work fit in with the company's own schedules and priorities?

1.3   Are the arrangements for the external audit of group companies and divisions appropriate?

1.4   Are materiality levels reassuring where there is no local audit requirement? For instance, where there is no statutory audit requirement in a particular country, is the audit performed to a local materiality level or to overall group materiality?

1.5   Are materiality levels reassuring where consolidation occurs at individual operating company level? For instance, where group companies operate through a number of divisions, is the external audit of the separate divisions performed to a divisional materiality level, to a local company materiality level, or to overall group materiality?

1.6   Are there effective relationship and access arrangements with other auditors in the group as well as with auditors of associates and joint ventures?

1.7   Is audit evidence readily available, for instance from service organisations supplying outsourced functions?

1.8   What additional assurance services needed and is the approach satisfactory to (a) their provision and (b) the nature of any reports required in addition to the statutory audit report – for example on corporate governance matters, or on the company's environmental or ethical policies and procedures?

**2.   Audit effectiveness**

2.1   Does the audit effectively cover the key operations of the group?

2.2   Does the audit effectively address the main issues facing the group and the key areas of business and audit risk?

2.3   How strong is (a) the quality of the audit planning process and (b) the retrospective assessment of whether the audit achieved what was intended?

2.4   How proactive have the auditors been requesting discussion with, and in questioning, the appropriate level of management in relation to matters arising?

2.5   How appropriate has been the external auditors' reliance on management representations?

2.6   How well have audit issues arising, especially contentious matters, been handled?

2.7   What has been the quality of the auditors' assessment of the group's systems and controls, and the effectiveness of their recommendations for improvement?

2.8   What has been the quality of the external auditors' ideas for improvements to business practices and procedures?

**3.   Company action to facilitate audit efficiency**

3.1   To what extent has external audit efficiency been facilitated by the company – eg in providing correct information in an appropriate format at the right time?

**4.   Relationship with internal auditors**

4.1   What has been the role and scope of internal audit and the extent of any reliance placed by the external auditors?

**5.   Information technology**

5.1   What impact does the nature of the company's systems have upon the external audit, and how appropriate has been the external auditor's approach to the company's use of IT?

## 6. Treasury functions

6.1 What impact does the nature of the company's treasury operations have upon the external audit, and how appropriate has been the external auditor's approach to the company's treasury functions?

## 7. Communications with the audit committee

7.1 To what extent are current standards on communication between external auditors and audit committees followed – especially in relation to regularity of meetings?

## 8. Provision of other services

8.1 Does the provision of non-audit services (such as those listed below) threaten the independence and objectivity of the auditors?

- Compliance with corporation tax legislation;
- filing of company tax returns;
- tax planning including VAT;
- due diligence investigations;
- work on profit-related pay (awarded after a presentation by rival firms of auditors);
- minor training services for the internal audit department;
- Year 2000 compliance work and review;
- ad hoc recruitment services; or
- corporate finance.

## 9. Other auditor independence issues

9.1 Does the audit committee have concerns in relation to the external audit firm's independence and professional objectivity?

## 10. Liability and risk profile of the firm

10.1 Are the external audit firm's litigation record, financial position and professional indemnity insurance cover satisfactory?

## 11. Personnel involved in the audit and issues of rotation

11.1 Is the external audit staffed appropriately (eg the different levels of staff on the audit team, and the nature of their experience)?

11.2 Are the number and expertise of partners involved in the audit satisfactory?

11.3 Are there unacceptable personality clashes?

11.4 What is the frequency of rotation of the audit engagement partner and other members of the audit team, are these satisfactory and has such rotation been handled well?

# Appraising your auditors – a guide to the assessment and appointment of auditors
B6.10

We are very grateful to The Institute of Chartered Accountants of Scotland for permission to reprint their excellent new guidance on the approach which may be taken to select and appraise the performance of external auditors. Published originally in 1998, this edition first appeared in June 2003. No responsibility for loss occasioned to any person acting or refraining from action as a result of any material in this publication can be accepted by the authors or the publishers. All rights reserved. No part of this publication may be reproduced, stored in a retrieval system, or transmitted in any form or by any means, electronic, mechanical, photocopying, recording or otherwise, without the prior permission of the publisher.

Additional printed copies in booklet form are available at a price of £5 from The Institute of Chartered Accountants of Scotland, 21 Haymarket Yards, Edinburgh EH12 5BH. Tel: 0131 347 0240. Fax: 0131 347 0110. E-mail: accountingandauditing@icas.org.uk. The booklet can be downloaded without charge from the Institute's website at www.icas.org.uk.

David Wood at ICAS would be pleased to hear from readers with any enquiries about this guidance. He is Deputy Director, Accounting and Auditing, The Institute of Chartered Accountants of Scotland, 21 Haymarket Yards, Edinburgh EH12 5BH (tel: +44 (0)131 347 0233; fax: +44 (0)131 347 0105; e-mail: dwood@icas.org.uk.

*Acknowledgements*

The Institute's Business Law Committee would like to thank the members of the Working Party for taking part in this initiative. The members were:

| | |
|---|---|
| Ian Paterson-Brown (Chairman) | Finance DirectorISIS Asset Management plc |
| Bryan Rankin | Finance DirectorCaledonian Trust plc |
| Alan Thomson | Finance DirectorSmiths Group plc |
| Andrew Walker | Senior Technical ManagerPKF |
| David Wood | Deputy Director, Accounting and AuditingSecretary to the Business Law CommitteeThe Institute of Chartered Accountants of Scotland |

It should be noted that the members of the Working Party were acting in their personal capacity and were not representing the organisations for which they work.

*Foreword by Sir Robert Smith, Chairman of Weir Group plc, Chairman of the Financial Reporting Council-appointed Group which developed proposed Guidance for Audit Committees, and Past-President of The Institute of Chartered Accountants of Scotland*

I am pleased to support this publication by The Institute of Chartered Accountants of Scotland. It has addressed the much written about and much discussed issues of auditor independence and objectivity and the role of the audit committee from a very practical and different standpoint, and will add to the ongoing debate on the subject.

The practical aspects of this publication, which is aimed at providing audit committees with detailed assistance in evaluating the audit issues, are contained in the flow diagram and the detailed guidance questions which are split into three helpful checklists. These checklists, or sets of guidance questions, should provide useful and practical assistance to audit committees in implementing the proposed guidance developed by the FRC appointed group which I chaired and which was published in January 2003.

**The guidance questions are drawn up as three specific checklists.**

1) Trigger points from the audit committee's ongoing review of the auditors, which may indicate that an assessment of the auditors should be undertaken.

2) Points to consider in a full annual assessment of the auditors.

3) Procedural matters for addressing during the audit tender process.

However, their purpose is very much aimed at creating practical guidance and direction for audit committees seeking to discharge their duties. To treat these checklists as another tick box exercise will neither meet the requirements of demonstrating that the audit committee has discharged their duties, nor do credit to the significant work in preparing this practical guidance.

As audit committees are being given additional responsibilities and are being required to perform an even more critical role in the relationship between company and external auditor, the guidance should provide assistance to them in performing this very important duty. Furthermore, in highlighting factors which might be relevant to the audit committee's consideration of the audit relationship, this publication should create a catalyst for rigorous discussion and debate. It should also help develop the audit trail for audit committees by establishing the validity, effectiveness and professionalism with which they discharge their obligations of assessing auditor independence and objectivity.

*Sir Robert Smith*

*4 June 2003*

# Introduction

## Introduction to the checklists

The Institute of Chartered Accountants of Scotland is pleased to publish this short paper, and hopes that the guidance questions set out in the appendices will be of assistance to audit committees in the application of best practice and, in particular, in following the Combined Code guidance developed by the FRC-appointed group chaired by Sir Robert Smith.

While the guidance questions have been prepared in the form of three user friendly checklists, which should provide practical guidance for audit committees, they are not intended to create a 'tick box' exercise. It is anticipated that, used sensibly, they will stimulate questioning and debate. If they are to provide an audit trail, they should be accompanied by suitable supporting documentation.

We have deliberately avoided the development of large sections of text, in order not to duplicate material in the Combined Code guidance or in guidance available from numerous other sources. Instead, we have sought to provide a flowchart and three practical checklists which can be readily used by company audit committees in managing and reviewing their relationship with their auditors. The three checklists cover:

- trigger points from the audit committee's ongoing review of the auditors, which may indicate that an assessment of the auditors should be undertaken;

- points to consider in a full annual assessment of the auditors; and

- procedural matters for addressing during the audit tender process.

The guidance questions are designed to highlight the issues which should be considered by the audit committee when monitoring its auditors and formally reviewing them prior to recommending re-appointment and, where necessary, provide assistance on the audit tender process. They might form part of the documentary evidence of the work of the audit committee. The questions could also be of use to others in the company, to professional firms with an interest in the audit process, and other parties.

Although designed to reflect the Combined Code guidance for audit committees developed by Sir Robert Smith's group, the guidance questions also reflect our own views on matters of best practice and, to that extent, we hope they make a useful contribution to the ongoing debate on the role of audit committees in the framework of corporate governance.

The checklists are intended as a means of bringing rigour to the matters to be considered by audit committees and to the judgements which need to be made. We are not advocating that a 'tick box' mentality be adopted by audit committees, but instead emphasise that judgement must be applied in relation to each question raised.

Whilst these guidance questions are designed to be applicable to the largest of listed groups, it is hoped that they will also be of assistance to other, smaller, listed and unlisted companies and groups, whether or not they have a formal audit committee, and indeed in any company where the management is separated from the ownership. Accordingly, the term 'audit committee' in the following text and in the questions should be taken to mean 'audit committee or other appropriate persons'.

In addition to explaining about guidance questions, this introduction seeks to raise some issues which are worth consideration and debate by audit committees – relating to auditor independence, the company – auditor relationship and the tender process. We have not sought to replicate what has already been written on these subjects from a technical or guidance standpoint. Rather, we have preferred to raise a few practical issues which are worthy of debate and which should provide some background information to the audit committee on the professional framework against which the checklists or guidance questions can be implemented.

**Auditor independence**

In today's business climate, boards and audit committees must not lose sight of the need, not only to ensure independence, objectivity and effectiveness of auditors, but also to be able to demonstrate that they have done so. In order to secure the primary objective of auditor objectivity, there are various provisions relating to independence which auditors are required to follow. For the audit committee, the concept of auditor independence needs to be looked at from two standpoints.

- First, the relationship that the auditors have with senior management and, in particular, the finance department and whether the relationship has become compromised due to familiarity, excessive awards of non-audit work, or other factors.

- The second issue is the processes and procedures that are in place within the audit firm to ensure that they not only provide a professional and independent service but can provide the necessary audit trail to demonstrate to the respective company's audit committee, and if ever challenged, the external world, that they provided a professional and independent service. For auditors and companies this has moved following the Enron debacle to one of reputational risk management. Neither can afford to allow a 'cosy' relationship to be created or exist.

Companies may wish to consider with their auditors procedures for ensuring both audit continuity and independence. This could be achieved by having a lead partner and a continuity partner. Each would serve a set term but with a significant degree of overlap. The newly appointed partner would be the lead partner providing the 'fresh' approach. Following his period as lead partner, he or she would become the continuity partner for a further period whilst a new partner serves as lead partner.

The subject of auditor independence underlies many of the guidance questions, in all three checklists.

### Company-auditor relationship

Equally important for the audit committee is the culture of senior management and in particular the finance department. With the issue of independence goes the important values of transparency, honesty, accountability and integrity. If all these exist then the environment is created for a good working relationship (mutual trust) which provides a value added service to the shareholders and a professional relationship between senior management, the finance department, the audit committee and the auditors.

The monitoring of the ongoing relationship between the auditors and the company is fundamentally important and one in which both the executive directors and the non-executive directors have important roles to play.

While much of this is about independence, it is also about transparency and trust. A relationship which is independent without the ingredients of transparency and trust will not necessarily provide short or long term benefits. What the audit committee requires to address is both the independence of the auditor, the culture of the management and the level of transparency and trust that exists between management and the auditors.

Management for their part should be prepared to engage, and openly discuss issues, with the auditors, and should seek to work with them in a professional manner. If the auditors are objective and are providing an independent sounding board then this provides a source of valuable assistance for management. If management cannot convince the auditors that a proposed course of action is appropriate, then they will need to consider an alternative course of action.

The acid test for management, boards and auditors should be – would they be happy to explain fully what they are doing to the shareholders? If the answer is no then they probably shouldn't be doing it!

The importance of the company-auditor relationship and, in particular, open and honest communication between the auditors and audit committee is emphasised throughout the guidance questions.

### The tender process

Audit tenders are costly exercises for both management and the audit firms. They tie up significant amounts of time and both parties incur significant costs. That said, the occurrence of a tender should only be needed on a very occasional basis and, in such cases, the time and cost will normally be fully justified.

The audit tender process is a very important process and one which should be planned and executed by the audit committee and executive management.

Prior to entering into a tender process, careful consideration needs to be given as to what the board is seeking to achieve. Indeed, consultation with the major shareholders prior to commencing the process is an action that all boards should consider as the auditors are shareholder appointed and, as such, consultation is the appropriate way to proceed under best corporate governance practice.

Indeed, it is highly likely that certain major institutional shareholders will develop their own internal policies or procedures linked to their interpretation of best practice and, as such, issues such as audit tenders will be issues upon which institutions will not only have a view but will wish to have input into prior to the tender process being commenced.

Having determined the purpose of the tender process and the possible entrants, the audit committee may require to reduce this to a feasible number of audit firms. It is suggested that less than three participants, particularly if the current auditors are part of the process, would not provide a robust tender. However, more than four would tend to become unwieldy. After the initial stages of the process, the audit committee would seek to reduce the prospective firms to a shortlist, with whom more detailed discussions could be held.

These matters are reflected in the guidance questions on the selection and appointment of a new audit firm.

**Practical approach – how to use this guide**

Our model for assessing the company's auditors is set out in the flowchart.

The checklist on ongoing auditor review sets out some trigger points which may indicate to the audit committee that it needs to consider, through a limited scope review or a full annual assessment, the position of the auditors and whether they should be replaced. It is recommended that the chairman of the audit committee uses this checklist in the context of his or her regular discussion with company executives and the finance department, and as an aide-memoire for reporting back to audit committee meetings. The audit committee could also use this as a checklist to be reviewed at some or all of its meetings throughout the year.

The extent of any limited scope review will be dependent on the issue which has arisen and the nature of what needs to be addressed. It is suggested that this review could be undertaken using the appropriate section or sections of the full annual assessment checklist, but without using all the guidance questions contained therein.

The annual audit assessment checklist provides guidance to audit committees when performing the annual assessments as required by Sir Robert's Combined Code guidance. This checklist is framed in the context of the assessment taking place after the conclusion of the annual audit. Where this checklist is used at an earlier stage, possibly as a result of the occurrence of some trigger point during the year, a number of the guidance questions may not be directly applicable or may be applicable only in the context of the previous year's audit.

**B6.10**  *Appraising your auditors*

An unsatisfactory conclusion on the incumbent auditors arising from the annual audit assessment would be likely to lead to a tender process for the selection and appointment of a new audit firm. The checklist for selection and appointment of a new audit firm provides guidance to the audit committee on this process.

It should be recognised that, whilst the guidance question in these checklists have been drawn up in the context of a company, many businesses operate through groups of companies. The application of the checklists to group situations will depend on the individual circumstances of the company and the group, the degree to which the audit of the group is undertaken by the parent company auditors, and the approach taken by the parent company audit committee in its relationship with the respective auditors of the group.

## Conclusion

We hope that these guidance questions are found to be helpful for audit committees in their relationship with their company's auditors. We would be grateful for any comments, so that we can update and improve these in future.

*Auditor Assessment (1)*

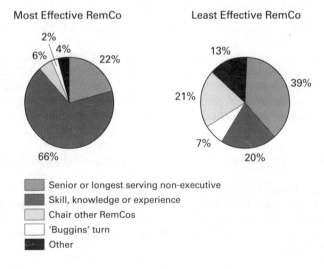

Most Effective RemCo    Least Effective RemCo

Senior or longest serving non-executive
Skill, knowledge or experience
Chair other RemCos
'Buggins' turn
Other

*Auditor Assessment (2)*

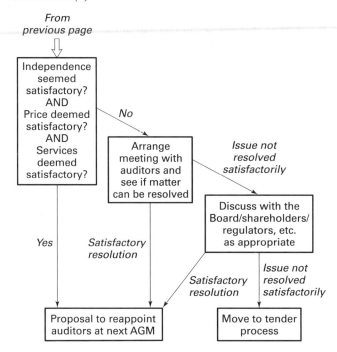

## Audit committee guidance questions

### Possible trigger points from ongoing auditor review

| | No Issue | Issue to be Addressed |
|---|---|---|
| **Internal Procedural Issues** (which could indicate a breakdown in independence) | | |
| 1. Company policy for award of non-audit work to auditors does not exist, is out of date or has not been reviewed within the last 15 months. | | |
| 2. Award of non-audit work is made which is outwith the policy | | |
| **Change in Relationship** | | |
| 3. Did the audit team comprise audit partner(s) and staff at appropriate levels of seniority, audit qualification, relevant industry experience and expertise? | | |

|  | No Issue | Issue to be Addressed |
|---|---|---|
| 4. Has the audit partner or a senior member of the audit team left the audit engagement or the audit firm, and are future audit staffing arrangements deemed satisfactory? | | |
| 5. Has the firm withdrawn from an activity or location which was core to the original appointment, or changed its business arrangements such that possible conflicts of interest may arise? | | |
| 6. Has the company recruited a key member of the audit engagement team to a senior position in the company's finance function? | | |
| 7. Has there been a communication breakdown between a key member of the audit engagement team and the company, in particular, its key executives, its finance department or the chairman of its audit committee? | | |
| 8. Has there been any disagreement between management and the auditors of a material nature? | | |
| 9. Has there been any unscheduled non-attendance by the auditor at an audit committee meeting? | | |

## Change in Independence

|  | No Issue | Issue to be Addressed |
|---|---|---|
| 10. Does the company policy ensure that the audit firm is not engaged to provide non-audit services where this would result in: | | |
| • the auditors auditing their own firm's work; | | |
| • the audit firm making management decisions; | | |
| • a joint interest between the company and the auditors; or | | |
| • the audit firm acting in the role of advocate for the company; and | | |
| • has the company complied with this policy in the awarding of all non-audit engagements to the auditors? | | |
| 11. Have there been personnel changes in the audit team or company which could create a perception that the auditors are no longer independent? | | |

|  | No Issue | Issue to be Addressed |
|---|---|---|
| 12. Have there been changes in the nature of the audit firm's or the company's businesses which could create a perception that the auditors are no longer independent? |  |  |
| 13. Have any of the company's accounting policies or disclosures been brought into question or publicly challenged (eg by the Financial Reporting Review Panel or in adverse press comment) such that the auditors' independence is questioned? |  |  |
| 14. Have any comments or questions been raised by regulators or shareholders regarding issues of auditor independence? |  |  |
| 15. Is the relationship between auditors and management deemed too close, eg are corporate hospitality levels such that independence must be questioned? |  |  |
| 16. Have any other matters arisen or been notified to the audit committee which cast doubt on the independence of the auditors or individual members of the audit team? |  |  |

**Change in Competence**

|  | No Issue | Issue to be Addressed |
|---|---|---|
| 17. Have any key staff members departed from the audit firm such that this calls into question the ongoing competence of the auditors? |  |  |
| 18. Have there been any changes in the nature or size of the audit firm's or the company's business which indicate that the auditors may no longer have the necessary competence or specialist expertise to perform the audit? |  |  |
| 19 Has any material error or sequence of errors been discovered which should have been identified previously as part of the audit process? |  |  |
| 20. Has any control breakdown been discovered which could have resulted in a material error, and which should have been identified previously as part of the audit process? |  |  |

|  | No Issue | Issue to be Addressed |
|---|---|---|
| **Communication** | | |
| 21. Have the auditors communicated with the audit committee according to their timetable and on a timely basis, or have the communications been late or the information incomplete? | | |
| 22. Were issues arising from the audit raised with management or the appropriate person within the finance team in an appropriate and timely manner? | | |
| 23. Have the auditors reported all significant issues, or adverse or unexpected findings, to the audit committee on a timely basis? | | |
| 24. Have there been any material fee overruns in any area of work being conducted by the auditors which have not been communicated or explained to the audit committee in advance of the work being concluded? | | |
| **Other Matters** | | |
| 25. Has the audit firm been involved in an issue which causes it reputational damage and which could bring into question the auditors' professionalism and independence, or the firm's financial stability? | | |
| 26. Have any incidences of whistleblowing occurred which may call into question the independence, professionalism and objectivity of the auditors or the effectiveness of the audit process? | | |
| 27. Have any issues been referred from divisional controllers or subsidiaries which may call into question the appropriateness of the company or group auditors? | | |
| 28. Has there been any other issue, the outcome of which causes the audit committee concern? | | |
| 29. There is no prescribed list of other issues which the chairman of the audit committee or the audit committee itself should monitor on an ongoing basis. However, they should be ever vigilant to any factor which could bring into question the independence, objectivity and effectiveness of the auditors. | | |

**Annual audit assessment**

|  | No Issue | Issue to be Addressed |
|---|---|---|

**Independence and Objectivity**

1. Has the audit committee received documented reassurance that the auditors and their staff have no family, financial, employment, investment or business relationship with the company?

2. Has the audit committee received from the audit firm on an annual basis, in writing where appropriate, information about policies and processes for maintaining independence and monitoring compliance with relevant requirements, to enable it to monitor the group's auditors' compliance with professional ethical guidance and in particular has this covered the following:

   • the rotation of audit partners and staff?

   • the level of fees that the company pays in proportion to the overall fee income of the firm, office and partner?

   • the nature of other services provided to the company?

   • any relationships between the audit firm and its staff and the company?

   • office and business procedures including partner and senior manager incentive arrangements?

   • overall confirmation of the auditors' independence and objectivity?

3. Have the auditors met with the audit committee and discussed their objectivity and independence in an appropriately open and straightforward manner?

4. Have the auditors provided information, including the number of former employees currently employed in senior positions in the company, to enable the audit committee:

   • to monitor application of the company policy on employment of former employees of the audit firm?

**B6.10** *Appraising your auditors*

|  | No Issue | Issue to be Addressed |
|---|---|---|
| • to consider whether there has been any impairment, or appearance of impairment, of the auditors' judgement or independence in respect of the audit? |  |  |
| • to ensure compliance with the board approved company policy for the employment of former employees of the audit firm, who were part of the audit team and moved directly to the company? |  |  |
| 5. Has the audit committee taken into account best practice regarding the provision of non-audit services by the auditors and satisfied itself that: |  |  |
| • the auditor does not audit its own firm's work? |  |  |
| • the auditor does not make management decisions for the company? |  |  |
| • no joint interest between the company and the auditors is created? |  |  |
| • the auditor is not put in the role of advocate for the company? |  |  |
| 6. Notwithstanding the above, does the audit committee regard the relationship between auditors and management as too close, such that the auditors may lack, or appear to lack, the required degree of objectivity? |  |  |
| 7. Have any other matters arisen or been notified to the audit committee which cast doubt on the independence of the auditors or individual members of the audit team? |  |  |

**Financial Stability and Risk Profile of the Firm**

| | No Issue | Issue to be Addressed |
|---|---|---|
| 8. By reference to the auditor's litigation record, financial assets, the structure of the firm and its professional indemnity insurance cover, has the audit committee considered the firm's financial stability and whether it has the ability to meet any claims which might arise from the audit engagement? |  |  |

| | No Issue | Issue to be Addressed |
|---|---|---|

**Audit Strategy**

9. Did the auditors communicate their strategy for the audit to the audit committee, and did that communication include the undernoted, where relevant:

- terms of reference including an engagement letter or letters covering the statutory audit and corporate governance, and an independence letter?

- a relationship chart summarising the key auditor -company/group relationships by division and function?

- relationship to any other auditor in the UK or overseas?

- the appointment of an independent review partner who has not had any prior involvement with the company or group?

- the audit approach?

- audit arrangements for other group companies and divisions?

- audit arrangements in relation to service organisations supplying outsourced functions?

- the auditors' assessment of company or group treasury operations and the proposed audit arrangements?

- the level of audit materiality adopted for the audit, and justification for this amount?

- the timetable for the audit and for verbal and written communication to the audit committee?

- the role and scope of internal audit and the extent of any reliance to be placed by the auditors on the internal audit function?

- the auditors' understanding of the company's IT strategy and their approach to the audit of IT systems?

| | No Issue | Issue to be Addressed |
|---|---|---|
| • accounting developments and financial reporting? | | |
| • an assessment of group accounting and business risks, both qualitative and quantitative, and how they will be addressed as part of the audit approach, including use of experts in specialist or complex areas? | | |
| • additional assurance services and the nature of any reports required in addition to the statutory audit report, eg on corporate governance matters or on environmental or ethical policies and procedures? | | |
| • outline of fee proposal including reasons for major changes from prior year and fee analysis by scope and hours? | | |
| • key aspects of the auditors approach to ensuring continuous audit quality? | | |
| 10. In determining their audit strategy, did the auditors state that they would ensure that: | | |
| • they would evaluate the key risks of misstatement in the financial statements and allocate resources and focus their work accordingly? | | |
| • they would maintain an open and regular dialogue with management so that issues are identified and dealt with early? | | |
| • where the company's own internal controls are considered effective they would place reliance on them where appropriate to maximise the cost/benefit of the audit? | | |
| • there is a good working relationship with the company's internal audit function? | | |
| • they would maintain an appropriate level of continuity of all key personnel worldwide and would manage the audit on a basis that mirrors the company's or group's own structure? | | |
| they remain independent and objective in their assessment of the company or group financial statements and the issues which arise? | | |

| | No Issue | Issue to be Addressed |
|---|---|---|
| 11. Was the audit approach at each group company or division agreed in advance with the divisional controllers and determined by materiality of the company or division to the group, local legislative requirements or an assessment of the audit risks inherent in and specific to that company or division? | | |
| 12. Where a significant part of the group's operations is audited by a firm other than the parent company auditors, has the audit committee satisfied itself that: | | |
| • The parent company auditors are satisfied with the existing audit arrangements as a basis for their audit opinion on the consolidated group accounts? | | |
| • The audit arrangements do not contravene the rules of any relevant regulatory body (such as the US Securities and Exchange Commission, in relation to US listings)? | | |
| 13. Was the scope of the audit work at each entity categorised under broad headings such as full scope, limited scope and high level visit, with appropriate category description? | | |
| 14. Was the timing of the auditors procedures and their communication with the audit committee tailored to the annual reporting cycle? | | |
| 15. Did the auditors explain what would be communicated to the audit committee and when, eg the audit strategy, any half year review report, adverse and unexpected findings, and the final report to the audit committee? | | |

**Communication of Adverse or Unexpected Findings**

| | No Issue | Issue to be Addressed |
|---|---|---|
| 16. Were issues, including adverse or unexpected findings, communicated on a timely basis? | | |
| 17. Did the auditors identify the extent to which anticipated audit and accounting issues might have an impact on the year-end process? | | |
| 18. Was the actual or potential resolution of significant audit and accounting issues discussed and agreed with division, company and group management and documented for audit committee consideration? | | |

| | No Issue | Issue to be Addressed |
|---|---|---|
| 19. Did the auditors report on the companies or divisions where there were either new concerns regarding the control environment or update the position where there had been historic concerns? | | |
| 20. Did the auditors provide an update on new exposure drafts and financial reporting developments and identify those which were applicable to the company? | | |

**Finalisation of the Audit**

| | | |
|---|---|---|
| 21. Did the auditors provide the audit committee with a final report on the full year audit in advance of the board meeting to approve the annual accounts? | | |
| 22. Did the audit scope and fees change from that reported at the previous audit committee meetings and have such changes been satisfactorily explained in the report? | | |
| 23. Has a schedule of fees for non-audit services been provided in the report, and has this been approved by the audit committee? | | |
| 24. Did the report summarise the key features of the final phase of the audit cycle? | | |
| 25. Did the report provide an overview of results and report upon significant audit and accounting issues; particularly those of a subjective or judgemental nature? | | |
| 26. Did the auditors provide details of unadjusted misstatements or errors? | | |
| 27. Did the auditors ask for written representations as to the reasons why these errors were not adjusted? | | |
| 28. Did the auditors provide details of any occurrences of material fraud or errors and discuss these with the audit committee? | | |
| 29. Did the auditors request from the management, board of directors or audit committee details of any suspected or actual non-compliance with laws and regulations, and were any material matters discussed with the audit committee and appropriately taken forward? | | |

| | No Issue | Issue to be Addressed |
|---|---|---|
| 30. Did the auditors properly address the issue of going concern with the audit committee? | | |
| 31. Did the auditors provide their views on the qualitative aspects of the company's accounting practices and financial reporting? | | |
| 32. Did the auditors identify significant issues relating to accounting treatments where management's view of the preferred treatment differed from their own? | | |
| 33. Did the auditors confirm to the audit committee that they were satisfied that the procedures adopted by the company were sufficient to meet the relevant corporate governance requirements, including the provisions of the latest applicable code(s) and guidance, and were any recommendations for improvement considered to be practical and effective? | | |
| 34. Did the final phase of the audit reveal any significant audit and accounting issues which had not been identified in earlier communications to the audit committee? | | |
| 35. Did the auditors carry out a thorough and robust subsequent events review, including enquiry of, and discussion as appropriate with, management or the audit committee? | | |
| 36. Did the auditors request details of related parties and controlling parties, including enquiry of, and discussion as appropriate with, management or the audit committee? | | |
| 37. Did the auditors identify any areas for improvement in their audit approach and discuss these with the audit committee? | | |
| 38. Did the auditors make constructive recommendations on improving the company's control environment? | | |
| 39. Did the auditors provide details of significant weaknesses in the accounting and internal control systems found during the audit, and were their recommendations for improvement considered to be practical and effective? | | |

|  | No Issue | Issue to be Addressed |
|---|---|---|
| 40. Did the auditors consider the appropriateness and effectiveness of the company's broader risk management processes, and were any recommendations for improvement considered to be practical and effective? |  |  |
| 41. Did the auditors' letter of representation address appropriate issues, and had due consideration been given by the auditors to the appropriateness of their reliance on management representations? |  |  |
| 42. Did the auditors confirm that their independence had continued throughout the audit? |  |  |
| 43. Did the auditors issue a standard unqualified audit opinion on the financial statements or, if the opinion was non-standard (qualified or subject to a fundamental uncertainty), was the issue of concern and the impact on the audit report identified at a sufficiently early stage in the audit and discussed with the audit committee? |  |  |

**Concluding Matters**

| | | |
|---|---|---|
| 44. Did the audit team comprise audit partner(s) and staff at appropriate levels of seniority, experience and expertise? |  |  |
| 45. Has there been a good working relationship between the members of the audit engagement team and the company, in particular, its key executives, its finance department and the chairman of its audit committee? |  |  |
| 46. Has the Finance Director, Head of Internal Audit and other members of senior management provided positive feedback on the quality of the audit work? |  |  |
| 47. Has the auditor been sufficiently robust in dealings with the finance director and other company management? |  |  |
| 48. Has the auditor attended meetings with the audit committee without management present, and been sufficiently transparent and incisive? |  |  |

|  | No Issue | Issue to be Addressed |
|---|---|---|
| 49. Has the auditor notified and discussed with the audit committee any problems arising in dealings with the finance and other directors and other company or group management, including concerns as to the competence and integrity of these individuals? | | |
| 50. Does the audit committee consider that the audit was effective? | | |
| 51. Does the audit committee recommend to the board the reappointment of the incumbent auditors? | | |

**Selection and appointment of new audit firm**

Actioned?

**Audit Tender Consideration Process**

1. Have the reasons for putting the audit out to tender been clearly debated so the committee can discuss why it intends to do so with the board, major shareholders and other appropriate parties, such as regulators in regulated industries, prior to starting the process?

2. Have views been sought from major shareholders, regulators, and other appropriate parties independent of the board?

**Background Information**

3. Has an industry analysis been performed to ascertain who it would be appropriate to invite to participate in the tender process?

4. Does this include:

    (a) Reputations of firms?

    (b) Industry knowledge?

    (c) Any past experience of firms?

    (d) Financial stability, risk profile and litigation record?

    (e) Any personal references?

5. Has a list of necessary skills and services been prepared?

**Current Capabilities**

6. Do any potential conflicts exist, such as existing relationships or engagements with the company, which could exclude a particular firm from the tender process?

7. Does the firm have the size, resources and coverage required to audit the company or group?

8. Does the company's audit or other assurance requirement necessitate specialist skills – e.g. actuarial skills, and does the audit firm possess these skills?

## The Initial Tender Process – Phase 1

9. Have management prepared and the audit committee reviewed an invitation to tender which will allow all parties to tender on an equal footing? Have detailed specifications been prepared as to the desired content of the written proposals to be received by the audit committee?

10. Does the invitation to tender provide the following information to the prospective audit firms:

   (a) Financial performance?

   (b) Control framework?

   (c) Previous audit committee minutes?

   (d) Previous audit committee papers?

   (e) Organisation structure charts?

   (f) Prior year accounts?

   (g) Accounting procedures manuals?

   (h) Reporting procedures manuals?

   (i) Other relevant information?

11. Have the relevant parties signed a confidentiality letter prior to receiving information?

12. Have the relevant parties provided a draft statement of independence which will require to be signed if they are successful?

13. Has a timetable been prepared for the process, including adequate access to senior management, finance personnel and the audit committee? Is the timetable feasible?

14. Has it been agreed that a member of the audit committee should attend some of the meetings with senior management?

15. Has a checklist for scoring each firm's written submission been prepared?

16. Have plans been made for determining the shortlist, the likely number of firms involved, and what format phase 2 of the tender process will take?

## The Due Diligence Tender Process – Phase 2

17. Have plans been made for the shortlisted firms to visit selected typical company or group operations?

18. Has it been agreed whether these visits will result in expanded written submissions or only a final presentation?

19. Has a process been established for the management of the visited operations to score the shortlisted firms?

20. Has a list of questions been prepared to be addressed in the final presentations? Has a list of subjects been prepared for the prospective audit firms to address in their final written submissions?

21. Will the shortlisted auditors be asked to comment on the group's accounting and financial reporting manuals, consolidation pack, and other relevant documentation used by all company or group operations?

22. Has it been decided who from the company should attend the face to face presentations – audit committee, management, others – and have dates been reserved for these? Has it been decided who will consider the prospective audit firms' final written submissions?

23. Has a checklist for scoring each firms' submission or presentation been prepared?

24. Are the people presenting to the audit committee those that will conduct the audit?

25. Are expected audit hours and scale rates comparable with other firms?

26. Is the audit firm willing to disclose its percentage recovery on chargeable time, and if so, what does this indicate?

27. Has a draft joint press communication been prepared and agreed in advance with the shortlisted parties on a confidential basis, together with the intended timing of its release after the final selection process has been completed?

28. Have the following factors been considered in making the final decision on the appointment of the auditors:

    (a) Reputation and financial stability of the firms?

    (b) Views of shareholders, regulators and financiers?

    (c) Previous experience and recommendations from others?

    (d) Value for money?

    (e) Personality and experience of the key audit staff?

    (f) Depth of audit team expertise and technical back-up?

    (g) Industry expertise?

    (h) Geographic service capability?

    (i) Independence and objectivity?

    (j) Procedure for ensuring continuing independence and objectivity?

29. If the decision is made following a tender process to change the current auditor and appoint new auditors, then there will be various legal and procedural matters which will need to be addressed. For companies which

do not have in-house legal departments, this may involve seeking external advice. This should be undertaken once a decision has been made but prior to any public announcement.

# Hermes on auditor independence                                    B6.11

The following statements are included by permission of Hermes. They are at Lloyds Chambers, 1 Portsoken Street, London, E1 8HZ (tel: +44 (0)20 7680 2322; fax: +44 (0)20 7680 2477; www.hermes.co.uk and www.hermes.co.uk/ corporate-governance) where the latest version of this and their other contributions to corporate governance thinking can be found.

Further corporate governance guidance can be obtained from the Hermes website. This handbook carries certain Hermes guidance and discussion as follows.

- 'Hermes: Statement on UK Corporate Governance and Voting Policy' (2001) (**B7.7**).

- 'Hermes Guide for Shareholders and Independent Outside Directors' (**B10.79**).

- 'Not Badly Paid, But Paid Badly?' (**B15.15**).

- 'Value Drivers: Paying a Fair Price for Non-executive Directors' (Michelle Edkins) (**B15.16**).

- 'Hermes International Corporate Governance Principles' (**B26.8**).

## Auditor independence

The Enron debacle has reopened the public debate on the role of auditors and whether their independence can be called into question in certain circumstances. The chief executive of Andersen, Enron's auditor, admitted honest errors in the accounting work his firm did for the now bankrupt energy trader. 'Faith in our firm and in the integrity of the capital market system has been shaken', Joseph Berardino told the US Congress in December 2001.

Being able to rely on the accounts produced by a company is a fundamental requirement of shareholders. The published accounts are their main insight into a company's financial position, and as such they provide basic data on the health of existing investments and for the decision to make an investment in the first place. Shareholders therefore need to be able to rely on the accuracy and independence of published accounts. That is why public companies are required to have their accounts audited by an independent professional firm. Generally speaking public faith in the audit has diminished over the years not least because of the scale of some of the sums involved.

The question is whether this system works. Following a series of mergers, there are now only five firms – the Big Five – with the scale effectively to audit the largest global public companies. In recent years, all the auditing firms have progressively diversified their operations away from audit towards other revenue streams: management consulting, tax and legal advice, IT consultancy, corporate finance and other fields. Some of these fields, such as tax accounting and merger-related work interrelate closely with auditing – and so, we believe, should give rise to fewer concerns among shareholders (see below) – while others are clearly much more divorced from the audit.

Audit clients are an obvious target for these non-audit services; this breeds suspicions, particularly where non-audit fees are substantial in relation to audit fees, that auditing standards may be compromised. The fact that suspicions exist can lead to two very damaging things. First, it lowers the auditing profession in the public perception; and second, it undermines shareholder confidence in the figures they are presented with.

The scale of the questions raised by this diversification was shown by a recent study of the FTSE 100 companies by *Financial Director* magazine, published in January 2002. This found that the average audit fee paid by the UK's largest companies was £2.21 million. The average level of fees these companies pay to their auditors for non-audit work is over £6.5 million. This divergence reflects an earlier study of the FTSE 350 by Brand Finance, a brand valuation company. A couple of years ago the firm found that overall audit fees paid by these companies to the 'Big Five' were £300 million while at the same time non-audit fees paid by the companies to their auditors were worth nearly £500 million. These overall figures mask some extreme cases. There were a number of instances where the non-audit fees to a company's auditor do not just equal the audit fee, but are ten to twelve times as big. The survey uncovered two still more remarkable examples, where the figures were 47 and 78 times. It is not surprising that perceptions exist of substantial conflicts of interest. Audit firms will have to work very hard to overcome these.

These concerns about loss-leading on audit fees and cross-subsidy are widely acknowledged and have given rise to a slew of initiatives in recent years. The most substantial have come from the US's Securities and Exchange Commission (SEC) and from the European Commission in Brussels. After much debate, the SEC published its revised rules on auditor independence in November 2000 (see www.sec.gov/rules/final/33–7919.htm). The European Commission launched a consultation on the issue in December of the same year (it, and other documents on the topic, can be found at www.europa.eu.int/comm /internal_market/ en/company/audit/news/index.htm). There have also been moves by various professional bodies – such as work by the American Accounting Association, the Institute of Chartered Accountants in England and Wales, the International Federation of Accountants, and by professional bodies from countries as diverse as the Czech Republic and Brazil. Most recently in the UK, the issues were raised once again in the final report on the Maxwell affair.

The auditing firms themselves have come up with their own proposed solutions to the issue, largely as a result of the SEC's attentions. In three cases, these amount to the splitting of their businesses, with auditing and certain allied businesses remaining in one firm and management consulting and other services in one or more others. Ernst & Young has completed the sale of its consulting business to France's Cap Gemini and KPMG has spun off KPMG Consulting with a Nasdaq listing. PricewaterhouseCoopers is also taking steps along this route, though its initial planned sale to Hewlett Packard was abandoned. Arthur Andersen's split from Andersen Consulting (now Accenture) was a particularly public and messy affair. However, Arthur Andersen (now just Andersen) has stated its intention to keep its remaining consulting capacity in-house, as has rival Deloitte & Touche.

While Hermes agrees that the issue of audit independence is fundamental, we are not sure that the current moves and proposals offer the best solutions to the existing problem. Hermes does not agree that audit firms should be barred from giving other advice. For example, the close links between tax and accounting issues mean that it is often wasteful for companies to seek tax advice from a firm other than the auditors. The same argument applies in a number of areas. We are not keen to encourage financial waste for the sake of purely cosmetic effects on apparent independence. In addition, such moves add to one of the risks of the auditor independence problem, because pure audit firms seem likely to be far less attractive to clever young staff than more generalist firms which offer greater scope for career and personal development.

Rather, Hermes believes that the duty to ensure that accounts showing a true and fair view are prepared with the necessary detail and rigour falls squarely on companies themselves and in particular on the independent non-executive directors on their audit committees. They have a duty to oversee the accounts process and to ensure that the auditors are not perceived to lack full independence. That is why Hermes has in recent years become more forthright in its discussions with companies whose audit committees continue to include executives. While executive directors can provide useful input and comment to the committee, they should certainly not be members. The independent non-executive members of the committee should have scope to build trust with the auditors directly and so ensure that any threats to a full, independent and detailed audit are discussed in full. We acknowledge the work that the Blue Ribbon Committee in the US has done on the financial abilities of audit committee members (see www.nasd.com/docs/textapp.pdf), and believe that UK audit committees should live up to similar standards.

We believe that as part of their oversight role, the audit committee should assess any major non-audit contracts with their company's auditors, and have the power to veto them. The committee should assure itself that any awards of substantial non-audit contracts are made on a competitive basis. The disclosure of non-audit fees should also be broken down more effectively in the notes to the accounts, particularly where there are substantial fees paid for services not closely related to auditing accounts, tax or regulatory reporting. Halifax Group plc is one UK company whose annual report disclosures have revealed a policy along the lines which Hermes is recommending.

There is one other possible way out of the auditor independence problem which we at Hermes have been discussing. That is the forced rotation of auditors, after say five years. Already, audit firms rotate the staff assigned to a particular audit to ensure there are fresh eyes which may spot a problem and to ensure that the audit partner maintains a distance from the company under review. Requiring there to be a change of audit firm takes this a whole stage further. The regular need to tender for the work might lead to an increase in the fees for audits, but that in itself may not be a bad thing. The fees would begin more accurately to reflect the costs of the skilled staff needed, the profession would rise in public estimation and be a more attractive career. Also, knowing that the fresh eyes of a new auditor will be checking your work might spur the current auditors to be even more thorough. Most importantly, investors and prospective investors would receive information they were more confident in relying on. If this raised the cost of the annual audit, that ought to be a price which investors would be happy to pay. Financial director calculates the average FTSE 100 audit fee per £1 million of turnover is £466. Even if some increase on this current level was necessary, it might well be a price worth paying for enhancing the confidence that investors have in the audited accounts.

# Auditor Independence – A Global Best Practice Outline From Institutional Investors B6.12

The attached is a document aimed at promoting and ensuring auditor independence that has been developed by members of the Global Institutional Governance Network (GIGN), an informal international group of investment institutions which seek to promote good corporate governance at those companies in which they invest.

The document is intended as a minimum best practice standard. Some GIGN members are keen to establish higher standards in their home jurisdictions, but are content to set this as the minimum level internationally.

The following members of the GIGN have agreed to back the document publicly:

ABP, the Netherlands

Alecta Investment Management, Sweden

California Public Employees' Retirement System (CalPERS), US

Hermes Investment Management Ltd, UK

Morley Fund Management, UK

Ontario Teachers' Pension Plan, Canada

PGGM, the Netherlands

SPF Beheer, the Netherlands

Standard Life Investment Management, UK

TIAA-Cref, US

We hope that the companies in which we invest on our own behalf or for clients will regard this as a useful contribution to the debate, and as helpful in laying out the expectations of their major international investors.

## Auditor Independence – A Global Best Practice Outline From Institutional Investors

We, as large institutional investors, regard the independence of auditors, both in reality and perception, as of paramount importance to maintaining both the confidence of shareholders, who rely on audited financial statements, and the stability of global financial markets.

In this regard, we expect the corporations in whose securities we invest, or might invest, to give careful consideration to the following guidelines.

- Corporations should have effective audit committees, which are genuinely independent of both management and auditors. Such committees should:

  o annually conduct a meaningful evaluation of the audit services and the relationship between the auditor and the corporation's directors and officers.

  o ensure they establish and maintain independent channels of communication with the auditors, including other members of the audit team in addition to the engagement partner when appropriate.

  o have a clear policy, supported by effective processes, to ensure the provision of non-audit services by the auditor and its affiliates does not affect the auditors' independence, perceived or real.

  o annually consider the re-appointment of the auditors, and make an appropriate recommendation to the Board and or to the shareholders as appropriate.

  o consider the benefits of seeking tenders for the audit at regular and appropriate intervals. In evaluating such tenders we expect audit committees to pay particular regard to the quality of the audit and not just its cost.

  o have access to independent sources of advice, including but not limited to technical accounting advice. This advice should be sought and obtained when the audit committee deems it necessary.

  o approve employment policies designed to prevent conflicts of interest arising from the interchange of personnel between the audit team and corporation's audit related staff.

- Corporations should, subject to constraints of commercial confidentiality, disclose:

  o the nature and quantum of audit and non-audit services provided by the auditor, analysed in sufficient detail to enable shareholders to make an informed decision in respect of the resolution to re-elect the auditors.

○   a summary of the audit committee's charter

○   a commentary on the audit committee's composition and activities, up to and including the date of the audit report. This could include

☐   the number of meetings held;

☐   the factors that influenced the balance of the committee and the selection of its members;

☐   a summary of the process used to control the provision of non-audit services by the auditor and its affiliates.

• Corporations should promptly inform investors when there has been a change of auditors, and explain why the change was made.

• Corporations should have processes designed to ensure the competence of their audit committee and its members and when appropriate, they should provide independent training to ensure that competence is maintained.

• When appointing new auditors, regard should be had to any conflicts of interest arising from pre-existing relationships between the corporation and the proposed new firm of auditors.

At our discretion, we will use best endeavours to communicate to corporations when we have concerns about the independence of the auditors. We may reinforce our concerns, especially if such concerns have not been addressed to our satisfaction.

**Notes**
1.   The Combined Code: Requirements Of Auditors Under The Listing Rules Of The London Stock Exchange, (November 1999), Bulletin 1999/5 of The Auditing Practices Board, ISBN 1–85355–055–8. [Accountancy Books, PO Box 21375, London, WC1N 1QP. Tel: +44 (0)20 7920 8991. Fax: +44 (0)20 7920 8992. E-mail: abgbooks@icaew.co.uk; www.accountancybooks.co.uk.
2.   The Smith guidance suggests means of applying this part of the Code.

# Voting Policies

## Responsible voting – a joint ABI/NAPF statement                          B7.1

We reproduce here the joint statement by the Association of British Insurers and the National Association of Pension Funds dated 19 July 1999. Enquiries to should be made to (ABI) Michael McKersie (020 7216 7659) or (NAPF) David Gould (020 7808 1300).

Note that ABI/NAPF criteria for independence are given at the end of this statement. Readers may also wish to refer to the Combined Code – IVIS monitoring checklist (**B7.3**), and to the section entitled 'Criteria for defining independence' (**B10.54**).

### 1. Introduction

1.1   The Hampel Committee's Report on Corporate Governance confirms the principle that boards are accountable to shareholders of companies. Share ownership also gives rise to governance responsibilities which have, for many years, been acknowledged by a large number of institutional shareholders. In addition, institutional investors have an overriding fiduciary responsibility to those on whose behalf they are investing.

1.2   The ABI and the NAPF fully support the principles of good governance recommended by the Hampel Committee, which in many respects build on those evolved by the earlier Cadbury Committee. This joint statement responds to Hampel's proposal that 'the ABI and the NAPF should examine the problem caused by the existence of different and incompatible shareholder voting guidelines' (Hampel 5.8). The ABI and the NAPF recognise that responsible shareholders may wish to brief boards of directors on their particular expectations but recommend that, when voting policies are introduced, or such policies are reviewed, due account is taken of the guidance below.

### 2. The need for joint guidance

2.1   Between them, ABI and NAPF members own or manage shareholdings representing by value more than half the UK stock market. Additionally, overseas institutional shareholders are increasingly investing in the UK and are seeking guidance on UK corporate governance practices. For UK investors, corporate governance is seen as a core issue and many recognise that a joint authoritative exposition of investor views could be helpful.

## 3.   Why voting is important

3.1   Shareholders' ability to influence management depends to a considerable degree on the proportion of the votes which they can exercise and the use they make of these votes. Indeed, voting rights and the exercise thereof, in pursuit of responsible and effective corporate governance and the achievement of long-term shareholder value, may be recognised as an important and integral part of the investment management function. A considerable number of institutional investors have made an active and considered voting policy a priority and this is reflected in their creditable voting record in recent years.

3.2   The right to vote is, as the Hampel Report identifies, an asset and institutional investors owe it to their clients to make considered use of it. The responsibility for voting is also one which, increasingly, ultimate beneficiaries are expecting to see fulfilled. Voting, though, is only part of the dialogue that should exist between investors and boards of directors. The report of the Myners Working Group sets down the principles to be followed.

## 4.   The need for responsible voting

4.1   Responsible voting involves the application of informed decisions reached within the framework of a considered corporate governance policy. The ABI has long-established guidelines on a range of shareholder issues and ABI members will, in the main, reflect these in the application of their voting policies. The NAPF also strongly encourages its members to vote responsibly, and whenever reasonably possible. The ABI and the NAPF believe that the requirements of the Combined Code should become a starting point for these policies.

4.2   A simple 'box-ticking' approach to corporate governance, by contrast, does not lead to considered and responsible voting. The Hampel Report also recognised the strong arguments against making voting compulsory since this would be unlikely to improve overall standards of corporate governance.

4.3   It is important that institutional shareholders support boards by a positive use of their voting rights unless they have good reasons for doing otherwise. Where a board has received steady support over a period of time, it should become a matter of concern to the board if that support is not forthcoming on a particular matter.

4.4   Where an institutional investor would judge it appropriate to vote against a proposal which it considers undesirable, it is important that, wherever possible, representations are made in time for the problem to be considered and for consultation to take place with a view to achieving a satisfactory solution.

4.5   The ABI and the NAPF liase closely with their members through their respective voting services to provide relevant information about resolutions and related corporate governance issues. These services are now being widely used within the investment community as investors increasingly realise that considered advice is needed to secure responsible voting decisions.

**5. Composition of the board**

5.1 The composition, balance and effectiveness of a company's board must be a matter of legitimate concern to shareholders. They have the opportunity to confirm all appointments to the board and to re-elect directors as, routinely, they retire by rotation. Shareholders will be particularly concerned to ensure the appointment of a core of non-executives of sufficient number and of appropriate calibre, experience and independence and to identify where there may be undue concentrations of decision-making power not formally constrained by checks and balances appropriate to the particular company. The ABI's and the NAPF's voting services have an agreed definition of independence (see Appendix 1).

5.2 Institutional shareholders fully support the appointment of audit, remuneration and nomination committees, and the value of these committees and the importance of the role played generally by non-executive directors are increasingly widely recognised.

**6. Emoluments of directors and senior managers**

6.1 Institutional shareholders support the key recommendations of the study group under the chairmanship of Sir Richard Greenbury and the framework this has provided for shareholders to vote on share-based long-term incentive schemes, which involve either dilution or the commitment of shareholders' equity.

6.2 Overall remuneration strategy as it affects executive directors and other senior executives, including the proportions of fixed and performance-related variable components of pay, should be dealt with by a remuneration committee which, in accordance with the Greenbury and Hampel recommendations, should be composed wholly of non-executive directors. It is essential that shareholders are, through the annual report on remuneration, informed clearly and concisely of the principles upon which directors' emoluments are determined, the details of performance-linked contracts and the potential for compensation on premature termination of contract.

6.3 It is considered essential that challenging performance criteria should govern the vesting of awards or the exercise of options under any form of long term share-based incentive scheme. Investors will expect these criteria to demonstrate the achievement of a level of performance or rate of growth in a defined financial measure which is demanding in the context of the prospects for the company and the wider economic environment in which it operates.

6.4 Remuneration committees may propose performance criteria requiring, as the primary focus, outperformance on the chosen financial measure (or total shareholder return where this is supported by underlying financial performance) of the mean or median achieved within a defined peer group. Where consideration is given to devising other types of performance criteria these will need to be fully explained, demonstrated to be robust and demanding, and linked clearly to the achievement of enhanced shareholder value.

6.5 When considering remuneration policies, the ABI and NAPF voting services have regard to the above considerations and seek to assess the extent to which the stated aims are relevant and likely to be achieved. The ABI has detailed guidance on a number of aspects of remuneration policy, including share schemes and incentive elements of pay, with which the NAPF is in broad agreement. Both associations welcome the opportunity to discuss remuneration policies at an early stage.

6.6 While directors' service contracts are available for inspection in all instances, shareholders do not generally have the opportunity to vote on these. There has been a clear trend towards shorter length contracts. However, a particular area of concern is in circumstances of early termination, especially where the duration of the contract is in excess of one year, leading either to a perception of payment for failure, or concern where the individual commences new employment, often shortly after receiving a very substantial compensation payment. There are a number of ways of addressing the problem of early termination. One which deserves careful consideration is to phase compensation payments over the length of the notice period, with these payments ceasing when the individual concerned commences alternative employment.

## 7. Takeover bids

7.1 The greatest potential for tension between management and shareholders arises when a company becomes the object of a takeover bid which is launched without prior agreement of the incumbent board. However, where a company has kept its shareholders informed of its long-term plans, confidence and understanding will have developed between management and shareholders, making it less likely that a contested bid will succeed. Where shareholders understand the long-term objectives of management, they are more likely to support the incumbent board in its resistance to an unwelcome bid.

## 8. Conclusion

8.1 The overall objective of ABI and NAPF members is to achieve, on behalf of those for whom they act, a competitive return on the funds invested. The exercise of their voting policy, in respect of the range of matters on which shareholder decisions are sought, will be in support of the proper management of companies and directed towards the enhancement of long-term shareholder value and the wider economic benefits which this should also engender.

8.2 Corporate governance practices, both in the UK and overseas, are evolving rapidly and it is likely that the ABI and the NAPF will continue to develop further guidance as necessary.

# Directors' independence B7.2

The issue of a non-executive director's independence has been highlighted by the Hampel Committee and a company's viewpoint on an individual's status is likely to be challenged from time to time. The ABI and the NAPF suggest the criteria set out below as the minimum likely acceptable to institutional investors. This is not, though, necessarily an exhaustive list of factors in the nature of significant financial or personal ties to a company or its management, the existence of which may lead to a perception of lack of genuine independence on the part of the non-executive director concerned.

An individual director's integrity is highly relevant and it is understood that the level of a director's independence can vary, depending on the particular issue under discussion. In assessing the independence of a non-executive director, the assumption is that the individual is independent unless, in relation to the company, the director:

- was formerly an executive;

- is, or has been paid by the company in any capacity other than as a non-executive director;

- represents a trading partner or is connected to a company or partnership (or was prior to retirement) which does business with the company;

- has been a non-executive director for nine years – ie three three-year terms;

- is closely related to an executive director;

- has been awarded share options, performance-related pay or is a member of the company's pension fund;

- represents a controlling or significant shareholder;

- is a new appointee selected other than by a formal process;

- has cross-directorships with any executive director;

- is deemed by the company, for whatever reasons, not to be independent.

# Combined Code – IVIS monitoring checklist B7.3

The Association of British Insurers runs The Institutional Voting Information Service. Further particulars can be found on www.ivis.computasoft.com. Here we reproduce the IVIS checklist for monitoring company compliance with the Combined Code. The checklist can be compared with the voting template given at **B7.4 NAPF's voting policy**. The checklist ends with the criteria for assessing the independence of non-executive directors.

# Introduction

The following is a copy of the corporate governance checklist which forms the basis for the IVIS Corporate Governance Report. At the time of going to print, this checklist had not been updated for the 2003 Combined Code.

Detailed analysis is provided in the Notes after each subsection. See the 'Sample Report' which can be accessed from the homepage of the website (www.ivis.computasoft.com) for a live example.

# XYZ plc

## Compliance with the Combined Code

**Compliance statements (Rule 12.43A Listing Rules)**

1      Is there a narrative statement which adequately explains how the Company has applied the Principles of the Code?

Is there *any* statement of how the company has applied the Principles of the Code?

2      Has the company made a statement of full          Note 1
compliance with Section 1 of the Code?

Has the company made a statement of *limited* compliance with Section 1 of the Code, [which includes the approved transitional arrangements for reporting own internal controls?] (The transitional period has now passed, so this no longer applies.)

**Note 1 – Combined Code compliance**

Further details of the compliance statement made by the company.

*Code requirements*

*Board composition and balance*

3(a)   Have the chairman, chief executive and senior independent NED been identified?

Has a senior Independent director been nominated?

(b)    Are these three separate people?

Are the roles of chairman/chief executive separated?

Has the decision to combine been explained in the report and accounts?

(c)   Is the senior independent director independent?

4     Do NEDs comprise at least one-third of the Board?

5     Are a majority of NEDs independent?                    Note 2

6     Is there a nominations committee?

Are a majority of its members NEDs?

Is its chairman either the chairman of the board
or a NED?

No nominations committee because company
regard board as small?

7(a)  Is there a statement that all directors are subject
to re-election every three years?

(b)   Are there sufficient biographical details of
directors submitted for election?

**Note 2 – Independence of non-executive directors**

See Appendix 1 for details of criteria used to help assess independence of non-
executives.

*Remuneration packages and procedures*

8(a)  Is the remuneration committee made up entirely
of NEDs?

(b)   Are the NEDs on the committee regarded as
independent?

9     Have the performance targets attached to the
vesting of long-term incentives been disclosed?      Note 3

10    Is only basic salary pensionable?

11    Are the following details of all directors' service
contracts disclosed:

(a)   details of notice periods in excess of twelve
months; and                                          Note 4

(b)   a stated objective that notice periods will be
reduced to one year or less.

8(a)  Is the remuneration committee made up entirely
of NEDs?

(b)   Are the NEDs on the committee regarded as
independent?

9     Have the performance targets attached to the
vesting of long-term incentives been disclosed?      Note 3

10    Is only basic salary pensionable?

11    Are the following details of all directors' service
contracts disclosed:

(a)    details of notice periods in excess of twelve
months; and                                                    Note 4

(b)    a stated objective that notice periods will be
reduced to one year or less.

## Note 3 – Long-term incentive arrangements

Details are given of all long-term incentives, including size of conditional
awards, and performance criteria.

## Note 4 – Directors' service contracts

Details of all contracts in excess of one year.

*Accountability and audit*

12    Have the directors stated that they have
reviewed the system of internal controls?

Have the directors stated that they have
reviewed the system of internal financial controls?

Does the company have an internal audit
function?

Has the company reviewed the need for an
internal audit function?

13    Is there an audit committee with at least three
members confined to NEDs?

Are the majority of NEDs on the committee
independent?

Is there an audit committee of two members?

If so, is it confined to independent NEDs?

14    Are audit fees equal to or greater than non
audit fees?

*Supplementary questions*

## Board composition

> *Executives*
>
> *Independent NEDs*
>
> *Non-independent NEDs*

**Environmental report:**

> *see page ...*

**Year 2000 report:**

> *see page ...*

**Auditors:**

*Audit fees: (£)*     Current year

            Last year

*Non-audit fees: (£)*   Current year

            Last year

**CE basic salary per annum (£):**


# Appendix 1

## Independence of NEDs

In assessing the independence of a non-executive director we try to be as objective as we can and, in particular we start with the assumption that he/she is independent unless, in relation to the company:

- was formerly as executive;

- represents a trading partner or is connected to a company or partnership (or was prior to his/her retirement) which does business with the company;

- is, or has been, paid by the company in any capacity other than as a NED;

- new appointees selected other than by a formal process;

- has been a NED for nine years – i.e. we allow three three-year terms;

- is closely related to an executive director;

- has been awarded share option, performance related pay or is a member of the company's pension fund;

- represents a controlling or significant shareholder;

- has cross directorships with any executive director; or

- the company, for whatever reason, says he/she is not independent.

There may be other circumstances which lead us to doubt the independence of a non-executive director.

However, we will outline our reasons for doubting independence in every case where it occurs in the IVIS report.

# NAPF's voting policy **B7.4**

We reproduce here *verbatim* NAPF's published voting policy on general meetings, which ends with their template, or checklist for assessing companies' governance. This Voting Template can be compared with the checklist in **B7.3** COMBINED CODE – IVIS MONITORING CHECKLIST. The independence criteria given here correspond to those given in **B7.1** RESPONSIBLE VOTING – A JOINT ABI – NAPF STATEMENT and **B7.3** COMBINED CODE – IVIS MONITORING CHECKLIST, but need slight revision to bring into line with Provision A.3.1 of the 2003 Combined Code (see PART A).

# NAPF voting issues service – voting policy on general meeting resolutions

## Introduction

In July 1999 a joint ABI/NAPF statement, Responsible Voting, was issued in response to the Hampel Report's proposal that 'the ABI and the NAPF should examine the problem caused by the existence of different and incompatible shareholder voting guidelines' (Hampel 5.8). Copies of Responsible Voting are available from either body, on request.[1]

Also in July 1999, the Report of the Committee of Inquiry into UK Vote Execution, chaired by Yve Newbold, was published. One of the recommendations was that the NAPF Investment Committee should develop 'a voting "template" to encourage considered voting'.

The template is an important element in the drive towards UK electronic vote execution as it is part of the process enabling subscribers to the Voting Issues Service (VIS) to access electronic proxy cards with supporting analysis. When VIS subscribers access the system[2], the electronic proxy card will normally have been provisionally completed on the basis of the VIS voting template. VIS reports issued by post or accessed *via* the VIS website will also reflect that template.

VIS reports, incorporating voting recommendations, are compiled following extensive consultation with companies. This is known as the 'engagement partnership'. This engagement between companies and VIS provides subscribers with analysis on Combined Code compliance, environmental engagement and social responsibility issues. The partnership relies for its success on co-operation between companies and investors. It is in such a context that the following voting template has been devised. Further information about the engagement partnership is available from VIS[3].

## Summary of template

The template will support board resolutions and strategy unless there are very good reasons for doing otherwise. In seeking to support incumbent management, VIS will consider carefully how the board concerned is meeting the expectations of institutional investors.

If it appears to VIS that these are not being fully met, VIS will seek to discuss with the company concerned any special circumstances that would justify its viewpoint. If VIS can establish that there are reasonable grounds for the company's position, the template will support the relevant resolution(s). If VIS remains dissatisfied, the template will indicate that subscribers should either abstain or vote against the relevant resolution(s). This will also apply if, having found shortcomings, VIS then finds it impossible to engage with the company[4].

As company law currently stands, an abstention indicated on a proxy card need not be registered as a vote. A handful of companies do provide an abstention box on proxy cards and the NAPF supports this practice. The NAPF is also pressing the DTI, as part of the Review of Company Law, to ensure that a registered abstention is recognised as a vote, which would indicate to incumbent management shareholder concern regarding a particular resolution(s). As with any vote against management, institutional shareholders should ensure that their concerns are fully explained to the company.

Should VIS believe that implementation of a resolution would seriously diminish shareholder value or otherwise not be in the interests of existing shareholders, VIS will seek to discuss with the company the issues underlying the board's position with the aim of understanding fully the reasons behind the stance. The template would indicate a vote against a board resolution, once informal discussions had taken place, where management remained unwilling to change its proposals within an agreed timescale.

## Investor expertise

Recommendations made on the template will be based primarily on the analysis of relevant governance issues by VIS and voting decisions can be changed by subscribers as they wish.

**Notes on VIS voting template relating to common resolutions**

**1.   Company's report and accounts**

Whilst the Companies Act requires only that accounts are 'laid before' the annual general meeting (AGM) and the Combined Code (D.2.2) (**A1 THE 2003 COMBINED CODE**) requires that companies 'should in particular propose a resolution … relating' to them, the decision taken routinely by companies to seek the adoption of their report and accounts by shareholders at the AGM is strongly supported.

*Template recommendation: support the adoption of the report and accounts in normal circumstances.*

**2.   Final dividends**

Only the payment of a final dividend requires shareholder approval and some boards of directors choose to announce and pay a series of interim dividends instead. Shareholders are most usually concerned where there is a lack of dividends; this, of course, is not a voting issue.

*Template recommendation: support, in normal circumstances.*

**3. Directors**

Appointing directors to sustain an effective board is a key element in delivering shareholder value and arguably the most important routine responsibility placed upon a company's shareholders.

VIS will check whether boards have established and developed procedures capable of securing compliance with best practice guidance as set down in the Combined Code. In seeking to support selected candidates for board appointments, VIS will compare a candidate's background and experience against existing board composition and the suitability of its non-executive directors (NED), in particular, to fulfil their expected committee responsibilities. VIS will also check that the individual(s) has been selected by a formal, recognised process such as a nominations committee and has been offered a contract consistent with good practice. VIS would be most reluctant to recommend support for the appointment of an individual combining the roles of chairman and chief executive.

*Template recommendation: support the appointment of executive directors, dependent upon the foregoing.*

## Independent directors

The question of a NED's independence has become an issue in recent years. The VIS position on this, agreed with the ABI, is set out below and forms part of Responsible Voting.

The issue of a director's independence has been highlighted by Hampel and a company's viewpoint on this is likely to be challenged from time to time. VIS suggests that the following criteria may be the minimum acceptable to some institutional investors.

'An individual director's integrity is highly relevant and the NAPF understands that the level of a director's independence can vary depending on the particular issue under discussion.

In assessing the independence of a NED the assumption is that the individual is independent unless, in relation to the Company, the director:

- was formerly an executive

- is, or has been, paid by the company in any capacity other than as a NED

- represents a trading partner or is connected to a company or partnership (or was prior to retirement) which does business with the company

- has been a NED for nine years – i.e., three 3-year terms
- is closely related to an executive director
- has been awarded share options or performance-related pay or is a member of the company's pension fund
- represents a controlling or significant corporate shareholder
- is a new appointee selected other than by a formal process
- has cross-directorships with any executive director
- for whatever reasons, is said by the company not to be independent'

There may be other circumstances which could cast doubt on the independence of a NED.

Template recommendations will reflect both the degree of independence shown by a NED proposed for appointment or re-appointment and the strength of independence – or lack of it – amongst non-executive board members collectively.

*Template recommendation: normally support the appointment of properly selected non-executive directors. A recommendation would normally be made to abstain on the initial appointment or re-election of non-executive directors where the individual(s) is known to have board committee responsibilities as an independent and fails on one or more of the above criteria.*

#### 4. Age of directors

The voting template has adopted the advice of the Institutional Shareholders' Committee that reasons should be offered as to why directors aged over 70 should be re-appointed to the board.[5]

*Template recommendation: abstain where adequate reasons are not provided.*

#### 5. Directors' remuneration

### Remuneration policy

Where shareholder approval is sought for this, VIS will assess whether the policy meets good practice as set down in the Combined Code.

*Template recommendation: support remuneration policies that meet Combined Code requirements.*

### Incentive reward

The likely level of shareholder support for executive share scheme proposals and for long-term incentive plans could depend upon many factors but, in the case of institutional investors, these are likely to include the following:

- how well the proposals are explained to shareholders and relate to the development of overall corporate strategy and the delivery of shareholder return; and

- the extent to which performance targets are judged to be relevant and challenging.

Executive incentive arrangements, to the extent that they are subject to shareholder approval, will be assessed on their merits by VIS in conjunction with a specialised remuneration consultancy. Meis Ltd is currently retained by VIS for this purpose.

*Template recommendation: support proposals for incentive remuneration that are believed by VIS to operate in the best long-term interests of shareholders and are consistent with the principles set down in relevant ABI guidelines.*

## 6. All-employee share schemes

These schemes are broadly supported. Any proposals will be assessed, particularly those affecting the dilution of existing shareholdings and the grant of options at a discount to market price.

*Template recommendation: support.*

## 7. Appointment, re-appointment and remuneration of auditors

Independent audit is a cornerstone of good governance and a safeguard for the shareholder. A change of auditor, usually by tender process, need not necessarily be regarded, therefore, as a governance concern. The practice amongst audit firms of earning very substantial consultancy fees from amongst audit clients has led to some questions concerning the independence and rigour of the audit process itself.

VIS will report on the reasons underlying the payment to the audit firm of substantial fees for non-audit work. Normally, these relate to significant business developments and are unlikely to compromise the audit process itself.

*Template recommendation: support the (re-)appointment of the proposed auditor and delegate the determination of the auditor's remuneration to the directors, provided VIS is satisfied as to the independence of the audit process.*

## 8. Memorandum and articles of association

As a company's memorandum and articles protect the interests of shareholders, any proposed changes should be fully explained and clearly drafted. Where significant, non-routine changes are proposed, these should not be 'bundled' into a single resolution.

*Template recommendation: support, provided that any changes will not detract from shareholder value or significantly reduce shareholder rights.*

## 9. Scrip dividends

*Template recommendation: support, provided shareholders receive a cash dividend unless they opt for the scrip alternative.*

## 10. Share buy-backs

*Template recommendation: support, provided the requirements of the Listing Rules and relevant shareholder guidance are met.*

## 11. Authority to issue shares

*Template recommendation: support the disapplication of pre-emption rights for new issues of shares within current guidance from the Pre-emption Group.*

## 12. Political donations

Following the recommendations of the Neill Committee on the Funding of Political Parties in the United Kingdom, companies wishing to make political donations may be more likely to seek shareholder approval for the policy on a regular basis. Companies will be expected to justify any proposals.

*Template recommendation: assess on merits.*

## 13. Non-routine resolutions

*Template recommendation: assess on merits.*

## 14. Extraordinary general meetings

Whilst EGMs are held for a variety of reasons, such as changes to memorandum and articles, they are frequently called to seek shareholder approval of investment issues such as takeovers, mergers or capital reorganisations. In such circumstances, investment professionals will make voting recommendations and decisions based on their investment expertise.

*Template recommendation: voting recommendations will not be made on investment issues but VIS will alert subscribers to such non-governance matters.*

# NAPF voting issues service B7.5

## Example of typical voting template

| | Nature of resolution | For | Against | Abstain | Case by case | Alert only |
|---|---|---|---|---|---|---|
| 1 | **Adoption of report and accounts** | ✓ | | | | |
| 2 | **Final dividend approval** | ✓ | | | | |
| 3 | **(a) Appointment of new directors** | | | | | |
| | Combined Chairman/CEO | | ✓ | | | |
| | Executive director: | | | | | |
| | ● 3-year contract | | ✓ | | | |
| | ● 2-year contract | | ✓ | | | |
| | ● 2-year contract reducing | ✓ | | | | |
| | ● 1-year contract[6] | ✓ | | | | |
| | Independent non-executive director | ✓ | | | | |
| | Non-independent[7] | | | ✓ | | |
| | Non-independent[8] | | | | ✓ | |
| | **(b) Reappointment of directors** | | | | | |
| | Combined Chairman/CEO | | | | ✓ | |

| | Nature of resolution | For | Against | Abstain | Case by case | Alert only |
|---|---|---|---|---|---|---|
| | Executive director: | | | | | |
| | ● 3-year contract | | √ | | | |
| | ● 2-year contract (recommenda-tion might change where contract provides for longer termination period in the event of change of control) | | | √ | | |
| | ● 1-year contract (recommenda-tion might change where contract provides for longer termination period in the event of change of control) | √ | | | | |
| | Independent non-executive director | √ | | | | |
| | Non-independent[7] | | | √ | | |
| | Non-independent[8] | | | | √ | |
| 4 | **(Re)appoint-ment of directors aged over 70** | | | | | |
| | ● Valid reasons | √ | | | | |
| | ● Invalid reasons or no reasons | | | √ | | |

| | Nature of resolution | For | Against | Abstain | Case by case | Alert only |
|---|---|---|---|---|---|---|
| 5 | **Directors' remuneration** | | | | | |
| | (a) Remuneration policy approval | | | | | |
| | • Policy consistent with good practice | √ | | | | |
| | • Policy not consistent with good practice | | √ | | | |
| | **(b) Incentive reward** | | | | | |
| | • Proposals consistent with good practice | √ | | | | |
| | • Proposals not consistent with good practice | | √ | | | |
| 6 | **All-employee share schemes** | √ | | | | |
| 7 | **(Re)appoint-ment of 'independent' auditors etc.** | √ | | | | |
| 8 | **Changes to company's memorandum and articles** | | | | | |
| | • Shareholder value and rights protected | √ | | | | |
| | • Shareholder value and rights in question | | | | √ | |
| 9 | **Scrip dividends** | √ | | | | |

| | Nature of resolution | For | Against | Abstain | Case by case | Alert only |
|---|---|---|---|---|---|---|
| **10** | **Share buy-backs** | | | | | |
| | ● Listing Rules/ shareholder guidance met | √ | | | | |
| | ● Listing Rules/ shareholder guidance not met | | √ | | | |
| **11** | **Authority to issue shares** | | | | | |
| | ● Within pre-emption guidelines | √ | | | | |
| | ● Not within re-emption guidelines | | | | √ | |
| **12** | **Authority to make political donations** | | | | √ | |
| **13** | **Non-routine resolutions** | | | | √ | |
| **14** | **EGM 'investment' resolutions** | | | | | √ |

# The NAPF current policy position on corporate governance   B7.6

This was revised late 2001. Here it is reprinted *verbatim*. Some changes are suggested to bring this policy in line with the 2003 Combined Code (see PART A).

# NAPF – Towards better corporate governance

## Foreword

Since the National Association of Pension Funds (NAPF) published *Good Corporate Governance* in 1996, the debate on the role of institutional shareholders in UK quoted companies has progressed substantially. The incorporation of the Hampel Committee's recommendations into the Combined Code, which is appended to the Listing Rules, is one of a number of major developments. The range of issues on which shareholders may vote has increased. Indeed, the Government has taken a keen interest in corporate governance issues, looking to shareholders to play a more active part in ensuring that boards steer their companies forward to achieve long-term shareholder value. In line with this aim, it has urged institutional shareholders to make greater use of their rights to vote.

For its part, the NAPF has continued to develop its corporate governance service through the Voting Issues Service (VIS), which remains the leading provider of its kind for pension funds. The VIS has sought to assist pension schemes to make more effective use of their voting rights by providing timely information of forthcoming resolutions. It has extended its range of information to cover background on directors' remuneration and on the environmental record of companies.

This document, *Towards better corporate governance*, sets out the current NAPF policy positions on a wide range of corporate governance issues, many of which are fully in step with the Principles set out in the Combined Code. On a number of issues, however, the NAPF has gone further by setting out more details of the process and, in some cases, has tackled issues which currently lie outside the scope of the Combined Code.

The emergence of this comprehensive policy document, which both updates the NAPF's policy positions and is in line with modern thinking on the need for voting rights to be exercised, provides the platform for the VIS to move forward and make recommendations as to how their subscribers should vote. To further assist VIS subscribers, the Service will offer templates, based on the NAPF policy, enabling them to vote with greater frequency and ease.

The NAPF's Investment Committee will be keeping these policy positions under regular review, notifying NAPF Members and VIS subscribers as and when changes occur.

It is our ardent hope that the introduction of clear policy positions, agreed by the NAPF, together with templates to assist voting, will go a long way towards helping pension funds achieve a higher level of active participation in the governance of UK companies, to their and the whole economy's benefit.

Alan Rubenstein Chairman, NAPF Investment Committee

## Introduction

This document sets out the NAPF's corporate governance policy for UK listed companies. Good corporate governance is not just for boards of directors. It is essential to ensure a close relationship between companies and investors.

Shareholders have a vital role to play in encouraging a higher level of corporate performance. Pension funds in particular are long-term investors, with significant exposure to and interest in the well being of many of the companies which drive the UK economy forward.

Boards of directors are subject both to statutory obligations under the Companies Act and to the Combined Code appended to the Listing Rules. These require them to get approval for certain decisions. Following the recommendations of a number of committees of inquiry into corporate governance, the range of issues on which boards must seek shareholder approval has expanded. The NAPF, for its part, considers that there are further areas where companies have a responsibility to put matters before shareholders and these are also included in this document.

Whilst the policies set out in this document reflect the NAPF's current stance on corporate governance, the NAPF will keep them under regular review as law, codes and best practice evolve, and will provide its members with updated information on a timely basis. For example, this document already reflects the changes to the *Pensions Act 1995*, which from 3 July 2000 will require trustees to set out their voting policy in their Statements of Investment Principles. Looking ahead, the range of issues, and appropriate recommendations, may be widened further following the Review of Company Law, currently in progress.

There is a clear Government expectation that shareholders, particularly institutional investors, will exercise their corporate governance rights, including voting. The NAPF supports this stance and encourages pension funds, in their capacity as major investors in the UK economy, to make use of the power derived from those voting rights.

The policy statements, which follow in this document, are accompanied by references to their basic sources:

**Key to basic sources:**

| | |
|---|---|
| CA85 | *Companies Act 1985* (including *Table A*) as amended by *Companies Act 1989*. |
| PA95 | *Pensions Act 1995 s35* as amended by *The Occupational Pension Schemes (Investment) Regulations 1996*. |
| ISC | Institutional Shareholders' Committee – The Role and Duties of Directors 3.2(f)(1993). |
| Hampel | Committee on Corporate Governance, Final Report (1998) chaired by Sir Ronald Hampel. |
| CC | Combined Code (appended to Listing Requirements)(1998). |
| ABI | Association of British Insurers Share-based Incentive Schemes – Guideline Principles (1999). |
| NAPF | National Association of Pension Funds policy. |
| ABI/NAPF | Responsible Voting – a joint ABI/NAPF Statement (1999). |

*Please see the important disclaimer at the end of this document*

# NAPF corporate governance policy

## The board

| 1 | General | Basis of policy |
|---|---|---|
| | An effective board is essential to lead and control each listed company. | Combined Code A.1 |
| | One of the major duties of the board is to agree corporate strategy and, thus, the frequency of board meetings must be sufficient to ensure that the directors, including the non-executive directors, can direct that corporate strategy, as well as monitoring performance and risk. | NAPF |
| | Whilst boards should meet regularly, each must decide its frequency. | CC A.1.1 |
| | Where an 'executive committee', comprising both directors and senior management, meets regularly to implement board strategy, the board may be content to meet at relatively infrequent intervals provided that the board as a whole is satisfied that agreed strategy is being followed. | NAPF |

| | Basis of policy |
|---|---|
| The board should adopt a formal schedule of matters specifically reserved for board decisions. This should include major strategic concerns likely to impact on the direction of the company, setting strategic benchmarks and the assessment of management achievement against them. This would normally include, for example, decisions on acquisitions and mergers. | CC A.1.2 |
| All directors, particularly when first appointed to the board of a listed company, should receive appropriate training. | CC A.1.6 |

**2    Board balance**

| | |
|---|---|
| An effective board is essential to deliver shareholder value. | NAPF |
| The approval of the appointment of directors to the board is, arguably, the most important routine responsibility placed upon a company's shareholders. | NAPF |
| The board should be composed of both executive and non-executive directors (including independent non-executives) such that no individual or small group of individuals can dominate the board's decision-making. | CC A.3 |
| Non-executive directors should comprise not less than one-third of the board with a minimum of three. | CC A.3 |
| Non-executive directors have the capacity to look at the interests of the company as a whole over the longer term and should be capable, therefore, of exercising independent judgement with an ability to influence board decision-making. | NAPF.1 |

**3    Independent directors**

| | |
|---|---|
| Independent directors play an essential role by using their unfettered judgement on the issues of strategy, performance, resources, key appointments and standards of conduct. Such independent assessment of strategic direction is probably the greatest value to be derived from an independent non-executive director. | NAPF |
| The majority of non-executive directors should be independent of management and identified as such in the annual report. | CC A.3.2 |

|  | **Basis of policy** |
|---|---|
| Independence can be determined by the following criteria: | ABI/NAPF |

An individual director's integrity is highly relevant and the level of a director's independence can vary, depending on the particular issue under discussion. In assessing the independence of a non-executive director the assumption is that the individual is independent unless, in relation to the company, the director:

- was formerly an executive;

- is, or has been, paid by the company in any capacity other than as a non-executive director;

- represents a trading partner or is connected to a company or partnership (or was prior to retirement) which does business with the company;

- has been a non-executive director for nine years – i.e. three 3-year terms;

- is closely related to an executive director;

- has been awarded share options, performance-related pay or is a member of the company's pension fund;

- represents a controlling or significant shareholder;

- is a new appointee selected other than by a formal process;

- has cross-directorships with any executive director; or

- is deemed by the company, for whatever reason(s), not to be independent.

**4        Chairman and chief executive officer**

There are two discrete roles which must be performed by those leading a company. Firstly, the board requires a chairman to guide it and, secondly, a chief executive officer who will understand the business, formulate proposals on strategy for the board and implement its decisions. There should be a clear division of these responsibilities at the head of the company to ensure a balance of power and authority, such that no one individual has unfettered control.        CC A.2

| | | **Basis of policy** |
|---|---|---|
| | The different functions of chairman and chief executive officer must not be confused. Therefore, it is generally preferable for different people to perform the two functions. The Combined Code (A.2.1) allows one person to fulfil both roles, provided this is publicly justified. The NAPF rejects this as a valid option. | NAPF |
| **5** | **Supply of information** | |
| | The board requires appropriate and timely information sufficient to enable it to discharge its duties. It is the responsibility of company management to ensure that all directors are supplied with the information necessary to make informed judgements on matters affecting the company. | CC A.4/A.4.1 |
| **6** | **Dialogue with institutional shareholders** | |
| | Boards should maintain a dialogue with institutional shareholders based on a mutual understanding of objectives. | CC C.1 |
| **7** | **Appointments to the board** | |
| | There should be a formal and transparent procedure for the appointment of new directors to the board. | CC A.5 |
| | Boards should establish a sub-committee (normally called the nomination committee) to deal with director appointments. The nomination committee's role is to filter proposals and recommend candidates to the board. Final appointments are the responsibility of the whole board. Where boards are very small, say five or less, there is likely to be a case for the entire process to be undertaken by the board itself, dispensing with the need for a nomination committee. | CC A.5.1 |

## Directors

| **8** | **Directors' election and re-election** | |
|---|---|---|
| | All directors must be put forward for election by shareholders at the first AGM after their appointment. | CC A.6.2 |
| | All directors should be subject to re-election at intervals of no more than three years. | CC A.6.2 |
| | The names of directors submitted for election or re-election should be accompanied by sufficient biographical details to enable shareholders to take an informed decision on their election. | CC A.6.2 |

| | | Basis of policy |
|---|---|---|
| | Where the company identifies a non-executive director as independent, the independence test should be applied to those seeking re-election on each and every occasion. | NAPF |
| | The annual report should disclose the ages of all directors and, in the cases of those aged over 70 on the occasion when they stand for election or re-election, provide an explanation of why it is felt appropriate that such directors be retained. | ISC |
| **9** | **Directors' remuneration** | |
| | **(i)   Procedure on directors' remuneration** | |
| | Policy on executive remuneration should follow a formal and transparent procedure. | CC B.2 |
| | No director should be involved in deciding his or her own remuneration. | CC B.2 |
| | Each board should establish a remuneration committee. | CC B.2 |
| | The remuneration committee should consist solely of independent non-executive directors and be responsible for making recommendations to the board. | CC B.2.2 |
| | The remuneration committee requires a minimum of three independent non-executive directors. | NAPF |
| | Non-executive directors should be rewarded commensurate with their responsibilities. | NAPF |
| | A proportion of non-executive pay can be made in the form of shares, provided these are not leveraged options. | Hampel 4.8 |
| | Independent non-executive directors should not take "significant" holdings in the companies in which they are directors because this reduces their independence. | NAPF |
| | **(ii)   The level and make-up of remuneration** | |
| | Executive directors' remuneration should be related to the performance of the company. | CC B.1.2 |
| | Levels of remuneration should be sufficient to attract and retain the directors needed to run the company successfully, but companies should avoid paying more than is necessary for this purpose. | CC B.1.1 |

| | | Basis of policy |
|---|---|---|
| | The remuneration of each individual director, together with the components that form his/her pay package, should be tabulated and explained in a form that can be easily understood by shareholders. | CC B.3 |
| | Remuneration committees must set, and take responsibility for, reward levels. Guidance from institutional shareholders can only be general in nature and should be so regarded by companies. | CC B.1.2 |
| | It is unrealistic to expect institutional shareholders to have sufficient knowledge of the business to set specific performance hurdles for incentive reward.This is clearly a matter for the board itself. | NAPF |
| | An executive director's remuneration should be structured so that a proportion links reward to corporate and individual performance. | CC B.1.4 |
| | Remuneration committees should be sensitive to the wider scene, including pay and employment conditions elsewhere in the group, especially when determining annual salary increases. Performance-related elements of remuneration should form a significant proportion of the total remuneration package of executive directors and should be designed to align their interests with those of shareholders and to give those directors keen incentives to perform at the highest levels. The balance between the performance and salary-related elements will depend on the nature of the underlying business. | CC B.1.3<br><br>CC B.3.2<br><br>NAPF |
| | The important factor is the need for a balance that is relevant to the company's business development. The structure adopted can also give a clear message to the market. A high level of incentive-related pay with challenging performance hurdles indicates that a company believes it can significantly improve shareholder value. In the present climate of shareholder opinion, boards would be well advised to determine the most appropriate and challenging performance criteria for themselves. Boards must, therefore, explain and justify the proposed scheme to their shareholders. | |

|  |  | Basis of policy |
|---|---|---|
|  | Directors' and shareholders' interests should be aligned and the NAPF therefore supports grants of options to directors as part of their overall package. However, the NAPF will not agree to the re-pricing of share options due to the underperformance of the company share price. | NAPF |
|  | **(iii)   Service contracts and compensation** |  |
|  | Any rolling contract should not exceed one year. If, on first appointment, an initial longer period is deemed essential by the board, this would generally be acceptable provided that shareholders are given an explanation in the annual report. | CC B.1.7/8 |
|  | There should be no advance agreement for special compensation arrangements (including enhanced pension arrangements, deferred options etc.) for those cases where executive directors' contracts are terminated early. If a director's contract has to be terminated and an element of compensation is agreed, staged payments should be made to mitigate loss. These should cease on a subsequent new appointment. | NAPF |
|  | **(iv)   Remuneration disclosure** |  |
|  | The report of the remuneration committee should be submitted to shareholders each year for their approval. | NAPF |
|  | Long-term incentive schemes must be put to shareholders for approval. Performance hurdles should be set before incentive scheme grants are made. | CC B.3.4 |
|  | Remuneration committee reports should be relevant to corporate objectives, and communicated in a clear and transparent manner. | NAPF |

**Accountability and relationships**

| 10 | Constructive use of the annual general meeting |  |
|---|---|---|
|  | The results of all proxy votes should be published during or shortly after the AGM. This could be done most cost effectively as a matter of routine on the company website. | CC C.2.1 |
|  | Resolutions should cover separate issues and should not be 'bundled'. | CC C.2.2 |

| | | Basis of policy |
|---|---|---|
| | Notice of the AGM and related papers should be sent to shareholders at least 20 working days before the meeting. | CC C.2.4 |
| **11** | **Accountability and internal control** | |
| | Good quality accounts are essential if investors are to understand where the company is today and where it is going. The board should present a balanced and understandable assessment of the company's position and prospects. | CC D.1 |
| | The board should ensure that the management establishes and maintains a sound system of internal control to safeguard shareholders' investments and the company's assets. | CC D.2 |
| **12** | **Audit committee** | |
| | Each board should establish an audit committee, comprising a majority of non-executive directors. The audit committee should report to the board. | CC D.3.1 |
| | The audit committee is responsible for ensuring that management applies financial reporting and internal control Principles. The committee must maintain an appropriate relationship with the company's auditors. This will include reviewing the scope and results of the audit, its cost-effectiveness and the independence and objectivity of the auditors. | CC D.3.2 |
| **13** | **Auditors** | |
| | Any change of auditors, agreed by the board as part of a periodic planned review, or for any other reason, should be explained and justified to shareholders. | NAPF |
| | There should be full disclosure of any non-audit fees charged by a related company of the auditors in the annual report and accounts. | NAPF |
| **14** | **Internal control and risk management** | |
| | The NAPF has noted and, in principle, supports the proposals in 'Internal Control: Guidance for Directors on the Combined Code' formulated by a working party of the Institute of Chartered Accountants in England & Wales, chaired by Nigel Turnbull. The requirements have been incorporated into the Combined Code and companies must comply for accounting periods ending on or after 23 December 1999. However, transitional arrangements apply for the first year. | NAPF |

| | | Basis of policy |
|---|---|---|
| **15** | **Donations to UK political parties** | |
| | The NAPF would not normally support the policy of making UK political donations. However, companies wishing to make such donations should seek shareholder approval at general meetings. In-line with the Neill committee recommendations on *'the funding of political parties in the United Kingdom'*, such resolutions, once passed, should be voted on by shareholders at least every three years. | NAPF |
| **16** | **Institutional investors** | |
| | Institutional investors should engage in regular dialogue with investee companies. | |
| **17** | **Company's report and accounts** | |
| | A resolution to adopt the report and accounts must be presented at the AGM. | *Companies Act 1985 s 234/ s 241* |
| | | CC C.2.2 |
| **18** | **Memorandum and articles of association** | |
| | As a company's memorandum and articles protect the interests of shareholders, any proposed changes should be fully explained and clearly drafted. Significant, non-routine changes should not be 'bundled' into a single resolution. | NAPF CC C.2.2 |
| **19** | **Final dividends** | |
| | Where a final dividend is proposed, shareholder approval must be sought. | *Companies Act 1985* |
| | | Table A |

**Shares**

| | | |
|---|---|---|
| **20** | **All-employee share schemes and dilution limits** | |
| | **(i)   All-employee share schemes** | |
| | The NAPF supports all-employee share schemes because they serve to align the interests of both employees and companies. Any such schemes should be assessed by the investor, particularly those affecting the dilution of existing shareholdings and the grant of options at a discount to market price. | NAPF |

|  | | **Basis of policy** |
|---|---|---|
| **(ii)** | **Dilution limits** | |
| | Where the terms of any incentive scheme provide that entitlements may be satisfied through the issue of new shares then the rules of that scheme must provide that, when aggregated with awards under *all* of the company's other schemes, commitments to issue new shares must not exceed 10% of the issued ordinary share capital of the company (adjusted for scrip/bonus and rights issues) in any rolling 10 year period. Remuneration committees should ensure that appropriate policies regarding flow-rates exist in order to spread the potential creation of new shares more evenly over the life of relevant schemes. | ABI |
| | In addition, commitments to issue shares under discretionary or executive schemes, except to the extent that vesting will be dependent on the achievement of more stretching performance criteria, should not exceed 5% of the issued ordinary share capital of the company (adjusted for scrip/bonus and rights issues) in any rolling 10 year period. | |
| **21** | **Scrip dividends** | |
| | In accordance with company law, companies must secure shareholder approval to offer scrip dividend programmes. | *CA 1985 Table A* |
| | Shareholders should not be forced to accept a scrip dividend. Cash should always be offered as a choice. | NAPF |
| **22** | **Authority to issue shares** | |
| | In accordance with company law, companies must secure shareholder approval to be able to issue new shares. | *CA 1985 s 80* |
| | The NAPF supports the issue of shares provided, where there is a proposed disapplication of pre-emption rights, these are within the current guidance of the Pre-emption Group. | CA 1985 s 95 |
| **23** | **Authority to buy back shares** | |
| | Companies are permitted to make market purchases of their own ordinary shares. | *CA 1985 s 162* |
| | Provided the requirements of the Companies Act, Listing Rules and relevant shareholder guidance are met, the NAPF will support share repurchases. | NAPF |

|  |  | Basis of policy |
|---|---|---|
|  | **Broader governance developments** |  |
| **24** | **Socially responsible investment** |  |
|  | As well as summarising their voting policies in Statements of Investment Principles (SIPs), pension fund trustees are now required, under Pensions Act regulation, to state in the SIP the extent, if at all, that social, environmental and ethical considerations are taken into account in connection with their investment strategy. | *Pensions Act 1995* |
|  | Over time, this requirement is likely to have a significant impact on UK governance practices as institutional investors seek to establish the extent and nature of corporate activity in these areas in order that their impact on long-term shareholder value can be better assessed. At the same time, boards of directors will increasingly incorporate these concepts into corporate strategy and companies will strive to respond to investor concerns. |  |
|  | Companies should now ensure that they report to shareholders on these developments. |  |

---

**Important notice**

# Hermes: Statement on UK Corporate Governance and Voting Policy (2001)   B7.7

## Introduction

Hermes Investment Management is the principal fund manager for the UK's largest pension scheme, owned by BT. It also manages portfolios for the Post Office Pension Plan and a number of other major corporate and public pension schemes. These corporate governance guidelines explain in detail how Hermes exercises its clients' ownership rights in practice. The guidelines are intended as a basis for dialogue between companies and shareholders. The guidelines are applied giving due consideration to the specific circumstances of individual companies, and adopting a pragmatic approach where appropriate.

## 1. Statement of general principle

1.1 Directors of public companies are responsible for running companies in the long-term interests of shareholders. Shareholders and their agents have responsibilities as owners to exercise stewardship of companies. Corporate governance should provide a framework where both parties can fulfil these responsibilities.

1.2 A company run in the long-term interests of its shareholders will need to manage effectively relationships with its employees, suppliers and customers, to behave ethically and to have regard for the environment and society as a whole. Hermes' approach to social, environmental and ethical matters is explained in Appendix 4 to this piece.

1.3 Non-executive directors (NEDs) should work co-operatively with their executive colleagues and demonstrate objectivity and robust independence of judgement in their decision-making.

1.4 A remuneration committee of independent NEDs is best placed to decide executive remuneration on behalf of the board. Actual and potential awards should not be excessive and should be directly related to the success of the company and aligned over time to the returns achieved by shareholders. Hermes encourages companies to put the board's remuneration report to a vote at the AGM, particularly where significant changes are made to policy or controversial issues arise during the year. A more detailed explanation of Hermes' views on remuneration is at Appendix 1 to this piece.

1.5 Hermes supports a standard approach to corporate governance. Hermes welcomes the publication of the Combined Code and will normally apply its recommendations. Consideration will also be given to the fuller discussions in the Cadbury, Greenbury and Hampel Reports that underlie the Combined Code. Where relevant, reference will be made to the policies of the National Association of Pension Funds and other related bodies. There are some issues that Hermes believes, primarily because of its investment policies, require greater emphasis or an alternative approach. In addition, the Hampel Report left open some matters of detail for shareholders to resolve with company boards. This supplementary statement is intended to assist directors' understanding of Hermes' views on these issues.

## 2. The board

2.1 Composition

The precise number of executive directors (EDs) and NEDs for any company is for its board to determine with the approval of its shareholders. It is the overall balance of the board that is important. Not all NEDs need to be independent but there should be a strong core of NEDs that are both independent and seen to be independent.

## 2.2 Role of NEDs

The key role of NEDs is to ensure that the chief executive and the board as a whole concentrate on maximising long-term shareholder value. There are three aspects of this for which NEDs should expect to be held accountable.

**Strategic function** – Bringing their independent judgement to strategic decision-making.

**Expertise** – Providing skills and experience that may not otherwise be readily available to the company. This applies particularly to small and medium-sized companies.

**Governance function** – Ensuring compliance with best practice, participating in the appointment of new directors and monitoring the performance of NEDs. The number of NED positions held by any individual should reflect the need to ensure that adequate attention can be given to every office, particularly at times of corporate turbulence.

## 2.3 Independence of NEDs

The board should have a core of at least three vigorously independent directors on whom shareholders can rely for the independence of their judgement and who can act as agents for change should the need arise. Hermes endorses the Cadbury Committee's definition of independence: that NEDs 'should be independent of management and free from any business or other relationship that could materially interfere with the exercise of their independent judgement'.

Hermes will interpret this to mean that to be considered independent a NED must not:

- be or have been an employee of the company;

- serve as a director for more than ten years or be over 70 years of age;

- represent significant shareholders or other single interest groups (e.g. supplier, creditor);

- receive an income from the company other than NED fees;

- participate in the company's share option or performance-related remuneration schemes

- have conflicting or cross directorships; or

- have any other significant financial or personal tie to the company or its management which could interfere with the director's loyalty to shareholders

Hermes accepts that not all NEDs need to be independent in accordance with this definition and that there can be a role for other NEDs providing a majority of NEDs satisfy the above test of independence. We believe that the final decision on whether NEDs are independent lies with the shareholders who elect them. There should be full disclosure in the annual report of any factors to be taken into account in judging an individual's independence in accordance with the above criteria.

2.4   Chairman/chief executive

Hermes favours separation of the roles of chairman and chief executive and is generally opposed to a chief executive becoming chairman in the same company. Hermes prefers to discuss any departure from this guideline in advance of decisions being taken. The over-riding consideration will be whether the composition and balance of the board will ensure that no individual can wield undue influence on board.

2.5   Senior NED

Hermes supports the appointment of a senior NED and sees the role as an extension of that of deputy chairman. This is an important position; Hermes' detailed views on the role of the senior NED are at Appendix 2.

2.6   Succession

The expression of fresh views and genuine debate across the board table are of considerable value and importance. For this reason at least one new independent NED should join the board every three years and NEDs should not normally serve for more than ten years.

2.7   Nomination committee

Hermes' views on the role and constitution of this committee are given at Appendix 3 to this piece.

2.8   Performance assessment and development of NEDs

It is good practice for all boards to conduct an annual review of the performance of NEDs and the chairman and to consider the effectiveness of the board as a whole. The role of NED is becoming increasingly complex and Hermes recommends that companies encourage NEDs to participate in the range of seminars and workshops offered by organisations such as Cranfield School of Management, Henley Management College, Institute of Directors and Spencer Stuart.

Hermes contributes to several of these development fora, which encourage a participatory approach and include case studies illustrating difficult situations.

**3.   Voting**

3.1   Hermes believes that a separate resolution seeking approval of the annual report and accounts should be tabled at all AGMs.

3.2   Hermes welcomes the introduction of electronic proxy voting and encourages companies to adopt this as soon as practicable.

## 4. Share structure

4.1 A split share capital structure often disadvantages the majority of shareholders. Hermes will not support the issue of shares with reduced or no voting rights and is likely to withhold support for other capital raising exercises by companies with such capital structures. Support for a company with an unequal capital structure would be qualified in the event of it becoming a take-over target.

## 5. Pre-emption

5.1 Existing shareholders should be offered right of first refusal when a company issues shares exceeding 5 per cent of the existing shares in issue. Only in exceptional circumstances would Hermes approve the waiver of clients' pre-emption rights.

## 6. Donations

6.1 It is inappropriate that any of the return that is rightfully shareholders' should be diverted to political donations. Donations to charities are acceptable within reason.

## 7. Hostile take-overs

7.1 Take-overs are an important part of an efficient and competitive corporate environment but do not always add to shareholder value, particularly for the bidding company. Hermes' predisposition in a hostile bid is to support existing management, but this support is conditional. It does not apply where confidence has been lost in management nor for example where synergistic or strategic benefits clearly justify a bid premium. Unreasonable or unjustifiably expensive defence tactics will not be supported.

## 8. Investment trusts

8.1 At least three, and a majority, of the directors of an investment trust should be clearly independent. The tests of independence in paragraph 2.3 above apply to investment trusts. In addition, directors who are not considered independent include employees or former employees of the trust's fund manager or of related group or associated companies and directors of more than one investment trust managed by the same fund management company. The chairman should always be fully independent and there should be no more than one representative of the trust's fund manager on the board.

8.2 Management contracts should have notice periods of no more than one year.

# Appendix 1 – Remuneration

## 1. General principles

1.1 Performance-related remuneration is the principle means by which EDs are motivated to achieve greater shareholder value and are rewarded for doing so. It is therefore an area of company policy in which shareholders have a valid role.

1.2 Remuneration committees of independent NEDs are best placed to decide the remuneration packages necessary to recruit, retain and motivate executives. They should take professional advice as necessary. Where independent advisers are appointed they should be responsible to the remuneration committee and not the company EDs. Consideration should be given to naming the advisers in the board's remuneration report. Hermes encourages companies to put the board's remuneration report to a vote at the AGM, particularly where significant changes are made to policy or controversial issues arise during the year.

1.3 Remuneration is a package. Actual and potential rewards should not be excessive; scrutiny from informed observers should not diminish the legitimacy of the executive team in the eyes of shareholders or employees. Performance-related remuneration should be aligned over time with returns earned by shareholders. Increases in remuneration should be driven by improved performance and should not just be a matter of annual appreciation.

1.4 Companies should require all directors to build over a period of time a substantial shareholding, say to the value of at least one year's emoluments. For NEDs, one way of achieving this is to pay them partly in shares which must be retained whilst they hold office. NEDs who are executives elsewhere, and whose fees are paid to their primary employer, should receive the share component of their fee. NEDs should not participate in performance-related pay or incentive schemes.

1.5 Hermes recognises the difficulty faced by companies with international operations when designing remuneration packages, particularly incentive schemes. Although it is accepted that companies have to offer packages that are competitive in the local market there are certain features that should be universal.

1.6 Hermes will assess all schemes individually, taking into account the particular circumstances of the company, but sound reasons would need to be given by a remuneration committee proposing a scheme that did not comply with the spirit of the above principles.

## 2. Contracts

2.1 Hermes prefers that executives be appointed on one-year rolling contracts. Executives appointed on a two-year fixed contract that subsequently reduces to a one-year rolling contract will also be supported. Hermes does not currently vote against existing directors with two-year rolling contracts but recommends that these be reduced to one year, without compensation, as a show of leadership. Contracts with a clause that increases compensation paid for early termination in the event of a take-over are not supported.

## 3. Incentive scheme principles

3.1 Incentive schemes should be designed to reward exceptional performance. Awards should be scaled against achievement of performance criteria, with a relatively low payout if the minimum target is achieved and full payout only for truly exceptional performance. No award should be made where targets are not met. The measure used will vary depending on the type of incentive but performance should be compared to an appropriate benchmark or peer group. Awards should not be made unless there has been improvement in the underlying real financial position of the company. Where comparative performance against a peer group is used as the measure awards should generally not be made when company performance is below median. Earnings per share growth of RPI+2 per cent a year is not a suitably challenging performance target for the majority of companies.

3.2 Performance measurement and vesting periods should ideally be five years although a minimum of three years will be considered. A further holding period between vesting and sale is encouraged.

3.3 Share matching schemes should be subject to challenging performance criteria and grants made should not be overly generous.

3.4 Remuneration committees should explain proposed schemes clearly to shareholders, justifying the structure of the scheme and the relevance of the performance criteria chosen. Schemes should be structured as simply as possible to ensure they can be understood by participants and monitored by shareholders. The link between company performance and executive reward should be clear. The effect of the scheme should be illustrated with examples showing rewards at various performance levels for one of the participants, say, the chief executive.

3.5 The dilution guidelines published by the Association of British Insurers should be observed.

3.6 Where annual grants are made there should be no re-testing period; if the performance targets are not met the award for that year should be foregone.

3.7 Where remuneration committees have authority to vary incentive schemes they should only do so in exceptional circumstances and to ensure that the scheme continues to motivate executives. All changes should be reported and justified to shareholders.

3.8 Companies should confirm continuing shareholder support for a scheme during its lifetime, giving shareholders an opportunity to reassess the scheme in light of actual payout levels.

3.9 Companies should have only one executive long-term incentive scheme in place; exceptions should be justified in the remuneration report. Executives should not be rewarded twice for the same performance. Remuneration committees should take into consideration the number of options outstanding and the remaining period for which they are exercisable when making grants under a newly introduced performance share scheme.

3.10 The annual report should disclose the level of recent grants made under any existing incentive scheme, the performance criteria applied to the grants, and any payouts resulting from grants made in previous years. The actual performance resulting in the vesting of grants should be disclosed and clearly explained.

## 4. Incentive scheme structures

### 4.1 Share option schemes

Share option schemes are both popular and widely criticised. Participants can be rewarded for market rises on which they had no influence, they bear no risk (unprofitable options are simply not exercised) and seldom retain shares they exercise. Requirements for the share price to exceed a benchmark and for executives to retain a minimum shareholding partly address these points.

### 4.2 Performance share plans

In Hermes view, schemes based on the grant of shares are preferable to many share option schemes. It is difficult to specify an appropriate level of grant (e.g. 50 per cent or 100 per cent of base salary) because companies give different weights to base salary and performance pay. Remuneration committees should be mindful that, unlike options, the full value of the shares (less tax) will be received by the participants if the performance criteria are met. The over-riding principle, that grants should not be excessive, should be observed. Performance should be measured on a total shareholder return basis against a suitable peer group, either a public index or a specially constructed one.

## Appendix 2 – The role of the senior non-executive director

In many respects Hermes sees the role as an extension of that of deputy chairman and supports combining the roles of independent deputy chairman and senior non-executive director. Hermes believes that the main responsibilities of the role are to ensure that the views of each NED are given due consideration and to provide a communication channel between NEDs and shareholders. This communication channel should be in addition to and not replace existing channels. For many companies this new channel may have only occasional and irregular use. Hermes proposes the following job description for the senior NED:

1. The senior NED should chair some (or all) of the board sub-committees. Where the board chairman either combines the role of chairman and chief executive or has at any time been an executive director of the company then the senior NED might chair both the nomination committee and the remuneration committee.

2. The senior NED should make himself available for confidential discussions with other non-executive directors who may have concerns which they believe have not been properly considered by the board as a whole.

3.   The senior NED should have the authority to call a meeting of the NEDs if, in his opinion, it is necessary.

4.   The senior NED should be responsible for completing a periodic performance appraisal of the company chairman.

5.   Where the company chairman combines the role of chairman and chief executive or has at any time been an executive director of the company then the senior NED should take a major part in the performance appraisal of the board as a whole and of individual directors.

6.   If requested by major shareholders, the senior NED should ensure that he is available for consultation and direct communication. At present such communication is rare. When it does occur it is invariably because of a crisis' situation. Establishing direct channels as a matter of routine should enable difficult issues to be aired before a crisis develops.

This job description should be amended depending on the particular circumstances of each company and the overall composition of its board.

## Appendix 3 – The nomination committee

The Combined Code recommends that ' … a nomination committee should be established to make recommendations to the board on all new board appointments' but does not define the role or constitution of the committee. Hermes recommends that:

1.   The nomination committee should comprise a minimum of three directors, a majority of whom should be independent non-executive directors. Membership of the committee should be disclosed in the annual report.

2.   The chairman of the company and the senior independent NED should always be members of the committee.

3.   The nomination committee should be formally constituted as a sub-committee of the main board to whom it is answerable and to whom it should report. It should be given written terms of reference which deal adequately with its membership, authority and duties.

4.   The chairman of the nomination committee should normally be a fully independent NED.

5.   Hermes recommends that the nomination committee be responsible, after consultation with other directors, for finalising the candidate specification for all board appointments and for approving the process by which suitable candidates are identified and shortlisted, including choosing a third party advisor where appropriate. Confirmation of the appointment should be the responsibility of the board as a whole.

6.   The nomination committee should ensure that all board appointees undergo an appropriate induction programme. These guidelines should be amended depending on the particular circumstances of each company with significant departures being explained in the annual report.

## Appendix 4 – Guidelines for reporting on social environmental and ethical matters

These guidelines are intended to assist the companies in which Hermes invests on behalf of its clients meet the concerns of those clients on social, environmental and ethical (SEE) matters. These guidelines reflect both the need for pension fund trustees to take SEE matters into consideration in investing the funds entrusted to them and the disclosure recommendations of the Turnbull Report on financial and non-financial risks. They are intended to complement existing standards to which companies might already be working (e.g. the Global Reporting Initiative, ISO standards, or Department of Trade and Industry recommendations) and were drafted by a committee of institutional investors of which Hermes was a member. Underlying these guidelines is an assumption that the effective management of the risks associated with SEE matters can lead to long-term financial benefits for the companies concerned. Hermes will monitor the performance of boards in respect of these disclosure requirements and will engage with companies who in our view could improve the quality of their disclosures. Hermes will apply these guidelines with thought and will adopt a pragmatic approach where the unique circumstances of a company make that appropriate.

### 1. The board

The company should disclose in its annual report whether:

1.1 The formal schedule of matters reserved to the board takes account of SEE matters.

1.2 The board has identified and assessed the significant risks to the company's short and long-term value arising from SEE matters.

1.3 Account is taken of SEE matters in the training of directors.

1.4 The board has received adequate information about SEE matters that may affect the company's short and long-term value.

1.5 The remuneration committee, in designing and implementing performance related remuneration schemes, has considered the effect on the company's performance of SEE matters.

### 2. Policies, procedures and verification

The annual report should:

2.1 Include information on SEE matters that significantly affect the company's short and long-term value.

2.2 Describe the company's policies and procedures for managing risks to the company's short and long-term value arising from SEE matters. If the annual report and accounts states that the company has no such policies and procedures, the board should provide reasons for their absence.

2.3 Include information about the extent to which the company has complied with its policies and procedures for managing risks arising from SEE matters.

311

2.4   Describe the procedure for verification of SEE disclosures (we are interested to know if there is a verification procedure and, if so, where responsibility for verification lies, for instance, with the company's internal auditors, audit committee or external advisors such as auditors or consultants). The verification procedure should be such as to achieve a reasonable level of credibility.

**Hermes' code of conduct in support of companies**

We are interested to know if there is a verification procedure and, if so, where responsibility for verification lies, for instance, with the company' s internal auditors, audit committee or external advisors such as auditors or consultants.

For further information contact Michelle Edkins (tel + 44 (0)20 7702 0888; www.hermes.co.uk).

1.   Hermes acknowledges, on behalf of its clients, that shareholders have responsibilities as owners to participate in the stewardship of companies.

2.   Management of companies run in the long-term interests of shareholders can be confident of Hermes' continuing support.

3.   Hermes will normally support incumbent management in hostile take-over situations, but the support is conditional (as explained in paragraph 7.1 above). Hermes generally prefers change from within rather than hostile bids.

4.   Hermes will lodge proxies at AGMs and EGMs in accordance with the principles outlined in this document.

5.   Hermes will contact companies to explain its reasons for voting against or abstaining on any resolutions. Hermes prefers these discussions to be kept private.

6.   Hermes supports a standard approach to corporate governance. Hermes welcomes the publication of the Combined Code and will normally apply its recommendations. Consideration will also be given to the fuller discussions in the Cadbury, Greenbury and Hampel Reports that underlie the Combined Code. Where relevant, reference will be made to the policies of the National Association of Pension Funds and other related bodies. There are some issues that Hermes believes, primarily because of its investment policies, require greater emphasis or an alternative approach. In addition, the Hampel Report left open some matters of detail for shareholders to resolve with company boards. This supplementary statement is intended to assist directors' understanding of Hermes' views on these issues.

7.   Codes of best practice and supplementary guidelines provide the base from which to build dialogue between companies and shareholders. Hermes is committed to applying its corporate governance and voting policies with thought, giving due consideration to the specific circumstances of individual companies, and will adopt a pragmatic approach where appropriate. Hermes will consider, at the request of a

company, any company-specific circumstances that may make it inappropriate to apply Hermes' standard policies.

8.    Hermes is always prepared to discuss companies' affairs with their boards and management. As this can, and on occasion does, make Hermes an insider, active fund management is foregone for the relevant period. Formal communication channels with NEDs are encouraged.

# Corporate governance and social, environmental and ethical performance: the policies of the UK's leading investment institutions    B7.8

This research was conducted by David Ladipo and Merlin Underwood of Lintstock assisted by Bryn Hughes. Lintstock Ltd is at 42 Borough High Street, London SE1 1XW. Tel: +44 207 089 9464. Fax: +44 207 089 9474. E-mail: contact@lintstock.com. Website: www.lintstock.com". Lintstock is a London-based consultancy that provides independent corporate governance advice. Their analysis enables companies to strengthen their governance system, meet the needs of financial regulators and enhance their profile with the investor community. For copies of the report or comment and feedback, contact David Ladipo or Merlin Underwood.

# Executive summary

In September 2001, Hermes commissioned an analysis of the policies adopted by the UK's leading investment institutions with respect to voting and engagement on issues of corporate governance and social, environmental and ethical performance, the results of which were carried in the first edition of this Handbook. This study, conducted by Lintstock, revisits the twenty institutions that participated in the 2001 study and expands the sample to include five new participants. In total, the sample comprises 22 of the UK's largest investment managers, two trade associations (the National Association of Pension Funds and the Association of British Insurers) and one of the more prominent proxy voting advisers (Institutional Shareholder Services).

In the report that follows, we examine a broad range of policy issues and, in each case, highlight the differences of opinion and/or emphasis exhibited by the investment institutions. In doing so, we also highlight the extent to which these policy statements are in accordance or at variance with the views expressed in both the 'old' and the 'new' Combined Codes on Corporate Governance. Amongst the more topical findings are the following:

**CEO becoming Chair**: Only eight policy statements comment on one of the more controversial topics raised by the Higgs Review. Of these, one considers that the practice is acceptable provided there is a clear majority of independent directors; five are 'generally opposed' to the practice and would seek 'persuasive justification' were it to occur. The remaining two express a 'strong' opposition to this practice, one of which makes it clear that they would not expect a retiring CEO to retain a seat on the board as a non-executive director (let alone sanction their appointment to the Chair).

**The appointment of a Senior Independent Director (SID)**: Twenty policy statements venture an opinion on the role of SID – whose cameo appearance in the Higgs Review elicited a surprising amount of ill-tempered debate. Of these, fifteen statements support the provisions of the new Combined Code viz. that a Senior Independent Director be appointed irrespective of whether the roles of Chair and CEO are combined.

**The composition of the Nomination Committee**: In their policy statements, twenty of the institutions in our study express a view which runs directly counter to that expressed in the EU Corporate Governance Action Plan. Whereas the Action Plan suggests that the group responsible for board nominations be comprised mainly of executive directors, these twenty institutions all insist that the nomination committee be comprised of a majority of non-executives (with many insisting that these non-executives be demonstrably *independent*).

**Director term limits**: Does long tenure compromise the independence of a non-executive director? It is a subject which attracts comment in fourteen of the policy statements we reviewed, most of which suggest – in line with the new Combined Code – that a non-executive director will not 'normally' be considered independent after nine years continuous service.

**'Rewards for failure'**: Reflecting the highly publicised 'shareholder revolts' against companies employing directors on notice periods of more than one year (most notably Glaxo SmithKline), twenty three of the policy statements indicate a preference for notice periods of one year or less. But there is less agreement with regard to the use of liquidated damages clauses in directors' contracts – a subject on which the tide of opinion appears to be flowing away from that articulated by the Hampel Committee and back to that expressed in the Greenbury Report.

**Publication and verification of SEE reports**: All but four of the institutions make clear their expectation that listed companies annually disclose their performance on social, environmental and ethical matters. Of these, nine suggest that listed companies should abide by the disclosure guidelines issued by the Association of British Insurers. A small number of institutions have also started to recommend the Sustainability Reporting Guidelines developed by the Global Reporting Initiative.

**Putting policy into practice**: With UK investment institutions under growing pressure to detail the actions they have taken in support of their corporate governance and SRI policies, six of the twenty two investment managers in this study made a commitment (in their governance and/or SRI policies) to report to their clients on a quarterly/regular basis on both their voting and engagement record. And the responsibility for monitoring the effectiveness of their activism was mentioned, in a variety of statements, by ten other investment managers.

# Detailed Findings

## Board Balance

### Combining the roles of Chair and CEO

All the policy statements discuss the acceptability of board positions that combine the roles of Chair and CEO. Ten of these statements are 'strongly opposed' to such combinations with their opposition couched in language that considerably exceeds that expressed in the old Combined Code[9]. A further eight express a 'general opposition' to the combination of these roles with the other seven indicating a 'preference' for the roles to be kept separate (in tones that echo the principles of the old Combined Code). However, over the course of the next year, we expect the tone of these more softly expressed statements to harden in line with the language adopted in the new Combined Code[10].

*Fig 1: Combining the roles of Chair and CEO*

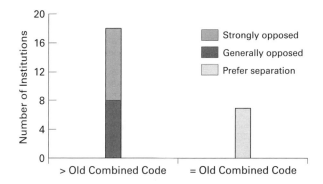

### CEO becoming Chair

Eight of the policy statements express a view on the acceptability of retiring CEOs moving on to become Chair of the same company. One considers that the practice is acceptable provided there is a clear majority of independent directors; five are 'generally opposed' to the practice and would seek 'persuasive justification' were it to occur. The remaining two express a 'strong' opposition to this practice, one of which makes it clear that they would not expect a retiring CEO to retain a seat on the board as a non-executive director (let alone sanction their appointment to the Chair).

The transition from CEO to Chair was not an issue touched on by the old Combined Code but the new Code has clearly stated that: 'A Chief Executive should not go on to be Chairman of the same company. If exceptionally a board decides that a chief executive should become Chairman, the board should consult major shareholders in advance and should set out its reasons at the time of the appointment and in the next annual report'. In light of this new Code provision, we expect that a greater proportion of investors will declare their stance on this issue over the course of the coming months. In doing so, they will no doubt be mindful of the views garnered by the Confederation of British Industry (CBI) in their recent poll of FTSE 100 Chairs[11] (see Figure 3).

*Fig 2: CEO becoming Chair*

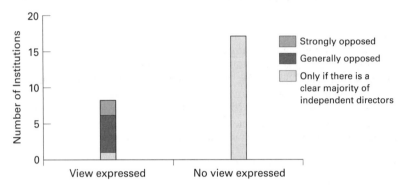

*Fig 3: CBI Poll of FTSE Chairmen ('Disallowing a CEO to become Chairman of the same company will lead to better Board performance')*

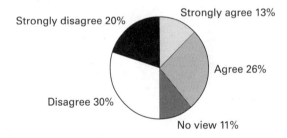

**The appointment of a Senior Independent Director**

The role of the Senior Independent Director (SID) has been the subject of bitter controversy since the publication of the Higgs Review which suggested that SID:

* chair meetings between non-executive directors where the chairman does not attend;

* be available to shareholders, if they have reason for concern that contact through the normal channels of chairman or chief executive has failed to resolve;

- attend sufficient of the regular meetings of management with a range of major shareholders to develop a balanced understanding of the themes, issues and concerns of shareholders; and

- communicate these views to the non-executive directors and, as appropriate, to the board as a whole.

In the CBI poll of FTSE 100 Chairs which followed the publication of the Higgs Review, 82% of respondents felt strongly that the role of the Chairman was undermined by what the Review said about the Senior Independent Director. Commenting on these findings, Digby Jones, the CBI's director-general suggested that the responses were reflective of a widespread fear (amongst the FTSE 100 Chairs) that SID would open up 'a separate and potentially divisive channel of communication with shareholders'. Notwithstanding these deep throated growls of disapproval, the role of SID as expressed in the new Combined Code is little changed from that outlined in the draft provisions of the Higgs Review[12].

*Fig 4: CBI Poll of FTSE Chairmen ('The Higgs Report undermines the role of Chairman, by what it says about the role of SID')*

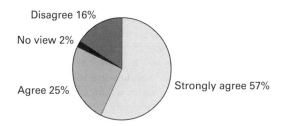

In light of the controversy generated by SID, the policy statements we have examined make for interesting reading (see Figure 5). Five institutions suggest that such appointments are necessary where there is a joint Chair/CEO (in line with the provisions of the old Combined Code) but fifteen expect companies to appoint a senior independent non-executive irrespective of whether the roles of Chair and CEO are combined (in line with the provisions of the new Combined Code). Nevertheless, of these fifteen, several stress their belief that, notwithstanding the value of SID, a Chairman who is independent of management should be 'the normal channel of communication' between shareholders and the board.

*Fig 5: Appointing a Senior Independent Director*

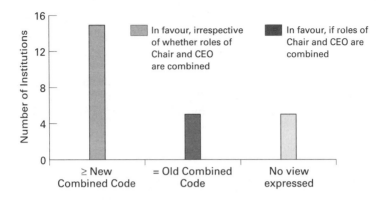

Also included in the text of the new Combined Code is the suggestion that SID, together with the other non-executive directors should meet at least once a year without the Chairman present 'to appraise the chairman's performance and on such other occasions as are deemed appropriate'. This suggestion is echoed in the 'Corporate Governance Rule Proposals' submitted to the SEC by the NYSE on August 1, 2002. The third of these proposals suggests that: 'To empower non-management directors to serve as a more effective check on management, the non-management directors of each company must meet at regularly scheduled executive sessions without management[13]'. This is not a suggestion which appears in the policy statements we have examined; but over the coming months we expect that some institutional investors will wish to revise their statements to include commentary on this issue – not least because of the disparity of opinions which this subject has already elicited (see Figure 6).

*Fig 6: CBI Poll of FTSE 100 Chairmen ('The proposal for NEDS to meet in the absence of the Chairman will be useful for good Corporate Governance')*

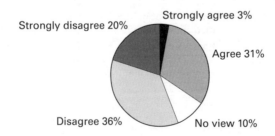

**Percentage of NEDs on Board**

With regard to the ratio of non-executive directors (NEDs) to executive directors, only five policy statements go beyond the provisions of the old Combined Code (which recommended that non-executive directors comprise not less than one third of the board and that the majority of non-executive directors be independent). And, of these five, only two match the provisions of the new Combined Code (which provides that except for smaller companies, at least half the board, excluding the Chairman[14], should be comprised of independent non-executive directors).

*Fig 7: Board Composition*

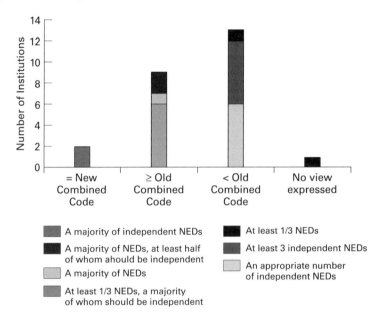

## The Audit Committee

Twenty two of the policy statements discuss the role of the audit committee. Of these, only twelve statements match the provisions of the new Combined Code which provides that *all* members of the committee should consist of independent non-executive directors. Eight match the provisions of the old Combined Code which recommended that the committee consist of a *majority* of independent non-executives. As indicated in Figure 8, two statements adopt a less stringent threshold and three do not express a view.

## The Remuneration Committee

Unlike the policies expressed with respect to the composition of the audit committee, all but three of the policy statements insist that the remuneration committee be comprised solely of independent non-executive directors – a position that matches that expressed in both the old and new Combined Codes (see Figure 9).

*Fig 8: Composition of Audit Committee*

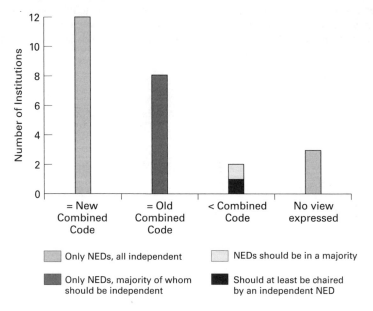

*Fig 9: Composition of Remuneration Committee*

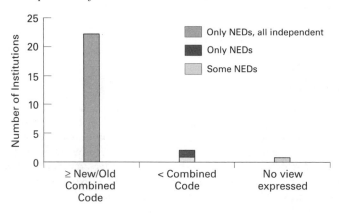

**Nomination Committee**

Twenty of the policy statements discuss the role of the nomination committee. Five go beyond the provisions of the new Combined Code by insisting that the committee be comprised *solely* of non-executive directors. And one statement, although it echoes the language of the new Code[15] by suggesting that the committee be comprised of a *majority* of independent non-executive directors, also recommends that it be chaired by an independent non-executive director. This suggestion that the committee be chaired by an independent non-executive director (as opposed to the Chairman), when made in the Higgs Review, met with a considerable degree of antagonism from FTSE 100 Chairs (see Figure 11) and was eventually watered down in the provisions of the new Combined Code.

Four of the policies reflect the position expressed in the new Combined Code guidelines whilst the remaining policies are less prescriptive. Eight of these suggest that the committee be comprised of a majority of NEDs (without specifying that these NEDs need necessarily be 'independent') and two simply recommend that NEDs 'play a key role'. The diversity of positions – with respect to the appropriate composition of the nomination committee – is reflected in the views of the FTSE 100 Chairs polled by the CBI. As shown in Figure 11, more than half of these individuals disagreed with the suggestion that the appointment of an independent NED to chair the nomination committee would strengthen the independence of the board. In light of this disparity of opinion – and the debate that is currently surrounding the recommendations of the EU *Corporate Governance Action Plan*[16] – we expect that many institutional investors will wish to tread carefully when revising their policy positions with respect to the procedures by which directors are nominated to the board.

*Fig 10: Composition of Nomination Committee*

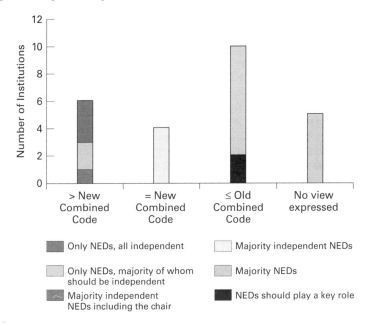

*Fig 11: CBI Poll of FTSE 100 Chairmen ('The recommendation that the Nomination Committee should be chaired by an independent NED will strengthen the independence of the Board')*

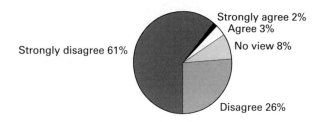

Strongly agree 2%
Agree 3%
No view 8%
Strongly disagree 61%
Disagree 26%

# Directors' Time Commitments and Suitability for Election

## Directors' attendance record

In its discussion of the 'role of the board', the Higgs Review bemoaned the fact that: 'information on the number of board and committee meetings held, and on attendance by individual directors, is not routinely published by all companies and would help shareholders judge the extent of directors' participation'. The Review recommended that the new Combined Code include a new provision requiring companies to publish, in their annual reports, the number of meetings of the board (and its committees) and the individual attendance thereat by company directors. This recommendation has been duly adopted by the Financial Reporting Council and, over the course of the coming months, we expect this guidance to find an echo in the policies of institutional investors. At present, only six of the policies contained in our sample make mention of this topic. At the most prescriptive end, one institution threatens to withhold votes for directors who attend less than 75% of meetings. Two indicate that they will not support the re-election of a director with a 'poor' attendance record. One recommends that sanctions for non-attendance should be provided for in companies' articles and two content themselves with the recommendation (akin to that of the new Combined Code) that board meeting attendance be fully disclosed.

## Number of directorships

As revealed in the Higgs Review and contrary to popular perceptions (that there are a large number of people holding multiple non-executive directorships), less than one-fifth of the NEDs surveyed by the Higgs Review held more than one non-executive directorship in a UK listed company, only 13 individuals held five or more such posts and only one in 14 non-executive directors also held an executive director post. Derek Higgs acknowledged that many non-executive directors may also hold appointments in unlisted or non-UK companies as well as charitable, public sector or other roles. Nevertheless, the conclusion he arrived at was that 'the variety of different appointments and individual circumstances means that it is arbitrary and unrealistic to set a prescriptive limit for the number of non-executive directorships any individual not in full time employment may hold'[17].

But prescriptive advice was not long arriving. The National Association of Pension Funds (NAPF), for example, made clear in its response to the Higgs Review that it would expect directors holding purely non-executive positions to justify how they can manage more than five posts (including the boards of charities etc):

> 'Whilst the NAPF would not wish to discourage directors from taking on work for charities or public boards, any such non-plc work should nevertheless be taken into account when assessing workloads, as some may require time commitments that are every bit as demanding as those of plc boards ... in respect of individuals with more than five directorships, the NAPF recommends that each listed company, for which that NED holds a directorship, should be required to include a brief statement in their annual reports to the effect that the NED in question is able to devote the agreed amount of time to the company.'

In light of this guidance, we expect to see more institutional investors declaring their views on this subject. At the time of writing, it was an issue touched on by only six of the policies in our study. Two (including the NAPF) suggest that individuals should not (normally) hold more than five non-executive directorships[18]. One goes a little further by declaring that it will not normally support the re-election of a director who has too many other commitments; and three confine themselves to statements suggesting that NEDs must ensure they have 'adequate time' to properly discharge their role.

As for the number of outside directorships that should be permitted an executive director, this issue was not addressed by any of the policies in our study. But as institutional investors revise their policy statements over the coming year, we expect that several of them will wish to comment upon it – not least because the new Combined Code has adopted one of the more contentious recommendations of the Higgs Review, viz. that boards: 'should not agree to a full time executive director taking on more than one non-executive directorship in a FTSE 100 company nor the chairmanship of such a company'.

**Director Term Limits**

Fifteen of the policy statements express a view on the time period beyond which they would normally expect a non-executive director to resign his/her appointment. Only one statement goes beyond the provisions of the new Combined Code and makes an unqualified declaration that independent NEDs should retire after 6 years. Six are in line with the new Combined Code[19] and suggest that after nine years, an NED will not normally be considered 'independent'; six set the limit at ten years rather than nine years; one sets the bar at 12 years; and one policy does not express a view on the matter other than to declare its opposition to proposals which seek to limit NED tenure. The rest of the policy statements (ten in total) do not address the subject.

*Fig 12: NED Term Limits*

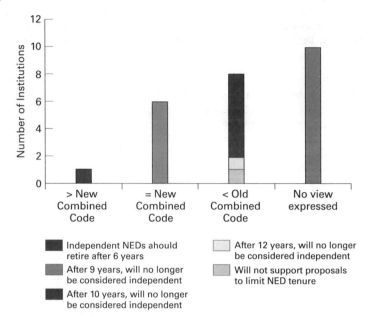

**Director Turnover**

In his review of the role and effectiveness of NEDs, Derek Higgs argued that limits on board tenure would help to secure not just the *independence* but also the *freshne*ss of a board's non-executive directorship[20]. This observation is reflected in provision A.7.2 of the new Combined Code which states that: 'any term beyond six years (e.g. two three-year terms) for a non-executive director should be subject to particularly rigorous review, and should take into account the need for *progressive refreshing* of the board'. In light of this guidance, we expect that many institutional investors will wish to declare their views on what could well prove a rather contentious issue[21]. At the time of writing, it was an issue touched on by only five policy statements. Two indicate that – in the interests of fresh thinking and genuine debate – they expect one new independent NED to be elected to the board at least once every three years. The other three statements register their approval of succession plans designed to encourage the expression of 'fresh views' but make no specific comment on the form such plans should take.

**Age of Directors**

As revealed in the findings of the Higgs Review, in 2002 the average age of a non-executive director in the FTSE 100 was 59, with over three-quarters 55 or over. The average age of a FTSE 100 Chairman was 62 and almost 40 per cent were 65 or over. Whilst the Higgs Review did not make any recommendations as to the age at which directors should be retired, twelve of the policies in our study express their views on this subject. As shown in Figure 13, one states quite categorically that non-executive directors should retire at age 70. Two make clear that they will only support the re-election of a director aged 70 or over if there is a clear statement from the company as to the need for the individual. Three acknowledge that each re-appointment should be judged on its own merits but recommend that, in cases where the individual is aged 70 or over, the company should provide an explanation as to the 'appropriateness' of his/her appointment. By contrast, four statements strongly endorse the principle that directors' suitability for election should *not* be judged by reference to their age but should be evaluated on the basis of their individual skills and abilities.

*Fig 13: Age of Directors*

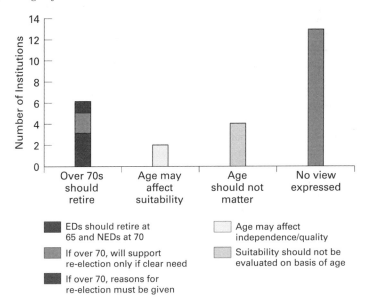

## Director Education and Evaluation

### Directors' induction and professional development

In their policy statements, seven of the institutions covered by this study make clear that they expect directors to be provided with appropriate training/induction upon first appointment, six of which echo the language of the old Combined Code by providing that 'subsequent' training should also be provided. Over the course of the next year, we expect a greater proportion of institutional investors will wish to declare their stance on this issue. It is a subject which has received a considerable amount of attention since the publication of the Higgs Review, which revealed that two-thirds of non-executive directors 'had not received any training or development' in their capacity as board members. The weight of attention given to this issue is also reflected in the structure of the new Combined Code. For, although the new Combined Code contains a much larger number of Code 'provisions' than its predecessor, it has added only two new 'main principles'. These relate, respectively, to 'information and professional development' and 'performance evaluation'[22].

**Performance evaluation**

The subject of board performance evaluations is discussed by only six of the policy statements covered in this study. Four make it clear they expect boards to conduct regular performance evaluations; and two institutions go further by suggesting that the board evaluation process should be fully disclosed to shareholders. Here again, we expect that many institutional investors will be revising their policy statements over the coming year – to take account of the guidance on board performance evaluations contained in the new Combined Code. In line with the recommendations of the Higgs Review, the new Code establishes as a new 'main principle' that a board should 'undertake a formal and rigorous annual evaluation of its own performance and that of its committees and individual directors'. The new Code also provides that the board should state in the annual report how the performance evaluations have been conducted.

The suggestion that performance evaluations should extend, not just to the board (and its committees) *as a whole* but to *individual* members thereof, has already elicited a disparity of opinion[23]. As more companies begin to disclose the processes by which their performance evaluations have been conducted, institutional investors will begin to acquire a better understanding of what constitutes 'good' and 'bad' practice in this area.

# Audit and Internal Control

### The provision of non-audit services

The issue of auditors' remuneration for non-audit services is discussed by eighteen of the policy statements in our study. Five are restricted to an endorsement of the recommendations contained in the old Combined Code, viz. that 'where the auditors also supply a substantial amount of non-audit services to the company, the company should keep the nature and extent of such services under review'. Four go slightly further, by insisting that companies should not only keep the extent of such services 'under review' but should also disclose the fees paid for such services. Another four insist that companies not only disclose these fees but explain why they do not compromise the auditors' independence – a stance which reflects the provisions of the new Combined Code[24]. More prescriptive yet are the four statements which warn of active opposition to the re-appointment of auditors whose fees for non-audit services appear 'excessive' and the one statement which insists (without further qualification) that non-audit fees should not exceed audit fees by more than 100%.

*Fig 14: Non-Audit Fees*

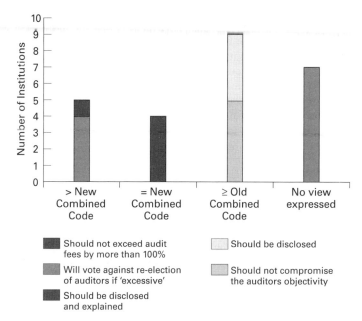

**Rotation of auditors/audit partners**

In light of the 'auditor capture' evidenced in some of the more egregious governance failures (most notably in the case of Enron), recent years have seen companies faced with a growing demand that they rotate their lead audit partner or, indeed, their audit firm itself. The Smith Guidance on Audit Committees does not proffer any prescriptive advice in this respect but it does recommend that: 'The audit committee should seek from the audit firm, on an annual basis, information about policies and processes for maintaining independence and monitoring compliance with relevant requirements, including current requirements regarding the rotation of audit partners and staff.' Over the coming months, it will be interesting to note the extent to which institutional investors choose to express a view on this matter. At the time of writing, it was an issue on which only three of the policy statements ventured an opinion. One suggests that the lead audit partner (if not the audit firm itself) should be rotated at least every five years. Another indicates that it will vote for shareholder proposals asking for audit firm rotation provided that the rotation period is not too short (i.e. less than five years). The third endorses the suggestion that there be a mechanism to ensure that 'within the audit firm' the responsibility for the audit changes hands but makes clear its belief that 'systematic rotation of audit firms' is neither 'intrinsically desirable nor in the best interests of shareholders'.

## Internal control

The role of a company's internal control system is discussed by eleven policy statements, all of which endorse the provisions of the old Combined Code recommending that directors conduct an annual review of their companies' internal control systems (and report to shareholders that they have done so). In the wake of the provisions contained in the new Combined Code[25] and the recommendations set forth in the Smith Guidance on Audit Committees, we expect that a growing number of institutional investors will declare their position on this issue in their statements of corporate governance policy.

## Shareholder Rights

### Frequency of director re-elections

In his review of the 'terms of engagement' on which directors should join the boards of listed companies, Derek Higgs accepted the argument that annual re-election of all directors could be 'potentially damaging to a company' in so far as it 'might encourage short-termism or leave a vacuum at the top of a company if an entire board is voted out in a protest by a minority of shareholders'. This view is reflected in the new Combined Code which leaves unchanged the provisions of the old Code with regard to director re-elections, viz. that directors be subject to re-election at intervals of *no more than* three years. It is also the view most commonly reflected in the policy statements covered by this study (see Figure 15).

*Fig 15: Frequency of Directors' Re-elections*

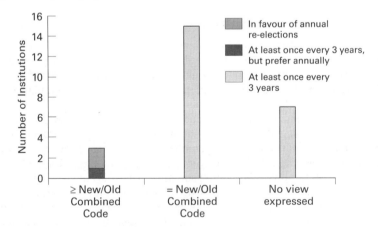

### Dis-application of pre-emption rights

In their policy statements, nineteen institutions discuss the dis-application of pre-emption rights. These statements all endorse the limits established by the Pre-emption Group of the London Stock Exchange and the Association of British Insurers (ABI), viz. that an annual dis-application of pre-emption rights is acceptable, provided it is restricted to an amount of shares not exceeding 5% of the company's issued ordinary share capital. The only significant variation between the statements is in respect of the tone in which this injunction is couched. Eight institutions express their intention to *vote against* waivers of pre-emption rights in excess of the 5% limit 'other than in exceptional circumstances'; the remainder express their disapproval in less categorical fashion (e.g. 'we will not generally support' such practices).

### Share repurchases

In their policy statements, thirteen institutions address the issue of share repurchases, all of which indicate their support for such progammes provided they work to the best interests of shareholders 'as a whole'. Of these thirteen, six declare that they expect companies to comply with the Listing Rule guidelines on share repurchases (e.g. that a general authority to repurchase shares should be limited to 15% of the issued share capital). Five also make it clear that they will not support share repurchases in circumstances where the buy-back is considered a defensive manoeuvre or an attempt to entrench management. Three of the statements also recommend that, in the event of a buy-back, the performance targets in executive bonus or share incentive schemes should be adjusted to take account of the increase in earnings per share caused by the share repurchase.

### Restricted voting rights

Eleven of the policy statements discuss the practice of issuing shares with restricted voting rights, all of which express their disapproval of such measures. Some of these statements reiterate a belief in the fundamental principle of 'one share, one vote'. Others suggest a more qualified opposition to variations in voting rights. For example, one statement recommends that any change in voting rights 'should be subject to a shareholder vote'. Another statement suggests that, although the institution will vote against proposals to create a class of shares with superior voting rights, it will support proposals to create a new class of non-voting or sub-voting shares where such measures are 'intended for financing purposes with minimal or no dilution to current shareholders' and/or are 'not designed to preserve the voting power of an insider or significant shareholder'.

### The use of anti-takeover measures

In their policy statements, eight institutions discuss the use of anti-takeover devices. The hardest stance is taken by the three institutions which declare their intention to 'vote against' the insertion of any mechanisms which are intended to defer a takeover bid. A softer stance is adopted by the four institutions which do not express an explicit intention to 'vote against' anti-takeover mechanisms but indicate, rather, a more qualified disapproval of such devices. For example, one of these four institutions states that although 'takeovers do not always maximise shareholder value', it will 'not generally support the creation or continuation of poison pill arrangements, take-over defences or other equivalent arrangements, unless fully justified and time limited'. The eighth institution merely recommends that companies seek shareholder approval 'for any action which alters the fundamental relationship between shareholders and the board ... this includes anti-takeover measures'.

## Directors' Remuneration

In the two years since this study was last conducted, we have witnessed a lively debate about the level and make-up of directors' remuneration. This debate has been fuelled by the disparity between the pay increases enjoyed by company directors and the share price declines suffered by their shareholders (see Figure 16). It also reflects the impact of the Directors Remuneration Report Regulations (DRRR) which came into force in August 2002 and introduced, amongst other things, an annual shareholder vote on the remuneration report. Prior to the introduction of the DRRR, in most cases shareholder dissent on remuneration issues could only be registered in respect of share option schemes (requiring shareholder approval) and/or the re-election of members of the remuneration committee (too blunt and bloody an instrument to appeal to most institutional shareholders). But the 'advisory vote' on the remuneration report which is now mandated by the DRRR affords shareholders the opportunity to 'safely' express their dissatisfaction on directors' contracts/notice periods, pay rates and pension arrangements (i.e. without having to fire the 'de-selection' blunderbuss). As shown in Figure 17, during the first six of months of 2003, shareholders have made rapid use of this opportunity.

In the sub-sections that follow, we compare the stated positions of the 25 institutions covered by this study on: the length of directors' notice periods; the use of liquidated damages; the level of shareholdings expected of both executive and non-executive directors; and the design and implementation of share option and other 'long-term' incentive plans.

*Fig 16: Change in Boardroom Pay, Share Prices and Avg Earnings during the 2002 Financial year*

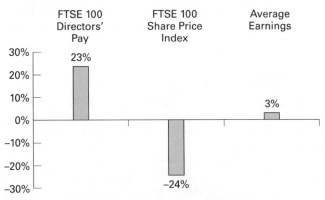

Source: Guardian Executive Pay Survey (July 2003)

*Fig 17: Rates of opposition/Abstention on Remuneration Reports, Jan–June 2003 (FTSE 100)*[26]

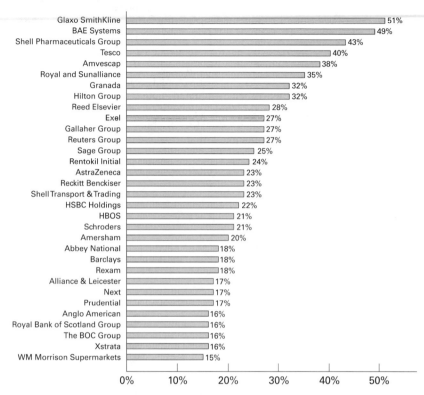

*Source:* PIRC Evidence to the Trade & Industry Committee (June 2003)

**Directors' Notice Periods**

As was reflected in the highly publicised 'shareholder revolt' at the 2003 Glaxo SmithKline AGM, institutional investors are increasingly reluctant to support contractual provisions that allow for lengthy notice periods (and entail the concomitant risk of directors receiving substantial 'rewards for failure'). Faced with this reluctance, the directors of UK listed companies have – for several years now – been witnessing a general reduction in their notice periods (a trend accelerated in 2002 by the imminent arrival of the annual vote on the remuneration report). As shown in the evidence presented by Pensions & Investment Research Consultants (PIRC) to the Trade & Industry Committee enquiry into directors' remuneration, the number of FTSE 350 directors with a notice period in excess of one year fell from 69% in 1994 to just 16% in 2002 (see Figure 18).

This trend towards shorter notice periods is reflective of the policy statements we examined. Twenty three of the statements in our sample express a view on this issue, all of which indicate a preference for contracts of one year or less.

These expressions are, however, made in a wide variety of tones: fourteen make clear that they will not 'normally support' notice periods in excess of one year whilst the remaining ten express a general preference for one year contracts but emphasise the need for flexibility[27] in circumstances where contracts of longer duration might be necessary to attract and retain executives of 'sufficient calibre'. Moreover, as a consequence of the DTI's consultation on *Rewards for Failure* (which ends on September 30 2003) we may find a greater number of institutional investors beginning to voice their concerns over the 'unintended' consequences of shortened notice periods, namely the demand for more generous up front payments ('golden hellos') and/or increases in basic remuneration by directors wishing to protect themselves against the added 'risk' of termination with a smaller compensation package.

*Fig 18: 5 of Executive Director Notice Periods in Excess of 1 Year, 1994–2002 (FTSE 350)*

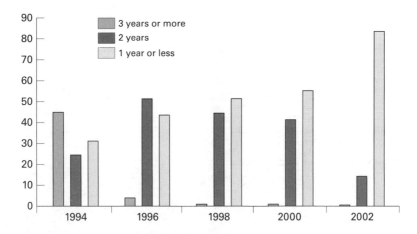

*Reproduced from PIRC's 'Evidence to the Trade & Industry Committee' (June 2003)*

**The use of liquidated damages**

In their evidence to the Trade & Industry Committee enquiry into directors' remuneration, PIRC have pointed out that despite the general contraction in notice periods, compensation payments on departure have not exhibited the decline expected (and wished for) by many investors. By way of example, they point to the fact that in 1999, compensation payments paid to departing FTSE 100 directors averaged 90% of total annual cash remuneration, a figure which had increased to 100% by 2001. PIRC suggest that the explanation for this trend may lie in the fact that:

- the directors who have been paid compensation may have been those longer-standing directors who still retained longer notice periods;

- the compensation now includes a greater number of remuneration elements; and

- the compensation is often being based on a pre-determined formula (liquidated damages) which guarantees a certain proportion of salary and other entitlements, rather than resulting from a negotiated process (mitigation)

The latter explanation touches on an issue – frequently addressed in the policy statements we have examined – that has long been the subject of contention amongst institutional investors and corporate governance policy makers. Compare, for example, the different stances advocated by the Greenbury and Hampel Committees. Whereas the Greenbury Committee emphasised the need for companies to reduce compensation 'to reflect departing directors' obligations to mitigate damages by earning money elsewhere', the Hampel Committee advocated the use of liquidated damages as a way to avoid the 'problems of mitigation and inevitably subjective arguments about performance'.

As for the tide of current opinion, it appears to be flowing away from Hampel and back to Greenbury. The NAPF and the ABI have now issued a joint statement on 'Best Practice on Executive Contracts and Severance' in which they argue that 'shareholders do not believe the liquidated damages approach is generally desirable'. Other parties, such as PIRC, have indicated that although they accept the rationale for liquidated damages[28], the amounts provided for have not reflected the spirit of the Hampel Code.

The 'return to Greenbury' is also reflected in the wording of the new Combined Code provisions on 'service contracts and compensation' which departs, rather noticeably, from the wording put forward by Derek Higgs. In his suggested Code revisions, Higgs had recommended that a rider be attached to the injunction to companies to 'consider the advantages of providing explicitly in the initial contract' for compensation commitments. This rider was to have been worded as follows: 'In doing so, they should bear in mind the need to ensure that such provisions do not have the effect of rewarding poor performance which would not amount to misconduct or otherwise entitle the company to terminate the contract'. The Financial Reporting Council however, when they published the new Combined Code, decided to drop all mention of the use (let alone the 'advantages') of liquidated damages whilst retaining the exhortation that 'companies take a robust line on reducing compensation to reflect departing directors' obligations to mitigate loss'.

Meanwhile, a possible compromise between the two approaches (mitigation/arbitration vs. liquidated damages), is proposed by the DTI consultation document on 'rewards for failure', viz. that there be a restriction, or 'cap' on the level of damages set at, for example, six months of basic salary.

In light of these debates, we expect that many institutional investors will wish to clarify their position with regard to liquidation/mitigation of damages. Of the policy statements included in our study, two fund managers express their approval of the ABI and NAPF joint statement on executive contracts and severance and a third indicates that it will usually oppose 'advance agreement' for special compensation for those cases where executive directors' contracts are terminated early[29]. Seven statements shy away from an express disapproval of liquidated damages but do insist that companies should press for full mitigation (see Figure 19). Four statements, although they do not insist upon the need for mitigation, suggest that the amount of liquidated damages agreed upon should be less generous than that which might be paid out under a standard notice period (i.e. one year's remuneration). One, rather more generously, recommends that an 'acceptable parachute' should not exceed three times base salary plus guaranteed benefits and one simply endorses the provisions of the old Combined Code (which clearly favoured the use of liquidated damages). The seven remaining statements do not express a view on this issue.

*Fig 19: The Use of Liquidated Damages*

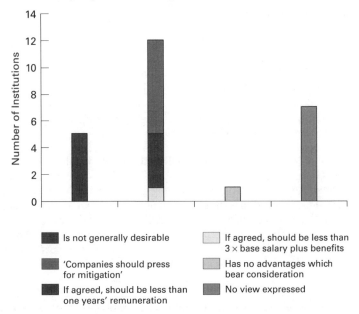

**Directors' shareholdings**

Fifteen policy statements express a view on the extent to which *executive directors* ought to hold shares in the companies they govern. Of these statements, three suggest that executive directors should acquire a shareholding equivalent to a least one year's salary. Eleven statements encourage directors to build up (and retain) 'meaningful' shareholdings but do not specify a threshold below which the shareholdings will not be considered 'meaningful'. The last statement indicates that although the institution is generally 'in favour' of share ownership on the part of executive directors, the determination of the 'appropriate ownership requirement' should be left to the individual company.

Ten policy statements also voice an opinion on the holding of shares by *non-executive directors*. Only one statement suggests that non-executive directors should be 'required' to hold shares in the companies they govern. Six endorse the view that 'shares could be helpful in aligning the interests of the [non-executive] director with the long-term interests of shareholders'. Two do not go so far as to suggest that the practice would be 'beneficial' but they do indicate their willingness to accept it. The last statement also accepts that a proportion of non-executive pay can be made in the form of shares but insists that non-executive directors should not take 'significant' holdings in the companies in which they are directors (a statement which mirrors that expressed in the Higgs Review[30]).

*Fig 20: NEDs Holding Shares in the Companies They Govern*

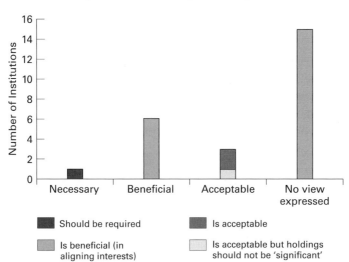

On the related question of whether non-executive directors should participate in share option or other long-term incentive schemes, nineteen policy statements express a view. Eleven of these statements enjoin non-executives not to participate in such schemes (for whatever reason). Seven adopt a more qualified position by suggesting that non-executive should refrain from participation in share option or other performance-related remuneration *if they wish to be seen as independent*. And one institution indicates that, on rare occasions, it has supported NED participation in share option plans when 'other safeguards were in place'.

**Performance hurdles for peer group comparisons**

In their discussion of long-term incentive plans, all but three of the policy statements express a view on the height of the performance hurdles that should be applied to such plans. Of these, all specify the need for 'challenging' and 'demanding' performance criteria but some are more proscriptive than others (see Figure 21). For example, seven statements insist that when the criteria involve measurement against a comparator universe (eg a sector or index), awards under incentive schemes should be made only for *above median* performance. And six adopt a slightly softer stance in suggesting that awards should not be made for *below median* performance (and that awards for median performance should not be 'excessive').

*Fig 21: Performance Hurdles in Peer Group Comparisons*

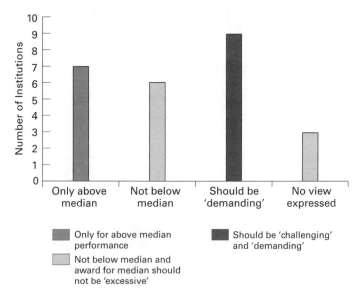

## The use of underlying financial measures in share incentive schemes

Only ten of the policy statements suggest that the performance conditions for share option and other long-term incentive plans should not be restricted to share-price based measures (such as total shareholder return) but should include at least one item measuring the underlying financial performance of the company (eg return on capital employed or the weighted average cost of capital). Of these ten statements, six express this view in terms of a definite 'expectation' while four couch it in terms of a general 'preference'.

### Re-pricing of share options

Seventeen of the policy statements express their opposition to the practice of re-pricing share options in response to falling share prices. There is, however, some interesting variation in the tone in which this opposition is expressed. As illustrated in Figure 22, some make clear that they will 'vote against' re-pricing, some are 'strongly' opposed, others are 'generally' opposed and some simply indicate their belief that such practices should 'not be necessary'.

*Fig 22: Re-pricing of Share Options*

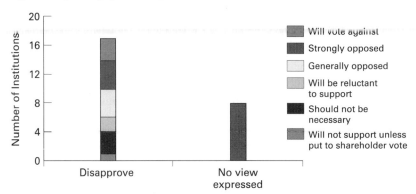

### Re-testing of performance conditions and the issuance of discounted stock options

Thirteen statements express a view on the re-testing of performance conditions[31]. Of these, five statements are unequivocal in their insistence that when performance targets are not met, there should be no re-testing period. Three make clear that they will support re-testing 'only in exceptional circumstances'; two suggest that they will 'not normally' support this practice and three simply insist it be accompanied by 'careful justification'. Eleven policy statements also discuss the issuance of discounted stock options, all of which express their opposition to this practice.

### Measurement and vesting periods

Of the nine statements that discuss the length of measurement periods for share incentive schemes, five make clear their belief that it should be a 'minimum of 3 years' and four go beyond that by emphasising that they 'strongly encourage' longer periods (eg 5 years). And of the twelve statements that discuss the vesting periods for incentive schemes: eight indicate their opposition to vesting periods of less than 3 years from the date of grant; two recommend that companies employ staggered vesting periods of beyond 3 years; one insists on a 4 year period; and one suggests that 5 years would be the 'ideal'. Twelve policy statements also recommend that the grant of share incentive awards and option grants be phased over time rather than awarded in one large block (of which two suggested that this should thereby remove the need for the re-pricing of share options).

## Social, Environmental & Ethical (SEE) Performance

### Publication and verification of SEE reports

Reflective of the growing concern with the social, environmental and ethical practices of listed companies, all but four of the institutions make clear their expectations with regard to the form in which their investees should disclose information about their SEE performance. Of these, the majority stick to the view expressed in the ABI's *Disclosure Guidelines on Socially Responsible Investment*, viz. that the annual report should:

'Describe the company's policies and procedures for managing risks to short and long-term value arising from SEE matters. If the annual report and accounts states that the company has no such policies and procedures, the board should provide reasons for their absence. The company should [also] include information about the extent to which the company has complied with its policies and procedures for managing risks arising from SEE matters.'

Four statements go beyond the ABI guidelines and recommend that larger companies and/or those operating in sectors with high environmental impacts publish a separate SEE report but only one statement indicates that a separate report will be expected of *all* listed companies (see Figure 23). In line with the ABI's Disclosure Guidelines, nine of the policy statements also insist that each listed company describe in its annual report the procedures for verification of SEE disclosures and that these procedures 'should be such as to achieve a reasonable level of credibility'. And two institutions go a step further by suggesting that a company should not just 'verify' its SEE disclosures but should also 'audit' the extent to which it has complied with its stated SEE policies.

*Fig 23: Publication of SEE Reports*

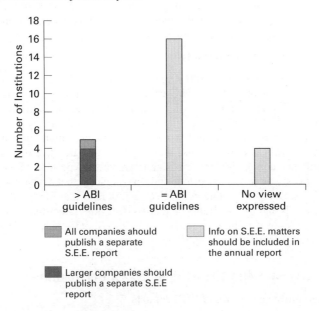

**Recommended disclosure guidelines**

Ten policy statements state the SEE disclosure guidelines with which they expect UK listed companies to comply. In most of these cases, the only expectation is that companies comply with the Disclosure Guidelines on Socially Responsible Investment issued by the ABI in October 2001 (guidelines which were modeled on those previously developed by the Socially Responsible Investment Forum). But four of these statements also commend the *Sustainability Reporting Guidelines* developed by the Global Reporting Initiative[32] and two also recommend the SEE reporting standards expressed in the *Global Sullivan Principles* and *ISO 14001* (see Figure 24).

*Fig 24: Recommended SEE Disclosure Guidelines*

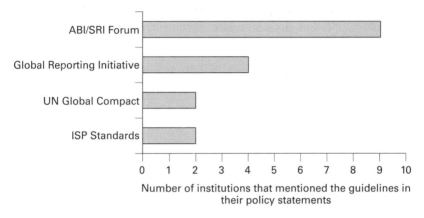

Number of institutions that mentioned the guidelines in their policy statements

**Linking SEE performance to executive compensation**

Ten policy statements register their belief that the pay of a company's executive directors should be linked (in some way) to the achievement of the company's SEE objectives. In doing so, two employ the wording adopted by the SRI Forum in its (November 2000) draft *Guidelines for Reporting on Social, Environmental and Ethical Matters*. This wording states that 'The company should disclose in its Annual Report whether the Remuneration Committee, in designing and implementing performance related remuneration schemes, has considered the effect on the company's performance of SEE.' Seven employ the revised (and slightly more circumlocutory) wording used by the ABI's *Disclosure Guidelines on Socially Responsible Investment*[33] and one suggests that it will 'vote on a case by case basis on proposals to review ways of linking executive compensation to social factors'.

In light of the public interest in both the 'social responsibilities' of listed companies and the compensation payments made to their directors, we expect that institutional investors will increasingly be asked to clarify their expectations with regard to the means by which the two should (or should not) be linked. And we will be curious to see how many adopt the position expressed in the *Sustainability Reporting Guidelines* issued by the Global Reporting Initiative viz. that companies should clearly describe the 'linkage between executive compensation and achievement of the organisation's financial and non-financial goals (eg, environmental performance, labour practices)'[34].

**Political and charitable donations**

Seventeen of the institutions in our sample state their views on the (in)appropriateness of political donations by listed companies. Of these, seven register their opposition to 'political donations of any kind', three suggest that they will only support such donations in 'exceptional circumstances', six merely require that such donations be made dependent upon shareholder approval, and one declares that it will vote against proposals to disallow political contributions (on the grounds that barring contributions might put a company at a 'competitive disadvantage'). By contrast, only four of the policy statements express a view on the acceptability of charitable donations, all of which indicated that such donations are acceptable 'within reason'.

*Fig 25: Political Donations by Listed Companies*

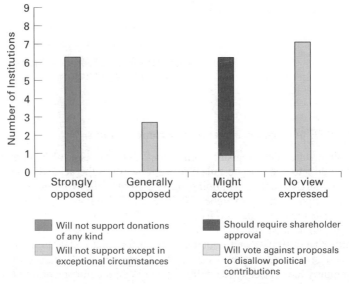

**Conclusion: Putting Policies into Practice**

In the two years since this study was last conducted, the UK's investment institutions have been called upon to provide more detailed information about the actions they have taken in support of their corporate governance and SRI policies. As described below, this call has come from the government, from the trade unions and from within the investment industry itself.

The Government is currently undertaking its 'two year review' of the Myners Investment Principles (a process that began in March 2003 and will run until the end of the year). Amongst other things, this review will address the recommendation that UK law incorporate a duty – to be laid upon both pension fund trustees and their fund managers – to intervene in the companies in which their money is invested 'as one of the means of adding value for their clients'. Although the sentiment within the Department of Work & Pensions (DWP) is that a legal 'duty to intervene' will 'not be required'[35], the DWP has confirmed that the government is planning to include in the new Pensions Bill, legislation that will enshrine the principle that 'where trustees are taking a decision, they should be able to take it with the skill and care of someone familiar with the issues concerned'.

Interestingly, the government insists that it 'does not believe that it is necessary or desirable to set out in further detail what being "familiar" involves or what must be done in order to comply with the new standard of care' – on the grounds that 'to do so would constrain the flexibility of the standard of care' and that 'its interpretation is best left to the Courts'. Not so long ago, pension fund trustees could have argued that the governance and CSR practices of the companies in which their stock was invested were not amongst the issues with which they need concern themselves. But in the wake of the recent high profile corporate governance failures – entailing the loss of billions of dollars of 'pension fund value' – pension fund trustees know that, in order to fulfil (and *be seen to* fulfil) their trustee obligations they must: a) familiarise themselves with the governance and CSR practices of investee companies; and b) familiarise themselves with the governance and CSR policies (and engagement record) of the fund managers with whom they contract. As expressed in the 'Statement of Principles' published last year by the Institutional Shareholders Committtee[36]:

'Institutional shareholders and agents have a responsibility for monitoring and assessing the effectiveness of their activism[37]. Those that act as agents will regularly report to their clients details on how they have discharged their responsibilities. This should include a judgement on the impact and effectiveness of their activism. Such reports will be likely to comprise both qualitative as well as quantitative information.'

This responsibility – for assessing and reporting upon their activism – is clearly acknowledged in most of the policy statements that we examined. As shown in Figure 26, of the twenty two investment managers included in our study, six made a commitment (in their governance and/or SRI policies) to report to their clients on a quarterly/regular basis on both their voting and engagement record. And the responsibility for monitoring the effectiveness of their activism was mentioned, in a variety of statements, by ten other investment managers.

**B7.8** *Corporate governance and social, environmental and ethical performance*

*Fig 26: Stated Policy on Voting and Engagement*

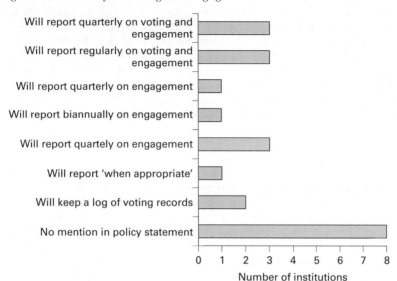

Number of institutions

In addition, our enquiries suggest that several of the institutions covered by this study have begun to disclose their engagement record not just to their clients but to the public as a whole. To date, seven of the twenty two investment managers have posted details of their engagement record on their website and one institution, the Co-operative Insurance Society, details the way it has voted at the AGMs of each of its UK investee companies since January 2002 – together with brief explanations of each instance in which it has voted against or abstained on a management resolution.

Over the coming months, Lintstock will keep track of the changes to the corporate governance and SRI policies adopted by each of the institutions in this study. And as more investment institutions begin to reveal their proxy voting records, we hope to return in twelve months time with a clearer understanding of the extent to which these policies have translated into practice.

## Institutions Covered in this Study

1.  Association of British Insurers

2.  Baillie Gifford & Co

3.  Barclays Global Investors

4.  Co-operative Insurance Society

5.  ISIS Asset Management

6.  Gartmore Investment Management

7.  Henderson Global Investors

8. Hermes Investment Management

9. HSBC Asset Management

10. Insight

11. Institutional Shareholder Services

12. JP Morgan Fleming Asset Management

13. Jupiter Asset Management

14. Legal & General Investment Management

15. M & G Investment Management

16. Merrill Lynch Investment Management

17. Morley Fund Management

18. National Association of Pension Funds

19. Newton Investment Management

20. Railways Pension Trustee Company

21. Schroders Investment Management

22. Scottish Widows Investment Partnership

23. Standard Life Investments

24. Threadneedle Investments

25. Universities Superannuation Scheme

**Notes**

1. NAPF, NIOC House, 4 Victoria Street, London SW1H 0NE, 020 7808 1300; The Association of British Insurers, 51 Gresham Street, London EC2V 7HQ, 020 7700 3333
2. Provided by E-Vote, Aldgate House, 33 Aldgate High Street, London EC3N 1DL, 020 7369 7000
3. NAPF Voting Issues Service, NIOC House, 4 Victoria Street, London SW1H 0NE; 020 7808 1340
4. As Company Law currently stands, an abstention indicated on a proxy card need not be registered as a vote. A handful of companies do provide an abstention box on proxy cards and the NAPF supports this practice. The NAPF is also pressing the DTI, as part of the Review of Company Law, to ensure that a registered abstention is recognised as a vote, which would indicate to incumbent management shareholder concern regarding a particular resolution(s). As with any vote against management, institutional shareholders should ensure that their concerns are fully explained to the company.
5. Institutional Shareholders' Committee: current membership comprises ABI, NAPF, FMA (Fund Managers' Association), AUTIF (The Association of Unit Trusts and Investment Funds) and AITC (The Association of Investment Trust Companies).
6. Recommendation might change where contract provides for longer termination period in the event of change of control.
7. Using ABI/NAPF definition

8. VIS would normally recommend support for the appointment of such a director where a board contains an adequate number of independent non-executive directors.

9. References to the 'old Combined Code' refer to 'The Combined Code-Principles of Good Governance and Code of Best Practice' May 2002. References to the 'new Combined Code' refer to 'The Combined Code on Corporate Governance' which was published by the Financial Reporting Council on 23 July 2003. The Financial Services Authority has said that it will replace the old Code with the new Code and will seek to make consequential Rule changes. There will be consultation on the necessary Rule changes but not further consultation on the Code principles and provisions themselves.

10. Whereas the text of the old Combined Code provided that 'a decision to combine the posts of chairman and chief executive officer in one person should be publicly justified', the new Code states that 'the roles of chairman and chief executive should not be exercised by the same person'.

11. Of the 100 questionnaires issued by the CBI, 61 questionnaires were completed, three of them by Chairmen representing two companies.

12. The new Combined Code has dropped the suggestion that SID 'communicate [the issues and concerns of shareholders] to the non-executive directors and, as appropriate, to the board as a whole'; but elsewhere the wording of the provisions pertaining to the role of SID has remained largely unchanged from that contained in the revisions suggested by the Higgs Review.

13. N.B. the term 'executive sessions' can be a little confusing for many UK investors where the distinction between management and non-management directors is usually expressed in terms of 'executive' vs. 'non-executive'.

14. Provision A.2.2 of the new Combined Code states that the Chair should, on appointment, meet the independence criteria established in Provision A.3.1 but thereafter the test of independence 'is not appropriate in relation to the chairman'.

15. The provisions of the new Code are expressed as follows: 'A majority of members of the nomination committee should be independent non-executive directors. The chairman or an independent non-executive director should chair the committee.'

16. With respect to the procedures by which directors should be nominated the Plan states that: 'The responsibility for identifying candidates to fill board vacancies should in principle be entrusted to a group composed mainly of executive directors, since executive directors can usefully bring their deep knowledge of the challenges facing the company and of the skills and experience of the human resources grown up within the company.' (Communication from the Commission to the Council and the European Parliament: Modernising Company Law and Enhancing Corporate Governance in the European Union – A Plan to Move Forward, May 5, 2003). It is a recommendation that has met with squeals of indignation from many British commentators. Take, for example, the reaction of the FT journalist, John Plender, who suggested (under the byline 'Stop loopy Frits') that the EU Commissioner be told that independence is needed more than inside knowledge when it comes to performing the nomination task: 'For without it, executive directors will have the happy chore of appointing those responsible for monitoring their own performance. Institutional investors should move fast to stop this anti-governance initiative. Whatever next from Mr B?' (Financial Times, Aug 25, 2003).

17. However, the new Combined Code (in line with the Higgs Recommendations) does include a new provision (A.4.4) stating that: 'The terms and conditions of appointment of non-executive directors should be made available for inspection. The letter of appointment should set out the expected time commitment. Non-executive directors should undertake that they will have sufficient time to meet what is expected of them. Their other significant commitments should be disclosed

to the board before appointment, with a broad indication of the time involved and the board should be informed of subsequent changes.'

18. It should be noted, however, that the NAPF's corporate governance policy is currently undergoing substantial revision in light of the publication of the new Combined Code. The NAPF have indicated that the revised policy will not specify a particular number of directorships beyond which extra disclosure/justification is required but will, instead, reflect the provisions of the new Combined Code which state that 'non-executive directors should undertake that they will have sufficient time to meet what is expected of them'.

19. The new Code states that 'non-executive directors may serve longer than nine years (e.g. three three-year terms), subject to annual re-election' but provides that: 'the board should state its reasons if it determines that a director is independent notwithstanding the existence of relationships or circumstances which may appear relevant to its determination, including if the director has served on the board for more than nine years from the date of their first election'.

20. 'Inevitably, the effectiveness of a non-executive director's contribution will change over time. Non-executive directors should be willing and able to acknowledge when their individual contribution is no longer fresh, and should make way for newcomers in an orderly and managed way' (paragraph 6.18 of the Higgs Review).

21. As was acknowledged in the Higgs Review, there is a strong case to be made that, given that a new NED often faces a 'lengthy learning curve', a long tenure should be of benefit to a company. At the very least, the advantages of a long tenure need to be carefully weighed against the potential disadvantages (e.g. a reduction in independence and/or 'freshness').

22. In light of these developments, Lintstock – in conjunction with the Judge Institute of Management at the University of Cambridge – has been conducting a survey of the continuing professional development needs of UK NEDs (in the FTSE 350). The results of this survey, which are due for publication in October 2003, may prompt further reflection amongst UK fund managers as to the practices and disclosures (with respect to director education) they expect from the companies in which their assets are invested. Copies of the survey can be obtained from the Lintstock website www.lintstock.com/news13.php).

23. See, for example, the articles in Financial News by Michael Hoare ('Higgs "misses the point"', 21 Apr 2003) and Kit Bingham ('UK firms play board games', 29 June 2003) and Matthew Gower's article in the June 2003 issue of IR Magazine ('The trouble with Higgs').

24. Provision C.3.7 of the new Code requires that: 'The annual report should explain to shareholders how, if the auditor provides non-audit services, auditor objectivity and independence is safeguarded'.

25. Provision D.2.2 of the old Code provided that: 'Companies which do not have an internal audit function should from time to time review the need for one'. In the new Code, this provision has been replaced by the more stringent Provision C.3.5 which states that: 'Where there is no internal audit function, the audit committee should consider annually whether there is a need for an internal audit function and make a recommendation to the board, and the reasons for the absence of such a function should be explained in the relevant section of the annual report'.

26. Figure 17 is drawn from the evidence presented to the Trade & Industry Committee enquiry into directors' remuneration by PIRC. Of the 58 FTSE 100 companies whose voting results (during the period Jan-June 2003) were supplied to PIRC, 32 companies experienced against/abstain votes on their remuneration reports in excess of 15%. By comparison, PIRC notes that the opposition recorded against remuneration reports (that were voluntarily submitted for a vote) in 2002 averaged around 4%.

27. This acceptance of the need for 'flexibility' mirrors the language of the old rather than the new Combined Code. Whereas the old Code suggested that 'there was a strong case for setting notice periods at, or reducing them to, one year', the new Code simply states that 'notice or contract periods should be set at one year or less'. The old Code also added a rider to the effect that 'boards should set this an objective; but they should recognise that it may not be possible to achieve it immediately' – a rider which has been excised from the new Code.

28. PIRC's acceptance of the rationale for liquidated damages is based on their observation that 'few companies have been rigorous in applying the principle of mitigation'.

29. Because the NAPF and ABI are amongst the 25 institutions covered by this study, the first column in Figure 19 shows a total of 5 institutions whose view on the use of liquidated damages is closer to that of Greenbury than Hampel.

30. The Higgs Review suggested that 'although there is merit in the current practice of some companies giving their non-executive directors the opportunity to take part of their remuneration in the form of shares in lieu of cash', it would be 'undesirable, however, for any shareholdings to represent a large proportion of the individual non-executive director's financial wealth'.

31. For example, in the case of a share option plan where the performance measurement period is set at 3 years, re-testing occurs if the targets are not met in that 3 year period (hence no bonus is due) but the bonus is still awarded if the targets have been met over 4 years or over 5 years from the same base date, i.e. the conditions are 're-tested' in years 4 and 5.

32. The Global Reporting Initiative was started in 1997 by the Coalition for Environmentally Responsible Economies (CERES) and is, to date, the most comprehensive attempt to develop and disseminate globally applicable SEE guidelines.

33. 'The company should state in its annual report whether the Board has ensured that the company has in place effective systems for managing significant risks, which, where relevant, incorporate appropriate remuneration incentives.'

34. See Reporting Element 3.5 of the Sustainability Reporting Guidelines.

35. The DWP has suggested that the government is not minded to incorporate an 'activist duty' into UK law because the force of the 'voluntary' Myners principles will already have proved sufficient

36. The Institutional Shareholders Committee comprises the Association of British Insurers, the National Association of Pension Funds, the Association of Investment Trust Companies and the Investment Management Association.

37. It is a sentiment that also finds expression in the recent TUC survey of Fund Manager Voting which concludes that: 'As Myners has made clear, the right to vote is an asset of a pension fund and is subject therefore to fiduciary duties. Trustees would be negligent if they disregarded fund managers' approach to activism in making selection decisions.'

# Risk Management and Internal Control

## Developments in internal control concepts and definitions over time B8.1

Internal control is a complex, carefully thought-out concept. We tend to take its meaning for granted. Here, we explore the development of the definition and framework of internal control over the last century. A summary table at **B8.25** gives an overview.

'Control' divides into *external control* by the stakeholders of an entity (such as the shareholders, debenture holders, creditors) and *internal control* by the board, management and other personnel. (See **B5** EXTERNAL CONTROL for a consideration of external control.)

Internal control has often been seen as synonymous with *management control* – control by management of the internal affairs of the entity. Now it is more clearly understood that the board has overall oversight and monitoring responsibilities for internal control and that all members of staff, especially in empowered entities, have roles to play in achieving effective internal control.

## The meaning of internal control B8.2

Some important concepts can contribute to our understanding of internal control. We can summarise them as follows.

- Control consists of *external* as well as *internal* control.

- Internal control is broadly synonymous with *management control*, subject to oversight by the board and inputs from other members of staff.

- Management is primarily responsible for internal control;[1]

- Internal audit is the independent appraisal of the effectiveness of internal control on behalf of management;[2]

- Management control is achieved by the judicious application of *all* of the elements of management – planning, organising, directing, staffing, controlling and coordinating.

Control is analogous to the process of a central heating or air conditioning thermostat, which:

- has a planned temperature (e.g. 24°C);

- takes measurements of actual performance;

- compares actual against plan;

- notes the variance between actual and plan; and

- makes a decision whether to switch on the pump (or fan) to keep actual performance within a tolerable range of planned performance.

With this model of control it is clear that first there is a need for a plan against which to control. The development of policies on business conduct and the design of detailed procedures are both aspects of planning. Secondly, control entails monitoring. Thirdly, control requires decision taking: decision taking is usually associated with planning but it is also right at the heart of controlling – an indication that it is impossible neatly to unravel planning from controlling.

## The first definition of internal control (AICPA)   B8.3

A seminal definition of internal control dates back to 1948 though it has now been generally replaced by the COSO definition which we look at later. In 1948, AICPA defined internal control in a way which they acknowledged was 'broader than the meaning sometimes attributed to the term', as follows:

> 'Internal control comprises the plan of organisation and the co-ordinate methods and measures adopted within a business to safeguard its assets, check the accuracy and reliability of its accounting data, promote operational efficiency, and encourage adherence to prescribed managerial policies.'[3]

Two key points to note about this definition are first that it identified planning, organisational arrangements and procedures as being basic to internal control, and secondly that it gave four objectives of internal control which were to do with:

- safeguarding assets;

- reliability of accounts;

- operational efficiency; and

- effectiveness (achievement of policies).

The definition also characterised internal control more as a 'state of affairs' than as a 'process' (which is the emphasis in the more recent COSO definition).

## Administrative and accounting control   B8.4

A significant milestone in the development of conventional wisdom about internal control came in 1958 when AICPA divided internal control into (a) administrative control, and (b) accounting control[4]. This distinction has been with us ever since[5]. The motivation for the distinction was an awareness on the part of public accountants acting as external auditors that their primary concern was with the controls which contribute to the reliability of the accounts (or published financial statements) and that they as external auditors were not so concerned with so-called 'administrative controls' over operations. Dividing internal control into administrative and accounting controls was intended to allow external auditors to largely restrict their interest in internal control to the accounting controls only.

AICPA made the distinction as follows:

'Accounting control comprises the plan of the organisation and the procedures and records that are concerned with the safeguards of assets and the reliability of financial records' and

'Administrative control includes, but is not limited to, the plan of organization and the procedures and records that are concerned with the decision processes leading to management's authorization of transactions. Such authorization is a management function directly associated with the responsibility for achieving the objectives of the organization and is the starting point for establishing accounting controls of transactions.'[6]

## Traditional UK definitions of internal control                           B8.5

In the UK a broadly similar understanding about the nature of internal control emerged. The generally accepted UK definition of internal control was:

'the whole system of controls, financial and otherwise, established by the management in order to carry on the business in an orderly and efficient manner, ensure adherence to management policies, safeguard the assets and secure as far as possible the completeness and accuracy of the records.[7]

At about that time, an alternative UK definition of internal control (which did not replace the above definition) was:

'The regulation of activities in an organisation through systems designed and implemented to facilitate the achievement of management objectives.'[8]

## IIA definitions of internal control                                       B8.6

We must make reference to the position of the Institute of Internal Auditors. Until the adoption of their new Standards in 2002, The IIA had a straightforward definition of internal control which could be reconciled to the definitions we have already used. The IIA identified five objectives of control in contrast to the four explicit in the AICPA/CCAB pronouncements we have already considered and the three objectives in the COSO framework to which we turn our attention shortly. Until 2002 The IIA continued to adhere to their position that internal control exists to achieve these five objectives in contrast to COSO's three objectives[9] notwithstanding that the IIA was one of the five COSO bodies. By 2002 The IIA had come into line with COSO except that it continues to show *safeguarding of assets* as a separate objective of internal control. It is generally regarded as to have been a mistake by COSO not to have done so.

Until the adoption of the new IIA Standards, the IIA definition of internal control was as follows:

'The overall system of internal control is conceptual in nature. It is an integrated collection of controlled systems used by an organization to achieve its objectives and goals.'[10]

Now, their definition has become more complex (see Row 12 of the table at **B8.25**, and also **B23.4** which is the new IIA Standards):

> '**Control** – Any action taken by management, the board, and other parties to enhance risk management and increase the likelihood that established objectives and goals will be achieved. Management plans, organizes, and directs the performance of sufficient actions to provide reasonable assurance that objectives and goals will be achieved.'

And the IIA's old five objectives of control, which were:

> '(a) the reliability and integrity of information;
>
> (b) compliance with policies, plans, procedures, laws and regulations;
>
> (c) the safeguarding of assets;
>
> (d) the economical and efficient use of resources;[and]
>
> (e) the accomplishment of established objectives and goals for operations or programmes.'[11]

have now been rejigged to four.

- 'Reliability and integrity of financial and operational information.

- Effectiveness and efficiency of operations.

- Safeguarding of assets.

- Compliance with laws, regulations, and contracts.'

# Treadway, COSO and the UK equivalents                                    B8.7

During the 1980s five US bodies[12] known as COSO (Committee of Sponsoring Organizations) invited Treadway to head a commission of enquiry in the wake of concern about fraudulent financial reporting. The so-called Treadway Report[13] was published in 1987 and even today can be downloaded from the web (www.coso.org). Treadway recommended that management should include a report on internal control with their published financial statements. Adoption of this proposal was initially deferred pending clarification of the meaning of internal control and the form and process of any such report by management: it never became mandatory in the US though it is a practice frequently followed. To provide this clarification, COSO funded a further project, the fieldwork of which was conducted by Coopers & Lybrand, which led to the publication in 1992 of 'Internal Control – Integrated Framework'[14] (known as 'The COSO Report'). This gave us a new definition of internal control which is supplanting the 1948 AICPA definition and its derivatives. COSO also gives guidance on how internal control is achieved by means of five interrelated control components. Finally, COSO gave guidance on the process and form of public reports by management on internal control. One limitation of the 1992 COSO internal control framework was that within the COSO definition itself there was no acknowledgement that today's outsourcing means that so much of what contributes to an organisation's effective internal control now occurs within the activities of business partners (see **B8.26** on internal control when activities are outsourced).

## The COSO definition of internal control                    B8.8

'Internal control is broadly defined as a process, effected by the entity's board of directors, management and other personnel, designed to provide reasonable assurance regarding the achievement of objectives in the following categories:

- Effectiveness and efficiency of operations.

- Reliability of financial reporting.

- Safeguarding of assets.

- Compliance with applicable laws and regulations.'

COSO recognises that the three objectives of control are 'distinct but overlapping categories [which] address different needs and allow a directed focus to meet the separate needs'. It is easier to reconcile these three categories of objectives with the four objectives of control in the 1948 definition if one bears in mind that the drafters of the COSO definition intended that safeguarding of assets against unauthorised use (etc.) should be regarded as part of the effectiveness and efficiency of operations objective, whereas in the UK, Rutteman was to classify this as part of internal financial control.

The COSO definition puts stress on 'process' though this is a largely cosmetic change of nomenclature from the earlier uses of the expressions 'methods and measures' and 'system' which we referred to earlier. (The UK continues to use the expression 'system').

'Internal control is not an event or circumstance, but a series of actions that permeate an entity's activities. These actions are pervasive, and are inherent in the way management runs the business.'[15]

The COSO definition also usefully stresses that internal control cannot *guarantee* the achievement of control objectives – but can give reasonable assurance of doing so.

**Approximate matching of principal classifications of stated
objectives of internal control**                                       **B8.9**

| Old AICPA/CC AB | IIA (1978 to 2001) | COSO (1992) | IIA (2002) |
|---|---|---|---|
| 1  Safeguarding assets | The safeguarding of assets | (COSO intended this to be subsumed within row 3) | Safeguarding of assets |
| 2  Reliability of accounts | The reliability and integrity of information | Reliability of financial reporting | Reliability and integrity of financial and operational information |
| 3  Operational efficiency | The economical and efficient use of resources | Effectiveness and efficiency of operations | Effectiveness and efficiency of operations |
| 4  Effectiveness | The accomplishment of established objectives and goals for operations or programmes | ('Effectiveness' is included in Row 3 above) | ('Effectiveness' is included in Row 3 above) |
| 5 | Compliance with policies, plans, procedures, laws and regulations | Compliance with applicable laws and regulations | Compliance with laws, regulations, and contracts |

# Components of internal control                                       B8.10

COSO goes on to provide a classification of the ways in which internal control is
achieved which they term the five interrelated control 'components' and
COSO's extensive discussion of the nature of these components is extremely
useful.

- Control environment       for instance, the ethical tone set by the Board

- Risk assessment           for instance, it is necessary for management to
                            assess relative risk as a prerequisite for
                            developing and maintaining commensurate
                            effective internal control

- Control activities        for instance, segregation of duties

- Information and          for instance, exception reports
  communication

- Monitoring               for instance, by internal audit

## The Rutteman Report on internal control                    B8.11

A parallel development took place in the UK. The Cadbury Report[16] recommended that directors of listed companies should report publicly on internal control, and guidance was prepared on this[17].

This guidance defined internal control as:

'The whole system of controls, financial and otherwise, established in order to provide reasonable assurance of:

1.  effective and efficient operations;

2.  internal financial control; and

3.  compliance with laws and regulations.'

The UK therefore perpetuated the 1972 suggestion that it is possible and helpful to distinguish between financial and other controls whereas COSO really makes the distinction only at the level of the *objectives* of control, not the *process* of control. In other words COSO is saying internal control can give reasonable reassurance of the achievement of three categories of objectives, whereas Rutteman agreed that there are these three aims but suggested further that there are also at least two sub-sets of internal controls (one of which comprises the *internal financial controls*), and that control over the reliability of financial statements is achieved by the internal financial controls subset.

COSO does not go so far as to claim there are two sub-sets of internal control. COSO only goes as far as to recognise, with regard to the three categories of objectives of control, that

'these distinct but overlapping categories address different needs and allow a directed focus to meet the separate needs'[18].

Until the Turnbull Report, the UK also placed less emphasis upon *process*.

Rutteman replaced the five US components by which control is achieved by five similar *criteria*, taking exception to the word *components*. The criteria were:

- control environment;

- identification and evaluation of risks, and control objectives;

- information and communication;

- control procedures; and

- monitoring and corrective action.

Rutteman described these as 'criteria' in order to emphasise that the quality of these internal control components should be assessed in order to evaluate the effectiveness of internal control. In other words, it is not enough to consider whether there have been any significant breakdowns in internal control as a means of concluding on internal control effectiveness, although this must be done. Even if there have been no breakdowns in internal control, the system of internal control may still be defective – it may be just that its weaknesses have not yet been exploited.

## The Turnbull Report on internal control                                B8.12

The Turnbull guidance, which replaces the Rutteman guidance, gives us a new definition of internal control:

'An internal control system encompasses the policies, processes, tasks, behaviours and other aspects of a company that, taken together:

- facilitate its effective and efficient operation by enabling it to respond appropriately to significant business, operational, financial, compliance and other risks to achieving the company's objectives. This includes the safeguarding of assets from inappropriate use or from loss and fraud, and ensuring that liabilities are identified and managed;

- help ensure the quality of internal and external reporting. This requires the maintenance of proper records and processes that generate a flow of timely, relevant and reliable information within and outside the organisation;

- help ensure compliance with applicable laws and regulations, and also with internal policies with respect to the conduct of business.'

(The Turnbull Report is reproduced in PART A.)

Turnbull also carries forward the COSO/Rutteman components/criteria of internal control, though for a reason which is not very clear, Turnbull has combined two of the five so that we now have:

- risk assessment;

- control environment and control activities;

- information and communication; and

- monitoring.

The author does not consider it wise for committees convened for a particular purpose to redefine an important concept which has been meticulously considered by another committee with that specific remit. COSO remains the authoritative definition of internal control, and is widely accepted throughout the world as such.

# Would a more modest paradigm of internal control be better?   B8.13

The generally accepted COSO definition of internal control states that internal control is the process that gives reasonable assurance of the achievement of objectives. COSO gave three categories of objectives – effectiveness and efficiency of operations, reliability of financial reporting, and compliance with applicable laws and regulations.

Does this mean that internal control comprises *all* of the processes that management applies to achieve the organisation's objectives, or just those processes which are designed to *assure* (i.e. confirm, attest) that management are doing what is necessary to achieve objectives? If so, how can one distinguish between the two? The external audit profession uses the word 'assurance' in the latter sense of 'confirming' or 'attesting' – they talk about 'assurance services'; might we not also do so when we are defining the scope of internal control? Would this not help to keep the concept of internal control more modestly confinable and practical – rather than making it appear to be *all*, or at least *most*, of management? Indeed, what did COSO mean the scope of internal control to be regarded as? How could we apply a more modest concept of the boundaries of internal control while still holding to the COSO framework?

## How COSO described the overlap between 'management' and 'internal control'   B8.14

In the final COSO Report, the authors stated:

> 'Some respondents [to the COSO exposure draft] said that internal control is only a part, albeit an important part, of the management process, and that the exposure draft incorrectly defines internal control in a way that encompasses or appears to encompass the entire management process. They believe this implies that internal control can ensure management's achievement of the entity's objectives, which implication could continue or aggravate the existing expectation gaps.

> To address these comments, the final report more clearly distinguishes internal control from other aspects of the management process. It makes it clear that many management responsibilities such as establishing objectives, making business decisions, executing transactions and carrying out plans are among the management activities that are integrated with, but not a part of, the internal control system.'[19]

COSO went on to state that:

> 'Internal control can be judged effective in the case of each of the three categories[20] respectively, if the board of directors and management have reasonable assurance that:
>
> • They understand the extent to which the entity's operations objectives are being achieved.

355

- Published financial statements are being prepared reliably.

- Applicable laws and regulations are being complied with.[21']

and:

> 'Even effective internal control can only help an entity achieve [the basic business objectives]. It can provide management information about the entity's progress, or lack of it, toward their achievement. But internal control cannot change an inherently poor manager in to a good one. And, shifts in government policy or programs, competitors' actions or economic conditions can be beyond management's control. Internal control cannot assure success, or even survival.'[22]

and:

> 'achievement of operations objectives – such as a particular return on investment, market share or entry into new product lines – is not always within the entity's control. Internal control cannot prevent bad judgements or decisions, or external events that can cause a business to fail to achieve operations goals. For these objectives, the internal control system can provide reasonable assurance only that management and, in its oversight role, the board are made aware, in a timely manner, of the extent to which the entity is moving toward those objectives.'[23]

COSO accepted that not everything management does is an element of internal control. Establishment of objectives, for example, while an important management responsibility is not part of internal control, but is a precondition to internal control. Similarly, many decisions and actions by management do not represent internal control.

COSO considered that establishing objectives was a prerequisite to effective internal control, objectives providing measurable targets toward which the entity moves in conducting its activities.[24] However, although an entity should have reasonable assurance that certain objectives are achieved, COSO pointed out that that might not be the case for all objectives.

On the other hand, COSO suggested that an effective internal control system should provide reasonable assurance that an entity's financial reporting objectives are being achieved. Similarly, there should be reasonable assurance that compliance objectives are being achieved. This is because both of these categories are primarily based on external standards established independently of the entity's purposes, and achieving them is largely within the entity's control.

COSO pointed out:

> 'there is a difference when it comes to operations objectives. First, they are not based on external standards. Second, an entity may perform as intended, yet be out-performed by a competitor. It could also be subject to outside events – a change in government, poor weather and the like – that it cannot control. It may even have considered some of these events in its objective-setting process and treated them as low probability, with a

contingency plan in case they occurred. However, such a plan only mitigates the impact of outside events. It does not ensure that the objectives are achieved. Good operations consistent with the intent of objectives do not ensure success.

The goal of internal control in this area focuses primarily on: developing consistency of objectives and goals throughout the organization, identifying key success factors and timely reporting to management of performance and expectations. Although success cannot be ensured, management should have reasonable assurance of being alerted when objectives are in danger of not being achieved.'

COSO provided a quite useful table, reproduced here, which sought to show how internal control was not all of management.

**Internal control and the management process**                                **B8.15**

| Management Activities | Internal Control |
|---|---|
| Entity-level objective setting – mission, value statements | |
| Strategic planning | |
| Establishing control environment factors | √ |
| Activity-level objective setting | |
| Risk identification and analysis | √ |
| Risk management | |
| Conducting control activities | √ |
| Information identification, capture and communication | √ |
| Monitoring | √ |
| Corrective actions | |

While this limits internal control to something less than all of management, it is not so clear whether it limits internal control to 'assurance' activities. Indeed, it is a challenge to separate those activities of management which are assurance activities from other things which managers do.

The Canadian CoCo programme excludes decisions from internal control, thus making internal control certainly less than *all* of what management does. The classic work on management control by Anthony (1965) defined management control as 'the process by which managers assure that resources are obtained and used effectively and efficiently in the accomplishment of the organization's objectives'. So CoCo and Anthony both lend weight to the suggestion that internal control is an 'assuring' or supportive process or processes. If this is so, then the challenge is to logically demarcate the assurance processes from the other processes within the business – or perhaps this cannot be done.

*Risk assessment*                                                                **B8.16**

COSO also made a distinction between risk assessment, which COSO classified as part of internal control, and the resulting plans, programmes or other actions deemed necessary by management to address the risks. COSO regarded the actions undertaken to be a key part of the larger management process, but not an element of the internal control system.[25]

Topical today, in the light of Turnbull, COSO regarded risk analysis not as a theoretical exercise but as often critical to the entity's success, and most effective when it includes identification of all key business processes where potential exposures of some consequence exist. The COSO report suggested that risk analysis might involve process analysis, such as identification of key dependencies and significant control nodes, and also the establishment of clear responsibility and accountability. COSO suggested that effective process analysis directs special attention to cross-organisational dependencies, identifying, for example, where data originate, where they are stored, how they are converted to useful information and who uses the information; and that large organisations usually need to be particularly vigilant in addressing intra-company and inter-company transactions and key dependencies. These processes can be positively affected by quality programmes which, with a 'buy-in' by employees, can be an important element in risk containment.

*A directed focus*                                                               **B8.17**

COSO also accepted that the COSO definition of internal control accommodated subsets of internal control, so that those who wish to can focus separately, for example on controls over financial reporting or on controls related to compliance with laws and regulations, are able to do so. Similarly, a directed focus on controls in particular units or activities of an entity can be accommodated.'[26]

**Recent UK perceptions**                                                        **B8.18**

*Rutteman*                                                                       **B8.19**

UK perceptions have not been entirely consistent. Rutteman's definitions of internal control[27] and of internal *financial* control left open the possibility that his working party was restricting the scope of internal control to those elements which provided *assurance* of the achievement of objectives, *viz.*

*Internal control:*
'The whole system of controls, financial and otherwise, established in order to provide reasonable assurance of:

1.   effective and efficient operations.

2.   internal financial control.

3.   compliance with laws and regulations'.

*Internal financial control:*
'The internal controls established in order to provide reasonable assurance of:

(a) the safeguarding of assets against unauthorised use or disposition; and

(b) the maintenance of proper accounting records and the reliability of financial information used within the business or for publication.'

## *Hampel* B8.20

The Hampel Report was even more ambiguous on the matter:

'The board should maintain a sound system of internal control to safeguard shareholders' investment and the company's assets.'

## *Turnbull* B8.21

On the other hand, the most recent UK report to attempt a definition of internal control, the Turnbull Report[28], perhaps almost unwittingly comes down unambiguously on the side of internal control being all those things that management does to ensure the achievement of objectives, not just those things which provide reassurance that objectives are being achieved:

'An internal control system encompasses the policies, processes, tasks, behaviours and other aspects of a company that, taken together:

• facilitate its effective and efficient operation by enabling it to respond appropriately to significant business, operational, financial, compliance and other risks to achieving the company's objectives. This includes the safeguarding of assets from inappropriate use or from loss and fraud, and ensuring that liabilities are identified and managed;

• help ensure the quality of internal and external reporting. This requires the maintenance of proper records and processes that generate a flow of timely, relevant and reliable information within and outside the organisation;

• help ensure compliance with applicable laws and regulations, and also with internal policies with respect to the conduct of business.'

(The Turnbull Report is reproduced in PART A.)

## Internal control in the context of management theory B8.22

It is difficult to separate out internal control from the other elements or functions of management, *viz.*[29]

• Planning.

• Organising.

• Staffing.

• Directing and leading.

- Controlling.

- Co-ordinating.

These functions interact, overlap and coalesce. Control is an important set of threads woven through the tapestry of management. It is beguiling but misleading to consider internal control to be *all* of management.[30]

The arguments in favour can be summed up as follows.

1.   Many of the definitions of internal control are very broad so as apparently to leave little space for any other managerial functions.

2.   Control depends upon each of the other functions of management. There is no control without:

- Planning:

  ○   For instance, design of the right procedures (which is part of planning) is essential for effective control.

  ○   There has to be a plan against which to exercise control. Without a plan there can be no control.

- Organising:

  ○   For instance, structuring the business into subdivisions and determining reporting arrangements31

- Directing and leading:

  ○   Few would question that the quality of leadership impacts upon control.

- Staffing:

  ○   Too few or too many staff can lead to things getting out of control – as can incompetent, disloyal, dishonest or lazy staff.

- Coordinating:

  ○   The art of ensuring that happenings occur in harmony with each other – without which things will be out of control.

Despite these beguiling arguments, it is more prudent to acknowledge that whilst planning, organising and the other functions of management are mechanisms by which the board and management achieves control, managers also achieve other objectives apart from control by the judicious application of these elements of management. For instance, they may develop effective long-term plans; or they may make excellent staffing arrangements so that not only control but other elements of management are better handled.

**Implications for internal audit scope**                                        **B8.23**

If internal auditors interpret their mission as to conduct an independent appraisal of the effectiveness of internal control, it is true that they may be drawing management's attention to weaknesses in planning, organising, directing, staffing and co-ordinating which may account for control weaknesses. It would not therefore be beyond the scope of internal auditing to raise audit points which relate to weaknesses in planning, staffing, directing and so on. Conventionally this would be done when these weaknesses provide an explanation for actual or potential breakdowns of control. There may be other weaknesses in planning, staffing and so on which do not impinge directly upon control and would therefore be beyond the scope of internal audit to detect or comment upon – if we define internal auditing as being the review of internal control.

On the other hand the terms of reference of many internal auditors require them to draw management's attention to *anything* they detect during the course of their internal auditing work which is commercially unsound and so not too much ceremony may be attached to whether an audit finding is, or is not, a control point.

Nevertheless the generally accepted emphasis of internal audit is the review of internal control so it is perhaps less likely that internal audit will detect weaknesses in the other elements of management which do not have a significant control impact.

## Enterprise risk management (COSO)      B8.24

Late in 2001 COSO let to Pricewaterhouse Coopers (PWC) the contract to research and report on enterprise risk management. (Coopers & Lybrand had been the firm that undertook the work to develop the 1992 COSO framework). PWC initially committed 10,000 professional hours to this project. Mid-2003 COSO published their exposure draft of this study (Executive Summary, and Enterprise Risk Management Framework) (http://www.coso.org). We consider this new study will be as influential as the 1992 COSO study Internal Control – Integrated Framework. In the new Exposure Draft (p18) COSO states that:

> 'Because Internal Control – Integrated Framework is the basis for existing rules, regulations and laws, that document remains in place as the definition of and framework for internal control. The entirety of *Internal Control – Integrated Framework* is incorporated by reference into this framework [ie into COSO's new enterprise risk management exposure draft].'

Rather than the five essential components of internal control in COSO's 1992 internal control framework, COSO is proposing eight components of enterprise risk management:

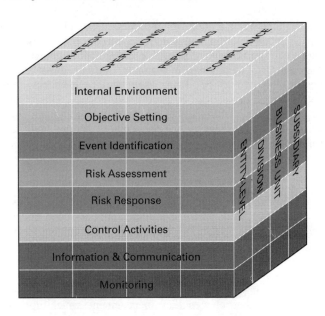

In COSO's Enterprise Risk Management exposure draft, ERM is defined as follows (p3):

> 'Enterprise risk management is a process, effected by an entity's board of directors, management and other personnel, applied in strategy setting and across the enterprise, designed to identify potential events that may affect the entity, and manage risks to be within its risk appetite, to provide reasonable assurance regarding the achievement of entity objectives.'

COSO describes internal control as part of enterprise risk management (p18):

> 'Internal Control is an integral part of enterprise risk management. This enterprise risk management framework encompasses internal control, forming a more robust conceptualization and tool for management. Internal control is defined and described in Internal Control – Integrated Framework.'

In **B26.21** we draw attention to the SEC's recognition by name of three internal control frameworks for the review of internal control effectiveness – CoCo, Turnbull and COSO (1992). We can expect the new COSO Enterprise Risk Management framework to be accorded similar recognition – both on merit and because of the statement (see above) that:

> 'The entirety of *Internal Control – Integrated Framework* is incorporated by reference into this framework [ie into COSO's new enterprise risk management exposure draft].'

In time, we suggest that directors' reports on internal control will be superseded by directors' reports termed 'resorts on risk management' or 'reports on risk management and internal control'. They will include but not be limited to internal control. The UK's *Combined Code* Provision on directors internal control reviews (C.2.1 in the 2003 *Code*) has, since 1998, included risk management within the scope of those reviews. The rewording of this provision as it appears in the 2003 UK Code, from 'risk management' to 'risk management systems' gives a better indication of what it is that the directors are reviewing.

**How definitions of internal control have developed over the years    B8.25**

|    | Date | Source | Definition of internal control |
|----|------|--------|-------------------------------|
| 1. | 1916 | Henri Fayol: *Administration Industrielle et Générale.* | Control as one of the elements of management. |
| 2. | 1948 – publication. 1949 | American Institute of Certified Public Accountants: *Internal Control – Elements of a Co-ordinated System and its Importance to Management and the Independent Public Accountant,* New York. | 'Internal control comprises the plan of organisation and the co-ordinate methods and measures adopted within a business to safeguard its assets, check the accuracy and reliability of its accounting data, promote operational efficiency and encourage adherence to prescribed managerial policies.' |
| 3. | 1980 and 1992 | Consultative Committee of Accounting Bodies, Auditing Practices Committee: *Auditing Guideline* [1980, s3]; and Chartered Institute of Management Accountants: *A Framework for Internal Control* | 'the whole system of controls, financial and otherwise, established by the management in order to carry on the business in an orderly and efficient manner, ensure adherence to management policies, safeguard the assets and secure as far as possible the completeness and accuracy of the records.' |
| 4. | 1972 and 1988 | AICPA, 1972 and AICPA: *Professional Standards, Volume 1* (June 1, 1988). | 'Accounting control comprises the plan of the organisation and the procedures and records that are concerned with the safeguards of assets and the reliability of financial records' |

|   | Date | Source | Definition of internal control |
|---|------|--------|-------------------------------|
|   |      |        | Administrative control includes, but is not limited to, the plan of organization and the procedures and records that are concerned with the decision processes leading to management's authorization of transactions. Such authorization is a management function directly associated with the responsibility for achieving the objectives of the organization and is the starting point for establishing accounting controls of transactions.' |
| 5. | 1983 | IIA Inc: *Control: Concepts and Responsibilities* [Statement on Internal Auditing Standards (SIAS), No. 1 [July 1983], and Standard 305. | The overall system of internal 'control is conceptual in nature. It is an integrated collection of controlled systems used by an organization to achieve its objectives and goals.'<br><br>'The primary objectives of internal control are to ensure:<br>(a) the reliability and integrity of information;<br>(b) compliance with policies, plans, procedures, laws and regulations;<br>(c) the safeguarding of assets;<br>(d) the economical and efficient use of resources;<br><br>(e) the accomplishment of established objectives and goals for operations or programmes. |
| 6. | 1990 | CCAB: Auditing Guideline 308: *Guidance for Internal Auditors* (Glossary of Terms section) [1990]. | The regulation of activities in 'an organisation through systems designed and implemented to facilitate the achievement of management objectives.' |

| | Date | Source | Definition of internal control |
|---|---|---|---|
| 7 | September 1992 | *Internal Control – Integrated Framework*, published by The Committee of Sponsoring Organizations of the Treadway Commission, obtainable from American Institute of Certified Public Accountants, Harborside Financial Center, 201 Plaza III, Jersey City, NJ 07311–3881. Their new (1999) website: www.coso.org. | 'Internal control is broadly defined as a process, effected by the entity's board of directors, management and other personnel, designed to provide reasonable assurance regarding the achievement of objectives in the following categories:<br><br>• Effectiveness and efficiency of operations;<br>• Reliability of financial reporting<br>• Compliance with applicable laws and regulations.' |
| 8. | December 1994 | *Internal Control and Financial Reporting* ('The Rutteman Report') (ICAEW). | **Internal control:**<br>'The whole system of controls, financial and otherwise, established in order to provide reasonable assurance of:<br>1. effective and efficient operations.<br>2. internal financial control.<br>3. compliance with laws and regulations'.<br><br>**Internal *financial* control:**<br>'The internal controls established in order to provide reasonable assurance of:<br>(a) the safeguarding of assets against unauthorised use or disposition; and |

**B8.25**  *How definitions of internal control have developed over the years*

| Date | Source | Definition of internal control |
|---|---|---|
| | | (b)  the maintenance of proper '  accounting records and the reliability of financial information used within the business or for publication.' |
| 9.  November 1995 | Guidance on Control, Control and Governance – Number 1, ('The CoCo programme'), The Canadian Institute of Chartered Accountants, ISBN 0–88800–436–1. | Control comprises those *'elements* of an organization (including its resources, systems, processes, culture, structure and tasks) that, taken together, support people in the achievement of the organization's objectives. These objectives fall into one or more of the following categories: <br> • **Effectiveness and efficiency of operations** includes objectives related to an organization's goals, such as customer service, the safeguarding and efficient use of resources, profitability and meeting social obligations. This includes the safeguarding of the organization's resources from inappropriate use or loss and ensuring that liabilities are identified and managed. <br> • **Reliability of internal and external reporting** includes objectives related to matters such as the maintenance of proper accounting records, the reliability of information used within the organization and of information published for third parties. This includes the protection of records against two main types of fraud: the concealment of theft and the distortion of results. |

| | Date | Source | Definition of internal control |
|---|---|---|---|
| | | | • Compliance with applicable laws and regulations and internal policies includes objectives related to ensuring that the organization's affairs are conducted in accordance with legal and regulatory obligations and internal policies. |
| 10. | 1997/1998 | The Hampel Report and The Combined Code. | 'The board should maintain a sound system of internal control to safeguard shareholders' investment and the company's assets.' |
| 11. | September 1999 | Internal Control – Guidance for Directors on the Combined Code, ('The Turnbull Report'), the Institute of Chartered Accountants in England & Wales, ISBN 1–84152–010–1 | 'An internal control system encompasses the policies, processes, tasks, behaviours and other aspects of a company that, taken together: <br><br> • facilitate its effective and efficient operation by enabling it to respond appropriately to significant business, operational, financial, compliance and other risks to achieving the company's objectives. This includes the safeguarding of assets from inappropriate use or from loss and fraud, and ensuring that liabilities are identified and managed; <br> • help ensure the quality of internal and external reporting. This requires the maintenance of proper records and processes that generate a flow of timely, relevant and reliable information within and outside the organisation; |

**B8.25** *How definitions of internal control have developed over the years*

| Date | Source | Definition of internal control |
|---|---|---|
| | | • help ensure compliance with applicable laws and regulations, and also with internal policies with respect to the conduct of business.' |
| 12. Effective January 2002 | Standards for the Professional Practice of Internal Auditing (Standards), the Institute of Internal Auditors Inc, available on their website: www.theiia.org. | **New *Standard* 2110.A2** 'The internal audit activity should evaluate risk exposures relating to the organization's governance, operations, and information systems regarding the<br>• Reliability and integrity of financial and operational information.<br>• Effectiveness and efficiency of operations.<br>• Safeguarding of assets.<br>• Compliance with laws, regulations, and contracts.'<br><br>**New *Standard* 2120.A1:** 'Based on the results of the risk assessment, the internal audit activity should evaluate the adequacy and effectiveness of controls encompassing the organization's governance, operations, and information systems. This should include:<br>• Reliability and integrity of financial and operational information.<br>• Effectiveness and efficiency of operations.<br>• Safeguarding of assets.<br>• Compliance with laws, regulations, and contracts.'<br><br>**From the Glossary to the new *Standards*:** 'Control – Any action taken by management, the board, and other parties to enhance risk management and increase the likelihood that established objectives and goals will be |

| Date | Source | Definition of internal control |
|------|--------|-------------------------------|
|      |        | achieved. Management plans, organizes, and directs the performance of sufficient actions to provide reasonable assurance that objectives and goals will be achieved.'<br><br>'**Adequate Control** – Present if management has planned and organized (designed) in a manner that provides reasonable assurance that the organization's risks have been managed effectively and that the organization's goals and objectives will be achieved efficiently and economically.'<br><br>'**Control Environment** – The attitude and actions of the board and management regarding the significance of control within the organization. The control environment provides the discipline and structure for the achievement of the primary objectives of the system of internal control. The control environment includes the following elements:<br>● Integrity and ethical values.<br>● Management's philosophy and operating style.<br>● Organizational structure.<br>● Assignment of authority and responsibility.<br>● Human resource policies and practices.<br>● Competence of personnel.'<br><br>'**Control Processes** – The policies, procedures, and activities that are part of a control framework, designed to ensure that risks are contained within the risk tolerances established by the risk management process.' |

| | Date | Source | Definition of internal control |
|---|---|---|---|
| 13. | July 2003 (in Exposure Draft form) | Enterprise Risk Management Framework, published by The Committee of Sponsoring Organisations of the Treadway Commission obtainable from www.coso.org | 'Enterprise risk management is a process, effected by an entity's board of directors, management and other personnel, applied in strategy setting and across the enterprise, designed to identify potential events that may affect the entity, and manage risks to be within its risk appetite, to provide reasonable assurance regarding the achievement of entity objectives.' |

## Internal control when activities are outsourced   B8.26

Outsourcing means business objectives are more dependent on suppliers and service providers than ever before. Investment institutions rely on custodians; businesses rely on internet service providers; environmentally managed businesses depend on the responsibility of their suppliers – and so on.

Throughout the 1990s standard-setting and other bodies have been active in defining internal control and its necessary components, its evaluation and its reporting. Undoubtedly this has enhanced our appreciation of internal control in the contemporary environment.

One major contribution has been to develop approaches to reviewing and reporting upon internal control. At a more fundamental level has been the development of definitions of internal control and explanations of its characteristics which have been more in harmony with modern business needs and practices. It is not that the older definitions and insights were wrong – just that they did not overtly refer to matters which became important since those definitions and insights were developed.

### An altered definition for changing times   B8.27

[**B8.25** traces the development of internal control concepts and definitions]. The replacement of the 1948 AICPA definition of internal control by the 1992 COSO definition, in particular has had a profound impact. This impact has particularly been felt in the more acute appreciation that risk assessment (while COSO termed this 'Risk assessment', the Rutteman guidance (commendably succinct in other respects) preferred 'Identification of risks and control objectives') is an essential component of any system of internal control. The subsequent contemporary and ubiquitous development of business risk consulting groups in most large professional firms has been a direct consequence. Of equal impact has been the overt recognition that monitoring (the Rutteman guidance termed this 'Monitoring and corrective action') is also an essential component of internal control – a focus which could be claimed to be closely linked to the developing interest in controls assurance reports and control opinion assignments.

The COSO definition has also captured for the first time the sense that internal control is a dynamic 'process' rather than an inert state of affairs; that it is a collaborative responsibility not just of management but also of the board and other personnel; and that it provides reasonable assurance, though not an absolute guarantee, of the achievement of objectives.

Clearly, these sentiments, encapsulated within the COSO internal control definition, have caught the mood of the times, but the phrasing of the definition in this way has also arguably contributed to giving these sentiments more expression in reality. We are suggesting that the wording of definitions can influence, not merely reflect, practice. For instance there has been considerable post-1992 stress on the overall responsibilities of the board for internal control. There is now also more emphasis in practice upon the contribution that members of staff other than management can and should make to the development of more effective systems of internal control – for instance through their participation in control risk self assessment workshops.

# Post-1992 COSO                                                    B8.28

Whether in the past the evolution of internal control definitions has given the impetus to the development of new practices, or *vice versa* is a mute point. In reality it has probably been a bit of both. The new pronouncements have caught the tide of events and shaped them. The same will happen again.

Now, there is a need for a further evolution, beyond COSO, in internal control definition and emphasis – which will lead to a further wave of developments – including the development of professional pronouncements to take account of this new focus and perhaps a fresh orientation and designation for internal control specialists in the large professional firms (the 'business risk' designation becoming passé already).

It was remarkable that the AICPA internal control definition of 1948 survived for 44 years. It is true that it was modified a little before its passing. It does seem that the life of the 1992 COSO definition will be shorter, very influential though it has been.

COSO and Rutteman overlooked *external* internal control – the need to control what happens 'outside' the entity which contributes to the achievement of the entity's objectives. The COSO text which supports the COSO internal control definition similarly overlooks the externalities of internal control.

Take, for instance, these abstracts from COSO:

'Internal control is effected by a board of directors, management and other personnel in an entity. It is accomplished by the people of an organization, by what they do and say. People establish the entity's objectives and put control mechanisms in pace.' (*Internal Control – Integrated Framework* ('The COSO Report), 'Framework' volume, p11.)

'Control environment – The core of any business is its people – their individual attributes, including integrity, ethical values and competence – and the environment in which they operate. They are the engine that drives the entity and the foundation on which everything rests.' (COSO, 'Framework' volume, p12.)

'The control environment sets the tone of an organisation, influencing the control consciousness of its people. It is the foundation for all other components of internal control, providing discipline and structure. Control environment factors include the integrity, ethical values and competence of the entity's people; management's philosophy and operating style; the way management assigns authority and responsibility, and organises and develops its people; and the attention and direction provided by the board of directors.' (COSO, 'Framework' volume, p19.)

It is not that the COSO definitions are inconsistent with the fact that some internal control is 'external' to the entity. The same can be said of Rutteman. It is more a matter that the COSO and Rutteman definitions and discussions largely or completely overlook that such is the case and therefore do not address the issue. For instance, companies' codes of business conduct and, where applicable, codes of ethical (or scientific) conduct should enjoin contractors and other business partners to observe the same principles and approaches as those that apply to in-house personnel.

There is increasing reliance on external providers contributing to the achievement of an entity's objectives and the internal control implications of this need to be addressed openly.

## What is 'external' internal control?                    B8.29

By external control we mean the internal control which takes place, at least in part, outside the entity itself. A key issue is whether controls within supplier organisations can be regarded as either (a) outside an entity's system of internal control as they function within the supplier organisation, or (b) of no concern to the entity for other reasons. This would be likely to be the case if one or more of the following applies:

- the goods or services supplied did not contribute to the achievement of the entity's objectives – which would be very unlikely;

- the goods or services being supplied were commodities whose quality is always standard or readily discernible before supply;

- alternative sources of supply were readily available which would be satisfactory with regard to quality, delivery, etc;

- internal control mechanisms within the entity were a satisfactory alternative to internal control procedures within the supplier organisation with respect to safeguarding the quality of goods or services being supplied, in that they permit or ensure the detection and rectification (without significant disruption or cost, and without significant impediment to the achievement of the entity's objectives) of substandard provision.

It is entirely mistaken to regard the controls within the supplier organisation as *external* controls. 'External control' is control by the stakeholders – often principally the shareholders – over management. Internal control is management control – the arrangements that management puts in place and operates to give the entity reasonable assurance of the achievement of objectives.

From an outsourced supplier's perspective, the control that their client exercises over their affairs may be regarded as external control over the supplier; but from the client's perspective it is part of their internal control. This may apply to some extent even to the supply of what may appear, *prima facie*, to be commodity products. For instance, B&Q, Marks and Spencer, Bodyshop and others are famous for their monitoring of what happens within their suppliers' businesses as it impacts upon the achievement of their own objectives. In reality these are not commodity supplies as their special characteristics cannot be relied upon without client involvement which is likely to include supplier monitoring by the client.

Many corporate objectives are planned, direct commercial outcomes. Other objectives are indirect: stories are rife of western multinationals whose images and even businesses have been tarnished by exploitative labour practices within their supplier organisations.

## JIT                                                                B8.30

JIT (just in time management) makes businesses more dependent on internal controls in their suppliers' businesses, and the integration of those controls with the entity's own controls.

## Outsourcing                                                       B8.31

The allure of outsourcing is hard to resist. It makes the entity smaller at its core, easier for it to change direction, easier in many other respects to manage, often easier for management to vary production to match demand, and with a smaller fixed overhead cost. In addition, there is the presumption that outsourcing will be to a specialist provider who can offer better value for money than the in-house alternative, and thus contribute to the bottom line.

Against the allure of outsourcing must be set the overhead, and sometimes the impracticality, of putting in place mechanisms to monitor the internal controls within the supplier entities. Where these mechanisms are impractical, the entity has, in effect, lost control and for security reasons the activity should not have been outsourced.

There is a general trend towards outsourcing anything that is not 'core'. We would define 'core' as being the business activities which should be kept in-house because they can be done better (more economically, efficiently or effectively) in-house, or because they need to be kept in-house for security reasons. Security considerations include the long term viability of outsourcing a service, the future difficulties of bringing it back in-house, and the extent to which outsourcing weakens the entity for instance by stripping out in-house systems, staff resources and skills. Anything else is a candidate to be outsourced to a provider who can perform the service more economically or more effectively – often because the provider specialises in that provision. It is a major challenge for a business to determine what is 'core' – what it can do as well as or better than outside providers. To continue to keep in-house what is not 'core' is a recipe for medium to long term decline.

The issue of outsourcing is of course not new: businesses have always had suppliers. But what is new is the *extent* of outsourcing of many non-core activities which have traditionally been regarded as being close to the heart of the business; and the *extent* to which many basic business service functions (such as accounting, IT services, internal auditing) have become candidates for outsourcing. There are internal control implications here as more and more of the essential internal controls of an entity may be designed, operated and monitored by new-style suppliers who may be providing similar services to many other entities.

**Outsourcing checklist**                                                              **B8.32**

- Do the tender document and the subsequent contract specify an adequate minimum standard of service, and ensure that unanticipated contingencies will be serviced effectively?

- Are the contracting procedures for outsourcing adequate to ensure the contractor is selected objectively, and are these procedures followed?

- Is it evident that contracted out services are value-for-money?

- Has management considered, and are management managing, the security risk associated with utilisation of outsiders for contracted out work?

- Is contracted out work periodically market tested so as to ensure the service is provided competitively?

- Are all services currently performed by in-house personnel considered on an impartial basis for market testing?

- Has management and the board a clear strategic grasp of what is its core activity/ies which are not to be regarded as candidates for outsourcing?

- Is partial outsourcing (whereby contract staff work alongside in-house staff) rationally considered as an option wherever it may be applicable?

- Is contracting-out leading to excessive dependence on one supplier, and does management and the board regularly consider this risk?

- Does management review the discharge of contracts for outsourced services with a view to learning lessons from cost overruns, etc.?

## Internal auditing for the outsourced entity    B8.33

In a highly outsourced entity it may be more likely that internal auditing along with many other key business activities has been outsourced. The entity then needs to consider whether it has lost control. There may be special vulnerabilities in outsourcing the review of internal control over other outsourced activities.

Through the outsourcing of so many non-core processes we are seeing the transfer of more of the internal control system to outside the core business. Third party reviews of internal control, arranged by outsourced suppliers on behalf of their clients, will become more important, but are often inadequate. Amongst the potential defects of third party reviews are that they may be conducted at an inappropriate time from the perspective of the party that needs to rely on the third party review. They are likely to be conducted with inadequate awareness on the part of the reviewer of the controls which are important to a particular entity that needs to rely on the third party review: this being so because the entity may have considerable discretion as to the extent to which it achieves internal control in-house (via the inputs to, and outputs from, the service provider) or relies on internal controls within the service organisation.

An entity must negotiate rights of audit access to a service provider at the pre-contract stage. The wording and content of service level agreements becomes very important. The development of collaborative systems which integrate the businesses of the entity with that of the service provider may be an effective way of addressing many of the internal control challenges of reliance upon service providers. Of course, collaborative systems have to be designed with care as they need to integrate in a controlled way with the already existing systems of the various parties.

As a last resort, the risks associated with making significant use of service providers may be covered by insurance. Care should be taken to ensure that necessary insurance cover is in place. It is all too easy to assume without checking that a service provider has appropriate classes of sufficient insurance cover in place.

## Contractors and joint ventures    B8.34

Much outsourcing is to do with the provision of services which, while often important, are ancillary to the main mission of the entity. The provision of inputs, such as materials or sub-assemblies would be examples. Even the outsourcing of IT and accounting services might fall into this category.

Other outsourcing occurs when the entity entrusts to another the responsibility of interfacing with the customer. For instance, a financial institution might entrust the administration of a mortgage book, including collections, to another. UK Training & Enterprise Councils usually subcontracted with training companies and others to deliver many of the training programmes which the TECs were under contract with government to deliver.

Where the performance and management of key relationships with 'end clients' is entrusted to outsourced service providers, it is usually particularly important that the monitoring of internal control within the service providers' businesses is not neglected. Thus, for instance, TECs instituted a special FAM (Financial Appraisal and Management) audit to evaluate the standard of service provision of their contractors.

Joint ventures are a special case. A useful publication by the Institute of Internal Auditors Research Foundation ('Internal audit involvement in the joint-venture process' – see the Bibliography at **APPENDIX 1**) points out that reporting and review mechanisms such as internal audit or independent auditor review should be specified within the terms of the legal agreement of the joint venture, and might cover the following.

- What areas or activities are to be audited?

- What are the record-retention guidelines, including audit working papers retention?

- Type and timing of notice required prior to the start of the audit.

- Communication channel for audit status and subsequent audit findings.

- Statement on use of auditing standards (eg the Institute of Internal Auditors).

- Responsibility assignment for corrective action of audit findings.

An SRI International Report[32] drew attention to *two* critical areas for joint venture monitoring:

- the joint venture activities; and

- the partner(s) in the joint venture.

## The importance of customers                                    B8.35

Here we have been assuming that 'external' internal control is within the supplier organisations of the entity. Thought should be given to whether the internal control within the customer organisations of the entity may not also be relevant. Where vertical integration is quite complete then sources of supply and outlets for products and services may be more under control – though often at a cost. Even where there is no vertical integration, the entity should be concerned about the reliability of all organisations in the chain.

Entities may also need to be concerned about the quality of internal control in organisations which are not, directly or indirectly, suppliers or customers of the entity.

# Millennium risk                                                    B8.36

At the time of the 'Millennium challenge' there were concerns about the possible breakdown of public infrastructure systems. We would generally characterise these types of risk as being external, but they are nevertheless risks to the achievement of corporate objectives; and systems of internal control are intended to provide reasonable assurance of the achievement of objectives.

The reliance that entities have upon software and hardware suppliers with regard to 'millennium compliance' was an example of how businesses achieve their objectives, or fail to do so, through dependence upon control within supplier entities; and the difficulties of assessing the compliance characteristics of supplied hardware and software. The millennium challenge was not much broader than this, and illustrated vividly the extent to which the achievement of corporate objectives is dependent upon what happens external to the entity – in telecoms, electricity supply, public transport systems and so on (Vide, eg The Year 2000 Issue – Supplementary Guidance for Auditors, The Auditing Practices Board, June 1998).

# Internal control in cyberspace                                     B8.37

With the galloping development of the use of the internet for business purposes, how we develop satisfactory monitoring of our internal control arrangements which exist within cyberspace now represents a particularly acute challenge. Just as with in-house computer systems, we are sure a 'black box' approach of auditing around the internet system will not be adequate. The 'black box' approach to monitoring depends upon matching output with input so as to conclude that nothing has gone wrong within the system. It is a tempting approach when it is difficult to review the system itself. The best the 'black box' approach can achieve is to indicate that nothing observable has gone wrong *to date*: it provides virtually no assurance that the system is sufficiently controlled to prevent things from going wrong tomorrow. The 'black box' approach may therefore have the potential to provide more audit assurance for the external auditor of historical financial statements than for the internal auditor of internal control as it is operating currently and can be expected to operate in the future. The Institute of Internal Auditors has produced a useful guide to internet security (see the Bibliography at **APPENDIX 1**).

# Scope of directors' public reports on internal control when internal control is outsourced            B8.38

A related issue is whether controls within supplier organisations are beyond the scope of the directors' public reports on internal control. For the UK, the current scope requirement is to report on internal control over the *whole* of the business for the *whole* of the period under review, though in the US, under the SEC interpretation of *Sarbanes-Oxley*, it is 'point of time' reporting. It is idiosyncratic if a policy of outsourcing should radically alter the scope of the directors' report – but this issue has not been tackled head-on in the guidance which has been developed.

## Conclusions B8.39

A root and branch revamp of our definitions and expositions of internal control is needed. To date, standard setting and other bodies are addressing 'external' internal control in a piecemeal way. For instance, ICAEW's Audit Faculty has quite recently revised its guidance on reporting on the internal controls of investment custodians to third parties.[33]

APB's excellent briefing paper on providing assurance on internal control[34] describes a framework for forming an opinion on the effectiveness of internal control suitable for reporting to third parties on internal control adequacy. The framework illustrates the separate elements of an engagement to provide assurance on internal control, the range of considerations that apply to each process, and, consequently, the inherent complexity of engagements to provide assurance about the effectiveness of internal control. APB's recent publication on audit evidence considerations when an entity uses a service organisation is useful but entirely from the external audit angle[35]. Their new briefing paper on communication between external auditors and audit committees (see the Bibliography at **APPENDIX** 1) largely overlooks the external auditor's 'management letter' and does not address the externalities of internal control.

## Internal control and risk management in the Combined Code B8.40

The July 1998 amendment (12.43A) to the UK Listing Rules specified listed companies' obligations with respect to the Combined Code. The general obligations read:

'In the case of a company incorporated in the United Kingdom, the following additional items must be included in its annual report and accounts:

(a) a narrative statement of how it has applied the principles set out in Section 1 of the Combined Code, providing explanation which enables its shareholders to evaluate how the principles have been applied;

(b) a statement as to whether or not it has complied throughout the accounting period with the Code provisions set our in Section 1 of the Combined Code. A company that has not complied with the Code provisions, or complied with only some of the Code provisions or (in the case of provisions whose requirements are of a continuing nature) complied for only part of an accounting period, must specify the Code provisions with which it has not complied, and (where relevant) for what part of the period such non-compliance continued, and give reasons for any non-compliance ... '

### Internal control B8.41

In the March 1998 consultation document (*proposed changes to the Listing Rules – Corporate Governance (principles of good governance and Code of best practice: consultation document* (March 1998)) of proposed changes to the Listing Rules relating to the Combined Code, the Code Provision D.3 had read:

> 'The directors should review the effectiveness of the company's system of internal control and should report to shareholders. This report should cover all controls, including financial, operational and compliance controls and risk management.'

The final form of the 1998 Combined Code used a revised numbering system for the Principles and Provisions. What had been Provision D.3 in the consultation document became Provision D.2.1 in its 1998 form. This sits beneath D.2 which is the overarching Principle on 'Internal Control', the wording of which is unchanged in its final form from the consultation draft, viz:

> 'The board should maintain a sound system of internal control to safeguard shareholders' investments and the company's assets.'

and remains unchanged in the revised 2003 Code.

## Last minute changes to the Code Provision on internal control

**B8.42**

What is significant is that the wording of what had been Code Provision D.3 (see above) became amended in what has become D.2.1 in the 1998 Code to read:

> 'The directors should, at least annually, conduct a review of the effectiveness of the group's system of internal controls and should report to shareholders that they have done so. The review should cover all controls, including financial, operational and compliance controls and risk management ["risk management systems" in 2003 version].'

So there has been a tightening up in that it is now unequivocally stated that the review should be 'at least annual'.

Readers can infer what they like (or nothing at all!) from the change to the plural from 'system of internal control' to 'system of internal controls' and the author confesses as to having no clue as to why this change was made.

It can now be construed that it is only the directors' *review* (and not necessarily also their *report* on that review) which should cover *all* controls, including financial, operational and risk management. This ambiguity may be taken advantage of by some companies who would like to continue to restrict the contents of their directors' internal control reports which are published to the minimum content prescribed by Rutteman (*Internal control and financial reporting: Guidance for directors of listed companies registered in the UK*, (December 1994), 'The Rutteman Report', ICAEW) which related only to internal *financial* control. In practice, an examination of annual reports shows that directors' published reports on internal control have not taken advantage of this possible loophole, but have covered all aspects of internal control.

The revised wording of Provision D.2.1 (1998), now C.2.1 (2003), made it transparently clear that directors are not required to report on the results of their review of internal control – just that they have conducted a review – an approach which was not clear in the draft wording (see above). This has been the approach taken by listed companies in implementing this provision.

## Risk management                                                      B8.43

While, apart from Code Provision D.2.1, there was no other reference to 'risk management' in the 1998 Combined Code, this was an issue which was elaborated upon considerably in the Turnbull Report which provided guidance to directors on implementing Principle D.2 and Provisions D.2.1 and D.2.2 (C.2, C.2.1 and C.3.5 in the 2003 Code). We address this in **B8.58–B8.62**.

### Effectiveness                                                       B8.44

Although the directors' review of internal control must cover 'effectiveness', their report had not in the past needed to disclose their opinion on effectiveness; and the Combined Code Provisions make no change to that. In addition, if literally interpreted, there also continues to be no requirement for directors even to come to a private (not for publication) opinion on effectiveness – just to *review* effectiveness.

Nevertheless, the word 'effectiveness' has survived from Cadbury through to the new 2003 Combined Code, notwithstanding the challenges to it along the way, and notwithstanding that in 1994 Rutteman gave directors a way to opt out of disclosing an opinion on effectiveness.

# Understanding risk assessment and risk management                     B8.45

Years ago Drucker said, in effect, that it is not the task of boards to avoid risk but rather to be able to take bigger risks but more safely. While, in a sense this is a contradictory statement, it places stress on the relationship between risk taking and the development of successful enterprises. It rightly implies that risks should be managed.

## What do we mean by risk?                                             B8.46

Risk has been defined as:

> The uncertainty of an event occurring that could have an impact on the achievement of objectives. Risk is measured in terms of consequences and likelihood. (This is the definition of risk in the Glossary to the new Standards of the Institute of Internal Auditors, see **B23.3**.)

A recent Australian/New Zealand standard defines risk management as:

> 'the culture, processes and structures that are directed towards the effective management of potential opportunities and adverse effects'[36]

Already this definition of risk management is being applied in the UK, for instance in the NHS[37].

Risk may be considered in terms of *outcomes*:

'A possible outcome which cannot be predicted with certainty and which would be unwelcome because it would be counter-productive.'

Or in terms of *process*:

'Factors which could affect the achievement of objectives, or the likelihood of unwanted consequences occurring.'

Risks in the context of *process* are often referred to as *risk factors*. In essence the difference between risk which is viewed in terms of *outcomes* and risk which is considered in terms of *process* is a matter of the perspective of the observer. For a staff operative a successful *outcome* of the operation may be the avoidance of an unwanted result, but for senior management and the board the risk of that unwanted outcome will be seen as a risk factor – a risk associated with the *process*.

## Components of risk                                           B8.47

Different parties have different risks and consequently see risk as having different components. For instance, external auditors regard *audit risk* ('audit risk' for the external auditor being the risk of a significant misstatement in the financial results of the entity not being detected and corrected (or reported) as a result of the audit) as having three components: inherent risk, control risk and detection risk.(Auditing Practices Board (March 1995), Statements of Auditing Standards, (London, CCAB).) There is common ground that the components of risk are:

● inherent risk – the risk which is intrinsically bound up with the activity;

● control risk – the scope to reduce inherent risk through the application of control; and

● residual risk – the extent of the risk after the application of control.

The degree of residual risk which is acceptable is for the board to decide, and will depend on a number of considerations. One is the possible overall consequences to the enterprise if the risk materialises. Another is the general attitude of the entity to risk taking, which should be determined by the board. We can call this the *risk appetite*. Risk appetite may also vary between entities for a number of reasons, which can be contradictory. For instance, public entities tend to be *risk averse* as they are custodians of the public purse. On the other hand they often take on the management of risks which are unacceptably great for the private sector to be willing to assume.

Because it is most generally accepted that 'inherent risk' comprises the 'size' or 'impact' which is inherent in the activity and also that part of the 'system' or 'likelihood' component which is also considered to be inherent in the activity (ie uncontrollable), that is the approach we take in this handbook. Thus, for instance, trading in derivative futures may be inherently risky both on account of how much is at risk and also, even the application of the best processes to handle these trades will not successfully control the risks.

In essence, this generally accepted view of inherent risk is subdividing the 'system' or 'process' contributor of risk into that which is deemed uncontrollable and that which is controllable; and it is bracketing the former with the 'size' risk to provide this composite measure of inherent risk. The graphical matrix approach we suggest later is an illustration of this. If this approach is followed, care must be taken not to concede with too much alacrity an inevitable, inherent vulnerability which is then not focused on with the intention of improving control. Essentially, there are these three components of risk:

● 'size' (of risk before the application of control);

● 'process' or 'system' risk; and

● residual risk – the extent of the risk after the application of control.

## Components of risk management                               B8.48

Risk management comprises:

● risk identification;

● risk measurement;

● risk control; and

● risk taking.

The term 'risk assessment' (one of the five COSO components of effective internal control, and thus one of the five Rutteman criteria for assessing the effectiveness of internal control) focuses mainly on risk identification and measurement.

## Why this emphasis on 'risk'?                                 B8.49

Spectacular corporate collapses or near collapses (Enron, Marconi, for instance) can be attributed to failures of risk management. The message of the Turnbull Report is that the board has overall responsibility for risk management – the board itself should be engaged in assessing overall risks and in effective oversight of risk management. A 'top-down' assessment of risk should feed down from the board to the businesses and operations within the entity. Secondly, the board should be satisfied about the embedded processes for the review of risk and control within the enterprise, the results of which should be fed up to the board for board consideration.

Another, less worthy, reason for the focus on risk management is the too frequent unwillingness of boards and senior management to invest in effective internal control to the extent that managements and boards would have done so in the past. It is tempting to factor into the price of the product or service the cost associated with weak control. Delayered, downsized, re-engineered entities have taken out many of the opportunities to achieve control in traditional ways. Major change, including significant redesign of systems, tends to introduce control vulnerabilities which had been progressively reduced until the reorganisation of the business. Management is less willing to invest in comprehensive internal control to reduce risk and this has not been a priority with those who design new systems. Unwilling to lose the cost advantages of re-engineered business approaches, management seeks to justify investment in control in terms of the relative degrees of risk that control mitigates. The pursuit of annually increasing returns for the shareholders make boards of companies reluctant to saddle the business with the costs of more watertight controls. There are, in itself, risks associated with this. The best approaches to risk assessment are highly subjective. They may overlook major risks or fail to assess them reliably. Major risks may be 'buried in the woodwork' perhaps not readily amenable to identification by top management and the board, nor to reliable assessment if they are identified. Take, for instance, the falsification of quality data by four production workers at BNFL, or the sales cut-off problem which led to the collapse of a retailer. So a 'top-down' approach to risk management is not enough on its own: intelligence about risk and control vulnerabilities needs to be gathered at the grass roots level of the business, synthesised and fed upwards to top management and the board.

Another justification for contemporary focus on risk management is that businesses are changing fast. The half-life of business systems is relentlessly getting shorter as the nature of business activities changes. It is not so much that control is costly, but that the finite resources of senior executive, systems designer and internal auditor time are limited and need to be directed to the areas of the business where the need is greatest to achieve effective internal control. It follows that a pre-requisite is risk assessment – both to identify the areas of greatest need and also to identify the greatest vulnerabilities in these areas which need fixing.

# Matrix and risk register approaches for the board to assess risk                              B8.50

A picture is worth a thousand words. This simple matrix allows risks to be noted down according to their potential impact as well as the probability of them occurring. When this technique has been applied at the level of the board, the number of risks plotted should be limited to perhaps the 20 to 24 major risks that the company faces, otherwise too much detail obscures the big picture. Similarly, if this matrix technique is used at divisional or departmental level, focus on just the major risks is usually desirable.

If this is done first *before* taking account of the effectiveness of the controls upon which the company is currently relying, it can be used to indicate where and how management and the board needs to focus on implementing effective controls. A corollary of this is that it can be used to indicate where the controls upon which management and the board are currently relying are too elaborate (in view perhaps of the modest inherent risk) or inappropriate (in view of the characteristics of the inherent risk).

Then the risks can be plotted again on the matrix to show where the principal risks are *after* the application of internal control. Management and the board then need to judge whether the risks are acceptable in view of their 'risk appetite'.

The division of the graph into labelled quadrants suggests, in broad brush terms, the appropriate control responses to risks recorded in each of the quadrants, according to the key:

| Matrix key | |
|---|---|
| **Primary:** | Risks which must be focussed upon continuously by top management to minimise the likelihood of them occurring and the impact of them if they do occur. |
| **Contingency:** | Requires carefully pre-designed and tested contingency plans to be in place to cater for the eventuality if it occurs (but note that 'risk avoidance' might be preferred to a contingency approach to managing these risks). |
| **Housekeeping:** | Sufficiently regular and careful attention by way of effective internal control to minimise the likelihood of this unwanted outcome. |
| **Monitoring and review:** | Provision of periodic information to confirm the containment of this risk within acceptable levels, together with assigned responsibilities to keep this periodic information under review. |

HM Treasury's '4 Ts' are useful as an alternative guide to the options available to manage risk[38].

● Transfer

● Tolerate

● Treat

● Terminate

Of course there is a lot of subjectivity in this approach – as in any other approach to risk management. The identification of which risks to plot on the matrix is a matter of judgment Where to plot them is also a matter of judgement. Revising the plotting of the risks to take account of the effectiveness of introduced controls is also a matter of judgement. Finally, it is a matter of judgement to decide whether the residual risks are acceptable.

The use of this technique *before* the application of control gives a picture which corresponds to an external auditor's view of inherent risk – which combines a consideration of the likely impact (in their case upon the reliability of the financial statements) with a consideration of the degree of probability of it happening.

**Risk assessment matrix**                                                    **B8.51**

*(Before taking account of controls)*

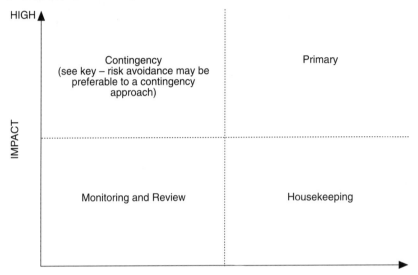

*(then plot risks again* after *taking account of control)*

A modified approach to using this graph is to (a) *possibly* omit the quadrants, and (b) use circles of varying size according to 'Impact' and of different colours according to 'Likelihood *after* control', viz.

● Green (rare) – no problem.

● Amber – some risk.

● Red – danger!

Many businesses classify risks – for instance according to whether they are funding risks, personnel risks, competitor risks – and on. Our discussion later in this chapter of a tabular approach to top-down risk assessment goes into this in more detail (see **B8.53–B8.57**). The above graphical matrix approach works well when applied to each of the classes of risks.

The simple matrix shown above, we have encountered an elaboration of the same approach. The graph is divided into more sections and colour coding (red, amber and green) used to flag up degrees of relative seriousness, as shown in the following chart.

## Risk assessment matrix

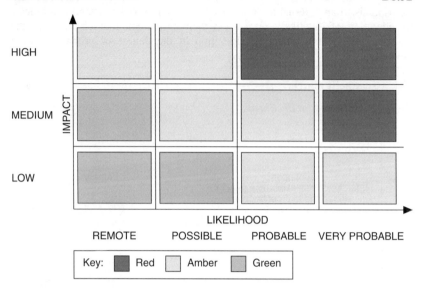

With the addition of one further one, the labels used in the simple matrix with which we started, can be applied to the above chart as shown below:

| Matrix key | |
|---|---|
| **Showstopper:** | Continuous focus, as with 'Primary' risks (below), supplemented by regular attention of the board. The intention is to eliminate as far as possible the risk of this unwanted outcome materialising, which would prudently involve avoidance of risk taking in this area. |
| **Primary:** | Risks which must be focussed upon continuously by top management to minimise the likelihood of them occurring and the impact of them if they do occur. |
| **Contingency:** | Requires carefully pre-designed and tested contingency plans to be in place to cater for the eventuality if it occurs (but note that 'risk avoidance' might be preferred to a contingency approach to managing these risks). |
| **Housekeeping:** | Sufficiently regular and careful attention by way of effective internal control to minimise the likelihood of this unwanted outcome. |
| **Monitoring and review:** | Provision of periodic information to confirm the containment of this risk within acceptable levels, together with assigned responsibilities to keep this periodic information under review. |

**Risk assessment matrix** **B8.53**

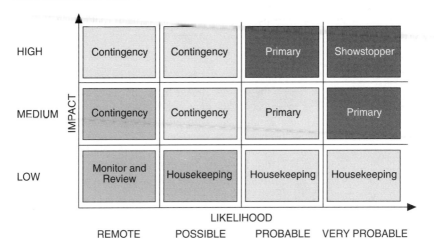

**Using a risk register approach to business risk assessment** **B8.54**

In the following pages we offer three examples of risk registers. In both examples 1 and 2 below, it is noteworthy that the company entrusted to the chief audit executive the tasks of developing these risk tables (ie 'risk register') and presenting them respectively to senior management, the audit committee and then the board. In this, he was playing a major role in the risk management of the company – a challenging role in view of the need for the risk management process to be audited independently. This is illustrative of the enhanced role that internal audit is now often playing in the wake of the Turnbull Report. In the third example, the government agency concerned had neither a risk management function nor its own internal audit function (internal audit was centralised at sponsoring departmental level above the level of the agency) and so the task of facilitating the development of the risk register was entrusted to a member of the agency's quality assurance function.

For the board to be actively involved in oversight of risk management, an appropriate approach may be for an overall presentation to be made to the board once a year – which summarises the content of the risk tables (see below) and gives the board the opportunity to contribute to the consideration of risk management. Then, at subsequent board meetings, the subject matter of one table can be opened up in detail. The overall presentation may be made by the chief audit executive, but could be made by the chief executive. The subsequent detailed presentations could be made by the respect responsible executives – for instance, the finance director, the director of human resources, the company lawyer, etc. Clearly, the board will need to balance their more detailed involvement in this way against other board priorities: time is always of the essence.

Now that colour laser and other colour printers are plentiful and economic to use, colour has now arrived for internal management reports. Risk register entries can with advantage use colour coding to indicate degrees of risk – usually utilising the 'red, amber, green' indicators.

# Example 1 B8.55

We set out below an early attempt developed by a UK listed manufacturing company to give effect to aspects of the approach for assessing internal control as set out in the Turnbull guidance. Altogether, by considering the risks outlined in these tables, the board was considering just over 30 major risks. This was not too inconsistent with our earlier advice, in the context of the risk matrix discussed before in this section, that the number of risks the board should address needs to be limited if the board is to avoid becoming immersed in too much detail.

Although not given in this example, it is important that this exercise commences with an agreed statement of corporate objectives, and that each risk in the tables should be cross referenced to the objective(s) it threatens. It is best that specific performance indicators (key performance indicators – KPIs) are identified and associated with each of the objectives and each of the risks in the tables wherever possible, and that the monthly management accounting pack which goes to the board should have a section showing performance against each of the KPIs so that the board can track the containment of risk.

In this example, the risks are classified into eight main areas but they are not related directly to the stated objectives, as we believe they should be – perhaps by use of an additional column to cross reference to a separate statement of major corporate objectives. Usually it is sufficient if major corporate objectives are expressed as between four and six objectives at the most.

An important issue is whether or not the company truly has identified the right risks. Another issue is the relative ranking by importance of each of the identified risks – which these schedules do not indicate, but a later example does.

In the full example before we abbreviated it, it was noticeable that specific controls and actions had not been identified to mitigate certain of the risks, and in some cases no review body had been identified.

Establishing ownership of risk is important. Some of the identified 'controls' referred to the monitoring role of external bodies – such as regulators or trade associations – which was inappropriate as, at best, these were 'review bodies' rather than 'controls'. These external bodies are not a front line control and at best are likely to be only an erratic 'back stop' control. And they are more by nature *of external* controls than *internal* controls. We think they should be shown in the right hand column as a 'Review Body' rather than in the column titled 'Controls'.

*Example 1*  **B8.55**

The appearance again and again of the same bodies in the 'Review Body' column raises the question as to whether each of these can always be depended upon to exercise effective review of the particular risks: rules should be developed to prescribe more tightly whether it is reasonable to show a body in this column – for instance, internal audit should perhaps only be shown if an audit which covers this risk is scheduled to be conducted within the next twelve months (or has been conducted in the previous twelve months) without significant audit scope limitations.

Presenting to the board tables such as this is likely to generate the sort of discussion alluded to immediately above – which means that they are starting to work effectively to get the board involved in a top level assessment of risk and control.

---

**The XYZ Group plc**

*Business Risk Assessment*

*(date) – initial output*

Following a series of discussions with the Group's senior management a range of identifiable risks have been established. Given the rate of consolidation in the sector, the intensely competitive market, and the downwards pressures on prices, XYZ's major risks come from the actions of both our suppliers and our competitors. The risk assessment process has therefore highlighted the need to keep a close watch on input costs as well as market and competitor developments, however its main focus has been on areas where management actions can alleviate risks in order for the Group to achieve its business objectives.

This process has resulted in eight main groups of risks which are discussed in details below. It should be noted that some risks could appear in more than one category.

The risks are summarised as:

1. strategic;
2. structural;
3. people related;
4. general systems;
5. regulatory and legal;
6. new business and markets;
7. the market and competition; and
8. funding.

**B8.55**   *Example 1*

## 1.   Strategic risks

|  | Risk | Controls | Review Body |
|---|---|---|---|
| 1.1 | It is important for the group to have a clear medium/long term strategy to avoid the danger of market initiatives being made with a short term focus that may act against the long term interests of the Group's shareholders. | Forecasting Budgets/Variance Analysis Formally documented strategy. Sales and marketing strategy. | Executive Operational board Internal audit Main board |
| 1.3 | XYZ is a medium sized operator in big markets and our strategies, structure, systems, cost base etc. should reflect this; the risk being that we could be squeezed out by big competitor manufacturers. | Niche market strategy Forecasts/ budgets and reviews. Cost Control. | Executive Operational board Monthly divisional board Internal audit Main board |

## 2.   Structural issues

|  | Risk | Controls and Actions | Review Body |
|---|---|---|---|
| 2.1 | The organisation of the Group's operating divisions and their management via the operational and executive boards needs constant attention to avoid the problems outlined in 1.3 above and to ensure new developments make full use of existing resources rather than duplicate management, people and processes where this may be unnecessary. | Formal documentation Budgetary reviews | Executive Operational Board Internal audit Main board |

*Example 1* **B8.55**

| | Risk | Controls and Actions | Review Body |
|---|---|---|---|
| 2.3 | The non executive directors (NEDs) should not become 'stale' and should continue to provide new ideas and their experience to the Group as well as providing an appropriate challenge to management. The experiences of other companies (such as Marconi) indicate the importance of effective challenge by NEDs of strategic proposals of the executive. | | Executive Operational Board Internal audit Main board |

### 3. People-related risks

| | Risk | Controls and Actions | Review Body |
|---|---|---|---|
| 3.1 | Without a medium to long term view of succession planning and resourcing, the Group faces the risks of a lack of continuity and knowledge if key individuals leave. Also there is a risk associated with making inappropriate appointments from outside the Group to fill gaps that could potentially be more efficiently filled from within.<br><br>Careful consideration should be given to succession planning and bolstering resourcing in key areas. | Formal consideration of succession planning. Development plans for managers. | Executive Operational Board Business Heads Internal audit Main board |

**B8.55**   *Example 1*

|  | Risk | Controls and Actions | Review Body |
|---|---|---|---|
| 3.7 | Poor communication between HQ and divisional sites may impede business objectives and/or sour relations between staff in the locations. | Team Talk Databases Regular visits by Group staff to divisional sites. | Executive Operational Board Internal audit Main board |

**4.   General systems-related risks**

|  | Risk | Controls and Actions | Review Body |
|---|---|---|---|
| 4.1 | Systems priorities may not reflect Group priorities for the business lines. | Functional heads are responsible for determining their priorities clearly. | Executive Operational Board Internal audit Main board |

|  | Risk | Controls and Actions | Review Body |
|---|---|---|---|
| 4.7 | Staffing requirements may not be assessed appropriately. | Cost benefit analysis | Operational Board Internal audit Main board |

**5.   Regulatory and legal risks**

|  | Risk | Controls and Actions | Review Body |
|---|---|---|---|
| 5.1 | Health and safety requirements are becoming increasingly demanding and the consumer lobby is also getting stronger. Non-compliance may cause business objectives to suffer or costs to increase to ensure compliance. | Health and safety function Trade Association membership obligations and review | Executive Operational Board Internal Audit Main board |

*Example 1* **B8.55**

|  | Risk | Controls and Actions | Review Body |
|---|---|---|---|
| 5.5 | Empowerment has its risks. Where mandates for human resources-related issues are not clear there is a danger that local management make mistakes. | Human Resources Ensure that Team Leaders/Team Directors are fully aware of their responsibilities with regards to staff issues and when they should seek advices/ confirmation to be taken with HR | Executive Operational Board Internal audit Main board |

## 6. New business and markets

|  | Risk | Controls and Actions | Review Body |
|---|---|---|---|
| 6.1 | There are risks in developing new products, entering new markets or opening new distribution sources, there is a risk that product delivery is of unacceptable quality or at higher cost than anticipated. | Market Analysis/Research | Executive Group marketing Internal audit Main board |
| 6.3 | Staff and management in front line as well as in support areas must have sufficient skills and experience to ensure that new markets and products are fully understood, or business objectives may not be met | Ensure the relevant experience/ knowledge is in place – either through recruitment of these skills or specific training programmes | Operational board Internal audit Main board |

## 7. Market and competitive changes

|  | Risk | Controls and Actions | Review Body |
|---|---|---|---|
| 7.1 | While in the businesses we are in there are significant barriers to entry, there is relatively little customer loyalty and a need always compete on price. | Carefully watch market developments (particularly in our niche markets) and defend our position where possible | Executive Operational board Divisional boards Internal audit Main board |
| 7.2 | Consolidation in the market brings both risks and opportunities. There is a risk of big players competing us out of the market – niche strategies can counter some of this if we can be swift and accurately identify our chosen markets and customers. | Continue to develop new niches. | Executive Operational board Divisional boards Internal audit Main board |

## 8. Funding

|  | Risk | Controls and Actions | Review Body |
|---|---|---|---|
| 8.3 | Risk of tightening of borrowing criteria leading to working capital constraints . | Optimise relationships with providers of working capital and carefully monitor performance of existing credit lines. Group Accounting and Structured Finance work together to ensure a workable solutions are achieved | Finance director Internal audit Main board |

*Example 2*   **B8.56**

# Example 2 **B8.56**

In this example, the listed manufacturing company sought to implement Turnbull's recommendations through a series of interviews/brainstorms with the group's directors, the creation of a risk framework or register, a series of bi-monthly reports/presentations to formal board meetings, and the development of an operational audit plan for the following year consistent with this risk assessment. The approach is better than that shown in Example 1 in that a ranking of each risk, which takes account of impact and probability, has been attempted.

*Inter alia,* this assisted the board in determining:

- whether all the questions set out in the Turnbull guidance are being taken into account;

- the wording of any risk management policy document the board may wish to disseminate;

- the approval of any new procedures that need to be in place; and

- the appropriate level of disclosure in the annual report and accounts.

## Risk Assessment Framework

The interviews/discussions with the group's directors revealed the following generic risk areas.

- Strategic
- Marketing
- People-related
- Credit
- Legal and Regulatory
- Operations
- Treasury and Funding
- Technology

In the interests of conciseness, we show below an abstract from the first of these tables only. Of course these are not all the risks found, but give examples and summarise the impact on objectives and the appropriate monitoring and review mechanisms.

The assessment relates primarily to the group's ability to meet its corporate objectives and has taken into consideration the potential severity of the risk to the group and also, without appropriate control processes, the likelihood of the risk occurring. Whilst this is clearly a subjective area, we have tried to create a methodology to rank both risk and security, with 0 being low and 5 being high. The internal control processes relating to each risk has been established, early warning mechanisms discussed and accountable individuals/committees identified.

**B8.56** *Example 2*

In simple terms, the main and operational boards are responsible for strategic risks and marketing/people risks directly. credit committee is the point of focus for credit risks, health and safety management largely covers legal and regulatory risks, internal audit review and report on operational risks and a finance committee oversees treasury and, funding risks. Technological risks also fall to the executive directors.

The board had separate formal discussions of the different generic risk areas and the audit committee receives regular operational reports from internal audit.

In addition to this, the board regularly reviews other standing committee minutes as well as the group's monthly 'management accounting pack' (MAP) and market/competitor analysis.

| 1 | Risk Strategic risks | Control Processes | Likelihood | Severity | Review Body |
|---|---|---|---|---|---|
| 1.1 | In inadequate formalised (and regularly reviewed) group strategy could lead to short-term, sub-optimal decisions being made. | Regular business and strategic planning reviews, together with clear statements of group objectives to limit the scope for decisions to be made which do not fall within our strategic framework. | 2 | 4 | Main Board |
| 1.4 | Share price/ sector risks. Movements in prices of either just this company or the sector as a whole create issues with regard to financing, acquisitions and even predatory activity by other players. | Close management public relations and regular dialogue with major shareholders and brokers. | 3 | 4 | Executive |

Key:  **0 = Low**
      **5 = High**

396

*Example 3* **B8.57**

# Example 3 B8.57

The Combined Code[39] provision D.2.1 and the 'Turnbull Report'[40] guidance on this provision have had a significant impact upon the formality with which boards and top management teams assess risk and associated controls. It was the last three words of Combined Code provision D.2.1 which jump started this process:

'D.2.1    The directors should, at least annually, conduct a review of the effectiveness of the group's system of internal controls and should report to shareholders that they have done so. The review should cover all controls, including financial, operational and compliance controls and risk management.'

One consequence has been the development in many entities of risk registers. High level risk registers are often developed in more detail as they cascade down from the level of the board to lower levels of the business. These registers are maintained and developed further over time.

The public sector has been particularly diligent in developing these risk registers, usually taking their cue from the HM Treasury guidance.

### Example 3 as an approach to developing a risk register, starting with an 'awayday'

At the end of this paragraph we show the first two pages of a sixteen-page risk register which is a first attempt by an entity to develop their risk register. The extract from the register has been altered to preserve confidentiality. The approach taken was to spend a day away as a top executive team, facilitated by their designated risk management function. In their case the risk management function, at least temporarily, is the responsibility of a nominated member of their quality assurance function. In other entities the responsibility is often given to the internal audit function. In others there is a separate risk management function. Of course it is important to put across the perspective that *management* owns risk – any specialist risk management function should *facilitate* the effective ownership of risk by management

At least one cell of their risk register format has a dual use – a simple technique which we consider quite effective. The third column is used both to indicate 'risk category' (External, Operational, Technological or Resource risk). They distinguish between 'risk sponsor' and 'risk owner' although the form only shows the 'risk owner'. All risks categorised as 'external risks' are 'sponsored' by their chief executive whereas all their technological risks are 'sponsored' by their IT Strategy Group. The other categories of risk have their respective sponsors too. Sponsors may assign 'ownership' of individual risks to managers within the entity who then have the responsibility to monitor and control the risks so assigned. But overall responsibility remains with the risk sponsor.

Their awayday brainstormed (or is it more correct now to say 'word-stormed' or 'brain-showered'?) in order to identify the principal risks they consider the entity faces. During the course of the day and in the days following they determined the ownership of each of the risks and the approach to be taken in controlling each risk. With respect to the latter, they settled on the HM Treasury's classification:

- Treat

- Tolerate

- Transfer

- Terminate.

**More stress on 'likelihood' than on 'impact' in Example 3**

The entity has designed a form which allows them to indicate their judgement of likelihood of the risk occurring and the probable impact if it does. These are ranked High (Red), Medium (Amber) and Low (Green) and shown in the risk register in descending order according to Likelihood. It is ambiguous as to whether this ranking is of *inherent* risk before the application of control, or of *residual* risk after the application of control but ideally it should be the former. The ranking takes account only of the perceived degree of *likelihood* whereas we consider it should be based on the combined effect of 'likelihood' *and* probable 'impact'.

**Further points on approach used in Example 3**

Since this is the entity's first version of their risk register, and since the table ranks risks in order of priority, the serial number assigned to each stated risk and the risk priority number are the same – but this will change over time. Being the first version of their risk register, none of the risks has been closed off in the sense of no longer being a current risk on their risk register.

This entity has chosen to use the colour coding also to express their judgement of the quality of control over each of the given risks – Uncertain (Red), Inadequate (Amber) and Adequate (Green). An important column is the one where they record their agreed action – often cross referencing to a separate 'risk assessment plan' (RAP).

A point to bear in mind is that risks, like buses, tend to arrive together: a risk register approach such as this may too easily allow management to overlook the potential challenges to the business if several risks materialise at the same time. An effective risk assessment should nevertheless assess that possibility.

The annual cycle applied by this entity to updating their risk register is intended to start with the completion of the corporate planning process for the coming year. Once the plan has been agreed, the risks associated with the plan are to be assessed using the methodology described in this article. One implication of this is that the year will well advanced before this risk assessment is completed. Another associated implication is that the entity cannot rely upon this process to assess the risk associated with different strategic options before the annual plan for the year is settled upon.

**Use of software in the context of Example 3**

Currently the entity holds this risk register as a straightforward Word file. Spreadsheet software could have been used. However, formatting the register as a Microsoft Word table does allow rows to be sorted into ascending or descending sequence according to the entries in the cells of columns selected to be sorted upon. If sorting is to be done of rows within a Word table it is of course important to take care that the data entered in the cells to be used for the sort is capable of being interpreted as having the intended sort order. For instance where a cell is split so that it can be used for two purposes, as is the case with the cells in row 3, it is unlikely that a useful sort could be undertaken using those cells as the basis of the sort. There would be scope for more sophisticated software to be used.

# Board approach to implementing the Turnbull Report

**B8.58**

[Note that the Turnbull Report is reproduced in PART A.]

Hermes Guide for Shareholders and Independent Outside Directors (see **B10.79**) has some useful discussion on questions on audit and risk management.

Boards of listed companies are now required to report on their compliance or otherwise with the internal control requirements of the *Combined Code* as detailed in the Turnbull Report. In practice this often means:

- an increase in the accountability of the board for the internal control processes and structures that exist within the company;

- the board must perform an assessment of internal controls at least annually, and consider reports relating to risk and internal control regularly during the year;

- a review process is required that enables the board to assess the risks that exist in the business and the effectiveness of the internal controls designed to limit these risks; and

- in providing a statement on internal control which complies fully with Turnbull, the directors need to be able to conclude that there is an ongoing process that has been in place for the year under review, and up to the date of approval of the annual report and accounts, which accords with the guidance.

## What the board should do

**B8.59**

In a well managed business most of the elements of risk management and internal control may already be in place through committee structures and line functions tasked with monitoring compliance with the company's risk policies. However, on an ongoing basis the board will need to:

- consider whether there are any gaps in control against significant risks;

- redirect, where necessary, monitoring and reporting; and

- consider the implications of any control failings and weaknesses.

## An approach the board might take                                    B8.60

Here we provide an example set of guidance notes on the process to be followed to give effect to these Turnbull requirements. They are designed with a view to being applicable for a listed group of companies which has one or more operational boards under the group board. We are assuming a December 31 year end. In our example (for instance in the table) we are assuming that the group of companies is in the financial sector, but we suggest that a closely similar approach can be applicable for companies in other sectors.

Much of the process is likely to be facilitated by internal audit, including the discussions, the drafting of reports and the presentation of outcomes at board meetings, all of which are integral parts of the process. There is no doubt that the Turnbull initiative has often had the effect of placing internal audit more alongside the board and top management than had been the case before.

### Process                                                            B8.61

- Summarise the group objectives and clearly identify the divisional objectives that underpin the group results.

- Conduct a series of brainstorming sessions with the executive directors, operational board members and non-executive directors to identify key risks to achieving objectives and to rank them (perhaps as 'low', 'medium' or 'high' risk). The internal control processes relating to each risk should be established, early warning mechanisms discussed, and accountable individuals/committees identified.

- From this, prepare a draft paper to be presented and discussed at the board about six months before the commencement of the new company year. This should establish a clear risk management policy and formalise control strategies.

- The internal audit plan for the year will also be generated by this approach and should be placed before the audit committee for their discussion and approval prior to the commencement of the year.

- The formal review process will then need to be established; our proposal at present would look as follows: It could follow lines similar to those suggested in Table 1. In each case, the board would receive a presentation delivered by the person indicated in parentheses. It may be appropriate for the audit committee to follow the same approach before these matters come through to the main board as suggested in the table.

**Table 1**                                                    **B8.62**

| March Board | Discussion of legal/regulatory risks (Company solicitor) |
|---|---|
| June Board | Consideration of the risk assessment process (Head of internal audit) |
| August Board | Review of credit risks (Head of credit risk) |
| October Board | Review of treasury risks (Head of Treasury function) |
| December Board | Review of operational risks (Internal Audit) |
| January/February Board | Formal review of the process (Internal audit) |

- Where necessary, additional resources should be put in place to ensure procedures, timetables and reviews are completed on time.

- Ahead of the year end (probably following the June board), the board should set aside time to consider:

  o whether all the questions set out in the Turnbull guidance are being taken into account;

  o the wording of any risk management policy document the Board wish to disseminate; and

  o the approval of any new procedures that need to be in place at the time of the approval of the annual report and accounts.

# How non-executive directors may view risk   B8.63

Turnbull is certainly impacting upon how companies consider risk. One approach is for the board to set aside time at almost every board meeting to consider one major aspect of risk – so that all aspects are reviewed over the course of the year. We discussed this under Examples 1 and 2 at **B8.55** and **B8.56**. What each of these major aspects is will depend upon the nature of the business: one might be legal risks, another might be 'regulatory' another 'funding', another 'competitive', and so on.

It is wise for the company to set aside time to be spent with each director, including especially each of the non-executive directors, to explore individual directors' own perceptions of risk. The executive involved in this can be the risk manager of the entity, the chief audit executive or the chief executive or his/her assistant. It may entail visiting the non-executive directors at their usual places of work or, occasionally, setting up a telephone or video conference where this has not been feasible.

The outcomes of these meetings will be a report to the board which may be presented making use of risk matrices or of risk tables as explained in this chapter.

Non-executive directors often have different perceptions of risk from those typically held by executives. A possibly not entirely anticipated consequence of the Turnbull process is the focus on external risks which non-executive directors may bring, whereas Hampel and Turnbull had both bracketed risk management with internal control, suggesting more of a focus on internal rather than external risks. It is true that an effective system of internal control provides reasonable assurance of the achievement of corporate objectives, and this includes safeguarding against external risks.

## Illustrative risks from a non-executive perspective        B8.64

Based on a specific case, here are some of the risks than a non-executive director identified when he participated in this process. We have amended this account to ensure confidentiality.

1.  There is a risk that a top-down assessment of risk and control, emanating from the group board, will overlook key risks within the individual businesses of the group. It is important that each divisional board (etc) conducts a similar review and assessment.

2.  There is a real risk that the focus on 'top-down' assessment of risk and control will overlook major risks and control weaknesses which may be concealed within the systems of the business. Detailed auditing and monitoring, with systematic coverage, remain very important.

3.  We should be open to the possibility of referring in our published internal control statement to areas we have identified where there is scope for improvements which we intend to make. One of the risks a business faces is a loss of stakeholder confidence that the board really knows what is happening within the business. This is more likely if the board always reports in a bland, flawless way.

4.  A critical area of risk is in that of 'competencies' – does the company have the competencies it needs, and will it do so into the future? Do we know what *are* our key competencies?

5.  What is the internal audit risk? How do we measure internal audit performance?[41]

6.  Any overall 'top down' assessment of risk should start by defining the objectives of the enterprise – perhaps just four to six principal objectives. Risks should be related to these objectives.

7.  Where possible, KPIs (Key Performance Indicators) for each of the major risks should be established to measure whether or not these risks are under adequate control. The board's monthly MAP (management accounting pack) should report performance against these KPIs.

8.    The simple risk matrix (shown in **B8.51**) is an attractive aid to assessing and representing risks.

9.    As this NED saw it, these were some of the major risks the company faced:

- reputational risk;

- risk of profits stagnation or decline;

- economic cycle risks';

- share price/sector risk;

- board competence and succession planning risks;

- loss of top executives (including the level(s) below the top level) risks;

- risk of top executive exhaustion, getting into a rut, loss of enthusiasm or surrender into an 'end game' scenario for personal reasons not closely related to the company's prospects;

- risk of irrational prejudice (eg 'anti-Microsoft', 'www a waste of time');

- regulatory risk;

- unprovided-for liabilities, and contingent liabilities;

- potential future impact of clauses within contracts which are unknown to the board;

- lack of a directors' manual/insufficient board use of technology; and

- risk from inadequate embedded monitoring of internal control.

# Control environment checklist                            B8.65

(Based on a checklist which appears in Chambers, A D and G V Rand (1997): 'The Operational Auditing Handbook: Auditing Business Processes', [John Wiley & Sons, Chichester, England], 530 large format pages £75 hardback including diskette in WORD format of the book's extensive checklists and appendices. ISBN 0471 97060 3. Order from Wiley's Customer Services. Tel: +44 (0) 1243 779777. Fax: +44 (0)1243 820250.

# Objectives                                               B8.66

To ensure that management conveys the message that integrity, ethical values and commitment to competence cannot be compromised, and that employees receive and understand that message. To ensure that management continually demonstrates, by word and action, commitment to high ethical and competence standards.

**Checklist** **B8.67**

| 1. | Key Issues |
|---|---|
| 1.1 | Are there in place satisfactory Codes of Conduct and other policies which define acceptable business practice, conflicts of interest and expected standards of integrity and ethical behaviour? |
| 1.2 | Do management (from the *top* of the business downwards *to all levels*) clearly conduct business on a high ethical plane, and are departures appropriately remedied? |
| 1.3 | Is the philosophy and operating style of management consistent with the highest ethical standards? |
| 1.4 | Do the human resource policies of the business adequately reinforce its commitment to high standards of business integrity, ethics and competence? |
| 1.5 | Has the level of competence needed been specified for particular jobs, and does evidence exist to indicate that employees have the requisite knowledge and skills? |
| 1.6 | Are the Board and its committees sufficiently informed and independent of management such that necessary, even if difficult and probing, questions can be explored effectively? |
| 1.7 | Is the organisation structure such that (a) all fully understand their responsibilities and authorities, and (b) the enterprise's activities can be adequately monitored? |
| 2. | Detailed Issues |
| 2.1 | Are Codes of Conduct comprehensive, addressing conflicts of interest, illegal or other improper payments, anti-competitive guidelines and insider trading? |
| 2.2 | Are Codes of Conduct understood by and periodically subscribed to by all employees? |
| 2.3 | Do senior managers frequently visit outlying locations for which they are responsible? |
| 2.4 | Is it the impression that employees feel peer pressure 'to do the right thing'? |
| 2.5 | Is there sufficient evidence that management moves carefully in assessing potential benefits of ventures? |
| 2.6 | Do management adequately deal with signs that problems exist (eg hazardous by-products) even when the cost of identification and remedy could be high? |
| 2.7 | Are sufficient efforts made to deal honestly and fairly with business partners (eg employees, suppliers etc.)? |

| 2.8 | Is disciplinary action sufficiently taken and communicated in the case of violations? |
|---|---|
| 2.9 | Is management override of controls appropriate when it occurs; and sufficiently authorised, documented and explained? |
| 2.10 | Are there job descriptions (which adequately define key managers' responsibilities) and performance appraisals with follow-up action to remedy deficiencies? |
| 2.11 | Is management and staff turnover not excessive? |
| 2.12 | Are staffing levels adequate but not excessive? |
| 2.13 | Do staff recruitment procedures sufficiently enhance the enterprise's commitment to high standards of integrity, ethics and competence? |
| 2.14 | Do training programmes sufficiently enhance the enterprise's commitment to high standards of integrity, ethics and competence? |
| 2.15 | Do sufficient lines of communication exist to obviate the temptation of 'whistleblowing'? |

# Organisation checklist                                              B8.68

(Based on a checklist which appears in Chambers, A D and G V Rand (1997): 'The Operational Auditing Handbook: Auditing Business Processes', [John Wiley & Sons, Chichester, England], 530 large format pages £75 hardback including diskette in WORD format of the book's extensive checklists and appendices. ISBN 0471 97060 3. Order from Wiley's Customer Services. Tel: +44 (0)1243 779777. Fax: +44 (0)1243 820250.

## Objectives                                                         B8.69

(a) To ensure that the organisational structure is appropriate to the business and the achievement of strategic objectives.

(b) To ensure that the organisational structure is determined by the business and operational needs and avoids needless sub-divisions and excessive levels.

(c) To ensure that the structure enables the flow of key information upwards and outwards within the organisation and across all the business activities.

(d) To ensure that relevant responsibilities, authorities and functional terms of reference are defined and in place.

(e) To ensure that responsibilities and authorities are adequately segregated in order to avoid conflicts of interest and the potential for fraudulent practices.

(f) To ensure that the structure is periodically reviewed and any changes are agreed and authorised at a senior level.

(g) To ensure that each manager's span of control is optimised and avoids either over- or under-utilisation.

(h) To ensure that adequate staff resources are determined, authorised and provided in order to achieve the functional and business objectives.

(i) To ensure that the prevailing organisational structure is suitably documented and communicated to all relevant staff.

(j) To ensure that the organisational structure and the related functional divisions of responsibility are accurately and adequately reflected in the accounting and management information systems.

**Checklist**                                                                     **B8.70**

| 1. | Key Issues |
|---|---|
| 1.1 | How does management ensure that the organisational structure is optimised and appropriate for the achievement of strategic objectives? |
| 1.2 | Has the prevailing structure been ratified and authorised by senior management, and are all suggested changes assessed and authorised? |
| 1.3 | Is the organisation structure regularly reviewed for its relevance and in order to rationalise and streamline its form? |
| 1.4 | Have documented terms of reference, responsibilities and authorities been agreed, authorised and implemented for all functions and departments, and they maintained up-to-date? |
| 1.5 | How does management ensure that the organisational structure incorporates adequate segregation of key activities and duties? |
| 1.6 | Are management and staff establishment levels reliably determined, agreed and authorised (and what measures ensure that actual staffing levels are maintained within establishment)? |
| 1.7 | How can management be sure that the prevailing organisational structure is accurately reflected in both the accounting and management information systems? |
| 2. | Detailed Issues |
| 2.1 | Is the structure of the organisation based upon the operational characteristics of the underlying business activities? |
| 2.2 | Are organisation charts maintained up-to-date and adequately circulated? |
| 2.3 | Are reporting, functional and line relationships clearly defined? |
| 2.4 | What mechanisms enable the identification of unnecessary or superfluous structural elements (or those with the potential for amalgamation)? |
| 2.5 | Are there sufficient reporting and information channels to senior management level? |

| 2.6 | Are suitably approved authority limits (and mandates) in place? |
| 2.7 | How is the accuracy of data input from other systems (i.e. long-term planning considerations) confirmed? |
| 2.8 | How is the accuracy of data output to other systems (i.e. manpower and succession planning or the management information system) confirmed? |

# Management information checklist  B8.71

## Objectives  B8.72

To ensure:

(a)  that management satisfactorily utilises information (which is timely, complete, accurate, consistent, clear, concise, relevant, secure and economic) in assisting them to meet their objectives; and

(b)  that opportunities are taken to gain a competitive advantage through the strategic use of information.

## Checklist  B8.73

| **1.** | **Key Issues** |
|---|---|
| 1.1 | Is there a clear association between (a) the *objectives* of management, and (b) the information available to management – so that the latter can inform management of their progress in achieving the former? |
| 1.2 | Some businesses have plentiful data but too little information derived from that data; others have plentiful information but too little analysis performed on that information; others have plentiful analysis but too little decision and action following the analysis. Is the availability and balance right in this case? |
| 1.3 | Is applicable external information (e.g. about the market) available – as well as internally generated information about business performance? |
| 1.4 | Is there satisfactory security over the collection, processing, retention and disposal of information? |
| 1.5 | Are data protection principles complied with, with regard to personal data? |
| 1.6 | Has the business considered the scope to develop strategic information systems (targeted at suppliers and/or staff & customers) which achieve a competitive advantage by reducing costs and/or improving service and reliability? |

| 2. | Detailed Issues |
|---|---|
| 2.1 | Has responsibility for management information been formally assigned to one or more managers who is/are formally responsible for appraising its quality and utilisation? |
| 2.2 | Is information *timely* – produced and distributed promptly at the most appropriate intervals from up-to-date data? |
| 2.3 | Is information clearly and reliably dated with no risk of out-of-date reports being used as if current? |
| 2.4 | Is information retained no longer than necessary? |
| 2.5 | Is the information *complete* enough to meet the operational needs of managers? Does it adequately inform as a basis for necessary management action? Does it cover all operational areas of the business? |
| 2.6 | Is the information *accurate* enough to be used reliably by management? |
| 2.7 | Are management reports *consistent* (a) between each edition, and (b) between different reports which relate to associated issues? Is *cut-off* handled reliably? |
| 2.8 | Is *clarity* achieved in that management reports are (a) clearly titled, dated and captioned, and (b) attractive, unambiguous and easy to use? |
| 2.9 | Where figures are presented which relate to each other, is *clarity* achieved in that comparison is facilitated? |
| 2.10 | Are management reports *concise* without being too brief? Is proper use made of reporting by exception only? |
| 2.11 | Is all the information *relevant* to the business and to those who receive it (who fully appreciate its purpose)? |
| 2.12 | Is management information satisfactorily and promptly *acted upon* by those who receive it? |
| 2.13 | Are exception reports all followed up? |
| 2.14 | *Security:* Is an inventory maintained of confidential and sensitive corporate information, and is the handling and issuance of this information subject to proper authorization controls? |
| 2.15 | Are company secrets kept securely? |
| 2.16 | Are there satisfactory access controls to (a) the site, (b) the buildings, (c) departmental information stores, and (d) computers? |
| 2.17 | Is data adequately secure while being transmitted (e.g. by making use of encryption)? |

# Risk management checklist  **B8.74**

Based on a checklist which appears in Chambers, A D and Rand G V (1997): 'The Operational Auditing Handbook. Auditing Business Processes', (John Wiley & Sons, Chichester, England), 530 large format pages £75 hardback including diskette in Word format of the book's extensive checklists and appendices. ISBN 0471 97060 3. Order from Wiley's Customer Services. Tel: +44 (0)1243 779777. Fax: +44 (0)1243 820250.

## Objectives  **B8.75**

(a)  To ensure that management are aware of all the relevant commercial and operational risks.

(b)  To ensure that an effective risk management strategy is defined, authorised and implemented in order to counteract. avoid and minimise applicable risks.

(c)  To ensure that the business operations and financial success of the organisation are neither disrupted nor adversely affected by disasters and problems.

(d)  To ensure that adequate precautions are taken to protect assets, persons and the organisation's reputation.

(e)  To ensure that the potential for accidents and losses is prevented or reduced.

(f)  To ensure that adequate contingency plans have been developed to provide continuity of the business in the event of any form of disaster.

(g)  To ensure that contingency arrangements are tested to confirm their effectiveness and relevance.

(h)  To ensure that adequate and cost effective insurance cover is provided.

(i)  To ensure that insurance costs are minimised.

(j)  To ensure that insurance claims are made whenever relevant, and duly settled.

(k)  To ensure that all relevant legislation and regulations are complied with.

**Checklist**  **B8.76**

| 1. | Key issues |
|---|---|
| 1.1 | What steps has management taken to accurately identify potential risks? |
| 1.2 | Has a documented business impact review been undertaken as the basis for determining the action required? |
| 1.3 | Have adequate plans been developed to counteract, reduce or avoid risks to assets, persons and the organisation's reputation? |

| 1.4 | How can management be assured that the plans in place remain relevant and adequate? |
|---|---|
| 1.5 | Have the risk assessment and action plans been suitably authorised (and how is this evidenced)? |
| 1.6 | Are contingency plans regularly and adequately tested in order that they remain effective? |
| 1.7 | Are all affected staff aware of their responsibilities in the event of a significant disaster or risk situation (and how is their effectiveness assessed)? |
| 1.8 | Are all insurance requirements subject to appropriate assessment and authorisation, and how can management be certain that insurance cover is appropriate and adequate? |
| 1.9 | What steps are taken to minimise and contain insurance costs? |
| 1.10 | How can management be assured that all the relevant legislation, regulations and preventative requirements are complied with? |
| **2.** | **Detailed issues** |
| 2.1 | What measures ensure that the assessment of risks is accurate and realistic? |
| 2.2 | Are all new projects and ventures adequately assessed for risks, and are action and contingency plans accordingly updated? |
| 2.3 | What mechanisms prevent any business activity or project being overlooked for risk assessment purposes? |
| 2.4 | Have the business impact review and risk management strategy been authorised, documented, and circulated? |
| 2.5 | Are non-financial risks (i.e. damage to commercial reputation, public image, etc.) also taken into account? |
| 2.6 | Are adequate measures in place to protect employees, visitors, etc. from injury or death? |
| 2.7 | Where the organisation is heavily dependent upon the use of information technology, has specific consideration been given to the effects on the business of a loss of computing facilities? |
| 2.8 | Have documented contingency plans been developed for all relevant business activities, and what measures ensure that the plans are maintained up-to-date? |
| 2.9 | Are staff made aware of their roles and responsibilities within the contingency arrangements? |
| 2.10 | Are contingency plans regularly tested for effectiveness (and how are amendments identified, authorised and applied)? |

| 2.11 | Have appropriate insurance arrangements been made to cover the following areas: |
|------|---------------------------------------------------------------------------------|
|      | • product liability; |
|      | • loss due to business interruption; |
|      | • loss of funds due to malpractice; and |
|      | • damage and injury to persons and property |
| 2.12 | Are all hazardous processes identified and subject to all the relevant precautions and safety measures (how is this evidenced)? |
| 2.13 | Has an effective Health & Safety Policy been implemented? It is suitably tested and how is it maintained up-to-date? |
| 2.14 | Are staff adequately trained in safety matters, and how can their understanding and proficiency be confirmed? |
| 2.15 | Are accidents and incidents fully investigated and shortcomings identified and satisfactorily addressed? |
| 2.16 | Are all claims against the organisation fully investigated and only settled when duly authorised? |
| 2.17 | What measures ensure that insurance costs are competitive? |
| 2.18 | Are insurance arrangements subject to regular review and are changes suitably authorised? |
| 2.19 | How is the accuracy of data input from other systems (i.e. planning) confirmed? |
| 2.20 | How is the accuracy of data output to other systems (i.e. insurance department) confirmed? |

# Control risk self assessment B8.77

A strong programme of control risk self assessment (CRSA) can contribute significantly to the confidence that the board may have that the risk management and internal control arrangements within the business are sound so as to give reasonable assurance that corporate objectives are being achieved, and that there are strong risk management processes embedded within the business, per the Turnbull guidance.

## Introducing CRSA B8.78

CRSA (or control self assessment (CSA) as it often termed), is highly packaged by consultants. It can be difficult to break through the hype to understand its essential nature and whether it can be of continuing value within a business. Just to ask this question risks the wrath of those who promote CRSA! Now, coming through as a new wave promoted equally heavily by management consultants, is an approach labelled 'enterprise-wide risk management'.

**Defining CRSA**                                                                    **B8.79**

So what *is* CRSA? We can describe it as simply the assessment of risk, and
controls over risk by staff at all levels for themselves. Beyond that, CRSA has
been dressed up with protocols and magic tricks which have become the
preserve of a small cognoscenti and are serving to exclude the uninitiated – just
what is not required if CRSA is to gain ground. It is a shame that the mysteries
of CRSA are too often, and too much, shrouded behind issues of intellectual
property rights rather than being in the same open domain as most other
professional concepts and approaches.

In a broad sense, any approach to the self assessment of risk and internal
control is CRSA – it may range from occasional completion by line managers
of a business controls certificate, through to the use of letters of representation
on risk and control or the completion of questionnaires – all the way up to
participative workshops using anonymous voting approaches. At the end of this
section (**B8.80**) we provide a sample business controls certificate, a standard
'boilerplate' form of wording for a letter of representation on risk management
and internal control and an example of a questionnaire.

## Letters of representation on risk management and internal control                                         **B8.80**

The use of letters of representation or questionnaires has its limitations, but then
so do all other approaches to self assessment. The concept is that all managers
with key responsibilities for risk management and internal control make a
return on their awareness and performance, usually once a year. The content of
the return is then assessed by more senior management and/or by internal audit
in order to identify areas of probable relative risk and control weaknesses where
further investigative and remedial work appears to be needed – perhaps by way
of internal audit 'fieldwork'. Summaries of the returns are fed through to the
audit committee of the board, usually by internal audit, and serve to add to the
degree of confidence that the board attains with respect to its oversight of risk
management and internal control.

Some managers are likely to refuse to return a letter of representation, claiming
there is no way they can commit themselves to the sentiments they are being
asked to express, or claiming to be perplexed by the terminology of the return.
It should be made clear to managers that they should modify the wording of
their return to make it consistent with what they feel they can confidently
associate themselves with. Other managers are likely to wish to clear their in-
trays as quickly as possible and may not take the exercise sufficiently seriously.
But the majority will enter into the spirit of things in a responsible way, with
most of the rest of the managers resolving to put themselves into a better
position to be able to approach the exercise more responsibly the following
year. Top management support for the approach is essential if it is to work in a
valuable way.

Undoubtedly, as with so many other things, with the support of the board and
the audit committee, top management must champion CRSA, and staff at all

levels and in all areas may engage in it. It is likely that internal audit will need to facilitate and monitor CRSA if it is to survive and prosper. 'Facilitation' is one of the forms of consultancy that the new internal auditing *Standards* regard as authentic internal auditing (see the Glossary to the new Standards at **B23.4**, and the discussion on internal audit consulting in at **B23.31**). CRSA is not a sufficient substitute for traditional internal auditing of the 'assurance' variety, but the mix of internal audit work will change dramatically in a CRSA-oriented enterprise.

# Why CRSA? B8.81

What is new about CRSA? Line management have always been responsible for internal control. Indeed self assessment programmes have been in place in some corporations[42] for many, many years – and these have often embraced an assessment of issues beyond a narrow view of control – such as quality, safety, equity, environmental management, etc.

Contemporary paradigms of internal control all avow that the monitoring of internal control is an essential part of internal control itself, as is the process of risk assessment (see **B8.10**). In the past, management has often found that the monitoring of internal control has been done best when it has been delegated on their behalf to an internal audit function. An internal audit function has the specialist skills to conduct reviews objectively. Its relative freedom from other duties means that the monitoring of internal control is not so likely to be put on the back burner.

So, can the monitoring of internal control be left to line management and staff? Or, put another way, what has changed which makes CRSA attractive today? As we have said, CRSA is unlikely to flourish without internal audit to give it a helping hand. An important issue can be the degree to which internal audit is independent enough of the CRSA programme so as to be able to provide top management and the audit committee with objective reassurance about the CRSA programme's effectiveness. Too much internal audit independence from the CRSA programme may mean CRSA is likely to fail; too little and CRSA is just a tool for internal audit. Indeed, a hybrid approach, combining both internal audit and CRSA, is sometimes applied: in this approach the fieldwork of an internal audit engagement commences, and perhaps also ends, with a CRSA workshop.

Top management and the audit committee will want advice from internal audit as to where to first introduce CRSA. In its participative workshops form, CRSA works best in non-threatening, non-hierarchical parts of the business. Top management and the audit committee will ask for periodic reports from internal audit on CRSA's effectiveness. So CRSA is more likely to run in parallel with internal audit in all but the smallest enterprises that may not have internal audit.

CRSA is very much a response to, some would say, an essential component of, the modern re-engineered business. Downsized, delayered businesses have empowered staff to control the destinies of their business activities. They have more authority as well as more responsibility. It is in keeping with empowerment that they should monitor their own risk and control arrangements, and that control should be tightly focused on the achievement of key objectives. Nowhere is this more important than in the re-engineered business where the development and implementation of new management processes can, of itself, have such a detrimental effect on risk and control.

Certainly it ill behoves anyone to denigrate this new enchantment with assessing the effectiveness of internal control. Introducing CRSA through participative workshops, perhaps aided by anonymous voting, which is fun and can be an important and regular way of giving practical substance to the re-engineered, empowered and participative business.

## The role of internal audit in control risk self-assessment B8.82

Embedding the review of control and risk within the business, as Turnbull stipulates (We reproduce the Combined Code and the Turnbull Report in PART A). Here we are referring to 2003 Combined Code Provisions C.2.1, C.3.5 and C.2.1, is giving a new impetus to control risk self assessment in many enterprises. Turnbull's guidance on implementing the Combined Code provision on internal audit is also putting the spotlight on internal auditing generally. So it is not inappropriate to review the relationship between internal audit and control risk self assessment.

The prudent corporate approach is not to see CRSA as an alternative to internal audit, but rather to co-ordinate CRSA with the internal audit process and see them as complementary ways of assessing risk and control. Conventional internal auditing has the advantage that audit findings are supported by evidence which internal auditing standards require to be contained within the records of the audit engagement. 'Evidence' in CRSA programmes is, in the main, vested in the knowledge and experience which the participants bring to the CRSA workshops – which has its own advantage as their 'know-how' is likely to exceed that which can be acquired by a sole internal auditor or by an internal audit team during the brief fieldwork of an audit assignment.

The closeness of the CRSA participants to the activities they are considering has the possible disadvantage, compared with conventional internal auditing, of a relative lack of objectivity perhaps because of excessive familiarity or because of a reluctance to admit to weaknesses. Internal auditors also have the edge in the quality of their professional skills in conducting reviews of activities. Furthermore, summary reports on internal auditing engagements to the audit committee from a properly constituted internal auditing function will be perceived by the audit committee as being more independent of management and thus potentially more dependable than those which are generated through the CRSA programme.

Internal audit can facilitate the CRSA process in a number of important ways. A successful CRSA programme can also provide valuable reassurance to internal audit.

## Internal audit as a facilitator of control risk self-assessment   B8.83

Internal audit should be a respected advisor to management and the board on risk, control and governance matters. It is natural that management will turn to internal audit for assistance in the following ways with respect to CRSA.

- Advice as to which parts of the organisation CRSA should be introduced into first. CRSA works best in non-hierarchical, non-threatening parts of the entity where the culture is open to the acknowledgement, without penalty, of control weaknesses. There are also likely to be some parts of the entity which have a greater need for CRSA in the sense that conventional internal audit review is difficult – perhaps because of the highly technical nature of the activity – but nevertheless risk is believed to be high and internal control is believed to be weak.

- Advice on the preparation of the training sessions for those who will be involved in CRSA. Internal audit involvement may go beyond an advisory role, to become the sole or principal provider of this training. Training will be needed in the principles of internal control and risk management as well as the approach to be followed in the CRSA programme.

- Review of the CRSA work completed by individual line managers and emerging from CRSA workshops.

- Facilitation of the CRSA workshops themselves.

- Guidance on the consolidation upwards of the results of CRSA, and possibly an active role in making these consolidations through to top management and the audit committee of the board.

- Advice to top management and to the audit committee as to the effectiveness of CRSA, so that they receive reliable advice on the extent to which they can rely upon the CRSA programme.

- Review of the follow up of agreed actions to be taken resulting from CRSA, though ideally responsibility for the follow up process should be with management, not with internal audit.

Management and administration of the CRSA programme by internal audit threatens a conflict of interest for internal audit. Internal auditing standards require internal audit to be independent of the activities they audit. For executive responsibility to be given to internal audit for the CRSA programme challenges internal audit independence and hence internal audit objectivity. For instance, there is the problem of the reliability of internal audit advice to top management and to the audit committee as to the effectiveness of the CRSA process if internal audit have, in effect, been championing and managing it.

### Control risk self assessment as reassurance to internal audit   B8.84

The results of the CRSA can be utilised by internal audit where the head of the internal auditing unit is satisfied that the quality of CRSA work means that it can be relied upon. Internal audit has always had a professional obligation to avoid duplication of audit work where the work of others can be relied upon to meet internal audit objectives at least in part. Involvement of internal audit as an advisor in the CRSA process will provide internal audit with the confidence to draw conclusions as to the effectiveness of CRSA and the extent to which it can be relied upon to meet internal audit objectives.

## Dealing with concerns about CRSA                    B8.85

The concerns about CRSA are best resolved if we allow that CRSA should be an additional and *not* an alternative approach (to internal audit) to the monitoring on risk management and internal control. It is hard to be confident that management and staff, who have never been busier, can be relied upon exclusively as the mechanism for monitoring risk and control arrangements effectively.

Senior managers in several businesses have said there is no way they could entertain the introduction of CRSA if this were to involve training sessions followed by annual, participative workshop sessions. They consider their managers and staff are either too busy, or could not safely take their eyes of real time problems for the duration, or both. For them, CRSA has to be implemented in a less demanding way – through letters of representation on internal control or through self assessment questionnaires possibly completed online through the company's network and returned to internal audit for review.

Of course, as we suggested in **B8.80**, internal control comfort letters and questionnaires may not be taken seriously – there is always a risk that they are just another document to get off the desk (or screen) as quickly as possible.

CRSA gurus propound an annual cycle for CRSA although it is not entirely clear why necessarily this should be so. Certainly, conventional forms of internal audit rarely work to a one-year cycle. Is there not a risk that staff at all levels will resent the time it takes as CRSA quickly recycles a second and a third time? If they do not resent it, they will surely find it harder to take it so seriously. On the other hand, they will become more adept at working CRSA.

It was striking that a March 1994 survey of internal auditing in the pharmaceutical sector found that eight of the twenty-two respondent companies had by then introduced CRSA with a further six then planning to set it up. A repeat survey in 1997 found CRSA present in only five surveyed companies – some indication that CRSA is not always standing the test of time.

## Objectivity                                          B8.86

There is also the challenge of objectivity. To what extent will managers and staff be candid about control deficiencies? Certainly CRSA works best in a culture where acknowledgement of deficiencies incurs brownie points rather than black marks. A participative workshop approach to CRSA makes it harder for a more senior member of staff to avoid unwelcome candour – particularly if the workshop is enabled by anonymous voting.

Possibly managers and staff, even with the best wills in the world, may be too close to their responsibilities to be able to assess their affairs with a high degree of objectivity or to have a clear view of their control interfaces with other business activities. But nobody would surely suggest that that they should not endeavour to do so. Here again the participative workshop approach to CRSA scores heavily over the more pedestrian letter or questionnaire-based approaches – especially if members are chosen who cut across departmental frontiers and levels.

The determination of each activity to be the subject of a participative workshop must also be done imaginatively so that it is not a mere reflection of the way the business is structured. Control is usually relatively strong within a group of people put together to work on a common or a series of closely related tasks: they very often have well developed formal procedures reinforced by informal ones as well as by a strong sense of group commitment. Control is usually weakest where there is a need for co-ordination between separate parts of the business. We need to be sure that CRSA addresses this issue – in particular through the determination of the workshops which will take place and their membership. Traditional internal auditing is also quite well placed to address this issue as internal auditors have the rare authority and opportunity to step across departmental frontiers to explore control issues wherever they spread. Even so, internal auditors prefer to audit business activities which correspond to the work responsibilities of a formal sub-division of the business – they know where to go to do the audit and which manager will take ownership of the issues raised as a result of the audit. CRSA is ideally suited to be applied to a business process which cuts across departmental frontiers, as the members of the CRSA workshop can be carefully selected to be representative of the different facets of that activity.

## The CRSA workshop B8.87

Our preference is for a workshop to take a short working day – perhaps commencing mid-morning and ending mid-afternoon. Those invited to attend will be the key players in the different facets of the activity which is the subject of the CRSA. This does not necessarily mean that only senior staff and managers will be present – it all depends on how crucial to the activity is the work of more junior members of staff.

Anonymous voting hardware and software may be used. This can comprise of cordless key pads which allow the workshop members to vote anonymously on issues which arise during the workshop. This makes for more candid expressions of view – especially when otherwise a junior member of staff might otherwise be constrained by his or her perception of the expectations of others present at the workshop. Anonymous voting breaks through log jams and enables the workshop to make progress more quickly. But it is a mistake to believe that it allows consensus views to gel – instead it implies that the majority view prevails.

Where the cordless keypads are connected to a peripheral devise of a computer which accepts the voting signals, the computer software can be organised to immediately display the results of voting anonymously using a computer projector, and to store the results so that the report of the workshop can be generated quickly and attractively after the workshop has ended.

It is likely that one or two internal auditors will facilitate the CRSA workshop – one as the main facilitator and the other to take notes.

The approach to the conduct of the workshop may entail these stages:

- brainstorm on what are the objectives for the activity which is the subject of the CRSA;

- brainstorm on what are the perceived major risks to attaining these objectives (and also the perceived major risks of unwanted consequences possibly occurring in parallel with the achievement of these objectives);

- consider whether the risk profile can be improved by, for instance, risk avoidance or risk transfer

- consider the adequacy of controls and where and how they can be improved; and

- develop an action plan to implement to proposed changes to risk and control.

A variant of this approach is to utilise a standard set of questions as the agenda of the workshop. In our experience this leads to similar workshop outcomes. A suggested list of questions was developed by CoCo and is given below at **B8.89**.

After the conclusion of the workshop, the report of the workshop is written, including the action plan. The action plan then has to be approved by senior management and it then usually falls to those who attended the CRSA workshop to implement the changes outlined in the action plan. The CRSA may be repeated twelve months later to review progress and to repeat the process.

## Conclusion                                                         B8.88

CRSA, like the quality circles of perhaps a decade ago, has caught the mood of the times. If we dissect it we discover an amalgam of traditional practices often overlaid by modern technology. It may not last for ever. It is likely to reinvent itself – perhaps now the form of enterprise-wide risk management. Despite the pros and cons, it is easier to espouse CRSA in principle than to give it ensuring substance in practice. But then, the effective monitoring of internal control has never been straightforward.

## CoCo's Sample Assessment Questions                    B8.89

This is copyright of the Canadian Institute of Chartered Accountants and is reproduced with their kind permission. It formed Exhibit C of their 'Guidance on Control' [November 1995] which was Number 1 in their 'Control &

Governance' series. CICA offers this, together with Number 2 'Guidance for Directors – Governance Processes for Control' [December 1995], a binder and a subscription to subsequent exposure drafts and guidance issued by their Criteria for Control (CoCo) Board.

# Sample assessment questions

To assess the effectiveness of control, an organization may find it helpful to express the criteria as questions tailored to its circumstances. The following is a simple example of questions a group might use to conduct a self-assessment. They have been tailored by drawing on some of the explanatory material in this guidance ('Guidance on Control', Control and Governance No. 1, (Toronto, CICA, November 1995). In each case, the answer to the question would be followed up by 'How do we know' to trigger identification and discussion of the control processes.

## Purpose

- Do we clearly understand the mission and vision of the organization?

- Do we understand our objectives, as a group, and how they fit with other objectives in the organization?

- Does the information available to us enable us to identify risk and assess risk?

- Do we understand the risk we need to control and the degree of residual risk acceptable to those to whom we are accountable for control?

- Do we understand the policies that affect our actions?

- Are our plans responsive and adequate to achieve control?

- Do we have manageable performance targets?

## Commitment

- Are our principles of integrity and ethical values shared and practised?

- Are people rewarded fairly according to the organization's objectives and values?

- Do we clearly understand what we are accountable for, and do we have a clear definition of our authority and responsibilities?

- Are critical decisions made by people with the necessary expertise, knowledge and authority?

- Are levels of trust sufficient to support the open flow of information and effective performance?

## Capability

- Do we have the right people, skills, tools and resources?

- Is there prompt communication of mistakes, bad news and other information to people who need to know, without fear of reprisal?

- Is there adequate information to allow us to perform our tasks?

- Are our actions coordinated with the rest of the organization?

- Do we have the procedures and the processes to help ensure achievement of our objectives?

## Monitoring and learning

- Do we review the internal and external environment to see whether changes are required to objectives or control?

- Do we monitor performance against relevant targets and indicators?

- Do we challenge the assumptions behind our objectives?

- Do we receive and provide information that is necessary and relevant to decision-making?

- Are our information systems up to date?

- Do we learn from the results of monitoring and make continuous improvements to control?

- Do we periodically assess the effectiveness of control?

## Business controls certificate – example wording                    B8.90

**To:**   The Director of Internal Audit
The Finance Director – Operating Group

We confirm to the best of our knowledge and belief that operations at
_____ comply with the business controls set
out in the attached self-certification questionnaire except as noted. Additionally, we are not aware of any fraudulent transactions or any irregularities involving management or employees who have significant roles in the system of internal control.


_____


_____
General Manager/Chief Executive                              Finance Director

## Letter of representation on risk management and internal control – standard form of wording                    B8.91

From:   A Line Manager

To:   Internal Audit, or to:_____

Line Manager immediately senior (copy Internal Audit), or to:_____

The Audit Committee (copy Internal Audit) in the case of the most senior executive management

Re.:     Representations on internal control

Date:

_____

_____

I confirm that the objectives I am responsible for achieving are clearly defined. I acknowledge that the identification, assessment and control of risks to the achievement of these objectives, and the maintenance of effective internal control to provide reasonable assurance of the achievement of these objectives, are amongst my key managerial responsibilities. I am confident I understand what this entails and have been given the necessary authority to achieve these outcomes.

I have agreed with responsible management the risk appetite which should be applied to my area of responsibilities, and I believe I am managing operations within these parameters.

Having monitored achievement of my objectives and the functioning of the risk management and internal control arrangements in place within my area of responsibilities I consider that throughout 20XX risks have been satisfactorily managed and internal control has been adequate to provide reasonable assurance of effective and efficient operations, of internal financial control, and of compliance with laws and regulations; and that these arrangements have been complied with in all material respects throughout this period.

I have communicated to my staff the essential elements of an effective system of risk management and internal control and have ensured that: (a) they are aware of their responsibilities especially in areas of potential critical risk; and (b) they have been empowered to operate appropriate control procedures effectively.

All staff within my area of responsibility, at all levels, have been appraised of their duty to report upwards unresolved matters of concern about risk and control and to deal expeditiously and effectively with such matters reported to them. In reporting upwards, staff have been empowered, without risk of victimisation, to by-pass intermediate levels of management where they consider this to be necessary. I have taken appropriate steps to confirm that no matters remain unresolved as a result of this process. All such matters drawn to my personal attention by staff have been dealt with to my satisfaction.

No issues remain outstanding related to risk or control in my areas of my responsibility, which have been communicated to me by internal or external audit or by others.

I have considered whether significant changes have been made to business practices in my area of responsibility which may have impacted upon risk or weakened internal control and believe that this is not the case. Furthermore our plans for future change have been appraised in the context of their potential risk and internal control impacts and I believe these issues have been addressed satisfactorily.

I am unaware of any weaknesses in risk management and internal control or irregularities in accounting practices which should be drawn to your attention.

# Self-check questionnaire on internal control for managers to use
B8.92

The questionnaire which ends this section was included in a guide to internal control for management and staff of a multinational company. We reproduce here both the guide and the questionnaire.

### Internal control – a guide for management and staff            B8.93

*Why internal control?*                                          **B8.94**

- Four in five organisations in the UK have suffered a breakdown in their IT systems during the past two years at an annual cost of £1.2 billion and increasing. A quarter of the incidents led to serious losses.

- Age Concern, the UK's leading charity for the elderly, ground to a halt after theft of computer chips.

- In February 1995 the UK's oldest merchant bank, Barings, collapsed. When Leeson had joined Barings, he had two outstanding County Court judgements against him. Because of this record, Barings had failed to get Leeson a trading license in the UK, but they had not disclosed his record to the Singaporean authorities. An ignored internal audit report in August 1994 had concluded that there was 'a significant general risk that the controls could be over-ridden by Nick Leeson as he is the key manager in the front and the back office'. He was also not only trading but was supervising the trading function (ie the 'front room') as well.

- On 26 September 1995, criminal complaints were filed against a rogue trader, Mr. Iguchi, for running up £700m losses over eleven years in the New York trading arm of Daiwa Bank (Japan's tenth biggest commercial bank), through unauthorised trading of American Treasury bonds and falsification of the bank's books and records to conceal the losses. Mr Iguchi had been in charge of front and back office operations.

At least half of large companies are victims of fraud more than once a year, and in most cases an employee is involved. Fraud is avoidable loss due to an inadequate system of internal control. Other avoidable losses, including accidental errors or omissions, may be even more damaging, for example flood.

Internal control is not designed just to prevent these sorts of unwanted consequences. Internal control, probably designed and observed, provides *reasonable assurance* of the achievement of objectives – not an *absolute guarantee* as a business may be thrown off course by external events. Without effective internal control no enterprise is likely to achieve its objectives.

## *What is internal control?*                              **B8.95**

Internal control is control by management of what happens within the business. It is *management control.*

Internal control is broadly defined as a process, effected by the entity's board of directors, management and other personnel, designed to provide reasonable assurance regarding the achievement of objectives in the following categories:

- effectiveness and efficiency of operations;

- reliability of financial reporting;

- compliance with applicable laws and regulations.

'Effectiveness and efficiency of operations' includes the safeguarding of assets, that is the prevention or timely detection of unauthorised acquisition, use or disposition of the entity's assets.

Internal control is much more than internal (cross) check. It is the totality of methods that management has introduced to provide reasonable assurance of the achievement of objectives and the avoidance of unwanted outcomes. As such, internal control is the essence of good management. The classic view of management is that it comprises effective planning, organising, staffing, directing and controlling. Each of these must be done well if there is to be effective internal control.

We can distinguish between (a) *preventative controls* designed to avoid the non-achievement of objectives or to avoid the occurrence of unwanted outcomes and (b) *detective controls* to inform management and others when things have gone wrong.

## *Practical advice on internal control*                    **B8.96**

Internal control should assist management to achieve their objectives. These objectives must be clear when an internal control framework is established.

There is no such thing as 100 per cent effective control. The allocation of additional resources to improve control may have inadequate marginal benefit. Whether that is so is a matter of management judgement in the light of:

- the importance of the objectives, and the degree of risk of not achieving them;

- the seriousness of the potential exposures, and the degree of risk of them occurring; and

- the cost, if any, of additional control measures.

Control must be cost-effective – tailored to a realistic assessment of need and appropriate for the purpose. Control will be more cost-effective if:

- complex controls are rejected in favour of simple ones which have the same control effect;

- redundant controls are jettisoned;

- compensating controls are rationalised; and

- checks are performed on *samples* where appropriate.

Much can be done in a well controlled way with no additional use of resources. For instance, dividing work between two members of staff will not necessarily be costly.

It is best to place control as early as possible within the system. Until control has been established there is a greater possibility of error or loss which may go undetected.

Where control depends upon a reconciliation of figures, the reconciliation should be performed or supervised by someone who is (a) competent and (b) independent of the generation of any of the figures which are to be reconciled.

Where control depends upon supervision it is important that this is taken seriously. Delegation is an important and valid management approach but it should not be abdication. Authority, rather than responsibility, is delegated.

A well designed system of internal control is worse than worthless unless it is complied with, since the semblance of control may lead to a false assurance. Senior management should set a good example with regard to control compliance.

While control serves a much broader purpose than the prevention and detection of fraud, this is nevertheless an important aspect. But fraud often involves the circumvention of controls through deception and/or collusion. Management and staff must be encouraged to watch out for tell-tale signs of both fraud and error.

Broadly, a 25–50–25 per cent rule applies. 25 per cent will be honest in all circumstances. 25 per cent dishonest whenever circumstances permit. 50 per cent are easily swayed. Few will be able to resist the temptation to defraud if they have an unsharable financial problem, there is opportunity and very little risk of detection, and the consequences upon detection would be modest.

We should take a lot of trouble to recruit trustworthy staff. But thereafter systems of internal control should confirm they are working in a trustworthy way. This is in the interests of staff themselves – otherwise the finger of suspicion is likely to start pointing at them. A good system of internal control reduces the opportunity for fraud and makes detection more likely. It has been said that the best form of prevention (of fraud) is detection.

### *Key controls which should be in place*  **B8.97**

There are five necessary components of a system of internal control.

*Control environment* **B8.98**

- Commitment to competence and integrity.

- Communication of ethical values and control consciousness.

- Appropriate organisational structure.

- Appropriate delegation of authority with accountability.

*Risk assessment* **B8.99**

- Identification of key business risks in a timely manner.

- Consideration of the likelihood of risks crystallising and their likely impact.

- Prioritising allocation of resources for control.

*Control activities* **B8.100**

- Procedures to ensure completeness and accuracy of transactions, accounting, data processing and information reports.

- Appropriate authorisation limits.

- Controls to limit exposure to loss of assets or to fraud.

- Procedures to ensure compliance with laws and regulations.

*Information and communication* **B8.101**

- Performance indicators to monitor activities, risks and progress in meeting objectives.

- Systems which communicate relevant, reliable and up-to-date information.

*Monitoring* **B8.102**

- A monitoring process to give reasonable assurance to the Board of appropriate control procedures in place.

- Identification of business change which may require modification of the system of internal control.

- Formal procedures for reporting weaknesses and for ensuring appropriate corrective action.

In the following table at **B8.106** is a checklist of some of key control issues likely to be relevant in most contexts.

*Control risk self assessment* **B8.103**

Contemporary management approaches risk effective internal control. De-layering broadens the *span of supervisory control* of remaining management layers and empowers staff to make more decisions; replacing hierarchical management by project-based management may have the effect of increasing individual authority and weakening reporting.

Any process of business re-engineering must preserve the essential internal control framework both *during* the process of re-engineering (when the attention of staff to internal control matters may be diverted) and *after* processes have been re-engineered (when essential controls may have been superseded inadvertently).

In an environment of empowered staff management and staff may assume more responsibility for identifying risks and improving internal control – through a process of control risk self assessment – especially where delegation of this to internal audit results in only incomplete coverage on an annual basis.

(Also see **B8.92–B8.111**.)

### *Internal control for the smaller operating unit*      B8.104

In a small business there is less opportunity to rely on forms of segregation to achieve internal control at minimal or no cost. On the other hand the closeness to operations of the small unit's senior management, means that they may be more sensitive to control problems as they develop. Where control cannot be achieved by segregation it has to be achieved by supervision. Parts of the supervisory control process may be automated using the computer.

It is the control risk rather than the number of staff employed which should determine the controls which are appropriate even for the operating unit which employs few people.

### The questionnaire      B8.105

### *Key control issues*      B8.106

| | Yes | No |
|---|---|---|
| 1. Is there shared responsibility for all important parts of the accounting system – so that absolute and independent control by any one person is avoided? | | |
| 2. Have you avoided giving any one person custody or control of (a) assets (such as cash or stock), or (b) operations (such as Purchasing) – where that person *also* has involvement in accounting for those assets or operations? | | |
| 2.1 If this is unavoidable, is there frequent, independent review of the accounting records? | | |
| 3. Is authorisation of (a) the acquisition, use or disposal of an asset, or (b) the initiation of any operation or programme – segregated from those who have custodial or operational responsibilities for these matters? | | |

|  | Yes | No |
|---|---|---|
| 4. Do two people always work together when handling significant qualities of cash and other attractive assets? | | |
| 5. Where control depends upon a reconciliation of accounting and other data, is it always conducted by someone independent of the generation of any of the data being reconciled? | | |
| 6. Have you avoided situations where a single person or department inappropriately is allowed to handle all or several phases of a transaction or operation? | | |
| 7. Wherever possible is the work of one employee complementary to (i.e. serves as a check upon) that of another so that a continuous audit is made of the details of the business? | | |
| 8. Do staff who have been assigned to segregated duties also use adequately segregated office facilities (such as office, telephone, filing cabinet, e-mail)? | | |
| 9. Do you successfully avoid staff standing in for other staff when their respective duties are meant to be segregated for control purposes? | | |
| 10. Are authorisation limits and methods of authorisation (sole, dual, by committee, etc) appropriate to the risks involved in every case? | | |
| 10.1 Is 'third level' authorisation applied where risks of collusion are greatest? | | |
| 10.2 Is 'after the event' authorisation applied where prior authorisation may not be effective? (For instance, changes to computer-based customer credit limits may require prior authorisation; but additionally it may be helpful for a changed credit limit *not* to be applied by the computer until an appropriate manager has had it displayed on his or her screen and has approved the new value. This acts as an additional safeguard against unauthorised or invalid computer input.) | | |
| 11. Is full use made of the potential of exception reports, and are these reports followed up? | | |
| 12. Are physical security controls applied wherever necessary and are they satisfactory in the light of the risks involved? | | |
| 13. Do personnel controls maximise the opportunities for recruiting and retaining trustworthy staff? | | |

|  | Yes | No |
|---|---|---|
| 13.1  Are procedures upon dismissal adequate to minimise the security risks associated with terminated staff? |  |  |
| 14.  Are all managers capable of supervising effectively the number of staff for which they are directly responsible? |  |  |
| 14.1  Is the supervision of contractors, suppliers etc. similarly effective? |  |  |
| 15.  Are adequate records created and retained in accessible form for a sufficient period of time? |  |  |
| 16.  Is all information necessary for management control available promptly (e.g. no later than one-third of way thru' the next period so that timely corrective action is possible)? |  |  |
| 17.  Is there satisfactory control over who can add, delete, amend and interrogate computer-based corporate data? |  |  |
| 18.  Where appropriate, as a last resort to achieve satisfactory internal control, is certain knowledge segregated on a need to know basis? |  |  |
| 19.  Are there effective procedures to ensure the validity of payments? |  |  |
| 20.  Is there effective physical and accounting control over returns from customers, and over the payment of refunds? |  |  |
| 21.  Is there effective custody and control (including accurate accounting for) all promotional vouchers (and other 'accountable documents' with potential value)? |  |  |
| 22.  Is the control over non-standard transactions effective? |  |  |
| 23.  Are all staff required to take their holidays? |  |  |
| 23.1  Do all staff take at least one holiday of at least two weeks' duration each year? |  |  |
| 23.2  Are duties re-assigned to other staff when staff are on holiday? |  |  |
| 24.  Is excessive dependence upon key members of staff avoided? |  |  |
| 24.1  In every case are there substitute staff ready to step in promptly to perform competently the duties of staff who become unavailable? |  |  |
| 25.  Are duties rotated where appropriate? |  |  |

| | Yes | No |
|---|---|---|
| 26. Is original documentation (such as expenses vouchers) required to support claims – to avoid the risk of multiple presentation? | | |
| 27. Is all documentation stamped appropriately – e.g. with 'Date Received' or with a cancellation stamp? | | |
| 28. Are there adequate arrangements to protect corporate data and data processing? | | |
| 28.1 Where appropriate, are they tested? | | |
| 29. Are there adequate arrangements to protect corporate data and data processing? | | |
| 29.1 Where appropriate, are they tested? | | |
| 30. Are all important procedures fully documented? | | |
| 30.1 Are the procedures known to those who apply them? | | |
| 30.2 Is the documentation of procedures kept up-to-date? | | |
| 31. Is there an effective internal audit with unrestricted scope and unrestricted rights of access? | | |

**Notes**

[1] In the UK, the 1990 CCAB: Auditing Guideline 308: Guidance for Internal Auditors put it like this:

'It is a management responsibility to determine the extent of internal control in the organisation's systems which should not depend on internal audit as a substitute for effective controls. Internal audit, as a service to the organisation, contributes to internal control by examining, evaluating and reporting to management on its adequacy and effectiveness. Internal audit activity may lead to the strengthening of internal control as a result of management response.'

[2] This conveniently concise definition of internal auditing now has to give way to the new definition of The Institute of Internal Auditors:

'Internal auditing is an independent, objective assurance and consulting activity designed to add value and improve an organization's operations. It helps an organization accomplish its objectives by bringing a systematic, disciplined approach to evaluate and improve the effectiveness of risk management, control, and governance processes.'

[3] American Institute of Certified Public Accountants: Internal Control – Elements of a Co-ordinated System and its Importance to Management and the Independent Public Accountant, AICPA, New York, 1948, pub. 1949.

[4] American Institute of Certified Accountants: Statement on Auditing Procedure No. 29, AICPA, New York, October 1958.

[5] Vide, eg American Institute of Certified Public Accountants: SAP 54 (Statement on Auditing Procedure, No. 54), November 1972; also AICPA SAS No. 1 and No. 55 ; and more recently the distinction is continued in the US COSO report, Internal Control – Integrated Framework [1992] and in the Rutteman Report [1994].

6.    AICPA, 1972 and AICPA, Professional Standards, Volume 1 (June 1, 1988).
7.    Consultative Committee of Accounting Bodies, Auditing Practices Committee: Auditing Guideline [1980, §3]; and Chartered Institute of Management Accountants: A Framework for Internal Control [1992].
8.    CCAB: Auditing Guideline 308: Guidance for Internal Auditors (Glossary of Terms section) [1990].
9.    This was discussed and agreed at the mid-year meeting of the Internal Auditing Standards Board off IIA Inc (December 1993).
10.   IIA Inc, Control: Concepts and Responsibilities, Statement on Internal Auditing Standards (SIAS), No. 1 [July 1983].
11.   IIA Inc, Standard 305.
12.   American Institute of Certified Public Accountants, American Accounting Association, The Institute of Internal Auditors, The Institute of Management Accountants, The Financial Executives Institute.
13.   Report of the National Commission on Fraudulent Financial Reporting, National Commission on Fraudulent Financial Reporting, New York, 1987 ('The Treadway Commission Report').
14.   Internal Control – Integrated Framework, known as 'The COSO Report' (September 1992), Framework volume (published by The Committee of Sponsoring Organizations of the Treadway Commission, obtainable from American Institute of Certified Public Accountants, Harborside Financial Center, 201 Plaza III, Jersey City, NJ 07311–3881, p111. Their new (1999) website: www.coso.org. (Committee of Sponsoring Organizations of the Treadway Commission, AICPA, September 1992).
15.   Internal Control – Integrated Framework, Framework volume, p10.
16.   Report of the Committee on the Financial Aspects of Corporate Governance, Gee, December 1992 ('The Cadbury Report').
17.   Internal Control and Financial Reporting, 'The Rutteman Report', (ICAEW, December 1994).
18.   Eg by auditors.
19.   Internal Control – Integrated Framework, p111.
20.   The three categories are: effectiveness and efficiency of operations; reliability of financial reporting; Compliance with applicable laws and regulations.
21.   Internal Control – Integrated Framework COSO, Executive Summary, p4.
22.   Internal Control – Integrated Framework, Executive Summary, p4.
23.   Internal Control – Integrated Framework, Framework volume, p12.
24.   Internal Control – Integrated Framework, Framework volume, p35.
25.   Internal Control – Integrated Framework, Framework volume, p39.
26.   Internal Control – Integrated Framework, Framework volume, p10.
27.   Internal Control and Financial Reporting, December 1994, 'The Rutteman Report', (ICAEW).
28.   Internal Control – Guidance For Directors On The Combined Code, (September 1999) ('The Turnbull Report'), The Institute of Chartered Accountants in England & Wales, ISBN 1–84152–010–1.
29.   Henri Fayol first described the elements or functions of management in 1916 in his classic book Administration Industrielle et Générale and he was the first to identify "controlling" as a function of management. His book did not appear in English until published in Geneva in 1929 by the International Institute of Management-but this was a limited edition and it only became widely read in English with the Pitman (London) edition of 1949. Fayol, who then became acknowledged as the father of management theory described the functions of management in terms which to us now appear dated:

- Planning
- Organising
- Commanding
- Co-ordinating
- Controlling

Had Fayol been widely read soon after he wrote his book, perhaps the concepts of internal control would have been established much sooner – and perhaps the Institute of Internal Auditors would have been established earlier than 1941.

30. Chambers A.D., G.M. Selim and G. Vinten: Internal Auditing, [Pitman, London, 2nd edition, 1987], vide Chapter 4, also in first edition (1981).

31. To illustrate the proximity between organising and controlling it is illuminating to remember that Fayol used the label 'span of control' to describe the issue of how many subordinates one boss might supervise – yet this is clearly a matter of organisation as well as of control.

32. Gorbis, Marina and York, Karen: Strategic partnerships: a new corporate response, SRI International, Report 730, Winter 1985–86.

33. Reports on Internal Controls of Investment Custodians Made Available to Third Parties, Audit Faculty Technical Release FRAG 21/94 (Revised); available from The Audit Faculty, Chartered Accountants' Hall, PO Box 433, Moorgate Place, London, EC2P 2BJ (Tel: 0171 920 8526; Fax: 0171 638 6009). The Audit Faculty of the Institute of Chartered Accountants in England and Wales issued this revised 17 page Technical Release in September 1997 to assist reporting accountants who are requested to report in accordance with the framework for reporting which is set out in this Release. The Release points out that increased usage of reports on internal controls in this area has resulted in the recipients identifying more precisely the information they need, and that at the same time reporting accountants have gained experience in assessing the risks to them of issuing reports that relate to what are often very significant levels of customer assets. The Release provides an illustrative report and also an attachment of illustrative tests performed by the reporting accountants. While the Release stresses that the latter should not be regarded as a specimen work programme, both the latter and the former will undoubtedly be valuable for those who need to construct their own internal control review programmes to cover this important area.

34. Providing assurance on the effectiveness of internal control (July 2001), The Auditing Practices Board, £5.50 each, post-free from ABG Professional Information, PO Box 21375. London, WC1N 1QP. Tel: +44 (0)20 7920 8991. Fax: +44 (0)20 7920 8992. E-mail: info@abgpublications.co.uk.

35. Audit evidence when an entity uses a service organisation, Statement on Auditing Standards No. 480, The Auditing Practices Board, April 1998, 15 pps, £5, Accountancy Books, PO Box 620, Central Milton Keynes, MK9 2JX. Tel: + 44 (0)1908 248000.

36. Australia/New Zealand Standard 4360: 1999 Risk Management – joint standard prepared by the Joint Standards Australia/Standards New Zealand Committee OB/7 on Risk Management as a revision of AS/NZS 4360: 1995 on Risk Management.

37. NHS Executive (May 1999): Governance in The new NHS: Controls assurance statements 1999/2000: risk management and organisational controls, [HSC 1999/123], available on the website http://tap.ccta.gov.uk/doh/coin4.nsf.

38. HM Treasury, (June 2001): 'Management of Risk – A Strategic Overview – With Supplementary Guidance for Smaller Bodies', known as 'The Orange Book'.

39. The Combined Code, (July 1998) originally an appendix to The Stock Exchange Listing Rules ('the Yellow Book') and then also available from Gee Publishing Limited, 100 Avenue Road, Swiss Cottage, London, NW3 3PG, England. Tel: +44 (0)207 393 7400. Fax: +44 0()207 722 4762.

40. Internal Control – Guidance to Directors on the Combined Code, ('The Turnbull Report'), published by The Institute of Chartered Accountants in England & Wales, ISBN 1 84152 010 1. The guidance can be downloaded from ICAEW's website: www.icaew.co.uk/internal control.
41. See February 2000 article in The Institute of Internal Auditors Inc's bi-monthly journal, 'Internal Auditor'.
42. Vide, eg IBM, BP.

# Corporate Governance In The Public Sector

## Corporate governance in Whitehall and Westminster: the role of non-executive directors   B9.1

*Dr Mark Egan contributed this leading article. Mark can be contacted at markegan@sand-dancer.co.uk*

### 1.  Introduction

1.1  Many of the features of private sector corporate governance, such as audit committees, risk management and non-executive directors (NEDs), are now becoming familiar in the public sector. Much of the attention on public sector corporate governance has, hitherto, focused on bodies such as NHS trusts, housing associations, and non-departmental public bodies, rather than central government departments and parliamentary bodies. This paper aims to assess the prevalence of, and reasons for, the appointment of NEDs in central government departments and parliamentary bodies, as a case study of public sector corporate governance issues.[1] It begins by deriving from theories of corporate governance the reasons why NEDs might be appointed in the private sector, before discussing how such theories might be applied in the public sector. Having established the theoretical background, it presents the results of a survey of the numbers of NEDs appointed to the boards of central government departments and parliamentary bodies, and the reasons given for their appointment. Some conclusions are drawn about the robustness of theories of corporate governance.

### 2.  Methodology

2.1  The collection of primary data was based on two surveys: first of the websites of central government departments, which all include information about how departments are managed; and secondly, of the secretariats of select committees, to find out what information departments had given them about the role of their NEDs. This work was supplemented by semi-structured interviews with a number of officials who support the work of management boards. The interview sample was based on the availability of contact data. This may limit the reliance which can be placed on the results: given the small number of departments, a more comprehensive study in this area should involve interviews with staff in each. Interview data must always be treated with caution, given its inherent subjectivity, and published information about the reasons for appointing NEDs might not always tell the full story; these warnings should be borne in mind when reading the results of the surveys.

## 3.   Non-executive directors: theoretical framework

### 3.1   Private sector

#### *3.1.1   Principal theories of board governance*

3.1.1.1   There are three main theories of how private sector boards of management operate. The most well-known is agency theory, in which 'the directors of a company are seen as agents of the owners and are duty bound to act so as to maximise the interests of those owners'.[2] Agency theory places the onus on managers to act in the best interests of the owners, and on the owners to oversee the actions of management effectively. If managers maximise their self-interest at the expense of profitability, and this is not quickly detected by shareholders, the owners' interests may be compromised.

3.1.1.2   In contrast, stewardship theory suggests that managers act as 'good stewards of corporate assets, loyal to the company'.[3] It argues that managers are motivated by a wider range of factors than those relating to financial gain and that, consequently, the goals of shareholders and management are less likely to diverge than is suggested by agency theory.

3.1.1.3   The development of stakeholder theory is more recent and seeks to place firms in a wider context. It suggests that a variety of stakeholders are affected by a board's decisions and that stakeholders' interests are factors in the decision-making process.

#### *3.1.2   Non-executive directors in the private sector: theory*

3.1.2.1   Fitting NEDs into the theoretical frameworks described above is not necessarily straightforward. Tricker gives a colloquial definition of a NED as a board member 'who has no day-to-day executive role and is not an employee of the company' but that does not necessarily imply independence from the firm.[4] The Combined Code puts particular emphasis on independent NEDs and gives seven criteria, relating, for example, to family ties, past links with the firm, and shareholdings, by which independence may be judged.[5] Firms subject to the Code are required to identify genuinely independent NEDs in their annual reports, but the same requirement is not made of central government departments. All NEDs in the departments and parliamentary bodies shown in Table 1 (below) are assumed to be independent.

3.1.2.2   The main theoretical underpinning for the appointment of NEDs is 'to provide, and be seen to provide, a counterweight to managerial power'.[6] The NED is thus seen as a representative of shareholder interests, placed on boards to ensure that the managers are acting in the interests of shareholders rather than following their own agendas. Firms have traditionally sought NEDs with considerable social status – 'the titled gentlemen of the nineteenth and twentieth century' – as a signal of probity to potential investors.[7]

3.1.2.3   A second rationale for the appointment of NEDs, stemming from stewardship theory, is to provide 'an objective force on the board, able to offer independent criticism of the company's performance and future plans'.[8] If managers are acting as stewards of their firms, and are motivated by factors such as good corporate performance, then they may seek to recruit NEDs to help improve the board's decision-making capabilities.

3.1.2.4   A third reason for appointing NEDs is to ensure that the views of stakeholders – such as major suppliers or customers – are represented on the board. This would explain the appointment of NEDs under the stakeholder theory of board governance. Tricker, in his 1978 survey of private sector NEDs, found no evidence that appointments were made for this reason; the Higgs Report did not mention the stakeholder rationale. As will be seen below, however, there is evidence of this approach being used in central government departments.[9]

### 3.1.3   From Cadbury to Higgs

3.1.3.1   Corporate governance, including the role of NEDs, has been in the spotlight for much of the last ten years, particularly as a result of high-profile evidence of managerial failure and dishonesty, including, for example, the Enron affair. The 1992 Cadbury Report, which focused on financial aspects of corporate governance, raised the profile of NEDs. Its conclusions were combined with those of the 1995 Greenbury Report and the 1998 Hampel Report to form the Combined Code. A further review in this area was published by Higgs in 2003. Taken together, these reports were intended by the government to provide a non-statutory, voluntary framework for private sector corporate governance; firms must either comply with it or explain to investors the reasons for non-compliance.

## 3.2   Public sector

### 3.2.1   Introduction

3.2.1.1   The debate about the extent to which private sector practices are applicable to the public sector has run for some time and is largely focused on the different functions and structures of public sector organisations. For the most part, public sector organisations do not aim to maximise profit and nor are they owned by shareholders. Through an accounting officer, public sector organisations are responsible to Parliament for their expenditure; and politicians are, directly or indirectly, involved in their management. Successive governments in the UK have extended the use of private sector techniques, such as competitive tendering, into the public sector. Consequently, public sector organisations have been required to consider the applicability of private sector corporate governance best practice, and adopt the same 'comply or explain' regime.

3.2.1.2   One of the problems encountered in applying private sector norms to the public sector is that the public sector is a 'collection of widely diverse public services, each of which has unique features, which require special attention, and each of which is governed by different statutory and managerial frameworks, which impose different sets of accountabilities'.[10] Van der Walt, Ingley and Diack identified in 2002 that 'there have been few attempts to develop a typology of governance structures by sector and ownership type', and their own attempt to do so neglected to mention central government departments, or parliamentary bodies.[11]

### 3.2.2   Applying theories of corporate governance to the public sector

3.2.2.1   In order to understand how the theories of corporate governance might be applied to public sector institutions, models of their corporate governance must be developed. Percy has used diagrammatic models to contrast the structure of some basic private and public sector organisations.[12] Figure 1 shows a simple model for a company. Agency theory would suggest that the lack of overlap between shareholders and directors is problematic: one option for overcoming this would be the appointment of NEDs, although another would be for executive directors to receive share options as part of their remuneration package.

*Figure 1: Simple model of private sector corporate governance*

3.2.2.2   Figure 2 is a model of local authority governance. Service provision is managed both by senior managers and elected councillors. Outside of the organisation, stakeholders include auditors – whose relationship with public sector entities is usually statutory and less close than the relationship between a firm and its auditors – other service providers – such as those which have been contracted out – and electors.

*Figure 2: Model of local authority corporate governance*

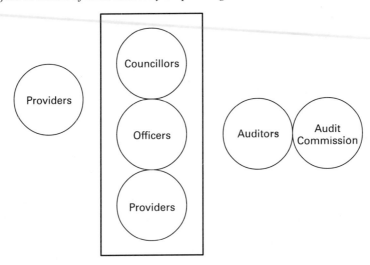

3.2.2.3 These models are not without their flaws. For example, Percy's depiction of local authority governance omits to mention central government, which provides the majority of the funding for such bodies. The models usefully help clarify discontinuities in principal-agent relationships, and identify key stakeholders, however. Simple models for the governance of a central government department, and a parliamentary body, the House of Commons, derived from Percy's approach, are suggested below.

3.2.2.4 Figure 3 is a model of the governance of a central government department. Unlike in the local authority model, the politicians in charge of policy do not play an active role in managing the service providers, and are therefore portrayed as stakeholders. This accurately describes the situation in many departments; but in others, such as the Department of Trade and Industry, a two-tier board structure includes ministers.[13] The key feature of this model is the number of types of stakeholder. Some categories may be subdivided – for example customers might include businesses (large and small, or different sectors) and trade unions.

*Figure 3: Model of central government department corporate governance*

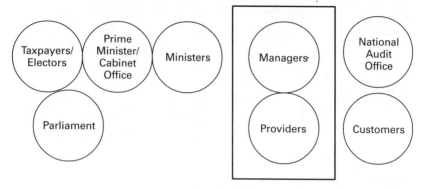

3.2.2.5    Figure 4 provides a simplified model of the governance of a parliamentary body, in this case the House of Commons. In contrast to most central government departments, politicians play an important role in the management of the House. The House of Commons Commission determines the strategy of the House service; the Board of Management oversees the implementation of that strategy, but also exercises authority over matters delegated to it by the Commission, including staff management. The range of stakeholders shown in Figure 4 is smaller than that in Figure 3, mainly because Members of Parliament are the main customers of the House service, and there are fewer direct links with other outside groups.

*Figure 4: Model of House of Commons service corporate governance*

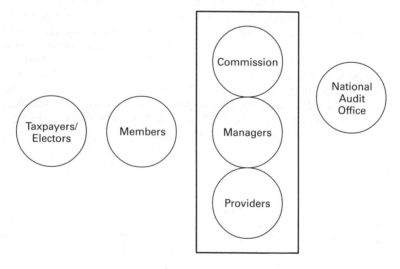

### *3.2.3* *Non-executive directors in the public sector: theory*

3.2.3.1 There are few analyses of the rationale for NEDs outwith the private sector and those which exist focus on charities or local, service-driven organisations, such as NHS trusts, rather than central government. Nevertheless, theories of corporate governance can be used to identify reasons for appointing NEDs in central government and parliamentary bodies.

3.2.3.2 Identifying the agent which delegates the management of a department to civil servants is not simple: three possible options exist. Taxpayers may sometimes be regarded as the shareholders in government but they can only influence departments through electing politicians to the House of Commons. Ministers, who owe their positions both to their electors and the strength of their party in the Commons, have opportunities to influence the management of their departments, but these are constrained by civil service rules. The Prime Minister, through the Cabinet Secretary, who is head of the civil service, is in a strong position to issue directions to departments, for example on the need to focus on achieving key targets, but cannot closely manage how such directions are implemented.

3.2.3.3 Stakeholder theory suggests that boards might seek to recruit NEDs to represent major stakeholders, so that their views are, or are seen to be, taken into account. Many departments' main stakeholders are their customers – whether schools, universities and teachers for the Department for Education and Skills, or patients and health professionals for the Department of Health. Stakeholder theory would suggest representatives of such groups would sit as NEDs on departmental boards.

3.2.3.4 Stewardship theory applies equally to public sector organisations and the private sector. Managers might seek to add to the range of skills available to them by recruiting NEDs, in order to run public sector organisations more successfully. Management boards might also seek to appoint NEDs in order to counter or ward off criticism that career public servants are not equipped with the management competencies needed to run a modern department and deliver the policy priorities set by politicians.

3.2.3.5 Corporate governance theories may apply in much the same way to parliamentary bodies, although agency and stakeholder theories would both point towards representatives of their Members being appointed as NEDs on management boards, and Figure 4 shows that there are few other stakeholder interests.

## 4.   Non-executive directors in central government: practice

### 4.1   History

4.1.1   The appointment of NEDs to the boards of central government departments began in the early 1990s. The 1999 Wilson Report on civil service reform recommended that all departments should appoint NEDs, although without giving any argument for doing so.[14] In 2000 it was reported that 'non-executive directors have either been appointed to, or are being sought for, the management boards of all the main departments'.[15] The Sharman Report into audit and accountability for central government welcomed the appointment of NEDs to departmental boards and made some modest suggestions about their recruitment, to which the government did not respond in its reply.[16] Guidance on the recruitment, appointment and development of NEDs in central government departments first emerged from the Cabinet Office in draft in June 2003.

### 4.2   Prevalence

4.2.1   Table 1 shows the numbers of NEDs appointed to the management boards of central government departments and parliamentary bodies.

*Table 1:  Prevalence of non-executive directors in central government departments and parliamentary bodies*

| Organisation | Number of NEDs on management board | NEDs as a percentage of whole board (%) |
|---|---|---|
| Cabinet Office | 2 | 18.2 |
| Department for Constitutional Affairs | 1 | 16.7 |
| Department for Culture, Media and Sport | 2 | 25.0 |
| HM Customs and Excise | 5 | 27.8 |
| Ministry of Defence | 2 | 20.0 |
| Department for Education and Skills | 2 | 20.0 |
| Department for Environment, Food and Rural Affairs | 3 | 23.1 |
| Foreign and Commonwealth Office | 2 | 15.4 |
| Department of Health | None | – |
| Department for International Development | 2 | 33.3 |
| Home Office | 3 | 33.3 |

| Organisation | Number of NEDs on management board | NEDs as a percentage of whole board (%) |
|---|---|---|
| House of Commons | None | – |
| House of Lords | None | – |
| Inland Revenue | 4 | 44.4 |
| Northern Ireland Office | 2 | 20.0 |
| Office of the Deputy Prime Minister | 2 | 16.7 |
| Scottish Parliament | None | – |
| Department of Trade and Industry | 3 | 27.3 |
| Department for Transport | 2 | 25.0 |
| HM Treasury | 2 | 22.2 |
| National Assembly for Wales | 2 | 10.0 |
| Department for Work and Pensions | None | – |

4.2.2   The table shows that almost all central government departments now have NEDs on their management boards. The two exceptions are departments with large managerial boards which cover several major agencies, as well as the central department, and, in the case of the Department of Health's board, include quasi-independent figures such as the Chief Medical Officer. Only one parliamentary body has recruited NEDs, although the issue is under active consideration in others. The National Assembly for Wales combines both executive and parliamentary functions: the two NEDs mentioned in Table 1 sit on the board managing the executive branch and a third sits on the subsidiary board which oversees the parliamentary branch.

4.2.3   The table also shows that there are no departmental management boards in which NEDs form a majority: the mean proportion of NEDs is 23.4%. This is in contrast to the situation Higgs discovered in surveying listed companies: excluding chairmen, NEDs make up 47.4% of such firms' boards, and 57.1% of the boards of FTSE 100 companies.[17]

**4.3     Role**

4.3.1   Information about the role and effectiveness of NEDs on the boards of central government departments can be hard to find. Some departments have published little or nothing about the reasons for appointing NEDs or about their activities. Others have restricted themselves to general statements, buried away in annual reports. The discussion below of the role of NEDs in central government

441

departments is based on evidence given to select committees; interviews conducted with civil servants working for departmental boards; and presentations made by Home Office and Department of Trade and Industry officials about the work of their NEDs.

4.3.2   Three main reasons have been given to explain why NEDs have been appointed to departmental management boards. Firstly, NEDs are expected to challenge existing business processes and 'interrogate and question' senior managers to help departments 'become more effective'.[18] Emphasis is placed on the fresh perspectives that NEDs can bring to public sector management, especially if they are recruited from beyond the civil service.

4.3.3   Secondly, NEDs are often recruited by departments to enhance the skills and expertise collectively available to the board. This can involve helping board members to improve their management skills as well as contributing to board discussions and advising the accounting officer at other times. Areas of expertise in which NEDs specialise include strategic thinking, internal consultancy, business planning, risk management and change management.[19]

4.3.4   Finally, the Office of the Deputy Prime Minister recruited one of its NEDs 'to help us understand how local government responded to some of the actions we took',[20] suggesting that his role was primarily to represent one of the department's key stakeholders. The Department of Trade and Industry's highly publicised decision to recruit business leaders as NEDs in 2001 attracted criticism from trade union leaders who felt that they too should be enlisted to ensure their views were taken into account in the management of the department. The Secretary of State later denied that she sought to recruit stakeholder representatives as NEDs, arguing that business leaders were needed for their experience of managing change.[21]

4.3.5   The draft Cabinet Office guidance on NEDs suggests that they could be appointed in order to make management boards more diverse.[22] The Tyson report on the recruitment of NEDs made the same point, arguing that this could improve decision making, 'contribute to a better understanding by the company's leadership of the diverse constituencies that affect its success' and 'send a positive and motivating signal' to customers and employees.[23] No department has publicly stated that it has appointed a NED to improve the diversity of its board.

## 4.4   Does practice support theory?

4.4.1   The reasons given for the appointment of NEDs in central government departments and parliamentary bodies provide support for stewardship theory. Senior managers themselves have sought to recruit NEDs to help improve the management of their organisations, both by adding to the range of skills which boards can draw upon and by introducing an element of constructive challenge.

4.4.2 The reasons given for appointing NEDs do not strongly support the agency or stakeholder theories of corporate governance, however. It might be thought that the appointment of NEDs to challenge management demonstrated the validity of agency theory. With the exception of the Department of Trade and Industry, however, senior management teams, not ministers, appear to have been responsible for recruiting NEDs. Further research is necessary into ministerial input into the decisions to recruits NEDs in departments. Finally, although there are examples of NEDs being recruited by departments to represent stakeholder interests, these form only a small minority of cases.

# 5. Conclusions

5.1 Over the last few years, several elements of private sector corporate governance have been introduced at the heart of government, the latest being the appointment of NEDs to management boards. This change has occurred quietly and has not previously been the subject of analysis, but it is intended to have significant positive implications for the way in which government departments are managed. Both in the public and private sectors, NEDs tend to be sought by senior managers in order to improve a board's decision-making capability. Although this provides some support for stewardship theory, in that it shows executives acting in support of corporate rather than individual goals, those testing stewardship theory have argued that the appointment of NEDs might be correlated with poor corporate performance.[24] Ministerial roles in advocating the appointment of NEDs to improve the management of departments may also have been more significant than has subsequently been portrayed. More research on how boards operate in practice is required to investigate further the validity of the theories of corporate governance.

5.2 Another area in which more work is required is research into whether or not NEDs add any value to the organisations they serve. Anecdotal evidence, for example the responses of those interviewed for this paper, is often extremely positive, but the academic studies are mixed.[25] There has perhaps been too much emphasis on econometric analyses of links between board structure and some measures of corporate performance in the private sector, when a more valuable approach might be to study in depth how the performance of NEDs is evaluated in practice, to find specific examples of how they can make a difference.

**Notes**

[1.] Table 1 shows the departments and bodies covered in this paper.

[2.] Mullins, L., *Management and Organisational Behaviour*, 6th edition, Prentice Hall, 2002, pp148–49.

[3.] Muth, M. M., and Donaldson, L., 'Stewardship Theory and Board Structure: a Contingency Approach', *Corporate Governance*, Vol. 6, No. 1, 1998, (hereafter M&D) p6.

4. Tricker, R. I., The Independent Director, Tolley, 1978, (hereafter Tricker) p45.
5. Financial Services Authority, Combined Code on Corporate Governance, draft, June 2003, (hereafter Combined Code) A.3.1.
6. Tricker, p46.
7. British Institute of Management, The Board of Directors, Management Survey Report No. 10, 1972, p12.
8. Ibid. For a fuller statement see Combined Code, p63 (excerpt from Higgs Report).
9. It may also explain the appointment of suppliers to project boards.
10. Percy, I., and Hepworth, N. P., Corporate Governance in the Public Sector, CIPFA, 1994, (hereafter Percy and Hepworth) p10.
11. Van der Walt, N. T., Ingley, C. B., and Diack, G., 'Corporate governance: Implications of ownership, performance requirements and strategy', Journal of Change Management, Vol. 2, No. 4, 2002, pp321, 328 (Table 1).
12. Percy and Hepworth, chapter 1 by Percy.
13. Trade and Industry Committee, Minutes of Evidence, 12 December 2001, HC (2001–02) 454 (hereafter TISC), Q1.
14. Cabinet Office, Civil Service Reform, Report to the Prime Minister from Sir Richard Wilson, head of the Home Civil Service, December 1999.
15. Cabinet Office, Civil Service Reform Programme: Annual Report, 2000, paragraph 1.6.
16. Sharman of Redlynch, Lord, Holding to Account: the review of audit and accountability for central government, Feb 2001, paragraphs 3.23–3.25.
17. Higgs, D., Review of the Role and Effectiveness of Non-Executive Directors, Department of Trade and Industry, Jan 2003, section 3.
18. For example, see TISC, Ev, p1, paragraph 14 and Treasury Committee, Minutes of Evidence, 26 June 2002, HC (2001–02) 1011, Q26.
19. For example, see TISC Qq15, 16, 19 and Treasury Committee, Third Report, HM Treasury, HC (2000–01) 73-I, 2001, paragraph 59.
20. Committee on the Office of the Deputy Prime Minister: Housing, Planning, Local Government and the Regions, Minutes of Evidence, 1 July 2003, HC (2002–03) 900-I, Q33.
21. TISC, Q5.
22. Cabinet Office, Guidance on the recruitment, appointment and development of non-executive directors on civil service boards, Cabinet Office, draft, June 2003, paragraph 2.1.
23. Tyson, L., Report on the Recruitment and Development of Non-Executive Directors, DTI, June 2003, p1.
24. M&D.
25. For example, Beasley, M. S., 'An empirical analysis of the relation between the Board of Director composition and financial statement fraud', Accounting Review, Vol. 71, No. 4, Oct 1996, 443–465 and Korac-Kakabadse, N., Kakabadse, A. K., and Kouzmin, A., 'Board Governance and Company Performance: Any Correlations?', Corporate Governance, Vol. 1, No. 1, 2001, 24–30.

# The Nolan Principles                                                  B9.2

We reprint here what have become known as 'the Nolan Principles' which have been widely adopted, especially in the UK public sector, as indicative of the highest standards of certain aspects of corporate governance.

The Committee on Standards in Public Life ('the Nolan Committee') was set up in October 1994 by the UK government as a standing body:

*Table 1*   **B9.3**

'To examine concerns about standards of conduct of all holders of public office, including arrangements relating to financial and commercial activities, and make recommendations as to any changes ... to ensure the highest standards of propriety in public life.'

Its first report[1] was published in May 1995. In that report the Committee restated the general principles of conduct which the Committee considered underpin public life, and these are set out here in Table 1 (see **B9.3**). The Committee recommended that all public bodies should draw up codes of conduct incorporating these seven Principles. For the Principle of 'openness' the Committee suggested a Standard, which we reproduce as Table 2 (see **B9.4**).

It is interesting to note that in 1992 the Report of the Committee on the Financial Aspects of Corporate Governance ('the Cadbury Committee') had stated that their Code of Best Practice was based on three of these principles – 'openness, integrity and accountability'[2].

## Table 1                                                                  B9.3

| |
|---|
| **The seven principles of public life** |
| **Selflessness** – Holders of public office should take decisions solely in terms of the public interest. They should not do so in order to gain financial or other material benefits for themselves, their family, or their friends. |
| **Integrity** – Holders of public office should not place themselves under any financial or other obligation to outside individuals or organisations that might influence them in the performance of their official duties. |
| **Objectivity** – In carrying out public business, including making public appointments, awarding contracts, or recommending individuals for rewards and benefits, holders of public office should make choices on merit. |
| **Accountability** – Holders of public office are accountable for their decisions and actions to the public and must submit themselves to whatever scrutiny is appropriate to their office. |
| **Openness** – Holders of public office should be as open as possible about all the decisions and actions they take. They should give reasons for their decisions and restrict information only when the wider public interest clearly demands. |
| **Honesty** – Holders of public office have a duty to declare any private interests relating to their public duties and to take steps to resolve any conflicts arising in a way that protects the public interest. |
| **Leadership** – Holders of public office should promote and support these principles by leadership and example. |
| *These principles apply to all aspects of public life.* |
| *The Committee has set them out here for the benefit of all who serve the public in any way.* |

# Table 2 **B9.4**

---

**A standard of best practice for openness in executive non-departmental public bodies (NDPBs) and National Health Service (NHS) bodies access to information.**

- Adoption of a specific code on access to information incorporating the government's Code[3], and building on it where possible.

- Clear and published procedures for implementing the Code, including:

  o well-defined criteria for information that will be withheld, which should be cited whenever a request for information is refused;

  o standards for speed of response to enquiries (eg information to be provided normally within 21 days or correspondent informed of likely date);

  o an appeal mechanism, within the organisation initially and then either to the Ombudsman, or (where the body does not come under the Ombudsman's jurisdiction) to another independent person appointed for the purpose; and

  o a policy on charging for information provided (with requests requiring only a reasonable amount of work incurring no charge).

**Meetings**

- Opening meetings to the public or making minutes of meetings (and main committees) available for public inspection or describing key discussions and decisions in newsletters etc. after each meeting. Some items may be deemed confidential, but the criteria for doing so should be published.

- A well publicised annual general meeting open to public and media, allowing an opportunity to question the board members on the performance and activities of the body.

- Other opportunities taken to involve and inform the public and organisations with a major interest, through consumer groups or user forums; or public meetings on major issues.

**Publications**

- Annual report and accounts, including information on the role and remit of the body, long term plans or strategy; membership of the board, performance against key targets; targets for the forthcoming year; their commitment and approach to open government; and where further information can be obtained (including how to inspect the register of board members interests and how to pursue complaints).

- Other important information to be routinely published. Depending on the body this might include key statistics; the results of consultation

---

> exercises; details of key procedures (eg criteria for allocating public
> funds); reports of regulatory investigations etc.
>
> - All publications should be made as widely available as possible, such
>   as through public libraries, and all annual reports and accounts should
>   be deposited in the parliamentary libraries.

## Policy principles for audit committees in central government  B9.5

These principles were published by HM Treasury in December 2000. They are
an annex to their statement in **B9.6** CORPORATE GOVERNANCE: STATEMENT ON
INTERNAL CONTROL and are referred to in **B9.7** GOVERNMENT INTERNAL AUDIT
STANDARDS.

To check for updates, visit

www.hm-treasury.gov.uk/Documents/Public_Spending_and_Services/
Guidance_for_Government_Departments/

For audit committees these policy principles were due to be revised by
31 October 2003.

The purpose of an audit committee is to give advice to the accounting officer on
the adequacy of audit arrangements (internal and external) and on the
implications of assurances provided in respect of risk and control in the
organisation. The following principles are provided to facilitate the
establishment of audit committees that will be well equipped to meet that
purpose.

*Some bodies, particularly NDPBs, are already required by Cabinet Office or
by sponsoring bodies to have an audit committee in accordance with other
guidance. This document does not amend or supersede such requirements;
rather it provides for a minimum position in the absence of any other
applicable guidance. In particular the board structures of some NDPBs will
tend to favour particular approaches to the establishment and membership of
the audit committee*

1. Audit committees are strongly encouraged as best practice in all central
   government bodies (departments, executive agencies and non-
   departmental public bodies). If it is decided not to have an audit
   committee, there should be clearly identified circumstances justifying the
   decision.

2. In bodies that have a management board structure, the audit committee
   should be a committee, or a sub-committee, of the board. In some bodies
   that have numerically small boards, the board may sit separately as the
   audit committee.

3.  In bodies that have non-executive or independent members on the management board, these non-executive or independent members should form at least part of the membership of the audit committee (subject to appropriateness of numbers).

4.  In bodies that have no non-executive or independent management board members, appropriate individuals should be sought for appointment as external members of the audit committee. Ideally two or three independent members should be sought.

5.  In medium and large organisations the audit committee should ideally have no fewer than five and no more than ten members. For smaller bodies a minimum membership of three may be more practicable.

6.  The audit committee is appointed to give advice to the accounting officer. Although the accounting officer may chair the audit committee, the objectivity of the advice given can be enhanced if another member (particularly a non-executive) is the chair of the audit committee.

7.  Members of the audit committee who have executive responsibility in the body (in those organisations which have a sufficiently large number of senior executive staff) should be rotated on an appropriate cycle (three years will generally be appropriate) to provide for objectivity in the long-term and to avoid over or under representation of particular aspects of the body's business and administrative interests.

8.  Audit committees should have documented terms of reference from the accounting officer/board, which should include a remit to consider the adequacy of risk management and internal control through reviewing (*inter alia*):

    ●  the mechanisms for the assessment and management of risk;

    ●  the planned activity of internal audit;

    ●  the results of internal audit activity;

    ●  the planned activity of external audit;

    ●  the results of external audit activity;

    ●  adequacy of management response to issues identified by audit activity; and

    ●  assurances relating to the corporate governance requirements for the organisation.

9.  The head of internal audit and the senior member of the external audit team should have the right of access to the audit committee and should normally be present at meetings (as attendees rather than members).

10. The audit committee should meet regularly and at least three times a year.

# Corporate governance: Statement on Internal Control

**B9.6**

This is a reproduction of a letter dated 29 May 2003 sent to all government Accounting Officers by Brian Glickman, Treasury Officer of Accounts, HM Treasury, Room 505, Allington Towers, 19 Allington Street, London, SW1E 5EB. Tel: 020 7270 1683. Fax: 020 7270 4311. E-mail: gordon.adam@hm-treasury.gov.uk; www.hm-treasury.gov.uk.

The Policy Principles for Audit Committees in Central Government, due to be revised by 31 October 2003, are reproduced at **B9.5**. The Government Internal Audit Standards are also reproduced at **B9.7**.

To check for updates, visit www.hm-treasury.gov.uk/Documents/Public _Spending_and_Services/Guidance_for_Government_Departments/,

### Purpose of this letter

The purpose of this letter is to:

- Remind Accounting Officers what they were expected to have achieved by the end of March 2003 to comply with DAO(GEN)13/00[4] (and advise on the actions to be taken if this has not been achieved);

- Provide a revised proforma 'Statement on Internal Control' (SIC) applicable from 2003/4 (some bodies which have met the requirements of DAO(GEN)13/00 for 2002/3 may have to develop their processes further to comply with this letter for 2003/4). The new proforma includes:

  o a requirement for the SIC, from 2003/4 and subsequently, to confirm that the results of the Accounting Officer review of the effectiveness of internal control has been discussed with the Board, Audit Committee (and the Risk Committee, where applicable);

  o an expectation for a reference in the SIC to ongoing maintenance and development of risk management and review processes.

- Advise on the interpretation of a 'significant internal control problem' which requires commentary in the SIC on the actions taken, or proposed, to deal with it.

2. The National Audit Office's (NAO) approach to the review of the SIC remains unchanged from that outlined in DAO(GEN)13/00, the relevant elements of which are reproduced in Annex 1.

### Background

3. The subject of risk management in Central Government has developed considerably since the issue of DAO(GEN)13/00. That letter was primarily concerned with adapting private sector requirements into the central government sector. Since then there has been a Public Accounts

Committee report on risk (following the hearing on the 2000 NAO report 'Supporting Innovation: Managing Risk in Government Departments'). More recently the Strategy Unit published their report 'Risk: Improving Government's Capability to Handle Risk and Uncertainty', which has led to a programme of work, called 'The Risk Programme'. This is being steered by a sub-group of the Civil Service Management Board.

4. Risk management is now firmly at the heart of the management of the business of government bodies. In particular risk is being embedded into the highest level delivery planning mechanisms. As risk sets the context for internal control, it is important that the SIC should reflect these developments and the provisions of this letter aim to ensure that the SIC process is firmly and clearly linked to the continuing development of risk management in central government.

**Expectations under the provisions of DAO(GEN)13/00**

5. Achievement of the deadline set in DAO(GEN)13/00 required that 'all relevant risk management and review processes' be in place by the end of March 2003. We have been asked to clarify how this should be interpreted. Annex 2 of this letter offers a range of elements which are relevant in a body's consideration of whether it has the relevant processes in place. It is based on the risk management guidance set out in the Orange Book ('Management of Risk – A Strategic Overview', HM Treasury, 2001) and the Annex itself provides further guidance on the way in which it may be used.

6. Information collected by the Treasury and by the NAO indicates that at least 80% of bodies expected to have the required processes in place by March 2003. Any that have not done so should take the actions set out in Annex 3 to this letter.

7. When drafting the SIC for 2002/3, those bodies which will have completed the implementation of appropriate risk management and review processes during the year 2002/3 should follow the model of the proforma SIC at Annex A1 of DAO(GEN)13/00[5]. They should record at what stage in the year key elements of the processes were implemented if they have not been in place for the full year.

**Maintenance and development of risk management and review processes**

8. Once a body has the appropriate risk management and review processes in place, it is important that they are maintained and developed to ensure their continuing effectiveness. The SIC should record the key elements of the way in which this is done, whether as part of a 'planned maintenance' programme or in response to problems or significant external developments (for example, machinery of government changes). It is also expected that bodies will be developing and improving their existing risk management capability as a result of the risk improvement programme resulting from the Strategy Unit's risk report. However, ability to make an

SIC compliant with the provisions of this DAO is not dependent on further improvements arising from the Risk Improvement Programme.

**'Significant internal control problems'**

9. The proforma SIC promulgated with DAO(GEN)13/00 includes a requirement to disclose 'details of actions taken, or proposed, to deal with material internal control aspects of any significant problems disclosed in the annual report and accounts'. This requirement has caused some bodies to request more detailed guidance on what should be reported here.

10. The proforma SIC attached to this letter now refers to 'significant internal control problems'. This change is intended to clarify the expectation that the SIC only need make reference to significant problems arising from internal control issues. A 'significant internal control problem' cannot be centrally defined; the same essential problem may or may not be significant depending on circumstances. The following indicators (which are not exhaustive) may be helpful in considering whether or not an internal control problem is significant enough to be reported in the SIC:

- it seriously prejudiced or prevented achievement of a PSA target;

- it has resulted in a need to seek additional funding from Treasury/the sponsoring department to allow it to be resolved, or has resulted in significant diversion of resources from another aspect of the business;

- the external auditor would regard it as having a material impact on the accounts;

- the Audit Committee advises it should be considered significant;

- the Head of Internal Audit reports on it as significant in their annual opinion on the whole of risk, control and governance.

**Revised proforma SIC**

11. The proforma SIC to be used from 2003/4 has been revised. It has been approved in principle by the Financial Reporting Advisory Board (FRAB) and is attached at Annex 4. There are two reasons for the revisions:

- both Treasury and NAO reviews of the 2001/2 SICs indicate a high level of 'boiler plating', reproducing the example SICs at Annexes A2 and A3 of DAO(GEN)13/00 rather than providing a tailored portrayal of the actual processes in the particular body; and

- as referred to earlier, it is intended to align the processes underpinning the SIC as closely as possible with the work being carried out to implement the recommendations of the Strategy Unit's 2002 report 'Risk: Improving Government's Capability to Handle Risk and Uncertainty'.

12. Whilst the new proforma format is *required* for 2003/4, bodies are encouraged to adopt it for their SIC for 2002/3 (if doing so, the last

sentence of the wording in the section headed 'Review of effectiveness' ['*I have been advised on the implications ... continuous improvement of the system is in place*' is optional for this year).

13. The mandatory elements of wording are not materially changed from those required by DAO(GEN)13/00. However the 'freeform' elements are now specified by rubrics requiring bodies to 'describe *an aspect of risk management*'. These aspects of risk management pick up both the 'Orange Book' stages of the risk management lifecycle and the risk management themes emerging from the Strategy Unit report.

**Effectiveness of internal control**

14. It is implicit in the provisions of DAO(GEN)13/00 that the process of reviewing the effectiveness of internal control generates in some shape or form a documented assessment of effectiveness. Given the complexity of most government bodies this may well consist of a number of documents resulting from the review process, including the Head of Internal Audit's annual assurance, the sequence of stewardship reports (where such a process is implemented), documentation surrounding the maintenance of the risk register and notes from meetings of the Board/Audit Committee/Risk Committee on risk and control issues.

15. A criticism of SICs is that they inform the reader that a review of effectiveness has been undertaken but do not give any assurance that action is taken in response to the assessment of effectiveness generated by the review. To increase the assurance delivered by the SIC the new proforma includes a requirement to record that the Accounting Officer has taken advice on the implications of the assessment of effectiveness from the Board and the Audit Committee (and the Risk Committee, where applicable) and, if appropriate, action has been taken or is planned to address issues arising from it.

**Enquiries**

16. Any enquiries on the content and application of this letter should be addressed in the first instance to Gordon Adam in the Assurance, Control and Risk Team in the Treasury (Room 1/21, 1 Horseguards Road, London SW1A 2HQ, telephone 020 7270 1683, gordon.adam@hm-treasury.gsi.gov.uk).

**Further action**

17. The provisions of this letter apply to departments, Executive Agencies, trading funds, executive NDPBs, white paper accounts and accounts produced by departments relating to transactions with public corporations and the National Loans Fund. Departments should ensure that their

Executive Agencies, trading funds and executive Non-Departmental Public Bodies are aware of the requirements of this letter.

Yours sincerely

Brian GlicksmanTreasury Officer of Accounts

# Annex 1

## NAO's approach to the review of statements on internal control

### *Review procedures*

1. The NAO's approach to the review of internal control statements remains unchanged from that detailed in DAO(GEN)13/00. The relevant part of the Comptroller and Auditor General's certificate will read along the following lines:

   'I review whether the statement on page – reflects the [name of audited body]'s compliance with Treasury's guidance, "Corporate Governance: Statement of Internal Control". I report if it does not meet the requirements for disclosure specified by Treasury, or if the statement is misleading or inconsistent with other information I am aware of from my audit of the financial statements'.

2. The NAO review procedures draw on the relevant section of the Auditing Practices Board's guidance, Bulletin 5/99 'The Combined Code: Requirements of Auditors Under the Listing Rules of the London Stock Exchange', tailored as appropriate for a central government context. The objective of the review is to assess whether the audited body's description of the processes adopted in reviewing the effectiveness of the system of internal control appropriately reflects that process. This involves:

   • Consideration of whether the disclosures are consistent with the NAO's review of board and committee minutes and their knowledge of the audited body obtained during the audit of the financial statements;

   • NAO attendance at audit committee meetings at which corporate governance, internal control and risk management matters are considered;

   • Consideration of the process adopted by the Accounting Officer for his/her effectiveness review, and of the documentation prepared to support the statement.

3. The NAO's work on internal control will not be sufficient to enable them to express any assurance on whether the audited body's controls are effective. In addition, the financial statement audit should not be relied

upon to draw to the Accounting Officer's attention all matters that may be relevant to their consideration as to whether or not the system of internal control is effective. Auditors are not expected to actively search for mis-statements or inconsistencies, but if they become aware of such a matter they will discuss it with senior management to establish the significance of the lack of proper disclosure.

### The NAO's work on understanding the business and controls

4. As noted above, the auditor's work on the financial statements audit is not driven by the requirement for an internal control statement and cannot be relied upon to indicate that controls are effective. Nevertheless the NAO audit approach, 'Audit 21', is a risk based approach based upon obtaining a good understanding of the business, the risks that it faces and how those risks are managed. Although the emphasis remains to an extent on financial risks and controls, this work should provide a sound base for the auditor's consideration of the Accounting Officer's internal control statement. It should also provide opportunities to make recommendations for improvements to internal controls.

5. Risk management and internal control issues are often a feature of the NAO's wider Value-for-Money audit role. The NAO recognise that risk-taking is essential if public bodies are to innovate and improve and have stated that they will support well thought through risk taking and innovation.

## Annex 2

### Elements relevant in considering whether appropriate risk management, control, and review processes are in place to support the sic

A body should have risk management, control and review processes in place, appropriate to the circumstances and business of the body. The detail of these processes will vary from one body to another depending on circumstances such as the size the body and the complexity of the risks which it faces.

This Annex offers a summary of detailed characteristics (italic text) under six high level elements (bold text) to help with consideration of the completeness of the processes which have been put in place in a particular body.

In respect of the 2002/3 SIC, this Annex is provided as a tool which bodies *may* adopt in the preparation of their SIC. For 2003/4, these characteristics are included in a 'Risk Management Assessment Framework' which is being developed by the Treasury Risk Support Team. Whilst the use of that *particular* tool will not be mandatory, bodies should ensure that they have evidence which they deem sufficient to demonstrate that they have implemented processes appropriate to their circumstances under each of the high level elements to support their SIC for 2003/4.

## 1. Leadership and strategy

There should be a risk management strategy.

1.1 There should be a risk management strategy which:

- is endorsed by the Accounting Officer/Board/Audit Committee/ Risk Committee;

- sets out the organisation's attitudes to risk;

- defines the structures for the management and ownership of risk and for the management of situations in which control failure leads to material realisation of risks;

- specifies the way in which risk issues are to be considered at each level of business planning ranging from the corporate process to the setting of individual staff's objectives;

- specifies how new activities will be assessed for risk and incorporated into risk management structures;

- ensures common understanding of terminology used in relation to risk issues;

- defines the structures for gaining assurance about the management of risk;

- defines the criteria which will inform assessment of risk and the definition of specific risks as 'key';

- defines the way in which the risk register and risk evaluation criteria will be regularly reviewed.

1.2 Whether the strategy is set out in a single document or in a series of related documents or resources, it should be easily available to all staff and reviewed at least annually to ensure it remains appropriate and current.

## 2. Context for risk management

The context in which risk has to be managed should be identified.

Identifying the context for risk management should include consideration of:

- Stakeholders, including:

  o ministerial interests;

  o public interests;

  o service user interests;

  o wider societal interests.

- Risk aspects of relationships inside and outside of government (including key suppliers of goods and services), including:

- ○ ways in which the behaviour of 'partners' affects the organisation;

- ○ ways in which the behaviour of the organisation affects the 'partners';

- ○ the risk priorities of 'partners'.

## 3.   Risk identification and evaluation

Risk should be identified and evaluated in a structured way.

There should be documentation which:

- Records identified risks in a structured way to:

  - ○ record dependencies between risks;

  - ○ record linkages between lower level risks and higher level risks;

  - ○ identify key risks;

  - ○ facilitate assignment of ownership at a level which has authority to assign resources to the management of the relevant risk;

  - ○ evaluate risks using defined criteria which are applied consistently;

  - ○ provide evaluation of inherent risk (before any control implemented) and residual risk (risk remaining after planned controls are implemented).

- Evaluates risk taking account of both:

  - ○ the likelihood of the realisation of the risk; and

  - ○ the impact of the realisation of the risk

- Identifies assigned ownership of the risk at a level or grade with sufficient authority to assign appropriate resources to control the risk.

- Records, in as far as it can be defined:

  - ○ the acceptable level of exposure in relation to each risk;

  - ○ why it is considered that the defined acceptable level of exposure can be justified.

## 4.   Criteria for evaluation of risk

There should be specific criteria for evaluating risk encompassing a range of factors.

4.1  Criteria for evaluating risk should give consideration to:

- financial/value-for-money issues;

- service delivery/quality of service issues;

- reversibility or otherwise of realisation of the risk;

- the quality or reliability of evidence surrounding the risk;

- the impact of the risk on the organisation/stakeholders/partners/others;

- defensibility of realisation of the risk.

4.2 The criteria should be applied consistently and methodically across the whole range of risks.

## 5.   Risk control mechanisms

Appropriate controls should be in place in relation to each risk:

5.1 The controls should be:

- Based on active consideration of the options for controlling that risk to an acceptable level of residual exposure.

- Promulgated to all those who need to know about the controls.

- Regularly reviewed to consider whether they continue to be

○   Effective

○   The best value for money response to the risk

○   Documented by the relevant managers.

5.2 In respect of key risks, including those which lie beyond the control of the organisation, plans should be developed and documented contingent against the risk being materially realised despite the controls which are in place?

## 6.   Review and assurance mechanisms

Review and assurance mechanisms should be in place.

Review and assurance mechanisms should ensure that:

- Each level of management, including the Board, regularly reviews the risks and controls for which it is responsible.

- These reviews are monitored by/reported to the next level of management.

- Any need to change priorities or controls is clearly recorded and either actioned, or reported to those with authority to take action.

- Lessons which can be learned, from both successes and failures, are identified and promulgated to those who can gain from them.

- An appropriate level of independent assurance is provided on the whole process of risk identification, evaluation and control.

- The methodology for gaining independent assurance is defined with particular reference to the role of internal audit and to the role of any other review bodies working within the organisation.

# Annex 3

**Provisions for those not able to make an sic for 2002/3 recording that all processes are in place by the end of the year**

1.  Information collected by the Treasury and NAO indicated that a small but significant number of bodies still had work to do after 31st March 2003 before all their risk management and review processes would be in place. This annex makes provision for these bodies to complete implementation of their processes during 2003/4 whilst still being compliant with Treasury guidance. It should be noted that this provision is a concession against the requirements of DAO(GEN)13/00, made to recognise the reality of the situation of a number of bodies at this stage.

2.  By Friday 27 June 2003 they should notify Treasury of their position. This notification should be addressed to Gordon Adam in the Assurance, Control and Risk team (contact details in the final paragraph of this letter), copied to the NAO Director responsible for the audit of the particular body's financial statements. The notification should include a summary of work remaining to be done along with a proposed timetable for completion of the work. This timetable should not extend past March 2004. This will allow Treasury to consider ways in which appropriate support can be delivered to the bodies involved; ongoing monitoring procedures will be notified by Treasury to all bodies concerned

3.  Executive Agencies and NDPBs should copy their notification to their sponsoring department in order that sponsoring departments can consider the implications of the position of the body for the departmental SIC and what actions they might take to encourage and assist the body to complete the implementation of its risk management and review processes.

4.  When preparing their SIC for 2002/3 they should follow the principles of Annex A3 to DAO(GEN)13/00, except that they should add a broad timetable to the statements of the actions planned for 2003/4.

# Annex 4

**Proforma statement on internal control**

(The wording which is not in italic script in this proforma SIC should be replicated in every SIC, the words in italic script being amended as appropriate to the body in question. Bold italic script indicates a rubric which should be fulfilled in a way appropriate to the actual processes in place in the body to which the SIC relates.)

## 1.  Scope of responsibility

As Accounting Officer, I have responsibility for maintaining a sound system of internal control that supports the achievement of *Department Yellow's* policies, aims and objectives, whilst safeguarding the public funds and departmental assets for which I am personally responsible, in accordance with the responsibilities assigned to me in Government Accounting.[6]

*(Accounting Officers should add to this paragraph to provide an explanation of the accountability arrangements surrounding their role. In particular they should comment on*

●  Processes in place by which they work with / involve Ministers on managing risk

●  Inter-relationship of department /Executive Agency/ NDPB)

## 2.  The purpose of the system of internal control

The system of internal control is designed to manage risk to a reasonable level rather than to eliminate all risk of failure to achieve policies, aims and objectives; it can therefore only provide reasonable and not absolute assurance of effectiveness. The system of internal control is based on an ongoing process designed to identify and prioritise the risks to the achievement of *departmental* policies, aims and objectives, to evaluate the likelihood of those risks being realised and the impact should they be realised, and to manage them efficiently, effectively and economically. The system of internal control has been in place in *Department Yellow* for the year ended 31 March 200x and up to the date of approval of the annual report and accounts, and accords with Treasury guidance.

## 3.  Capacity to handle risk

*(Describe the key ways in which*

●  leadership is given to the risk management process

●  staff are trained or equipped to manage risk in a way appropriate to their authority and duties. Include comment on guidance provided to them and ways in which you seek to learn from good practice)

## 4.  The risk and control framework

*(Describe the key elements of the risk management strategy including the way in which risk (or change in risk) is identified, evaluated, and controlled. Include mention of how risk appetites are determined.[7])*

*(Describe key ways in which risk management is embedded in the activity of the organisation)*

*[This section should only be inserted by those bodies to which it is relevant.*

*(Describe the key elements of the way in which public stakeholders are involved in managing risks which impact on them)]*

### 5.  Review of effectiveness

As Accounting Officer, I have responsibility for reviewing the effectiveness of the system of internal control. My review of the effectiveness of the system of internal control is informed by the work of the internal auditors and the executive managers within the *department* who have responsibility for the development and maintenance of the internal control framework, and comments made by the external auditors in their management letter and other reports. I have been advised on the implications of the result of my review of the effectiveness of the system of internal control by the Board, the Audit Committee (*and Risk Committee, if appropriate*) and a plan to address weaknesses and ensure continuous improvement of the system is in place.

(Describe the process that has been applied in maintaining and reviewing the effectiveness of the system of internal control, including some comment on the role of:

- the Board;
- the Audit Committee;
- if relevant, the Risk Committee/Risk managers/Risk Improvement Manager;
- Internal Audit;
- Other explicit review / assurance mechanisms).

### 6.  Significant internal control problems *(if applicable)*

(If there are significant internal control problems, record here an outline of the actions taken, or proposed, to deal with them. The wording should be tailored to reflect the circumstances of the case.)

(Signature of Accounting Officer and date of signature)

# Government Internal Audit Standards            B9.7

The Standards for the Professional Practice of Internal Auditing of The Institute of Internal Auditors Inc are reproduced at **B23.4**.

The following is the finalised version of standards published by the Audit Policy and Advice Unit in HM Treasury, July 2001. Policy Principles for Audit

Committees in Central Government , published by HM Treasury – December 2000 are reproduced at **B9.5**. Similarly the Corporate Governance: Statement on Internal Control appears at **B9.6**.

To check for updates, visit www.hm-treasury.gov.uk/Documents/Public _Spending_and_Services/Guidance_for_Government_Departments/, and for this guidance in particular see www.hm-treasury.gov.uk/Documents/Public _Spending_and_Services/Guidance_for_Government_Departments/pss_ggd_gi as.cfm?

## Contents

**Introduction**

**Definition of internal audit**

**Code of ethics**

**Organisational Standards**

**Operational Standards**

## Introduction

Government accounting requires Accounting Officers, in accordance with their terms of appointment, to make provision for internal audit in accordance with the standards set out in the Government Internal Audit Manual.

The definition of internal audit, code of ethics and accompanying Standards for the professional practice of internal audit in central government organisations which are subject to the provisions of government accounting, are addressed to both accounting officers and to heads of internal audit. The definition and Standards have been updated to reflect the Institute of Internal Auditor's new

Standards, so aiming to minimise any possible conflict for internal auditors in government who are members of the Institute. They nevertheless continue to reflect both the unique accountability structures of central government, and the developing nature of internal audit as it continues, in a context of rapid change and development, to add value[8] to the organisations it serves (see below for a definition of internal audit).

We hope they will also prove beneficial (as have previous Standards and versions of the Government Internal Audit Manual) to the wider public sector.

The Standards define the way in which the internal audit service should be established and undertake its functions. They cover both assurance-related and consultancy work. They apply equally to internal audit services which are provided by in-house audit units, by in-house audit units under service level agreements following market tests, and by external contractors who provide either partial services in support of an in-house team or the whole internal audit service.

The Standards form two groupings. The first encompasses the organisational and structural aspects of internal audit; the second encompasses the activity and operation of internal audit:

| Organisational Standards | Operational Standards |
|---|---|
| 1. Scope of internal audit | 6. Audit strategy |
| 2. Independence | 7. Management of audit assignments |
| 3. Audit committees | 8. Due professional care |
| 4. Relationships with management, other auditors and other review bodies | 9. Reporting |
| 5. Staffing, training and development | 10. Quality assurance |

If any organisation subject to these Standards knowingly (unavoidably or deliberately) does not comply with them on a long-term basis, the reasons for the non compliance should be documented and discussed with HM Treasury.

# Definition of internal audit

Internal audit is an independent and objective appraisal service within an organisation.

- Internal audit primarily provides an independent and objective opinion to the accounting officer[9] on risk management, control and governance, by measuring and evaluating their effectiveness in achieving the organisation's agreed objectives[10]. In addition, internal audit's findings and recommendations are beneficial to line management in the audited areas. Risk management, control and governance comprise the policies, procedures and operations established to ensure the achievement of objectives, the appropriate assessment of risk, the reliability of internal and external reporting and accountability processes, compliance with applicable laws and regulations, and compliance with the behavioural and ethical Standards set for the organisation.

- Internal audit also provides an independent and objective consultancy service specifically to help line management improve the organisation's risk management, control and governance. The service applies the professional skills of internal audit through a systematic and disciplined evaluation of the policies, procedures and operations that management put in place to ensure the achievement of the organisation's objectives, and through recommendations for improvement. Such consultancy work contributes to the opinion which internal audit provides on risk management, control and governance.

## Code of ethics for internal auditors in central government

The purpose of this code of ethics is to set the central and local Standards for the performance and conduct of the staff and units to which it applies. This code is intended to clarify the standard of conduct expected from all members of the internal audit unit when carrying out their duties. The code applies to all staff and units who are required to comply with the Government Internal Audit Standards, but does not supersede or replace the Civil Service Code.

There are four main principles that should be observed:

- integrity;
- objectivity;
- competency; and
- confidentiality.

### Integrity

All members of the internal audit team should demonstrate integrity in all aspects of their work. The relationship with fellow colleagues and external contacts should be one of honesty and fairness. This establishes an environment of trust which provides the basis for reliance on all activities carried out by the internal audit team.

### Objectivity

Objectivity is a state of mind that has regard to all considerations relevant to the activity or process being examined without being unduly influenced by personal interest or the views of others. Members of the internal audit team should display appropriate professional objectivity when providing their opinions, assessments and recommendations.

## Competency

Members of the internal audit team should apply the knowledge, skills and experience needed in the performance of their duties. They should carry out their work to the Standards set out in the Government Internal Audit Standard. They should not accept or perform work that they are not competent to undertake unless they receive adequate advice and support to competently carry out the work.

## Confidentiality

Members of the internal audit team should safeguard the information they receive in carrying out their duties. There should not be any unauthorised disclosure of information unless there is a legal or professional requirement to do so.

Confidential information gained in the course of audit duties should not be used to effect personal gain.

# Organisational Standards

## 1. Scope of internal audit

### 1.1 Provision of terms of reference

1.1.1 The purpose, authority and responsibility of internal audit should be formally defined by the accounting officer in terms of reference set out below.

(a) Are consistent with the definition of internal auditing and with these Standards.

(b) Specify the requirements for the appointment of the head of internal audit and their staff, including professional skills and experience.

(c) Establish the responsibilities and objectives of internal audit.

(d) Establish the relationship of the head of internal audit with the accounting officer and audit committee.

(e) Establish the relationship between the head of internal audit and accounting officers or third parties to be reported to11. The terms of reference should specify that heads of internal audit should review any such report with their accounting officer and audit committee prior to publication.

(f) Establish the organisational independence of internal audit, including the direct accountability of internal audit to the accounting officer and make appropriate provision for the objective assessment of the resource requirements of internal audit.

(g) Embrace the risk management, control and governance processes of the organisation including all its operations, resources, services, and responsibilities for other bodies.

(h) Enable the head of internal audit to deliver an audit opinion of the nature specified by the accounting officer.

(i) Define the consultancy role of internal audit.

(j) Establish internal audit's right of access to all records, assets, personnel and premises, and its authority to obtain such information as it considers necessary to fulfil its responsibilities.

1.1.2    The head of internal audit should advise the accounting officer on the content of the terms of reference and should regularly consider whether any amendment is required.

## 1.2    Scope of work

1.2.1    Internal audit should fulfil its terms of reference by systematic review and evaluation of risk management, control and governance which comprises the policies, procedures and operations in place to:

(a) Establish, and monitor the achievement of, the organisation's objectives.

(b) Identify, assess and manage the risks to achieving the organisation's objectives.

(c) Advise on, formulate, and evaluate policy, within the responsibilities of the accounting officer.

(d) Ensure the economical, effective and efficient use of resources.

(e) Ensure compliance with established policies (including behavioural and ethical expectations), procedures, laws and regulations.

(f) Safeguard the organisation's assets and interests from losses of all kinds, including those arising from fraud, irregularity or corruption.

(g) Ensure the integrity and reliability of information, accounts and data, including internal and external reporting and accountability processes.

1.2.2    Internal audit should devote particular attention to any aspects of the risk management, control and governance affected by material changes to the organisation's risk environment.

1.2.3    If the head of internal audit or the audit committee consider that the level of audit resources or the terms of reference in any way limit the scope of internal audit, or prejudice the ability of internal audit to deliver a service consistent with the definition of internal auditing, they should advise the accounting officer in a formal minute, emphasising the consequent limitations to the scope and value of the head of internal audit's opinion and the risks which may arise as a result. If the accounting officer decides to accept any such limitation, this decision should be recorded formally. (Standard 6.1.10.)

### 1.3 Responsibilities in respect of other bodies

1.3.1 The head of internal audit should make provision for the derivation of appropriate opinion about:

(a) control over any subsidiary bodies;

(b) the adequacy of the arrangements for internal audit in any subsidiary bodies (Standard 10.1);

(c) control in inter-departmental or cross-cutting systems; and

(d) control in contractors or service providers where that control is material to the achievement of organisational objectives.

1.3.2 Internal audit should decide whether to conduct the work to derive the required opinions themselves or rely on the opinions provided by other auditors.

1.3.3 The head of internal audit should advise on the provision of relevant access rights in the drafting of contracts let by the organisation.

### 1.4 Fraud

1.4.1 Audit procedures alone, even when performed with due professional care, cannot guarantee that fraud will be detected. Internal audit should not have responsibility for the prevention or detection of fraud. However internal auditors should be alert in all their work to risks and exposures that could allow fraud.

1.4.2 Managing the risk of fraud is the responsibility of line management. Line management may establish a functionally independent fraud detection and prevention organisation. Where they establish a separate fraud unit, the relationship between this organisation's head and the head of internal audit should be formally defined.

1.4.3 The head of internal audit should arrange to be informed of all suspected or detected fraud so that they can consider the adequacy of the relevant controls, evaluate the implication of the fraud for their opinion of the risk management, control and governance, and consider making recommendations to line managers regarding any need for more detailed investigation and improvement in control.

**2.      Independence**                                                    **B9.36**

**2.1      The principles of independence**

2.1.1      Internal audit should be sufficiently independent of the activities which it audits to enable auditors to perform their duties in a manner which facilitates impartial and effective professional judgements and recommendations. They should have no executive responsibilities.

2.1.2      Accountability for the response to the advice and recommendations of internal audit lies with the line managers who either accept and implement the advice or formally reject it. Audit advice and recommendations are without prejudice to the right of internal audit to review the relevant policies, procedures and operations at a later date.

**2.2      Organisational independence**

2.2.1      Internal audit is primarily a service to, and should report directly to the accounting officer. Internal audit may also have additional or secondary reporting lines to other accounting officers for the audit of cross cutting projects or to external bodies in cases where internal audit is appointed for the delivery of compliance and other assurances required by regulators or other authorities.

2.2.2      The accounting officer should be advised on the discharge of their responsibilities in respect of internal audit by their audit committee. In particular (amongst its other responsibilities) (see **B9.5** POLICY PRINCIPLES FOR AUDIT COMMITTEES IN CENTRAL GOVERNMENT), the audit committee should advise on internal audit in accordance with Standard 3.2. The audit committee should not obstruct the head of internal audit's direct access to the accounting officer (Standard 9.1.6).

2.2.3      The accounting officer should make appropriate arrangements for the routine provision and management of the budget and resources of internal audit (including staff appraisal arrangements) without prejudice to the direct accountability of internal audit to the accounting officer. These arrangements will normally involve delegation of these particular responsibilities to the principal finance officer.

**2.3      Status of the head of internal audit**

The head of internal audit should be graded with sufficient status to facilitate the effective discussion and negotiation of the results of internal audit work with senior management in the organisation. Evaluation tools used to grade the post should give due weight to the influence of the head of internal audit on the risk management, control and governance of the organisation.

**2.4      Independence of individual auditors**

2.4.1      Individual auditors should have an impartial, unbiased attitude, characterised by integrity and an objective approach to work, and should avoid conflicts of interest. They should not allow external factors to compromise their professional judgement.

2.4.2 Objectivity is presumed to be impaired when individual auditors review any activity in which they have previously had executive responsibility, or in which they have provided consultancy advice. Auditors should not be assigned to assurance work in business areas where they have had an executive or other involvement, and where the head of internal audit deems that this may impair their objectivity, until a suitable period has elapsed. The head of internal audit should develop appropriate guidelines for determining the duration of such periods.

2.4.3 Long term responsibility for the audit of a particular aspect of an organisation can also affect independence; assignment of ongoing audit responsibilities should be rotated from time to time.

**2.5 Independence of audit contractors**

Objectivity could be impaired if an audit contractor also provides other services to the organisation. Steps should be taken to avoid or manage such conflicts of interest.

**2.6 Declaration of conflict of interest**

2.6.1 Individual auditors should declare any conflicts of interest arising from audit work assigned to them by the head of internal audit. Such potential conflicts of interest include previous executive or consultancy responsibilities and personal relationships with staff with current executive responsibilities.

2.6.2 Internal audit should plan the allocation of audit work to minimise the risk of conflicts of interest whenever possible.

**3. Audit committees**

*This Standard only encompasses internal audit issues and does not define the full role or constitution of an audit committee.*

**3.1 Principles of the audit committee**

The 'Policy Principles for Audit Committees in Central Government'[12] provide that the accounting officer should establish an audit committee unless there are clearly identified reasons for the decision not to.

**3.2 Internal audit issues on which the accounting officer should seek the audit committee's advice**

The accounting officer should ask the audit committee to advise them on:

(a) the skill, experience and competency requirements for the post of head of internal audit;

(b)   the terms of reference for internal audit;

(c)   the effectiveness of the internal audit strategy and periodic plan in addressing the organisation's risks;

(d)   the resourcing of internal audit;

(e)   the periodic work plans of internal audit, and material changes to these plans the head of internal audit's annual and interim audit report(s) and any implications arising from their findings and opinion;

(f)   the arrangements for and the results of quality assurance processes;

(g)   the adequacy of management response to internal audit advice and recommendations; and

(h)   the arrangements made for co-operation between internal audit, external audit and other review bodies.

## 3.3   The head of internal audit's relationship with the audit committee

3.3.1   The head of internal audit should attend audit committee meetings unless, exceptionally, the audit committee decides they should be excluded from either the whole meeting or particular agenda item(s). The reasons for any such exclusion should be made known to the accounting officer.

3.3.2   The head of internal audit should have a right of access to the chair of the audit committee to discuss any issues they wish to raise.

## 4.   Relationships with management, other auditors and other review bodies

4.1   Principles of good relationships

Heads of internal audit should co-ordinate internal audit plans and activities with line managers, other internal auditors, external audit and other review agencies to ensure the most effective audit coverage is achieved and duplication of effort is minimised.

## 4.2   Relationships with management

4.2.1   Internal audit provides a service to management. Its strategy, planning and delivery should aim to maximise the value added for management without jeopardising internal audit's responsibilities to the accounting officer.

4.2.2   Management and staff at all levels of the organisation should have complete confidence in the integrity, independence and capability of internal audit. The relationship between internal auditors and line managers is a privileged one, and information gained in the course of audit work should remain confidential to those with a legitimate interest within the organisation.

4.2.3   Co-operative relationships with line management enhance the ability of internal audit to achieve its objectives effectively. Audit work should be planned in conjunction with management as far as possible, particularly in respect of the timing of audit work (except where unannounced visits are essential to the achievement of the audit objectives).

4.2.4   When fraud is suspected or detected, decisions to involve external agencies such as the police should be taken by line management. If internal audit does not consider that line management have made appropriate decisions in this respect, this should be reported internally to the accounting officer.

**4.3   Relationships with other internal auditors**

Where internal auditors need to work with internal auditors of another organisation (for example, in interdepartmental systems or cross cutting projects), the roles and responsibilities of each party should be agreed and endorsed by each accounting officer. Whenever possible agreement to joint working or to placing professional reliance on work carried out by one party should be sought.

**4.4   Relationships with external auditors[13]**

4.4.1   Internal audit should seek to meet regularly with the external auditor to consult on audit plans, discuss matters of mutual interest, discuss common understanding of audit techniques, methods and terminology, and to seek opportunities for co-operation in the conduct of audit work. In particular, internal audit should offer the external auditor the opportunity to rely on their work where appropriate, provided this does not prejudice internal audit's independence.

4.4.2   In any case of conflict with the external auditor, the head of internal audit will consult with, or refer the matter to, the accounting officer.

**4.5   Relationships with other review bodies**

4.5.1   Where other assurance and review bodies such as management inspection or compliance teams are in place, internal audit should look for opportunities to gain assurance from, and place reliance on, their work. If it is intended to place formal reliance on work by such bodies, an appropriate audit or quality assurance exercise should be carried out to ensure that each body's work is carried out to a suitable standard to enable reliance.

4.5.2   The head of internal audit should establish a means to gain an overview of other assurance providers' work to enable them to identify and consider individual or common material issues or themes emerging. If appropriate, they should be reported to the accounting officer.

**5.**     **Staffing, training and development**

**5.1**     **Principles of staffing, training and development**

Internal audit should be appropriately staffed in terms of numbers, grades, qualification levels, and experience, having regard to its objectives and to these Standards. Internal auditors should be properly trained to fulfil their responsibilities and should maintain their professional competence through an appropriate ongoing development programme.[14]

**5.2**     **The Government Internal Audit Certificate**

5.2.1     The Government Internal Audit Certificate (GIAC) defines the minimum level of skill, knowledge and experience required of an internal auditor.

5.2.2     The head of internal audit should be both GIAC-qualified and have a wide experience of management.

5.2.3     All internal audits should be led or supervised by internal auditors who hold the GIAC.

**5.3**     **Staffing the internal audit unit**

5.3.1     The head of internal audit is responsible for ensuring that they have access to the full range of knowledge, skills, qualifications and experience to meet the unit's audit objectives and these Standards. In addition to internal audit skills, the head of internal audit should specify any other professional skills which may be needed by the internal audit unit. They should also make provision for appropriate administrative support.

5.3.2     The head of internal audit is responsible for recruiting staff with the appropriate intellectual qualities, personal attributes, and qualifications (or perceived ability to undertake professional training).

5.3.3     The head of internal audit may appoint non GIAC-holders to the internal audit unit where they deem such appointees' specialist knowledge, training and experience enhances the organisation's overall audit capability, and does not jeopardise its compliance with these Standards.

5.3.4     The head of internal audit should set criteria for the appointment of the more senior staff in the internal audit unit based on demonstration of training and experience in accordance with the competencies framework in the 'Internal Audit Training and Development Handbook'.

**5.4**     **Continuing professional development**

5.4.1     All internal auditors should undertake a programme of continuing professional development to maintain and develop their skills. They should maintain a record of such training activities.

5.4.2 Heads of internal audit should ensure that appropriate provision is made for maintaining and developing the competence of audit staff. They should monitor the ongoing training activity of all staff in their internal audit unit.

## Operational Standards

**6. Audit strategy**

**6.1 Developing the internal audit strategy**

6.1.1 The head of internal audit should develop and maintain a strategy for providing the accounting officer, economically and efficiently, with objective evaluation of, and opinions on, the effectiveness of the organisation's risk management, control and governance arrangements[15]. The head of internal audit's opinions are a key element of the framework of assurance and the accounting officer needs to inform their completion of the annual Statement of Internal Control (SIC).[16]

6.1.2 The strategy should also aim to add value for the organisation's line managers by providing them with audit analyses, findings and recommendations. In addition, where internal audit judge it appropriate, they can offer consultancy to support management in implementing the recommendations.

6.1.3 The strategy should be developed to meet the audit needs of the organisation, as assessed by the head of internal audit, using the organisation's objectives and risk assessment as a primary resource.

6.1.4 The strategy should include provision for the head of internal audit to consider, at least annually, the adequacy of the organisation's risk assessment and, if necessary, make recommendations for its review.

6.1.5 The strategy should include a systematic and prioritised review of how effectively the organisation's risks are managed by its policies, procedures and operations.

6.1.6 The head of internal audit should consider any risk which they think may be material to the organisation's risk management, control and governance, even if it is not included in management's risk priorities.

6.1.7 The strategy should establish the resources and skills required for its delivery.

6.1.8 The strategy should describe the audit techniques selected as the most effective for delivering the audit objectives.

6.1.9 The strategy should set out the relative allocation of audit resources between assurance work and consultancy work. The exact allocation will be determined in the periodic plans.

6.1.10 The strategy should be approved by the accounting officer. This approval should include acceptance of risks or other areas of potential audit coverage which cannot be resourced, and identification of consequent residual risk exposure. The accounting officer should be advised by the head of internal audit that they are responsible for that residual exposure. (Standard 1.2.3).

## 6.2 Developing the periodic audit plans

6.2.1 Internal audit should prepare periodic work plans, designed to implement the audit strategy, for approval by the accounting officer.

6.2.2 The periodic plans should set out details of the assignments to be carried out in the period covered by the plan, providing sufficient detail for the accounting officer and management to understand the assignments' purpose and scope. They should establish the broad resources and skills required for each assignment, and should set relative priorities for each assignment. These periodic plans should be approved by the accounting officer.

6.2.3 The periodic audit plans should be kept under review to identify any amendment needed to reflect changing priorities and emerging audit needs. They should make provision for an element of contingency to accommodate audit assignments which could not have been reasonably foreseen. Material changes to the periodic audit plans should be approved by the accounting officer.

## 7. Management of audit assignments

## 7.1 Planning

7.1.1 For each audit assignment a detailed plan should be prepared and discussed with relevant line managers. These plans should establish detailed objectives for the assignment, the level of assurance that management wishes to derive from the opinion to be delivered, resource requirements, audit outputs and target dates. They should set out:

(a) The scope and objectives and timing of the work to be done, allocating internal audit resources and establishing their targets;

(b) Any requirements for participation by line management including supplying IT system or other data to the auditors;

(c) The schedule and timing of the assignment; and

(d) To whom the assignment findings will be disclosed (without prejudice to the right of disclosure of all audit findings to the accounting officer). For audits of cross cutting projects, the assignment plan should clearly identify the reporting lines to each accounting officer involved.

7.1.2 Internal audit should seek a 'sponsor' for each assignment. This will normally be the manager with overall responsibility for the business risk area to be audited.

7.1.3    Assignment plans should be agreed with the sponsor before work is done, and the agreement recorded. They should take account of any concerns of the sponsor about aspects of the policies, procedures and operations within the area to be audited. Any material objection to the assignment plans which cannot be resolved by negotiation should be referred to the accounting officer.

## 7.2    Approach

7.2.1    Assignments intended to provide an audit opinion should be approached using a risk based systematic approach which should clearly:

(a)   identify and record the objectives, risks and controls;

(b)   establish the congruence of the objectives with higher level corporate objectives;

(c)   evaluate management's risk analysis, taking account of their acceptance of specific risks;

(d)   evaluate the controls in principle to decide whether or not they are appropriate and can be reasonably relied upon to achieve their purpose;

(e)   identify any instances of over-control;

(f)   evaluate the impact of any decision by management to accept risk(s) rather than transfer or control them;

(g)   determine an appropriate strategy to test the effectiveness of risk management and controls; and

(h)   arrive at conclusions and report, making recommendations as necessary and providing an opinion on the effectiveness of risk management and control in the audited area.

7.2.2    The scope and objectives, timing, and reporting arrangements should be defined and agreed for consultancy assignments in the same way as for assurance assignments. The objectives should make it clear that the internal auditors' involvement is in a consultancy role. The head of internal audit will reserve the right to audit any risk management, control and governance processes developed with internal audit acting in its consultancy role.

7.2.3    Internal auditors should apply the risk-based systematic audit approach by independent acquisition and examination of relevant evidence or by using risk and control evaluation methods[17]. At each stage of the assignment, auditors should consider what specific audit work needs to be conducted or to what extent review of evidenced management activity is sufficient to support an independent and objective audit opinion.

7.2.4    Audit opinion can also be derived by the use of supplementary audit techniques and approaches.[18]

7.2.5   The head of internal audit should develop local policies for the way in which assignment level opinion will be expressed, including definition of any terms of quantification.

7.2.6   Auditors should obtain and record sufficient relevant evidence to support their conclusions and to demonstrate the adequacy of evidence obtained to support professional judgements.

7.2.7   Internal audit should review their findings with the sponsor, making recommendations for dealing with any weaknesses and offering consultancy support if appropriate.

7.2.8   The head of internal audit should inform the accounting officer of any remaining material weaknesses. The head of internal audit should develop standards and retention requirements for all audit records and documentation, whether they are held on paper or electronically. They should control access to audit records and should obtain the approval of relevant management before releasing records to external parties (except where the National Audit Office has a right of access).

**7.3      Follow-up**

7.3.1   Internal audit should follow-up assignments. Follow-up will be a review of the effectiveness of management's response to assignments' findings and recommendations. The follow-up findings should be reviewed with the sponsor before being reported.

7.3.2   The head of internal audit should develop escalation procedures for any management responses which they judge to be inadequate in relation to the identified risk. These procedures should ensure that the risks of not taking action have been understood and accepted at a sufficiently senior management level.

7.3.3   Where follow-up reveals a change in the audit opinion, this change should be reported to the sponsor.

**8.       Due professional care**

**8.1      Principles of due professional care**

8.1.1   Due professional care is the care and skill that a reasonably prudent and competent internal auditor will apply in performing their duties.

- Due care is working with competence and diligence. It does not imply infallibility or extraordinary performance.

- Due professional care is the use of audit skills and judgement based on appropriate experience, training (including continuing professional development), ability, integrity and objectivity.

8.1.2   Due professional care should be appropriate to the objectives, complexity, nature and materiality of the audit being performed.

8.1.3   Due professional care is achieved by adherence to these Standards.

## 8.2 Conduct of the individual auditor

**Individual auditors are responsible for ensuring that they conduct their own work with due professional care. They should:**

    (a) be fair and not allow prejudice or bias to override objectivity;

    (b) declare any conflicts of interest;

    (c) not accept any gifts, inducements, or other benefits from employees, clients, suppliers or other third parties;

    (d) consider and document the work needed to achieve audit objectives and the work which they perform in the course of an audit;

    (e) consider and document the management or other criteria which they use in evaluation of audit findings;

    (f) use all reasonable care in obtaining sufficient, relevant and reliable evidence on which to base their conclusions;

    (g) be alert to the possibility of intentional wrongdoing, errors and omissions, inefficiency, waste, lack of economy, ineffectiveness, failure to comply with management policy, and conflicts of interest;

    (h) have sufficient knowledge to identify indicators that fraud may have been committed;

    (i) disclose any indicators identified that fraud may have been committed and recommend any further investigation which may be appropriate;

    (j) disclose all material facts known to them which if not disclosed could distort their reports or conceal unlawful practice;

    (k) disclose in reports any non-compliance with these Standards; and

    (l) not use information which they obtain in the course of their duties for personal benefit or gain.

## 8.3 Organisational arrangements for due professional care

8.3.1     The head of internal audit should develop a programme of review to ensure that due professional care is achieved. This will principally be achieved through quality assurance methodologies (Standard 10).

8.3.2     The head of internal audit should ensure that appropriate processes are available for individual auditors to disclose any suspicions of fraud or improper conduct.

8.3.3     The head of internal audit should make provision in their plans for the basic training and continuing professional development of all internal audit staff, including themselves (Standard 5).

## 9. Reporting

### 9.1 Principles of reporting

9.1.1 The head of internal audit should determine the way in which audit findings will be reported, subject to the provisions of these Standards and the requirements of the accounting officer and any third parties.

9.1.2 The head of internal audit should set local Standards for all reports.

9.1.3 Internal audit should agree with report recipients the form and medium of those report(s), without prejudice to Standards 9.1.1 and 9.1.2.

9.1.4 All audit findings should be promptly reported to the sponsor.

9.1.5 A written audit report should be issued to the sponsor, at the close of each individual audit assignment undertaken in accordance with Standard 9.2.

9.1.6 The head of internal audit should provide a written report to the accounting officer timed to support their Statement of Internal Control.

9.1.7 The head of internal audit should be entitled to report any risk management, control or governance issue directly to the accounting officer.

### 9.2 Assignment recording and reporting

9.2.1 Internal audit's records of each assignment should include:

(a) the objectives and scope of the assignment;

(b) how these objectives have been achieved;

(c) a description of the objectives of the business area covered by the assignment;

(d) the risks, controls and all other material factors examined by the assignment; together with the evaluation criteria employed by the auditors (including an explanation of criteria formulated by the auditors rather than by management);

(e) an evaluation of the effectiveness of the risk management, disclosing weaknesses and non-effectiveness, over-control and poor value-for-money;

(f) the opinion given;

(g) any recommendations for improvement;

(h) any areas of disagreement between the auditor and management which cannot be resolved by discussion;

(I) disclosure of any relevant non-compliance with any of these Standards in the conduct of the audit and the reasons for the non-compliance;

(j) any indicators of fraud which may have been detected; and

(k) a record of how all these have been reported to the sponsor.

9.2.2   The head of internal audit should set Standards for reporting and should make arrangements for the review and approval of reports by audit management before issue.

9.2.3   A written report or reports should be issued to the sponsor at the conclusion of the assignment, encompassing at least (c), (d), (e), (f) and (g) from 9.2.1 above. Any audit findings presenting material concerns should be reported to the sponsor as soon as possible.

9.2.4   Reports should be clear, concise, and constructive. They should be issued promptly and within laid down timescales.

9.2.5   Reports should be security classified in accordance with organisational policies and with the material covered by the report to avoid unauthorised disclosure of material which would otherwise be subject to a security classification.

9.2.6   Reports should not be issued to third parties without the knowledge of relevant management.

9.2.7   In the event of a material error being discovered in a report this should be corrected and communicated to all who received copies of the report.

**9.3      Annual reporting and presentation of audit opinion**

9.3.1   The head of internal audit's formal annual report to the accounting officer should present their opinion of the overall adequacy and effectiveness of the organisation's risk management, control and governance processes. It should also:

(a) disclose any qualifications to that opinion, together with the reasons for the qualification;

(b) present a summary of the audit work undertaken to formulate the opinion, including reliance placed on work by other assurance bodies and accredited by internal audit;

(c) draw the accounting officer's attention to any issues the head of internal audit judges particularly relevant to their preparation of the Statement on Internal Control;

(d) compare work actually undertaken with the work which was planned and summarise performance of the internal audit function against its performance measures and criteria; and

(e) comment on compliance with these Standards and communicate the results of the internal audit quality assurance programme.

9.3.2   In addition to the formal annual report, the head of internal audit should make arrangements for interim reporting to the accounting officer in the course of the year. Such interim reports should address emerging issues in respect of the whole range of areas to be covered in the formal annual report. The head of internal audit should also provide information required by the accounting officer or audit committee on an *ad hoc* basis.

## 10.  Quality assurance

### 10.1  Principles of quality assurance

10.1.1 The work of internal audit should be controlled at each level of operation to ensure that a continuously effective level of performance, compliant with these Standards, is being maintained.

10.1.2 The head of internal audit should develop a quality assurance programme designed to gain assurance by both internal and external review that the work of internal audit, including internal audit within their organisation's subsidiary bodies, is compliant with these Standards and achieves its objectives, and to sustain a commentary on compliance with these Standards in the annual audit report.

### 10.2  Management of internal audit

10.2.1 The head of internal audit should establish policies and procedures in a local audit manual to guide staff. The form and content of this manual should be appropriate to the size of the audit unit. At a minimum the manual should include audit's role and responsibilities, documentation Standards, local reporting Standards and targets, training requirements and expectations, and audit performance measures and indicators.

10.2.2 The head of internal audit should ensure that internal audit staff at all levels are appropriately supervised throughout all audit assignments to monitor progress, assess quality and coach staff. Supervision should include:

(a)  ensuring compliance with these Standards and local manuals;

(b)  providing suitable instructions at the outset of an audit;

(c)  approving audit objectives and work plans;

(d)  ensuring audits are conducted as planned or that variations are approved;

(e)  ensuring that appropriate audit techniques are used;

(f)  ensuring that audit findings, conclusions and recommendations are adequately supported by relevant and sufficient evidence;

(g)  ensuring that reports are accurate, objective, clear, concise and timely; and

(h)  ensuring that work is achieved within resource budgets, or variations are approved.

10.2.3    The extent of supervision will depend on the experience and training of the individual auditor. Particular care should be taken to ensure that all work by trainee auditors is subject to comprehensive supervision and that trainee auditors never work without the supervision of a professionally qualified auditor.

10.2.4    The head of internal audit should establish a set of performance measures and criteria for the internal audit function. Where there is a service level agreement or a contract, the performance measures and criteria should be contained within it. These measures and criteria should be approved by the accounting officer.

10.2.5    Supervisors should regularly discuss auditors' performance with them and identify any areas in which improvement or training is required.

## 10.3    Internal quality review

10.3.1    The head of internal audit should make provision for internal quality reviews to be undertaken periodically by experienced members of the internal audit function. These reviews should be undertaken at least every other year.

10.3.2    Internal reviews should appraise:

(a)  the quality of audit work;

(b)  the quality of supervision;

(c)  compliance with these Standards;

(d)  compliance with the local audit manual;

(e)  the ways in which the internal audit function adds value to the organisation; and

(f)  achievement of performance standards/indicators.

10.3.3    The sponsor for internal reviews should be the head of internal audit who should include comment on the results of such reviews in the annual audit report. Following an internal quality review the internal auditors involved should develop an action plan for addressing any weaknesses identified.

10.3.4    Internal reviews should be conducted by reviewing a range of completed and current audit assignments.

10.3.5    Internal reviews should be conducted according to a review programme approved by the head of internal audit, and should themselves be subject to the principles of objectivity and the acquisition of evidence contained in these Standards.

## 10.4    External quality review

10.4.1    The head of internal audit should make provision for external quality reviews to be commissioned periodically from appropriately qualified and independent reviewers. These reviews should be undertaken at least once every five years. External quality reviews should appraise:

(a) the terms of reference for the internal audit function;

(b) the independence and objectivity of internal audit;

(c) the efficiency and effectiveness of the approach to formulating the audit strategy and plans;

(d) the quality of supervision;

(e) compliance with these Standards;

(f) compliance with the local audit manual; and

(g) achievement of performance Standards/indicators.

10.4.2 The sponsor for external quality reviews should be the accounting officer, who should discuss the results with the head of internal audit. Following an external quality review the head of internal audit should develop a programme for addressing any weaknesses identified and agree an action plan with the accounting officer. Progress against any such action plans should be reported upon in the annual audit report.

# National Health Service corporate governance     B9.8

The corporate governance debate for private sector entities has been driven by such matters as boardroom excess (Tyco, GlaxoSmithKline and so on), fraudulent financial reporting (Enron, WorldCom and so on), failures in internal control, and spectacular failures of policy and strategy (Marconi springs to mind).

## Boardroom excess     B9.9

Indeed, one lamentable philosophy is that 'greed is good'. Agency theory suggests to us that there will always be a tension between the interests of the shareholders and the interests of their management teams, who are the shareholders' agents. Both behave to maximise their own rewards. In 2003 the GlaxoSmithKline shareholders organised themselves sufficiently to strike a blow against boardroom excess. Some of the Principles and Provisions of the UK's Combined Code address the responsibilities of stakeholders, and rightly so; they have an essential role to play in corporate governance. While the perception is that stakeholders of listed companies have been too uninvolved, this cannot be said of the NHS where the problem, if anything, has been, and promises to be, the opposite. Furthermore, the governance of the NHS has been driven by dedication and commitment for modest personal rewards.

'Boardroom greed' is not an NHS ailment. From time to time politicians score points about management costs in the NHS, but professional management is necessary and it would not be right for doctors and nurses to be diverted significantly from clinical matters. Certainly, every entity should monitor total boardroom costs. Taken in aggregate it is likely that the total boardroom costs are high in the NHS compared to a hypothetical private sector entity of similar size. That is because the NHS has so many boards, and also so many central specialist and oversight functions serving NHS boards in a broader sense – not because individual board members are excessively rewarded.

Cynics might say it is right that NHS directors (whether executive or non-executive) are only modestly rewarded since profit is the reward for risk, and it is not clear, for instance, what personal risk an NHS non-executive director is taking. On the other hand Cadbury, in the context of PLCs, said that the financial rewards of non-executive directors should be commensurate with the value of their time commitment and the expertise they bring to the board: on that basis non-executive directors in the NHS are very good value for money. Neither can chief executives of NHS trusts and those who report to them be accused of feathering their nests – especially when measured against their time commitment.

Indeed, stewardship theory (which emphasises the trustee relationship of directors to stakeholders) rather than agency theory is the better model to describe what we see in place in the NHS. When we observe NHS corporate governance in action we see stewardship theory (where directors and managers are trustees) rather than agency theory (where they compete with stakeholders to maximise their personal returns) as the dominant corporate governance paradigm. The governance ethic in the NHS is, to my mind, therefore much more healthy than that of the with-profit sector of our economy.

It is notable that the NHS generally has balanced boards – balanced between executive and non-executive directors with an avoidance of excessive concentration of power at the top. The roles of chief executive and chair are separated. As yet these qualities do not always characterise listed company boards. While I was active in the NHS I also experienced the admirable practice of each non-executive director shadowing a particular executive director – giving the non-executives an opportunity to get involved and giving each executive director a sympathetic, independent ear.

## Fraudulent financial reporting                                    B9.10

If 'boardroom greed' is not an issue in the NHS, then neither is 'fraudulent financial reporting'. Off-balance sheet special purpose partnerships, artificial related party transactions, premature recognition of income, or delayed or inadequate accounting for liabilities are not significant NHS problems. How often has the NHS and its parts had to significantly restate their past, audited financial statements, for instance? Certainly most rarely due to fraudulent financial reporting.

Reliability of NHS financial reporting is not an issue in the *public mind*, and this is most likely because 'creative accounting' is not a material issue *in reality*. There are however concerns about off-balance sheet liabilities associated with the Private Finance Initiative (PFI). Just as Lord Stockton memorably described privatisation as 'selling the family silver', so PFI (and the way PFI is being accounted for) looks like pawning new family silver which has only just been acquired.

Good corporate governance demands full accountability by boards to stakeholders. Directors should account publicly and clearly for whatever they are responsible for; and mechanisms must be in place which enable stakeholders to exercise effective *control from outside*. We might call this *external* control to distinguish it from *internal* control. If directors have a responsibility, then there should be a matching accountability – otherwise how are we to know that directors are discharging their responsibilities? Secrecy engenders irresponsibility; transparency is a key principle of corporate governance.

Transparency does not mean you see nothing at all because you are looking straight through a clear piece of glass into a void beyond. It means you see it all clearly, not opaquely. Of course, public disclosure is not worth the paper it is written on; indeed, it is positively harmful if the disclosure is unreliable.

With respect to openness, the NHS is light years in front of the for-profit private sector. The Nolan Principle of Openness[19] and its interpretation in the Nolan 'Standard of Best Practice for Openness in Executive NDPBs and NHS Bodies'[20] does not remotely have a counterpart in the private sector. For instance, what public company holds its board meetings in public!

As far back as 29 September 1997 the NHS Financial Development Branch announced its approach[21] to requiring all authorities and trusts within the NHS to publish annual controls assurance statements which now parallel quite closely, with some significant differences, the practice that has been in place for UK listed companies since 1995. Indeed NHS directors go further than those in listed companies by disclosing publicly their conclusions about the appropriateness of internal control – operational, financial and compliance. The liability risk may be greater for directors of NHS authorities compared to directors of NHS trusts. Internal financial control of trust monies depends largely upon the systems *within* the trust under the overall direction of its board. A matter for clarification in the context of internal control assurance statements is the nature and extent of the responsibilities of directors of an NHS *authority* for the quality of internal financial control within an NHS *trust* over the funds provided to the trust by the authority. This issue is now even more important as the scope of internal control assurance reports has broadened to cover operational matters (such as clinical risk and control).

## Breakdowns of internal control                                        B9.11

Sir Adrian Cadbury said that 'If you look at all the failures of quoted companies in the past, they have all been failures of internal control'. Yes, there have been breakdowns in internal control within the NHS, but again nowhere near the level we have seen in private sector entities – where the scale of breakdown has led even to the complete collapse of multinational corporations. Internal control is taken seriously in the NHS. Read any NHS annual report and there is much more disclosure about internal control than you will find in the annual reports of listed companies. The *applied* control standards are disclosed and described and the NHS Executive is demandingly prescriptive as to what the *minimum* of these control standards is to be. Then, NHS chief executives and chairs of NHS boards publicly express their opinions, on behalf of their boards, on the *appropriateness* of their internal control systems – this goes much further than the private sector where the internal control report just states that the directors have reviewed the effectiveness of internal control – not whether they have drawn a conclusion from that review; nor what that conclusion on effectiveness, if indeed they came to such a conclusion, had been.

Of course, the NHS has seen occasional instances of top management greed, fraudulent financial reporting and so on – but they have been few and far between, minor in scale and certainly not indicative of systemic failings in NHS governance. The NHS should be immensely proud of this tradition. As a nation we might reflect on how fortunate we are, for the inherent potential for abuse is huge in view of the scale of the resources at stake.

# Formulation of policy and strategy                                    B9.12

So, many, indeed most, of the fundamentals of corporate governance best practice are exemplified par excellence in the NHS. Where there are concerns about corporate governance in the NHS they are to do with: first, the formulation of policy and strategy; secondly: accountability for what really matters; thirdly: the exercise of external control; fourthly, culture; and last of all, structure.

With respect to policy and strategy, the politicisation of the NHS is a tragedy. Even politicians agree with this but their agendas mean they cannot resist exacerbating the problem. The NHS should not be allowed to be a political football. Neither should we give time of day to trendy gurus peddling their latest theories of organisational design and what have you. Even before the ink was dry on the internal market of the 1980s and early 1990s, it was being dismissed as a failure. But, was it a failure in itself, or was it other more long term, fundamental matters which were letting down the NHS? In any case it was too early to tell.

The NHS internal market had the potential for addressing many of the problems of the NHS – just as foundation trusts have a similar potential: 'Plus ça change, plus c'est la meme chose'.[22] But the last thing which should be happening in the NHS is to repeatedly pull up saplings planted just a few years earlier, before they have had the chance to mature into oak trees. This is a serious, abject failure of NHS corporate governance. It is a too meddlesome interference by categories of NHS stakeholders – in striking contrast to the spectator mentality of many listed companies' shareholders. And it diverts the best NHS managers to building their careers on their track records for so-called successful reorganisations rather than for delivering better patient care.

## Accountability for the right things                    B9.13

The second concern about corporate governance in the NHS is the state of accountability. That may seem surprising in view of the quality of NHS annual reports even when compared with leading listed companies. But it is mainly a matter of what you are accounting for. The principal body of stakeholders of a company, that is the shareholders, are primarily interested in their financial return – the bottom line is economic performance. The financial statements are therefore the key report – they contain the account they need – if it is reliable. This account tells them what they 'need to know' in order to exercise control from outside – at the annual general meeting and so on.

But it is not like that for the NHS. Or rather, it is like that but it should not be. What should be regarded as 'the primary stakeholders' of the NHS have little interest in the financial performance of the various parts of the NHS. It is operational performance which is key to them. It is clinical governance which allows NHS boards to attest reliably for their operational performance. But there is much less emphasis on clinical reporting in the annual reports of NHS trusts than there is on financial reporting. Openness and rigor is impressive in financial reporting – not so much in operational reporting.

As we have said, directors should be accountable for what they are responsible for. And accountability should be proportionate to stakeholder perceptions of importance. With the past focus on financial reporting perhaps it is small wonder that the concerns that are insufficiently addressed are about operational performance. Stakeholder pressure is targeted at NHS operational performance – hence the temptation to cheat with operational target data just as top management teams of listed companies are tempted to cheat with their financial data – especially if their targets are not being met. Of course, since financial resources follow operational performance in the NHS, there are also indirect financial reporting implications in massaging performance data.

What should this mean in practical terms? First, there should be more serious attempts to develop a standard, informative way of reporting on clinical performance. NHS annual reports should include, in addition to financial statements, a set of statements on operational performance prepared in accordance with generally accepted standards for reporting on clinical operational performance. Just as numbers feature prominently in financial statements, so they should in operational statements: narrative is important but not enough. Reporting on clinical performance is a matter of reporting on clinical outcomes – in part in relation to the nature of the inputs. The bottom line which interests a company shareholder is economic profit – a measure of the success of the company to add economic value – to achieve economic results in excess of the cost of their inputs. By analogy, that is how we must measure NHS clinical performance. It is a matter of reporting on individual and group productivity. These clinical reporting standards still largely need to be developed and applied. Logically these public accounts of clinical performance, being of more interest to stakeholders than the account of financial performance, need to be at least as detailed – probably even more so. But it is important that the reader should be able to see the wood despite the trees.

Just as listed companies report at the interim (that is every six months), and US listed companies report quarterly, so consideration should be given to public clinical reporting of the component parts of the NHS to be more frequent than annual, albeit with the interim reports being less detailed and perhaps just reviewed rather than being comprehensively audited.

By analogy with the financial reporting of listed companies, it should not be for the NHS itself to publish comparative evaluations of the operational performance of different parts of the NHS – league tables, starred ratings and so on spring to mind. Rather it should be a matter for the market in health care to make their own assessments of relative performance based on published operational results which are reliably prepared, consistently stated and subject to independent audit. Reporting on clinical performance should be just that. Comparative data, such as league tables, are another matter. It would be better to leave such comparisons to 'the market' (as do companies with respect to comparative analyses of their financial statements with those of other companies) rather than to develop and apply standard approaches to such comparative operational analysis as a requirement of public reporting of the parts of the NHS. League tables are open to misinterpretation and can be demoralising in the extreme. They are bound to be damaging and misleading unless and until they are comparisons of operational performance which has been reported according to satisfactory generally accepted standards for reporting on clinical operational performance.

## Match audit with accountability                                        B9.14

As an eminent professor once said:

> 'Without audit, no accountability;without accountability, no control;and if there is no control, where is the seat of power? ... great issues often come to light only because of scrupulous verification of details.'[23]

The need for an independent audit of clinical governance statements is even greater than the need for an independent audit of NHS financial reports. If there are inadequate reports of clinical performance, or if they are inadequately audited, or if the auditors inadequately report on the results of their audit – then there is no effective accountability for operational performance. The temptation to cheat becomes irresistible. And thus there can be no effective stakeholder control. The Audit Commission is concerned that Foundation Trusts may be subject to an audit only of their financial statements to be published. They should be concerned too about the extent to which the various parts of the NHS (whether Foundation trusts or not) account for their operational performance, the extent to which there are generally accepted standards to govern the preparation of operational reports, and the extent to which those reports are audited independently. There are no annual, or more frequent, external and independent audit report and audit opinion on a comprehensive statement of operational, or clinical performance – communicated to the stakeholders.

## Clinical governance       B9.15

Thirdly, there must be clinical governance committees of boards mirroring board audit committees but focussing on clinical risk, clinical control and clinical reporting rather than on accounting and financial risk, control and reporting. As with audit committees, membership of clinical governance committees would be exclusively non-executive directors and they would be chaired by a non-executive director with a clinical rather than financial background. As with audit committees their minutes would be reported regularly to the board. Those in attendance at clinical governance committee meetings (but not as members) would be the medical and nursing directors and the clinical risk managers rather than the finance director and so on who attend audit committee meetings.

## External control of boards       B9.16

The board is at the hub of effective corporate governance. The important external aspects of corporate governance, which are to do with the accountability of the board to the stakeholders so that they can exercise effective external control from outside, are one important part of corporate governance.

Not much confidence can be placed in the mechanisms for local accountability being built into the Foundation Trusts model. Their governing bodies are unlikely to be effective at representing stakeholders' interests and exercising external control. The prospect of local politicians being a part of this process is horrific if it means that health care priorities will come to be determined by the number of local votes at stake. NHS Foundation Trusts are to be 'modelled on co-operative societies and mutual organisations'[24]. Their members will mostly live locally, being largely patients and staff. There will be a Board of Governors (elected by the members from the members) to represent them[25] and with a proper balance between different interest groups in the membership. There will also be a Board of Directors[26], the chair and non-executive directors of which are to be elected by the Board of Governors[27]. Prima facie, it does appear that this two-tier board system – reminiscent of German or Danish companies – is a cumbersome and costly overhead. While some local accountability and local dialogue is useful, local stakeholder control is not apposite for the NHS.

## Boards' internal oversight       B9.17

The fourth important part of corporate governance is its internal aspects: they relate to the formulation of policy by the board and the oversight by the board of management's implementation of board policy. The quality of information that the board receives and also all the other aspects of internal control including culture are vital elements of these internal aspects of corporate governance.

(Although not addressed here, we should also realise that there is another essential aspect of corporate governance, which is how the board is run (the scheduling, staging and number of meetings, board committees and their terms of reference, attendance at meetings, quality of chairmanship, quality of directors, etc).)

There is a culture problem within the NHS. Directors are overall responsible for culture. It has often been described as being, at least in part, a culture of 'fear'. In any safety conscious industry a command culture ruled by fear is the opposite of what is needed. Staff should get brownie points for drawing attention to failure. Fear manifests itself in a variety of ways – in particular in terms of 'productivity' and 'service'. In the NHS one rarely observes more than just a very few of staff working briskly. It seems the only way we could achieve more output is to negotiate extra shifts, or to hire more locum or agency people. So this means that some people are working ridiculously long hours. Productivity as an individual obligation seems so often absent as a consideration. In the private sector people know they have to raise their act to clear backlogs and meet deadlines – even working into the evening or over weekends without extra reward. Their jobs depend on it. This sense of responsibility should be shared by all categories of worker. In the private sector, staff car parks are not half empty over school half terms. This is a real and multi-faceted problem for the NHS – easy (though politically incorrect) to express, difficult to get consensus over and much more difficult to deal with.

Herein is the main governance challenge in the NHS. Foundation Trusts have some potential to address this challenge. Small is beautiful. The larger the bureaucracy, the larger the morale problem and the lower is individual productivity. NHS trusts under the internal market model were starting to address this – before the market was scrapped, the trusts were merged, chief executives were reapplying for jobs and executive and non-executive directors were out on their ear with hardly a word of thanks.

But Foundation Trusts will fail if the weight of oversight, of control and of demanding new initiatives by the NHS Executive is not significantly relieved, and if the seemingly unremitting rejigging of policy by ministers is not more restrained.

Even apart from the development of Foundation Trusts, the NHS is so divided in its structure as to be significantly impeded. It is endeavouring to be a centralised and a decentralised business at the same time. A much lighter central touch on the tiller is needed – and this will be the more so if the new Foundation Trusts are to succeed. The alternative would be the abandonment of decentralised governance at the level of Trusts, in favour of full centralisation. That is not the course that has been embarked upon; neither is it the preferable one. But it must be the one course or the other – not both at the same time.

**Notes**

1. Standards in Public Life, First Report of the Committee on Standards in Public Life (Chairman: Lord Nolan), Volume 1: Report, May 1995, Cm 2850–1, 109 pps, price: £11.80. (The second volume was evidence submitted to the Committee), Available from HMSO Publications Centre, PO Box 276, London, SW8 5DT. Tel: +44 (0)207 873 9090. Fax: +44 (0)207 873 8200).

2. Committee on the Financial Aspects of Corporate Governance (1 December 1992), chaired by Sir Adrian Cadbury; Gee Publishing Ltd, 100 Avenue Road, Swiss Cottage, London, NW3 3PG, Freephone: +44 (0)345 573113. Fax: +44 (0)207 393 7463. ISBN 0 85258 913 1 (Report). ISBN 0 85258 915 8 (Report with Code of Best Practice), 91 A5 pages, $3.2 – 3.3.

3. The Government's Code of Practice on Access to Government Information (1994). This Code also applies to NDPBs which are subject to the jurisdiction of the Ombudsman.

4. DAO(GEN)13/00 introduced the requirement for a Statement on Internal Control to be made alongside the accounts of central government bodies.

5. Alternatively, bodies may, and are encouraged to, adopt the new proforma SIC when preparing their SIC for 2002/3 (see paragraph 10).

6. In NDPBs where responsibility for risk management is shared by the Board and the Accounting Officer, the SIC may be made jointly by the Accounting Officer and the Chair of the Board. Some NDPBs may be required to do this under other provisions by which they are governed. For example, the Charities Statement of Recommended Practice (SORP) 2000 requires the trustees of charitable bodies to be jointly responsible for the preparation of accounts and annual reports. Consequently, for charitable NDPBs one or more of the trustees should sign the foreword to the accounts, the balance sheet and the SIC along with the Accounting Officer.

7. It will be helpful if indication can be given here of the generic risk priorities of the body during the period covered by the SIC. For example, a body might indicate that its risk priorities are in the areas of personnel and project management whilst another might indicate that its priorities are IT infrastructure and external economic circumstances

8. The way in which internal audit adds value is set-out in the 'Definition of Internal Audit'.

9. In the case of NDPBs the opinion may also be given to the statutory board where it has an executive function.

10. Audit work designed to deliver opinion on the risk management, control and governance of the organisation is referred to in these Standards as 'assurance work' because management use the audit opinion to derive assurance about the effectiveness of their controls.

11. Heads of Internal Audit in Executive Agencies or NDPBs may also be required to provide reports to the Accounting Officer of the sponsoring department. Again, some departmental Heads of Internal Audit may be required to report to the EC on aspects of their departments' control of expenditure of European funds.

12. Published by HM Treasury, December 2000

13. Detailed guidance on co-operation between internal and external auditors is contained in a good practice guide published jointly by the National Audit Office and HM Treasury

14. Detailed guidance on training requirements for Internal Auditors in central government is contained in the 'Internal Audit Training and Development Handbook' published by HM Treasury.

15. Where the Head of Internal Audit must also report to another Accounting Officer or to a third party the strategy should also set out how this requirement is to be met, including the timing of any such reports.

16. The Statement of Internal Control requires Accounting Officers to acknowledge their personal responsibility for the effective governance of their organisation; to confirm that they have, within the period covered by the Statement of Internal Control, reviewed the adequacy and effectiveness of the controls, and that any material weaknesses identified by the review have been addressed.

17. Such methods include Control and Risk Self-Assessment.

18. The full range of such techniques available to the internal auditor are described in the GIAM Best Practice guides which support these Standards.

19. 'Holders of public office should be as open as possible about all the decisions and actions they take. They should give reasons for their decisions and restrict information only when the wider public interest clearly demands.'

20. Standards in Public Life, First Report of the Committee on Standards in Public Life (Chairman: Lord Nolan), Volume 1: Report, May 1995, Cm 2850–1, 109 pps, price: £11.80. (The second volume was evidence submitted to the Committee). Available from HMSO Publications Centre, PO Box 276, London, SW8 5DT. Tel: +44 (0)207 873 9090. Fax: +44 (0)207 873 8200.

21. Corporate Governance in the NHS: Controls Assurance Statements, EL(97)55 (September 29, 1997), Financial Development Branch, NHS Executive, Quarry House, Leeds, LS2 7UE. Tel: +44 (0)113 254 5483. Fax: +44 (0)113 254 5534.

22. 'The more things change, the more they are the same.' Alphonse Karr 1808–90, French novelist and journalist.

23. Professor W.J.M. Mackenzie in the foreword to The Accountability and Audit of Governments, by E.L. Normanton, Manchester University Press (1966), pvii. Also published by Frederick A. Prager, New York (1966).

24. A Guide to NHS Foundation Trusts, December 2002, p3

25. A Guide to NHS Foundation Trusts, December 2002, p10

26. I understand The Department of Health has dropped the Foundation Trust term 'Management Board' in favour of 'Board of Directors'.

27. A Guide to NHS Foundation Trusts, December 2002, p10.

# Being A Director

## Qualifications for directors                                    B10.1

In this section we outline two qualifications in directorship and corporate governance – the Chartered Director qualification of The Institute of Directors and the Diploma in Corporate Governance of The Association of Chartered Certified Accountants.

## Chartered Director (CDir) qualification of the IoD          B10.2

This is claimed by the Institute of Directors to be the world's first professional qualification for directors.

### Summary                                                      B10.3

The Chartered Director qualification is available to directors who have demonstrated the requisite knowledge and experience to act in this professional capacity. IoD claims this to be the only award that recognises capabilities as a director. Being a chartered director shows a possession of all the key skills to be an effective and dynamic member of a board. The IoD is working with government, regulators, executive search agencies, companies and the public sector to promote the value of the Chartered Director qualification.

### Eligibility                                                   B10.4

Candidates must be:

- members or fellows of IoD;

- a practising director, and have been so for at least three years in the last five (seven years in the last nine if the candidate does not have a degree or professional qualification);

- aged at least 28 at date of registration;

- proposed and seconded; and

- a member of a board that meets at least four times a year, having at least three directors and focusing on the governance,. not management, of the organisation.

### Structure and syllabus                                       B10.5

To qualify, candidates must pass a formal examination and also a peer review interview.

**Aims and objectives**                                                                    **B10.6**

Chartered directors are able to:

- attract interest and support from investors and banks;

- demonstrate to clients or customers that their organisation is professional;

- operate at a strategic and tactical level to establish and sustain growth;

- appreciate all aspects of effective business leadership and sound corporate governance;

- improve the board's effectiveness and their personal contribution; and

- enhance their career prospects as an executive director or non-executive director.

**Syllabus content**                                                                       **B10.7**

The syllabus for the examination in company direction assesses competence in:

- director duties, liabilities and responsibilities;

- finance;

- strategy and setting strategic direction;

- human resource strategy;

- leading change;

- decision making; and

- performance management.

**Study**                                                                                  **B10.8**

Candidates decide for themselves how to prepare for the examination. There is an interactive practice exam to help in assessing knowledge in all area of the programme and to assist in deciding which study route is best suited (www.iod.com/practiceexam). There are three study routes offers to the exam:

- the study route (all seven courses – **B10.7**);

- the partial study route (one or more of the courses); or

- the 'no study route' (none of the courses).

IoD offers a company direction programme as seven discrete courses each running for one to three days and available on several dates each month throughout the year throughout the UK. The total time commitment to study all seven courses is 15 days.

**Assessment**                                                                             **B10.9**

The first stage is to pass the IoD examination in Company Direction. Secondly, candidates must also demonstrate experience via a professional review which consists of a history and self evaluation of the candidate's boardroom work which then forms the basis of a one hour interview with two of the candidate's peers.

### Registration and fees                                              **B10.10**

Contact the Chartered Director programme on +44 (0)20 7766 2601. E-mail: chartered.director@iod.com.    Website:    www.iod.com/chartered    (also www.iod.com/courses).

# Diploma in Corporate Governance (DipCG of ACCA)   **B10.11**

The qualification was launched at the end of 2001.

### Summary                                                            **B10.12**

The Association of Chartered Certified Accountants is the largest global professional accountancy body, with nearly 300,000 members and students in 160 countries. ACCA's headquarters are in London and it has 31 staffed offices around the world. ACCA's mission is to provide quality professional opportunities to people of ability and application, to be a leader in the development of the global accountancy profession, to promote the highest ethical and governance standards and to work in the public interest.

In October 2001 ACCA launched a Diploma in Corporate Governance (DipCG) designed for executive and non-executive directors who are responsible for the management and direction of their organisations and senior managers who are involved in establishing governance procedures. The qualification covers the theoretical and practical aspects of corporate governance and is assessed by two 5,000 word projects. It is a six-month web-based course with online access to a mentor. It is a comprehensive qualification covering both the theoretical and practical aspects of the subject. It demonstrates that a positive approach to corporate governance is entirely compatible with and supportive of responsible entrepreneurship and public service.

### Structure and syllabus                                             **B10.13**

The diploma course is divided into eight modules, designed both for convenience of study and for progress smoothly from basic principles to more complex issues.

### Aims                                                               **B10.14**

To develop knowledge and understanding of the main theoretical perspectives and frameworks of corporate governance, integrating regulatory, international, ethical, environmental and social dimensions.

To enable candidates to identify and manage corporate governance issues and to implement and control corporate governance procedures within their organisations, whether they operate in the corporate or public sector.

**Objectives**                                                      **B10.15**

On completion of the diploma candidates should be able to:

● appreciate the range and scope of topics and issues contributing to the area of corporate governance;

● understand the role which corporate governance plays in maintaining the stability of markets and retaining public confidence in public institutions;

● describe the principal elements which constitute corporate governance frameworks;

● explain the role of audit in corporate governance;

● compare approaches to corporate governance internationally;

● understand the implications of the nature and scope of social and environmental accountability for corporate governance practice;

● understand the roles and responsibilities of executive directors, non-executive directors, company secretaries and auditors in ensuring effective corporate governance;

● understand the ethical responsibilities of senior management, describe key ethical theories and discuss their relevance to ethical dilemmas in practice;

● understand the external reporting requirements relating to corporate governance to which an organisation is subject; and

● assist the board and the executive team of an organisation in developing appropriate corporate governance procedures to achieve organisational objectives and to ensure regulatory compliance.

**Syllabus – content**                                              **B10.16**

*An overview of corporate governance*                              **B10.17**

● What is corporate governance?

● How do the definitions of corporate governance differ and what do they have in common?

● The history of corporate governance.

● Issues in corporate governance.

*Corporate governance concepts and theories*                       **B10.18**

● Stewardship theory;

● agency theory;

● stakeholder theory;

● corporate control;

- corporate governance and performance; and
- accountability and enterprise.

### The role of the regulatory framework                          B10.19

- Legislation;
- financial reporting;
- audit; and
- voluntary codes.

### Models of corporate governance                                B10.20

- Around the boardroom table.
- Governance and management.
- International differences.
- Do international differences matter?

### The board of directors                                        B10.21

- The board of directors;
- who controls the board;
- the role of the non-executive director; and
- board committees.

### Social and environmental issues                               B10.22

- What is corporate social responsibility?
- Issues of social and environmental responsibility.
- How can companies demonstrate socially responsible behaviour?

### Ethical issues in corporate governance                        B10.23

- Ethical aspects of corporate governance;
- ethical theories;
- case study 1: practical application of ethical theories;
- case study 2: practical application of ethical theories; and
- corporate code of ethics.

### Corporate governance issues in practice                       B10.24

- Demonstrating high standards of corporate governance.
- Corporate governance failure – on the decline?
- The Combined Code in the UK.
- Future issues.

**Study**                                                                 **B10.25**

Study for the diploma is through a web-based course, with full online support from a mentor. The course is designed to take between six and nine months to complete, depending on prior experience. Access to online facilities is essential for the duration of the course. Candidates can register online at www.accademy.com in order to access all support material and advice. The course is designed to help candidates identify further relevant material and develop their understanding of the topics covered through background reading.

**Assessment**                                                            **B10.26**

The diploma is assessed by two 5,000 word written projects submitted online. The first project is set on completion of the first five modules and enables candidates to demonstrate understanding of the theoretical background to corporate governance. The second project is set at the end of the course and evaluates ability to apply the principles studied within the context of your own organisation. Projects are completed in candidates' own time, provided they are submitted within the duration of the course. Individuals who fail to achieve the required standard in a project are be permitted one re-submission.

**Registration and fees**                                                 **B10.27**

*How to register*                                                         **B10.28**

Register for the diploma is via www.accaglobal.com/students/dicg.

*Entry requirements*                                                      **B10.29**

The recommended entry standard to the diploma course is a recognised degree, HND/HNC, NVQ Level 4 or membership of a professional body. Individuals may also be admitted to the course on the basis of their work experience.

*Fees*                                                                    **B10.30**

The following fees were applicable in 2002 (subject to change without written notice):

- Course fee: £590 (including VAT). Fees must be paid online by credit card.

- Re-submission fee: £90 (if applicable).

**Mentoring**                                                             **B10.31**

Mentors on the Diploma in Corporate Governance have two main roles.

- Direct student support.

    o   A mentor is allocated to individual students who may contact the mentor through the course to ask for help and advice on particular aspects of corporate governance. Students can join the course at any time during the year, so the diploma course does not operate cohorts or tutorial groups. Mentors are not required to conduct any formal teaching sessions, to answer any queries relating to the administration of the course, to carry out marking or to help students in preparing their projects.

- Mentor contributions to the 'CourseRoom'.

  o In the 'CourseRoom' students and mentors can discuss topics of general interest and exchange information. Mentors are expected to:

    □ be familiar with the content and philosophy of the course;

    □ log on to the course at least twice a week;

    □ reply to your students' queries within five working days; and

    □ make at least two contributions per month to the general 'CourseRoom' discussions e.g. introduce a topic to stimulate discussion or present useful references.

### *Mentor profile*                           **B10.32**

Mentors have a relevant professional or post-graduate qualification or have at least five years senior management experience in the area of corporate governance, a keen interest in and knowledge of developments within corporate governance, computer equipment adequate to access the diploma course on a twice weekly basis; and it is desirable that mentors also have mentoring or teaching experience.

### *Applications to become mentors*              **B10.33**

Applications should be sent to Lis Hristova, Education Adviser, ACCA, 29 Lincoln's Inn Fields, London WC2A 3EE, UK.

# Joining a board – how to decide         **B10.34**

In this section we suggest a careful approach a prospective director might follow if invited to join a board of directors. At the end of this section there is a checklist which summarises the main points made. Our recommendation is that prospective directors weigh up the offer carefully before deciding, and use their own judgement as to whether the advice given in this section of the handbook is directly applicable to the circumstances.

How should you react to an approach to join a board? Of course, you may be flattered and keen to accept the challenge for the experience that it promises to bring. You should not allow that excited reaction to colour your judgement.

On the other hand, if you are predisposed to decline the invitation, probably you should heed your inclination if it has anything to do with a lack of motivation, for, certainly, being a successful director requires more commitment, energy and focus (not to mention skills, experience and integrity) than you might at first anticipate.

But if your cautious reticence is a matter of concern about the risks you may be taking, then there may be much you can do to allay or confirm your anxieties before you have to make a decision. No worthwhile company would wish you to give a snap response and, if circumstances mean that time is the essence, then a worthwhile company will be keen to address the issues you raise quickly, before you have to make your decision.

## What can you bring to the board? B10.35

Your analysis will need to have two facets. First, will you be able to make the contribution to the board that the board believes you can? Secondly, can you afford to take the risk of joining the board?

As far as the first is concerned, you already have an indication that someone (perhaps a number of people) believes you are likely to be the right person. It seems you have a good reputation which takes time to build but can be quickly lost. But you may know more about yourself than others do! You should know more than most others would about your personal impediments to being an effective director at this time and on this board. Especially you more than anyone is privy to your present and future circumstances, to those aspects of your business and personal life which are currently unfolding. For instance, if the board is intent upon you being one of their independent directors, do you know of any present of likely future impediment to you being so regarded?

While there is much contemporary criticism of how boards are perceived to select directors from a rather 'incestuous' closed circle of cronies, there is an almost forgivable rationale for this. Prospective directors have to be very careful about what boards they join, and companies equally have to be very cautious as to whom they welcome onto their boards. When the parties have known each other for a long time, they are less likely to make mistakes. When most of the parties are relative strangers, then there is a need for extra caution.

Being a director carries weighty responsibilities. In principle, each director is fully responsible for the direction and control of the company and for breaches in company and other law by the company. It is true that when courts apportion damages between directors they may take account of a director's background, qualifications and expertise which he or she held out as having. For instance, if you are a qualified accountant you may be judged as having a special responsibility for the financial and accounting affairs of the company, notwithstanding that you might be inclined to plead that you were 'only' a non-executive director.

## Personal risk B10.36

By joining a board you are risking your fortune as well as your reputation. You could find yourself party to behaviour which also could lead you to being disqualified from being a director. If you are already active in business you will know that you are often required to fill in forms which enquire whether you have been a director of a company than has gone into liquidation.

It may be appropriate for you to make arrangements to place your assets beyond the reach of any who may have claims against you for your involvement as a director of this company. In some circumstances, transfer of assets into a trust fund or into the name of your spouse, may achieve this, although perhaps not without some disadvantages and usually involving a time delay before this transfer is effective.

From your experience of running a business you know that management is not about taking no risks, but of taking risks in a controlled way. A pre-requisite is to know what are the risks. You should follow this same line of enquiry before accepting a position on a board. The risk you will be taking in joining a board will be all the greater if the company has no directors' indemnity insurance cover in place: you should enquire about this, the terms of the insurance policy and also consider whether the limit of the cover is likely to be sufficient. It would be wise to ask for a copy of the policy. When you have joined the board you should enquire regularly to ensure that this insurance cover remains in place.

Blue chip companies may be very well run and almost risk free for their directors, in comparison with small, private or start-up companies. It is usually true that the smaller company is unable to remunerate its directors (especially its non-executive directors) to the same extent as the blue chip company, despite the bigger risks involved for each director.

## The 'compensation package' B10.37

Best practice is that directors' remuneration is proportionate to the expertise and experience the director brings to the board, and his or her time commitment. It is not necessary that all non-executive directors receive the same remuneration though it is not uncommon that they do. Frequently a non-executive director will receive extra for membership of chairmanship of a board committee. Total boardroom costs should be proportionate with other business costs and with company performance. The prospective director should learn about these matters before accepting an appointment on a board and shy away from board involvement where the board is rewarding itself extravagantly.

You need to know what salaries and other elements of compensation which the other directors receive. You should also know about any outstanding loans to directors and whether any directors have unreasonably large outstanding expenses advances or significant unexplained company credit card transactions which may indicate an anarchic situation.

The solution for the small company which is unable to afford to compensate its non-executive directors for the extra risks they are taking, and often for the extra involvement they are expected to make, is often to allocate to a new director a small proportion of the company's equity. So, for instance, whereas a large listed company might pay a non-executive director an annual fee of £35,000 to £50,000, a very small company might pay an annual fee of £5,000 or £10,000 and provide an equity stake of between 1 per cent and 3 per cent of the issued share capital. It would be reasonable for the company to reserve the right to buy back this equity stake from the new non-executive director if his or her appointment on the board was terminated early due to unsatisfactory performance, but it is important that the terms of this buy-back are set out in advance. The director who is allocated this small equity stake will need to have a exit route defined which will allow him or her to realise the value of these shares at some future date.

## Tax implications                                        B10.38

You should budget personally for any income tax implications of receiving an equity stake in the company in lieu of director's fees. The tax authorities are likely to value this stake for income tax purposes according to their estimate of its value at the time it was allocated to you, which is not easy to determine for a company that is not listed. Any other purchases of shares in the company by other people at about the same time may be held by the tax authorities as an indication of the value of your stake —so be aware of the possible implications of the value of your small stake if any investor has invested heavily in the company recently but been granted only a modest equity stake – as may be the case if a new executive director has recently joined the board.

## Shareholders' agreement                                 B10.39

The issue of shareholdings in private companies should be covered in the shareholders' agreement. For instance, this agreement will set out the circumstances and terms under which a shareholder's shares will be bought back from the shareholder in the event that the person's involvement with the company is ended. The right time to ensure that there is a satisfactory shareholders' agreement is when the company is set up in the first place, and a prospective director should be very cautious about accepting a position on the board if there is no shareholder's agreement, or if it is inadequate. So the prospective director should be given a copy of the shareholders' agreement and should study it before accepting a position on the board – whether or not he or she is being offered a shareholding. The prospective director should similarly require a copy of the memorandum and articles of association.

## Learning about the company                              B10.40

You need to learn as much as you can about the company who wants you on their board, before you decide whether to accept their invitation.

As soon as the invitation reaches you, you should not overlook that, in the invitation itself you are starting to learn significant things about the company.

First, who was it who invited you to join the board? If it was not the chairman, was there a good reason why the task was deputed to another? Or does it mean that the chairman is not in control of the board which is possibly indicative of a poorly run, disunited board. If it is the chairman who has approached you, try to ascertain whether the rest of the board has given prior concurrence to the approach: if not, it could be a warning that all is not well with the board.

## Why you? B10.41

If, however, the way the overture has been made to you does not sound any alarm bells as a bad omen for the future, you can immediately pursue the matter further by enquiring why the board wants you to join them. No worthwhile company will approach someone to join the board without very careful analysis of the company's requirements and the qualities of the prospective director. In your estimation, do you fit that profile?

You should not be put off if you are one of a shortlist being approached about just one vacancy on the board – this reveals prudent caution by the board and a determination to have both the strongest and most compatible board possible.

You should also be able quickly get a feel as to why the board thinks you are the right person. What particular skills and experience of yours are they looking for? You need to learn about the skills and experience of the other board members and satisfy yourself that what you will bring to the party is not already provided in abundance by other board members. This gives you the opportunity too to satisfy yourself that the board is a balanced board which is likely to meet the needs of the business into the future.

## The right skills B10.42

Apart from the skills and experience that the board is looking for in yourself, the board may also be intending that you take on special responsibilities, such as the chairing of a board committee, and you should consider whether their intention, and the timing of it, are appropriate in view of your strengths, weaknesses and initial time availability. Furthermore, if there are other members on the board who appear to have the requisite skills and experience for this additional responsibility, what is the significance that they are being passed over?

## Time commitment B10.43

Clearly you need to assess the time commitment which will be involved. In addition to scheduled board meetings and board committee meetings there are likely to be unscheduled board meetings and informal board meetings to attend, and you may be required to attend at the company for other reasons. For instance, the chairman of the audit committee may wish to meet with internal and external auditors and with the secretary of the committee between meetings on occasion. If a change of external auditor is contemplated, there are likely to be presentations to attend from the firms tendering for the work and so on. Many companies have a weekend away for the board once a year to consider strategy.

A practical problem may be that you have other regular commitments which clash with the companies standard date for board meetings, for example, too many companies seem to choose the last Friday of the month for this purpose! If you are right for the company and the company needs you, then the company is likely to be willing to try to rearrange their preferred date for board meetings so as to avoid clashes with your prior appointments. It is not unreasonable for you, as a prospective director, to point out that there you have diary clashes at least initially. It is certainly important that you 'come clean' in advance of accepting a board position if it appears that there will be significant clashes with other commitments into the future, and this needs to be resolved before you accept the invitation to join the board. It is a sensible idea for the company to issue its planned board and board committee dates on a rolling basis for as full year forward. You will find as a director that careful diary maintenance is important

## Is the board in control?                                               B10.44

In getting to grips with the issue as to whether you will be able to give the company the attention you should, you will also be able to assess whether the board meets sufficiently often to discharge its responsibilities thoroughly, which is essential. This will vary between companies, but a fairly standard norm is a monthly board meeting or possibly a formal board meeting every other month, alternating with an informal board meeting in each of the intervening months. Audit committees which meet fewer times than four a-year may be ineffective and it is certainly unwise that they should meet, for instance, at nine in the morning before the main board meets on the same morning at ten.

You would be imprudent not to enquire whether any of the directors has a criminal record or has in the past been a director of a company that have failed, or has been declared bankrupt or come to an arrangement with his or her creditors. This is one of the many issues you will want clarification about before you join the board, and will need to have it in writing for it to be worthwhile.

## Succession planning                                                     B10.45

If from your enquiries you form the view that the board is being forward looking in its succession planning, then this is good news. The corollary will be concerning: a board that has no planned turnover of its membership is likely to be an ossified board. So it is reasonable to enquire about planned board succession, and about the duration and end dates of directors' contracts.

In general a well run board will have arranged things so that something like one-third of the board appointments come up for termination or renewal annually, and it would be a matter of concern if a director's contract allowed compensation amounting to more than one year's compensation. You should enquire as to the significant terms within each director's contract, and ascertain whether, when you join a board, a copy of each director's contract will be made available to you.

## Financial and management accounting matters          B10.46

Once you are a member of the board, you will quickly appreciate how important the accounting processes and accounting information of the business are to its board of directors. 'Flaky' management accounts can mean that the board is uncertain whether or not the business is solvent and thus whether the company is trading illegally – which is a solemn responsibility of each director to avoid. 'Flaky' management accounts will be an inadequate basis for decision making at the board and will almost inevitably lead to the decline of the company.

There is much that you can do before you join the board to assess whether you are likely to have problems with management accounts and financial statements when you are a member of the board. It would be sensible to ask for a copy of the last two sets of audited financial statements; this will give you comparative figures for the past three years. If the company has a very small turnover, in some legislations it may have chosen not to have an annual audit, in which case this leaves you, as a prospective director in a vulnerable position unless you can satisfy yourself in other ways as to the reliability of the financial statements. Without an audit, all you can be reasonably sure about is that the financial statements which have been returned to the authorities are compiled consistently with the underlying accounting records, not that those accounting records are reliable.

Except for the smallest of companies, it should not improve your confidence if the annual audit has been done by a very small firm, or perhaps by a sole practitioner.

Of course you will endeavour to interpret the audited financial statements. Any qualification to the audit opinion will weigh upon you. If the date of the audit report is more than three months after the end of the year, you may interpret this as being inefficient and worrying: if such a practice continued after you joined the board it would mean that you would be delayed in getting the reassurance that the audited financial statements may give you. You will look for trends over the years for which you have been given the figures. You will observe the level of profitability of the company and the extent to which its assets exceed its liabilities, having regard to the size of the business. It would be wise, if possible, to work out a few key accounting ratios and to observe the trends in these over time. If you decide to join the board, you can be surprisingly effective at board meetings if you continue to monitor changes in these key ratios over time.

The quality of the regular monthly management accounts is very important. You should ask to see examples from the recent past, including the most recent. For a small company, at a minimum they should include an up-to-date balance sheet, profit and loss account, cash flow projection; and, for each of the important items for this company, the management accounts should show monthly results and 'cumulatives' for the year-to-date compared to budgets, with projected outturns for the financial year.

You should have regard for how long it appears to take to produce these monthly accounts, whether a following month's management accounts appear to start with the closing figures reported for the previous month, and for the quality of the chief accountant's or financial director's narrative interpretation of these figures. Be particularly wary of any indications that the company has become too tightly extended with regard to its cash flow: indications of this may include the factoring of its debts, high levels of loans, overdue accounts, etc. Although it should not be your chief concern, if cash flow is unhealthy, it could mean that you will experience difficulty in extracting from the company your agreed director's fees. It would be sensible to ensure that you have in writing what your remuneration will be and the dates on which payment will be made.

You should be worried if tax payments are being delayed: check if the company is incurring any penalties from the taxation authorities. What you are less likely to learn about from scrutiny of management accounts is the possibility of unrecorded liabilities, but you can ask the chief executive and the finance director directly for assurances on this score. You should also check if the company is engaged in any significant legal disputes or is aware that it has breached any covenants in its contracts or of any significant claims made, or likely to be made against the company. Ask the company if they have a disputed accounts file and, if so, request to peruse it. Be wary of accounting practices which seem dubious and too clever by half.

Remember, financial statements which are published are the directors' financial statements (not the auditors') and so, if you join the board you will shortly be subscribing to a set of annual financial statements. You should be very cautious about joining if the monthly accounts to the board give you little confidence about the company's capability to prepare reliable accounts.

# Conduct of board meetings B10.47

In general it should be entirely reasonable for you to ask to see the agenda papers and minutes of recent board meetings. You may leave this request until just before you are ready to accept the invitation to join the board as companies may reasonably be reluctant to share this information with a distant, uncommitted suitor. There may be justification for certain items to be omitted from what you are permitted to see, but it is desirable that you know the general nature of these and the reasons why they were omitted. For instance, one agenda item is likely to have been the board's consideration of the pros and cons of inviting you to join the board; you should be concerned if that were not the case as it means that the board minutes are an incomplete record of the directors' deliberations on board business.

When you study these agenda papers and minutes you will learn much about the affairs of the company which will help to get you up to speed more quickly.

You will also have the opportunity to conclude much about how the board conducts its business by asking the following questions.

- Do agenda papers reach board members in sufficient time before meetings for them to be thoroughly prepared?

- Do the executive directors regularly provide written reports to the board within the agenda pack which is circulated to directors in good time in advance of the meetings?

- Do agenda papers appear to be competently written and cover in sufficient detail the items upon which the board needs to be informed and as a basis for the decisions to be taken?

- Do the board agenda papers include minutes of the board committees?

- Are the right sort of items on the agendas of board meetings? For instance, is the board attending to its core business, or is it preoccupied with other matters such as new ventures, etc.

- Are the minutes of the board issued reasonably promptly?

- Do the board minutes and board committee minutes appear to cover in sufficient detail the key points of discussion that took place in the meetings, in addition to decisions arrived at?

- Do later meetings appear to adequately follow-up upon items outstanding from earlier meetings and decisions taken at earlier meetings?

- Is attendance by directors good?

Every board should have a schedule of matters reserved to the board, and this should have been adopted by formal board resolution. You should ask for a copy of this and ask yourself whether there are any significant omissions from it. Bear in mind that matters not contained therein may be matters which will not come to the board for decision. The board needs to be in control of the company.

Some companies get into difficulties through failing to keep abreast with statutory requirements such as registering promptly with the authorities any changes in board membership, failing to issue share certificates in accordance with board decisions to issue shares, and failing to lodge annual financial statements within the stipulated time. Your own search where financial statements, etc. are lodged may be informative.

You will want to meet most or all of the directors individually before you accept the invitation to join the board. They should wish to meet you. Try to discern if there is tension between board members; a board riven with dissent is best avoided. Discretely try to gauge the opinion of board members as to the calibre and commitment of their colleagues.

Clearly you will need to see and finalise your director's contract before joining the board. This should not be a problem, but if it is, then there is probably a deeper problem within the company.

If you decide to join the board, you will probably be aware of your limitations as a new board member. With the chairman and chief executive, you should endeavour to identify the training you need, and obtain their agreement to that taking place. It may involve attendance at outside courses, not just initially but at other times during the tenure of your directorship. You should also ask that an induction programme for you should be arranged so that you can meet the key players within the company and visit the key operations within the first month or two of you joining the board.

## Considering joining a board? B10.48

**Checklist of matters to be considered** **B10.49**

| **Suggested principal** | Y = | **Your responsibility to ascertain/decide** |
|---|---|---|
| **method of enquiry:** | W = | **In writing from the company** |
| | V = | **Verbally from the company** |

| | Timing and method of enquiry | | |
|---|---|---|---|
| **Issue to be addressed** | **At outset** | **During negotiations** | **Before acceptance** |
| **1.    You personally** | | | |
| 1.1    Ascertain why you are being asked to join the board. | | W | |
| 1.2    If you are being sought because of a particular expertise, will you be able to give that expertise to the company in the way they need it? | | | Y |
| 1.3    Have you the motivation for this appointment? | | | Y |
| 1.4    Will you be able to devote the required time, not just for meetings but for preparation as well? | | | Y |
| 1.5    Obtain dates of future meetings and check and resolve any significant diary clashes. | | W | |

| Issue to be addressed | Timing and method of enquiry | | |
|---|---|---|---|
| | At outset | During negotiations | Before acceptance |
| 1.6 Do you think you have, or can acquire, the skills you will need? | | | Y |
| 1.7 Is there anything in your background which makes you unsuitable to accept a directorship? | Y | | |
| 1.8 Is there anything in your circumstances which you should draw to the attention of the board before accepting, such as a potential conflict of interest? | | Y (in writing) | |
| 1.9 If the board is relying upon you to be an independent non-executive director, would that be the case? | | Y | |
| 1.10 Are your personal assets sufficiently protected from being claimed against in the case of legal actions against the directors of the company whose board you are considering joining? | | | Y |
| 1.11 Have you planned for your tax liabilities which may result from accepting this position (eg liability to pay tax on any share allocation you may be granted)? | | | Y |
| 1.12 Does the company have sufficient directors' indemnity insurance cover? | | | W |

| | Timing and method of enquiry | | |
|---|---|---|---|
| **Issue to be addressed** | **At outset** | **During negotiations** | **Before acceptance** |
| **2.   Your duties and your development** | | | |
| 2.1   Are you clear, and are you satisfied, as to the board's intentions of the contribution you can make? | | W | |
| 2.2   Have you been told which board committees you will be asked to belong to, and whether it is the intention that you will chair any of these, initially or later? | | V | |
| 2.3   Is the company arranging an induction programme for you? | | V | |
| 2.4   Is the company committed to developing you through training courses, and have your development needs been identified? | | V | |
| 2.5   Even as a non-executive director, will your performance be subject to annual appraisal? | | V | |
| **3.   Contractual matters** | | | |
| 3.1   Is the intended compensation package for you (fees, allocation of shares, etc) appropriate? | | | Y |
| 3.2   Is there a written contract covering your post as director, and is it satisfactory? | | | W/Y |
| 3.3   Does the intended contract specify the duration of your appointment and whether it is open to renewal thereafter? | | | W |
| 3.4   Does the intended contract specify the fees you will receive and their dates of payment? | | | W |

| | Timing and method of enquiry | | |
|---|---|---|---|
| **Issue to be addressed** | **At outset** | **During negotiations** | **Before acceptance** |
| 3.5 Are there any matters in the contracts of other directors of the company which cause you concern? | | W/Y | |
| 3.6 Is there a shareholders' agreement, and is it satisfactory? | | W/Y | |
| **4. The company** | | | |
| 4.1 Are you clear as to the principal risks the company faces? | | | Y |
| 4.2 Have you visited the company and its key sites? | | | Y |
| 4.3 Have you inspected the constitutional documents of the company (eg, Memorandum and Articles of Association)? | | | Y/W |
| **5. The board** | | | |
| 5.1 Was it the board that has decided you should be invited to join the board? | Y | | |
| 5.2 Have you met the board members prior to making a decision to join the board, and learnt about their backgrounds? | | | Y |
| 5.3 Do you consider the board to be balanced, competent and committed? | | Y | |
| 5.4 Does the board have proper succession planning for board positions? | | Y/V | |
| 5.5 Do the board and its committees meet sufficiently frequently, and for sufficient time? | | Y | |

|  | Timing and method of enquiry | | |
|---|---|---|---|
| **Issue to be addressed** | **At outset** | **During negotiations** | **Before acceptance** |
| 5.6  Is there a schedule of matters reserved to the board, and does it seem appropriate? |  | W/Y |  |
| **6.  Board agendas and minutes** |  |  |  |
| 6.1  From what you have seen, does attendance at board meetings seem good? |  | Y |  |
| 6.2  Do agenda papers appear to reach board members in sufficient time before meetings for them to be thoroughly prepared? |  | Y |  |
| 6.3  Do the executive directors appear to regularly provide written reports to the board – within the agenda pack which is circulated to directors in good time in advance of the meetings? |  | Y |  |
| 6.4  Do agenda papers appear to be competently written and cover in sufficient detail the items upon which the board needs to be informed and as a basis for the decisions to be taken?  Do the board agenda papers include minutes of the board committees? |  | Y |  |
| 6.5  Are the right sort of items on the agendas of board meetings? For instance, is the board attending to its core business, or is it preoccupied with other matters – such as new ventures, etc. |  | Y |  |

| | Timing and method of enquiry | | |
|---|---|---|---|
| **Issue to be addressed** | **At outset** | **During negotiations** | **Before acceptance** |
| 6.6  Are the minutes of the board issued reasonably promptly? | | Y | |
| 6.7  Do the board minutes and board committee minutes appear to cover in sufficient detail the key points of discussion that took place in the meetings, in addition to decisions arrived at? | | Y | |
| 6.8  Do later meetings appear to adequately follow-up upon items outstanding from earlier meetings and decisions taken at earlier meetings? | | Y | |
| **7.  The financials of the company** | | | |
| 7.1  Have you seen and studied the last two years audited financial statements, and do they indicate any matters of concern? | | Y | |
| 7.2  Are total boardroom costs reasonable? | | Y | |
| 7.3  Are there any outstanding loans and advances to other directors which should cause you concern? | | | W/Y |
| 7.4  Does the board receive regular, up-to-date, sufficient and apparently reliable management accounts with a narrative interpretation of their key points? | | Y | |

| Issue to be addressed | Timing and method of enquiry | | |
|---|---|---|---|
| | At outset | During negotiations | Before acceptance |
| 7.5  Do the financial statements and the latest management accounts of the company indicate a healthy position and prospects? | | | Y |
| 7.6  Does the company have any significant outstanding claims or contingent liabilities? | | | W/Y |
| 7.7  Does the company have a cash flow problem? | | Y | |
| 7.8  Is the company solvent? | | Y | |
| 7.9  Is the company up-to-date with its payment of tax liabilities? | | | W/Y |

'Hermes Guide for Shareholders and Independent Outside Directors' (see **B10.79**) has some useful advice on induction meetings and meetings subsequent to induction.

# Outside advice for directors at the company's expense
**B10.50**

The Principles and Supporting Principles within the 2003 Combined Code (see PART A) are intended to be mandatory for UK listed companies. The more detailed Provisions of the Combined Code, which nest below the Principles are not mandatory. The Listing Rules require a statement in the annual report explaining how the Principles and Supporting Principles have been followed. The Listing Rules also require a statement explaining whether or not all of the Provisions have been observed and, if not, which Provisions have not been followed and why not.

For most companies, observing the Provisions is likely to be appropriate as contributing to adhering to the Principles, though the Hampel Committee was at pains to point out that 'box ticking' compliance with Provisions will not amount to adherence to the Principles. Nevertheless, most companies take the line that compliance with the Provisions is sensible. Indeed, in the previous Cadbury Code there were no Principles, only Provisions which carried the same optional status as the Provisions in the Combined Code.

To obtain an understanding of what is regarded as best practice, it is still now necessary to draw upon both the Cadbury and Hampel Committees' Reports and respective Codes. This is in part because it appears that Hampel omitted, while not apparently intending to overturn, certain content of Cadbury, which we refer to below. of course, it is also necessary to draw upon the FRC's new 2003 Code publication which we reproduce in **PART A**.

Principle A.1 of the 2003 Combined Code stipulates that:

'Every listed company should be headed by an effective board which is collectively responsible for the success of the company.'

Provision A.5.2 reads:

'The board should ensure that directors, especially non-executive directors, have access to independent professional advice at the company's expense where they judge it necessary to discharge their responsibilities as directors. Committees should be provided with sufficient resources to undertake their duties.'

Note that the first part of this Provision is targeted at each individual director – whether executive or non-executive, but especially the non-executive directors. Note too that there are also other Provisions designed to ensure that individual directors perform in a competent way; a major feature of the 2003 Code is the new stress that is placed on the selection, competence, commitment and evaluation of the performance of individual directors.

Note further that board committees, not just individual directors, should be mandated to seek independent advice in the furtherance of their responsibilities. However, there was no reference in any part of the 1998 Combined Code, nor in the Hampel report itself, to the nominations and audit committees needing to be empowered to take outside professional advice, though such authority would certainly be desirable. n the other hand, the Cadbury Report (though not its Code of Best Practice) contained the following:

'The audit committee should have explicit authority to investigate any matters within its terms of reference, the resources which it needs to do so, and full access to information. The committee should be able to obtain external professional advice and to invite outsiders with relevant experience to attend if necessary.'

and, within the specimen terms of reference for an audit committee, which the Cadbury Report recommended:

'The Committee is authorised by the Board to obtain outside legal or other independent professional advice and to secure the attendance of outsiders with relevant experience and expertise if it considers this necessary.'

and, for remuneration committees:

'We recommend that boards should appoint remuneration committees, consisting wholly or mainly of non-executive directors and chaired by a non-executive director, to recommend to the board the remuneration of the executive directors in all its forms, drawing on outside advice as necessary.'

In one respect the Combined Code is an advance from the earlier Cadbury Code. While there were these recommendations within the body of the Cadbury Report that remuneration and audit committees should be empowered to take outside advice at the company's expense, there was no provision on this in the Cadbury Code whereas the Hampel Committee's Combined Code does provide for this, but only in the context of remuneration committees.

The Combined Code Provision that

'There should be a procedure agreed by the board for directors in the furtherance of their duties to take independent professional advice if necessary at the company's expense.'

represented a sharpening of the wording of the equivalent Provision' in the Cadbury Code, which had read:

'There should be an agreed procedure for directors in the furtherance of their duties to take independent professional advice if necessary, at the company's expense.' [1]

So it is now clear from the Combined Code Provision that the procedure must be agreed by the board in some way. The Cadbury report had indicated as much in the body of that report, though not in the Cadbury Code, in wording (or equivalent wording) which is absent from the Hampel report, *viz:*

'**Professional Advice**

Occasions may arise when directors have to seek legal and financial advice in the furtherance of their duties. They should always be able to consult the company's advisers. If, however, they consider it necessary to take independent professional advice, **we recommend** that they should be entitled to do so at the company's expense, through an agreed procedure laid down formally, for example in a Board Resolution, in the Articles, or in the Letter of Appointment.' [2]

The 1998 Code ( Provision B.2.5) with respect to remuneration committees had stated:

'Remuneration committees should consult the chairman and/or chief executive officer about their proposals relating to the remuneration of other executive directors and have access to professional advice inside and outside the company.'

But this specific wording has been lost from the 2003 Code where Provision A.5.2 merely states (see above):

' ... Committees should be provided with sufficient resources to undertake their duties.'

It is true that the Smith Report, in guidance which has not been incorporated into the 2003 Code itself states (see paragraph 2.15 of the Smith Report contained in PART A):

> 'The board should make funds available to the audit committee to enable it to take independent legal, accounting and other advice when the audit committee reasonably believes it necessary to do so.'

And the new Code publication includes, in its 'Summary of the principal duties of the nomination committee' (see PART A):

> 'The committee should make a statement in the annual report about its activities; the process used for appointments and explain if external advice or open advertising has not been used ... '

and in a similar section on remuneration committees, that:

> 'The committee should be exclusively responsible for establishing the section criteria, selecting, appointing and setting the terms of reference for any remuneration consultants who advise the committee.'

To sum up, in earlier Codes there has been more stress than in the present 2003 Code on the need for board committees to be empowered to take outside advice. Such a suggestion has now been relegated to the level of supporting guidance with respect to each of the three standard board committees (audit, remuneration and nomination).

Here we reproduce the policy statement which one UK listed company has developed to cover the issue of individual directors taking independent professional advice if necessary at the company's expense. The footnotes are our elaboration upon some of the content of the policy statement, but they did not form part of the policy statement itself. In particular we draw readers attention to footnote 14 on whether the scope of the advice which may be sought under this policy should be restricted in any way – perhaps to advice on one's responsibilities in law as a director, or advice only of legal and accounting matters in general.

## Independent professional advice for directors    B10.51

### Standing guidelines    B10.52

(Adapted from existing guidelines of a major multinational company)

1.  The board recognises that as is recommended in corporate governance best practice, directors should be able to take independent professional advice, at the expense of the company, in the event that circumstances warrant it.

2.  This facility is intended to provide directors with a 'safety net' to be used when they feel that a second opinion is necessary on a particular matter, over and above the advice available to them through the normal channels.

3. This facility should not be used lightly, and consequently it is difficult to anticipate all the circumstances under which a director would find it necessary to seek independent counsel. Whilst it is not mandatory, a director who finds him or herself in a position which, in the director's judgement, warrants independent advice being taken, should consider first raising the matter with the chair of the audit committee who may be in a position to resolve the matter through the channels of that committee.

4. The limit on the amount of costs which may be incurred by any director on an annual basis is £10,000. This amount may be varied at any time by board resolution.

5. There is no obligation for a director to disclose the nature of the advice sought or given. He or she is only obliged to confirm that the advice was sought in the context of his or her position as a director of XYZ Ltd.

6. A director who seeks to invoke this policy should instruct the independent advisor (law firm etc) to address invoices to:

c/o the Secretary to the Audit Committee

The Group Chief Audit Executive,

XYZ Ltd,

(Address).

## Further information

1. In this policy statement, the term 'directors' referred exclusively to members of the board of XYZ Ltd and not to directors of any other group companies.

2. It was the Cadbury Code of Best Practice which first used the expression 'independent professional advice' (provision 1.5 at **B3.4**) in this context, but elsewhere in the Cadbury Report (paragraph 4.18) this was referred to as 'legal or financial advice'. It is up to boards to decide whether the scope of this advice should be broader than legal and financial: in view of the terms of reference of Cadbury it is reasonable to take the view that Cadbury's recommendation was limited to 'legal and financial' advice but this is not to say that Cadbury would have disapproved of a company broadening the scope beyond 'legal and financial'. It may be, for instance, that a director in the furtherance of his or her duties might feel a need for independent advice on human resource or IT issues: couching the query in legal and/or financial terms he or she could consult lawyers and/or accountants to obtain this advice. They in turn might consult other specialists. Or authority might exist for the director to consult the appropriate specialist directly.

3. Resolution in this way may either be that the audit committee takes the professional advice itself (perhaps by action of the chair) or that the chair prevails upon the director concerned that the advice should be taken openly at the company's expense and available to all board members.

4. In addition, some companies permit a higher spend subject to prior approval of the company chairman.

5. The implication of this address is that the secretary to the audit committee is the group chief audit executive. Ideally the secretary of the audit committee should be the company secretary as (a) the committee is a committee of the main board and (b) it is preferable that the secretary to this committee is not a person whose performance it is critical that the audit committee appraises.

6. It is not necessary that the audit committee need be involved as per para 3 (above) or with respect to payment. It could alternatively be the company chairman, or the senior non-executive director (where there is one) or the company secretary.

# Criteria for defining independence          B10.54

The ABI/IVIS criteria for assessing non-executive director independence are also to be found with slightly different wording in Appendix One of the section of this handbook, 'Combined Code – IVIS monitoring checklist' (see **B7.3**) and the similar NAPF ones in the section entitled 'NAPF's voting policy' (see **B7.4**).

Except in the most general of terms, even Cadbury sold the pass on defining independence, explaining only that independent directors are 'independent of management and free from any business or other relationship which could materially interfere with the exercise of their independent judgement' and that 'it is for the board to decide in particular cases whether this definition is met'.[3] The Hampel Report concurred, adding that the board 'could be called on to justify its decision'.

'The Cadbury Committee recommended that a majority of non-executive directors should be independent, and defined this as 'independent of management and free from any business or other relationship which could materially interfere with the exercise of their independent judgement' (report 4.12). We agree with this definition, and after careful consideration we do not consider that it is practicable to lay down more precise criteria for independence. We agree with Cadbury that it should be for the board to take a view on whether an individual director is independent in the above sense. The corollary is that boards should disclose in the annual report which of the directors are considered to be independent and be prepared to justify their view if challenged. We recognise, however, that non-executive directors who are not in this sense 'independent' may nonetheless make a useful contribution to the board.' [4]

Sir Adrian Cadbury has said (1998):

'The presence of independent members of boards does not imply that they have inherently higher standards of morality than their executive colleagues. It is simply that it is easier for them to take an objective view of whatever matters are under review. They stand further back from the

517

action, they bring outside standards to bear on the issues and their interests are less directly at stake. The argument for independent members of professional disciplinary bodies rests on the same grounds.'

There is nothing quite like the notion of 'independence' to rattle the timbers of the non-executive director. To pin it down has been like nailing a jelly to the ceiling. Higgs noted that so many different and often inconsistent lists of criteria of independence had been developed by institutional investors and others that it was time to incorporate a standard list into the revised Combined Code content itself with the rather general wording which used to be contained within Provision A.3.2 of the 1998 Code:

'The majority of non-executive directors should be independent of management and free from any business or other relationship which could materially interfere with the exercise of their independent judgement. Non-executive directors considered by the board to be independent in this sense should be identified in the annual report.'

## The 2003 Code on independence                                       B10.55

We reproduce here the Principles and Provisions in the 2003 Combined Code which relate most directly to the concept of director independence.

---

**A.1     The board**

**Main Principle   Every company should be headed by an effective board, which is collectively responsible for the success of the company.**

**Code Provisions**

**A.1.2**   The annual report should identify the chairman, the deputy chairman (where there is one), the chief executive, the senior independent director and the chairmen and members of the nomination, audit and remuneration committees. It should also set out the number of meetings of the board and those committees and individual attendance by directors.

**A.1.3**   The chairman should hold meetings with the non-executive directors without the executives present. Led by the senior independent director, the non-executive directors should meet without the chairman present at least annually to appraise the chairman's performance (as described in A.6.1) and on such other occasions as are deemed appropriate.

**A.2     Chairman and chief executive**

**Main Principle   There should be a clear division of responsibilities at the head of the company between the running of the board and the executive responsibility for the running of the company's business. No one individual should have unfettered powers of decision.**

---

518

A.2.2[5]   The chairman should on appointment meet the independence criteria set out in A.3.1 below. A chief executive should not go on to be chairman of the same company. If exceptionally a board decides that a chief executive should become chairman, the board should consult major shareholders in advance and should set out its reasons to shareholders at the time of the appointment and in the next annual report.

## A.3     Board balance and independence

**Main Principle**   **The board should include a balance of executive and non-executive directors (and in particular independent non-executive directors) such that no individual or small group of individuals can dominate the board's decision taking.**

### Supporting Principles

To ensure that power and information are not concentrated in one or two individuals, there should be a strong presence on the board of both executive and non-executive directors.

### Code provisions

A.3.1   The board should identify in the annual report each non-executive director it considers to be independent[6]. The board should determine whether the director is independent in character and judgement and whether there are relationships or circumstances which are likely to affect, or could appear to affect, the director's judgement. The board should state its reasons if it determines that a director is independent notwithstanding the existence of relationships or circumstances which may appear relevant to its determination, including if the director:

- has been an employee of the company or group within the last five years;

- has, or has had within the last three years, a material business relationship with the company either directly, or as a partner, shareholder, director or senior employee of a body that has such a relationship with the company;

- has received or receives additional remuneration from the company apart from a director's fee, participates in the company's share option or a performance-related pay scheme, or is a member of the company's pension scheme;

- has close family ties with any of the company's advisers, directors or senior employees;

- holds cross-directorships or has significant links with other directors through involvement in other companies or bodies;

- represents a significant shareholder; or

- has served on the board for more than nine years from the date of their first election.

**A.3.2**   Except for smaller companies[7], at least half the board, excluding the chairman, should comprise non-executive directors determined by the board to be independent. A smaller company should have at least two independent non-executive directors.

**A.3.3**   The board should appoint one of the independent non-executive directors to be the senior independent director. The senior independent director should be available to shareholders if they have concerns which contact through the normal channels of chairman, chief executive or finance director has failed to resolve or for which such contact is inappropriate.

**Principle**   **Companies should establish a formal and transparent procedure for developing policy on executive remuneration and for fixing the remuneration packages of individual directors. No director should be involved in deciding his or her own remuneration.**

**Code Provisions**

**B.2.1**   To avoid potential conflicts of interest, boards of directors should set up remuneration committees of independent non-executive directors to make recommendations to the board, within agreed terms of reference, on the company's framework of executive remuneration and its cost: and to determine on their behalf specific remuneration packages for each of the executive directors, including pension rights and any compensation payments.

**B.2.2**   Remuneration committees should consist exclusively of non-executive directors who are independent of management and free from any business or other relationship which could materially interfere with the exercise of their independent judgement.

**Principle**   **The board should establish formal and transparent arrangements for considering how they should apply the financial reporting and internal control principles and for maintaining an appropriate relationship with the company's auditors.**

**Code Provisions**

**D.3.1**   The board should establish an audit committee of at least three directors, all non-executive, with written terms of reference which deal clearly with its authority and duties. The members of the committee, a majority of whom should be independent non-executive directors, should be named in the report and accounts.

It is notable that absent from the 2003 Code's list of criteria is the age bar (age 70) which many other lists of criteria had included.

## Cadbury Committee survey                                           B10.56

When the Cadbury Committee reconvened to review compliance with its Code it cited the following barriers to independence while conceding that this view of independence might run contrary to the views of some boards and their auditors:

- a close relative of an executive director;

- a connection with the company exceeding 20 years;

- formerly an executive director; or

- an employee of the company.

Its survey also concluded rather bravely that the majority of non-executive directors are independent.

In the interests of pragmatism, Cadbury had compromised on the principle of independence by conceding that independent directors might hold shares in the enterprise and receive directors' fees. Of course, there are examples of non-executive directors receiving no fee. Take, for instance, those on the boards of Training and Enterprise Councils which existed until 2001. It is difficult to avoid the conclusion that the government deemed it unnecessary to offer them fees as many TEC directors had an interest in their TEC through their positions in the local community – often as directors of major, local business partners of their TEC. Do related party transactions impede independence? 1998 Combined Code Provision A.3.2 (see **B3.11** above) implied that they might, as does A.3.1 in the 2003 Code (see **B10.55** above).

## Non-director independence                                          B10.57

We sometimes use the expression 'outside director' to lay emphasis upon the independent credentials of most non-executive directors. In some contexts the complete outsider (who is not also a director) may bring an even greater degree of independence. For instance, for several years until 2002 the audit committee of the church commissioners had a chairman who was not a member of the board. The chairs of many audit committees in the public sector are often not members of the board, and indeed the responsibilities carried collectively by the board of a company are often enshrined within the personal responsibilities of a single accounting offer. Cadbury and Hampel made no provision for any non-director to be a member of an audit committee. Note that the 2003 Combined Code includes at the level of a Provision, a 'requirement' that every member of the audit committee should be an independent director whereas previously, while all should have been non-executive, only a majority were 'required' to be independent. Undoubtedly, the complete outsider who is not a member of the board brings to bear an extra degree of independence, but has the disadvantage of not necessarily being privy to all aspects of board business, and thus having an extra challenge to be fully aware of all the issues which may be of importance to the audit committee. Such an independent chairman of the audit committee would need to be 'in attendance' at board meetings, or parts thereof, in order to present the report of the audit committee. Many audit committees report to the board by tabling their minutes as part of the board agenda papers. In addition, or alternatively, audit committees may make to the board an 'annual report of the audit committee' or a six-monthly report.

It is considered that an independent director is always, by definition, a non-executive director. It is implied as being axiomatic that being an executive clouds one's independence of judgement, though in reality this may depend more upon personality, attitude of mind, background, ability and access to information. At the board every director is required to put partisan executive interest to one side. The true independence of the executive director may only become apparent following resignation on a point of principle. Here we reach another truism: independence is in the eye of the beholder: independent directors must be seen and believed to be independent. Of course, no-one would argue that an executive director is entirely independent of the executive, but many would argue that there is no such thing as complete independence for anyone and that independence depends upon much else besides the formal role of the individual concerned.

## Tests of independence                                    B10.58

Most understand that the independent director is something more than a non-executive director. What exactly, defies definition? However, the new 2003 Code now gives us a standard list of criteria (see above). We might cheerfully conclude that the non-executive director who is the spouse of the chief executive is not independent of the executive; but who is to say? What of the non-executive director who went to school or college with the chief executive; or who is the godmother of the chief executive's daughter; or who is an executive director on a second board to which the chief executive of the first board belongs in a non-executive capacity?

In truth non-executive directors who fail most of the formal tests of independence may still in reality be the most independent of directors who are often much more capable of standing up to over-powerful, misguided executives. Their closer social ties to one or more executives may have removed their fear of taking a stand at odds with the viewpoint of those people. And personality and other personal attributes can in practice by far outweigh impediments to independence posed by social and other ties.

Contrariwise, the non-executive director who has no links with any executives may in practice be far from independent. This might be so if he or she did not have the personal courage to stand up and be counted; possibly through a meek temperament or on account of significant dependence upon the income which the directorship attracts.

Not least of the threats to effective independence is an incapability to master the issues that confront the board. This leads to dependency upon an executive who may be pulling the wool over that director's eyes. Failure to master issues may be a consequence of several factors. Incomplete information may be given to the board which could be too late to influence decisions: in such cases executive directors may be better placed than non-executive directors to form objective judgements. So, independence does not necessarily enhance objectivity, though it is largely for that reason that independence is valued. So much information might come to the board that core issues are obscured. The background of the non-executive director may be inappropriate to master technical fundamentals. Or the non-executive director may be unwilling or unable to put in the time to master the affairs of the business and the business of board meetings.

Higgs has endeavoured to cover these concerns in Provision A.3.1 by stressing that, in addition to the list of independence criteria, an independent director is one who is 'independent' in character and judgement' and it is 'for the board to determine' this based, of course, upon their knowledge of the personal attributes of the individual director concerned.

A non-executive director who passes these tests with flying colours as far as main board business is concerned may fail lamentably when it comes to the intricacies of audit committee business. Of course, it is true that those with a non-financial, non-accounting background can achieve a workable degree of independent judgement even when quite technical accounting matters are being debated and decided upon. Yet audit committees are frequently addressing frontier issues, for instance the impact of new accounting standards, and it may be too much to expect the lay person to follow the arguments. Indeed if lay people insist on preserving their independence by taking advice from no-one, they may be more likely to come to wrong conclusions. And, in a sense, as soon as we open our mouths we have lost a degree of independence. It is not without significance here that the Cadbury Code provided for directors to take independent professional advice if necessary, at the company's expense in the furtherance of their duties. In the 1998 Combined Code the wording was as follows.

---

**Principle**  **Every listed company should be headed by an effective board which should lead and control the company.**

**Code Provision**

A.1.3  There should be a procedure agreed by the board for directors in the furtherance of their duties to take independent professional advice if necessary at the company's expense.

---

Equivalent wording in the 2003 Code reads (Provisions A.5.2):

'The board should ensure that directors, especially non-executive directors, have access to independent professional advice at the company's expense where they judge it necessary to discharge their responsibilities as directors. Committees should be provided with sufficient resources to undertake their duties.'

Proximity to the executive also may impede effective independence. We are all social animals and value our membership of groups.

## Best corporate governance requires that the controlling shareholder is not also the chairman    B10.59

Stelios Haji-Ioannou, the founder of EasyJet, announced on 18 April 2002 that he was standing down as chairman of EasyJet.[8] Sir Colin Chandler becomes deputy chairman for a year before succeeding Haji-Ioannou as chairman at the company's next AGM in March 2003. On Sky News Haji-Ioannou said 'Best corporate governance requires that the controlling shareholder is not also the chairman'. EasyJet is Europe's second largest low cost carrier, after Ryanair: on 18 April 2002 EasyJet had a market capitalisation of £1.49bn while Ryanair's market cap was larger than British Airways.

This is an interesting case of the need to make changes in order introduce best practice corporate governance in enterprises built up rapidly by successful entrepreneurs.

It is also an interesting case of the practical impact on corporate governance of judgements being made by interested parties about adherence with the Combined Code 'Principles' – even though in this case none of the more detailed 1998 Code 'Provisions', which are interpretative of the 'Principles', had been breached. For instance, Haji-Ioannou was not both chairman *and* chief executive. Institutional investors are (as they are entitled to do) making their own interpretations as to whether 'Principles' have been violated, and are not content to use the 'Provisions' as a sufficient guide of this.

In part this change shows that modest pressure from institutional investors can influence the composition of boards: only a handful of shareholders voted against Haji-Ioannou at the March 2002 AGM. Indeed it is apparent that EasyJet was already looking for a new chairman before that AGM – not doubt in part in anticipation of modest shareholder disapproval.

At EasyJet's March 2002 AGM, of the institutional investors it was only one with a small holding (the Co-operative Insurance Society with 17,205 shares out of the total issued shares of 292 million[9]) that had voted against EasyJet's report and accounts because of concerns about EasyJet's corporate governance – both the independence of non-executive directors and the ability of Haji-Ioannou's EasyGroup, the biggest shareholder with 58.5% of the equity, to appoint the chairman. However, it is thought that other shareholder groups may have exerted 'behind the scenes pressure' on EasyJet – which might have become more vociferous at the next AGM, had Haji-Ioannou not acted.[10]

One wonders whether the decision of institutional investors to take a stand might have been accentuated by the colourful non-establishment character at the top of EasyJet, and whether it would have been the same had EasyJet's leader been more conventional. However, it is fair to point out that it had been pressure from institutional investors which recently led to the replacement of the 'establishment figure' chairman of outstandingly successful Manchester United, Roland Smith, due to their perception of the excessive length of time he had been at the helm of that company.

It remains to be seen the extent to which this will alter following the changes announced on 18 April – the new chairman may not find it easy to exert his independence. However, Haji-Ioannou also announced his intention to unload some of his EasyJet stock, saying 'I need to sell my past to finance my future', and that starting a company 'requires a very different skill set to those needed to chair a major PLC and I consider my strengths are in the former. I am a serial entrepreneur.' It is to his credit that that he has this insight which is so sorely lacking in many successful entrepreneurs.

**ABI and NAPF on what constitutes independence**      **B10.60**

The concept of independence is very subjective but the Association of British Insurers (ABI) and the National Association of Pension Funds (NAPF) have established a set of broad principles that shape their definition of independence.

In assessing the independence of a non-executive director, the ABI and NAPF assume that the individual is independent unless the director falls into one or more of the categories listed below.

*[Ie If the answer to any of the following questions is yes, then the ABI and NAPF will regard the non-executive director as not being independent.]*

**Checklist**      **B10.61**

**Note:** This checklist was decided upon before the 2003 Combined Code included a set of independence criteria, reproduced earlier in this chapter.

| Name: [Mr. A]     Company: [company] | Yes/No? |
|---|---|
| 1. Were they formerly an executive director of [company]? | |
| 2. Have they or are they being paid by [company] in any capacity other than as a non-executive director? | |
| 3. Do they represent a trading partner or are they connected to a company or partnership (or were prior to retirement) which does business with [company]? | |
| 4. Have they been a non-executive director for nine years – i.e. three three-year terms | |
| *[NB of all of these criteria probably the most common area of non-compliance is the nine-year service limit]* | |
| 5. Are they closely related to a current executive director of [company]? | |

| Name: [Mr. A]        Company: [company] | Yes/No? |
|---|---|
| 6. Have they been awarded:<br>• share options/incentives under LTIPs;<br>• performance related pay ;or<br>• are they members of the [company]'s pension fund?<br><br>*[NB Non-executives can receive a proportion of their pay in shares, rather than options, as long as their shareholding does not become 'significant']* | |
| 7. Do they represent a controlling or 'significant' shareholder? | |
| 8. Are they a new appointee selected other than by a formal process (eg through a nominations committee)? | |
| 9. Do they have cross directorships with any other director *(ie are they executives in a company where executives in [company] are also non-executive directors in that company?* | |
| 10. Are they deemed by [company] for whatever reason[s] not to be independent? | |

NB There is potential for some discussion and flexibility with the ABI/NAPF on the above points in individual director's cases.

*For reference*                                                    **B10.62**

- The statutory guidelines on independence are far less clear-cut than those established by the institutional shareholders. The Combined Code defines independence as being 'independent of management and free from any business or other relationship which could materially interfere with the exercise of their independent judgement'.

- When disclosing in the report and accounts which non-executives are independent and which are not, companies do not have to follow the institutional shareholders' definition of independence and can instead apply the statutory definition set out above.

- As a consequence it is only against this much looser definition of independence that the non-executives need to be judged for disclosure purposes.

- There is, however, obviously nothing to stop companies applying the stricter definition and it is likely to be seen as a favourable step by institutional shareholders where they to do so.

*What are the consequences of not being an independent non-executive?*                                              **B10.63**

As already noted, the fact that the institutional shareholders deem a non-executive not to be independent need not necessarily be reflected by disclosure in the accounts.

It's also important to stress that the institutional shareholders do not insist that every single non-executive director is independent and do acknowledge that there is value in having non-independent non-executives for certain roles on the board.

So when does it matter if the institutional shareholders deem a non-executive not to be sufficiently independent?

The institutional shareholders, having assessed each non-executive using their independence criteria, will review the make-up of the board as follows.

| Source of recommendation | Company [company] | Yes/No |
|---|---|---|
| CC.A3.2 | Are the majority of non-executive directors independent? | |
| CC.B2.2 | Does the remuneration committee consist exclusively of independent non-executive directors? | |
| AB.NAPF | Does the remuneration committee consist of at least three independent non-executive directors? | |
| CC.D3.1 | Does the audit committee consist of at least three non-executive directors, a majority of whom are independent? | |
| ABI.NAPF | Is the Senior Independent Director independent? | |

Only if the answer to *all* of these questions is yes will the institutional shareholders be satisfied. Otherwise they will recommend a no vote whenever the breach involved is relevant to a proposal put before shareholders.

Examples of where this could become relevant include:

- opposing the introduction of a new option scheme because the remuneration committee isn't sufficiently independent;

- opposing the election/re-election of a non-executive director at the AGM because they're not considered suitably independent given their role on the Board (eg head of remuneration committee);or

- opposing the entire Remuneration Report (when legislation requiring a shareholder vote on the Report is introduced in 2002/3) because of insufficient independence on the Board or specifically in the remuneration committee.

# Overseas conventions                                        B10.64

Elsewhere there has been more prescription. For instance, Malaysia's Kuala Lumpur Stock Exchange directed that all listed companies should set up an audit committee within a year of August 1 1993, and companies seeking to go public must have an audit committee. The composition and functions of the audit committee are specified in the KLSE Listing Requirements, and the independence criteria of the members of the audit committee are given as follows:

- a majority of members shall not be executive directors of the company or any related corporation;

- a majority of members must not be a spouse, parent, brother, sister, son or adopted son or daughter or adopted daughter') of an executive director or of any related corporation; and

- a majority shall not have any relationships 'which, in the opinion of the board of directors, would interfere with the exercise of independent judgement in carrying out the functions of an audit committee.

It is a shame that on 4 May 1998, Singapore cut back on their corporate governance requirements, especially with respect to audit committees. The principal rationale seems to have been that the economic crisis called for a streamlining of the overheads imposed upon Singaporean companies in order to maintain or improve competitiveness, but there was the added risk of widespread failure by Singaporean listed companies to comply with these new and demanding provisions. It is unfortunate that this lends inappropriate weight to the sentiment that corporate governance requirements are an impediment to corporate prosperity. Until 4 May 1998, the Stock Exchange of Singapore's rules on audit committees required that the majority of members must be independent, which was defined as meaning:

- no direct or indirect financial or other interest other than the receipt of fees as an independent director;

- this to have been so over at least the last twelve months unless the board is satisfied that such relationships would not affect the director's exercise of independent judgement;

- not a relative of (a) an executive director, (b) an executive or (c) a substantial shareholder; and

- not a nominee of any director or substantial shareholder.

Certain specific business or other relationships of a member with the listed issuer were specified as not considered to make the member non-independent, per pre-May 4 1998 Practice Note 9j, as follows:

- goods or services are sold or rendered based on a fixed or graduated scale which is publicly quoted, and the scale prices are applied consistently to all customers or classes of customers;

- the receipt of fees or payment for professional services or business services that amounts to $30,000 or less, in respect of each transaction;

- the receipt by the member of financial services from the listed issuer in the latter's ordinary course of business as a financial institution;

- the receipt by the member of financial services from the listed issuer in the latter's ordinary course of business as a financial institution;

- purchases of residential property where the terms of such transaction have been specifically approved by shareholders;

- an interest of the member of less than 5 per cent of the total issued share capital of any of those companies; and

- a member of a listed issuer is not regarded as being not independent by the mere fact that he is an independent director of the listed issuer's listed substantial shareholder or of a substantial shareholder's listed associates, or of the listed issuer's subsidiaries and associated companies.

As an example, suppose Listed A is a substantial shareholder of Listed B, a person who is an independent director on Listed A does not by itself disqualify him from being an independent director in listed B's audit committee. Similarly, if Listed C is a subsidiary of Listed A, a person being an independent director in Listed A is not disqualified from being an independent director in Listed C's audit committee. However, a person who qualifies by virtue of the above criteria, will not be considered an independent director with regard to interested part transactions between Listed A and Listed B, or between Listed A and Listed C.

From 4 May 1998 the rules were simplified and the requirement now is simply that:

'The Board can consider a director as independent if any relationship he may have would not, in the individual case, be likely to affect the director's exercise of independent judgement.'

## Auditor independence                                      B10.65

Auditors face similar dilemmas. We talk of the independent auditor; in part to discriminate from the internal auditor. But no external auditor is entirely independent. The profession's rules on the proportion of fees which may be earned from one client, the length of time a partner may head an audit, and so on, are designed to buttress actual and perceived independence which must also depend upon technical and professional skills and personal character.

## PIRC survey of independence and other issues             B10.66

Research by PIRC found 593 non-executive directors of UK listed companies who had personal or commercial links with the company which meant, PIRC concluded, that they could not be deemed to be independent. Of these only 33 'owned up' to not being independent. 104 were ex-employees, 16 were related to board members, 47 were linked to the firm's professional advisors, 19 were employed as consultants and 92 had been on the board for more than 20 years.

Study of the wording of the now superseded 1998 Combined Code (see box below) does however show that PIRC is taking a much more stringent line than the Code intended with respect to most of these matters. A reasonable interpretation of the Code on 'independence' allows that it is for the board to decide whether a past or even a present relationship (with management, the business or with anyone or anything else) is an impediment to the exercise of independent judgement. In defence of PIRC, the Hampel Committee was at pains to assert that it is the spirit of the Principles contained within the Combined Code that it is appropriate for companies to adhere to, and of course it becomes a matter of judgement as to how such adherence can be achieved.

---

**From the 1998 Combined Code**

**A.3      Board balance**

**Principle   The board should include a balance of executive and non-executive directors (including independent non-executives) such that no individual or small group of individuals can dominate the board's decision taking.**

**Code Provisions**

**A.3.1**   The board should include non-executive directors of sufficient calibre and number for their views to carry significant weight in the board's decisions. Non-executive directors should comprise not less than one-third of the board.

**A.3.2**   The majority of non-executive directors should be independent of management and free from any business or other relationship which could materially interfere with the exercise of their independent judgement. Non-executive directors considered by the board to be independent in this sense should be identified in the annual report.

---

## Components of compensation as factors affecting independence

It is regarded as best practice that non-executive directors' compensation should be limited to the fee they receive for being a non-executive director, though in the UK the 1998 Hampel Report saw no objection to a proportion of their compensation being in the form of shares in the company. Unlike US practice, participation by non-executive directors in share option schemes is not approved in the UK on account of the risk that the 'leverage effect' of these schemes could cloud the exercise of independent judgement by non-executive directors when making decisions, especially decisions that impact upon share price or on the option schemes themselves. However, it is accepted that UK non-executive directors may (but are not required to) hold shares in the company and that this can be positively desirable as it will mean that the directors identify more closely with the interests of the shareholders. But it should be pointed out that the right decision for a board to come to is not always the decision that maximises share price (as for instance when the board decides it should disclose that it is probably in breach of a key funding covenant).

The 2003 Code, reflecting Higgs' recommendations, makes two changes to this. First, it is not inconsistent with the 2003 Code for non-executive directors to have share options, although the 2003 Code, is restrictive in the circumstances in which this would be reasonable. Provision B.1.3 reads:

> 'Levels of remuneration for non-executive directors should reflect the time commitment and responsibilities of the role. Remuneration for non-executive directors should not include share options. If, exceptionally, options are granted, shareholder approval should be sought in advance and any shares acquired by exercise of the options should be held until at least one year after the non-executive director leaves the board. Holding of share options could be relevant to the determination of a non-executive director's independence (as set out in provision A.3.1).'

Secondly, since non-executive directors' fees should be proportionate to their responsibilities and their time commitment, it is in order for an additional amount of fee to be paid for, for instance, chairing a board committee. Their total compensation should always be known to the board and disclosed in the annual report.

## Composition of audit committees B10.68

An effective way of strengthening the outside and independent element on the board, is to ensure that the business has an audit committee with at least three members, none of whom should be executive directors and all of whom, under the 2003 Code, should be genuinely independent of the business, as per Provision D.3.1 of the Combined Code (see **A1** and **B10.55** above). While executive directors and others (such as other executives, the head of internal audit and the external auditor) may be in attendance at audit committee meetings, this should be at the discretion of the committee's chairman who may require them to leave during all or part of certain agenda items.

Of course, the audit committee has a specific purpose apart from this indirect benefit of strengthening the composition of the board. Its responsibilities are to monitor, on behalf of the board:

- the financial statements for publication;
- the quality of internal control;
- the quality of the external, statutory audit; and
- the quality of internal audit.

The chair of the business, whether executive or non-executive, should not also be the chair of the audit committee. This is another way of assisting to avoid an excessive concentration of power at the top of the business.

## Deciding directors' remuneration independently          B10.69

A key principle is that no director should participate in the determination of his or her own compensation package. Thus, the compensation of executive directors should be recommended to the board by a remuneration committee of non-executive directors; and the fees of the non-executive directors should be recommended to the board by a committee of executive directors. The remuneration committee of the board may also be charged with the responsibility of determining the remuneration of the most senior executives below the level of the executive directors.

## Directors obtaining independent advice          B10.70

It is good practice that board committees and individual directors should be empowered to take independent professional advice at the company's expense on matters relating to their responsibilities. The arrangements for this should be set out in a formal board resolution. Features of this resolution might include:

- the circumstances in which such advice might be sought;

- the nature of such advice which is included within this authority;

- the annual financial limit of the cost of this advice without specific board or chairman approval;

- arrangements for payment, and whether disclosure of the nature of the advice sought and given is required;

- whether the chairman should be consulted first; and

- that the choice of professional advisor is at the discretion of the individual director or the board committee seeking the advice.

## Nominated directors' conflict of loyalty between their nominator and the company          B10.71

While there are notable examples of investment institutions who are active shareholders but would not seek to place their people on the boards of companies in which they invest (Hermes is one example) this is often not the case. Pension funds, insurance companies and some other institutional investors would prefer to retain the freedom which comes from not having their representatives on the boards in which they are investing significantly. But venture capitalists and banks very frequently make board appointments and are quite pragmatic about being there to protect their investments. They might argue that it would be negligent to take a major stake in a company and not to monitor it. Protecting the stakes of shareholders and other investors can however be done in other ways than by having one or more seats on the board (eg by careful monitoring from outside, by applying the law, by the stakeholder clearly making known their viewpoint as an active shareholder etc).

A broadly parallel situation exists when a representative of a dominant shareholder (perhaps a family or founder of the company) sits on the board; or when one or more members of a board sit on the board of a subsidiary company which is listed.

Where the practice on nominating directors for boards is followed, the nominating institution is likely to be nervous about conflicts of interest but to take the view that these rarely occur and can be managed when they do, especially if the investing institution has a clearly worked out policy on this matter.

There is a fundamental flaw in the concept of nominated directors on boards of publicly held companies. The flaw exists when the intention or the effect is to make inside knowledge available to the investing institution so as to optimise their potential to safeguard their interests.

In the UK, *Part X* of the *Companies Act 1985* stipulates that directors should seek shareholder approval in circumstances where a director's personal interests might conflict with his or her duty to the company. More generally, a board of directors is accountable to the shareholders as a whole for its stewardship of the company.

If, as we shall suggest later, it is necessary for a nominated director not to participate in board business where there is a conflict of interest, then (assuming this is successful) the presence of the nominated director cannot serve the intended purpose. Paragraph 8 of the Preamble to the new 2003 Combined Code (see **PART A**) acknowledges that all shareholders should have similar access to information:

> 'Nothing in this Code should be taken to override the general requirements of law to treat shareholders equally in access to information.'

The 'Sample letter of non-executive director appointment', drawn from the Higgs Report and now part of the 2003 Code publication (see **PART A**) reminds non-executives directors that:

> 'All directors must take decisions objectively in the interests of the company'

and

> 'It is accepted and acknowledged that you have business interests other than those of the company and have declared any conflicts that are apparent at present. In the event that you become aware of any potential conflicts of interest, these should be disclosed to the chairman and company secretary as soon as apparent.'

and

> 'All information acquired during your appointment is confidential to the Company and should not be released, either during your appointment or

following termination (by whatever means), to third parties without prior clearance from the chairman.

Your attention is also drawn to the requirements under both legislation, and regulation as to the disclosure of price sensitive information. Consequently you should avoid making any statements that might risk a breach of these requirements without prior clearance from the chairman or company secretary.'

Note that acting in the interests of the company is not the same as acting in the best interests of the shareholders as a body, let alone the best interests of a faction of shareholders. Sometimes boards have to make decisions which do not maximise shareholder value – for instance when it is a matter of observing the law or observing terms entered into by the company in contracts.

The focus of much of the 2003 Code on careful selection of board members, using a nomination committee, makes no allusion to the circumstances in which a third party nominates their representative(s) to join the board, and indeed the general tenor of the Code (especially with respect to independence) does not provide any support for nominee directors. The Code is, of course, targeted primarily at listed companies, but has been adopted much more widely. The concerns about nominated directors do not apply only to listed companies although they are more pronounced for companies which are not closely held.

## Motivations of nominee appointments                         B10.72

A key question is the motivation to nominate a director. If the motivation is to ensure that the company has scarce expertise available to it, then that is less problematic than alternative motivations. But it would be disingenuous to suggest that the scarce expertise sought is only available in the form of a nominated director. If the motivation is that the company has at least one director who is well informed about the policies of a major shareholder, then that could also be construed as desirable. But chairmen and chief executives of companies without nominated directors resort to other much more effective ways of sounding out the opinions of their major shareholders. If the motivation is that the nominating entity thereby gains inside and fast track knowledge of the affairs of the nominee company, that is less defensible. Any non-executive director must ensure he manages the conflict in the interests of the company on whose board he serves. Perhaps it is impossible to manage the conflict if the director also serves on the board of the entity which nominated him or her for this other board as their representative.

To some extent, where nominee directorships pertain, some reliance can be placed on the fact that the directors were elected by the shareholders in general meeting. If, at that time, the shareholders were clear as to the nominee relationship, it could be harder for those shareholders to subsequently object to the conduct of the nominee director when he appeared to be placing first the interests of the nominating company. But that would not, in all circumstances, be an adequate defence in an action against the nominee director for breach of trust. In practice, an action may be by the company against the board of directors as a whole; such an action may be inspired by the conduct of the individual nominee director if that is construed as having been against the interests of the shareholders or against the interests of the company. There is also the matter that the board initially appoints the director and it is only later that the shareholders vote to confirm his or her appointment: so there is a period of time when the shareholders have not been consulted about the appointment, during which the board might be vulnerable to shareholder action because of the effect of its decision to welcome the nominee onto the board.

## Board balance and independence                                    B10.73

It needs to be understood that a nominee director may be non-executive but is certainly not independent. It would be ironic if investment institutions, who exert pressure on companies to conform to corporate governance best practice, were to make it harder for companies to do so by nominating non-executive directors who are not independent to the boards of companies in whom they have invested. Investment institutions today, however, are sticklers for companies in which they are invested to comply with the Combined Code in all respects – extending to the Provisions and their own interpretations as to what are the criteria to be applied (such as with respect to 'Independence') to determine whether the Provisions are being complied with.

The nominee director is not independent because he is an executive or is otherwise significantly associated with a related party (for instance, an investor or a parent company). The relevant part of the Combined Code states, at Provisions A.3.1:

> 'The board should identify in the annual report each non-executive director it considers to be independent[11]. The board should determine whether the director is independent in character and judgement and whether there are relationships or circumstances which are likely to affect, or could appear to affect, the director's judgement. The board should state its reasons if it determines that a director is independent notwithstanding the existence of relationships or circumstances which may appear relevant to its determination, including if the director:
>
> ● has been an employee of the company or group within the last five years;
>
> ● has, or has had within the last three years, a material business relationship with the company either directly, or as a partner, shareholder, director or senior employee of a body that has such a relationship with the company;
>
> ● has received or receives additional remuneration from the company apart from a director's fee, participates in the company's share option or a performance-related pay scheme, or is a member of the company's pension scheme;

- has close family ties with any of the company's advisers, directors or senior employees;

- holds cross-directorships or has significant links with other directors through involvement in other companies or bodies;

- represents a significant shareholder; or

- has served on the board for more than nine years from the date of their first election.'

It is of course the penultimate bullet point which is most relevant in this context.

A slightly different slant was given by the Cadbury Committee who used the phrase 'related party transactions' as an indicator as to whether a non-executive director should be regarded as independent. Association with a significant supplier of the company would mean that the director was linked with a related party and thus not independent. An investing institution is clearly a related party as a supplier of capital to the company.

In our view it is likely to be impractical for companies to find much space on their boards for nominee directors since they cannot be regarded as independent. Modern boards are modest in size – both in the interests of effectiveness and in order to control total boardroom costs. Total boardroom costs are related to board size, and an investing institution or parent company should be reluctant to burden the company with extra board costs. Except for companies outside the FTSE 350, at least half of the board, excluding the chairman, is to be independent, as per 2003 Code provision A.3.2:

'Except for smaller companies, at least half the board, excluding the chairman, should comprise non-executive directors determined by the board to be independent. A smaller company should have at least two independent non-executive directors.'

The 2003 Code also states as supporting principles on board balance and independence that:

'The board should not be so large as to be unwieldy'

and

' … there should be a strong presence on the board of both executive and non-executive directors.'

While the Combined Code is strictly applicable to listed companies, not their subsidiaries and not those companies in which a listed company has investments (unless listed), it is regarded as best practice much more generally. We should say here that, under Listing Rules, it is the Principles, not the Provisions, which are intended to be mandatory (although there is little or no evidence that they are enforced by the regulators): listed companies may depart from the Provisions if they disclose and explain their departure.

In general it is not best practice to appoint non-executive directors to the board who cannot be regarded as independent at the time of their appointment. Since today's board is usually small, and there will be a need to have a proportion of the board today who satisfy the independence tests into the future, it is likely to be problematic to appoint non-executive directors who are not independent even at the time they are appointed. A strict reading of Provisions A.3.1 allows that a non-executive director could become independent when particular impediments to that director's independence (ie some of the bullet points of A.3.1) no longer apply; but that is unlikely and, where it could be held to apply, it would not do so for long as a director is not to be regarded as independent if he or she has served on the board for longer than nine years since first appointed (vide. last bullet point of Provision A.3.1)

We should not overlook that some directors appointed as independent may lose that status in the future and yet still be desirable members of the board. In practice, therefore, it is not easy for board composition to be managed in order to ensure an adequate independent element, and appointments which may impede this objective are usually best avoided.

## Declaring an interest                                     B10.74

One way of handling the conflict which may arise is for a nominated director not to participate in board business when there is a conflict of interest. This is not ideal. First, it is highly unlikely in practice that the non-participating director will be unaware of the nature of the item of business: he would need to be aware of it in order to be able to opt out of becoming further involved. Awareness of the nature of the item is often enough to influence the market, for instance in the case of a possible takeover bid. The nominated director will also almost certainly have knowledge before the market as a whole of the outcome of the board's decision on such a matter.

Other relevant points here are that boards do not need unproductive directors; and that non-participation would not obviate the director's share of responsibility for the decisions the board came to. With respect to the latter, the director may therefore feel constrained to become involved, notwithstanding the conflict of interest.

We have a situation here where the director concerned may be at risk of using his or her knowledge against the best interests of the company on whose board he has been nominated to sit; arguably in breach of his or her fiduciary duties to that company of shareholders as a whole.

## The nominee's duties to the nominator                     B10.75

The issues of conflict, which we are discussing here, apply whether or not the nominee director is also a director of the entity which nominated him or her. Where the individual is also on the board of the entity which nominated him or her, an additional conflict factor comes into play. It is that the director is likely to have inside knowledge of the affairs of the company on whose board he has been nominated to sit (whether a subsidiary (which may be listed separately from the parent) or a company invested in by an investment fund). The director may find that he is unable to discharge his or her fiduciary responsibilities to the latter nominating company, due to unwillingness to make disclosure to that board of matters relating to the former company.

A board and its individual members must act in the interests of all the shareholders, and not preferentially in the interests of any group of shareholders. Minority shareholders, for instance, need their interests to be looked after by the board; but, again, not preferentially. No director is to use inside knowledge for his/her personal benefit or for the benefit of others with whom they are associated, or indeed for the benefit of other parties. There should be no director (or director-inspired) dealings in shares of the company when inside knowledge applies or may apply (eg during a close period). This would apply to dealings in the investor company shares when that company's appointee had inside knowledge about the company on whose board he sits. Having a nominee on the board can cramp the style of the investment institution who may feel unable to deal in the shares, or to act in other ways, because of their inside position on the board of the company.

## Creating a shadow director situation   B10.76

We should not overlook that in some circumstances, if a lender interferes in the direction of company in which the lender has invested, the lender could be construed as at least a shadow director, and the loan might then regarded as equity. *Prima facie* this situation is more likely to pertain when the lender has a representative on the board.

## Elements of a policy for handling these conflicts of loyalty   B10.77

- Accept the need at times to formally declare an interest and ensure the declaration is minuted.

- On occasion exercise the option of not voting on an issue.

- Even on occasion exercise the option of not attending a board or board committee meeting.

- In the case of a smaller, non-listed company, make sure the Shareholders' Agreement gives shareholders the right to see all information made available to the directors; and make sure there is a mechanism in place that allows for a flow of information from subsidiaries/investee companies to the main board, so that the type of situation where a representative director is privy to information at subsidiary/investee company level that he might not feel comfortable to disclose to the parent company/majority shareholder, should not arise. This mechanism has to accommodate the need for outside shareholders to be privy to the same information if it is price sensitive with respect to the share price.

- Make it clear that the director must resolve any conflict in favour of the company on whose board he sits at the time, although he must take into account the impact on shareholders/other group companies.

# Director search firms

All the firms listed are strong in the recruitment of non-executive directors and will also handle executive director assignments. The list is not intended to be exhaustive.

| Firm | Contact details | Notes |
| --- | --- | --- |
| Boyden International Limited | Harriet Tupper Consultant Director Appointments Boyden International Limited 24 Queen Anne's Gate London SW1H 9AA Tel: 020 7222 9033 Fax: 020 7222 8838 Email: london@boyden.com or harriet.tupper@ boyden.com Website: www. Boyden.com | Boyden provides senior-level executive recruitment services across all positions (including Board level) and industries. There is also a significant interim management business. Non-Executive Director and Chairman recruitment for all industry sectors is handled by Harriet Tupper who has specialised in this area for over five years, working with all sizes and types of company and organisation. Director Appointments used to be based at the Institute of Directors and remains the NED recruitment service recommended by the IoD. |

| Firm | Contact details | Notes |
|---|---|---|
| Egon Zehnder International | Tony Couchman and Julia Budd Egon Zehnder International Devonshire House Mayfair Place London W1X 5FH Tel: 020 7493 3882 Fax: 020 7629 9552 www.zehnder. comezilondon@ezi.net | Egon Zehnder International is one of the worlds leading executive search firms with over 300 consultants operating out of 55 offices in 35 countries. In addition to its core activity of executive search, the firm is a leader in consulting to boards and in particular the recruitment of chairmen and non-executive directors. In the UK the firm undertakes approaching 100 assignments each year at the top end of the plc market and for a number of specialist organisations, government organisations, mutuals, private companies, etc. |
| Hanson Green | Peter Waine Esq., and Barry Dinan Esq., Directors, Hanson Green 43 North Audley Street London W1Y 1WH Tel: (0)20 7493 0837 Fax: (0)20 7355 1436 E-mail: pwaine@ hansongreen.co.uk, bdinan@hansongreen.co.uk www.hansongreen.co.uk | Hanson Green specialises in the recruitment of independent chairmen and non-executive directors and has no 'off limits'. They publish a useful guide for non-executive directors, developed by them in conjunction with Ashurst Morris Crisp, Solicitors: *The Guide for Non-Executive Directors,* (2000). |

| Firm | Contact details | Notes |
|---|---|---|
| Heidrick & Struggles International Inc | Dr John Viney<br>Chairman, Europe<br>Heidrick & Struggles International Inc<br>3 Burlington Gardens<br>London<br>W1S 3EP<br>Tel: (0)20 7074 4000<br>Tel: (0)20 7491 5904<br>(John Viney)<br>Fax: (0)20 7075 4179<br>Fax: (0)20 7409 2767<br>(John Viney)<br>E-mail: jcv@h-s.com<br>(John Viney)<br>www.heidrick.com | |
| KPMG Search & Selection | Colin Grant-Wilson<br>KPMG Search & Selection<br>PO Box 730<br>20 Farringdon Street<br>London<br>EC4A 4PP<br>Direct + 44 (0)20 7694 5047<br>Internal 783 5047<br>colin.grantwilson@kpmg.co.uk<br>www.kpmg.co.uk/searchandselection<br>Also:<br>Geoffrey Mathur, | |
| SpencerStuart | Ms Sue Mandelbaum<br>SpencerStuart<br>16 Connaught Place<br>London<br>W2 2ED<br>Tel: (0)20 7298 3333 | |
| Springman, Tipper Campbell Partnership | Malcolm Campbell<br>Springman, Tipper Campbell Partnership<br>Bond Street House<br>14 Clifford Street<br>London<br>W1S 4JU<br>Tel: (0)20 7499 9892<br>Fax: (0)20 7499 7546 | |

| Firm | Contact details | Notes |
|---|---|---|
| The Independent Directors | Website: www.non.exec.com | They describe themselves as 'the leading recruiter of non-executive directors for unlisted entities'. |
| Whitehead Mann | Gerard Clery-Melin Chief Executive Whitehead Mann 11 Hill Street London W1J 5LG Tel: (0)20 7290 2000 Fax: (0)20 7290 2050 E-mail: uklondon@ wmann.com www.wmann.com | Whitehead Mann enables clients to fulfil their strategic ambitions by cultivating leadership. They approach what they do from the perspective of the organisation; its business, its culture, its value, using this perspective to shape leadership performance to drive long term organisational success. The group delivers this 'organisation-first' philosophy through and integrated approach that identifies, benchmarks and develops world class talent. The success of this holistic approach is manifested in the dominance they have achieved in their key market: the main boards of FTSE 100, Fortune 500 and CAC 40 companies. |

# Hermes' Guide for Shareholders and Independent Outside Directors
B10.79

This Hermes guidance was produced alongside Hermes response to the initial Higgs consultation. Further corporate governance guidance can be obtained from the Hermes website: http://www.hermes.co.uk/corporate-governance" This Handbook carries certain Hermes guidance and discussion as follows:

- 'The Value of Corporate Governance' (see **B1.44**).

- 'Hermes on Auditor Independence' (see **B6.6**).

- 'Hermes: Statement on UK Corporate Governance and Voting Policy (2001)' (see **B7.7**).

- 'Not Badly Paid, But Paid Badly' (see **B15.15**).

- 'Value Drivers: Paying a Fair Price for Non-executive Directors (Michelle Edkins)' (see **B15.16**).

- 'Hermes International Corporate Governance Principles' (see **B26.8**).

Hermes welcomes the debate on the role of non-executive directors sparked by comments by Paul Myners and government interest aroused by the events at Enron, giving rise to the current Higgs Review. Hermes has for a long time argued that there should be direct contacts between investors and independent outside directors, and has emphasised the importance of the senior independent director role.

We sometimes find that companies and outside directors become uncomfortable about requests from Hermes for meetings. There seems to be a belief that our intention is somehow to circumvent the usual channels of communication between investors and investee companies, the executive team principally, and the chair. This is certainly not our intention. For us, outside directors are a parallel channel of communication and not one used on a regular basis, but it is important to us that this parallel channel is open at companies about which we have concerns, to enable us properly to exercise our stewardship obligations in respect of those companies.

This document aims to set out our guidelines as to the nature of conversations between Hermes (or other involved institutional investors) and outside directors. We hope thereby to avoid companies and directors being uncomfortable about meeting requests and ensure that they start on the right footing. As part of this, we think it is useful to clarify our view of the role of the senior independent director, who will necessarily be the first port of call for contact between investors and the independent outside directors.

## Role of the senior independent director

To our minds, the term senior independent director has caused unfortunate opposition to the creation of the role among some investors and companies. As our Statement on Corporate Governance puts it: 'In many respects Hermes sees the role as an extension of that of deputy chairman and supports combining the roles of independent deputy chairman and senior independent director. Hermes believes that the main responsibilities of the role are to ensure that the views of each outside director are given due consideration and to provide a communication channel between outside directors and shareholders. This communication channel should be in addition to and not replace existing channels.'

Among the roles of the senior independent director should be to be available for consultation and direct communication in response to requests from major shareholders. At present such communication is rare. When it does occur it is almost invariably because of a crisis situation. Establishing direct channels as a matter of routine should enable difficult issues to be aired before a crisis develops.

In particular, this alternative route of investor-company discussion will be used where the more natural and standard routes of meetings with the executives or with the chair are not appropriate, for whatever reason. It would only rarely be used, but it is valuable for investors to have such an alternative way of raising concerns.

## Induction meetings

We believe that independent outside directors should make themselves available for meetings with their top investors as part of their induction process on appointment, and when the occasion demands while they are in office. The induction meetings are likely to be relatively brief and provide an opportunity for an introduction to the views of each party about the company, and how they see it developing over the years of the director's term and beyond. If investors have substantial concerns about the conduct of the company, its strategy or its board structure, these should be discussed fully and frankly so that there are no misunderstandings.

The number of shareholders that it is appropriate for the incoming outside director to meet will vary according to the shareholding structure of the company but the director should be confident following the series of meetings that he or she has a thorough understanding of the range of views about the company in the investment community. If the outside director does not have time available for this number of brief discussions, investors will find it hard to understand how he or she will have the appropriate amount of time to devote to the company to satisfy the responsibilities of the director's role.

Below are the key issues and the specific questions which investors are likely to seek to discuss in these induction meetings. They are not the only questions which might be raised, and though they are written in question format, we see them as an opportunity for starting a two-way discussion rather than an interrogation.

**Key issues at induction**

- Appointment process and future appointments

- Positives and negatives about the company

- Skills and attitude the outside director brings to the company

- Nature of investment

- Offer of help in the future

## Questions at induction

### Key issues

- Appointment process and future appointments
- Positives and negatives about the company
- Skills and attitude the outside director brings to the company
- Nature of investment
- Offer of help in the future

### Likely questions

- Who made the first contact with you about becoming an outside director?
- Did you know any of the other board members before the appointment process started?
- Do you expect further changes on the board?
- How will succession planning be approached?
- Do you believe your appointment process worked well?
- Are there ways in which it could be improved for future board members?
- Is there a board statement of the roles and responsibilities of outside directors?
- Is there a system of regular outside director and whole board appraisal?
- What attracted you to the company?
- What do you think attracted the company to you?
- What unique skills and perspectives do you bring to its board?
- How many days a year do you expect to be able to devote to the company?
- Will you be able to increase that if some crisis were to emerge?
- Do you expect to take on a specific role on the board?
- What does the company currently do well?
- Do you perceive there to be any current problems at the company?
- How can these be addressed?
- Over what timescale?
- What do you believe is the company's current competitive advantage?
- Is this being exploited to the full? Are there investment opportunities to develop it further?
- Is the company the best parent of all its operations?
- Where do you see the company in ten years' time?
- How many shares in the company do you currently hold?

- Do you expect to add to your holding in due course?

- How many other shareholders are you seeing?

- Explanation of the nature of the shareholder's investment (passive/active, long/short-term) and reasons for holding company. Approach to stocklending and short-selling.

- How can we assist you to do your job better?

## Meetings subsequent to induction

We do not believe that after the induction it is necessary for there to be regular (some have proposed annual) meetings between investors and outside directors – the directors are time-limited individuals and we would not seek to use up some of their remaining time without good reason. However, where investors do have genuine concerns, they will expect outside directors to make themselves available within a reasonable timeframe to discuss them. Hopefully, directors will see this as a natural part of their role.

Usually, such meetings would be with the independent chair. If the chair is executive, or is in some way conflicted over the issues to be discussed, shareholders would contact the independent deputy chair or senior independent director, but other independent directors should also be prepared to receive requests for meetings on occasion. In particular, at times there will be more appropriate individuals for shareholders to approach – for example, the chair of the audit committee in relation to accounting or risk management issues, or the chair of the remuneration committee on matters of executive pay. Where a board has decided not to appoint a senior independent director, investors are likely to use their discretion to decide which outside director(s) to approach on an issue of concern.

Shareholders should recognise this as a two-way process, and make appropriate staff available promptly when an independent outside – or any other – director requests a meeting. One of the main roles of the meetings we hold is to establish contact and to offer investor support if the outside director would find that useful. Investors will of course need to consider any such request for support on its individual merits.

Below are samples of key issues and likely questions which investors might ask the independent outside directors for each of the most likely forms of meeting. Again, though they are written in question format, we see them as an opportunity for starting a discussion rather than an interrogation. It should be noted that we are not trying to gain specific information about the company, and certainly not inside information about issues such as trading. Rather, we are seeking to understand the functioning of the board and its procedures to ensure that it works to drive long-term value for shareholders.

| Key issues for general meetings | Key issues on audit/risk |
|---|---|
| Positives and negatives about the company | management |
| | Structure of audit committee |
| Functioning of the board and succession planning | Activities and success in risk management |
| Strategic work by the board | Audit committee role in maintaining |
| Role and involvement of the outside directors | auditor independence |
| | Any difficult accounting issues |
| Offer of help in the future | Offer of help in the future |
| **Key issues on remuneration** | **Key issues on SEE matters** |
| Structure of remuneration committee | Structure of board committee |
| Link between pay structures and strategy, and pay with performance | Attitude of the board and company as a whole |
| Mitigation policy | Whatever key investor SEE |
| Independence of advice received | concerns are |
| Options valuation and value to shareholders | Offer of help in the future |
| Offer of help in the future | |

**Questions for general meetings**

**Key issues**

- Positives and negatives about the company
- Functioning of the board and succession planning
- Strategic work by the board
- Role and involvement of the outside directors
- Offer of help in the future

**Likely questions**

- What excites you most about the company?
- What disappoints you most?
- How often and for how long does the board meet?
- How many meetings do you attend?
- To what extent do you have contact with the company between meetings?
- How many days a year do you devote to the company's affairs?

- How far in advance of meetings do you receive board papers?

- How much time is involved in advance preparation for the meeting?

- Does the advance briefing provide enough information?

- How is board time split between discussing operational matters and strategy?

- Do you believe that enough time is set aside for discussing strategy?

- What is the nature of discussions? Are they constructive?

- What would you do if you felt that the current strategy was not working yet the chair and/or chief executive did not agree with your view?

- What do you believe is the company's current competitive advantage?

- Is this being exploited to the full? Are there investment opportunities to develop it further?

- By what mechanisms does the company assess investment opportunities in advance, in particular their capacity to provide returns in excess of the cost of capital?

- How are investments reviewed after the event to judge their success?

- How is the company's capital structure reviewed to minimise the cost of capital?

- Is the company the best parent of all its operations?

- How effective are board meetings? Do you leave with a sense of achievement?

- Do you think that the board has an appropriate balance of skills and appropriate perspectives to provide full insight into all aspects of company business?

- Does the current balance between executives and independent outside directors work?

- Is there a clear division of responsibilities, especially between chair and chief executive?

- How are the independent outside directors kept appraised of shareholders' views, comments and feedback?

- Do you have regular contact with shareholders independently of the executives?

- Do you attend the AGM? Are board members told of the outcome of AGM votes?

- If there is a senior independent director, what does he or she do?

- If there is not one, why does the board believe the role is unnecessary?

- Do the independent outside directors meet, either formally or informally, without (a) the executives and (b) the chair being present? How often?

- Who arranges these meetings and takes responsibility for them?

- If such meetings have not yet happened, what circumstances can you envisage where one might be necessary?

- If the circumstances were such that you felt it was necessary to remove an under-performing chair or chief executive, what would you do?

- How are potential independent outside directors identified and recruited?

- Is the process formalised and open?

- Is there any formal evaluation of the executives, the chair, the independent outside directors or the overall effectiveness of the board?

- If not, has this been considered by the board?

- Is there a formal assessment of the skill gaps on the board taking into account the strategy planned for the company?

- What, if any, consideration is given to succession?

- Which of your skills, experience and personal attributes do you think add particular value to the company?

- What do you see as your role on the board?

- Are independent outside directors encouraged to develop their skills through attending seminars or other training? Are they given a budget to do so?

- Do the outside directors call on the services of independent, external advisers?

- In what circumstances? Do they need to seek any authority before doing so?

- Do executives below board level brief the board and/or the independent outside directors in person? On what type of issues?

- Are they available to answer independent outside directors' questions?

- To what extent do independent outside directors have contact with other employees below board level?

- How often do the independent outside directors visit sites other than the head office?

- Is this done without executive board members being present?

- How many of the group's operations have you personally visited?

- Is the level of the fee you receive as a independent outside director appropriate?

- What value of the company's shares do you own?

- How would you feel about being paid partly in shares?

- What proportion of your fee would you be prepared to receive in shares?

- Do you believe independent outside directors bear too much responsibility under the current regime? How would you change it?

- How can we assist you to do your job better?

**Likely questions on audit and risk management**

**Key issues**

- Structure of audit committee
- Activities and success in risk management
- Audit committee role in maintaining auditor independence
- Any difficult accounting issues
- Offer of help in the future

**Likely questions**

- How is the audit committee constituted? How are the individual members chosen?

- What skills do they bring? Is there at least one audit committee member who has expertise in financial reporting or interpretation of accounts?

- Does the committee have access to fully independent advice on accounting and risk management matters?

- Is there scope for committee members to receive special training on relevant issues?

- How has the board gone about identifying the key areas of greatest risk to the company?

- How frequently will that process be repeated?

- Once identified, how does the board go about managing the risks?

- How have any deficiencies in internal control been dealt with?

- Is there a board member (executive or not) with responsibility for risk management?

- How often do the outside directors meet the audit partner and audit staff?

- Are any executives present at such meetings? Are there sufficient opportunities for the auditors to raise concerns with the audit committee without executives being present?

- How does the committee assess the independence/robustness of the audit process?

- Is the proposed appointment or retention of the outside auditors the responsibility of the audit committee or the finance director? Is reappointment formally considered each year?

- Does the audit committee negotiate the annual audit fee with the auditor?

- Is the need for a new tender for auditing services considered regularly?

- Is the committee confident the balance between audit and non-audit fees is appropriate? Does the committee oversee the award of non-audit assignments to the auditors?

- Does the committee oversee any transfer of staff from the audit team to the company?

- Do the accounts contain any areas where difficult judgements are required, such as provisions, valuations or revenue recognition?

- How has the audit committee gained confidence that the necessary judgements have been exercised with due prudence so that the result accurately reflects reality?

- Would the accounts be substantially different if the company used an available alternative under accounting standards?

- Why is the option now in use the best representation of the company's current status?

- How can we assist you to do your job better?

**Likely questions on remuneration**

**Key issues**

- Structure of remuneration committee

- Link between pay structures and strategy, and pay with performance

- Mitigation policy

- Independence of advice received

- Options valuation and value to shareholders

- Offer of help in the future

**Likely questions**

- How is the remuneration committee constituted?

- How are the individual members chosen?

- What skills do they bring?

- How does remuneration policy fit in with and drive the company's strategic aims? Do the performance hurdles the committee has set match with the board's strategy?

- Are they stretching enough to ensure that the strategic aims are achieved, and that payments are only triggered if this occurs? If not, why not?

- Will the executives be able to achieve substantial rewards without driving strong returns for shareholders and without having moved the company forward strategically?

- Is the remuneration committee happy to justify such payments?

- What is the remuneration committee's position on payments for departing executives, particularly where they leave after a period of underperformance?

- Does the committee understand that it is the departing executive's legal duty to mitigate the costs to the company in such circumstances?

- How does the committee ensure that the departing individual is held to that legal duty?

- From whom does the remuneration committee seek independent advice on pay matters?

- Is the committee confident that advice is genuinely independent and not coloured by a desire to win wider business?

- Has the committee considered seeking advice from a consultant without any other links to the company who would be answerable to the remuneration committee alone?

- What degree of discretion does the remuneration committee have? Why?

- How has that discretion been used to date?

- What is the committee's current method of estimating the value of the share options it awards to executives and other staff?

- What would be the impact on the profit and loss account of share option expensing on the model proposed by accounting bodies?

- Is the committee confident that it is deriving shareholder value from that expenditure?

- How can we assist you to do your job better?

**Likely questions on social, environmental and ethical (SEE) matters**

These will tend to be built around whatever SEE issues have caused investors to take an interest, but the following considers the procedural questions likely to be asked.

**Key issues**

- Structure of board committee

- Attitude of the board and company as a whole

- Whatever key investor SEE concerns are

- Offer of help in the future

## Likely questions

- How is the relevant committee constituted?

- How are the individual members chosen?

- What skills do they bring?

- If the relevant skills and background knowledge are not available among the committee's members, does it have scope to seek external advice?

- Has it ever done so?

- Does the committee have regular access to staff below the executive level – for example, those in internal audit, health & safety and HR?

- Is this done outside the presence of more senior executives?

- Are the committee's decisions on SEE matters definitive or can the full board override them? Has this ever happened?

- Does the board pay adequate attention to these matters in your opinion?

- Which of these issues do you see as being most significant to the company?

- Which does the company deal with well?

- Which require some improvement?

- Is there an attitude of continual improvement? How is this manifested?

- How can we assist you to do your job better?

### Notes

1. Provision 1.5 of The Cadbury Code of Best Practice
2. Para 4.18, p24
3. The Committee on the Financial Aspects of Corporate Governance, December 1992, Report of the Committee, London: Gee & Co., ISBN 0 85258 913 1 or 915 8, paras 4.12 & 4.13.
4. Committee On Corporate Governance – The Hampel Committee (January 1998), Final Report, chaired by Sir Ronald Hampel, Gee Publishing, London, ISBN 1 86089 034 2, para. 3.9.
5. Compliance or otherwise with this provision need only be reported for the year in which the appointment is made.
6. A.2.2 states that the chairman should, on appointment, meet the independence criteria set out in this provision, but thereafter the test of independence is not appropriate in relation to the chairman.
7. A smaller company is one that is below the FTSE 350 throughout the year immediately prior to the reporting year.
8. Kevin Done and Andrea Felsted, (19 April 2002): 'Stelios to step down as EasyJet chairman', Financial Times, p21 (and Lex Column, p14).
9. Alistair Osborne, 19 April 2002, 'EasyJet's Stelios takes a back seat', Daily Telegraph, p40.
10. Kevin Done and Andrea Felsted, 19 April 2002, 'EasyJet founder resigns as chief', Financial Times, p1.
11. A.2.2 states that the chairman should, on appointment, meet the independence criteria set out in this provision, but thereafter the test of independence is not appropriate in relation to the chairman.

# The Effective Board

## The importance of quality information for the board

Much more focus is being given to the importance of the quality of information that the board receives. This was covered only briefly in the 1998 Combined Code, as follows.

### A.4    Supply of Information

**Principle    The board should be supplied in a timely manner with information in a form and of a quality appropriate to enable it to discharge its duties.**

### Code Provision

**A.4.1**    Management has an obligation to provide the board with appropriate and timely information, but information volunteered by management is unlikely to be enough in all circumstances and directors should make further enquiries where necessary. The chairman should ensure that all directors are properly briefed on issues arising at board meetings.'

The 2003 Code has expanded on the above.

### A.5    Information and professional development

**Main Principle    The board should be supplied in a timely manner with information in a form and of a quality appropriate to enable it to discharge its duties. All directors should receive induction on joining the board and should regularly update and refresh their skills and knowledge.**

### Supporting Principles

The chairman is responsible for ensuring that the directors receive accurate, timely and clear information. Management has an obligation to provide such information but directors should seek clarification or amplification where necessary.

The chairman should ensure that the directors continually update their skills and the knowledge and familiarity with the company required to fulfil their role both on the board and on board committees.

The company should provide the necessary resources for developing and updating its directors' knowledge and capabilities.

**B11.1**   *The importance of quality information for the board*

Under the direction of the chairman, the company secretary's responsibilities include ensuring good information flows within the board and its committees and between senior management and non-executive directors, as well as facilitating induction and assisting with professional development as required.

The company secretary should be responsible for advising the board through the chairman on all governance matters.'

Board members need to be provided with adequate information, made available to them in time to properly influence decisions rather than to merely ratify courses of action which the company has, in effect, been committed to by the executive prior to the board meeting. It is more likely that the non-executive directors will be inadequately informed, but this can also apply to the board as a whole. Executive directors may not be in a strong position to protest about this if it is the chief executive who is being selective in feeding information to the board. It is a key responsibility of the non-executive board members to insist upon, and probe with respect to, the quality of information the board receives.

In determining what information the board needs to receive, and the timing of it, consideration needs to given to the distinction between those matters which are reserved to the board and those which have been delegated by the board (**B11.7** and **B11.10** address these topics).

A key anxiety of boards, especially the non-executive members, is whether the board is informed on all matters which it should know about. Frequently there are cases where it is apparent that the board has, at least initially, been kept in the dark, for instance with respect to:

- off balance sheet transactions;
- contingent liabilities;
- expected or current litigation;
- contractual breaches and compensation claims;
- undisclosed liabilities;
- late payment of tax; and
- unprovided losses,

and so on. Once the bond of trust has been broken between on the one hand the chief executive and finance director in particular and on the other hand the non-executive directors, it is very hard to mend. The bond is threatened both by withholding information from the board and also by providing the board with information which subsequently is shown to have been unreliable. Non-executive directors have a solemn responsibility to ask the right questions, to probe when they have concerns and not to be content with unclear explanations.

It may not be that the executive is deliberately misleading the board: it might be that the executive are not in possession of the facts. What is not clearly understood cannot be clearly expressed. Or they may be guilty of oversight or denial.

A recent development in practice is for the audit committee to review the quality of information that the board receives:

> 'One of the major requirements for good corporate governance is that the board of the company receives the information it needs to take the decisions it has to take; that this information is reported in a digestible form and that it is accurate. This is something the audit committee looks at on a regular basis, though it is equally a concern of the whole board who take great interest in this matter.'[1]

This chimes with the Hampel Committee's observation that:

> 'We endorse the view of the Cadbury committee (Report 4.14) that the effectiveness of non-executive directors (indeed, of all directors) turns, to a considerable extent on the quality of the information they receive.'[2]

However, beyond highly specific obligations to review information (for instance with respect to the financial statements of the company, or with respect to whistleblowing), neither the Smith Report nor the 2003 Combined Code give the audit committee a specific remit to review the quality of information which the board receives. This is not to say that the audit committee should not undertake this – we would suggest usually an agenda item once a year.

With respect to information on internal control, in the US the Public Oversight Board has recently advised that audit committees should:

> 'obtain a written report from management on the effectiveness of internal control over financial reporting and establish specific expectations with management and the internal and external auditors about the qualitative information needs of the committee related to internal control. Discussions of internal control should include the effects of technology on current and future information systems.'

In **B4** REPORTING ON INTERNAL CONTROL AND THE TURNBULL REPORT we suggested that, especially in the context of implementing Turnbull, the board should receive regular information on the performance of the entity with respect to the key risks of the business. This is in addition to regular management accounting information which should come to the board.

Good practice is for an attractively presented, bound set of management accounts to be produced monthly and to be circulated to board members. If the board meets monthly, this 'MAP' (Management Accounting Pack) can be presented to the board monthly by the finance director. We suggest it is likely that it should include the section shown in this table:

## Contents of MAP for the board                                   B11.2

- Performance summary

- Key financial indicators

- Key risk indicators

- Group Profit and Loss

- Segmental Profit & Loss

- Margins analysis

- Cashflow analysis

- Headcount

- Other financial information

- Performance summary for each business segment

- Treasury

- Share performance and market comparables

Each section should commence with a narrative summary highlighting the main points and trends contained within the data which should follow. The use of colour and graphical representations will improve the clarity of the MAP, and is to be recommended.

As with other board papers, it is important that board members receive the MAP a few days before the board meeting so that they can prepare themselves properly.

## Schedule of matters to be reserved to the board   B11.3

It is good practice for a company to know what decisions need to be made by the board itself. The UK Cadbury Code of Best Practice for corporate governance included a Code provision that stated:

'The board should have a formal schedule of matters specifically reserved to it for decision to ensure that the direction of the company is firmly in its hands.'[3]

After the Hampel Committee reported[4], the Cadbury Code has recently been replaced in the UK by the 1998 Combined Code which includes a Code Provision that states:

'The board should have a formal schedule of matters specifically reserved to it for decision.'[5]

Provisions of the Combined Code are subordinate to overarching Principles. In this case, the Principle is that:

'Every … company should be headed by an effective board which should lead and control the company.'[6]

The new 2003 Combined Code expresses it like this.

## A.1    The Board

**Main Principle**    **Every company should be headed by an effective board, which is collectively responsible for the success of the company.**

### Supporting Principles

As part of their role as members of a unitary board, non-executive directors should constructively challenge and help develop proposals on strategy. Non-executive directors should scrutinise the performance of management in meeting agreed goals and objectives and monitor the reporting of performance. They should satisfy themselves on the integrity of financial information and that financial controls and systems of risk management are robust and defensible. They are responsible for determining appropriate levels of remuneration of executive directors and have a prime role in appointing, and where necessary removing, executive directors, and in succession planning.

### Code Provisions

A.1.1    The board should meet sufficiently regularly to discharge its duties effectively. There should be a formal schedule of matters specifically reserved for its decision. The annual report should include a statement of how the board operates, including a high level statement of which types of decisions are to be taken by the board and which are to be delegated to management.

Strictly, all of the above applies only to UK listed companies who must disclose in their annual reports how they are ensuring they comply with the Principles and whether or not they comply with the Provisions (and, if not, why not). But the Combined Code is sound counsel even for smaller companies, if applied flexibly, and certainly the sentiments reproduced in bold above are important even for the smallest non-listed company.

Company law dictates that some matters are the responsibility of the board. Good corporate governance dictates that other matters should be. Companies' own memoranda and articles of association may add further matters.

The two examples given at the end of this section of schedules of matters reserved to the board are attempts to produce practical, useful guidance. They are not complete lists of the important responsibilities of a board although they relate very closely to these. The responsibilities of a board include those matters which the board may delegate to others – authority, not responsibility, is delegated. The lists are restricted to those matters which it is likely that a board will decide not to delegate – in other words those matters on which the board is likely to wish to reserve to itself the powers of decision.

## General responsibilities of boards B11.4

More general, more comprehensive advice on the responsibilities of boards can be found elsewhere[7][8]. For instance, a board's responsibilities include[9]:

- the legal requirement for directors to prepare financial statements for each financial year which give a true and fair view of the state of affairs of the company (or group) as at the end of the financial year and of the profit and loss for that period;

- the responsibility of the directors for maintaining adequate accounting records, for safeguarding the assets of the company (or group), and for preventing and detecting fraud and other irregularities;

- confirmation that suitable accounting policies, consistently applied and supported by reasonable an prudent judgements and estimates, have been used in the preparation of the financial statements;

- confirmation that applicable accounting standards have been followed, subject to any material departures disclosed and explained in the notes to the accounts.

Neither should these example lists be interpreted as comprehensive guides to the responsibilities of individual directors.

## Schedules of matters reserved to the board B11.5

**Example 1**

*This schedule was drafted by a recently appointed non-executive chairman, for his second board meeting in mid-September 1998. At that meeting the suggested schedule was adopted by the board.*

At a meeting of the board on [date] it was resolved by the Board that only the Board can approve:

| | Reserved items: |
|---|---|
| **1. Strategy** | |
| 1.1 | Strategic decisions which are, or may be significant, in terms of future profitability. |
| 1.2 | Any decision to commence, discontinue or modify significantly any business activity or to enter or withdraw from a particular market sector. |
| **2. Capital & finance** | |
| 2.1 | Decisions on share capital changes (authorised and/or issued). |
| 2.2 | Decisions on investments or capital projects by the company or its subsidiaries where the principal sum or cost exceeds £n. |

| | **Reserved items:** |
|---|---|
| 2.3 | Decisions to acquire or dispose of company assets where the acquisition cost, disposal proceeds or profit or loss on disposal exceeds £n, or which would be likely to be regarded as significant by the board. |
| 2.4 | Decisions over new borrowing or significant amendments to the terms and conditions of existing borrowings. |
| 2.5 | Decisions on the adoption of treasury and risk management policies. |

**3. Terms of reference etc**

| | |
|---|---|
| 3.1 | Decisions on the wording of any changes to be recommended to the memorandum and articles of association and any other constitutional documents of the company. |
| 3.2 | Decisions on the creation, maintenance, terms of reference, leadership and membership of board committees. |
| 3.3 | Initial consideration of any matter (such as a company name change) which has to be decided by special resolution of the company. |

**4. Delegation of authority**

| | |
|---|---|
| 4.1 | Deciding delegation of authority to board and other committees such as an Assets & Liabilities Committee. |
| 4.2 | Decisions to grant, or vary, power, role, responsibilities and authority levels to individual directors, especially the chairman and the managing director; and in so doing to specify by implication the ones that the board reserves to itself. |

**5. Appointments**

| | |
|---|---|
| 5.1 | Decisions to appoint or remove a member of the board, or the company secretary, or the head of the internal audit function, following proper procedures agreed by the board. |
| 5.2 | Decision to appoint or remove a director from the chairmanship of the board. |
| 5.3 | Decisions to appoint or remove the auditors or other professional advisors. |

**6. Contracts and transactions etc**

| | |
|---|---|
| 6.1 | Decisions to commit the company to directors' contracts, including the terms of their appointment and remuneration. |
| 6.2 | Decisions to enter into any other significant contracts. |
| 6.3 | Significant decisions relating to any transaction in which a director has a direct or indirect material interest. |

|       | **Reserved items:**                                                                                                                        |
| ----- | ------------------------------------------------------------------------------------------------------------------------------------------ |
| 6.4   | Any matter where a director's (or directors') personal interests might conflict with his or her duty to the company. eg a political donation.[10] |
| 6.5   | Significant decisions on any contract or transaction material to the company falling outside the above categories.                         |
| **7. Disclosure** | |
| 7.1   | Decisions to adopt financial information for publication (eg the annual financial statements, prospectuses etc).                           |
| 7.2   | The presentation of reports and accounts to shareholders at the Annual General Meeting.                                                    |
| 7.3   | Decisions on anything that is likely to generate significant publicity and affect the image of the company.                               |
| **8. Meetings** | |
| 8.1   | Deciding policy governing the frequency, notice, purpose, conduct, duration and reporting of board meetings; and, especially, the setting of agendas. |

## Example 2

|       | **Reserved items:**                                                                                                                        |
| ----- | ------------------------------------------------------------------------------------------------------------------------------------------ |
| In compliance with Provision A.1.1 of the 2003 Combined Code as attached to the Listing Rules published by the Financial Services Authority, it was resolved by the board that: | |
| **1.** | Only the board can approve:                                                                                                               |
| 1.1   | The acquisition and disposal of group assets where the acquisition cost, disposal proceeds or profit or loss on disposal exceeds £5m, or would be likely to be regarded as significant by the board. |
| 1.2   | Strategic decisions which are, or may be significant, in terms of future profitability.                                                   |
| 1.3   | Investments or capital projects by a member of the group where the principal sum or cost exceeds £5m.                                      |
| 1.4   | Any decision to commence, discontinue or modify significantly any business activity or to enter or withdraw from a particular market sector. |
| 1.5   | Any significant contracts.                                                                                                                 |
| 1.6   | Decisions over new borrowing or significant amendments to the terms and conditions of existing borrowings.                                 |

| 1.7 | The appointment or removal of auditors or other professional advisors. |
|---|---|
| 1.8 | Any transaction in which a director has a direct or indirect material interest. |
| 1.9 | Anything which is likely to generate significant publicity and affect the image of the group. |
| 1.10 | Any transaction material to the Group falling outside other categories. |
| 1.11 | The granting to, or variation of, authority levels for executive directors. |
| 1.12 | The implementation or operation of group treasury and risk management policies including the delegation of authority to an Assets & Liabilities Committee. |
| 1.13 | The appointment or removal of a member of the board or the company secretary.[11] |
| 2. | Any three of the chairman and the non-executive directors be appointed a Nomination Committee.[12] |
| Only candidates nominated by the Committee shall be appointed as members of the board. | |
| 3. | That, in addition to any expenses payable in accordance with the Company's Articles of Association, the Company will reimburse directors for the reasonable costs of obtaining independent professional advice on matters directly connected with their directorship of the Company up to a limit of £5,000 per director per annum (or such greater sum as the Chairman may approve).[13] |
| See also **B10.50** OUTSIDE ADVICE FOR DIRECTORS AT THE COMPANY'S EXPENSE | |
| 4. | That the Terms of Reference of the Audit Committee, as approved by the board on 28 April 1991, should be extended by including the following: |
| | 'The Committee is able to obtain outside professional advice and, if necessary, to invite outsiders with relevant experience to attend its meetings.'[14] |
| 5. | It was noted that in compliance with the Code, James Green has been nominated the senior non-executive member of the board.[15] |

# Further reading

'Good Practice for Directors – Standards for the Board', Institute of Directors in association with Henley Management College, 1995, IoD, Mountbarrow House, 12–20 Elizabeth Street, London, SW1W 9RB. Tel: 0207 730 6060. Fax:

0207 235 5627.'The Company Chairman', Sir Adrian Cadbury 1990, published by Director Books in association with the Institute of Directors, UK. ISBN 1–870555–26–0.

# Delegation of authority guidelines B11.7

Delegation of authority guidelines (which, alternatively, may be called Authorisation guidelines or Concurrence guidelines) are the policies of the company on delegation of authority. They specify where decisions should be taken on important matters and whether these decisions are to be taken upon the recommendation of another or after consultation with another. That they are adopted by formal board resolution is a valuable way of contributing to the board being in effective overall control of the business. We suggest they should be reviewed by the board annually – both to remind the board of what is board policy and to provide an opportunity for amendment.

## How authority guidelines follow corporate governance best practice B11.8

There has been much recent interest in the broad subject of corporate governance and the establishment of effective systems of internal control. In the United States the Committee of the Sponsoring Organisations of the Treadway Commission prepared a comprehensive report titled 'Internal Control – An Integrated Framework'. This was followed, in December 1992, by the publication of the equivalent UK report of the Cadbury Committee. Both these reports set out best practices in relation to the composition and functioning of the board of directors, in reporting practice and in control matters. The Cadbury Code of Best Practice required that there should be a formal schedule of matters reserved to the board for its decision to ensure that the direction and control of the company is firmly in its hands. (An example of such a policy statement is given in **B11.5**.) Note 2 to the Cadbury Code had suggested that the board should lay down rules to establish the materiality level for each type of transaction and that there should be formal procedures to be followed when a decision is required between board meetings. These matters should all be addressed in formal board resolutions.

When considering the necessity and justification for establishing and implementing a policy on delegated authorities, the underlying principles of creating a valid and realistic internal control environment should be borne in mind. Whether or not it ever becomes mandatory for organisations to report upon the effectiveness of their systems of internal control (see **B4** REPORTING ON INTERNAL CONTROL AND THE TURNBULL REPORT), there is still value in defining realistic limits for operational, financial and accounting decision making. The board still needs to know that there is effective internal control, even though they rarely publish their opinion on this. Such an approach can give management greater assurance as to the accuracy and reliability of corporate accounting data, and reinforce the concept of the board and senior management being in overall control of the total business and its development.

## Approach to developing guidelines                    B11.9

The nature and form of a business organisation is naturally subject to ongoing development and change; accordingly the contents of these authority delegation policies should be subject to periodic review in order to ensure that they remain relevant and realistic.

Guidelines such as these may usefully be classified into major areas and documented in table form (with a table for each major area).

It is of course important that companies make sure that any guidelines they develop are tailored to their requirements, but this example may be a useful starting point.

## Example of authority guidelines                    B11.10

The following tables represent the Board Policies on Delegation of Authority recently drafted for use within a large company. They have been developed in relation to both the prevailing organisational structure and the spirit of the company's original 'Concurrence guidelines'. The relative financial limits have also been reviewed and updated where necessary. The old Concurrence guidelines indicated that concurrence was not required with respect to transactions and decisions which had already been approved as part of a budget or business plan; that concept, though entirely valid, has not been carried through to these guidelines. The company was a German-based multinational, and the two-tier board structure shows through to a limited extent – requiring minor modifications (referred to in the footnotes) for a unitary board situation. The German approach to directing and managing tends to be more thoroughly controlled than the UK approach, but UK companies should consider whether they might benefit from adopting a rather similar approach.

In this example, the nominated Authorisation Responsibility for each of the noted activities can be defined under any of the headed columns which the tables use. The nature of the responsibility is denoted by use of the alphabetic coding which is explained in the following paragraph. Whenever necessary, the coding is augmented by specific, stated limit values or by more discursive explanatory notes.

The alphabetic codes used in the authorisation responsibility columns, have the following meanings:

**O – Originated by**   This denotes the potential point of origin for a requirement, transaction, etc. It is possible to use this code in combination with others where alternative courses of action are possible. Additionally, a specific economic event may have a number of potential points of origin within the organisation. Where there are either a number of potential points of origination or all the points may apply, we have avoided illustrating every combination for the sake of clarity.

**R – On Recommendation of**

This normally relates to a proposal or activity, which may have originated elsewhere, which should be subject to formalised assessment and authorisation before progressing to the next authority stage. An example would be the recommendation of an appropriate committee prior to submission to the board of directors for final sanction.

**C – After Consultation with**

At any stage prior to final concurrence it may either be desirable or necessary to obtain the views of affected parties. Beyond the obvious benefit of involving and motivating those affected, this process can add quality to the understanding of the relative situation and the solution being proposed.

**D – Decision**

The use of this category indicates where the responsibility for the final decision lies. Ideally there should be a formal process of signifying and documenting that actions, transactions, projects, etc. are officially authorised to proceed.

The delegations of authority have been classified into nine sets, each corresponding to one of the tables. The tables are as follows.

Table 1  Board affairs

Table 2  Strategy

Table 3  Communications

Table 4  Accounting and variances

Table 5  Variances

Table 6  Published statements and other key documents

Table 7  Audit and control

Table 8  Personnel

Table 9  Appointments

# Authorisation tables

**Table 1**

*Board affairs*

| 1. | Board Affairs | Chairman | Board | Board Committee | Executive Committee | Country Manager | Divisional Manager | Regional or Functional Head |
|---|---|---|---|---|---|---|---|---|
| 1.1 | Amendments to the company's constitution (Memorandum & Articles of Association, or equivalent) | | R Decision of members in general meeting | | | | | |
| 1.2 | Whether the posts of Chairman and Chief Executive should be combined or separate.[1] | | D | | | | | |

---

[1] Where a Board is entirely non-executive this is not an issue. The *Combined Code* reads:

A.2   Chairman and CEO

Principle   There are two key tasks at the top of every public company - the running of the board and the executive responsibility for the running of the company business. There should be a clear division of responsibilities at the head of the company which will ensure a balance of power and authority, such that no one indi-vidual has unfettered powers of decision.

Code Provision:

A.2.1   A decision to combine the posts of chairman and chief executive officer in one person should be publicly justified. Whether the posts are held by different people or the same person, there should be a strong and independent non-executive element on the board, with a recognised senior member other than the chairman to whom concerns can be conveyed. The chairman, chief executive and senior independent director should be identified in the annual report.

| | | | | | | | |
|---|---|---|---|---|---|---|---|
| 1.3 | Where the posts of Chairman and Chief Executive are combined, which director is to be the recognised senior member.[2] | | D of non-executive directors only | | | | |
| 1.4 | The appointment and replacement of the Chairman of the Board. | | D | | | | |
| 1.5 | The number of non-executive and executive main Board directors. | | D with effective ratification by members | | | | |
| 1.6 | The appointment and removal of a Board director, together with severance terms. | | D with effective ratification by by members | | | | |
| 1.7 | Severance terms on removal of a director | | D | | | | |
| 1.8 | What shall be the standing committees of the Board, e.g.:<br>– Audit committee<br>– Assets & Liabilities committee | | D in all cases | | | | |

[2] To review all policy matters not specifically reserved to the Board or to another Board committee

| 1. | Board Affairs | Chairman | Board | Board Committee | Executive Committee | Country Manager | Divisional Manager | Regional or Functional Head |
|---|---|---|---|---|---|---|---|---|
|  | – Chairman's committee<br>– Community Affairs committee<br>– Group Operations committee<br>– Ethics committee<br>– Finance committee<br>– Nominations committee<br>– Remuneration committee<br>– Personnel committee<br>– Standing Orders committee |  |  |  |  |  |  |  |
| 1.9 | Who shall be the chairman of the Board committees. | (R)[3] | D | (D or R)[3] |  |  |  |  |
| 1.10 | Who shall be the members of the Board committees | D |  |  |  |  |  |  |

[3] Board may wish to consult with, or follow the recommendation of (a) the Chairman of the Board, or (b) the committee itself. Sometimes the committee itself is authorised to appoint its own Chairman.

| No. | Item | | | | | | |
|---|---|---|---|---|---|---|---|
| 1.11 | Policy on Board members, as individual directors, seeking outside professional advice, including the financial limits set to this. | | D | | | | |
| 1.12 | The frequency and scheduling of the meetings of the Board. | D | | | | | |
| 1.13 | The frequency and scheduling of the meetings of the Board's committees. | | | D by the committee chairman | | | |
| 1.14 | Agenda of Board meetings | D | | | | | |
| 1.15 | The appointment and removal of the secretary to the Board. | | D | | | | |

**Table 2**

*Strategy*

| 2. Strategy | Chairman | Board | Board Committee | Executive Committee | Country Manager | Divisional Manager | Regional or Functional Head |
|---|---|---|---|---|---|---|---|
| 2.1 Major decisions on strategy, reorganisation/ restructuring | | D | | R | | | |
| 2.2 Board policies on delegation of authority | | D | | C | | | |
| 2.3 The nature of the business, including adoption of new technologies | | D | | R | | | |
| 2.4 Approval of significant transactions which have material financial, political, commercial, legal, employee relations or environmental implications now or in the future. | | D | R | R | | | |

| | | | | |
|---|---|---|---|---|
| 2.5 | Transactions which have a significant effect on entities outside the Area executing the transaction. | | | D |
| 2.6 | Policy re. future acquisitions and divestments | D | | R |
| 2.7 | Actual acquisitions, mergers and divestments. | D | | R |
| 2.8 | Significant disposals of assets | D | R Assets & Liabilities committee | C |
| 2.9 | Management buy-outs | D | R[4] | C |
| 2.10 | Business principles and ethics, including approval of a written Code of Corporate Conduct | D | R[5] | R/C |

[4] Only if the Board has an Ethics committee.
[5] Only if the Board has an Ethics committee.

| 2. | Strategy | Chairman | Board | Board Committee | Executive Committee | Country Manager | Divisional Manager | Regional or Functional Head |
|---|---|---|---|---|---|---|---|---|
| 2.11 | Insurance cover policy: | | | | | | | |
| | 1 Directors' liability insurance | | D | R Finance committee | | | | |
| | 2 Officers' liability insurance | | D | R Finance committee | | | | |
| | 3 Fidelity bonding insurance (limit of cover, and posts to be covered) | | | D | R Finance committee | | | |
| | 4 Key person cover | | D | R Finance committee | | | | |
| | 5 General insurance | | | | D | | | |
| 2.12 | Arrangements for the management of land, buildings and other assets. | | | | | D | | |
| 2.13 | Management and control of stocks | | | | | | | D |
| 2.14 | Health and safety arrangements | | D | | R | | | |

**Table 3**

*Communications*

| 3. | Strategy | Chairman | Board | Board Committee | Executive Committee | Country Manager | Divisional Manager | Regional or Functional Head |
|---|---|---|---|---|---|---|---|---|
| 3.1 | Communication of policies (especially those covered in Table 2) | | | | D | R | R | |
| 3.2 | Determining the Terms of Reference for each of the Board committees. | | D | R[6] | | | | |
| 3.3 | Determination of Minutes of Board meetings | | D | | | | | |
| 3.4 | Management and control of computer systems and facilities | | | | D | | | R Head of I.T. etc |
| 3.5 | Data protection arrangements | | | | D | | | R Head of I.T. |

---

[6] Optional to ask for Recommendation of the committee itself.

**Table 4**

*Accounting and variances*

| 4. | Strategy | Chairman | Board | Board Committee | Executive Committee | Country Manager | Divisional Manager | Regional or Functional Head |
|---|---|---|---|---|---|---|---|---|
| 4.1 | Review and acceptance of outturns, in general | | | | $D^7$ | $D^7$ | $D^7$ | $D^7$ |
| 4.2 | Post investment appraisal | | | | $D^7$ | $D^7$ | $D^7$ | $D^7$ |
| 4.3 | Post project evaluation | | | | $D^7$ | $D^7$ | $D^7$ | $D^7$ |
| 4.4 | Negative variances of >5% from the net income of an approved budget or business plan: – >$1million[8] | | | | Must be specifically identified and brought to the attention of the Executive Committee | | | |

[7] Depending upon their nature and scale.

[8] Previous Concurrence Guidelines required concurrence of the Executive Committee upon identification if >5% of net income, and additionally required it to be brought to the attention of the Board if >10% of net income.

| | | | Must be specifically identified and brought to the attention of the Board Executive Committee B | |
|---|---|---|---|---|
| | – >$1 million | | | |
| 4.5 | Excess from an approved capital investment budget[9]:<br>– >10%<br>– >20% | | D | D |
| 4.6 | Consideration as to whether the company remains a going concern | D | R<br>Finance committee | |

[9] Previous Concurrence Guidelines required concurrence of the Executive Committee upon identification if variance was >10%, and additionally it had to be brought to the Board's attention if >20%.

**Table 5**

*Variances*

| 5. | Strategy | Chairman | Board | Board Committee | Executive Committee | Country Manager | Divisional Manager | Regional or Functional Head |
|---|---|---|---|---|---|---|---|---|
| 5.1 | Review of outturns | | | | | | | |
| 5.2 | Post investment appraisal | | | | | | | |
| 5.3 | Post project evaluation | | | | | | | |

**Table 6**

*Published statements and other key documents*

| 6. | Strategy | Chairman | Board | Board Committee | Executive Committee | Country Manager | Divisional Manager | Regional or Functional Head |
|---|---|---|---|---|---|---|---|---|
| 6.1 | The timing of publication of published statements | | D | R Finance committee | | | | |
| 6.2 | The timing of statutory general and other shareholder meetings | | D | | C | | | |
| 6.3 | Approval of the confidential annual report and accounts | | D | R Audit committee | | | | |
| 6.4 | Approval of any other published reports and accounts - such as prospectuses. | | D | R Audit committee | | | | |
| 6.5 | Approval of the less confidential Annual Review | | D | R | C | | | |
| 6.6 | Signing and sealing of documents | | | | $D^{10}$ | $D10^{10}$ | $D10^{10}$ | $D10^{10}$ |

[10] Depending upon their nature and the size of any commitment which is involved

**Table 7**

*Audit and control*

| 7. | Strategy | Chairman | Board | Board Committee | Executive Committee | Country Manager | Divisional Manager | Regional or Functional Head |
|----|----------|----------|-------|-----------------|---------------------|-----------------|--------------------|-----------------------------|
| 7.1 | The appointment and removal of the Group Chief Internal Auditor | | | D<br>Audit committee | | | | |
| 7.2 | The appointment and removal of the external auditors | | D<br>to be ratified by the members | R | | | | |
| 7.3 | Compensation for the external auditors | | D<br>to be ratified by the members | | | | | |
| 7.4 | Review and approval of the plans, scope, quality and report of the external auditors | | | D<br>Audit committee | | | | |
| 7.5 | Plans and scope of internal audit work | | | D<br>Audit committee | | | | R<br>Chief Internal Auditor |

| | | | | D<br>Audit committee | C | | | C<br>Chief Internal Auditor |
|---|---|---|---|---|---|---|---|---|
| 7.6 | Review of the adequacy of the company's systems of internal control, including computerised information system controls and security | | | | C | | | C |
| 7.7 | Review and acceptance of the external auditors' management letters | | | D<br>Audit Committee | | | | |
| 7.8 | Review and acceptance of the results of internal audit work | | | D<br>Audit Committee | C | C | C | C |

580

**Table 8**

*Personnel*

| 8. Strategy | Chairman | Board | Board Committee | Executive Committee | Country Manager | Divisional Manager | Regional or Functional Head |
|---|---|---|---|---|---|---|---|
| 8.1 The appointment and removal of the Chief Executive, together with severance terms. | | D | C Personnel and Nominations committee | | | | |
| 8.2 Approval of Chief Executive's expenses claims | D[11] | | | | | | |
| 8.3 Approval of expenses of the Chairman of the Board | | | D by chairman of the Remuneration committee | | | | |
| 8.4 Approval of expenses of directors | D | | | | | | |

[11] Or by chairman of the Remuneration committee, or another non-executive director approved for this purpose by the Board.

| | | | | | |
|---|---|---|---|---|---|
| 8.5 | Compensation packages of non-executive directors: <br> – Service contracts <br> – Fees <br> – Other benefits | D[12] | | | |
| 8.6 | Personnel policies to be used for determining pay and other terms and conditions of key staff. | | D <br> Personnel committee | R | |
| 8.7 | Actual salaries and emolument packages of executive directors: <br> – Service contracts <br> – Salaries <br> – Profit sharing <br> – Bonuses <br> – Other incentives <br> – Pension contributions <br> – Other benefits | | | | |
| 8.8 | Salaries and emolument packages of senior executives[13] | | D <br> Remuneration committee | | |

[12] Where the Board has executive directors it would be usual that the latter would recommend on this to the Board.

[13] If the company had executive directors it would be usual for decisions on 8.8 and 8.9 relating to more junior staff to be made by the Executive committee which would comprise the executive directors.

| | Strategy | Chairman | Board | Board Committee | Executive Committee | Country Manager | Divisional Manager | Regional or Functional Head |
|---|---|---|---|---|---|---|---|---|
| 8. | – Service contracts<br>– Profit sharing<br>– Bonuses<br>– Other incentives<br>– Pension contributions<br>– Other benefits | | | | | | | |
| 8.9 | General staff bonus schemes | | | D<br>Remuneration committee | | | | |
| 8.10 | Engagement in, or having an interest in, any business similar to the company's business or representing a potential conflict of interest, by:<br>– a director<br>– a member of the Executive Committee<br>– another | | D<br>D | | D | | | |

| 8.11 | Significant redundancies | | D Personnel committee | R | C | C | C |
|---|---|---|---|---|---|---|---|

**Table 9**

*Appointments*

| 9. | Strategy | Chairman | Board | Board Committee | Executive Committee | Country Manager | Divisional Manager | Regional or Functional Head |
|---|---|---|---|---|---|---|---|---|
| 9.1 | Appointment of the official stockbroker to the company. | | D | R Finance committee | C | | | |
| 9.2 | Appointment of the principal form of lawyers to the company. | | D | | C | | | |
| 9.3 | Appointment of the company's merchant bankers. | | | D Finance committee | C | | | |
| 9.4 | Issuing, receiving and opening of tenders, appointment of contractor(s), and post tender negotiations. | | | | D | D14 | D14 | D14 |

© Andrew Chambers
August 2000

# Shadowing of executive directors by non-executive directors B11.12

Some boards apply the practice, formally or informally, of nominating a non executive director to 'shadow' a particular executive director.

If the board is a balanced board numerically, between executive and non-executive directors, then a fairly comprehensive system of shadow partnering can usually be worked out. Each executive directors can be 'shadowed' by a non-executive director.

## A 'shadow director' B11.13

This is of course completely distinct from the concept of a 'shadow director' which occurs when someone passes him or herself off as being a board director of the company and thereby assumes the responsibilities of a director and incurs the potential liabilities. Someone can be cast in the role of being a 'shadow director' if he or she can be shown to have been culpable in allowing others to believe that he or she was a member of the board.

## Example B11.14

For instance, one might shadow the finance director: he or she would be chosen for his or her financial acumen; would focus on financial, accounting and audit issues; and would be relied upon by the board to have prepared, particularly thoroughly, for any board agenda items in these areas. This 'shadow' might, for instance, receive a full copy of each internal audit report whereas the other directors on the audit committee might usually receive very high level summaries only. This 'shadow' would routinely discuss issues of concern with the finance director prior to board and audit committee meetings – which can be an excellent way of ensuring that the non-executive directors become more fully involved and better informed.

## Approach to 'shadowing' B11.15

Generally, the approach to follow is that if the shadow has any particular queries on agenda items relating to the work of the executive director being shadowed, then in advance of the board or board committee meeting these should be raised and discussed (usually with that executive director) to the shadow's satisfaction.

## Pros and cons of 'shadowing' B11.16

This shadowing approach provides an excellent opportunity for non-executive directors to get actively involved – not as executives, but in an active non-executive capacity. It avoids inactivity of non-executives between board meetings. It assists a new non-executive director to get 'up to speed' quickly.

The 'shadow' can be a valuable ally and source of counsel and advice for the executive director being shadowed. The approach can contribute to team building at the level of the board, but of course there is a risk that it could contribute to divisive coalitions forming.

'Shadowing' in this way has to handled carefully. In some circumstances a 'shadow' may be held to be more culpable for any negligence of the board in the area being shadowed. So the shadow must be chosen with care. The rest of the board should understand that a shadowing arrangement does not absolve them, collectively and individually, of their usual responsibilities: there will always be a risk that the other directors might tend to assume that the non-executive shadow can be relied upon to keep on top of issues within his or her area of shadowing responsibility – to the extent that the rest of the board might neglect to master those agenda items.

# Tracking shareholder value B11.17

In an individual case, the right decision for a board to come to may not be the decision which maximises shareholder value. This will be so, for instance, when the decision which might maximise shareholder value would be in breach of a law, a regulation or a covenant entered into by the company under the terms of a contract. If a company is in breach of a funding covenant, it is right that the board should disclose this to the parties involved rather than pretend that the problem does not exist – even if, in extreme cases, this might cause the collapse of the share price and even of the company itself.

In such a case directors are in an invidious position: if their precipitate action is ill founded, they could find themselves sued by the shareholders for the value they have lost. On the other hand, if they fail to act in accordance with law, regulation or covenant, they will be in breach of their duty to so act and so vulnerable from other parties. Clearly the board needs to weigh things up very carefully and will be likely to need expert advice.

So it is true that in an individual case, the right decision for a board to come to may not be the decision which maximises shareholder value. However, in the generality of board decisions taken over time, and also with respect to the majority of individual decisions the board makes, the guiding principle above all others should be the intention of the board – the firm determination and indeed the effect – to maximise shareholder value while acting 'within the rules of the game'. In the words of Milton Friedman:

> 'There is one and only one social responsibility of business – to use its resources and engage in activities designed to increase its profits so long as it stays within the rules of the game ... '

Almost certainly the board will fail in this if the information it receives on shareholder value is inadequate. This useful schematic expresses well the relationship between 'information' and 'shareholder value':

Data > ('informationalise') > Information > Knowledge > Strategy > Action > Shareholder value

## Categories of information the board needs            B11.18

In today's environment the information the board needs goes well beyond conventional management accounting information, important though that is. Sometimes other forms of information are even more important. Of these, there are four categories which stand out in terms of being essential, but all too often are inadequate:

• Key performance indicators (KPIs) designed to enable the board to monitor the success of the executive in managing the risks which the board considers to be the major risks facing the business.

• Information on board performance. Other categories of information (such as management accounting information, risk management KPIs, and the type of information discussed in this section) all throw light on board performance. In addition the board needs other information more directly focused on how the board conducts itself – such as the attendance record of individual directors.

• Information which tracks corporate reputation and the quality and importance of relationships with stakeholders (see **B22** STAKEHOLDERS AND REPUTATIONAL MANAGEMENT). For a listed or other company, the principal stakeholder is the shareholder (see below).

• Information which tracks the board's success in delivering value to the shareholders, which is the subject of this section.

(We consider management accounting packs (MAPs) in **B11.2**.) We recommend that the traditional MAP which the board regularly receives should be extended to include key information in the above categories. If this information is not reaching the board it is likely that the board is not giving these important matters sufficient focus. One can measure the importance the board is giving to a matter by the quality of the information the board receives regularly on it, and the extent to which that information is discussed at the board.

A quick self-test, that any director can do, is to consider whether he or she knows how the company shapes up with respect to the performance measures on delivering value to shareholders discussed in this section.

## Historic data, projections and peer group data            B11.19

Beyond bringing information to the board about shareholder value, the board should set targets to achieve in this area, approve strategy designed to deliver on these targets, and monitor success at doing so.

Much more so than with conventional management accounting information, measures on delivering value to shareholders are particularly illuminating when historical data stretching back a number of years[16] and forward projections[17] are placed before the board alongside current information. Care must be taken to account for the distortion of the statistics which may result, for instance, from an acquisition, a change in the issued share capital, and so on. We should also be alert to the sensitivity of the numbers to the particular date on which the data is struck – for instance, market capitalisation can fluctuate widely in response to volatility of share price. Share price volatility in turn may be a consequence of low volumes of trading when there are not many buyers or sellers in the market.

Much of the information on shareholder value discussed in this section is more informative if comparable data of a peer group of companies is also presented. This is particularly the case with respect to information on current and projected performance.

There are many different facets to measuring shareholder value. As with so many performance measures, it is necessary to look at performance across an array of pertinent measures as relative success in one may be at the expense of relative failure in another – it is the entire tapestry that gives the picture, not the individual threads.

## Graphical representations of shareholder value      B11.20

Graphical representations provide a useful visual impression. In Chart 1, for a hypothetical listed company we show past trends in market capitalisation[18], P/E ratio[19] and profit before tax.

**Chart 1**                                                         **B11.21**

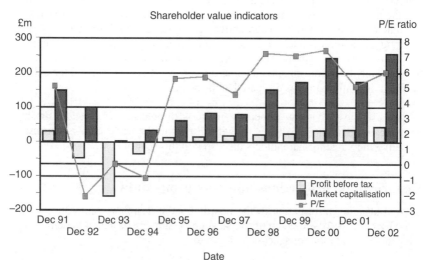

The same basic data is presented in a different way in Chart 2 to reveal how closely, for this fictional company, share price tracks profitability. The charts also show that profit before tax has, for this company, grown quite steadily.

**Chart 2**                                                                 **B11.22**

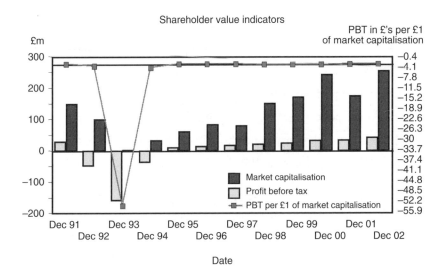

Shareholder value indicators

Date

## Information on shareholder value                                          **B11.23**

We give below a checklist of information which relates closely to whether the board is delivering value to shareholders. Our suggestion is that boards select from these types of information, the information they will monitor and interpret regularly in order to satisfy themselves that they are performing well in terms of shareholder value. Most of these measures should be applied over time, with historical data going back four years or so, and projections forward also by four years or so.

1.  **General company performance data which impacts directly or indirectly on shareholder value**

    1.1   Profit before tax

    1.2   Profit after tax

    1.3   Net assets (per balance sheet)

    1.4   Total shareholder value

    1.5   Cost to income ratio

    1.6   Share of market

    1.7   Revenue gains plus cost savings

1.8    Free cash

1.9    Projected tax rate

1.10   Peer group comparisons with respect to most of the above

**2.    Share information**

2.1    Shareholder concentration (50% in hands of top 5 institutional investors; 75% in hands of top 15)

2.2    Volumes of trading in shares (share price volatile if volumes small)

2.3    Peer group comparisons with respect to the above

**3.    Share performance**

3.1    Share price

   - Graph showing monthly movements for the last four years

   - Graph showing 90 day average movements over last four years

3.2    Earnings per share (EPS) – P/E ratios (based on profit before tax) – and minimum and maximum P/E ratios over the past 12 months

3.3    Projected growth rate in earnings per share

3.4    Price to book (market capitalisation, divided by net worth (a common measure in financial companies.

3.5    Net assets per share (excluding goodwill)

3.6    Return on equity (RoE) (Profit after tax divided by opening shareholder funds (capital and reserves) at the start of the period)

3.7    Declared dividend

3.8    Yield (total dividend as a percentage of market capitalisation)

3.9    Total shareholder return (comprises Yield (annualised dividend yield over time, at present value), plus Movement in market capitalisation (annualised change in 'share price x number of shares on issue' at present value, after adjusting for the impact of new share issues during the measurement period), adjusted for Changes in share capital either by new issues or company buy back of its share capital apportioned annually over the measurement period, expressed at present value).

3.10   Peer group comparisons with respect to most of the above

**4.    Brokers' reports** (brokers' forecasts can be shown separately and also the consensus view of the brokers taken together)

4.1    Brokers' forecasts of target market price of shares over the next three years

4.2    Brokers' forecasts of profit before tax over the next three years

4.3    Brokers' forecasts of earnings per share over the next three years

4.4    Brokers' forecasts of target price in 12 months time

4.5    Brokers' recommendations on 'Strong buy', 'Buy', 'Add', 'Hold' or 'Sell', etc

4.6    Brokers' recommendations on whether 'Undervalued' …

4.7    Plot for comparable group the PE ratio (vertical axis) against EPS increase (% – horizontal axis).

4.8    Peer group comparisons with respect to most of the above

**Shareholder value information which could usefully appear in the management accounting pack which the board receives**                     **B11.24**

1.    Commentary (anything on movements, comparables, etc):

  ●  Major movements in the month

  ●  New/exiting institutional investors

  ●  New broker reports

  ●  Comparables moves

2.    Measures, selected from the Table (above)

3.    Comparables

With respect to comparable companies (peer group) 6 month relative price movements, price:book, prospective PE and projected EPS growth rates.

# Company secretarial function checklist          **B11.25**

## Objective                                      **B11.26**

To ensure that the board and its committees are served by competent secretarial assistance in general and with regard to meetings and statutory/regulatory matters.

## Checklist                                      **B11.27**

**1.   Key Issues**

  1.1    Are the board and its committees provided with adequate secretarial support?

  1.2    Do the secretarial arrangements for the board and its committees preserve due business confidentiality?

  1.3    Is there maintained satisfactorily by the secretarial function a guide (or guides) accessible to members to regulate the conduct of board and committee business, covering terms of reference, standing orders, resolutions of continuing significance, etc.?

1.4 Do minutes sufficiently and promptly record the discussion and resolutions of meetings, are they signed by the chairperson, and are they maintained in an orderly, accessible yet secure fashion.?

1.5 Are there procedures which ensure that statutory and regulatory returns are submitted correctly and on time.?

1.6 Do board members and senior executives receive appropriate and timely advice on matters of a statutory or regulatory nature?

# Sound arrangements for meetings B11.28

1. There should be a meetings calendar so that business is executed at appropriate times.

2. Board committees should meet approximately ten days before the associated board meeting so that the draft minutes of a committee meeting can be an agenda paper at the following board meeting.

3. Adequate notice of meetings should be given so as to ensure good attendance.

4. Draft agenda should be approved by the committee chair before issuance.

5. Agendas and agenda papers should be approved by the board or committee chairman and circulated to members at least one week in advance.

6. Agenda papers should be fully informative.

7. Draft minutes should be approved by the board or committee chairman before issuance.

8. The approval of minutes should be taken seriously, will usually occur at the next meeting of the board or committee concerned, and will be indicated by the dated signature of the board or committee chairman on a copy of the approved minutes.

9. Minutes should fully describe the discussion which ensured at the meeting.

10. Follow-up of committee and board decisions is the responsibility of the committee or board concerned, and is facilitated by careful attention to 'matters arising' and by carrying forward open items to the agendas of subsequent meetings.

11. Chairs of meetings should not stifle contributions from members, but should facilitate full discussion of agenda items to the satisfaction of the board or committee members.

12. A copy of all agendas, agenda papers and approved minutes should be retained indefinitely in a secure and accessible place.

# Directors' handbook **B11.29**

A major challenge for most boards is for their members to be able readily to recall all past resolutions of the board. Usually these were originally resolved upon for good reason and after careful consideration: not only should they be regarded as binding upon the board until rescinded but they are likely to represent prudent practice. Of equal difficulty is for the board to be sure that they are fully aware of all material contract terms which the entity has entered into and which, if breached, would place the company and the board in default of their duties – either by virtue of the breach or by failure to disclose the breach to the other parties. An example would be a clause in a financing agreement which requires any 'material adverse change' to be drawn to the attention of the other party/ies. Another, sometimes related, example would be a clause in a contract which makes it an automatic breach of the terms of the contract if an accommodation is made with a party to another contract, or if a disclosure is made to a party to another contract of a material adverse change.

It is sound practice for each director to have an up-to-date directors' handbook giving them ready access to documents and information of continuing importance to the board. The handbook will be maintained by the company secretariat function. Here we suggest the contents of this manual.

The suggestion of a directors' handbook is included in the questionnaire on 'Auditing the Board at **B11.30**.

## Example contents of the directors' manual

1. A copy of the constitutional documents of the entity (memorandum of association, articles, etc)

2. A copy of the terms of reference of all board committees.

3. A copy of policy statements such as the entity's Statement of Corporate Principles, Code of Business Conduct, Code of Ethical Conduct, Fraud Policy Statement, Environmental Policy Statement.

4. A copy of the resolution authorising board members to take individual professional advice at company's expense

5. A copy of all other resolutions of the board with continuing effect.

6. A précis of all decisions of continuing significance made by the board under their reserved powers.

7. A copy of any established Delegation of Authority Guidelines (see **B11.7**).

8. Terms of appointment of board members: an up-to-date and complete copy of the service and employment contracts with the company of all directors.

9. A statement of the general and specific responsibilities of the directors.

10. A copy of declared (a) conflicts of interest and (b) related party transactions of directors and senior executives.

11. A copy of the key terms of the contracts between the company and its professional advisors.

12. Details of key contract terms the breach of which could conceivably lead to action against the directors.

13. The calendar of future company, board and board committee meetings and, where appropriate, an outline of their planned agendas.

14. Details of contingent liabilities of the company.

15. A schedule setting out the composition of the shareholders of the company, especially naming the principal shareholders.

# Auditing the board                                                 B11.30

It is a paradox of business that, while nothing is more important to the success of the business than the conduct of the board, the board itself is possibly the least likely of all parts of the business to be subject to independent review. But it can be done!

And it should be done. The board sets the tone for the business. Tight control should not be regarded as an irksome and counterproductive impediment for the board, while being an important feature for the rest of the business. Neither need control impede the flair of boards; rather, board internal control provides the framework in which board creativity can blossom to its fullest extent.

While it is true that the board is subject to external control by the stakeholders, this does not diminish the need for it to have effective internal control for its own purposes. Whatever the business activity, the primary justification for a satisfactory system of internal control is to ensure that the activity is likely to be done well; the secondary justification is to provide reassurance to those external to the activity that the task is under control. Either way, the board needs good internal control. And we now understand that the review, or monitoring of internal control is an essential feature of an effective system of internal control.

Where auditing the board does occur it is likely to be occasional rather than continuous. As such it is likely to be only reactive to a particular concern about board performance rather than being a periodic 'health check' of an unlimited scope ultimately determined by the reviewer.

In these respects it is often very different from the classic model of an internal audit which suggests that, after consultation, internal audit determines its programme of work having regard to risk. So management consultants and external auditors rather than internal auditors will often be used for this purpose. The checklist we provide here is intended as an *aide memoire* for whichever agency is entrusted with the task.

## A task for internal audit? **B11.31**

The traditional rationale for not using internal audit for this review centres upon the position of internal audit within the business. To be most effective, internal audit needs to be independent. Of course there is no such thing as complete independence.

One important aspect of effective independence is that the most senior point to whom internal audit reports must be able to be confident of the objectivity which underpins the determination of (a) audit scope, and (b) the content and emphasis of audit reports. That means, for instance, that it must be confident that the scope of internal audit reviews has been the professional judgement of the internal auditor. If, for instance, internal audit reports to an audit committee, that committee must be confident that no one beneath the audit committee has been unduly influential in deflecting internal audit away from investigating certain areas and into other areas against internal audit's better judgement. It also means that the most senior point to which internal audit reports must be confident that the content of internal audit reports is determined by internal audit and not, in effect, censured, by anyone beneath the level of the audit committee which relies upon the objectivity of internal audit.

Certain safeguards can provide reassurance to the audit committee as to internal audit independence, but these safeguards will not necessarily ensure effective independence for internal audit from the board itself and from the audit committee.

## Adapting the audit approach **B11.32**

Applicable safeguards can, however, be developed. They require the board to recognise that the board too can benefit from an independent review. Ideally they require the board to allow internal audit to determine the scope of its work when it audits the board. They require the content of resulting audit reports to be unexpurgated, for instance by executive directors, prior to being presented to the board.

## Web-based approaches to evaluating the board **B11.33**

All human societies need governing, wherever power is exercised to direct, control and regulate activities that affect people's interest. Governance involves the derivation, use and limitation of such powers. It identifies rights and responsibilities, legitimises actions and determines accountability. (ref RI Tricker) In recent years in the UK, much attention has been paid to governance in the UK company and much board time is concerned with complying with regulations.

The challenges are to ensure that, in a rapidly changing business climate:

- **Strategic management** can benefit synergistically from the demands of Governance on the one hand, dealing with accountability and supervision;

and the needs of management on the other, dealing with executive decision making and operational management,

- **An auditable focus** on the needs of the shareholders and other stakeholders can be utilised for the benefit of the business, where a company depends more than ever on its capacity for sustained learning.

Web based systems are now available that can help company secretaries, company boards, executives and staff at any location create, contribute, record, safeguard and exploit information of value as well as demonstrate via auditable trails that needed information has been developed, distributed, accessed and acted upon. Groups of participants can collaborate at a distance to achieve specific tasks within a short time frame or cultivate and learn at a slower pace the new knowledge that winning companies find critical. Winning boards can use this approach to monitor and reward, invite feedback, value relationships, innovate, explore, pioneer, discover and shape the future. Information management can replace information overload.

One such system is enable2, developed by Fount Solutions, supporting both collaboration and communities of learning. Further information can be obtained from David Meggitt or Colin Macklin on 0121 683 7906.

Whilst the foundations for fair and accurate reporting can be in place, fully auditable trails of information and document flow can provide the assurance of corporate governance compliance. The move to web based collaboration methods can be used to cultivate a learning organisation directed by a winning Board.

# Reporting arrangements                               B11.34

The management grade of the head of internal audit is a factor in influencing the likely effectiveness of internal audit's review of board level matters. CIMA, in their submission to Hampel, went as far as to suggest to Hampel that heads of internal audit should have equal status with executive directors. ICSA asserted to Hampel that in many companies the company secretary, particularly if a Chartered Secretary, is probably the most suitable officer to head up the internal audit function. On the other hand there can be a conflict if the head of internal audit is also secretary to the audit committee of the board, one of whose responsibilities is to monitor on behalf of the board the effectiveness of internal audit.

Neither CIMA's nor ICSA's suggestion was picked up by Hampel[20].

Certainly, for internal audit to report organisationally to the company secretary may give internal audit an apt degree of independence from the finance and accounting functions whose activities so often comprise so large a part of internal audit programmes. The Company Secretary usually already has the confidence of the board and is better placed to engineer an internal audit of board business.

# Other sources                                    **B11.35**

Readers may also like to consult other sources on good board practice, such as the following.

- Henley Management College, 'Good Practice for Directors – Standards for the Board', Institute of Directors, March 1995, ISBN 0–901–23045–6, 58 pps.

- Audit Commission, 'Taken on Board – Corporate Governance in the NHS: Developing the Role of Non-Executive Directors', HMSO, 1995, ISBN 011 886 403 3, 27 pps.

- Criteria of Control Board (COCO), 'Control and Governance No. 2: Guidance for Directors – Governance Processes for Control', (Canadian Institute of Chartered Accountants, 1996), 32 pps. Vide: Exhibit 7: 'Sample Questions about the Board's Effectiveness'.

---

**Control Objectives:** To ensure the enterprise has a high quality board of directors. To ensure that the board effectively sets the strategic direction of the business and is in control of its execution. To ensure effective corporate governance within the business. To ensure that board business is conducted efficiently. To ensure that overall board costs are reasonable.

---

| Key issues | | Illustrative scope or approach |
|---|---|---|
| | **Risk/Control Issue** | **Current Control/Measure** |
| 1.1 | How does the board ensure that its constitution, composition and organisation address its responsibilities effectively? (see also 1.2 below) | Terms of Reference of the board, explicitly adopted by the board and reviewed periodically. Appropriate main board committees with Terms of Reference which have been explicitly adopted by the board and are periodically reviewed by the board. Appropriate mix of executive and non-executive directors as members of the board and its committees. A formal and appropriate selection and performance review process re: the chair of the board, including approval by the board. A formal and appropriate selection and performance review process of chairs for the board committees, including approval by the board of these appointments |

| Key issues | | Illustrative scope or approach |
|---|---|---|
| | **Risk/Control Issue** | **Current Control/Measure** |
| 1.2 | How does the board address the matter of ensuring that its membership is suitable (in its size, composition and other respects) to the needs of the business? (see also 1.1 above) | Formal contracts for all directors. Directors' contracts are for a satisfactory fixed term. There is a board Nominations Committee which: <br>• determines board need; <br>• is responsible for succession planning; and <br>• recommends appointees to the board. <br>A sufficient degree of independence amongst the non-executive directors. The record shows that the board determines that the majority of its audit committee members are regarded by the board as being independent. Analysis of need, and a matching of background and skills to need. The board itself resolves on appointments and terminations of board members. Periodic comparison of board composition with that of similar enterprises. A record is kept of attendance of directors at board and board committee meetings, tabled to the board periodically. Attendance has been good (better than 80%). |
| 1.3 | How does the board ensure that there is not excessive concentration of power at or near the top of the business? | Separation of the roles of: <br>• chief executive <br>• chair of the business <br>or nomination of a suitable non-executive director to be the senior non-executive director. Non-executive directors meet alone from time to time, in addition to their time together at certain board committee meetings. Sufficient access for the board and its members to management, in addition to the MD. Close liaison between the chairs of board committees and the relevant, responsible manager(s) &/or other parties – for instance between: <br>• the chair of the audit committee; <br>• the head of internal audit; <br>• the head of compliance (if applicable); and <br>• the external auditor. <br>The record shows that board members at board meetings are encouraged to challenge management proposals. |

| Key issues | | Illustrative scope or approach |
|---|---|---|
| | **Risk/Control Issue** | **Current Control/Measure** |
| 1.4 | How does the board ensure it has taken charge of the ethical values of the business? | The board has adopted, as corporate policy statement(s), one or more of the following, as appropriate:<br>●    Statement of Corporate Principles;<br>●    Code of Business Conduct;<br>●  Code of Scientific Conduct;<br>●  Code of Ethical Conduct;<br>●  Code of Environmental Conduct; and<br>●  Fraud Policy Statement.<br>The board sets an appropriate and consistent example.<br>The board follows the principle of openness, and the other Nolan Principles where appropriate.<br>There is a satisfactory policy and procedure for taking ethical violations to the board.<br>The board is in overall control of the business's policy and practices with respect to equal opportunities. |
| 1.5 | How does the board ensure that its business is conducted efficiently and effectively, both at the board and in committee? | Scheduling of board and board committee meetings ensures that board committee minutes (at least in draft) are promptly available to the board as board agenda papers.<br>Chairs of board committees speak to their committee minutes at board meetings.<br>Adequate time is allowed for board and board committee meetings, and apt allocation of time between agenda items.<br>There are sufficient refreshment breaks within long meetings, and between meetings which follow on from each other.<br>Adequate notice of board and board committee meetings. Future schedule of meeting dates prepared and issued to members on a rolling annual basis.<br>Adequate timing of distribution of agenda papers, for members to prepare thoroughly.<br>Quality of agenda papers, including their reliability, sufficiency and clarity.<br>Freedom of undue filtering of information placed before the board.<br>Avoidance at the board of excessive involvement in detail and in management matters. |

| Key issues | | Illustrative scope or approach |
|---|---|---|
| | **Risk/Control Issue** | **Current Control/Measure** |
| 1.6 | How does the board ensure that the total compensation packages of executive and non-executive directors are appropriate? | An effective remuneration committee of non-executive directors to determine executive directors' compensation. Non-executive directors' compensation determined by the executive directors. |
| 1.7 | How does the board ensure that the right items are placed on board agendas, on a timely basis? | The board has an Agenda Committee (or a Chairman's Committee with, *inter alia*, agenda setting responsibility). |
| 1.8 | How does the board ensure that matters which require board approval are brought to the board? | Regular written reports from each executive director to the board, presented orally by the director and fully discussed at the board. Maintenance of a formal schedule of matters reserved to the board for its decision (see 1.11 below). |
| 1.9 | How does the board ensure that its members are fully appraised of the continuing information they need to discharge their responsibilities as directors effectively? | There is a tailored, on-going induction and training programme for each board member. Regular presentations are made to the board of important aspects of the business. Each director has a copy of a Directors' Manual containing, *inter alia*, a copy of: <br>• the memorandum of association; <br>• the articles of association; <br>• each director's contract; <br>• the terms of reference of board committees; <br>• delegation of authority guidelines; <br>• standing orders; <br>• all past board policy decisions not yet rescinded (see 1.10 below); <br>• essential extracts from all critical contracts, including significant covenants in financing and other agreements[21]; and <br>• copy of policy statement on directors taking independent professional advice (see 1.14 below). |

| Key issues | | Illustrative scope or approach |
|---|---|---|
| | **Risk/Control Issue** | **Current Control/Measure** |
| 1.10 | How does the board ensure that earlier formal resolutions it has taken will always be recalled, when appropriate, as being board policy – until rescinded or replaced? | There is a complete and up-to-date Guide to board policy decisions which have not been rescinded. (see 1.9 above) Minutes are thorough. Matters arising from past Minutes are identified and carried forward until addressed fully. |
| 1.11 | How does the board ensure that it is in control of the business? | There is a formal schedule of matters reserved to the board for its decision. (see 1.8 above) There are Delegation of Authority Guidelines, and they are clear and comprehensive. Do the right things get placed on board and board committee agendas – in time to determine outcomes? The board receives a regular MAP (Management Accounting Pack) which allows board members to monitor performance against plan, in all areas of the business. The MAP is: <br>• comprehensive; <br>• reliable; <br>• clear; <br>• timely; and <br>• not misleading. |
| 1.12 | How does the board ensure its decisions are implemented? | There is a monitoring procedure for follow-up of decisions, which is applied. It includes a schedule of decisions whose implementation must be ensured. There is evidence that this monitoring procedure is being applied. |
| 1.13 | How does the board ensure that its business, and that of its committees, is managed efficiently and effectively? | A qualified company secretariat, independent of other responsibilities, services the board and its committees. |

| Key issues | | Illustrative scope or approach |
|---|---|---|
| | **Risk/Control Issue** | **Current Control/Measure** |
| 1.14 | How does the board ensure that directors have adequate access to information and advice? | The company secretariat is available to the board, its committees and to individual board members in order to provide information and address issues of concern brought to the secretariat.<br>Board members need access to members of management in addition to the chief executive.<br>Board committees and individual board members are formally empowered to take independent, professional advice at the business's expense (see 1.16). |
| 1.15 | How does the board ensure it is appraised of shareholder, customer, supplier and other stakeholder complaints and concerns? | There is an established reporting system through to the board on these matters.<br>Non-executive directors serve on panels which deal with these matters.<br>These panels have appropriate terms of reference and standing orders, and their proceedings are thoroughly minuted.<br>Records of these panels show they work well. |
| 1.16 | How does the board protect itself and its members against the risk of negligent performance and/or possible litigation? | Thorough minuting of all board and board committee meetings.<br>Directors' liability insurance.<br>At their own discretion, individual directors, and board committees (per their terms of reference) are authorised to take professional advice at the business's expense, on matters relating respectively to their duties as directors or to their committee responsibilities (see 1.14). |
| 1.17 | How does the board secure its records? | Permanent retention of 100% of board and board committee agenda papers and minutes.<br>Duplicate (separate and secure) storage of these records.<br>Records are readily accessible by those who are authorised to access them, but safeguarded against unauthorised access.<br>Access to records is logged, and the log is kept secure.<br>Storage method(s) is proof against deterioration. Archives are inspected for quality periodically. Electronic records are checked periodically for continued accessibility and are refreshed periodically to avoid deterioration. |

| Key issues | | Illustrative scope or approach |
|---|---|---|
| | **Risk/Control Issue** | **Current Control/Measure** |
| 1.18 | How does the board monitor that the business continues to be a going concern? | The MAP (see 1.11 above) covers this with respect to liquidity, solvency, etc.<br>The audit committee of the board regularly addresses going concern.<br>The board, or the audit committee on behalf of the board, reviews the adequacy of the business's disaster recovery plan. |
| 1.19 | Is the board determining effectively the nature and content of corporate information which is published? | The audit committee considers the reliability of all information from the directors which is published.<br>The board consciously determines its policy with respect to the content of the Annual Report and Accounts – particularly with regard to disclosures over which there is no mandatory requirement, such as:<br>• environmental statements; and<br>• Corporate governance statements beyond minimum requirements. |
| 1.20 | Is the board approaching its legal responsibilities effectively? | The board has appointed a senior executive as compliance officer.<br>The board, through its audit committee, ensures that there is an effective internal audit, including:<br>• staff and other resources;<br>• qualifications;<br>• reporting relationships;<br>• programme of audits;<br>• completion of planned programme of audits; and<br>• content of audit reports.<br>The board, through its audit committee, ensures that there is an adequate external audit, headed by an appropriate audit partner.<br>In non-financial, non-accounting respects, the information and reporting system through to the board is sufficient to enable its directors to be reassured that they are meeting their legal responsibilities.<br>The Code of Business Conduct, approved by the board, specifically bans illegal acts by representatives of the business. |

| Key issues | | Illustrative scope or approach |
|---|---|---|
| | Risk/Control Issue | Current Control/Measure |
| 1.21 | Is the board pro-active? | The board and its committees (such as the audit committee) must consider future issues. Significant time at meetings should be spent on future prospects. |
| 1.22 | Are board members properly prepared for their duties? | There should be a tailored induction programme for each new board member, covering: <br> • the affairs of the business; and <br> • the characteristics of this board. <br> The responsibilities, duties and practice of directors (except for already experienced directors). |

# Board performance, not just board conformance

B11.36

EBF's Spring 2001 Forum asked contributors to consider whether corporate governance is delivering value for company stakeholders. A range of articles traced the origins of the main ideas, debated whether there is a distinct and emerging European governance model, and highlighted flaws in current systems. The article here by Bob Garratt – a reaction to the Forum – is a timely reminder that corporate governance is something much more dynamic than a set of rules which have to be observed. Bob Garratt is the chairman of two companies and a visiting Professor at Imperial College, London. He can be contacted at garratts@btconnect.com.

*This article appeared in European Business Forum (EBF) Issue 7, Autumn 2001, pp 36–37; ISSN 1469 6460.*

*European Business Forum, c/o PriceWaterhouseCoopers, Plumtree Court, London, EC4A 4HT, London, UK. Subscription service: Tel: + 44 (0)20 8597 0181. E-mail: subscription@ebfonline.com, www.ebfonline.com*

The EBF Spring 2001 issue 'Is Corporate Governance Delivering Value?' signals a refreshing approach to the rather stalled debate on how corporate governance will develop. But there were still hints in some articles of what one might term the conformance-based mindset which most directors find too restrictive and which I certainly believe is too narrow. The comments from Valter Lazzari – that 'corporate governance can be seen as the set of institutions, practices and rules to prevent expropriation of outside investors by insiders or dominant shareholders' and (elsewhere) that 'most major insights into corporate governance, and contributions to the debate, have come from the finance field' – are symptomatic of current thinking. I would argue, by contrast, that until the study and practice of appropriate behaviour and values behind the boardroom door is elevated to equal status with the compliance issues then we will not have effective corporate governance.

As a speaker at a conference on corporate governance in Paris not long ago I was hissed as I started to speak and was told by members of the rather irate audience, ENArques and French senior politicians, that 'corporate governance' is well-known as an Anglo-Saxon plot to destabilise La Francophonie. This is patent nonsense.

The issue of effective board performance is not simply a US versus Europe battle, it is a universal struggle. Indeed, the US and UK models differ significantly so the notion of an 'Anglo Saxon' bloc fails. The issues, especially the abuse of directoral office, are global and are found daily on the front pages of newspapers and on TV screens in both the developed and developing world, in the private and public sectors, in not-for-profit and in non-governmental organisations.

Effective corporate governance is about the exercise of the complex relationships between ownership, power, trust and anti-corruption processes in the boardroom. To be effective it must be as much concerned with generating wealth for society (board performance) as about staying rigidly within the rules (board conformance). Board conformance is necessary but not sufficient. Sufficiency comes through the exercise of appropriate values, structures and processes in a board to generate added value for the owners, private or public, to achieve their purpose within the laws of their country. As demands for greater transparency in the board's risk-taking and decision-making processes become more common, increasingly backed by legislation and through the use of internet technology by stakeholders, so the focus of the corporate governance debate will change from the present over-emphasis on basic compliance to the regular assessment of effective board and individual directoral behaviours and the consequent performance of their organisation. This is being driven both by directors' own needs to understand better the roles and tasks of the board in adding shareholder value, and by the need to combat the many abuses of directoral office for personal gain. Both can be countered by annual (or possibly more frequent) appraisal of the board and of individual directors' performance.

What would effective board performance look like? I will show two processes which have proved effective in developing more effective board behaviour in diverse countries. The first is the draft list of Ten Duties of an Effective Director which I have produced for discussion at the Commonwealth Association for Corporate Governance. This is a distillation of Commonwealth Law (based on its 54 country members) and highlights the ten most commonly misunderstood aspects of a director's role under that law. My work focused on ensuring each director, and each board, understood and acted on the three fundamental values to the owners of Corporate Governance:

- accountability;

- probity; and

- transparency.

It then lists the Duties.

1.  Ensuring Legitimacy (staying within the law).

2.  Upholding their Primary Obligation (to the company not the shareholders).

3.  Upholding their Primary Role (to drive the enterprise forward whilst keeping it under prudent control).

4.  Holding the company in Trust (for future generations).

5.  Ensuring critical review and debate (around the boardroom table).

6.  Upholding a duty of Care (in risk assessment and decision-taking).

7.  Upholding the three values of Effective Corporate Governance (Accountability, Probity, and Transparency).

8.  Upholding the rights of Minority Owners.

9.  Ensuring Corporate Social Responsibility.

10. Ensuring the board learns, develops and communicates.

For these Duties to be respected, lived and monitored it is essential that a director is inducted, included and brought to directoral competence. This is the responsibility of the Chairman, not the Chief Executive. A director must be respected for his or her individual inputs and encouraged to exercise personal judgement. The law holds them both jointly and individually liable for their decisions and actions although most directors do not understand this. Neither do they appreciate that they are not the representative of any grouping inside or outside the organisation. Because this so seldom understood, directors then adopt odd behaviours to please their non-existent 'masters'. They do not understand that at the very moment of their appointment as a director the law insists that their loyalty switches from those who appointed them to the company as a separate legal personality. Too many directors feel that this is a career-limiting approach. But legally they have no option.

The second process for effective board performance is to adopt the Learning Board Model which I have developed over the past ten years (see Figure 1).

Using a quadrant model, comprising on the horizontal axis the short-term and long-term perspectives, and on the vertical axis the external and internal perspectives, I have constructed the following sequential flow of work for any board of directors.

●  Policy Formulation/foresight.

●  Strategic Thinking (not Strategic Planning).

●  Supervising Management.

●  Accountability.

The details are discussed in my book 'The Fish Rots From The Head: The Crisis In Our Boardrooms'. I would stress here that this is a sequential process which gives an intellectual discipline to a board's cycle, annual or shorter. Board Performance is determined on the right side of the model – Policy Formulation and Strategic Thinking – and Board Conformance is determined on the left side – Supervising Management and Accountability. The quality of board critical review and debate, under a neutral chairman, is essential as the external and internal worlds change frequently and the complex interactions between the two need constant monitoring for the board to be able to make business sense of the political, physical, economic, social, technological, trade and legal worlds.

From my empirical observations I have found that the key problem points for boards are the debates that are needed where 'monitoring the external environment' and 'positioning in the changing markets' meet. This provides the strategy of the organisation – the broad deployment of scarce resources to achieve its purpose. Underperformance here prejudices the organisation's future. Yet equally important is the debate around 'implementing the strategy' and 'assessing organisational capability'. My research into directors' thinking styles shows that this is the major weakness in their thinking – they do not enjoy the process of implementing a strategy, and are particularly bad at receiving hard facts that show things are not working as planned. The discipline of working through the Learning Board model helps overcome this, as well as giving each board meeting a different focus, thus stopping it becoming a rubber stamp of executive actions.

The public is becoming more demanding of the need for competent directors, rather than managers. In the UK the publication of the Turnbull Report for listed companies in 1999, and the Rutteman Report for the public sector, has helped concentrate minds wonderfully. Listed companies are now obliged to explain to their owners their processes for risk assessment and decision-taking in their annual reports, or explain why they are not doing so. This is causing concern in many boardrooms as it throws up difficult questions of how precisely they do this now. Owners are beginning to ask just what does happen behind the boardroom door. So for directors to just carry on following a powerful Chairman or Chief Executive's gut feel will no longer be enough. Aspects of directoral professionalism and competence are raising their heads.

The assessment of directoral questions follow quickly from the owners. This goes way beyond the issues of Board Conformance and deeply into Board Performance. The practice of using 360 degree appraisals for all board members has started. This involves both peer and outsider review of the total Board Performance; and individual director assessment through a mixture of Chairman review, peer review, direct-report review, and on occasions customer or shareholder review. I have handled recently the review of the Chairman of one of the UK's major retail banks. Despite the trepidation on all sides beforehand the Chairman found it much less threatening, and more helpful, than he had anticipated. Indeed he has gone public in the bank's newsletter and published a synopsis of the findings and encouraged the staff to help him when he is under-performing in these areas – to the shock of many.

The cosy world of the non-performing director is ending, and quickly. Now boards are under scrutiny from many sides on both their conformance and their performance. The spotlight from investors, pensioners, and the pressure groups will not go away. Indeed it will become more closely focused. In future boards are likely to have to report on a 'triple bottom line' – financial, physical environmental, and corporate social responsibility. To do that board conformance will certainly not be sufficient.

# Corporate performance is closely linked to a strong ethical commitment
B11.37

Dr Curtis C Verschoor, CPA, CMA, CIA, CEE, who wrote this article, is the Ledger & Quill Research Professor at DePaul University, Chicago, and recently completed this significant study outlined in this article. He would be interested in hearing from any who comments to make, or who would like more information. E-mail: cverscho@condor.depaul.edu. Tel: +00 847 381 8115. Fax: +00 847 381 2310.

Greater recognition of the relevance of codes of ethics to corporate governance as well as intangible corporate assets like a highly motivated workforce, trustworthy suppliers, a loyal customer base, and most important, a reputation for fair dealing has significantly increased the focus on ethics as a mainstream driving force in business. This study demonstrates a strong positive link between a corporation's performance using three published unrelated financial and non-financial measures and a public commitment by its management to follow a code of ethical corporate conduct. Statistically, the level of significance of the difference is very high as the probability that the better performance results are due to chance is 1 per cent or less.

Approximately three-quarters of the 500 largest publicly held US corporations voluntarily make a formal public assertion of their management's responsibilities for properly reporting financial results and also maintaining an effective system of internal control. Virtually all of these companies report that the same strategies are used to execute these responsibilities. However, in spite of the significance that ethics is assuming as a strategic component of internal control, my study shows only about 25 per cent make a public representation that an expectation of ethical behavior or conformity to a code of ethics or corporate code of conduct is an aspect of their internal control system. Further analysis shows that about 14 per cent had an extensive or more explicit commitment to ethical accountability.

My research found that companies publicly committing to follow an ethics code as an internal control strategy achieved significantly higher performance using three published measures. These are the Business Week financial ranking, the Fortune survey of 'most admired' corporations, and the Stern Stewart analysis of Market Value Added. Statistically, the significance of the differences is very high as the probability that the better performance results are due to chance is one per cent or less.

Using membership in the Ethics Officers Association as a proxy for the completeness of a company's ethics program and commitment to its success, my analysis shows that these factors do not result in superior performance. Rather, the most plausible cause of superior performance is that certain organisations set an ethical tone at the top whose values permeate all levels. Based on interviews with representatives of a number of the high-performing companies, I believe superior performance relates to the nature of the values that management and the board of directors have infused into an organisation over time. The resulting code of conduct is merely a reflection of these values. This conclusion is consistent with the results reported by other recent academic studies.

An emphasis on proper values deals with setting examples, interpreting ethical principles, and structuring appropriate reward systems. An ethical culture spreads from clear and unequivocal goal setting at the top and openness throughout the organisation. On the other hand, a code of conduct with a compliance orientation has to do with rules, hierarchy, and sanctions. Legalistic codes of conduct designed only to protect an organisation from conflicts of interest or rogue managerial behaviors are unlikely to motivate loyal employee behavior and result in long-term retention of favorable relationships with suppliers, customers, and other stakeholders. The latter factors are what result in long-term profitability and corporate success.

In summary, there is clear evidence of a very strong connection between superior corporate performance and a public statement by corporate management of a strategic reliance on ethics as an element of internal control and corporate governance. However, the mere presence of an ethics code or even a well-executed ethics program does not itself cause superior performance. The most critical factors appear to be both the nature of the values upon which the corporate culture is based as well as the strength of a top management commitment to ethical treatment of stakeholders that is expressed in actions and not just in words.

**Notes**

1. John Baden (see **B15.36–B15.49**).
2. Final Report: Committee on Corporate Governance ('The Hampel Committee'), p17.
3. Report of the Committee on the Financial Aspects of Corporate Governance (1 December 1992), known as The Cadbury Report, chaired by Sir Adrian Cadbury; Gee [as Footnote 2], ISBN 0 85258 913 1 (Report); ISBN 0 85258 915 8 (Report with Code of Best Practice), 91 A5 pages.
4. Final Report of the Committee on Corporate Governance, (January 1998), chaired by Sir Ronald Hampel; Gee Publishing Ltd, 100 Avenue Road, Swiss Cottage, London, NW3 3PG. Freephone: +44 (0)345 573113. Fax: +44 (0)171 393 7463. ISBN 1 86089 034 2. Price: £10; 66 A5 pages.
5. The Combined Code, (June 1998), Committee on Corporate Governance, Gee Publishing Ltd, 100 Avenue Road, Swiss Cottage, London, NW3 3PG. Tel: 0345 573113. Fax: 0207 722 4762. ISBN 1 86089 036 9, 29 pages, £10. p. 13. Code Provision A.1.2.
6. Ibid, Principle A.1
7. Vide, eg: Good Practice for Directors – Standards for the Board: Institute of Directors in association with Henley Management College, 1995, IOD, Mountbarrow House, 12–20 Elizabeth Street, London, SW1W 9RB. Tel: 0207 730 6060. Fax: 0207 235 5627.
8. Sir Adrian Cadbury: The Company Chairman, 1990, published by Director Books in association with the Institute of Directors, UK. ISBN 1–870555–26–0.
9. Drawn from The Cadbury Report, (see footnote 1, above), p66.
10. In the UK, Part X of The Companies Act 1985 stipulates that directors should seek shareholder approval in circumstances where a director's personal interests might conflict with his or her duty to the company. More generally, a board of directors is accountable to the shareholders as a whole for its stewardship of the company.
11. 2003 Combined Code Provision A.5.3 reads:
    'All directors should have access to the advice and services of the company secretary, who is responsible to the board for ensuring that board procedures are complied with. Both the appointment and removal of the company secretary should be a matter for the board as a whole.'

12. 2003 Combined Code Provision A.4.1 reads:
     'There should be a nomination committee which should lead the process for board appointments and make recommendations to the board. A majority of members of the nomination committee should be independent non-executive directors. The chairman or an independent non-executive director should chair the committee, but the chairman should not chair the nomination committee when it is dealing with the appointment of a successor to the chairmanship. The nomination committee should make available its terms of reference, explaining its role and the authority delegated to it by the board.'

13. 2003 Combined Code Provision A.5.2 reads:
     'The board should ensure that directors, especially non-executive directors, have access to independent professional advice at the company's expense where they judge it necessary to discharge their responsibilities as directors. Committees should be provided with sufficient resources to undertake their duties.'
     See also **B10.50–B10.52**.

14. Curiously, the Hampel Committee was silent on this, although the 1998 Combined Code specified that the remuneration committee should be empowered to seek outside advice. On the other hand, the earlier Cadbury committee had recommended that audit committees should be able to seek outside advice, and we assume that not to do so was an oversight of the Hampel committee.

15. Although some had considered that the Cadbury Code guidance on this could lead to divided boards, the Hampel Committee continued with the guidance in the Combined Code and indeed strengthened it so that even when the posts of chairman and chief executive are not combined, it is recommended that there should be a recognised senior non-executive director. Despite opposition to Higgs proposals on this, the 2003 Combined Code has strengthened the role of the senior non-executive director still further. Provisions A.1.3 and A.3.3. now read respectively:
     'The chairman should hold meetings with the non-executive directors without the executives present. Led by the senior independent director, the non-executive directors should meet without the chairman present at least annually to appraise the chairman's performance (as described in A.6.1) and on such other occasions as are deemed appropriate.
     and
     'The board should appoint one of the independent non-executive directors to be the senior independent director. The senior independent director should be available to shareholders if they have concerns which contact through the normal channels of chairman, chief executive or finance director has failed to resolve or for which such contact is inappropriate.'

16. For about four years.

17. Also perhaps for four years.

18. Total issued shares, multiplied by today's market price.

19. The number of times market capitalisation exceeds annual profit.

20. Committee On Corporate Governance – The Hampel Committee, January 1998, Final Report, chaired by Sir Ronald Hampel, Gee Publishing, London. ISBN 1 86089 034 2.

21. Just one example here would be financing contracts which contain clauses that the board must disclose any material adverse change in the business's circumstances to the other parties to the contract, and perhaps that such a material adverse change represents a breach in the terms of the contract. The key point here is that the board needs to be confident that it is keeping on top of the business's contracting arrangements – at least to the extent that they have a potential material impact upon the welfare of the business.

# Board Policies and Policy Statements

## Oversight and control – board policy statements   B12.1

A sound control environment is now universally recognised to be an essential component of effective management[1] or, put another way, an essential to give reasonable assurance that corporate objectives will be achieved. Included within the control environment is the example set by the board of directors. It should go without saying that the board must display impeccable standards of integrity in the ways they conduct themselves collectively and individually. It is also important that the board and its members are consistent, not least in their dealings with staff and business partners.

More and more businesses are developing a code of business conduct, which COSO, Rutteman and Turnbull would all regard as part of the 'control environment' of a business. Doing so provides a good opportunity to crystallise the business's attitudes and practices with respect to many matters that have ethical implications. While often the result will be a formalisation of what is already custom and practice; it is surprising how the development of a code is likely to confront the organisation with anomalies and dilemmas to be resolved before consensus emerges. A code of business conduct can provide an agreed, communicable and understandable framework to govern the conduct of staff. They know where they stand. They know what is expected of them. They know what their responsibilities and opportunities are to raise as matters of concern.

Of course, it is important that the code is developed through a process of wide consultation. The well meaning sentiments of a consultant or even of the chairman of the board will be quite inadequate. The code should encapsulate the practical values of the business as a whole. While the development of the code will undoubtedly give some opportunities to improve on current practice, fundamentally it should be a code which reflects the best practices and the best principles currently at work within the enterprise. It will need to be communicated effectively. Of vital importance is that it is applied consistently in practice.

While a code may have real value in public relations terms, it should not be seen as a promotional tool to be ignored in practice. It can be an integral part of the open, empowered, participative and motivated enterprise. In developing a code which can be workable in practice, it may be necessary to settle for something less than the ideal. We believe that this is preferable to developing a code which in some respects is an aspiration only, to be honoured in the breach rather than the observance.

We recommend that the code of business conduct should be adopted by formal board resolution as the policy of the board for the company as a whole.

**B12.1**   *Oversight and control board policy statements*

(Sir Adrian Cadbury provides powerful justification for company codes at **B2.26** and **B2.27**).

# Examples                                                            B12.2

It is of course at the discretion of the board to decide what policy statement should be developed, adopted by the board and effectively communicated and followed throughout the business and by business partners such as contractors. In the following sections we give examples of these policy statements.

- Vision, promise and values (**B12.3–B12.4**).

- Who are our stakeholders and what do they want? (**B12.5–B12.6**)

- Statement of corporate principles (**B12.7**).

- Code of business conduct (**B12.8**).

- Code of ethical conduct on scientific and environmental matters (**B12.9**).

- Product supply chain ethical principles (**B12.10**).

- Risk strategy policy statement (**B12.11**)

- Internal audit charters (**B12.12–B12.15**).

- Whistle-blowing (**B12.16–B12.22**).

- Harassment (**B12.23–B12.24**).

- Environment and health (**B12.25**).

- Information security (**B12.26–B12.28**).

- E-mail internet and telephone (**B12.29**).

- Fraud (**B12.30**).

- Pension plan investment principles (**B12.31**).

The statement of corporate principles, code of business conduct and code of ethical conduct on scientific and environmental matters were developed as a set for a multinational pharmaceutical group whose board considered there was an overarching requirement for a statement of principles, to be interpreted separately with respect to commercial and scientific rules of conduct. This approach is discussed in more detail in the preamble to the Statement of Corporate Principles at **B12.7**.

# Statements of vision, promise and values    B12.3

## XYZ Group plc    B12.4

---

**Vision**

- To become the UK's most highly rewarded specialist provider of finance for people.

- As such, we will assist our customers to achieve their lifestyle ambitions and be an organisation of which employees can be proud.

---

**Promise**

- Deliver product value with excellence.

- Work together as a team.

- Invest in staff to enable them to achieve their career potential.

- Seek constant improvement – never being satisfied.

- Produce value and results that are both pleasing and rewarding to shareholders.

---

**Values**

- **Team work**
  To work in harmony in our respective teams and collectively towards the delivery of the overall objectives

- **Creativity**
  To identify and create new business opportunities and to apply creative and effective solutions to problems.

- **Integrity**
  To be ruthlessly honest and open in everything we do.

- **Respect**
  To treat people as individuals and to listen to their views.

- **Commitment**
  To drive the business forward with determination and to do so with effort and enthusiasm.

- **Professionalism**
  To maintain the highest standards and to deliver our products and services with care and accuracy.

- **Humour**
  To ensure we have fun while achieving success.

# Who are our stakeholders and what do they want?  B12.5

## ABC plc  B12.6

| Major stakeholders | What do they want? |
|---|---|
| Shareholders | Depends on shareholder Generally above average earnings per share growth over time |
| Staff<br><br>Directors | Security<br>Job satisfaction<br>Rewards |
| Customers | Service<br>Relationship |
| Suppliers | Future business<br>Paid on time |
| Funders | Low risk<br>Additional business |

# Statement of corporate principles  B12.7

A multinational pharmaceutical company set to work to develop their code of business conduct. It was not long before they determined that their approach should be to develop an overarching statement at the level of general principles to which the business subscribed, which they called their statement of corporate principles. We reproduce it here. They then developed two codes at a lower level. The two codes were more at the level of being rules to be followed, and were intended to be consistent with the overarching principles. They were:

- code of business conduct; and

- code of ethical conduct on scientific and environmental matters.

These are reproduced in **B12.8** and **B12.9**.

Space does not allow us to analyse in detail the statement of corporate principles and the code of business conduct. We would say that the company intended to develop a code which really could be observed in practice rather than being a statement of theoretical aspiration to be used for PR purposes with no intention that it should be complied with in reality. In view of this, the reader may think that some ethical compromises have been made. For instance, there is no unequivocal statement that company personnel would never break the law in the context of their activities. Neither do staff have a stated duty to report on wrongdoing unless they are personally involved in it; if they are not personally involved, they are accorded a right rather than a duty. Codes of business conduct in other companies make it a duty in both cases.

XYZ
XYZ London Limited
150 River Walk
London WC2 3XD

(Chairman's name)
Chairman

(Date)

## Statement of corporate principles

This policy statement addresses the general principles of our corporate life. Our separate code of business conduct sets out the rules which govern our application of these principles. Our code of ethical conduct applies our policy principles to scientific and environmental issues in particular. You will find some wording in common between the statement and the two codes where similar principles and practices are set out.

Copies of these three documents are available to all staff – from regional and country managers, and from divisional and business unit heads. They are also available from environmental affairs staff or through internal audit locally or at group level, from whom guidance on interpretation and application may be sought.

XYZ operates responsibly and with integrity, avoiding even the suggestion of impropriety. There should be no risk to our reputation if any details about our affairs became public knowledge. It is our policy to operate worldwide in a manner which protects the environment and the health of our employees and of those in the communities where we have an impact. We conduct our business honestly, scrupulously and free of deception or fraud. We observe applicable laws and regulations. We endeavour to ensure that equivalent standards are followed in companies in which XYZ has an interest but does not have control and also in those businesses with whom XYZ has contractual relationships.

The board of XYZ regards it as the duty of every individual employed by or acting for XYZ to observe the principles set out here. Any individual has a right to raise concerns about apparent breaches of these principles directly with senior management or with the group director of internal Audit.

### Conflicts of interest

XYZ's staff are to avoid any real or apparent conflict between their personal interests and those of XYZ. XYZ's assets and other resources are for use in XYZ's business only.

**B12.7**  *Statement of corporate principles*

## Business gifts, favours and entertainment

XYZ does not encourage the practice of giving or receiving gifts, even of nominal value. This also applies to gifts etc. made indirectly by another on XYZ's behalf. We believe that commercial criteria, rather than the influence of gifts, etc., best serve XYZ's interests. When gifts etc. are made they should be lawful and ethical, necessary and appropriate, of nominal or moderate value, capable of reciprocation, and properly authorised and recorded. They should not be interpretable as an improper inducement, nor be extravagant or too frequent.

## Confidentiality

XYZ's information is handled with discretion. It is not to be misused nor disclosed so as to place XYZ at a potential or actual commercial disadvantage, or for the benefit of another who is not entitled to receive it. Rights and responsibilities under privacy and other data legislation are to be observed.

## Internal control

XYZ acknowledges its duty to maintain an effective system of internal control which provides reasonable assurance of the achievement of business objectives, of the reliability of information used for reporting, of the safeguarding of resources, and of compliance with laws and regulations.

## Operational and accounting records

It is company policy (a) that the operational records and accounts of the business are to be reliable, truthful, accurate, complete, up-to-date and in compliance with prescribed standards and regulations, and (b) that there shall be no falsification. There are to be no secret or unrecorded activities, bank accounts, funds of money or other assets; no liabilities are to go knowingly unrecorded or unprovided for; and there are to be no off-books transactions.

## Relationships with suppliers

The viability of our suppliers is a key concern of XYZ. We set out to observe the terms of purchase orders and contracts, including the payment of suppliers according to agreed payment terms. We give weight to the quality of past service to XYZ while ensuring that transactions are justified on commercial grounds, and while actively considering alternative sources of supply. We avoid excessive dependence upon particular sources of supply when possible.

## Political activities and contributions

XYZ companies are authorised to make political donations in the countries where they operate in so far as the objective is to facilitate a healthy political process and to the extent that the contributions are lawful and meet our other criteria relating to purpose, amount, transparency and authorisation.

We have an interest in communicating relevant, reliable and responsible information and views on issues of public concern which impact upon our business.

XYZ strives to be a good employer with regard to individual staff who are actively involved in politics as private individuals.

**Conduct towards employees**

XYZ is committed to its employees. We seek to maximise the extent to which employees achieve their personal potential through their work with XYZ. We do this in part through appropriate commercial policies so that employees share in the company's success, and in part through policies which relate to health and safety. We believe in the inalienable right of every person to their personal dignity and do not allow practices which infringe upon this. All XYZ employees have equal opportunity in their employment. Staff are recruited for their relevant aptitudes, skills, experience and ability. Discrimination or harassment on grounds of race, colour, marital status, religion, sex, sexual orientation, ethnic or national origin, or legal political activity is not permitted. Treatment at all times shall be fair in terms of compensation, job security, work experiences, recognition of achievement and opportunities for advancement.

**Conduct in the community, and charitable contributions**

Our business is dedicated to the well-being of individuals. We have a duty to avoid conduct prejudicial to the communities where we do business and to enhance community life where practical. Our community support is targeted to improve economic or social well-being.

**Customer relations and product quality**

We strive to ensure that our products and services meet or exceed customer and statutory requirements at economical price; that our product information is reliable, and that we are responsive to customers' enquiries.

Please use your best endeavours to bring this statement to the attention of all personnel and to any with whom we are associated or do business.

# Code of business conduct                                    B12.8

This code is one of a set of three statements reproduced in this handbook, the others being THE STATEMENT OF CORPORATE PRINCIPLES (at **B12.7**) and THE CODE OF ETHICAL CONDUCT ON SCIENTIFIC AND ENVIRONMENTAL MATTERS (at **B12.9**).The relationships between the three are explored in the preamble to the former.

We consider this code of business conduct is strong in the avenues of communication which staff are authorised to use in order to express their concerns on matters of conduct. For instance, they may by-pass their immediate boss; or they may communicate directly with the head of internal audit.

Notice too the efforts that this company is taking to endorse this code at the highest level and to ensure that it is disseminated throughout the business. Note too that they expect their contractors and business partners to comply with this code.

XYZ

150 River Walk
XYZ London Limited
London WC2 3XD

(Chairman's name)
Chairman

(Date)

## Code of business conduct

XYZ is a major multinational corporation whose business partners range from governments and multinationals through to small suppliers, and whose ultimate customers are the many individuals who rely on the quality of our products for their well-being. So it is appropriate that we are seen to operate responsibly and with ethical integrity in our business conduct and in our corporate governance – to a standard which would usually be associated with the major public, listed companies who are so often our competitors; and we should avoid even the suggestion of impropriety. This should be so even when the law is permissive. In principle, there should be no risk to our local or international reputation if any details about our business affairs were to become public knowledge. At all times our business must be conducted honestly and scrupulously, free of deception and fraud.

To these ends, this code provides detailed guidance on the application to issues of business conduct of the policies outlined in XYZ's statement of corporate principles. A separate code of ethical conduct applies those policies to scientific and environmental issues in particular. You will find some wording in common between the statement and the two codes where similar principles and practices are set out.

Copies of the three documents are available at all locations to all staff, from regional and country managers, and from divisional and business unit heads. They are also available from environmental affairs staff or through internal audit locally or at group level, from whom guidance on interpretation and application may be sought by staff.

This document has been approved by the executive committee and adopted by the board of XYZ. The executive committee reviews annually the code's appropriateness and effectiveness, and advises the board accordingly. As part of this review, line managers annually are required to formally monitor their and their staff's performance in observing the requirements of this code within their areas of responsibility and, where judged appropriate, to develop initiatives to provide reasonable assurance of future compliance.

The board places particular importance upon timely actions to be taken whenever necessary to identify, contain and eliminate illegal acts.

A fundamental principle of the way XYZ conducts its business affairs is that applicable laws and regulations are to be scrupulously observed at all times. Practical difficulties may arise in many cases, such as when there are conflicts between the law of different countries, when local business custom and practice is inconsistent with local law or when there is ambiguity as to the legal position. Any case of actual or prospective non-compliance with law should be raised urgently with management and, if material, with the group chief executive.

The XYZ person responsible should endeavour to ensure that equivalent standards to those set out in this code are followed in companies in which XYZ has an interest but does not have control and also in those businesses with whom XYZ has contractual relationships. Where they are not, the XYZ person responsible should refer the matter upwards within XYZ.

The board of XYZ regards it as the duty of every individual employed by or acting for XYZ to follow all the requirements of this code. Any proposed action which appears to be in breach of any requirement of this code should not be progressed without full disclosure to and prior approval of the group chief executive or as delegated to the group financial controller or the group director of internal audit. Appropriate behaviour by individuals which is in compliance with this code and also specifically approved departures from this code will be supported by the company under the principle of collective responsibility.

Your duty to comply with this code includes a duty both to yourself and to XYZ to raise any concerns you may have on any matter of business conduct which appears to be a violation of this code and in which you are actively involved. In addition you have a right to raise similar concerns about the conduct of others even where you are not directly involved. Usually you should first raise a matter of concern with your line manager and you should do so at the earliest opportunity. At your discretion you may raise your concerns directly with senior management, with local internal audit or with the group director of internal audit and you should do so where an issue remains unresolved to your satisfaction after you have consulted your immediate management about it.

**Conflicts of interest**

Directors and employees of XYZ are responsible to avoid any real or apparent conflict between their own personal interests and those of XYZ. This may be at risk with respect to:

- dealings with suppliers, customers and other parties doing, or seeking to do, business with XYZ;

- transactions in securities of XYZ or of any company with whom XYZ has or is likely to have a business relationship; and

- acceptance of outside positions whether or not for a fee.

In appropriate circumstances XYZ encourages its directors and staff to be active outside the company.

XYZ's assets and other resources should not be used for any purpose other than for XYZ's business. They are not to be used for personal gain. These resources include but are not limited to staff time, materials, property, plant, equipment, cash, software, trade secrets and confidential information.

In cases of doubt, an employee should discuss the matter with his or her manager.

### Business gifts, favours and entertainment

XYZ operates in many host countries of the world with widely differing laws, regulations, customs and business practices. As a multinational XYZ is expected by its host in each case to conform to local societal norms and values whether enshrined in their laws, regulations, customs or business practices. Ethical dilemmas abound and have to be managed in harmony with the requirements of this code.

By way of illustration these may be some of the dilemmas:

- inconsistency between different applicable laws within one country;

- inconsistency between the laws of different countries involved in a transaction;

- inconsistency between law on the one hand and customs and practice on the other hand;

- an opportunity to achieve a considerable social good (such as by successfully marketing an effective product) but only at an ethical cost (such as by making a facilitating payment);

- the difficulty of distinguishing convincingly between on the one hand facilitating payments which may in some circumstances be permissible (to facilitate a legal right which might otherwise be withheld or delayed) and bribes which should not be permissible even when legal (to influence a business decision or gain an unfair commercial advantage which is not a right); or

- at what level a payment becomes extravagant.

As a general rule XYZ does not encourage the practice of giving or receiving gifts, even those of nominal value. Employees should use their best endeavours to ensure so far as is possible that commercial criteria, rather than the influence of gifts, favours or entertainment, best serve XYZ's business interests and their ongoing maintenance.

In determining whether any given or received business gift, favour and/or entertainment is permissible under this code each occurrence (and all connected ones taken together) are required to pass all of the following tests unless a requirement is specifically waived by the group chief executive or his or her delegatee. These tests should also be applied equally to gifts etc. made indirectly by another party such as by an agent using funds which could be construed as having originated in XYZ.

The tests:

- it could not be interpreted reasonably as an improper inducement;

- it is necessary;

- it would be considered nominal or moderate, and neither extravagant nor too frequent;

- it would be considered appropriate to the business responsibilities of the individual concerned;

- in the case of a gift etc. received, it would be capable of reciprocation as a normal business expense;

- unless of nominal value, there is appropriate prior specific approval usually of regional management;

- it is properly recorded, whether given or received;

- the group financial controller and the group director of internal audit have both been made fully aware of it beforehand;

- it is lawful and ethical.

## Confidentiality

All of XYZ's employees and contractors have a general duty to ensure that all XYZ's data and information which they encounter is handled with discretion.

XYZ personnel are not permitted to use confidential price sensitive information or to engage in other ways with competitors or others to fix the market price for products.

XYZ's information (whether technical, commercial, financial, personnel or other) must not be disclosed so as to place XYZ at a potential or actual commercial disadvantage, or for the benefit of another party who is not entitled to receive it.

Employees and contractors must ensure they act so as not to jeopardise (a) the rights of staff and others under privacy legislation and (b) the responsibilities and restrictions which apply to XYZ under data protection and other legislation.

## Internal control

All businesses and projects owned, managed or controlled by XYZ must maintain an adequate system of internal control which is in accordance with XYZ's control policies. Management and staff are responsible to ensure that, within their respective areas of responsibility, necessary arrangements at acceptable cost are in place and are complied with to give reasonable assurance that the objectives of internal control are met. These objectives include:

- the achievement of business objectives efficiently and economically;
- the reliability of information used internally and for external reporting;
- the safeguarding of corporate resources; and
- compliance with laws, regulations and policies of the company.

The necessary arrangements comprise proper attention to the following:

- the control environment;
- information and communication;
- risk analysis;
- control activities or procedures; and
- monitoring.

All incidents involving a breakdown of control leading to any actual or potential losses should be reported upwards immediately to management and to internal audit. For companies in which XYZ has an interest but does not have control, the XYZ person responsible should endeavour to ensure that equivalent standards are applied and should refer the matter upwards within XYZ when they are not.

### Operational and accounting records

Responsible staff must ensure that all the operational records and books of account of the business represent a reliable, truthful, accurate, complete and up-to-date picture in compliance with prescribed corporate procedures and external standards and regulations; and that they are suitable to be a basis for informed management decisions. The prompt recording and proper description of operations and of accounting transactions is a duty of responsible staff. Falsification of records and books is strictly prohibited.

No secret or unrecorded bank accounts, funds of money or other assets are to be established or maintained; no liabilities should knowingly go unrecorded or unprovided for; and there should be no off-books transactions.

### Relationships with suppliers

It is as important for XYZ to secure satisfactorily its sources of supply as it is for XYZ to achieve and maintain market penetration. To this end, the viability and well-being of XYZ's suppliers must be a key concern of XYZ's management and staff. Employees have a duty to ensure that XYZ observes the terms of purchase orders and contracts, including the payment of suppliers according to agreed payment terms.

While it is appropriate that due weight be given to the quality of past service to XYZ rendered by a supplier, the placing of an order for goods or services should always be demonstrably defensible on commercial grounds, and as a general principle XYZ's employees should be active in seeking new sources of supply. Excessive dependence upon particular sources of supply should be avoided whenever possible.

## Political activities and contributions

XYZ recognises that a healthy political climate is, in the long-term, an essential attribute of a prosperous and stable society as well as a key ingredient for the long-term success of XYZ whose mission is to improve the quality of life of ordinary people through the responsible application of its expertise. XYZ acknowledges that a healthy political climate depends in part upon adequate funding of the political process, upon there being active participation by many in the political process, and upon open and well informed debate on societal issues.

XYZ group companies are authorised to make political donations in the countries where they operate in so far as the objective is to facilitate a healthy political process by contributing to the adequacy of funding, by raising the level of participation or by enhancing the quality of informed debate on issues related to the XYZ business; but only to the extent that such contributions are:

● entirely lawful;

● in the public domain;

● modest in amount and not disproportionate in size to local conditions and to XYZ's public profile;

● not designed to prejudice political or commercial outcomes;

● properly recorded in the accounting records; and

● authorised in advance by the appropriate managing director.

XYZ has an enlightened self interest in communicating information and views on issues of public concern which have an important impact upon the XYZ business: management should be active in looking for appropriate opportunities to do so. The information and views so communicated must be relevant, reliable and responsible.

XYZ strives to be a good employer with regard to individual staff who are actively involved in politics. Accordingly XYZ management should facilitate and not unnecessarily impede the process when individual XYZ staff exercise their legal rights to become actively involved in local or national politics. In turn, staff who are politically active, or minded to become so, should be candid with their XYZ management so that management are best able to be cooperative and difficulties are more likely to be avoided. Staff so involved have an obligation to XYZ to weigh carefully their obligations to XYZ when actual or potential conflicts of interest arise; in their use of time, in campaigning of issues of relevance to the XYZ business, and so on. Employees engaging in political activity do so as private individuals and not as representatives of XYZ.

## Conduct towards employees

XYZ is committed to its employees. An underlying principle is to maximise the extent to which all employees have the opportunity to achieve their personal potential through their work with XYZ. XYZ believes that it succeeds through the dedication of all its employees. Their motivated involvement, work satisfaction and security are high priorities. In part this depends upon the implementation of appropriate commercial policies so that employees share in the company's success; in part upon policies which relate to health and safety. Apart from the inalienable right of every person to their personal dignity, practices which intentionally or unintendedly infringe upon personal dignity are likely to interfere with an individual's work performance.

In the conduct of his or her business responsibilities every XYZ employee is expected to apply the principle of equal opportunity in employment. No member of staff shall discriminate so that another member of staff (or a member of staff of a contractor, supplier or customer) is victimised or less favourably treated than another on grounds of race, colour, marital status, religion, sex, sexual orientation, ethnic or national origin, or legal political activity. Treatment shall at all times be fair in terms of compensation, job security, work experiences, recognition of achievement and opportunities for advancement.

Staff shall be recruited for their relevant aptitudes, skills, experience and ability; and their advancement shall be on the same grounds according to the opportunities available within XYZ.

Employment practices including recruitment practices, contract terms and working conditions shall be sensitive to the culture of the country concerned so as to ensure that company conduct does not contribute to unacceptable social tensions or malaise. At the same time, care must always be taken to ensure so far as is reasonably possible (a) that no harm occurs to those whose services the company employs while they are engaged in work-related activity, and (b) that the equal opportunity principles outlined in the preceding two paragraphs are applied.

XYZ seeks to ensure that employees have and exhibit mutual respect for each other at all times, both at work and also at business-related functions. XYZ staff are expected to behave in this way towards other employees, contractors, suppliers and customers. Harassment is unacceptable. Discrimination, in action, writing or through remarks, is a form of harassment. Unwelcome verbal and physical advances and derogatory remarks are other forms of harassment. It is a duty of all XYZ employees to ensure that their behaviour at no time contributes towards the creation of an intimidating, offensive or hostile work environment.

For staff to identify with XYZ and for XYZ to benefit most from the potential within its staff, the approach to their staff of XYZ's managers and supervisors must be as open and candid as possible. Staff also must be made to feel that they can communicate upwards without formality, rebuff, rancour or victimisation. While not abdicating their personal responsibility, managers should delegate downwards to as great an extent as possible so as to empower and develop their staff. Rigid hierarchical styles of management should be discouraged and staff may address any issues directly above the level of their immediate supervisor if they judge this to be appropriate.

## Conduct by people acting on XYZ's behalf

In the introduction to the code I indicated that the XYZ person responsible should endeavour to ensure that equivalent standards to those set out in this code are followed in companies in which XYZ has an interest but does not have control, and also in those businesses with whom XYZ has contractual relationships. I also stated that it is the policy of the board of XYZ that those employed by or acting for XYZ should follow all the requirements of this code. For instance, contractors working on behalf of XYZ must ensure they act in accordance with this code with respect to confidentiality, conflicts of interest, the making and receiving of gifts and with respect to their and their employees' conduct towards XYZ's employees and towards those whom the contractors employ on XYZ's business.

It is not accepted that management and staff of XYZ circumvent their obligations under this code by deputing unacceptable practices to intermediaries acting directly or indirectly on XYZ's behalf so that XYZ may achieve a desired end while endeavouring to avoid any opprobrium.

## Conduct in the community, and charitable contributions

XYZ accepts that it has community obligations where it does business. We have a general duty to avoid conduct prejudicial to the best interests of the communities where we do business. We have a positive duty as well as a self interest, as corporate citizens committed within our business to improving the well-being of individuals, to use our best endeavours to enhance community life. Apart from altruistic motivations which are important, we believe that a positive approach to our community relations is in the best long term interests of our company, of those who work within it, and of our present and future customers.

Staff are asked to assist XYZ to be proactive in searching out appropriate opportunities to contribute positively to community affairs and staff will be encouraged by XYZ to do likewise as individuals. Our contributions may be in leadership by initiating or steering community projects; they may be supportive in terms of donations of facilities, equipment, materials, time or cash.

To avoid waste, our community support should be targeted to improving economic or social well-being in demonstrable ways with a particular emphasis upon improving the quality of life of ordinary people. In nature and scale our support should be appropriate in each community while bearing favourable comparison with other companies of similar standing. Our support should be consistent with XYZ's business interests and corporate image, and should have a clear potential to enhance both of these.

## Customer relations and product quality

XYZ has no future unless it continues to satisfy customer needs in a competitive environment characterised by rapid technological advances. The company acknowledges the primacy of the following business principles which it expects its staff, as of duty, to apply consistently in practice and to encourage those who supply our ultimate customers to do likewise:

- we strive to ensure that the specifications of our products meet or exceed customer requirements at economical price;

- we strive to provide services which are excellent value-for-money and are delivered courteously and with sensitivity to our clients' requirements;

- we endeavour in all circumstances to ensure that all information about our products and services is reliable and a sufficient basis for fully informed customer decision making and customer use;

- we will be truthful and not misleading in our public relations, marketing and advertising;

- we are committed to satisfying enquiries, complaints and suggestions thoroughly and promptly; and

- we are committed to meeting or exceeding all statutory requirements with regard to our products and services as well as to their marketing, sale, distribution and subsequent after-sales support.

**Grievance procedures**

Every XYZ operating unit must have in place and comply with suitable procedures to ensure that the concerns of staff on any issue related to this code are considered promptly and thoroughly, and that remedial action is taken where appropriate.

Please use your best endeavours to bring this code appropriately to the attention of all personnel, to all new employees, to our business partners and contractors as well as their staff and to any others with whom we are associated or do business.

# Code of ethical conduct on scientific and environmental matters
B12.9

This code is one of a set of three statements reproduced in this handbook, the others being THE STATEMENT OF CORPORATE PRINCIPLES (at **B12.7**) and THE CODE OF BUSINESS CONDUCT (at **B12.8**). The relationships between the three are explored in the preamble to the former.

XYZ

150 River Walk
XYZ London Limited
London WC2 3XD

(Chairman's name)
Chairman

(Date)

# Code of ethical conduct on scientific and environmental matters

XYZ is a major multinational corporation operating in many countries, impacting upon the environment in many ways, employing many people and whose ultimate customers are the many individuals who rely on the quality of our products for their well-being. So it is appropriate that we are seen to operate responsibly and with ethical integrity in our scientific conduct and our environmental responsibility.

Our guiding principle is that we should endeavour at all times to maximise community benefit while never doing any harm. We should avoid even the suggestion of impropriety. This should be so even when the law is permissive. There should be no risk to our local or international reputation if any details about our affairs were to become public knowledge. We should aim to adopt the highest available scientific and environmental standards. At all times our business must be conducted honestly and scrupulously, free of deception.

To these ends, this code provides detailed guidance on the application to issues of scientific and environmental responsibility of the policies outlined in XYZ's statement of corporate principles. A separate code of business conduct applies those policies to commercial issues in particular. You will find some wording in common between the statement and the two codes where similar principles and required practices are set out.

Copies of the three documents are available at all locations to all staff; from regional and country managers, from divisional and business unit heads. They are also available from environmental affairs staff or through internal audit locally or at group level, from whom guidance on interpretation and application may be sought by staff.

This document has been approved by the executive committee and adopted by the board of XYZ. The executive committee reviews annually the code's appropriateness and effectiveness and advises the board accordingly. As part of this review, line managers annually are required to formally monitor their and their staff's performance in observing the requirements of this code within their areas of responsibility and, where judged appropriate, to develop initiatives to provide reasonable assurance of future compliance. Line managers are responsible to foster a sense of responsibility for the environment amongst employees at all levels. The board places particular importance upon timely actions to be taken whenever necessary to identify, contain and eliminate irresponsible or illegal acts; especially having regard to changes in technology, industrial practices, product design and trends in legislation.

A fundamental principle of the way XYZ conducts its affairs is that applicable laws and regulations are to be scrupulously observed at all times. Practical difficulties may arise in many cases, such as when there are conflicts between the law of different countries, when local business custom and practice is inconsistent with local law or when there is ambiguity as to the legal position.

Any case of actual or prospective non-compliance with law should be raised urgently with management and, if material, with the group chief executive.

The XYZ person responsible should endeavour to ensure that equivalent standards to those set out in this code are followed in companies in which XYZ has an interest but does not have control and also in those businesses with whom XYZ has contractual relationships. Where they are not, the XYZ person responsible should refer the matter upwards within XYZ.

The board of XYZ regards it as the duty of every individual employed by or acting for XYZ to follow all the requirements of this code. Any proposed action which appears to be in breach of any requirement of this code should not be progressed without full disclosure to and prior approval of the group chief executive or the group head of environmental affairs. Appropriate behaviour by individuals which is in compliance with this code and also specifically approved departures from this code will be supported by the company under its principle of collective responsibility.

Your duty to comply with this code includes a duty both to yourself and to XYZ to raise any concerns you may have on any matter of scientific or environmental conduct which appears to be a violation of this code and in which you are actively involved. In addition you have a right to raise similar concerns about the conduct of others even where you are not directly involved. Usually you should first raise a matter of concern with your line manager and you should do so at the earliest opportunity. At your discretion you may raise your concerns directly with senior management, with local internal audit or with the group head of environmental affairs and you should do so where an issue remains unresolved to your satisfaction after you have consulted your immediate management about it.

### Conduct in the community

XYZ accepts that it has community obligations wherever XYZ sources its supplies, conducts its business and where its products are used. We have a general duty to avoid conduct prejudicial to the best interests of these communities. We have a positive duty as well as a self interest, as corporate citizens committed within our business to improving the well-being of individuals, to use our best endeavours to enhance community life. Apart from altruistic motivations which are important, we believe that a positive approach to our community relations is in the best long term interests of our company, of those who work within it, and of our present and future customers and users of our products.

Staff are asked to assist XYZ to be proactive in searching out appropriate opportunities to contribute positively to community affairs and staff will be encouraged by XYZ to do likewise as individuals. Our contributions may be in leadership, by initiating or steering community projects; they may be supportive, in terms of responsible donations of facilities, equipment, materials, time or cash.

To avoid waste, our community support should be targeted to improving economic or social well-being in demonstrable ways with a particular emphasis upon improving the quality of life of ordinary people. In nature and scale our support should be appropriate in each community while bearing favourable comparison with other companies of similar standing. Our support should be consistent with XYZ's business interests and corporate image, and should have a clear potential to enhance both of these.

XYZ has an enlightened self interest in communicating information and views on scientific and environmental issues which should be of public concern which have an important impact upon the XYZ business: management should be active in looking for appropriate opportunities to do so. The information and views so communicated must be relevant, reliable and responsible. We should seek to co-operate with official bodies and technical organisations in the formulation of standards and the means of complying with them.

XYZ strives to be a good employer with regard to individual staff who are actively involved in community life, including involvement in politics. Accordingly, XYZ management should facilitate and not unnecessarily impede the process when individual XYZ staff exercise their legal rights to become actively involved in local or national affairs and politics. In turn, staff who are so active, or minded to become so, should be candid with their XYZ management so that management are best able to be cooperative and difficulties are more likely to be avoided. Staff so involved have an obligation to XYZ to weigh carefully their obligations to XYZ when actual or potential conflicts of interest arise; in their use of time, in campaigning on issues of relevance to the XYZ business, and so on. Employees engaging in political activity do so as private individuals and not as representatives of XYZ.

**Business and product development**

The environmental impact and potential health effects of all new corporate activities, acquisitions, projects, processes, products and services shall be assessed in advance by responsible staff. XYZ accepts a responsibility to evaluate the 'cradle-to-grave' impacts of our products and services. All investment decisions are to take account of environmental and health considerations. There is an *a priori* assumption that clean technologies shall be chosen. The environmental impact of facilities shall be assessed with regard *inter alia* to site appearance, effect on local and remote ecological systems, and storage safety and access. XYZ's transport strategy shall be determined having due regard to its environmental soundness.

**Conduct towards employees**

XYZ is committed to its employees. An underlying principle is to maximise the extent to which all employees have the opportunity to achieve their personal potential through their work and in the rest of their lives. XYZ believes that it succeeds through the dedication of all its employees. Their work satisfaction, security and safety are high priorities. In part this depends upon the implementation of appropriate policies which relate to health and safety.

Employment practices including recruitment practices, contract terms and working conditions shall be sensitive to the culture of the country concerned so as to ensure that company conduct does not contribute to unacceptable social tensions or malaise. At the same time, care must always be taken to ensure so far as is reasonably possible that no harm occurs to those whose services the company employs while they are engaged in work-related activity.

For staff to identify with XYZ and for XYZ to benefit most from the potential within its staff, the approach to their staff of XYZ's managers and supervisors must be as open and candid as possible. Staff also must be made to feel that they can communicate upwards without formality, rebuff, rancour or victimisation. While not abdicating their personal responsibility for scientific and environmental matters, managers should delegate downwards to as great an extent as possible so as to empower and develop their staff. Rigid hierarchical styles of management should be discouraged and staff may address any issues directly above the level of their immediate supervisor if they judge this to be appropriate.

## Supply

XYZ is concerned about the sources and methods of production of the raw materials and components it acquires, and the environmental conditions of service providers. XYZ subscribes to the principle of sustainable development, development which meets the needs of the present without compromising the abilities of future generations to meet their own needs. Wherever possible we use renewable, recycled and recyclable materials and components. Responsible XYZ staff should enquire so as to ascertain the extent to which elements of XYZ's suppliers' environments, products and services are hazardous, toxic, over-packed, non-renewable or not re-usable.

## Production and administration

In designing and operating production and administrative processes, XYZ staff shall endeavour to maximise efficiency by minimising or eliminating waste in all parts of the business with respect to materials, supplies, energy and other inputs and processes. Excess production is to be avoided. Where available 'waste free' processes and business practices shall be chosen in preference to others. Wherever possible XYZ reuses and recycles by-products of production. Hazardous substances, discharges, emissions, activities, practices and equipment are formally identified and necessary measures (including satisfactory plant maintenance and quality control) introduced and followed to prevent unwanted outcomes.

## Product quality and customer relations

XYZ aims to provide eminently usable products which function for users efficiently and reliably and without harmful effects. They are, where possible and appropriate, to be reusable and repairable. At the time of production there must be sufficient opportunities to ensure ultimate safe and environmentally friendly disposal of our products and their parts including packaging; and wherever practical our products and their components shall be recyclable.

Appropriate advice shall be provided to customers on all relevant environmental aspects of the handling, use and disposal of the products made or distributed by the company.

XYZ has no future unless it continues to satisfy customer needs in a competitive environment characterised by rapid technological advances. The company acknowledges the primacy of the following environmental and technical principles which it expects its staff, as of duty, to apply consistently in practice and to encourage those who supply our ultimate customers to do likewise:

- we strive to maximise the operational efficiency and reliability of all products we supply;

- we strive to eliminate all possible hazards arising from the use of the products we supply;

- wherever possible we intend to provide products which are environmentally friendly through their reliability, reparability, reusability and recyclability;

- we ensure that our products and packagings can be disposed of safely;

- we endeavour in all circumstances to ensure that all information about our products and services is reliable and a sufficient basis for fully informed customer decision making and customer use;

- we are committed to satisfying enquiries, complaints and suggestions thoroughly and promptly; and

- we are committed to meeting or exceeding all statutory requirements with regard to our products and services as well as to their marketing, sale, distribution and subsequent after-sales support.

**Internal control**

All businesses and projects owned, managed or controlled by XYZ must maintain an adequate system of internal control which is in accordance with XYZ's control policies. Management and staff are responsible to ensure that, within their respective areas of responsibility, necessary arrangements at acceptable cost are in place and are complied with to give reasonable assurance that the objectives of internal control are met. These objectives include:

- the achievement of business objectives efficiently and economically;

- the reliability of information used internally and for external reporting;

- the safeguarding of corporate resources; and

- compliance with laws, regulations and policies of the company.

The necessary arrangements comprise proper attention to the following:

- the control environment;

- information and communication;

- risk analysis;
- control activities or procedures; and
- monitoring.

All incidents involving a breakdown of control leading to any actual or potential breaches of the code should be reported upwards immediately to management and to internal audit. For companies in which XYZ has an interest but does not have control, the XYZ person responsible should endeavour to ensure that equivalent standards are applied and should refer the matter upwards within XYZ when they are not.

**Records**

Responsible staff must ensure that all the operational records of the business represent a reliable, truthful, accurate, complete and up-to-date picture in compliance with prescribed corporate procedures and external standards and regulations; and that they are suitable to be a basis for informed management decisions. The prompt recording and proper description of operations is a duty of responsible staff. Falsification of records is strictly prohibited.

No secret or unrecorded scientific activities are to be established or maintained.

**Conduct by people acting on XYZ's behalf**

In the introduction to code I indicated that the XYZ person responsible should endeavour to ensure that equivalent standards to those set out in this code are followed in companies in which XYZ has an interest but does not have control, and also in those businesses with whom XYZ has contractual relationships. I also stated that it is the policy of the board of XYZ that those employed by or acting for XYZ should follow all the requirements of this code. For instance, contractors working on behalf of XYZ must ensure they act in accordance with this code.

It is not accepted that management and staff of XYZ circumvent their obligations under this code by deputing unacceptable practices to intermediaries acting directly or indirectly on XYZ's behalf so that XYZ may achieve a desired end while endeavouring to avoid any opprobrium.

**Grievance procedures**

Every XYZ operating unit must have in place and comply with suitable procedures to ensure that the concerns of staff on any issue related to this code are considered promptly and thoroughly, and that remedial action is taken where appropriate.

Please use your best endeavours to bring this code appropriately to the attention of all personnel, to all new employees, to our business partners and contractors as well as their staff and to any others with whom we are associated or do business.

# Example of product supply chain ethical principles

## Introduction

This document details the ethical principles of the ABC Group in respect of the product supply chain. It should be read in conjunction with the 'code of business conduct', the 'environmental protection principles and guidelines' and the group personnel policies (this latter document currently under development). These four policy statements together dictate our behaviour towards our stakeholders, competitors, customers and the community in general.

We are a unique healthcare company and proud of our tradition of supplying high quality products and services developed through the application of our scientific and technical expertise.

As a general principle, the safety of our end users is of paramount importance and decisions in respect of all of all products and services we supply are taken with safety as the overriding criteria.

The embodiment of current best practices within ABC into these principles, demonstrates the importance that the top management of our group give to the ethical principles of our product supply chain. All our people are required to live these principles. These principles were developed by a working party which included representation from the ultimate holding company of the ABC Group.

## Part A – Summary

### A.1 Research and development

Research and development carried out by the ABC Group is directed at new products which serve the health of our customers.

Our goal is to offer extensive health concepts for disease management, from research to routine applications, covering diagnosis through to therapy, monitoring and patient training.

The use of biotechnology is particularly important for this and we are aware of the concerns that some people have in respect of this subject. We therefore attach great importance to behaving in a responsible and ethical manner in this, as well as all other areas.

### A.2 Products and services

ABC is involved in some or all stages of development, manufacture, marketing and sale of therapeutic, diagnostic and biochemical products and services. These products and services are aimed at improving the quality of life of the individuals who are treated with them.

## A.3 Production

Quality, a high degree of employee and plant safety, and respect for the environment, are the cornerstones of our manufacturing philosophy. We have mechanisms in place to ensure that our production processes are critically examined to keep risks as low as is possible. In addition, we recognise that different types and levels of risk will exist in different geographic and cultural environments and we will balance these with the techniques used in our production facilities.

## A.4 Marketing and customers

The ABC Group markets a range of high-quality diagnostic, therapeutic, and biochemical products and services of high value to our customers.

These products are aimed at improving the well-being and quality of life of a variety of end users and are developed and produced in an ethical manner.

## A.5 Other policies

ABC is committed to environmental protection, and our policy in this respect is detailed in a separate document entitled 'Environmental Protection Principles and Guidelines' issued in June 1995.

In addition to the importance that we place on acting responsibly and ethically in respect of our Product supply chain, and Environmental matters, we also have a 'code of business conduct', issued in October 1996 which describes our standards in respect of the conduct of our business affairs.

ABC is also in the process of developing 'personnel policies' which will codify our principles in respect of personnel matters.

# Part B – Detail

## B.1 Research and development

### B.1.1 Introduction

Research and development with the ABC Group is aimed at using our technological and scientific expertise to meet current and future needs for high quality products and services to improve the well being and quality of life of our various end users.

The scientific standards that we apply are amongst the highest in our industry, taking into consideration the competitive environments that exists.

We undertake to communicate any research results which are of direct significance to our customers without delay. However, the scientific knowledge gained through our research forms the basis for the development of new products and the international competitive situation requires us to treat this information confidentially. We are aware of the contradiction between the economic need for confidentiality and giving appropriate access to the results of research and we acknowledge our obligations in this respect.

The following statements refer to some specific aspects of research and development within the ABC Group.

### B.1.2 Gene technology

Methods such as gene technology, which are enhancing our knowledge on the causes of illnesses, are being used to develop methods of diagnosis and treatment. In addition, gene technology also enables us to produce proteins and other biological substances with increased efficiency and in an environmentally friendly manner. Gene technology is also essential in the production of many human proteins which are used for therapeutic purposes. Furthermore, it has become possible to modify the DNA sequence coding for proteins, thereby resulting in improvements to aspects of the product such as the pharmacological properties.

ABC is aware of the concerns associated with gene technology and this technology is used responsibly and ethically in the field of medicine with the clear objective of increasing our ability to improve the health, well-being and quality of life of our customers.

### B.1.3 Gene therapy

The development of somatic gene therapies to treat genetic diseases is one of the main focuses of our work. The dignity of human life is paramount and at ABC we are opposed to any form of interference in the human genotype.

### B.1.4 Animal experiments

Animal experiments are essential for the development and introduction of new therapeutic products. In many countries, it is a legal requirement for new products to have been tested on animals, prior to their being registered and sold in the marketplace. Animal experiments are used to evaluate dangers, side effects and risks to humans and to test the efficacy of the product.

At ABC we have undertaken to carefully review the necessity for animal experiments, to limit animal experiments in research and development of new drugs and treatments to a bare minimum, and to resort to alternative test procedures wherever possible. We also make every effort to use alternatives which contribute to a reduction in animal experimentation, and wherever possible to develop alternatives to animal experimentation ourselves.

### B.1.5 Transgenic animals

Transgenic animals make possible the creation of more specific and accurate pathological models than previously available, and therefore lay the scientific foundations for the future treatment of illnesses such as cancer and cystic fibrosis.

Furthermore, the use of Transgenic animals allows a drastic reduction in animal experiments.

## B.1.6 Technology transfer

Technology transfers and co-operation with research institutes and universities is a major key to our success. For this reason, it is extremely important for the ABC Group to allow our joint-venture partners an appropriate share of this success. This is also true of scientific publications and patents. The terms and conditions of such ventures are negotiated fairly and in a timely manner with our partners.

## B.1.7 Resources from developing countries

The use of biological resources, including those from developing countries, makes an important contribution to our research for new medical substances. We do of course observe all legal requirements in each of the countries concerned and ensure that we deal with any joint-venture partners equitably and reward them fairly for their assistance. We also act in full awareness of the importance of preserving biodiversity and strive to pass this awareness on to our joint-venture partners.

## B.1.8 Risk/benefit analysis

We try to analyse potential risks and dangers which could arise in the development or later application of our products before they are developed. We only develop a product when the expected benefits outweigh the potential risks.

## B.2 Products and services

## B.2.1 Introduction

As a unique healthcare company, our aim is to improve the quality of life of the persons being treated with our products and services through the application of our scientific and technical expertise.

Our business comprises diagnostic, therapeutic and biochemical products.

## B.2.2 Diagnostics

The ABC Group is involved in the development and sale of diagnostic products for various illnesses. Ethical problems do exist in certain areas of this science, for example tests for the diagnosis of non-treatable diseases, the area of genetic diagnosis (also known as DNA diagnosis), or tests which indicate increased disposition to illnesses. For this reason, we will only work in these areas if we, or other firms, are also working on the development of treatments for the diseases concerned, or if the tests for diseases with no means of treatment are still of high value, for example proof of pathogens in stored blood.

## B.2.3 Therapeutics

In the development of therapeutic products the guiding principle of the ABC Group is to offer a high degree of efficacy together with the highest possible safety.

In the therapeutics division we have established principles that we are involved in the development of drugs and services which provide the population with good and affordable health care; and our products are aimed at the prevention and/or treatment of illnesses.

We aim to prevent off-label use of our products by the provision of clear and comprehensive information. Any side effects, contra-indications and possible dangers of off-label use of our products are explained in unambiguous terms.

### B.2.4 Biochemicals

At the ABC Group, we also undertake manufacture and sale of biochemical products which are needed for research and medical application. We are aware that these reagents can also be used for purposes other than those intended by us and we therefore reserve the right to refuse to sell these products if there is reasonable grounds for suspicion that their ultimate use will not be in accordance with our ethical principles.

### B.3 Production

We continually strive to improve our production processes, for example by reducing energy consumption. In the manufacture of our products, we try to use scarce resources with care and we develop processes for recycling raw materials wherever practical. It is our stated objective to keep environmental impact caused by production to the minimum possible.

In respect of plant safety, our production sites are governed by standards which satisfy all legal requirements, and exceed them wherever practical and possible.

When building new production sites we choose suitable sites world-wide which meet economic, social and ecological criteria, taking into consideration factors such as the impact on the community and existing workforce, the existing infrastructure, waste disposal capacities and the availability of suppliers.

### B.4 Marketing and customers

Our objective is to offer high quality health-care products of the maximum possible customer value, which have been developed and produced in an ethical manner.

We carry out targeted market research which guarantees that the products which we develop are oriented to the needs and wishes of our customers.

We strive to bring new diagnostic and therapeutic principles to the market as quickly as possible, without compromising safety or quality. We undertake not to delay the market launch of new developments which could contribute to better health care solely for business reasons.

Information about our products will be scientifically accurate, open, and easy to comprehend. We will inform customers and end-users honestly about any risks in respect of our products, particularly in the case of misuse.

Our products will meet and, wherever possible, exceed all legal requirements in respect of safety of use both for the consumer and for the environment. Our products are subject to continuous quality control to ensure that this requirement is met.

Employees with an appropriate degree of technical knowledge will be available to answer any legitimate questions concerning our products. Complaints will be promptly investigated and courteously resolved.

We offer our customers an extensive service oriented towards their needs including training for doctors and patients, provision of comprehensive information material, and consultation in respect of problems, servicing of appliances etc.

We conduct ongoing reviews with the objective of determining ways by which our products can be further improved so as to provide increased value to our customers and end-users.

# Risk strategy policy statement                                   B12.11

Today, the conscious focus of boards and management is very much on risk strategy and risk management. Turnbull stipulates a 'top down' assessment of risk and control starting at the level of the board, and that processes for the review of risk and control should be embedded within the business and reviewed by the board. New, consultant driven, approaches to 'enterprise risk management' are being rolled out – with the contemporary accent of the gurus now being more on 'enterprise risk management' than on 'control risk self assessment'. 'ERM' is the new bandwagon to jump on!

So it is appropriate, indeed necessary, that the board formulates a policy on risk for the enterprise. This statement is contributed by Kelsey Beswick of Network Housing Association. E-mail: Kelsey_Beswick@networkha.org.uk. Tel: 020 8903 1339. Termed their 'risk strategy' it is nevertheless a useful example of a high level policy on risk management.

## Background

Risk is defined as 'Any event or action that effects Network's ability to meet its key business objectives and deliver its strategies effectively'.

## Housing Corporation Requirements – Regulatory Code

'Housing Associations must operate a framework which effectively identifies and manages risks…identifying all risks which might prevent it achieving its objectives…with the necessary arrangements to manage risks and mitigate their effects.'

The risk assessments usually cover about an 18-month period, however medium terms risks also need to be considered.

## Risk appetite

Network's risk appetite centres on the types and level or risk the organisation is prepared to take. It is based on the premise that calculated risk-taking is essential for ongoing success and that prudence is naturally required in situations where there are uncertainties over the outcome and where public money is at stake.

The types of risks Network are willing to take are covered by the organisational objectives. We will not take risks which fall outside of our objectives without prior Board approval. Our approach remains one where significant new types of risk will be managed by creating specialist teams or subsidiaries when the activity level is sufficient to warrant such action.

Each year we will review our business activities and the Board will decide whether it is appropriate to set activity limits to determine the level of risk we are prepared to take. Consideration will be given to turnover, property numbers, subsidy and resource capability.

Network will use external scanning and market analysis tools to identify risk areas and long term financial modelling to quantify financial risks.

## The risk management framework

Managing risk is a continuous process which needs to be embedded into Network's systems to aid decision making, accountability and systems improvement.

Risks are identified and prioritised at two key stages during the year, before and after the production of the Business Plan and monitored regularly to take into account the impact of new risks and changes in priority.

An assessment of the effectiveness of the controls in place to mitigate risks is carried out as an integral part of the process and actions to correct weaknesses are identified and implementation monitored.

The risk management framework and outputs are reviewed by the Risk Panel reporting to EMT and by the Group Audit Committee reporting to the Board.

## Responsibilities

The table below shows responsibilities for Network Housing Association. The Group Strategy Board and Group Management Team responsibilities are also noted to demonstrate how Group Risks are managed. The Risk Panel may be asked by GMT to co-ordinate Group Risk Management activities.

| Board/GSB | Group Audit Committee | Management/ GMT | Specialist Risk | Risk Panel/ GMT | Internal Audit |
|---|---|---|---|---|---|
| Determine risk appetite | Review approach | Identify risk | Insurance | Risk Strategy | Maintain risk map |
| Approve and Review strategy | Review risk management | Evaluate risk | Development | Risk Framework | Independent audit |
| | Monitor actions | Manage risk | Health & Safety | Monitor and co-ordinate | Assurance and opinion |
| | | Take risk | Business Continuity | Risk reporting | |
| | | Own risk | | Facilitate improvements Proactive advice and support | |

## Strategic approach to risk management

Network will employ the following strategies to ensure effective risk management:

- Carry out risk assessments before and after the production of the Business Plan, taking into account external and operational risk factors

- Carry out !s yearly reviews of the risk assessment recording changes in risks and priorities

- Monitor actions agreed to improve control effectiveness on a half yearly basis

- Provide an annual evaluation of control effectiveness to the Board via the Group Audit Committee

- Carry out annual Departmental Risk Assessments

- Carry out Risk Assessments on all significant projects

- Monitor overall impact to ensure that we do not attempt to introduce too many risks at once

- Implement a policy on reporting control failures

- Maintain the risk map and Risk Strategy on @Work (intranet)

- Carry out risk / control workshops with Board and Managers

- Focus committee papers on risk issues where relevant

- Register our risk management procedures to ISO9001

- Identify Group and cross-collateral risks and monitor at GMT

# Internal audit charters

The Standards of The Institute of Internal Auditors are at **B18.9–B18.13**.

Standard 1000 **'Purpose, Authority, and Responsibility' reads:**

'The purpose, authority, and responsibility of the internal audit activity should be formally defined in a charter, consistent with the Standards, and approved by the board.'

Standard 1000.A1 reads:

'The nature of assurance services provided to the organization should be defined in the audit charter. If assurances are to be provided to parties outside the organization, the nature of these assurances should also be defined in the charter.'

and Standard 1000.C1:

'The nature of consulting services should be defined in the audit charter.'

The Glossary to these Standards defines 'Charter' as:

'The charter of the internal audit activity is a formal written document that defines the activity's purpose, authority, and responsibility. The charter should (a) establish the internal audit activity's position within the organisation; (b) authorise access to records, personnel, and physical properties relevant to the performance of engagements; and (c) define the scope of internal audit activities.'

and 'Board' is defined to include audit committees working on behalf of boards and also sole individuals upon whom are vested the responsibilities more usually carried by directors collectively, viz:

'A board of directors, audit committee of such boards, head of an agency or legislative body to whom internal auditors report, board of governors or trustees of a non-profit organisation, or any other designated governing bodies of organisations.'

# Example 1

Here we provide a revised charter for an internal audit activity[2], giving effect to the new requirement that the nature of consulting services provided by an internal audit activity should be defined in the charter.

**Internal Audit Charter 1**

**ABC Holdings plc**

**CHARTER**

**OF**

**GROUP INTERNAL AUDIT**

**B12.13**  *Example 1*

In this charter the following words and terms have these respective meanings.

| | |
|---|---|
| 'The Entity' | The group of businesses within this plc; |
| 'The Board' | The Board of directors of the entity; |
| 'The Group' | All operations, investments and obligations which are the responsibility of the Board; |
| 'Audit Committee' | A committee of directors of the entity appointed by the Board as provided for in 'Terms of Reference of the Audit Committee' formally adopted by the Board; |
| 'Group Internal Audit' | The function which provides internal audit services to Group Management and to the Board through the Audit Committee. |

This charter identifies the purpose, authority and responsibility of the Group Internal Auditing Unit.

## Purpose

The Group Internal Auditing Unit is responsible to advise all levels of management, and the Board through its Audit Committee, on the quality of the Group's operations with particular emphasis on systems of control. It is a review activity which does not relieve line management of their responsibility for effective control. It functions by conducting independent appraisals leading to reports on its findings and recommendations addressed, as appropriate, to (a) the levels of management who need to know and are capable of ensuring that appropriate action is taken, and (b) the Audit Committee of the Board.

Subject to not prejudicing its assurance activity, the internal auditing unit may undertake consulting engagements the nature and scope of which are agreed upon with management and which are intended to add value and improve the organization's operations. Such consulting engagements will generally apply internal audit's competence in risk management, internal control and/or governance, and involve the provision of counsel, advice, facilitation, process design, and/or training.

The Board requires the Group Internal Auditing Unit to function professionally, adhering to the Code of Ethics, Standards and Guidelines of The Institute of Internal Auditors and meeting the requirements of regulatory authorities in those areas which are within the Group Internal Auditing Unit's responsibility.

## Authority

The Group Internal Auditing Unit derives its authority from senior management and from the Board to whose Audit Committee it has open access. The entity has also given the Group Internal Auditing Unit, for the purpose of its audit work, unrestricted access at any time to all the records, personnel, property and operations of the entity with strict responsibility for safekeeping and confidentiality.

*Example 2* **B12.14**

The Audit Committee of the Board reviews the scope and nature of the work of the Group Internal Auditing Unit to confirm its independence, and receives and reviews its reports to the Committee.

The Group Internal Auditing Unit does not perform line tasks as this would impair its objectivity; neither has it any direct responsibility for, nor authority over, the activities it reviews.

**Responsibilities**

The Group Head of Internal Audit is responsible for determining the Group Internal Auditing Unit's programme of work, so that management and the Board can have assurance as to the objectivity of audit reports. To provide this reassurance to management and the Board, the scope of the Group Internal Auditing Unit's work includes ascertaining, at home and abroad and at all levels of the entity, that the assets of the Group are being safeguarded; that operations are conducted effectively, efficiently and economically in accordance with Group policies and procedures as well as with laws and regulations; and that records and reports of the Group are accurate and reliable. The review of systems under development is part of the Group Internal Auditing Unit's responsibilities. In addition the Group Internal Auditing Unit may perform special reviews requested by management or the Board.

The Group Internal Auditing Unit is not relieved of its responsibilities in areas of the Group's business which are subject to review by others; but should always assess the extent to which it can rely upon the work of others and co-ordinate its audit planning with those other review agencies.

**[Signed]**

# Example 2           B12.14

This charter has been contributed by Kelsey Walker, Head of Audit and Consultancy at Network Housing Group. Kelsey can be contacted by e-mail at: KWalker@networkhg.org.uk" or by phone: 020 8903 1339.

**Internal Audit Charter 2**

*Purpose and scope of work*

The purpose of the Internal Audit service is to provide independent, objective assurance and consulting services designed to add value and improve the organisation's operations. It helps the organisation accomplish its objectives by bringing a systematic, disciplined approach to evaluate and improve the effectiveness of risk management, control and governance processes.

The scope of work of the Internal Audit service is to determine whether the organisation's network of risk management, control and governance processes, as designed and represented by management is adequate and functioning in a manner to ensure:

- Risks are appropriately identified and managed.

- Significant financial, managerial and operating information is accurate, reliable and timely.

- Employees' actions are in compliance with policies, standards, procedures and applicable laws and regulations.

- Resources are acquired economically, used efficiently and adequately protected.

- Programmes, plans and objectives are achieved.

- Quality and continuous improvement are fostered in the organisation's control process.

- Significant legislative or regulatory issues impacting the organisation are recognised and addressed appropriately.

- Opportunities for improving management control, profitability and the organisation's image may be identified during audits. They will be communicated to the appropriate level of management.

*Accountability*

The Head of Audit and Consultancy is accountable to management and the Group Audit Committee to:

- Provide annually an assessment on the adequacy and effectiveness of the organisation's processes for controlling its activities and managing its risks in the areas set forth under the Purpose and Scope of Work.

- Report significant issues related to the processes for controlling the activities of the Group, including potential improvements to those processes and provide information concerning follow up and implementation of agreed action.

- Periodically provide information on the status and results of the annual audit plan and the sufficiency of department resources.

- Co-ordinate with and provide oversight of other control and monitoring functions (risk management, external audit, internal quality auditing).

*Independence*

To provide for the independence of the Internal Audit service, staff report to the Head of Audit and Consultancy, who in turn reports functionally and administratively to the Chief Executive, and periodically to the Group Audit Committee (see Accountability section). Included in the reporting is a regular report to the Group Audit Committee on internal audit staff resources.

*Responsibility*

The Head of Audit and Consultancy and staff of the Internal Audit service have responsibility to:

*Example 2*  **B12.14**

- Develop a flexible annual audit plan using an appropriate risk-based methodology, including any risks or control concerns identified by management and submit that plan to the audit committee for review and approval as well as periodic updates.

- Implement the annual audit plan, as approved, including as appropriate any special tasks or projects requested by management and the audit committee.

- Maintain a professional audit staff with sufficient knowledge, skills, experience and training to meet the requirements of this Charter.

- Evaluate and assess significant new or changing services, processes, operations and control processes coincident with their development, implementation and/or expansion.

- Issue periodic reports to the Group Audit Committee and management summarising results of audit activities.

- Keep the Group Audit Committee informed of emerging trends and successful practices in internal auditing.

- Provide significant performance measurement targets and results to the Group Audit Committee.

- Assist in the investigation of suspected fraudulent activities within the organisation and notify management and the Group Audit Committee of the results.

- Consider the scope of work of the external auditors, internal quality auditors and regulators, as appropriate, for the purposes of optimal audit coverage, to the organisation at a reasonable overall cost.

### *Authority*

The Head of Audit and Consultancy and staff of the Internal Audit service are authorised to:

- Have unrestricted access to all functions, records, property and personnel.

- Have full and free access to the Group Audit Committee.

- Allocate resources, set frequencies, select subjects, determine scopes of work and apply the techniques required to accomplish audit objectives.

- Obtain the necessary assistance of personnel in departments of the organisation where they perform audits, as well as other specialised services from within or outside the organisation.

The Head of Audit and Consultancy and staff of the Internal Audit service are *not* authorised to:

- Perform operational duties inconsistent with the Audit and Consultancy role for the Association or the Group.

- Initiate or approve accounting transactions external to the Audit & Consultancy department.

647

**B12.14**  *Example 2*

### Standards of audit practice

The Internal Audit service will meet or exceed the Standards for the Professional Practice of Internal Auditing of The Institute of Internal Auditors and abide by the Code of Ethics.

SIGNED _____

Head of Audit & Consultancy

SIGNED _____

Chief Executive

SIGNED _____

Chair of Group Audit Committee

# Example 3

This is the sample Internal Audit Department Charter of The Institute of Internal Auditors Inc.

### Mission and scope of work

The mission of the internal audit department is to provide independent, objective assurance and consulting services designed to add value and improve the organization's operations. It helps the organization accomplish its objectives by bringing a systematic, disciplined approach to evaluate and improve the effectiveness of risk management, control, and governance processes.

The scope of work of the internal audit department is to determine whether the organization's network of risk management, control, and governance processes, as designed and represented by management, is adequate and functioning in a manner to ensure:

- Risks are appropriately identified and managed.
- Interaction with the various governance groups occurs as needed.
- Significant financial, managerial, and operating information is accurate, reliable, and timely.
- Employees' actions are in compliance with policies, standards, procedures, and applicable laws and regulations.
- Resources are acquired economically, used efficiently, and adequately protected.
- Programs, plans, and objectives are achieved.

*Example 3* **B12.15**

- Quality and continuous improvement are fostered in the organization's control process.

- Significant legislative or regulatory issues impacting the organization are recognized and addressed appropriately.

Opportunities for improving management control, profitability, and the organization's image may be identified during audits. They will be communicated to the appropriate level of management.

## Accountability

The chief audit executive, in the discharge of his/her duties, shall be accountable to management and the audit committee to:

- Provide annually an assessment on the adequacy and effectiveness of the organization's processes for controlling its activities and managing its risks in the areas set forth under the mission and scope of work.

- Report significant issues related to the processes for controlling the activities of the organization and its affiliates, including potential improvements to those processes, and provide information concerning such issues through resolution.

- Periodically provide information on the status and results of the annual audit plan and the sufficiency of department resources.

- Coordinate with and provide oversight of other control and monitoring functions (risk management, compliance, security, legal, ethics, environmental, external audit).

## Independence

To provide for the independence of the internal auditing department, its personnel report to the chief audit executive, who reports functionally to the audit committee and administratively to the chief executive officer in a manner outlined in the above section on Accountability. It will include as part of its reports to the audit committee a regular report on internal audit personnel.

## Responsibility

The chief audit executive and staff of the internal audit department have responsibility to:

- Develop a flexible annual audit plan using an appropriate risk-based methodology, including any risks or control concerns identified by management, and submit that plan to the audit committee for review and approval as well as periodic updates.

- Implement the annual audit plan, as approved, including as appropriate any special tasks or projects requested by management and the audit committee.

- Maintain a professional audit staff with sufficient knowledge, skills, experience, and professional certifications to meet the requirements of this Charter.

- Evaluate and assess significant merging/consolidating functions and new or changing services, processes, operations, and control processes coincident with their development, implementation, and/or expansion.

- Issue periodic reports to the audit committee and management summarizing results of audit activities.

- Keep the audit committee informed of emerging trends and successful practices in internal auditing.

- Provide a list of significant measurement goals and results to the audit committee.

- Assist in the investigation of significant suspected fraudulent activities within the organization and notify management and the audit committee of the results.

- Consider the scope of work of the external auditors and regulators, as appropriate, for the purpose of providing optimal audit coverage to the organization at a reasonable overall cost.

## Authority

The chief audit executive and staff of the internal audit department are authorized to:

- Have unrestricted access to all functions, records, property, and personnel.

- Have full and free access to the audit committee.

- Allocate resources, set frequencies, select subjects, determine scopes of work, and apply the techniques required to accomplish audit objectives.

- Obtain the necessary assistance of personnel in units of the organization where they perform audits, as well as other specialized services from within or outside the organization.

- The chief audit executive and staff of the internal audit department are not authorized to:

  o Perform any operational duties for the organization or its affiliates.

  o Initiate or approve accounting transactions external to the internal auditing department.

  o Direct the activities of any organization employee not employed by the internal auditing department, except to the extent such employees have been appropriately assigned to auditing teams or to otherwise assist the internal auditors.

## Standards of audit practice

The internal audit department will meet or exceed the *Standards for the Professional Practice of Internal Auditing* of The Institute of Internal Auditors.

SIGNED _____

Chief Audit Executive

SIGNED _____

Chief Executive Officer

SIGNED _____

Audit Committee Chair

Dated _____

# Whistleblowing and whistleblowing policy statements  B12.16

At the end of this section we provide an example of a whistleblowing policy statement.

## The UK Public Interest Disclosure Act 1998  B12.17

The *Public Interest Disclosure Act 1998* (*PIDA 1998*) came into effect on 1 July 1999[3]. UK employers risk heavy penalties and media attention if they discourage or attempt to cover up staff warnings about malpractice.

Under *PIDA 1998*, employees are able to claim full compensation if they are sacked or otherwise victimised for disclosing perceived malpractices to their employer or to an approved outside organisation. As there is no limit imposed on the level of compensation that can be awarded by a tribunal, the government hopes that this may encourage senior managers to blow the whistle on unscrupulous employers.

The purposes of *PIDA 1998* are to protect an individual who makes certain disclosures of information in the public interest; and to allow such an individual to bring action (including claims for compensation for wrongful dismissal) in respect of victimisation on the ground that the worker has made a protected disclosure. The relevant failure may have occurred within the UK or elsewhere, and the law applying to it may be the law of any country.

A qualifying disclosure to a person other than to the worker's employer is regarded as a disclosure to the employer if it is in accordance with a procedure authorised by the employer. The same rights apply to workers in government bodies if the disclosure is made to a minister or to a person prescribed for the purpose by the Secretary of State.

Under this Act, contractual duties of confidentiality are void insofar as they purport to preclude a worker from making a protected disclosure. *Section 43K* of *PIDA 1998* extends the Act in certain circumstances to freelance workers, contractors and subcontractors and those on work experience, etc.

*PIDA 1998* uses the expressions 'qualifying disclosure', 'relevant failures' and 'protected disclosures'. A 'qualifying disclosure' is any legal disclosure of information which, in the reasonable belief of the worker making the disclosure, tends to show one or more of these 'relevant failures':

(a) that a criminal offence has been committed, is being committed or is likely to be committed;

(b) that a person has failed, is failing or is likely to fail to comply with any legal obligation to which he is subject;

(c) that a miscarriage of justice has occurred, is occurring or is likely to occur;

(d) that the health or safety of any individual has been, is being or is likely to be endangered;

(e) that the environment has been, is being or is likely to be damaged; or

(f) that information tending to show any matter falling within any one of the preceding paragraphs has been, is being or is likely to be deliberately concealed,

unless the disclosure is made by a person to whom the information has been disclosed in the course of obtaining legal advice, about which a claim to legal professional privilege could be maintained in legal proceedings.

A 'protected disclosure' is a 'qualifying disclosure' made by the worker in good faith to his employer, or in some cases to another, so long as the following apply:

(a) the worker makes the disclosure in good faith;

(b) he reasonably believes that the information disclosed, and any allegation contained within it, are substantially true;

(c) he does not make the disclosure for purposes of personal gain;

(d) a number of conditions are met; and

(e) in all the circumstances of the case, it is reasonable for him to make the disclosure (what constitutes reasonableness is spelt out in *sections 43G(3)(a)* to *(f)* of *PIDA 1998*.

## UK whistleblowing cases following the Public Interest Disclosure Act 1998 B12.18

Employees are protected if they make a qualified disclosure in good faith.

Other workers (such as sub-contractors) must also pass the test that the disclosure was based on a reasonable belief in the truth of the matter disclosed.

A qualifying disclosure is one which tends to show (a) that a criminal offence is being or will be committed, (b) some other legal obligation such as a statutory duty or contract is being or will be breached, (c) the health and safety of a person is being or will be put in danger, (d) the environment is being or will be damaged, or (e) any of the above are the subject of a cover up.

### *Fernandes v Netcom Consultants (UK) Limited*      **B12.19**

An industrial tribunal awarded compensation of £293,441 to Fernandes who was dismissed after blowing the whistle to Netcom's parent company that £300,000 of expenses claims by the MD of Netcom did not have the necessary supporting documentation. The tribunal judged that the reasons given for Fernandes dismissal were a smokescreen, and the intention was to cover up the financial irregularities which had taken place.

### *Azmi v Orbis Charitable Trust*      **B12.20**

Mrs Azmi's appointment was not confirmed. This occurred after she had disclosed her concern about allegedly improper payments to (a) the external auditors, (b) the charity commissioners, (c) the charity's US associate organisation, and (d) Orbis's executive director. The tribunal found that (a) and (b) did not amount to a protected disclosure as (a) had been careful to ensure that these outside bodies kept her disclosures to them confidential. (c) was also not a protected disclosure because (c) was a separate organisation, not the parent of Orbis. But (d) was a protected disclosure and so Mrs Azmi won her case, the tribunal not believing Orbis's explanation for her termination.

### *Bladon v ALM Medical Services Limited*      **B12.21**

A matron disclosed his concern about the standard of nursing care to (a) management, and then, when no action followed, to (b) Social Services who investigated and found the allegations largely justified. The tribunal found that he was entitled to go outside the organisation in view of the nature of the complaint, the lack of action and the fact that the employer had no disclosure policy operating to act as guidance. If there had have been such a policy which was being followed, the employer may have been able to argue that the disclosure was unprotected, or the damages awarded may have been less. His disclosure was protected as he had first brought his concerns to the attention of his employer. The tribunal dismissed as 'fabricated' the employer's given reasons for dismissing him for 'dereliction of duty'. Damages of £23,000, including £10,000 for aggravated damages were awarded.

### Whistleblowing policy statement – 'doing the right thing' (Network Housing Association)      **B12.22**

Here we reproduce a whistleblowing policy statements by Kelsey Beswick and her colleagues in Network Housing Association, with the assistance of the charity Public Concern at Work.

There are a number of key elements to this policy statement.

The scope of the statement is given and covers frauds, corruption and malpractice, criminal or illegal behaviour, miscarriage of justice, danger to health and safety, abuse or neglect of vulnerable people, failure to deliver proper standards of service, damaging personal conflicts at senior level, and bullying, discrimination, harassment or victimisation in the work place. The organisation commits generally to the highest standards and specifically to involve staff in the development of its procedures on confidential reporting. It undertakes to monitor the policy, keeping confidential records of all matters raised through the whistleblowing policy and ensuring that an appropriate committee receives reports with an assessment of the effectiveness of the policy and any emerging patterns.

The policy encourages employees to express concerns suggesting they might like to come forward with a colleague or another person. There is a promise of support and confidentiality where possible, and describing it as a disciplinary offence to discourage staff from expressing concerns or victimisation following expression of a concern. There is specific commitment to ensuring that expressing concerns will not affect careers.

Staff are encouraged to 'blow the whistle' within the organisation rather than overlooking a problem or raising the issue outside. Staff are reminded that organisational rules require staff not disclose confidential, false or misleading information. So, in considering whether to take a concern outside the organisation staff are reminded of their duty of confidentiality and that they should ensure that the matter is raised without confidential information being divulged. The policy statement points out that *PIDA 1998* gives legal protection to whistleblowers who honestly and reasonably believe that the information they disclose or the allegations they make are substantially true.

A flexible route for communicating concerns is allowed for, in most cases to the immediate manager but with allowance for the concern to be expressed at the discretion of the concerned person direct to the internal audit service, or to a senior officer, or to the central services director, or even to the chief executive. Staff are given the right to ask a confidential meeting and are reminded that both parties should treat such contacts in confidence.

There is specific reference to the view that if the organisation's policy and procedures are working properly, there should be no need to contact one of the organisation's board members, or some external agency, to express concerns. But it is recognised there may be exceptional or urgent circumstances where it might be best to contact an external agency, and examples are given of the circumstances and what external people might be contacted. Reference in this context is made to Public Concern at Work who assisted this organisation to draw up this policy statement. Staff are, however, reminded that abuse of this confidential reporting process, for instance by maliciously raising unfounded allegations, will be treated as a disciplinary matter, but the statement seeks to assure that no-one who comes forward in good faith will have anything to fear.

The conduct of an investigation is covered within the general assurance that it will be looked into carefully and thoroughly, and acted upon appropriately. Provision for either internal or independent investigation is made. Fairness to all parties is warranted. If requested, the organisation agrees to try to let the concerned person know the results of the investigation and the action proposed.

The policy provides that concerns which fall within the scope established procedure will be referred for consideration under those procedures.

The organisation commits to acknowledging a communicated concern within seven days, with an indication of how the organisation proposes to deal with the matter and likely timescale. If a decision is made not to investigate, the reasons will be given. The concerned person is assured of as much information as possible on the outcomes of the investigation, subject to certain constraints.

## 1. Introduction

1.1 Network Housing Association is committed to the highest standards of quality, probity, openness and accountability.

1.2 As part of that commitment, we encourage employees or others with serious concerns about any aspect of our work to do the right thing and come forward and express those concerns. In many cases, concerns or complaints will be dealt with through our normal procedures. However, in some cases, we recognise that employees will need to come forward on a confidential basis. We want to make it clear that they can do so without fear of reprisal or victimisation.

1.3 This statement to our employees is intended to underline our commitment, and our support to those who come forward to express their concerns. Staff are often the first people who realise that there may be something seriously wrong within the organisation, but may not express their concerns. This could be for a number of reasons; because speaking up might be regarded as disloyal by colleagues or the organisation, because of fear that they may be victimised, doubts about reporting what might only be a suspicion, or because it might seem easier to ignore it and not get involved.

1.4 'Whistleblowing' is often understood as reporting a concern outside the organisation because, for various reasons, the employee does not wish or feel able to raise the matter internally. This whistleblowing policy aims to encourage and enable staff to raise serious concerns by 'blowing the whistle' within the Association, rather than overlooking a problem or raising the issue outside.

1.5 There are existing procedures in place to enable staff to raise concerns (the fraud policy), be it about the conduct of a service, or in order to protect service users from abuse and other forms of ill treatment. In addition, there are procedures to enable staff to complain on behalf of service users on more general matters relating to the provision of services. This policy has a wider application and is intended for any form of malpractice and cover-up of any of these.

## 2. Consultation and information

2.1   We will consult and involve you as we develop our procedures and practises on confidential reporting. We will also consult the staff association and recognise trades unions, as well as using our normal staff briefing and consultation procedures. We hope to get wide backing for and promotion of our approach.

2.2   Through our staff induction and briefing, we will make sure that you know how to recognise the following problems, and that you understand the effects they may have on the organisation, your job, and the service you provide:

- frauds, corruption and malpractice;

- criminal or illegal behaviour;

- miscarriage of justice;

- danger to health and safety;

- abuse or neglect of vulnerable people;

- failure to deliver proper standards of service;

- damaging personal conflicts at senior level; and

- bullying, discrimination, harassment or victimisation in the work place.

2.3   We will make sure that you know what is expected of you, and what practises you regard as unacceptable. You should study our staff guidance carefully, and discuss anything that seems unclear with your manager. If you are not sure what to do in a given situation, ask before taking any action.

2.4   When we find a problem, we will always deal with it seriously. We know that we cannot expect you to practise higher standards than those we apply. We will always pursue fraud and serious abuse as vigorously as possible through out disciplinary procedures, or if necessary, through the courts; frauds are always reported to the police. We hope that you will feel confident in doing the right thing by coming forward, that we share your sense of right and wrong and act on what you tell us.

## 3. Confidential reporting

3.1   We know that it is never easy to report a concern, particularly one which may relate to fraud or corruption. We urge you to come forward with any concerns at an early stage, and before problems have a chance to become serious.

3.2   If you prefer, we are happy for you to come forward with another colleague, a friend, trades union representative or other advisor to report a concern.

3.3   We will support concerned employees and protect them from reprisals or victimisation. If you come forward with a concern, you can be confident that this will not affect your career, or your enjoyment of your job. This applies equally if you come forward in good faith with a concern which turns out later not to be justified.

3.4 We will do anything we can to respect your confidentially, if you have requested this.

3.5 If anyone tries to discourage you from coming forward to express a concern, we will teat this as a disciplinary offence. In the same way, we will deal severely with anyone who criticises or victimises you after a concern has been expressed.

3.6 The association's disciplinary rules and staff conduct requires that you do not disclose confidential, false or misleading information. In considering taking a concern outside the association you should be aware of your duty of confidentiality and ensure that the matter is raised without confidential information being divulged.

3.7 The Public Interest Disclosure Act 1998 (which came into force in January 1999) gives legal protection to whistleblowers who honestly and reasonably believe that the information they disclose or the allegations they make are substantially true.

## 4. Who to contact

4.1 In most cases, you should be able to raise your concerns with your immediate manager or his supervisor. If for some reason this is not possible, you should speak to the internal audit service, a senior officer, the central services director, or the chief executive. And if necessary, your should ask for a confidential meeting. All such contacts should be treated in confidence.

4.2 If our policy and procedures are working properly, you should not need to contact one of the organisation's board members, or some external agency, to express concerns. But there may be exceptional or urgent circumstances where it might be best to contact an external agency. It is not possible to give precise examples but, for instance, relevant situations might be:

- if the problem involved very senior member of the organisation, the Chair or another board member;

- in the case of a criminal offence, the police;

- in the case of abuse of vulnerable people in a residential home;

- the local authority social services department

- in the case of abuse of public funds, the Housing Corporation, which is responsible for regulating all registered social landlords

- In the case of any fraud, the association's external auditors; or

- regional office of the Housing Corporation.

We hope that none of these will ever prove necessary.

4.3 You can also approach Public Concern at Work for confidential and independent advice at the following address: Lincoln's Inn House, 42 Kingsway, London WC2B 6EX. E-mail: whistle@pcaw.demon.co.uk.

4.4 Performance audit staff in the relevant regional office of the Housing Corporation are also able to advise on a confidential basis if you are not sure whom to contact about a particular problem. As regulators, they may need to follow up on any potential problems identified.

## 5. Network's response

5.1 If you come to us with a concern, we will look into it carefully and thoroughly. We have to be fair to you, but also to any other person involved. If someone is potentially being accused of misconduct, we have to find out their side of the story as well. In our investigation, we will respect any concerns you have expressed about your own safety or career.

5.2 If you request, we will try to let you know the results of our investigation and about any action that is proposed. However, in doing this, we have to respect the confidentiality of other employees as well.

5.3 The action that will be taken by Network will depend on the nature of the concern. The matters raised may be investigated by management, by internal enquiry or through the disciplinary process. Alternatively, they may be subject to independent enquiry. Relevant matters may also be subject to investigation by the police. However, in order to safe guard both Network and individuals, initial enquiries will be made to determine whether the commitment of resources to any form of investigation would be appropriate. These initial enquiries would also assist in determining the most appropriate process for the consideration of the concern. Any necessary action that is required urgently would be carried out ahead of any assessment/investigation process.

5.4 Concerns or allegations raised which fall within the scope established procedure will be referred for consideration under those procedures.

5.5 A referral of a concern will be acknowledged within seven days, with an indication of how the association proposes to deal with the matter and likely timescale. If it is not possible to complete the initial enquiries within the seven days, the letter of acknowledgement will explain. If a decision is made not to investigate, the reasons will be given.

5.6 Some matters may be investigated without the need for initial enquiries to be made. Similarly, some concerns may be capable of resolution by agreed action without the need for investigation.

5.7 The level of contact between you and whoever is considering the issues will depend on the nature of the matters raised, the potential difficulties involved as well as the clarity of the information provided. Further information may be sought from you.

5.8 The association will take appropriate steps to minimise any difficulties that you may experience as a result of using the whistleblowing policy.

5.9 You will be given as much information as possible on the outcomes of the investigation, subject to the constraints of the association's duty of confidentiality to service users, staff or board members or any other legal constraint. The objective of the various responses would be to assure you that the matter has been addressed.

5.10 If you have abused the confidential reporting process, for instance by maliciously raising unfounded allegations, we will treat this as a disciplinary matter. But no-one who comes forward in good faith has anything to fear.

## 6. Monitoring the policy

6.1 Confidential records will be kept of all matters raised through the whistleblowing policy and the appropriate Network committee will receive reports with an assessment of the effectiveness of the policy and any emerging patterns.

# Harassment policies                                    B12.23

Increasing attention is being given to the need to make the workplace a safe and supportive environment. Here we reproduce a harassment policy, together with guidelines for managers investigating allegations of harassment which has recently been agreed between management and trades union colleagues, and formally adopted by the board.

The underlying theme is that harassment as defined is unacceptable, whether by other staff or by representatives of business partners (especially suppliers and customers) or by other parties (for instance visitors). The policy and guidelines reproduced here define the action which will be taken where inappropriate behaviour is found to have taken place.

In this organisation, the board considered harassment to be a priority area for action, including the need for the implementation of policies and procedures to tackle harassment and for arrangements to monitor progress. They have arranged that the policy and guidelines will be reviewed periodically and performance will be monitored.

Readers should note that harassment is not the same thing as victimisation. The word 'harassment' appears 27 times but 'victimisation' only twice. Arguably this or another statement should also address victimisation to a greater extent.

Readers of this statement have pointed out that the requirement to write a letter could be difficult, even intimidating, in these circumstances, and that perhaps a form could be designed to be used instead. Another observation on this statement is that the phrase 'putting someone down' is ambiguous.

A practical suggestion is that this statement would be improved if the organisation's policy provided for a 'mediation service' to resolve tensions, especially where complaints appear to be malicious or otherwise unjustified, and if this mediation service was covered within this statement.

# Harassment – policy statement                                    B12.24

## Introduction

The company believes that employees have the right to be treated with dignity and respect at work and to carry out their employment without any form of harassment.

This policy applies to all persons employed by the company and also to those other persons who work within the company and make decisions on behalf of the company, where such decisions affect any matter set out within this policy and could give rise to any unacceptable practice.

The company will not condone or accept trade union, employment agency or service contractor policies and practices which it considers constitute any form of harassment.

The company also considers that all employees, customers, suppliers and associates have a responsibility to treat others with consideration, dignity and respect.

## What is 'harassment'?

Harassment is behaviour which may involve unwelcome, unreasonable and offensive physical, verbal or non-verbal conduct, where the individual is intimidated, humiliated, threatened, bullied, abused, patronised or where their privacy is invaded in some way. This may be on the grounds of race, gender, sexuality, religion, ethnic origin, marital status, disability, age, expired convictions or health.

Harassment is defined by the impact on the recipient not the intention of the perpetrator. The person whose course of conduct is in question ought to know that it amounts to harassment of another, if a reasonable person in possession of the same information would think the course of conduct amounted to harassment of the other.

It may be the result of a single act or repeated inappropriate behaviour.

### *Examples*

- Unwanted physical contact, including unnecessary touching, patting or pinching, brushing against another person's body;

- shouting or swearing at someone;

- assault;

- personal insults;

- coercing sexual intercourse, unwelcome sexual advances;

- suggestive remarks, innuendoes, lewd comments, discriminatory or personal remarks;

- treatment detrimental to professional status and credibility;

- display of racist, pornographic or sexually suggestive pictures, objects or written materials;

- leering, whistling or making sexually suggestive or insulting gestures;

- non-co-operation or exclusion from conversation and activities; or

- putting someone down.

### Informal remedy

Employees who are victims of harassment should make it clear to the harasser that the behaviour is unacceptable and must stop. The employee may wish to seek advice from their manager, personnel officer or staff side representative before doing so.

### Formal procedure

If the informal remedy fails to resolve the situation or the harassment is too serious to be dealt with this way, the victim should submit a formal written complaint to their immediate manager, or their staff representative may do it on their behalf. This should contain:

- the name of the harasser;

- the nature of the harassment;

- dates and times when harassment occurred;

- names of witnesses to any form of harassment; and

- any action taken by the complainant to stop the harassment.

In some circumstances it may not be appropriate to send this complaint to the immediate manager and if this is the case it should be submitted to a more senior line manager or to a personnel manager.

As harassment is a disciplinary offence, the complaint should be investigated and dealt with under the company's disciplinary procedure. Whilst an investigation is taking place it may be necessary to suspend the alleged harasser from duty or remove them to a different area of work. However, a person accused of harassment may not necessarily be guilty and has a right to support and to know of what they are accused.

The complaint should be investigated within ten working days wherever possible. All employees involved in the investigation will be expected to maintain confidentiality. Failure to do so may be considered a disciplinary offence.

An employee who makes a complaint will not suffer victimisation for having done so. However, if the complaint is untrue and has been made in a malicious way, disciplinary action will be taken against the complainant.

### Alleged harassment of staff by representatives of customers and suppliers, and by visitors

Staff have the right to be treated with respect and dignity at all times and it is unacceptable for others external to our company to harass staff.

Staff should initially raise any concerns they may have about harassment from this source with the appropriate manager. The content of any discussion should be kept confidential unless further action is considered necessary. Staff may also discuss the matter in confidence with their personnel officer or staff representative to obtain further advice. The manager should carry out a full investigation and keep a written record which may be used in evidence in case the member of staff complaining of harassment becomes the subject of a complaint by the other party. Where the problem is of a serious or persistent nature the alleged harasser of the member of staff must be made aware that such behaviour is unacceptable and that the company may take legal action. In some cases it may be appropriate to review the company's business relationship with a supplier or customer or to arrange for changes in personnel to minimise the future risk.

### Duty of supervisors and managers

All supervisors and managers have a duty to take all reasonable action to ensure that harassment does not occur in work areas for which they are responsible.

Managers should be responsive and supportive to any members of staff who complain about harassment, provide full and clear advice on the procedure to be followed, maintain confidentiality and ensure there is no further problem or any victimisation after a complaint has been resolved

### Duty of employees

All employees have a clear role to play in creating a climate at work in which harassment is unacceptable. They must take all reasonable steps to prevent this through awareness and sensitivity towards the issue and by ensuring that standards of conduct and behaviour for themselves and for colleagues do not cause offence.

Appropriate disciplinary action, including dismissal for serious offences, will be taken against any employee who breaches this policy.

### Review

Implementation of this policy will be monitored by personnel and a review undertaken from time to time to ensure that it continues to meet the needs of the company and its staff.

**Management of harassment guidelines for managers investigating allegations of harassment**

Complaints should be investigated in accordance with the company's disciplinary procedure, within ten working days of the complaint being made.

*Interviewing the complainant*

- Explain the process to be followed and reassure them regarding confidentiality;
- allow plenty of time and be prepared for the complainant to become emotional;
- do not express any personal views or opinions;
- try to establish the following:
  - what actually took place, where and when,
  - the frequency of the alleged harassment,
  - whether there were any witnesses,
  - what was said or done by whom and to whom,
  - how the complainant felt at the time,
  - what the complainant has done to stop the alleged harassment,
  - whether they have notes or copy letters to support the allegations or demonstrate any action they have taken,
  - whether they have discussed the alleged harassment with anyone else,
  - whether they are aware of anyone else being subjected to the same treatment,
- finally, reassure the complainant and clarify the process again; and
- retain full and clear notes which reflect the discussion.

*Interviewing the alleged harasser*

- Explain the allegations that have been made against them and the process to be followed;
- reassure them regarding confidentiality;
- allow plenty of time and be prepared for the individual to become emotional or aggressive;
- listen with an open mind and remain impartial;
- try to establish and corroborate the facts;
- give the individual adequate opportunity to respond to all the allegations;
- clarify the process again for the individual; and
- retain full and clear notes which reflect the discussion.

# Policy statement on environment and health    B12.25

XYZ will ensure that all its activities worldwide are conducted safely; the health of its employees, its customers and the public will be protected; environmental performance will meet contemporary requirements, and that its operations are run in a manner acceptable to the local communities.

In particular we will:

- comply with relevant laws and regulations and take any additional measures we consider necessary;

- ensure that all our activities are being carried out in accordance with the XYZ Group safety, health and environment standards;

- set demanding targets and measure progress to ensure continuous improvement in safety, health and environmental performance;

- require every member of staff to exercise personal responsibility in preventing harm to themselves, others and the environment, and enable them to contribute to every aspect of safety, health and environmental protection;

- manufacture only those products that can be transported, stored, used and disposed of safely;

- seek to develop new or modified products which assist in conserving the environment and lead to sustainable development;

- provide appropriate safely, health and environmental training and information for all our staff, contractors and others who work with us, handle our products, or operate our technologies;

- communicate openly on the nature of our activities and report progress on our safety, health and environmental performance;

- promote the interchange of safety, health and environmental information and technology throughout the XYZ Group and make our expertise and knowledge available to relevant statutory authorities; and

- encourage, through positive interaction within the industry, the worldwide development and implementation of the principles of the International Chamber of Commerce's 'Business Charter for Sustainable Development';

This policy applies throughout XYZ and our subsidiaries worldwide.

We encourage our related companies to adopt policies which accord with this policy.

# Information security policy statements          B12.26

In the following two sections of this handbook we provide respectively example IT SECURITY GUIDELINES FOR STAFF (at **B12.27** and **B12.28**) and an example of an E-MAIL, INTERNET AND TELEPHONE USAGE POLICY STATEMENT (at **B12.29**).

The UK's Department of Trade and Industry has given us permission to reproduce their 'boilerplate' information security policy statement. Copies of this free publication can be obtained by phoning DTI on +44 (0)870 1502 500 quoting reference *URN 96/702*, or fax +44 (0)870 1502 333.

DTI's website (www.dtiinfo1.dti.gov.uk/security/ contents.htm) holds a wealth of information put together by DTI's information security policy group, under the contents sections.

- What is information security?

- Why is information security important to me?

- What is the best approach to provide security?

- What roles and responsibilities should I consider?

- What security do I need?

- How do I develop my security policy?

- How do I provide security solutions?

- What further help is available to me?

Within the DTI, this development work is done by their information security policy group, CII Directorate, Department of Trade and Industry, 151 Buckingham Palace Road, London, SW1W 9SS. Tel: +44 (0)20 7215 1962. Fax: +44 (0)20 7931 7194.

DTI points out that an information security policy provides an opportunity for top management to set a clear direction and demonstrate their support for and commitment to information security. It should complement the organisation's 'mission' statement and reflect the desire of the business to operate in a controlled and secure manner.

As a minimum, the information security policy should include guidance on the following areas:

- the importance of information security to the business process;

- a statement from top management supporting the goals and principles of information security;

- specific statements indicating minimum standards and compliance requirements for:

- ○ legal, regulatory and contractual obligations,

- ○ security awareness and educational requirements,

- ○ virus prevention and detection,

- ○ business continuity planning,

- ○ definitions of responsibilities and accountabilities; and

- ○ details of the process for reporting suspected security incidents.

## Information security policy statement B12.27

### Policy

The purpose of the policy is to protect the company's information assets[4] from all threats, whether internal or external, deliberate or accidental.

- the chief executive has approved the information security policy;

- it is the policy of the company to ensure that:

  - ○ information will be protected against unauthorised access,

  - ○ confidentiality of information will be assured[5],

- integrity of information will be maintained[6];

- regularity and legislative requirements will be met[7];

- business continuity plans will be produced, maintained and tested[8];

- information security training will be available to all staff;

- all breaches of information security, actual or suspected, will be reported to, and investigated by the information security manager;

- standards will be produced to support the policy which may include virus control, passwords and encryption;

- business requirements for the availability of information and information systems will be met;

- the role and responsibility for managing information security, referred to as the information security manager, will be performed by whom[9];

- the information security manager has direct responsibility for maintaining the policy and providing advice and guidance on its implementation;

- all managers are directly responsible for implementing the policy within their business areas, and for adherence by their staff; and

- it is the responsibility of each employee to adhere to the policy.

## Objective

The objective of information security is to ensure business continuity and minimise business damage by preventing and minimising the impact of security incidents.

Signed: _____

Title: _____

Date: _____

(The policy will be reviewed by the information security manager, usually plus one year from the date signed.)

# Information security – guidelines for staff          B12.28

In the previous sections of this handbook we provided another example INFORMATION SECURITY POLICY STATEMENT at **B12.27**; in the following section of this handbook we provide an example of an E-MAIL, INTERNET AND TELEPHONE POLICY STATEMENT at **B12.29**.

## Introduction

The growth of PCs, networks, applications and data accessible to employees means that information is available to a wide audience in XYZ plc. It is essential that this information is kept:

● confidential; and

● protected from damage or abuse.

The company managers are clearly accountable for ensuring that there is a secure process for staff to operate; however, there are some things for which every employee must take individual accountability.

### Objective

The objective of this leaflet is to set out for XYZ's employees and associated staff, the standards and practices for which they must take personal accountability and where failure to observe them will be regarded as a serious breach of trust.

### Security policy

XYZ maintains as information security policy, agreed by the directors, that embodies industry best practice. Some of the requirements in the policy are repeated in this booklet. Others are the responsibility of identified directors or managers.

You are responsible for reading and understanding the policy and bringing to your manager's attention any serious breach of its requirements. The policy can be obtained via your manager.

You are responsible for understanding and adhering to any formal procedures that are put in place and documented or the implementation of the policy.

### Taking care of assets

Most staff have important assets in their personal custody. Typically these are such things as:

- personal computers (equipment, files, software) and documents;

- security 'tokens' (keys, access cards, passwords, etc); and

- mobile phones.

You are responsible for ensuring these items are not:

- passed to third parties;

- misused or damaged;

- used for the purposes other than XYZ's business; or

- removed from company premises without authority.

### Access

Many operational areas have special access rules. You are responsible for abiding by them.

You must ensure the following points are carried-out.

- Escort any external visitor until they leave or are handed over to another member of staff.

- Challenge unauthorised 'intruders' or report them to the manager of the area.

- Lock away confidential items (documents, PC diskettes etc) when the area is unattended. No business information should be available for casual inspection by visitors. Workstations should not be left unattended in a state where applications could be accessed by unauthorised individuals.

A 'clear desk' policy is followed by XYZ.

### Operating procedures

Operating procedures are written to help safeguard XYZ's assets. You are responsible for following them and bringing to your manager's attention any errors they contain.

## Viruses

Viruses and other types of malicious software are a serious threat, particularly to personal computers.

You must not carry-out the activities below.

- Load illegal copies of software or any games or 'shareware' on to any computer. Even spreadsheets or documents are a risk. If you are importing files from third parties raw data files are preferable.

- Use any disk that you know has not been virus checked.

- Interrupt the 'boot-up' sequence.

You must ensure the following.

- Report any symptom that might indicate your PC is 'infected'.

- Understand and adhere to the company's formal virus avoidance procedure. This will include the procedure for implementing legal code (eg software fixes) from insecure sources (e.g. the internet).

## Communications

Most public communication services (eg e-mail, telephone) are inherently insecure. When using the internet add the following text to any of your e-mails which might amount to 'business letters':

XYZ plc

Registered office:

[Address]

Registered in England no. XXXXX

This basic corporate information is required by law to be given on business letters and order forms. When sending e-mails which contain sensitive information, it is worth adding the following text:

> This e-mail is confidential and may contain privileged information. If you are not the addressee it may be unlawful for you to read, copy, distribute, disclose or otherwise use the information in this e-mail. If you are not the intended recipient please notify us immediately.

## System access controls

All applications should have access controls (e.g. passwords) to prevent unauthorised use or access to data. This applies equally to personal computer applications.

You must not:

- use another employee's password or user identity without management authority;

- access or change any application or data that you are not authorised to do;

- input information that you know to be incorrect; and

- write down, display or disclose your user identity or password.

You must:

- adhere to password standards, e.g:

  - use more than six characters,

  - change it regularly varying at least three characters,

  - do not use user-ID or name,

  - avoid all numeric passwords where possible,

  - get your user-id deleted if you no longer need it; and

  - report any violation of these guidelines or any attempt to persuade you to provide access or information to an unauthorised person.

**Purchasing**

XYZ has a formal purchasing process. This requires that goods and services that are required are sourced and provided by the IT department.

**Legislation and contracts**

XYZ is committed to adhere to legislation and contract conditions.

You must not:

- create unauthorised copies of copyright software, documents or customer data;

- hold personal data other than is allowed by our entry on the data protection register, as held by group secretariat; or

- use software except as allowed under the terms of the license purchased.

As an individual, the following legislation applies to you personally:

- the *Copyright, Design and Patents Act 1988* (this outlaws illegal copying of software);

- the *Computer Misuse Act 1990* (this defines 'hacking' and deliberate virus contamination as criminal offences); and

- the *Data Protection Act 1998* (this covers the conditions under which personal data can be held).

## Housekeeping

Data owners are responsible for deleting unnecessary files to avoid retention of out of date information and wasting of vulnerable storage resources. For individuals this is particularly relevant for their 'C', 'D' and network drives.

The IT department take back up copies of all data stored on the network drives every night but individuals have the responsibility for ensuring that proper back-ups of their data stored on local drives ('C' or 'D') are taken and securely stored.

## Insurance

The use of equipment at home for XYZ work should be notified to your household buildings and contents insurers as this may well affect the cover under your policy.

## Internet

Access to the Internet must be authorised by a head of department and must be used for company purposes only.

# E-mail, internet and telephone policy statement B12.29

In the previous two sections of this handbook we provide respectively an example of a general IT policy statements (at **B12.27**), and of guidelines to staff on IT security (at **B12.28**).

This statement of policy aims to explain briefly:

- how employees are allowed to use e-mail, telephones and the internet using the company's facilities;

- how employees or the company may be liable in law for misuse of e-mail or the internet; and

- how the employee's interests and the company's interests can be protected.

This policy is not a definitive statement of what the company's facilities must not be used for. Employees must conduct themselves in a trustworthy and appropriate manner so as not to discredit or harm the company or its staff and in accordance with the spirit of this policy statement.

This policy applies to all telephone and computer users within the company (including, without limit, all directors, employees and third parties) who use e-mail, bulletin boards, the world wide web and the internet through computers based at the company's premises or through any computers located at other sites (including private equipment) via the company's network or using the company's telephone lines. A breach of or refusal to comply with this policy is a disciplinary offence and is liable to result in disciplinary penalties including instant dismissal.

## Authorised use

### E-mail and internet

The company encourages staff to use e-mail as a method of communication in appropriate circumstances within the office and with third parties by the internet. It will not always be appropriate to communicate by e-mail and staff should always consider whether there is a more suitable method (for example in circumstances where there is a need to preserve confidentiality or in the case of sensitive issues which should be communicated face-to-face).

Employees use of e-mail and the internet is only authorised for *bona fide* purposes directly connected with employers' work or the company's business. Employees are expected to exercise responsible and appropriate behaviour when using the company's computers and when sending e-mail, whether internally within the company or externally using the internet.

Unauthorised use of the internet may expose both employees personally and the company to court proceedings including criminal liability. An employee will be held responsible for any claims made against the company arising out of any legal action brought as a result of the employee's unauthorised use of the internet. Unauthorised use of the internet and the company's computer system or breach of this policy is a disciplinary offence, which may lead to dismissal.

### Telephone use

No personal calls should be made or received except in an emergency, when permission should be first obtained from a manager.

Employees should be aware that mobile telephones can be disrupting and distracting, and personal mobile phones should either be turned off or diverted during working hours.

### Monitoring

The company reserves the right to listen to or have access to read any communication made or received by an employee using its computers or telephone system without notice for the following purposes:

- to establish the existence of facts;
- to ascertain compliance with regulatory or self regulatory practices;
- for quality control and staff training purposes;
- to prevent or detect crime;
- to investigate or detect unauthorised use of the company's telecommunication system;

- to intercept for operational purposes, such as protecting against viruses and making routine interceptions such as forwarding e-mails to correct destinations; or

- to check voice mail systems when staff are on holiday or on sick leave.

The company also reserves the right to make and keep copies of telephone calls or e-mails and data documenting use of the telephone, e-mail and the internet systems, for the purposes set out above, and if it sees fit to use the information in disciplinary proceedings against employees. The company may bypass any password you set. You may only set passwords and security codes for your computer, the system or any part of it or documentation held on it in accordance with company policy from time to time.

All communications and stored information sent, received, created or contained within the company's systems are the property of the company and accordingly should not be considered as private.

## Software

The company licenses computer software from a variety of outside sources. The company does not own this software or related documentation and, unless authorised by the software developer, does not have the right to reproduce it. The software used on the local area network or multiple or individual machines should have the appropriate licence(s) and employees should only use it according to the licence agreement.

Employees should notify their departmental manager or the IT manager of any misuse of software or associated documentation.

## Security

The accessibility of the internet is both an advantage and disadvantage of the system. Whilst employees can access a huge amount of information via the internet, information and e-mails sent across the internet may be read by persons unknown to the sender. Potentially anyone could read private and confidential information transmitted on the internet. Even if some information has been deleted from your screen it may not necessarily be deleted from the internet system which provides back up saving mechanisms. It is therefore essential that you notify any third party with whom you are communicating via the internet that any e-mail exchanged is transmitted over the internet in an interceptable form. Any message or information requiring security or confidentiality should be distributed by an alternative means of communication.

Employees must not put on the internet any material, which incites or encourages or enables others to gain unauthorised access to the company's computer system. It is vital that all staff take all necessary steps to safeguard the company's computer system from viruses. Accordingly, employees should not exchange executable programs using internet e-mail and discard any documents or attachments which employees receive unsolicited. Employees must not introduce new software onto the company's system without written authorisation from the IT department and employees must always ensure that the appropriate virus checking procedures have been followed.

## Courtesy

As e-mails can easily be misconstrued, employees must consider carefully whether e-mail is the appropriate form of communication in particular circumstances and if employees decide that it is; consider carefully the content of the e-mail and who the recipients should be. It is inappropriate to send e-mails and or attachments to people (whether they are other employees of the company or third parties) if the e-mail does not relate to them or if the attachment cannot be read by them. In addition, sending e-mails needlessly to other people wastes their time and needlessly sending long files or attachments will cause delays in the system.

## Defamation

The internet is considered to be a form of publication and accordingly is within the scope of legislation relating to libel. Both words and pictures produced on the internet are capable of being libellous if they are untrue, ridicule a person and as a result damage that person's reputation. Employees must not put any defamatory statement onto the internet or on the company's computer system. As well as the employee being liable, the company can also be liable as an online provider.

## Obscenity

The internet has been abused by the distribution of child and other pornography. It is an offence to publish or distribute obscene material and this includes possessing, showing or distributing any indecent photographs or pseudo-photograph of a child, (this includes a computer-generated photograph on the internet). It is also an offence to display indecent material in public. The internet qualifies as a public place. Employees must not send any such material using the company's system.

## Discrimination and harassment

The company does not tolerate discrimination or harassment in any form whatsoever. This principle extends to any information distributed on the company's system or via the internet. Employees may not put on either system any material which discriminates or encourages discrimination or harassment on racial or ethnic grounds or on grounds of gender, sexual orientation, marital status, age, ethnic origin, colour, nationality, religion or disability. To do so will lead to disciplinary action up to and including dismissal. Please also bear in mind the company's policy on discrimination and harassment.

## Data protection

If employees are required to put information (including photographs) onto the company's system or the internet containing personal data other than their own, employees must have the express written consent of the individuals to whom the personal data relates.

## Board policy statement on fraud                                    B12.30

The XYZ Group will deal with fraud within the framework of its statement on business ethics, and its security policy, which require a secure working environment to protect people, capital information and the assets from the risk of deliberate harm, damage or loss.

In particular:

- we require all employees to act honestly and in the best interests of the company at all times, and to ensure that XYZ acts with integrity in its dealings with third parties;

- we will ensure that effective controls and procedures are in place for preventing, detecting and dealing with fraud;

- we will ensure that all employees are aware of their responsibility to report details immediately to their line manager (or next most senior person) if they suspect that a fraud has been committed or see any suspicious acts or events;

- we will ensure that the controller is advised of any significant fraud or attempted fraud;

- we require management to investigate any allegations or evidence of fraud in consultation with the relevant security adviser and internal audit manager;

- we require employees to assist in investigations by making available all relevant information and by co-operating in interviews; and

- in appropriate cases, and after proper investigation, we will dismiss without notice employees who are found to be defrauding the company and, where appropriate, press for criminal prosecution and to seek financial recovery through civil proceedings.

All businesses and subsidiaries shall establish, and audit, procedures to ensure that this policy is fully implemented.

## Pension plan – statement of investment principles                  B12.31

The trustees of the ABC pension plan ('the plan') have drawn up this statement of investment principles ("the statement') to comply with the requirements of the *Pensions Act 1995* (*PA 1995*). As required under *PA 1995*, the trustees have consulted a suitably qualified person in obtaining written advice from the XYZ Investment Consulting Practice. The trustees in preparing this statement have also consulted ABC plc ('the sponsoring company'), in particular on the trustees' objectives and on their policy on compliance with the Minimum Funding Requirement ('the MFR') as set out in *PA 1995*.

Overall investment policy falls into two parts. The strategic management of the assets is fundamentally the responsibility of the trustees acting on advice from their investment consultant, XYZ, and is driven by their investment objectives as set out below. The remaining elements of policy are part of the day-to-day management of the assets that is delegated to professional investment management.

## Investment objectives, risk and the Minimum Funding Requirement

### Investment objectives

To guide them in their strategic management of the assets and control of the various risks to which the plan is exposed, the trustees have considered their objectives and adopted the following points.

- The trustees' overall investment policy is guided by an objective of achieving, over the long-term, a return on the investments that is consistent with the long-term assumptions made by the actuary in determining the funding of the plan.

- Over the shorter term, the objective is to maximise the return above the performance benchmark set out in Section 3 without exceeding the limits of prudent pension fund investment. The trustees believe the investment strategy adopted will be appropriate also for achieving the further objective of avoiding the need for additional contributions arising from the MFR.

The trustees appreciate that the sponsoring company wish to avoid significant volatility in their contribution rate, but such volatility will be tolerated if it is deemed necessary in the achievement of other objectives.

### Risk

There are various risks to which any pension scheme is exposed. The trustees have considered the following risks.

- The risk of a deterioration in the plan's funding level.

- The risk of a shortfall of assets relative to the value of liabilities as determined if the plan were to wind up.

- The risk that the day-to-day management of the assets will not achieve the rate of investment return expected by the trustees. They recognise that the use of an active investment manager involves such a risk. However, they believe this risk is outweighed by the potential gains from successful active management.

### Policy on compliance with the Minimum Funding Requirement

*PA 1995* introduced the MFR with which all pension schemes must comply, although full implementation of the MFR is deferred until 2002.

The trustees have sought expert advice on the potential development of the MFR position and been advised by the actuary that the position is currently above 100 per cent. The trustees' general policy on complying with the MFR is:

- to create and maintain an adequate funding 'cushion' such that the risk of deterioration of the MFR ratio to below 100 per cent is reduced to an acceptable level; and

- to accept the risk that a significant deterioration in the MFR ratio may require additional contributions from the sponsoring company as determined by legislation.

### Investment strategy

The trustees have determined, based on expert advice from XYZ, a benchmark mix of asset types and ranges within which the investment manager may operate with discretion; these guidelines are set out in *section 3* of *PA 1995*.

The trustees believe that the resulting asset mix is currently appropriate for controlling the risks identified in *sections 2(2)* and *2(3)* of *PA 1995*.

# Day-to-day management of the assets

### Main assets

The trustees invest the main assets of the plan solely in pooled fund arrangements operated by FGH Asset Management (the 'investment manager'). The investment manager has responsibility for the day-to-day discretionary management of those assets, subject to the guidelines set out below.

The trustees are satisfied that the spread of assets by type and the investment manager's policy on investing in individual securities within each type provides adequate diversification of investments.

The investment manager's mandate includes the following guidelines and restrictions:

### *Asset allocation guidelines*

|  | % |
|---|---|
| UK equities | 49.5 –69.5 |
| Overseas equities | 14–28 |
| North American equities | 3.5–13.5 |
| European equities | 3.5–13.5 |
| Pacific Basin equities | 3.5–13.5 |
| **Total equities** | **70–100** |
| Index-linked gilts | 0–30 |
| Other assets | 0–10 |

## Investment restrictions

Direct self-investment and borrowing are prohibited (although a temporary overdraft of up to 2 per cent of the portfolio's market value is permitted).

## Investment performance benchmark

The performance of the investment manager is compared with the Performance Benchmark set out below:

|  | % | Benchmark |
|---|---|---|
| UK equities* | 59.5 | CAPS Trustee Service UK Equities Median |
| Overseas equities | 25.5 |  |
|   US equities | 8.5 | CAPS Trustee Service US Equities Median |
|   European equities | 8.5 | CAPS Trustee Service European Equities |
|   Pacific Basin equities | 8.5 | Median |
|   Total | 85.0 | CAPS Trustee Service Pacific Basin Equities |
| Total equities |  | Median |
| Index-linked gilts | 15.0 | FTSE A Index-linked Gilt (over 5 year) Index |
| Total | 100.0 |  |

\* Currently invested in FGH Life's UK Equity Fund

The Performance Objective is to outperform the Performance Benchmark return by 1 per cent p.a. over rolling five year periods.

### Additional assets

Assets in respect of members' additional voluntary contributions are held in deposit accounts, discretionary managed and with-profit finds operated by [name] Insurance Limited and [name] Pension & Life Assurance Society.

### Realisation of investments

There is no current policy on realising assets as the plan's cash flow is positive at present. In general, the investment manager has discretion in the timing of realisations of investments and in considerations relating to the liquidity of those investments, but would be responsible for generating any cash required for benefit outgoings and other expenditure on the instruction of the trustees.

### Monitoring the investment manager

Performance of the investment manager is not measured independently by the trustees although performance of the underlying funds is monitored by the

Combined Actuarial Performance Services Limited ('CAPS') survey of UK pooled pension funds.

The trustees meet the investment manager at least two times each year and scrutinise reports issued by them to review the investment manager's actions together with the reasons for and background behind the investment performance. XYZ are retained as investment consultants to assist the trustees in fulfilling their responsibility for monitoring the investment manager.

**Policy on socially responsible, environmental and ethical investment (SRI) and corporate governance**

*Socially responsible investment*

As the assets of the plan are managed in pooled arrangements, the trustees accept that the assets are subject to the investment manager's own policies on social, ethical or environmental considerations relating to the selection, retention or realisation of investments.

The trustees monitor the investment manager's policies on a regular basis and are satisfied this corresponds with their responsibilities to the beneficiaries of the plan.

*Corporate governance*

Similarly, the trustees accept the assets are subject to the investment manager's own policies on corporate governance and the exercise of rights (including voting rights) attaching to investments

The trustees expect their investment manager to update them on any changes to their corporate governance or socially responsible investment policies. The trustees will review these policies on an annual basis, or more often if necessary.

The trustees are satisfied this corresponds with their responsibilities to the beneficiaries of the plan.

**Compliance with this statement**

The trustees will monitor compliance with this statement annually. In particular they will obtain written confirmation from the investment manager that they have complied with this statement as supplied to them and the trustees undertake to advise the investment manager promptly and in writing of any material change to this statement.

**Review of this statement**

The trustees will review this statement in response to any material changes to any aspects of the plan, its liabilities, finances and the attitude to risk of the trustees and the sponsoring company that they judge to have a bearing on the stated Investment policy.

This review will occur no less frequently than every three years to coincide with the actuarial valuation or other actuarial advice relating to the MFR. Any such review will again be based on written, expert investment advice and the sponsoring company will be consulted.

**Notes**

1. Vide, eg Internal Control and Financial Reporting – Guidance to Directors of Listed Companies Registered in the UK [ICAEW, December 1994].

2. Note that the terminology of the new (2201) Standards means that 'an internal audit' is no longer an internal audit 'activity', it is now an 'engagement'. New terminology uses 'activity' in a different context, dispensing with terms such as 'Unit' or 'Department' in favour of:

   **'Internal Audit Activity** – A department, division, team of consultants, or other practitioner(s) that provides independent, objective assurance and consulting services designed to add value and improve an organization's operations. The internal audit activity helps an organization accomplish its objectives by bringing a systematic, disciplined approach to evaluate and improve the effectiveness of risk management, control, and governance processes.'

   (Glossary of Terms to the new Standards of The Institute of Internal Auditors).

3. Public Interest Disclosure Act, 2 July 1998, London, The Stationery Office, £2.85, ISBN 0–10–542398-X.

4. Information takes many forms and includes data stored on computers, transmitted across networks, printed out or written on paper, sent by fax, stored on tapes and diskettes, or spoken in conversations and over the telephone.

5. The protection of valuable or sensitive information from unauthorised disclsure or intelligible interruption.

6. Safeguarding the accuracy and completeness of information by protecting against unauthorised modifications.

7. This applies to record keeping and most controls will already be in place; it includes the requirements of legislation such as the *Companies Act 1985* and the *Data Protection Act 1998*.

8. This will ensure that information and vital services are available to users when they need them.

9. This may be a part or full-time role for the allocated person.

# Remuneration Packages

We are grateful to Cliff Weight for strengthening this handbook by providing authoritative content on remuneration packages to supersede much of that we carried in the first edition. Cliff is a Director of Independent Remuneration Solutions, who provide advice on Executive Directors' Remuneration packages, Annual and Long Term Incentives and Non-Executive Directors' Fees. He can be contacted at IRS at 9 Savoy Street, London WC2R 0BA. Tel: 020 7836 5831. E-mail: cliffweight@msn.com.

The current framework for corporate governance of remuneration in the UK is an amalgam of Company Law, the Combined Code, FSA rules and guidance and guidelines of the various UK institutional investors. It is complex, confusing, sometimes contradictory and seemingly forever changing. My challenge in this section of the book is to produce something that is both rigorous and helpful to the reader. So:

- **B13** REMUNERATION PACKAGES – THE CORPORATE GOVERNANCE FRAMEWORK provides the framework;

- **B14** REMUNERATION DISCLOSURE REQUIREMENTS provides detailed disclosure requirements;

- **B15** BEST PRACTICE GUIDANCE describes best practice guidance from investors;

- **B16** THE REMUNERATION COMMITTEE describes the Remuneration Committee role and how it works in practice, including some unique survey data from IRS;

- **B17** THE TOTAL REMUNERATION PACKAGE describes the remuneration package- its history, each of its components in detail and the market practices; and

- **B18** COMMUNICATING DIRECTORS' PAY explains what and how to communicate to stakeholders and gives a checklist for remuneration design and communication.

# Remuneration Packages – The Corporate Governance Framework

## Corporate governance requirements B13.1

Corporate governance can be split between what must be done, what is good practice and what organisations think is good practice. Company law must always be followed, and company law requirements relating to remuneration are described in detail in **B14 REMUNERATION DISCLOSURE REQUIREMENTS**. The main requirements are set out in *Schedules 6* and *7* to the *Companies Act 1985 (CA 1985)*, and the *Directors' Remuneration Report Regulations 2002 (SI 2002/1986)*. The Combined Code describes best practice. Institutional investors, their representative bodies and the intermediaries also offer further guidance and guidelines to companies, and their advice is described in some detail in **B15 BEST PRACTICE GUIDANCE**.

This chapter explains the background to the rules, regulations and guidance governing directors' remuneration and explains which are most important.

## Introduction B13.2

Remuneration of directors is a key area of corporate governance. Patricia Hewitt, the Secretary of State for Trade and Industry, in her Foreword to the 2001 proposals on directors' remuneration described it thus:

> 'Directors' remuneration lies at the heart of the debate on effective corporate governance. This is the issue, above all others, on which directors face a conflict of interest; it is also one in which there is a real need for non-executive directors to exercise independent judgment. Indeed, some commentators have suggested that non-executive directors who are unable to ensure proper performance linkage in respect of executive directors' remuneration are unlikely to respond effectively to strategic proposals generated by the chief executive and management.'

The major corporate governance reports (Cadbury, Greenbury, Hamper, Turnbull and Higgs) have all commented on remuneration. Greenbury was solely concerned with remuneration, as was the 2001/2002 DTI consultation on directors' remuneration.

**The Cadbury Report** restricted itself to three paragraphs about remuneration (see **B3.9**) Cadbury reduced the maximum contract length to three years (previously it was five years); required full and clear disclosure of directors' total emoluments, including pension contributions and stock options; and recommended a remuneration committee made up wholly or mainly of non-executive directors.

**The Greenbury Report** was published on 17 July 1995. The backcloth was of large gains from share options in newly privatised companies and the terms of reference to Greenbury referred to unjustified compensation packages in privatised utilities. The Greenbury Report set out three fundamental principles of accountability, transparency and performance linkage. Greenbury developed a detailed code (see **B3.10–B3.13**) which has now been superceded by some of the contents of the Combined Code.

**The Hampel Report** suggested three broad principles for remuneration (the level and make up of remuneration, procedure and disclosure) and these were incorporated in the Combined Code (see **B3.14–B3.32**). With regard to 'the level and make-up of remuneration', Hampel commented:

> 'The wording makes it clear that those responsible should consider the remuneration of each director individually, and should do so against the needs of the particular company for talent at board level at the particular time.'

**The Turnbull Report's** focus was on risk and internal control. Turnbull set some questions for the board to consider (see **B4.30**) including the following:

> 'Do the company's culture, code of conduct, human resource policies, and performance reward systems support the business objectives and risk management and internal control systems?.'

**The DTI consultation on directors' remuneration** concluded that remuneration was a matter for shareholders, but the legal framework could be improved to help the shareholders exert their responsibility. The Government enacted the *Directors Remuneration Report Regulations 2002 (SI 2002/1986)* with the aim of improving transparency and accountability. The new Regulations required:

- more and better disclosure of remuneration and its link to performance; and

- a vote at the AGM on the Remuneration Report.

**The Higgs Report** made a number of recommendations that affected remuneration.

- Only independent directors should sit on the Remuneration Committee.

- The remuneration committee's terms of reference were extended to include the chairman, who he did not regard as independent. Higgs also widened the responsibility of the remuneration committee to set the executive directors and chairman's remuneration, whereas Hampel had felt that the overall policy should be a matter for the board as a whole.

- Training of directors and the performance evaluation of the board, its committees and its individual directors were stressed. A performance appraisal of the remuneration committee must be done and how it is conducted must be reported in the annual report.

- Notice or contract periods should be set at one year or less and if longer notice or contract periods were needed to recruit new directors from outside these should reduce after the initial period.

- The remuneration committee should also be responsible for appointing consultants in respect of executive director remuneration. This last point was in response to research which had confirmed the worries of many directors that compensation consultants were often perceived to be too close to executive management and too ready to encourage companies to position their remuneration policy in the 'upper quartile' of their peer group comparators.

**The FRC Review** of Higgs made minor changes to the wording regarding remuneration, but said:

'Remuneration committees should take a robust line on reducing compensation to reflect departing directors' obligations to mitigate loss thus removing the alternative of liquidated damages in contracts.'

## Shareholder views                                              B13.3

Ultimately it is the shareholders who approve the remuneration of the directors. Historically it was left to their representative bodies, the Association of British Insurers and the National Association of Pension Funds, to represent institutional shareholders. More recently a number of leading investment houses have issued their own guidelines on remuneration.

Small shareholders can air their views at the AGM and frequently do at great length. This can be embarrassing to the directors and lead to bad press the next day. However as they own few shares in total they rarely influence the voting.

## Other interested parties                                       B13.4

The list of other interested parties is long: the Institute of Directors, the CBI, the Government, employees, the TUC and trade unions, PIRC, Manifest, nearly all the major consultants, lawyers, accountants and actuaries, the press. It seems nearly everyone has a view on directors' pay. Directors' pay attracts huge interest in the media and can cause substantial damage to the company's reputation.

# Principles of remuneration                                      B13.5

## Managing conflicts of interest                                 B13.6

No director should be involved in setting his or her own pay. Directors do have a conflict of interest and there is a danger that they may seek excessive remuneration, and do so in ways which are not in the best interests of the company. Where there is a major or controlling shareholder they may seek to influence remuneration so that their wider interests are maximised. Major shareholders have a legitimate interest in how the directors are remunerated, but they should not be allowed to decide. For this reason the setting of executive directors' remuneration is best done by a remuneration committee made up exclusively of independent directors.

The remuneration committee should seek the views of the chairman, the chief executive, internal management, shareholders, external advisers and consultants, but ultimately they must make the decisions themselves.

# Disclosure                                                                 B13.7

The Combined Code, company law and Financial Services Authority rules all require the disclosure of how and how much directors are paid. If this information is available to shareholders, then they are in a position to decide if the remuneration is appropriate.

# Transparency and accountability                                           B13.8

Transparency and accountability were two of the main Greenbury principles and underpinned the *2002 Regulations*. If the remuneration is fully disclosed (in a way that interested parties can see exactly how and how much directors are paid) then those people setting the remuneration can be held accountable for the consequences of their decisions. The additional requirements have added length but not clarity to the disclosures. The preamble to the 2003 Combined Code does, however, make it quite explicit what is expected:

'Para 11: It is important that this [remuneration] report is clear, transparent and understandable to shareholders.'

Accountability is achieved ultimately through the vote at the AGM on the remuneration report resolution. However, key shareholders will make their views known well before this if they are unhappy with the company's proposal. This is an area where much discussion and negotiation happens behind the scenes.

# Performance linkage and alignment to shareholders          B13.9

Agency theory says that management are the agents of shareholders and should manage the company in the best interests of shareholders. In order to do so, they need to be incited to do so. The rational economic person will try to maximise his or her wealth with minimum risk. This is, however, totally different to what shareholders want. Therefore agency theory says that the management needs to be incited to manage the company in the best interests of shareholders. Remuneration therefore needs to be linked to shareholders' interests of long term share price appreciations and dividends. Management will discount any pay that does not pay out until some years ahead and which is dependant on factors many of which they feel are beyond their control.

## Window on corporate governance                B13.10

How directors and senior managers are remunerated provides an important window on corporate governance more generally.

- If the process is well-managed, with a properly constituted remuneration committee which operates fully independently, appoints expert, professional, independent remuneration consultants to assist them, listens to shareholders and management and evaluates their inputs, then this is a good sign that other corporate governance will be effective. If however the reverse is true, eg remuneration committee members are seen to be too close to the chief executive, consultants are appointed by and are too close to management, shareholder concerns are ignored and excessive remuneration is awarded, then this is a sign that other corporate governance may be poor.

- The choice of performance measures and their relative importance in the delivery of performance-related pay is the second window on corporate governance, as they indicate what is felt to be important in the company. The exclusive use of profit in annual bonus plans is a warning sign. The performance measures that determine the remuneration of the management of the company should be those that drive the future business success, eg customer satisfaction, customer retention, customer growth, average revenue per customers, employee satisfaction, staff turnover and average length of service, environmental and social responsibility measures, health and safety, effective relationships with regulators etc. If these measures are not part of the incentive plans, then the company may be saying one thing to its shareholders but internally may be behaving quite differently. Hence this is a crucial window on what is happening inside the company.

# The roles of the intermediaries                B13.11

Who are the intermediaries and what do they do?

- There are 2,700 listed companies in the UK and over 200 fund managers. Each company cannot talk to each fund manager about every aspect of corporate governance. They use intermediaries to assist and to make the process manageable. Also, the cost of analysing the remuneration and other corporate governance items is such that it is more efficient for institutional shareholders to sub-contract out much of this analysis to the intermediaries.

- For a long time, the ABI have provided services to the fund management arms of insurance companies. They provide general guidance on corporate governance and have a separate (for profit) voting issues service, for which clients pay an annual subscription. The NAPF provide general guidance on corporate governance, mainly to pension funds, and have a separate (for profit) voting issues service called IVIS, for which clients pay an annual subscription. PIRC, set up in 1992, provides a range of corporate governance services and its main clients are local authority pension funds. Manifest, set up in 1995, provides a range of corporate governance services to fund managers and other clients. ISS, IRRC, GovernanceMetrics and Deminor provide similar services but are US-based and have small operations in the UK and Europe. ISS and NAPF announced a link up in 2003, as did Manifest and GovernanceMetrics.

- When a company sends out the remuneration committee report, or a proposal for a new remuneration plan to shareholders, the intermediaries will analyse the proposals and report on them to their clients the shareholders. They will flag up areas of concerns and may in some cases recommend abstention from or even voting against an AGM/EGM resolution. The press regularly use their reports or quote these intermediaries. It should be noted that most fund managers are extremely reluctant to be quoted as saying anything negative about a company as this may be detrimental to the share price and their personal relationships with directors and senior management. Access to these people is crucial for them to do their job of analysing the company. Thus the intermediaries perform an important role.

- When a company wishes to test the reaction of its shareholders to a remuneration proposal, the ABI will organise a subcommittee of (usually three) major shareholders in the company to consider and report back on the proposals on behalf of the ABI. More recently, many companies have started to go directly to their major shareholders rather than via the ABI.

# Remuneration Disclosure Requirements

*This chapter is based on material that appeared in Chapter 9 – Directors'
Remuneration and Benefits of Tolley's Non-Executive Directors Handbook
(2003), written by Patrick Dunne, 3i and Glynis D. Morris BA, FCA. This
material is used by permission of LexisNexis UK.*

## Disclosure of directors' remuneration B14.1

## At a glance B14.2

- *CA 1985* requires detailed disclosures on directors' remuneration to be given in the notes to the accounts.

- Separate disclosure requirements apply for quoted and unquoted companies.

- Additional requirements also apply to listed companies under the FSA Listing Rules and the Combined Code.

- Aggregate disclosures must be given in respect of emoluments, contributions to defined contribution retirement schemes, share options, amounts payable under long-term incentive schemes and the number of directors accruing benefits under defined benefit retirement schemes.

- Slightly reduced disclosure requirements apply in the case of small companies.

- Additional aggregate information must be given by quoted and AIM companies.

- The auditors are required to include any missing information in their audit report.

- The money value of any benefits in kind must be included in emoluments.

- Bonus payments that require shareholder approval should normally be included in emoluments in the year in which they are approved.

- Details of directors' share options must also be given in the directors' report.

- Awards under long-term incentive schemes are disclosable when the director becomes entitled to receive payment.

- All pension schemes must be classified as either defined contribution or defined benefit for disclosure purposes.

- Amounts paid to or receivable by, a person connected with a director must be included in the disclosures.

- Particular difficulties can arise in groups of companies, especially if all directors' remuneration is paid by the holding company.

## Disclosure under the Companies Act 1985    B14.3

A company's annual accounts must include detailed information on remuneration paid to, or receivable by, anyone who was a director during the year. The disclosure requirements cover all amounts receivable by the directors in respect of their services as directors of the company (and, where relevant, of its subsidiaries), regardless of who actually makes the payment. The legislation requires basic disclosures to be given by all companies, and then makes a clear distinction between quoted and unquoted companies in requiring more detailed information to be given. The requirements are broadly similar for accounting periods ending before 31 December 2002, although greater detail is required in the case of quoted companies, but the *Directors' Remuneration Report Regulations 2002 (SI 2002/1986)* introduce some significant changes to the disclosure requirements for quoted companies for accounting periods ending on or after 31 December 2002. For these purposes, a quoted company is defined as a company whose equity share capital is:

- included in the Official List of the London Stock Exchange;

- officially listed in an EEA State; or

- admitted to dealing on the New York Stock Exchange or the Nasdaq Exchange.

Thus, AIM listed companies do not have to report under the *Directors' Remuneration Report Regulations 2002 (SI 2002/1986)*, but should view compliance as best practice.

## Basic accounts disclosures for all companies    B14.4

The basic requirement is that every company should disclose in the notes to the accounts:

- the aggregate of the emoluments paid to, or receivable by, the directors in respect of their qualifying services (which include services as director of a subsidiary or in the management of the company or group);

- the aggregate value of any contributions paid by the company in respect of directors into a pension scheme where the benefits depend on the level of contributions paid (i.e. defined contribution schemes;

- the number of directors who are accruing retirement benefits under money purchase schemes; and

- the number of directors who are accruing retirement benefits under defined benefit schemes.

The contributions made during the year to defined benefit retirement schemes do not have to be disclosed. Slightly reduced disclosure requirements apply in the case of small companies. Emoluments are defined in *CA 1985* as including salary, bonus, fees, benefits in kind, expense allowances (if these are chargeable to UK income tax) and amounts paid on acceptance of office as director. This list is not intended to be exhaustive and any other similar amounts paid to, or receivable by, directors will therefore be disclosable. Share options, pension contributions and amounts payable under long-term incentive schemes are specifically excluded from the definition of emoluments as they are subject to separate disclosure requirements.

## Quoted and AIM companies                                              B14.5

In addition to the above aggregate information, quoted companies and those whose equity share capital is listed on the Alternative Investment Market (AIM) must disclose:

- the aggregate gains made by directors on the exercise of share options; and

- the aggregate of the amounts paid to, or receivable by, directors under long term incentive schemes in respect of qualifying services and the net value of any assets (other than cash or share options) receivable by directors under such schemes.

## Avoiding duplication                                                   B14.6

If any of the required details are readily ascertainable from other information included with the accounts, such as a remuneration report (see **B14.24** below), they generally do not have to be disclosed again. The one exception is aggregate gains on the exercise of share options that must always be shown separately in the notes to the accounts. In practice, if the detailed information is included in a separate directors' remuneration report, it is helpful for the notes to the accounts to include a cross-reference.

## Audit requirements                                                     B14.7

If the accounts do not include all of the required disclosures in respect of directors' emoluments and other benefits, or transactions between the company and its directors or other officers, the auditors must include a statement of the missing details in their audit report, so far as they are reasonably able to do so. In the case of listed companies, the FSA has extended this requirement to cover disclosures required under the Listing Rules and it also applies to certain elements of the information that must be included in the directors' remuneration report (see **B14.24** below).

## Benefits in kind                                        B14.8

Emoluments specifically include the estimated money value of benefits in kind received by a director otherwise than in cash. The most common benefits in kind are:

- company car;

- free or subsidised accommodation;

- insurance for the benefit of the director (eg private health cover, indemnity insurance, personal accident cover);

- loans at preferential interest rates;

- relocation costs (unless the relocation is clearly for business purposes).

Some of these may also be disclosable in the annual accounts as loans or transactions with directors. Share options are subject to separate disclosure requirements and are therefore specifically excluded from emoluments for disclosure purposes. The main difficulty with benefits in kind is establishing an appropriate and realistic money value for the benefit. In most cases, market value will provide the best estimate of money value.

## Bonus payments                                          B14.9

Provision should usually be made in the accounts for bonuses in the year in which they are earned. Where a bonus payment to directors requires approval by the shareholders before the directors are entitled to receive it, it is usual to treat the bonus as being receivable by the directors (and therefore disclosable within directors' emoluments) in the year in which shareholder approval is given, even though the bonus may have been charged to the profit and loss account in an earlier period.

## Share options                                           B14.10

In addition to the disclosures on share options referred to in **B14.3** above, the directors' report (or the notes to the accounts) must give detailed information on directors' interests (including options) in the shares in or debentures of the company or any other body corporate in the same group. Interests include those held by the directors' close family. Certain exemptions apply in the case of wholly-owned subsidiaries. In the case of listed companies, extensive disclosures must also be given in the directors' remuneration report (see **B14.24** below).

## Long-term incentive schemes                          B14.11

Under *CA 1985*, amounts payable under long term incentive schemes are disclosable when they are paid to or receivable by the director. The director must therefore have the right to receive a sum before it becomes disclosable. Amounts should therefore normally be disclosed in the year in which the director becomes entitled to receive payment. In the case of a long term incentive scheme, the director will not usually be entitled to receive payment until all the specified conditions have been met.

Further disclosures on long term incentive schemes must be given in the directors' remuneration report (see **B14.24** below).

## Pension arrangements                                  B14.12

For the purposes of the *CA 1985* disclosures referred to in **B14.3** above, all pension schemes must be classified as either defined contribution or defined benefit schemes. Any death in service benefits are to be disregarded when classifying a pension scheme for disclosure purposes. A pension scheme under which a director will be entitled to receive both money purchase benefits and defined benefits is classified as a defined benefit scheme for disclosure purposes. Where a scheme provides for the director to receive money purchase benefits or defined benefits, whichever is the greater, the company is allowed to assume for disclosure purposes that the benefits will be whichever appears more likely at the end of the financial year in question. Listed companies must also give additional details on directors' pension arrangements in the directors' remuneration report.

## Payments to and from other parties                    B14.13

Amounts paid to or receivable by a person connected with a director or a body corporate controlled by him are specifically included within the disclosure requirements. Disclosure therefore cannot be avoided by arranging for the payment to be made to a connected party. In the case of payments to a company owned by the director, the emoluments note to the accounts usually includes an explanation that some or all of the payments have been made through the company. Emoluments also include all relevant amounts in respect of a director's services paid by, or receivable from the company, the company's subsidiary undertakings and any other person, unless the director must in turn account to the company or any of its subsidiary undertakings for the amounts received.

## Payments to third parties                             B14.14

The accounts must also disclose the aggregate amount paid to, or receivable by, third parties for making available the services of any person as a director of the company or otherwise in connection with the management of the affairs of the company or group. The most common example of this is an arrangement whereby a substantial investor in a company (eg a bank or venture capital company) has the right to appoint a director to the board of the investee company and payment for the services of this director is made to the investor rather than to the director himself.

## Disclosure in holding companies                               B14.15

Directors' remuneration in the accounts of the holding company will comprise:

- remuneration paid to directors of the holding company in respect of their services to the company and management of the company and group; and

- if any holding company directors are also directors of one or more of the subsidiaries, remuneration paid to them for their services in relation to these companies.

Remuneration paid to those who are directors of subsidiaries but who are not directors of the holding company is not disclosable in the accounts of the holding company. The same disclosure requirements apply in the holding company's accounts, regardless of whether some or all of the remuneration costs are recharged to the subsidiaries.

## Disclosure in the accounts of subsidiaries                    B14.16

Where the holding company recharges the subsidiaries with the cost of remunerating their directors, each subsidiary should disclose as directors' remuneration the amount paid to the holding company in respect of directors' services to the company. If the holding company makes a global recharge to the subsidiaries to cover general management costs, including directors' remuneration, but the element for directors' remuneration cannot be separately identified, an appropriate apportionment should be made for disclosure purposes. Where the holding company does not recharge the subsidiaries with the costs of remunerating their directors, the costs borne by the holding company are still disclosable as directors' remuneration in the accounts of the subsidiary – it is not acceptable to simply disclose the fact that the directors have been remunerated by the holding company and not quantify the amount that they have received. However, it may be helpful to explain that this cost has been borne by the holding company and is not charged in the subsidiary's accounts.

Where directors of a subsidiary are also directors or employees of the holding company, it is sometimes argued that the holding company remunerates them only for their services to the holding company and that they receive no remuneration in respect of their services as directors of the subsidiary. The validity of this argument will usually depend on the amount of time that the director or employee devotes to the subsidiary company. If the time is relatively small it may be acceptable that he/she does not receive remuneration for services as a director of the subsidiary. In this case, a brief explanation should be included in the subsidiary's accounts.

## Compensation for loss of office                                      B14.17

The aggregate compensation for loss of office paid to, or receivable by, directors and former directors must also be disclosed. Compensation for loss of office constitutes a separate category of payment to directors and should not be included in the figure for directors' emoluments for the period. Where compensation payments include non-cash benefits, these should be included in the disclosures at their estimated money value and the nature of the benefit must be disclosed. Many compensation payments to directors will also require shareholder approval under *CA 1985*, although this is not usually required for genuine payments in respect of damages for breach of contract or for pensions in respect of past services. If significant non-cash items are included, the compensation payments may also require approval under the provisions on substantial property transactions in *section 320* of *CA 1985*. Where a retired director continues to have an involvement with the company in a part-time or consultancy capacity, any payments in excess of normal market rates for the work performed may well include an element of compensation for loss of office, in which case the details should be disclosed.

# Directors' service contracts                                          B14.18

## Service contracts for executive directors                            B14.19

Where a director has a written contract of service with the company, *section 318* of *CA 1985* requires the company to retain a copy of the contract at one of the following locations:

- the company's registered office;

- the place where the register of members is kept (if this is not the registered office); or

- the company's principal place of business (provided that this is in the part of Great Britain where the company is registered).

If a director does not have a written contract of service, the company must keep a written memorandum of the terms of his/her appointment. The same rules apply to a variation of a director's contract. A parent company is also required to keep copies of service contracts between its subsidiaries and their directors, or a written memorandum of the terms if these contracts are not in writing. Copies of all contracts and memoranda must be kept in the same place. If they are not kept at the registered office, the company must notify the Registrar of Companies of where they are held and of any changes in location. *Section 318(6)* of *CA 1985* emphasises that these arrangements apply equally in the case of shadow directors. However, there is no formal requirement for a company to retain a copy of a contract, variation or memorandum when the unexpired term is less than 12 months, or where the contract can be terminated by the company within the next 12 months without the payment of compensation.

## Director working outside the UK                                    B14.20

Where a director of the company, or of one of its subsidiaries, is required under his/her contract to work wholly or mainly outside the UK, the company is not required to keep a copy of the contract, but it must keep a memorandum giving the director's name and the provisions of the contract relating to its duration. In the case of a contract for a director of a subsidiary, the name and place of incorporation of the subsidiary must also be recorded in the memorandum. These memoranda must be kept in the same place as the contracts and memoranda relating to the other directors.

## Inspection of contracts                                            B14.21

Under *section 318(7)* of *CA 1985*, any member of the company is entitled to inspect the copies of the directors' contracts of service (or the memoranda where there is no written service contract) without charge. If the company refuses to allow a member to inspect a contract or memorandum, the court can require immediate inspection.

## Shareholder approval for contracts for more than five years        B14.22

Under *section 319* of *CA 1985*, a director cannot be given the right of employment with the company (or, where relevant, with the group) for a period of more than five years under an agreement which does not allow the company to give unconditional notice at any time, unless this term of the contract has been first approved by the company in general meeting (or, in the case of a private company, by written resolution). Employment is defined as including employment under a contract for services. Where the director is also a director of the company's holding company, prior approval to the arrangement must normally be given by the shareholders of both the subsidiary and the holding company (unless the subsidiary is wholly-owned, in which case prior approval of the arrangement by the shareholders of the subsidiary is not required).

A written memorandum setting out the proposed agreement must be available for inspection by the members at the company's registered office for a period of at least 15 days before the meeting and at the meeting itself. In the case of a private company where agreement is to be by written resolution, a copy of the memorandum must be sent to each member before, or at the same time as, the resolution is provided for signature.

A term included in a director's contract in contravention of *section 319* of CA *1985* is void, and the agreement is deemed to include a term entitling the company to terminate the agreement at any time by the giving of reasonable notice.

## Series of agreements B14.23

*CA 1985* includes special provisions to prevent a company entering into a series of shorter agreements with the same director in an attempt to avoid the requirement for shareholder approval of a contract that in effect extends for more than five years.

# Directors' remuneration report B14.24

## At a glance B14.25

- For accounting periods ending on or after 31 December 2002, the directors of a quoted company are required to prepare a separate directors' remuneration report.

- Certain elements of the directors' remuneration report are subject to audit.

- The general meeting at which the annual reports and accounts are laid must include a resolution inviting the shareholders to approve the directors' remuneration report.

- The content of the directors' remuneration report is specified in the legislation and includes:

  ○ the name of each director who was a member of the committee, the name of any person who materially assisted the committee and, if they are not a director, the nature of other services provided to the company and whether they were appointed by the committee.

  ○ detailed information on the remuneration paid to each individual director;

  ○ a statement on the company's future remuneration policy;

  ○ an explanation of any performance-related elements of remuneration;

  ○ details of pension entitlements earned under a defined benefit retirement scheme;

  ○ details of service contracts and any related compensation commitments; and

> ○   comparative information on shareholder return for the last five years.
>
> ●   The legislation also specifies which elements of the directors' remuneration report should be included in summary financial statements.

## Requirements of CA 1985 B14.26

For accounting periods ending on or after 31 December 2002, the directors of a quoted company are required to prepare a directors' remuneration report containing the detailed information specified in a new *Schedule 7A* to *CA 1985*. Current directors and those who have served as director in the preceding five years are given a specific duty to disclose relevant information to the company to enable the report to be prepared. The report must be formally approved by the directors and must be signed on behalf of the board by a director or by the company secretary. A signed copy must be delivered to the registrar as part of the company's annual reports and accounts. The auditors are required to report on the auditable part of the report (which is defined as the part covering the detailed disclosures on remuneration received by the directors) and to include any missing information in their audit report, so far as they are reasonably able to do so.

## Comparison to Combined Code recommendations B14.27

The preparation of a separate directors' remuneration report had been a recommendation under the Combined Code for a number of years and, for listed companies, a requirement of the FSA Listing Rules. The contents of the report required under the new legislation are similar to those previously required by the Code and the FSA rules, but include some additional disclosures. In particular:

●   An annual vote at the AGM on the remuneration report

●   A 5 year performance graph showing the total shareholder return

●   Disclosure of the proportion of remuneration that is performance related

●   Disclosure of the transfer value of the accrued pension

●   Disclosure of the names of consultants advising the remuneration committee, who appointed them, together with details of any other services they provide.

## Shareholder approval B14.28

Under the legislation, the general meeting at which the annual reports and accounts are laid must include a resolution enabling the shareholders to approve the directors' remuneration report, and details of the resolution must be set out in the notice of the meeting. However, the legislation notes that this requirement does not mean that the entitlement of any individual to the remuneration shown in the report is conditional on the resolution being passed. For accounting periods ending before 31 December 2002, there was no requirement for the report prepared under the Combined Code recommendations or FSA Listing Rules to be formally approved by the shareholders.

## Contents of the remuneration report                  B14.29

The detailed contents required by *CA 1985* are set out at **B14.43** below in the form of a disclosure checklist. The contents are divided into two sections in the legislation (those subject to audit and those not subject to audit). The legislation generally requires the detailed information to be given in tabular form and in a way that links the information to each director by name. A limited degree of aggregation is permitted in the disclosure of information on share options where the required details would otherwise result in a disclosure of excessive length.

One of the potential problems here is the considerable amount of detail that may need to be given in the report. In presenting the disclosures, companies need to make a particular effort to ensure that the information that is likely to be of most interest to shareholders does not become obscured by the sheer volume of detail. The preamble to the Combined Code refers to this explicitly – 'It is important that this [remuneration] report is clear, transparent and understandable to shareholders.'

## Pension entitlements                                 B14.30

Defined benefit retirement schemes usually link pension entitlement to final salary or average salary over a fixed period (eg the last three years). Two separate disclosures are required for each director.

The *Directors' Remuneration Report Regulations 2002 (SI 2002/1986)* require:

- the accrued benefit and the increase in the accrued benefit in the year; and

- the transfer value of the accrued benefit at the end of the year and of the preceding year and the increase in the year. The transfer value should be calculated in accordance with Actuarial Guidance Note 11 (GN11). Any contributions made by the director should be deducted from the increase in accrued benefit.

Paragraph 12.43 of the Listing Rules has different requirements:

(a) details of the amount of the increase during the period under review (excluding inflation) and of the accumulated total amount at the end of the period in respect of the accrued benefit to which each director would be entitled on leaving service or is entitled having left service during the period under review;

(b) and either:

(i) the transfer value (less director's contributions) of the relevant increase in accrued benefit (to be calculated in accordance with Actuarial Guidance Note GN11 but making no deduction for any underfunding) as at the end of the period; or

(ii) so much of the following information as is necessary to make a reasonable assessment of the transfer value in respect of each director:

(A) current age;

(B) normal retirement age;

(C) the amount of any contributions paid or payable by the director under the terms of the scheme during the period under review;

(D) details of spouse's and dependants' benefits;

(E) early retirement rights and options, expectations of pension increases after retirement (whether guaranteed or discretionary); and

(F) discretionary benefits for which allowance is made in transfer values on leaving and any other relevant information which will significantly affect the value of the benefits.

Voluntary contributions and benefits should not be disclosed.

Both require the same disclosure for money purchase schemes (as in *Part I* of *Schedule 6* to *CA 1985*) ie details of the contribution or allowance payable or made by the company in respect of each director during the period under review.

## Disclosure of transfer value                                      B14.31

Where a transfer value is disclosed, it should be calculated in accordance with Actuarial Guidance Note 11 (GN11) but should not include any deduction for underfunding. The Combined Code notes that companies may wish to make clear in the report that transfer values represent a liability of the company, not sums paid (or due) to the individual directors.

## Share performance graph                                           B14.32

The share performance graph must show TSR for five years compared to a relevant index. There is no requirement to disclose information for periods before the company came into effect – in the early years, therefore, information will be given for one to four years as appropriate. The legislation includes detailed guidance on calculating total shareholder return for this purpose.

## Summary financial statements

The provisions of *CA 1985* on summary financial statements are amended to require, in the case of a quoted company, the inclusion of either the whole of the directors' remuneration report or, as a minimum:

- aggregate information on directors' remuneration (see **B14.3** above);

- the statement of the company's policy on directors' remuneration for future years; and

- the performance graph summarising shareholder return.

## The Combined Code for Remuneration

The preamble to the July 2003 draft of the Combined Code on Corporate Governance states:

'11. The revised Code does not include material in the previous Code on the disclosure of directors' remuneration. This is because "The Directors' Remuneration Report Regulations 2002" are now in force and supersede the earlier Code provisions. These require the directors of a company to prepare a remuneration report. It is important that this report is clear, transparent and understandable to shareholders.'

Section B of Part 1 of the Combined Code sets out the following main principles, supporting principles and Code provisions regarding remuneration. Companies must report to their shareholders on how they apply the main principles and supporting principles and either comply with the Code provisions or explain why they do not.

# Remuneration

## B.1 The level and make-up of remuneration

> **Main Principles**
>
> Levels of remuneration should be sufficient to attract, retain and motivate directors of the quality required to run the company successfully, but a company should avoid paying more than is necessary for this purpose.
>
> A significant proportion of executive directors' remuneration should be structured so as to link rewards to corporate and individual performance.

---

**Supporting Principle**

The Remuneration Committee should judge where to position their company relative to other companies. But they should use such comparisons with caution, in view of the risk of an upward ratchet of remuneration levels with no corresponding improvement in performance.

They should also be sensitive to pay and employment conditions elsewhere in the group, especially when determining annual salary increases.

---

## Code Provisions

### Remuneration policy

B.1.1    The performance-related elements of remuneration should form a significant proportion of the total remuneration package of executive directors and should be designed to align their interests with those of shareholders and to give these directors keen incentives to perform at the highest levels. In designing schemes of performance-related remuneration, the Remuneration Committee should follow the provisions in Schedule A to this Code.

B.1.2    Executive share options should not be offered at a discount save as permitted by the relevant provisions of the Listing Rules.

B.1.3    Levels of remuneration for non-executive directors should reflect the time commitment and responsibilities of the role. Remuneration for non-executive directors should not include share options. If, exceptionally, options are granted, shareholder approval should be sought in advance and any shares acquired by exercise of the options should be held until at least one year after the non-executive director leaves the board. Holding of share options could be relevant to the determination of a non-executive director's independence (as set out in provision A.3.1).

B.1.4    Where a company releases an executive director to serve as a non-executive director elsewhere, the remuneration report should include a statement as to whether or not the director will retain such earnings and, if so, what the remuneration is.

### Service Contracts and Compensation

B.1.5    The Remuneration Committee should carefully consider what compensation commitments (including pension contributions and all other elements) their directors' terms of appointment would entail in the event of early termination. The aim should be to avoid rewarding poor performance. They should take a robust line on reducing compensation to reflect departing directors' obligations to mitigate loss.

B.1.6    Notice or contract periods should be set at one year or less. If it is necessary to offer longer notice or contract periods to new directors recruited from outside, such periods should reduce to one year or less after the initial period.

# B.2 Procedure

**Main Principle**

There should be a formal and transparent procedure for developing policy on executive remuneration and for fixing the remuneration packages of individual directors. No director should be involved in deciding his or her own remuneration.

**Supporting Principles**

The Remuneration Committee should consult the chairman and/or chief executive about their proposals relating to the remuneration of other executive directors.

The Remuneration Committee should also be responsible for appointing any consultants in respect of executive director remuneration. Where executive directors or senior management are involved in advising or supporting the Remuneration Committee, care should be taken to recognise and avoid conflicts of interest.

The chairman of the board should ensure that the company maintains contact as required with its principal shareholders about remuneration in the same way as for other matters.

**Code Provisions**

B.2.1    The board should establish a Remuneration Committee of at least three, or in the case of smaller companies two, members, who should all be independent non-executive directors. The Remuneration Committee should make available its terms of reference, explaining its role and the authority delegated to it by the board. Where remuneration consultants are appointed, a statement should be made available of whether they have any other connection with the company.

B.2.2    The Remuneration Committee should have delegated responsibility for setting remuneration for all executive directors and the chairman, including pension rights and any compensation payments. The committee should also recommend and monitor the level and structure of remuneration for senior management. The definition of 'senior management' for this purpose should be determined by the board but should normally include the first layer of management below board level.

B.2.3    The board itself or, where required by the Articles of Association, the shareholders should determine the remuneration of the non-executive directors within the limits set in the Articles of Association. Where permitted by the Articles, the board may however delegate this responsibility to a committee, which might include the chief executive.

B.2.4    Shareholders should be invited specifically to approve all new long-term incentive schemes (as defined in the Listing Rules) and significant changes to existing schemes, save in the circumstances permitted by the Listing Rules.

# Performance-related remuneration B14.35

Schedule A to Part 1 of the Combined Code comprises the guidance originally set out in the Greenbury Code of Best Practice on Directors' remuneration, with a number of minor wording changes.

### Schedule A: Provisions on the design of performance related remuneration

1. The Remuneration Committee should consider whether the directors should be eligible for annual bonuses. If so, performance conditions should be relevant, stretching and designed to enhance shareholder value. Upper limits should be set and disclosed. There may be a case for part payment in shares to be held for a significant period.

2. The Remuneration Committee should consider whether the directors should be eligible for benefits under long-term incentive schemes.

Traditional share option schemes should be weighed against other kinds of long-term incentive scheme. In normal circumstances, shares granted or other forms of deferred remuneration should not vest, and options should not be exercisable, in less than three years. Directors should be encouraged to hold their shares for a further period after vesting or exercise, subject to the need to finance any costs of acquisition and associated tax liabilities.

3. Any new long-term incentive schemes which are proposed should be approved by shareholders and should preferably replace any existing schemes or at least form part of a well considered overall plan, incorporating existing schemes. The total rewards potentially available should not be excessive.

4. Payouts or grants under all incentive schemes, including new grants under existing share option schemes, should be subject to challenging performance criteria reflecting the company's objectives. Consideration should be given to criteria which reflect the company's performance relative to a group of comparator companies in some key variables such as total shareholder return.

5. Grants under executive share option and other long-term incentive schemes should normally be phased rather than awarded in one large block.

6. In general, only basic salary should be pensionable.

7. The Remuneration Committee should consider the pension consequences and associated costs to the company of basic salary increases and any other changes in pensionable remuneration, especially for directors close to retirement.

# Disclosure of corporate governance arrangements    B14.36

Schedule C of the Combined Code includes the following that relate to remuneration.

The Listing Rules require a statement to be included in the annual report relating to compliance with the Code, as described in the preamble. For ease of reference, the specific requirements in the Code for disclosure are set out below: The annual report should record:

- a statement of how the board operates, including a high level statement of which types of decisions are to be taken by the board and which are to be delegated to management (A.1.1);

- the names of the members of the Remuneration Committee (A.1.2);

- the number of meetings of the Remuneration Committee and individual attendance by directors (A.1.2);

- how performance evaluation of the Remuneration Committee has been conducted (A.6.1);

- the steps the board has taken to ensure that members of the board, and in particular the non-executive directors, develop an understanding of the views of major shareholders about their company (D.1.2).

The report should also include a description of the work of the Remuneration Committee as required under the *Directors' Remuneration Reporting Regulations 2002*, and including, where an executive director serves as a non-executive director elsewhere, whether or not the director will retain such earnings and, if so, what the remuneration is (B.1.4)

The following information should be made available (which may be met by making it available on request and placing the information available on the company's website):

- the terms of reference of the Remuneration Committee, explaining their role and the authority delegated to them by the board (B.2.1);

- where remuneration consultants are appointed, a statement of whether they have any other connection with the company (B.2.1).

# New share schemes    B14.37

New long term incentive schemes must be approved by shareholders. This is a requirement of the Listing Rules (paragraph 13.13). There are two exceptions to this:

'13.13

(a) an arrangement under which participation is offered on similar terms to all or substantially all employees of the issuer or any of its subsidiary undertakings whose employees are eligible to participate in the arrangement (provided that all or substantially all employees are not directors of the issuer); and

(b)  an arrangement in which the only participant is a director of the issuer (or an individual whose appointment as a director of the issuer is in contemplation) and the arrangement is established specifically to facilitate, in unusual circumstances, the recruitment or retention of the relevant individual. In these circumstances the following information must be disclosed in the first annual report published by the issuer following the date on which the relevant individual becomes eligible to participate in the arrangement: all of the information prescribed in paragraph 13.14(a) to (d); the name of the sole participant; the date on which the participant first became eligible to participate in the arrangement; explanation of why the circumstances in which the arrangement was established were unusual; the conditions to be satisfied under the terms of the arrangement; and the maximum award(s) under the terms of the arrangement or, if there is no maximum, the basis on which awards will be determined.'

## Contents of accompanying circular

13.14

A circular to shareholders in connection with the approval (as required by paragraph 13.13) of an employees' share scheme or a long-term incentive scheme must:

(a)  include either the full text of the scheme or a description of its principal terms;

(b)  include, where directors of the company are trustees of the scheme, or have a direct or indirect interest in the trustees, details of such trusteeship or interest;

(c)  state that the provisions (if any) relating to:

(i)  the persons to whom, or for whom, securities, cash or other benefits are provided under the scheme (the "participants");

(ii)  limitations on the number or amount of the securities, cash or other benefits subject to the scheme;

(iii) the maximum entitlement for any one participant;

(iv) the basis for determining a participant's entitlement to, and the terms of, securities, cash or other benefit to be provided and for the adjustment thereof (if any) in the event of a capitalisation issue, rights issue or open offer, sub-division or consolidation of shares or reduction of capital or any other variation of capital: cannot be altered to the advantage of participants without the prior approval of shareholders in general meeting (except for minor amendments to benefit the administration of the scheme, to take account of a change in legislation or to obtain or maintain favourable tax, exchange control or regulatory treatment for participants in the scheme or for the company operating the scheme or for members of its group);

(d) state whether benefits under the scheme will be pensionable and, if so, the reasons for this;

(e) if the scheme is not circulated to shareholders, include a statement that it will be available for inspection:

(i) from the date of the dispatch of the circular until the close of the relevant general meeting, at a place in or near the City of London or such other place as the UK Listing Authority may determine; and

(ii) at the place of the general meeting for at least 15 minutes prior to and during the meeting; and

(f) comply with the relevant requirements of paragraph 14.1 (contents of all circulars).

13.15

The resolution contained in the notice of meeting accompanying the circular must refer either to the scheme itself (if circulated to shareholders) or to the summary of its principal terms included in the circular.

13.16

A resolution approving the adoption of an employees' share scheme or long-term incentive scheme under paragraph 13.13 may authorise the directors to establish further schemes based on any scheme which has previously been approved by shareholders but modified to take account of local tax, exchange control or securities laws in overseas territories, provided that any shares made available under such further schemes are treated as counting against any limits on individual or overall participation in the main scheme.'

# Accounting for share options           B14.38

Recently there has been a great deal of interest and comment about accounting for share options. Of course, the information on awards of options, exercise price, exercise periods and vesting conditions have been available for many years. And yet how and when this appears on the face of the accounts is felt by many commentators to affect the value of the company and the future of remuneration! As the old saying goes 'You cannot fatten the pig by weighing it'; or can you?

There is at the time of writing no requirement for UK companies to account for the cost of share options. But UK companies with listings in the US will need to follow GAAP in this regard. For example BT in their 2003 Annual Report state:

'**Extract from BT Annual Report note 34**

The weighted average fair value of share options granted during the year ended 31 March 2003 has been estimated on the date of grant using the Black-Scholes option pricing model. The following weighted average assumptions were used in that model: an expected life extending one month later than the first exercise date; estimated annualised dividend yield of approximately 5% (2002 – 5%, 2001 – 2%); risk free interest rates of approximately 5% (2002 – 6%, 2001 – 7%); and expected volatility of approximately 40% (2002 – 34%, 2001 – 41%).

The weighted average fair value of the share options granted in the year ended 31 March 2003 was 55p (2002 – 55p, 2001 – 329p) for options exercisable three years after the date of grant and 72p (2002 – 55p, 2001 – 424p) for options exercisable five years after the date of grant. The weighted average fair value of options granted under the BT Group Global Share Option Plan has been estimated as 24p. The total value of share options granted by BT in the year ended 31 March 2003 was £41 million (2002 – £88 million, 2001 – £168 million).

In accordance with UK accounting practices, no compensation expense is recognised for the fair value of options granted where the exercise price equals the market price at date of grant or options granted under approved Sharesave schemes. See United States Generally Accepted Accounting Principles – IV Accounting for share options for the treatment under US GAAP

**IV. Accounting for share options**

Under UK GAAP, the company does not recognise compensation expense for the fair value, at the date of grant, of share options granted under the employee share option schemes. Under US GAAP, the company adopted the disclosure-only provisions in SFAS No. 123 "Accounting for Stock-Based Compensation". Accordingly, the company accounts for share options in accordance with APB Opinion No. 25 "Accounting for Stock Issued to Employees", under which no compensation expense is recognised. Had the group expensed recognised compensation cost for options granted in accordance with SFAS No. 123, the group's pro forma net income (loss), basic earnings (loss) per share and diluted earnings (loss) per share under US GAAP would have been £4,127 million (2002 – £792 million loss, 2001 – £2,419 million loss), 47.9p (2002 – 9.5p loss, 2001 – 33.2p loss) and 47.6p (2002 – 9.5p loss, 2001 – 33.2p loss), respectively. The SFAS No. 123 method of accounting does not apply to share options granted before 1 January 1995, and accordingly, the resulting pro forma compensation costs may not be representative of that to be expected in future years. See *!!!!!!!!!!ˇ÷"http://www.btplc.com/report/report03/Consolidatedfinancialst atements/Employeeshareschemes.htm" ˇ≠note 34ˇ§* for the SFAS No. 123 disclosures of the fair value of options granted under employee schemes at date of grant.'

# International Accounting Standards Board (IASB)  B14.39

The IASB, which remains committed to the development of a single set of global accounting standards, has placed the issue of share-based payments high on its agenda. It considers the point to be of growing international importance.

The IASB's current timetable envisages a final standard being issued towards the end of 2003 and the standard coming into effect from 1 January 2004. This is an issue with which companies must become familiar. Understanding the implications may prove critical to both immediate and future financial success, and will affect the operation of existing schemes and the design of new share-based incentives.

On 7 November 2002, the IASB produced an Exposure Draft proposing significant changes to accounting for share schemes which the Accounting Standards Board (ASB) have supported. Under existing UK accounting standards, many companies do not have to recognise the cost of providing stock options to their employees in the way that salary and other remuneration costs are accounted for.

## The accounting issue  B14.40

At present, it is suggested that many companies are overstating their profits because share-based payments (eg share options) are not accounted for in the company's profit and loss account, thereby making the company appear more profitable than it actually is.

The great investment guru Warren Buffett came up with the definitive comment on stock options almost ten years ago. He asked 'If options aren't a form of compensation, what are they?' 'If compensation isn't an expense, what is it?', was his second question. 'And if expenses shouldn't go into the calculation of earnings, where in the world should they go?', was his third. QED, as the Romans used to say.

## The proposals  B14.41

The IASB Exposure Draft has proposed that:

- there should be a profit and loss charge to reflect the value of the resources that the employees have contributed to the company in exchange for the shares or options, regardless of the actual cash expenditure made by the Company in satisfying the share awards;

- using an option pricing model, the charge should reflect the estimated fair value of the shares or options issued and should take into account vesting and performance conditions;

- the date at which the fair value of the shares or options issued is estimated should be the date of grant; and

- the charge should be spread over the period between issue and vesting, so that the charge will only be finalised at the vesting date.

**B14.41**   *The proposals*

The Draft contains stringent disclosure requirements about the assumptions used to calculate the profit and loss expense.

**The debate**                                                                                    **B14.42**

Reaction to the proposals has been mixed and there are a number of arguments both for and against the introduction of this new standard. Concerns have been raised that the new standard will discourage the use of share based incentive schemes (particularly all-employee schemes) because, assuming the standard proves to decrease company earnings, it could increase the cost of raising capital. However, it is argued in the alternative that share-based payments are a form of remuneration, a transfer of value from shareholders to employees, and should therefore be treated as an expense. The American corporate sector has never liked the idea of accounting for share options. In 1994 the American standard-setters, the FASB, put forward proposals for showing options as an expense. In response, corporate America put together some $70m as a fighting fund to get the idea over-turned.

You can argue all manner of different issues as to the calculation of the value of options. The point is the Buffett point. Does explaining why you should not account for share options as an expense really stand up? There are many examples, eg Yahoo, the internet company, has, on its last figures, an astonishing $409,556 per employee undisclosed as stock options. Explaining to the Board, investors and analysts that this is now going to have to be taken as a hit on earnings is an unenviable task.

One of the other problems is that share options were seen as a 'good thing'. It was argued that they made employees feel good throughout the company and increase loyalty and morale. But the reality is that this never happened. There are companies, particularly in the UK, where company-wide share option schemes have worked well, eg Asda and Tesco. However, significant share options have generally been only given to the few at the top of companies. Figures for America show that 75% of all options go to people classified as being among the top five executives at their company. The next 50 executives in the pecking order scooped 15%. And the rest of the employees accounted for the final 10%.

We are now in an era when being seen to be bending not just the rules but investors' credulity is not good from the corporate governance point of view. The consensus is that Buffett has prevailed. In 2002, 200 of the Dow 350 announced they would expense stock options.

# Checklist for the remuneration report                            **B14.43**

The following checklist is based on the requirements of *CA 1985* (which apply for accounting periods ending on or after 31 December 2002), the recommendations in the Combined Code and current FSA Listing Requirements. The second column indicates the origin of the disclosure requirement. Additional details may need to be given, depending on the specific circumstances of the company. There are three types of disclosures:

A.  Contents Subject to audit

B.  Contents not subject to audit

C.  Items required by the Combined Code or FSA

## A:  Contents subject to audit                    B14.44

The following information must be disclosed and is subject to audit.

| | |
|---|---|
| ● For each director who served during the financial year, the total amount of: | FSA Listing Rules |
|    – salary and/or fees; | |
|    – bonuses; | |
|    – expense allowances that are chargeable to UK income tax; | |
|    – any compensation for loss of office and similar payments; | |
|    – the estimated money value of any benefits in kind; and | |
|    – the sum total of all these amounts, and the equivalent total for the previous financial year. | *CA 1985, Sch 7A* |
| ● The nature of any element of a remuneration package which is not cash. | *CA 1985, Sch 7A* Combined Code, FSA Listing Rules |
| ● For each director who served during the financial year, the number of shares subject to a share option (distinguishing between those with different terms and conditions) at: | *CA 1985, Sch 7A* Combined Code |
|    – the beginning of the year, or the date of appointment if later; | |
|    – the end of the year, or the date of ceasing to be a director if earlier. | *CA 1985, Sch 7A* Combined Code, FSA Listing Rules |
| ● Information on share options awarded, exercised and lapsed during the year, and any variations to terms and conditions. | *CA 1985, Sch 7A* Combined Code, FSA Listing Rules |

- For each share option that was unexpired at any time during the year:

  - the price (if any) paid for its award;

  - the exercise prices;

  - the date from which the option can be exercised; and        *CA 1985, Sch 7A*

  - the date on which the option expires;

- A summary of any performance criteria upon which the award or exercise of a share option is conditional, and any changes made in the year.     *CA 1985, Sch 7A* Combined Code, FSA Listing Rules

- For any share option exercised during the year, the market price at the time of exercise.     *CA 1985, Sch 7A* Combined Code, FSA Listing Rules

- For each share option that was unexpired at the end of the financial year:

  - the market price at the year-end date; and

  - the highest and lowest market price during the year;     *CA 1985, Sch 7A* Combined Code, FSA Listing Rules

- For each director who served during the financial year, details of interests in long-term incentive schemes, showing:

  - interests at the beginning of the year, or the date of appointment if later;

  - awards during the year, showing whether they crystallise in the year or in subsequent years;

  - the money value and number of shares, cash payments or other benefits received during the year; and

  - interests at the end of the year, or on ceasing to be a director if earlier;     *CA 1985, Sch 7A*

- For each disclosed interest in long-term incentive schemes, the date by which the qualifying conditions have to be fulfilled and details of any variations in the terms and conditions madeduring the year.     *CA 1985, Sch 7A*

- For each scheme interest that has vested during the year, details of any shares, the amount of any money and the value of any other assets that have become receivable as a result.     *CA 1985, Sch 7A* Combined Code, FSA Listing Rules

- For each director who served during the financial
  year and has rights under a defined benefit
  retirement scheme:

  - details of any changes during the year in their
    accrued benefits under the scheme;

  - the accrued benefits at the end of the year;

  - the transfer value of the accrued benefits,
    calculated as recommended by the Institute
    of Actuaries and Faculty of Actuaries
    (see **B14.30**); and

  - the equivalent transfer value at the end of the
    previous year and the difference between this
    and the current transfer value, after deducting
    any contributions made by the director in the
    current year;

- For each director who served during the financial
  year and has rights under a money purchase
  retirement scheme, details of the contributions
  paid or payable by the company during the year.
  *CA 1985, Sch 7A,*
  *FSA Listing Rules*

- Details of certain excess retirement benefits paid
  to directors or former directors.
  *CA 1985, Sch 7A*

- Details of any significant awards to former
  directors (eg compensation for loss of office,
  pensions).
  *CA 1985, Sch 7A,*
  *FSA Listing Rules*

- For each director who served during the financial
  year, the aggregate amount of any consideration
  (including any benefits in kind) paid to, or
  receivable by, a third party for making available
  the services of the individual as a director.
  *CA 1985, Sch 7A*

# B: Contents not subject to audit                **B14.45**

The following information is required to be disclosed, but is not subject to
audit.

- The name of each director who was a member
  of any committee that considered directors'
  remuneration, the name of any person who
  materially assisted the committee and, if they
  are not a director, the nature of other services
  provided to the company.
  *CA 1985, Sch 7A*

| | |
|---|---|
| • The names of remuneration consultants who materially assisted any committee, what other services they have provided to the company and whether appointed by the company. The Combined Code also requires details of any other connection with the company to be made available (ie in the report or on the company website). | *CA 1985, Sch 7A*<br><br><br><br><br><br>CC B2.1 |
| • A statement of the company's policy on directors' remuneration for the forthcoming year and for subsequent financial years, drawing attention to any factors specific to the company – this must include for each individual who has served as a director between the end of the financial year under review and the date on which the annual reports and accounts are laid before the members: | *CA 1985, Sch 7A*<br>Combined Code,<br>FSA Listing Rules |
| – a detailed summary of any performance conditions in respect of awards under share option or long-term incentive schemes; | |
| – an explanation of why these performance conditions were chosen; | |
| – a summary of the methods used in assessing whether the performance conditions are met, and why those methods were chosen; | |
| – if any performance condition involves comparison with external factors, a summary of the factors to be used and the identify of any companies or index used for comparison purposes; | *CA 1985, Sch 7A* |
| • The relative importance of elements of remuneration that are related to performance and those that are not. | *CA 1985, Sch 7A* |
| • A statement of the company's policy on the granting of options or awards under employee share schemes and other long term incentive schemes and an explanation and justification of any departure from that policy during the year. | *CA 1985, Sch 7A* |
| • A description of, and explanation for, any significant changes to the terms and conditions of entitlement under share option or long-term incentive schemes. | *CA 1985, Sch 7A* |
| • An explanation of why any entitlements under share option or long-term incentive schemes are not subject to performance conditions. | Combined Code,<br>FSA Listing Rules |

- An explanation of, and justification for, any grants   *FSA Listing Rules*
  under share option or other long term incentive
  schemes that are awarded in one large block.

- A summary of the company's policy on the
  duration of directors' service contracts and on
  notice periods and termination payments under
  those contracts.

- The following information on the contract of
  service, or contract for services, of each person
  who served as a director during the financial year:

  - date of the contract, the unexpired term and
    any notice period;

  - any provision for compensation on early
    termination; and

  - sufficient information on any other provisions   FSA Listing Rules
    to enable a member to estimate the company's
    liability in the event of early termination of
    the contract;

- The unexpired term of any directors' service         Combined Code,
  contract of a director proposed for election or      FSA Listing Rules
  re-election at the forthcoming AGM, and if any
  such director does not have a service contract,
  a statement of that fact.

- An explanation of any service contracts which        *CA 1985, Sch 7A*
  provide for, or imply, notice periods in excess      FSA Listing Rules
  of one year, or which include provisions for
  pre-determined compensation which exceeds
  one year's salary and benefits.

- An explanation for any significant awards during     Combined Code
  the year to former directors (eg compensation
  for loss of office, pensions).

- An explanation of, and justification for, any annual  *CA 198, 5Sch 7A*
  bonuses or benefits in kind that are pensionable.

- A line graph showing the total shareholder return
  for the last five years on:

  - a holding of the class of equity shares whose
    public trading has resulted in the company
    meeting the definition of a quoted company; and

  - a hypothetical holding of shares, based on a       *CA 1985, Sch 7A*
    broad equity market index, together with the
    name of index and why it was chosen.

# C:  Items required by the Combined Code or FSA    B14.46

---

**Combined Code (as drafted by the FRC in July 2003)**

- The contents must explain how it applies                Combined Code,
  the principles in the Code, both main and               FSA Listing Rules
  supporting principles, including any special
  circumstances that have led to a particular
  approach.

- The company must comply with the provisions             Combined Code,
  of the Code or ,where it does not, provide an           FSA Listing Rules
  explanation.

  - Performance related elements of remuneration   CC B1.1
    should form a significant proportion of
    remuneration.

  - Performance related remuneration should        CC B1.1 and
    follow the provisions of Schedule A to the      Schedule A
    Code.

  - Executive Share options should not be          CC B1.2
    offered at a discount.

  - Where an executive director serves as         CC B1.4
    a non-executive director elsewhere, it
    should be stated whether the director
    retains such earnings and if so what
    the remuneration is.

  - Contracts should be set at one year or less,   CC B1.5 and 1.6
    with a robust line regarding mitigation. It
    may be necessary to offer longer periods
    but this should reduce after the initial
    period.

  - Remuneration Committee should consist of       CC B2.1 and A1.2
    at least 3 (2 if outside FTSE350) members,
    who should all be independent directors.
    Meeting frequency and attendance should
    be stated.

  - Term of reference and delegated authority      CC B2.2
    should be available and should include
    setting the remuneration for the chairman
    and executive directors and the structure
    and level for senior management.

  - Explanation of who sets non-executive          CC B2.3 and 1.3
    directors' remuneration. If options are
    granted shareholder approval should be
    sought in advance.

---

| | |
|---|---|
| – Significant changes to existing and all new long term incentives should be approved by shareholders, except as provided in the Listing Rules | CC B2.4 and Listing Rules 13.13 and others. |
| – How performance evaluation of the Remuneration Committee has been conducted | CC A.6.1 |
| – The steps the board has taken to ensure that members of the board, and in particular the non-executive directors, develop an understanding of the views of major shareholders about their company. | CC D.1.2 |

# Best Practice Guidance

*This chapter has been compiled by Cliff Weight of Independent Remuneration Solutions.*

## Introduction

This chapter details the best practice guidance from investors and their intermediaries, including:

- ABI;
- NAPF;
- Hermes;
- Morley;
- Standard Life;
- Manifest;
- PIRC; and
- US Conference Board.

## ABI guidelines and guidance

The ABI, with around 440 members, is the trade association for authorised insurance companies operating in the United Kingdom. Between them, Association members account for over 95% of the business of UK insurance companies. ABI members manage assets of some £1000 billion including one quarter of all UK equities (1999). In December 2002 they published the following 'Guidelines On Executive Remuneration'.

### Contents

- Introduction
- Executive Remuneration – Principles
- Guidelines for the Structure of Remuneration
- Guidelines for Share Incentive Schemes
- Best Practice on Executive Contracts and Severance – A Joint Statement by The Association of British Insurers and The National Association of Pension Funds

# Introduction

The ABI Guidelines have sought to provide an appropriate framework for share incentive schemes. The introduction of new government legislation has, however, now broadened the scope of both disclosure and voting on remuneration, which necessitates a fresh approach.

To act as a reference point both for shareholders in making voting decisions and for companies in the design of their remuneration policy, the ABI has therefore supplemented its guidelines with additional papers: 'Executive Remuneration – Principles', 'Guidelines for the Structure of Remuneration', and 'Best Practice on Executive Contracts and Severance'[1]. Together with the existing guidance on share incentive schemes these papers now constitute the ABI Guidelines on Remuneration. The papers will be refreshed regularly to reflect changing market practice.

Institutional shareholders continue to expect companies to follow good practice under the Combined Code by establishing remuneration committees comprised of non-executive directors with sufficient and appropriate qualities of independence. They will also expect companies to demonstrate best practice as regards disclosure as well as compliance with statutory regulation.

Shareholders recognise that employment costs represent a substantial outgoing for the companies in which they invest and that, through their remuneration strategy, companies recruit, retain and incentivise individuals to create shareholder value. The structures of remuneration packages will be a key determinant of whether this is achieved.

Remuneration policy should aim to establish a clear link between reward and performance. Effective consultation by companies when formulating policy can help to avoid inappropriate outcomes. It is preferable for companies to ensure that an appropriate policy is in place and followed, rather than to risk controversy when remuneration outcomes are disclosed in the annual report.

19 December 2002

# Executive remuneration – principles

Remuneration committees should maintain a constructive and timely dialogue with their major institutional shareholders and the ABI about remuneration policies including issues relating to share incentive schemes.

Boards should demonstrate that performance based remuneration arrangements are clearly aligned with business strategy and objectives. Simple structures assist with motivation and enhance the prospects of successful communication with shareholders.

Companies should establish properly constituted remuneration committees having delegated authority from company boards.

The remuneration report should set out principles which have been followed and describe the approach used when putting into place the different components of total remuneration.

Remuneration should reflect market requirements and take business size, complexity and geographical location into account, when appropriate.

Remuneration committees should have regard to pay and conditions elsewhere in the company. They should pay particular attention to arrangements for senior executives who are not board directors but have a significant influence over the company's ability to meet its strategic objectives. There should be appropriate disclosure, which may be best achieved through disclosing the number of executives with specified levels of remuneration on a banded basis.

Contemplated changes to remuneration policy and practice should be discussed with shareholders in advance.

All new share-based incentive schemes should be subject to approval by shareholders by means of a separate and binding resolution whether or not they are dilutive. Furthermore where the rules of share-based incentive schemes, or the basis on which the scheme was approved by shareholders, permits some degree of latitude as regards quantum of grant or performance criteria it is expected that any changes will be detailed in the remuneration report. Any substantive changes in practical operation of schemes resulting from policy changes or modifications of scheme rules as previously approved should be subject to prior shareholder approval.

Any proposed departure from the stated remuneration policy should be subject to prior approval by shareholders.

Where there is performance-linked enhancement or matching arrangements in respect of shares awarded under deferred bonus arrangements, there should be a separate shareholder vote.

Boards should review regularly the potential liabilities associated with all elements of remuneration including share incentive participation and pension arrangements and should make appropriate disclosures to shareholders.

There should be transparency on all matters relating to the remuneration of present and past directors and where appropriate other senior executives. Shareholders' attention should be drawn to any special arrangements and significant changes since the previous remuneration report.

# Guidelines for the structure of remuneration

1.  Remuneration packages should achieve an appropriate balance between fixed and variable pay as well as between long and short-term incentives.

    When setting salary levels remuneration committees should take into consideration the requirements of the market, bearing in mind competitive forces applicable to the sector in which the company operates and to the particular challenges facing the company. Disclosure of policy in this regard, for example that base pay is designed to be at median level, is helpful to shareholders. It is also appropriate to evaluate other elements of the overall remuneration package, which are usually expressed by reference to base salary.

    A policy of setting salary levels below the comparator group median can provide more scope for increasing the amount of variable performance based pay and incentive scheme participation. Where a company seeks to pay salaries at above median, justification is required.

2.  Annual bonuses, normally payable in cash, can provide a useful means of short-term incentivisation, but should be related to performance. Both individual and corporate performance targets are relevant and should be tailored to the requirements of the business and reviewed regularly to ensure they remain appropriate.

3.  The performance targets should generally be disclosed in the remuneration report, subject to commercial confidentiality considerations. Shareholders understand that commercial confidence may prevent disclosure of specific short-term targets, but they expect to be informed of the basic parameters adopted in the financial year being reported on.

4.  Shareholders are not supportive of **transaction bonuses** which reward directors and other executives for effecting transactions irrespective of their future financial consequences. Any material payments that may be viewed as being **ex-gratia** in nature should be subject to shareholder approval prior to payment.

5.  Institutional shareholders recognise that pension entitlements accruing to directors represent a significant, and potentially costly, item of remuneration. There should be informative disclosure identifying incremental value accruing to pension scheme participation or from any other superannuation arrangements, relating to service during the year in question. This should include the cost to the company, the extent to which liabilities are funded and aggregate outstanding unfunded liabilities.

6.  Remuneration committees should scrutinise all **other benefits**, including benefits in kind and other financial arrangements to ensure they are justified and appropriately valued.

# Guidelines for share incentive schemes

1.1 Institutional shareholders generally support share incentive schemes that link remuneration to performance and align the interests of participating directors and senior executives with those of shareholders.

1.2 The implementation of such schemes involves either the commitment of shareholder funds or the dilution of shareholders' equity. It is important, therefore, that they be objectively costed, well-designed and form a coherent part of the overall remuneration package.

1.3 Shareholders expect all share incentive schemes to follow the spirit of the Guidelines.

## 2. General principles

2.1 Institutional shareholders rely on a number of principles when evaluating share incentive schemes and determining their voting intentions.

2.2 Share incentive schemes should emphasise the importance of linking remuneration to performance, limits on dilution and individual participation, and a structure that effectively aligns the long-term interests of management with those of shareholders, having due regard to the cost of the schemes, which should be disclosed.

2.3 Shareholders strongly encourage the adoption of phased grants and welcome the trend towards awards being applied on a sliding scale in relation to the achievement of demanding and stretching financial performance against a target group or other relevant benchmark

2.4 Dilution is a matter of particular concern to investors. These Guidelines re-affirm the basic principle that dilution should not exceed 10 per cent in any 10-year period (see section 13).

2.5 Schemes should be designed to encourage share retention so that directors and other senior executives build up and maintain shareholdings which are meaningful in the context of their remuneration.

## 3. Scope

3.1 These Guidelines apply to all share incentive schemes or arrangements sponsored by UK listed companies whether option-based or involving conditional awards of shares, and including arrangements whereby awards on vesting or exercise are made in cash, or the transfer of shares to the value of the imputed gain at vesting date. Other companies should have regard for them, whenever possible.

## 4. Remuneration committees

4.1 Remuneration committees should:

- regularly review share incentive schemes to ensure their continued effectiveness and compliance with current Guidelines;

- obtain prior shareholder authorisation for any substantive or exceptional amendments to scheme rules and practice including changes to limits and changes which make it easier to achieve performance targets, also where significant exercise of discretion is proposed by the remuneration committee.

## 5. Disclosure

5.1 Companies must make full and relevant disclosure in their remuneration reports and in new proposals regarding share incentive schemes. Their rationale should be fully explained in order to enable shareholders to make informed decisions. In the absence of clear disclosure, shareholders may not be able to take the informed decision that will enable them to give their support.

5.2 Scheme and individual participation limits must be fully disclosed in share incentive schemes. Disclosure should, *inter alia*, cover performance conditions and related costs and dilution limits as set out in the relevant sections below. The reasons for selecting the performance conditions and target levels, together with the overall policy for granting conditional share or option awards, should be fully explained to shareholders.

## 6. Performance conditions

6.1 It is now widely recognised that the desired alignment of interests is best achieved through the vesting of awards under share incentive schemes being conditional on satisfaction of performance criteria. These should demonstrate the achievement of demanding and stretching financial performance over the incentivisation period.

6.2 Challenging performance conditions should govern the vesting of awards or the exercise of options under any form of long term share-based incentive scheme. These should:

- relate to overall corporate performance;

- demonstrate the achievement of a level of performance which is demanding in the context of the prospects for the company and the prevailing economic environment in which it operates;

- be measured relative to an appropriate defined peer group or other relevant benchmark;

- be disclosed and transparent.

The reasons for selecting the performance condition(s), together with the overall policy for granting conditional share or share option incentive awards, should be fully explained to shareholders.

6.3 Share-based performance awards should not be made for less than median performance. Initial vesting levels should not be significant in relation to annual salary.

6.4 The greater the level of potential reward to individual participants the more stretching and demanding the performance conditions should be. Companies should explain clearly how this is achieved, especially when annual grants of options in excess of one times salary, or equivalent long term share incentive awards, are made.

6.5 Sliding scales that correlate the reward potential with a performance scale that incorporates the provisions of these Guidelines are a useful way of ensuring that performance conditions are genuinely stretching. They generally provide a better motivator for improving corporate performance than a 'single hurdle'.

6.6   When share schemes provide for awards of matching shares in respect of annual bonuses further performance conditions should be satisfied before the matching shares are permitted to vest (see paragraph 14.4).

## 7. Performance criteria

7.1   Total shareholder return (TSR) relative to a relevant index or peer group is generally acceptable as a performance criterion. However, the remuneration committee should satisfy itself that the recorded TSR is a genuine reflection of the company's underlying financial performance. In circumstances where there appears to be a divergence, the remuneration committee should explain its reasoning.

7.2   Innovative types of performance criteria will need to be fully explained. It should be demonstrated that they are robust and demanding, and linked clearly to the achievement of enhanced shareholder value.

7.3   Shareholders need to have sufficient data to judge the appropriate size of the award for any given performance level. They also expect a maximum level of grant to be disclosed.

7.4   Other than in exceptional circumstances, the setting of a premium exercise price is not of itself a substitute for the adoption of relative performance conditions in accordance with these Guidelines.

## 8. Retesting of performance conditions

8.1   It is increasingly recognised that retesting of performance conditions for all share-based incentive schemes is unnecessary. Consequently any facility for extending the performance measurement period needs careful justification, should be of limited duration and of a sufficiently demanding nature to ensure that genuine performance has been achieved over the extended period. The stipulated performance conditions should not combine a fixed performance hurdle with measurement from a variable base date.

8.2   It is unlikely that the criteria described in 8.1 will be met for retesting proposals for long term incentive plans (LTIPs) and similar nil-priced option schemes.

## 9. Vesting of awards

9.1   Performance conditions should be measured over a period of three or more years. Strong encouragement is given to use of longer performance measurement periods of more than three years and deferred vesting schedules, in order to motivate the achievement of sustained improvements in financial performance.

## 10. Performance on grant

10.1 The linking of grants of awards to satisfaction of performance conditions may contribute to the effectiveness of incentive schemes in addition to the application of targets at vesting. Exceptionally, remuneration committees may consider the application of challenging performance conditions to govern the grant instead of the vesting of options, but only provided that at least the following conditions have been met.

- The company has clearly demonstrated to the satisfaction of shareholders that it is operating in a global environment which genuinely requires it to pay attention to global remuneration practices. Furthermore, that the scheme is tailored to executives who are exposed to those remuneration practices. This approach should not be applied automatically to UK-based participants. Comparisons with overseas companies should take account of the different practices for setting remuneration, including pension provision, when compared with UK practices.

- Performance conditions covering the grant should refer to overall corporate performance as a reference, not just individual performance of the grantee.

- The basis of performance criteria should be fully disclosed and explained.

- Performance-linking at grant does not alter the requirement that the minimum period for exercise of options should be three years from the date of grant.

- The dilution limits set out in section 13 are adhered to.

- Participants in schemes are expected by the board to build up a significant and disclosed shareholding through retention of awards that vest. Holding share options is not a substitute for share ownership in meeting ownership targets.

- Disclosure concerning the scheme should comply with the highest standards relevant to the other jurisdictions in which the company operates eg those applied by the US Securities and Exchange Commission.

## 11. Change of control provisions

11.1 Scheme rules should state that there will be no automatic waiving of performance conditions either in the event of a change of control or where subsisting options and awards are "rolled-over" in the event of a capital reconstruction, and/or the early termination of the participant's employment.

11.2 In the event of change of control, share incentive awards should vest on a pro-rata basis ie taking into account the vesting period that has elapsed at the time of change of control, though making due allowance for the reduction in value resulting from truncation of the life of the option.

## 12. Cost

12.1 The cost of share incentive schemes (and any amendments to existing schemes) should be disclosed at the time shareholder approval is sought in order that shareholders can assess the benefits of the proposal against the total costs and award justification. The following information should be disclosed.

- The total cost of all incentive arrangements.

- The potential value of awards (see Note 1) due to individual scheme participants on full vesting. This should be expressed by reference to the face value of shares or shares under option at point of grant, and expressed as a multiple of base salary.

- The expected value (see Note 2) of the award at the outset, bearing in mind the probability of achieving the stipulated performance criteria.

- The maximum dilution which may arise through the issue of shares to satisfy entitlements.

12.2 There should be prudent and appropriate arrangements governing acquisition of shares, and financing thereof, to meet contingent obligations under share-based incentive schemes.

12.3 The use of phased grants of share options and restricted shares, and utilisation of both new and purchased shares to satisfy the vesting of awards, requires a comprehensive approach to valuation. Assessment should focus on expected value, which should be disclosed, and it should take account of the performance vesting schedule which is adopted as well as the existence of any 'retesting' and 'replacement option' facilities such as have been prevalent under traditional schemes. Shareholders are helped in this task by disclosure of face value of any share award or option grant as well as of expected value.

## 13. Dilution limits

13.1 Where the terms of any incentive scheme provide that entitlements may be satisfied through the issue of new shares, then the rules of that scheme must provide that, when aggregated with awards under *all* of the company's other schemes, commitments to issue new shares must not exceed 10% of the issued ordinary share capital (adjusted for scrip/bonus and rights issues) in any rolling 10 year period. Remuneration committees should ensure that appropriate policies regarding flow-rates exist in order to spread the potential issue of new shares over the life of relevant schemes in order to ensure the limit is not breached. As an alternative, remuneration committees may give consideration to market purchases of shares in order to meet share incentive scheme liabilities.

13.2 Commitments to issue shares under executive (discretionary) schemes should not exceed 5% of the issued ordinary share capital of the company (adjusted for scrip/bonus issues) in any rolling ten year period. This may be exceeded where vesting is dependent on the achievement of more stretching performance criteria with full vesting typically requiring at least top quartile performance.

13.3 For small companies, up to 10% of the ordinary share capital may be utilised for executive (discretionary) schemes, provided that the total market value of the capital utilised for the scheme at the time of grant does not exceed £500,000.

## 14. Participation

14.1 Participation in share incentive schemes should be restricted to bona fide employees and executive directors, and be subject to appropriate limits for individual participation which should be disclosed.

14.2 It is considered beneficial for non-executive directors to have share-holdings and this may be achieved through having their fees paid in the form of shares at the full market price. However they should not participate in any form of share incentive scheme.

14.3 Participation in more than one share incentive scheme must form part of a well-considered remuneration policy, and should not be part of a multiple arrangement designed to raise the prospects of payout.

14.4 Institutional shareholders are not supportive of arrangements whereby shares or options may, in effect, be granted at a discount. This principle applies in circumstances where Remuneration Committees provide for awards of matching shares in respect of annual bonuses payable in the form of shares where these are then held for a qualifying period of, say, three years. In these cases, institutional shareholders will generally expect that satisfaction of further performance criteria will be required in order for the matching element to vest (see paragraph 6.6).

## 15. Phasing of awards and grants

15.1 The regular phasing of share incentive awards and option grants, generally on an annual basis, is encouraged because:

- It reduces the risk of unanticipated outcomes that arise out of share price volatility and cyclical factors.

- It eliminates the perceived problem that a limit on subsisting options encourages early exercise.

- It allows the adoption of a single performance measurement period

- It lessens the possible incidence of 'underwater' options, where the share price falls below the exercise price.

The phased vesting of awards in specific tranches following the minimum three year performance measurement period is not an alternative to phased grants. However, it can help to enhance the linking of vesting of awards to sustained performance and maintain incentivisation.

## 16. Pricing of options and shares

16.1 The price at which shares are issued under a scheme should not be less than the mid-market price (or similar formula) immediately preceding grant of the shares under the scheme.

16.2 Options granted under executive (discretionary) schemes should not be granted at a discount to the prevailing mid-market price.

16.3 Repricing or surrender and regrant of awards or 'underwater' share options is not appropriate.

## 17. Timing of grant

17.1 The rules of a scheme should provide that share or option awards normally be granted only within a 42 day period following the publication of the company's results.

## 18. Life of schemes and incentive awards

18.1 No awards should be made beyond the life of the scheme approved on adoption by shareholders, which should not exceed ten years.

18.2 Shares and options should not vest or be exercisable within three years from the date of grant. In addition, options should not be exercisable more than ten years from the date of grant.

18.3 Where a company is taken over (except where arrangements are made for a switch to options of the offer or company) or in the event of the death or cessation of employment of the option holder, outstanding options may be exercised (or lapse) within twelve months. Any performance conditions attaching to the exercise of options should normally be fulfilled prior to exercise.

18.4 Any shares or options that a company may grant in exchange for those released under the schemes of acquired companies should normally be taken into account for the purposes of dilution and individual participation limits determined in accordance with these Guidelines.

## 19. Retirement

19.1 Options or other conditional share awards should not be granted within 6 months of a participant's anticipated retirement date. In determining the size and other terms of a grant made within three years of the anticipated retirement date, Remuneration Committees should have regard to the executive's ability to contribute to the achievement of the performance conditions.

19.2 Any unvested options or other conditional share awards which are outstanding at a participant's retirement date should be subject to performance measurement over the original stipulated period. Where the rules of the scheme require early exercise on retirement, performance should be pro-rated over the shorter period. In any event options should vest no later than the end of the initial performance measurement period, and should be finally exercisable no later than twelve months following the date of vesting.

## 20. Personal shareholding requirements

20.1 Institutional shareholders are generally supportive of companies which encourage their senior executives to build up meaningful shareholdings in the companies for which they work. The rules of incentive schemes should incorporate the requirement to retain a significant proportion of shares to which participants become entitled and the targets for shareholding should relate to the reward potential. This is particularly important in the case of awards where performance conditions apply principally at the point of grant.

## 21. Subsidiary companies and joint venture companies

21.1 It is generally undesirable for options to be granted over the share capital in a joint venture company.

21.2 In normal circumstances grants over the shares in a subsidiary company should not be made. However shareholders may consider exceptions where the condition of exercise is subject to flotation or sale of the subsidiary company. In such circumstances, grants should be conditional so that vesting is dependent on a return on investment that exceeds the cost of capital and that the market value of the shares at date of grant is subject to external validation. Exceptions will apply in the case of an overseas subsidiary where required by local legislation, or in circumstances where at least 25% of the ordinary share capital of the subsidiary is listed and held outside the group.

## 22. All-Employee schemes

22.1 All-Employee schemes, such as SAYE schemes and Share Incentive Plans (SIPs) (formerly known as AESOPs) should operate within an appropriate best practice framework. If newly issued shares are utilised, the overall dilution limits for share schemes should be complied with. Guidelines relating to timing of grants (except for pre-determined regular appropriation of shares under SIPs) apply.

## 23. Employee Share Ownership Trusts (ESOTS)

23.1 ESOTs should not hold more shares at any one time than would be required in practice to match their outstanding liabilities, nor should they be used as an anti-takeover or similar device. The prior approval of shareholders should be obtained before 5% or more of a company's share capital at any one time may be held within ESOTs.

### Note 1 – Potential value of the award

Shareholders are likely to have regard to the potential value of the award assuming full vesting. This should be expressed on the basis that a conditional award is made of shares, or options over shares, with a face value, at current prices, equal to a given percentage of base salary. However the potential value will also be a function of share price at the time of vesting and illustrative disclosures of potential outcomes may also be helpful. Full vesting of awards of higher potential value should require the achievement of commensurately greater performance.

## Note 2 – Expected value

The concept of expected value (EV) should be central to assessment of share incentive schemes. Essentially, EV will be the present value of the sum of all the various possible outcomes at vesting or exercise of awards. This will reflect the probabilities of achieving these outcomes and also the future value implicit in these outcomes. The calculation of the EV of share schemes is often complex and relies on a range of assumptions, and reliance on this concept by Remuneration Committees will require a sufficient measure of disclosure to enable shareholders to make informed judgments about such arrangements.

The nature of performance hurdles governing exercise is also crucial to calculations of EV and it must also be recognised that any facility for "retesting" will also increase the EV of the award whereas in contrast if the exercise price is set at a premium to the share price at the outset, this will reduce the value of the EV of the instrument.

Institutional investors welcome efforts towards ensuring that accounting for share options and other share-based payment awarded under incentive schemes fully reflects the true cost to shareholders.

# Best practice on executive contracts and severance

A joint statement by the Association of British Insurers and the National Association of Pension Funds

## 1. Introduction

1.1 Institutional shareholders believe top executives of listed companies should be appropriately rewarded for the value they generate. However, they are also concerned to avoid situations where departing executives are rewarded for failure or under-performance. This is a matter of good governance, about which the ABI and NAPF have been concerned for many years.

1.2 It is unacceptable that failure, which detracts from the value of an enterprise and which can threaten the livelihood of employees, can result in large payments to its departing leaders. Executives, whose remuneration is already at a level which allows for the risk inherent in their role, should show leadership in aligning their financial interests with those of their shareholders.

1.3 Our two organisations, whose members are leading institutional investors in UK markets, are therefore publishing this statement of best practice, which sets out the expectations of shareholders that boards will give careful consideration to the risk that negotiation of inappropriate executive contracts can lead to situations where failure is rewarded.

1.4 If companies are to recruit executives of sufficient calibre, boards must bear in mind the basic demands of the market. These require them to offer incoming executives a degree of protection against downside risk. Contract law also provides employees with certain rights that must be respected.

1.5 However, shareholders also believe it is the duty of boards to develop and implement recruitment and remuneration policies which will prevent them being required to make payments that are not strictly merited. When companies recruit senior executives, they do so in a mood of optimism and expectation of success. They may therefore tend to overlook the consequences of failure, which is clearly inappropriate.

1.6 At the outset, boards should calculate the potential cost of termination in monetary terms. This should cover all elements of the severance package, including any property liabilities the company may be required to assume on behalf of the departing executive. They must also consider and avoid the serious reputational risk of being obliged to make and disclose large payments to executives who have failed to perform.

1.7 Shareholders will hold boards accountable for the design and implementation of appropriate contracts. The primary responsibility resides, however, with Remuneration Committees.

1.8 Remuneration committees should have the leeway to design a policy appropriate to the needs and objectives of the company, but they must also have a clear understanding of their responsibility to negotiate suitable contracts and be able to justify severance payments to shareholders.

1.9 This statement provides a reference point, both to make companies aware of the reasonable expectations of shareholders and to inform voting decisions under the new legislation giving shareholders an annual vote on the remuneration report. We expect that this guidance will be reviewed periodically and refreshed as necessary to take account of changing market circumstances.

## 2. Basic principles

2.1 The design of contracts should not commit companies to payment for failure. Shareholders expect boards to pay attention to minimising this risk when drawing up contracts. They should bear in mind that it may be in the interest of incoming executives and their personal advisers to exaggerate their potential loss on dismissal. Boards should resist consequent pressure to concede overly generous severance conditions.

2.2 Choices made when the contract is agreed have an important bearing on subsequent developments. Companies should have a clear, considered policy on directors' contracts which should be clearly stated in the remuneration report. Boards should calculate and take account of all the material commitments which the company would face in the event of severance for failure or underperformance. The nomination committee needs to see through the process of appointment by working with the remuneration committee to ensure that the contract is fair to all parties.

2.3 Objectives set for executives by the board should be clear. The more transparent the objectives, the easier it is to determine whether an executive has failed to perform and therefore to prevent payment for failure. Wherever possible, objectives against which performance will be measured should be made public.

2.4 It should be clearly understood that investors do not expect executives to be automatically entitled to bonuses. Bonuses should be cut or eliminated when individual performance is poor. From the outset, boards should therefore establish a clear link between performance and bonus as well as other aspects of variable pay.

2.5 Compensation for risks run by senior executives is already implicit in the absolute level of remuneration. Boards should ensure that there is an appropriate balance between contractual protection and total remuneration and be able to justify their policies to shareholders. Shareholders prefer short contracts of one year or less, and boards must be able to justify the length agreed. The one-year period provided for under the Combined Code best practice should thus not be seen as a floor. Shorter periods would be appropriate if other remuneration conditions would mean that a one-year contract period would lead to excessive severance payment.

2.6 In highly exceptional circumstances – for example, where a new chief executive is being recruited to a troubled company – a longer initial notice period may be appropriate. These cases should be justified to shareholders and the longer notice period should apply to the initial term only with reversion to best practice at the earliest opportunity.

2.7 Experience suggests that courts take account of some elements of variable pay, such as bonuses, when making awards to departing executives. This can be limited through the attachment of clear performance conditions to variable pay. Boards may also wish to specify that a proportion of the bonus is for retaining the executive and this should fall away in the event of severance. A remuneration policy that favours relatively low base pay and a higher proportion of variable pay is a good way of linking remuneration to performance.

## 3. Contract Setting

3.1 There is no standard form of contract that can apply in all circumstances. Companies have taken a number of different approaches to severance in the past. These include phased payments, liquidated damages, and reliance on mitigation. It is important that Boards consider the relative merits of different approaches as they apply to their own company's situation, follow their chosen approach consequentially and are able to justify it to shareholders.

3.2 A welcome recent innovation has been the use of phased payments, which involve continued payment, eg on a normal monthly basis to the departing executive for the outstanding term of his or her contract. Payments cease when and if the executive finds fresh employment. Shareholders believe this approach has considerable advantages, which deserve the active consideration of boards, but this approach does need to be specifically provided for in the contract. It does not involve payment of large lump sums, which cannot be recovered. In many cases, executives will wish to seek further employment rather than remain idle till the monthly payments lapse. Allowing the contract to run off may also obviate the need for pension enhancement (see below).

3.3 The liquidated damages approach involves agreement at the outset on the amount that will be paid in the event of severance. It is clear from the beginning how much will be paid, but the amount cannot be varied to reflect under-performance. Shareholders do not believe the liquidated damages approach is generally desirable. Boards, which adopt it, should justify their decision, and should therefore consider a modified approach. This would involve reaching agreement in advance that, in the event of severance, the parties would go to arbitration to decide how much should be paid. This approach needs to take account of the likely cost of arbitration.

3.4 The concept of mitigation refers to the legal obligation on the part of the outgoing director to mitigate the loss incurred through severance, for example by seeking other employment and reducing the need for compensation. Where this is the sole approach, shareholders expect reassurance that the board has taken steps to ensure that the full benefit is obtained. As with liquidated damages, boards need to have considered at the outset what the cost of severance would be under the proposed contract as well as the relative merits of arbitration as opposed to litigation.

3.5 An essential problem is that it is not normally possible for under-performance to be established as a ground for summary dismissal without compensation. Under the *Employment Act 2002*, however, a statutory disciplinary procedure will be implied into every employment contract, including those of executive directors. Boards should be aware of this and be prepared to use disciplinary procedures if warranted.

3.6 In the wake of this legislation contracts should also make clear that, if a director is dismissed in the wake of a disciplinary procedure, a shorter notice period than that given in the contract would apply. A reasonable period would be the statutory period, comprising one week for each year's service up to a maximum of twelve weeks. Without such a provision the full notice period would continue to apply even after dismissal following a disciplinary procedure.

3.7 Companies should also consider including in contracts a safeguard for more extreme cases, for example, that compensation would not be payable in case of dismissal for financial failure such as a very significant fall of the share price relative to the sector. This would help deal with particularly egregious cases.

3.8 Other than in highly exceptional circumstances, such as the recruitment of a new chief executive of a troubled company, contracts should not provide additional protection in the form of compensation for severance as a result of change of control if this would result in potential compensation exceeding the one year maximum payable under Combined Code best practice. Where exceptional circumstances apply, any additional protection should relate to the initial contract term only and not be a rolling provision.

3.9 Companies may consider other options, including a provision for compensation to be paid by reference to shares with the amount of shares set at the outset of employment. Where such an option is proposed it should, however, be clearly explained both as to purpose and to the details of its operation. Remuneration committees should satisfy themselves that it is workable and will yield advantages greater than the phased payment and other approaches outlined above. Compensation paid by reference to shares should be paid in cash rather than directly in shares to prevent unmerited windfall gains.

3.10 The use of shareholding targets for senior executives and directors is likely to be a powerful and therefore more effective means of aligning the financial interests of executives with those of shareholders.

## 4. Pension arrangements and other remuneration issues

4.1 Pension enhancements can represent a large element of severance pay and involve heavy cost to shareholders, the full extent of which may not be immediately evident. It is important that boards state the full economic cost for pension enhancement at the earliest opportunity. Discipline is crucial if boards are to avoid rewarding failure. Boards should not support enhanced pension payments without making themselves fully aware of the costs.

4.2 A large liability looms in the future where companies choose not to fund an enhanced pension liability but to pay it as it arises. In all cases, whether the pension is funded or not, Boards must disclose the cost, justify their choice to shareholders and demonstrate that they have chosen a route that involves the least overall cost to the company.

4.3 An important principle with regard to pensions is that boards should distinguish between the amount that is a contractual entitlement and the amount of discretionary enhancement agreed as part of a severance package. Contracts should state clearly that the pension would not be enhanced in the event of early retirement unless the board was satisfied that the objectives set for the executive had been met or that the enhancement was merited. Shareholders are likely to question enhancement decisions when they are doubtful of the merit and, if not satisfied with the board's justification, they may vote against the remuneration report.

## 5. General considerations and conclusion

5.1 Boards should have a clear and explicit policy on contracts and on how Remuneration Committees will play a primary role. It should include calculation of the cost of severance at the time the contract is drawn up and an approach to implementation which ensures that all payments made on severance take account of performance in relation to objectives set for the departing executive by the board.

5.2  Contracts should be readily available for shareholders to inspect, together with any side letters relating to severance terms and pension arrangements. Shareholders will take account of contracts and the way they are implemented in considering their vote on the remuneration report.

19 December 2002

# The ABI Institutional Voting Information Service                                                                B15.3

The Institutional Voting Information Service (IVIS) is produced by the ABI. First published in January 1993, the service has been developed to advise Association members on aspects of corporate governance of UK companies in which they invest. Through consultation with members it seeks to represent the consensus view of UK insurance companies on these matters.

## What does IVIS do?                                                      B15.4

IVIS reviews UK company annual reports and accounts and company meeting notices for compliance with corporate governance best practice. The service has developed from the low key, proactive but non-confrontational approach to corporate governance adopted by the ABI.

Its benefits are fourfold. It:

● does the essential groundwork in the review of reports and accounts and meeting notices;

● identifies matters of concern, particularly to insurers (who hold 25% of the UK equity market), and seek resolutions prior to voting at meetings;

● provides the relevant information in a focused way and in a standardised user-friendly format; and

● contributes to the audit trail on voting policy.

IVIS covers all the companies which comprise the UK FTSE All Share Index. Other companies are monitored on an ad hoc basis when requested by members. The ABI guidelines and the Stock Exchange Combined Code, which comprise the recommendations of the Cadbury, Greenbury and Hampel Committees, provide the basis for the monitoring service. Matters of concern are dealt with in liaison with ABI members who tend to be major shareholders in the companies they monitor.

IVIS covers a number of areas of concern regarding corporate governance. The ones which relate to remuneration packages and procedures are:

8.  (a)  Is the remuneration committee made up entirely of NEDs?

    (b)  Are the NEDs on the committee regarded as independent?

9.  Have the performance targets attached to the vesting of long term incentives been disclosed (ie are details given of all long term incentives, including size of conditional awards, and performance criteria)?

10. Is only basic salary pensionable?

11. Are the following details of all directors' service contracts disclosed:

    (a) details of notice periods in excess of twelve months;

    (b) a stated objective that notice periods will be reduced to one year or less.

## NAPF guidelines and guidance                                   B15.5

The NAPF are at the time of writing reviewing their corporate governance guidelines and the new guidelines should be available on their website (www.napf.co.uk) later in 2003.

The NAPF issued in December 2002 a joint statement with the ABI regarding executive directors' contracts (see **B15.2** above).

The NAPF support the ABI Guidelines on Share Incentive Schemes.

## The NAPF Voting Issues Service                                 B15.6

The NAPF Voting Issues Service (VIS) (a subsidiary business of the NAPF) analyse companies in the UK FTSE All Share Index, approx 800 companies. They issued a Company Secretary's Aide-Memoire 2003. They stressed that the highlighted issues are relatively new to the corporate governance agenda and may be of more interest to readers than the reiteration of previously documented issues. The parts pertinent to remuneration were as follows.

**1.  Remuneration Report**

The 2003 AGM season will see every company putting the directors' remuneration report to a shareholders' vote and disclosing the information required by the *Directors' Remuneration Report Regulations 2002*.

In order to provide voting recommendations on such resolutions, VIS will look for clarity of purpose and expression within the Remuneration Report as well as evidence that the incentive arrangements for directors appear to relate to the achievement of corporate objectives. Ideally, VIS would like to recommend support for all companies' Remuneration Reports, but recognises that in reality this is unlikely to occur. Areas which could cause concern and produce a voting recommendation of 'abstain' or 'against' include:

(i)  the payment of transaction bonuses;

(ii) any variation made in the performance criteria attached to a long-term incentive scheme which, in the view of VIS, is not justified or fully explained;

(iii) insufficient information concerning award levels, performance criteria and comparator groups used in long-term incentive schemes;

(iv) performance conditions which appear insufficiently challenging, are below currently accepted norms and are not adequately justified by the remuneration committee;

(v) any deviations from the ABI's Guidelines for Share Incentive Schemes which are not fully explained and justified;

(vi) the existence of any ED service contract containing a notice period in excess of one year or enabling the recipient to receive compensation in excess of one year's remuneration. VIS will take a particularly strong line against service contracts that contain a provision allowing for additional compensation and/or an extended notice period in the event of a change of control.

It is not possible to list all the eventualities which might cause concern, but it is believed that the majority of areas which have recently provoked institutional investors' disapproval are listed above. One of the most important aspects is the level of transparency and clarity provided in a remuneration report. Companies should ensure that the majority of shareholders will be able to understand the remuneration arrangements and that the level of awards made to individual directors can be supported and justified in order to avoid a charge of excess.

**The appointment/re-election of directors**

(i) Change of control provisions: VIS will take a strong line where a service contract contains a provision allowing for additional compensation and/or an extended notice period in the event of a change of control. Unless the existence of such an arrangement is fully explained and accepted by VIS, a vote recommendation will be issued AGAINST the appointment of a new director with a service contract containing this type of provision. In the case of existing directors, a recommendation to ABSTAIN will be issued.

# Individual institutional investors' guidelines    B15.7

A number of leading shareholders have published their own guidance on remuneration. Below are the guidance of Hermes, Morley and Standard Life.

# Hermes    B15.8

Hermes, formerly PosTel, is a large UK fund manager. Hermes have published their corporate governance Principles. Hermes' overriding requirement is that companies be run in the long term interest of shareholders. Hermes Principle 5 relates to remuneration: 'Companies should have performance evaluation and incentive systems designed cost effectively to incentivise managers to deliver long-term shareholder value.'

In the Hermes UK guidance they state the following.

1.4 A remuneration committee of independent NEDs is best placed to decide executive remuneration on behalf of the board. Actual and potential awards should not be excessive and should be directly related to the success of the company and aligned over time to the returns achieved by shareholders. Hermes encourages companies to put the board's remuneration report to a vote at the AGM, particularly where significant changes are made to policy or controversial issues arise during the year. A more detailed explanation of Hermes' views on remuneration is at Appendix 1.

## Appendix 1 – Remuneration

### *1. General principles*

1.1 Performance-related remuneration is the principle means by which EDs are motivated to achieve greater shareholder value and are rewarded for doing so. It is therefore an area of company policy in which shareholders have a valid role.

1.2 Remuneration committees of independent NEDs are best placed to decide the remuneration packages necessary to recruit, retain and motivate executives. They should take professional advice as necessary. Where independent advisers are appointed they should be responsible to the remuneration committee and not the company EDs. Consideration should be given to naming the advisers in the board's remuneration report. Hermes encourages companies to put the board's remuneration report to a vote at the AGM, particularly where significant changes are made to policy or controversial issues arise during the year.

1.3 Remuneration is a package. Actual and potential rewards should not be excessive; scrutiny from informed observers should not diminish the legitimacy of the executive team in the eyes of shareholders or employees. Performance-related remuneration should be aligned over time with returns earned by shareholders. Increases in remuneration should be driven by improved performance and should not just be a matter of annual appreciation.

1.4 Companies should require all directors to build over a period of time a substantial shareholding, say to the value of at least one year's emoluments. For NEDs, one way of achieving this is to pay them partly in shares which must be retained whilst they hold office. NEDs who are executives elsewhere, and whose fees are paid to their primary employer, should receive the share component of their fee. NEDs should not participate in performance-related pay or incentive schemes.

1.5 Hermes recognises the difficulty faced by companies with international operations when designing remuneration packages, particularly incentive schemes. Although it is accepted that companies have to offer packages that are competitive in the local market there are certain features that should be universal.

1.6 Hermes will assess all schemes individually, taking into account the particular circumstances of the company, but sound reasons would need to be given by a remuneration committee proposing a scheme that did not comply with the spirit of the above principles.

## 2. Contracts

2.1 Hermes prefers that executives be appointed on one-year rolling contracts. Executives appointed on a two-year fixed contract that subsequently reduces to a one-year rolling contract will also be supported. Hermes does not currently vote against existing directors with two-year rolling contracts but recommends that these be reduced to one year, without compensation, as a show of leadership. Contracts with a clause that increases compensation paid for early termination in the event of a take-over are not supported.

## 3. Incentive scheme principles

3.1 Incentive schemes should be designed to reward exceptional performance. Awards should be scaled against achievement of performance criteria, with a relatively low payout if the minimum target is achieved and full payout only for truly exceptional performance. No award should be made where targets are not met. The measure used will vary depending on the type of incentive but performance should be compared to an appropriate benchmark or peer group. Awards should not be made unless there has been improvement in the underlying real financial position of the company. Where comparative performance against a peer group is used as the measure awards should generally not be made when company performance is below median. Earnings per share growth of RPI+2% a year is not a suitably challenging performance target for the majority of companies.

3.2 Performance measurement and vesting periods should ideally be five years although a minimum of three years will be considered. A further holding period between vesting and sale is encouraged.

3.3 Share matching schemes should be subject to challenging performance criteria and grants made should not be overly generous.

3.4 Remuneration Committees should explain proposed schemes clearly to shareholders, justifying the structure of the scheme and the relevance of the performance criteria chosen.

Schemes should be structured as simply as possible to ensure they can be understood by participants and monitored by shareholders. The link between company performance and executive reward should be clear. The effect of the scheme should be illustrated with examples showing rewards at various performance levels for one of the participants, say, the chief executive.

3.5  The dilution guidelines published by the Association of British Insurers should be observed.

3.6  Where annual grants are made there should be no retesting period; if the performance targets are not met the award for that year should be foregone.

3.7  Where remuneration committees have authority to vary incentive schemes they should only do so in exceptional circumstances and to ensure that the scheme continues to motivate executives. All changes should be reported and justified to shareholders.

3.8  Companies should confirm continuing shareholder support for a scheme during its lifetime, giving shareholders an opportunity to reassess the scheme in light of actual payout levels.

3.9  Companies should have only one executive long-term incentive scheme in place; exceptions should be justified in the remuneration report. Executives should not be rewarded twice for the same performance. Remuneration committees should take into consideration the number of options outstanding and the remaining period for which they are exercisable when making grants under a newly introduced performance share scheme.

3.10 The annual report should disclose the level of recent grants made under any existing incentive scheme, the performance criteria applied to the grants, and any payouts resulting from grants made in previous years. The actual performance resulting in the vesting of grants should be disclosed and clearly explained.

### 4. Incentive scheme structures

4.1  Share option schemes: Share option schemes are both popular and widely criticised. Participants can be rewarded for market rises on which they had no influence, they bear no risk (unprofitable options are simply not exercised) and seldom retain shares they exercise. Requirements for the share price to exceed a benchmark and for executives to retain a minimum shareholding partly address these points.

4.2  Performance share plans: In Hermes' view, schemes based on the grant of shares are preferable to many share option schemes. It is difficult to specify an appropriate level of grant (eg 50% or 100% of base salary) because companies give different weights to base salary and performance pay. Remuneration committees should be mindful that, unlike options, the full value of the shares (less tax) will be received by the participants if the performance criteria are met. The over-riding principle, that grants should not be excessive, should be observed. Performance should be measured on a total shareholder return basis against a suitable peer group, either a public index or a specially constructed one.

# Morley

Morley is a large fund manager. Morley have issued a paper, 'Corporate Governance and Voting Policy 2003' which contained detailed guidance on directors' remuneration, as follows.

## General principles

22.1 MFM's normal practice is not to be involved in debates about absolute levels of remuneration since, as an institutional investor, MFM is not in the best position to make these decisions.

22.2 The level of pay and structure of executive pay packages should be the responsibility of remuneration committees comprising independent non-executive directors.

22.3 Incentive pay should be explicitly linked to the performance of the company.

22.4 Our view is that alignment of interests with shareholders is likely to be strongest where a proportion of the participant's wealth is invested in their company. We would therefore encourage directors to expose a reasonable degree of their assets to the performance of their company by holding shares.

22.5 Compliance with the *Directors' Remuneration Report Regulations 2002* should be transparent and aim to meet the spirit of the regulations rather than the requirement of the rules.

22.6 There is increasing political pressure on institutional investors to actively participate in executive pay issues. MFM will continue to express its views to companies at regular meetings with senior executives and by actively considering and voting on remuneration issues.

## Voting on the remuneration report

22.7 The *Directors' Remuneration Report Regulations 2002* provide that, from the end of 2002, UK listed companies will be required to prepare a detailed directors' remuneration report and seek shareholder approval for it. The vote will be advisory i.e. payments made or promised to directors will not have to be repaid if the ordinary resolution is not passed. The Government's objective is to promote transparency and accountability to shareholders.

22.8 Morley will assess board pay as a total package, ie basic pay, bonuses, incentives, pensions and take a view of these arrangements judged against company performance.

22.9 Voting decisions on the remuneration report will be taken on the basis of an overall assessment. In doing so it will be necessary to have regard to the significance of issues i.e. it will be a weighted decision as to whether a particular concern is sufficiently important for us to vote against the report.

22.10    As a general principle we expect companies to comply with the 'spirit' of established guidelines. As a minimum, we would consider best practice to mean compliance with the new legislation, Association of British Insurers' guidelines on remuneration and share schemes1 and the Combined Code, Compliance with our own guidelines will also, of course, influence our voting decisions.

22.11    We will continue to vote against resolutions to appoint and re-appoint directors and other resolutions in addition to voting against the resolution to approve the remuneration report where concerns are warranted to be sufficiently significant.

## Share Incentive Schemes – general guidelines

23.1 MFM's approach to share Incentive Plans is to assess each case on its own merits. In general, we would expect long term incentive schemes to comply with the Combined Code recommendations and industry guide-lines, unless there are very good reasons not to do so.

23.2 Share incentive schemes should comply with ABI dilution limits.

23.3 Some share option schemes allow for options to be surrendered and re-granted at a lower price. We discourage this practice.

23.4 Share option grants should be phased rather than awarded in one large block. Where grants are not phased, the remuneration report should explain and justify.

## Performance targets

24.1 Where grants are made annually, schemes should not include a facility for extending the period over which performance is tested as this may result in a number of grants vesting as a result of just one year's good performance.

24.2 There should be differing levels of performance targets so that the largest rewards are made for exceptional performance.

24.3 Performance targets must be disclosed, ie we would not support schemes based on internal performance arrangements.

24.4 Performance conditions should continue to apply in the event of a takeover or reconstruction.

24.5 Where schemes have a facility for matching shares, awards should generally be subject to performance conditions.

24.6 Our preferred performance criterion as between Total Shareholder Return and Earnings Per Share is Total Shareholder Return (share price plus dividends). It is also our view that a relative target, eg against an index or sector is preferable to an absolute performance target. We would normally support schemes only where, in MFM's opinion, the criterion is appropriate and the target is sufficiently demanding.

24.7 MFM will approve schemes only where performance conditions reflect above-average performance. Therefore, we would not generally consider the Earnings Per Share figure of 2% above RPI per annum over three years as acceptable performance.

24.8 Where the company is being compared to an index or sector, we would expect its performance to be above median, that is, 50th percentile and above. Ideally, there should be a secondary financial measure to ensure that awards are made only where there has been an improvement in the company's underlying performance.

### Directors' service contracts

25.1 The Combined Code states 'there is a strong case for setting notice or contract periods at, or reducing them to, one year or less. Companies should set this as an objective.

25.2 MFM's current practice is to:

- vote in favour of any existing fixed or rolling contracts of one year or less

- vote against the remuneration report and vote against directors with contracts in excess of one year, unless there are special reasons

25.3 The broad aim of dealing with early termination cases is to avoid rewarding poor performance while dealing fairly with cases where departure is not due to poor performance. Companies should take a robust line on reducing compensation to reflect departing directors' obligations to minimise their loss (i.e. companies should have a sensible mitigation policy).

25.4 Where companies provide explicitly in the initial contract for compensation commitments (except in the case of removal for misconduct), we would expect such payments to reflect less than one year's remuneration.

25.5 MFM would not generally support change in control provisions that are more advantageous than standard provisions specified in the service contract.

25.6 MFM reviews its policy on service contracts on a regular basis to ensure that it reflects best practice.

**Note:** The joint ABI/NAPF paper 'Best Practice on Executive Contracts and Severance' states that shareholders prefer short contracts of one year or less and boards must be able to justify the length agreed.

### Special payments

26.1 The fundamental principle which governs our approach to directors' pay is that exceptional pay should only be for exceptional performance. Therefore any payment made to directors should be proven to have added value for shareholders. For example, a completed transaction may not, in itself, be value enhancing. We would only support special discretionary payments if they are:

- justified;
- closely aligned to performance over a measurable period after the event;
- subject to a shareholder vote.

# Standard Life                                                            B15.10

Standard Life is a large fund manager. Standard Life have published the following principles relating to remuneration.

- A company's board should have a Remuneration Committee which is chaired by an independent non-executive director and comprises a majority of such directors.
- Exceptional levels of remuneration should be available for the achievement of exceptional performance.
- Directors' service contracts should have notice periods which do not exceed twelve months.
- Companies should be open in their disclosures to shareholders.

Their guidelines in relation to remuneration are as follows.

Levels of remuneration should be sufficient to attract and retain the directors needed to run the company successfully. The component parts of remuneration should be structured so as to link rewards to corporate and individual performance.

We expect companies to have a formal and transparent procedure for developing executive remuneration policy and for fixing the remuneration packages of individual directors. No director should be involved in fixing his or her own remuneration.

Standard Life believes that directors' service contracts should have notice periods which do not exceed 12 months unless there is special justification or a well-defined and acceptable mitigation policy. We generally oppose the award of unmitigated and liquidated damages in the event of early termination of directors' service contracts or a change of control of the company if the amounts involved exceed 12 months' basic salary.

Standard Life supports the payment of exceptional levels of remuneration for the achievement of exceptional performance, provided that the basis for determining performance is acceptable and can be justified by the board having regard to levels of remuneration within and outwith the company. We oppose the use of total shareholder return and other share price based performance measures if they are not underpinned by a challenging measure of underlying financial performance.

**B15.10**  *Standard Life*

On share incentive schemes, Standard Life:

- opposes provisions for early release of rewards unless the spirit of the performance condition has been, or is likely to be, met;

- opposes re-testing of performance conditions when grants of conditional awards are being made on a rolling basis;

- encourages vesting of awards three years or longer after the period of grant;

- encourages phased granting of awards;

- encourages the use of staggered vesting of awards.

Also, Standard Life support, in principle, the use of share-save and profit participation schemes.


# Manifest                                                        B15.11

Manifest analyse approx 1,300 companies. Manifest have a different approach than the ABI and NAPF. They allow their clients to decide what criteria they wish to use when assessing the corporate governance of a company. They provide a service to their clients by assessing whether each company has met the client's template. They also provide in depth analyses of each company. For example their 2003 report on Cable & Wireless was 28 pages and their one on BA was 17 pages. The key issues they consider in relation to remuneration are if:

- the remuneration committee is not considered to be independent;

- a director's service contract may on termination be greater than 12 months;

- a proposed new option scheme does not contain an overall 10% dilution limit in 10 years;

- a proposed new incentive scheme:

   o   has maximum annual participation limits over 100% salary,

   o   allows bailing out of underwater options,

   o   has performance targets that do not include a comparator group,

   o   allows awards within two years of retirement,

   o   allows preferential vesting of awards in the event of a change in control.

Manifest announced a link up with GovernanceMetrics International in July 2003 and in future will have the ability to score the FTSE 100 companies on the basis of a highly detailed 600 question analysis and supporting computer algorithm. GMI have pioneered this approach in the USA and are now rolling it out throughout the world in partnership with local institutional investment advisory companies.

# PIRC                                                    **B15.12**

PIRC analyse companies in the UK FTSE All Share Index, approx 800
companies. The PIRC voting guidelines are more onerous in a number of cases
than those of the Combined Code and the ABI/NAPF.

The PIRC Shareholder Voting Guidelines 2003 on directors' remuneration are
as follows.

Directors face a clear conflict of interest when setting their remuneration in
terms of their duty to the company, their accountability to shareholders and
their own self-interest. The perceived failure to balance these interests is largely
responsible for the recurrent controversies over directors' remuneration.

Directors' pay is not just an issue of the cost to the company, but also has
serious implications for corporate performance.

It is important that remuneration packages are structured in ways that provide
the right incentives to senior management, whether this is through fixed
remuneration or variable, incentive-based pay. Performance targets should not
reward underperformance, but also should not incentivise executives to take
undue risks or take short-term decisions.

Boardroom pay also is a leadership issue and will affect the morale and
motivation of employees, and the attitude of customers. Corporate reputation
among the public as a whole is also influenced by remuneration practices. It is
in shareholders' interests to see this issue dealt with satisfactorily if the integrity
and reputation of business is not to be undermined.

For these reasons, the way in which remuneration is handled can be seen as an
indicator of the overall integrity, accountability and governance standards
applied by the board.

**Remuneration reports**

With the passage of the *Directors' Remuneration Report Regulations 2002*, all
listed companies are required to publish a remuneration report and to put this to
the vote at their annual general meeting. This will provide shareholders with
additional disclosures and with the opportunity to hold directors directly
accountable for remuneration policies and practices.

This requirement does not supplant the role of the remuneration committee. All
companies should still have a remuneration committee comprising solely
independent directors whose role is to determine policy ahead of endorsement
by shareholders. The Remuneration Committee should not rely solely on advice
from executives within the company, and should have the ability and funding
available to take independent advice.

## B15.12   *PIRC*

When analysing remuneration reports PIRC provides a rating of the quality and depth of disclosure, the balance of performance requirements and potential rewards for long term incentive plans, and directors' service contract policy.

**Disclosure**

In order to ensure accountability over this sensitive issue, there should be full disclosure of all elements of pay. Shareholders need to be able to assess the value of the whole package.

A clear valuation of benefits received during the year, including share options, other conditional share awards and pension benefits, should be provided.

The performance basis of all such incentive schemes under which benefits are potentially payable should be clearly set out each year, together with the actual performance achieved against the same targets. Any discretionary or unusual payments should be fully described and justified.

The full scheme rules for new and existing schemes should be available on request as well as being on display at the AGM.

Most companies justify their remuneration policy in the general terms of the need to 'to attract, retain and motivate' executives. However, companies have different circumstances, structures and outlooks. Their policies should reflect this. Financial rewards need to be seen in the context of the director's other terms and conditions, the company's culture and its aims and objectives. The statement of remuneration policy should clearly explain the rationale behind the remuneration structure and should describe all the elements. This statement should include a description and explanation for all elements of pay, justification for the choice of performance criteria and the level of targets, a description of how the remuneration strategy fits with overall corporate strategy and the drivers behind corporate performance, and should make explicit reference to the relationship (with evidence) between directors' remuneration and company performance and employee remuneration levels. Factors specific to the company should be emphasised rather than relying on a general market rationale.

The main terms of directors' contracts including notice periods on both sides, non-compete clauses and any fixed compensation should be summarised in the annual report.

Copies of all contracts should be sent to shareholders on request.

Policy should also deal with non-executive directors' remuneration in terms of how their pay is set and its components, including an explanation for any differences between fees for various directors. Non-executives should not receive any form of performance-related remuneration, such as bonuses or share options.

## Balance of performance and reward

Shareholders are concerned that overall remuneration levels are reasonable and that any incentive remuneration is based on relevant and challenging performance targets. Tougher performance requirements are necessary for progressively higher potential rewards.

All share-based incentives should use at least two performance criteria, one of which should be measured against a peer group in order to demonstrate relative out-performance.

The choice of performance criteria should be justified. The specific target or range of targets attached to a performance criterion should be justified in order to explain how it encourages out-performance.

All schemes should use a vesting scale in order to allow for differential rewards for improving performance levels. Maximum vesting should only be possible for significant out-performance against market forecasts. For the very highest payouts (*e.g.* annual options awards of more than two times salary), performance significantly in excess of market expectations or set at above upper quintile performance relative to a comparator group, should be required in most cases.

Minimum vesting should be dependent on the achievement of market forecasts or at least median performance against a comparator group.

## Excessiveness issues

As most incentive awards are based on multiples of salary, the level of base salary is relevant. In general, salaries should not be significantly higher than comparable companies within the sector. Equally, potential excessiveness should be assessed in terms of the interplay of various incentive schemes, including annual bonus plans. As a general rule, potential incentive rewards should not represent more than two times salary levels.

It is important that executive directors are encouraged to build up a significant shareholding in the company in order to more closely align their outlook with that of shareholders.

This is especially the case when directors are to participate in share-based incentive schemes.

Finally, remuneration structures should recognise the contributions made by all employees to corporate success. In order to avoid the impression that only senior executives can benefit from good company performance, schemes should be in place that recognise the efforts of all employees.

## Contracts

Lengthy rolling contracts remain a controversial issue for many shareholders. If directors are dismissed, shareholders can be in the position of paying large sums by way of compensation, even though an executive may have failed to perform well.

We consider that the maximum length of notice periods should be one year and preferably shorter. We also support the rigorous application of mitigation and arrangement for phased payment of compensation. The basis of any compensation paid in the year should be clearly identified and explained, together with the level of mitigation applied. Notice periods or payments should not be extendable for any reason.

## Voting on remuneration reports

PIRC uses our rating derived from the assessment of the above issues to inform our voting advice. PIRC reserves the right to override our general position in exceptional or unusual circumstances. In particular, major concerns over the operation of remuneration policy or unacceptable practices, such as option repricing, will have a material effect on our voting advice.

## New share incentive schemes

Most incentive schemes of longer than one year are share based.

Directors and shareholders have different interests which can be more closely aligned by the use of share schemes. However, it should be recognised that a share scheme will not automatically create convergence of interest and that any transfer of equity to directors should be clearly justified by performance. Equally, it should be recognised that the value of share-based rewards will be mediated by market sentiment, over which directors may have little control.

Thus, share based schemes can produce perverse results. These sorts of schemes should form only a part of an overall remuneration package, rather than dominating potential reward structures.

All new share incentive schemes in which any director may participate should be put to the vote. The Remuneration Committee's discretion to change the rules of the scheme should only relate to technical amendments. Any changes to performance targets, comparator groups or award levels should be put to shareholders.

For new schemes, the following information should be provided in full in the proxy material.

- A full explanation of the basis on which awards will be made (either of options or restricted shares), together with the level of maximum award.

- Full information on performance targets which determine exercise of options or vesting of shares together with a justification of why these are viewed as stringent.

- Full details of any retesting provisions.

- Full details of any comparator groups used.
- Full details of any voting scales:
  - information on change-in-control or retirement provisions;
  - information on the source of shares to be used, either newly issued or market purchased;
  - Information on limits to the number of shares which can be awarded (whether new shares or purchased shares) or the proportion of equity which may be issued over various timescales;
  - a calculation of the expected value of potential awards.

PIRC provides a rating of the scheme based on consideration of the quality of disclosure, the scale of rewards relative to the performance conditions required, general excessiveness issues (as described above) and other elements of scheme structure such as dilution levels and the need for financial commitment from participants. The rating informs PIRC's voting advice.

**Executive remuneration should be determined by a formal and independent procedure**

1. *Remuneration committee exists comprising wholly independent directors:* The remuneration policy for executive directors and the chairman should be determined by a remuneration committee which is free from executive influence and the members of which are independent by PIRC guidelines.

2. *Remuneration Committee receives independent advice:* The remuneration committee should have the resources and the ability to seek advice from independent sources. It should not rely on advice from within the company, though input from senior managers will be appropriate. The names of advisers should be disclosed.

**There should be full and transparent disclosure of directors' remuneration**

3. *All elements of each director's cash remuneration is disclosed:* In disclosing remuneration, companies should provide figures for each element of director's cash remuneration. Explanation for any major changes should be provided.

4. *All share incentive awards are fully disclosed with award dates and prices:* For each director, companies should disclose all separate awards of options, conditional, matching or bonus shares together with dates of award, vesting status and exercise price. Average exercise prices are not acceptable.

5. *Expected values are disclosed for all share incentive awards for each director:* For share-based incentive schemes, companies should provide a full individual breakdown of all awards which have not yet fully vested or been exercised, together with a fair valuation of the value of such awards using an option pricing model.

**B15.12** *PIRC*

The basis of the option pricing model chosen should be explained.

6. *Pension contributions and entitlements are fully disclosed:* For each director and all relevant pension plans, contributions made by the company should be disclosed along with the increase in the transfer value of accrued pension benefits after inflation, in line with Institute of Actuaries /Faculty of Actuaries guidance. Only base salary should be pensionable.

7. *Pay policy aims are fully explained in terms of the company's objectives:* The Remuneration Committee should explain how the remuneration policy is aligned with the specific business objectives of the company or how it relates to factors affecting the company, rather than simply repeating the standard 'attract, retain and motivate' explanation.

8. *Pay elsewhere in the company is considered in determining director's remuneration:* It should be clear that directors' remuneration is not considered in isolation from other employees and that it forms part of a coherent policy that is consistent with the company's goals and culture. Examples of disclosure could be policy on limiting differentials or multiples of salary, uniform increases across the company, other statements which explain the relationship.

9. *All the individual components of the pay package are fully described:* Each element within the overall remuneration structure should be identified and explained. The relative importance of each element should also be explained.

10. *There is information on the composition of the NEDs' remuneration and how it is determined:* The remuneration report should disclose both the level of NED fees, their composition and the process by which they are set.

Linkages to time commitments should be explained together with an explanation for any disparities between directors.

11. *Duration of contracts and company liabilities on termination are given:* For all service contracts, there should be clear disclosure of the contract length, the length of notice period required on either side, any circumstances that affect the notice period, any predetermined damages provisions, the circumstances in which such payments might be made, the company's policy on mitigation (if any) and how compensation payments might be phased.

12. *Compensation payments or significant changes in policy are fully explained:* Divergences from previously stated remuneration policy or changes in policy from previous years should be clearly identified and explained. Any compensation payments made or committed to during the year should be disclosed, the components explained and basis for the payments (*e.g.* degree of mitigation, contractual obligation) explained.

13. *Future performance conditions and/or past targets for annual bonuses paid are stated:* Annual bonuses can result is significant payments and have an important role in incentive structures. The performance criteria and targets should be disclosed. If provision of forward looking targets is

deemed commercially sensitive, the targets achieved which resulted in payments during the year should be disclosed.

14. *Maximum potential awards under annual bonuses are stated:* The maximum amount that may be earned under annual bonus schemes should be disclosed, together with any performance scales.

15. *Performance conditions for long term incentive schemes are disclosed:* The performance criteria chosen and the targets relating to the criteria for all share-based incentive plans or other long term incentive plan should be disclosed together with the reasons for their choice. Performance achieved against the targets used should be disclosed. Where relative or comparative performance measures are being used, the company's performance ranking should be provided each year.

16. *Maximum awards for long term incentive schemes disclosed:* The maximum awards that may be made under individual schemes annually should be disclosed. Where these vary from normal award levels, the circumstances in which larger awards might be made should be explained.

17. *Vesting scale for long-term incentives schemes is clear:* The performance required for maximum and minimum vesting should be clearly stated together with the relevant awards.

The scale between these points should be disclosed.

### Longer term incentives should provide rewards scaled towards superior performance

18. *Maximum vesting targets are challenging relative to performance required:* Shareholders have a reasonable expectation that directors should perform competently. Additional cash or share-based incentives should be available only for outstanding performance beyond that which may be expected of directors as part of their normal responsibilities. In this context, performance targets should be stringent, relevant to the company and should reflect the executive's role in the business rather than external factors beyond the executive's influence.

Options should never be issued at a discount.

The performance target required for the achievement of maximum rewards should be significantly in excess of market expectations in the case of an internal performance measure, or should represent at least upper quintile performance in the case of a relative performance measure. Higher than average base awards should require tougher performance conditions.

19. *Minimum vesting targets are challenging relative to performance required:* The performance target required for the achievement of minimum rewards should be at least in line with market expectations or set at least at median performance. Higher than average base awards will require tougher performance conditions.

Any amounts vesting for median performance should be minimal.

20. *Vesting scales are sufficiently broad and geared towards better performance:* Vesting scales should cover a range of different performance
outcomes. While payments may start for average or median performance,
such rewards should be extremely limited with significant payments
reserved for demonstrably superior performance.

21. *There are at least two performance criteria, one of which uses a
comparator group:* All long term share incentive schemes should base
rewards on at least two performance criteria which apply to all possible
rewards under the scheme, rather than parts of awards being dependent on
separate criterion. One criterion may be a hurdle target, with the second
determining the vesting scale.

However, both should be challenging. Consideration should be given to non-
traditional performance indicators so long as these are verifiable by independent
bodies. Examples might include personal targets, environmental targets,
investment, innovation, market share, customer satisfaction, achievement of
regulatory targets or health and safety.

**Remuneration structure as whole should not be excessive**

22. *Total potential rewards under all incentive schemes are not excessive:*
Incentive rewards should not be excessive in terms of delivering potential
value which is out of line to the real contribution made by individuals and
senior executives, or which is regarded as excessive compared to the
performance required, base salary, market norms or rewards available to
other employees. Often, the existence of multiple long term share based
incentive schemes will provide excessive rewards, though the total potential payments and performance targets will be the key issue.

In general, annual and long term awards with an expected value of no more
than 200% of salary should be made in any one year, unless performance
targets are exceptionally challenging or base salaries are relatively low.

23. *Average salaries are broadly in line with the sector:* Companies should
avoid contributing to an inevitable pay spiral that occurs when all seek to
pay salaries of median or above. While sector comparison is appropriate, it
is reasonable to benchmark salaries at below median. Any variation from
sector trends should be explained.

24. *Directors are required to build up a significant shareholding:* Share-based
incentive schemes which do not include an element of capital commitment
on the part of the participant do not align the interests of participant and
shareholder in terms of downside risk. We consider that there should be a
real financial commitment by participants which is subject to the same
investment risks that shareholders face. The simplest way of achieving this
is to require participants to hold substantial numbers of shares in the
company prior to participation in a scheme. Such holdings should not be
achievable simply through the exercise of previously held share options.

Holdings should be built up over a limited time period. A deferred bonus will
be regarded as a capital commitment for such schemes, so long as participation

is optional and any matched awards are subject to a suitable performance hurdle.

25. *Share incentive schemes conform with dilution guidelines:* The dilution limits linked to all option schemes should be clearly disclosed. No more than 10% of issued share capital should be available for issue under all employee share schemes, and no more than 5% of issued share capital should be issuable under any single discretionary share option scheme in any ten year period. These limits should apply whether or not new shares are being issued.

26. *Schemes are available to enable all employees to benefit from business success:* Remuneration structures should reward the efforts of all staff since a motivated and well-rewarded workforce is an important component of company performance. Such structures also reduce the perceptions of unfairness about directors' pay. Companies should have bonus and incentive structures which reward all employees for business success, albeit with differing levels of reward and participation. These should not be limited to SAYE option schemes. Such schemes should be fully disclosed as part of the directors' reporting on companywide remuneration structures.

27. *Other remuneration practices do not raise concerns:* Discretionary or exceptional bonus payments should be fully described and explained. Incentive awards should be phased to avoid distorted or unsustainable gains. Payments which are unjustified in terms of policy or performance such as 'golden hellos' or guaranteed bonuses will be regarded as unacceptable.

### Contracts policy should balance potential costs to shareholders with directors' interests

28. *No current directors have rolling contracts of longer than one year:* A notice period of no longer than one year should be the maximum which balances the interests of shareholders and the company with those of the director. Shorter notice periods should be considered. In exceptional circumstances, a longer initial fixed contract period may be necessary in order to recruit a new executive. Such circumstances may involve international relocation or a high-risk move to a problem company.

In such cases, the most important factor is for the directors (or the remuneration committee) to explain the circumstances effectively. Fixed initial notice periods should not exceed two years and it should be clear that these reduce to a period of no more than one year after the initial period.

Should it be necessary to reduce the notice period of contracts to comply with best practice, we do not consider that compensation should be payable.

29. *Statement on application of mitigation made:* There should be a formal statement of how the company applies the principle of mitigation in cases of termination of contracts. This should be coupled with phased payment for any compensation paid, which should be terminated upon suitable employment being found by the individual.

30. *Contracts do not provide for liquidated damages or automatic payments in excess of one year in any circumstances:* Any contractual clauses which imply fixed compensation equivalent to more than one year's salary and benefits will be viewed as a breach of best practice. These could include liquidated damages provisions paying more than one year's remuneration (including bonuses) or change-in-control provisions which extend a notice period beyond one year.

31. *Future bonuses are not taken into account in determining compensation:* Contracts should specifically exclude any future or potential bonus payments from the calculation of compensation, whether predetermined or not.

**PIRC Ratings Service**                                                          **B15.13**

PIRC provide a 'Ratings Service for New Share Incentive Schemes and Remuneration Reports', which they explain as follows.

For the 2002 proxy season, PIRC launched a significant new enhancement to our Corporate Governance Service by providing a rating of new directors' share incentive schemes and proposals to approve remuneration reports.

The overall aim of the Remuneration Rating Service is to provide a comparative assessment of the positive and negative features of any new share incentive scheme and/or remuneration report, benchmarked against standards of best practice, and to use this analysis to come to an overall determination of the proposal.

PIRC continues to provide a voting recommendation based on the policy positions set out in our Shareholder Voting Guidelines alongside the Remuneration Rating.

The key issues contributing to the rating are:

- the performance targets required to be achieved for maximum and minimum payouts. A high rating will only be awarded where the highest payouts are dependent on performance which is substantially ahead of market expectations (in the case of a financial target) or in the top quintile compared to a peer group, if used; and where the vesting scale does not allow for significant proportions of salary to be potentially payable for average or median performance or below market expectations;

- the level of base salaries compared to industry peers and the total sums available for incentive rewards relative to salaries;

- the quality and depth of disclosure of remuneration figures, policy and performance targets;

- the length of directors' service contracts (in the case of a remuneration report vote).

## 1. New share incentive schemes

For new share options schemes, conditional share schemes or deferred bonus schemes, we provide a two-letter rating, each scored from A to D. The first letter relates to the balance of performance targets and reward; the second relates to the quality of disclosure, type of performance criteria and other structural issues.

### i) *Balance of performance and reward*

The primary element analysed is the balance between performance required and the potential rewards available. A higher rating is given to schemes with demonstrably tougher performance targets for the release of higher awards.

As is our current practice, the level of rewards is calculated on an expected value basis. In the absence of company disclosure of an expected value, PIRC assumes that an option award has an expected value of approximately 35% of the award price, while a conditional share has a value of 100% of the price at the date of award.

The appropriateness of performance targets is assessed according to the type of target used. Where companies use a financial target such as EPS, we assess the stringency of the target against brokers' consensus forecasts. If a comparator group is used, we look at the vesting scale.

PIRC advocates the use of at least two performance criteria, one of which should be measured against a peer group in order to demonstrate relative out-performance.

At *maximum vesting*, a high rating is achieved by targets which require significant out-performance against market forecasts. The greater the potential reward in relation to base salary, the tougher the performance target required. For the very highest payouts (eg annual options awards of two or three times salary), performance significantly in excess of brokers' forecasts or set at above upper quintile performance relative to a comparator group, is required in most cases.

At *minimum vesting*, a high rating is dependent upon the achievement of market forecasts or at least median performance against a comparator group.

### *Excessiveness issues*

As well as comparing payouts against performance targets, various excessive-ness issues contribute to the rating. These include whether:

- salaries are broadly in line with the company's sector;
- no more than 200% of salary is available in annual and long-term incentive bonuses in any year;
- schemes are available enabling all employees to benefit from business success (e.g. a profit share scheme).

These issues contribute to an overall rating on the scheme's performance/ reward structure on a scale of A-D.

### ii) New share incentive schemes: other issues

The second letter of the rating is derived from a range of other issues central to a scheme's structure. These include:

- the quality of disclosure of the operation of the scheme. A high rating is achieved by full disclosure of the performance conditions, vesting scale, normal and exceptional awards, expected valuation, takeover provisions and dilution provisions.

- the type of performance conditions attached. A higher rating will be awarded to schemes which use a comparator group and which use more than one performance condition concurrently.

- the level of discretion enjoyed by the remuneration committee in amending or operating the scheme. A high rating is dependent on there being a requirement for shareholders to be consulted an any major amendment to a scheme's operation.

- observation of dilution limits. Both an overall 10% limit for all schemes and an individual limit to awards of 5% for a single discretionary scheme are necessary.

- the length of the performance period and any holding or retesting period. A high rating depends on a performance period in excess of three years or a combined performance period and additional holding period in excess of three years.

- the level, if any, of any financial commitment required of participants (eg a shareholding requirement).

### iii) Voting advice on new share schemes

The two-letter rating contributes to PIRC's overall voting advice. To support a new scheme, we require a rating of not less than AB. A rating of D for either category always leads to an Oppose recommendation.

### 2. Voting on remuneration reports

For proposals to approve remuneration reports, PIRC provides a three letter rating focusing on disclosure, the balance of performance and reward for the share based incentive schemes in operation, and contracts policy.

### i) Disclosure

The factors below contribute to an A–D rating for quality of disclosure.

*Figures*

Issues assessed include:

- clear reporting of each director's cash remuneration;

- expected value figures for outstanding option or LTIP awards;

- clear explanation of the components and calculation of any compensation paid;

- clear disclosure of pension contributions and benefits with transfer values for accrued benefits under defined benefit schemes.

*Policy*

Issues assessed include whether there is:

- a statement explaining the aims and objectives of the policy as a whole, beyond a boiler plate statement;

- a description of the role of individual components of the package and their relative importance;

- an explanation for the choice of performance targets and their role in contributing to business objectives;

- evidence that pay for other employees in the company has been considered when determining that of the directors;

- explanation of the method for determining non-executives' remuneration and its composition;

- any serious concern about aspects of policy which is not in line with good practice.

*Performance targets*

Issues assessed include whether there is:

- full description of performance criteria, targets and maximum payouts under annual bonus schemes;

- full description of performance criteria, targets, vesting scales, maximum and minimum award levels for longer term incentive plans.

## ii) Balance of performance and reward

The same criteria, as applied to new incentive plans, are employed for existing incentive plans in order to arrive at an A–D rating for the balance of performance and reward. Tougher performance requirements are necessary for progressively higher potential rewards.

## iii) Contracts

PIRC analyses existing contracts on the following issues in order to arrive at a rating for contracts policy. Whether:

- all rolling contracts are set at one year or less;

- any fixed term contracts revert to one year rolling or less;

- any liquidated damage provisions are limited to the payment of one year's salary and benefits;

- the company is committed to applying mitigation;

- notice periods or payments cannot be extended in a takeover situation.

### iv) Voting on remuneration reports

This produces a three letter rating referring to disclosure, balance of performance and reward, and contracts.

A rating of D or a C in any category will usually lead to an Oppose vote recommendation. Advice to vote For or Abstain will depend on the combination of As and Bs achieved.

In all cases, both for new share schemes and for remuneration reports, PIRC reserves the right to override our general position in exceptional or unusual circumstances.

For more details, please contact PIRC Ltd, Cityside, 40 Adler Street, London E1 1EE. Website: www.pirc.co.uk. Tel: 020 7247 2323

# The Conference Board Commission on Public Trust and Private Enterprise     B15.14

The Conference Board convened the 12-member Commission in June 2002 to address the causes of declining public and investor trust in companies, their leaders and America's capital markets. The members include prominent leaders from business, finance, public service, and academia. The Commission was co-chaired by Peter G. Peterson, Chairman of The Blackstone Group and Chairman of the Federal Reserve Bank of New York; and John W. Snow, Chairman and CEO of CSX Corporation and former Chairman of The Business Roundtable. Members included Arthur Levitt Jr. Former Chairman U.S. Securities and Exchange Commission and Paul A. Volcker Former Chairman Board of Governors of the Federal Reserve System. Their report has no formal status in the UK but is included here as it indicates what best practice may become in the US. The Commission provided the following principles in relation to compensation (ie remuneration).

## Principles

### Principle 1: The compensation committee's role and responsibilities

A strong, independent Compensation Committee should take primary respons-ibility for ensuring that the compensation programs and values transferred to management through cash pay, stock and stock-based awards, are fair and appropriate to attract, retain and motivate management, and are reasonable in view of company economics, and of the relevant practices of other, similar companies. The Committee should be held accountable for the decisions they make. The Compensation Committee should also recognize the potential conflict of interest in management's recommending its own compensation levels

## *Specific best practice suggestions*

1. The Compensation Committee should retain any outside consultants who advise it, and the outside consultants should report solely to the Committee.

2. The Compensation Committee should be comprised solely of directors who are free of any relationships with the company (except for compensation received in their role as directors) and its management and who can act independently of management in carrying out their responsibilities.

3. The Compensation Committee should vigorously exercise continuous oversight over all matters of executive compensation policy. In addition, the Chair of the Compensation Committee should "take ownership" of the Compensation Committee's activities and be available at shareholders' meetings to respond directly to questions about executive compensation.

4. No compensation arrangement should be permitted that creates an incentive for top executives to act contrary to the company's best interests or which could be interpreted as an attempt to circumvent either the requirements or the spirit of the law or accounting rules.

5. The Compensation Committee should be responsible for all aspects of executive officers' compensation arrangements and perquisites, including approval of all employment, retention, and severance agreements.

6. The Compensation Committee should approve any compensation arrangement for a senior executive officer involving any subsidiary, special purpose entity (SPE) or other affiliate. Because of the significant potential for conflicts of interest, these compensation arrangements should be permitted only in very special circumstances and only when of benefit to investors. They should also be disclosed in filings with the SEC.

7. The Compensation Committee should exercise independent judgment in determining the proper levels and types of compensation to be paid unconstrained by industry median compensation statistics or by the company's own past compensation practices and levels, which, in certain companies, have been excessive. The Committee should also be mindful of the differences in compensation levels throughout the corporation in setting senior executive compensation levels.

8. The Compensation Committee should hold executive sessions as required (for example, to determine CEO pay and stock option grants) and the Committee should exercise its power to schedule meetings and set its own agenda.

## Principle 2: The importance of performance-based compensation

Performance-based compensation tied to specific goals can be a powerful and effective tool to advance the business interests of the corporation, and the use of performance-based compensation tools should be encouraged in a balanced and cost-effective manner.

*Specific best practice suggestions*

1.  Compensation policies should meet the unique needs of each corporation in the market in which that corporation competes for executive talent.

2.  The Compensation Committee should establish, with the concurrence of the board, performance-based incentives that support and reinforce the corporation's long-term strategic goals set by the board (for example, cost of capital, return on equity, economic value added, market share, quality goals, compliance goals, environment goals, revenue and profit growth, cost containment, cash management, etc.) and whose award is linked to achievement of specific strategic goals.

3.  The Compensation Committee should adopt specific policies and programs to recapture incentive compensation from executives in the event that malfeasance on the part of such executive or executives results in substantial financial harm to the corporation.

**Principle 3: The role of equity-based incentives**

The use of high levels of equity-based compensation, particularly in the form of fixed-price options, has been at the heart of much of the recent controversy over corporate compensation. The Compensation Committee should endeavor to use all equity-based compensation arrangements in a reasonable and cost-effective manner.

*Specific best practice suggestions*

1.  Equity compensation, including stock options, can be an effective form of incentive compensation, particularly if it is designed to promote the type of performance goals being encouraged.

2.  Consistent with its duty to preserve long-term value for the corporation, the Compensation Committee should establish compensation policy and arrangements that appropriately consider and balance the relationship between the perceived value of equity compensation and the costs of that compensation to the corporation.

3.  A broad distribution including non-executive employees of properly structured equity-based compensation may be desirable for various reasons, for example in start-up companies with limited cash, in industries in which equity-based compensation has become a part of accepted broad-based compensation packages or for companies where an important portion of intellectual capital resides with employees.

4.  The Compensation Committee must disclose in conspicuous ways the effective costs passed on to shareholders through dilution or any direct costs associated with shares acquired in the open market to limit that dilution.

## Principle 4: Creating a long-term focus

Compensation policies should encourage a meaningful financial stake in the corporation through long-term 'acquire and hold' practices by key executives and directors, while insuring that any contribution by the company to creating that stake is done in a reasonable and cost-effective manner.

*Specific best practice suggestions*

1. The Compensation Committee should:

   1) require senior management to accumulate a meaningful amount of company stock on a long-term basis; and

   2) specify substantial minimum holding periods for equity received as compensation, in each case in order to align the interests of management with those of the corporation. Holding periods for senior executives and directors should generally not be less than the holding periods for other employees under 401(k) or similar retirement plans

2. While recognizing that director compensation involves policy issues different from those in management compensation, directors nonetheless should own and retain substantial amounts of company stock they receive as compensation or otherwise acquire. Furthermore, at a minimum, required retention and holding levels by directors should also be established

## Principle 5: Accounting neutrality

Compensation decisions should be based on the effectiveness of various forms of compensation to achieve company goals and their respective relative costs, rather than simply on their accounting treatment. The costs associated with equity-based compensation should be reported on a uniform and consistent basis by all public companies in order to provide clear and understandable comparability.

*Specific best practice suggestion*

1. To eliminate accounting bias in favor of one form of equity-based compensation, fixed-price stock options should be expensed on financial statements of public companies.8 The Financial Accounting Standards Board (FASB) and the International Accounting Standards Board (IASB), as organizations with technical expertise in this area, should move expeditiously in order to determine appropriate accounting treatment for equity-based compensation including a uniform and broadly accepted method of valuing options.

## Principle 6: Shareholder rights

Shareholders should have control over potential equity dilution resulting from compensation practices.

*Specific best practice suggestions*

1.  Equity-based compensation should be made through plans approved by shareholders.

2.  Existing equity compensation arrangements should not be materially modified, including the re-pricing of options, without shareholder approval.

**Principle 7: Transparency and disclosure**

Shareholder and market interests are best served through transparent and readily understandable disclosure of executive compensation and the economic impact of such compensation. Public trust would be enhanced if the Compensation Committee took specific steps and implemented policy to further reassure the public that senior management is not engaged in stock transactions involving the company in advance of material information being available to the public.

These policies should be disclosed in filings with the SEC.

*Specific best practice suggestions*

1.  A corporation's public disclosures should include a conspicuous statement highlighting both earnings per share after dilution and the proportion of future shareholder value that equity-based compensation plans would provide to executives and employees.

This disclosure should illustrate in plain language the percentage of total equity (market overhang) represented by unexercised options.

2.  Executive officers should be required to give advance public notice of their intention to dispose directly or indirectly (eg by hedging or other similar arrangement) of the corporation's equity securities.

In this connection, the Compensation Committee, with the assistance of experts as required, should develop and publish appropriate methods by which disclosure of such intentions must be made.

3.  Companies should be required to disclose publicly employment agreements entered into with executive officers promptly following their execution.

A company's disclosure should include a summary in plain English of the significant terms of the agreement when the agreements are filed with regulatory authorities.

# Not badly paid, but paid badly                                    B15.15

*This article by Paul Lee of Hermes was the winner of the second PricewaterhouseCoopers European Shareholder Value Award, held in conjunction with Financial News and the European Business Forum: Compensation*

*Revisited – Are Managers Paid Too Much – Or Too Little? More information on Hermes can be found in* **B6.11** *on* **HERMES ON AUDITOR INDEPENDENCE.**

Executive managers are not, in general, badly paid, but many of them are paid badly. Executives deserve to be well paid, because the good ones are capable of creating enormous value for the companies and underlying shareholders that employ them. Most are in fact well paid, but there is an increasing disconnection between that pay and the shareholder value that the executives create.

To pick just a few examples, when shareholders have egged on German prosecutors to investigate Mannesmann's former executives over pay-offs received following its takeover by Vodafone, because investors fear that their motives in eventually accepting the takeover may have been clouded by the payments; when 40 per cent of UK independent institutional investors – usually so proud of their ability to reach compromises with companies behind the scenes – vote against or abstain on pay issues at Schroders, one of their own; and when a US company, Warnaco, cannot sack the chief executive that has brought it to the brink of ruin because the compensation she would receive at such a departure is more than the cash left in the company, there is clearly a major problem of disconnection between the interests of shareowners and executives. At the very least, some shareholders perceive that there is a disconnection between executive pay and shareholder value creation. That's a huge problem.

How did we get in such a mess?

## The three Ts

Let's start by thinking about what executive pay is all about and why it is structured as it is. Typically, there are three aspects of pay (leaving pension payments to one side – these are surely just delayed payments of salary, deferred into the future, largely for tax reasons specific to the country of residence). These aspects are: salary, bonus and long-term incentives, typically options or some other equity-linked remuneration. These aim to do different things. The salary should compensate executives for their time and efforts over each year. The bonus aims to provide an incentive to hit clearly specified targets which help ensure that each year the company moves towards its strategic aims. The third should provide incentives for more long-term good performance, as reflected in the share price – hence the emphasis here on equity-based incentives. All are intended to reflect shareholder value creation, but the last most transparently so because it is equity-linked.

Why is there a need for the different forms of remuneration? Would it not be simpler just to pay executives a flat fee? There are three reasons why the different forms of incentive have developed: tax, time-scales and trust, what I call the three Ts. The sums of money involved are such that tax issues will always be a major factor. If companies can use tax-efficient structures to pay their executives, they will be able to provide the same financial rewards at lower cost, which is clearly good for their results and good for shareholder value. Tax issues are increasingly dictating the structures of executive pay, often in negative ways, as I will discuss below.

The issue of time-scales is a simple one: most investors (such as pension funds, life assurers) are long-termist and recognise that only long-term strong performance is to their benefit. The danger with a single fee is that it might create false incentives for executives to create short-term good performance, often to the detriment of long-term shareholder value.

This problem of trying to create the right incentives to match the performance time-scales that shareowners are looking for – and that corporate investments often require – leads naturally to the trust issue. In formal economic terms, this is called the agency problem. Shareholders are the owners of the business and they employ the executives as their agents to run the business. The agency problem captures the idea that those agents may on occasions act in their own interests rather than in the interests of the owners. This could happen, say, where executives over-pay for an acquisition whose main benefits will be to make them seem more important because they are running a bigger business and will help protect them from losing their jobs because a hostile takeover is much less likely.

The area where the agency problem arises most clearly, however, is in executive remuneration. This is the direct payment of shareholders' money to their agents. Even where those payments are mediated through a committee of independent non-executive directors (something I will come back to), there is real scope for conflicts of interest here. That is why shareholders have increasingly sought to use equity-based incentives, in the hope that ensuring that a large bulk of executives' remuneration is in the form of – or linked to – the company's stock will encourage their agents to act very deliberately and clearly in the long-term interests of shareholders as a whole, rather than in their own interests.

## The imperfect market

Within this general structure, a market for talent operates, at least in theory. There are, however, a number of reasons why this market is imperfect. First, it does not operate transparently and without negative influences. While in theory pay is administered by remuneration committees made up exclusively of independent non-executive directors, the theory does not necessarily lead to a properly functioning market. Even in those cases where these non-executives are genuinely independent, the majority of them, particularly in the US, are executive directors at other companies. Thus, they can influence the overall structure of the pay market from which they themselves benefit.

Second, there are valid questions to ask whether executives are truly globally mobile. Clearly, those at the head of genuinely multinational companies are already internationally footloose and so are likely to see little change if they formally move the base of their activities. But there are far fewer genuinely multinational companies than is generally assumed, and this global flexibility does not really apply to executives at the bulk of the world's companies.

Third, international borders introduce not only cultural differences (which create a historical context for current pay practices) but most importantly tax differences. These make certain forms of executive pay more attractive in some countries than others, and make some schemes simply impossible. The most important tax regime in this context is that in the US, because practice there seems to be the magnet for practice elsewhere in the world.

That there is not a truly international market for executives is clear from the vast discrepancies in remuneration paid in different countries, mainly for tax and historical reasons. In general, pay surveys (conducted by consultants such as William M Mercer) reveal that continental Europe pays its executives far more in the way of salary and bonus than do either the US or the UK – often because more complex forms of payment have not been possible nor part of corporate culture.

In contrast, in the US and UK, there is more of an emphasis on equity-linked incentive pay. While the levels of salary and bonus are pretty much comparable in these two countries, US incentives are far in excess of anything seen in the UK. The largest and most international companies in all these countries are beginning to move towards pay structures closer and closer to the US model.

The driver for this move to US structures, they explain, is 'globalisation'. By this, they mean that their US rivals are offering options on hugely attractive terms – wherever in the world they are operating – and their competitors from other countries feel forced to move towards matching those US-style terms in order to remain attractive employers. The extent to which these pressures are having an impact is hard to judge from the outside, but whether they are actually being forced to or not, companies around the world are moving towards US-style remuneration packages.

## The American way

If companies are tending to move towards the US model of pay, the question naturally arises as to whether this model is sustainable and whether it drives shareholder value creation. The evidence suggests not. The evidence in the US is of many companies having given away 10 per cent, and in some cases as much as 30 per cent, of their equity to executive directors and other staff in just the last five years or so. That is clearly not sustainable into the future: there wouldn't be any companies left in public hands if it were. Already, executive directors – and not just those who have genuinely created the companies, but also those who are hired hands brought in to run existing businesses – are among the largest shareholders of many US companies. The evidence is of monstrous payments being made, even in years where all that has happened is stagnation in company financial performance and stagnation in the share price, and even in years of underperformance. The scale of rewards for failure is monumental – even in cases where the total contracted golden parachute does not amount to four times the cash left in the business, as was the case at Warnaco. For example, US shareholders have filed a case against the board of Mattel for wasting corporate assets in paying outgoing chief executive Jill Barad – ousted for her perceived failure to perform – 'grossly excessive and unjustifiable' severance payments which have been estimated to amount to around $50 million.

The evidence in the US is that options (and for accounting, and to an extent tax, reasons, options are the predominant form of equity-based incentive in use there) are used to hide the genuine cost of employing staff. A study produced by HSBC in June indicates that if equity-based incentives are accounted for through the profit and loss account, as accounting standards boards are now proposing, many UK and European companies would face substantial reductions in their headline profitability. Applying the method proposed by the UK Accounting Standards Board, HSBC found that in the case of ARM Holdings, the figure would more than wipe out the company's current profits; in most cases, the number is between 2 per cent and 10 per cent of profits.

As far as I am aware, similar studies have not been conducted in the US market, but given the fact that equity-linked incentivisation has been more widely spread throughout companies there, is more generously structured and has been in place for more years, it seems likely that the average levels of profitability which would be seen under the proposed accounting changes would be around 20–25 per cent lower than currently. That is certainly the order of magnitude found by HSBC at those UK and European companies that have used equity-based remuneration in ways most similar to those in the US.

The fact that it seems to many investors in the US that it is standard practice to reprice options – something which in itself undermines the concept of aligning the interests of executives with those of shareowners, who don't have the chance to reprice their shares – indicates that the attitude of the accounting standards boards is correct. Options are being used by companies as an alternative way to remunerate their staff. The fact that companies are seen to reprice almost automatically means that they regard the lure of options as a necessary part of the pay of those staff in order to retain them. As such, the cost should appear transparently on the profit and loss accounts of the company, just as other staff costs do. At the moment, the cost of options is not totally transparent in the US; the fact that detailed and complex disclosures are made in the notes to the accounts does not create full transparency even for sophisticated investors.

As an aside, it is worth noting the new accounting rules in the US on repricing: in theory, these mean that the cost of any repricing must be expensed. However, if companies leave six months and a day between the cancellation of options and their replacement with cheaper ones, this does not fall within the scope of the accounting rules. Companies are therefore simply repricing with this six-month delay (Lucent is just one company to have done so this year).

To an extent, the huge spiral in executive pay has been justified by the increasingly revolving-door nature of executive tenure. In the UK a couple of years ago, Cranfield University found that the average length of time that a chief executive holds that post is just four years and two months. According to Murray Steele, head of strategic management at the university, that time period is likely to be still less now. In the US, it is far lower – around three years, or even less. This is clearly a hugely negative development where shareholders are seeking to align the interests of managers with their own. Chief executives only have the scope to be short-termist – often to the detriment of long-term shareholder value – where they aren't in the role for anything other than the very short term.

So, the evidence is that pay structures and systems in the US are not sustainable, that they seem to reward failure as well as success, and are not efficient and transparent in aligning executive interests with those of share-owners. Furthermore, the main justification for the system having developed in this direction in recent years also runs contrary to the long-term interests of shareowners. And yet it seems that the remuneration schemes of companies elsewhere in the world are moving towards these US-style schemes.

## Problems, problems

Before we discuss what can be done to move in more advantageous directions, it is instructive to seek the reasons why US remuneration structures became so far removed from the ideal. The first major reason is that US shareholders rarely have an opportunity to approve or disapprove of pay schemes. While the listing rules of the main US markets do state that companies should put equity-based incentive schemes to shareowner votes, there is a wide exemption for 'broadly based' schemes, where at least half the options go to the wider employee-base. Most schemes are designed to fall into this category and so are exempt from shareholder oversight. In these circumstances, it is perhaps unsurprising that little limit has been placed on the generosity of option schemes. Earlier this year, one institutional investor (in a written response to Nasdaq consultation on this issue) went so far as to suggest that there was an equivalence between this appropriation of shareowners' funds without their consent and theft.

Even where US shareholders do have a vote on these issues, they are faced by an extraordinary situation whereby brokers – who have no beneficial interest in the stock at all – are allowed to vote unvoted stock as they see fit. This stock tends to be voted in support of management, whether or not that is in the interests of shareholder value. Because voting is not an option, the main weapon of US shareholders against excessive pay is lawsuits for wasting company money. As well as being expensive and clumsy, this method has not proved particularly efficient. Few such cases have succeeded.

US companies have been enabled to maintain the illusion that options are not a cost borne by the shareowners because of the second major problem with US structures, lax accounting standards. I have discussed the proposed move

769

towards accounting for options through the profit and loss account. In contrast, the costs of the current situation are so opaque that it is hard even for sophisticated shareholders to judge whether they are getting value for money. The limited moves to make the costs of option repricing transparent contain the six month loophole that I have also discussed above.

US accounting, and to an extent tax, rules have a further negative impact. Technical provisions make it prohibitive to offer any equity-linked scheme other than options. This means that little consideration is given, for example, to schemes involving free shares, which some investment institutions believe are more advantageous, because they do not amount to a one-way bet in the same way that options do (particularly options where there is an expectation of repricing). US accounting standards also effectively bar the attachment of any performance conditions to the vesting of share options. According to the 'Fit Cats' report produced by Deutsche Bank last year, equity-based incentive schemes with performance criteria are much more effective at linking executive pay to shareholder value creation (after all, the purpose of equity-linked schemes) than those without performancing. This means that schemes with performancing can drive the same level of alignment of interests much more cheaply than those without. The fact that the US accounting, and to an extent tax, regimes effectively act as a barrier to the use of performance criteria in option schemes is clearly therefore hugely negative for the creation of shareholder value.

The fourth major problem is cultural. It is perfectly acceptable for US executives to convert their options directly into cash, rather than holding on to at least some of the shares that the options convert into. This helps to divorce their interests from those of genuine shareholders. Some companies require their executives to hold some equity stock, but the amounts are often limited and the practice is not widespread either across companies or deeply into companies. The simplest way for executives to be driven to create shareholder value is for them to act like shareholders, and the simplest way for them to act as shareholders is for them to hold substantial quantities of stock. Options should be converted and the shares retained at least for a decent period of time.

It remains to be seen how the US fad for options – fuelled at least in part by the long bull run on Wall Street – plays out in the more difficult markets of future years. It is clear that the explosion in the use of options has happened without much thought or understanding. A study last year by OppenheimerFunds in the US found that 11 per cent of respondents had allowed in-the-money options to lapse, effectively throwing money away. This is one sign of a wider problem: incentive schemes are increasingly complex. If they become so complex that it is difficult for their beneficiaries to understand them, they cannot be acting as an incentive to perform at all.

We will also see within the next few years how some of the perverse incentives fuelled by the option boom pan out when markets turn adverse. For example, many commentators have noted that in recent years US companies have been issuing new debt and buying back their own shares at a time when those shares already seemed overpriced. One reason for this buyback boom, commentators have suggested, was the desire on the part of executives to keep the share price stoked upwards – a desire not unrelated to thoughts of their own stock options. These moves have introduced significant additional gearing into most US companies, putting them at greater financial risk in a downturn. It seems likely that in the current downturn, some companies will sink under the weight of their extra debt.

## Moving on

The problems are therefore threefold: companies around the world are feeling forced by competitive pressures into offering pay schemes which are similar to those offered by US companies; the structures of those schemes has largely been dictated by factors other than shareholder value creation, such as accounting rules, tax and lack of shareowner oversight; and the result is that the schemes currently being introduced and many of those in use are not designed to link executive rewards to shareholder value creation in the most efficient way possible. In its most simple form, the question which arises is: is it right that US accounting and tax structures, which are not advantageous to those who are footing the bill, should dictate best practice in executive remuneration in Europe and Asia?

What is the way forward from this unsatisfactory position? Equity-linked remuneration can be a tremendous tool for incentivising executives to create shareholder value. But most structures seem likely to reward executives no matter what. Stiff performance conditions (ones that are directly linked to the aims and strategy of the business rather than the generic ones which are becoming the norm in the UK), preferably explicitly linked to some shareholder value measure such as total shareholder return, should become standard. For the US accounting and tax regimes to be driving the world in a direction which wastes shareholder value is absurd. Fit cats perform better if they have performance hurdles to aim for and which they have to stretch to reach. If accounting and tax rules in the US and elsewhere need to be changed for this to happen, then that needs to be done rather than let bureaucratic rules continue to interfere with the creation of shareholder value.

There could also be a move away from options. Again, this is difficult in the US at the moment because of accounting and tax rules. Nevertheless, there are signs that option schemes are not efficient at linking executive pay to shareholder value. While the technology boom was an extreme case, it demonstrates the problems well. The tremendous sums of money made by many managers through exercising options in the boom had little to do with their own qualities as managers: their sector as a whole was in favour and their performance as managers was irrelevant. To an extent, they were simply in the right place at the right time. That money was lost to shareholders, and many US managers are now enjoying the benefit of option repricing. Thus, the managers benefited from the upside of the extreme valuations – which had little to do with their personal performance – and yet are protected from the downside of the share price collapses. None of this aligns their pay with the shareholder value that they themselves have created. Relative performance measurements against the rest of the sector would provide better measures of the actual performance of those managers.

In addition, companies should introduce shareholding requirements, not just steep ones for board members (of several multiples of salary), but as far down the organisation as possible – certainly as far down as equity-linked incentives are on offer. Where executives are themselves shareholders, they will clearly be more attentive to shareholder value creation and destruction. These three steps will not by themselves turn the current problems around, but they should begin to create a system whereby executives are much more clearly driven to create shareholder value, and will not receive generous pay when shareholder value has been destroyed. That should begin to turn around the situation of share-holder suspicion and concern, something which is becoming more pervasive and is eating away at what should be the positive relationships between shareowners and the managers that run their companies.

# The value of non-executive directors and why they should be paid more     B15.16

*The following article was written Michelle Edkins, Corporate Governance Director at Hermes ([tel: +44 (0)20 7702 0888; fax: +44 (0)20 7680 2477); e-mail: M.edkins@hermes.co.uk; www.hermes.co.uk and www.hermes.co.uk/corporate-governance. More information on Hermes can be found in* **B6.11** HERMES ON AUDITOR INDEPENDENCE.

## Value drivers: paying a fair price for non-executive directors

It has been said that economists are people who know the price of everything and the value of nothing. The same could perhaps be rephrased and applied to those of us who monitor directors' pay from outside the boardroom: we can easily assess the price paid for directors but not the value they create. This is even more true of the non-executive directors (NEDs) on the board, who are arguably the foundation stone of the self-regulatory corporate governance practised in the UK, because they operate largely out of the limelight.

When NEDs were first mooted as being the key to good corporate governance and should therefore be a significant presence on the board Sir Tiny Rowland famously said that NEDs were little more than baubles on a Christmas tree. And his view was probably quite widely held at that time. Perhaps Sir Tiny's view was informed by the type of NED Agatha Christie wrote about:

> '(Coote) got me in as a director of something or other. Very good business for me –nothing to do except go down to the City once or twice a year to one of those hotel places – Cannon Street or Liverpool Street – and sit around a table where they have some very nice new blotting paper.

Then Coote or some clever Johnny makes a speech simply bristling with figures, but fortunately you needn't listen to it – and I can tell you, you often get a jolly good lunch out of it '

But things have moved on and the contribution that NEDs make to the work of the board is recognised, anecdotally at least. Although the monitoring role still exists, the involvement of NEDs in 'issues of strategy, performance, resources, including key appointments, and standards of conduct', to quote the Cadbury Report, has increased considerably. Correspondingly, the type of person sought now for NED roles is not a 'friend of Coote' but someone who is most likely a senior executive director at another quoted plc, or has been recently and has moved to working part-time on a portfolio of interests.

Such a person is already going to have considerable demands on his or her time. Add to this legal liability, the fact that it can easily take a day or more to prepare properly for a board meeting, particularly for the chairmen of the board sub-committees on audit, remuneration and nomination, visits to production sites or subsidiaries, the potential for criticism in the press, and needing the capacity immediately to focus 100 per cent on any extraordinary developments such as a takeover bid, it's hardly surprising that recruitment consultants report difficulties in finding candidates. Indeed, we often hear from very suitable candidates that they would far rather act as freelance consultants than NEDs. And they would be better remunerated: average NED fees per day at large companies are approximately £2,000, at smaller companies approximately £1,000 (*The Independent Chairman and Non Executive Director Survey 2001* [The Top Pay Research Group]). Not many senior consultants would take on assignments at that rate.

Another obstacle seems to be that NEDs are not good at pricing themselves. A basic economic premise is that when the price is right demand and supply will be equal. But we have heard from recruitment consultants that NEDs who have turned down an offer on the grounds of fee levels often will not specify the fee for which they would join a board. An explanation for this reticence to name their price could be that people at this level do not necessarily work for the money. But equally, everybody wants to feel valued and remuneration is often a proxy (especially in terms of public recognition and comparability) for the value placed on the individual's contribution or worth.

There are concerns that the fees paid to NEDs are generally too low as, without a sufficient pool of suitably talented people to join boards in a non-executive capacity the UK system of corporate governance will flounder. Perhaps surprisingly, the author is therefore in favour of higher fees being paid to NEDs. The public perception of institutional investors active in corporate governance as foes of high pay is erroneous. Hermes has always maintained that it is not the amount *per se* that is the issue but the link to long term shareholder value creation.

So how can we deepen the pool of prospective NEDs? Arguably by increasing the fees offered to reflect the greater time commitment and increased responsibility involved and to reward NEDs for their contribution to the long-term performance of the company. For NEDs probably the best way of achieving this goal is to grant them shares in addition to a cash fee. In effect, this is the same as directors being paid more cash and then using it to buy shares in the market each year.

Why shares and not share options? After all, options are commonly used for executive directors here and for all directors in the US.

Stock options are a contingency payment and, in Hermes' view, align the interests of the NEDs with the executives rather than with shareholders. Holding an option is very different to holding a share. Put crudely, the holder of a share is a part-owner of the company, the holder of an option is taking a punt that the company's share price will appreciate. Shares will have a value, unless the company folds, while an option is a one-way bet. When options are 'in the money', i.e. when the share price is higher than it was when the option was granted, directors will be rewarded. When options are out of the money directors have lost nothing but a paper profit, and in our experience, frequently receive further grants of options to 'compensate' them on the grounds that the outstanding options are not motivating. However, shareholders are not in the same fortunate position – when the share price goes below the price that we paid we have quite simply made a loss. No-one is willing to compensate us for the drop in value of our holding.

It is widely accepted that the point of stock-based incentive plans is to align the interests of shareholders and directors. The most obvious way to get directors to think like shareholders is for them to be shareholders. Intuitively, it comes down to that old adage of putting your money where your mouth is. But there are also a number of academic papers that make a connection between NEDs (or outside directors, as they're known in the US) holding a significant personal stake in the company and that company's performance. One in particular, 'Outside Directors with a Stake: the Linchpin in Improving Governance' by Donald Hambrick and Eric Jackson of the Columbia University Graduate School of Business, puts the case succinctly. It compares 40 'star' companies in their fields with 40 'laggards' over the ten years from 1987–96 and finds director stakes to be strikingly different in the two groups. Outside directors of the 'star' companies held as much as five times the number of shares as those of the 'laggards'.

As one outside director interviewed for the study observed:

> 'I'm convinced that having a significant financial stake in the company affects the alertness and behaviour of directors. I've seen it in others, and I've seen it in myself. You seek more information, you spend more time with the information, you ask more questions, you probe much more. And, best of all, the CEO knows you're super-interested, and so he does a better job too. .

> 'I've been on several boards. I've always held small, token amounts. But now I'm on a board where the CEO encouraged us to buy and hold

significant shares. I'm in for about half a million dollars, and I can tell you I'm a heck of a lot more attentive to this company than I have been to the others. If this company faces a challenge, I lose sleep at night – which is what you want from your directors. '

This highlights a number of issues for UK companies and directors. First, how much is significant? Clearly, half a million dollars is, but it is also probably a little unrealistic in the UK context. The Colombia study defined significant in the context of the individual's personal financial position rather than in terms of issued capital of the company. Hermes believes, and has long advocated, that all directors should have a shareholding in the company to the value of approximately one year's emoluments. This seems to us both a realistically achievable and significant level of share ownership.

Secondly, when should such a holding be acquired? Some argue that it should be from the day of appointment. But we believe it should be built over time. Requiring NEDs to buy a significant holding before joining the board would potentially exclude suitable candidates. And as we've already noted, those who are willing and able to take up NED posts seem to be scarce enough as it is.

Thirdly, should such shareholdings be mandatory or merely actively encouraged? It would be contrary to the best practice approach taken in the UK to compel directors to hold shares. But a number of larger UK companies are making retention of shares a condition of participation by executives in their share-based incentive schemes.

Similarly, we believe boards should use 'moralsuasion' to set a precedent for NEDs to hold shares. Clearly, if a share grant were made in lieu of cash fees this would help NEDs to build their stake. NEDs who choose not to take shares and who do not have a sizeable shareholding should expect to be asked by shareholders to explain and justify their reluctance to be shareholders themselves.

And ultimately, that is where the buck stops. It is for shareholders to monitor the executive directors and to hold them accountable for their actions and the resultant long-term impact on company performance. When directors, both executive and non-executive, are also shareholders the accountability is internal as well as external.

NEDs are on the whole doing a fine job for shareholders. Paying them partly in shares will recognise this contribution in a way that both aligns their interests with ours and makes a direct connection between their contribution and the long-term performance of the company.

# The Remuneration Committee

*This chapter has been compiled by Cliff Weight of Independent Remuneration Solutions.*

## Terms of reference

The main board will usually delegate to the remuneration committee authority with regard to the remuneration of the executive directors, the chairman and usually some senior executives. The remuneration committee will propose its terms of reference which will be approved by the board. These terms of reference will be summarised in the annual report to shareholders.

The Higgs Report suggestions for good practice, which were published by the FRC along with the revised Combined Code in July 2003, include the following.

### 'Summary of the principal duties of the remuneration committee

The Code provides that the remuneration committee should consist exclusively of independent non-executive directors and should comprise at least three or, in the case of smaller companies[1], two such directors.

### Duties

The committee should:

- determine and agree with the board the framework or broad policy for the remuneration of the chief executive, the chairman of the company and such other members of the executive management as it is designated to consider[2]. At a minimum, the committee should have delegated responsibility for setting remuneration for all executive directors, the chairman and, to maintain and assure their independence, the company secretary. The remuneration of non-executive directors shall be a matter for the chairman and executive members of the board. No director or manager should be involved in any decisions as to their own remuneration;

- determine targets for any performance-related pay schemes operated by the company;

- determine the policy for and scope of pension arrangements for each executive director;

- ensure that contractual terms on termination, and any payments made, are fair to the individual and the company, that failure is not rewarded and that the duty to mitigate loss is fully recognised[3];

- within the terms of the agreed policy, determine the total individual remuneration package of each executive director including, where appropriate, bonuses, incentive payments and share options;

- in determining such packages and arrangements, give due regard to the contents of the Code as well as the UK Listing Authority's Listing Rules and associated guidance;

- be aware of and advise on any major changes in employee benefit structures throughout the company or group;

- agree the policy for authorising claims for expenses from the chief executive and chairman;

- ensure that provisions regarding disclosure of remuneration, including pensions, as set out in the Directors' Remuneration Report Regulations 2002 and the Code, are fulfilled;

- be exclusively responsible for establishing the selection criteria, selecting, appointing and setting the terms of reference for any remuneration consultants who advise the committee;

- report the frequency of, and attendance by members at, Remuneration Committee meetings in the annual reports; and

- make available the committee's terms of reference. These should set out the committee's delegated responsibilities and be reviewed and, where necessary, updated annually.

This guidance has been compiled with the assistance of ICSA who have kindly agreed to produce updated guidance on their website www.icsa.org.uk in the future.'

# The ICSA guidance                                                        B16.2

The ICSA have developed draft terms of reference for the remuneration committee and these are reproduced below.

### Terms of reference – remuneration committee

Following the review of the Higgs proposals[4] the Financial Reporting Council revised Combined Code in July 2003. This Guidance Note advises on best practice in light of the recommendations contained in the Higgs Review and has been redrafted using the provisions in the suggested code.

The Combined Code states as one of its principles that:

'Companies should establish a formal and transparent procedure for developing policy on executive remuneration and for fixing the remuneration packages of individual directors. No director should be involved in deciding his or her own remuneration.'[5]

As with most aspects of corporate governance, the above stated principle makes it clear that, not only should companies go through a formal process of considering executive remuneration, but also they must be seen to be doing so in a fair and thorough manner. It is, therefore, essential that the remuneration committee is properly constituted with a clear remit and identified authority.

The Combined Code recommends that the remuneration committee should consist of at least three independent[6] non-executive directors; larger companies may wish to increase the number. The chairman should not be a member of the committee but may be asked, as the Chief Executive may, to attend on occasion to assist in the discussions.

Although not a provision in the code, the Higgs Review, states as good practice, in its Non-Code Recommendations, that the company secretary (or their nominee) should act as secretary to the committee. It is the company secretary's responsibility to ensure that the board and its committees are properly constituted and advised. There also needs to be a clear co-ordination between the main board and the various committees where the company secretary would normally act as a valued intermediary.

The frequency with which the committee needs to meet will vary considerably from company to company and will no doubt change from time to time. It is, however, clear that it must meet at least once each year prior or close to the year-end; its purpose at this meeting should be to prepare the remuneration report which the Combined Code and now the Directors' Remuneration Report Regulations require to be submitted to shareholders with or as part of the company's Annual Report. The Remuneration Report must be put to the share-holders for approval at the AGM.[7]

The reporting requirements suggested by Higgs and expanded on in Schedule B to the Combined Code, mean that the following has to be disclosed by the board each year within the Annual Report.

- The chairman and members of the committee need to be identified.

- The terms of reference need to be explained, to an extent that the role and authority is clearly demonstrated.

- The number of committee meetings and attendance level by members.

- The company's policy with regard to both executive and non-executive pay.

- The information required under Schedule B and the Directors' Remuneration Report Regulations 2002.

The list of duties we have proposed are those contained within the Summary of Principle Duties of the Remuneration Committee which ICSA helped compile for the Higgs Review and which we believe all remuneration Committees should consider. Some companies may wish to add to this list and some smaller companies may need to modify it in other ways. The chairman of the committee should attend the Annual General Meeting (AGM) and be prepared to respond to any questions which may be raised by shareholders on the committee's report or other matters within the committee's area of responsibility.

These recommendations and explanations clearly show the need for there to be a guiding document and the provisions of the Combined Code also advocate terms of reference for a remuneration committee. This has led the ICSA to produce this Guidance Note proposing model terms of reference for a remuneration committee. The document draws on the experience of senior company secretaries and best practice as carried out in some of the country's leading companies.

### Terms of reference of remuneration committee

References to 'the committee' shall mean the remuneration committee.

References to 'the board' shall mean the full board of directors.

The square brackets contain recommendations which are in line with best practice but which may need to be changed to suit the circumstances of the particular organisation.

1. **Membership**

    1.1 The committee shall comprise of at least [3] members, each of whom shall be appointed by the board.

    1.2 All members of the committee shall be non-executive directors who are independent of management and free from any business or other relationship which could interfere with the exercise of their independent judgement.

    1.3 The board should appoint the committee chairman and determine the period for which they shall hold office. The chairman of the company shall not be eligible to be appointed as chairman of the committee.

    1.4 Care should be taken to minimise the risk of any conflict of interest that might be seen to give rise to an unacceptable influence. (It is recommended that, where possible, the chairman and members of the committee should be rotated on a regular basis.) No member of the committee shall also be a member of both the audit and nomination committee.[8]

2. **Secretary**

    2.1 The company secretary or their nominee shall act as the secretary of the committee.

3. **Quorum**

    3.1 The quorum necessary for the transaction of business shall be [2]. A duly convened meeting of the committee at which a quorum is present shall be competent to exercise all or any of the authorities, powers and discretions vested in or exercisable by the committee.

## 4.  Meetings

4.1  The committee shall meet [not less than once a year][quarterly on the first Wednesday in each of January, April, July and October] and at such other times as the chairman of the committee shall require.[9]

## 5.  Notice of meetings

5.1  Meetings of the committee shall be summoned by the secretary of the committee at the request of any member thereof.

5.2  Unless otherwise agreed, Notice of each meeting confirming the venue, time and date together with an agenda of items to be discussed, shall be forwarded to each member of the committee, any other person required to attend and all other non-executive directors, no fewer than [5] working days prior to the date of the meeting.

5.3  The chief executive [and personnel director] shall have the right to address any meeting of the committee; others may be called upon or shall able to speak by prior arrangement with the chairman of the committee.

## 6.  Minutes of meetings

6.1  The secretary shall minute the proceedings and resolutions of all committee meetings, including the names of those present and in attendance.

6.2  Minutes of committee meetings shall be circulated to all members of the committee and to all members of the board.

## 7.  Annual General Meeting

7.1  The chairman of the committee shall attend the annual general meeting prepared to respond to any shareholder questions on the committee's activities.

## 8.  Duties

The committee shall:

8.1  Determine and agree with the board the framework or broad policy for the remuneration of the chief executive, the chairman of the company and such other members of the executive management as it is designated to consider[10]. The remuneration of non-executive directors shall be a matter for the executive members of the board. No director or manager shall be involved in any decisions as to his or her own remuneration. In order to assure his independence, the committee will also review and recommend to the board the remuneration of the company secretary;

8.2  In determining such policy, take into account all factors which it deems necessary. The objective of such policy shall be to ensure that members of the executive management of the company are provided with appropriate incentives to encourage enhanced performance and are, in a fair and responsible manner, rewarded for their individual contributions to the success of the company. It shall also liase with the nomination committee to ensure that the remuneration of newly appointed executives is within the company's overall policy;[11]

8.3 Determine targets for any performance related pay schemes operated by the company and asking the board, when appropriate, to seek shareholder approval for any long term incentive arrangements;[12]

8.4 Within the terms of the agreed policy, determine the total individual remuneration package of each executive director including, where appropriate, bonuses, incentive payments and share options;

8.5 Determine the policy for and scope of pension arrangements, service agreements for the executive director, termination payments and compensation commitments;

8.6 In determining such packages and arrangements, give due regard to the comments and recommendations of the Combined Code[13] as well as the UK Listing Authority's Listing Rules and associated guidance;

8.7 Review competitor companies but insure that automatic increases are not implemented, thereby avoiding the "ratchet" effect;

8.8 Be aware of and oversee any major changes in employee benefit structures throughout the company or group;

8.9 Vet and authorise the reimbursement of any claims for expenses from the chief executive and chairman of the company;[14]

8.10 Ensure that provisions regarding disclosure of remuneration including pensions, as listed in the Directors' Remuneration Report Regulations 2002, are fulfilled; and

8.11 Produce an annual report of the committee's remuneration policy.

## 9. Authority

9.1 The committee is authorised by the board to seek any information it requires from any employee of the company in order to perform its duties.

9.2 In connection with its duties the committee is required by the board to select, set the terms of reference and appoint remuneration consultants, at the company's expense.

# US practice regarding CEO pay and performance    B16.3

The terms of reference of US Compensation Committee tend to be similar to those of UK companies, with the notable exception that in the US the requirements regarding the CEO are usually explicit and imply an assessment of performance, which should link into the CEO compensation. The New York Stock Exchange's new regulations (August 2003) regarding compensation committees are as follows.

**Require listed companies to have a compensation committee composed entirely of independent directors.**

We believe it is essential that each listed company have a compensation committee, and that the committee's membership be confined to independent directors.

The compensation committee must have a written charter that addresses:

- the committee's purpose – which, at minimum, must be to discharge the board's responsibilities relating to compensation of the company's executives, and to produce an annual report on executive compensation for inclusion in the company's proxy statement, in accordance with applicable rules and regulations.

- the committee's duties and responsibilities – which, at minimum, must be to:

  o review and approve corporate goals and objectives relevant to CEO compensation, evaluate the CEO's performance in light of those goals and objectives, and set the CEO's compensation level based on this evaluation. In determining the long-term incentive component of CEO compensation, the committee should consider the company's performance and relative shareholder return, the value of similar incentive awards to CEOs at comparable companies, and the awards given to the listed company's CEO in past years.

  o make recommendations to the board with respect to incentive compensation plans and equity-based plans.

- an annual performance evaluation of the compensation committee.

We believe the compensation committee charter should also address the following items: committee member qualifications; committee member appointment and removal; committee structure and operations (including authority to delegate to subcommittees); and committee reporting to the board. Additionally, if a compensation consultant is to assist in the evaluation of director, CEO or senior executive compensation, the compensation committee charter should give that committee sole authority to retain and terminate the consulting firm, including sole authority to approve the firm's fees and other retention terms.

# Membership and skills

B16.4

The remuneration committee should be comprised entirely of independent directors.

The Higgs Report stated that the chairman, even if independent when appointed, should not be considered as independent and should not sit on the remuneration committee. The FRC revision to the Combined Code in July 2003 said that all members of the remuneration committee should be independent and that the chairman should be independent on appointment, but thereafter the test was not appropriate. Higgs also required the remuneration committee to set the pay of the chairman and the FRC confirmed this.

The chairman works closely with the CEO and is best placed to assess the CEO's performance, his current motivation and the risk he may be lured elsewhere and hence the remuneration required to retain the CEO's services and motivate him to achieve tough performance goals and high standards of performance. It is therefore vital that the chairman attends the remuneration committee, but withdraws when his own remuneration is discussed.

Similarly the CEO is best placed to provide input on the executives who report to him and he should also attend remuneration committee meetings, but withdraw when his own remuneration is discussed.

Committee members require considerable background knowledge and skills with regard to remuneration, including:

- statistics to interpret market data;

- business acumen regarding performance measures, including but not limited to accounting knowledge;

- financial theory to understand option valuation and risk;

- pensions and actuarial knowledge;

- tax, both personal and company tax that is pertinent to remuneration issues;

- trust law;

- employment law.

A good working knowledge of the above is essential in order to be able to participate in the remuneration committee debate. Expert skills are not needed if the remuneration committee has access to independent expert advice.

Members also require the ability to read and digest long complex reports.

# Advisers

B16.5

The company secretary or an external independent adviser should be the secretary of the remuneration committee. The HR director should never perform this role as he/she works for the CEO and is conflicted.

The chief executive and the chairman (if not a member of the committee) will usually attend remuneration committee meetings (in a non-voting capacity) and withdraw when their own pay is discussed. They provide valuable input to the committee on the performance of individuals, the risk of them leaving and how easily they could be replaced either internally through normal succession plans or by external recruitment.

The HR director and/or the remuneration and benefits director may be invited to remuneration committee meetings. Their input about remuneration elsewhere in the group is particularly valuable. They may also have considerable knowledge of the history of directors' remuneration and of practices in other companies. The HR director or remuneration and benefits director often will also be involved in preparing papers for the committee. They will reflect the views of the chief executive and the other executive directors. Few HR or remuneration and benefits directors are prepared to disagree with or disappoint their CEO. There will however be times when the remuneration committee wish to discuss items without internal management present.

External consultants are used to provide market data, commentary on trends, latest best practice, to design new incentive arrangements, both short and long-term and to provide legal, tax and accounting advice. Most of the large accountancy firms have executive compensation consulting arms. For them this is a natural extension of their work in tax, share schemes, HR and audit. Most of the large actuarial firms also have executive compensation consulting arms. In their case it is a natural extension of their work in pensions, benefits and HR consulting. There are also a small number of specialist executive remuneration firms.

The remuneration committee must disclose the names of their advisers, who appointed them and what other services they provide to the company.

The remuneration committee should appoint its own independent remuneration consultants. This is an essential pre-requisite for promoting transparency and accountability to shareholders regarding directors' remuneration. Shareholders and other interested parties will continue to be concerned if companies seek advice from consultants who are dependent on executive management for fees for other services to the company. The Enron debacle is only the latest and largest example of the conflict of interest when advisers are not independent.

There is always a danger that a remuneration committee is merely asked to rubber stamp management's proposals. At present, executive directors have huge internal resources and pay large fees to their management consultants to prepare and justify their case for more money, bigger bonuses, increased incentives and better benefits. The scales are not evenly balanced. Remuneration committees need to take the lead and appoint their own independent advisers who can comment objectively on management's proposals.

Consultants often call themselves *management* consultants, which in this case is all too often true. Almost all consultants predicate their business strategy on developing good relationships with executive directors and senior executives and then cross-selling their other consulting services. It is worth noting that the fees for other consulting services will generally dwarf the fees for remuneration committee consultancy.

# The remuneration setting process                    B16.6

Companies have boards of directors who delegate the remuneration setting process for directors and usually some senior executives to the remuneration committee, made up wholly of independent non-executive directors.

The chairman of the remuneration committee sets the agenda and dates of the meetings, having consulted with the secretary of the committee, the company chairman, CEO, HR director/remuneration and benefits director, and the committee's adviser. The committee chairman commissions research and position papers relevant to the agenda items. He briefs other committee members of any contentious issues for the next meeting and obtains their views.

The chief executive and the chairman (if not a member of the committee) will usually attend remuneration committee meetings (in a non-voting capacity) and withdraw when their own pay is discussed. They provide valuable input to the committee on the performance of individuals, the risk of them leaving and how easily they could be replaced either internally through normal succession plans or by external recruitment.

The HR director or remuneration and benefits director often will also attend the remuneration committee and/or be involved in preparing papers for the committee.

External consultants may also be used to provide data and advice across a range of remuneration issues.

Using all of this advice and assistance, the remuneration committee will set the remuneration strategy for the executive directors and senior executives. Typically this will include:

- selection of appropriate comparator group of companies;
- identification of desired pay market position and linkage to performance;
- mix of fixed and variable compensation;
- alignment to shareholders' interests.

Consultants perform another role in this process: they are aware of what is and is not acceptable to shareholders. Some consultants will talk to shareholders and their representatives on behalf of their clients, explain the new remuneration proposals and seek to persuade the shareholders that the new plans are acceptable. In some cases a negotiation ensues and a compromise deal is done. In some companies the chairman of the remuneration committee or the chairman will talk to the key shareholders.

Finally, the company will vote in general meeting on new long term incentive plans and the remuneration committee report. Some shareholders may vote against the appointment of individual directors because of remuneration issues.

# Survey data                                          **B16.7**

Independent Remuneration Solutions (IRS), in association with 3i, The Independent Directors Programme, surveyed the views of non-executive directors regarding fees, board practices and remuneration committees. The survey was conducted in November/December 2002. The results related to remuneration committees were as follows.

IRS asked some special questions on our data collection form to provide readers with an insight into aspects of independent directorship that they may find particularly interesting. The questions were aimed at directors who are chairmen or members of a remuneration committee. IRS received replies from 283 members of remuneration committees plus a further 25 who told us that in their companies, remuneration is not settled by a committee but by the chairman, the CEO or the board direct. These latter are predominantly private or venture capital backed companies who do not have to operate under quoted rules.

In each section of this survey IRS give the answers in terms of percentages as a different number of respondents answered the different sections of the survey and the most useful way to demonstrate the differentials weight of response seemed to be percentages based on the respondent level to each question.

The breakdown in terms of chairmanships, memberships and the number of remuneration committees on which they serve are as follows.

| Of how many committees are you the chairman? | |
|---|---|
| 1 | 40 |
| 2 | 16 |
| 3 | 9 |
| 4 | 3 |
| 5+ | 1 |
| or a member? | |
| 1 | 51 |
| 2 | 28 |
| 3 | 10 |
| 4 | 3 |
| 5+ | 1 |

In each section of the questionnaire IRS asked respondents how the committee handles the issue in the most effective remuneration committee and the least effective committee on which they sit. IRS thought this approach would provide the most interesting editorial for readers and indicate differences between effective remuneration committees compared to those judged to be less so.

The first question related to the critical issue of choosing a chairman. Attitudes are shown in the following table where on the most effective remuneration committees skill, knowledge and experience are seen as the most important criteria for the chairman whereas in the least effective committees it is simply the senior or longest serving non-executive or the 'Buggins turn' member who is likely to get the nod.

***How is the Chairman of the RemCo chosen?***

Most Effective RemCo          Least Effective RemCo

- Senior or longest serving non-executive
- Skill, knowledge or experience
- Chair other RemCos
- 'Buggins' turn
- Other

The second question related to the secretary to the remuneration committee. IRS think this is an area which will come under increasing scrutiny as the secretary of the committee clearly needs to be entirely independent and should probably not be expected to participate in the debate.

Current practice in this area is extremely mixed. IRS know several companies where a non-executive plays the role of committee secretary. This is obviously undesirable because they cannot concentrate upon being a contributor to the discussion. IRS think it is very important that the secretaries' of the committee are entirely independent and cannot be bullied by the executive directors, particularly the CEO, who do not sit on the committee. For this reason the company secretary probably needs to split his role in the sense that as a company secretary and secretary to the remuneration committee he is answerable to the board via the chairman while for his executive tasks, which may include insurance, personnel issues and running the pension scheme, he is answerable to the finance director or the CEO.

It is becoming increasingly apparent in some companies that this split responsibility is not working and the company secretary, who see themselves as a member of the executive team needs assistance to become a fully paid up member of the independent corporate governance operation. IRS are slightly surprised by the findings below as IRS would have expected that a higher percentage of committees would have the company secretary as their secretary.

*Who is the secretary to the RemCo?*

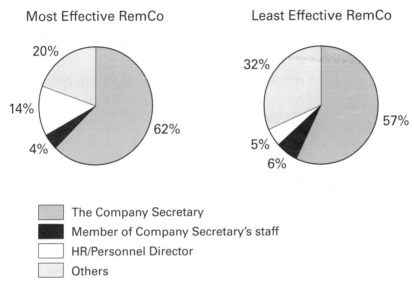

The situation between effective and less effective committees is not very dramatic as most independent directors are satisfied that the secretary of the committee is sufficiently independent. However, this is not so in 20% of less effective committees.

*Are you satisfied with the independence of the committee secretaries, who may see themselves as answering to the executive team rather than the RemCo?*

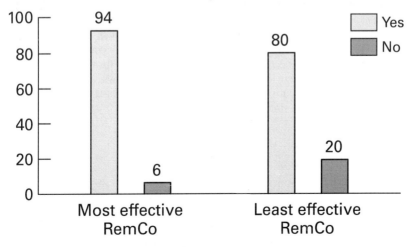

**B16.7** *Survey data*

On the same tack IRS asked whether or not remuneration committee papers are properly prepared for the chairman and members.

There is a very marked difference between effective and ineffective committees as on less effective committees it is quite clear that the papers are not properly presented which may be a reason for their underperformance. Looking at the overall figures, this is an area in which committee chairmen need to become more active in insisting their proper papers and briefing notes are prepared. A score of only 72% for most effective committees does not look adequate for such a crucial part of the committee's modus operandi.

*Are committee papers and outside consultants' reports properly prepared and on time?*

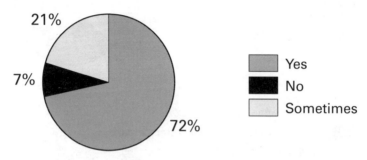

It has been obvious to all those involved in remuneration committees that the time commitment for members has been increasing significantly over the past three years.

IRS give below a breakdown of the time spent on the 283 directorships analysed in this appendix which shows that on average the chairman is spending 8–9 days a year on this responsibility and members between 4 and 5. The principal time driver is the number of committee meetings.

IRS have been suggesting for some time that the committee should have one meeting in which there are no specific items on the agenda, when members can discuss the strategic development of remuneration within the senior ranks of the company and possibly have a presentation from consultants on what's going on in the outside world. In our experience the two or three formal meetings each year are fully occupied in deciding on annual salary reviews, allocating options, the agreement of executive bonuses and other items that do not allow for a general strategic discussion.

| How many days per year do you spend on committee work? | | |
|---|---|---|
| **Formal meeting days** | **Chairman** | **Member** |
| 1 | 5 | 23 |
| 2 | 41 | 27 |
| 3 | 17 | 13 |
| 4 | 17 | 19 |
| 5+ | 20 | 18 |
| **Informal contact meetings/phone calls between members** | **Chairman** | **Member** |
| 1 | 16 | 40 |
| 2 | 33 | 22 |
| 3 | 18 | 14 |
| 4+ | 33 | 24 |
| **Preparing for meetings** | **Chairman** | **Member** |
| 1 | 36 | 50 |
| 2 | 31 | 35 |
| 3 | 13 | 7 |
| 4+ | 20 | 8 |

IRS were very interested to know for how long remuneration committee members were appointed. The table below gives the answers, IRS were slightly surprised to see such a high percentage with no fixed term appointment.

*For how many years are RemCo members appointed?*

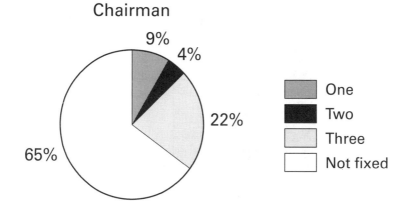

Chairman

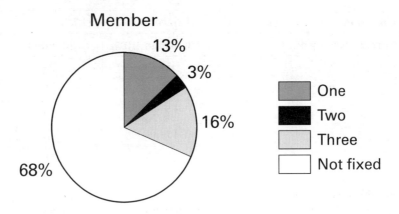

Member

*Do you feel this is the best approach?*

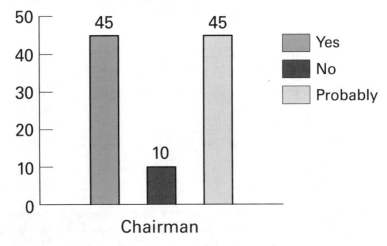

Chairman

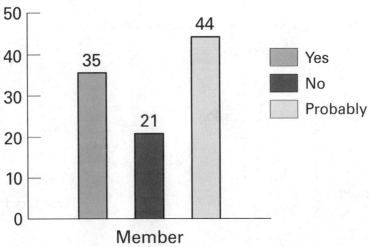

Member

There is general satisfaction with the terms of appointment under which members serve which is probably the best criteria for accepting that the current system is working well.

In the general survey IRS lump together all special committee fees received by independent directors whether they are for audit, remuneration, environmental, nominations or in the case of financial companies, the investment committee. Below IRS give information on remuneration committee fees. It is quite interesting that the majority of the respondents do not receive specific payment for either chairing or being a member of the remuneration committee. This is something IRS highlight in the main survey as committee fees are being wrapped up in a single independent director payment.

*Do you receive separate fees for chairing or being a member of the committee?*

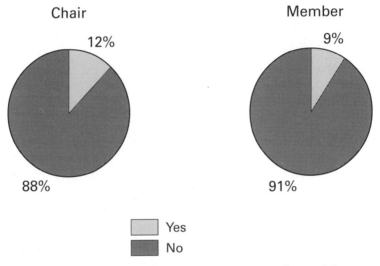

Larger companies are much more likely to pay separate fees and the research highlights the most popular fee for a remuneration committee chairman of £5,000 with between £2–£4,000 paid to members. Despite the increase in the workload there is general satisfaction with the fairness of this payment as 65% of the sample indicated that these levels were about right.

| Amount in £'000 | Chairman % | Member % |
|---|---|---|
| £1–2000 | 11 | 12 |
| £2–3000 | 12 | 38 |
| £3–4000 | | 38 |
| £5–6000 | 55 | 12 |
| £6–7000 | 11 | |
| more | 11 | |

| Is this amount: | % |
|---|---|
| Too little | 35 |
| About right | 65 |
| Or generous | 0 |

With the London Stock Exchange recommending that quoted companies should have three independent directors it is not so surprising that this is a most popular number. The size of the committee to some extent reflects the size of the company as very major groups are likely to have committees of five or six. IRS were slightly surprised to see the number of members on such committees who are not non-executive directors. This may indicate that some of the respondents have assumed that the CEO and maybe the personnel or finance directors who attend are actually members of the committee. Under corporate governance guidelines they cannot, of course, be full voting members and IRS suspect that this statistic slightly exaggerates the number of those who are not non-executives sitting on committees.

*How many directors are on the RemCo?*

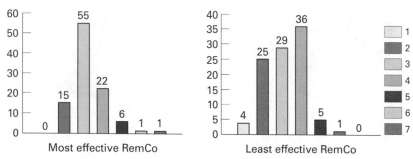

Most of the respondents feel that the makeup is approximately correct. A small percentage see the size of some less effective remuneration committees as one of their problems with 4% indicating they have too many members.

*Are they all independent or non-executive directors*

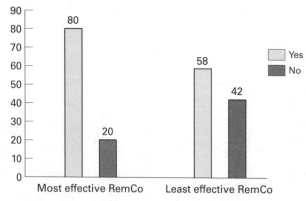

It is interesting that on the most effective remuneration committees 20% of the members are not independent directors with the number rising to 42% on less effective groups.

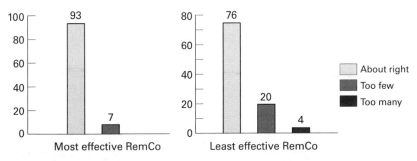

There has been intense interest over the last year in the training of independent directors. IRS highlight the issue as 93% of members of effective and 96% of less effective remuneration committees do not receive any training to help them undertake their duties.

|  | **Most effective RemCo** | **Least effective RemCo** |
|---|---|---|
| **Does the company offer training to RemCo members?** | | |
| Yes | 7 | 4 |
| No | 93 | 96 |
| **Do you think they would benefit if it were available?** | | |
| Yes | 27 | 34 |
| No | 32 | 30 |
| Maybe | 41 | 36 |

IRS all know there is a resistance from experienced executives who sit on other boards accepting that they might need some high level training for their ID responsibilities. This is reflected in the figures below which show about the same number of independent directors who feel they might benefit from further training as those that do not.

In most cases the committees seem to be happy with their size and composition. In IRS experience remuneration committee meetings are usually run on fairly tight timescales on a day where there are several other meetings to be slotted into the board schedule. This can lead to a less than full examination of all the issues. IRS can see that directors might feel that additional members would simply slow down the agenda. IRS do question whether the attitude shown by the respondents to this survey to training and committee membership is adequate in a situation where remuneration and particularly directors' remuneration is seen as a touchstone of good corporate governance. Perhaps the most interesting finding in the tables below is that a third of the most effective committees used more than one consultant.

*Does the RemCo use more than one consultant?*

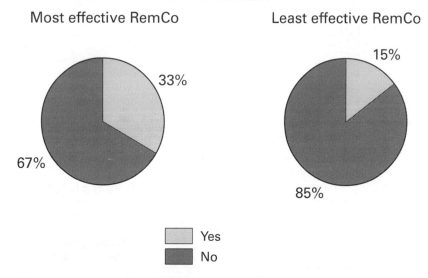

Most effective RemCo                    Least effective RemCo

33%

67%

15%

85%

Yes
No

IRS suspect that the second consultant may often be an option or a pension specialist, but there is no doubt that the use of two specialist consultants for main board directors' remuneration is an increasingly favoured option. Remuneration committee chairmen clearly want an alternative opinion on the increasingly complex issue of balancing the interest of shareholders and their executive cadre.

There is relatively little difference between the appointment procedures, length of service and re-appointment system for consultants of the most effective and the least effective remuneration committees.

| Independent consultants – What kind? | Most effective RemCo | Least effective RemCo |
|---|---|---|
| Use traditional consultants who have serviced the company for years | 17 | 19 |
| Use consultants linked to accountants, actuaries, solicitors or other professional adviser | 10 | 12 |
| Recommended consultants by committee members | 40 | 32 |
| Independent consultants not associated with other professional advisers | 33 | 37 |

Perhaps the fact that the most effective committees use the same consultant for three years or more shows a consistency of remuneration strategy that is likely to bring benefits to the shareholders.

| | Most effective RemCo | Least effective RemCo |
|---|---|---|
| Consider formally appointing new consultants every: | | |
| 1 year | 10 | 33 |
| 2 years | 20 | 33 |
| 3 years | 70 | 34 |

In contrast, a third of consultants servicing less effective committees only last a year, suggesting there is a fair amount of dissention between the consultants and members or between the members of the committee itself.

| | Most effective RemCo | Least effective RemCo |
|---|---|---|
| If appointing new consultants we would carry out a 'beauty parade' | | |
| Yes | 75 | 65 |
| No | 25 | 35 |
| We take out references with consultants current clients | | |
| Yes | 66 | 52 |
| No | 33 | 48 |

One of the areas in which there is a significant difference between most and least effective committees is the dependency of the committee on the consultant's advice. The figures for the most effective committee, showing 13% very dependent and 83%, as you would expect, quite dependent reflecting the experience and skill of the members of the committee who ultimately determine the director's remuneration package. The comparator figures for least effective committees are quite interesting as they show both excessive dependence at 28% with 19% deriving very little benefit from outside advice.

**B16.7**   *Survey data*

*How dependent is the committee on consultants' advice?*

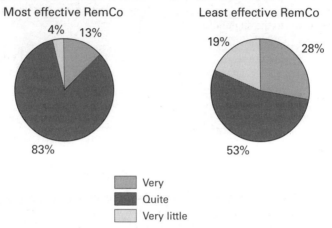

Most effective RemCo

4%   13%

83%

Least effective RemCo

19%   28%

53%

Very
Quite
Very little

The percentages for the length of appointment and the dependency on the consultant's report suggests that in some less effective committees outside consultants are used as a necessary evil as their input is not seen as particularly relevant to what may be entrenched attitudes.

In terms of challenging consultants' reports, a question never asked before, the figures are extremely interesting The most effective remuneration committee pattern with 21% often challenged, 23% seldom challenged and 56% never challenged probably indicates that consultants have been fully briefed so that their report does cover the ground required. On the other hand, when the percentage of reports that are never challenged goes to 80% I think it is fair to suggest that the remuneration committee does not feel confident to debate any of these suggestions with the consultants or, alternatively, that they plan to ignore the report so any challenge is pointless.

*How often have you seen consultants' reports challenged and significantly changed for the better by the RemCo's input?*

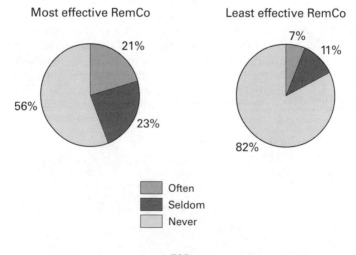

Most effective RemCo

21%

56%

23%

Least effective RemCo

7%   11%

82%

Often
Seldom
Never

The final question assesses the relationship between consultants and executive directors and whether this could lead to less than fully objective reports has not been posed in any other survey. The fact that 47% of respondents think that there is or may be too close a relationship is concerning when for the past three years remuneration committees has been urged to appoint consultants who are totally independent of the executive team.

***Do you feel consultants are often too close to executive directors to be able to give really objective independent advice?***

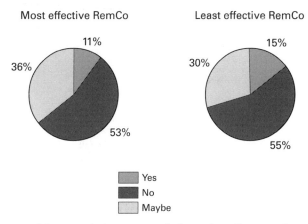

Most effective RemCo          Least effective RemCo

There was surprising unanimity amongst independent directors that consultants should not be named in the remuneration committee's report. Protecting anonymity obviously reduces the chance that individual shareholders may try and discuss issues with the consultants direct or call for copies of their report. On the other hand, it does allow consultants whose advice shows a consistent pattern which may not be seen as acceptable to institutions to disguise the fact that they are advising a high proportion of companies where remuneration is a very contentious issue.

***Should companies name their remuneration consultant(s)?***

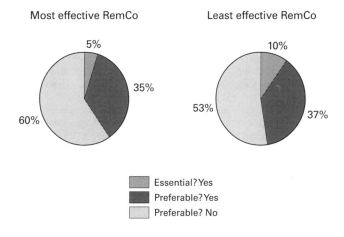

Most effective RemCo          Least effective RemCo

Finally, who writes the remuneration committee report? IRS offer the results without comment but would suggest that the full committee should always approve the draft. This only seems to happen in 50% of companies.

| | Most effective RemCo (%) | Least effective RemCo (%) |
|---|---|---|
| Who writes the Remuneration Committee's report in the annual accounts? | | |
| Committee Chairman | 40 | 36 |
| Chief Executive | 8 | 6 |
| HR Director | 7 | 8 |
| Committee Secretary or other | 45 | 50 |
| Is it approved by: | | |
| Committee Chairman? | 43 | 50 |
| Whole committee? | 57 | 50 |

**Summing up**

The special questions have highlighted three issues that are very much in the news.

1. The choice of remuneration committee chairman is critical if the committee is going to be fully effective.

2. There is some reluctance among remuneration committee members, most of whom will be widely experienced, to accept that training or maybe additional members of the committee would increase its competence.

3. It is of some concern that a high percentage of remuneration committee members feel that their consultants, who are meant to be completely independent are or could be too close to the executive team.

**Notes**
1. A smaller company is one that is below the FTSE 350 throughout the year immediately prior to the reporting year .
2. Some companies require the remuneration committee to consider the packages of all executives at or above a specified level such as those reporting to a main board director whilst others require the committee to deal with all packages above a certain figure.
3. Remuneration committees should consider reviewing and agreeing a standard form of contract for their executive directors, and ensuring that new appointees are offered and accept terms within the previously agreed level.
4. Review of the role and effectiveness of non-executive directors, published January 2003.
5. Principles of Good Governance and Code of Best Practice, (The Combined Code), B.2
6. An Independent non-executive director, is one that satisfies Combined Code Provision A.3.4

7. The *Directors' Remuneration Report Regulations 2002 (SI 2002/1986)*.

8. It is recognised that small companies who do not have sufficient NED's may not always be able to comply with this rule. Although not stated in the Code, ICSA consider it best practice that no member of the nomination committee be a member of the remuneration committee, so that no conflict of interest can arise following a new appointment.

9. The frequency and timing of meetings will differ according to the needs of the company. Meetings should be organised so that attendance is maximised (eg by time-tabling them to coincide with board meetings).

10. Some companies require the remuneration committee to consider the packages of all executives at or above a specified level such as those reporting to a main board director whilst others require the committee to deal with all packages above a certain figure.

11. Combined Code Provision B.1.10 specifically refers to termination provisions within a service contract, but the Higgs Review refers to an obligation to consider that all incentives are properly structured.

12. A long term incentive is defined as an arrangement, whereby a payment either in shares or in cash, is paid to an executive at least two years after he was invited into the scheme and is not based on that year's performance.

13. In particular Schedule A of the Combined Code which details Provisions on the design of performance-related remuneration.

14. It is suggested that the more common arrangement is for the chairman to vet and authorise the chief executive's expenses and for the chairman of the remuneration committee to vet and authorise the company chairman's claim. Whilst this may be more appropriate where remuneration committees do not meet that frequently we believe that the recommended provision is preferable.

# The Total Remuneration Package

*This chapter has been compiled by Cliff Weight of Independent Remuneration Solutions.*

## A short history of remuneration in the UK  B17.1

History helps us to understand why we have got to where we are today and how we got there. It also helps in making informed decisions for the future.

### 1970s  B17.2

The 1970s are remembered for the three day week, power cuts, 83% rate of income tax and a stock market low of 146 for the FT30 Index and 62 for the All Share. There was a banking crisis and the Chancellor had to ask the International Monetary Fund for a loan. Unions were strong and managers' jobs were difficult. It was also a time of pay freezes, applying to all employees including directors. High inflation and stock losses destroyed profits and bonus plans did not pay out. The highest rate of tax of 83% was a big disincentive, but only applied to the top slice of income. Below that there were a series of lower rates which applied to different layers of income. Creative minds spent their time devising ways to avoid tax rather than improve business performance. Consequently pension plans were extremely popular, as executives could expect a lower rate of taxation after they retired. There was brief flurry of interest in options under Ted Heath's Government between 1970 and 1974, but for most of the decade the tax environment was not favourable. Some company perks were not taxed as income, so some companies went to great lengths to provide employee benefits, eg free suits. Performance-related pay dropped off the agenda.

The Conservatives, under Margaret Thatcher, were elected in 1979 and this was the start of change.

### 1980s  B17.3

The 1980s saw the Thatcher revolution, which transformed the business landscape. Union power was curtailed. Uncompetitive practices were changed. Unemployment rose to 3 million. Much of UK manufacturing moved overseas, where products could be made cheaper and often better. The stock market took off, with the All Share rising to 1238 on 16 July 1987, four and a half times its level on 4 May 1979 when Margaret Thatcher took power and some 20 times its 1974 low of 62.

The top rate of tax was reduced to 60%. Incentive plans to motivate top management were introduced. Salary differentials between directors and employees which had shrunk in the 1960s and 1970s widened again.

The biggest change came in 1984 with the removal of income tax on share options and gains subject to capital gains tax at the then highest rate of 30%. This was a huge tax bias in favour of share options over cash remuneration. A £100 gain from share options netted the executive £70, whereas £100 of cash pay would deliver only £40 net of tax. The same £100 share option gain would cost shareholders £100 through dilution (but have no profit impact and result in a cash inflow equal to the exercise price), whereas the £100 cash would cost the company £110, as NIC would be payable on cash but not on share options. As the Bill went through Parliament, one Labour MP, who saw the potential bonanza, proposed a limit on the amount of share options that could be awarded. This limit was set at four times remuneration face value of options, ie number of shares under option times the exercise price, which would be the market price at the date of grant. As all too frequently happens when politicians intervene, things did not go as planned. Companies and their executives realised that:

- if these new options were such a good thing that there had to be a limit on the number they could have, then they had to have a scheme as soon as possible; and

- if there was a limit then they better fill their boots with them quickly, so most companies granted the maximum at the earliest opportunity.

98% of FT100 companies adopted executive share option plans within one year of Royal Assent to the *Finance Act 1984*.

There were other factors which conspired against share options. To receive the favourable capital gains tax treatment options could not be exercised until three years after the date of grant and not until three years after the previous grant. This meant that executives tended to exercise as soon as the three years were up and then expected the company to grant them another set of options. This problem, like the four x remuneration limit, could have been avoided by better design.

However the 1980s was a rampant bull market. Many directors and executives had large gains (some had realised them, whilst for others they were only on paper). In 1987 the stock market crashed and 30% of the value was wiped off stocks in a few days in October. Directors and executives who had exercised and sold their shares had made considerable sums. Those who had not were most unhappy. Many people started to say that options were a lottery.

In 1988 income tax was reduced to 40% and capital gains tax increased to 40%. So the huge tax bias in favour of share options largely evaporated – there still remained a small bias as options were still treated as a benefit and not subject to national insurance.

The Finance Act 1988 introduced a limit on the amount of pension that could be provided through an approved scheme. The limit for the final pensionable salary was set at £60,000, and would increase with RPI. In 2003 the limit is now £97,600. Indexing the limit in line with RPI meant that more and more people would be affected over time. Most companies reacted by pretending the new law did not exist, ie they gave executives subject to the cap the same benefits as those who were not. Some did this via a promise, by what came to be known as an Unfunded Unapproved Retirement Benefit Scheme (UURBS). Others set money aside to guarantee the benefit using Funded Unapproved Retirement Benefit Scheme (FURBS). Although the pension cap was not a large problem initially, it was going to slowly and inevitably become a much bigger one in the future.

Companies became more global. Many UK companies made acquisitions in the US. US pay levels, which were much higher than the UK, began to be cited as justification for increases in UK remuneration. Dick Giordano, an American, was appointed CEO of BOC, with a US style package and this set a new level for other UK plcs to aspire to.

The ABI published their first set of guidance on remuneration but this was limited to share schemes and mainly focussed on dilution. The dilution limit for executive share options set by the ABI was 5% over 10 years. This meant that the maximum a prudent company would grant was an average of 0.5% a year.

To judge from the press at the time, one would have thought UK pay was surging ahead. However there were three factors which held back executive directors' remuneration:

- the conservatism of non-executive directors;

- the limit on executive share options of 4 x remuneration;

- the dilution limit for executive share options set by the ABI and NAPF of 5% over 10 years.

# 1990s                                                             B17.4

The FTSE 100 more than tripled, from 2,000 to almost 7,000. The 14 year bull market led to enormous wealth creation. This was particularly the case in the United States where executive compensation reached levels which many commentators called obscene. Wall Street compensation levels reflected profits and both were high. These levels of expectation flowed into most other areas of business. US corporations who had always been keen on granting share options now fell in love with them. S&P data show that 79% of the increase in median CEO compensation from 1992 to 2000 was due to growth in long term incentives, primarily stock options. In 1992 options were 27% of median CEO compensation, whereas by 2000 options were 60% of median CEO compensation. A proposal to account for stock options in the profit and loss account was strongly resisted and the eventual compromise was that the cost of options had to be shown in a footnote to the accounts. Leading companies were granting options over as much as 2% or even 3% of their shares each year. Appointing a good CEO led to a huge surge in the share price and a poor choice could negatively impact the share price. Thus CEOs had huge leverage when asking for higher compensation. The US passed a law, S162, intending to curtail pay – any pay above $1 million, unless it was performance-elated, was non-deductable for tax. As often happens when Governments intervene in executive pay, there were unexpected consequences. $1 million salary became the norm for a CEO of a large US company and there was a huge surge in the options awarded.

Globalisation of business continued, with more pressure to increase UK levels to be competitive with the US. Few UK executives went to the US to head up US corporations. However a number of UK FTSE plcs recruited US and other nationals to lead their companies and they expected remuneration commensurate with what they would receive in their home country. This increased the expectations of the UK nationals.

Directors were caricatured as 'fat cats' smoking cigars and licking the cream. There was particular concern about newly privatised industries. These were still regulated and therefore the future share price was dependent on a beneficial regime operated by the regulator. There were however gross inefficiencies in the utilities and with the benefit of hindsight they were sold too cheaply. Share options were granted at privatisation. The rationale was that executive directors and senior managers now had to think and act like the private sector and it was believed that options would help this. Salaries were increased as executives from the private sector were recruited and it was felt divisive if existing employees were not paid at a similar level. Annual bonus plans were introduced. Share prices roared ahead. Water and electricity companies share prices trebled, which was rather surprising as they were privatised with high yields and low risk and modest expectations of share price growth (they were meant to be safe 'granny shares'). Executive directors became rich beyond their wildest dreams. Public sector managers of utilities who were perfectly happy earning £40,000 plus a good pension in the public sector were now millionaires leading large quoted companies, and were then courted by their advisers to expand overseas. After all, how else were they going to get the share price to grow in the future? The excesses of remuneration led to political action and the Greenbury Report. The growth strategies led to many dubious acquisitions, investments and higher risk.

The Greenbury Report criticised the use of share options and proposed in their place awards of shares contingent on other performance measures such as total shareholder return (TSR) compared to a comparator index or group of companies. The Conservative Government removed capital gains tax relief on executive share options on awards of shares above £30,000, thereby reversing its policy of 1984 where it had granted favourable tax treatment to options.

Many companies had already found the limit of options that any single executive could receive, of 4 times remuneration, somewhat restrictive. A number had used super options which were allowed under the ABI guidelines. Super options were a further 4 times remuneration of options, but exercise of this was contingent on being in the top 25% of companies over a 5 year period.

Companies realised that by switching to use restricted shares in place of options they could avoid the 4 times limit of options. Award levels of 1 times salary of options had become typical practice. A similar limit of 1 times salary of shares rapidly became the norm. Even with a discount for the performance conditions the award was probably worth twice as much as the option award. Such comparisons are difficult because of the different risk profile of the two incentives. Whether it was convenience or careful planning or luck one can only guess. The result was that in the UK, options fell out of favour and restricted shares became the hot form of long term incentive and they got a new name – LTIPs.

In 1997 a Labour Government was elected, the first since 1979. One of their first acts was a windfall tax on privatised electricity and water companies. Their share prices declined and executives option gains disappeared. Most of these companies had (with the Government's encouragement) strongly encouraged their employees to buy shares via SAYE share option plans and IR approved Profit Sharing Plans. Employees now began to realise the truth in the statement that share prices can go down as well as up.

The Labour Government also removed the tax credit on dividends. Relatively little criticism was made at the time, but as the impact became more apparent more and more criticism was levied and it became known as the pension tax. It levelled the field in terms of dividends or capital growth. Dividends which were particularly attractive to some shareholders now lost their favourable tax bias. Dividends in the UK had always been higher than in the US, but had always been partly driven by the dividend tax credit. Would this now result in lower dividends and would this lead to a swing back towards options? (note: options only deliver the capital growth to executives whereas LTIPs give executives the benefit of share price changes and dividends.)

In the 1990s in the US, as noted above, there had been a massive growth of in the use of options. This led to a number of leading UK plcs to revert in the late 1990s to granting options to be competitive.

## 2000s

The 2000s started with the dot.com boom and bust. Looking back with the benefit of hindsight, we wonder why all those fabulous growth projections were accepted and why the stock market ratings of technology shares were so high. As companies announced bigger and bigger losses, their share prices seemed to go higher and higher as this was viewed by analysts as a signal of investment for the future. Hi-tech companies paid low salaries, few benefits and compensated with lots of options. There was an exodus of bright young people from traditional companies to dot.com startups where they hoped to make their millions. The traditional companies made attempts to retain staff by themselves offering more and more options. Dilution and overhang in large technology companies grew and grew, for example Microsoft issued options over 30% dilution.

The dot.com boom became a bubble and burst. The outcome resembled the Tulip bulb bubble, the South Sea Bubble and the Crash of 29. The Nasdaq (which was heavily biased towards technology stocks) went from a high of 5000 to a low of 1200, losing over 70% of its value. As the stock market fell many companies options went underwater. They were left with the choice of granting more or letting their employees leave and get buckets of options from their new employer. They chose to grant more options and many cancelled options and re-loaded. The above is primarily a US story. It did filter through to the UK, but what occurred was much more extreme in the US than in the UK.

The scandals at Enron, WorldCom, Tyco and elsewhere led to a decline in stock markets worldwide. Excessive executive compensation and greed were cited as causes. Compensation consultants had got too close to management and had not worked in the best interests of the company. They had in all too many cases colluded with management to design and recommend schemes whereby executives got rich at the expense of the company. This was a low point in business morality. The US enacted Sarbanes-Oxley, which was far reaching. In addition, the Conference Board of America formed the Commission on Public Trust and Private Enterprise. They noted that the general public felt they could trust CEOs less than used car salesmen. They said that CEO compensation and the use of stock options had got out of control and made proposals to improve the situation. (see **B15.14**).

In the UK the Government announced a consultation exercise in July 2001 regarding directors' remuneration. This was in response to the continued highly critical press coverage of directors' remuneration. This resulted in the *Directors' Remuneration Report Regulations 2002* (*SI 2002/1986*) which came into effect for any company year ends on or after 31 December 2002

The 2003 reporting season led to massive publicity about pay and shareholder rebellions at many leading plcs including voting down of remuneration report at GSK. PIRC have provided the following data of the lowest votes in favour of remuneration reports January–June 2003 of FTSE 100 companies.

| Company | For | Abstain[1] | Oppose |
|---|---|---|---|
| GlaxoSmithKline | 49% | | 51% |
| Bae Systems | 51% | | 49% |
| Shire Pharmaceuticals | 57% | 3% | 40% |
| Amvescap | 62% | 8% | 30% |
| Tesco | 60% | 23% | 17% |
| Royal & Sun Alliance | 65% | 7% | 28% |
| Hilton | 68% | 7% | 25% |
| Granada | 68% | 10% | 22% |
| Reed Elsevier | 72% | | 28% |
| Reuters | 73% | 5% | 22% |
| Gallaher | 73% | 12% | 14% |
| Exel | 73% | 15% | 12% |
| Sage | 75% | 16% | 9% |
| Rentokil Initial | 76% | 17% | 7% |
| Reckitt Benckiser | 77% | 10% | 14% |
| Shell Transport & Trading | 77% | | 23% |
| Astra Zeneca | 77% | 6% | 17% |
| H Holdings | 78% | 8% | 14% |
| Schroders | 79% | 7% | 14% |
| Bos | 79% | | 21% |
| Amersham | 80% | | 20% |
| Rexam | 82% | 11% | 7% |
| Abbey National | 82% | 9% | 8% |
| Barclays | 82% | | 18% |
| Prudential | 83% | 14% | 4% |
| Next | 83% | 9% | 8% |
| Alliance & Leicester | 83% | 5% | 11% |
| BOC | 84% | 9% | 8% |
| Royal Bank of Scotland | 84% | | 16% |
| Anglo American | 84% | 6% | 10% |
| Xstrata | 84% | 4% | 12% |
| Wm Morrison Supermarkets | 85% | 10% | 5% |

PIRC requests results of proxy votes from each of the companies on which they report. To the end of June this year, they had recorded the results of 58 AGMs held by FTSE 100 companies. The table shows that 32 companies received positive support of 85% or less on the required vote on its remuneration report. For comparison, in a survey PIRC carried out last year average opposition recorded against remuneration reports at All Share Companies (not just the FTSE 100) was around 4%.

In 2003, the DTI announced another consultation exercise – this time into directors' contracts and severance packages.

200 of the Dow 350 announced that they would expense stock options in their accounts. In August 2003, Microsoft announced it was stopping granting employee options. In place it would issue restricted stock. It also announced a plan to buy out existing options, partly to ensure employees understood the value of their options.

# Why total remuneration is important                    B17.6

Salaries make up on average only 15% of the total remuneration of the CEO ten largest companies quoted in the UK, according to a survey by Independent Remuneration Solutions of remuneration reports published in 2003. It should be noted that smaller companies in general set salaries that comprise a higher proportion of total remuneration. However, these ten largest companies comprise about one quarter of the UK stock market capitalisation, are highly visible and tend to set trends for other companies to follow.

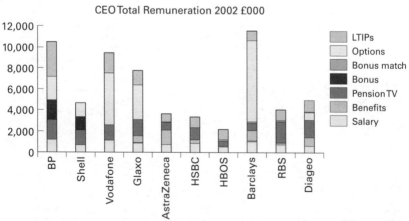

Other findings of the IRS survey were as follows.

- The survey analyses total remuneration: this is the total value of salary, benefits, the transfer value of the increase in accrued pension, annual bonus and the expected value of long term incentives, shares and share options awarded during the year.

- It is unclear how much CEOs are actually paid. Although companies have to disclose each of the elements of remuneration, they spread the data over numerous pages of the remuneration committee report. Some do not include the expected value of long term incentives and none state the total remuneration.

- The lack of data on the expected value and potential value of share options and share plans makes it difficult to understand most companies' remuneration plans. IRS made estimates of the expected value in order to calculate total remuneration.

- Total remuneration for 2002 ranged from £2 million to £12 million. There is evidence of company culture having a moderating effect, with Shell paying half the BP rate and AstraZeneca paying half the GlaxoSmithKline rate.

- Although salary on average comprise only 15% of total remuneration, most other elements of remuneration are set as percentages or multiples of salary, so any increase in salary has a knock on effect on total remuneration.

- Different companies have different proportions of the various elements of remuneration.

- The new rules on disclosure of pensions have shown the value of this important benefit.

# Developing remuneration policy         B17.7

The Combined Code is a good starting point. It states the following.

'● Levels of remuneration should be sufficient to attract, retain and motivate directors of the quality required to run the company successfully, but a company should avoid paying more than is necessary for this purpose.

- A significant proportion of executive directors' remuneration should be structured so as to link rewards to corporate and individual performance.

- The remuneration committee should judge where to position their company relative to other companies. But they should use such comparisons with caution, in view of the risk of an upward ratchet of remuneration levels with no corresponding improvement in performance.

- They should also be sensitive to pay and employment conditions elsewhere in the group, especially when determining annual salary increases.'

Agency theory says that management are the agents of shareholders and should manage the company in the best interests of shareholders. The rational economic man will try to maximise his or her wealth with minimum risk. This is, however, totally different to what shareholders want. Therefore agency theory says that management need to be incited to manage the company in the best interests of shareholders. Remuneration therefore needs to be linked to shareholders' interests of long term share price appreciations and dividends. Management will discount any pay will does not pay out until some years ahead and is dependant on factors many of which they feel are beyond their control. A remuneration policy should reflect these issues and should therefore cover four key elements.

---

1. The selection of appropriate comparator companies should reflect:

   types of executives required

   importance of individual executives to delivery of business strategy

   size of talent pool

   comparator companies location UK, Europe, Global

   comparator companies size – sales, market cap, employees, assets, profits, etc

2. Pay market position(s) and linkage of pay market position to performance

3. Mix of performance related and not-performance related elements

4. Alignment to shareholders' interests. Issues to be covered include:

   upside and downside alignment

   share ownership guidelines

   alignment to business strategy

   performance measures

---

In order to develop a remuneration policy, remuneration committees need to take account of a wider range of issues than those mentioned in the Combined Code, as illustrated below.

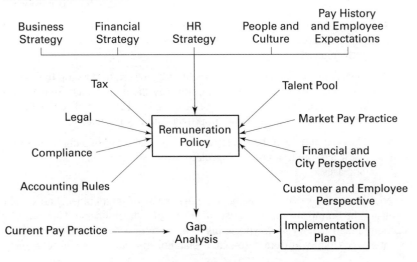

Detailed scenario analyses of remuneration proposals must be carried out, which:

- illustrate a range of possible outcomes;

- consider *all* elements of remuneration;

- consider *all* historic awards of medium and long term incentives as well as the current proposals; and

- are presented in an easily understood format.

Remuneration advice should be based upon rigorous, detailed, precise analysis undertaken by experienced consultants. Remuneration committees should challenge such advice and ensure it is not slanted in favour of the executive directors. Appointing consultants who are independent of any other fee based relationship with the company or the management is an important step in ensuring that the consultants advice is in the best interests of the company.

External consultants will also be used to provide market data, commentary on trends and latest best practice and to design new and ever more complex incentive arrangements, both short and long-term. Surprisingly, although this is an area where one could argue that it has all been done before, there is often a search for the mystical solution and the latest and 'best' plan or scheme. This tends to create complexity and confusion, leading to less transparency. Consultants perform another role in this process: they are aware of what is and is not acceptable to shareholders.

Using all of this advice and assistance, the remuneration committee will set the remuneration strategy for the executive directors and senior executives. In deciding remuneration strategy, remuneration committees should consider carefully the business environment in which they operate and how they aim to deliver shareholder value. The business environment may well impact on how the remuneration committee structure the mix of the remuneration package and how performance measures are used to trigger payment of both long- and short-term incentives. For example, in a company which has been under-performing for some time, more shareholder value may be delivered by being at lower quartile for a particular performance measure against a group of comparator companies than a successful company delivers at median against a similar group. A second example is when a company needs to hire a new CEO to turn around an under performing business: this may require a higher total package with a high potential upside to attract the new hire and to make it worth him/her taking on a high profile and high risk job.

In the UK, most remuneration is driven off base salary – pension is a percentage of salary, contractual compensation is a number of years and months of salary (plus other pay and benefits), annual bonuses are calculated as percentage of salary and long term incentive awards are made as multiples of salary. So setting salary at an appropriate level, and the annual salary review are crucial.

Recruitment, retention and motivation are key goals of remuneration policy. To achieve these goals, remuneration must be competitive with appropriate comparator companies, ie companies of similar size and complexity, operating, probably, in similar sectors or environment. Companies should not compare themselves with larger companies as this is inflationary, but should look to those companies and countries to which they lose their best talent or from which they recruit.

# Remuneration comparisons and the use of surveys
B17.8

The Combined Code says:

> 'Levels of remuneration should be sufficient to attract, retain and motivate directors of the quality required to run the company successfully, but a company should avoid paying more than is necessary for this purpose.'

> The remuneration committee should judge where to position their company relative to other companies. But they should use such comparisons with caution, in view of the risk of an upward ratchet of remuneration levels with no corresponding improvement in performance.

> They should also be sensitive to pay and employment conditions elsewhere in the group, especially when determining annual salary increases.

> B.1.1 The performance-related elements of remuneration should form a significant proportion of the total remuneration package of executive directors ... '

Hampel urged caution in the use of comparisons with other companies including remuneration surveys:

> 'Few Remuneration Committees will want to recommend lower than average salaries. There is a danger that the uncritical use of comparisons will lead to an upward ratchet in remuneration with no corresponding improvement in corporate performance.'

The remuneration committee needs to be aware of what other organisations are paying. Of most relevance will be organisations from where the company typically recruits or those to which executives have moved or could potentially move to.

Care must be taken to ensure that the comparisons are with companies of the same size and characteristics. Size can be measured in terms of sales, market cap, employees, assets, profits, etc. Market cap can be highly volatile and comparisons on this basis can be used to justify higher pay when the company is performing well compared to the comparator companies. However few companies reduce pay when the market cap reduces and this point illustrates the dangers of using simplistic comparisons. Remuneration committees should review the comparative size statistics using at least turnover and market cap, but preferable also consider other measures such as number of employees, assets, profits, etc. Geography scope (eg % of turnover outside UK) and business complexity (eg high or low tech, speed of change, scope to create shareholder value) also need to be considered. Having reviewed this data, judgement is required.

Comparisons of CEO remuneration are particularly difficult. Often each individual's remuneration is a result of history. CEOs who are recognised as highly successful may command a premium. New internal appointments may be paid less than the 'market rate'.

Care must be taken when comparing other executive directors that the comparisons are of similar jobs with similar responsibilities. Job titles can be misleading, particularly if there are different structures, eg contrast one Divisional Director reporting to the CEO with one who reports to a COO who reports to the CEO.

Comparisons should be based on total remuneration. Different companies have different amounts of remuneration linked to performance, eg it is wrong to compare the salary of a low salary, low pension, big incentive package with the salary of a package made up to an average salary, generous pension and average incentives.

Surveys are another source of data. Monks (now part of PWC), Towers, Mercer, Watson Wyatt, Hay, Reward and many others conduct and publish surveys. Some require participation in order to purchase the survey. Many surveys have a large number of participants and this is helpful in seeing the wider picture. However, care must be taken in interpreting such surveys as your own company will be either bigger or smaller than the survey sample. Special cuts of data to suit companies needs may be available. Some surveys do not include all elements of total remuneration, so using such surveys can be misleading.

Bespoke surveys where the company designs the survey can be very useful, but only if sufficient of the desired companies can be persuaded to participate.

Personal contact with other non-executives in other organisations can provide confidential information that might not be available through surveys. However, such information may be incomplete or selective and is not usually statistically significant.

# The mix of performance and non-performance-related remuneration                                    B17.9

B1.1 of the Combined Code says:

> 'The performance-related elements of remuneration should form a significant proportion of the total remuneration package of executive directors and should be designed to align their interests with those of shareholders and to give these directors keen incentives to perform at the highest levels.'

However, no guidance is given on what is significant.

**B17.9**  *The mix of performance and non-performance-related remuneration*

The CEOs of the ten largest UK companies have an average of 70% of total remuneration that is performance related and the performance related elements have an estimated value of 350% of salary. However, PIRC suggest that the performance related elements should not be more than 200% of salary. The average FTSE100 CEO mix in 2002 was (source Manifest and IRS):

## FTSE CEO Renumeration Mix 2002

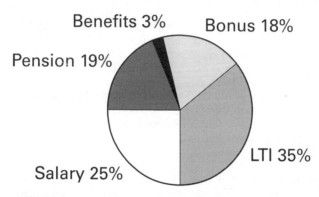

Benefits 3%     Bonus 18%

Pension 19%

LTI 35%

Salary 25%

In August 2003 Mercer published the following data.

| Chief Executive pay in FTSE 100 companies (£ in 000s) (Source: Mercer) | | | | | | |
|---|---|---|---|---|---|---|
| | Lower Quartile | | Median | | Upper Quartile | |
| Pay component | % | £ | % | £ | % | £ |
| Base salary | | 500 | | 600 | | 738 |
| Bonus · | 40% | 183 | 63% | 400 | 101% | 701 |
| Total Cash Pay | | 744 | | 989 | | 1,337 |
| Performance Shares | 24% | | 49% | | 102% | |
| Share Options | 23% | | 51% | | 111% | |
| Total Long-Term Incentive | 45% | 248 | 95% | 544 | 159% | 1,028 |
| Total Pay (w/o pension) | | 1,069 | | 1,525 | | 2,350 |
| Pension | 28% | 181 | 75% | 440 | 121% | 808 |
| Total Pay (w/pension) | | 1,602 | | 2,048 | | 2,951 |

Figures have been calculated separately and therefore are not additive.

Percentages are of base salary.

Bonus = short term incentive

Total cash pay = base salary plus bonus

Performance shares, share options, and total long term incentives percentages are expected values discounting for performance conditions

Total pay = base salary plus short term incentives plus expected value of long term incentives

# Salary   B17.10

The Combined Code states. 'They should also be sensitive to pay and employment conditions elsewhere in the group, especially when determining annual salary increases.' No other explicit guidance is given on salaries but of course the comments about total remuneration need to be considered, eg:

> 'Levels of remuneration should be sufficient to attract, retain and motivate directors of the quality required to run the company successfully, but a company should avoid paying more than is necessary for this purpose.'

Institutional investors in quoted companies are very keen that remuneration packages are in line with comparator groups.

The annual guaranteed salary is the basic system through which all executives are remunerated. It is the foundation of the executive remuneration package. Base salary is often a key factor in determining the level of other elements of the package, defined benefit pension is based on final salary, money purchase is a % salary, annual bonus is usually calculated as a % of salary and the value of awards of LTIPs and options are set as a % of salary. Getting the salary right is therefore the most important remuneration issue facing most employers in the UK.

Salary agreements for managers and directors are universally based upon payment monthly in arrears, with the employer being responsible for the necessary deductions of employee and employer's national insurance and any tax, so that an individual receives a net sum each month from which no further deductions will be made.

# Annual salary reviews   B17.11

It is normal for salaries to be reviewed once a year. Main board salaries in quoted companies are reviewed by the remuneration committee, other salaries in such groups tend to be reviewed by the chief executive, divisional director or head of department. In private companies, senior salaries are normally reviewed by the chief executive or chairman and then approved by the board, with the same below board levels as used in fully quoted groups.

Most companies are increasingly using an overall review grid, whereby the board agrees how much they can afford next year in terms of an increase in salaries, which is a fixed overhead once it has been agreed. The chief executive would therefore issue a note to all those reviewing their subordinates' salaries in which he makes it clear that the total increase in the salary bill for each department could be no higher than, say, 4% and within this discretion can only be used over half the amount, ie 2%. In practice this means that the best performers could get an increase of 6% and the worst performers could only get an increase of 2%. The use of this system has increased but some companies they allow the differential to range, say 8% in the case above, to 0%. However, people not given a salary review, whereas others in the department have received an increase, are likely to be fairly disaffected. If they are not worth a review, it might be better to bite the bullet and allow them to go before the review takes place.

In the decade since 1993, there have been sustained year-on-year increases in directors' salaries among the largest companies. Among current constituents of the FTSE 100 for which PIRC have records over the period, the median base salary for the highest paid director (either the CEO or the executive chairman) increased from £301,000 to £579,000, some 92%. In that time inflation has increased by 25%, and average wages by 44%[2].

*Highest-paid directors median base salaries 1993–2002 (FTSE100) (Source: PIRC)*

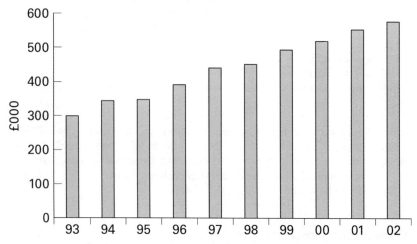

There are many exceptions to this. Some companies in expanding industries will have paid significantly higher figures than this, whereas other employers in contracting or static industries will have reviewed at the bottom end of these figures.

Because the media tend to highlight high pay increases as part of the media story in UK limited, there is a danger that boards are panicked into feeling that they have got to offer much too high a basic salary increase to keep directors happy. Staff do of course feed this particular fear.

The Combined Code states 'They should also be sensitive to pay and employment conditions elsewhere in the group, especially when determining annual salary increases'. The increase in the RPI has traditionally been used as a benchmark for the setting of salaries amongst lower paid and support staff. Any increase that does not match the RPI is likely to mean the employee is slightly worse off in the following year than he was in the one just past. Unions and other collective organisations are, of course, extremely keen to use this as the bottom line in any negotiations. Boards setting salaries need to be aware that this is not so commonly used in private sector organisations as it was in the inflationary 1980s and 1990s. It is fairly easy to review salaries when the company has had a good year. You would probably review at RPI +4–5%. The problem comes when the company has had a bad year and profits barely cover the cost of capital or, even worse, is making a loss.

In this situation it is very unlikely any bonuses will be paid and the natural feeling for colleagues who have worked well, despite the lack of corporate success, is that they deserve an increase. This is where independent directors can earn their corn, because it is obviously necessary to put a break on any increase in fixed central costs, such as salaries. One solution is to phase increases so that you, for instance, give an increase of 2% with a promise of a second review in, say, four to six months if trading starts to improve, at which point you would possibly give another 2% increase. The use of more frequent reviews is one way to take account of turnaround situations when a company simply cannot afford to be as generous as it might like on the normal review date.

## The use of comparator groups   B17.12

Institutional investors in quoted companies are very keen that remuneration packages are in line with comparator groups. This can be an extremely dangerous practice when it comes to base salaries as the comparator group chosen for a particular organisation will often, at the urging of the chief executive, include businesses rather larger than the company itself.

This can result in companies feeling they have to increase the remuneration of their directors to the median level of the comparator group. Effectively you get locked into what might be called an 'upper quartile syndrome' in which everybody is trying to pay slightly higher than their competitors in the comparator group. This is an inevitably inflationary spiral and has led to significant overpayment of boards in some large quoted plc groups.

## Differentials   B17.13

Salary differentials should reflect the added value the individual can make, the job responsibilities and the market practice. Manifest data for FTSE100 companies for 2002 show the following average salaries.

| Chief executive | 640,073 |
|---|---|
| Other executive directors | 330,142 |
| Differential | 94% |

At lower levels, a 30% to 50% premium between subordinate and boss might be typical, although on promotion a rise of 10% to 15% might be awarded as this will allow further progression over time to the market rate.

A problem facing companies with significant overseas interests is that the key executive cadre running the American, German and maybe Japanese divisions might well earn salaries above those paid for the main board in the UK. This anomaly is usually over-turned in terms of total remuneration, as the main board are entitled to higher bonuses and much bigger share or option allocations. Most groups have come to terms with the reality of international trade, when the head office in the UK, is not one of the world's highest salaried executive societies and it is not unknown for group chief executives to be paid less in salary terms than the American, German and Japanese divisional heads who report to them.

# Owner-managed companies                               B17.14

There is a danger in owner-managed companies that the proprietor, probably the chairman/CEO, earns significant dividends from his stake in the company. For this reason he may not maintain his own salary at the level he would need to pay if he hired an outside professional.

The danger is that he then tries to preserve normal differentials so that directors on the main board and subsidiary, may be significantly under salaried because of the depression created by the view of the owner-manager.

In such a situation, the danger is that staff will leave for higher paid jobs in more traditionally remunerated companies.

The incidence of this type of underpayment is more common than is often supposed. The reason given by the owner-manager is that the company simply cannot afford more, and this may knock on in terms of the business plan, because the company may not be pricing its products at a sufficient level to support a necessary salary structure for the type of skills they need.

This is one of the areas in which independent directors on private company boards can play a significant part by suggesting a review of the company's entire business plan, with a principal objective of raising salaries to competitive rates so that key executives and technical staff are not tempted to leave the company for bigger groups.

# Pension                                              B17.15

Pension is deferred pay. It is important to think of it as such and as just one part of the total remuneration package.

The Combined Code says in Appendix A:

'Para 6. In general, only basic salary should be pensionable.

7.   The Remuneration Committee should consider the pension consequences and associated costs to the company of basic salary increases
and any other changes in pensionable remuneration, especially for
directors close to retirement.'

The transfer value of the accrued pension and the increase in the transfer value
now have to be disclosed. This has increased the transparency of pension.
Pension is not performance-related pay, so any excessive pension benefits will
attract criticism.

There are two main categories of pension plan, defined benefit and defined
contribution (often referred to as money purchase plans).

**Defined benefit plans** promise a pension after retirement calculated as a
proportion of the final pensionable salary (which can comprise salary plus
bonus and benefits, but the Combined Code says should be salary only). The
proportion is the number of years service divided by the accrual rate. Most
employee pension plans have an accrual rate of 60ths or 80ths. However
some directors have 45ths or 30ths. The combination of faster accrual rates
and higher than average salary increases means the defined benefit plan is
worth much more to directors than it is to the average employee. It is only
since the *Directors' Remuneration Report Regulations 2002 (SI 2002/1986)*
that the transfer value of pension had to be disclosed. The transfer value will
depend on:

- final pensionable salary;
- years service;
- accrual rate;
- discount rate;
- rules for indexation of pension after retirement; and
- widows pension.

Increases in the transfer value will depend on the above and the salary
increase.

**Defined contribution plans** are much simpler than defined benefit plans. A
sum of money is contributed to the plan on behalf of the participant and this is
invested generally in accord with their wishes. The value on retirement will
depend on investment returns.

**Hybrid plans** are combinations of defined contribution plans and defined
benefit plans.

# The value of pension

The IRS survey of the CEOs of the 10 largest UK companies showed the following.

|  | Transfer value of total accrued pension £million | Transfer value of increase in accrued pension in 2002 £million | Increase in transfer value of accrued pension in 2002 as a multiple of salary |
|---|---|---|---|
| BP | 12.8 | 1.88 | 147% |
| Shell | 7.9 | 1.48 | 198% |
| Vodafone | 6.5 | 1.36 | 114% |
| Glaxo | 5.6 | 0.61 | 63% |
| AstraZeneca | 9.7 | 1.42 | 166% |
| HSBC | 5.5 | 0.46 | 49% |
| HBOS | 3.8 | −0.06 | −9% |
| Barclays | 1.4 | 0.99 | 90% |
| RBS | 1.9 | 0.3 | 36% |
| Diageo | 6.7 | 0.8 | 108% |
| average | 6.19 | 0.92 | 96% |

Mercer surveyed the annual value of FTSE100 CEO pensions as follows

|  | Lower Quartile | | Median | | Upper Quartile | |
|---|---|---|---|---|---|---|
|  | %salary | £000 | %salary | £000 | %salary | £000 |
| Pension | 28% | 181 | 75% | 440 | 121% | 808 |

## The pensions cap

The *Finance Act 1988* introduced a limit on the amount of pension that could be provided through an approved scheme. The limit for the final pensionable salary was set at £60,000, and would increase with RPI. In 2003 the limit is now £97,600. Indexing the limit in line with RPI meant that more and more people would be affected over time.

There are a number of strategies to deal with the cap:

- give executives subject to the cap the same benefits as those who were not. Some do this via a promise, using an Unfunded Unapproved Retirement Benefit Scheme (UURBS). Others set money aside to guarantee the benefit using Funded Unapproved Retirement Benefit Scheme (FURBS).

- Maximise the benefits under the IR approved plan and:

  ○ give a FURB or UURBS above this; or

  ○ give a cash supplement; or

  ○ give additional remuneration to ensure the total remuneration is competitive.

## Pensions policy                                           B17.18

As the real cost of directors' pensions now have to be revealed following the new disclosure rules in 2003, the rationale for pension needs to be revisited. Previously it was a convenient and effective way for companies to reward their senior executives and directors that was not transparent to shareholders. With the current tax regime, if we did not have pensions then no one would invent them as they do not make sense. Imagine your boss saying to you 'I am going to hold some of your salary until you are 60 and then the amount you get will depend on your salary at age 60 if you are still here. But don't worry, if you leave early then I will index your leaving salary at RPI. And when you do get it you will have to pay tax on it. And if it is a FURB you will have to pay tax now on the pay I have not given you. But if it is an UURB then you won't pay any tax now, but if we go bust before you are 60 then we won't have to pay you.' However, changing pension plans is difficult and requires expert advice on both total remuneration strategy and pensions technical issues.

# Performance-related pay                                     B17.19

How much, what for and when should it be paid? These are the three key questions.

The Combined Code recommends 'keen incentives to perform at the highest levels' for executive directors and gives detailed guidance on each of annual bonus, LTIPs and options in its Appendix A. Greenbury referred to incentive plans as being part of a 'cohesive, integrated reward strategy'. Those words are no longer part of the Code, although whether this is by design or by chance is not clear. Appendix A.3. to the Code merely states 'any new long term incentive plan should form part of a well considered overall plan.'

Institutional shareholders and their intermediaries give plenty of guidance about individual plans but not on the interaction of plans.

The how much question, the proportion of performance related pay was discussed above in **B17.3**. The what for question (ie performance measures) is discussed below.

# Performance measures – an introduction     B17.20

Understanding performance measures is key to a well-designed cohesive integrated reward strategy. In the long term shareholders want share price appreciation and dividends. However, share price movements can be capricious. Share prices can be driven by fear and greed, particularly in the short term. Over the medium to long term the following affect share prices:

- interest rates;

- market sentiment;

- sector sentiment;

- company management actions.

Companies with high Beta will have share prices which change faster than the market average. Volatility in theory should not affect the share price over the medium to long term, but option theory tells us that an option over a volatile share is worth more than one over a less volatile share.

A company can be performing well but this might not be reflected in the share price. Over the long term the company's performance will drive the share price, but how do we design incentive plans that motivate in the short and medium term?

Another problem is that internal performance measures may be achieved but this may not translate to the share price performance. Companies should nevertheless choose performance measures for annual bonus plans that if achieved should translate into long term share price performance. It is up to the remuneration committee to justify annual bonus payments in the remuneration report to shareholders. They are accountable to shareholders and if they approve large annual bonuses for a number of years that do not translate into share price performance they can expect criticism from shareholders.

Another issue is that the share price already discounts future performance. It expects a certain amount of performance and if that is not achieved then the share price will decline (subject to any concomitant changes in interest rates, market and sector sentiment).

There should be a balance of incentive between annual and long term incentives to reflect that no-one can be sure that the annual performance measures will translate into long term performance. So some incentive should be linked more directly to share performance.

If we knew for sure what the measures of annual performance should be in the annual bonus plan then we would not need to have long term incentives. From a governance viewpoint, some would say that long term incentives developed because shareholders were not satisfied with the way annual bonus plans were operating, eg they were paying out year after year with no improvement in the share price.

Another problem is that most long term incentive plans are not long term at all – they are three year medium term incentive plans.

Implementation of strategy and the rewards for success may take several years to be reflected in the share price. However, the remuneration committee should ensure the executives are rewarded for the successful implementation of the strategic goals and milestones. This is best done through the annual bonus plan. Bonus deferral/matching can provide a kicker when the strategy results in subsequent increases in shareholder value. Although the board as a whole is collectively responsible for strategy, it is appropriate that a considerable part of total remuneration package is linked to the share price performance, either through LTIPs or options or both.

Share price will grow over the long term if the profits generated are higher than the cost of capital. There is a danger of incentivising executives to beat the competition – they can achieve this but the share price may reduce. It may have been a better strategic decision to not invest rather than compete.

Most fund managers measure themselves on relative performance, as they market their services to clients as being better than their competitors. To sell retail funds requires top decile or even top three performance. The wholesale funds market is more sophisticated and recognises that beating the median over the long term is a significant achievement. However below median performance is unacceptable. As most fund managers' personal bonus depends on relative performance this has become inbred in their culture and they tend to be in favour of such approaches for executive directors.

## A model of performance and rewards   B17.21

| Do these operational things in the short term | ▶ | Beat the competitors in the medium term | ▶ | Share price growth in the long term |
|---|---|---|---|---|
| Rewarded by | | Rewarded by | | Rewarded by |
| Annual Bonus and Bonus Matching | | LTIPs and Bonus Matching | | Options and Share Ownership |

Readers may find the above model useful. There are however a number of difficulties in its implementation. Institutional shareholders prefer only one type of long term incentive plan. They also prefer share options with three year performance measures attached to them, which turns a ten year incentive plan into a complex hybrid of three year dash followed by a long term share appreciation incentive. It is difficult to find comparator companies in the same business, at similar stages of development with similar gearing. Data on key performance measures may not be readily available or sufficiently robust. Executives will wish to diversify their portfolios and not have too large a proportion tied into the performance of their employer.

# Annual bonus plans                                    B17.22

The Combined Code in Appendix 1 says:

> '1.  The remuneration committee should consider whether the directors should be eligible for annual bonuses. If so, performance conditions should be relevant, stretching and designed to enhance shareholder value. Upper limits should be set and disclosed. There may be a case for part payment in shares to be held for a significant period.'

The annual cash bonus is the longest established system of providing additional incentive to staff in the UK. It is the way management specifically rewards those who have made a greater than normal contribution to the results of the year and most directors are very jealous of their right to award such bonuses, which is a critical part of their control/incentive mechanism of their staff.

Whereas thirty years ago bonuses were discretionary within an overall budget figure, so that the boss had the right to discriminate very significantly between people within his department, modern practice is to make some of the bonus specific and linked to the achievement of certain departmental or corporate targets, leaving a rather smaller amount to the managers' discretion.

Independent Remuneration Solutions has developed a 70/30 model, whereby 70% of a bonus is delivered automatically if the group of which the individual is a member has delivered profits in line with or above the business plan. 30% is left as a discretionary reward so that individuals working extremely effectively can be acknowledged in the discretionary reward which is not linked to salary. The automatic award is nearly always linked to salary so that the higher paid get a higher bonus.

Bonuses are usually linked, though they shouldn't be awarded at the same time, to the annual appraisal. Good practice indicates that the appraisal interview should normally take place three to four months before the annual bonus announcements are made.

## Quantum                                              B17.23

Main board directors of quoted British companies can normally earn annual cash bonuses up to 50% of their salary if they have out-performed against budget. Directors of subsidiary companies usually have bonuses capped at 30–40% of salary. PIRC provided the following data:

> 'The maximum that may be earned as an annual bonus is usually set at a proportion of salary. Five years ago, the majority of FTSE100 companies set the upper limit for annual bonuses at between 40% and 60% of salary. By this year, these ceilings had increased in almost a third of cases to 100% of salary, with some companies going even higher. So the trend is clearly towards the potential payment of higher proportions of bigger salaries.

Of course, it may be that the performance targets required for these higher sums to be earned have also toughened. However, as annual performance targets are rarely disclosed and are not required to be reported under the Regulations, it is not possible to assess this.'

***Annual bonus schemes: Maximum % of salary awardable 1999–2003 (FTSE100) (Source: PIRC)***

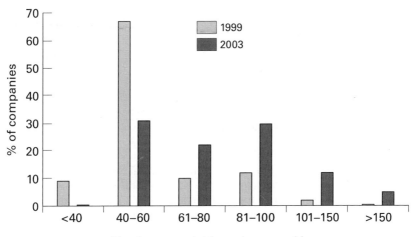

Manifest data show the increase in the average amounts paid to FTSE100 CEOs. It should be noted that FTSE dropped in value by 40% over the period 2000 to 2002. One would expect therefore that bonus payments were less than the target level.

| Year | Salary | Bonuses | % salary |
|------|--------|---------|----------|
| 1998 | £424,919 | £187,891 | 44% |
| 1999 | £443,743 | £213,820 | 48% |
| 2000 | £499,429 | £344,579 | 69% |
| 2001 | £525,262 | £368,670 | 70% |
| 2002 | £569,442 | £408,459 | 72% |

**Performance measures** **B17.24**

Profit has traditionally been the favourite performance measure in annual bonus plans. However it is a lagging indicator of shareholder value and, as has been seen in the US, capable of accounting manipulation. Statistical studies show that it is poorly correlated to share price movements. Nevertheless it is an important cornerstone of almost any annual incentive plan.

The choice of performance measures and their relative importance in the delivery of performance related pay is a window on corporate governance, as they indicate what is felt to be important in the company. The exclusive use of profit in annual bonus plans is a warning sign. The performance measures that determine the remuneration of the management of the company should be those that drive the future business success, eg customer satisfaction, customer retention, customer growth, average revenue per customers, employee satisfaction, staff turnover and average length of service, environmental and social responsibility measures, health and safety, product development, brand management, effective relationships with regulators, etc. If these measures are not part of the incentive plans, then the company may be saying one thing to its shareholders but internally may be behaving quite differently. Hence, this is a crucial window on what is happening inside the company.

Cash Flow, ROCE and EVA are also common financial measures. Like profit they are lagging indicators. The remuneration committee should also consider using leading indicators of shareholder value. These will often be company or sector specific.

A well designed plan may have financial, non-financial operational measures as well as strategic goals. Evaluation of the bonus award in such plans requires judgement by the remuneration committee as well as a good understanding of the business, its strategic challenges and competitors' performance.

**Bonus design**                                                    **B17.25**

A classic bonus pattern would be that if the department, division or group achieves 90–95% of the annual target, whether these are profits before tax or some other measure, managers would start to earn a small bonus of 5%, which would increase steadily as the results exceed budgets. In most companies the bonus would be capped at about 120% of target.

Whether or not annual cash bonuses should be capped is an ongoing argument. IRS are in favour of this system because if, a group can exceed their budgets by more than 20%, the chances are there has been very loose budgeting or an unexpected movement not anticipated when the budget was set, ie the cost of some input material has collapsed, one of your competitor's factories has burned down, or the currency in which you trade has moved favourably against those of competitors.

The purpose of capping the bonus is to ensure that lucky breaks do not create very large payments, when the management may not have to try very hard to enjoy a windfall bonus.

On the other side there are those who believe that you should always pay for out-performance. There are some companies in which bonus expectations can be as high as 200% of salary. These tend to be financial service organisations, eg dealer teams who often have relatively low salaries with the whole remuneration package tilted towards the bonus. This approach can be dangerous in many companies as it can lead to managers trying to pack additional profits into the final months of the year so that they earn a higher bonus. The inevitable consequence is under-performance against budgets for the first three months of the next year, but by then several of the beneficiaries of the bonus may have left the company or moved to other departments.

**Payment of the bonus**                                        **B17.26**

Traditionally bonuses were paid once the accounts have been published and all the figures were out in the open. They were then paid as a single lump sum with the next month's salary. More sophisticated companies are now paying bonuses on a phased basis, whereby 25–50% is paid at the end of the year, 25–50% is paid three months later and a final tranche is paid after the end of the year. The beauty of this approach is that if there is any creative accounting, it will tend to come out before the second tranche has been paid and, at the same time, it does not encourage key staff to leave after receiving a very big single payment.

With younger staff it is quite important to ensure that they are not encouraged to start a life-style that can only be supported by continuous high bonuses. Phasing tends to reduce the risk of their over-trading as well as looking for an alternative employer and claiming they think can meet inflated expectations.

**Taxation**                                                    **B17.27**

Cash bonuses are treated as part of the individual's normal remuneration. Full tax and if necessary national insurance is deducted by the employer before the payment is made to the employee.

**Bonus banks**                                                 **B17.28**

This is a system whereby a high bonus over, equalling say, 50% of salary or more is earned in a particular year but only half is paid, with the other half put into a bonus bank payable, say, in two tranches 12 and 24 months later.

While the bonus is in the bank it earns interest because the company has the use of the money and it may also attract performance bonuses in subsequent years if the executive continues to be successful.

This type of a bonus bank creates a long term incentive and handcuff for key executives and is one answer for companies who cannot use options because they are subsidiaries, private or family groups who do not have or wish to use equity options as long term incentives.

**Bonus deferral and bonus matching**                           **B17.29**

In these plans part of the bonus is deferred and used to buy shares which vest usually in three years. Deferral may be mandatory or voluntary. The participant may be given extra shares after three years to encourage him to defer the bonus. There may be extra matching shares which vest according to performance over the next three years. Like the bonus bank, this type of a creates a long-term incentive and handcuff for key executives. The downside is that there is no long term incentive when no bonus is awarded, so such plans are usually combined with options and/or LTIPs to make a cohesive and integrated approach.

# Long term incentives B17.30

Long term incentive payments fall into the following categories: options, share based (LTIPs) and cash. By long term, most organisations mean incentive bonuses measured over three years that are then paid in a single or a phased number of payments.

Most quoted companies tend to base a percentage of such payments on shares or share options, but this is not so easy for private companies who do not have an open market for their equity.

The use of medium- to long-term incentives of this kind has been increasing for the past fifteen years as they tie the management to a shareholder value-based bonus system.

The size of potential payments under long-term incentive plans have created a significant amount of shareholder, media and political comment over the past three years.

It is an area where remuneration committees have a particularly important part to play to ensure that:

- the performance triggers for long-term incentives are sufficiently demanding and clearly add shareholder value;

- that the payment currency, whether cash, shares or options can only be encashed over time, so that executive beneficiaries are not tempted to leave the company after a significant pay-out;

- that creative accountancy has not been used so that the company appears to have exceeded certain trigger targets for very large pay-outs when under strict accounting rules, the targets would not have been met.

The availability of a long term performance payment system is fairly critical when executives are considering whether or not to join a company. They may well be walking away from options in their existing employer worth several hundred thousand pounds which is one of the reasons for 'golden hellos' when a recruit is offered a large number of options by his new employer to compensate for those he would sacrifice.

## Quantum B17.31

Note: market data on individual plans is potentially misleading as some companies only award LTIPs, some only options and some a mixture. Thus it is best to review data for the expected value of all types of long term incentive plans. Manifest have provided the following data, which show the rapid 5-fold increase in the importance of this element of the remuneration package:

| Year | Salary | ESOS average Expected Value | LTIP average Expected Value | LTI total average Expected Value | LTI Expected Value % salary |
|------|--------|------|------|------|------|
| 1998 | £424,919 | £87,754 | £62,208 | £149,963 | 35% |
| 1999 | £443,743 | £145,315 | £127,801 | £273,116 | 62% |
| 2000 | £499,429 | £208,589 | £246,323 | £454,911 | 91% |
| 2001 | £525,262 | £251,919 | £230,671 | £482,590 | 92% |
| 2002 | £569,442 | £475,946 | £262,530 | £738,476 | 130% |

The Mercer August 2003 survey gave broadly similar results, but are somewhat different because of differing assumptions for calculating expected values:

*Chief Executive pay in FTSE 100 companies (£ in 000s) (Source: Mercer)*

| | Lower Quartile | | Median | | Upper Quartile | |
|------|------|------|------|------|------|------|
| Pay component | % | £ | % | £ | % | £ |
| Base salary | | 500 | | 600 | | 738 |
| Performance Shares | 24% | | 49% | | 102% | |
| Share Options | 23% | | 51% | | 111% | |
| Total Long-Term Incentive | 45% | 248 | 95% | 544 | 159% | 1,028 |

# Share options                                    B17.32

The Combined Code says:

> 'B.1.2 Executive share options should not be offered at a discount save as permitted by the relevant provisions of the Listing Rules.'

And in Appendix A:

> '2. Traditional share option schemes should be weighed against other kinds of long-term incentive scheme. In normal circumstances, shares granted or other forms of deferred remuneration should not vest, and options should not be exercisable, in less than three years. Directors should be encouraged to hold their shares for a further period after vesting or exercise, subject to the need to finance any costs of acquisition and associated tax liabilities.

3.   Any new long-term incentive schemes which are proposed should be approved by shareholders and should preferably replace any existing schemes or at least form part of a well considered overall plan, incorporating existing schemes. The total rewards potentially available should not be excessive.

4.   Payouts or grants under all incentive schemes, including new grants under existing share option schemes, should be subject to challenging performance criteria reflecting the company's objectives. Consideration should be given to criteria which reflect the company's performance relative to a group of comparator companies in some key variables such as total shareholder return.

5.   Grants under executive share option and other long-term incentive schemes should normally be phased rather than awarded in one large block.'

Institutional investors have more specific guidance on quantums and performance measures, which are complex and sometimes contradictory. Most of those who have guidelines expect that any award of more than 1 times salary (face value of options) will have tougher performance targets attached and any award above 2 times salary will have significantly tougher targets. The ABI guidelines allow global companies to use performance targets on grant rather than on exercise.

The ABI guidelines limit dilution to 10% for all schemes and 5% for executive schemes, both over ten years. The limits should be spread over the ten years, so the limit for executive schemes is an average of 0.5% per annum. In contrast the median dilution in the US is 1.9% per annum, which creates a problem for any UK employer wishing to compete with US corporations.

The ABI guidelines also require companies to report the expected value and projected value of long term incentives including share options. Few companies comply with this particular guidance.

The IASB has announced proposals that the cost of options have to be shown as an expense, which will highlight the real cost of options and lead companies to re-evaluate if this remuneration expense could be better spent in different ways.

Share options had a brief flurry under Ted Heath's government between 1970 and 1974 and were reintroduced by Mrs Thatcher in the early 1980s. This was part of the Conservatives' plan to increase the commercial effectiveness of the nation and was highly successful in improving the performance of quoted and private companies, most of whom had introduced option schemes by the early 1990s. The schemes have gone through a maturing process against a background of an Inland Revenue requirement that they cannot be triggered outside an encashment window three to ten years from grant. Early approved schemes had to be cleared with the Inland Revenue and were taxed as capital gains with no national insurance costs for the employee or the employer. These schemes still exist but are limited to £30,000 worth of options per executive and have been by-passed by unauthorised schemes. Unapproved schemes are taxed as income on exercise and involve the individual and the company paying National Insurance contributions. Because the encashment of such options could have bankrupted some of the dotcom companies faced by huge national insurance charges, companies are allowed to pass on employer national insurance costs to the employee. This means that the total potential tax on option encashment is about 52% which tends to make these schemes slightly unattractive unless the executive is very certain that the underlying shares are going to appreciate by a significant percentage.

## Quantums                                                    B17.33

Prior to 1999, most discretionary option schemes in which directors participate had rules limiting the holding of options to the equivalent of four times a director's remuneration in any ten year period. While one undesirable side-effect of this rule was that an award of the whole amount could be made in one block, no more options could then be issued. In 1999, the Association of British Insurers (ABI) amended its rules by removing this limit and replacing it with guidance that awards should be made annually. It suggested that an equivalent award level would be options with a face value of one times salary[3].

The result was an immediate change in new schemes. In 2000, PIRC found that 65% of new option schemes used a new style annual award limit. Initially, one times salary was the most popular limit. However, by 2002, the ceiling had been raised so that 47% of new schemes specified a limit of two times salary[4].

As with annual bonuses, these higher multiples of salary are themselves based on larger salaries, creating a powerful multiplier effect through executive director remuneration structures.

As noted above, market data is potentially misleading as some companies only award LTIPs, some only options and some a mixture. Thus it is best to review data for the expected value of all types of long term incentive plans.

## Performance measures                                        B17.34

PIRC report that there has been some movement to toughen performance conditions. In 1996, 67% of new share option schemes used a measure of earnings per share (EPS) to determine the exercise of options and of these, 48% of new schemes required EPS growth of 2% in excess of inflation for full vesting. In 2002 EPS was still the most popular performance condition with 58% of new option schemes using it. However, most schemes (72%) now have a vesting scale whereby different levels of options become exercisable for gradually tougher performance. PIRC have found that in most cases, the required EPS targets are relatively weak compared to market expectations of the company's performance.

**EMI** **B17.35**

The best scheme of all was introduced in the 2000 Budget and subsequently enhanced in the 2002 Budget. However, it is only available to companies with a gross asset value of less than £30 million, who can offer Enterprise Management Incentive (EMI) options to up to thirty members of their staff, with no individual entitled to options worth more than £100,000 at the date of grant.

These options are taxed as capital gains tax and, in addition, benefit from taper relief so that if they are encashed three years after grant, the tax may only be 10% of the profit realised.

Any quoted company with a gross asset value inside this limit should consider issuing such options to the most important members of your executive team, keeping some available for future recruits. If you are running a private company up to this size, the EMI scheme is still very attractive but a buyer for the shares needs to be in place when the option beneficiary wishes to encash his entitlement.

# Share-based plans (LTIPs) B17.36

The Combined Code guidance is in paragraphs 2 to 5 of Appendix 1 and is quoted above in **B17.32**.

The use of shares rather than options was encouraged by institutions in the middle nineties as they were worried there was no downside risk to an executive granted options who simply let them lapse if the shares had collapsed.

The company needs to establish an Employee Share Ownership Plan (ESOP) which purchases shares in the market and holds them for subsequent issue. The company has to finance the ESOP or alternatively provide a guarantee so a bank will finance the ESOP which is simply a warehouse of the company's own shares. Shares can be issued in a much more flexible way than options as there are no Revenue concerns unless shares are issued below current market price, in which case the executive faces an immediate demand for income tax on the difference. The use of ESOP schemes has become very sophisticated and can provide the ideal flexible long-term incentive currency for executive teams. Shares can be allocated without actually vesting so that an executive only has to pay for the shares when they take up and probably sell some of them in the market, to finance the purchase.

Reading the remuneration committee's report in the accounts of any major FTSE company, shows a bewildering variety of incentive schemes based upon options and ESOP-type shares. This is an area of some complexity but it is worth considering with outside consultants how such schemes can bring benefits to the company.

Long term incentive schemes normally run alongside an annual cash bonus though in some companies all incentives are based on long-term results.

## Quantum

PIRC has tracked the structure of new share schemes in which directors will participate since 1996. Awards of conditional shares and/or share options are usually expressed as a multiple of base salary. In 1997 (the first year after the Greenbury Report became effective), 68% of new conditional share plans made awards worth less than 100% of salary each year. By 2002, only 17% of new schemes awarded less than 100% of salary, with 24% offering more than 145% of salary each year[5].

*Maximum initial awards of new long term incentive plans (Source: PIRC)*

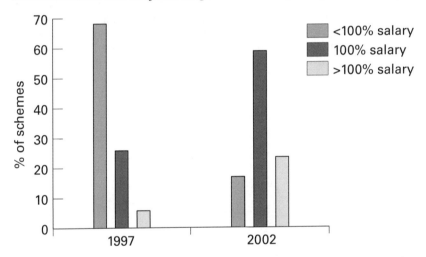

As noted above, market data is potentially misleading as some companies only award LTIPs, some only options and some a mixture. Thus it is best to review data for the expected value of all types of long term incentive plans.

## Performance measures

The usual measure is TSR compared to a comparator group of companies, with a secondary measure of financial performance, usually EPS. There are, however, a wide range of alternatives that might be appropriate to a company's particular circumstances. It is often difficult to find a good comparator group. Acquisitions and mergers deplete comparator groups, so at least 12 and preferably 20 are needed. Sometimes this is not possible, eg BP compared itself with the seven sister oil multinationals.

**B17.38**  *Performance measures*

A typical vesting schedule would be:

| Performance | % of award vesting |
|---|---|
| Below median | nothing |
| Median | 25% of target award |
| Upper Quartile | 100% of target award |
| Upper Decile or above | 100% or 150% or even 200% of target award |

There would be a sliding scale of payments between these points. It should be noted that the practice has become to announce an award figure of say 100% of salary, which would be paid at Upper Quartile performance. However there may be additional rewards above this level, eg the Upper Decile multiplier maximum could be 200% of salary. It should be further noted that these percentages are based on current salary and share price at award. If the share price has gone up so will the percentage. If upper decile performance is achieved the share price is likely to have grown substantially, eg if the share price doubled and Upper Decile performance was achieved, the so called maximum award of 100% of salary would be worth 400% of salary after three years.

## Retention period

B17.39

Some plans have a further mandatory retention period after the three year vesting, with the aim of retention/handcuffs. Other plans make awards in the form of nil-price options, which enable the executive to choose when to exercise after the award vests.

## Bonus matching

B17.40

This requires the executive to defer his bonus and they will then receive matching shares if performance targets are achieved. Usually the targets are similar to the LTIP targets described above, but companies are free to choose whatever targets they feel are appropriate. The main difference is that the award in the LTIP is not linked to the annual bonus amount, but tends to be a fixed amount.

## Communicating LTIPs

B17.41

Many employees find it quite complex to understand how well they are doing with their LTIPs. This is less so in the first year of a plan, but when three cycles are running, often with different comparator groups, this can be much less clear than working out the 'in the money' value of options.

# Cash long term incentive plans                B17.42

These payments systems normally pay out three years from inception and are often overlapping so each year a new three year cycle is started. They are normally measured against more demanding and wide-ranging targets than annual cash bonuses. A normal range of trigger targets for a three year bonus would be 'earnings per share' (EPS) plus control of cash flow against three year budgets and possibly return on capital employed.

One of the purposes of a longer term bonus is to ensure executives use the assets of the company as well as its revenue to best effect. Schemes often therefore involve specific targets to sell off surplus property, inventory or other non-core assets over the three years of the programme. Remuneration committees normally insist that any such scheme is self-financing, the bonus becoming a revenue cost.

# Share ownership guidelines                B17.43

Share ownership guidelines, like other parts of remuneration, have been imported from the US. The idea is that directors must build and hold a substantial stake in shares in the business. Most shareholders like to see directors with significant personal investment in the company. Companies need to consider whether their guidelines are mandatory or advisory and what penalties for non-achievement are to be applied.

Some companies expect executives to retain a minimum of shares which vest through share plans so as to build up towards the share ownership target.

The scandals in the US will increase the pressure for directors to hold shares for a minimum period of one or two years after exercise, after selling shares to pay taxes.

# Retention incentives ('handcuffs')                B17.44

When the market for good people is particularly vibrant, it may be necessary to offer retention incentives to ensure that enough good people stay to manage the company. It is usually better to offer performance-related incentives.

If a company is potentially going bust or is going to be sold, then incentives to tie in the key players may be appropriate if the business will be worth less if these people were to leave. In such circumstances, the payment of guaranteed amounts may be more effective in retention than incentives where people are unsure of payments and feel they have little effect on the end results.

If a key executive announces they are going to leave, it may be appropriate to negotiate with them and offer them a better offer to stay. In such circumstances then payment of guaranteed amounts may be more effective in retention than incentives, although a mixture of both and possibly a salary rise may be the optimum solution. Remuneration committees should have flexibility in their remuneration policy to manage such situations and can use Rule 13.13 of the Listing Rules for a special LTI plan.

# Benefits and perquisites                                    B17.45

Widow's (surviving spouse) pension and life insurance are typically provided as part of the pension plan. Holidays, private medical and directors' indemnity insurance are also normal benefits. A company car and use of a chauffeur whilst on company business is also normal. Larger companies with overseas operations may find it cost effective to have a company plane. Payment of club membership fees is also a common benefit.

CEO expenses are usually signed off by the chairman of the remuneration Committee.

# Directors' service contracts                                B17.46

*This section is based on material that appeared in Chapter 9 – Directors' Remuneration and Benefits of Tolley's Non-Executive Directors Handbook (2003), written by Patrick Dunne, 3i and Glynis D. Morris BA, FCA. This material is used by permission of LexisNexis UK.*

## At a glance                                                B17.47

---

- The Combined Code includes specific provisions on the notice periods and compensation arrangements for directors.

- The ABI/NAPF have jointly issued detailed guidance on contracts.

- A comprehensive service contract for each executive director can help to prevent misunderstandings.

- Each non-executive director will usually have a contract for services.

- *CA 1985* includes provisions on the retention and location of directors' service contracts (see **B14.17**).

- Members of the company are entitled to inspect directors' service contracts. Details have to be disclosed in the remuneration report (see **B14.24**).

- Shareholder approval is required for any contract giving a director a right of employment for more than five years, unless the company can give unconditional notice at any time.

- Consultation announced by the Department of Trade and Industry.

---

## Service contracts and compensation                B17.48

The Combined Code as revised by the FRC in July 2003 following the Higgs Report, includes the following provisions:

> 'B.1.5 The Remuneration Committee should carefully consider what compensation commitments (including pension contributions and all other elements) their directors' terms of appointment would entail in the event of early termination. The aim should be to avoid rewarding poor performance. They should take a robust line on reducing compensation to reflect departing directors' obligations to mitigate loss.
>
> B.1.6 Notice or contract periods should be set at one year or less. If it is necessary to offer longer notice or contract periods to new directors recruited from outside, such periods should reduce to one year or less after the initial period.'

The Code drafting is quite specific and stronger than the previous wording. Large payoffs for failure have consistently attracted negative publicity. In December 2002, in response to continuing concern, the ABI and NAPF issued a joint statement with specific and detailed guidance (see **B15.2**). When companies did not follow the new guidance, both the ABI and NAPF were vocal in criticising companies and this led to much negative publicity and some large percentages votes against the remuneration report resolutions at AGMs in 2003. The Government responded by issuing another consultation document, 'Rewards for Failure: Directors' Remuneration – Contracts, Performance and Severance' (June 2003). Views have been sought by the Department of Trade and Industry by 30 September 2003 on whether, and if so how, further measures are required to enable shareholders to ensure that compensation reflects performance when directors' contracts are terminated.

## Service contracts for executive directors            B17.49

An executive director is in effect an employee of the company and it is appropriate that the terms and conditions of his/her appointment should be set out in a written contract of service between the director and the company. A comprehensive service contract can help to prevent misunderstandings and provides a useful point of reference if problems arise. Non-executive directors have a very different role to executive directors and the terms and conditions of their appointment will usually be set out in a contract for services. A service contract for an executive director should normally include:

- specific duties of the director, including the amount of time to be spent on company activities (this may be particularly important where the individual also holds posts such as non-executive directorships in other businesses);
- remuneration, including details of any arrangements involving:
  - benefits in kind (eg private health cover, accommodation, company car);

**B17.49**  *Service contracts for executive directors*

- ○   bonus schemes;
- ○   long term incentive plans;
- ○   share options;
- •   holiday entitlement;
- •   arrangements in the case of prolonged absence through illness;
- •   pension arrangements;
- •   required notice period, and procedures in the case of dismissal;
- •   compensation arrangements in the event of early termination of the contract;
- •   compensation and other arrangements in the event of change in control;
- •   confidentiality arrangements; and
- •   restrictions after employment,

Other issues may need to be covered, depending on the circumstances.

Shareholders have been concerned about contractual provisions that can lead to substantial severance payments after a period of poor performance for more than a decade. In the early 1990s Hermes Asset Management (then PosTel) wrote to FTSE 100 companies threatening to vote against three year rolling contracts. In 1995, the Greenbury Committee recommended that companies should aim to have contracts with a notice period of no longer than one year rolling.

Most contracts with notice periods of longer than one year tend to be held by chief executives or finance directors with other executive directors on one year or less. Around 4% of directors have six month rolling notice periods.

*Notice periods for executive directors 1994–2002 (FTSE350) (Source: PIRC)*

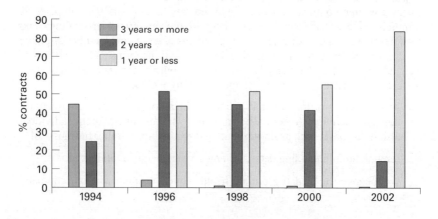

# Liquidated damages and mitigation B17.50

Liquidated damages clauses do not comply with the July 2003 Code, which specifies that companies should take a robust line regarding the departing executive's obligation to mitigate their loss.

The concept of mitigation is that the departing executive is expected to seek and find alternative employment with a similar level of remuneration as soon as possible. It may take several months and the executive may have to accept a lower level of remuneration. Thus an executive on a years notice might be expected to find similar employment in six to nine months. It will of course depend on particular circumstances and the company must take care not to make statements that impact on the executive's reputation and ability to secure another similar job.

# Conclusions regarding contracts B17.51

The issue of compensation associated with notice periods and contracts cannot be looked at in isolation from other elements of directors' remuneration. Salary, bonus, benefits and pension also impact on compensation levels. Therefore as well as looking at the issue of 'rewards for failure' in relation to contracts, the wider issue of remuneration packages unrelated to any past or future improvements in company performance should also be addressed. The remuneration committee needs to consider the total remuneration that may be earned over a number of years under a number of performance scenarios and confirm that the contractual compensation is not an excessive part of this total remuneration.

Shareholder pressure has been successful in reducing notice periods. This suggests that contractual terms are not the outcome of the 'market for executives' but are as much influenced by what is acceptable to shareholders and other interested parties. Shareholders can be expected to be more assertive in enforcing their interests. But in clamping down on one aspect of 'excessive' pay, shareholders must ensure that other payments are not made. In this respect, complexity is a barrier. Shareholders should be analysing remuneration packages in the round, rather than in a fragmentary way, but this is not easy for them to do with complex remuneration structures.

The use of phased payments and/or linking payments to changes in the share price since appointment is generally supported.

Reducing compensation following poor performance is an entirely reasonable concept, though open to considerable legal debate. However, poor performance has wider ramifications than just its impact on compensation levels. All boards should be approaching appraisal and competence issues in a far more professional and consistent way than at present. In this context, IRS commend the recommendations of the Higgs Report on board and individual director appraisal. If this process is being conducted effectively, poor performance would be identified and dealt with at an earlier stage and would not necessarily be an issue for negotiation in a severance situation.

Experience suggests that disclosure of contractual provisions could be improved to build on the new regulations. The simplest solution would be for companies to disclose the maximum compensation payable to each director if their contract was terminated, with a note saying the amount would be subject to mitigation.

## Contracts for services of non-executive directors      B17.52

Higgs provided guidance on the role of the non-executive director and also provided a sample letter of non-executive director appointment, as follows.

On [date], upon the recommendation of the nomination committee, the board of [company] ('the Company') has appointed you as non-executive director. I am writing to set out the terms of your appointment. It is agreed that this is a contract for services and is not a contract of employment.

**Appointment**

Your appointment will be for an initial term of three years commencing on [date], unless otherwise terminated earlier by and at the discretion of either party upon [one month's] written notice. Continuation of your contract of appointment is contingent on satisfactory performance and re-election at forthcoming AGMs. Non-executive directors are typically expected to serve two three-year terms, although the board may invite you to serve an additional period.

**Time commitment**

Overall we anticipate a time commitment of [number] days per month after the induction phase. This will include attendance at [monthly] board meetings, the AGM, [one] annual board away day, and [at least one] site visit per year. In addition, you will be expected to devote appropriate preparation time ahead of each meeting.

By accepting this appointment, you have confirmed that you are able to allocate sufficient time to meet the expectations of your role. The agreement of the chairman should be sought before accepting additional commitments that might impact on the time you are able to devote to your role as a non-executive director of the company.

**Role**

Non-executive directors have the same general legal responsibilities to the company as any other director. The board as a whole is collectively responsible for the success of the company. The board:

- provides entrepreneurial leadership of the company within a framework of prudent and effective controls which enable risk to be assessed and managed;

- sets the company's strategic aims, ensures that the necessary financial and human resources are in place for the company to meet its objectives, and reviews management performance; and

- sets the company's values and standards and ensure that its obligations to its shareholders and others are understood and met. All directors must take decisions objectively in the interests of the company.

In addition to these requirements of all directors, the role of the non-executive director has the following key elements.

- **Strategy:** Non-executive directors should constructively challenge and help develop proposals on strategy.

- **Performance:** Non-executive directors should scrutinise the performance of management in meeting agreed goals and objectives and monitor the reporting of performance.

- **Risk:** Non-executive directors should satisfy themselves on the integrity of financial information and that financial controls and systems of risk management are robust and defensible.

- **People:** Non-executive directors are responsible for determining appropriate levels of remuneration of executive directors and have a prime role in appointing, and where necessary removing, executive directors and in succession planning.

**Fees**

You will be paid a fee of £[amount] gross per annum which will be paid monthly in arrears, [plus [number] ordinary shares of the company per annum, both of] which will be subject to an annual review by the board. The company will reimburse you for all reasonable and properly documented expenses you incur in performing the duties of your office.

**Outside interests**

It is accepted and acknowledged that you have business interests other than those of the company and have declared any conflicts that are apparent at present. In the event that you become aware of any potential conflicts of interest, these should be disclosed to the chairman and company secretary as soon as apparent.

[The board of the Company have determined you to be independent according to provision A.3.1 of the Code.]

**Confidentiality**

All information acquired during your appointment is confidential to the company and should not be released, either during your appointment or following termination (by whatever means), to third parties without prior clearance from the chairman.

Your attention is also drawn to the requirements under both legislation and regulation as to the disclosure of price sensitive information. Consequently you should avoid making any statements that might risk a breach of these require-ments without prior clearance from the chairman or company secretary.

## Induction

Immediately after appointment, the company will provide a comprehensive, formal and tailored induction. This will include the information pack recom-mended by the Institute of Chartered Secretaries and Administrators (ICSA), available at www.icsa.org.uk. We will also arrange for site visits and meetings with senior and middle management and the company's auditors. We will also offer to major shareholders the opportunity to meet you.

## Review process

The performance of individual directors and the whole board and its committees is evaluated annually. If, in the interim, there are any matters which cause you concern about your role you should discuss them with the chairman as soon as is appropriate.

## Insurance

The company has directors' and officers' liability insurance and it is intended to maintain such cover for the full term of your appointment. The current indemnity limit is £ [amount]; a copy of the policy document is attached.

## Independent professional advice

Occasions may arise when you consider that you need professional advice in the furtherance of your duties as a director. Circumstances may occur when it will be appropriate for you to seek advice from independent advisors at the company's expense. A copy of the board's agreed procedure under which directors may obtain such independent advice is attached. The company will reimburse the full cost of expenditure incurred in accordance with the attached policy.

## Committees

This letter refers to your appointment as a non-executive director of the company. In the event that you are also asked to serve on one or more of the board committees this will be covered in a separate communication setting out the committee(s)'s terms of reference, any specific responsibilities and any additional fees that may be involved.

This sample appointment letter has been compiled with the assistance of ICSA who have kindly agreed to produce updated guidance on their website www.icsa.org.uk in the future.

## Special arrangements for recruitment      B17.53

It may not be possible to follow the normal remuneration practice when recruiting a new director, particularly a new CEO. In order to persuade an established director to move company he will need to be offered more than he currently receives. Moving company entails additional risk and risk requires additional compensation. In addition, he may have unvested long term incentives and be giving up the time value of options. The recruiting company has two alternatives, either to buy out these options and incentives or to recruit someone who is cheaper!

If the recruiting company buys out the oldco incentives, it needs to decide the form in which to compensate. This might be in the form of a guaranteed bonus, a payment of deferred shares or an additional option award. One creative approach is to persuade the recruit to buy some shares in newco and award a matching number, some contingent only on service and some performance linked.

## Special considerations for large global companies      B17.54

Global companies have to compete globally for customers and employees. They will need to pay rates that are locally competitive, not necessarily the top of the market, but not at the bottom. The issue is not just about salary, but about the structure of the package. For example if the company has operations in the US and all their competitors issue lots of options then granting small amounts of LTIPs is not competitive and may breed dissatisfaction in local employees unless the company can communicate very clearly why it wishes to pay differently to everyone else.

## Special considerations regarding CEO pay      B17.55

The CEO is the most visible executive in the company to the outside world. Thus the CEOs pay is open to particular scrutiny.

The nature of the role is such that there can be great scope to create or destroy value. This is reflected in the differentials in pay of the CEO versus other directors.

There is however a problem of short tenure. The average CEO tenure is four years, but 'of course that won't happen to us'. Whilst taking all steps to ensure that the appointment is the right one, the remuneration committee must consider all scenarios and ensure that the CEO package is skewed in the best interests of the company and not one-sided in favour of the CEO.

# Non-executive directors' remuneration                    B17.56

The Combined Code says:

> 'B.1.3  Levels of remuneration for non-executive directors should reflect the time commitment and responsibilities of the role. Remuneration for non-executive directors should not include share options. If, exceptionally, options are granted, shareholder approval should be sought in advance and any shares acquired by exercise of the options should be held until at least one year after the non-executive director leaves the board. Holding of share options could be relevant to the determination of a non-executive director's independence (as set out in provision A.3.1).

> B.2.3 The board itself or, where required by the Articles of Association, the shareholders should determine the remuneration of the non-executive directors within the limits set in the Articles of Association. Where permitted by the Articles, the board may however delegate this responsibility to a committee, which might include the chief executive.'

The FRC wording permits the grant of options to non-executive directors (NEDs), albeit under strict rules. This is a softening of the wording proposed by Higgs that options should be avoided. There is a variety of views on linking NEDs remuneration to share price movements. The majority view is in favour. The granting of options in small companies is often appropriate. In larger companies options may be in special circumstances, for example, in 2003 Cable and Wireless introduced a co-investment plan for NEDs, which had a similar design to share options and this was approved by the majority of their shareholders.

## Background                                              B17.57

NEDs need to be seen as independent of the company and therefore receive fees, not a salary. Pluralist non-executives with several directorships will often have set up a service company to which these fees are paid gross.

Individuals who only have one or two non-executive directorships may choose to have their fees paid via the company payroll with national insurance and tax deducted but they are still being paid fees, not a salary.

The Independent Chairman And Non-Executive Director Survey, which IRS edit, shows that 98% of independent directors have a letter of appointment, of which 25% are for one year, 33% are for two years and 40% are for three years.

However, a NED is always entitled to resign immediately if he has a disagreement with the board or feels there is a point of principle involved.

In most cases, non-executive directors who lose their appointments following a takeover or merger would be entitled to between three and six months' fees as compensation for loss of office.

It is very important that non-executive candidates check the directors' indemnity insurance policy in the light of an increasing number of shareholder and other actions against companies and their boards, this is probably the most important issue before accepting a non-executive directorship.

Survey data from the IRS Independent Chairman and Non-Executive Director Survey follows together with an extract from the report.

| Company Turnover £M | <10 | 11–30 | 31–100 | 101–500 | 501–1000 | 1000+ |
|---|---|---|---|---|---|---|
| **Independent Director** | | | | | | |
| Formal Meeting Days | 12 | 13 | 13 | 13 | 15 | 16 |
| Preparation and Travel Time | 4 | 6 | 6 | 6 | 6 | 7 |
| Plant visits and other non-formal occasions | 1 | 2 | 2 | 2 | 2 | 3 |
| Total | 17 | 21 | 21 | 21 | 23 | 26 |
| **Chairman** | | | | | | |
| Formal Meeting Days | 14 | 14 | 15 | 15 | 16 | 18 |
| Preparation and Travel Time | 9 | 12 | 12 | 12 | 13 | 14 |
| Plant visits and other non-formal occasions | 2 | 4 | 4 | 3 | 4 | 5 |
| Investor Relations and ambassadorial days | 8 | 10 | 12 | 21 | 18 | 16 |
| Total | 33 | 40 | 43 | 51 | 51 | 53 |

*\*Formal meetings include the AGM and Away/Day Strategy Meetings*

**Fees**

| Company Turnover £M | <10 | 11–30 | 31–100 | 101–500 | 501–1000 | 1000+ |
|---|---|---|---|---|---|---|
| Chairmen £'000 | | | | | | |
| Fees | 35–40 | 40–50 | 60–70 | 80–100 | 100–120 | 150–200 |
| Independent Director £'000 | | | | | | |
| Main Board Fees | 8–15 | 15–20 | 15–25 | 18–25 | 20–35 | 35–40 |
| Committee Fees | - | - | 2–5 | 3–5 | 5–10 | 5–10 |

**B17.57** *Background*

Very few chairman are paid sub-committee fees and in quoted companies should not chair their own sub-committees. It has been fairly common practice in medium-sized and smaller quoted companies to roll up committee fees in a single overall non-executive fee, covering membership of both the audit and remuneration committees. When they were quoted they averaged £2000 per committee and £2500 per committee chairmanship.

In larger groups, with a wider choice of independent directors, many do not sit on any committee and others only sit on one. As a high percentage of increasing governance takes place in the audit, remuneration and nominations committee, respondents on large company boards indicated the fee rates they are now receiving for work on these committees. As we have banded annual fee rates, we also use this system for the per diem rates which include committee fees where relevant.

| Daily Rates | <10m | 11–30m | 31–100m | 101–500m | 500–1000m | 1000m+ |
|---|---|---|---|---|---|---|
| Chairman £ | 1060–1400 | 1000–1250 | 1400–1630 | 1570–1960 | 1960–2350 | 2830–3775 |
| Independent Director £ | 470–880 | 710–950 | 810–1420 | 1000–1420 | 1090–1959 | 1540–1920 |

We think it is quite likely based on recent assignments that an increase in remuneration over the next year will not necessarily affect base fees, unless corporate performance improves, but we suspect there will be a significant increase in sub-committee fees, whether these are paid separately or rolled into a single overall figure. Although we have no evidence of this from our survey, we suspect that in the minds of non-executive directors, the make up of the fee equation is beginning to change to something like the following.

| Factors in the equation (£000) | Large Cap | Small Cap | Unquoted |
|---|---|---|---|
| The personal risk and responsibility of accepting a directorship | 25 | 12 | 1 |
| Fees for attending formal meetings | 15 | 12 | 8 |
| Preparation and informal discussion time | 8 | 5 | 3 |
| **Total** | 48 | 29 | 12 |

Shareholders and pressure group class actions against directors are sharpening candidates' perceptions of the risk as well as the increasing time commitment of ensuring corporate governance compliance and dealing with the increasing tide of Westminster and EEC regulators. Per diem rates that are now below and often well below 50% of managers' as well as partners' day rates charged by professional advisers.

**Payment in shares or options**

The table below shows the percentage of independent directors holding shares or options in their company. Not surprisingly, option holding is much more prevalent among directors of smaller companies where they probably play a greater part in the commercial strategy of the group as well as maintaining a monitoring function in line with independent directors on the boards of the larger groups.

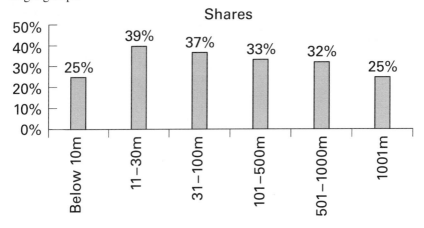

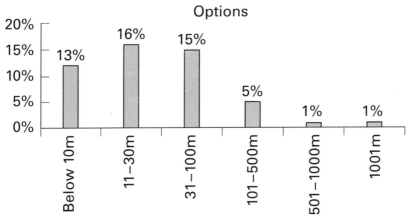

IRS have consistently argued for options to be available in certain situations to, particularly, the chairmen of smaller companies who may well spend two days a week on their responsibilities. Many companies are introduced to the main or AIM markets with independent director option schemes in place but as a number of those directors holding options for some years may well have realised all or part of their holding, directors holding options in quoted companies are likely to decrease. A certain number of companies are now making it clear that they would like independent directors to purchase a shareholding, but very few companies make this a condition.

**Notes**
1.  Although investors often use abstentions as a means of expressing discontent companies do not have to disclose figures for these and this column has been left blank where we do not have the relevant figure. The figures in the table are as recorded on our database from figures provided to us, on request or disclosed to the stock exchange by the company in question. Figures may not add up to 100 because of rounding
2.  Source: Average Earnings Index, ONS.
3.  Share Based Incentive Schemes – A Statement of Principles and Guidelines, ABI July 1999.
4.  Corporate Governance 2000 – PIRC Annual Review (PIRC Ltd); Corporate Governance Annual Review 2002 (PIRC Ltd).
5.  Fair Shares?: Long term incentive plans and Executive Share Option Schemes 1996–97 (PIRC Ltd), Corporate Governance Annual Review 2002 (PIRC Ltd).

# Communicating Directors' Pay

*This chapter has been compiled by Cliff Weight of Independent Remuneration Solutions.*

## Introduction                                                    B18.1

78% of people believe directors of large companies are overpaid, according to a UK MORI poll commissioned by the Financial Times (30 June 2003), and 80% think that top company directors cannot be trusted to tell the truth. Public opinion polls in the US provide comparative data. For example, in a Gallop poll in July 2002, 79% of people, when asked if corporate executives take improper actions to benefit themselves at the expense of their corporation, responded that this practice was very or somewhat widespread. 73% thought that CEOs of large corporations could not be trusted.

Does it matter what the general public think about directors' pay? It does, because the issue is in the political arena. If UK and US companies cannot 'clean up their act', then the governments may be forced to legislate. In addition there is research which shows that excessive pay and poor ethics impact on customers' views of brands.

Do people believe directors are overpaid because they are or because of the way pay is communicated? Directors' pay is complex and traditionally it has not been transparent. The way it is communicated suggests there is something to hide. There is, however, a systemic problem here. If a company communicates more clearly than anyone else, it will be easier for journalists to write about that company and they may draw unwelcome and unwarranted attention to themselves. Thus no one company wants to be leading in this respect.

Historically a major problem has been that the press have not reported directors' remuneration in a balanced responsible manner. Instead they have sought out the easy story and looked for controversy. Many organisations in the remuneration arena have an agenda and have sought publicity for their views. Consequently the best approach for most companies has been to adopt a low profile and disclose as little as possible. Less information meant less ammunition.

## The issues                                                      B18.2

● Remuneration attracts publicity. It is an easy story and nearly always negative. The PR and investor relations could be managed better.

- Remuneration is high profile and increasingly high risk. Recent examples include GlaxoSmithKline, Vodafone and Prudential. In some cases it is potentially damaging to the brand as well as to investor relations. Companies and individuals who attract negative PR on pay issues often find their shareholders less willing to support them on other issues.

- The government's new regulations mean all companies have to put their remuneration report to a vote at their AGM and also require better, more transparent remuneration committee reports. Consequently remuneration will attract even more publicity.

- Graphs of total shareholder return(TSR) over the past five years have to be included in the remuneration report, but no companies give explanations of the variations in CEO pay over the same period. The shareholders are left to work this out for themselves. This lack of clarity reduces accountability.

- TSR comparisons have in some cases been against a general index, whereas companies say they are comparing their remuneration against a specific market. Many companies in other parts of their annual report comment on measures of performance other than TSR, but do not include such data in the remuneration report. Since they link remuneration to more than just TSR, it would be logical to report on the other measures and such explanation would help justify changes in remuneration levels.

- Remuneration is complex. This is one area where the saying 'the devil is in the detail' is true. For example, problems often arise many years in the future because of seemingly innocuous small print.

- In order to manage the financial PR of directors' remuneration, detailed analysis is required, underpinned by up to date knowledge of the various stakeholder views.

- It is not only the high profile cases who need help. All companies would benefit from a risk assessment and analysis of the strengths and weaknesses of their remuneration arrangements – from a shareholder perspective.

# How to communicate with shareholders     B18.3

This is emerging as increasingly important. Most remuneration committee reports are impenetrable. Is this what companies and shareholders want? Remuneration committees must decide.

The history of alignment of pay and performance should be also be tested. Since a five year performance graph is now required, it is essential that the last five years of remuneration awarded and paid out should be reviewed by the remuneration committee and possibly disclosed. This analysis will reveal how successful the remuneration committee has been in:

- implementing its stated policy; and

- linking pay and performance.

Going forward, companies have to convince their shareholders to vote for their AGM remuneration committee report resolution and as well as new share schemes. Companies who are open and fully transparent will receive a better reception from their major shareholders than those who only partially disclose or try to pull the wool over the eyes of their shareholders. IRS research ('A New Paradigm for Directors' Remuneration', April 2002) shows that shareholders want to have collaboration with companies about pay. They want constructive dialogue. They do not want public spats all over the newspapers.

Some companies' proposals are like a red rag to a bull. A number of the institutions have their own agenda and the company should not feed them ammunition for them to publicise their agendae. If the minutiae have not been addressed, the company is always going to be on, in cricketing terms, a sticky wicket.

The mantra should be 'collaboration not conflict' with shareholders. To do so requires a better understanding of each others' points of views. The checklist at the end of this chapter (see **B18.7**) is a good starting point.

# The communication process                                    B18.4

**Step 1:** Assess where you are. IRS have developed a 180 question questionnaire to undertake a detailed assessment of a company's current arrangements to identify their strengths and weaknesses. In particular it considers the impact of the directors' remuneration report regulations.

## Impact Assessment – Directors' Remuneration Report Regulations

Part of this assessment should include detailed scenario analyses which:

● illustrate a range of possible outcomes;

● consider *all* elements of remuneration; and

- consider *all* historic awards of medium and long term incentives as well as the current proposals.

**Step 2:** Develop a communication plan, eg:

- plan what you want to say;

- assess the likely reaction;

- modify your strategy and if necessary change your remuneration policy;

- test your proposal with informal discussions;

- understand the likely objections an arguments and decide how to address them;

- decide what are must haves and where you can be flexible if you have to be;

- refine your messages;

- decide who should communicate to who and in what order;

- consult, listen and react.

**Step 3:** The remuneration committee report needs to be drafted so that it meets the new Regulations and achieves the optimum impact with shareholders and other target audiences.

**Step 4:** Once the above steps have been completed, the company has to publish its remuneration report and share plan proposals. These will be analysed by the intermediaries, the ABI, NAPF, Manifest, PIRC etc. They may already have been consulted as part of your communication plan. At this stage it may be necessary to issue them with some questions and answers to give further explanation and background data on top of what is in the remuneration report and shareholders' circular. The intermediaries will send the company copies of their report in draft form to ask for confirmation it is factually correct. This is another opportunity for the company to explain itself.

Through this process there may be leaks to the press. When the intermediaries issue their reports and voting guidance they may also comment to the press.

**Step 5:** Companies need to prepare thoroughly for the AGM with questions and answers for the chairman and/or chairman of the remuneration committee, so they can answer accurately and confidently.

Companies should expect some shareholders to vote against their proposals. They need to take a view about what is acceptable and manage either their remuneration policy or communication strategy accordingly, or preferably both together.

# The press and how to work with them          **B18.5**

Most companies fail to educate the press, some of whom are not very knowledgeable about these issues. The companies with problems generally need to be much more open and be more detailed in what it communicated. To do so successfully needs good initial assessments of the likely reactions to the company's proposals.

# How to communicate directors' pay to employees          **B18.6**

It is not just shareholders who have a view about directors pay. It can be highly demotivational and bad for morale if the CEO and directors are getting large bonuses, pay rises and awards of options and LTIPs when staff are being made redundant and asked to work harder. Before pay decisions are made, remuneration committees should consider how those decisions can be explained to employees and their likely reactions.

# Checklist          **B18.7**

---

1. Process

☐ Remuneration committee

- Does the remuneration committee make a report to shareholders and is it signed off by a member of the committee?

- Are all members independent?

- Are terms of reference defined, clear and in line with the Combined Code?

- Are the remuneration committee advisers independent:

  ○ what other services do they provide; and

  ○ what are their fees for remuneration committee advice and other work?

  Is the chairman a member of the remuneration committee?

  Do the chairman and CEO attend the remuneration committee and withdraw when their own pay is discussed?

  Is the remuneration committee secretary the company secretary or HR director?

☐ Is the remuneration committee report put to the vote at the AGM:

- Are there separate votes for forward looking policy and on the actual practice and payments for the previous year?

---

|   |
|---|
| • Are substantive changes in remuneration policy explained to shareholders and voted upon at the AGM?<br><br>• Are all new share schemes and incentives over more than one year put to a vote? |
| 2. Remuneration Policy |
| ☐ Is there a remuneration policy? |
| ☐ Is it stated in the remuneration report? |
| ☐ Does the remuneration policy cover the four key elements:<br><br>  1. Selection of appropriate comparator companies:<br>    • types of executives required;<br>    • importance of individual executives to delivery of business strategy;<br>    • size of talent pool;<br>    • comparator companies location UK, Europe, Global;<br>    • comparator companies size – sales, market cap, employees, assets, profits etc.<br><br>  2. Identifies pay market position(s) and linkage of pay market position to performance.<br><br>  3. Mix of performance related and not-performance related elements.<br><br>  4. Alignment to shareholders' interests:<br>    • upside alignment;<br>    • downside alignment:<br>      ○ contracts,<br>      ○ LTIPs/options;<br>    • share ownership guidelines;<br>    • alignment to business strategy;<br>    • performance measures:<br>      ○ are KPIs included,<br>      ○ can they be massaged in the short term,<br>      ○ is there a good mix of leading and lagging indicators. |
| ☐ Detailed remuneration policy issues:<br><br>  • Is there a graph/table to show total remuneration at different performance levels?<br><br>  • Relativities of CEO to other executive directors – are they justifiable/ sensible? |

- Is there flexibility to adjust the remuneration policy in special circumstances:

  ○ to retain those who have been offered jobs elsewhere?

  ○ to attract key hires (eg using rule 13.13 of the Combined Code)?

  ○ to adjust future award levels if market practice changes?

  ○ adjust performance targets if special circumstances arise?

- Annual bonus:

  ○ Target and maximum annual bonus?

  ○ Are the annual bonus performance measures drivers of long term shareholder value or short term focused?

  ○ Bonus deferral and matching:

    – performance condition for minimum match;

    – performance condition for maximum match;

    – are expected value and potential value disclosed.

- Options:

  ○ Are face value and expected value disclosed?

  ○ Are potential gains disclosed?

  ○ Are performance conditions sufficiently stretching?

  ○ Are higher awards subject to tougher performance conditions?

  ○ Are higher awards part of a cohesive integrated reward strategy?

  ○ Can options vest for below median/RPI performance?

  ○ Is exercise subject to an underlying improvement in financial performance?

  ○ Length of time until vesting and performance period length?

- LTIPs (restricted share plans):

  ○ Are face value and expected value disclosed?

  ○ Are potential gains disclosed?

  ○ Are performance conditions sufficiently stretching?

  ○ Are higher awards subject to tougher performance conditions?

  ○ Are higher awards part of a cohesive, integrated reward strategy?

  ○ Can LTIPs vest for below median/RPI performance?

  ○ Is exercise subject to an underlying improvement in financial performance?

  ○ Threshold performance for payment?

|  |
|---|
| ○ % of award paid at threshold? |
| ○ Award at Q3 performance? |
| ○ Maximum performance level? |
| ○ Award at maximum performance level? |
| ○ Length of performance period and subsequent holding period? |
| ● Combined long term incentive plans (bonus matching, options and LTIPs): |
| ○ Are combined Face Value and Expected Value disclosed? |
| ○ Are combined potential gains disclosed? |
| ○ Are the combined schemes excessive? |
| ○ Are the combined schemes part of a cohesive integrated reward strategy? |
| ● Share ownership guidelines: |
| ○ Is the policy disclosed? |
| ○ Level? |
| ○ Years to achievement? |
| ○ Which shares are included? |
| ○ Penalties for non-achievement? |
| □ Does directors' remuneration take account of pay conditions within the company: |
| ● Is there information on employee remuneration policy? |
| ● Is pay elsewhere in the company considered in determining directors' pay? |
| ● Do all employees benefit from business success? |
| 3. Remuneration Practice, ie how much was paid/awarded for the previous year |
| □ Are all remuneration figures clearly disclosed: |
| ● Full table of option awards -not average issue price |
| ● Pension transfer value |
| ● Salary increase and new salary for present year |
| ● Is the total remuneration awarded and received disclosed? |
| ● Is performance basis for all incentives clearly set out? |
| □ Salary: |
| ● Level |

- Position v comparators
- Relativities – ie internally
- % increase on previous year
- Alignment of performance and salary % increase

☐ Pension:

- Level of benefits
- Transfer value £, as % salary
- Treatment of pay above the cap
- Definition of final salary – is only basic salary pensionable?
- Early leaver provisions?

☐ Other benefits:

- Benefits disclosed £, as % salary
- Housing allowance
- Access to exotic benefits such as planes, yacht, company mansion etc

☐ Contracts:

- Notice period – is the policy for one year or less?
- If notice periods are greater than 1 year are they satisfactorily explained?
- Mitigation (including statement of policy) or liquidated damages
- 'Pay as you go' or lump sum
- Treatment of bonuses and incentives including guarantees and early vesting
- Enhanced pension provision

☐ Annual bonus (including special one off bonuses):

- Actual amount £, %?
- Performance measures – are they what the City looks at?
- Bonus matching and deferral
- Alignment of performance and bonus paid – are targets stretching?

☐ Options:

- Level of award £, % salary
- Are Face Value and Expected Value disclosed?
- Are potential gains disclosed?

- Are (paper) gains to date shown?
- Performance measures:
  - Is the expected probability of performance measures disclosed?
  - Is it transparent how the measures align to shareholder value?
  - Threshold for grants above 1x salary p.a.
  - Degree of stretch for maximum award
  - Can options vest for below median/RPI performance
  - Is exercise subject to an underlying improvement in financial performance?
- % dilution
- Number of shares over which options awarded each year including those bought in the market – % total
- P&L impact disclosed (as per FAS123 of ASB25)
- % of all options granted that are granted to CEO
- % of all options granted that are granted to top five executives
- Is the full history of awards and performance achievement and expected payout disclosed?

☐ LTIPs

- Level of award £, % salary
- Are face value and expected value disclosed?
- Are potential gains disclosed?
- Performance measures:
  - Is the expected probability of performance measures disclosed?
  - Is it transparent how the measures align to shareholder value?
  - Threshold for grants above 1x salary p.a.
  - Degree of stretch for maximum award
  - Can options vest for below median/RPI performance?
  - Is exercise subject to an underlying improvement in financial performance?
- % dilution
- Number of shares over which LTIPs awarded each year including those bought in the market – % total
- P&L impact (as per FAS123 of ASB25)
- % of all LTIPs granted that are granted to CEO

- % of all LTIPs granted that are granted to top five executives
- Is the full history of awards and performance achievement and expected payout disclosed?

☐ Mix of remuneration:

- Is the mix of remuneration disclosed?
- Is pension included?
- Does the mix of remuneration contain too much or too little performance-related?

☐ Total remuneration:

- Is the total remuneration disclosed?
- Is it possible to calculate the total remuneration from the disclosed data:
  - ○ Total of actual cash pay and benefits received plus the expected value of long term incentives
  - ○ Total of actual cash pay and benefits received plus the paper gains in the year on the long term incentives awarded in the year and in previous years plus the gains on actual shares owned
  - ○ Total of actual cash pay and benefits received plus the amounts realised from the exercise of long term incentives

☐ Share ownership

- How big is the shareholding?
- Was the SOG policy achieved?
- Does level of share ownership (plus other remuneration) provide alignment with shareholders?

4. PR and investor relations perceptions

☐ Transparency of remuneration committee report

☐ Sensitivity of remuneration committee report:

- Are remunerations levels high?
- Alignment of remuneration and performance
- Previous history and sensitivity to pay issues
- Company performance this year, last three years and last five years:
  - ○ TSR
    - – absolute

      versus comparators

      versus FTSE100

| |
|---|
| ○  EPS |
| absolute |
| versus comparators |
| versus FTSE100 |
| versus inflation |
| □  Media views: |
| ●  On the company |
| ●  On remuneration in the company |
| □  Fund managers views: |
| ●  On the company |
| ●  On remuneration in the company |
| □  Compliance with corporate governance guidance on remuneration: |
| ●  Combined Code |
| ●  ABI |
| ●  NAPF |
| ●  PIRC |
| ●  Manifest |
| ●  Hermes |
| ●  Standard Life |
| ●  Morley |

# Board Committees

## Introduction B19.1

Standing committees of the board are a useful means of ensuring that the board gives in-depth consideration to all matters for which it is responsible. The time available at board meetings may make this difficult or impossible to achieve. The appropriate timing when matters need to be considered and decisions made may make it more efficient for the matters to be considered first by a board committee rather than by the board as a whole which may not be meeting at the appropriate time. Some matters, such as the remuneration of executive directors, may be best determined by a committee comprising only some of the board members.

Entities in compliance with all the Provisions of the Combined Code will have an audit committee, a remuneration committee and a nominations committee. Beyond that, entities will need to exercise their discretion to determine whether further board committees are appropriate.

## Arranging meetings B19.2

Adequate time must be allowed for board committee meetings, adequate notice given and adequate agenda papers circulated sufficiently in advance to allow for thorough preparation by the committee members.

Generally board committees should schedule their meetings so that their minutes are available to become agenda papers of an appropriate main board meeting. Thus the audit committee will meet shortly before the board approves the financial statements for publication.

### Reporting to the board B19.3

The chairperson of a board committee will usually speak to the committee's minutes that are tabled at the board meeting. Frequently these will be draft minutes since by then the committee may not have met subsequently to approve those minutes, but in practice this is rarely an impediment to the efficient conduct of business. Usually the members of board committees will also be members of the board – so a committee member will be able, if necessary, to use the board meeting to dissent from a committee minute which is tabled to the board in draft form.

Board committee minutes, as well as board minutes, should be sufficiently comprehensive to be an adequate record not only of recommendations made to the board but also of the process followed in arriving at those recommendations. There may be a need to refer back to minutes to show that the committee, and thus the board, had conducted its affairs diligently and not negligently.

Occasionally there may be outside membership of a board committee, and there are even instances where the chair of the audit committee is not a member of the board.

Because board committees are established to assist the board to despatch board business efficiently and effectively, their decisions are only advice to the board, potentially to be overturned at that level. Yet it would not be appropriate to have such committees if the main board routinely reopened all matters which had been considered at committee meetings.

In some cases it may even be regarded as preferable that the board routinely opts for *the decisions themselves* of a committee (such as the remuneration committee's determination of executive compensation) not even to be disclosed to the board. Of course there is no doubt that the board always has a right to this information but the board may choose not to ask for it. In a culture of openness and fuller public disclosure it is less likely that there will be matters to be decided in this way.

**Terms of reference**                                                          **B19.4**

The authority, responsibilities and membership of each board committee should be outlined in the committee's terms of reference which should be adopted by the board.

In some cases this would clearly be counterproductive, as, for instance, the attendance of an executive director at a remuneration committee which is determining his or her compensation package. Best practice is that no director should participate in the determination of his or her own remuneration. The membership of a board committee should be set out in its terms of reference which will also cover its responsibilities and membership. The terms of reference should be adopted by the board. The terms of reference are likely to empower the chairperson of the committee to invite others who are not members (whether other directors, senior and other executives, or outsiders) to be in attendance for part of all of meetings and should empower the chairperson to require those in attendance to leave the meeting when he or she considers it appropriate. While technically within his or her rights, any director who was not a committee member and yet insisted upon attending against the wishes of the chair should be brought to realise that he or she is also acting against the wishes of the board and should be prepared to face the consequences.

Some companies make provision in their constitutional documents for the existence of a remuneration and some other standing committees of the board; others by detailing the membership and responsibilities of these committees in minuted board resolutions.

## Annual review of terms of reference                              **B19.5**

It is good practice that an audit committee should review its terms of reference annually. This ensures that committee members are reminded of their responsibilities and powers. It also provides an opportunity for the committee to draw the board's attention to desirable modifications.

## Assistance for board committees                                 **B19.6**

Increasingly board committees are being empowered to take outside professional advice at the company's expense in connection with the discharge of their responsibilities. Board committees may also commission work to be done directly on their behalf by executives of the business. A 1997 survey found that audit committees of a sample of multinational companies typically commission one assignment each year to be conducted directly on the committee's behalf by the company's internal audit function (1997 Internal Audit Survey – Health Care Companies, Management Audit Ltd. Tel: +44 (0)1529 413344. Fax: +44 (0)1529 413355. E-mail: email@management-audit.com). However, in many cases it will be normal practice for a board committee to work through the responsible executive directors to arrange for specific tasks to be undertaken to meet the committee's needs. The nominations and remuneration committees are likely to need to conduct their business discretely.

In most cases it is sound that secretarial support for committees of the board should be provided by the secretary of the board, but it would be acceptable if necessary for someone such as the assistant company secretary to act as secretary to a board committee. It would not, for instance, be sound for the head of internal audit to act as secretary of the audit committee.

## Treading on executive toes                                      **B19.7**

We must also distinguish between the responsibilities of board committees for particular issues and the responsibilities of the executive for the same issues. Generally board committees are responsible to the board for the development of policy on particular issues whereas the executive (rather than the board or the board committee) is likely always to be responsible for the implementation of that policy which has been developed.

In **B21** BOARD COMMITTEES – TERMS OF REFERENCE the proposed draft terms of reference of the audit (second example) and remuneration committees include wording which specifies the committee is not an executive committee. Further consideration would need to be given as to whether the distinction between 'executive' and 'non-executive' in the context of committee powers, responsibilities and duties is valid, and, if so, which (if any) committees are to have executive powers.

## Selecting the committee chair                                   **B19.8**

It is general practice that the board determines who shall be the chairman of these board committees, often on the recommendation of the chairman of the entity whose overall responsibility it is to ensure the effective functioning of the board and its committees. A usually less satisfactory alternative would be for the committee itself to select its own chairman from those appointed by the board to be members of the committee. Many UK entities deem the gender-specific term 'chairman' to be both acceptable and indeed required, but progressive companies might alternatively opt for the rather ungainly expressions 'chairperson' or just 'chair'.

**Other related material**                                            B19.9

Under each of the sample terms of reference of board committees reproduced in **B21 BOARD COMMITTEES – TERMS OF REFERENCE**, the committee is authorised to engage professionals as the committee sees fit to provide independent counsel and advice and to assist in any review or investigation on such matters as the committee deems appropriate. A related topic is that individual directors should be empowered to obtain independent professional advice in the further-ance of their responsibilities as directors; advice on the standing guidelines that regulate the conduct of board business may be shown as a responsibility of the standing orders committee which may also be the committee with the responsibility to ensure that there is maintained an up-to-date board manual, available to all board directors. The standing orders committee is also shown as being responsible to advise the board on matters to be reserved to the board and on delegation of authority guidelines.

**Overlap**                                                          B19.10

In **B21 BOARD COMMITTEES – TERMS OF REFERENCE** we reproduce sample terms of reference for board committees developed in draft for one client. In their draft form there is some overlap between the terms of reference of three of the committees – nominations, personnel and remuneration. Here we summarise the overlap contained within these three draft terms of reference.

With the client for whom these terms of reference were developed, the suggestion arose internally for a personnel committee and this has been developed into proposed terms of reference which include certain duties also within the recommended terms of reference of the remuneration and nomina-tions committees. This overlap would need to be corrected if the board decided to go ahead and establish a personnel committee of the board.

Potential overlap between the nominations, remuneration and personnel committees can be summed up as follows.

- From the **nomination committee** draft terms of reference:

     '6.6 Nominating suitable people for the most senior executive positions, including that of chief executive.'

- From the **remuneration committee** draft terms of reference:

     '6.1 The committee's purpose is to ensure that … and senior executives are fairly rewarded for their individual contributions to overall performance . … '

'6.2 The duties of the committee shall be to recommend to and advise the board on the remuneration (in all its forms) and associated matters of the … senior executives. This requires the committee to:

1  Determine appropriate remuneration in all its forms (including pension arrangements within the discretion of the company's scheme) of the … senior executives, as defined from time to time. This will bear in mind differentials between levels of personnel and market relativities.

2  Ensure there is good succession planning and management development at senior executive levels, and to review specific development plans for the top *n* executives in the group.

3  Measure the performance of key senior executives as a prelude to determining their annual remuneration, bonus rewards and award of long term incentives.

4  See that, in exercising the rights to performance related compensation, benefits are related to the performance both of individuals and the group, and that they provide a long term incentive.

5  Ensure that the committee only makes recommendations which it can justify to shareholders and staff alike and that the criteria on which performance is measured can be clearly explained.'

- From the **personnel committee** draft terms of reference:

'1  Ensure that the company has a satisfactory personnel function covering all aspects of personnel management including succession planning and career development.

6  Ensure there is good succession planning and management development at senior executive levels; and review specific development plans for the top executives in the group.

7  Recommend to and advise the board on the remuneration (in all its forms) and associated matters of the senior executives.

8  Review the performance of key senior executives.

9  Ensure that, in exercising the rights to performance related compensation, benefits are related to the performance both of individuals and the group, and that they provide a long term incentive.

10 Ensure that the committee only makes recommendations which it can be justified to shareholders and staff alike and that the criteria on which performance is measured can be clearly explained.

11 Nominate suitable people for senior executive positions.'

# Deciding what board committees to have B19.11

Boards should be economical in the number of board committees they establish. Half a dozen is likely to be on the high side – especially for anything other than very large companies with large boards. Those which are appropriate will vary according to statute, regulation, nature of business, corporate culture and the inclination of the principal players.

Specifying in a committee's terms of reference that committee duties are additional makes it practical for supplementary fees to be paid to directors for their committee duties, where appropriate. This is likely to be appropriate in the case of non-executive directors. Some companies settle for paying a supplementary fee only to their chairs of board committees, and then only where they are non-executive.

A key point to remember is that an audit committee should be as independent as is practical of finance and accounting decisions. It is therefore unsound in principle for there to be a single 'Finance and audit committee' or for any other committee to have oversight of both (a) investment and other financial matters and (b) audit matters.

In **B21** BOARD COMMITTEES – TERMS OF REFERENCE we consider in more detail the role of audit, remuneration and nominations committees – each of which will be in place for any company complying with all the Combined Code Provisions. We provide sample terms of reference for these committees and also for board committees on finance, personnel and standing orders.

## Some possible board committees B19.12

Here we list some of the committees we have noted as being in place in medium to large corporations.

- Acquisitions and disposals
- Agenda committees
- Appraisal and remuneration
- Assets & liabilities (ALCO)
- Audit
- Board business
- Capital resources
- Chairman's
- Community affairs
- Compliance
- Due diligence

- Environmental
- Ethical
- Ethics & standards
- Group operations
- Human resources
- Legal
- Management development
- Manufacturing
- Marketing (domestic)
- Marketing (overseas)
- Nomination(s)
- Personnel
- (New) Product development
- Remuneration
- Resources
- Standing orders
- Strategic planning
- Treasury

# Audit Committees

## Audit committees – best practices[1]                    B20.1

'Since I joined my first audit committee, about ten years ago, the scope of the work done by the audit committee, in my experience, has greatly deepened and widened. In those days, the audit committee tended to look mainly at the annual accounts, and most of its work was related to that. Nowadays, the matters looked at by the audit committee are vastly broader than they used to be and the time involved as a member of the audit committee must have at least doubled.'[2]

Since John Baden spoke these words in London in mid-1998, the pressures on audit committee time have increased still further in the wake of the Turnbull Report in the UK[3], the Blue Ribbon Report in the US[4], the Sarbanes-Oxley Act in the US (see **B26.13–B26.24**) and the Smith Report and 2003 Combined Code in the UK. Consultancy firms are being hired to revamp audit committee processes so as to contain the exercise of their expanding responsibilities within a reasonable annual time frame. At **B20.12** we map out the historical development of audit committees.

## Cadbury, Hampel and Smith in the UK                    B20.2

The Code of Best Practice of the Cadbury Committee[5] first made it virtually mandatory for UK listed companies to have audit committees, by virtue of the Provision within the Code which read:

'The board should establish an audit committee of at least 3 non-executive directors with written terms of reference which deal clearly with its authority and duties'[6]

Audit committees are not a new innovation, but it is only recently that they have become ubiquitous and their roles regarded as essential. Bearing in mind that in 1992 only approximately two-thirds of the top UK listed companies had audit committees, Table 1 shows the immediate impact which the Cadbury Code Provision on audit committees had on UK practice. It also had the indirect, 'hidden agenda' impact of virtually ensuring that the boards of listed companies became balanced through having a significant number of non-executive directors.

**Table 1**                                                                 **B20.3**

*UK audit committees in June 1995* [7]

|  | Number of companies with an audit committee | Average size of an audit committee | Average number of non-executive directors as audit committee members | Number of audit committees without executive members |
|---|---|---|---|---|
| **FTSE 100 companies** | 100 | 4.24 | 4.05 | 92 |
| **Mid 250 companies** | 245 | 3.95 | 3.53 | 207 |

Source: 1995 Price Waterhouse Corporate Register, publ. By Hamilton Scott.

The Cadbury Committee's more detailed guidance, which was appended to the Cadbury Code, is reproduced at **B20.13** and also in Note 11 of the Cadbury Code itself (at **B3.4**).

In June 1998 the Combined Code replaced the Cadbury Code in the UK. So, the equivalent Provision was reworded to read:

'The board should establish an audit committee of at least three directors, all non-executive, with written terms of reference which deal clearly with its authority and duties. The members of the committee, a majority of whom should be independent non-executive directors, should be named in the report and accounts.' [8]

And the duties of the audit committee were spelt out in another Provision within the Combined Code:

'The duties of the audit committee should include keeping under review the scope and results of the audit and its cost effectiveness and the independence and objectivity of the auditors. Where the auditors also supply a substantial volume of non-audit services to the company, the committee should keep the nature and extent of such services under review, seeking to balance the maintenance of objectivity and value for money.' [9]

Other related Provisions within the 1998 Combined Code included that non-executive directors should comprise not less than one third of the board [10], that the majority of these should be independent [11] and that those directors considered by the board to be independent should be identified in the annual report [12]. Now, under the 2003 Combined Code a majority of board members (excluding the chairman) should be independent, as should every member of the audit committee.

For conciseness we are not reproducing here extensively from the Smith Report, nor on audit committees from the 2003 Combined Code – both of which can be found in PART A.

## Membership of audit committees                               B20.4

Until 2003, in the UK all members of the audit committee should have been non-executive directors with a majority of them being 'independent', Verschoor points out that

> 'in the US the NYSE rules resulting from the Blue Ribbon committee's recommendations stress that in order for the committee to function as representatives of the shareholders and not management, the audit committee must consist of at least three members, all of whom must be independent of management and financially literate. At least one member must have accounting or related financial management expertise. These characteristics are required so audit committees can perform the new oversight and review functions concerning financial accounting and reporting, controls. ... The NYSE listing rule states that the company's board of directors in its business judgement can interpret the financial literacy qualification.'[13]

The Sarbanes-Oxley Act endorses the Blue Ribbon Committee's sentiments, and the UK has also come into line.

In other jurisdictions across the world it is regarded as permissible for a proportion of the members of the audit committee to be executives. There are also examples of outstanding audit committees which have outside members, even as chairman of the committee, who are not directors of the entity. Many public sector audit committees have at least a proportion of their members who are executives, and often also contain complete outsiders who are not board members.

## External reporting by audit committees                       B20.5

In the UK there is no requirement for a report from the audit committee to appear in the annual report of the company, though audit committees are usually deeply involved in the development of the directors' statements on corporate governance which are required to be published in the annual report. However, the chairman of the audit committee (as well as the chairmen of the remuneration and nominations committees) should be available to answer questions at the annual general meeting of the company[14]: the Hampel Committee considered this should be at the company chairman's discretion in that it should be for the chairman of the meeting to decide which questions to answer himself or herself and which to refer to any colleague[15]; and the members of the committee should be named in the annual report[16]. The Smith Report and the 2003 Combined Code are not inconsistent with Hampel in this regard.

Baden has drawn attention to …

> 'A fairly recent innovation has been the Bank of England requirement to see the chairman of the audit committee at various regulatory and prudential meetings … the Bank … [is] pleased they could ask questions of a non-executive to confirm the answers they were getting from the executives who normally attend such meetings'[17]

## Committee reporting to the board                                    B20.6

The audit committee is a committee of the board. It exists to assist the board to discharge certain of its responsibilities. As such, it is wise that the minutes of audit committees should be tabled as 'above the line' agenda items at the following board meeting ('above the line' being for discussion and/or decision), and that the chairman of the audit committee will speak to those minutes at that board meeting

> 'to draw to the attention of the board any particular items which give him cause to worry or which might be of particular interest to the board.'[18]

This way, the board learns of audit committee deliberations promptly.

In practice it is not a problem that the audit committee minutes the board thereby receives are only draft minutes. Every member of the audit committee is likely to be a member of the board and so each has his or her opportunity to indicate needed corrections at the board meeting.

Audit committee meetings should be scheduled to take place about two weeks before the 'associated' board meeting – so that the committee's minutes can form part of the board papers circulated to directors some five days before the board meeting to allow the directors to prepare thoroughly. If a rolling calendar of board and board committee meetings is scheduled for about one year forward, it will be found that this sequencing usually can be adhered to, even with respect to the audit committee meeting which scrutinises the year end financial statements prior to approval by the board – as everyone will adjust to working to this calendar.

Audit committee minutes should be quite comprehensive not just of outcomes but of discussion which took place; and they should be retained indefinitely. It may be necessary to look back and show that, while a wrong decision may have been made, for instance relating to the treatment of a contentious matter in the financial statements, there had not been negligence but that the matter had been considered carefully from all angles before coming to a finely judged decision.

In addition to regular reporting through to the board following each audit committee meeting, it is good practice for the audit committee to provide a special annual report to the board. Some boards may consider this annual report to be a satisfactory alternative to regular reporting through to the board following each audit committee meeting, although there is an obvious need for the audit committee to report to the board on its scrutiny of interim and final financial results. The annual report will cover the committee's activities over the year. It may also incorporate the committee's overall opinions on the quality and effectiveness of the entity's financial accounting, risk management, internal control and governance processes.

## Taking charge of the committee's agenda  B20.7

Errors in audit committee minutes are usually errors of omission rather than mistaken minuting. Immediately after a meeting of the audit committee a chairman may draft out the headings he or she expects the minutes to cover, and then match those notes against the first draft which the committee secretary sends to the chairman for approval. That way, there is a better chance of the chairman spotting omissions. It is important that the chairman of the audit committee (not its secretary and certainly not the finance director or the chief executive) is effectively in control of both the agendas and the minutes of the committee. One current, draft recommendation of the Public Oversight Board's Panel on Audit Effectiveness is that an audit committee:

'take charge of their agenda and assure, in particular, that it focuses on, among other matters, financial statement risks, key controls, interim financial information, policies and practices for management's communications with analysts, and the qualitative aspects of financial reporting.'

Apart from the challenge to control its own agenda, which this draft recommendation makes, as Verschoor points out:

'This recommendation could be far-reaching if it results in the interjection of the audit committee into matters concerning the type and timing of earnings forecasts and other information that the company disseminates to investment analysts and others between quarterly earnings releases.'[19]

Having a standard schedule of matters to be on the agenda of particular audit committee meetings throughout the year will assist the committee to be in control of its agenda. An example is given at **B20.14**). This is consistent with the US Public Oversight Board's new recommendation that the committee should

'develop a formal calendar of activities related to those areas of responsibility prescribed in the committee charter, including a meeting plan that is reviewed and agreed to by the entire board. The meeting plan should include communications between the committee chair or full committee and the auditors before the release of interim or year-end financial data. In addition, the Panel recommends a minimum of two face-to-face meetings during the year with the external auditors and at least one executive session with the internal and external auditors without management's presence.'

A merely token commitment to audit committees is certainly no longer apt. This means for instance that the days should be long past when the audit committee met at 9 am with the main board scheduled for 10am. About half a day typically needs to be set aside for an audit committee meeting and it is doubtful that these meetings should be scheduled to take place on the same day as board meetings, if meeting fatigue is to be avoided. While the Cadbury Committee recommended that the audit committee should normally meet at least twice a year, this is rarely sufficient. Four or five meetings will typically be needed over the year. Since the committee's opinion on the effectiveness of internal control is now coupled with the formulation of the wording of the directors' internal control report which is published within the annual report, today's audit committee needs to address the effectiveness of internal control at about the same time as it scrutinises the draft final accounts. It is likely to be too much for a single audit committee meeting to conclude on internal control effectiveness and also to scrutinise the annual financial statements properly, so the committee needs to meet twice at about the same time, shortly after the year end.

Since it is a board committee, the secretary to the audit committee should be the person who is secretary to the board – or perhaps the assistant secretary to the board – and a full range of secretariat services should be available to the committee and its members. It is not satisfactory for the audit committee secretary to be the head of internal audit as one of the responsibilities of the audit committee is to advise the board as to whether the arrangements for internal audit within the business are satisfactory. Similarly, the committee's secretary should not be the finance director since the committee scrutinises all financial information which is to be published by the board. Where the finance director is also the secretary to the board, this poses a challenge.

Nevertheless, behind an effective audit committee is likely to be an excellent finance director as well as an excellent head of internal audit. As John Baden put it:

'For an audit committee to operate effectively, it needs two things – a first class executive finance director and a first class internal auditor … who needs to hold not only the confidence of the audit committee, but also the confidence of his executive colleagues.'[20]

The audit committee should review its own terms of reference at least once a year: this both facilitates appropriate revision and also keeps committee members mindful of their responsibilities. Again, the US position is that:

'annually, audit committees are to assert that they have reviewed and assessed the adequacy of their charter.'

*Verschoor, ibid*

Most internal audit functions also have charters, or formal terms of reference. Examples are to be found at **B12.13**, **B12.14** and **B12.15**. One audit committee agenda item, at least once a year, should be to review this charter and recommend to the board any changes.

## The audit committee's oversight responsibility for risk management and internal control      B20.8

The committee's relationship with internal audit is quite key. One of the responsibilities of the audit committee is to advise the board on the effectiveness of risk management and internal control and so the committee needs to be able to place reliance upon internal audit. This means that not only does an audit committee receive reports from internal audit on risk management and internal control, but that the committee has a responsibility to advise the board as to whether the entity's arrangements for the review of risk management and internal control are sound. This includes advising the board on the adequacy of internal audit after coming to a considered view.

It is best practice that the appointment or removal of the head of internal audit should have the prior approval of the audit committee. The head of internal audit should have unrestricted access to the chair of the audit committee at all times and the right to ask for items to be placed on the agenda of audit committee meetings. Baden's experience as chairman of an audit committee is that

'High risk/high probability reports from the internal auditor are immediately circulated to the members of the committee. It does not wait for the next committee meeting.'[21]

The head of internal audit will usually attend audit committee meetings and arrangements should be made for the committee to spend committee time alone with the head of internal audit without any other executives being in attendance at that time. Some audit committee chairmen spend time with the head of internal audit prior to an audit committee meeting: this can be a useful opportunity for the head of internal audit to ask the chairman of the audit committee to raise a particular direct question during the meeting, when the auditor considers it would be easier to respond to a direct question than for the auditor to raise the contentious issue 'cold'. Baden, again:

'the internal auditor will talk to the chairman of the audit committee before each meeting is case there are any worries on any items of the agenda or to give him any special background to an item which might be helpful to him when chairing the meeting.'[22]

It is a good idea for the chair of an audit committee to spend a day with the internal audit function once or twice a year: This is 'to get under the skin of things', and to break down any barriers between internal audit and the audit committee. An issue here is whether direct communication between junior internal auditors and the audit committee should be allowed for: there have been too many examples of heads of internal audit trying to suppress expressions of concern made by a junior internal auditor so that these do not reach the audit committee on a timely basis. This will be guarded against, to some extent, if all the internal auditors individually have access to the chair of the audit committee at all times.

As part of the committee's review of internal control, the committee receives reports from internal audit and from other review functions on reviews that these parties have conducted. As a prelude to receiving these reports, the audit committee should have had the opportunity to review and approve the planned future programme of work of these review functions. It is also important that the committee monitors the execution of these programmes of work, understands deviations from what was planned and draws the appropriate conclusions therefrom.

Largely as a result of the Turnbull Report, a significant change in the UK is that many internal audit functions are abandoning their own risk-based ways of conducting an audit needs assessment and are instead developing a programme of audit assignments which is based on the 'top down' assessment of risk which Turnbull enjoins upon the board. Internal audit is often now assisting the board and its audit committee in the development of this top-down assessment of risk. So, an impact of the Turnbull Report within the UK has been that internal auditors are working alongside the board to a greater extent than they did before. Even before Turnbull there was a trend in this direction, as Baden reported:

> 'We believe that internal audit, as a separate discipline, is no longer cost-effective or efficient --it is, instead, an essential element of the overall corporate risk management system. Good internal auditors must be risk and control consultants. Their job, in part, is to help the business make more accurate assessments as a basis for commercial decisions.'[23]

There is however a particular risk in this. A top-down assessment of risk by the board may overlook major risks perhaps as yet unearthed by top management and the board because they are still buried in the woodwork of the company. Detailed auditing at the level of the systems of the business is needed to uncover these risks. An audit needs assessment based exclusively on the board's own 'top down' assessment of risk is therefore a risk in itself. One enterprise insists that no more than two thirds of internal audit assignments are based on the board's 'top down' assessment of risk, leaving significant internal audit time for more detailed, systematic coverage of the enterprise. The Institute of Internal Auditors' new definition of internal auditing reminds us that internal auditing should continue to be 'systematic', but does not tell us what this means ('Systematic' in the context of internal auditing might mean that internal audit coverage is systematic, or it might mean that an audit assignment is conducted systematically (i.e. that a system is followed in the conduct of an audit assignment)).

In essence in the UK the Turnbull Report 'requires'[24] that, at least annually, the board:

1.   conducts a top down assessment of risk and control;

2.   ensures that there are satisfactory processes for the review of risk and control embedded into the business; and

3    the board reviews these embedded processes.

The Turnbull Report also requires that the board at least annually reviews the adequacy of the internal audit function or, whether there is no internal audit, considers whether internal audit should be set up. Much of the detail in implementing these Turnbull 'requirements' is being delegated to audit committees (often with consequential impacts upon their workloads) but it is important that the board is 'kept within the loop' as it were.

Most audit committees want concise reports to the committee on internal audit reviews conducted. Just one or two paragraphs on each audit assignment may be enough for a busy audit committee – so long as these summaries get the main messages across. The committee does not want to get bogged down in the detail, but can ask for that detail when they need it. Where a board operates the practice of a non-executive director 'shadowing' an executive director, it may be that one of the non-executive directors (most likely the one who shadows the finance director, who will almost certainly be a member of the audit committee) routinely receives the full version of each internal audit assignment report.

Usually summary reports on completed internal audit assignments will be combined into an operational report from the head of internal audit to each audit committee meeting and this report will also include an analysis of progress against the audit plan. Care must be taken that protocol is not allowed to unduly extend the time it takes for internal audit to report to the audit committee on an internal audit assignment. For instance, sometimes management may use as a delaying tactic a requirement that management respond to an audit assignment report before it reaches the audit committee, ostensibly so that management's response can reach the audit committee at the same time as the auditor's report itself.

Related to this is Baden's practical advice that …

> 'if there is something wrong, [the audit committee is] likely to ask [the] executive for a deadline by which the problem will be put right and that it will be monitored thereafter. We are also told when the problem has been finally solved so that we do not have to worry about it any more.'[25]

Care also must be taken to ensure that management does not in effect censor, or edit out, the impact of what internal audit tells the audit committee. The audit committee needs to be confident that both the scope and content of internal audit work as well as the wording of internal audit reports is in essence the professional judgement of internal audit – otherwise the audit committee will not be able to place so much reliance on what internal audit tells the committee, which will therefore not be so useful to the committee in formulating the committee's own opinion on the effectiveness of internal control for communication to the board who have ultimate oversight responsibility for the effectiveness of internal control.

Since it is now generally understood that audit committees and boards must come to opinions on the effectiveness of internal control, more audit committees are asking internal audit to formulate its own overall opinion on the effectiveness of internal control and to express such an opinion once or twice a year to the audit committee. We give example wording in **B23.14–B23.16**. The requirement to give such an opinion may have a significant impact on how internal auditing is approached. Undoubtedly, internal audit is now serving two masters – management and the audit committee.

Verschoor drew attention to a recommendation of the Public Oversight Board that audit committees should:

'obtain a written report from management on the effectiveness of internal control over financial reporting and establish specific expectations with management and the internal and external auditors about the qualitative information needs of the committee related to internal control. Discussions of internal control should include the effects of technology on current and future information systems.'

He goes on to point out that:

'Public comments to the Panel have recommended the desirability of a report that would encompass additional controls. Of particular importance to internal auditors are those controls over the validity of information used by management and the board, over safeguarding of assets and over compliance with laws and regulations. The Institute of Internal Auditors Professional Practices Pamphlet entitled Assessing and Reporting on Internal Control recommends the director of internal auditing issue an annual opinion on the adequacy of design and effectiveness of operation of the system of internal control. The opinion should be based on work performed by internal auditing and on information available from other sources.'

Another development in audit committee responsibilities is to review the quality of information that the board receives:

'One of the major requirements for good corporate governance is that the board of the company receives the information it needs to take the decisions it has to take; that this information is reported in a digestible form and that it is accurate. This is something the audit committee looks at on a regular basis, though it is equally a concern of the whole board who take great interest in this matter.'[26]

This chimes with the UK Hampel Committee's observation that:

'We endorse the view of the Cadbury committee (Report 4.14) that the effectiveness of non-executive directors (indeed, of all directors) turns, to a considerable extent on the quality of the information they receive.'[27]

The external auditor's management letter is one of the inputs that the audit committee should use in coming to the committee's opinion as to the effectiveness of internal control. It is now more generally understood that the committee needs the external auditor's management letter shortly after the year end, before the board approves the final accounts – not a few months' later as has so often been the practice in the past. This is because the external auditor's management letter assists the audit committee to come to a conclusion on the effectiveness of internal control.

It is not just for internal *financial* control that the board has control oversight responsibility. A key question is how does a board satisfy itself that there is effective *operational* and *compliance* control as well as effective *financial* control (that is, controls that give reasonable assurance of compliance with laws and regulations)? The board should certainly be 'in the know' about this – whether or not the directors intend to publish their opinion about it. Can the board reasonably ask its audit committee to advise the board as to whether there is effective operational and compliance control? It is less controversial that the audit committee can advise the board on whether there is effective internal financial control. If the audit committee takes on the oversight of *all* of internal control, it can have significant implications for the workload of the audit committee and the type of directors who are needed to belong to the committee.

Some organisations are establishing additional committees of the board, mirroring quite closely the structure and functions of the audit committee, but focusing on operational risk and control. For instance, many UK hospital boards of directors now have clinical governance committees reporting to the board on clinical risk and control – which, by and large, is their equivalent of operational control. Arguably, clinical matters would be beyond a typical audit committee to cope with – especially on top of everything else. But there is a risk in separating the oversight of internal financial control from the oversight of internal operational control. They do not separate naturally and risks may be overlooked unless a holistic view is taken. Cross-membership between committees can help here. Another option is for the board to retain for itself the detailed oversight of operational risk and control and not delegate it to their audit committee or to any other committee – but there is a risk that long board agendas will mean that the board is incapable of attending to this thoroughly.

Occasionally, in our experience typically once a year, an audit committee may commission an audit assignment to be conducted by internal audit specifically on behalf of the audit committee, with the full report going direct to the committee. This is different from the audit committee influencing, usually with the full concurrence of management and internal audit, the choice of internal audit assignments to be conducted. Audit committees are now being empowered to commission assignments and to take advice from outside parties – such as from consultancies and public accounting firms: the authority to do so should be built into the committee's terms of reference. This matter was addressed by the Cadbury Committee, for instance in their note on the Code Provision on audit committees (see **B20.15–B20.16**). Most probably by oversight, the matter of audit committees obtaining outside professional advice where necessary was omitted, we think through oversight, from both the Hampel Report itself and also from the Hampel Committee's 1998 Combined Code.

The 2003 Code also fails to give the audit committee an unequivocal mandate to seek outside advice when necessary, stating merely that (Provision A.5.2) board committees should be provided with sufficient resources, albeit that individual directors should be empowered to get outside advice when necessary:

> 'The board should ensure that directors, especially non-executive directors, have access to independent professional advice at the company's expense where they judge it necessary to discharge their responsibilities as directors. Committees should be provided with sufficient resources to undertake their duties.'

The Smith Report, in its introduction (paragraph 1.10), went a bit further:

> 'However, the high-level oversight function may lead to detailed work. The audit committee may intervene if there are signs that something may be seriously amiss. For example, if the audit committee is uneasy about the explanations of management and auditors about a particular financial reporting decision, there may be no alternative but to grapple with the detail and perhaps to seek independent advice.'

A number of different inputs may be utilised by the audit committee to assist the committee to form an opinion on the effectiveness of internal control. We have already referred to some of these. They are elaborated upon at **B20.15**, and listed here.

- Intelligence gathered as board members during the year.

- Confirmation that key line managers are clear as to their objectives.

- A report from the Executive on key risks.

- A report from the Executive on the key procedures which are designed to provide effective internal control.

- The committee's assessment of the effectiveness of internal audit.

- Reports from internal audit on scheduled audits performed.

- Reports on special reviews commissioned by the committee from internal audit or others.

- Internal audit's overall summary opinion on internal control (see **B23.13**).

- The overall results of a control self assessment process.

  o Letters of representation ('comfort letters') on internal control from line management.

  o The external auditors' management letter.

  o A losses report from the CEO or FD.

- An Executive report on any material developments since the b/s date and the present.

- The Executive's proposed wording of the internal control report for publication.

## The audit committee's oversight responsibility for internal audit   B20.9

We should distinguish between the audit committee's responsibilities with respect to the oversight of internal control and its oversight responsibilities for internal audit and other review functions. We need to do so as otherwise it is likely that one or other will not be done properly.

It is not a new practice for audit committees regularly (perhaps once a year and certainly as a significant, specific agenda item) to review the adequacy of the internal audit function. In the UK, the Turnbull Report has put a new focus on this – which is carried forward into the 2003 Combined Code. It is important to realise that this review does not happen automatically as a by-product of the committee receiving regular reports on internal audit assignments undertaken, or even as a by-product of the committee considering the internal audit planned programme of work and then monitoring its execution and progress, or as a consequence of the committee asking for an overall report and opinion from internal audit on enterprise-wide risk management and internal control. All of these will provide helpful inputs to the committee's consideration of the adequacy of the internal audit function. But other essential considerations include:

- Is the complement of internal auditors sufficient?

- Are the experience and qualifications of the internal auditors appropriate?

- Is the scope of internal audit unrestricted?

- Is internal audit sufficiently independent of management?

- Is the charter of the internal auditing function appropriate?

- Is internal auditing conducted with due professionalism?

- What is the level of acceptability within the organisation of internal audit?

- Has the risk profile of the entity changed so as to impact on the adequacy of internal audit?

Benchmarking internal audit externally can be useful for the audit committee; and, at intervals, the audit committee may commission external reviews of the internal audit function.

Both the charter of the internal audit function as well as the terms of reference of the audit committee may sensibly stipulate that internal auditing should be performed in accordance with the Standards of The Institute of Internal Auditors since these standards represent best practice internal auditing.

We have mentioned earlier that the audit committee should spend time alone with the internal auditor without other executives being in attendance. It is best that this happens at most or all audit committee meetings. But at least once a year the committee should meet without internal audit present, for part of the committee's consideration of the adequacy of the internal audit function. This is one reason why it is not ideal for the head of internal audit to be the secretary of the audit committee. For some of this committee time it may be best that other executives are also not present since the adequacy and effectiveness of internal audit is related to the attitudes of management.

The 2003 Combined Code includes, at the level of a provision (C.3.5) and for this first time, a requirement for boards to publicly justify a decision not to have an internal audit function:

> 'The audit committee should monitor and review the effectiveness of the internal audit activities. Where there is no internal audit function, the audit committee should consider annually whether there is a need for an internal audit function and make a recommendation to the board, and the reasons for the absence of such a function should be explained in the relevant section of the annual report.'

Generally, audit committee chairmen need to be much more assertive in controlling who is in attendance at audit committee meetings, and for which agenda items.

## The audit committee's oversight responsibility for public reporting                                                    B20.10

So far we have focused on the audit committee's evolving responsibilities for the oversight of risk management and internal control and for its oversight of internal audit. The committee has two further responsibilities which are also closely related to each other but which need to be handled separately if they are to be handled effectively: these are the committee's oversight of financial reporting and its oversight of the external audit.

Financial statements which are published are the board's, not the auditor's, financial statements and each director needs to confident about their reliability. Busy board agendas mean that the detailed scrutiny of draft financial statements, prior to their adoption by the board for publication, needs to be entrusted to the audit committee of the board. An emerging issue is 'when is "information" *financial*?'. It can be said to be financial information if it communicates a financial message to the reader, whether or not it is expressed in monetary units. Another issue is 'what constitutes *publication*?' This certainly includes year end financial statements, interim statements and quarterly statements which are published. It should also be regarded as including financial information in prospectuses, and returns made to regulators or to parent bodies – for instance in the case of government agencies to central government departments.

Verschoor reminds us that the Blue Ribbon Committee recommended, and the SEC has since made it a requirement, that companies must have their external auditors perform a review of quarterly financial results. On those occasions the auditor is required to attempt to discuss with the audit committee chair the same matters of accounting quality and other issues required by GAAS as is required at year end.[28]

The new SAS on audit committees is also relevant[29]. SAS 90 is in response to recommendations 8 and 10[30] of The Blue Ribbon Committee on Improving the Effectiveness of Corporate Audit Committees. The auditor is now required to discuss certain information relating to the auditor's judgements about the quality, not just the acceptability, of the company's accounting principles with the audit committee of SEC clients. Three-way discussion is encouraged between the auditor, management and the audit committee. There is a requirement that the auditor should communicate to the audit committee or be satisfied, through discussions with the audit committee, that matters described in SAS 61 have been communicated to the audit committee by management when they have been identified in the conduct of interim financial reporting; and there is a requirement that the auditor of an SEC client attempts to discuss these matters prior to fling Form 10-Q.

Another emerging issue is how the board secures the confidence it needs to publish in its name non-financial information – such as environmental statements. Should the detailed scrutiny of non-financial information which is to be published by the board be entrusted to the board's audit committee or placed elsewhere?

There is general acceptance that financial statements in annual reports should be examined by the audit committee. The committee should focus in particular on items the valuation of which entails a significant degree of management judgement: these are the areas where management has the opportunity to indulge in creative accounting or merely to exercise bad judgement. Verschoor points out that:

> 'Suggesting that internal auditors should be involved with audit committee candid discussions of financial reporting issues implicating accounting judgment and impacting reporting quality may be new areas of responsibility for many internal auditing functions.'

The committee should also focus on any changes in accounting practice which management is intending to introduce, so that the committee is satisfied the changes are reasonable and are being introduced properly.

It is a good idea for the audit committee to probe the external auditor to discover which areas within the accounts were the subject of contention between management and the auditor during the course of the audit, notwithstanding that those matters are likely to have been resolved before the audit committee meeting – they are likely to be matters of which the audit committee needs to be aware.

Furthermore, the audit committee should review the management of the information flow from management to the external auditor, because late disclosure towards the end of the audit can mean it is effectively too late for the external auditor to deal with it. Cynics might say that, in practice, audit materiality tends to be, say, 'three times the audit fee divided by the number of days left to complete the audit'!

Changes in accounting standards which will have a bearing on the financial statements should be brought to the audit committee's attention as early as possible in the year and their impact modelled in anticipatory form so that difficulties can be identified and resolved well before the year end.

A practice which is developing at the audit committee meeting which considers the final accounts is for the external auditor to table and talk through a report which covers the main points considered during the course of the audit. This can be an excellent way for the committee to make sure it focuses on the right issues.

Just as the committee will meet with the internal auditor without other executives being in attendance, so, at least once a year, the audit committee will meet with the external auditor without any executives (including internal audit) being present. This is an opportunity for the auditor to talk confidentially and also for the audit committee to sound out the external auditor on any matters of concern to the committee. The committee should also ask the external auditor for a frank view about the audit committee itself.

## The audit committee's oversight responsibility of external audit

**B20.11**

(Readers are also referred to **B6.8** REVIEWING THE PERFORMANCE OF THE EXTERNAL AUDITOR – in particular the need for the audit committee to consider the auditor's concept of materiality, and the need for the committee to consider the timing of the release of relevant information to the external auditor by management – and to the section on the US *Sarbanes-Oxley Act 2002* (see **B26** INTERNATIONAL DIMENSIONS)).

The fourth and final responsibility of the audit committee is *oversight of the external audit*. It is now much more widely accepted that an enterprise has an interest in the quality, not just the price, of the audit and can reasonably challenge the external auditor to justify the external audit approach. Clearly, the right time for the committee to consider this is at a meeting far removed from the year end, at which the external auditors will table an agenda paper outlining their proposed approach to the forthcoming audit.

Verschoor, again, points out that a US Public Oversight Board recommendation designed to give specific prominence to the audit committee's responsibility to represent shareholders and other stakeholders rather than management, explains more clearly the new NYSE rule regarding the fact that the outside auditor should be accountable to the board of directors rather than management. The statement says that audit committees should:

'review the internal and external auditors' performance on an annual basis; exercise the committee's responsibility, as the auditors' primary client, to assess the auditors' responsiveness to the committee's and board of directors' expectations; and be satisfied that the auditors are appropriately compensated for performing a thorough audit.'

Verschoor points out that:

'By lumping together a responsibility for both internal and external auditors, this recommendation gives specificity to the closeness of a direct relationship between audit committees and internal auditors. It also suggests that adequate resources need to be provided to internal as well as external auditors. Unfortunately, there does not appear to be widespread understanding of the appropriate methodology or criteria that should be used for auditor performance evaluations or who should provide assistance to the committee to perform them.'

Relevant issues here, in the context of the audit committee's oversight of the external audit, are:

- the timing of audit work;
- the extent to which the external auditor places reliance is placed on internal audit and other internal review agencies;
- the continuity of the audit team from one audit to the next;
- the qualifications and experience of the audit team;
- the price of the audit; and
- whether there are any factors which may significantly compromise the independence, or perceived independence, of the external auditors.

This last matter has recently been addressed in the UK by the Stock Exchange, in the US by the SEC and now by the European Commission (European Commission, (December 2000), *Consultation paper* on audit independence regulations, based on principles rather than detailed rules).

Again, Verschoor is useful here. He tells us that:

'On the subject of auditor independence, the stock exchange listing rules clarify the objective of the discussions with the external auditors previously required by Independence Standards Board Statement No.1. … According to the NYSE listing rule, the audit committee is responsible for:

'actively engaging in a dialogue with the outside auditor with respect to any disclosed (by the auditor) relationships or services that may impact the objectivity and independence of the outside auditor and for recommending that the Board of Directors take appropriate action in response to the outside auditors' report (of relationships) to satisfy itself of the outside auditor's independence.

'The counterpart NASD Market Rule is phrased somewhat differently. It requires the audit committee to take, or recommend that the full board take, appropriate action to "oversee the independence of the outside auditor." Both of these requirements raise questions of implementation and compliance risk for audit committees. They also provide opportunities for internal auditing to assist the audit committee.

'Although not taking a position on the sensitive aspects of auditor independence, the POB panel draft report does recommend that audit committees should pre-approve non-audit services that exceed a threshold amount and should consider the nature of the service when doing so. It calls on the Independence Standards Board (ISB) to provide guidance. It also notes that the proposed SEC ruling to revise auditor independence guidelines will serve as an appropriate forum for debate.'[31]

It will be the audit committee's responsibility to recommend to the board either the continuation of the external auditor, or to embark on a process of considering competing bids for the annual statutory audit – with or without the existing firm being given the opportunity to tender. If the existing firm is not going to be reappointed, it should not be trifled with by inviting it to tender for the future – as this is a costly. time consuming business.

Attending presentations given by bidding firms will fall largely upon audit committee members with other directors and executives likely to be in attendance. The challenge here is to initiate proper consideration of the need to change auditors, and to complete the process in time for the next audit to take place seamlessly. Because this is so difficult to achieve, inertia often reigns and so the audit committee often never gets round to considering properly the need for change.

In the US, Stock Exchange rules resulting from the Blue Ribbon Committee recommendations:

'articulate more specifically the audit committee and board of director responsibility and authority to select, evaluate, and replace the outside auditor. This is as a result of the specific acknowledgement that the outside auditor for the company is ultimately accountable to the board and audit committee ...

The rules state a new requirement that audit committees should represent in the company's proxy statement that they have accomplished several newly-instituted functions:

- reviewed and discussed the audited financial statements with management;

- discussed with the independent auditors the matters required to be discussed by a new revision to GAAS, primarily the auditor's judgements about the quality, not just the acceptability, of the entity's accounting principles; and

- based on these reviews and discussions, recommended to the Board of Directors that the audited financial statements be included in the company's Annual Report on Form 10-K. This is tantamount to a warranty asserting that they are in accordance with GAAP. Since all directors have been required for some time to sign the Form 10-K, this new requirement appears to give clarity to what the directors' responsibilities actually are.'[32]

# Appendix A: History of audit committees    B20.12

| | |
|---|---|
| 19th century | In the 19th century audit committees existed, as this extract from the minutes of one of Britain's great railway companies indicates. It is interesting to observe that within this brief extract are suggestions that this audit committee discharged three of the four contemporary roles of audit committees, *viz.* oversight of financial reporting, oversight of external audit arrangements, oversight of internal control including operational control. The fourth responsibility of the today's audit committee, oversight of internal audit, is not indicated. |

The extract from the minutes[33]:

---

'Great Western Railway

'Report of the Audit Committee

'The auditors and Mr. Deloitte attended the Committee and explained the various matters connected with the Finances and other departments of the railway, which explanations were highly satisfactory.

'The Committee consider the Auditors have performed their arduous duties with great care and intelligence and therefore confidently recommend that they be continued in office.

Benjamin Lancaster
Chairman
Paddington Station

22nd February, 1872'

---

*Tricker, R.I. (1978): The Independent Director, [Tolley, Croydon, England, ISBN 0 510 49378 5], 104 pages, minute quoted on p.56*

| | |
|---|---|
| 1939 | Audit committees were proposed by the New York Stock Exchange as a direct result of the McKesson & Robbins scandal; and by the Securities and Exchange Commission in 1940. |
| 1967 | The Executive Committee of the American Institute of Certified Public Accountants recommended: |

'that publicly-owned corporations appoint committees composed of outside directors (those who are not officers or employees) to nominate the independent auditors of the corporation's financial statements and to discuss the auditor's work with them.'

| | |
|---|---|
| Late 1960s –<br>early 1970s | As a result of several highly publicised corporate failures (notably Atlantic Acceptance) audit committees (with a *majority* of non-executive directors) become mandatory under the Canadian province laws of Ontario and British Columbia and under Canadian Federal law. |
| 1972 | The US Securities and Exchange Commission's Accounting Series Release No. 123 (23 March 1972) ended as follows: |

'To this end, the Commission, in the light of the foregoing historical recital, endorses the establishment by all publicly-held companies of audit committees composed of outside directors and urges the business and financial communities and all shareholders of such publicly-held companies to lend their full and continuing support to the effective implementation of the above-cited recommendations in order to assist in affording the greatest possible protection to investors who rely upon such financial statements.'

| | |
|---|---|
| 1975 | 89% of the *Fortune* top 500 industrials had audit committees and 77% of heads of internal audit met regularly with them (Mautz, R.K. and F.L. Neumann, (1977): Corporate Audit Committees: Policies and Practice, [Ernst & Ernst, US]). |
| 1977 | Sir Brandon Rhys Williams, MP for Kensington, unsuccessfully put to the House of Commons a 'Companies (Audit Committee) Bill' which would have applied to listed companies employing more than 1,500 people or having total net assets in excess of £5 million. The 'Explanatory Memorandum' to this bill stated: 'In requiring major public companies to set up audit committees the Bill follows a practice now well established in Canada and the United States.'. The Bill would have required such companies to have at least three non-executive directors, and also to have had an audit committee at least half of whose members would have been at least three non-executive directors. The chairman of the audit committee was to have been chosen by the audit committee members. The members of the audit committee were termed 'audit directors' in this Bill. The Bill set out the proposed duties of audit committees in some detail, which included a responsibility of the audit directors to make a statement, signed by each audit director, to be attached to the balance sheet and read by the chairman of the audit committee at the AGM. The Bill proposed that, with the approval of the AGM, audit directors would be paid an additional fee. |
| 1978 | Every domestic company listed on the New York Stock Exchange required to have an audit committee consisting wholly of outside (non-executive) directors with an outside chairman. |

---

1981    Sir Brandon Rhys Williams unsuccessfully proposed amendments to the 'Companies (No. 2) Bill, which again would have required listed companies to have had at least three non-executive directors (this time if the company turnover exceeded £25m, or the balance sheet total exceeded £50m or the number of employees exceeded 2,500). The Bill also again promoted the idea of audit committees this time for listed companies with turnovers in excess of £200m, balance sheet total in excess of £400m or more than 50,000 employees. The Bill proposed that such companies should be required to consider the appointment of an audit committee at each AGM and if the AGM resolved to appoint an audit committee it would be a committee with particular characteristics as defined in the Bill, which included:

- Such companies to have had at least three non-executive directors, and also to have had an audit committee at least half of whose members were to have been at least three non-executive directors.

- At least two audit committee meetings per annum, convened by the committee's chairman.

- The external auditors to have been notified of the meetings, with a right to attend them, but not as members.

- A copy of the minutes of each audit committee meeting to have been given to each director of the company within seven days of the meeting.

- The audit committee to have recommended on the appointment of the auditors and their remuneration.

- The audit directors to have made a statement, signed by each audit director, to have been attached to the balance sheet and to have been read by the chairman of the audit committee at the AGM

- With the approval of the AGM, audit directors to have been paid an additional fee.

During the debate in the House of Commons, at 11:30pm on 19 October 1981, Sir Brandon said:

---

'I am reminded of a famous quotation from Bryce:

"But while they talked the heavens darkened, and the flood came and destroyed them all."

'I am afraid that while we are talking about the possibility of introducing audit committees in many of our large companies they will go bankrupt, or the whole social scene will change so much that the issue will die on its feet. Although I have had the assurances if Ministers and experts – Establishment figures particularly – that everything is going along quite all right and that there is no need for legislation, I do not think that there is any evidence that we are making significant progress in this area.'

| 1992 | Approximately two-thirds of the top UK listed companies had audit committees. |
| --- | --- |
| 1993 | London Stock Exchange requires UK listed companies to disclose in their Annual Reports if they do not have audit committees of the main board comprising at least three non-executive directors, and to explain why not. |
| 1995 | All the FTSE 100 companies had an audit committee as had 245 of the mid 250 FTSE companies (Source: 1995 Price Waterhouse Corporate Register, publ. By Hamilton Scott) |
| 2002 | The Sarbanes-Oxley Act makes audit committees of US issuers responsible for the appointment of their companies' external auditors and for approving on an 'item by item' basis any non-audit work undertaken by the auditor for an audit client. Certain categories of non-audit work are banned. |
| 2003 | The 2003 Combined Code brings the UK into line with the US by 'requiring' that all (not just a majority of) members of the audit committee should be independent non-executive directors. The 2003 Code, by adopting the Smith Report proposals, has markedly increased content on audit committees than the 1998 Code. |

# Appendix B: The Cadbury Committee's note on their Code Provision on audit committees B20.13

The Committee's recommendations on audit committees are as follows.

'(a) They should be formally constituted as sub-committees of the main board to whom they are answerable and to whom they should report regularly; they should be given written terms of reference which deal adequately with their membership, authority and duties; and they should normally meet at least twice a year.

(b) There should be a minimum of three members. Membership should be confined to the non-executive directors of the company and a majority of the non-executives serving on the committee should be independent of the company, as defined in paragraph 2.2 of the Code.

(c) The external auditor and, where an internal audit function exists, the head of internal audit should normally attend committee meetings, as should the finance director. Other board members should also have the right to attend.

(d) The audit committee should have a discussion with the auditors at least once a year, without executive board members present, to ensure that there are no unresolved issues of concern.

(e) The audit committee should have explicit authority to investigate any matters within its terms of reference, the resources which it needs to do so, and full access to information. The committee should be able to obtain outside professional advice and if necessary to invite outsiders with relevant experience to attend meetings.

(f) Membership of the committee should be disclosed in the annual report and the chairman of the committee should be available to answer questions about its work at the Annual General Meeting.

Specimen terms of reference for an audit committee, including a list of the most commonly performed duties, are set out in the Committee's full Report.'

# Appendix C: Illustrative timing and content of audit committee meetings, showing the committee's consideration of internal control　B20.14

The Head of Internal Audit was asked to advise the audit committee on the timing and content of their meetings. The company year end is 31 December. It is a small listed company.

This is the essence of the advice which the Head of Internal Audit developed:

Notwithstanding that Cadbury allows the committee to meet only twice a year, at a minimum this committee will need to meet four times a year. We are showing the agenda for the February meeting as dealing, *inter alia*, with the financial statements for publication as well as with the assessment of the effectiveness of internal control. With two heavy items like this it is likely that one will be dealt with inadequately unless adequate committee time is safeguard. Accordingly we are suggesting a full day meeting but an alternative would be two separate meetings at approximately the same time during February. Further meetings should be arranged as required.

In each case we recommend that the audit committee's meeting is scheduled eight to ten days before the associated board meeting so that its draft minutes may be tabled at the board meeting and spoken to by the chair of the audit committee.

These are the meetings we suggest, together with their principal agenda items:

**July meeting** (eight to ten days before the associated Board)

1.  Interim results

2.  Summary reports on internal audit work done.

    (i)   Including internal auditor time alone with the committee.

3.  Consideration of anticipated impact of changes in accounting standards and in accounting treatment upon the next set of annual financial statements, including s simulated set of financial statements.

**November meeting** (eight to ten days before the associated board meeting)

1.  Summary reports on internal audit work done.

    (i)   Including internal auditor time alone with the committee.

2.  Discussion and approval of the internal audit plan of work to be conducted in the coming financial year.

**February meeting(s)** (likely to be a full day's meeting, or preferably two separate half day meetings, ideally about eight days before the associated Board).

**Part 1**

1. Final results

    (i) Consideration of external auditor's report of audit now completed.

2. External audit time alone with the committee.

3. Committee's recommendation, for transmittal to the board, on the appointment of the external auditors for the current year's audit.

**Part 2**

4. Summary reports on internal audit work done.

    (i) Including committee time alone with the internal auditor.

5. Concluding the committee's review of internal control.

    (i) External auditor's draft management letter.

    (ii) Committee's consideration of the Executive's Losses Report.

    (iii) Committee's review of internal audit's overall summary opinion on internal control.

6. Formulation and adoption of the committee's opinion of the effectiveness of internal control over the year under review, and their draft internal control report for publication (both for communication the board) etc.

**April, May or June meetings** (eight to ten days before the associated board meeting)

1. The committee's review of its own terms of reference.

2. Consideration of planned external audit approach.

3. Preliminary review of whether to consider appointing alternative external auditors for the *following* financial year.

4. Summary reports on internal audit work done.

    (i) Including committee time alone with the internal auditor.

5. Receive a report on an external quality assurance review of the internal audit function (once every three years).

6. Committee conclusions on the present and planned future adequacy of the internal audit function.

    (i) Including time *without* the internal auditor being present.

    (ii) Including review of the internal audit function's 'charter' or 'terms of reference'.

# Appendix D: Audit committee inputs for assessing internal control effectiveness  B20.15

(This summary is slightly oriented to the UK position)

After the year end, but shortly before finalising the Annual Report, the audit committee should meet to consider internal control. In some cases, their scope may be limited to internal financial control.

The committee's formal review of internal control will benefit from a number of inputs to it. To a small extent what will be appropriate will depend upon whether the audit committee's review of internal control is restricted to just internal financial control or whether it also covers the other aspects of internal control (control for operational efficiency and effectiveness and control for legal and regulatory compliance). However, in practice it is hard to separate these out.

Companies have considerable discretion in their approach which is likely to make use of some of the following inputs (ie evidence on internal control for the committee to consider). For the UK, in general these inputs should relate to the period under review. The US guidance envisages that the published report on internal control will relate only to control in place *as of the year end date* whereas Rutteman ('Internal Control and Financial Reporting – Guidance to Directors of Listed Companies Registered in the UK', ICAEW, December 1994) required that:

> 'The directors' statement should cover the period of the financial statements and should also take account of material developments between the balance sheet date and the date upon which the financial statements are signed.'

- **Intelligence gathered as board members during the year**

Many of the agenda items of board meetings, and of the meetings of other board committees over the previous year, will have informed the audit committee members about matters which have internal control implications. Indeed, many board decisions will have had impact upon internal control. Of course audit committee members would be unlikely to exclude this intelligence from their deliberations on internal control, but we are suggesting that a written summary of these matters should be prepared for the audit committee most probably by the finance director or by the company secretary. It should also cover matters aired at board committees which have no non-executive representation.

- **Confirmation that key line managers are clear as to their objectives**

Contemporary definitions of internal control acknowledge that internal control is intended to provide reasonable assurance of the achievement of objectives. It follows that to assess whether internal control has been effective, management should be clear as to their objectives and whether they have been achieved. Failure to achieve objectives might not be a consequence of defective internal control; for instance it may be due to external events. Succeeding in achieving objectives might not be a consequence of effective internal control since control weaknesses might not have been exploited. So it is wise to consider both the extent to which objectives have been achieved as well as to framework of internal control in coming to an opinion on the effectiveness of internal control.

- **A report from the executive on key risks**

Internal control must be proportionate to relative risk. It is important that the business has a clear idea of the risks it faces – risks of failing to achieve objectives; and risks of unwanted outcomes. The audit committee needs this to be clear when its considers the effectiveness of internal control.

- **A report from the executive on the key procedures which are designed to provide effective internal control**

A summary of this had to be included in the internal control report for publication in order to comply with the old Rutteman guidance, now superseded by the Turnbull guidance. Here we are looking for something more detailed. Clearly the arrangements the business has in order to achieve effective internal control are absolutely crucial to determining whether or not there has been, and will be, effective internal control. So the audit committee needs to be clear about them. The audit committee may have recommendations to make to management.

Common examples are:

- ○ the audit committee itself;
- ○ a code of business conduct;
- ○ the budgetary control system;
- ○ a formal process of risk assessment;
- ○ internal audit;
- ○ a credit committee; and
- ○ control (and risk) self assessment.

- **The committee's assessment of the effectiveness of internal audit**

COSO (US) and Rutteman (UK) rightly elevated the monitoring of internal control to the status of, respectively, an essential component of internal control and an essential criterion for assessing internal control effectiveness, it follows that this traditional interest of the audit committee becomes an important input to their assessment of internal control effectiveness. The committee will be concerned to satisfy itself that the internal audit function is properly resourced. Also of concern will be the scope of internal audit work which should be at least as broad as the committee's own review of the effectiveness of internal control. The committee will wish to monitor the completion of internal audit's planned programme of audits against their earlier approved plan.

The committee's assessment of internal audit should (a) be done carefully, (b) lead to a definite conclusion and (c) be documented. The Internal Auditing

Standards guide that periodically the internal audit function should audit itself and also that external reviews should be conducted of internal audit: these can be valuable sources for the committee's assessment of internal audit effectiveness ('Standards for the Professional Practice of Internal Auditing', (1995), Altamonte Springs, Florida: Institute of Internal Auditors Inc.).

- **Reports from internal audit on scheduled audits performed**

During the year most audit committees receive a summary report on each internal audit performed. Taken separately and together these reports help the audit committee build a picture of the effectiveness of internal control within the business. Some audit committees nominate one of their members to 'shadow' the head on internal audit and this person may receive a full copy of each detailed internal audit report. An agenda item of most audit committee meetings will be a report from the head of internal audit, and perhaps at the end of each meeting the committee should arrange to meet this person without any other member of the executive being present.

- **Reports on special reviews commissioned by the committee from internal audit or others**

In the UK the Cadbury Report stipulated that the audit committee should be empowered to take independent professional advice. Before going outside, the committee may consider commissioning internal audit to conduct specific assignments on the committee's behalf, reporting to directly to the committee. Survey data shows this is happening occasionally – perhaps once a year on average. This goes further than merely influencing the content of internal audit's planned programme of work.

- **Internal audit's overall summary opinion on internal control**

See **B23.14–B23.15**.

If the audit committee of non-executive directors is expected to come to an opinion on the effectiveness of internal control – either for publication or for confidential transmission to the board, then it is not unreasonable for the committee to expect the head of internal audit to formally express in writing his or her opinion on this. Usually it will be unacceptable for this opinion to be qualified by protestations about inadequate internal audit resources and coverage – the audit committee itself will not wish to qualify its opinion on internal control in these ways.

- **The overall results of a control self assessment process**

If the business has put in place a process of control and risk self assessment by management and staff, then the results of this should be a valuable additional monitoring of internal control effectiveness available to the audit committee over and above the inputs they receive from internal audit. Internal audit's own opinion of the effectiveness of the CSA programme should also be obtained. The audit committee will be particularly interested in the most significant outputs from the CSA programme and will need to know of any limitations in its coverage, with explanations.

- **Letters of representation ('comfort letters') on internal control from line management**

A minimalist approach to CSA will be to rely on letters of representation about internal control from line managers. Even with a full CSA programme in place, these can be a useful supplement. It would not be usually for these to be addressed to the audit committee, but the audit committee should receive a report upon this process and the matters arising therefrom.

- **The external auditors' management letter**

The report from the external auditors on internal control now becomes centre stage as an important part of the audit committee's deliberation of the effectiveness of internal control. Of course it should not be regarded as comprehensive and would, in any case, major on internal financial control. It now needs to be available no later than the audit committee meeting which formulates the directors' internal control report for publication.

- **A losses report from the CEO or FD**

Losses are likely to be indicative of ineffective internal control. If the audit committee does not ask for a regular report on losses from the executive, then this may be the reason why the committee does not learn of control breakdowns. It is best not to call this an 'avoidable losses' report as the committee should not risk the executive holding back information about an event on the grounds that the executive does not think it could have been avoided. What should be covered in this report are:

  ○ an account of losses which were exceptional in size;

  ○ an account of losses which were exceptional in character; and

  ○ an account of any other losses of which the Executive should understand that the audit committee would wish to be told.

- **An executive report on any material developments since the b/s date and the present**

Rutteman stipulated that any such events should be taken into account when the internal control report for publication is being formulated.

- **The executive's proposed wording of the internal control report for publication.**

It is much better not to undertake initial drafting in committee, although the committee is likely to wish to adapt the wording which the executive suggests.

What is essential is that the audit committee, on behalf of the board, makes a carefully considered judgement about internal control. The more comprehensive the array of inputs available, the more likely that the committee will not come to faulty judgements about internal control quality and thus not mislead either the directors or readers of published accounts. Of course, the inputs need to be of high quality.

# Checklist on general audit committee issues   B20.16

This is intended as a checklist of questions audit committee members might like to use to reconsider how well their committee is functioning. It is not comprehensive.

## Checklist of general audit committee issues

### Committee terms of reference

- Does the committee have written terms of reference covering its authority and duties?

- Does the committee have the authority to invite outsiders with relevant experience to attend its meetings?

- Do the terms of reference of the committee give the chair of the committee the right to require executives to be in attendance for particular meetings or particular agenda items?

- Do the terms of reference of the committee empower the chair of the committee to require that some of those usually in attendance are absent for particular meetings or agenda items, and is this functioning effectively?

- Is the concurrence of the audit committee required prior to the appointment or dismissal of the head of internal audit?

### Risks to committee effectiveness

- Is the audit committee a barrier between the auditors and the executive directors on the main board?

- Does the audit committee mean that the main board abdicates its responsibilities in the audit area, so weakening the board's collective responsibility for reviewing and approving the financial statements?

- Is the audit committee under the influence of any dominant personality on the main board?

- Does the audit committee get in the way and obstruct executive management, and stifle entrepreneurial skills?

### Membership

- Do minutes of the main board show that the board appointed the members of the audit committee, as well as its chairman?

- Does the audit committee have a strong chairman, who has the confidence of the board and of the auditors?

- Do the members of the audit committee have sufficient understanding of the auditing, accounting and control issues to be dealt with by the committee to take an active part in its proceedings?

## Training

- Is there a programme of training for audit committee members?

## Responsibilities

- Does the board or the audit committee review rigorously and approve all financial statements which are to be published?

## Minutes

- Are audit committee minutes a reasonably full record of the discussion that took place as well as the final views taken on all key matters?

- Does the chair of the audit committee approve the audit committee minutes before they are circulated?

- Are audit committee minutes tabled promptly at a main board meeting which takes place shortly after the audit committee meeting, and does the chair of the audit committee speak to those minutes at the board meeting?

- Are the audit committee minutes tabled for approval by the audit committee at the next audit committee meeting?

## Committee meetings

- Does the frequency, timing and duration of audit committee meetings allow the committee to effectively discharge its responsibilities?

## Attendance at meetings

- Is the attendance record of directors at board and board committee meetings (to which they belong) tabled as an agenda item once a year?

- Does the external auditor normally attend committee meetings?

- Does the head of internal audit normally attend audit committee meetings

- Does the finance director normally attend audit committee meetings?

- Is it understood that other board members also have the right to attend, but in practice is their actual attendance counter-productive to the effective functioning of the committee?

# Issues impacting audit committee effectiveness    B20.17

Audit committees are now established in most listed companies throughout the world, though less so in countries where companies have a two-tier board structure. A properly constituted audit committee, with all or a majority of its members being non-executive independent directors, can assist in achieving better balance of power 'at the top' as well as greater stakeholder confidence. A properly functioning audit committee can markedly assist the board in the discharge of its responsibilities.

In the UK the Combined Code for corporate governance has extended the defined duties of audit committees and has introduced other 'requirements' relevant to audit committees. The full Code appears in **B3** CORPORATE GOVERNANCE PRONOUNCEMENTS – UK, as does the useful Cadbury Committee's guidance on audit committees. We reproduce a small part of the Combined Code here.

## Extracts from the Combined Code                    B20.18

---

### D. Accountability and audit

D.1  Financial Reporting

> **Principle**    **The board should present a balanced and understandable assessment of the company's position and prospects.**

#### Code Provisions

**D.1.1**    The directors should explain their responsibility for preparing the accounts and there should be a statement by the auditors about their reporting responsibilities.

**D.1.2**    The board's responsibility to present a balanced and understandable assessment extends to interim and other price-sensitive public reports and reports to regulators as well as to information required to be presented by statutory requirements.

**D.1.3**    The directors should report that the business is a going concern, with supporting assumptions or qualifications as necessary.

### D.2  Internal Control

> **Principle**    **The board should maintain a sound system of internal control to safeguard shareholders investment and the company's assets.**

#### Code Provisions

**D.2.1**    The directors should, at least annually, conduct a review of the effectiveness of the group's system of internal controls and should report to shareholders that they have done so. The review should cover all controls, including financial operational and compliance controls and risk management.

**D.2.2**    Companies which do not have an internal audit function should from time to time review the need for one.

---

---

**D.3  Audit Committee and Auditors**

| Principle | The board should establish formal and transparent arrangements for considering how they should apply the financial reporting and internal control principles and for maintaining an appropriate relationship with the company's auditors. |
|---|---|

**Code Provisions**

**D.3.1**   The board should establish an audit committee of at least three directors, all non-executive, with written terms of reference which deal clearly with its authority and duties. The members of the committee, a majority of whom should be independent non-executive directors, should be named in the report and accounts.

**D.3.2**   The duties of the audit committee should include keeping under review the scope and results of the audit and its cost effectiveness and the independence and objectivity of the auditors. Where the auditors also supply a substantial volume of non-audit services to the company, the committee should keep the nature and extent of such services under review, seeking to balance the maintenance of objectivity and value for money.

---

As with the earlier Cadbury Code the new Code is having a wide influence beyond the UK.

An old, cynical view was that audit committees were unlikely to be effective in the companies that needed them most, and were unnecessary for well run companies. We rarely hear that view expressed today. Today it is appreciated that the audit committee has a pivotal role in a modern business. In any case, it is wise for a business to establish effective approaches to corporate governance 'in the good times' when it may be less obvious that they are needed, so as to be an effective buttress against compromising on standards when the going gets hot. The audit committee is one such buttress.

It is convenient to represent the responsibilities of the audit committee, on behalf of the board as being fourfold:

☐   scrutiny of financial statements before their publication;

☐   review of the effectiveness of management's internal control;

☐   oversight of the external audit; and

☐   oversight of the internal audit.

Important contemporary issues for audit committees are whether their missions extend to the review of non-financial statements which are published (such as the chairman's report) and to the oversight of non-financial audit (such as quality, environmental, health and safety and other audits).

There are also challenges in co-ordinating the responsibilities of management with those of the audit committee. This challenge is likely to be experienced when an audit committee commissions work to be done directly on the committee's behalf. It is also likely to be experienced in the direct reporting to the audit committee of the internal audit function, of the compliance function and of others.

Below, we set out some of the areas for attention in order to assess whether an audit committee is, and indeed is capable of, performing well.

1. The composition of the board.

2. The board committees and their duties.

3. The means of appointing audit committee members, and the term of their appointment.

4. The experience and independence of audit committee members.

5. The training and development of audit committee members.

6. The means of appointing a chair for the audit committee, and the term of this appointment.

7. The terms of reference of the audit committee, in particular the committee's responsibilities and authorities.

8. Appropriateness of the responsibilities of the audit committee and the responsibilities of other board committees.

9. The means of reporting by the audit committee to the board.

10. General administration of the committee's business.

11. The servicing of the committee's needs (secretarial etc).

12. Access by others to audit committee members between meetings.

13. Audit committee members' involvement between meetings.

14. The number, timing and duration of audit committee meetings.

15. The timeliness within the company's year of the committee's agenda items.

16. Regularity of attendance of audit committee members at committee meetings.

17. Whether appropriate non-committee members are in attendance at audit committee meetings when required.

18. Quality of audit committee agenda, agenda papers and minutes.

19. The degree of correspondence between the committee's responsibilities and the record of its meetings.

20. The committee's approach to its scrutiny of the financial statements.

21. The committee's approach to its review of the effectiveness of management's internal control.

22. The committee's approach to the oversight of the external audit.

23. The committee's approach to oversight of the internal audit.

24. The committee's approach to meeting the requirements of regulators.

25. The thoroughness of the board's approach to its oversight responsibilities generally.

26. Whether the committee has the authority to seek professional advice from outside the company, and whether the committee exercises such a right appropriately.

27. The approach to setting up and running audit committees in groups of companies, where each subsidiary may have an audit committee.

28. Determining the membership of subsidiary company audit committees.

29. Effective relationships between subsidiary audit committees and the main audit committee.

## The developing role of audit committees                    B20.19

*John Baden, who wrote this article, was chief executive of Girobank and chaired the audit committee of Alliance & Leicester where he is deputy chairman. He was a member of the 'Rutteman Working Party' which, in December 1994 published the current guidance to UK directors on reporting on internal control. He famously dissented from the working party's conclusion that directors could reasonably restrict their report to internal financial control rather than cover the wider aspects of internal control as well. Recently John's dissenting view has been endorsed in the Hampel Report and the Combined Code.*

During 1993 and 1994 I very much enjoyed working on the Rutteman Working Party on Internal Control and Financial Reporting.

The Working Party, in my view, chickened out by deciding, with the help of the Cadbury Committee, that where the Cadbury Committee used the words 'internal control', they actually meant internal financial control and not internal control in the wider sense. I was one of the minority on the Working Party who wanted to broaden the concept to internal control in the wider sense; but, as always, one of the first worries is the question of liability and the practising members of the Working Party were unanimous in wishing to keep the concept as narrow as possible to avoid possible liability.

Since I joined my first audit committee about ten years ago, the scope of the work done by the audit committee, in my experience, has greatly deepened and widened. In those days, the audit committee tended to look mainly at the annual accounts and most of its work was related to that. Nowadays, the matters looked at by the audit committee are vastly broader than they used to be and the time involved as a member of the audit committee must have at least doubled.

My recent experience has been as a member of the Alliance & Leicester audit committee, which consists entirely of non-executive directors, and for some time as chairman.

## Audit committee pre-requisites

For an audit committee to operate effectively, it needs two things – a first class executive finance director and a first class internal auditor – both of which, I am happy to say, we undoubtedly have at Alliance & Leicester. Just as the role of the audit committee has changed over the years, so has the role and status of the internal auditor. When I first joined the board of Alliance & Leicester in 1990, the internal audit function was extremely low key and tended to concentrate on counting the cash in branches etc, rather than looking at the larger picture. It is now completely changed.

An audit committee is undoubtedly hampered unless it has a first class chief internal auditor who needs to hold not only the confidence of the audit committee, but also the confidence of his executive colleagues. In our case, the chief internal auditor can only be appointed or removed with the agreement of the audit committee and the chief internal auditor reports to the company secretary. His role is now seen as being as much involved in helping management, particularly from the risk point of view, as in reporting to the audit committee – and this is a very important step forward.

Internal audit and executive management tended, in the past, to be somewhat adversarial, but we have got over this particular problem and they now work together smoothly.

### NED induction

New non-executive directors of Alliance & Leicester have an induction course. Additionally, all non-executive directors are strongly encouraged to visit branches and other offices of the Group and most board meetings include a presentation by an executive of his or her particular area of business. So we do our best to ensure that the non-executive directors understand the business.

### Audit committee meetings

The audit committee meets four or five times a year and certainly meets to approve the interim and annual accounts. At all its meetings, various executives would be present to answer questions or to take part in any discussion. Once a year, however, all executives and the external auditor leave the room while the company secretary gives his appraisal of the chief internal auditor.

Additionally, once a year, the executives leave the room so that the external auditors have a chance to talk in confidence with the members of the audit committee and raise any worries they might have. We also ask them for a frank view of the effectiveness of the audit committee, which, so far, I am glad to say, has been very positive.

Equally, once a year, the external auditors leave the room and the executives stay while we discuss the performance of the external auditors.

We now have an assessment form which is operated at the end of each audit which assesses the work of the external auditors. This is supplied to the external auditors for their comments and, with the assessments and comments alongside each other, is then placed in front of the audit committee. This is a fairly new development for us, but it seems to be a really effective discipline and I think is helpful for both sides. It is obviously the finance director who plays the leading role in this assessment.

While the external auditors are out of the room, we also look at the relationship of the audit to non-audit fees and need to feel happy that the balance between these is correct. In our case, we use several firms, other than our auditors, for specialist work outside the audit – which reduces the possible problems of conflicts of interest between the audit and non-audit fees. We also consider, from time to time, whether we should put our audit out to tender. From this point of view, we deprecate the tendency of major audit firms to merge as this reduces our choice.

**Audit committee coverage apart from accounts and audit**

In our case, we cover the whole gamut of internal control. It is in no way limited to internal financial control. In this, we were helped by having been a building society because, while the Building Society Commission was much more difficult to work with than the Bank of England, the *section 71* assessment of controls under the *Building Societies Act 1986*, was actually rather helpful. I was Chief Executive of Girobank before and during the takeover by Alliance & Leicester, and I thought I was running quite an efficient business. When Girobank became a subsidiary of Alliance & Leicester, the *section 71* process was applied to Girobank and it actually brought out a whole series of weaknesses, of most of which I and my senior management were unaware.

The board of Alliance & Leicester has agreed that, while now as a bank we are not subject to Section 71, we should nevertheless keep the *section 71* practice in being as a valuable way of ensuring that our processes are being properly managed.

Compliance is treated in a similar fashion. The responsibility for compliance remains in the line and they have to report as to whether they have been compliant. The compliance officer is responsible for ensuring that compliance reports are given in and that they are, on the face of it, accurate; but the compliance officer is not responsible for compliance as such. We find that this works very successfully.

Fraud is always a worry and we have in place a formal procedure for 'whistleblowing'.

### Risk management

Risk management is a line function and we have a head of risk management who reports to the audit committee perhaps twice a year on various aspects of risk so that we can be happy that all aspects are being looked at and properly dealt with. But, it is one of internal audit's functions to check that line management has identified the risks and taken the necessary action.

We have adopted a major programme of risk and control self assessment, driven by internal audit, from which we expect considerable business benefits. This extends, for example, into the questions of contingency and the ability to continue in business under various disaster scenarios. Earlier this year, the audit committee had a presentation from the head of risk management at the audit committee telling us what was the situation.

We have found it effective to name the individuals responsible for contingency in the various areas of the bank as this concentrates their minds, knowing that they are going to be asked about any weaknesses during a meeting of the audit committee and knowing also that the minutes of the audit committee go before the whole board.

We believe that internal audit, as a separate discipline, is no longer cost effective or efficient – it is, instead, an essential element of the overall corporate risk management system. Good internal auditors must be risk and control consultants. Their job, in part, is to help the business make more accurate assessments as a basis for commercial decisions.

### Millennium and Euro

This extends also to the question of the millennium, which is the responsibility of the executive in charge of risk management; and he, again, will report to the audit committee and the board on this on a regular basis.

I must say, in passing, that I do have worries that the British government is not taking this risk seriously enough or putting in sufficient funds to overcome the problem. In our own case, we reckon that the cost of being compliant for the millennium will be somewhere between £30–40 million – and probably nearer to the upper figure. We are also ensuring that our suppliers and our customers are going to be millennium compliant because, otherwise, we cannot operate. In general, and particularly looking across Europe, I think the dangers of the millennium are underestimated.

We have similar reports on preparation for the EMU which is the responsibility of the managing director of Girobank. Even though it seems unlikely that we will join the EMU in the immediate future, we are taking the longer term perspective on this as we view it likely that the UK will join in due course.

In any case, in the short term, we must be able to operate in, and to be able to deal with the Euro currency; and, as far as Girobank is concerned in its cash collection operation, to take in Euro coins and notes. If we do join the EMU, we believe our costs for that will be even greater than our millennium costs.

## The internal audit plan and reports

The audit committee approves the programme of the internal audit department and its staffing; and specifically ensures that there are adequately qualified staff for the different parts of the business in the internal audit department. The main specialisms we are interested in are computer audit and treasury audit. The chief internal auditor gives us a report approximately quarterly about the work he has been doing and what he has found, and raises with us any particular worries he might have. These are then discussed in the audit committee, with the executive in charge of the department concerned present to answer any questions and give his or her view on the situation. If there is something wrong, we are likely to ask that executive for a deadline by which the problem will be put right and, thereafter, that will be monitored. We are also told when the problem has been finally solved so that we do not have to worry about it any more.

If there are any high risk/high probability reports from the internal auditor, these are immediately circulated to the members of the audit committee. It does not wait for the next committee meeting.

### *Audit committee reporting to the board*

As mentioned above, the minutes (usually the draft minutes so that they reach the board in a timely fashion) are circulated to the whole board and included in the board papers as an *above the line item. Above the line* in our papers are items for decision; *below the line* are papers for information only. While the minutes of the audit committee do not normally call for any decision by the board, they are regarded as sufficiently important to be among the mandatory reading of the board, and the chairman of the audit committee will be asked by the chairman of the board to draw to the attention of the board any particular items which give him cause to worry or which might be of particular interest to the board. Among the recent items discussed in my own board was whether there was any sense in a bank having general provisions because we all know what happens in practice – that general provisions never get transferred to specific provisions, they tend always to go up, and when you need to use them, you are not allowed to. We are beginning to take steps to change this and this is a matter that has already been discussed twice in the audit committee.

## Co-ordination between internal and external audit

The relationship between the internal and external auditors is very close; they meet regularly and work harmoniously together. The external auditors attend every audit committee, receive a copy of every audit report, and the only time they are not present at the audit committee is when we are discussing their performance. The senior partner concerned will normally see, before the accounts are finalised, the chief executive, the chairman of the board and the chairman of the audit committee. Additionally, the internal auditor will talk to the chairman of the audit committee before each meeting in case there are any worries on any items of the agenda or to give him any special background to an item which might be helpful to him when chairing the meeting.

## Interfacing with the Bank of England

Another recent innovation has been the Bank of England requiring to see the chairman of the audit committee at various regulatory and prudential meetings. This is a comparatively recent development, but it strikes me as a sensible one. The times I have been present at such a meeting, I had the impression that the Bank of England was pleased that they could ask questions of a non-executive to confirm the answers they were getting from the executives who normally attend such meetings.

## ICAEW publications

There seems to be general acceptance of the need for greater emphasis on internal control. There is a very good newsletter, called 'Internal Control', published by the Institute of Chartered Accountants of England & Wales, and they also published a booklet on audit committees – 'A Framework for Assessment' – approximately a year ago, which is a useful work; and, more recently, one entitled 'Internal Audit and Its Value'. I am glad to say that the chief internal auditor of Alliance & Leicester was one of the Audit Faculty's Internal Audit Task Force which wrote the latter book.

## Quality of information

One of the major requirements for good corporate governance is that the board of the company receives the information it needs to take the decisions it has to take; that this information is reported in a digestible form and that it is accurate. This is something the audit committee looks at on a regular basis, though it is equally a concern of the whole board who take great interest in this matter.

## Interim and final accounts

Twice a year, when the interim and financial accounts are being considered, all non-executive directors of the board are invited to attend the meeting of the audit committee so that we can get input at that stage and so that the formal approval by the board becomes effectively a rubber stamp as the board, wearing a different hat (ie that of the audit committee) has already approved the accounts. In this way, any changes or amendments are produced earlier than they might otherwise be. This seems to work well.

### Should the board of the company report on the effectiveness of its internal control?

Finally – one of the most contentious points – should the board of the company report on the effectiveness of its internal control? Various views have been taken on this. We certainly consider it our responsibility to ensure that our internal control is effective. There is a continuing debate about whether we should report on this, particularly because of the difficulty of the definition of effectiveness, particularly because of the liabilities of the directors if there is then a glitch in the company and even more particularly because of worries from the auditors that they would have to confirm any such report as correct or not and thereby incur potential liabilities if we and they get it wrong.

My personal belief is that a board of directors should report on the effectiveness of internal control in the widest sense and if this opens them up to personal liability, they are likely to concentrate yet more attention on this matter and ensure that no liability will actually arise. In this year's report, we stated:

> 'The (Audit) Committee reviews the effectiveness of the Group's systems of internal control, and monitors compliance with regulatory requirements. To do this, the Committee approves the annual internal audit plan which is based on a thorough risk assessment of the full scope of the Group's business activities and monitors progress against the plan.'

**Notes**

1. We are grateful to Dr. Curtis C. Verschoor for material used in this part of the Handbook, especially on US developments. Curt is The Ledger & Quill Research Professor at DePaul University, Chicago (E-mail: cverscho@condor.depaul.edu. Tel: +00 847 381 8115. Fax: +00 847 381 2310). We are also grateful to John Baden upon whose experiences we have drawn. His article 'The Developing Role of Audit Committees' is included at **B20.36–B20.50**.

2. John Baden, (July 1998): 'The Developing Role of Audit Committees', Internal Control, pp 3– 6, Institute of Chartered Accountants in England & Wales, London, Issue 13, ISSN 1367 2517. Tel. +44 (0)207 920 8992.

3. Internal Control – Guidance to Directors on the Combined Code, (September 1999), published by The Institute of Chartered Accountants in England & Wales, ISBN 1 84152 010 1. Available from Accountancy Books, PO Box 21375, London, WC1N 1QP. Tel: +44 (0)20 7920 8991. Fax: +44 (0) 20 7920 8992. www.accountancybooks.co.uk. Currently the guidance can be downloaded from ICAEW's website: www.icaew.co.uk/internal control. The Turnbull Report is also reproduced in **PART A** of this handbook.

4. Report and Recommendations of the Blue Ribbon Committee on Improving the Effectiveness of Corporate Audit Committees, (1999), obtainable from Murray Teitelbaum at NYSE. Tel: (001) 212 656 2017) or the report may also be found on-line at www.nyse.com or www.nasd.com or www.nasdaq-amexnews.com. Curt Verschoor has explained to me that 'Blue Ribbon' is an American term that means 'best' or 'top-drawer', and that in other than Olympic contests, the winner is awarded a blue ribbon, the runner up a white ribbon, and third place a red ribbon.

5. Report of the Committee on the Financial Aspects of Corporate Governance ('The Cadbury Report'), (1 December 1992): The Code of Best Practice (The Cadbury Code'), Gee & Co., London, ISBN 0 85258 914 X.
6. Cadbury Code, provision 4.3.
7. Source: 1995 Price Waterhouse Corporate Register, published by Hamilton Scott.
8. Combined Code, provision D.3.1.
9. Provision D.3.2.
10. Provision A.3.1.
11. Provision A.3.2.
12. Provision A.3.2.
13. Curtis C. Verschoor (September/October 2000), 'New Audit Committee Responsibilities Provide Governance Opportunities for Internal Auditing', Internal Auditing, pp 35–38, Warren, Gorman & Lamont, New York, Volume 15, No. 5, ISSN 0897 0378. Tel: (001) 212 367 6425.
14. Provision C.2.3.
15. Final Report: Committee on Corporate Governance ('The Hampel Committee'), January 1998, Gee & Co, London, ISBN 1 86089 034 2, para 5.19, p 47.
16. D.3.1.
17. Baden, ibid.
18. Baden, ibid.
19. Verschoor, ibid.
20. Baden, ibid.
21. Baden, ibid.
22. Baden, ibid.
23. Baden, ibid.
24. The Turnbull Report is guidance to directors on implementing the section on 'Internal control' within the Combined Code.
25. Baden, ibid.
26. Baden, ibid.
27. Final Report: Committee on Corporate Governance ('The Hampel Committee'), ibid, p17.
28. Verschoor, ibid.
29. Statement on Auditing Standards No. 90 (SAS 90), (December 1999): Audit Committee Communications (at www.aicpa.org (then click on Teams, then Audit and Attest Standards Team, then Technical Activities and Publications, then Summaries of Recently Issue Standards). Guidance on the new auditor requirements is also in the SECPS Practice Alert 2000–2 (www.aicpa.org, then click on Online Publications, then click on The CPA Letter, then click on Practice Alert 2000–2). SAS 90 amdend SAS 61 (Communication with Audit Committees) and SAS 71 (Interim Financial Information).
30. Recommendation 8 (page 33 of the BRC Report):
'The Committee recommends that Generally Accepted Auditing Standards (GAAS) require that a company's outside auditor discuss with the audit committee the auditor's judgments about the quality, not just the acceptability, of the company's accounting principles as applied in its financial reporting; the discussion should include such issues as the clarity of the company's financial disclosures and degree of aggressiveness or conservatism of the company's accounting principles and underlying estimates and other significant decisions made by management in preparing the financial disclosure and reviewed by the outside auditors. This requirement should be written in a way to encourage open, frank discussion and to avoid boilerplate.'
31. Verschoor, ibid.
32. Verschoor, ibid.
33. Tricker, R.I. (1978): The Independent Director, Tolley, Croydon, England, ISBN 0 510 49378 5. 104 pages.

# Board Committees – Terms of Reference

## Audit committee terms of reference B21.1

Readers intending to use either of these samples as templates for developing their own terms of reference for audit committees may wish to consider three recent innovations in audit committee practice which are not fully covered in these sample terms of reference. First, audit committees, especially in the US, are increasingly being charged with the responsibility to consider the quality of information which the board receives, and to advise the board on the conclusions of this consideration. Secondly, audit committees, especially in the UK following the adoption of Turnbull, now more frequently have responsibility to advise the board on the quality of the entity's risk management and, on behalf of the board, to consider the major risks facing the entity and their management. Thirdly, again, particularly in the US, it is becoming accepted that the audit committee may have the responsibility to pro-actively and specifically consider the likely impact on risk, control and financial reporting of major changes planned, or being implemented by, the entity. These issues are discussed in **B20** AUDIT COMMITTEES.

## Terms of reference – 1 B21.2

**Terms of reference for an audit committee of a UK listed company revised in 2001**

> **XYZ plc**
>
> **Audit committee**
>
> **Terms of reference**

The audit committee (hereinafter 'the committee') is a committee of the group board (hereinafter 'the board'), comprising at least three non-executive directors with a quorum being any two committee members. Committee members are appointed by the board, the members being directors independent of management and free of any relationship that, in the opinion of the board, would interfere with the exercise of independent judgement as committee members. The chair of the committee, who shall not also be the chair of the board, is nominated by the chair of board and approved by the board.

At the request of the chair of the committee, the financial and other executive directors and further executives (in particular the chief audit executive) will be in attendance at committee meetings or for selected agenda items; and representatives of the external auditors may also be invited. The chief audit executive and the external auditor at their respective discretions also have direct access to the board.

The external auditor and the chief audit executive shall each, on separate occasions, have time alone with the committee at least once a year without members of the executive being present.

The committee meets at least three times a year (to scrutinise the interim and final accounts with the principal focus of the other meeting(s) being risk management, the quality of information the board receives, management control, internal audit and external audit).

The committee's minutes are an 'above the line' agenda paper for the next board meeting at which they are spoken to by the committee's chair.

The committee's purview extends to all the operations within the XYZ group of companies.

The committee at its own discretion is empowered to seek outside advice in the furtherance of its responsibilities, at the company's expense.

The secretary to the board shall also be secretary to this committee.

Consistent with section C of the 2003 Combined Code (**PART A**), the committee's responsibilities, on behalf of the board, are described in the following.

1. Ensure the board presents a balanced and understandable assessment of the company's position and prospects in all financial information which is published.

2. Ensure the board maintains a sound approach to risk management and to internal control.

3. Ensure that formal and transparent arrangements are established and followed for applying 1 and 2 above and for maintaining an appropriate relationship with the company's auditors, including keeping under review the scope and results of the external audit, its cost effectiveness and the independence and objectivity of the auditors.

4. Approve in advance the appointment and termination of employment of the chief audit executive who shall have a right of direct access to the chair of the committee at all times; review the quality, adequacy, resources, scope and nature of the work of the internal auditing function; recommend to whom it should report; receive and review reports (usually in summary form) from the chief audit executive; and on occasion commission audit assignments to be conducted on the committee's behalf.

**Formally adopted by the board of XYZ plc, 25 May 2001**

# Terms of reference – 2                                   **B21.3**

**Sample terms of reference from a listed company**

## 1. Constitution

1.1 At a meeting held at [location] on [date] the board of directors of [company name] resolved to establish a standing committee of the board without executive responsibilities, to be known as the audit committee, in accordance with these terms of reference which were adopted.

## 2. Membership

2.1 The membership of the committee shall be appointed by the board from amongst the non-executive directors of the company and shall consist of a minimum of three members and majority of whom should be independent of the company. A quorum shall be three members.

2.2 The duties and responsibilities of a member of the audit committee are in addition to those set out for a member of the board of directors.

2.3 The chairman of the committee, who shall not be the chairman of the company, shall be appointed by the board by formal board resolution.

## 3. Attendance at meetings

3.1 The chief financial officer, chief internal auditor and a representative of the independent accountant shall normally attend meetings. All other board members and the chief executive officer shall also normally have the right to attend.

3.2 The committee may instruct any officer or employee of the company to attend any meeting and provide pertinent information as necessary.

3.3 At least once a year, the committee shall meet with the chief internal auditor and the independent accountants respectively without the presence of executive management to discuss any matters that either the committee or these two believe should be discussed privately.

3.4 The company secretary shall be the secretary of the committee.

## 4. Frequency of meetings

4.1 Meetings shall be held at least three times yearly or more frequently as circumstances require.

4.2 The committee chairman shall convene a meeting upon request of any committee member who considers it necessary.

4.3 Whenever possible committee meetings shall be scheduled to allow for adequate time for committee business, and so that they can be reported promptly and effectively to the board.

## 5. Authority

5.1  The committee is authorised by the board to investigate any activity it deems appropriate. It is authorised to seek any information from any officer or employee of the company all of whom are directed to co-operate with any request made by the committee.

5.2  The committee is authorised to engage any firm of accountants, lawyers or other professionals as the committee sees fit to provide independent council and advice and to assist in any review or investigation on such matters as the committee deems appropriate.

5.3  The chief internal auditor reports functionally to the chairman of the audit committee (and administratively to the chief executive officer).

## 6. Duties

The duties of the committee shall be to as follows.

*General*

6.1  To ensure that there is an open avenue of communication between the internal auditors, the independent accountants and the board of directors.

6.2  Review annually and, if necessary propose for formal board adoption, amendments to the committee's terms of reference.

6.3  Consider, in consultation with the independent accountants and the chief internal auditor, the audit plans and scope of the independent accountants and internal auditors, ensuring that co-ordination of audit effort is maximised.

*Financial statements*

6.4  Review with management and the independent accountants at the completion of the annual examination:

  (a)  the company's annual financial statements and related footnotes;

  (b)  the independent accountants' audit of the financial statements and report thereon;

  (c)  any significant changes which have been required in the independent accountants' audit plan;

  (d)  any significant difficulties or disputes with management encountered during the course of the audit; and

  (e)  other matters related to the conduct of the audit which are to be communicated to the committee under generally accepted auditing standards.

*Internal control*

6.5  Enquire of management, the chief internal auditor, and the independent accountants about significant risks or exposures and evaluate the steps taken to minimise such risk to the company.

6.6 Consider and review with management and the chief internal auditor significant findings during the year and management's responses thereto.

6.7 Consider and review with the independent accountants and the chief internal auditor:

    (a) The adequacy of the company's systems of internal control including computerised information systems controls and security;

    (b) Any related significant findings and recommendations of the independent accountants and of the internal auditors, together with management's responses thereto; and

    (c) The contents of the independent accountants Management Letter, together with management's responses thereto.

*External audit*

6.8 Recommend to the board of directors the independent accountants to be appointed and their compensation; review and approve the scope and quality of their work, and their discharge or resignation.

6.9 Consider with management and the independent accountants the rationale for employing audit firms other than the principal independent accountants.

*Internal audit*

6.10 Review and approve, where possible in advance of the event, the appointment, replacement, reassignment, or dismissal of the chief internal auditor.

6.11 Consider and review with management and the chief internal auditor:

    (a) any difficulties encountered in the course of internal audits, and any restrictions placed on internal audit scope of work or access to required information or personnel;

    (b) the audit plan of future audits to be conducted;

    (c) the internal auditing department's budget and staffing;

    (d) any changes which have been required in the previously approved audit plan; and

    (e) the internal audit department's charter.

## 7. Reporting

7.1 The chairman of the committee shall report on committee business to the board of directors with such recommendations as the committee may deem appropriate.

7.2 The committee shall recommend approval of the annual report and accounts to the board of directors.

7.3 The secretary shall distribute copies of the minutes of meetings of the committee to all members of the board of directors, and the minutes shall be an agenda paper of next following board meeting.

# Remuneration committee sample terms of reference[1]

**B21.4**

There is some overlap of responsibilities between the nomination, personnel and remuneration committees, as set out in the sample terms of reference for those committees given in **B21.7** and **B21.11**. The overlap is set out in **B19.10**.

In a listed company the remuneration committee would always have responsibility for advising the board on the remuneration of the executive directors in all its forms, and would also frequently provide similar advice with regard to the most senior executives who are not board members. In the family controlled non-listed company for whom this sample terms of reference was developed, we have drafted the terms with a view to the remuneration committee also providing similar advice with regard to the compensation of members of the board and the remuneration in all its forms of the senior executives.

## Terms of reference

**B21.5**

### 1. Constitution

At a meeting held at [location] on [date] the board of directors of [company name] resolved to establish a standing committee of the board without executive powers to be known as the remuneration committee, in accordance with these terms of reference which were adopted.

### 2. Membership

2.1 The membership of the committee shall be appointed by the board by formal resolution from amongst the independent[2], non-executive directors of the company and shall consist of a minimum of three members. A quorum shall be two members.

2.2 The duties and responsibilities of a member of the remuneration committee are in addition to those set out for a member of the board of directors.

2.3 The chairman of the committee shall be appointed by the board by formal resolution.

### 3. Attendance at meetings

3.1 The committee may require the group's chief executive (and other executives) to attend its meetings for certain agenda items. No executive shall take part in decisions on his or her own remuneration.

3.2 At the discretion of the chairman of this committee, outside professional advisors may be in attendance for certain agenda items.

3.3 The company secretary shall be secretary to this committee.

## 4. Frequency of meetings

4.1 The committee shall meet at least twice a year and as frequently as is required.

4.2 The timing and agenda of meetings is the responsibility of the committee chairman, subject to the expressed wishes of committee members.

## 5. Authority

5.1 The committee is authorised to require the provision of such information[3], and access to such personnel, as it requires to discharge its responsibilities.

5.2 The committee is authorised to take outside professional advice as appropriate in particular to make external comparisons.

## 6. Duties

6.1 The committee's purpose is to ensure that the group directors and senior executives are fairly rewarded for their individual contributions to overall performance, and to demonstrate that the remuneration of senior executives is set by directors who have no personal; interest in the outcome of their decisions and who will give due regard to the interests of the shareholders and to the financial and commercial needs of the group.

6.2 The duties of the committee shall be to recommend to and advise the board on the remuneration (in all its forms) and associated matters of the directors and senior executives. This requires the committee to:

1. Determine appropriate remuneration in all its forms (including pension arrangements within the discretion of the company's scheme) of the group chairman, directors, chief executive and senior executives, as defined from time to time. This will bear in mind differentials between levels of personnel and market relativities.

2. Ensure there is good succession planning and management development at senior executive levels, and to review specific development plans for the top $n^4$ executives in the group[5].

3. Measure the performance of key senior executives as a prelude to determining their annual remuneration, bonus rewards and award of long term incentives.

4. See that, in exercising the rights to performance related compensation, benefits are related to the performance both of individuals and the group, and that they provide a long term incentive.

5. Ensure that the committee only makes recommendations which it can justify to shareholders and staff alike and that the criteria on which performance is measured can be clearly explained.

## 7. Reporting

7.1 The committee makes recommendations to the group board which either approves them or, stating its reasons for not doing so, asks the committee to reconsider them.

7.2 The chairman of the committee shall be available to answer members' questions at the annual general meeting.

# Nomination committee sample terms of reference[6]    B21.6

There is some overlap of responsibilities between the nomination, personnel and remuneration committees, as set out in the sample terms of reference for those committees given in **B21.5** and **B21.11**. The overlap is set out in **B19.10**.

A few director search firms are listed in **B10.78**.

The terms of reference for the nomination committee give to it responsibility for succession planning at board level while leaving to the remuneration committee the responsibility for ensuring that there is good succession planning and management development at senior executive levels. Alternative approaches would be to settle all these duties upon the nomination committee or to split them between the nominations committee and the senior executive team.

## Terms of reference    B21.7

### 1. Constitution

At a meeting held at [location] on [date] the board of directors of [company name] resolved to establish a standing committee of the board to be known as the nomination committee, in accordance with these terms of reference which were adopted.

### 2. Membership

2.1 Membership of the committee shall comprise a majority of the non-executive directors of the board with an emphasis on seniority[7], to be appointed to this committee by resolution of the board.

2.2 The chairman of the board shall be chairman of this committee.[8]

### 3. Attendance at meetings

3.1 The chairman of the committee may co-opt other directors to join the committee temporarily for particular specified purposes.

3.2 The committee may require the group's chief executive (and other executives) to attend its meetings for certain agenda items.

3.3 Directors (and senior executives in attendance) may be required by the chairman to leave the meetings of this committee when open discussion might be inhibited by their presence.

3.4 At the discretion of the chairman of this committee, outside professional advisors may be in attendance for certain agenda items.

3.5 The company secretary shall be secretary to this committee[9].

## 4. Frequency of meetings

4.1 The committee shall meet at least twice a year and as frequently as is required.

4.2 The timing and agenda of meetings is the responsibility of the committee chairman, subject to the expressed wishes of committee members.

## 5. Authority

5.1 The committee is authorised to require the provision of such information, and access to such personnel, as it requires to discharge its responsibilities.

5.2 The committee is authorised to take outside professional advice as appropriate.

## 6. Duties

**The committee is responsible for:**

6.1 proposing to the board the responsibilities of non-executive directors, including membership and chairmanship of board committees;

6.2 ensuring that there is a satisfactory, formal process for the selection of non-executive directors which it is the responsibility of this committee to follow;

6.3 proposing to the board any new board appointments, whether of executive or non-executive directors;

6.4 ensuring there is good succession planning at board level;

6.5 reviewing the effectiveness of non-executive directors; and.

6.6 nominating suitable people for the most senior executive positions, including that of chief executive.

## 7. Reporting

7.1 The committee makes recommendations to the group board which either approves them or, stating its reasons for not doing so, asks the committee to reconsider them[10].

# Finance committee sample terms of reference[11]   B21.8

## Terms of reference   B21.9

### 1. Constitution

At a meeting held at [location] on [date] the board of directors of [company name] resolved to establish a standing committee of the board to be known as the finance committee, in accordance with these terms of reference which were adopted.

## 2. Membership

2.1 The membership of the committee shall be appointed by the board from amongst the directors of the company and shall consist of a minimum of three members. A quorum shall be two members.

2.2 The duties and responsibilities of a member of the finance committee are in addition to those set out for a member of the board of directors.

2.3 The chairman of the committee, who shall not be the chairman of the company, shall be appointed by the board by formal board resolution.

## 3. Attendance at meetings

3.1 The chief executive officer and the chief financial officer shall normally attend meetings. All board members shall also normally have the right to attend.

3.2 The committee may instruct any officer or employee of the company to attend any meeting and provide pertinent information as necessary.

3.3 The company secretary shall be the secretary of the committee.

## 4. Frequency of meetings

4.1 Meetings shall be held at least three times yearly or more frequently as circumstances require.

4.2 The committee chairman shall convene a meeting upon request of any committee member who considers it necessary.

4.3 Whenever possible committee meetings shall be scheduled to allow for adequate time for committee business, and so that they can be reported promptly and effectively to the board.

## 5. Authority

5.1 The committee is authorised by the board to investigate any activity it deems appropriate. It is authorised to seek any information from any officer or employee of the company all of whom are directed to co-operate with any request made by the committee.

5.2 The committee is authorised to engage any firm of accountants, merchant bankers, lawyers or other professionals as the committee sees fit to provide independent council and advice and to assist in any review or investigation on such matters as the committee deems appropriate.

## 6. Duties

The purpose of this committee is to monitor the financial arrangements of the company; to decide upon financial issues of importance which have been delegated to this committee by the board; and to recommend to the board as appropriate on financial issues of more major importance which are reserved for board decision.

**The duties of the committee include, but are not limited to the following.**

*Going concern*

6.1 Formally considering and concluding upon whether the company remains a going concern.

*Capital issues*

6.2 Recommending to the board (a) any changes to the capital structure of the business, and (b) any arrangements with bankers and/or others for rescheduling long-term debt.

6.3 Recommending to the board appropriate dividend policy and appropriate dividends to be declared.

6.4 Approving borrowing limits of less than $50 million and recommending for board approval of borrowing limits greater than $50 million.

6.5 Recommending to the board approval of investments and expenditure of a capital nature greater or equal to $5 million, and approving similar expenditures between $1 million and £5 million.

*Liquidity and Solvency*

6.6 Reviewing and determining cash flow assumptions and projections.

6.7 Reviewing asset and liability positions.

*Treasury policies and treasury risk*

6.8 Approving treasury policies including the management of funds and investment policies, exposures to counter party risk, interest rate risk, liquidity risk, exchange risk, legal or compliance risk.

6.9 Reviewing currency positions.

*Variances*

6.10 Considering negative variances of more than 5 pr cent from the net income of an approved budget or business plan where these are greater than, or equal to, $1 million; and determining or approving appropriate action to be taken.

6.11 Considering overruns on approved capital investment budgets of more than 20 per cent.

*Contracts*

6.12 Approving (a) major contracts and agreements for services and consultancy (excluding those relating to directors and staff); (b) recommending to the board approval of commitment to spend which amount to $500,000 or greater; and (c) approving commitments to spend of between $100,000 and $500,000.

6.13 Monitoring major arrangements and contracts to ensure that company is not in default of significant financial and other contract terms; and decisions for remedial action where necessary.

## 7. Reporting

7.1 The chairman of the committee shall report on committee business to the board of directors with such recommendations as the committee may deem appropriate.

7.2 The secretary shall distribute copies of the minutes of meetings of the committee to all members of the board of directors, and the minutes shall be an agenda paper of next following board meeting.

# Personnel committee sample terms of reference                    B21.10

There is some overlap of responsibilities between the nomination, personnel and remuneration committees, as set out in the sample terms of reference for those committees given in **B21.5** and **B21.7**. The overlap is set out in **B19.10**.

## Terms of reference                    B21.11

### 1. Constitution

At a meeting held at [location] on [date] the board of directors of [company name] resolved to establish a standing committee of the board to be known as the personnel committee, in accordance with these terms of reference which were adopted.

### 2. Membership

2.1 The membership of the committee shall be appointed by the board from amongst the directors of the company and shall consist of a minimum of three members. A quorum shall be two members.

2.2 The duties and responsibilities of a member of the personnel committee are in addition to those set out for a member of the board of directors.

2.3 The chairman of the committee, who shall not be the chairman of the company, shall be appointed by the board by formal board resolution.

### 3. Attendance at meetings

3.1 The chief executive officer and the chief personnel officer shall normally attend meetings. All board members shall also normally have the right to attend.

3.2 The committee may instruct any officer or employee of the company to attend any meeting and provide pertinent information as necessary.

3.3 The company secretary shall be the secretary of the committee.

## 4. Frequency of meetings

4.1  Meetings shall be held at least three times yearly or more frequently as circumstances require.

4.2  The committee chairman shall convene a meeting upon request of any committee member who considers it necessary.

4.3  Whenever possible committee meetings shall be scheduled to allow for adequate time for committee business, and so that they can be reported promptly and effectively to the board.

## 5. Authority

5.1  The committee is authorised by the board to investigate any activity it deems appropriate and within its terms of reference. It is authorised to seek any information from any officer or employee of the company all of whom are directed to co-operate with any request made by the committee.

5.2  The committee is authorised to engage any firm of personnel consultants, management consultants, lawyers or other professional advisors as the committee sees fit to provide independent council and advice and to assist in any review or investigation on such matters as the committee deems appropriate.

## 6. Duties

The committee is responsible to ensure that the company follows best practice with regard to personnel matters. To this end it will:

6.1  ensure that the company has a satisfactory personnel function covering all aspects of personnel management including succession planning and career development;

6.2  approve all personnel policies of the company, including health and safety policies;

6.3  review to ensure that the company does not discriminate unfairly in personnel matters;

6.4  review to ensure that the company complied with all legal and regulatory requirements impacting upon personnel;

6.5  recommend to the board for board approval all significant staff redundancy plans;

6.6  ensure there is good succession planning and management development at senior executive levels; and review specific development plans for the top executives in the group.

6.7  recommend to and advise the board on the remuneration (in all its forms) and associated matters of the senior executives.

6.8  review the performance of key senior executives.

6.9  Ensure that, in exercising the rights to performance related compensation, benefits are related to the performance both of individuals and the group, and that they provide a long-term incentive.

6.10 Ensure that the committee only makes recommendations which it can be justified to shareholders and staff alike and that the criteria on which performance is measured can be clearly explained.

6.11 Nominate suitable people for senior executive positions.

### 7. Reporting

7.1  The chairman of the committee shall report on committee business to the board of directors with such recommendations as the committee may deem appropriate.

7.2  The secretary shall distribute copies of the minutes of meetings of the committee to all members of the board of directors, and the minutes shall be an agenda paper of next following board meeting.

# Standing orders committee[12] sample terms of reference

B21.12

## Terms of reference

B21.13

### 1. Constitution

At a meeting held at [location] on [date] the board of directors of [company name] resolved to establish a standing committee of the board to be known as the standing orders committee, in accordance with these terms of reference which were adopted.

### 2. Membership

2.1  The membership of the committee shall be appointed by the board from amongst the directors of the company and shall consist of a minimum of three members. A quorum shall be two members.

2.2  The duties and responsibilities of a member of the standing orders committee are in addition to those set out for a member of the board of directors.

2.3  The chairman of the committee, who shall not be the chairman of the company, shall be appointed by the board by formal board resolution.

### 3. Attendance at meetings

3.1  The chairman, the chief executive officer, the company secretary and the deputy company secretary shall normally attend meetings. All board members shall also normally have the right to attend.

3.2 The committee may instruct any officer or employee of the company to attend any meeting and provide pertinent information as necessary.

3.3 The company secretary shall be in attendance as secretary to the committee[13] except, at the discretion of the committee chairman, for agenda items where a frank discussion might be impeded by the company secretary's presence.

## 4. Frequency of meetings

4.1 Meetings shall be held at least twice yearly or more frequently as circumstances require.

4.2 The committee chairman shall convene a meeting upon request of any committee member who considers it necessary.

4.3 Whenever possible committee meetings shall be scheduled to allow for adequate time for committee business, and so that they can be reported promptly and effectively to the board.

## 5. Authority

5.1 The committee is authorised by the board to initiate any activity it deems appropriate and within its terms of reference. It is authorised to seek any information from any director, officer or employee of the company all of whom are directed to co-operate with any request made by the committee.

5.2 The committee is authorised to engage any firm of lawyers, accountants, merchant bankers, or other professionals as the committee sees fit to provide independent council and advice as the committee deems appropriate.

## 6. Duties

The committee is responsible to ensure that board business is conducted in an orderly way consistent with (a) best corporate governance practices and (b) the memorandum and articles of association of the company (or equivalent) and all existing resolutions of the board.

To these ends, the committee shall:

6.1 ensure that there is maintained an up-to-date board manual, available to all board directors, comprising:

- the memorandum and articles of association of the company;
- a copy of all past formal resolutions of the board which have continuing applicability;
- the terms of reference of all board committees;
- the terms of appointment of all current directors;
- the duties and responsibilities of members of the board;
- the authorities of individual directors to take advice at the company's expense;

- organisation charts of corporate structure and senior executive positions; and

- any other matters of constitution and procedure which directors need to continue to be aware of.

6.2 Advise the board on the appointment of members to, and chairmen of, board committees; and advise the board on changes to the terms of reference of board committees.

6.3 Ensure that due consideration is given to the implications for the company of developments in generally accepted approaches to corporate governance.

6.4 Advise the board on policy relating to the seeking by directors of independent professional advice, and the payment for such advice.

6.5 Ensure that there is an acknowledged senior member of the board[14].

6.6 Advise the chairman as appropriate on any matters relating to the orderly conduct of board and board committee meetings.

6.7 Advise the board on amendments to the schedule of matters reserved to the board for the board to decide upon.

6.8 Advise the board on delegation of authority ('Concurrence Guidelines').

6.9 Monitor the performance of the company secretariat function.

## 7. Reporting

7.1 The chairman of the committee shall report on committee business to the board of directors with such recommendations as the committee may deem appropriate.

7.2 The secretary shall distribute copies of the minutes of meetings of the committee to all members of the board of directors, and the minutes shall be an agenda paper of next following board meeting.

**Notes**

1. Generally, the remuneration committee comprises non-executive directors whose main mission is to recommend to the board the appropriate compensation for (a) the executive directors, and (b) most probably the executives immediately below the board level (who may be board members of group operating companies). Non-executive directors' fees would normally be recommended to the board by an executive committee of executive directors. In a case where the entire board is non-executive the remuneration committee is still an appropriate vehicle to arrive at recommendations on senior executive compensation; in the absence of executive directors on the board, it is also the best way of arriving at appropriate fee levels for the non-executive directors but there is a special need for the committee to take independent professional advice before reaching its conclusions. These terms of reference have been designed for a large, private company with a strong family element on a board which is entirely non-executive.

2. In the case of a private company where the majority of the shares are held by family or family trusts, it may not be feasible, even though desirable, to restrict membership of this committee to non-executive directors who are genuinely

independent. This will depend upon the composition of membership of the board. Independence for a non-executive director implies a freedom of relationships (such as family ties) with other directors and an absence of other business associations with the enterprise except for one's directorship.

3. Required information is likely to include a spreadsheet schedule which specified the monetary value for each director and senior executive within the purview of this committee, of the following components of compensation met by the company (as appropriate):
   - Basic pay (or fee)
   - National insurance
   - Tax paid by company on fees, etc
   - Pension contribution
   - Private medical insurance premium
   - Mortgage
   - Car
   - Free petrol
   - Last bonus
   - ESOP (applicable for a quoted company):
   - Share options allocated
   - Their current notional value

4. By way of illustration, the number here for Grandmet is 250.

5. The duty of nominating people for the most senior executive positions (including that of chief executive) has been accorded to the nominations committee in these terms of reference.

6. In these terms of reference, responsibility for succession planning at non-board senior executive level has been given to the remuneration committee. Alternatively it could be a responsibility of the nominations committee. However, the specific duty of nominating someone for one of the most senior executive positions (including that of chief executive) has been accorded to the nominations committee.

7. 'Seniority' may be determined by (a) existing role on the board – such as that of chairman or deputy chairman, (b) length of service as a non-executive director, (c) general reputation, or (d) through being formally nominated by the board to be regarded as the senior non-executive director.

8. In the UK, the Cadbury Report proposed that either the chairman of the board or a non-executive director should chair the nominations committee.

9. In view of the sensitivity and confidentiality of issues discussed, the company may take the view that the committee should appoint as secretary from amongst its members. However, on the whole boards operate better if the secretary to the board is also privy to the business of, and secretary to, the board committees. If the view is taken that the company secretary should not be privy to the business of this committee, it follows that the committee's secretary (a non-executive director of the company) should circulate the minutes privately to all the other board directors. Being a board committee all directors have a right and need to see the minutes.

10. The way this is handled will need to be considered if it is decided that the company secretary should not be secretary to this committee.

11. Some companies would have an assets and liabilities committee (ALCO) covering broadly similar issues. It would be unlikely to be appropriate to have both a finance and an ALCO committee.

12. This committee could alternatively be called 'the chairman's committee' (though this sometimes has a different meaning – or 'board business committee'.

13. f it is accepted that a duty of this committee is to review the company secretariat function, it may be desirable that the secretary of this committee is not a member of that function. Instead the committee may appoint its secretary from amongst its

members. This is analogous to the secretary of the audit committee not being the chief internal auditor since the audit committee has to review the effectiveness of the internal audit function. However, it is always more difficult to exclude the company secretary from knowledge of, and influence over board and board committee business: the decisions and recommendations of the standing orders committee ultimately reach the board for consideration.

14. Relevant only if the posts of chairman and chief executive are combined – in which case in the UK both Cadbury and Hampel recommended that a non-executive director is formally appointed as the senior member of the board (by formal board resolution). Indeed, the Combined Code has a provision which recommends that a non-executive director should be designated the senior non-executive director even when the posts of chairman and chief executive are separated.

# Stakeholders and Reputational Management

## Introduction

Reputational risk, reputational management and reputational audit are becoming an important area of focus for boards, senior managements and internal auditors. The spotlight is widening from the narrower focus of reputation to a broader spread on stakeholders. The goal should be that the stakeholder audit should become part of every company's system of internal control. Handling stakeholder relationships well is 'key' to achieving vital organisational objectives, and knowing whether this is being done should be regarded as essential. Internal control is defined as the processes, effected by the board, management and other personnel, which give reasonable assurance of the achievement of objectives. The monitoring of internal control is one of the essential components of effective internal control which Rutteman and Turnbull both included amongst the criteria an organisation should use to assess whether there is effective internal control. Any who are responsible for implementing Turnbull in a state of the art way are likely to find these challenging ideas of real value. In addition to chief executives, these issue are important for communication directors, strategy directors and finance directors.

Although here we take the 'for profit' company as the subject for a stakeholder audit, the approach is equally relevant for 'not-for-profit' organisations who, likewise, have their own but different bodies of stakeholders.

The stakeholder audit approach recognises that, increasingly, the worth of a company resides in its intangible assets. The recently published DTI report, 'Creating value from your intangible assets' has this to say:

> 'The combined impacts of globalisation, new technology and increased competition [mean] that all companies are facing the prospect of continual incremental and, occasionally, radical change. ... .ultimately, a company's ability to flourish in this environment will depend on its ability to create value from intangibles ... Ultimately, the ability of your organisation to meet not only its current goals and objectives, but also to grasp future opportunities, will depend on its ability to create value from its intangible assets. It is only by identifying, managing and developing the full spectrum of intangibles that you will be able to unlock your full potential.'
>
> *Department of Trade and Industry, (May 2001),*
> *'Creating value from your intangible assets'*

One of the greatest sources of intangible value resides today in a company's ability to **manage its relationships** with its various stakeholder groups.

## B22.1   *Introduction*

Relationships are the drivers of reputation. Failure to manage relationships effectively is a key area of risk many companies are overlooking.

If further persuasion is needed, the DTI study goes on to say:

'We ... highlight the need for organisations to improve the quality of dialogue with a variety of stakeholders, in communicating risks and uncertainties. Ultimately the quality of dialogue affects both 'licence to operate', which includes issues like consent to and support for activities from **non financial stakeholders,** and 'cost of capital' which is influenced by the attractiveness of the overall business proposition to **financial stakeholders'**.

*Department of Trade and Industry, ibid*

and:

'A successful company is one that looks constantly to build on its existing relationships, be they **external** (customers, suppliers or anyone else whose ideas and co-operation may assist in meeting goals and solving problems) or **internal** (different functions and their teams working together to seize opportunities and create value).

*Department of Trade and Industry, ibid*

and:

'For your company to reach its full potential in this area it is essential that you not only consider how you can develop and improve your current relationships, but that you also carefully consider how you can develop and improve the relationships necessary for your future success.'

*Department of Trade and Industry, ibid*

The stakeholder audit challenges us as to whether we can now answer these and other questions in the context of our businesses.

- Is responsibility for the management of stakeholder groups clearly delineated in the business?

- Do we know the state of health of each stakeholder relationship?

- Do we understand the risks inherent in these stakeholder relationships?

- Do we know which stakeholder groups represent the greatest opportunity for us?

- Is the amount of time and effort the business spends on managing stakeholder relationships roughly in proportion to their relative importance or intangible value?

- What listening mechanisms are in place to monitor these relationships on an on-going basis?

- How well do we integrate stakeholder relationship management? (There is too much potential for companies to give out conflicting messages through a lack of stakeholder communications integration.)

- How effective is our communication with each group?

- Have we checked that there is consistency between the way we perceive each stakeholder relationship, and how they see us?

## Compete successfully by being ahead in management thinking                                      B22.2

There are many battlefields on which companies compete. We compete aggressively for customers, for supplier commitment, for staff loyalty, for fast access to technology and innovation – and for many other valuable inputs and outcomes. There are also many different strategies for achieving competitive advantage – differentiation, price leadership, and so on.

Even more fundamental today, in terms of competitive advantage, is the quality and style of management that companies apply in all their battlefields. Throughout the 1990's companies re-engineered their cultures to secure competitive advantage in a changing world, and management generally has become much more professional. It seems that constant change in the business environment forces constant change of managerial approach upon businesses. A competitive edge comes to the leading business that is proactive in adapting to changing needs, not to the trailing business that tries to play the game of catch up.

New insights into what is required to achieve corporate success come through in waves that need to be harnessed quickly if a company is not to be left behind. Sometimes more than one wave strikes simultaneously. In the 1990s we have experienced the waves of empowerment, business process re-engineering, delayering, downsizing, corporate governance, internal control and risk management. In a sense, each of these has been a new lens through which management has needed to train their eye so as to gain, retain or recover a competitive edge. More recently, there has been the lens of reputational risk and the idea of reputational audit has been born.

In the UK, the Combined Code's Provision that directors should report on internal control and risk management, together with the 'Turnbull Report's' guidance on how boards should set about doing this, have led to a sea change in the focus that boards are placing on risk. Formal 'top-down' assessments of risk, starting at the level of the board, are now commonplace. They should certainly embrace considerations of reputational risk, though many still do not. They should now be adapted to focus, not exclusively but importantly, on stakeholder risk.

### 'Top-down' assessments of risk                                      B22.3

The obvious gap in most 'top-down' assessments of risk has been that they have not adequately reflected stakeholder risks. One of the greatest risks facing any business today is that of growing out of touch with, or otherwise failing to understand, what the market and other stakeholder groups expect, want and need. There have been a number of notable and dramatic cases recently, such as Marks & Spencer, BT and Railtrack, where a company appears to have grown out of touch with its various markets.

Now, the eye of the storm is shifting to focus more on the stakeholders themselves – and the very practical concepts of stakeholder risk, stakeholder control and stakeholder audit are moving centre stage. The stakeholder audit has been designed to meet boardroom and chief executive needs, for whom the interests of stakeholders of all sorts are becoming the major preoccupation.

**Image as reality**                                                                                     **B22.4**

For some years now, it has been accepted that both intangibles, such as 'image', along with hard commercial fundamentals are important ingredients for success. When we can look back we may conclude that year 2000 was about the time when perceptions of reality became the real reality, the main drivers of success and thus the necessary focus of successful management teams. There are already many businesses now whose market capitalisation owes more to brand image than to hard tangible assets.

So, building value for shareholders is becoming predominantly about developing and cherishing the corporate brand. In the last few years of the 20th century this became manifest in a focus on reputational management. In today's small, global, internet business world – subjected to intense media scrutiny – there are no hiding places for disreputable business practices. Truth will out – and often rapidly so. In an affluent society, consumer perceptions of quality increasingly factor in perceptions of brand ethics. In a world of brands, a tarnished brand image enhances no consumer's life style – which is image-based.

**Today 'reputation risk', tomorrow 'stakeholder risk'**                          **B22.5**

Risk management became reputational risk management. In a contemporary business, it has been argued, there are now no risks except for reputational risks – which need to be identified, assessed and managed. This has been interpreted as a matter of taking steps to enhance the corporate and product brand(s), to avoid events which would damage the brands, and to respond effectively and convincingly to crises which threaten the brands.

Now, the stakeholder audit is likely to take over from the reputational audit as the preferred approach for leading edge companies to use. The reputational audit approach constructively focussed on the criticality of reputation but it targeted the different stakeholder groups only in a scattergun way. In our experience, some key stakeholder groups were often largely overlooked in the reputational audit approach. Another change is that the stakeholder audit focuses more on relationships as the drivers of reputation, rather than more exclusively on reputation itself.

The stakeholder audit is a strategic management tool which enables companies consciously to identify and understand who are their stakeholders; then to assess and monitor the health or otherwise of their relationship and reputation with each key stakeholder group; and then to design and implement the necessary measures to create a better state of health in the future. In this way, the stakeholder audit helps to control, and thereby reduce, risks arising from relationships with various stakeholder groups.

Few companies today systematically consider their relationships with their true body of stakeholders. The body of stakeholders might resemble that shown in Figure 1 below.

## The stakeholder audit approach                                    B22.6

The stakeholder audit approach allows that this will vary from one company to another:

*Figure 1*

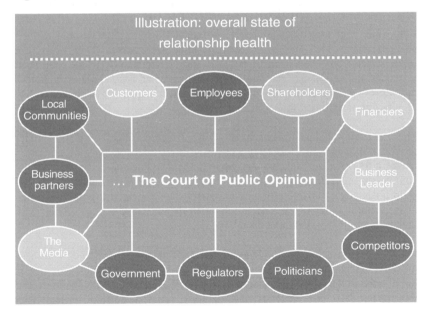

Whereas Figure 1 illustrates, for a hypothetical company, the assessed state of health with respect to each stakeholder relationship, Figure 2 additionally provides an indication of the relative importance to the company of each stakeholder relationship, on a numeric scale. Together they suggest where action is most needed and where are the best opportunities to leverage off relationships.

*Figure 2*

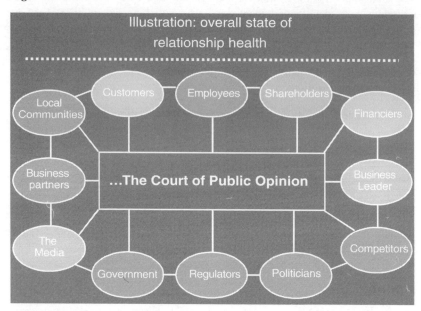

Companies need to achieve, preserve and enhance a strong reputation with each of their stakeholder groups. It is likely that even stakeholder groups not perceived as being 'key' can be serviced more satisfactorily to the long term benefit of the company. You can never be sure when a particular stakeholder relationship will assume more importance; and when it does it might be too late to put right past, long term neglect.

There is often a balance between satisfying the needs of different stakeholder groups. Company directors may not know how to reconcile the conflicting needs of their various stakeholders. Shareholders and customers appear to want completely opposite things. How do you reconcile these conflicting needs and keep all happy? But opportunities to satisfy one stakeholder group are often missed simply though lack of attention rather than because of any conflicts with the needs of other stakeholder groups.

In the last analysis it is not too fanciful to suggest that the conflicting interests of different stakeholders can be harmonised. For instance, in the long term it is likely to be in the best interests of staff to work for successful companies even if this means they experience the uncertainty of contested takeovers and other major changes. It is likely to be in customers' best interests to deal with suppliers who are generating a good return for their financial stakeholders. It is likely to be in an environmentally conscious community's best interests that a local employer is not having to cut corners to save costs. And so on. It is often a matter of managing stakeholder perceptions and expectations in order to reconcile conflicts between stakeholders for the better benefit of all; but, of course, a necessary pre-requisite is to understand what it is that has to be managed.

Satisfying stakeholders' perceived needs is not always costly nor resource intensive, but more a matter of doing 'appropriate things well' rather than 'inappropriate things badly'.

The stakeholder audit sets out to provide companies with an ongoing way of handling these challenges. It is designed to enable companies to strike the right balances between stakeholders. It should undoubtedly contribute to enhancing reputation across all stakeholder groups. Therefore, it optimises returns and creates conditions for sustainable success.

Identifying vulnerabilities in stakeholder relationships is important as it is a prerequisite to developing strategies to improve things. But as least as important is to ensure that we are exploiting for competitive advantage the particular strengths that we have in our stakeholder relationships. Businesses achieve their goals more by exploiting strengths than by avoiding vulnerabilities. The stakeholder audit facilitates both. There is little point in having an excellent stakeholder relationship if that is not turned to commercial advantage in the best possible way.

The stakeholder audit is multi-faceted and multi-staged. Initially, there is the high-level introductory questionnaire which sets out the proposition and flags up areas of opportunity. The CEO or one of his colleague directors could quite quickly complete this questionnaire. Alternatively, and preferably, internal audit could complete it in consultation with directors and senior staff, using the questionnaire as the basis of an audit assignment. If time permits, internal audit in the traditional way can look for sufficient evidence prior to homing on appropriate answers to the questions in this high-level questionnaire.

Areas identified as key in the completed high-level questionnaire can be drilled down in greater depth by using available more detailed 'facet-specific' questionnaires.

The approach outlined here has been developed by Bell Pottinger who have a number of more consultancy-based add-ons for interested clients. There is a workshop around how to run the stakeholder audit and how to evaluate and present the results. Bell Pottinger also provide intensive board-level seminars on stakeholder relationships and risk management. Finally there is the part of the stakeholder audit which is designed as an 'external stakeholder evaluation' process – to determine whether there is any mismatch between how we see ourselves and how others see us.

Further particulars from Kate Watts, Bell Pottinger Consultants, 14 Curzon Street, London, W1J 5HN. Tel: +44 (0)207 861 8587. Fax +44 (0)207 7861 8509. E-mail: kwatts@bell-pottinger.co.uk.

The checklist which follows is not based on the Bell Pottinger approach.

# Media, public and external relations checklist     B22.7

## Objectives

(a)  To ensure that the organisation projects a positive and high quality image to the public and through the media.

(b)  To ensure that all media and public relations are dealt with in accordance with defined and authorised policies.

(c)  To prevent *ad hoc*, unauthorised and potentially damaging output to the media and other external sources.

(d)  To ensure that the reputation and image of the organisation is effectively protected and defended whenever necessary.

(e)  To ensure that relevant members of management are suitably trained to deal with the media.

(f)  To ensure that plans are developed to effectively handle crisis situations (ie strikes, product concerns, etc).

(g)  To ensure that the organisation fosters good relationships with local communities.

(h)  To ensure that the organisation maintains an accurate awareness of relevant public opinion and takes the appropriate action.

(i)  To ensure that the organisation's business interests are supported by active participation in relevant trade associations or standards bodies.

(j)  To ensure that attempts to influence government polices and regulations are handled legally and effectively.

## Checklist

### 1. Key Issues

1.1  Has an agreed and authorised public and media relations policy been implemented, and if so how is management to be assured that the policy is always complied with?

1.2  Are the relevant employees and managers adequately trained to handle media and public relations, and how can management be sure that all external enquiries are correctly routed to the nominated individuals?

1.3  How does management remain aware of public opinion or media comment about the organisation, and what mechanisms are employed to effectively react to such comments?

1.4  Have contingency plans been developed in the event of crisis situations, and have specific responsibilities been allocated?

1.5  What steps does management take in order to remain aware of local community issues and to foster good relations with the local community?

1.6 What action does management take to ensure that the organisation is actively represented within the relevant trade and industry bodies?

1.7 Where there is a need to remain aware of, and attempt to, influence government policies in areas affecting the organisation, what steps are taken to ensure that lobbying is both legally conducted and effective?

## 2. Detailed Issues

2.1 What mechanisms prevent unauthorised statements being made to either the media or another external body?

2.2 Are named individuals made responsible for handling media and public relations matters, and are they appropriately experienced and trained?

2.3 Are all other staff made aware that they should not make comments or statements about the organisation to media representatives?

2.4 How does the organisation maintain an awareness of its public image, and does it have a structured approach to the projection of a positive corporate image?

2.5 How is the success of public relations activities monitored and evaluated (i.e. through the use of market research techniques)?

2.6 Are all media and public relations stances agreed and authorised by senior management, and how is this evidenced?

2.7 Are all company statements authorised and issued through an appropriate press officer?

2.8 In order to engender good local community relations, does the organisation become involved in local events and issues (and is such involvement subject to adequate justification and authorisation)?

2.9 How does management ensure that the impact of the organisation on the local community (i.e. through the appearance of its buildings or any potential environmental influences) is minimised and dealt with?

2.10 How does management ensure that enquiries or complaints from the local community are appropriately dealt with?

2.11 What steps does the organisation take to ensure that its opinion is effectively directed to influence the appropriate trade and industry bodies?

2.12 Have clear (and documented) guidelines been established regarding the methods to employ when seeking to influence government policies which could affect the organisation business interests?

2.13 How can management be assured that lobbying activities do not contravene either the law or ethical business practices?

2.14 Are all the costs associated with media, public and external relations accurately identified, authorised and reflected in the accounts?

2.15 Does management monitor the effectiveness of media, public and external relations in order to improve techniques and procedures?

2.16 How is the accuracy of data input from other systems (i.e. financial reporting) confirmed?

2.17 How is accuracy of data output to other systems (i.e. to industry regulators) confirmed?

# Corporate reputation – the role of measurement
B22.8

*This article is by Sir Geoffrey Chandler CBE. Sir Geoffrey was the Founder-Chair, Amnesty International UK Business Group 1991–2001 and former senior executive Royal Dutch/Shell Group. He can be contacted at Little Gaterounds, Parkgate Road, Newdigate, Dorking, Surrey, RH5 5AJ (tel: 01306 631612; fax: 01306 631361; e-mail: geoffchand@aol.com).*

Internal control and integrity of auditing and accounting are central to the reputation of business, but the real threats and the real risks to companies and their reputation today lie outside the traditional scope of internal control, auditing and accounting. They lie in companies' failure to give adequate care and measurement to the full range of their responsibilities in what is a too narrowly focused pursuit of profit. They lie in the failure of companies to match society's expectations in the way they deal with the human, physical and social environment in which they work and on which they depend for their success. While the accountancy profession is ensuring with increasing care and complexity the ordering of financial matters within the corporate fortress, the walls may fall as a result of assaults from without. In defending against these assaults, or rather in helping to remedy the self-inflicted wounds which allow the walls to be breached, the accountancy profession has a potential role to play and a commercial opportunity of which it is apparently, with a few exceptions, at present largely unaware.

The limited company has proved the most successful instrument the world has known for producing goods and services and creating financial wealth. But today we face a paradox. The demise of communism has extended the company's domain to most of the world and the company has never enjoyed greater opportunity or greater apparent success. But at the same time it has also never faced a greater challenge or been at greater risk.

The reason is that its economic reach has outstripped its moral reach and that it has failed to recognise the full range of its responsibilities. The world it has helped and is helping to create is one of increasing injustice and inequality. Injustice is exemplified by a growing violation of human rights in many countries; inequality by the increasing gap between rich and poor both nationally and internationally. This is inevitably a threat to the future of the company. The company is part of this world: it has a growing reach and a growing influence and therefore extended responsibilities.

In significant degree that threat lies within the company itself and in its actions. It is therefore also within its power to avert or diminish the threat by appropriate changes if it has the wit and wisdom to do so.

Companies are the servants of society. Not the reverse. The limited company is accorded privileges by society: society is therefore entitled to expect its values to be reflected in corporate practice. These values change over time. Companies which survive and flourish are those which keep up with those values, whose profits are underpinned by principle. But there is today the danger of a significant and perhaps growing gap between the legitimate expectations of society and corporate performance; a growing gap between corporate affluence and human poverty.

In the last two decades the context in which companies operate has changed faster than they have. The changes are familiar:

- the globalisation of the world economy;

- a communications revolution;

- a context of growing conflict and human rights violations in many countries; and

- critical consumers.

The implication of these changes has yet to be fully understood. Globalisation is a cliché, but reflects a reality. It has hugely extended the reach and influence of investing companies. It has increased opportunity for retailers who now source from thousands of producers in the Third World with little idea of the conditions in which these producers work. Globalisation is proving largely a one-way street in benefits brought. We have a world of increasing inequality, therefore an unstable one.

Immediacy of communications means that that there is no hiding place for company mistakes or misbehaviour. A critical consumer movement is interrogating not just *what* is produced, its price and quality, but *how*.

Companies create wealth, which is a good. But they cannot be permitted to do so at the cost of harm to those on whom they depend for their success or whom they affect through their operations. A company can only operate with the help or consent of others; employees, shareholders, the community and the social and physical environment in which it works. These are its stakeholders for which a company has responsibility and for its impact on which it is accountable. Shareholders are one, but only one such stakeholder. Stakeholders may not be an entirely apposite term since often only shareholders and employees have a direct stake in the business. But since the company cannot work without an impact on the social and physical environment and without the consent of the community, their overall designation as stakeholders has become a concept of central importance.

The challenge for companies today is to define these stakeholders, which will differ for each company, and to find an appropriate response to their needs. The challenge requires a new paradigm, a new pattern or framework of thought, if it is to find an effective response. It also requires new measurements for that response.

If companies accept this as their responsibility and apply their collective intellect and skills to interpreting it into action in regard to the full range of their stakeholders, while they cannot solve the problems of the world, they can make that world a better place for all of us and themselves. The trouble is that this is not accepted other than by a few far-sighted companies. Indeed the terminology which surrounds corporate responsibility today indicates the analytical confusion into which business thinking has retreated. Money and morality have become separated. For example the World Business Council for Sustainable Development[1], an organisation which includes some of the world's most distinguished companies, has just produced a report entitled 'Corporate Social Responsibility'. No other occupation talks of its social responsibility, its social utility is assumed to be inherent in what it does. The implication is that there is no social responsibility inherent in corporate activity, that it is an add-on. The report talks of the need for 'a corporate social responsibility strategy', something a company apparently adopts or adds on, rather than being inseparable from what it does. It argues that 'sound ethics and core values offer clear business benefits'. They may do. But the truth is that business should not exist, nor should any other occupation, without sound ethics and core values being their point of departure.

# What has gone wrong?

Throughout the history of the company there has been a conflict between the values of society and the assumed interests of business. The abolition of slavery in Britain was brought about by a pressure group in the face of commercial opposition that argued it would ruin the commercial interests of the country. The same was true of the 19th century Factory Acts which stopped small children being sent up chimneys. It has been true of the corporate response to the environment movement. More recently, it has been true in the resistance we have seen to the European Social Chapter and a minimum wage which will undoubtedly become part of the accepted scene here as they have for our major competitors.

History tells us that it is those companies which have adopted these values which have survived. Yet even they have followed rather than led; they have acted initially from external pressure rather than internal leadership.

**Why does appropriate corporate action have to be the result of pressure and not done spontaneously? And how do we change this?**

There are a number of answers to 'why?'. The insulation of top management is a real factor. Breadth of vision and open-mindedness tend to go in inverse ratio to hierarchical status. It is observable that perception and understanding of the real world are narrowed by the company car and chauffeur, the company aircraft and the corporate palaces which isolate top executives. The corporate instinct is to rebut, to look to public relations as a defence, not to change.

A further cause is adherence to the myth of the 'free' market. The market is not free: it has been constrained over time by the contemporary values of society which, without damaging the market's basic strength and utility, determine its parameters. Good companies will do more than the minimum prescribed by law. It is in their interest to have regulation to curb the practices of those who will try to do less. Yet corporate leaders and the institutions that represent them collectively have a hostile knee-jerk reaction to extending an established principle, a market with moral boundaries.

But the most fundamental cause lies in a false and misleading perception of the purpose of a company, in a confusion of ends and means, and from the fact that money has therefore become the sole measure of performance.

Many business schools teach, many company directors affirm, that the purpose of the company is 'to maximise value to shareholders'. The World Business Council Report states 'the rationale for the very existence of business is to generate acceptable returns for its shareholders and investors'. As a practising manager of many years I find this extraordinary, though it is sustained by UK company law to which I shall turn shortly. The satisfaction of shareholders is of course an essential *condition* of corporate success and survival, but it is a manifest nonsense both in practice and in principle to consider it a *purpose*. It is a hopeless guide to ethical behaviour in the complex situations that practising managers meet in the real world. It is demonstrably unjustifiable to claim that the pursuit of long-term shareholder interest leads inevitably to ethical behaviour throughout a company's operations.

But it is this misapprehension of corporate purpose that lies at the heart of the company's problem today. It is probably also the prime reason why in any survey of opinion business ranks near the bottom in public esteem, together with politicians and journalists.

Any thoughtful manager would define the purpose of a company to be to provide a product or service profitably. To do this it depends on its stakeholders. But because of the misinterpretation of company purpose, the interests of stakeholders, other than the interests of shareholders, have had to be fought for primarily from outside the company.

There has been a gradual acceptance of a company's direct responsibilities over the years as external pressure has been brought to bear. Health and safety of employees are now provided for. After some 20 years of pressure, responsibility for the corporate impact on the environment has been accepted in principle. Today a few companies have been forced to recognise that human rights are part of their direct responsibilities; to ensure that their supply chains are free of forced labour, exploitative child labour, discrimination and sweatshops; to ensure that security arrangements do not contribute to human rights violations as they have in Nigeria and Colombia with huge reputational damage to the companies involved; to accept that as corporate citizens of the countries in which they work the Universal Declaration of Human Rights (UDHR) calls on them to defend these rights.

These are all direct responsibilities, needing explicit policies and practices throughout the organisation. This is not a 'strategy' any more than we would consider honesty in an individual a 'strategy'. I would agree that honesty is the best policy for the individual. Also that these policies are essential for the long-term survival of a company. But, like honesty in the individual, they need to be done because they are right and reflect the values of society.

**It is fair to ask 'What society' and 'What values'?**

For the first time in history, internationally accepted values have been spelt out; in the UDHR, in the Convention on the Rights of the Child and in International Labour Organisation (ILO) conventions. There are complex issues here, for many of which companies have inadequate expertise. An important development has therefore been the growing constructive dialogue between non-governmental organisations (NGOs) and companies on issues such as child labour, Third World development, the environment and human rights.

NGOs do not uniquely hold the moral high ground and their only legitimacy and mandate lies in the extent to which they reflect the values of society and society supports their causes. But it is an irony today that it is the NGOs, more than corporate leadership, which are helping companies to secure their licence to operate in what will be a more critical 21st century.

**How do we change this?**

How do we encourage companies to respond constructively, not just defensively, to the values of society? And what has all this to do with the accountancy profession?

The potential incentives to change are the market, the law, and corporate leadership. Of these the market, with its all-pervasive impact, is the most important. There is a glib saying that what cannot be measured cannot be managed. While not wholly true this has some validity. What is wholly true is that the market only works effectively on what is measured. Since at present this is only money, the market is essentially short term in its impact. If we had comparable standards for the measurement of the quality and development of the human resource, something of far more importance to the long-term success of the company, the market would operate on a different time-scale and be a significant element in improving our inadequate international competitiveness as a country.

Measurement is also required for the environmental and social impact of company operations. Environmental reporting is already well established; social reporting in its infancy. Both will become central to the judgement of company performance in future. Both will become essential to securing a company's licence to operate. There is now growing activity, indeed com-petition, in the field. Individual accountancy firms, individual non-government organisations, international groupings such as the Global Reporting Initiative on Sustainability are all putting their toes in the water. But while diversity may be useful at this stage of the game, there is no doubt that measurement and reporting in these non-financial fields will need to be standardised across the board in order to provide a level playing field, to assist investors in their decision-making (and the fast growing area of ethical investment will undoubtedly demand this), and to prevent the irresponsible undercutting the responsible.

## The accountancy profession

It is vital that the accountancy profession plays its part in this. The 'triple bottom line', a phrase coined by John Elkington of SustainAbility for economic, environmental and social reporting, will become the essential shape of company reporting in the next century.

The revision of UK company law is also relevant. The government has recognised that this Victorian relic, designed to meet the needs of canal and railway developers, is seriously out of date. The concept of limited liability has served us well. But its central flaw is the designation of shareholders as the sole beneficiaries in law, meaning in practice that while one of the stakeholders, the shareholders, is protected by law, the interests of all the others have had to be fought for from outside, since in practice the belief that maximising shareholder value automatically brings good practice in its wake has proved a myth.

Central to the revision will be the choice between a law which continues to give the shareholder primacy, described in the Consultation Document as the 'enlightened shareholder value' approach; and a 'pluralist' approach which requires a company to serve a wider range of interests. Opponents of the latter approach, of which the backward-looking Hampel Report on governance is one, argue that accountability to many is accountability to none. But there is a difference between accountability *to* and accountability *for,* and it is the latter we need. And since the former, the 'enlightened shareholder value' approach, is dependent on the definition of corporate objective as being shareholder wealth maximisation which has served us ill, radical change is clearly essential. And in this the role the accountancy profession would be central in devising the appropriate standards by which performance in relation to other stakeholders would be measured.

But at the end of the day the initiative must lie with the companies. Corporate activities are diverse and complex. Law and regulation have a role and it would be wise for the good companies to support a legislative underpinning which enforces at least a minimum standard of behaviour on competitors who may be less scrupulous. But the law is not enough.

It is for individual companies to apply principles to the whole of their operations which encompass the totality of their stakeholders. Any new venture should be preceded not just, as now, by an economic and environmental assessment, but by an assessment which covers the whole spectrum of corporate responsibilities including human rights. And ultimately, in a world which will put no trust in anything that is not independently verified, companies will need to report on the whole of their activities in a manner that is open and comparable. It should be abundantly clear that it is in their self-interest to do so; the minimising of risk and the enhancement of reputation go together. Measurement is central to this.

The choice for companies is either a continuing rearguard action with loss of reputation, or what I have called a new paradigm, a new framework of thought, in which they take the initiative in meeting the full range of their responsibilities; not through external codes or as the outcome of external pressure, but as a result of their own internal imperative and corporate leadership.

If companies are seen to be wealthy islands in a sea of inequality and injustice, if the creation of financial wealth leads to the destruction of other forms of wealth, if that financial wealth is seen to benefit only a narrow section of national or international communities, then the company will not deserve to survive.

Without a radical change of thinking about the role and responsibilities of companies; without recognition in practice and in the law of the meaning of stakeholders, without established means of measuring the corporate impact on them, not only will the licence to operate of individual companies be at risk, we will jeopardise a remarkably effective mechanism for the creation of wealth. And we will do so because we have failed to understand that the point of departure must be morals, not money, principles not profit.

**Notes**

1. Contact details: 160, route de Florissant, CG-1231 Conches-Geneva, Switzerland, tel.: +41 (22)839 31 00; fax.: +41 (22)839 31 31, e-mail: info@wbcsd.ch

# Internal Audit

## Introduction **B23.1**

Internal auditing is globally organised with a single international professional body dedicated exclusively to internal auditing. Other professional bodies throughout the world, notably accountancy bodies, almost invariably accept as authoritative the Code of Ethics (see **B23.3**) and the standards of The Institute of Internal Auditors (see **B23.4**). These were radically redeveloped in 2001. Further major revisions to these Standards have been put out to exposure and are now due to be published by The Institute of Internal Auditors Inc in mid-November 2003 when they will be found on www.theiia.org. The exposure draft of these changes is at www.theiia.org/guidance/standards/Exposure_Draft_ED03S1/pdf.

One driver for the redevelopment of these Standards has been an acknowledgement that today's internal auditors spend significant time on work which does not fit into a classical view of the nature of internal auditing. Hence the new definition of internal auditing, and the new Standards, distinguish between the 'assurance' and the 'consulting' roles of internal auditors. The intention is to ensure that most, if not all, of the work that internal auditors undertake should fall within the scope of these official pronouncements of The Institute of Internal Auditors, and thus that internal auditors should be guided by their Standards in their approach to both their consulting and their assurance work. Whether today's internal auditor is being utilised as an assurance provider or as a consultant, he or she is deemed to be acting as an internal auditor. The proviso is that the nature of the internal auditor's consulting role should be set out in a charter for the internal auditing function. (Later in this chapter we examine in more detail the role of internal auditors as consultants at **B23.34–B23.61**, and three examples of internal audit charters are included in **B12.13**, **B12.14** and **B12.15**.)

Many entities have no mandatory requirement to have an internal audit function, and have complete discretion as to whom they appoint into their internal audit functions. It follows therefore that the enforcement role of The Institute of Internal Auditors is modest compared with professional bodies whose members alone are allowed to perform a professional service which is mandatory. Nevertheless, The Institute of Internal Auditors holds out its Code of Ethics and Standards as being applicable to any internal auditor or internal audit unit which provides an internal audit service which conforms to the Institute's definition of internal auditing, to be found at the start of both the new Code of Ethics and the new Standards, which reads:

> 'Internal auditing is an independent, objective assurance and consulting activity designed to add value and improve an organization's operations.

It helps an organization accomplish its objectives by bringing a systematic, disciplined approach to evaluate and improve the effectiveness of risk management, control, and governance processes.'

It may not be generally appreciated that the obligation to comply with the Code of Ethics follows an internal auditor out of his or her internal auditing job into other settings. This is illustrated by what the Institute of Internal Auditors gives as the correct answer (in bold) to the following question from the 2000 Model Examination paper for Part I of the Certified Internal Auditor qualification:

'A CIA, working as a director of purchasing, signs a contract to procure a large order from the supplier with the best price, quality, and perform- ance. Shortly after signing the contract, the supplier presents the CIA with a gift of significant monetary value. Which of the following state- ments regarding the acceptance of the gift is correct?

a)  Acceptance of the gift would be prohibited only if it were non- customary.

b)  **Acceptance of the gift would violate The IIA's Code of Ethics and would be prohibited for a CIA.**

c)  Since the CIA is not acting as an internal auditor, acceptance of the gift would be governed only by the organization's code of conduct.

d)  Since the contract was signed before the gift was offered, acceptance of the gift would not violate either The IlA's Code of Ethics or the organization's code of conduct.'

The Standards, as distinct from the Code of Ethics, would not be similarly binding upon Certified Internal Auditors (CIAs) not working as internal auditors, since the relevant rule in the Code of Ethics makes the Standards binding only in the context of internal auditing work:

'Internal auditors ...

4.2  Shall perform internal auditing services in accordance with the Standards for the Professional Practice of Internal Auditing.'

More internal auditing is being outsourced than ever before. The intention is therefore that the Code and Standards should be observed whether internal auditing is undertaken by 'in-house' staff, or whether it has been outsourced. In the latter case this may have implications for the wording of service level agreements and contracts with outside internal audit providers. (Later in this chapter we consider outsourced internal audit provision at **B23.62**.)

## Combined Code's reference to internal audit                         B23.2

The Provision in the Combined Code that companies without an internal audit function should from time to time review the need for one, was one of the two Provisions elaborated upon in the Turnbull Report. (Both the Combined Code and the Turnbull Report are reproduced in PART A.) Turnbull strengthened the import of this Provision by advising that it is the board who should do this, that it should be done at least once a year, and that the adequacy of an existing internal audit should also be reviewed annually by the board. There are some indications that the implementation of this 1998 Provision D.2.2, and also Provision D.2.1 (on board review and reporting on internal control and risk management) (in the 2003 Code these are Provisions C.2.1 and C.3.5 respectively) is impacting on internal auditing in the following ways.

- More entities are setting up internal audit functions where they did not have one before.

- The status of internal audit within the enterprise is being elevated, as internal audit assists the board in implementing Provision D.2.2.

- An unanticipated consequence of the first appearance in a UK corporate governance Code of reference to internal audit (in [Provision D.2.2) is that internal auditing is sometimes becoming optional in entities where it was previously mandatory, as for instance is now allowed by the Housing Corporation with respect to the housing associations it regulates. This is because internal audit is not expressed as being mandatory in Provision D.2.2 and the public sector (where internal audit had widely been mandatory) has the general intention of endeavouring to apply the Combined Code.

The adoption in the 2003 Combined Code as provisions C.3.5 of a Smith report recommendation has further tightened the obligations of boards with respect to internal audit in that compliance with the Code means that boards must now publicly explain why they have chosen not to have an internal audit function, if such is the case:

> 'C.3.5  The audit committee should monitor and review the effectiveness of the internal audit activities. Where there is no internal audit function, the audit committee should consider annually whether there is a need for an internal audit function and make a recommendation to the board, and the reasons for the absence of such a function should be explained in the relevant section of the annual report.'

# Code of Ethics                                                   B23.3

### The Institute of Internal Auditors

## Introduction

The purpose of the Institute's Code of Ethics is to promote an ethical culture in the profession of internal auditing.

> Internal auditing is an independent, objective assurance and consulting activity designed to add value and improve an organization's operations. It helps an organization accomplish its objectives by bringing a

systematic, disciplined approach to evaluate and improve the effectiveness of risk management, control, and governance processes.

A code of ethics is necessary and appropriate for the profession of internal auditing, founded as it is on the trust placed in its objective assurance about risk management, control, and governance. The Institute's Code of Ethics extends beyond the definition of internal auditing to include two essential components:

- Principles that are relevant to the profession and practice of internal auditing;

- Rules of Conduct that describe behaviour norms expected of internal auditors. These rules are an aid to interpreting the Principles into practical applications and are intended to guide the ethical conduct of internal auditors.

The Code of Ethics together with the Institute's Professional Practices Framework and other relevant Institute pronouncements provide guidance to internal auditors serving others. 'Internal auditors' refers to Institute members, recipients of or candidates for IIA professional certifications, and those who provide internal auditing services within the definition of internal auditing.

### Applicability and enforcement

This Code of Ethics applies to both individuals and entities that provide internal auditing services.

For Institute members and recipients of or candidates for IIA professional certifications, breaches of the Code of Ethics will be evaluated and administered according to the Institute's Bylaws and Administrative Guidelines. The fact that a particular conduct is not mentioned in the Rules of Conduct does not prevent it from being unacceptable or discreditable, and therefore, the member, certification holder, or candidate can be liable for disciplinary action.

### Principles

Internal auditors are expected to apply and uphold the following principles.

### Integrity

The integrity of internal auditors establishes trust and thus provides the basis for reliance on their judgment.

### Objectivity

Internal auditors exhibit the highest level of professional objectivity in gathering, evaluating, and communicating information about the activity or process being examined. Internal auditors make a balanced assessment of all the relevant circumstances and are not unduly influenced by their own interests or by others in forming judgments.

## Confidentiality

Internal auditors respect the value and ownership of information they receive and do not disclose information without appropriate authority unless there is a legal or professional obligation to do so.

## Competency

Internal auditors apply the knowledge, skills, and experience needed in the performance of internal auditing services.

Rules of Conduct

## 1. Integrity

Internal auditors:

1.1. Shall perform their work with honesty, diligence, and responsibility.

1.2. Shall observe the law and make disclosures expected by the law and the profession.

1.3. Shall not knowingly be a party to any illegal activity, or engage in acts that are discreditable to the profession of internal auditing or to the organization.

1.4. Shall respect and contribute to the legitimate and ethical objectives of the organization.

## 2. Objectivity

Internal auditors:

2.1. Shall not participate in any activity or relationship that may impair or be presumed to impair their unbiased assessment. This participation includes those activities or relationships that may be in conflict with the interests of the organization.

2.2 Shall not accept anything that may impair or be presumed to impair their professional judgment.

2.3 Shall disclose all material facts known to them that, if not disclosed, may distort the reporting of activities under review.

## 3. Confidentiality

Internal auditors:

3.1 Shall be prudent in the use and protection of information acquired in the course of their duties.

3.2 Shall not use information for any personal gain or in any manner that would be contrary to the law or detrimental to the legitimate and ethical objectives of the organization.

## 4. Competency

Internal auditors:

4.1. Shall engage only in those services for which they have the necessary knowledge, skills, and experience.

4.2 Shall perform internal auditing services in accordance with the Standards for the Professional Practice of Internal Auditing.

4.3 Shall continually improve their proficiency and the effectiveness and quality of their services.

Adopted by The IIA Board of Directors, June 17, 2000.

© The Institute of Internal Auditors

# Standards for the Professional Practice of Internal Auditing

*The Internal Auditing Standards developed to apply to government in the UK are reproduced at* **B9.25**.

THE INSTITUTE OF INTERNAL AUDITORS

**249 Maitland Avenue**

Altamonte Springs, Florida 32701–4201

ISBN 0–89413–454-X

October 18, 2001

# Introduction

Internal auditing is an independent, objective assurance and consulting activity designed to add value and improve an organization's operations. It helps an organization accomplish its objectives by bringing a systematic, disciplined approach to evaluate and improve the effectiveness of risk management, control, and governance processes.

Internal audit activities are performed in diverse legal and cultural environments; within organizations that vary in purpose, size, and structure; and by persons within or outside the organization. These differences may affect the practice of internal auditing in each environment. However, compliance with the Standards for the Professional Practice of Internal Auditing (Standards) is essential if the responsibilities of internal auditors are to be met.

The purpose of the Standards is to:

1.  Delineate basic principles that represent the practice of internal auditing as it should be.

2.  Provide a framework for performing and promoting a broad range of value-added internal audit activities.

3.  Establish the basis for the measurement of internal audit performance.

4.  Foster improved organizational processes and operations.

The Standards consist of Attribute Standards (the 1000 Series), Performance Standards (the 2000 Series), and Implementation Standards (nnnn.Xn). The Attribute Standards address the characteristics of organizations and individuals performing internal audit activities. The Performance Standards describe the nature of internal audit activities and provide quality criteria against which the performance of these services can be measured. The Attribute and Performance Standards apply to internal audit services in general. The Implementation Standards apply the Attribute and Performance Standards to specific types of engagements (for example, a compliance audit, a fraud investigation, or a control self-assessment project).

There is one set of Attribute and Performance Standards, however there may be multiple sets of Implementation Standards: a set for each of the major types of internal audit activity. Initially, the Implementation Standards are being established for assurance activities (noted by an "A" following the Standard number, e.g., 1130.A1) and consulting activities (noted by a "C" following the Standard number, e.g., nnnn.C1).

The Standards are part of the Professional Practices Framework. This framework was proposed by the Guidance Task Force and approved by The IIA's Board of Directors in June 1999. This framework includes the Definition of Internal Auditing, the Code of Ethics, the Standards, and other guidance. The Standards incorporate the guidance previously contained in the 'The Red Book', recasting it into the new format proposed by the Guidance Task Force and updating it as recommended in the Task Force's report, 'A Vision for the Future'.

The Standards employ terms that have been given specific meanings that are included in the Glossary.

The Internal Auditing Standards Board is committed to extensive consultation in the preparation of the Standards. Prior to issuing any document, the Standards Board issues exposure drafts internationally for public comment. The Standards Board also seeks those with special expertise or interests for consultation where necessary. The development of standards is an ongoing process. The Standards Board welcomes input from IIA members and other interested parties to identify emerging issues requiring new standards or revision to current standards. Suggestions should be sent to:

The Institute of Internal Auditors
Senior Manager Technical Services
249 Maitland Ave.
Altamonte Springs, Florida 32701
USA
E-mail: standards@theiia.org

Additional guidance regarding how the Standards might be put into practice can be found in Practice Advisories that are issued by the Professional Issues Committee.

## Attribute standards

## 1000 – Purpose, Authority, and Responsibility

The purpose, authority, and responsibility of the internal audit activity should be formally defined in a charter, consistent with the Standards, and approved by the board.

**1000.A1** – The nature of assurance services provided to the organization should be defined in the audit charter. If assurances are to be provided to parties outside the organization, the nature of these assurances should also be defined in the charter

**1000.C1** – The nature of consulting services should be defined in the audit charter.

## 1100 – Independence and Objectivity

The internal audit activity should be independent, and internal auditors should be objective in performing their work.

### 1110 – Organizational Independence

The chief audit executive should report to a level within the organization that allows the internal audit activity to fulfill its responsibilities.

**1110.A1** – The internal audit activity should be free from interference in determining the scope of internal auditing, performing work, and communicating results.

**1120** – Individual Objectivity

Internal auditors should have an impartial, unbiased attitude and avoid conflicts of interest.

**1130** – Impairments to Independence or Objectivity

If independence or objectivity is impaired in fact or appearance, the details of the impairment should be disclosed to appropriate parties. The nature of the disclosure will depend upon the impairment.

**1130.A1** – Internal auditors should refrain from assessing specific operations for which they were previously responsible. Objectivity is presumed to be impaired if an auditor provides assurance services for an activity for which the auditor had responsibility within the previous year.

**1130.A2** – Assurance engagements for functions over which the chief audit executive has responsibility should be overseen by a party outside the internal audit activity.

**1130.C1** – Internal auditors may provide consulting services relating to operations for which they had previous responsibilities.

**1130.C2** – If internal auditors have potential impairments to independence or objectivity relating to proposed consulting services, disclosure should be made to the engagement client prior to accepting the engagement.

## 1200 – Proficiency and Due Professional Care

Engagements should be performed with proficiency and due professional care.

**1210** – Proficiency

Internal auditors should possess the knowledge, skills, and other competencies needed to perform their individual responsibilities. The internal audit activity collectively should possess or obtain the knowledge, skills, and other competencies needed to perform its responsibilities.

**1210.A1** – The chief audit executive should obtain competent advice and assistance if the internal audit staff lacks the knowledge, skills, or other competencies needed to perform all or part of the engagement.

**1210.A2** – The internal auditor should have sufficient knowledge to identify the indicators of fraud but is not expected to have the expertise of a person whose primary responsibility is detecting and investigating fraud.

**1210.C1** – The chief audit executive should decline the consulting engagement or obtain competent advice and assistance if the internal audit staff lacks the knowledge, skills, or other competencies needed to perform all or part of the engagement.

**1220** – Due Professional Care

Internal auditors should apply the care and skill expected of a reasonably prudent and competent internal auditor. Due professional care does not imply infallibility.

**1220.A1** – The internal auditor should exercise due professional care by considering the:

- Extent of work needed to achieve the engagement's objectives.

- Relative complexity, materiality, or significance of matters to which assurance procedures are applied.

- Adequacy and effectiveness of risk management, control, and governance processes.

- Probability of significant errors, irregularities, or non-compliance.

- Cost of assurance in relation to potential benefits.

**1220.A2** – The internal auditor should be alert to the significant risks that might affect objectives, operations, or resources. However, assurance procedures alone, even when performed with due professional care, do not guarantee that all significant risks will be identified.

**1220.C1** – The internal auditor should exercise due professional care during a consulting engagement by considering the:

- Needs and expectations of clients, including the nature, timing, and communication of engagement results.

- Relative complexity and extent of work needed to achieve the engagement's objectives.

- Cost of the consulting engagement in relation to potential benefits.

**1230 – Continuing Professional Development**

Internal auditors should enhance their knowledge, skills, and other competencies through continuing professional development.

**1300 – Quality Assurance and Improvement Program**

The chief audit executive should develop and maintain a quality assurance and improvement program that covers all aspects of the internal audit activity and continuously monitors its effectiveness. The program should be designed to help the internal auditing activity add value and improve the organization's operations and to provide assurance that the internal audit activity is in conformity with the Standards and the Code of Ethics.

**1310** – Quality Program Assessments

The internal audit activity should adopt a process to monitor and assess the overall effectiveness of the quality program. The process should include both internal and external assessments.

**1311** – Internal Assessments

Internal assessments should include:

o Ongoing reviews of the performance of the internal audit activity; and

o Periodic reviews performed through self-assessment or by other persons within the organization, with knowledge of internal auditing practices and the Standards.

**1312** – External Assessments

External assessments, such as quality assurance reviews, should be conducted at least once every five years by a qualified, independent reviewer or review team from outside the organization.

**1320 – Reporting on the Quality Program**

The chief audit executive should communicate the results of external assessments to the board.

**1330 – Use of 'Conducted in Accordance with the Standards'**

Internal auditors are encouraged to report that their activities are 'conducted in accordance with the Standards for the Professional Practice of Internal Auditing.' However, internal auditors may use the statement only if assessments of the quality improvement program demonstrate that the internal audit activity is in compliance with the Standards.

**1340 – Disclosure of Non-compliance**

Although the internal audit activity should achieve full compliance with the Standards and internal auditors with the Code of Ethics, there may be instances in which full compliance is not achieved. When non-compliance impacts the overall scope or operation of the internal audit activity, disclosure should be made to senior management and the board.

**Performance standards**

**2000 – Managing the Internal Audit Activity**

The chief audit executive should effectively manage the internal audit activity to ensure it adds value to the organization.

**2010 – Planning**

The chief audit executive should establish risk-based plans to determine the priorities of the internal audit activity, consistent with the organization's goals.

**2010.A1** – The internal audit activity's plan of engagements should be based on a risk assessment, undertaken at least annually. The input of senior management and the board should be considered in this process.

**2010.C1** – The chief audit executive should consider accepting proposed consulting engagements based on the engagement's potential to improve management of risks, add value, and improve the organization's operations. Those engagements that have been accepted should be included in the plan.

### 2020 – Communication and Approval

The chief audit executive should communicate the internal audit activity's plans and resource requirements, including significant interim changes, to senior management and to the board for review and approval. The chief audit executive should also communicate the impact of resource limitations.

### 2030 – Resource Management

The chief audit executive should ensure that internal audit resources are appropriate, sufficient, and effectively deployed to achieve the approved plan.

### 2040 – Policies and Procedures

The chief audit executive should establish policies and procedures to guide the internal audit activity.

### 2050 – Coordination

The chief audit executive should share information and coordinate activities with other internal and external providers of relevant assurance and consulting services to ensure proper coverage and minimize duplication of efforts.

### 2060 – Reporting to the Board and Senior Management

The chief audit executive should report periodically to the board and senior management on the internal audit activity's purpose, authority, responsibility, and performance relative to its plan. Reporting should also include significant risk exposures and control issues, corporate governance issues, and other matters needed or requested by the board and senior management.

### 2100 – Nature of Work

The internal audit activity evaluates and contributes to the improvement of risk management, control and governance systems.

### 2110 – Risk Management

The internal audit activity should assist the organization by identifying and evaluating significant exposures to risk and contributing to the improvement of risk management and control systems.

**2110.A1** – The internal audit activity should monitor and evaluate the effectiveness of the organization's risk management system.

**2110.A2** – The internal audit activity should evaluate risk exposures relating to the organization's governance, operations, and information systems regarding the:

- Reliability and integrity of financial and operational information.

- Effectiveness and efficiency of operations.

- Safeguarding of assets.

- Compliance with laws, regulations, and contracts.

**2110.C1** – During consulting engagements, internal auditors should address risk consistent with the engagement's objectives and should be alert to the existence of other significant risks.

**2110.C2** – Internal auditors should incorporate knowledge of risks gained from consulting engagements into the process of identifying and evaluating significant risk exposures of the organization.

## 2120 – Control

The internal audit activity should assist the organization in maintaining effective controls by evaluating their effectiveness and efficiency and by promoting continuous improvement.

**2120.A1** – Based on the results of the risk assessment, the internal audit activity should evaluate the adequacy and effectiveness of controls encompassing the organization's governance, operations, and information systems. This should include:

- Reliability and integrity of financial and operational information.

- Effectiveness and efficiency of operations.

- Safeguarding of assets.

- Compliance with laws, regulations, and contracts.

**2120.A2** – Internal auditors should ascertain the extent to which operating and program goals and objectives have been established and conform to those of the organization.

**2120.A3** – Internal auditors should review operations and programs to ascertain the extent to which results are consistent with established goals and objectives to determine whether operations and programs are being implemented or performed as intended.

**2120.A4** – Adequate criteria are needed to evaluate controls. Internal auditors should ascertain the extent to which management has established adequate criteria to determine whether objectives and goals have been accomplished. If adequate, internal auditors should use such criteria in their evaluation. If inadequate, internal auditors should work with management to develop appropriate evaluation criteria.

**2120.C1** – During consulting engagements, internal auditors should address controls consistent with the engagement's objectives and should be alert to the existence of any significant control weaknesses.

**2120.C2** – Internal auditors should incorporate knowledge of controls gained from consulting engagements into the process of identifying and evaluating significant risk exposures of the organization.

## 2130 – Governance

The internal audit activity should contribute to the organization's governance process by evaluating and improving the process through which (1) values and goals are established and communicated, (2) the accomplishment of goals is monitored, (3) accountability is ensured, and (4) values are preserved.

**2130.A1** – Internal auditors should review operations and programs to ensure consistency with organizational values.

**2130.C1** – Consulting engagement objectives should be consistent with the overall values and goals of the organization.

## 2200 – Engagement Planning

Internal auditors should develop and record a plan for each engagement.

## 2201 – Planning Considerations

In planning the engagement, internal auditors should consider:

- The objectives of the activity being reviewed and the means by which the activity controls its performance.

- The significant risks to the activity, its objectives, resources, and operations and the means by which the potential impact of risk is kept to an acceptable level.

- The adequacy and effectiveness of the activity's risk management and control systems compared to a relevant control framework or model.

- The opportunities for making significant improvements to the activity's risk management and control systems.

**2201.C1** – Internal auditors should establish an understanding with consulting engagement clients about objectives, scope, respective responsibilities, and other client expectations. For significant engagements, this understanding should be documented.

## 2210 – Engagement Objectives

The engagement's objectives should address the risks, controls, and governance processes associated with the activities under review.

**2210.A1** – When planning the engagement, the internal auditor should identify and assess risks relevant to the activity under review. The engagement objectives should reflect the results of the risk assessment.

**2210.A2** – The internal auditor should consider the probability of significant errors, irregularities, non-compliance, and other exposures when developing the engagement objectives.

**2210.C1** – Consulting engagement objectives should address risks, controls, and governance processes to the extent agreed upon with the client.

## 2220 – Engagement Scope

The established scope should be sufficient to satisfy the objectives of the engagement.

**2220.A1** – The scope of the engagement should include consideration of relevant systems, records, personnel, and physical properties, including those under the control of third parties.

**2220.C1** – In performing consulting engagements, internal auditors should ensure that the scope of the engagement is sufficient to address the agreed-upon objectives. If internal auditors develop reservations about the scope during the engagement, these reservations should be discussed with the client to determine whether to continue with the engagement.

## 2230 – Engagement Resource Allocation

Internal auditors should determine appropriate resources to achieve engagement objectives. Staffing should be based on an evaluation of the nature and complexity of each engagement, time constraints, and available resources.

## 2240 – Engagement Work Program

Internal auditors should develop work programs that achieve the engagement objectives. These work programs should be recorded.

**2240.A1** – Work programs should establish the procedures for identifying, analyzing, evaluating, and recording information during the engagement. The work program should be approved prior to the commencement of work, and any adjustments approved promptly.

**2240.C1** – Work programs for consulting engagements may vary in form and content depending upon the nature of the engagement.

## 2300 – Performing the Engagement

Internal auditors should identify, analyze, evaluate, and record sufficient information to achieve the engagement's objectives.

## 2310 – Identifying Information

Internal auditors should identify sufficient, reliable, relevant, and useful information to achieve the engagement's objectives.

## 2320 – Analysis and Evaluation

Internal auditors should base conclusions and engagement results on appropriate analyses and evaluations.

## 2330 – Recording Information

Internal auditors should record relevant information to support the conclusions and engagement results.

> **2330.A1** – The chief audit executive should control access to engagement records. The chief audit executive should obtain the approval of senior management and/or legal counsel prior to releasing such records to external parties, as appropriate.

> **2330.A2** – The chief audit executive should develop retention requirements for engagement records. These retention requirements should be consistent with the organization's guidelines and any pertinent regulatory or other requirements.

> **2330.C1** – The chief audit executive should develop policies governing the custody and retention of engagement records, as well as their release to internal and external parties. These policies should be consistent with the organization's guidelines and any pertinent regulatory or other requirements.

## 2340 – Engagement Supervision

Engagements should be properly supervised to ensure objectives are achieved, quality is assured, and staff is developed.

## 2400 – Communicating Results

Internal auditors should communicate the engagement results promptly.

## 2410 – Criteria for Communicating

Communications should include the engagement's objectives and scope as well as applicable conclusions, recommendations, and action plans.

> **2410.A1** – The final communication of results should, where appropriate, contain the internal auditor's overall opinion.

> **2410.A2** – Engagement communications should acknowledge satisfactory performance.

> **2410.C1** – Communication of the progress and results of consulting engagements will vary in form and content depending upon the nature of the engagement and the needs of the client.

## 2420 – Quality of Communications

Communications should be accurate, objective, clear, concise, constructive, complete, and timely.

### 2421 – Errors and Omissions

If a final communication contains a significant error or omission, the chief audit executive should communicate corrected information to all individuals who received the original communication.

## 2430 – Engagement Disclosure of Non-compliance with the Standards

When non-compliance with the Standards impacts a specific engagement, communication of the results should disclose the:

- Standard(s) with which full compliance was not achieved,

- Reason(s) for non-compliance, and

- Impact of non-compliance on the engagement.

## 2440 – Disseminating Results

The chief audit executive should disseminate results to the appropriate individuals.

> **2440.A1** – The chief audit executive is responsible for communicating the final results to individuals who can ensure that the results are given due consideration.

> **2440.C1** – The chief audit executive is responsible for communicating the final results of consulting engagements to clients.

> **2440.C2** – During consulting engagements, risk management, control, and governance issues may be identified. Whenever these issues are significant to the organization, they should be communicated to senior management and the board.

## 2500 – Monitoring Progress

The chief audit executive should establish and maintain a system to monitor the disposition of results communicated to management.

> **2500.A1** – The chief audit executive should establish a follow-up process to monitor and ensure that management actions have been effectively implemented or that senior management has accepted the risk of not taking action.

> **2500.C1** – The internal audit activity should monitor the disposition of results of consulting engagements to the extent agreed upon with the client.

## 2600 – Management's Acceptance of Risks

When the chief audit executive believes that senior management has accepted a level of residual risk that is unacceptable to the organization, the chief audit executive should discuss the matter with senior management. If the decision regarding residual risk is not resolved, the chief audit executive and senior management should report the matter to the board for resolution.

## Glossary

**Add Value** – Organizations exist to create value or benefit to their owners, other stakeholders, customers, and clients. This concept provides purpose for their existence. Value is provided through their development of products and services and their use of resources to promote those products and services. In the process of gathering data to understand and assess risk, internal auditors develop significant insight into operations and opportunities for improvement that can be extremely beneficial to their organization. This valuable information can be in the form of consultation, advice, written communications, or through other products all of which should be properly communicated to the appropriate management or operating personnel.

**Adequate Control** – Present if management has planned and organized (designed) in a manner that provides reasonable assurance that the organization's risks have been managed effectively and that the organization's goals and objectives will be achieved efficiently and economically.

**Assurance Services** – An objective examination of evidence for the purpose of providing an independent assessment on risk management, control, or governance processes for the organization. Examples may include financial, performance, compliance, system security, and due diligence engagements.

**Board** – A board of directors, audit committee of such boards, head of an agency or legislative body to whom internal auditors report, board of governors or trustees of a nonprofit organization, or any other designated governing bodies of organizations.

**Charter** – The charter of the internal audit activity is a formal written document that defines the activity's purpose, authority, and responsibility. The charter should (a) establish the internal audit activity's position within the organization; (b) authorize access to records, personnel, and physical properties relevant to the performance of engagements; and (c) define the scope of internal audit activities.

**Chief Audit Executive** – Top position within the organization responsible for internal audit activities. In a traditional internal audit activity, this would be the internal audit director. In the case where internal audit activities are obtained from outside service providers, the chief audit executive is the person responsible for overseeing the service contract and the overall quality assurance of these activities, reporting to senior management and the board regarding internal audit activities, and follow–up of engagement results. The term also includes such titles as general auditor, chief internal auditor, and inspector general.

**Code of Ethics** – The purpose of the Code of Ethics of The Institute of Internal Auditors (IIA) is to promote an ethical culture in the global profession of internal auditing. A code of ethics is necessary and appropriate for the profession of internal auditing, founded as it is on the trust placed in its objective assurance about risk, control, and governance. The Code of Ethics applies to both individuals and entities that provide internal audit services.

**Compliance** – The ability to reasonably ensure conformity and adherence to organization policies, plans, procedures, laws, regulations, and contracts.

**Conflict of Interest** – Any relationship that is or appears to be not in the best interest of the organization. A conflict of interest would prejudice an individual's ability to perform his or her duties and responsibilities objectively.

**Consulting Services** – Advisory and related client service activities, the nature and scope of which are agreed upon with the client and which are intended to add value and improve an organization's operations. Examples include counsel, advice, facilitation, process design, and training.

**Control** – Any action taken by management, the board, and other parties to enhance risk management and increase the likelihood that established object-ives and goals will be achieved. Management plans, organizes, and directs the performance of sufficient actions to provide reasonable assurance that object-ives and goals will be achieved.

**Control Environment** – The attitude and actions of the board and management regarding the significance of control within the organization. The control environment provides the discipline and structure for the achievement of the primary objectives of the system of internal control. The control environment includes the following elements:

○  Integrity and ethical values.

○  Management's philosophy and operating style.

○  Organizational structure.

○  Assignment of authority and responsibility.

○  Human resource policies and practices.

○  Competence of personnel.

**Control Processes** – The policies, procedures, and activities that are part of a control framework, designed to ensure that risks are contained within the risk tolerances established by the risk management process.

**Engagement** – A specific internal audit assignment, task, or review activity, such as an internal audit, Control Self-assessment review, fraud examination, or consultancy. An engagement may include multiple tasks or activities designed to accomplish a specific set of related objectives.

**Engagement Objectives** – Broad statements developed by internal auditors that define intended engagement accomplishments.

**Engagement Work Program** – A document that lists the procedures to be followed during an engagement, designed to achieve the engagement plan.

**External Service Provider** – A person or firm, independent of the organiza-tion, who has special knowledge, skill, and experience in a particular discipline.

Outside service providers include, among others, actuaries, accountants, appraisers, environmental specialists, fraud investigators, lawyers, engineers, geologists, security specialists, statisticians, information technology specialists, external auditors, and other auditing organizations. The board, senior management, or the chief audit executive may engage an outside service provider.

**Fraud** – Any illegal acts characterized by deceit, concealment, or violation of trust. These acts are not dependent upon the application of threat of violence or of physical force. Frauds are perpetrated by individuals and organizations to obtain money, property, or services; to avoid payment or loss of services; or to secure personal or business advantage.

**Governance Process** – The procedures utilized by the representatives of the organization's stakeholders (e.g., shareholders, etc.) to provide oversight of risk and control processes administered by management.

**Impairments** – Impairments to individual objectivity and organizational independence may include personal conflicts of interest, scope limitations, restrictions on access to records, personnel, and properties, and resource limitations (funding).

**Internal Audit Activity** – A department, division, team of consultants, or other practitioner(s) that provides independent, objective assurance and consulting services designed to add value and improve an organization's operations. The internal audit activity helps an organization accomplish its objectives by bringing a systematic, disciplined approach to evaluate and improve the effectiveness of risk management, control, and governance processes.

**Objectivity** – An unbiased mental attitude that requires internal auditors to perform engagements in such a manner that they have an honest belief in their work product and that no significant quality compromises are made. Objectivity requires internal auditors not to subordinate their judgment on audit matters to that of others.

**Risk** – The uncertainty of an event occurring that could have an impact on the achievement of objectives. Risk is measured in terms of consequences and likelihood.

www.theiia.org

**The Institute of Internal Auditors**
**249 Maitland Avenue**
**Altamonte Springs, Florida 32701–4201, USA**
**+1–407–830–7600, Ext. 1**

# Chief audit executive reporting lines – the new Practice Advisory

There is now a new Practice Advisory 1110–2, released in December 2002, on 'Chief Audit Executive (CAE) Reporting Lines' to be found at http://www.theiia.org/ecm/printfriendly.cfm?doc_id=4043. Practice Advisories are non-mandatory guidance – in this instance the guidance is on Standard 1110–2 – 'Organizational Independence' which reads:

### '1110 – Organizational Independence

The chief audit executive should report to a level within the organization that allows the internal audit activity to fulfil its responsibilities.'

Although not referred to in this Advisory, there is a subordinate Assurance Standard which reads:

**'1110.A1** – The internal audit activity should be free from interference in determining the scope of internal auditing, performing work, and communicating results.'

Although 'non-mandatory', Practice Advisories reflect what is considered generally to be the best practice to be followed in order to fulfil the requirements of the Standards. The sentiment within the Practice Advisories is also regarded as being indicative of what would be a correct answers in the professional examinations of The Institute of Internal Auditors.

While this Advisory refers to 'audit committee', the Standards make it clear that for some this may mean the board itself, or a single person who has the responsibilities usually held collectively by the board. Indeed, the Standards always use the term 'board' while defining this to include audit committees. So, if a chief audit executive reports to the board of directors rather than to an audit committee, it is not in violation of the advice contained within this Advisory.

This new Advisory suggests that the reporting lines of internal audit should be appropriate to meet the increased needs of audit committees and other significant stakeholders as a stricter global climate of legislative, regulatory and financial reporting comes into force, and as internal audit plays a more significant role in the organization's governance and risk management activities.[1]

Internal audit reporting is complex. Other personnel in addition to the CAE may have multiplex reporting relationships, but it is unlikely that they would be more multiplex than those of the CAE. We have always taken the position that internal audit reports in three ways.

| Functional reporting: | to ensure that the professional service of the internal audit function is effective in meeting the entity's needs; |
|---|---|
| Administrative reporting: | for 'pay and rations' to ensure economic and efficient utilisation of internal audit resources; |
| Task reporting: | to communicate the results of audit engagements |

This Advisory takes the view that there are two forms of reporting for internal audit – 'functional reporting' and 'administrative reporting'. While acknowledging the legitimacy of differing reporting practices for internal audit, The IIA believes that functional reporting should *always* be clearly distinct from administrative reporting and *ideally* with the former to the audit committee and the latter to the CEO.[2]

We consider it is better to acknowledge a third type – reporting on audit work done – which we might call 'task reporting'; however, to the extent that this is covered in this Advisory, it is subsumed within 'functional reporting' to the audit committee. But clearly internal audit also reports elsewhere on individual audit engagements – both in detail and in summary form. The Advisory relies on appropriate and effective functional and administrative reporting for internal audit to take care of what needs to be achieved by what we call 'task reporting', but we think the latter deserves a focus on its own:

> 'CAE reporting lines are also critical to ensuring that the appropriate flow of information and access to key executives and managers that are the foundations of risk assessment and reporting of results of audit activities. Conversely, any reporting relationship that impedes the independence and effective operations of the internal audit function should be viewed by the CAE as a serious scope limitation, which should be brought to the attention of the audit committee or its equivalent.'[3]

The Advisory defines the 'functional reporting' for internal audit as that which gives internal audit:

> 'the ultimate source of its independence and authority.'

While the Advisory states that The Institute of Internal Auditors (The IIA) recommends that:

> 'the CAE report functionally to the 'audit committee, board of directors, or other appropriate governing authority'

since the Advisory is referring to a reporting *line*, it could possibly be argued that the *end* of the functional reporting line should be the audit committee but that the CAE will first report functionally to others beneath this – perhaps to the chief executive or to the finance director. While the Advisory does recommend that

> 'the functional reporting line should go directly to the Audit Committee or its equivalent to ensure the appropriate level of independence and communication'[4]

This does not unambiguously state that the 'direct' line means that the CAE might not first report functionally to someone below the level of the audit committee. 'Directly' is not defined. What CAE does not feel accountable to the executive for the quality of service the internal audit function provides? Is it not often the case that the CAE reports to the same executive both administratively and functionally, while also reporting functionally to the audit committee? The Advisory does not explore this. The difficulty seems to us to reside in the fact that the audit committee is not, and should not be, an executive committee. The executive has a legitimate, strong functional interest in internal audit. After all, as an essential aspect of 'monitoring'[5], management is responsible for internal audit, which is acknowledged in this Advisory.[6]

This is not discussed directly in the Advisory which does however state that the IIA's recommendation is for the audit committee (or other governing authority) to approve:

- the internal audit charter;

- the internal audit risk assessment and related audit plan;

- all decisions regarding the appointment or removal of the CAE; and

- the annual compensation pay adjustment of the CAE,

and:

- receive from the CAE the results of CAE activities or other matters the CAE deems necessary, including private meetings with the CAE without management present;

- inquire of management and the CAE as to scope or budgetary limitations that impede the ability of internal audit to execute its responsibilities.

This Advisory therefore goes further than PA 2060–2[7] which just requires the audit committee to review (rather than approve) the appointment, compensation, evaluation, retention, and dismissal of the CAE. Neither Advisory grasps the nettle of whether it is acceptable for these matters to be approved *after the event* – for instance after a CAE has been dismissed by the executive. However this Advisory does recommend that the CAE should have access to the audit committee when the CAE deems determines it to be necessary. It is noteworthy that CAE remuneration approval is given to the audit committee, as also in Advisory 2060.

In the last of the bullet points above, there is reference in very general terms to certain aspects of what are required to oversee the professionalism and the degree of effectiveness of the internal audit function. We concur with this as a key responsibility of the audit committee – not least because the audit committee needs this sort of confidence in the internal audit function in order to be in a position to rely on what internal audit reports through to the audit committee on the results of internal audit work. But there is more to the oversight of the professionalism of internal audit than a consideration of internal audit 'scope' and 'budgetary limitations'. For instance, the independence, qualifications, experience, training and methods of the internal auditors are also relevant. It is true that, as we have seen, this Advisory also recommends that the audit committee approve the audit committee charter – but that is unlikely to be adequate to pick up on all of these matters sufficiently. The Advisory does say that …

> 'The charter for the internal audit function should clearly articulate both the functional and administrative reporting lines for the function as well as the principle [sic] activities directed up each line.' [8]

The Advisory sums up 'administrative reporting' as including, for internal audit:

- budgeting and management accounting;
- HR admin including personnel evaluations and compensation;
- internal communications and information flows; and
- administration of the organization's internal policies and procedures.

The Advisory recommends that:

> 'Budgetary controls and considerations imposed by the administrative reporting line should not impede the ability of the internal audit function to accomplish its mission.' [9]

To whomsoever internal audit reports administratively, the Advisory stresses that the CAE should have sufficient independence from that individual, such as the Chief Financial Officer, in order to be able to audit activities for which that individual is responsible:

> 'The internal audit function should be free to audit and report on any activity that also reports to its administrative head if it deems that coverage appropriate for its audit plan. Any limitation in scope or reporting of results of these activities should be brought to the attention of the audit committee.' [10]

The Advisory further recommends that the following should be key aspects of functional reporting for internal audit.

- Private meetings between the CAE and the audit committee.
- The audit committee to have final authority over the annual audit plan and major changes to it.
- The CAE to have open and direct access to the chair of the audit committee and its members.
- The audit committee at least once a year review the performance of the CAE and approve the annual compensation and salary adjustment.

The Advisory sees Administrative reporting as not determining ultimate responsibility over audit scope or reporting of results, but needing to be appropriate to give internal audit sufficient authority and stature and to facilitate open and direct communications with any level of management. [11]

Finally, the Advisory appears to give internal audit a role in ensuring that the audit committee learns of material risk and control issues uncovered by other review agencies:

> 'CAEs should also consider their relationships with other control and monitoring functions (risk management, compliance, security, legal, ethics, environmental, external audit) and facilitate the reporting of material risk and control issues to the audit committee.' [12]

# Internal audit relationship with the audit committee – the new Practice Advisory   B23.6

There is now a new Practice Advisory 2060–2, released by The Institute of Internal Auditors (The IIA) in December 2002, on 'Relationship with the audit committee' to be found at http://www.theiia.org/ecm/printfriendly.cfm?doc_id=4044. Practice Advisories are non-mandatory guidance – in this instance the guidance is on Standard 2060 – 'Independence and Objectivity' which reads:

### 2060 – Reporting to the Board and Senior Management

The chief audit executive should report periodically to the board and senior management on the internal audit activity's purpose, authority, responsibility, and performance relative to its plan. Reporting should also include significant risk exposures and control issues, corporate governance issues, and other matters needed or requested by the board and senior management.

Although 'non-mandatory', Practice Advisories reflect what is considered generally to be the best practice to be followed in order to fulfil the requirements of the Standards. The sentiment within the Practice Advisories is also regarded as being indicative of what would be a correct answers in the professional examinations of The Institute of Internal Auditors.

This Advisory refers to a model charter for an internal audit function, available on http://www.theiia.org/ecm/guide-ia.cfm?doc_id=383 and reproduced at **B12.15**.

In keeping with the new Standards of the IIIA, this Practice Advisory allows that the term 'audit committee' should be regarded also as referring to any other 'governance body that is charged with oversight of the organization's audit and control functions.' [13] and thus the Advisory is offered as having applicability more broadly than just to relationships between internal audit and audit committees. In place of the audit committee, it could, for instance, be the board itself if the board has not delegated some aspects of audit and control oversight to an audit committee. It could also be the chief executive of a government agency if that individual had responsibilities which in other entities would be collectively borne by a board of directors and its audit committee.

The Advisory is not bashful in promoting the role of internal audit with respect to audit committees. In places it even creates the impression that internal audit may be in effective charge of the audit committee. For instance, the Advisory suggests that the chief audit executive (CAE) should be responsible for determining the content of the internal audit charter[14] and it gives the CAE a likely major role with respect to the charter of the audit committee itself …

> 'the CAE should assist the committee in ensuring that the charter, role and activities of the committee are appropriate for it to achieve its responsibilities.'[15]

The CAE is also given the role to review the completeness and accuracy of the information the audit committee receives – not just the information pertinent to its oversight of internal audit. This role for internal audit is more justifiable if, as in the Advisory, it is accepted that the CAE should be secretary of the audit committee.

The Advisory certainly gives internal audit the committee secretarial role. A contrary view would be that this is unsound in that the audit committee, being a committee of the board, should receive its secretarial support from the same source as the board itself. In the UK, this would mean that the company secretary would therefore usually be the secretary to the audit committee. If the CAE is secretary to the audit committee, it may make it more difficult for the audit committee to form an objective view of the professionalism, etc. of the internal audit function since most committees develop a 'cosy'; relationship with their secretary. It is also helpful for the secretary of the audit committee to be present at the board meeting when the chairperson of the audit committee speaks to the board on the audit committee's report to the board – this would happen naturally if the secretary to the audit committee were also the secretary of the board.

The Advisory classifies its content into:

> 'three areas of activities [which] … are key to an effective relationship between the audit committee and the internal audit function, chiefly through the Chief Audit Executive:
>
> - Assisting the audit committee to ensure that its charter, activities, and processes are appropriate to fulfil its responsibilities.
>
> - Ensuring that the charter, role, and activities of internal audit are clearly understood and responsive to the needs of the audit committee and the board.
>
> - Maintaining open and effective communications with the audit committee and the chairperson.'[16]

The first of these three, which is tantamount to advising that the CAE should be the committee's secretary, is elaborated upon in the Advisory as follows (which we set out here in abbreviated form):[17]

- Annually advise the audit committee on its charter (terms of reference).

- Maintain a planning agenda (pro forma agenda for committee meetings) for the audit committee.

- Draft meeting agendas, facilitate distribution of materials to committee members and write up audit committee minutes.

- Encourage the audit committee to benchmark itself against leading practices.

- Meet the committee chairman to discuss the informational needs of the committee.

- Find out if committee members need special presentations or training.

- Inquire whether the committee considers its frequency of meetings and their duration are sufficient.

The Advisory puts the second of these three areas of audit committee activity in the context that:

'the CAE's relationship to the audit committee should revolve around a core role of the CAE that the audit committee understands, supports, and receives all assistance needed from the internal audit function. The IIA supports the concept that sound governance is dependent on the synergy generated among the four principal components of effective corporate governance systems: boards of directors, management, internal auditors, and external auditors. In that structure, internal auditors and audit committees are mutually supportive. Consideration of the work of internal auditors is essential for the audit committee to gain a complete understanding of an organization's operations. A primary component of the CAE's role with the committee is to ensure this objective is accomplished and the committee views the CAE as their trusted advisor.'[18]

This is elaborated upon in the Advisory as follows (which we set out here also in abbreviated form):[19]

- Ask the committee to review and approve the internal audit charter, annually. (IIA's sample charter is reproduced as an Appendix here).

- Review with the audit committee that the functional and administrative reporting lines of internal audit allow adequate independence.

- Incorporate in the audit committee's charter the review of (a) the appointment, compensation, evaluation, retention, and dismissal of the CAE, and (b) review and approval of proposals to outsource any internal audit.

- Assist the committee to evaluate the scope, resources and results of internal audit activities.

- Inform the committee of internal audit coordination with, and oversight of other control and monitoring functions (e.g. management, compliance, security, business continuity, legal, ethics, environmental, external audit).

- Report to the committee significant control issues and opportunities for improvement across the organisation.

- Report progress against the approved annual audit plan and results; advise on the sufficiency of internal audit resources.

- Incorporate into the internal audit charter the responsibility of internal audit to report to the committee on suspected frauds and assist in their investigation if significant.

- Make the committee aware that quality assessment reviews of the internal audit function should be done every five years.

The essential elements of communication by the CAE to the audit committee are given as:

- regular private meetings between the CAE and the committee;

- an annual summary report and assessment of internal audit results;

- periodic reports to the committee of internal audit results;

- keeping the committee informed of emerging internal audit trends and practices;

- discussing with the committee its informational needs; and

- reviewing the completeness and accuracy of the information the committee receives.

The last could be construed as being a candidate to become a standard internal audit engagement included within the annual audit plan subject to qualifying for this attention as a result of an audit needs assessment.

# Not explored                                                                      B23.7

This Advisory is certainly not intended to be a comprehensive treatise on audit committees. It states that

> 'The Institute acknowledges that audit committee responsibilities encompass activities that are beyond the scope of this advisory, and in no way intends it to be a comprehensive description of audit committee responsibilities'[20]

But within its own more limited remit, to be useful guidance the Advisory needs more detail both with respect to the issues covered and the treatment of some of the issues which are referred to.

Internal audit/audit committee relationship issues not addressed include whether it is sufficient for just the CAE to have access to the audit committee: some would say that it is necessary for *all* the internal auditors in the function to have direct access to the chair of the audit committee, since there have been occasions when the CAE has sought to bury audit findings, perhaps in order not to embarrass a top management team with whom the CAE has a (too) close working relationship. Another matter not covered in this Advisory is whether the

CAE should have a right to request that items be placed on the agenda of the audit committee. We know that some chairs of audit committees make it a practice to spend perhaps a day or two a year within the internal audit function – in order to break down barriers and to get a better 'feel' of the risk and control issues of the organisation as well as the degree of freedom of the internal audit function to conduct itself independently: again there is no suggestion of this in the Advisory. Incidentally, 'risk' gets little attention in this Advisory. We would also have liked to see a recommendation that internal audit might report to the audit committee on the efficiency and effectiveness of the external audit, not just on the extent to which there is coordination between external audit and others.

Matters which could usefully have been discussed in more detail include aspects of committee secretariat support. We are referring not to the routine provision of secretarial services, but the need for audit committees and their members individually to have access to full secretariat support between meetings. Then there is the failure of the Advisory to do more than mention the need for audit committee to review the appointment and dismissal of the CAE. Practice Advisory 2060–2[21] goes further with the IIA's recommendation that the audit committee should:

'Approve all decisions regarding the appointment or removal of the CAE'

but neither Advisory is clear as to whether the *prior approval* of the audit committee should be obtained. Although 'special tasks or projects requested [of internal audit] by the audit committee' are mentioned, there is no further elaboration of the challenges associated with internal audit undertaking special engagements directly on behalf of the audit committee, with the engagement report going direct to the audit committee rather than to management as well. Finally, there was no discussion of the occasions when the CAE should *not* be present at audit committee meetings.

# The internal audit role in mergers and acquisitions   B23.8

The IIA is now defining internal audit as comprising both 'assurance' and 'consulting' services. The definition of internal auditing near the start of the Standards makes this clear, and both these services are defined in the Glossary which appears at the end of the Standards.

## Definition of 'internal auditing'   B23.9

'Internal auditing is an independent, objective assurance and consulting activity designed to add value and improve an organization's operations. It helps an organization accomplish its objectives by bringing a systematic, disciplined approach to evaluate and improve the effectiveness of risk management, control, and governance processes.'

## Definition of 'assurance services'                                B23.10

'An objective examination of evidence for the purpose of providing an independent assessment on risk management, control, or governance processes for the organization. Examples may include financial, performance, compliance, system security, and due diligence engagements.'

## Definition of 'consulting services'                               B23.11

'Advisory and related client service activities, the nature and scope of which are agreed upon with the client and which are intended to add value and improve an organization's operations. Examples include counsel, advice, facilitation, process design, and training.'

The above definition of assurance services classifies 'due diligence' investigations by internal auditors as belonging to the internal audit 'assurance' role. But **Practice Advisory 1000.C1–2 on 'Additional Considerations for Formal Consulting Engagements'[22] states in the section on 'Definition of consulting services' that the consulting role of internal auditors may include:**

'special consulting engagements – participation on a merger and acquisition team or system conversion team.'

(Compliance with Practice Advisories is discretionary, but adherence to the Standards is mandatory.)

A question is whether internal audit involvement in mergers and acquisitions fits into their 'assurance' or into the 'consulting' role, or both. The Institute of Internal Auditors is not being inconsistent here, as it is possible to reconcile the above apparently conflicting statements, as follows.

● When internal audit is involved in conducting a due diligence investigation, it could be said to fit into the 'assurance services' role since it contributes to providing assurance on the statements that are being relied upon by a party to the merger or acquisition. This might be what is being referred to as 'due diligence' in the IIA's Glossary definition on 'assurance services'.

● Internal audit may also be conduct audit engagements to provide assurance on the reliability of the due diligence process itself – in particular cases when due diligence is taking place, or of the due diligence process in general. This is different from internal audit being involved in performing the due diligence investigation. Undoubtedly such an audit engagement would be an example of internal audit discharging its 'assurance role', and this certainly must be included in what is meant by the reference to 'due diligence' in the IIA's glossary definition on 'assurance services'. Arguably this sort of involvement by internal audit is important for any company involved in mergers and acquisitions since such activities represent high risks for companies.

- Internal audit 'participation on a merger and acquisition team', which is referred to in Practice Advisory 1000.C1–2 as an example of a possible internal auditing 'consulting service', is presumably referring to *neither* internal audit involvement in a due diligence investigation, *nor* to an internal audit of the due diligence process itself. Instead it is referring to such activities as assisting in integrating the acquired business into the business of the acquirer.

# Overall opinions by internal audit     B23.12

Even though a board is likely to choose not to publish its opinion on internal control effectiveness, a board does need to oversee the effectiveness of internal control and it follows that it should have an informed view as to its effectiveness. Put another way, each director should have such an informed view. A board is likely to rely on its audit committee to a considerable extent to advise the board on this. In turn, it is reasonable for an audit committee to ask the chief audit executive to express to the audit committee his or her overall opinions on the effectiveness of internal control to the audit.

In some companies this expression of opinion by internal audit is made once a year, in others twice and in others at each audit committee meeting. In some cases the opinion is expressed to the group audit committee while similar opinions (though more focussed in scope, of course) are expressed to other audit committees at operating company level within the group.

Being required to express an opinion on internal control effectiveness presents a challenge to internal audit to maximise the reliability of that opinion by optimising the assurance that is attained from the audit work completed. It certainly suggests a risk-based method of determining audit scope, and it suggests the adoption of innovative ways of obtaining additional assurance as such:

- obtaining letters of representation from key line managers;

- checklists for managers to use to assess their control effectiveness;

- more extensive consideration of the extent to which internal audit can rely on the work of others; and

- more follow-up audit visits to assess how up-to-date is the internal audit assessment of internal control effectiveness.

Elsewhere in this handbook we cover the use of letters of representation on internal control (see **B8.80**, **B8.90–B8.91**) and checklists for managers to use to self assess control effectiveness (see **B8.92**). **B23.14 PUBLISHED REPORTS ON INTERNAL CONTROL BY INTERNAL AUDIT** takes the concept of internal audit opinions a stage further by applying it in a public reporting way.

The following example of an overall opinion by internal audit is modelled on an example contained in on an exposure draft Statement on Internal Auditing

Standards (SIAS) entitled 'Summary Reporting on Internal Control' (December 1994). The draft was re-exposed and subsequently abandoned as a proposed SIAS but appeared in modified form in the IIA Inc's Professional Practices Pamphlet 97–2 'Assessing and Reporting on Internal Control'. Appropriate adaptations to the UK situation have been made. It assumes the scope of this opinion is all of internal control, not just internal financial control.

Not least in view of the new definition of internal auditing and the new international internal auditing Standards (see **B23.4**) careful consideration now needs to be given to whether this opinion should be broadened to cover risk management and governance.

## Summary report on internal control — B23.13

To: the board of directors (or to the audit committee), the ABC Company

We have completed the programme of internal auditing coverage of internal control at the ABC Company for the year ended 19XX. The internal auditing work was performed in accordance with Standards for the Professional Practice of Internal Auditing and included such tests and appraisals of the competent policies, procedures, systems and processes as we considered necessary for the company and its business units.

The study and evaluation were made using the criteria for effective internal control developed by (cite criteria, for example the criteria established in Internal Control and Financial Reporting ie the 'Rutteman Report'). (Describe criteria as, for example, in the instance of the Rutteman criteria, a broad definition of the term internal control as the whole system of controls, financial and otherwise, established in order to provide reasonable assurance of:

- effective and efficient operations;
- internal financial control; and
- compliance with laws and regulations.

The scope of our coverage included (a) consideration of presentations made by the chief financial officer and other senior members of management regarding the design and operation of the internal control structure, (b) relevant work performed by X and Y, the independent accounting firm retained by the ABC company to perform the annual examination of ABC Company's financial statements, and (c) the performance of such internal audits of the internal control structure throughout the company as we considered necessary.

(Optional: Because of inherent limitations in the overall effectiveness in any system of internal control and the necessarily limited nature of the study and evaluation we designed and completed, it is conceivable that deficiencies may have existed during 19XX that were not detected and that errors, omissions or irregularities may have resulted which were not detected and corrected. Moreover, any internal control structure may be circumvented by actions of those members of management whose position and authority permit unrestricted freedom to act.)

In our opinion, the internal control structure in effect during 19XX conformed to and complied with the internal control criteria (such as Rutteman) in all material aspects. Specifically, the policies, procedures, systems and processes were designed and operated in order to achieve:

- effective and efficient operations;
- reliable financial reports
- compliance with laws and regulations.

James Smythe,

Chief Audit Executive.

# Published reports on internal control by internal audit      B23.14

In **B8 RISK MANAGEMENT AND INTERNAL CONTROL** we consider the internal use of overall opinions on internal control (and perhaps on risk management and wider aspects of governance) by internal audit.

Not least because of the reluctance of boards and of external auditors to become deeply involved in, respectively reporting publicly on internal control effectiveness and providing assurance on directors' corporate governance statements, perhaps in the medium term there could be a role here for internal audit. Notwithstanding any on-going external audit involvement here, internal auditors should nevertheless now be considering the case for their active involvement. Too little attention has been given to the merits of internal audit reporting publicly on internal control in the annual report.

It is not new for internal auditors to report publicly in the annual reports of entities. Here we reprint and analyse a set of such reports which appeared as early as the 1970s[23]. We do so as the approach taken by Anglian, although a long time ago, offers practical suggestions for internal auditors to approach this in the future.

These internal audit reports, which appeared in the annual reports of Anglian Water during the 1970s, have many points of interest. Clearly internal audit was primarily an audit of accounting and financial matters, under the direction and control of the director of finance (1974–75). But, as we shall see, its financial and accounting 'home base' was not allowed to be a significant restriction upon internal audit scope.

# Internal audit coverage                                          B23.15

Three years after being set up, internal audit was able to report that it had reviewed all financial systems in operation (1977–78), not a bad achievement although, admittedly, by the start of 1975 the department had its full complement of as many as 17 audit staff (1974–75), even though they regarded internal audit resources as being 'scarce' (1974–75). It is interesting to speculate how many internal auditors would be in post today in an equivalent but downsized function.

It is unlikely that the contemporary downsizing of internal audit can be attributed reasonably to either a more optimal allocation of internal audit resources to the areas of greatest relative need, nor to a better use of IT to assist in internal audit work by automating aspects of it.

## Risk assessment                                                 B23.16

With regard to the former, it looks as if internal audit in Anglian Water in the 1970s applied rather similar risk assessment methods in audit planning as we would today, take, for instance, their statements that:

> 'A formal system of audit planning and control has been instituted to ensure that the scarce audit resources are allocated to the best advantage of the Authority.'

> *(1974–75)*

## IT auditing                                                     B23.17

With regard to the latter it is striking that the internal audit function recruited a computer professional into it from its inception (1974–75). By 1977–78 the internal audit function had a computer audit terminal connected to Anglian Water's new mainframe and by then there is a clear suggestion that audit software was being built into the new IT systems being developed. The policy was:

> 'Wherever possible, use is made of the computer to aid audit work.'

> *(1977–78)*

A year later they were able to report in similar terms, this time that:

> 'Considerable use is made of the computer installation to aid audit work' and one notable example was the audit software built into their new direct billing applications.'

## A multi-disciplinary function                                   B23.18

Despite its financial and accounting orientation, it was clearly considered that internal audit should be a multi-disciplinary function, capable, for instance, of making a positive contribution in the areas of contracting and IT. Internal audit staff 'were recruited from a wide variety of sources'. Apart from an IT specialist, another internal auditor was an engineer (1974–75).

*Internal audit's mission*  **B23.19**

The first of this set of reports had outlined the role and responsibilities of internal audit (1974–75). As we have pointed out, its accounting and financial vantage point did not appear to have narrowed its scope significantly. Its mission, *inter alia*, was:

> 'to detect fraud, misappropriation, irregular expenditure and losses due to waste or extravagance' and 'to review the monitoring procedures in use … which ensure the physical security of assets and the privacy and confidentiality of information.'

*(1974–75)*

## Scope of internal audit work  **B23.20**

This must have allowed it a broad role. In 1977–78 they were starting to audit information relating to demand forecasting and to the formulation of the authority's capital development programme.

In 1978–79 we note an internal audit focus on (a) 'information systems that lead to decision making' and to (b) internal audit involvement at the development stage of an improved project appraisal system and in (c) the development of new controls over capital expenditure.

In 1976–77 internal audit had reported they conducted comprehensive examinations of capital spending and had also completed internal audits on 'energy' and 'research'. In 1976–77 internal audit was involved in the planning for the introduction of Anglian Water's new mainframe computer.

In 1978–79 we find them appraising every new IT application 'to ascertain whether all basic control requirements have been met'. As early as 1976–77 they make it clear that internal audit is concerned that Anglian Water's procedures and policies lead to 'best possible value for money'.

*'External' internal control*  **B23.21**

An organisation's internal control often extends to the systems in place within outside businesses, and that management and auditors should therefore consider the extent to which these should be reviewed before coming to an opinion on internal control. A foretaste of this appears in the 1976–77 internal audit report which describes a number of audits conducted by Anglian Water of District Councils who had an agency relationship with Anglian Water.

*Proactive role*  **B23.22**

Although internal audit is described as having a protective role (1976–77), it is also seen as being proactive in assisting in promoting improvements; whether financial, administrative or operational.

**The 'total audit'** **B23.23**

Commencing 1974–75, reference is made to the close liaison and co-operation between internal and external audit particularly with regard to the elimination of duplication (1977–78) and in 1978–79 the very modern concept of the 'total audit coverage' is introduced within internal audit's public report.

**The opinion on internal control** **B23.24**

Perhaps it is particularly interesting to see how internal audit expresses overall opinion on internal control in these published reports. Understandably, for a newly established function, it takes a few years before internal audit expresses such an opinion which first features in the 1977–78 report using the words:

> 'The standard of financial administration achieved throughout the Authority is now considered by the Chief Internal Auditor to be generally satisfactory.'

Internal audit points out that it had not expressed this opinion until they had been able to report that they had by then reviewed all financial systems in operation.

The following year (1978–79) the opinion was fleshed out:

> 'The standard of financial administration achieved is considered to be generally satisfactory. This opinion has been formed following reviews of all major financial systems, carried out in each division and at headquarters designed to ensure that systems, controls and procedures were effective, remained relevant in the light of changing circumstances and were adhered to in practice.'

It was in 1978–79 that the very modern phrase 'reasonable assurance' was used in connection with the objectives of internal control, as it is currently in both the COSO and Rutteman reports and thus in directors' internal control reports following the COSO[24] or Rutteman[25] guidance.

By 1979–80 there had been a refinement of emphasis in that the wording of the opinion joined internal audit and management together as endorsing the sentiment expressed:

> 'During the year all major financial systems have been audited sufficiently to satisfy management on the soundness, adequacy and application of controls, and that the assets and interests of the organisation have been accounted for and protected from serious losses due to any reason, including fraud and poor value for money.'

As with the 1990s reports on internal control, these opinions from Anglian Water were not 'point of time' opinions as of the year end date but rather related to the whole of the year being reported though perhaps without expressly stating so. They also, as with 1990s reports, tended to imply a current and even future assurance rather than merely assurance relating to the old year which was being reported. While they overtly focused upon internal financial control, arguably they were broader than that.

Unlike so many 1990s published reports on internal control, undoubtedly these statements included expressions of opinion on internal control in various terms – 'generally satisfactory', 'effective', 'relevant', 'adhered to', 'sound', 'adequate', 'applied', 'protected from serious losses', and 'value for money'.

### *Conclusion*   **B23.25**

So we have observed a thoroughly modern internal audit function in place a generation ago. Indeed in certain respects it was not only ahead of its time, but in advance of contemporary practice at the turn of the millennium.

### **Internal audit**   **B23.26**

> Under the *Accounts and Audit Regulations 1974* [superseded by *Accounts and Audit Regulations 1996 (SI 1996/590)*] the Authority was required to carry out, under the direction and control of the Director of Finance, an internal audit of the accounts of the Authority and of its officers.
>
> At its meeting in November 1974 the Authority agreed that the role and responsibilities of internal audit should be:
>
> (a) to secure the installation of soundly based systems of control within each area of directorate or divisional responsibility;
>
> (b) to review and where necessary make recommendations for the improvements of systems, controls and procedures in order to ensure that they are both efficient and effective, that they remain adequate in the light of changing circumstances and that they are adhered to in practice;
>
> (c) to assist in protecting the assets and interests of the Authority by carrying out a continuous examination of activities in order to detect fraud, misappropriation, irregular expenditure and losses due to waste or extravagance;
>
> (d) to review the monitoring procedures in use within the Authority which ensure the physical security of assets and the privacy and confidentiality of information.
>
> Internal audit is an integral part of the Finance Directorate, but to ensure its objectivity and independence in reviewing, appraising and reporting on systems and procedures it does not have any responsibility for developing and installing procedures, preparing records or engaging in any activity which will subsequently be subject to audit review and appraisal. The Chief Internal Auditor is directly responsible and reports to the Director of Finance personally, while all internal audit staff based either at

Headquarters or at four area offices located in various parts of the region are responsible to the Chief Internal Auditor and not to the Headquarters' directorates or divisions whose work they review and appraise.

A very close liaison has been maintained by internal audit with the Authority's external auditors, Price Waterhouse & Co, since the start.

Although recruitment of internal audit staff did not begin until a late stage, by 1st January 1975 all 17 audit staff were in post, and by the end of the financial year each division had been the subject of an audit visit, although inevitably the initial coverage could not be as extensive as would have been desired following the considerable changes which occurred at and after the 1st April 1974. Considerable emphasis has been placed on the internal training of audit staff, who were recruited from a wide variety of sources, and it is believed that this will provide to be a very sound investment for the future.

A formal system of audit planning and control has been instituted to ensure that the scarce audit resources are allocated to the best advantage of the Authority.

An unusual feature has been the recruitment of two non-accountants – an engineer and a computer professional – to ensure that the necessary expertise is available to enable internal audit to make a positive contribution in the vital areas of contract procedures and administration and of data processing.

*Anglian Water Annual Report 1974–75*

**Internal audit**                                                    **B23.27**

The Authority's internal audit staff carry out a continuous independent appraisal of accounting, financial and related processes to ensure that in all aspects of the Authority's work adequate internal controls are operating, and that where such controls are considered not to be operating effectively management are informed and appropriate action is taken. Internal auditors are expected to adopt a positive attitude and assist in promoting improvements to financial, administrative and operational procedures and policies so that the Authority may obtain the best possible value for the money it spends. This requirement to promote improvements arises out of internal audit's prime protective role and is not in substitution for it.

In addition to audits of divisional and headquarters activities, teams of internal audit and divisional staff carried out audits of expenditure incurred by district councils as agents of the Authority under Sections 7 and 15 of the Water Act 1973. In many cases these audits have resulted in the negotiation of substantial reductions in the amounts claimed from the Authority by the agent councils.

Other internal audit work during the financial year included planning for the introduction of the Authority's new computer, a comprehensive examination of capital spending and audits of spending on energy and research.

*Anglian Water Annual Report 1976–77. Part 6 – Finance*

## Internal audit                                                      B23.28

The Authority's internal audit staff carry out a comprehensive and independent appraisal of accounting, financial and related processes as a service to management. Internal audit is a managerial control which functions by measuring and evaluating the effectiveness of other controls. By the end of the financial year all financial systems in operation throughout the Authority had been reviewed and, in many cases, recommendations had been made and accepted for improvements to systems, controls and procedures to ensure that they remained both efficient and effective. The standard of financial administration achieved throughout the Authority is now considered by the Chief Internal Auditor to be generally satisfactory. Without losing sight of internal audit's prime protective role, increasing effort was devoted to appraising and evaluating information systems that lead to decision making in the Authority. A start was made in auditing the information relating to demand forecasting and the formulation of the Authority's capital development programme.

During the year, the internal audit headquarters team moved from Diploma House to Brook House, Huntingdon, and took delivery of the computer audit terminal connected to the new mainframe. This move was aimed at ensuring that the development of audit techniques in relation to the new systems, particularly direct billing, went in hand with the development of those systems themselves. Wherever possible, use is made of the computer to aid audit work.

Close co-operation between the Authority's internal auditors and the external auditors, Price Waterhouse and Co., has continued throughout the year, particularly in respect of the elimination, as far as has been possible, of duplication of work by the various teams.

*Anglian Water Annual Report 1977–78. Part 6 – Finance*

## Internal audit                                                      B23.29

The Authority has a system of internal control to provide reasonable assurance that its transactions are appropriately recorded and reported, its assets are protected, established policies are followed and costs are properly controlled and managed. This system is prescribed by the Financial Regulations, written delegation of duties to responsible officers and other clearly defined procedures. These are supplemented by a comprehensive internal audit appraisal of all accounting, financial and related processes.

The standard of financial administration achieved is considered to be generally satisfactory. This opinion has been formed following reviews of all major financial systems, carried out in each division and at headquarters designed to ensure that systems, controls and procedures were effective, remained relevant in the light of changing circumstances and were adhered to in practice.

Internal audit effort continued to be devoted to appraising and evaluating the information systems that lead to decision making. During the year a contribution was made to the introduction of an improved project appraisal system and to the development of controls over capital expenditure. With the publication of divisional revenue output measures a start was made on inter-divisional comparisons of performance.

Considerable use is made of the computer installation to aid audit work, and during the year an important innovation in the form of a special reports feature was developed jointly by the computer audit staff and Honeywell. This system is now operating on all direct billing applications. In addition, each new computer application is independently appraised by internal audit to ascertain whether all basic control requirements have been met.

The internal auditors liase with the external auditors, Price Waterhouse and Co., to ensure that total audit coverage is adequate and to eliminate any unnecessary duplication of work.

*Anglian Water Annual Report 1978–79. Part 6 – Finance*

**Internal audit**                                                                 **B23.30**

The scale and complexity of the Authority's organisation is recognised by the framework of control which is set down in Financial Regulations, Rules of Contract and the Schemes of Delegations. Within that structure management is responsible for ensuring that detailed systems of control exist to safeguard the Authority's assets, ensure reliability of records, promote operational efficiency and monitor adherence to policies and directives.

Management in turn relies on an effective internal audit to review, appraise and report on these systems of control.

During the year all major financial systems have been audited sufficiently to satisfy management on the soundness, adequacy and application of controls, and that the assets and interests of the organisation have been accounted for and protected from serious losses due to any reason, including fraud and poor value for money.

*Anglian Water Annual Report 1979–80. Part 6*

# Internal auditors as consultants                             B23.31

At the end of this section, we have included a checklist for internal auditors to use to assess whether their internal auditing activity is leading edge with respect to its involvement in consulting projects.

The second release of the new Standards dated 18 October 2001 contained the first roll-out of twenty 'consulting' Standards (indicated by the letter 'C' in their number) and also one additional assurance Standard (1000.A1) to match the new neighbouring 'consulting' Standard (1000.C1).

Specific consulting Standards include the letter 'C' within their Standard number. In every case, the new 'consulting' Standards interpret, in a consulting context, higher level Standards which have existed since the initial publication of the new Standards, and indeed are often a reformulation of the old 1978 Standards. Literally, therefore, it would not be true to say that 'consulting' is a late arrival into the Standards. More to the point, internal auditors engaging in consulting work should regard the higher level Standards, and the Standards as a whole (as well as the Code of Ethics) as essential guidance on their approach to consulting work, whether or not lower level 'consulting' Standards have been enunciated. Where these lower consulting Standards exist, they are inter-pretive of the higher level Standards in the context of consulting engagements. However, 'compliance with Practice Advisories is optional'[26].

By developing Standards on consulting separately from the assurance Standards, some avoidable duplication has sometimes crept in, since the mandatory guidance on both is sometimes identical in meaning if not in wording.

## Revised definition of 'consulting' in the context of internal auditing                                      B23.32

There is also a revised Glossary definition of 'consulting services' presumably suggested as the Standards setters developed the new 'consulting' Standards. The new definition of 'consulting Services' in the Glossary to the Standards refers to consulting engagements being 'agreed-upon', in nature and scope, between internal audit and the client; a meeting of minds which may not always be achieved with respect to assurance engagements:

> 'Advisory and related client service activities, the nature and scope of which are agreed upon with the client and which are intended to add value and improve an organization's operations. Examples include counsel, advice, facilitation, process design and training.'

### 'Consulting' in the first release of the new Standards        B23.33

The superseded definition of 'consulting services' had read:

> 'The range of services, beyond internal audit's assurance services, provided to assist management meeting its objectives. The nature and

scope of work are agreed upon with the client. Examples include facilitation, process design, training, and advisory services.'

The first release of the new Standards of The Institute of Internal Auditors, on June 17 2001, presaged the subsequent appearance of Standards specific to the internal auditor's consulting role, but contained none of these. They were not long in making their appearance.

Until the appearance of these consulting Standards, reference in the new Standards to consulting was in another context, but it was a new reference nevertheless, and relevant to the internal audit activity's approach to consulting work.

> *'Coordination*    *The chief audit executive should share information and coordinate activities with other internal and external providers of relevant assurance and consulting services to ensure proper coverage and minimize duplication of efforts.'* (2050)

The old Standard had read:

> *'External auditors*    *The director of internal auditing should coordinate internal and external audit efforts.'*

## Defining the consulting role of internal auditors                B23.34

With the new definition of internal auditing, which appears in both the new Code of Ethics and also in the preamble to the new Standards themselves, giving apparent equal stress to 'consulting' and 'assurance' activities for internal auditors, the profession clearly needs firm guidance on both:

> 'Internal auditing is an independent, objective assurance and consulting activity designed to add value and improve an organization's operations. It helps an organization accomplish its objectives by bringing a systematic, disciplined approach to evaluate and improve the effectiveness of risk management, control, and governance processes.'

The new Standards require that:

> 'The purpose, authority, and responsibility of the internal audit activity should be formally defined in a charter, consistent with the Standards, and approved by the board.' (1000)

And Implementation Standards stipulate that this applies to both the assurance (1000.A1) and the consulting missions of the internal auditing activity:

> 'The nature of consulting services provided to the organization should be defined in the audit charter.' (1000.C1)

**Practice Advisories on 'consulting'**                                **B23.35**

Of the sixty-two Practice Advisories released by 11 December 2001, only one (1000.C1–1: 'Principles Guiding the Performance of Consulting Activities of Internal Auditors' (May 15, 2001)) is on the subject of the internal auditor's consulting role, though a number of others are indirectly relevant to this, for instance:

- 1000–1: 'Internal Audit Charter' (Jan 5, 2001);

- 1130.A1–2: 'Internal Audit Responsibility for Other (Non-Audit) Functions' (Jan 5, 2001); and

- 2120.A1–2: 'Using Control Self-Assessment for Assessing the Adequacy of Control Processes' (June 18, 2001).

We have an indication in Practice Advisory 1000.C1–1 of the Institute's meaning of the phrase 'systematic, disciplined approach' which appears in the new definition of internal auditing. It could mean that the internal audit plan of engagements to be conducted is to be developed so as to cover the entity systematically over time; or it could mean that each engagement is to be conducted systematically. Practice Advisory 1000.C1–1 indicates that it is, at least, certainly the latter and that this 'systematic approach' is expected of consulting engagements as well:

> '**Consistency with Internal Audit Definition** – A disciplined, systematic evaluation methodology is incorporated in each internal audit activity. The list of services can generally be incorporated into the broad categories of assurance and consulting. However, the services may also include evolving forms of value-adding services that are consistent with the broad definition of internal auditing.'

**'Consulting' perceived as a central internal audit role**          **B23.36**

Of the twenty new 'consulting' Standards in the release of the Standards dated 18 October 2001, five belong to the 'Attribute' set, and fifteen to the 'Performance' set of Standards. This compares with twenty-six 'Assurance' Standards by 18 October 2001 (eight of which were 'Attribute' Standards and eighteen being 'Performance' Standards), most of which had been present since June 2001. If a simple numeric count is any indication, it is apparent that the internal audit 'consulting' role is today rivalling internal audit's traditional 'assurance' role.

Unlike certain other activities in which internal auditors become involved, it is important to stress that 'consulting' in accordance with the Standards ('consistent with the broad definition of internal auditing') is perceived as being, along with assurance activities, one of the two central pillars of authentic, contemporary internal auditing. Practice Advisory 1000.C1–1 appears to accord co-primacy to the assurance and consulting roles:

> 'A primary internal auditing value is to provide assurance to senior management and audit committee directors.'

**B23.36** *'Consulting' perceived as a central internal audit role*

It seems that the guidance is at pains to avoid describing the assurance role along the lines of being 'the primary role'. This Practice Advisory ends with a paragraph which states that the internal auditor is first and foremost an internal auditor, but this is not to imply that being an internal auditor only applies when the auditor is engaged in assurance work:

> '**Criteria for Resolving Conflicts or Evolving Issues** – An internal auditor is first and foremost an internal auditor. Thus, in the performance of all services the internal auditor is guided by The IIA Code of Ethics and the Attribute and Performance Standards of the Standards for the Professional Practice of Internal Auditing. Any unforeseen conflicts or activities should be resolved consistent with the Code of Ethics and Standards.'

When the internal auditor provides a consulting service consistent with the Standards, he or she is acting as a mainstream internal auditor, not discharging a non-audit role. The Standards identify other activities, which internal auditors sometimes become engaged in, which are not internal auditing; but this is not the case with 'consulting'. Practice Advisory 1000.C1–1 again:

> '**Audit Activities Beyond Assurance and Consulting** – There are multiple internal auditing services. Assurance and consulting are not mutually exclusive and do not preclude other auditing services such as investigations and non-auditing roles. Many audit services will have both an assurance and consulting (advising) role.'

There is a tautological confusion in the above statement as 'other audit services' are described as including 'non-auditing roles'. It is safest for us to regard internal audit involvement in activities beyond assurance and consulting activities as defined in the Standards, as being involvement in non-audit work, and that internal auditors are expected to abide by the Standards in all their work which is regarded as internal auditing work. We do not see anything in the Standards which bars an internal auditor from engaging in non-auditing work, but it must be clear to all parties that such work is not being done under the guise of being internal auditing.

Practice Advisory 1000.C1–1 acknowledges that:

> 'Internal auditors are expected to use professional guidance to determine the extent to which the guidance provided in this advisory should be applied in each given situation. Special consulting engagements, such as participation in a merger or acquisition project, or in emergency engagements, such as disaster recovery activities, may require departure from normal or established procedures for conducting consulting engagements.'

While both 'assurance' and 'consulting' should now be construed as essential roles for contemporary internal auditors to discharge, consulting engagements tend to be *ad hoc* and by invitation whereas assurance engagements are determined, largely, at the discretion of the chief audit executive, so as to provide systematic coverage of the entity having regard to relative risk. It is true that the new Standards exhort that the chief audit executive should consider the scale of the risk before deciding whether to accept a consulting engagement. And Practice Advisory 1000.C1–1 states, with respect to consulting engagements, that the chief audit executive:

'retains the prerogative of setting the audit techniques and the right of reporting to senior executives and audit committee members when the nature and materiality of results pose significant risks to the organization.'

## 'Scope limitations' in the context of the internal audit consulting role                                                                          B23.37

An issue here is whether internal auditors who do not undertake consulting engagements are effectively experiencing 'scope limitations'. By their very nature, consulting engagements are unlikely to provide the same sort of risk-based comprehensive coverage of the entity over time as is provided by assurance engagements, since the need for management to ask for this consulting advice will vary from area to area within the business and the initiation of an internal audit consulting assignment request is at the discretion of management rather at the discretion of the chief audit executive, who does however have the discretion to decline consulting requests.

The new definition of 'consulting' in the Glossary to the Standards is a useful starting point. It refers to consulting engagements being 'agreed-upon', in nature and scope, between internal audit and the client – a meeting of minds which may not always be achieved with respect to assurance engagements:

'Advisory and related client service activities, the nature and scope of which are agreed upon with the client and which are intended to add value and improve an organization's operations. Examples include counsel, advice, facilitation, process design and training.'

## Nature of internal audit 'consulting'                                                                          B23.38

A key issue is to understand the hallmarks of a consulting service which fits into the type of consulting that The Institute of Internal Auditors envisages as being authentic internal auditing.

Although not set out in this Glossary definition, the Standards make it clear that consulting services provided by internal audit should be targeted at risk management, control and governance matters. Being 'advisory and related', an internal auditing consulting assignment should not include the execution of operational tasks or executive duties. It may include advice on the design of processes relating to risk management, control and governance. Another hallmark of consulting engagements, which should also be shared with assurance engagements, is that they should be:

'intended to add value and improve an organization's operations'.

The definition distinguishes between 'advice' and 'counsel', making the point that internal audit consulting may entail the giving of either or both. Although not defined, to our knowledge, in the Standards or the supporting Practice Advisories, we define 'advice' as being practical proposals for solutions to day-to-day challenges. An examples of advice in the area of risk management would be a suggestion as to how to embed the review of risk within the business; in the area of internal control an example would be a suggested suitable procedure to avoid recurring errors, or in the area of governance an example would be a suggested solution to a practical problem of the board with regard to how it conducts its business. We define 'counsel' as expert opinion within one's professional competence, relating to a matter or matters on which there are independently established criteria (or frameworks, benchmarks, or bodies of knowledge) against which performance can be assessed. Examples of 'counsel' offered by internal auditors might include the substance of, and extent of compliance with, external regulations; appropriate use of statistical sampling; or the requirements and extent of adherence achieved in the areas of risk management, internal control and governance.

The definition of consulting in the context of internal auditing also includes 'facilitation' which we define as enabling others to achieve an agreed outcome well. An example would be facilitation of CRSA. Another example would be facilitation of risk management: Practice Advisory 2100–3: 'Internal Audit's Role in the Risk Management Process', paragraph 6 puts it in non-prescriptive terms like this:

> 'The internal audit activity's role in the risk management process of an organization can change over time and may be found at some point along a continuum that ranges from:
>
> No role; to
>
> Auditing the risk management process as part of the internal audit plan; to
>
> Active, continuous support and involvement in the risk management process such as participation on oversight committees, monitoring activities, and status reporting; to
>
> Managing and coordinating the risk management process.'

We think of 'process design', allowed in the definition as a feature of authentic internal audit consulting, as being to do with the determination of a set of procedures to be applied to a business requirement, or the revision of existing procedures. Examples would include participation in the design of new systems, advising on essential components of managing the change process effectively, or involvement in improving governance. Standard 2130 on internal audit involvement in the governance process, states:

> 'The internal audit activity should contribute to the organization's governance process by evaluating and improving the process through which (1) values and goals are established and communicated, (2) the accomplishment of goals is monitored, (3) accountability is ensured, and (4) values are preserved.' (2130)

Finally, the definition's inclusion of 'training' as a form of internal audit consulting is to do with developing competence in others. Appropriate examples might include developing and running case studies on risk, control and/or governance at management development programmes, or training executives and operational staff in CRSA.

## Internal audit professionalism when acting as consultants    B23.39

The relevant Standards read:

> '*Internal auditors should apply the care and skill expected of* a reasonably prudent and competent internal auditor. Due professional care does not imply infallibility.' (1220)

and:

> 'The internal auditor should exercise due professional care during a consulting engagement by considering the:
>
> □   Needs and expectations of clients, including the nature, timing, and communication of engagement results.
>
> □   Relative complexity and extent of work needed to achieve the engagement's objectives.
>
> □   Cost of the consulting engagement in relation to potential benefits.' (1220.C1)

## Relationships and conflicts between the 'assurance' and 'consulting' roles    B23.40

The definition of internal audit starts with the words:

'Internal auditing is an independent, objective assurance and consulting activity … ''Just as with external auditors, their assurance role can often lead to consulting opportunities. And, as with external auditors, there can be concerns about the maintenance of sufficient independence and objectivity when this is the case. External auditors attempt to make a positive virtue of the sufficiency of 'Chinese walls' between the consultancy and the assurance sides of their business, as a mechanism to assist in preserving audit independence. The position taken by The Institute of Internal Auditors is the opposite of this; there should be no Chinese walls' between information gathered in the course of consultancy work by the internal auditor, and information available to inform assurance work by the internal auditor:

> '**Communication of Fundamental Information** – A primary internal auditing value is to provide assurance to senior management and audit committee directors. Consulting engagements cannot be rendered in a manner that masks information that in the Chief Audit Executive's (CAE) judgment should be presented to senior executives and board members. All consulting is to be understood in that context.'

and:

> 'When the chief audit executive believes that senior management has accepted a level of residual risk that is unacceptable to the organization, the chief audit executive should discuss the matter with senior management. If the decision regarding residual risk is not resolved, the chief audit executive and senior management should report the matter to the board for resolution.' (2600)

Indeed, consulting Standards require that:

> 'Internal auditors should incorporate knowledge of risks gained from consulting engagements into the process of identifying and evaluating risk exposures of the organization.' (2110.C2)

and:

> 'During consulting engagements, risk management, control, and governance issues may be identified. Whenever these issues are significant to the organization, they should be communicated to senior management and the board.' (2440.C2)

Frequently an audit engagement will have elements of consulting as well as assurance:

> **Interrelationship between Assurance and Consulting** – Internal audit consulting enriches value-adding internal auditing. While consulting is often the direct result of assurance services, it should also be recognized that assurance could also be generated from consulting engagements.'

## Independence and objectivity in consulting                                    B23.41

While the same high level Standards 1100 and 1130 on 'independence' and 'objectivity' are applicable to both assurance and consulting work by internal auditors, the sentiment of associated Implementation Standards is markedly different:

The applicable Attribute Standards on 'independence and objectivity' read:

| | |
|---|---|
| **'Independence and objectivity** | *The internal audit activity should be independent, and internal auditors should be objective in performing their work.'* (1100) |

and:

| | |
|---|---|
| **'Impairments to independence or objectivity** | *If independence or objectivity is impaired in fact or appearance, the details of the impairment should be disclosed to appropriate parties. The nature of the disclosure will depend upon the impairment.'* (1130) |

While the associated Assurance Implementation Standards are prescriptive in a constraining way, the strictures are much less onerous with respect to consulting engagements:

> ***Assurance*** *'Internal auditors should refrain from assessing specific operations for which they were previously responsible. Objectivity is presumed to be impaired if an auditor provides assurance services for an activity for which the auditor had responsibility within the previous year.'* (1130.A1)

'Assurance engagements for functions over which the chief audit executive has responsibility should be overseen by a party outside the internal audit activity.' (1130.A2)

> ***Consulting*** *'Internal auditors may provide consulting services relating to operations for which they had previous responsibilities.'* (1130.C1)
>
> 'If internal auditors have potential impairments to independence or objectivity relating to proposed consulting services, disclosure should be made to the engagement client prior to accepting the engagement.' (1130.C2)

## What sort of consultant? B23.42

Although the conflicts between being providing assurance and providing consulting services can be managed effectively, there is no doubt that there are fundamental role conflicts which need to be managed. As with a policeman, a provider of assurance needs to have formal authority which is primarily vested in the office which the provider holds, and it is reinforced by the possibility of coercive sanctions. A glance at the charters of most internal auditing functions confirms these attributes of the internal audit role. On the other hand, a consultant usually has informal authority, vested primarily in the personal ability and reputation of the consultant, and it is reinforced not by the threat of coercion but by the consultant's powers of persuasion. It is necessary for internal auditors to carry these two distinct and often conflicting roles in harness, endeavouring to avoid conflict wherever this is practical.

The parent/child analogy has been used to suggest what sort of consulting relationship internal auditors should have with their consulting clients. Sarah Blackburn suggests that the internal auditor should be not merely an extra resource (where the client is, in effect, the parent, and the auditor is the child). She further suggests that neither should the auditor be the expert resource (where these roles are reversed, with the auditor being the parent and the client being the child. Rather, she suggests that it should be an adult to adult relationship where the internal auditor is the facilitator. While it is unlikely to be appropriate for internal audit to accept consulting assignments which fall into the first category of the auditor being 'the child' and the client being 'the parent', the IIA's definitional characterisation of internal audit consultancy as including, *inter alia*, the provision of counsel as well as facilitation indicates that the IIA sees the consultancy role as fitting into either or both of the remaining two categories.

**Proficiency**                                                                      **B23.43**

The general Attribute Standard on proficiency, applicable to both assurance and consulting internal audit work, reads:

'Internal auditors should possess the knowledge, skills, and other competencies needed to perform their individual responsibilities. The internal audit activity collectively should possess or obtain the knowledge, skills, and other competencies needed to perform its responsibilities.' (1210)

The Standard which elaborates on this for internal audit consulting allows the option that the chief audit executive may decline a consulting assignment where proficiency is in question an option which is not available for assurance work where the chief audit executive is expected to obtain the necessary proficient resources.

'The chief audit executive should decline the consulting engagement or obtain competent advice and assistance if the internal audit staff lacks the knowledge, skills, or other competencies needed to perform all, or part of the engagement.' (1210.C1)

**Due professional care**                                                           **B23.44**

'Due professional care' refers to the conscientiousness with which proficient internal auditors apply themselves. The general Attribute Standard, applicable to both assurance and consulting internal audit work, reads:

'Internal auditors should apply the care and skill expected of a reasonably prudent and competent internal auditor. Due professional care does not imply infallibility.' (1220)

The application of this, within the Standards, to consultancy work by internal auditors acknowledges that the needs and expectations of clients, including the nature, timing, and communication of engagement results may be, indeed should be, considered. The same does not apply within the Standards to assurance engagements where instead the ...

'extent of work needed to achieve the engagement's objectives [etc]'.

... are the considerations which apply. In other words, the internal auditor is more accommodating to client expectations in consultancy work and in this work the client may be more directive than would typically be the case with 'assurance' assignments:

'The internal auditor should exercise due professional care during a consulting engagement by considering the:

□ Needs and expectations of clients, including the nature, timing, and communication of engagement results.

□ Relative complexity and extent of work needed to achieve the engagement's objectives.

□ Cost of the consulting engagement in relation to potential benefits.' (1220.C1)

Even so, requiring the auditor to 'consider' the client's needs and expectations, is not to say that the internal auditor should subordinate his or her professional judgement to that of the client. Bearing this in mind, audit assignments which contain elements of assurance as well as consultancy objectives can be handled effectively.

**Planning**                                                                    **B23.45**

Notwithstanding that consulting engagements may not be initiated by internal audit, as they are an integral part of internal auditing, they (a) should, as with assurance engagements, be determined in part having regard to relative risk and (b) should be included within the overall internal audit activity plan:

'The chief audit executive should establish risk-based plans to determine the priorities of the internal audit activity, consistent with the organization's goals.' (2010)

'The chief audit executive should consider accepting proposed consulting engagements based on the engagement's potential to improve management of risks, add value, and improve the organization's operations. Those engagements that have been accepted should be included in the plan.' (2010.C1)

Note that the decision to accept a consulting engagement rests with the chief audit executive, and broadly similar acceptance criteria apply as for assurance audits?

**Risk management, control and governance**                               **B23.46**

The new definition of internal auditing sets out the nature of internal audit work as focusing on risk management, control, and governance processes:

'Internal auditing is an independent, objective assurance and consulting activity designed to add value and improve an organization's operations. It helps an organization accomplish its objectives by bringing a systematic, disciplined approach to evaluate and improve the effectiveness of risk management, control, and governance processes.'

For each of these in turn[27], and also for the various stages in performing an engagement, we set out the general Standard (as this has applicability to consulting work as well as to assurance work) and the related consulting Standards. In the interests of conciseness we do not provide here the parallel assurance Standards, though we do refer to the differences between the consulting and assurance Standards. Note that the approach to conducting a consulting engagement, as set out in the Standards, is closely similar to the approach for an assurance engagement, though with more deference to the needs and expectations of the client. Indeed, 'the client' is not a term used in the context of assurance engagements.

Note that whereas in the context of assurance work it is the professional responsibility of internal auditors to be effective generally in identifying risks, and control and governess weaknesses and in contributing to their improvement, in the context of consultancy work the requirement is not identical. In consultancy work it depends initially on the engagement's objectives although there is a stated supplementary obligation that internal auditors on consultancy assignments should have a wider alertness. It should be pointed out that consultancy assignments which it may be appropriate for internal audit to accept will be those in the areas of risk, control and governance, it should surely not be the case that any internal audit consultancy would not have a significant focus on one or more of these areas: Standard 2210.C1 reads:

> 'Consulting engagement objectives should address risks, controls, and governance processes to the extent agreed upon with the client.' (2210.C1)

### Risk management                                                    B23.47

> 'The internal audit activity should assist the organization by identifying and evaluating significant exposures to risk and contributing to the improvement of risk management and control systems.' (2110)

> 'During consulting engagements, internal auditors should address risk consistent with the engagement's objectives and should be alert to the existence of other significant risks.' (2110.C1)

> 'Internal auditors should incorporate knowledge of risks gained from consulting engagements into the process of identifying and evaluating risk exposures of the organization.' (2110.C2)

### Control                                                            B23.48

> 'The internal audit activity should assist the organization in maintaining effective controls by evaluating their effectiveness and efficiency and by promoting continuous improvement.' (2120)

> 'During consulting engagements, internal auditors should address controls consistent with the engagement's objectives and should be alert to the existence of any significant control weaknesses.' (2120.C1)

### Governance                                                         B23.49

> 'The internal audit activity should contribute to the organization's governance process by evaluating and improving the process through

which (1) values and goals are established and communicated, 92) the accomplishment of goals is monitored, (3) accountability is ensured, and (4) values are preserved.' (2130)

'Consulting engagement objectives should be consistent with the overall values and goals of the organization.' (2130.C1)

## Engagement planning  B23.50

While avoiding the word 'plan', a similar intention is expressed for consultancy assignments:

'Internal auditors should develop and record a plan for each engagement' (2200)

'Internal auditors should establish an understanding with consulting engagement clients about objectives, scope, respective responsibilities, and other client expectations. For significant engagements, this under-standing should be documented.' (2201.C1)

## Engagement work programs  B23.51

As in other respects, the Standards acknowledge a greater degree of variety with respect to work programs of consulting engagements than would be the case with assurance engagements:

'Internal auditors should develop work programs that achieve the engage-ments objectives. These work programs should be recorded.' (2240)

'Work programs for consulting engagements may vary in form and content depending upon the nature of the engagement.' (2240.C1)

## Engagement objectives  B23.52

The objectives of consulting engagements are expressed similarly to those of internal audit engagements generally, except that the needs and expectations of the client are factored in for establishing the objectives of consulting assignments:

'The engagement's objectives should address the risks, controls, and governance processes associated with the activities under review.' (2210)

'Consulting engagement objectives should address risks, controls, and governance processes to the extent agreed upon with the client.' (2210.C1)

## Engagement scope  B23.53

'The established scope should be sufficient to satisfy the objectives of the engagement.' (2220)

'In performing consulting engagements, internal auditors should ensure that the scope of the engagement is sufficient to address the agreed-upon objectives. If internal auditors develop reservations about the scope during the engagement, these reservations should be discussed with the client to determine whether to continue with the engagement.' (2220.C1)

**Performing the engagement – recording information**          **B23.54**

The Standards on custody and retention of engagement records are not very dissimilar between assurance and consulting engagements, though the phraseology is not identical.

'Internal auditors should record relevant information to support the conclusions and engagement results.' (2330)

'The chief audit executive should develop policies governing the custody and retention of engagement records, as well as their release to internal and external parties. These policies should be consistent with the organization's guidelines and any pertinent regulatory or other requirements.' (2330.C1)

**Communicating results**          **B23.55**

More flexibility is allowed by the Standards with respect to communicating results of consulting assignments.

'Internal auditors should communicate the engagement results promptly.' (2400)

'Communication of the progress and results of consulting engagements will vary in form and content depending upon the nature of the engagement and the needs of the client.' (2410.C1)

**Disseminating results**          **B23.56**

While the stress in the assurance Standard (2440.A1) is on communicating assurance engagement results 'to individuals who can ensure that the results are given due consideration', which is for the chief audit executive to decide upon, in the case of consulting assignments it is the client who is specified, but with an override allowed when a consulting assignment uncovers matters which need to be referred higher:

'The chief audit executive should disseminate results to the appropriate individuals.' (2440)

'The chief audit executive is responsible for communicating the final results of consulting engagements to clients.' (2440.C1)

'During consulting engagements, risk management, control, and governance issues may be identified. Whenever these issues are significant to the organization, they should be communicated top senior management and the board.' (2440.C2)

## Monitoring progress                                                   B23.57

Even the monitoring of how the results of a consulting assignment are used is made a requirement for an internal auditor who has conducted a consulting engagement, but only to the extent agreed upon with the client. Would that management consultants generally had standards which enjoined them not to walk away without any follow-up! Here we have an example of how the internal audit approach to consulting, drawing upon a tried and tested auditing approach is able to add value to the consulting process.

'The chief audit executive should establish and maintain a system to monitor the disposition of results communicated to management.' (2500)

'The internal audit activity should monitor the disposition of results of consulting engagements to the extent agreed upon with the client.' (2500.C1)

## Management's acceptance of risks                                       B23.58

There are neither assurance nor consulting Implementation Standards to interpret this general Standard. the general Standard itself therefore applies, without elaboration, for internal audit consulting work:

'When the chief audit executive believes that senior management has accepted a level of residual risk that is unacceptable to the organization, the chief audit executive should discuss the matter with senior management. If the decision regarding residual risk is not resolved, the chief audit executive and senior management should report the matter to the board for resolution.' (2600)

## Further guidance on internal auditors as consultants                   B23.59

This supplementary section attempts to assimilate a second Practice Advisory on consulting, released on 7 January 2002 (1000.C1.2: Additional Considerations for Formal Consulting Engagements). It had originally been intended that this would have been the first of the two Practice Advisories to date on consulting services, but difficulties in agreeing its wording led to its release being delayed.

This section presents further thoughts based on a study of the new Practice Advisory.

The launch of the consulting Standards has been made at an inauspicious time. Concerned parties, post-Enron, are stressing the importance of assurance services. At a time when the combination of auditing and consulting services by external auditors is being questioned, it not the ideal time to promote dual assurance and consulting roles for internal auditors.

Although the old Standards allowed that auditors provide advice ('recommendations', 'agreed action') which leads to improvements, many considered that much of what today's internal auditors do was not caught by the old Standards. It was considered inappropriate that the professional pronouncements of The Institute of Internal Auditors should cover only the assurance role of internal auditors, thereby treating everything else as being beyond internal auditing. So the attempt has been made to capture perhaps most of the non-assurance work that internal auditors do, within the category of 'consulting services'. An obvious question is therefore 'When is advice part of an assurance service and when is it part of a consulting service?'. A second obvious question is 'When is a non-assurance service provided by internal auditors an internal audsit consulting service and when is it a non-audit service?'.

The further we delve into these pronouncements on internal audit consulting services, the more questions we have to answer. From the new Standards and Practice Advisories released to date, it is extremely difficult to obtain a clear understanding of the intended nature and limits of the internal audit consulting role and its interface with the assurance internal auditing role. We consider this is due to a lack of clarity and consistency in these pronouncements – caused in part no doubt by a lack of agreement within the profession. What is not clearly understood and agreed upon cannot be clearly expressed. It is to be expected that greater clarity will emerge in time, and that this will need to be associated with significant redrafting of these pronouncements. While it is true that compliance with the Practice Advisories is optional, their content is not intended to be inconsistent with the Standards themselves – the latter being mandatory. Candidates for the Certified Internal Auditor qualification are examined on the basis that adherence to the Practice Advisories is the approach to be taken in order to observe the Standards. For the moment, readers will not find it easy to understand what The Institute of Internal Auditors is requiring and counselling with respect to the consulting role of internal auditors.

Leaving to one side the scope for disagreement between internal auditors as to what *should be* their consulting role, if any, we consider these to be some of the ambiguities in the Standards Framework with respect to consulting services by internal auditors:

- it is not clear that in practice it would be possible to conduct an assurance engagement which did not also have elements of consulting as defined, or *vice versa*;

- it is not clearly stated whether or not assurance services are the core internal auditing service, with consulting being a discretionary optional service;

- it is not clear whether a consulting engagement is always to be 'by invitation' and with an 'agreed upon' remit;

- it is not entirely clear whether *any* 'other activity' undertaken by internal auditors should be regarded as being the provision of a consulting service, nor how to differentiate those that *are* consulting from those that *are not*; especially what are the essential characteristics of an audit engagement which fits into the 'consulting' classification, as distinct from activities (other than assurance engagements) which do not?

- leaving aside 'assurance services', it is not entirely clear, though it appears to us to be probable, that the test of whether a service by an internal audit function is a 'consulting service' as distinct from a 'non-audit activity' is merely whether or not the type of consulting service is defined in the charter of the internal auditing activity.

As lower level, especially 'Implementation', Standards are released it is understandable that some revisions will be required to Standards that have appeared before. Hence, in addition to the already revised definition of 'Consulting Services' in the Glossary to the Standards on 15 January 2003 The IIA released the first 'omnibus' of proposed revisions to the new Standards.

'Consulting' in accordance with the Standards ('consistent with the broad definition of internal auditing.') is expressed in the new Standards in effect as being, along with assurance activities, one of the two central pillars of authentic, contemporary internal auditing. However, it is not clear what are the criteria to be used to determine whether a non-assurance service falls intrinsically into what may be regarded as a consulting service which may be provided by internal audit within the meaning of the Standards and the Practice Advisories, or falls outside the Standards and therefore outside the remit of internal audit. The description of internal audit consulting services is drawn very widely indeed – especially in Practice Advisory 1000.C1.2. The only unambiguous test we can discern is that if the type of consulting service falls outside what is allowed for in the internal audit activity's charter, then it is outside the scope of internal auditing for that particular internal audit function. This comes close to defining internal audit as being what internal auditors do.

Notwithstanding the almost equal emphasis upon 'assurance' and on 'consulting' internal audit services in the new Standards, we take it that the assurance role is a sine qua non and should almost always, if not always, comprise the majority of the internal auditing plan. The new Standards framework feels towards this perspective when it implies that the internal audit charter may even specify no involvement in consulting services – unthinkable for assurance services.

The sentiment in the new Standards is that when the internal auditor provides a consulting service consistent with the Standards, he or she is acting as a mainstream internal auditor, not discharging a non-audit role. The Standards refer to other activities, which internal auditors sometimes become engaged in, which may not be termed 'internal auditing' – but this is not intended to apply to 'consulting'. Practice Advisory 1000.C1–2 states that ...

'The internal audit activity's risk-based plan of engagements may incorporate and rely on consulting engagements, to the extent deemed appropriate, to provide necessary audit coverage to the organisation'.[28]

**B23.59** *Further guidance on internal auditors as consultants*

This may be interpreted to imply that internal audit consulting services contribute to the assurance objective of internal auditing.

Although formal consulting engagements are usually, or always, 'agreed-upon' between internal audit and the client, Practice Advisory 1000.C1–2 (which, note, is titled 'Additional considerations for Formal Consulting Engagements', rather than informal ones) states:

> 'Internal auditors may conduct consulting services as part of their normal or routine activities as well as in response to requests by management.'[29]

So, to some extent at least, internal audit is presented as being able to determine whether it provides consulting services as set out in the charter – the agreement of management does not appear always to be required – even for formal consulting engagements. If consulting services may be provided as part of normal,, routine internal audit activity this raises the question as to whether a recommendation made resulting from an assurance engagement means that the auditor is then working in consulting mode and the engagement is thereby to be regarded as a hybrid or blended one.

Even the use of internal auditors as firefighters confusingly appears to be regarded as 'consulting'. Practice Advisory 1000.C1–2 allows for 'emergency consulting engagements':

> 'Emergency consulting engagements – participation on a team established for recovery or maintenance of operations after a disaster or other extraordinary business event or a team assembled to supply temporary help to meet a special request or unusual deadline.'[30]

Practice Advisory 1000.C1.2 sees a potential for impairment of independence and objectivity if assurance services are provided within one year of a formal consulting engagement[31]. and the Advisory suggests ways in which this potential impairment can be managed. This risk to independence and objectivity is consistent with the Standards' guidance that assurance engagements should not be conducted by an internal auditor who has had operational responsibilities in that area of the business within the past twelve months. It does however leave us with a conceptual conundrum: if, in practice, all assurance engagements contain elements of consulting, then this impairment is omnipresent.

# Consulting activity by internal auditors

**B23.60**

**Checklist**

**B23.61**

| | Reference to Standards framework |
|---|---|
| **1. General** | |
| 1.1 Is it understood that the Attribute and Performance Standards relate to internal auditors performing both assurance and consulting engagements? | Practice Advisory 1000 C1–2 (Preamble) |
| 1.2 Does the role of internal audit include a consulting role in addition to an assurance role? | Definition of Internal Auditing |
| 1.3 If the role of internal audit includes a consulting role, has the chief audit executive confirmed that the board understands and approves the concept of providing these consulting services? | Practice Advisory 1000.C1–2, para 5. |
| 1.4 Is the nature of consulting services defined in the audit charter? | 1000, 1000.C1–1 |
| 1.5 Has the wording in the audit charter on internal audit consulting services been determined after considering that internal audit consulting services (a) may be formal (with written agreements) or informal, (b) may extend to some or all of process design, 'advice' and 'counsel', facilitation and training, and (c) should always have the expectation of adding value and improving the organization's operations? | Standards' Glossary definition of 'Consulting services'; Practice Advisory 1000.C1–2 (Preamble) |
| 1.6 Has consideration been given as to whether the execution of operational tasks or executive duties should be excluded from the scope of internal audit consulting, as set out in the Charter and in practice, except that 'emergency consulting engagements' by internal audit, for instance to recover or maintain operations after an extraordinary event, or to supply temporary help, are regarded as falling within the possible range of consulting services which internal audit may provide? | 1100, 1120, Practice Advisory 1000.C1–2, para 3, but see also para 8. |
| 1.7 Does the audit charter describe the nature of internal audit consulting activity as falling within the ambit of risk management, control and governance? | 2100, 2210.C1 |

|  |  | Reference to Standards framework |
|---|---|---|
| **1. General** *cont.* |  |  |
| 1.8 | Is the nature of consulting services defined in the audit charter, including the authority and responsibility of internal audit for consulting services; and are consulting engagements declined if prohibited by the charter? | 1000, 1000.C1, Practice Advisory 1000.C1–2, para 5 and 10. |
| 1.9 | Does the audit charter explicitly or implicitly set out that internal audit consulting work may entail process design, 'advice' and 'counsel', facilitation and training; and should always have the expectation of adding value and improving the organization's operations? | Standards' Glossary definition of 'Consulting services' |
| 1.10 | Has the possibility been considered that the internal audit activity may conduct hybrid engagements incorporating elements of both consulting and assurance activities, either in a blended or in a distinguishable way? | Practice Advisory 1000.C1–2, para 2. |
| 1.11 | Is it acknowledged that special consulting engagements, such as participation in a merger or acquisition or in an emergency engagement (for example, a review of disaster recovery activities) may require departure from normal or established procedures for conducting internal auditing consulting engagements? | Practice Advisory 1000.C1–2 (Preamble) |
| 1.12 | Has the chief audit executive determined the methodology for classifying different types of internal audit consulting engagement? | Practice Advisory 1000.C1–2, para 2. |
| 1.13 | Is the execution of operational tasks or executive duties excluded from the scope of internal audit consulting, as set out in the Charter, and in practice? | 1100, 1120 |
| 1.14 | Has the chief audit executive developed policies governing the custody and retention of consulting engagement records, as well as their release to internal and external parties; and are these policies consistent with the organization's guidelines and any pertinent regulatory or other requirements? | 2330.C1 |

| | Reference to Standards framework |
|---|---|
| **1. General *cont.*** | |
| 1.15 Does the chief audit executive share information and coordinate activities with other internal and external providers of relevant consulting services to ensure proper coverage and minimize duplication of efforts? | 2050 |
| 1.16 Is it the chief audit executive who decides whether to accept a consulting engagement? | 2010.C1 |
| 1.17 Is it acknowledged by internal audit that the independence and objectivity of an assurance engagement may be impaired if it is conducted within one year after a formal consulting engagement, and are steps taken to minimise the effects? | Practice Advisory 1000.C1–2, para 7. |
| 1.18 If there are potential impairments to internal audit independence or objectivity relating to a proposed consulting service, is disclosure made to the engagement client prior to accepting the engagement? | 1130.C1 |
| **2. Planning – General** | |
| 2.1 Are accepted consulting engagements included in the audit plan; and are the nature, extent and overall results of formal consulting engagements disclosed to management, the audit committee, board or other governing body along with other reports of internal auditing activities? | 2010.C1; 2060; Practice Advisory 1000.C1–2, para 17. |
| 2.2 Before a consulting engagement is embarked upon, is it always clear how the results may, in a worthwhile way, improve management of risks, add value and improve the organization's operations? | 2010.C1 |
| 2.3 Does the chief audit executive consider the scale of the risk before deciding whether to accept a consulting engagement? | 2010.C1 |
| 2.4 Is there an effective process which leads to making reliable decisions as to whether to decline a consulting engagement or obtain competent advice and assistance, in cases where internal audit staff lack the knowledge, skills, or other competencies needed to perform all, or part of the engagement? | 1210.C1 |

| | Reference to Standards framework |
|---|---|
| **2. Planning** *cont.* | |
| 2.5 Does the internal audit activity effectively incorporate knowledge of risks gained from consulting engagements into the process of identifying and evaluating risk exposures of the organization? | 2110.C2 |
| 2.6 Does the internal audit activity effectively factor into its assurance work the assurance which can be generated from the consulting engagements it has undertaken? | Practice Advisory 1000.C1–1 |
| **3. Engagement Planning** | |
| 3.1 Has the internal audit activity developed appropriate policies and procedures for conducting consulting engagements? | Practice Advisory 1000.C1–2, para 5. |
| 3.2 Are there clear consulting engagement objectives which address risks, controls, and governance processes to the extent agreed upon with the client? | 2210.C1 |
| 3.3 Is it established that the engagement objectives of the consulting engagement are consistent with the overall values and goals of the organization? | 2130.C1 |
| 3.4 For a consulting engagement in the area of governance, is it clear how the engagement results may improve in a worthwhile way the process through which (1) values and goals are established and communicated, (2) the accomplishment of goals is monitored, (3) accountability is ensured, and (4) values are preserved? | 2130 |
| 3.5 Are internal audit consulting engagements 'agreed-upon',in nature and scope, between internal audit and the client? | Definition of 'consulting services' in the Glossary |
| 3.6 How is it ensured that the intended scope of work will be sufficient to satisfy the agreed-upon objectives of the engagement? | 2220, 2220.C1 |
| 3.7 Does the client understand that the results of all consulting by internal audit may, at the judgment of the Chief Audit Executive, be presented to senior executives, board and audit committee members? | Practice Advisory 1000.C1–1 |

| | Reference to Standards framework |
|---|---|
| **3. Engagement Planning** *cont.* | |
| 3.8 How does the chief audit executive ensure that he or she retains the prerogative of setting the audit techniques to be used within a consulting engagement, and that there are no misunderstandings with respect to this between audit and the client? | Practice Advisory 1000.C1–1 |
| 3.9 Have the internal auditors established an understanding with consulting engagement clients about objectives, scope, respective responsibilities, and other client expectations? For significant engagements, has this understanding been documented? | 2201.C1 |
| 3.10 Is there a developed and recorded plan for the consulting engagement? | 2200 |
| **4. During a Consulting Engagement** | |
| 4.1 Is a disciplined, systematic evaluation methodology followed by internal audit in consulting work? | Practice Advisory 1000.C1–1 |
| 4.2 How is it ensured that due professional care is exercised during a consulting engagement with respect to (a) the needs and expectations of clients, including the nature, timing, and communication of engagement results, (b) the relative complexity and extent of work needed to achieve the engagement's objectives, and (c) the cost of the consulting engagement in relation to potential benefits? | 1220.C1 |
| 4.3 How is it ensured that during consulting engagements, internal auditors address risk consistent with the engagement's objectives and are alert to the existence of other significant risks? | 2110.C1 |
| 4.4 How is it ensured that during consulting engagements, internal auditors address controls consistent with the engagement's objectives and are alert to the existence of any significant control weaknesses? | 2120.C1 |
| 4.5 When significant risk management, control and governance issues are identified during a consulting engagement, how does internal audit ensure they are communicated to senior management and the board? | 2440.C2 |

| | Reference to Standards framework |
|---|---|
| **4. During a Consulting Engagement** *cont.* | |
| 4.6 | When internal auditors develop reservations about the scope during the engagement, are these reservations discussed with the client to determine whether to continue with the engagement? | 2220.C1 |
| 4.7 | Do the internal auditors record relevant information to support the conclusions and engagement results? | 2330 |
| **5. Towards the End of the Engagement** | |
| 5.1 | Does the chief audit executive ensure the final results of consulting engagements are communicated to clients? | 2440.C1 |
| 5.2 | Are consulting engagement results communicated by internal audit promptly and in appropriate form and content having regard to the nature of the engagement and the needs of the client? | 2400, 2410.C1 |
| 5.3 | Does the internal audit activity monitor the disposition of results of consulting engagements to the extent agreed upon with the client? | 2500.C1 |
| 5.4 | In the case of consulting engagements, when the chief audit executive believes that senior management has accepted a level of residual risk that is unacceptable to the organization, does the chief audit executive discuss the matter with the client and, if the matter is not resolved, ensure that the matter is reported to the board for resolution? | 2600 |

# Controlling the outsourced internal auditing contract    B23.62

*Geoffrey Clark has contributed this article. He is a director of Internal Audit Services Limited which offers a particularly interesting approach to the provision of outsourced internal auditing services. Internal Audit Services maintains a large database of skilled internal auditors and in our experience usually has been able to meet the needs of businesses for contracted out internal auditing using locally or semi-locally based internal auditors with the appropriate sector-specific backgrounds. This approach to outsourced internal audit provision very often results in mature internal auditors, perhaps early-retired people, being matched to client needs at very reasonable cost. It is surprising how much internal auditor expertise there is 'out there' which Internal Audit Services database is able to access.*

*These are intended as practical tips to purchasers on how to manage an outsourced contract. The perspective is that of a niche provider putting himself into the shoes of prospective purchasers. This is not an academic approach and there are no statistics. This article is based purely on personal experience and belief. For soundly based academic research, the right starting point would be 'The Outsourcing Dilemma: What's Best for Internal Auditing', by Larry E Rittenberg and Mark Covaleski, published in 1997 by The Institute of Internal Auditors Research Foundation (USA): ISBN 0–89413–384–5.*

# Background

Our experience is that the internal audit market is expanding steadily. It seems that with each passing year, more people can claim to be internal auditors; and there is a shortage of internal audit skills. Clearly, this is a very positive environment for all internal auditors. In terms of outsourced internal audit, the expansion is more uneven and is subject to flux.

The reasons for the steady expansion overall are well known. One is the stricter regulatory environment that has grown up over the last ten years. The same causes also may be attributed to the expansion of outsourced internal auditing; but outsourced internal auditing owes its development to other factors as well. One is the new wider availability; there are now a broader range of providers and more modes of provision existing in the marketplace. Providers range from 'one person bands' through to the very large firms of accountants, and down again to smaller specialist niche firms.

An increasing amount of marketing is being undertaken by all these providers. Although this marketing expenditure primarily is intended to feed opportunities through to individual firms, the expanded marketing effort has had the general effect of encouraging the take-up of internal audit, for the benefit of everyone engaged in this activity.

## Options

As regards mode of provision, the range of options has increased for purchasers. These are not restricted to a straight choice between in-house provision and a total outsourcing of the service. There are now many hybrids available, such as the outsourcing of certain skills, languages, countries, trading divisions or subsidiaries; or of particular parts of the work plan; or of the assessment of risk; or of the assessment of the performance of the internal auditing activity itself.

Some purchasers have outsourced the work of all except the head of audit, who remains as the only direct employee of the organisation. There are also examples of splitting higher level strategic work from field audit work: that is, outsourcing one while retaining the other in-house.

Thus the possible permutations have expanded greatly. Alongside all of these changes, the culture and attitudes of purchasers have changed. There is a great deal less reticence about hiring in whatever additional resources are needed on an *ad hoc* basis. This might be to catch up with a work plan that has fallen behind or to provide maternity leave cover, and so on.

All of these changes appear to have occurred mainly over the last ten years and they thus indicate a sea-change in attitudes and behaviour over that time.

**Outsourcing drivers**

We can sum up the drivers behind the expansion of outsourcing in general, as distinct from internal audit in particular, as being the following:

- import the culture of casual labour from other activities e.g. dock labour; legal, accountancy and other professions; building industry;

- external pressures e.g. legislative pressures such as the *Employment Protection Act (1974);*

- internal pressures e.g. the cost of internal resources needs to be reduced; or the size of the organisation is too small for internal auditing to be in-house;

- precedent; or trend set by others in other areas e.g. in manufacturing by Marks & Spencer since the 1930's; facilities management from the 1980s; IT from the 1990s;

- a need for a flexible resource or a different mix of skills; and

- the increasing availability of supply e.g. Brook Street Bureau formed in late 1940's; Manpower from the USA in 1964; Capita, sold off by CIPFA in 1988; and many others entering the market since then.

Most of the drivers imply that it is essentially labour that is being outsourced. However, in some instances it is know-how which is the sought after resource. Most of these drivers apply as much to the growth in outsourcing of internal audit as to the outsourcing of other activities.

Further factors specifically driving the expansion of outsourcing of internal audit have included:

- compulsion e.g. local government compulsory competitive tendering (1994), best value (1999); directives to NHS trusts to form audit committees; directives to housing associations by the Housing Corporation making internal audit mandatory (1995); other changes in the regulatory framework;

- as regards quoted companies, coercion or changes in best practice e.g. Cadbury (1992), the Combined Code (1999), the Turnbull Committee (1999), Smith (2003), Higgs (2003), Sarbanes-Oxley (2002, USA); the appointment of non-executive directors; the formation of audit committees; the need for improved internal controls;

- elevation in importance of corporate governance matters generally to the wider audience e.g. to bankers, suppliers, customers, regulators, shareholders, prospective investors/venture capitalists;

- 'bad news' events e.g. Barings, Maxwell, Enron, WorldCom etc.;

- perceptions of new risks and the need for an outside perspective;

- insufficient skills, or a need for a different mix of skills;

- a growing need for a truly independent view;

- a greater 'ability to let go': that is, the ability of purchasers to trust and have confidence in an alternative mode of supply, as manifested for instance by the esteem in which the provider is generally held, the quality of references from other clients, the quality of the tender submission (if applicable), adherence to standards and guidelines, adherence to quality standards (e.g. ISO 9001), membership of professional institutes and adherence to codes of professional ethics;

- supply availability e.g. from external auditors, from the 'Big Four' firms, from smaller and local accountancy practices, from specialist/niche providers, from consortium arrangements (common in the NHS), and from in-house departments seeking third party clients; and

- growth of joint ventures.

All of these drivers have worked powerfully together to build momentum to a point where expansion is now inevitable and unstoppable. However that expansion is not steady and rapid, but is rather characterised by a state of flux around a cycle.

**Advantages and disadvantages of outsourcing**

Dennis Cox from Prudential Fund Managers, and who gave the April 1999 Internal Auditing Moorgate Lecture, listed some advantages as being:

- introduces new skills;

- third party knowledge;

- resources when required; and

- total independence.

Note that these skills imply the provision of know-how rather than labour.

Cox listed these disadvantages:

- integration with suppliers;

- service level may fluctuate;

- loss of key skills;

- change to corporate culture; and

- price.

'Integration with suppliers' means there is a danger in treating the outsourced internal audit provider as just another supplier. We would not treat the statutory auditors or other professionals in this way, but rather as strategic advisers who provide important know-how and ongoing support.

Some of the disadvantages Cox mentions can also be advantages, for example bringing change to corporate culture, or a price advantage.

**Approaches to outsourcing**

Various approaches can be adopted by a purchaser, some of which have already been referred to. We can sum up the options with respect to approach as being:

- a work plan totally devolved on the provider to carry out;

- a work plan partially devolved on the provider; and

- secondments of staff to existing (perhaps reduced) in-house departments on a call-off basis.

The preparation of a work plan itself can be devolved on the provider, or can be produced prescriptively by the client. A consensus approach is preferable whereby the provider independently produces a draft work plan based on an assessment of risk, and then produces a definitive plan that takes into account the stated desires of the client including the client's audit committee.

As regards the composition of the plan, or the assignment brief, clients naturally do have their own agenda, even if sometimes that agenda is hidden. Motives differ, and may include that:

- the client seeks a good image for its corporate governance, perhaps above all else;

- the client has a minimalist approach, to be able to say 'we have internal audit' is enough!; or

- the client seeks ongoing comfort on very specific controls only – e.g. takings to bank, computer audit, etc.

These differing motives will inevitably affect the approach of the provider.

**Key features and principles of a contract**

In the contract itself it is better to err on the side of formality if in doubt. Of course, that requires a written contract. Whether this should be a document entitled 'contract', a written tender, or merely an exchange of correspondence is for the parties to determine. Apart from the actual selection process, these are some of the key points to consider and to cover when constructing a contract:

- an outsourced business is still your business;

- define the level(s) in the hierarchy at which the provider is to report;

- define the degree of autonomy to be granted to provider in assessing risk, compiling the work plan, setting objectives, and commencing audits;

- identify which skills are to be outsourced;

- define deliverables like audit reports, etc.;

- monitor supplier activity and performance;

- ensure there is a corrective mechanism for when things go wrong;

- ensure there is a cessation mechanism for when things go very wrong; and

- there must also be charging and invoicing mechanisms, including submission of detailed time sheets and expense claims.

## Controlling the internal audit contract

There are particular key control mechanisms to be used when controlling a contract, once it is activated. For instance:

- fix audit committee and other periodic review meetings, including dates;

- check invoices to time sheets and expenses claims;

- keep copies of all correspondence, faxes and e-mails;

- get feedback from audited entities on performance;

- complete customer satisfaction questionnaires when requested by the provider; it is helpful feedback to the provider;

- institute a formal annual performance appraisal including a written report.

## Summary

Internal auditing is expanding. Outsourcing of internal audit is expanding along with outsourcing generally. However, this is not 'mono-directional'; the mode of supply will change and go through cycles. Outsourcing is primarily a matter of outsourcing the provision of know-how, not just of labour. Of course, there are advantages and disadvantages; and the range of options and permutations available to purchasers is increasingly sophisticated. Invariably, the contract should be written; while it may take various forms, there are a number of key factors to remember and include when constructing a contract, and there are also certain important control mechanisms to help control the contract.

Internal Audit Services can be contacted at Hornefield House, David Street, Meopham, Kent, DA12 0BT (tel: +44 (0)1474 813052; fax: +44 (0)1474 812498; email: RGC@internalaudit.co.uk).

# Using knowledge within internal audit effectively

**B23.63**

*We suggest this article should be read in conjunction with* **B23.85** WISE INTERNAL AUDITORS MANAGE KNOWLEDGE WELL. *Mary Hardy wrote this article when she was Group Audit Director at Diageo where the experiences recounted in this article were then taking place. Mary is now Internal Audit Director for Transport for London and can be contacted at Windsor House, 42–50 Victoria Street, London SW1H 0TL. Tel: +44 (0) 20 7941 4087. Fax +44 (0)20 7941 4434. E-mail: maryhardy@tfl.gov.uk.*

Before we can consider how to use knowledge effectively in any context, we need to have a working definition. For the purpose of this paper I am defining knowledge as

'An accumulation of information about:

☐   Business strategies, operations and risks that is of relevance to enable the internal audit function to plan its work in a focused manner; and

☐   Audit processes and procedures to enable audit work to be carried out efficiently and effectively.'

It is very important to differentiate between 'knowledge', 'data', and 'information'. The amount of data available to us in this technological age is substantial and it is very tempting to build spreadsheets and databases and analyse this data to the ninth degree because we have the technology available to do it. However, we must constantly challenge whether the data is a mere collection of ciphers or whether it is information that is indeed adding to our knowledge and enabling us to do our job more effectively.

## Business knowledge

The key elements of knowledge that an internal auditor requires about the business are the strategic plans and objectives and the risks associated with those strategic plans. As companies' compliance with the Combined Code and Turnbull improves, the management and mitigation actions for risks as well as the sources of assurance should be documented and these will also be key pieces of knowledge for the internal auditor.

So armed with the above knowledge of the business, what does the internal auditor do next?

## Audit knowledge

The following example is based on how we manage knowledge in group audit in Diageo plc. At the moment these knowledge databases are on a variety of spreadsheets and linked Lotus Notes databases. We are, however, in process of installing an integrated software package, which will pull them together more effectively and give us search functionality, which will make the knowledge much more accessible and, therefore, valuable.

In order to understand what knowledge means to us in Diageo, I need to briefly introduce the group to you. Diageo was formed in December 1997 from a merger between Guinness and Grand Metropolitan. We have many, many well-known brands amongst which the key ones are Johnnie Walker, Smirnoff, Baileys, Guinness, Haagen-Dazs and Burger King. The Group operates in over 150 countries worldwide with two of the businesses headquartered in the US, (Pillsbury and Burger King), and two in the UK, (UDV and Guinness), along with the corporate headquarters. Annual revenues for the year ended 30 June 1999 were in the order of £12 billion.

As I write this article the group audit function is being decentralised so that each business will have its own business risk assurance team headed by a business risk assurance director with a central team who will have an ongoing coaching, quality assurance and co-ordination role. Prior to this decentralisation, the group audit function consisted of 45 staff based in five offices around the world. A similar number and distribution are anticipated once decentralisation has been completed.

In a group of this size and diversity, it is vitally important that the internal audit function has access to the right knowledge to enable it to operate effectively; it would be extremely easy to spend all the time analysing data!

There are eight segments to the knowledge databases within group audit in Diageo:

1.  standards database;

2.  audit universe;

3.  audit planner;

4.  skills database;

5.  electronic workpapers;

6.  audit reports;

7.  good practice database; and

8.  discussion database.

The contents and use of the each of these databases are described below.

## Standards database

In order to ensure consistency of quality of work throughout the audit group, we have a number of agreed standards that are followed on a worldwide basis.

| Audit methodology | This sets out the philosophy behind the audit approach as well as walking through the audit process from start to finish. |
|---|---|
| Master risk matrices | These are *not* audit checklists! However, they take each standard business process and identify the most common risks to those processes. They are only intended as a starting point to enable auditors to do their own thinking as the risks to any process will vary significantly depending on which of the four businesses are being audited and which part of the world the auditor is in. Alongside the common risks are the common controls you might expect to see. The auditor develops both the risk and the control aspects of this matrix before performing audit work. The matrix will then carry a summary of the audit work completed, and weaknesses identified which need to be included in the report will also be highlighted. |
| Reporting templates | We have a standard report format that is used by all of the auditors around the world. This is particularly important to ensure consistency of presentation for those people based at the corporate centre who receive copies of all reports issued. We also have standard wordings for conclusions with definitions included in the reports so there can be no misunderstanding of what the conclusions mean. |
| Distribution lists | Whilst this may seem a trivial point, in a group of 77,000 with constant turnover of staff and reorganisations, trying to keep track of who requires reports, where they are and what their current job title is can be something of a nightmare! By having the standard distribution lists on the database we can be sure that auditors use the current version and report distribution is accurate. |

## Audit universe

For every auditable entity in Diageo we have an entry on the audit universe. This does not incorporate an audit risk ranking and scoring system, which is what most people take an audit universe to mean. What it does contain is background information on the entity including business size, organisation charts and key players, major business/systems/personnel changes, major risks and then information on the entity's location and useful data on hotels, restaurants, bars, cinemas etc. Note that an auditable entity is not necessarily just a business unit, but it could be the functions within a large business unit, or possibly a major project.

## Audit planner

This is simply the forward schedule of staff and job planning. We always aim to have the planning fixed for the next three months and provisional for the three months afterwards.

## Skills database

On joining the department each member of staff is asked to fill in a skills database form which is updated annually. This gives us information on work experience, language skills and IT knowledge as well as career aspirations. The search functionality included in this enables managers to identify the individuals with the appropriate skills for the job they are trying to plan as well as to ensure that the planning, as far as is possible, meets career aspirations.

## Electronic work papers

The software package we are installing will enable all work papers to be reviewed remotely by managers and directors and so cut down on travel time, and improve response times should audit issues arise. There is also a capacity to scan documents into the work papers so that a complete file is available. The software will produce the detailed findings section of the audit report so that only the executive summary will need to be an original document.

## Audit reports

Copies of all audit reports will be maintained on the system. In the new system the important addition will be search functionality so that we will be able to analyse reports by business, risk category or finding.

## Good practice database

As we perform audits and identify examples of good business practice we not only highlight these in the executive summary of the audit reports to give credit to local management for the work they are doing, but we also add them to the good practice database.

## Discussion database

This is a free form Lotus Notes database which allows the audit staff to raise questions or start discussion topics as well as to put on to the system information that they believe will be of use to others in the department. Quite often this information will be a summary of a conference they have recently attended or maybe of some articles they have read in an industry magazine. At the end of each week an automatic e-mail is sent to all staff informing them what has been added to the discussion database during the course of that week to both encourage them to read the additions and remind them that the discussion database is there.

I hope the above outline of how we manage knowledge in Diageo Group Audit has been of interest and will help you to think about how you can use knowledge effectively within your internal audit department.

# Wise internal auditors manage knowledge well   B23.64

*We suggest this article should be read in conjunction with* **B23.73** USING KNOWLEDGE WITHIN INTERNAL AUDIT EFFECTIVELY. *Jeffrey Ridley wrote this article. Jeffrey is professor of auditing, attached to South Bank University Business School. He can be contacted as follows. Tel: +44 (0) 1526 354472. E-mail: profridley@btopenworld.com.*

Those who study and advise on knowledge management have written well on this subject over the past few years; both as a product of learning and as an important management tool to motivate and stimulate innovation. Knowledge management is a means of developing, capturing and communicating information. It is also about searching information to improve strategic thinking and decision-making processes. Most good knowledge management processes now use electronic methods to ensure all information available is being used to best advantage for the organisation and its entire staff.

Bill Gates (1999) of Microsoft discusses the value of the *electronic library* of knowledge in all organisations:

' ... to gather and organize information, disseminate the information to people who need it, and constantly refine the information through analysis and collaboration ... '

His simplified definition of knowledge management is:

' ... nothing more than managing information flow ... ' .

But is management of information enough and can it ever be simplified? In most organisations management of information is one of its most difficult tasks, too often disorganised and not used wisely.

All organisations have seen explosions of information. Storing and searching that information to achieve an organisation's two key objectives, its aims and improved performance, is not that easy. It requires good planning, efficient methods and a commitment to share knowledge. How often are all your information flows tested for the knowledge requirements of these two key objectives? Do you ever do this in your internal auditing function, your auditee's function or for the whole organisation? Such tests are becoming more and more important as volumes of information continue to grow. Internal auditors have a clear responsibility to address and evaluate knowledge management in their own functions and in all other areas of their organisations.

Auditing, as practised by internal auditors or any other type of auditor, is based on established principles that have been tested and developed over many years.

It has its own 'scientists' who have explored and developed better methods and opened up new boundaries of knowledge for those that practise its art. Committed practitioners have driven its development, either individually or in groups. Its principles have a universal acceptance. Its standards are continually being developed and revised to meet new demands by both practitioners and those who rely on its services. There is a continuous programme of research and development at academic and practitioner levels that documents and influences what is practised.

The IIA's 1941 Certificate of Incorporation sowed the seeds for a science of internal auditing. This stated that the IIA's then purpose as a profession was:

'To cultivate, promote and disseminate knowledge and information concerning internal auditing and subjects related thereto; to establish and maintain standards of integrity, honor and character among internal auditors; to furnish information regarding internal auditing and the practice and methods thereof to its members, and to other persons interested therein, and to the general public; to cause the publication of articles relating to internal auditing and practices and methods thereof; to establish and maintain a library and reading rooms, meeting rooms and social rooms for the use of its members; to promote social intercourse among its members; and to do any and all things which shall be lawful and appropriate in furtherance of any of the purposes hereinbefore expressed.'

The IIA has researched a common body of knowledge for internal auditing since the 1970s. Its knowledge framework, researched and published in the early 1990s, has this to say about internal auditing knowledge:

' ... internal auditors must possess skills and knowledge from several different disciplines. They must be excellent communicators, both orally and in writing. They must be well versed in computers and technology to be proficient in the new Information age. They must be logical thinkers. They must possess accounting, economics, finance, and other types of management knowledge to understand business and the context in which organisations operate. They must also have numerous other types of support knowledge, such as human relations, sampling, quantitative methods, and fraud detection abilities. Indeed, it appears that the knowledge required to be an effective internal auditor almost demands that one be 'superhuman' – an expert in numerous disciplines.'

Detail supporting this research was used to update the syllabus for the IIA Inc. Certified Internal Auditor (CIA®) examination programme as it is today. Further research by the IIA in the late 90's resulted in a new competency framework for internal auditing. Created from global research this framework identifies knowledge areas vital to internal auditing. Its guidance is now impacting much of the teaching and training in internal auditing today across the world. Its influence will grow, placing new demands on knowledge requirements for all internal auditors.

O'Regan (2001) recently studied the current professional status of internal auditing and recognises the IIA as:

' ... the driving force behind the increasing professionalisation of internal auditing over the last half-century.'

He lists amongst other attributes of the IIA:

' ... a defined body of examined and certified knowledge ... '

This attribute, more than any other, has driven the development of the profession and the science of internal auditing as we know it today. That defined body of knowledge is clearly stated in the current syllabi of the IIA Certified Internal Auditor (CIA) examination programme and the new international standards for the professional practice of internal auditing. Both are available in electronic form and provide a bank of knowledge that will grow, adding significant value worldwide to all internal auditing functions. Good knowledge management skills will be needed by internal auditors for these to be used to create best professional internal auditing practices. They should impact all internal auditors and provide continuous opportunities for performance improvement.

This year has seen a number of case studies being published showing how internal auditors are contributing to knowledge management in the organisations they serve. Four such studies developed by the IIA-UK (2001) demonstrate how internal auditors in Lex Services, Bank of England, Central Bank of Ireland and HM Customs & Excise have embraced knowledge management. Each is using electronic methods to store, manage and spread knowledge about their internal auditing to all audit staff and others in their organisations. Each is using their auditing to review how knowledge in their organisations is being managed.

A recent issue of the Institute of Internal Auditor's newsletter Auditwire (2001) also outlines how other North American based internal auditors are ' ... *getting involved and shaping key roles ...* ' in effective knowledge management. The article demonstrates how internal auditors in General Motors Corporation, Ford Motor Company, Xerox Corporation and Tosco Corporation are developing their knowledge management strategies and skills, as well as contributing to the dissemination of knowledge about control and risk across their organisations. All use databases linked to electronic communication systems to communicate their knowledge, both globally within their internal auditing functions and across their organisations. Each sees this as an added value to the services they provide. It improves the quality of audits and increases management awareness of best practices. For those internal auditing functions with a high turnover rate their planned and structured sharing of knowledge is seen to continuously improve the performance of all levels of staff, whether new or experienced, contributing to better teamwork, supervision and management of all resources.

It is not only large internal auditing functions that embrace the challenges of Intranet to spread knowledge throughout their services. The internal audit manager of Network Housing Association, London, has used her organisation's Intranet to establish a 'home site' for internal auditing. This site spreads up-to-date knowledge of its staffing, charter, audit planning, risk assessments, auditing procedures and quality assurance measures for all the organisations it serves. Capturing such knowledge, and keeping it up-to-date, provides an important stimulus and challenge for its internal auditing staff, as excellent learning processes.

But it is not just in-house Intranet knowledge that internal auditors should manage. Worldwide websites now provide large databases of knowledge with powerful search engines. There can be few internal auditing activities that could not benefit from knowledge freely available on websites set up outside the organisations they serve. All internal audits, risk assessments and consultancy activities need to manage and search this external knowledge. Any internal auditors today that do not reference into internet websites are weakened by a less than complete understanding of the knowledge available for the services they provide.

The IIA has also published guidance on the use of the internet by internal auditors. Written by an internal auditor this book provides:

> ' ... options for accessing the Internet, useful Internet tools and services for audit professionals, a comprehensive list of available resources, and case studies of how internal auditors use the Internet for audit-related work.'

The author, Jim Kaplan, has his own website www.auditnet.org providing useful references for all internal auditors seeking to increase their knowledge and the value of their services.

Creating frameworks for the implementation of good knowledge management practices has occupied many consultants over the past few years. Bain & Company's research lists knowledge management requirements as:

> '☐ Catalog and evaluate the organisation's current knowledge base;
>
> ☐ Determine which competencies will be key to future success and what base of knowledge is needed to build a sustainable leadership position therein;
>
> ☐ Invest in systems and processes to accelerate the accumulation of knowledge;
>
> ☐ Assess the impact of such systems on leadership, culture, and hiring practices;
>
> ☐ Codify new knowledge and turn it into tools and information that will improve both product innovation and overall profitability.'

Lloyd sees:

> ' ... a close link among data, information, knowledge and wisdom ... '

He argues that:

> ' … we start with wisdom and that provides the framework within which to manage knowledge … '

His definition of wisdom is the combination of knowledge and values. It is the use to which knowledge is put that is critical in all knowledge management processes. Being wise after the event is frequent. The art of good internal auditing must always be to be wise before the event. Being wise about knowledge before the event is a key to success in all internal auditing services.

Knowledge management will always be key to innovation and creativity in all sciences. Whether you view internal auditing as a profession, science or art, or none of these, there is no doubt that it requires well-managed knowledge to add value in all the services it provides. Knowledge not just of the organisation but also knowledge that is available outside the organisation. There are many roles for internal auditors to occupy in knowledge management; as a user, as a communicator and a provider of assurance. Roles that now require wise internal auditors to have the knowledge to be not only good auditors, but also to be good teachers and consultants.

**Notes**

1. Para 6.
2. Para 3.
3. Para 2.
4. Para 7.
5. COSO's Internal Control – Integrated Framework made 'monitoring' one of the essential components of an effective system of internal control. Although contentious, COSO also gave management, especially the CEO, 'ultimate responsibility' for internal control.
6. Para 8.
7. Practice Advisory 2060–2, also released in December 2002, on 'Relationship with the Audit Committee' to be found at http://www.theiia.org/ecm/printfriendly.cfm?doc_id=4044.
8. Para 7.
9. Para 7.
10. Para 5.
11. Para 7.
12. Para 8.
13. Para 1.
14. Penultimate bullet point in para 5.
15. Para 4 and third bullet point in para 5.
16. Para 3.
17. Para 4.
18. Para 5.
19. Para 5.
20. Para 2.
21. Practice Advisory 1110–2, also released in December 2002, on 'Chief Audit Executive (CAE) reporting lines' to be found at http://www.theiia.org/ecm/printfriendly.cfm?doc_id=4043.
22. Practice Advisory 1000.C1–2 on 'Additional Considerations for Formal Consulting Engagements' is an interpretation of Standard 1000.C1 (and other related Consulting Implementation Standards). Standard 1000.C1 reads:

23. We have not been able to obtain a copy of the 1975–76 report.
24. Internal control – integrated framework,(September 1992), [Committee of Sponsoring Organizations of the Treadway Commission (COSO), American Institute of Certified Public Accountants].
25. Internal control and financial reporting: guidance for directors of listed companies registered in the UK, (December 1994), 'The Rutteman Report', ICAEW.
26. As stated in each Practice Advisory, for instance Practice Advisory 1000.C1–1: Principles Guiding the Performance of Consulting Activities of Internal Auditors.
27. 'Risk management', 'control' and 'governance'.
28. Practice Advisory 1000.C1.2 (7 January 2002), para 10.
29. Practice Advisory 1000.C1.2 (7 January 2002), para 3.
30. Practice Advisory 1000.C1.2 (7 January 2002), para 3, last bullet point.
31. Practice Advisory 1000.C1.2 (7 January 2002), para 7.

# Fraud

## Defining fraud B24.1

'I can resist everything except temptation.'

*Lady Windermere's Fan (1892), Act 1, Oscar Wilde*

Whether or not an incident is a fraud is of secondary importance to professionals who have the responsibility to prevent and detect a wide range of varieties of abuse.

Fraud and abuse can be viewed as breakdowns in the system intended to implement policy set from the top. Frauds differ from accidental errors and losses due in particular to their deliberate intent. Perhaps, at its simplest, we can say that fraud is:

'dishonesty for gain with concealment'.

A recent definition is:

'any act which seeks a profit at the expense of another party through the practice of deception, collusion, or any other means of perpetuating unethical activity.'[1]

The new IIA Standards glossary at the end of **B23.4** defines fraud as:

'Any illegal acts characterized by deceit, concealment or violation of trust. These acts are not dependent upon the application of threat of violence or of physical force. Frauds are perpetrated by individuals and organizations to obtain money, property or services; to avoid payment or loss of services; or to secure personal or business advantage.'

Acts of theft may lack the element of deliberate concealment. Nevertheless many frauds are theft and may be proceeded against, through the courts, as such.

The Auditing Practices Board defines fraud as comprising:

'Both the use of deception to obtain an unjust or illegal financial advantage and intentional misrepresentations affecting the financial statements by one or more individuals among management, employees, or third parties. Fraud may involve:

- falsification or alteration of accounting records or other documents,

- misappropriation of assets or theft,

- suppression or omission of the effects of transactions from records or recording of transactions without substance,

- intentional misapplication of accounting policies, or wilful misrepresentation of transactions or of the entity's state of affairs.'[2]

The Audit Commission puts it this way:

'Intentional distortion of financial statements or other records by persons internal or external to the organisation, carried out to conceal the misappropriation of assets or otherwise for gain'[3]

## Defining corruption                                    B24.2

Corruption has a legal meaning in the public sector:

'When money or other consideration is paid, given to or received by a person in the employment of the Crown or of a Public Body by, or from, a person holding, or seeking to obtain a contract from the Crown, or Public Body such money or consideration shall be deemed to have been given, or received, corruptly unless the contrary is proved.'[4]

The Audit Commission describes corruption as:

'The offering, giving, soliciting or acceptance of an inducement or reward which may influence a person to act against the interests of the organisation.'[5]

# Incidence of fraud                                      B24.3

A Mori survey found that two-thirds of 100 leading UK finance directors admitted their companies had been the victim of fraud by employees and in two-thirds of the cases the perpetrator was a director or senior or middle manager. More than half of those who admitted they had been hit by fraud believed it might have been still taking place undetected.[6]

Another similar survey found that half of large companies had been victims of fraud more than once-a-year and in more than 70 per cent of the cases an employee had been involved; but fewer than 40 per cent of businesses had an explicit fraud reporting policy[7]. We give example fraud policy statements at **B12.30**.

A further survey[8] of 805 senior executives from eleven countries found:

- 90 per cent thought their companies were at a greater risk from fraud than five years ago;

- 25 per cent of companies had lost more than $1million from fraud over the past five years;

- 40 per cent had more than five frauds over the past five years;

- more than half the frauds were discovered by chance;

- three quarters of the frauds were committed by employees; and

- almost half the companies believed the courts failed to fully understand major fraud cases (in the UK just a quarter considered they understood).

A common feature of these surveys is that they date back three or four years; but only the most sanguine would consider the situation has improved. At that time, David Sherwin, head of fraud investigation and risk management at the accountants Ernst & Young, London, had this to say:

'Fraud is costing business more than $10billion (£6.6billion) per year world wide, taking account the costs of lawyers, accountants and investigators to deal with it.

'Unless senior managers take it seriously, and not just try to cover over the holes with sticking plaster, [fraud] will haunt businesses for many years to come. There will be more BCCIs and Barings.'

'It only takes one person in an organisation to decide they fancy putting their fingers in the till and the consequences can be catastrophic.'[9]

Today, there is a tendency to deride surveys of the incidence of fraud in business. The astronomic figures invite incredulity. Indeed, extrapolated in a statistical way they can only be rough estimates. What really matters is what is happening within the individual organisation. Almost certainly, much more is happening than meets the eye. A survey of IT fraud found that most were discovered by accident. They were not discovered by systems controls or by audit, whether internal or external. Indeed 'shopping' the culprit by a disgruntled or jealous friend associate was a more frequent source of information about fraud than was the work of auditors. Many of the frauds would not have been discovered had it not been for the carelessness of the defrauder.

# Discovery by accident                                       B24.4

This leaves us with a disconcerting question: if most frauds are discovered by accident, does this not make it likely that most frauds are not being discovered? It is unsafe to assume that if these frauds were large they would be bound to be noticed.

This survey of IT fraud also found that most were continuous, not 'smash and grab'. In other words, once set up most of them worked automatically and repeatedly on behalf of the defrauder. We accept that the proportion of IT frauds which can be classified as continuous is related to the proportions in the sample which are IT-dependent fraud (only possible because the computer is used), IT-assisted (traditional fraud but facilitated in perpetration or concealment by the use of the computer) or just IT-related (related to IT only because it is fraud where an IT system is in use).

Continuous frauds were often more vulnerable to detection when they were being set up or when the system was changed several years later, than they were when they were working automatically and continuously for the defrauder. If most IT frauds are discovered by accident and most are also continuous, does this not imply not only that most are not being discovered but that it may be the larger ones which are not being discovered, since these continuous frauds will get larger and larger? We cannot assume that the largest frauds are most likely to be discovered; the costs of these frauds may be written off regularly in the books of the company as if they were routine operating expenses, and so it is not necessarily the case that a larger and larger discrepancy between 'book' and 'actual' opens up until it becomes transparently obvious.

# Characteristics of recently reported US accounting malpractices[10]

B24.5

As the principal driver of the recently introduced US Sarbanes-Oxley Act and the new draft US corporate governance Standards, we thought it would be useful to provide this straightforward summary of some the most significant types of alleged accounting malpractices which have been reported from the US.

|   | Type of fraud or misstatement | Example | Basic tenet | Case |
|---|---|---|---|---|
| **1.** | Overstatement of sales; and also of margin | A broker, acting as a broker between sellers and buyers of energy, takes sales credit for the total size of the transaction, rather than only the fee involved, which makes the company's size and growth rate look much stronger than it really is. | A sale is made by a seller when title passes from the seller to the buyer. | Enron |
| **2.** | Overstatement of sales | Buying and selling telecoms capacity from each other and taking credit at both ends, thus overstating both companies' revenues. | Related party transactions provide an opportunity for artificial transactions. | Global Crossing and Qwest Communications |

| | Type of fraud or misstatement | Example | Basic tenet | Case |
|---|---|---|---|---|
| **3.** | Overstatement of income and also of long term assets (stock warrants) | 'Company A gives $9.5 million to Company B for $30 million of Company B stock warrants; and Company A books the difference – as advertising and commerce revenue.'[13] | Assets should be valued at lower of cost or market | AOL (Company A) and PurchasePro (Company B) |
| **4.** | Artificial inflation of revenue and net income through (a) secret side deals allowing customers to cancel contracts, (b) backdating contracts, (c) swapping inventory to increase revenue, and (d) using the company's acquisition reserves to reduce unrelated current expenses.\n\nThis happened prior to the company being acquired by another company who were unaware of the alleged fraud, but whose financials then became contaminated. | HBOS (the US medical information group), which McKesson (the US healthcare distribution group) acquired in 1999.[12] | *Inter alia,* thorough due diligence prior to an acquisition is essential. | Revenue had been artificially inflated by $330m and net income by $190m over a three year period leading up to HBOC's takeover by McKesson. Investors in the McKeeson lost $9bn when this alleged fraud in HBOS was revealed. Though unaware of the alleged fraud, McKesson's CEO and CFO reigned when it came to light.\n\nHBOC had been able to continually exceed analysts' quarterly earnings expectations through these |

|  | **Type of fraud or misstatement** | **Example** | **Basic tenet** | **Case** |
|---|---|---|---|---|
| 4. *cont.* |  |  |  | accounting irregularities. |
|  |  |  |  | The former chief executive of HBOC (who became chairman of McKesson after the takeover), HBOC's general counsel, and HBOC's president and chief operating officer were all three indicted on 4 June 2003. The SEC had filed civil fraud charges against six former HBOC executives in 2001 – three of whom pleaded guilty and provided crucial information for the criminal indictment. |
| 5. | Adjusting prior year's over-statement | A write-down of inventory means that profits had been overstated before the write-down | Inventory should be valued at the lower of cost or net realisable value. | Cisco wrote down more than $2bn early in 2001 |
| 6. | Adjusting provisions to improve results | Selling to very weak customers: booking the sales but inadequately reserving for the likely | Items based on the exercise of subjective judgement should be scrutinised carefully by | Lucent and other telecommunications equipment manufacturers. |

|   | **Type of fraud or misstatement** | **Example** | **Basic tenet** | **Case** |
|---|---|---|---|---|
| **6.** *cont.* | | failure to pay | external auditors and by the audit committee. | |
| **7.** | Failure to write down impaired assets so as to inflate results | | | SEC investigated Gateway for doing this to inflate results in third quarter of 2000. |
| **8.** | Premature recognition of revenue | Providing goods and services under a contractual lease-or-buy arrangement, and taking a large proportion of the arrangement's value immediately, even though there was a continuing obligation and the possibility of cancellation. | Income should be taken over the life of the commitment. | Xerox<br><br>Xerox is also investigating allegations that transactions by its South African affiliate were 'improperly recorded' and that a South American division made 'improper payments'. |
| **9.** | 'Channel stuffing' | Excessive despatches of product to wholesalers or retailers, regarding these despatches as sales in the period the goods were despatched, with inadequate provision for returns. | A sale should only be regarded as a sale when title passes and proper provision should be made for likely returns | Pharmaceutical companies, 'stuffing' wholesalers with as much as one year's supply of drugs, rather than the more usual one or two months' supply. Excessive stock at wholesalers and limited shelf life of drugs have meant that many of these supplies are now |

| | Type of fraud or misstatement | Example | Basic tenet | Case |
|---|---|---|---|---|
| **9.** *cont.* | | failure to pay | external auditors and | being returned by the wholesalers. |
| **10.** | Expense recognition | Fees paid every month to local carriers for line usage were treated as capital expenditure, not an operating expense | Expenses must be matched with their corresponding revenues.<br><br>Assets are an owned resource that has future value. | WorldCom<br><br>Prosecutors allege that Sullivan 'devised a scheme' to start reallocating as capital expenditure (which can be deducted over several years) costs of leasing the networks of rival companies – costs previously classified as expenses. |
| **11.** | Creating an artificial market | Arrange for acquisition candidates to take large profit write-offs before acquisition, so that profit improvement appears greater later on. | Collusion between acquirer and acquiree is against the interests of both companies' shareholders. | Tyco |
| **12.** | Creative accounting | Overstate acquisition expenses so as to improve performance post-acquisition (also improves pre-acquisition results of acquirer as | Expenses should be properly classified to provide a reliable picture. | Tyco |

|  | Type of fraud or misstatement | Example | Basic tenet | Case |
|---|---|---|---|---|
| **12.** *cont.* |  | normal operating costs of the acquirer are treated as acquisition expenses). |  |  |
| **13.** | Off balance sheet debt obligations | Off balance sheet special purpose entities (companies or partnerships) carry the debt (often collateralised with the company's stock) which unravels if the share price falls | The balance sheet should refer to all liabilities or contingent liabilities of the entity | Enron, collateralised with Enron stock.<br><br>Citigroup and J.P. Morgan Chase together structured 26 'pre-pay transactions' totalling $8.5 billion in which the banks put money up-front roughly equal to what specific energy trades might realise in the future. The key accounting question is whether this money should have counted as a loan, or as something closer to a payment for a future profit. If they were loans, Enron's debt would have risen by 40% while cash flow would have fallen by half, and this would have had a harsh impact of |

| | Type of fraud or misstatement | Example | Basic tenet | Case |
|---|---|---|---|---|
| **13.** *cont.* | | | | Enron's rating with the credit agencies. Citigroup funded these pre-paid transactions by issuing notes tied to Enron's creditworthiness (which was portrayed based on incomplete and misleading financial disclosures. |
| | | | | In November 2002 the SEC is investigating Elan the Irish drugs group, for excluding $1bn of off-balance sheet debt from its US accounts. |
| **14.** | Loss of pro-fessionalism by the accountants | Mandating the accounting function to generate better financial results by accounting contrivances – in other words regarding the accounting function as a profit centre. | One essential accounting principle is 'prudence'; another is 'objectivity'. | Xerox: James Bingham: 'Sometimes I fed the beast. … The beast was a Xerox culture that created an illusion of value'. The group overstated its profits by $1.4 billion between 1997 and 2001. |
| **15.** | Corruption | Bribes to secure overseas contracts | Foreign corrupt payments are outlawed in US under the 1977 Foreign Corrupt Payments Act. | Xerox admitted in a regulatory filing that, in an effort to push sales at its Indian unit, it had made 'improper |

| | Type of fraud or misstatement | Example | Basic tenet | Case |
|---|---|---|---|---|
| **15.** *cont.* | | | | payments over a period of years' to government officials there'. For instance, in 2000, when the bribery is said to have stopped, payments amounted to 'approximately $600,000 – 700,000'. |
| **16.** | Artificial related party transactions. | 'Round trip deals' to boost revenues and justify high share prices | | Veritas. A Wall Street listed software company, revealed late in 2002 in a regulatory filing that it had been asked by the SEC to hand over papers relating to a pair of deals with AOL in September 2000. Veritas had sold $50m in software and services to AOL while agreeing to buy $20m in internet advertising from AOL. |

# Fraud risk assessment and accountability  B24.6

Fraud now has become endemic and has developed a fresh momentum of its own, its ubiquitousness raises the level of temptation even for those who would otherwise have stood apart. The Association of British Insurers estimates that fraud costs the UK up to £12 billion a year, or at least one-third of the cost of all crime. As the Fraud Advisory Panel has put it:

'Fraud knows no boundaries. It afflicts both private and public sectors, small and large businesses. It hits the pensioner and the shareholder. Fraud leeches up to £12 billion a year from its rightful owners and it is uncomfortably apparent that current social and technological trends will facilitate its growth.'[13]

The Fraud Advisory Panel's 1999–2000 report reminds us that their own study in 1999 of published sources estimated fraud losses as up to £5 billion. They point out that the police in England and Wales recorded 312,151 fraud and forgery offences in the year ending September 1999, and that the Serious Fraud Office had 85 cases under investigation in March 2000, the highest total since its establishment in 1998, with a total value of over £2 billion. They remind us that the 1998 Ernst & Young survey found that two-thirds of British respondents had been defrauded in the previous 12 months and 84 per cent in the previous five years, and that a recent survey by Nottingham Business School revealed that there was no recovery of loss whatsoever in some 60 per cent of fraud cases.[14]

Moral constraints which mitigated against fraud have weakened; so that now, as Oscar Wilde would have said, it would seem that so many resist anything except for temptation.

## Fraud – a consequence of the way we run our businesses
B24.7

This is little surprise. Modern marketing makes that temptation irresistible. The open invitation to the light fingers of shoppers in supermarkets and department stores is emulated by so many other sectors. As never before, there is a perceived personal imperative for the acquisition of material things; but many are excluded from significant, legitimate participation in this rampant consumer society. In the market economy, the very level of economic prosperity which we enjoy has been achieved by the persuasiveness of a simple message; that we need to acquire more.

Of course, we are not saying that fraud is the preserve of a market economy. Fraud and corruption have been shown to be rife in many command economies. Absolute deprivation is also a driver of fraud. But is does seem undeniable that, in our society, escalating fraud is correlated to our growing prosperity in a free market economy. We rightly blame the perpetrator, but we should also be rooting out the other causes.

### Products and services conducive to fraud
B24.8

One of the causes is the introduction of products and services which are inherently prone to fraud. Or their hasty introduction before they have been made resistant to fraud, to steal a market advantage.

Supermarket display of goods would never have been acceptable business practice in Victorian England, on account of the theft risk. At that time, the level of credit card fraud accepted today by banks would have made these convenient slips of plastic an entirely unacceptable banking proposition, had the technology been available one hundred years earlier.

To take another example, in earlier times, the fraud risk would have made it unacceptable to set the level of medical prescription charges at often several times more than the 'over the counter' cost of purchasing the same medicines.

With breathtaking cynicism we build the cost of fraud into the price of our products and are often prepared to require our customers to pay 5 or 10 per cent more to subsidise the defrauder.

**Minimising fraud risk**                                              **B24.9**

Of course, this area of debate is shot through with moral tones. In particular, there is the immorality of the defrauder, notwithstanding that many defrauders find it hard to see that any individuals are hurt as a consequence of their frauds. But there is also the issue as to whether it is moral to launch new products and services which are prone to fraud. Do not enterprises have a moral obligation to minimise the temptation of fraud? Might this not also be in their enlightened self interest?

We suggest that the situation has now become so acute that it calls for urgent action at senior levels of government, by regulators and in the boardrooms of companies and other entities.

**Fraud risk management as part of corporate governance**      **B24.10**

Following the adoption of the Combined Code[15] and the Turnbull Report[16] by the London Stock Exchange, compliant boards are now certainly assessing the effectiveness of their internal control and risk management. At the level of the board, 'top down' assessments of risk are being undertaken. Boards are also assessing that the monitoring of control and risk management is effectively embedded throughout the business. In addition, boards are at least annually considering the adequacy of their internal auditing functions and, where they do not have an internal audit function, considering whether they should set one up appropriately.

Although specifically applicable to listed companies, the Combined Code and the Turnbull Report are being rolled out across the economy, impacting upon other private sector entities as well as upon public bodies.

It is significant to note that contemporary developments in corporate governance in both the US and the UK were born out of concern about fraud. In the US it was fraudulent financial reporting of Wall Street listed companies that led the Treadway Commission[17] being set up. In the UK, spectacular corporate collapses linked to fraud (for instance, Polly Peck, Maxwell Corporation, BCCI, etc) led to the Cadbury Committee whose conclusions[18] were to be reviewed six years later by the Hampel Committee[19].

The focus of concern in both the US and the UK was principally management fraud including fraudulent financial reporting, rather than employee fraud or the fraud risk inherent in products or services.

In view of their origins, it is perhaps surprising that the Combined Code and the Turnbull Report are silent on the question of fraud. But, clearly, proper risk management should include an assessment of the risk of fraud and the effectiveness of controls to mitigate that risk. Neither the Hampel Committee, which developed the new Combined Code, nor the Turnbull Working Party, which was asked to elaborate on part of the Combined Code, would have considered otherwise.

**Minimising fraud risk in new products or services**       **B24.11**

We would like to see a formal requirement that all new services and products intended to be launched should be assessed rigorously for their risk of fraud, with a presumption that systems controls must be able to contain the potential for fraud to within minimal levels before the product or service launch. Similar requirements should apply to public sector entities.

We note that new UK government initiatives must now be assessed for their bureaucratic impact upon business. Should not new products and services introduced by business as well as by government also be required to be properly assessed for their fraud risk?

We reject the contemporary view that a new product or service is a satisfactory proposition for an entity if the levels of fraud it allows or encourages are outweighed by the profits it generates. To launch such a product or service is to create a societal moral hazard, and a hidden tax directly on all of the entity's customers and indirectly on society as a whole. The test should be whether or not the risk of fraud is minimised at an acceptable level in absolute terms, not relative to the profits which the product or service will earn. Entities should be obliged to continue to invest in improving anti-fraud measures when the profitability of their products and services is excellent.

Neither is a 'top down' assessment of the risk of fraud by the board adequate on its own, important though it is. Opportunities for fraud may be buried in the woodwork of the entity, unknown to the board and unlikely to be revealed by the board's top down assessment of fraud risk. So we reject the alluring viewpoint that sees detailed controls as costly and perhaps ineffective. We see the detailed application of well-designed control procedures as being a key element in our fight against fraud and a necessary integral investment in all our systems.

## Accounting publicly on fraud policy and management      **B24.12**

We would also like to see statements in annual reports about the entity's policies with respect to its fraud risk tolerance/risk aversion, with respect to new products and services as well as with respect to other fraud-related issues including employee and management fraud. We would like to see companies report on the results of their own reviews of their compliance with their stated fraud policies.

While these statements would be part of the growing trend to report more fully on social responsibility and sustainability issues, they would also be of interest to those who read annual reports in order to maximise the returns on their investments. Indeed, the protagonists of sustainability reporting would argue that the most environmentally responsible companies will perform best in the medium to long term.

Some companies might choose to disclose the levels of fraud that they are experiencing. To some extent this is already caught by the requirements of accounting standards and of internal control reporting.

## Auditing the reports of directors on fraud      **B24.13**

Voluntarily, at least at first, we would like to see these directors' assertions on fraud reviewed and reported upon by independent auditors. The approach we are recommending here for fraud is closely similar to the approach taken on environmental issues by the European Community's Eco-Management and Audit Scheme (EMAS) or the ISO14000 environmental standard.

## Obligatory assignment of responsibilities      **B24.14**

Finally, we would like to see measures which obligate entities to clearly assign responsibilities for fraud prevention and fraud detection. We believe that the risk of fraud is greater because rarely do managers' job descriptions make them responsible for avoiding the risk of fraud. We believe frauds frequently go undetected because rarely is the responsibility to detect fraud formally assigned.

In assigning responsibilities for fraud prevention and detection, we consider that 'the buck stops at the board'. It needs to be clearly established that the board has specific overall responsibility for ensuring that the risk of fraud is managed.

## Conclusions      **B24.15**

If this all seems like a step too far, we would just say that, as we see it, fraud is now a serious sustainability matter, along with environmental and discriminatory issues. Active and pro-active fraud aversion is socially responsible behaviour for corporate entities. There needs to be transparent accountability about the exercise of this responsibility within corporate entities. With the majority of the largest world economies now being corporations not countries, participation of the former needs to be ensured, and we can no longer leave the containment of fraud to governments.

As with the development of environmental management and reporting, much will need to be done before an agreed framework for corporate fraud accountability can be established.

For well-known reasons, statutory auditors of financial statements have been reluctant to assume responsibilities for fraud detection as part of their annual statutory audit. The same audit profession is now developing agreed approaches to assurance services beyond the confines of the narrow annual audit of financial statements. This could be their way forward to providing audit services in the area of fraud. This way ahead would focus on attesting the assertions that directors make with regard to their anti-fraud policies. It may have the potential to close the audit expectations gap.

Notwithstanding the centrality of anti-fraud measures to effective corporate governance, effective accountability and effective audit, there remain crucial roles for government agencies and others to play. In particular there is a need for 'joined up thinking' and co-ordinated action across the piece. As the latest annual report of the Fraud Advisory Panel concludes[20]:

'The Panel believes that fraud, with all its damaging economic and social effects, will continue to grow unless a national effort is set on foot. We wish to see the principles of co-ordination and coherence underlying our own work to be given institutional form on the national stage.'

# Self-test checklist on managing the risk of fraud

**B24.16**

1. Do you know what is your enterprise's policy statement on fraud?

2. What are the rules on acceptance of gifts and hospitality?

3. Do you know what to do when a member of staff reports a suspected fraud?

4. Who would investigate a suspected fraud in the activities for which you are responsible?

5. Have you assessed the risk of fraud in those activities?

6. Do you include fraud risk assessment when you plan new systems or policies?

7. What checks do you administer to counter the risk of fraud?

8. Who can you turn to assist you to (a) assess fraud risk and (b) design countermeasures?

9. Have you been trained to manage fraud risk?

10. Do you know what frauds occurred within the business last year?

11. Do you have adequate information about frauds which have occurred within your sector recently?

12. What action are you going to take about fraud risks?

# Fraudulent financial reporting – COSO and ICAEW studies  B24.17

In the mid 1980s five US-based professional bodies[21] convened to consider their concerns about the level and nature of fraudulent financial reporting of Wall Street listed companies. The first report they commissioned addressed this in depth and gave the group of professional bodies their name – 'COSO', or the 'Committee of Sponsoring Organizations of the Treadway Commission'.

One of Treadway's recommendations which did not become a mandatory requirement in the US but is widely observed on an optional basis, was that directors should report on internal control. Indeed the Securities & Exchange Commission had much earlier suggested this following the enactment of the *Foreign Corrupt Practices Act 1977* which had drawn attention within the Act that boards are responsible for internal control[22]. If directors are responsible, they should render an account, the argument went. The suggestion was resisted, so COSO commissioned another study, researched by Coopers & Lybrand, which has become known as 'the COSO report', although COSO has commissioned several reports over the years. This report took our understanding of internal control to a new level and is still the most authoritative framework on internal control; although is currently subject to revision[23].

COSO is still active and recently published a research project to provide an extensive updated analysis of financial statement fraud occurrences, 'Fraudulent financial reporting: 1987–1997 – an analysis of US public companies'.

COSO sponsored this research project to provide an extensive updated analysis of financial statement fraud occurrences. While the work of the National Commission on Fraudulent Financial Reporting in the US in the mid-1980s had identified numerous causal factors believed to contribute to financial statement fraud, little empirical evidence had existed about factors related to instances of fraud since the release of the 1987 report. Thus, COSO commissioned this study to provide information to be used to guide future efforts to combat the problem of financial statement fraud and to provide a better understanding of financial statement fraud cases.

## COSO research objectives and scope  B24.18

The research had three specific objectives:

- to identify instances of alleged fraudulent financial reporting by registrants of the US Securities and Exchange Commission (SEC) first described by the SEC in an Accounting and Auditing Enforcement Release (AAER) issued during the period 1987–1997;

- to examine certain key company and management characteristics for a sample of these companies involved in instances of financial statement fraud; and

- to provide a basis for recommendations to improve the corporate financial reporting environment in the US.

The study analysed instances of fraudulent financial reporting alleged by the SEC in AAERs issued during the eleven-year period between January 1987 and December 1997. These AAERs, which contain summaries of enforcement actions by the SEC against public companies, represented one of the most comprehensive sources of alleged cases of financial statement fraud in the United States. The focus was on AAERs that involved an alleged violation of Rule 10(b) 5 of the *Securities Exchange Act 1934* or *section 17(a)* of the *Securities Act 1933* given that these represented the primary antifraud provisions in the US related to financial statement reporting. The study excluded restatements of financial statements due to errors or earnings management activities that did not result in a violation of the federal antifraud statutes.

Nearly 300 companies were found to have been involved in alleged instances of fraudulent financial reporting during the eleven-year period. From these a random selection of approximately 200 companies was examined in detail. Findings reported in this study were based on information obtained from reading (a) AAERs related to each of the sample fraud companies, (b) selected Form 10-Ks filed before and during the period the alleged financial statement fraud occurred, (c) proxy statements issued during the alleged fraud period, and (d) business press articles about the sample companies after the fraud was disclosed.

This was a penetrating study. Nevertheless, some of the observations about the profiles of fraudulent companies are not dissimilar from what one would expect in view of the sampling approach used. For instance, in any random sample of companies we would expect to find only a small proportion of large companies, and thus a bias towards the typical characteristics of the smaller company (such as dominant directors, family control, and so on), which this study found, applies to so many companies involved in falsifying financial statements. Nevertheless, it is helpful that COSO draws our attention to the dominance of small companies, with the structures and management styles which we associate with smaller companies, in fraudulent financial reporting.

The fact that most of the fraud companies were relatively small does throw a particular light on the campaign that was fought so strongly in the late 1990s for the UK code of best practice for corporate governance[24] to be streamlined for the smaller company. If the UK is similar to the US in respect of the incidence of fraud cases between small and large companies (and there is no reason to think it is not), then it would suggest that the need for rigorous approaches to corporate governance is as at least as great for the smaller company as for the larger. COSO touches on this, in a US context (see below). For the UK, Hampel[25] rejected the idea of a separate, simplified corporate governance code for the smaller company. His committee was able to point out that the mandatory 'Principles' should apply to all companies, whereas the more detailed 'Provisions', which are not mandatory, can be deviated from if the circumstances of a particular company made this desirable whilst not compromising adherence to the 'Principles'.

We would also challenge one or two of the inferences drawn by COSO from their analysis. For instance, they suggest that severe consequences awaited companies committing fraud; including bankruptcy, significant changes in ownership, and delisting by national exchanges, in addition to financial penalties imposed. But the issue is which was the 'cause' and which was the 'effect'? Bearing in mind that COSO also found that some companies committing fraud were experiencing net losses at the time, an alternative scenario would be that companies 'with their backs to the wall' are more likely to develop fraudulent ideas. Indeed COSO acknowledge that:

> 'pressures of financial strain or distress may have provided incentives for fraudulent activities for some fraud companies'.

In which case, it is probably too simplistic to claim that the unpleasant outcomes for so many of these companies were necessarily a consequence of the fraud

## Summary of COSO findings and implications on fraudulent financial reporting                     B24.19

COSO was able to generalise several key findings from the detailed analysis of the sample of approximately 200 financial statement fraud cases. They grouped these findings into five categories describing the nature of the companies involved, the nature of the control environment, the nature of the frauds, the consequences to the company and the individuals allegedly involved and issues related to the external auditor. Here we summarise the findings first, followed by the implications, with the exception that we leave until last the findings and implications relating to the external auditor, as they lead in well to the following part of this section on fraud.

### Nature of the companies involved                     B24.20

COSO found that most companies committing financial statement fraud were relatively small. The typical size of most of the sample companies ranged well below $(US)100 million in total assets in the year preceding the fraud period. Most companies (78 per cent of the sample) were not listed on the New York or American Stock Exchanges.

Some companies committing the fraud were experiencing net losses or were in close to breakeven positions in periods before the fraud. COSO consider that pressures of financial strain or distress may have provided incentives for fraudulent activities for some fraud companies. The lowest quartile of companies indicates that they were in a net loss position, and the median company had net income of only $175,000 in the year preceding the first year of the fraud period. Some companies were experiencing downward trends in net income in periods preceding the first fraud period, while other companies were experiencing upward trends in net income. Thus, the subsequent frauds may have been designed to reverse downward spirals for some companies and to preserve upward trends for others.

### Nature of the control environment – top management and the board                                                                          B24.21

Top, senior executives were frequently involved in the instances of fraud that COSO reviewed. In 72 per cent of the cases, the AAERs named the chief executive officer (CEO), and in 43 per cent the chief financial officer (CFO) was associated with the financial statement fraud. When considered together, in 83 per cent of the cases, the AAERs named either or both the CEO or CFO as being associated with the financial statement fraud. Other individuals named in several AAERs included controllers, chief operating officers, other senior vice presidents, and board members.

Most of the audit committees of the fraudulent companies met only about once-a-year or the company had no audit committee. 25 per cent of the companies did not have an audit committee. Most audit committee members (65 per cent) did not appear to be certified in accounting or to have current or prior work experience in key accounting or finance positions.

Boards of directors were dominated by insiders and 'grey' directors (ie outsiders with special ties to the company or management) with significant equity ownership and apparently little experience serving as directors of other companies. Approximately 60 per cent of the directors were insiders or 'grey' directors. Collectively, the directors and officers owned nearly one-third of the companies' stock, with the CEO/president personally owning about 17 per cent. Nearly 40 per cent of the boards had not one director who served as an outside or 'grey' director on another company's board.

Family relationships among directors and/or officers were fairly common, as were individuals who apparently had significant power. In nearly 40 per cent of the companies, the proxy provided evidence of family relationships among the directors and/or officers. The founder and current CEO were the same person or the original CEO/president was still in place in nearly half of the companies. In over 20 per cent of the companies, there was evidence of officers holding incompatible job functions (eg CEO and CFO).

### The nature of the frauds reviewed by COSO                                                 B24.22

Cumulative amounts of frauds were relatively large in view of the relatively small sizes of the companies involved. The average financial statement, misstatement or misappropriation of assets was $25 million and the median was $4.1 million. While the average company had assets totalling $533 million, the median company had total assets of only $16 million. Most frauds were not isolated to a single fiscal period. Most frauds overlapped at least two fiscal periods, frequently involving both quarterly and annual financial statements. The average fraud period extended over 23.7 months, with the median fraud being 21 months. Only 14 per cent of the sample companies engaged in a fraud involving less than 12 months.

Typical financial statement fraud techniques involved the overstatement of revenues and assets. Over half the frauds involved overstating revenues by recording revenues prematurely or fictitiously. Many of those revenue frauds only affected transactions recorded right at the period end (ie quarter end or year end). About half the frauds also involved overstating assets by under-stating provisions on receivables, overstating the value of inventory, property, plant and equipment and other tangible assets, and recording assets that did not exist.

## Consequences for the company and individuals involved B24.23

Severe consequences awaited companies committing fraud. Consequences of financial statement fraud to the company often included bankruptcy, significant changes in ownership, and delisting by national exchanges, in addition to financial penalties imposed. A large number of the sample firms (over 50 per cent) were bankrupt/defunct or experienced a significant change in ownership following disclosure of the fraud. 21 per cent of the companies were delisted by a national stock exchange.

Consequences associated with financial statement fraud were severe for individuals allegedly involved. Individual senior executives were subject to class action legal suits and SEC actions that resulted in financial penalties to the executives personally. A significant number of individuals were terminated or forced to resign from their executive positions. However, relatively few individuals explicitly admitted guilt or eventually served prison sentences.

### *Summary of implications*

The research team analysed the results to identify implications that might be relevant to senior managers, boards of directors and audit committee members, and internal and external auditors. The implications reflected the judgement and opinions of the research team, developed from the extensive review of information related to the cases involved.

## Implications related to the nature of the companies involved B24.24

The relatively small size of fraud companies suggested that the inability or even unwillingness to implement cost-effective internal controls may have been a factor affecting the likelihood of financial statement fraud (eg override of controls is easier). Smaller companies may be unable or unwilling to employ senior executives with sufficient financial reporting knowledge and experience. Boards, audit committees, and auditors need to challenge management to ensure that a baseline level of internal control is present.

The national stock exchanges and regulators should evaluate the trade-offs of designing policies that might exempt small companies, given the relatively small size of the companies involved in financial statement fraud. A regulatory focus on companies with market capitalisation in excess of $200 million may fail to target companies with greater risk for financial statement fraud activities.

Given that some of the fraud firms were experiencing financial strain in periods preceding the fraud, effective monitoring of the organisation's going-concern status is warranted, particularly as auditors consider new clients. In addition, the importance of effective communications with predecessor auditors is highlighted by the fact that several observations of auditor changes were noted during the fraud period.

**Implications related to the nature of the control environment
(top management and the board)**                                      **B24.25**

COSO considered that the importance of the organisation's control environment could not be overstated, as emphasised in COSO's 'Internal Control – Integrated Framework' (COSO, 1992). Monitoring the pressures faced by senior executives (eg pressures from compensation plans, investment community expectations etc) is critical. The involvement of senior executives who are knowledgeable of financial reporting requirements, particularly those unique to publicly traded companies, may help to educate other senior executives about financial reporting issues and may help to restrain senior executives from overly aggressive reporting. In other cases, however, board members and auditors should be alert for deceptive managers who may use that knowledge to disguise a fraud.

The concentration of fraud among companies with under $50 million in revenues and with generally weak audit committees highlighted the importance of rigorous audit committee practices, even for smaller organisations. In particular, the number of audit committee meetings per year and the financial expertise of the audit committee members may deserve closer attention.

It showed as important to consider whether smaller companies should focus heavily on director independence and expertise, like large companies are currently being encouraged to do. In the smaller company setting, due to the centralisation of power in a few individuals, it may be especially important to have a solid monitoring function performed by the board.

An independent audit committee's effectiveness can be hindered by the quality and extent of information it receives. To perform effective monitoring, the audit committee needs access to reliable financial and non-financial information, industry and other external benchmarking data, and other comparative information that is prepared on a consistent basis. Boards and audit committees should work to obtain from senior management and from other information providers relevant and reliable data to assist them in monitoring the financial reporting process.

Investors should be aware of the possible complications arising from family relationships and from individuals (founders, CEO/board chairs etc) who hold significant power or incompatible job functions. Due to the size and nature of the sample companies, the existence of such relationships and personal factors was to be expected. It is important to recognise that such conditions present both benefits and risks.

### Implications related to the nature of the frauds                    B24.26

The multi-period aspect of financial statement fraud, often beginning with the misstatement of interim financial statements, suggests the importance of reviews of interim financial statements and the related controls surrounding interim financial statement preparation, as well as the benefits of continuous auditing strategies.

The nature of misstatements affecting revenues and assets recorded close to or as of the fiscal period end highlights the importance of effective consideration and testing of internal control related to transaction cut-off and asset valuation. Based on the assessed risk related to internal control, the auditor should evaluate the need for substantive testing procedures to reduce audit risk to an acceptable level and design tests in light of this consideration. Procedures affecting transaction cut-off, transactions' terms, and account valuation estimation for end-of-period accounts and transactions may be particularly relevant.

## External audit findings and issues arising from the COSO study                    B24.27

### The external auditor                    B24.28

All sizes of audit firms were associated with companies committing financial statement frauds. 56 per cent of the sample fraud companies were audited by what was then a Big Eight/Six auditor during the fraud period, and 44 per cent were audited by non-Big Eight/Six auditors.

All types of audit reports were issued during the fraud period. A majority of the audit reports (55 per cent) issued in the last year of the fraud period contained unqualified opinions. The remaining 45 per cent of the audit reports issued in the last year of the fraud departed from the standard unqualified auditor's report because they addressed issues related to the auditor's substantial doubt about going concern, litigation and other uncertainties, changes in accounting principles, and changes in auditors between fiscal years comparatively reported. 3 per cent of the audit reports were qualified due to a GAAP departure during the fraud period.

Financial statement fraud occasionally implicated the external auditor. Auditors were explicitly named in the AAERs for 56 of the 195 fraud cases (29 per cent) where AAERs explicitly named individuals. They were named for either alleged involvement in the fraud (30 of 56 cases) or for negligent auditing (26 of 56 cases). Most of the auditors explicitly named in an AAER (46 of 56) were non-Big Eight/Six auditors.

Some companies changed auditors during the fraud period. Just over 25 per cent of the companies changed auditors during the time frame beginning with the last clean financial statement period and ending with the last fraud financial statement period, rather more than would be expected had the changes not been connected in some way with the fraud. A majority of the auditor changes occurred during the fraud period (e.g. two auditors were associated with the fraud period) and a majority involved changes from one non-Big Eight/Six auditor to another non-Big Eight/Six auditor.

### Implications regarding the roles of external auditors B24.29

COSO considered the study found that there is a strong need for the auditor to look beyond the financial statements to understand risks unique to the client's industry, management's motivation toward aggressive reporting, and client internal control (particularly the tone at the top), among other matters. As auditors approach the audit, information from a variety of sources should be considered to establish an appropriate level of professional scepticism needed for each engagement.

The auditor should recognise the potential likelihood for greater audit risk when auditing companies with weak board and audit committee governance.

### Better auditing and fraud detection and the auditor's fraud risk assessment B24.30

The Audit and Assurance Faculty of ICAEW has published a concise, accessible and very readable guide to better auditing[26] which, where appropriate, references into the more officially authoritative Statements of Auditing Standards (SASs) of the Auditing Practices Board.

In the context of fraud and the audit, relevant Statements of Auditing Standards referred to in this booklet include the following.

| SAS 110 | Fraud and error. |
| SAS 240 (revised) | Quality control for audit work. |
| SAS 601 | Imposed limitation of audit scope. |
| SAS 620 | The auditors' right and duty to report to regulators in the financial sector. |

'Towards Better Auditing' has chapters on:

- efficiency;
- developing people;
- change management;
- fraud;
- business Risk Assessment;
- analytical procedures;
- evidencing audit work; and
- review.

Apart from the chapter on fraud the other chapters which most closely relate to fraud and the auditor are the business risk assessment and review chapters, the latter in part because reviewers of audit work who are not sufficiently familiar with the business are more likely to miss warning signs of fraud which are present.

This chapter puts fraud in context by drawing attention to the Association of British Insurers' estimates that the direct costs of fraud in the UK increased from £3 billion in 1985 to £10 billion in 1995 and that the direct cost of fraud in the UK had reached £16 billion by 1999; and by pointing out that internet fraud and theft of intellectual property are now compounding the problem. We look at e-fraud at **B24.49**. This chapter views fraud from the perspective of the auditor, and especially from the perspective of audit risk. It deals with the possibility of materially misstated accounts, with the requirements for auditors to report suspicions of fraud to a number of different regulatory authorities and with public expectations in respect of fraud detection by auditors.

At least, on the face of it, it is surprising that the chapter on 'business risk assessment' largely overlooks fraud as a risk to be assessed by the auditor. Perhaps that is defensible since the issue is dealt with in some detail in the separate chapter on 'fraud', and this latter chapter recommends that the auditor's fraud risk assessment should be undertaken separately from the auditor's general business risk assessment, as we touch on later.

## The auditor's business risk assessment           B24.31

As far as fraud is concerned, it is relevant that the business risk assessment chapter points out that, in recent years, auditors' understanding of risk has widened to include the business risks affecting their clients. Instead of using the accounts to identify the risks of transactions and balances being misstated, today's auditor is likely to start with the business itself, and seek to identify the likelihood of misstatement in the accounts arising from risks originating in the business. This chapter goes on to suggest that it is useful to consider the audit planning implications of business risks in two stages,- for the company as a whole and secondly for individual audit areas. The advice is that the auditor should address the questions below.

Has anything emerged from the business risk assessment to indicate the following.

- A high risk of fraud?

- Previously unidentified related parties?

- The existence of third parties who might seek to place reliance on the accounts (for example, the company is being sold)?

- Deficiencies in the accounting system?

We could see no other reference to fraud and the auditor in the chapter on business risk assessment. But clearly a business risk assessment approach to audit planning does allow fraud risk to be put as 'centre stage' in the audit process as is necessary.

The move away from audit planning approaches driven by a focus on 'audit risk' towards audit planning based on a 'business risk' approach represents an interesting development with significant potential to make the audit more effective in detecting frauds

**The nature of fraud** B24.32

The section in the fraud chapter entitled 'Towards better auditing' further sets the fraud scene by pointing out that most corporate frauds are the work of insiders and that fraudulent employees, managers and owner-managers either work alone, or collude with each other, or more usually with outsiders, to perpetrate and conceal fraud[27]. On the other hand, while the number of frauds perpetrated by employees and managers is much greater than the number of frauds perpetrated by owner-managers or directors, nevertheless the losses suffered as a result of fraud perpetrated by owner-managers or directors tend to be much greater than the losses suffered when employees are involved. Fraudulent financial reporting springs to mind here. Larger frauds are claimed to be more likely to be well-hidden, to be material to the accounts and therefore to represent a real risk to auditors.

**Audit strategy and approach to counter the fraud risk** B24.33

In essence, the advice in the chapter on fraud on maximising the chances that an auditor will detect fraud partly relates to having an audit firm-wide strategy and partly to having an audit approach – particularly at the planning stage of the audit. With respect to the former, the advice is that particular emphasis in assignment acceptance and continuance procedures should be placed on checks into management integrity and fraud risk, including:

- an audit approach or system that puts sufficient emphasis on how best to comply with the requirements of SAS 110 'Fraud and error';

- training that helps ensure engagement teams can recognise fraud indicators and know how to respond to them;

- development programmes that encourage staff to learn from experience and which encourage the right sceptical attitude in audit personnel at all levels, to guard against complacency;

- a remuneration system, or rewards, that give sufficient incentive to partners and staff to adopt a robust attitude and to maintain their scepticism when there is pressure from clients to do otherwise; and

- appropriate independent reviews that provide extra assurance that teams maintain their objectivity and respond effectively to indicators of fraud risk.

An implication here that concerns us is that the degree of risk of fraud may be a routine consideration that the auditor bears in mind when deciding whether to accept or continue with an audit assignment. This places the audit service on a par, by analogy, with insurance cover which may or may not be provided by insurance companies. Would not a more appropriate analogy be with the medical profession? Are not the prospective clients who are most sick, most in need of a physician? In any case, is it not the stakeholders, primarily the shareholders, who are the clients rather than the management team who may be fraudulent? Is the audit profession being driven by commercial considerations rather than by the service ideal which should be a hallmark of the professions; and, if so, is this appropriate? It seems to us that this is an area deserving of much more attention by the auditing profession.

The chapter gives practical ideas and points of focus for audit teams and individual auditors, including that they must:

- understand the nature of fraud;

- conduct audits with a mindset that understands the risk of fraud and admits to the real possibility of its existence; and

- engage in thorough audit planning; here the advice is that the fraud risk assessment should preferably be carried out, concluded on and documented separately to the assessment of other risks 'because the thought processes required are different'.

Of course, there must be dangers in compartmentalising different aspects of the auditor's risk assessment, as 'joined up thinking' is sometimes more likely to reveal the warning signs. While we see great merit in the auditor carrying out a fraud risk assessment, we think it is just a matter of time before it is standard practice to integrate this with the other aspects of the auditor's business risk assessment.

## Fraud risk assessment                                          B24.34

The advice is that the auditor's fraud risk assessment should take account of all the matters which were, or should have been, considered when deciding on acceptance or continuance of the audit appointment, and that:

'because of the need to take into account the firm's accumulated knowledge and experience of client management and the client's activities, it is best to involve the engagement partner [in the fraud risk assessment] in an appropriate way.'

Practical advice on fraud risk factors includes that there will be an increase in audit risk if the audit team is faced with delays in obtaining important information, or where an audit client involved in negotiations regarding the sale of a business, a flotation, or the raising of finance, is tempted to accuse the auditors of jeopardising the whole deal if the auditors insist on more time to verify a late adjustment.

The chapter summarises some of the most important motives, opportunities and warning signs of fraud (ie 'fraud risk factors'), as:

● the presence of a dominant individual at the head of the business;

● laissez-faire, cynical or aggressive attitudes in directors or senior management;

● a willingness to bend the rules as far as they will go in order to achieve a particular aim; and

● an inability or unwillingness to make a proper distinction between personal and business affairs.

In Box 1 we reproduce the more extensive Box of fraud risk factors from Appendix 1 of SAS 110 Fraud and error.

---

## Box 1

### Part 1

**Examples of conditions or events which may increase the risk of fraud or error occurring.**

**(Reproduced from Appendix 1 of SAS 110 Fraud and error.)**

*Examples of conditions or events which may increase the risk of either fraud or error, or in some cases both. This is not an exhaustive checklist of such conditions or events.*

1. **Previous experience or incidents which call into question the integrity or competence of management**

   □ Management dominated by one person (or a small group) and no effective oversight board or committee.

   □ Complex corporate structure where complexity does not seem to be warranted.

---

☐   High turnover rate of key accounting and financial personnel.

☐   Personnel (key or otherwise) not taking holidays.

☐   Significant and prolonged under-staffing of the accounting department.

☐   Frequent changes of legal advisors or auditors.

2.   Particular financial reporting pressures within an entity

☐   Industry volatility.

☐   Inadequate working capital due to declining profits or too rapid expansion.

☐   Deteriorating quality of earnings, for example increased risk taking with respect to credit sales, changes in business practice or selection of accounting policy alternatives that improve income.

☐   The entity needs a rising profit trend to support the market price of its shares due to a contemplated public offering, a takeover or other reason.

☐   Significant investment in an industry or product line noted for rapid change.

☐   Pressure on accounting personnel to complete financial statements in an unreasonably short period of time.

☐   Dominant owner-management.

☐   Performance-based remuneration.

# Box 2

## Part 2

**3.   Weaknesses in the design and operation of the accounting and internal controls system.**

☐   A weak control environment within the entity.

☐   Systems that, in their design, are inadequate to give reasonable assurance of preventing or detecting error of fraud.

☐   Inadequate segregation of responsibilities in relation to functions involving the handling, recording or controlling of the entity's assets.

☐   Indications that internal financial information is unreliable.

☐   Evidence that internal controls have been overridden by management.

☐ Ineffective monitoring of the operation of systems which allows control overrides, breakdowns or weakness to continue without proper corrective action.

☐ Continuing failure to correct major weakness in internal control where such corrections are practical and cost effective.

4. Unusual transactions

☐ Unusual transactions, especially near the year end, that have a significant effect on earnings.

☐ Complex transactions or accounting treatments.

☐ Unusual transactions with related parties.

☐ Payments for services (for example to lawyers, consultants or agents) that appear excessive in relation to the services provided.

5. Problems in obtaining sufficient appropriate audit evidence

☐ Inadequate records, for example incomplete files, excessive adjustments to accounting records, transactions not recorded in accordance with normal procedures and out-of-balance control accounts.

☐ Inadequate documentation of transactions, such as lack of proper authorisation, supporting documents not available and alteration to documents (any of these documentation problems assume greater significance when they relate to large or unusual transactions).

☐ An excessive number of differences between accounting records and third party confirmations, conflicting audit evidence and unexplainable changes in operating ratios.

☐ Evasive, delayed or unreasonable responses by management to audit inquiries.

☐ Inappropriate attitude of management to the conduct of the audit — e.g. time pressure, scope limitation and other constraints.

6. Some factors unique to an information systems environment which relate to the conditions and events described above

☐ Inability to extract information from computer files due to lack of, or non-current, documentation of record contents or programs.

☐ Large numbers of program changes that are not documented, approved and tested.

☐ Inadequate overall balancing of computer transactions and data bases to the financial accounts.

The 'fraud' chapter we are reviewing here points out that the risk of fraud needs to be considered by the auditor separately at three levels; the entity level, the account balance level, and at the transaction level.

It is undoubtedly good advice that the auditor should 'think hard about whether exceptions are intentional' and that 'there is also a lot to be said for exceptions being discussed between the audit team' so that connections can be made and the possibility avoided of 'rationalising' or 'neutralising' indicators of fraud. The chapter counsels the need for a right balance between getting on with the audit and exercising appropriate professional scepticism, resisting easy acceptance of glib and plausible explanations. It is perceptive too to point out that …

> 'there is a risk that auditors assume that unless there are obvious indicators of potential fraud at the planning stage, then no further work is necessary and [the auditors] mentally dismiss the possibility of fraud.'

# Tell-tale signs of fraud                                    B24.35

It is a clichéd truism that business depends on trust, but a prudent interpretation of one aspect of this contention is that we should take abundant trouble to recruit trustworthy staff and business associates, and also abundant trouble to ensure that they then serve in a trustworthy way. We can say that while we must take infinite pains to recruit trustworthy people and to emphasise that our business depends upon their trustworthiness, nevertheless we should also ensure that we do not trust them!

This is as much in their interests as it is in the interests of the business. If we develop systems that prevent staff from conducting themselves in untrustworthy way, then the finger of suspicion will not point in their direction. If our controls could confirm the honesty of their conduct, members of staff would be exonerated more or less automatically. Nobody benefits from a suggestion of personal dishonesty.

One can sympathise with the catering manager, the contracts manager or the purchasing officer who is so routinely suspected of dishonesty because it has not been possible to design systems which prevent backhanders being made to these people by suppliers, or which detect that these have been made. It would be much better for staff if it were possible to devise systems which prevented or detected this type of fraud. Indeed, in practice there are many measures we can take to reduce the likelihood that such fraud will occur, but usually we cannot entirely eliminate the risk.

One practical outworking of a policy of ensuring that our security and control do not depend excessively upon assumed trustworthiness of staff, is to foster a climate of mutual suspicion. Clearly, this must not be taken out of proportion, but there is much that can be done before that becomes a risk.

Business policy statements have an important place in fraud containment. Amongst other things, they can define an employee's responsibility in the case of suspected fraud. The progressive stance here is that employees should be charged with a duty, not merely a right, to report suspected wrongdoing, even if they are merely bystanding observers and not otherwise personally involved. The ways in which suspected wrongdoing should be reported, and then dealt with, also need to be clearly worked out and defined.

We can go a step or two further by encouraging staff to look for explanations of behaviour which could amount to tell-tale signs of wrongdoing, rather than ignoring these possible indicators. Of course, there will often be innocent explanations for apparently errant behaviour. But even innocent explanations may need to be known about by a caring, supportive employer.

The following are some of the typical tell-tale signs of fraud.

## Altered attitudes                                        B24.36

It is hard to generalise as to what these may be. It could be a change in the level of the individual's commitment to the business. This may be an apparently enhanced level of commitment which may either be a smokescreen for untrustworthy conduct in progress, or an excuse for the extra level of involvement which is needed, perhaps out of usual working hours, to perpetrate and conceal the fraud.

Or, it may be a newly impaired level of commitment due to disillusionment with the employer. This sort of disillusionment can result from personal exploitation by the employer, whether actual or merely perceived; or it could be the result of some form of harassment. It could be a form of irrational self-justification for the fraudulent conduct which has been triggered perhaps by circumstances external to the business, thereby making it easier for the dishonest employer to square his or her conduct with their conscience.

Sometimes the tell-tale sign of a changed attitude may necessarily be a specific part of the process of concealing the fraud, as for example, with the previously prudent cashier who became a devotee of the betting shop.

## Extravagant lifestyle                                    B24.37

The employee who apparently lives beyond his or her means may have something to hide. Generally, explanations will be offered, such as betting winnings, inheritance, the wealth of a partner and so on. We take these at face value at our peril.

The author recalls one blatant case where a clerk dressed more smartly, acquired a toupee and an expensive partner, moved to a better home and even acquired the same model of car as the directors had. Amazingly, nobody thought it their business to query or confirm the clerk's explanations for this newly extravagant lifestyle, nor the clerk's decision to stay in that modestly remunerated job.

## Questionable friendships  B24.38

A close friendship is questionable if it is with a contractor or another party with whom the member of staff routinely, or even just occasionally, represents the business. It is important that these friendships are not secretive. The finger of suspicion will reasonably start pointing if the employee is not completely open about these relationships, so that management can ensue that no excessive risks to the business ensue.

Habitually mixing with people known or suspected of having criminal connections will also need to be explained, as will known friendships which appear to be strikingly unusual for a person in the employee's position.

## Self-contained behaviour  B24.39

Secretiveness can be a form of aid to concealment of fraud. Excessively self-contained behaviour can also be indicative of personal values and orientations which could indicate a compromised loyalty to the business. Excessively self-contained behaviour can point to personal circumstances or personality qualities which should be causes of concern. For instance, the employee who is preoccupied with a personal problem, such as an unsharable financial need, may seek to alleviate the problem deceitfully at the business's expense. Or the person with a personality under strain may be at risk of behaving irrationally in a dishonest way. Key positions of trust are best filled by employees of robust temperaments, all other things being equal.

## Excessive private phone calls and internet access  B24.40

Excessive private phone calls during working hours should be addressed as a specific cause of concern by a supervisor. Some businesses have policies to regulate private phone calls; others provide pay phones for employees to use for private calls; most leave it to the discretion of supervisors to ensure that the opportunity to make private calls is not abused by employees. Eaves-dropping on an employee's private calls is now regarded as a breach of the employee's rights to privacy, though it can be acceptable where it is required for business monitoring and control purposes, so long as employees know about it.

While excessive making of private calls may be a fraud issue in itself, it may also point to the on-going conduct of another more serious fraud, such as the running of a private business during work time. Certainly, it needs to be explained and understood.

Again, business policies vary with respect to internet access during working hours and via business IT equipment. Some businesses encourage it, whether or not the access is work-related, on the grounds that they wish their staff to become internet-literate for today's e-commerce world. Other businesses outlaw personal internet access via the businesses' IT systems: their main concern is usually not so much a matter of the line access costs but the cost of staff time consumed in this way during working hours. Web-based chat lines can be particularly addictive for some staff.

There is also the matter of staff access to undesirable websites which can be a form of harassment for other staff as well as tainting the business ethically for their permissive or negligent attitude to such access.

Similar challenges apply to personal internet access as to the making of private phone calls. We would certainly recommend that a business should have a specific internet access policy rather than leaving it to the discretion of supervisors to determine what is acceptable. Software can bar access to websites which are regarded as not permissible and can record attempts to visit those sites for management review.

## Irregular private life                                          B24.41

As with altered attitudes, an irregular private life could be suggestive of behaviour associated with the perpetration or concealment of fraud, or with the difficulty of living a personal life when one's nearest and dearest are aware or suspicious of the person's wrongdoing. So an irregular private life could be an effect of dishonest conduct at work. It could also be a cause of it; by placing the individual under mental or financial strain so that they may be more inclined to behave dishonestly.

Businesses need to have a good record of helping staff resolve their personal difficulties. Some staff will then be less likely to contemplate fraudulent ideas. And the business will be in a better position to know where are the fraud risks.

## Poor job performance                                           B24.42

Preoccupation with the perpetration and concealment of fraud can divert an employee from the demands of the job, leading to observable poor work performance. It may be a matter of the time consuming nature of the fraud. Or it may be a matter of the worry that the fraud is causing the perpetrator, so that he or she is diverted from focussing on the work at hand. Poor performance may also be indicative of fraud in the sense that targets are not met due to the diversion of company income for personal gain, or to the diversion of personal expenses so that they are accounted for as business operating costs.

## Appearance of being under pressure on the job                  B24.43

This tell-tale sign overlaps considerably with 'poor job performance' as well as with 'unclear explanations for exceptions' (see **B24.44**). Creating an aura or a reality of indispensability, drive and energy can be a smokescreen for ongoing fraud or even a necessary prerequisite for its perpetration or concealment. Undertaking the fraud on top of performing one's normal duties will undoubtedly add to the pressure the individual experiences and projects.

Appearance of excessive pressure on the job needs to be attended to by management, even apart from any concerns that it may be indicative of fraud: excessive pressure is counterproductive to efficient and effective operations. Excessive pressure is often caused by insensitive, perhaps autocratic top management imposing unrealistic targets upon staff: in itself this creates a fraud risk as it can lead to staff alienation and compromised levels of staff loyalty. It can also lead to creative accounting.

## Unclear explanation for exceptions B24.44

Auditors in particular quickly learn that when they do not understand an explanation it just may be because the explanation is not genuine. Independent confirmation of implausible explanations will often be needed. Not appearing to have time to provide satisfactory explanations for exceptions and showing irritation at being approached for explanations can be conscious tactics by the defrauder to put enquirers off the scent.

## Conclusions B24.45

Of course, nobody is saying that these tell-tale signs are entirely reliable signposts of dishonest conduct, or even of the risk of dishonest conduct developing in the future. But they should not be overlooked. As we have indicated, apart from the possibility of fraud, they often need to be followed up for reasons of operational efficiency and effectiveness as well as of good human resource management.

In today's business culture all members of staff have empowered roles to play 'outside their narrow box'. We have all known examples of where observed, possible wrongdoing has not been reported. In the empowered business culture no member of staff should be able to claim that it is 'not my business'. In practical terms the challenge may be that the observer has the merest suspicion but no hard evidence of wrongdoing and the concern is that the observed conduct may be entirely innocent. Good whistleblowing policies can come into play here.

Then again, fraud may occur with no revealing tell-tale signs of fraud. Nevertheless, many frauds are discovered by accident, often through the carelessness of the defrauder and the vigilance of observers. The carelessness of the defrauder often leaves behind a trail of highly visible tell-tale signs, which it is wise to formally try to capture.

# Areas vulnerable to fraud B24.46

It has been shown that 75 per cent of frauds involving theft also involve negotiable instruments of which, of course, cash is an obvious example. The defrauder is attracted to the opportunity which negotiable instruments provide to convert the theft into value of a different form, so making traceability more difficult. In principle, the more liquid (convertible) the commodity, the more potentially attractive it becomes to a defrauder and the tighter the controls therefore need to be. Forged inputs are often the means by which frauds are set up, and so inputs to cash payment routines need to be particularly closely controlled and monitored.

Most frauds involving theft also involve personal account manipulation. There are a number of different sorts of personal accounts which may offer fraud potential.

- An account of an employee. This may be an account of an employee who is a customer or a supplier of the business that employs him or her. Every employee has at least one account with the employer; their payroll account.

- A fictitious or unauthorised account. Pay particular attention to the risk that a genuine account which should be closed, is in fact modified so that it can be used for fraudulent purposes. An example would be the payroll account of an employee who leaves which is not removed or terminated from the computer. An allied risk is the new employee who declines to start employment but whose payroll record has already been set up.

- An account of an unwitting customer or supplier, or of a number of customers or suppliers. The teeming and lading fraud is an example of this. Another example would be the application of a balance on an apparently dormant account for fraudulent purposes, perhaps with the intention of using part of the proceeds of fraudulent activity to replenish the dormant account before anyone notices that it has been raided.

- Account of outside accomplice. For instance, a genuine account can be set up to be used by an inside employee as a channel to divert funds which are then withdrawn by the outside accomplice.

- Another example is the proper opening of a new customer account with a low credit limit. The customer manages the account immaculately and then applies for a larger credit limit which is granted on the strength of the customer's track record. The customer then quickly runs up debts for the full credit amount and absconds.

- Account of employer of outside accomplice. An example would be the use of this account to charge for goods or services enjoyed by the accomplices who, through their respective employments, may be in a position to initiate the accounting entries and approvals involved.

Other areas vulnerable to fraud include purchasing, catering, contracts. These come in various forms and are particularly pernicious since it is not possible by means of internal controls and internal checks to eliminate the possibility of backhanders being offered by suppliers or their agents to the employees with whom they deal.

Sales frauds are of course another problem area. It may be a matter of short deliveries, made possible by a failure to check at the point of delivery. Or it may be a matter of sales ledger frauds of which there are several types, including:

- unauthorised file or program amendment;

- low price for accomplice;

- altered credit limits;

- induced rejection and resubmission after false alteration;

- improper write-offs; and

- teeming and lading.

## Information which has been the object of fraud          B24.47

It is unlikely that there is any information in possession of a business which would not be of interest and value to outsiders who do not have a right of access to it. So all information is potentially vulnerable to fraud. The box gives a not exhaustive summary of some of the different sorts of business information which are known to have been the object of frauds.

The *Data Protection Act 1998* forces standards of conduct and security over personal data which businesses hold. It may be wise for a business to apply equivalent standards to all the data the business holds, whether it is personal data or not. First, this will ensure that no personal data is overlooked and not subjected to the regime which should apply to it. Secondly, all corporate data will benefit from the application of the data protection principles.

### Information which has been the object of fraud          B24.48

Payroll, trade secrets, patent applications, market research, sales analyses, complaints letters, forecasts, financial data, accounts, new products, pricing, tenders, customers, shareholders, proprietary programs, other software, engineering data, manuals and policies.

# E-fraud          B24.49

' ... in the e-world everything changes fast so the opportunities for fraud change at least as fast. ... The remoteness of many of the fraudsters ... may reduce the perceived chances of being caught. If it is true that about 5% of e-transactions are fraudulent, how will an organisation that does not know its customers make any money on increasingly tight margins? ... we have often seen a possibly unwitting increase in the risk appetite.'

A few years ago we noted that an increasing proportion of computer-based frauds, and then an increasing proportion of those frauds were related to real-time systems. On reflection, this was not surprising as, first, most business systems had become computer-based and, secondly, most computer systems had become online and real-time.

Now we are experiencing the rise and rise of e-fraud which is a reflection of the increasing rôle of e-commerce in business today. Even if e-fraud is unsurprising, this does not allow us to dismiss e-fraud as of no consequence.

# E-fraud facilitators
B24.50

It is of course true that many traditional types of fraud are now being given a new lease of life by the opportunities that the internet affords. Advance fee frauds are nothing new, but pose an extra risk in e-commerce. Likewise, the so-called 'pump and dump equity schemes' which utilise internet chat lines to deliberately talk up share prices, are a novel manifestation of what is in essence a traditional fraud. Recently, fictitious, misleading company announcements on websites have had dramatic impact on their share prices. These frauds have been all too successful on account of:

- the new remoteness of many customers and suppliers;

- the undue plausibility afforded to web-based information;

- the speed with which business is conducted over the internet, encouraging a less thorough approach to client authentication; due diligence of customers and suppliers is still important;

- the relative difficulty of seeking subsequent redress for breach of terms negotiated by e-mail.

The distinctive characteristics of e-commerce need to be understood as they provide the new means for perpetrating often traditional frauds in highly distinctive ways. New approaches to countering e-fraud are therefore necessary.

## E-fraud countermeasures
B24.51

Generally, the key to effective countermeasures is to harness the technology which is the basis of contemporary commercial systems so as to apply the same technology in the service of control and security. For instance:

- on-line and real time data processing needs online, real time auditing responses;

- e-commerce credit card transactions require online authentication by Worldpay, Europay or similar;

- website firewalls are essential; and

- embedded programming designed to detect fraudulent transactions is an important way ahead and so on.

The breakneck speed with which dotcom companies have been set up has often meant that dotcom companies and companies with e-business operations have neglected to put in place an appropriate control framework. Control frameworks tend to be established over time and 'time' is what has been in short supply. When there is major change, effective controls are even more important. For instance, internal audit is a comparative rarity in dotcom companies, but is vitally important:

> 'from the point of view of the internal auditor – as an expert in risk management – the issues are to ensure that the organisation is performing the fundamentals correctly and to facilitate the discussion of risk management with the right people.'

## E-fraud costs and risks                                         B24.52

One estimate is that internet fraud cost UK banks and retailers an estimated $15million in 2000. We believe this is probably a significant underestimate. Retail Decisions has concluded that fraud on the internet is running at 5–10 per cent of all internet credit card transactions. Experian, the credit and business information company, has claimed that while most websites currently report less than 1 per cent of fraudulent transactions, in some cases these losses are as high as 40 per cent.

The Financial Times reported that credit card fraud in general now costs $(US) 4 billion *per annum.* worldwide, or $2 per credit card issued, rising annually by one-third. An increasing proportion of credit card fraud will migrate to become e-fraud as e-commerce becomes more ubiquitous and as banks introduce security measures which promise to be quite effective in combatting fraud in traditional credit card transactions. Europay recently estimated that 6 per cent of credit card fraud was already internet-based in 2000, and that this type of fraud is rapidly becoming more common. Richard Fiddis, chief operating officer of Experian, has put it simply, like this:

> 'the internet is becoming the first choice for thieves.'

An issue of concern is the extent to which the potential of e-fraud is attracting both criminal elements as well as those with a record of sharp business practice. Kroll Associates, on the basis of their usual investigations of the backgrounds of executives and directors, has found that 39 per cent of dotcom executives and directors have 'unsavoury backgrounds', compared to a norm of about 10 per cent. Pre-employment screening standards should not be compromised; but they are of course no antidote to the risk of fraud in e-commerce operations which are being set up by untrustworthy people.

Apart from the senior executives and directors of dotcom companies, most of the other dotcom employees are too young to have much of a background either way, whether straight or unsavoury. So, we have a new sector staffed by young, inexperienced technical people balanced by older more experienced people at senior levels said to be disproportionately skewed towards being untrustworthy, compared to business in general. This is a recipe for fraud. It also augers badly for the future as young, inexperienced, high-flying dotcom personnel serve their business apprenticeships under less trustworthy management teams.

The crash in dotcom stocks is a further warning sign: the field of business history is littered with examples of management teams which have become engaged in fraud (especially, but not exclusively, fraudulent financial reporting) when the tide has turned against them and it is becoming harder to report results up to market expectations. The temptations are particularly acute in highly geared companies.

The breathtaking pace of the e-business revolution has often meant that basic controls, especially over the hiring of staff at all levels, have been overlooked:

'the whole effort has been to move at internet speed, which has meant not stopping to do careful checks on employees, or putting in place internal auditing or security.'

At present, the most costly type of internet fraud for banks is card theft and misuse. It is one manifestation of electronic impersonation (or 'identify theft') and is achieved in a variety of ways.

The fraud risks of traditional face-to-face credit card usage are well known. In New York city recently, some department store employees were caught illegally swiping customer credit cards into hand-held 'scanners'. The scanners captured the personal information from the 'strip' and this information was then illegally used to create fraudulent credit cards. A solution to this would be for the customer to request to swipe the card personally, but few customers are likely to insist on this on account of the embarrassment factor and also because most of the risk to customers is generally covered by the bank and the retailer. The initiative would need to be taken by the retailer to insist that customers swiped their cards personally.

Similar precautions are not available to reduce the risk of fraud in e-commerce credit card transactions, but there are promising alternative developments. The Secure Electronic Transaction (SET) scheme uses digital signatures to authenticate the identities of both cardholder and electronic retailer. Last December Egg became the first bank in Europe to sign up to this new Visa scheme. Visa, who claim to back over 50 per cent of online transactions, say they will oblige member banks to adopt the SET standard by October 2001 with Mastercard and Europay expected to follow suit.

In July 2000, the Electronic Signatures in Global and National Commerce Act became law in the US. It gives digital signatures the same legal standing as conventional ink-on-paper ones, and is seen as an essential step in the evolution of the internet.

www.FraudIndex.com: a weekly e-newsletter about fraud, with solutions to fraud scams and schemes making the news.

# Digital analysis tests and 'Benford's Law'   B24.54

'In any large database of naturally occurring numerical information, such as a list of cities ranked by population or islands ranked by surface area, the number "one" will probably be the first digit of 30.1 per cent of the database's numbers (1, 15, 199, 1003, and so on). A "two" will probably occur in 17.6 per cent of the numbers (2, 27, 200 and so on); and the probability reduces to 4.6 per cent for a "nine" appearing as the first digit.'

'Digital analysis is being used by listed companies, large private companies, professional firms and government agencies in the US and Europe – and by one of the world's biggest accounting firms.'

*(Mark Nigrini)*

Benford was a physicist working for General Electric when he discovered this 'first-digit phenomenon' in 1938. But as far back as 1881 one Simon Newcomb wrote a note to the American Journal of Mathematics pointing out that he had noticed that early pages of books of logarithms were more grubby than later pages, undoubtedly due to their more frequent use. More recently, Mark Nigrini showed how it could be applied to detecting fraud in his PhD thesis published in 1992. He is author and publisher of 'Digital analysis tests and statistics'.

Benford's Law holds because 'large things are made up of lots of little things', to quote Nigrini. For instance, there are thousands of small islands but only a few continents; thousands of tributaries but fewer rivers. Looked at another way, the 'gap' between 'one' and 'two' is greater than the gap between 'eight' and 'nine' in that, for instance, growing a business from a turnover of £1 million to a turnover of £2 million entails doubling its size, which is not the case with the incremental growth from £8 million to £9 million.

The law applies most faithfully when there is no natural limit to what is being measured, as there is with, for instance, the height or weight of people. It may not apply if numbers are, quite legitimately, rounded up or down. In business it can be expected to apply, for instance, to stock market prices, sales figures, payments, census data, ragbags of figures extracted from documents, declared income, suspicious data in clinical trails, suspicious data in quality assurance test results, data in laboratory notebooks, etc. Sometimes it may be possible to apply Benford's Law to optimising the use of space in warehouses, or storage space in computer systems.

Logic exists within ACL (Audit Command Language) to check quickly a large database for conformity to Benford's Law. ACL is one of the two leading generalised auditing packages, the other being IDEA (Interactive Data Extraction and Analysis). One group of auditors who are pursuing this approach is the North Yorkshire Audit Partnership based at Scarborough Borough Council where James Ingham is the audit manager involved. The technique is quite widely used, for instance within Proctor & Gambler, Colgate-Palmolive and American Airlines. In the US, the Institute of Internal Auditors Inc. now runs training courses on applying Benford's Law in fraud investigations, and have claimed it to be the biggest advance in the field for years.

References and contact details on Benford's Law:

- ACL Services Ltd, 575 Richards Street, Vancouver BC, V6B 2Z5, Canada (tel: +1 604 669 4225; www.acl.com).

- Robert Matthews (10 July 1999): 'The Power of One' (New Scientist).

- Mark Nigrini: mark_nigrini@email.msn.com. His publication on 'Digital Analysis Tests and Statistics'. He is professor of accountancy at Southern Methodist University, Dallas.

- James Ingham: jringham@ukonline.co.uk who is using the technique in audit contexts.

- Eric Weisstein: 'Treasure Troves of Science.'

# Balancing 'control by segregation' with 'control by supervision' B24.55

In the context of fraud prevention and fraud detection, it is helpful to consider that satisfactory control arrangements are likely to comprise an appropriate amalgam of different forms of what we may call 'segregation' (or 'separation') on the one hand, and different forms of 'supervision' on the other hand. If effective control cannot be achieved by taking advantage of opportunities for segregation, then more resort must be made to supervisory controls. Usually both will be needed, depending upon the circumstances.

Fraud is, in one sense, a form of breakdown in the system of control, a deliberate form of avoidable error and loss. Segregation and supervision controls will bear down upon accidental breakdowns in the system as well as fraudulent ones.

Segregation controls have the advantage that they are often, but not always, *preventative* rather than *detective* in nature, they prevent or deter frauds from occurring rather more than detecting them after they have occurred. Supervisory controls are preventative and detective in nature; preventative because the fact of supervision encourages staff to undertake their duties responsibly; detective because the act of supervision should detect errant performance by staff. Of course, supervision should be timely so that detection occurs before it is too late to achieve rectification.

Segregation controls may not cost anything to administer, it may be just a matter of organising how tasks are performed so that segregation controls are standard aspects of working practices. So it is not necessarily true that control has to be costly. Certainly the absence of control is likely to be more costly. It is too simplistic to argue that internal control must be cost effective; it is often impossible to quantify the costs and benefits of control; it is often impossible to anticipate the damage that may ensue from a breakdown in internal control. Effective control in some contexts, such as within the nuclear industry, has to be a *sine qua non* almost regardless of what it costs.

While segregation controls may not be costly, on the other hand supervisory controls invariably entail an overhead as they represent an extra task (or tasks) to be performed. They also have the disadvantage of being no more effective that the diligence of those entrusted to undertake the supervision. Too often 'delegation' is interpreted as 'abdication' and staff are just left to get on with things in an unsupervised way. Supervision entails conscious, defined activity. While authority can be delegated – to staff who therefore acquire their own responsibilities, it is sound to consider that responsibility is never delegated, only shared. So a failure by a junior member of staff to whom authority has been delegated is a failure of more senior staff who retain the overall responsibility even though the execution of the task has been delegated. It should rarely be regarded as acceptable for senior staff to attempt to avoid responsibility for an operational failure on the grounds that they are responsible for 'policy' not 'operations'.

Segregation and supervision controls may depend upon people to execute them, or they may be incorporated into IT systems. One person's work may be reconciled to another person's work manually or by using IT. Two segregated IT systems may produce output which is reconciled by a third IT system, or manually. Often segregation and supervisory controls are part IT-based and part people-based. For instance software may produce an exception report which must be followed-up by a supervisor.

Where resort has to be made to supervision to achieve control, it is usually necessary to ensure that the supervisory function has a sufficient degree of independence from the execution of the task being supervised.

Applying segregation and supervision approaches to the achievement of control can assist in the achievement of financial, operational and compliance control objectives. Financial control is the control over the reliability of financial information used within the business and for publication. Operational control is to do with assurance that operations are executed efficiently and effectively. Compliance control objectives are to do with ensuring adherence to regulations and laws.

In Table 1 we provide a classification of different available forms of segregation, and we offer a few further words of explanation here:

## Segregation of duties                                             B24.56

Sometimes our 'segregation of operations' (see **B24.58**) is alternatively termed 'segregation of duties'. Here, by 'segregation of duties' we mean that some very sensitive tasks will be better controlled if they are shared between more than one person, so that one person acts as an observer of, and a semi-automatic check over, the work of the other person. This also has the benefit of the business avoiding becoming excessively dependent upon one key member of staff. The 'downside' of this sort of control is that the business is entrusting control sensitive knowledge to a wider spread of staff.

### Segregation of fundamental responsibilities                      B24.57

Control will be improved if certain original operations are segregated from authorisation and both of these should be segregated from accounting. We call this a matter of making sure that fundamental responsibilities are segregated. Some of these original operations will be custodial in nature, such as the cashier function which keeps custody over cash, or the storekeeper who is custodian of stores. Other original operations are not custodial, for instance 'purchasing'. Control will be strengthened, for instance, if the person who authorises a purchase is different from the person who places the purchase order with the supplier, and both of these people should have nothing to do with accounting in the books of account for any aspect of the purchase. If this fundamental segregation is not followed, control will be weaker unless compensated by other appropriate segregation or supervision controls. One of the most frequent breaches of this segregation control is where managers have the authority to incur expenditure up to certain limits, so long as it is within their budget, without recourse to a purchasing officer to place the purchase with a supplier.

### Segregation of operations                                        B24.58

Some other operations are incompatible with each other in the sense that they should not be undertaken by the same person or section. For instance, it is widely held that control is improved if selling is segregated from credit control; or if IT systems development is segregated from IT operations. If this is not done, then supervisory controls will need to be relied upon more. For instance, one company allows sales staff to flex the levels of credit advanced to customers in order to maximise sales and because of the sales staff's local knowledge of their clients. But to compensate for the control weakness thereby created, the credit decisions of the sales staff are reviewed regularly (ie 'supervised') by a credit committee. Many companies have risk committees which review the levels of risk being taken by operational management.

### Segregation of staff                                             B24.59

This means of control refers to the need to ensure that the control effect of segregating operations is not negated by the reality of the situation. For instance, do staff engaged in segregated operations inappropriately share the same office, the same telephone or the same filing cabinet or computer, or inappropriately overhear what is happening in another operation which should be segregated from their work? Does one member of staff substitute for another during the latter's absence, and thereby engage in a task incompatible with their main operational tasks? Does one member of staff have a special personal relationship with another member of staff who is mainly engaged in other operations which should be segregated? And so on. It is not always possible to avoid these sorts of control weaknesses, but they should be identified and compensated for, by other segregation controls or by supervision, or both.

**Segregation of data**                                                            **B24.60**

Centralised databases require software walls to be built to restrict who is able to add, change, delete or merely use each item of data. This applies within a business and also to prevent hacking from outside, for which firewalls are important. Within a business it is necessary to define at the design stage of a database who needs the authority to add, change, delete or use each item of data to be held on the database and then to design the controls of the system to achieve these restrictions. Principally, control is achieved via a secure system of password access which restricts the access that individuals have to computer programs and to parts of the corporate database. Protocols should restrict the access of computer program modules to those parts of the database which those program modules should be expected to need to access, and should also restrict what activity the program modules can engage in with respect to the parts of the database which they are authorised to access. Individual computers on a network can be restricted to which computer programs on the network they can use, so, for instance, a computer in the payroll department would be barred from accessing computer-based customer records.

**Segregation of bookkeeping steps**                                               **B24.61**

Control will be improved if certain bookkeeping steps are segregated from other bookkeeping steps. An example might be the posting of a credit from the posting of a debit on a personal account.

PC-based accounting systems often make the segregation of bookkeeping steps a matter which is honoured more in the breach than in the observance. Where this is the case, businesses need to be aware of the risks they are running and to endeavour to compensate through the application of alternative segregation and supervisory controls.

**Segregation of data entry**                                                      **B24.62**

This is similar to segregating bookkeeping steps, but applicable to an IT environment.

For instance, an example might be the posting of an original entry from the posting of a correcting entry. It has been shown that many IT frauds involve the submission of fraudulent input data and that this fraudulent data is often incorporated into input data which has earlier been rejected as invalid and which is then 'corrected' for resubmission in a fraudulent way. Many businesses have tighter controls over the initial generation and submission of input data than over the correction and resubmission of input data which had earlier been rejected.

Sometimes a deliberate but innocent-looking error in input data can induce its rejection in order to facilitate its fraudulent alteration prior to resubmission. The risk of this can be avoided if the posting of an original entry is segregated from the posting of a corrected entry of that type. This also serves as a check on the quality of work of the staff who generated this data in the first place.

### 'Segregation' of authority to commit the business                B24.63

If authority to commit the business is vested in a sole individual, control will not be so strong as if it is dual authority (vested in two people). Control may be stronger still if authority to commit is vested in one person but has to be reviewed *ex post* by a supervisor or an independent person. Where authority to commit is vested in a committee it is likely to be stronger still. The best controlled situation is where nobody has authority to commit the business!

Applying the appropriate means to commit the business is not enough on its own to achieve effective control. What is also needed are established and applied authority limits coupled to the appropriate means of authority to commit the business.

### 'Segregation' of time                B24.64

Intelligent use of time, especially by building in considered delays, can improve control. For instance, it may be satisfactory to delay delivery of goods or services until a cheque has cleared. Computer terminal 'log off after time out' is another example. Times locks on safes or on access to other secure areas is yet another example. Barring client computers from accessing a server outside anticipated working hours may assist in preventing unauthorised activity on a computer network, and so on.

Rotating duties deters fraud if it is known to be company policy, as it makes it more likely that it will be detected. Closely related to this is a policy of transferring supervisors and managers between operating units every two or three years, where feasible.

Where staff work in pairs, as for instance in some delivery contexts, periodic changes in the pairing can be expected to enhance control as it reduces the risk of collusion occurring or continuing.

It is notable that many frauds come to light when the defrauding employee is absent, making the point that it is wise to insist that employees take at least one holiday of two weeks' duration each year. While they are away, their duties should be undertaken by a substitute. We should be wary of the employee who always comes in during their annual vacation on the pretext that they are indispensable, or 'just to check up that everything is okay'.

## Segregation of knowledge                                    B24.65

As a last resort, restricting knowledge on 'a need to know basis' will reduce the number of people who are informed about the control weaknesses within our systems, and thus who potentially are able to exploit those weaknesses. This may be both necessary and acceptable if we know that our systems in certain respects are inherently vulnerable to dishonesty in ways that cannot be rectified easily or at all, or at least have not been rectified.

But restricting knowledge often has unacceptable dysfunctional effects, and should therefore be regarded as a last resort when other forms of satisfactory control are not available. One dysfunctional effect is that staff are less able to use their initiative if they are restricted in what they know and understand. Another is the de-motivational impact.

## Segregation of 'operation' from 'review'                   B24.66

The monitoring (review) of control is an essential part of internal control, and needs to be done objectively. Independence of review from operations (as with a properly set up internal audit function) facilitates the achievement of this. Internal auditors cannot review with sufficient objectivity the operation of tasks which fall within their own remit to execute. One of the insidious mistakes that management often makes is to entrust to internal audit the execution of particularly control sensitive tasks, on the basis that internal auditors may be regarded, not always correctly, as trustworthy and as having sufficient independence to be able to conduct those important control-sensitive tasks objectively. This is counter-productive as it deprives those tasks from being audited effectively by internal audit.

The test to apply is whether internal audit is charged with the responsibility to execute anything which needs to be done for the business to function satisfactorily on a routine basis. if such is the case then, by definition, internal audit has responsibility for a task which is incompatible with its audit role. This would also be counter-productive as it would dilute management's own sense of responsibility for administering key controls, on the basis that they could leave it to the internal auditors, which of course they cannot safely do.

## Postscript on segregation                                  B24.67

Empowerment, downsizing and delayering have all made inroads into the traditional approaches to control set out in this article. Businesses today are more willing to take risks with control often with calamitous results in pursuit of enhanced performance. They do not see it as a matter of taking undue risks: they rationalise their approach as being a matter of establishing a control regime which is risk-based. The challenge is to make a realistic assessment of risk, and not to use the risk assessment as a pretext for cutting the investment in control to unacceptable levels.

**Table 1**                                                               **B24.68**

**Control by segregation (ie 'separation')**

|   | Type of segregation | Comments | Examples |
|---|---|---|---|
| 1. | **Duties** | Ensuring that control sensitive tasks are shared by two people who act as a cross check on each other, and excessive dependence on one member of staff is avoided. | Issuance of new passwords or; database administration; or credit control. |
| 2. | **Fundamental responsibilities** | Originating operations *from* authorisation of acquisition or use *from* accounting. | Cashier function *from* authorising use or replenishment of cash *from* accounting for cash; or storekeeping *from* authorising use; or replenishment of stores *from* accounting for cash; or (eg) purchasing *from* accounting *from* authorisation. |
| 3. | **Operations** | Separating out organisationally the execution of other incompatible activities which are incompatible with each other from a control perspective. | Sales *from* credit control; or IT programming *from* IT operations; etc. |
| 4. | **Staff** | Making sure that the impact of segregating 'fundamental responsibilities' and 'operations' is not invalidated by staffing arrangements. | For instance when staff engaged on segregated operations share the same office/phone/filing cabinet/computer; or staff are substituted by others who are usually engaged on segregated activities; or staff are transferred to segregated tasks. |

*Table 1*  **B24.68**

|    | Type of segregation | Comments | Examples |
|----|---------------------|----------|----------|
| 5. | **Data** | Centralised databases require electronic walls between different parts of the corporate database to prevent unauthorised access by staff and outsiders which might violate other segregation controls. | No staff should be able to access their payroll record. |
| 6. | **Bookkeeping** | Internal control will be improved by segregating certain bookkeeping operations. | Posting of debits *from* posting of credits on personal accounts. |
| 7. | **Data entry** | Consider whether the authority that individuals have to enter computer data has the effect of violating any of the segregation controls which are being replied upon. | Since many IT frauds are instigated by modifying data which has been rejected due to error, make sure that the correction and resubmission of rejections is performed by someone other than the staff member who entered the original data which was rejected. |
| 8. | **Means of authority to commit the company** | Authority to commit the entity is under progressively stronger control, as follows:<br><br>• vested in a sole individual;<br>• dual authority;<br>• sole authority, with prior approval at a higher level; and<br>• by committee. | Capital investments above a certain level are approved by a committee of the board on the recommendation of the executive. |
| 9. | **Time** | Time delays within processes may improve control if defects | Delay delivery until the cheque has |

|   | Type of segregation | Comments | Examples |
|---|---|---|---|
| 9. *cont.* | **Time** | may possibly reveal themselves after a short time.<br><br>Rotation of duties means that the work of one person will, in time, be subjected to the attention of another, making it less likely that fraud will be concealed, and thus deterring its perpetration.<br><br>A compulsory holiday of a fortnight's duration at least once a year, with duties being understudied by another member of staff during the absence on holiday. | cleared; or one clerk looks after one set of customer accounts for a month or two before exchanging these accounts with those of another clerk. |
| 10. | **Knowledge** | Segregation of knowledge on a 'need to know basis'. This should be a last resort when other forms of control are not available, since it restricts the extent that staff can take an intelligent interest the affairs of the business and tends to reduce job satisfaction and motivation. | Access to IT program documentation. Security code to activate a process. |
| 11. | **Review from operations** | Those responsible for review should not have operational responsibilities for what they review. | Internal audit should not design or operate systems. |

**Notes**

1. Glover, H.D. and J. C. Flagg, (1999), Effective Fraud Detection/Prevention Techniques, The Institute of Internal Auditors Inc. Tel: +1 770 442 8633, ext. 275. E-mail: iiapubs@pbd.com]
2. 'Auditing Practices Board (January 1995): Fraud and error, Statement of Auditing Standards SAS 110, issued by the Auditing Practices Board; the US equivalent is Consideration of Fraud in a Financial Statement Audit, Statement on Auditing Standard SAS 82, American Institute of Certified Public Accountants, 1997.
3. Audit Commission: Protecting the Public Purse 2: Ensuring Probity in the NHS, 1994
4. *Prevention of Corruption Act 1916*
5. Audit Commission: Protecting the Public Purse 2, p9.
6. Ian James, 'Ethics and Non-ethics Man', Computer Bulletin, [February 1996], pp 18–19. The Mori survey was commissioned by The Security Gazette and Control Risks.

*Table 1* **B24.68**

7. Ernst & Young, Survey of More than 100 Large Companies, January 1995, reported in The Financial Times, January 16 1995.
8. Ernst & Young, Fraud – The Unmanaged Risk: First International Fraud Survey, London, May 1996.
9. David Sherwin, head of fraud investigation and risk management at the accountants Ernst & Young, London, quoted in 'Business Hit by Rampant Fraud', The Sunday Times, 19 May 1996, p2.9, and in 'Staff Fraud Costing Companies Billions', Accountancy Age, 23 May 1996, p9.
10. Derived from Robert Howell, 13 August 2002, 'How accounting executives looked the wrong way', Financial Times, p11.
11. Alex Klein (of The Washington Post), 3/4 August 2002, 'AOL probe expanded to question more deals', International Herald Tribune, p9.
12. Scott Morrison, 5 June 2003, 'Former HBOC chiefs face fraud allegations', Financial Times, p29.
13. Second Annual Report (1999–2000), The Fraud Advisory Panel, Chartered Accountants' Hall, PO Box 433, Moorgate Place, London, EC2P 2BJ. Tel: +44 (0)202 7920 8721. E-mail: Sdiggens@icaew.co.uk. p1.
14. Second Annual Report (1999 – 2000), The Fraud Advisory Panel, p10, (see Footnote 13 above.
15. The Combined Code, July 1998 appendix to The London Stock Exchange Listing Rules, also available from Gee Publishing Ltd, 100 Avenue Road, Swiss Cottage, London, NW3 3PG. Tel.: 0345 573113. Fax: 0171 722 4762. ISBN 1 86089 036 9, 29 pages, £10.
16. Internal Control – Guidance For Directors On The Combined Code, September 1999 ('The Turnbull Report'), The Institute of Chartered Accountants in England & Wales, ISBN 1–84152–010–1
17. Report Of The Committee On Fraudulent Financial Reporting ('The Treadway Report') (1987), Committee Of Sponsoring Organizations Of The Treadway Commission, (COSO). This 200 page report can be downloaded even today from the new COSO website: www.coso.org.
18. Report Of The Committee On The Financial Aspects Of Corporate Governance ('The Cadbury Report'), (1 December 1992), published by Gee Publishing, London; Report only: ISBN 0 85258 913 1; Report with Code of Best Practice: ISBN 0 85258 915 8, 91 A5 pages; Code of Best Practice: ISBN 0 85258 914 X.
19. Committee On Corporate Governance – The Hampel Committee (January 1998), Final Report, chaired by Sir Ronald Hampel, Gee Publishing. ISBN 1 86089 034 2.
20. Second Annual Report (1999–2000), The Fraud Advisory Panel, p5, (see Footnote 13 above.
21. American Institute of Certified Public Accountants; American Accounting Association; The Institute of Internal Auditors; The Institute of Management Accountants; and The Financial Executives Institute.
22. Report of the National Commission on Fraudulent Financial Reporting, (1987), National Commission on Fraudulent Financial Reporting, New York, ('The Treadway Commission Report').
23. Internal Control – Integrated Framework, (September 1992), The Committee of Sponsoring Organizations of the Treadway Commission, available from AICPA, New York.
24. The Combined Code, (1998), Gee Publishing Limited, 100 Avenue Road, Swiss Cottage, London, NW3 3PG, England. Tel: +44 (0)20 7393 7400. Fax: +44 (0)020 7722 4762.
25. Final Report, (January 1998), Committee on Corporate Governance – chaired by Sir Ronald Hampel, Gee Publishing, London. ISBN 1 86089 034 2.

26. 'Towards better auditing', (December 2000), ISBN 1–84152–061–6, £10 including postage, Audit and Assurance Faculty, The Institute of Chartered Accountants in England & Wales, Chartered Accountants' Hall, PO Box 433, Moorgate Place, London, EC2P 2BJ.
27. A finding expressed in the Fraud Advisory Panel's 1999 report: Study of published literature on the nature and extent of fraud in the public and private sector'.

# Sustainability

## Complying with the ABI disclosure guidelines on social responsibility B25.1

With increasing numbers of companies embarking on social reporting, there has been a growing interest in how companies are viewing the UK Association of British Insurers guidelines on corporate responsibility. Dr Chris Moon, who wrote this section, is co-author of the Economist book 'Business Ethics' (reprinted in 2003) and Director of CSR Global. He can be contacted at !enquiries@csrglobal.com or by visiting csrglobal.com. This first appeared as an article in Ethical Corporation Magazine, January 2003. The Association of British Insurers' newly updated disclosure guidelines on social responsibility are reproduced in **B25.2**.

The Association of British Insurers (ABI) guidelines ask listed companies to include information in their annual report on significant social, environmental and ethical risks and opportunities and their possible impact on the business. They are also asked to report on the policies and procedures for managing these risks and the extent to which they comply with their own policies and procedures. Finally the report should describe any procedures for verification of social, environmental and ethical disclosures.

## Complying with the ABI guidelines – at a glance

| Boardroom challenge | Possible solution |
|---|---|
| Board takes regular account of the significance of social, environmental and ethical issues. Board identifies significant risks and opportunities arising from social, environmental and ethical issues. | This should be built into an annual risk management process. This can be tailor-made for the company or adapted from an off-the-shelf system like the GoodCorporation charter and verification. |
| Board has adequate information and directors are trained in social, environmental and ethical issues. | Training in social, environmental and ethical issues is underdeveloped a present. The Institute of Business Ethics has recently launched a training programme covering some of the issues. Training specifically for directors is offered by The Institute of Directors and by ACCA. |

**B25.1**  *Complying with the ABI disclosure guidelines on social responsibility*

| Boardroom challenge | Possible solution |
|---|---|
| Board should ensure effective systems in place to manage significant social, environmental and ethical risks. | In addition to the over-arching approaches, there are a number of tools that can be used to manage different social, environmental and ethical (SEE) risks. For example, Investors in People helps manage employee relationships, SA8000 manages risks of poor labour conditions in the supply-chain, ISO9001 manages aspects of customer relationships, EMAS/EMAP and ISO14001 manage environmental risks. The GRI framework covers the complete data set that a company might use, if it is looking to report on specific SEE issues. |
| Performance management systems and appropriate remuneration incentives in place. | Companies can adapt existing remuneration systems to reward social, environmental and ethical risk management. |

| Annual reporting issue | Possible solution |
|---|---|
| Include information on social, environmental and ethical related risks and opportunities. | The two main approaches to reporting on social, environmental and ethical risks are to produce a social report and publish verified data from it or to use a system like GoodCorporation and report on compliance with different sections of its charter. |
| Describe social, environmental and ethical risk management procedures. | There are a number of ways to report on risk management procedures. The most common approach is to report on company-specific systems. Alternatively the company can report using an off-the-shelf system. |
| Extent to which company has complied with its own policies on managing social, environmental and ethical risks. | Own codes allow a company to measure themselves against their own social, environmental and ethical policies and can allow a report on compliance. |

| Annual reporting issue | Possible solution |
|---|---|
| | Social reports allow a company to report on policies or principles and to assess effectiveness (usually by looking a data), although they do not normally look at what percentage of policies are being met. |
| | External codes can also be used as a benchmark. How many parts of the external code is the company meeting? |
| Procedures for verification of social, environmental and ethical disclosures | Own social reports can be combined with either external or internal verification. This is usually against social, environmental and ethical related data, but can also look at policies. |
| | GoodCorporation provides a ready-made external verification (of social,environmental and ethical policies) that can also be shadowed by internal audit. |

There are various ways that companies can comply with the guidelines, although as the table above shows, there is no single solution that meets all the requirements.

The ABI guidelines include case studies showing approaches taken by different companies, some of which have developed their own social and environmental reports. The AA1000 framework is mentioned as a tool that helps a company to assess its stakeholders' demands and to put systems in place to meet those demands.

The ABI's report also discusses the GoodCorporation framework developed by the Institute of Business Ethics. The GoodCorporation approach provides a ready-made and cost-effective system to help companies demonstrate responsible business practices and to comply with a significant part of the ABI guidelines. Already a number of companies have signed up to the charter and been verified (see the www.goodcorporation.com).

This still leaves some issues to address. The first of these is board level training in social, environmental and ethical issues. The Institute of Directors now offers training towards becoming a Chartered Director and ACCA offers a programme for Non Executive Directors.. The second issue is appropriate remuneration for managing social, environmental and ethical risks. Many businesses have developed multiple criteria for determining pay and rewards, often linked to 'soft' criteria like good team working. These systems should be able to be adapted towards social, environmental and ethical issues with little difficulty.

There are many other initiatives, codes and frameworks that can be used to help manage social, environmental and ethical risks. To take some examples:

- SA8000 can be used to manage labour conditions in the supply-chain;

- the Ethical Trading Initiative base code can also form the basis of an ethical procurement screening exercise;

- the UN Global Compact can be used to form some statements of over-arching principles;

- the responsible care charter can be used in the chemicals sector as a statement of principles;

- ISO quality and environmental standards can be used to manage these specific issues;

- UK Investors in People can be used to ensure that training and development of people is taking place and supports the company's strategy.

These types of initiatives are very useful either for managing specific risks, dealing with a specific set of functional issues, or establishing a set of global or sector based principles. The best starting point is either to develop a company-specific and verified social and environmental report or to use an off-the-shelf verified system. At present the reporting framework for corporate responsibility is ill-defined and leads to problems of interpretation and lack of comparability. Reports can also be hugely expensive. Many companies are therefore looking for more cost-effective approaches such as that of GoodCorporation.

In terms of timescale, the ABI has not set any deadline for companies to meet the disclosure requirements. However, they are expecting an increasing number of listed companies to report on social, environmental and ethical issues in their annual reports.. The Higgs Review of the Role and Effectiveness of Non-executive Directors has prompted further emphasis on director level development in advance of potential changes in Company Law.

# The ABI disclosure guidelines on social responsibility
B25.2

These guidelines form part of the Association of British Insurers' publication 'Investing in Social Responsibility' which can be viewed on www.ivis.co.uk. The article by Chris Moon, 'Complying with the ABI disclosure guidelines on social responsibility', is interpretative of these guidelines, appears at **B25.1** above. These guidelines were updated in February 2003, replacing the October 2001 version which we carried in the previous edition of this Handbook.

IVIS is the Institutional Voting Information Service produced by the Association of British Insurers (ABI). First published in January 1993, the service has been developed to advise Association members on aspects of corporate governance of UK companies in which they invest. Through consultation with members it seeks to represent the consensus view of UK insurance companies on these matters.

The ABI, with around 440 members, is the trade association for authorised insurance companies operating in the United Kingdom. Between them, Association members account for over 95% of the business of UK insurance companies.

ABI members manage assets of some £1000 billion including one quarter of all UK equities (1999).

# The ABI disclosure guidelines on socially-responsible investment

### 1. Background and introduction

Public interest in corporate social responsibility has grown to the point where it seems helpful for institutional shareholders to set out basic disclosure principles, which will guide them in seeking to engage with companies in which they invest.

In drawing up guidelines for this purpose they are mindful of statements made at multilateral level through the Guidelines for Multinational Corporations published in 2000 by the Organisation for Economic Cooperation and Development, as well as by the European Union and UK Government. These, coupled with legal disclosure obligations on UK pension funds and local authority investments, point to clear responsibilities both for companies and for institutions that invest in them.

Institutional shareholders are also anxious to avoid unnecessary prescription or the imposition of costly burdens, which can unnecessarily restrict the ability of companies to generate returns. Indeed, by focusing on the need to identify and manage risks to the long and short-term value of the business from social, environmental and ethical matters, the guidelines highlight an opportunity to enhance value through appropriate response to these risks.

It is not the intention of these guidelines to set a limit on the amount of information companies should provide on their response to social, environmental and ethical matters. Some shareholders with specific ethical investment objectives may seek more specific information. Some companies may choose to make additional information available in order to enhance their appeal to investors.

The ABI hopes that in elaborating these guidelines it will provide a helpful basic benchmark for companies seeking to develop best practice in this area.

## 2. The Disclosure Guidelines

The guidelines take the form of disclosures, which institutions would expect to see included in the annual report of listed companies. Specifically they refer to disclosures relating to Board responsibilities and to policies, procedures and verification.

*With regard to the board, the company should state in its annual report whether:*

1.1  The Board takes regular account of the significance of social, environmental and ethical (SEE) matters to the business of the company.

1.2  The Board has identified and assessed the significant risks to the company's short and long term value arising from SEE matters, as well as the opportunities to enhance value that may arise from an appropriate response.

1.3  The Board has received adequate information to make this assessment and that account is taken of SEE matters in the training of directors.

1.4  The Board has ensured that the company has in place effective systems for managing significant risks, which, where relevant, incorporate performance management systems and appropriate remuneration incentives.

*With regard to policies, procedures and verification, the annual report should:*

2.1  Include information on SEE-related risks and opportunities that may significantly affect the company's short and long term value, and how they might impact on the business.

2.2  Describe the company's policies and procedures for managing risks to short and long term value arising from SEE matters. If the annual report and accounts states that the company has no such policies and procedures, the Board should provide reasons for their absence.

2.3  Include information about the extent to which the company has complied with its policies and procedures for managing risks arising from SEE matters.

2.4  Describe the procedures for verification of SEE disclosures. The verification procedure should be such as to achieve a reasonable level of credibility.

*Towards best practice*

Institutional shareholders consider that adherence to the principles outlined above will help companies to develop appropriate policies on corporate social responsibility.

The principles should also provide a constructive basis for engagement between companies and their shareholders. Over time this will allow both parties jointly to develop a clear joint understanding of best practice in the handling of social environmental and ethical matters which will help preserve and enhance value.

It is the intention of the ABI to continue regular contact with companies and stakeholders with a view to refining the concept of best practice.

The principles should also provide a constructive basis for engagement between companies and their shareholders. Over time this will allow both parties jointly to develop a clear joint understanding of best practice in the handling of social environmental and ethical matters which will help preserve and enhance value.

It is the intention of the ABI to continue regular contact with companies and stakeholders with a view to refining the concept of best practice.

Current understanding of best practice leads to the following conclusions and indications as to how the guidelines should operate:

1.  The guidelines are intended to apply to all companies, including small and medium companies.

2.  The cost of managing risks should be proportionate to their significance. Ideally, procedures should be integrated into existing management structures and systems.

3.  Statements relating to the guidelines should be made in the annual report, and not separately as part of the summary accounts or on a web site dedicated to social responsibility. In view of the close philosophical linkage between these guidelines and Turnbull reporting, it would make sense to include a brief statement in the Internal Control section of the annual report, although this would not preclude a cross reference to other parts of the report where more detailed disclosure of the type of risks involved and systems for managing those risks may also fit with other content.

4.  With regard to the implementation, shareholders are anxious to leave leeway for companies to establish their own systems best suited to their business. However, they believe that, with regard to clause 1.1, best practice would require the full Board to consider the issues on a regular basis, although some on-going detailed work might be delegated to a committee. Disclosure should include a brief description of the process undertaken by the Board for identifying significant risks and indicate which risks are the most significant in terms of their impact on the business.

5.  Examples of initiatives for reducing and managing risks(see 1.4 and 2.2) include regular contact with stakeholders and mechanisms to ensure that appropriate standards are maintained in the supply chain. Evidence of such initiatives would be viewed positively by shareholders.

6.  Reporting on performance over time in complying with policies to reduce risk will help shareholders monitor improvement in compliance.

7.  Independent external verification of SEE disclosures would be regarded by shareholders as a highly significant advantage. Credible verification may also be achieved by other means, including internal audit. It would assist shareholders in their assessment of SEE policies if the reason for choosing a particular method of verification were explained in the annual report.

## Appendix 1

### *Questions on social, environmental and ethical matters*

Disclosure could be addressed by response in the annual report to the following questions:

1.  Has the company made any reference to social, environmental and ethical matters? If so, does the board take these regularly into account?

2.  Has the company identified and assessed significant risks and opportunities affecting its long and short term value arising from its handling of SEE matters?

3.  Does the company state that it has adequate information for identification and assessment?

4.  Are systems in place to manage the SEE risks?

5.  Are any remuneration incentives relating to the handling of SEE risks included in risk management systems?

6.  Does Directors' training include SEE matters?

7.  Does the company disclose significant short and long term risks and opportunities arising from SEE issues? If so, how many different risks/opportunities are identified?

8.  Are policies for managing risks to the company's value described?

9.  Are procedures for managing risk described? If not, are reasons for non-disclosure given?

10. Does the Company report on the extent of its compliance with its policies and procedures?

11. Are verification procedures described?

## Appendix 2

### *Questions for investment trusts*

1.  Is the voting policy of the trust publicly available?

2.  Does the voting policy make reference to SEE matters?

3.  Is the manager encouraged actively to engage with companies to promote better SEE practice?

# Environmental issues checklist

## Objectives

This checklist is based on one which appears in Chambers, A D & G V Rand (1997), 'The Operational Auditing Handbook: Auditing Business Processes' (John Wiley & Sons, Chichester, England, 530 large format pages £75 hardback including diskette in Word format of the book's extensive checklists and appendices, ISBN 0471 97060 3, order from Wiley's Customer Services on (Tel: +44 (0) 1243 779777, or Fax: +44 (0)1243 820250)). The objectives are:

(a) to provide an authorised and documented policy on environment issues as a framework for responsibly conducting related business activities;

(b) to minimise the impact of the organisation's activities on the environment;

(c) to ensure that the organisation's products are environmentally friendly;

(d) to ensure that waste is minimised and properly disposed of;

(e) to avoid pollution and environmental contamination;

(f) to assess, on an ongoing basis, the environmental impacts of business operations and define the requirements to be adhered to;

(g) to ensure that alternative and potentially environmentally friendly processes and technologies are considered and implemented where justified;

(h) to either minimise or avoid the use of scarce materials and non-renewable energy sources;

(i) to ensure that harmful or hazardous materials and waste products are safely and responsibly transported and disposed of;

(j) to ensure that all environmental legislation and regulations are fully complied with;

(k) to avoid adverse impacts upon the organisation's reputation and image; and

(l) to ensure that environmental issues are subject to monitoring and management.

## Checklist

### 1. Key Issues

1.1 Has an approved and documented environmental policy been established which defines the required approach for business operations?

1.2 What measures ensure that the principals of the environmental policy are complied with, and how would non-compliance be promptly detected?

1.3 Have production processes and other business activities been assessed for their environmental impacts (and how is the necessary corrective action evidenced)?

1.4 How does management ensure that all the relevant environmental legislation and regulations are fully complied with, thus avoiding penalties and adverse effects on the organisation's public image?

1.5 How can management be assured that all waste products are correctly and safely treated, discharged or disposed of?

1.6 What measures prevent the pollution and contamination of the environment?

1.7 Are the organisation's products assessed for 'environmental friendliness' (ie impact during production/use, potential to be recycled, safe disposal at end of product life, restricted use of scarce resources etc)?

1.8 Have management actively considered alternative and less environmentally harmful production/business processes?

1.9 Are measures in place which ensure that all environmental impacts are identified, monitored and effectively managed (and what is the evidence for this)?

1.10 Has management established a recycling policy and if so, how is compliance confirmed?

1.11 Have the full costs of adopting an environmental approach to the business been accurately identified, justified and authorised (and are they subject to monitoring and review)?

## 2. Detailed Issues

2.1 Is the environmental policy supported by the commitment of senior management and a suitable staff training/awareness programme?

2.2 Are all projects to reduce the impact of business activities on the environment subject to a full feasibility and cost appraisal, before being authorised?

2.3 Is the assessment of environmental impacts kept up-to-date in order that management action is relevant and targeted?

2.4 Where required, have measurements of environmental impact (ie water discharge, fume extraction, waste materials etc) been established (and are they checked for accuracy)?

2.5 How can management be certain that they remain aware of all the relevant environmental legislation and regulations?

2.6 Has responsibility for environmental management been defined and allocated?

2.7 What measures ensure that all waste products are identified, assessed for their environmental impact, and appropriately treated/processed?

2.8 Are all discharges of waste products subject to monitoring and permitted within the prevailing regulations (and how would non-compliance be detected)?

2.9  How can management be sure that all waste product treatment processes are operating correctly and efficiently?

2.10 Would management be made aware of all accidental and unintentional spillages of potentially harmful materials?

2.11 Are contingency plans and resources in place to effectively deal with the likely range of environmental accidents?

2.12 How can management be assured that waste disposal sites and operators are appropriately licensed to handle the specific by-products generated by the organisation?

2.13 Whenever necessary, are management considering utilising alternatives to either hazardous or scarce materials as a means of reducing the environmental impacts?

2.14 Are the potential long-term environmental liabilities adequately assessed for both newly acquired sites and those being disposed of?

2.15 Are environmental impact audits regularly conducted by appropriately experienced personnel and are their findings and recommendations effectively followed up?

2.16 Does the design and development of new products take into account the potential environmental impact of production, and what measures ensure that such impacts are minimised and contained?

2.17 Are the operating costs of any recycling programmes monitored, and are such programmes assessed for their effectiveness?

2.18 How can management be assured that the adopted environmental approach is justified (on either cost or company image grounds)?

2.19 Has management reviewed the type of packaging in use as the basis for adopting alternatives with a reduced environmental impact?

2.20 In the event of an environmental problem, are there mechanisms in place to deal effectively with media and public relations, so that the reputation of the organisation is protected?

2.21 How is the accuracy of data input from other systems (i.e. new product development or design) confirmed?

2.22 How is the accuracy of data output to other systems (i.e. industry regulation and compliance) confirmed?

# EMAS – Eco-management and audit scheme    B25.6

## General    B25.7

The 'competent body' in the UK is the Institute of Environmental Assessment (Tel: 01522 540069).

**B25.7**   *General*

EMAS is compatible with ISO14001 (which replaced BS7750 (1994)) except that the last two of the seven steps of EMAS are not in ISO14001.

More than one in two companies now claim to have an environmental policy. 'Pro-active' environmental management is necessary if an impact is to be made. Commitment from the top will be found to be essential for success.

**The steps**                                                                      **B25.8**

**1.    Environmental policy**

- Must be compliant with relevant environmental legislation.

- Commitment to continuous improvement.

**2.    Environmental review**

- Careful measurement and analysis.

**3.    Environmental programme**

- With quantifiable targets.

**4.    Environmental management system**

- Operational procedures and controls (can be based on ISO14001's model set, or can be specifically designed) are set out in detail.

**5.    Environmental audit**

- Measures progress against goals.

**6.    Environmental statement**

- It is published.

- Tells the public about the environmental impact of the entity.

- Enables reporting of environmental achievements to the entity's stakeholders.

**7.    Independent validation**

- ie external review.

Note that Steps 1–5 are shared with ISO14001 and therefore an entity's work for ISO14001 can be utilised for EMAS registration. Steps 6 and 7 are EMAS-specific and not parts of ISO14001.

**Typical environmental areas**                                      **B25.9**

**1.    Energy efficiency**

- Use and conservation

2. **Water efficiency**

- Reduction of water use

3. **Waste efficiency**

- Damaging emissions
- Recycling waste into production processes
- Crushing waste to compact it
- Incineration

4. **Noise efficiency**

- Noise reduction

5. **Accident procedures**

**Benefits**                                                                     **B25.10**

1. Keeping ahead of legislation and the regulator.

2. Improved staff and community relations.

3. Improved customer relations.

4. Significant bottom line cost savings

# The financial performance of large US firms and those with global prominence: how do the best corporate citizens rate?    B25.11

*We are pleased to reprint this article by Curtis C. Verschoor and Elizabeth A. Murphy which first appeared in Business and Society Review in 2002 (107:3 (371–380)). Verschoor and Murphy are professors at DePaul University. The article is copyright the Centre for Business Ethics at Bentley College. We suggest readers also consult 'Corporate performance is closely linked to a strong ethical commitment' at* **B11.37**.

For several years, Business Ethics magazine has announced its selections for the lOO Best Corporate Citizens incorporated in the US. In 2001, the designated lOO firms were chosen from the Standard and Poors 500 Index (S&P 500) plus 150 other public companies selected by KLD Research and Analytics (KLD), a leading provider of social research. Marjorie Kelly served as the project director, and Sandra Waddock and Samuel Graves of Boston College prepared the statistical analysis selecting the 100 best firms for 2001.[1] Waddock and Graves used publicly available financial information plus environmental and social information supplied by KLD to select companies where the board members and senior management have balanced the interests of multiple stakeholder groups, rather than considering only shareholders.

The strategy of public corporations having a broader appeal to many stake-holders has resulted in wider use of corporate performance measures that are both financial and social, like those used by Business Ethics. This paper uses publicly available information to examine the relationship between corporate social performance (CSP) and financial performance. It describes prior research on this subject and explains the selection process for the Best Corporate Citizens. The financial performance of Best Corporate Citizens in the US is compared to that of the remaining companies in the 5&P 500, using the 200 1 Business Week ranking of financial performance of companies in the 5&P 500. The same comparison is also made for those Best Corporate U .5. Citizens that are recognized as global leaders. Fortune's rankings in the Fortune 500 and Fortune's Most Admired (as well as their global equivalents) are also included in this empirical study.

## Linking financial and social performance measures

There have been a considerable number of theoretical studies that attempt to define the corporate social and environmental performance of corporations. These studies have applied various definitions of C5P and have found mostly positive linkages to financial and other performance measures. Margolis and Walsh[2] have compiled the results of many research studies dealing with the relationships between corporate performance variously defined under financial or other traditional measures and performance defined to include other aspects, such as environmental, social, or other objectives. Walker Information, a stake-holder research firm, summarized the results of 13 selected academic studies that showed a link between ethical corporate behavior or 'good corporate citizenship' and various positive outcomes.[3]

Prior studies have also examined the question of whether there is a link between a corporation's financial performance and their commitment to their code of ethical conduct[4] and diversity.[5] Franko found there was no evidence of a systematic tendency across industries toward negative relationships between multinational enterprise acceptance of minority positions and company under-performance. Verschoor's studies showed that there was a statistically significant linkage between management commitment to strong internal controls that emphasize ethical and socially responsible behavior on the one hand and favorable corporate financial performance on the other .

Waddock and Graves[6] have specifically addressed the relationship between CSP and financial performance. Their study found a positive, bi-directional relationship between CSP and financial performance. CSP appears to lead to improved financial performance, and positive financial performance apparently leads to improved CSP. These same researchers[7] argue that the question about the relationship between financial performance and CSP should emphasize instead the link between social performance and the way an organization is managed. Their findings support the idea that the quality of management of a company's stakeholders – owners, customers, employees, communities, and the environment – reflects the quality of its social performance.

Roman, Hayibor, and Agle[8] conducted an extensive review of other studies that also investigated the relationship between CSP and financial performance. Their review of over 50 articles found a positive correlation between CSP and financial performance by the vast majority of the studies reviewed. Simpson and Kohers[9] found a positive link in banks between financial performance and social performance using community investment as a surrogate for social performance. Orlitzky[10] posits that firm size may have an effect on the relationship between financial and social performance. Ruf, Muralidhar, Brown, Janney, and Paul11 found some support for a tenet in stakeholder theory that asserts that the dominant stakeholder group (shareholders) financially benefits when management meets the demands of multiple stakeholders.

'Socially responsible' or 'ethical' investing has gained considerable prominence as many fund families market mutual funds containing only investments that have been screened for various social and environmental issues. Waddock and Graves[12] found that screened-in and screened-out companies perform about the same financially and in market terms.

Similar to prior studies, this paper raises the question about the financial performance of firms considered 'Best Citizens'. Are these socially conscious firms also among the most profitable? The same question is also raised about the Best Corporate US Citizens that are also recognized as global leaders. This question is answered, using publicly available information.

## The selection process for best corporate citizens

Business Ethics measures the performance of the bets companies in terms of seven stakeholder groups. They include one financial performance measure and six social and environmental measures.

The financial performance measure is a three-year average of total return to shareholders taken from the CRSP database. Firms with a loss in 1999 were dropped from the list using Compustat. The social/environmental measures considered a company's impact on customers, employees, community, environment, minorities, and non-U.5. stakeholders. The KLD social/environmental measures involve the strengths and concerns for each category for the same years and encompass 650 companies – the 5&P 500 plus 150 other public companies. The scores for all seven variables were standardized by Waddock and Graves and given equal weighting when computing the single overall measure for each company.

KLD's performance definitions of the six attributes used by Waddock and Graves are as follows.

1.  Community relations refers to corporate response to the community by donations, contribution to the economically disadvantaged, and support of job training.

2.   Minorities and women refers to corporate hiring and promotion of women and minority employees, including family concerns such as child care and elder care.

3.   Employees refers to corporate policies of no lay-off plan, hiring and promoting the disabled, cash profit sharing, and good union relations.

4.   Environmental refers to corporate development, processing, and use of products or services that minimize environmental damage or are environmentally safe.

5.   Non-US stakeholders refers to corporate grant programs like those provided by Proctor and Gamble, including earthquake relief in Turkey, community building projects in Japan, contributions for school computers in Romania, and shore protection in France.

6.   Customer relations considers quality management programs, quality awards won, customer satisfaction measures, and so forth.[13]

A search of Lexis plus a review by a board of experts attempted to find any scandals or improprieties not contained in the KLD data. Several companies otherwise meeting the 'best' criteria were eliminated, including Microsoft for its antitrust conviction, Xerox for its financial reporting problems and Ben & Jerry's because of its acquisition by Unilever.

## Research methodology and empirical results

The information provided by the 2001 list of the Best Corporate Citizens published by Business Ethics allows a comparison of firms with an emphasis on corporate and social accountability to those perceived to have superior financial performance, based on the 2001 Business Week ranking.[14] A comparison is made of the rankings of the 100 Best Corporate Citizens and Business Week's rankings of the financial performance of each of the S&P 500 firms. Business Week uses the following eight criteria to rank the financial performance of each company in the S&P Index: (1) one-year total return, (2) three-year total return, (3) one-year sales growth, (4) three-year average annual sales growth, (5) one-year profit growth, (6) three-year average annual profit growth, (7) net profit margins, and (8) return on equity .Additional weight is given to a company's level of sales. Since firms with a 1999 loss are excluded from consideration as a Best Corporate Citizen, for comparison, any firm with a 1999 loss was also excluded from the S&P 500 listing of firms ranked by Business Week.

Table 1 shows that the majority (77 out of 100, or 77%) of the Best Corporate Citizens is also included in the S&P 500 Index. Table 1 also provides a second measure of corporate financial performance-the Fortune 500 ranking. Each year , Fortune magazine lists the financial data on the 500 largest US-incorporated companies as ranked by total operating revenues.[15] Table 1 demonstrates that 64% (64 out of lOO) of the Best Corporate Citizens are included in the 2001 Fortune 500 ranking compared to 77% that are in the S&P 500.

**Table 1: Comparison of 100 Best Corporate U.S. Citizens to Remaining S&P 500, Fortune 500 & Fortune's Most Admired US Firms**

|  | Mean Ranking* | No. of Companies |
|---|---|---|
| For firms ranked as Best Corporate Citizens: |  |  |
|   Business Week Ranking of Financial Performance | 198.6 | 77 |
|   Fortune 500 Ranking | 217.0 | 64 |
|   Fortune's Most Admired Ranking | 175.9 | 68 |
| For firms NOT ranked as Best Corporate Citizens:** |  |  |
|   Business Week Ranking of Financial Performance | 245.4 | 372 |
|   Fortune 500 Ranking | 247.7 | 393 |
|   Fortune's Most Admired Ranking | 267.6 | 415 |
| Probability that difference in ranking is due to chance: |  |  |
|   Business Week Ranking of Financial Performance | 0.0252 |  |
|   Fortune 500 Ranking | 0.1638 |  |
|   Fortune's Most Admired Ranking | 0.0001 |  |

\*    For each of these three rankings, the means for those ranked as Best Corporate Citizens are either the same (Fortune 500 Ranking) or statistically significantly better (Business Week Ranking of Financial Performance and Fortune's Most Admired) than the means for the firms NOT ranked as Best Corporate Citizens (based on Mann-Whitney U tests).

\*\*  Firms with losses in 1999 were removed from each of these three groups since firms with losses in 1999 were excluded from the 100 Best Corporate Citizens.

Each year , Fortune also surveys executives, directors, and security analysts to determine its list of 'most admired' companies. Responses on eight key attributes of reputation are averaged to determine an overall score that is used to rank the top firms in 61 industries.[16] The eight attributes include innovation, quality of management, employee talent, financial soundness, use of corporate assets, long-term investment value, social responsibility , and quality of products/services. The average scores reported by Fortune were used to rank all 535 firms considered 'most admired' with the highest score being assigned the highest rank. Those 2001 rankings were then compared to the firms ranked as Best Corporate Citizens by Business Ethics. As shown in Table 1, 68% of the Best Corporate Citizens are also ranked as Most Admired by Fortune.

To help answer the question as to whether the Best Corporate Citizens are also the most profitable ones, Business Week rankings for the S&P 500, the Fortune 500, and Fortune's Most Admired Firms (excluding those with 1999 losses) were analyzed. The mean rankings for the Best Corporate Citizens were compared to the mean rankings for the remaining firms. The Best Corporate Citizens were found to be the more profitable or had a better reputation of the two groups on two of the three performance measures. Based on a Mann-Whitney U test, the mean Business Week ranking and Fortune's Most Admired mean ranking are significantly better (statistically) for the Best Corporate Citizens than for those not selected as Best Corporate Citizens. Also, the mean of the raw scores for Fortune's Most Admired Firms rated as Best Corporate Citizens (6.58) is significantly higher than the mean score (5.97) for those not rated as best citizens that do not have 1999 losses, based on a one-factor ANOVA.

For the Fortune 500, the mean ranking of the two groups are not statistically different. Since the Fortune 500 ranking is based on total operating revenues, the larger firms rank higher than smaller firms. However, since there is no statistically significant relationship between the mean Fortune 500 ranking of the Best Corporate Citizens and the mean ranking for those not rated as Best Citizens, this is evidence that the largest firms do not dominate the lOO Best Corporate Citizens.

## Socially conscious firms that are prominent globally

From an international perspective, the Best U.S. Corporate Citizens were also compared to firms included on the equivalent global rankings by Business Week and Fortune. Business Week's Global 1000 ranks firms based on market capitalization.[17] Fortune's Global 500 ranks firms based on total revenue. For the Global Most Admired competition, Fortune consults with international business executives and analysts who rank firms based on the same eight criteria used for America's Most Admired corporations.[18] However, a ninth category of global business acumen is added when surveying the World's Most Admired Firms. The top 25 firms from each industry are included in the listing of Most Admired.

For this study, the scores obtained for the World's Most Admired survey were ranked in the same manner as the US Most Admired scores. For all three international performance measures, the firms chosen as Best US Corporate Citizens that are also on the international listings outperform those firms not ranked as Best US Corporate Citizens. In other words, the Business Week Global 1000, Fortune Global 500, and Fortune World Most Admired mean rankings were significantly higher (from a statistical perspective) for the US firms chosen as Best Corporate Citizens than those US firms not rated as Best Corporate Citizens, based on a Mann-Whitney U test (see Table 2).

**Table 2:  Comparison of 100 Best Corporate US Citizens to Remaining *Business Week Global 1000, Fortune's Global 500,* and *Fortune's World's Most Admired US Firms***

|  | Mean Ranking* | No. of Companies |
|---|---|---|
| For US firms ranked as Best Corporate Citizens | | |
| Business Week Global 1000 Ranking of Financial Performance | 283.74 | 68 |
| Fortune's Global 500 Ranking | 205.26 | 31 |
| Fortune World's Most Admired Ranking | 102.69 | 40 |
| For US firms NOT ranked as Best Corporate Citizens | | |
| Business Week Global 1000 Ranking of Financial Performance | 513.39 | 364 |
| Fortune's Global 500 Ranking | 239.82 | 136 |
| Fortune World's Most Admired Ranking | 133.11 | 85 |
| Probability that difference in ranking is due to chance: | | |
| Business Week Global 1000 Ranking of Financial Performance | 0.0001 | |
| Fortune's Global 500 Ranking | 0.0001 | |
| Fortune World's Most Admired Ranking | 0.0001 | |

\*   For each of the three rankings, the means for those ranked as Best Corporate Citizens are statistically significantly better than the means for the firms NOT ranked as Best Corporate Citizens (based on Mann-Whitney U tests).

\*\* Firms with losses in 1999 were removed from each of these 3 groups since firms with losses in 1999 were excluded from the 100 Best Corporate Citizens.

## Conclusions

Based on the findings in this study, there is unbiased and rather conclusive empirical evidence that demonstrates that firms that are simultaneously committed to social and environmental issues that are important to their stakeholders also have superior financial performance and superior reputations as well. These findings are based on publicly available information, which any stakeholder or investor can examine to evaluate corporate performance, and are not a theoretical construct.

These findings (like prior studies) should continue to encourage more corporations to increase their emphasis on accountability to all stakeholders, not just stakeholder profitability. They should also encourage the growth of investment in socially and ethically responsible corporations.

Corporations should integrate the same non-financial, social measures into their corporate culture as those used in the Best Corporate Citizen ratings. Firms taking this approach are not penalized with poorer financial performance. Instead, the Best Corporate Citizens outperform those firms that are not committed to a 'triple bottom line' approach to financial, environmental, and social objectives.

## Notes

1. Philip Johansson, 'The 100 Best Corporate Citizens for 2001 – America's Most Profitable and Socially Responsible Major Public Companies,' Business Ethics (March/April 2001), http:/ /www.business-ethics.com/ 100best.htm# Covero/020Story .

2. Joshua Daniel Margolis and James Patrick Walsh, People and Profits (Mahwah, NJ: Lawrence Erlbaum, 2001).

3. Curtis C. Verschoor, 'Ethical Behavior Brings Tangible Benefits to Organizations,' Strategic Finance 82(11) (May 2001), 20, 22.

4. Curtis C. Verschoor, 'A Study of the Link Between a Corporation's Financial Performance and Its Commitment to Ethics,' Journal of Business Ethics 17 (1998), 1509–1516; and 'Corporate Performance Is Closely Linked to a Strong Ethical Commitment,' Business and Society Review 104(4) (Winter 1999), 407–416.

5. Lawrence G. Franko, 'Use of Minority and 50–50 Joint Ventures by United States Multinationals During the 1970s: The Interaction of Host Country Policies and Corporate Strategies,' Journal of International Business Studies 20(1) (Spring 1989), 19–40.

6. Sandra A. Waddock and Samuel B. Graves, 'Finding the Link Between Stakeholder Relations and Quality of Management,' Journal of Investing 6(4) (Winter 1997), 20–24.

7. Sandra A. Waddock and Samuel B. Graves, 'The Corporate Social Performance-Financial Performance Link, ' Strategic Management Journal 18(4) (1999), 303–319.

8. Ronald M. Roman, Sefa Hayibor, and Bradley R. Agle, 'The Relationship Between Social and Financial Performance,' Business and Society 38(1) (March 1999), 109–125.

9. W. Gary Simpson and Timothy Kohers, 'The Link Between Corporate Social and Financial Performance: Evidence from the Banking Industry,' Journal of Business Ethics 35(2) (January 2002), 97–109.

10. Marc Orlitzky, 'Does Firm Size Confound the Relationship Between Corporate Social Performance and Firm Financial Performance?' Journal of Business Ethics 33(2) (September 2001), 167–180.

11. Bernadette M. Ruf, Muralidhar Krishnamurty, Robert M. Brown, Jay J. Janney, and Karen Paul, 'An Empirical Investigation of the Relationship Between Change in Corporate Social Performance and Financial Performance: A Stakeholder Theory Perspective,' Journal of Business Ethics 32(2) (July 2001), 143–156.

12. Sandra A. Waddock and Samuel B. Graves, 'Performance Characteristics of Social and Traditional Investments,' Journal of Investing 9(2) (Summer 2000), 27–38.

13. Johansson.

14. 'Performance Rankings of the S&P 500,' Business Week 3726A (Spring 2001), 58–80.

15. 'Fortune 5 Hundred: Ranked Within States,' Fortune 143(8) (16 April 2001), F33–F44.

16. 'Where Companies Rank in Their Industries,' Fortune 143(4) (19 February 2001), F-l, 6p, 5c.

17. 'The Business Week Global 1000,' Business Week 3689 (10 July 2000), 114–144.

18. Jeremy Kahn and Cait Murphy, 'The World's Largest Corporations,' Fortune 144(2) (23 July 2001), 144–152.

# Social responsibility – a challenge for organisations and internal auditing   B25.12

*This article was written by Jeffrey Ridley, professor of auditing, attached to South Bank University Business School. His article discusses the importance of social responsibility for organisations and internal auditing. It starts with John Humble's social audit of the 1970s and introduces some of the current developments in social and ethical accounting, auditing and reporting. It shows how social responsibility is now being integrated into economic and environmental performance measures: provides evidence that social responsibility is now an important part of the principles of good corporate governance, requiring both internal and external auditing: and, challenges internal auditors to take a more proactive role in how social responsibility is being managed and audited.*

## Management of social responsibility

Writing on the social responsibility audit in the 1970s John Humble cited Drucker's key areas in which an organisation must set objectives as:

- Business(es)

- Profitability

- Innovation

- Market standing

- Productivity

- Financial and physical resources

- Manager performance and development

- Worker performance and attitude

- Public (Humble preferred 'social') responsibility
  *Humble, John, (1973): Social Responsibility Audit, [Foundation for Business Responsibilities, London].*

Little has changed! Humble viewed the challenge of social responsibility at that time as follows.

'… one of the critical and difficult management tasks is balancing these objectives at any time, taking into consideration the changing requirements of stockholders, employees, customers and society generally … '.

He went on to define social responsibility as one of the key areas of the business:

' … typically concerned with the external environment problems of pollution, community and consumer relations, and the internal environment problems of working conditions, minority groups, education and training.'

His definition of the social responsibility audit and his analysis of its scope spanned both the external and internal environments of an organisation (Table 1).

## Table 1

**The social responsibility audit**

'Part of the strategic and operational planning process, to examine systematically on an organisation-wide basis the existing policies and practices relating to social responsibilities, internal and external to the organisation.'

It asks the right questions about:

| 1. | **Social responsibility: stewardship** |
|---|---|
| | • Is the business so organised that it makes the most effective and balanced use of its financial, physical and human resources? |
| | • Is there a full understanding within the business that long-term profitability, earned within the context of progressive social policies, is essential for all stakeholders … including society at large? |

| | |
|---|---|
| **2.** | **Social responsibility: policy & organisation** |
| | • Does the board/general management team recognise the need to look systematically at social responsibility as part of the planning process? |
| | • What problems/pressures/'felt needs' exist which would appear to make further studies worthwhile? |
| | • Which of the existing company policies are relevant to this field? When were they last reviewed and their inter-relationship examined in the light of changed circumstances? |
| | • Recognising that virtually every department/function is involved, is there, however, a single person/small group at Corporate level with the responsibility for a continuing overall review of developments? |
| | • If you have a public relations department, is it fully involved in the development and communication of social policies? |

It includes:

| | |
|---|---|
| **1.** | **Internal environment** |
| | • Physical environment |
| | • Working conditions |
| | • Minority groups |
| | • Organisation structure and management style |
| | • Communications |
| | • Industrial relations |
| | • Education and training |
| **2.** | **External environment** |
| | • Social responsibilities and new opportunities |
| | • Community relations |
| | • Consumer relations |
| | • Pollution |
| | • Packaging |
| | • Investment relations |
| | • Shareholder relations |

Source: Humble's Social responsibility audit (1973)

In many organisations some, if not all, of Drucker's key areas are now measured against new external standard initiatives, such as quality, environmental and best practice awards. Developing international standards also offer accreditation and auditing processes for quality and environmental management. Many of the requirements in these standards address social responsibility issues. The European Foundation for Quality Management's (EFQM) Excellence Model (European Foundation for Quality Management, (1999): The EFQM Excellence Model, [Belgium], www.efqm.org) is based on eight fundamental concepts, one of which is Public Responsibility (note the link to the Drucker key areas!). This concept states that the:

'  … long-term interests of the organisation and its people are best served by adopting an ethical approach and exceeding the expectations and regulations of the community at large.'

It requires that societal expectations are measured and actioned.

All organisations should review their conduct towards social responsibility issues on a regular basis and as part of their risk management. The questions in Table 2 provide a start. The results from such assessments will always require actions for control, monitoring and improvement.

## Table 2

How good is your conduct?

| |
|---|
| Is it: |
| ● required by your regulators? |
| ● led from the top – by style and values? |
| ● embedded in all strategies, plans and operations? |
| ● seen in all structures and systems? |
| ● communicated internally to everyone – staff and visitors? |
| ● communicated externally to all stakeholders? |
| ● known across all supply chains? |
| ● included in all review processes? |
| ● independently monitored? |
| Does it: |
| ● create/reduce wealth? |
| ● improve/reduce the quality of performance? |
| ● increase/decrease the efficiency and effectiveness of all staff? |
| ● increase/decrease customers' satisfaction? |
| ● improve/lower the organisation's reputation in society? |

---

- increase/decrease competitive edge?
- consider/ignore all stakeholders' needs?
- encourage/discourage good behaviour?

Do you have:

- a formal and published code of conduct?
- a procedure for dealing with all irregularities?
- a whistleblowing procedure?
- practical ethics training for all your staff?
- Environmental, health and safety policies?
- environmental, social and ethical accounting, auditing and reporting?

---

Source: J Ridley (2000)

Many organisations now report on social responsibility in audited annual statements, published with their annual reports or separately. This trend will increase. What is important is that these reports are related to all other objectives in the organisation, with clear links showing how the adoption of a high standard of social responsibility is contributing to all other achievements.

**Social responsibility and corporate governance**

The 1990s have seen an increasing focus on social responsibility, reporting and auditing, reflected in a growing number of governance principles. Most governance guidelines include references to social responsibility as an important part of risk management and control, across organisation supply chains. One of the latest of these governance guidelines is that adopted by the OECD for multinational enterprises, on 27 June this year (OECD, (June 2000): Guidelines for Multinational Enterprises, www.oecd.org). These are international recommendations that provide:

' ... voluntary principles and standards for responsible business conduct consistent with applicable laws. The Guidelines aim to ensure that the operations of these (multinational) enterprises are in harmony with government policies, to strengthen the basis of mutual confidence between enterprises and the societies in which they operate, to help improve the foreign investment climate and to enhance the contribution to sustainable development made by multinational enterprises.'

Table 3 sets out the policies that multinationals should take fully into account in the countries in which they operate. The first guideline establishes a commitment to contribute to economic, social and environmental progress with a view to achieving sustainable development. This is followed by other social and economic guidelines, including ...

'Support and uphold good corporate governance principles and develop and apply good corporate governance practices.'

All the guidelines encourage application across multinational supply chains as well as in the organisations they manage. The OECD also recognises that …

> 'Many enterprises have developed internal programmes, guidance and management systems that underpin their commitment to good corporate citizenship, good practices and good business and employee conduct … [including] consulting, auditing and certification services … '

There is a reference to the application of

> ' … high quality standards for disclosure, accounting and audit'

but despite the references to good corporate governance, internal auditing is not mentioned!

# Table 3

**OECD general policies for multinationals**

Multinational enterprises should:

| |
|---|
| 1.  Contribute to economic, social and environmental progress with a view to achieving sustainable development. |
| 2.  Respect the human rights of those affected by their activities consistent with the host government's international obligations and commitments. |
| 3.  Encourage local capacity building through close co-operation with the local community, including business interests, as well as developing the enterprise's activities in domestic and foreign markets, consistent with the need for sound commercial practice. |
| 4.  Encourage human capital formation, in particular by creating employment opportunities and facilitating training opportunities for employees. |
| 5.  Refrain from seeking or accepting exemptions not contemplated in the statutory or regulatory framework related to environmental, health, safety, labour, taxation, financial incentives, or other issues. |
| 6.  Support and uphold good corporate governance principles and develop and apply good corporate governance practices. |
| 7.  Develop and apply effective self-regulatory practices and management systems that foster a relationship of confidence and mutual trust between enterprises and the societies in which they operate. |
| 8.  Promote employee awareness of, and compliance with, company policies through appropriate dissemination of these policies, including through training programmes. |
| 9.  Refrain from discriminatory or disciplinary action against employees who make *bona fide* reports to management or, as appropriate, to the |

competent public authorities, on practices that contravene the law, the guidelines or the enterprise's policies.

10. Encourage, where practicable, business partners, including suppliers and sub-contractors, to apply principles of corporate conduct compatible with the guidelines.

11. Abstain from any improper involvement in local political activities.

Source: OECD Guidelines for Multinational Enterprises (June 2000)

Also in June, the Global Reporting Initiative (GRI) published international guidelines for the reporting and verification of sustainability:

'Since its inception in 1997, the GRI has worked to design and build acceptance of a common framework for reporting on the linked aspects of sustainability – economic, environmental and social.'

*Global Reporting Initiative, (June 2000): Sustainability Reporting Guidelines on Economic, Environmental and Social Performance, www.globalreporting.org*

This is a powerful and far-reaching initiative, creating principles that will encourage and drive debate on many governance and control issues related to sustainability – both as separate elements standing alone, but more and more as the elements are integrated in the practice, verification and reporting of sustainability.

The guidelines examine much that has been achieved already in the reporting of sustainability, albeit that this varies across organisations and sectors across the world. The GRI hopes that the principles in the guidelines will encourage development and integration of improved economic, environmental and social performance in future sustainability reporting. Table 4 shows the key GRI performance indicators for sustainability reporting. Compare these with Humble's scope of a social responsibility audit in Table 1.

# Table 4

**Key GRI performance indicators**

| Economic | Social | Environmental |
|---|---|---|
| Profit | Quality of management | Energy |
| Intangible assets | Health and Safety | Materials |
| Investments | Wages and benefits | Water |
| Wages and benefits | Non-discrimination | Emissions, effluents and waste |

**B25.12** *Social responsibility – a challenge for organisations*

| Economic | Social | Environmental |
|---|---|---|
| Labour productivity | Training and education | Transport |
| Taxes | Child labour | Suppliers |
| Community development | Forced labour | Products & services |
| Suppliers | Freedom of association | Land use/bio-diversity |
| Products and services | Human rights | Compliance |
| | Indigenous rights | |
| | Security | |
| | Suppliers | |
| | Products and services | |

*Source: Global Reporting Initiative Sustainability Reporting Guidelines
on Economic, Environmental and Social Performance (2000)*

On the independent verification of sustainability reports the GRI recognises that the:

' … quality, usefulness, and credibility … can be enhanced in several ways [one of which is the] internal auditing of systems and procedures for measuring, recording and reporting performance data.'

No mention is made of a possible role for internal auditing in advising or teaching organisations how to report on sustainability. Nor is the alignment of governance with the elements of sustainability explored in any great detail. These are clearly aspects that will evolve across sectors, as best practices develop, influencing and being influenced by government and regulatory requirements.

A current development in Europe is the drafting of a charter of fundamental rights of the European Union (the European Council, (2000): Draft Charter of Fundamental Rights of the European Union, www.db.consiliumeu.int/df). This charter will guarantee basic procedural human rights and freedoms as well as economic and social rights. Much of what it will contain is already established across Europe. However, publication of the charter and its promotion later this year, will impact strategies and practices in many, if not all, European organisations, increasing the adoption of social and ethical accounting, auditing and reporting policies. A recent UK appointment of a Minister for Corporate Social Responsibility is a sign of this government's interest and intent in social responsibility developments.

**Social responsibility and internal auditing**

The Institute of Social and Ethical AccountAbility (ISEA), combines the terms 'social' and 'ethical' to refer to:

'the systems and individual behaviour within an organisation and to the direct and indirect impact of an organisation's activities on stakeholders.'

Its new international standard, AccountAbility 1000 (AA1000), has at its core the importance of stakeholder engagement in the social and ethical accounting process. Its framework, incorporates auditing as an essential criterion in the:

i)    stand-alone implementation of its framework;

ii)   integration of its principles and guidelines into other standards and performance measurements used in organisations; and

iii)  accounting and reporting of social and ethical issues.

Auditing guidelines refer to:

'all assessment processes where the social and ethical, accounting, auditing and reporting process, including the social and ethical report(s), are examined by an independent body in order to provide assurance to the organisation and stakeholders as to the quality of the process and reports.'

AA1000 refers to the roles of both internal and external auditing. Internal auditing is recognised as providing:

'assurance to the organisation as to the quality of the social and ethical accounting, auditing and reporting (SEAAR) process and the organisation's social and ethical performance. It also provides support to the process of the external audit.'

External auditing is recognised as providing the same assurance and credibility to the organisation and its stakeholders.

A comparison between the AA1000 auditing principles and guidelines and the Institute of Internal Auditors' Professional Practices Framework shows strong links between each, both at the conduct and the audit engagement levels (see Table 5). Codes of conduct for both types of auditing are very similar.

# Table 5

**Links between AA1000 auditing principles/guidelines and the IIA Professional Practices Framework**

| AA1000 | IIA Professional Practices Framework |
| --- | --- |
| **Auditing Principles** | **Code of Ethics Principles** |
| Integrity | Integrity |
| Objectivity and independence | Objectivity |
| Professional competence | Confidentiality |

| Professional behaviour<br>Confidentiality<br>Due care | Competency |
|---|---|
| | **International Attribute Standards** |
| | 1100   Purpose, authority and responsibility |
| | 1200   Proficiency and due professional care |
| | 1300   Quality assurance and improvement programme |
| **Auditing Guidelines** | **International Performance Standards** |
| **1**   Audit engagement | **2300**   Performing the engagement |
| **2, 3**   Control environment | **2100**   Nature of work |
| **4, 5, 6**   Audit planning | **2200**   Engagement planning |
| **7**   Audit evidence | **2300**   Performing the engagement |
| **8, 9**   Use of experts | **2000**   Managing the internal audit activity |
| **10, 11, 12, 13**   Audit reporting | **2400**   Communicating results |
| **14, 15**   Audit documentation | **2300**   Performing the engagement |

Despite the importance now being given to social responsibility and its significance in good corporate governance there is still little evidence that many internal auditors are taking a proactive role in social responsibility auditing or reporting. Yet there can be few internal audits that do not touch on social responsibilities.

In a recent, revised exposure draft for a new Code of Ethics for professional internal auditors, The Institute of Internal Auditors sees the Code's purpose as:

' … to promote an ethical culture in the international profession of internal auditing.'
*The Institute of Internal Auditors Inc (2000), Code of Ethics (revised)*

The new code revises an existing code, providing guidance principles and rules of conduct for the proficiency of all internal auditors. The IIA-UK and Ireland recently published a professional briefing note on social and ethical responsibilities (IIA-UK & Ireland, (1999): Ethics and Social Responsibility, [Professional Briefing Note No. 15], www.iia.org.uk). This professional statement sees every corporate decision as having a social impact, for good or bad. It recognises economic implications in societal decision making and the increasing influence of governments, looking

' … to business to take a leading role in repairing and improving the basic fabric of society.'

The statement does not to set out to prescribe a role for internal audit in this area but rather to raise awareness of the issues. No attempt is made to recommend how internal auditors should audit or how they should otherwise become involved in social or ethical responsibilities.

ISEA has established an internal auditing learning network for internal auditors employed by its members. This group now meets quarterly to share their social and ethical responsibility practices and developments. A recent article in the ISEA journal AccountAbility demonstrated how one internal auditing group in the UK participated in a social accounting and reporting exercise in their organisation. Internal auditing reviewed the systems involved, provided advice during dialogue with all stakeholders and audited the collection and analysis of data. The resulting assurance and consulting work is stated as adding significant value to the final reporting (Birchmore, Ian (1st quarter 2000): 'The contribution of internal audit to stakeholder engagement', AccountAbility Quarterly, (the Institute for Social and Ethical Accountability (ISEA).).

The importance of social responsibility for good governance will continue to grow across the world. This is a high priority for most governments and global organisations and institutions. It is essential that all audit committees recognise this trend and ensure their internal auditors include these responsibilities in the scope of their charters and services they provide. The following actions should be pursued by all internal auditing functions:

1. Commit to a code of ethics for all internal auditing staff – one established by the organisation it serves or the IIA code for professional internal auditing, preferably both!

2. Understand what is meant by social responsibility across the supply chains in which the organisation operates. Create a learning programme for internal audit staff for this understanding. Keep it up-to-date.

3. Establish links between social responsibility and governance principles across the organisation, at strategic and operational levels. Assess the key risks associated with social responsibility. Ensure these are seen in all risk assessment processes and internal auditing scopes of work, audit tests and other services being provided to management and the board.

4. Look for ways to assist in the integration of economic, social and environmental issues in management, accounting, auditing and reporting activities.

5. Include social, environmental and health and safety policies and practices in every audit.

6. Be involved in any external social auditing of the organisation.

7. Benchmark internal auditing involvement in social and ethical management, accounting, auditing and reporting across the organisation's supply chain sector/s and nationally.

# International Dimensions

## Globalisation of corporate governance          B26.1

'The incentive to corporations and to those who own and manage them to adopt internationally accepted standards is that these standards will help them to achieve their corporate aims and to attract investment. The incentive for their adoption by states is that these standards will strengthen the economy and discourage fraud and mismanagement.

The foundation of any structure of corporate governance is disclosure. Openness is the basis of public confidence in the corporate system, and funds will flow to the centres of economic activity that inspire trust.'

An interesting issue is whether in the fullness of time we will see a global convergence of approach to corporate governance. By the start of 2000, some claimed that 51 of the top 100 economies in the world were corporations, not nation states, and thus the need for a global approach to corporate governance has become all the greater. (In **B1.7** we discuss a marginally more modest assessment of the relative scale of corporations when compared to countries.)

For instance, to refer to just one example, in February 2000, not for the first time Bernie Ecclestone's Formula One Administration, based in the UK, threatened it 'may quit Europe' over a dispute with the European Commission over the latter's threat to renegotiate the broadcasting rights for Formula One which, they claim, breach EU competition law. The Commission maintains that Bernie Ecclestone and Formula One Administration, the sport's world governing body, have abused their dominance of the sport to restrict competition by preventing motor racing circuits and related parties putting together their own media deals. Denys Rohan, chief executive of Silverstone Circuits was quoted as saying:

'The Commission ... seems to be forgetting that F1 has become a global TV circus, in which it doesn't really matter – except to the circuits and those immediately dependent on an event – where it is held. There is no reason why all the grands prix could not be held outside the EU.'

A 1995 international task force on corporate governance had this to say:

'The Task Force came to the conclusion that it was not appropriate, given the need to respect diverse cultures and legal structures, to prescribe an international standard for corporate governance. Instead it favoured a natural process of convergence, which is likely to flow from an informed global debate. To this end it saw transparency as the key and a move towards an internationally accepted regime for disclosure of different corporate governance practices as the important next step.'

# Diversity or uniformity? B26.2

On the other hand, contemporary research by leading academics is calling to question the aptness of developing a uniform approach to corporate governance – even in the long term. For instance, Carlin and Mayer have recently suggested that:

'there is not necessarily a dominant financial and corporate system that is appropriate to all economies or all industries within an economy. What may be right for a developed economy may be quite inappropriate for a developing one. What is suited to an innovative R&D intensive economy may be ill-suited to a more imitative one. There may be important trade-offs in matching systems with the industrial bases of countries and their stages of economic development and regulatory and legal policies towards financial and corporate systems needs to be sensitive to these potential impacts on corporate activities.'

And Turley and Zaman have had this to say about audit committees:

'The effects of audit committees need investigating both at the national and the international level. Research with an international scope has the potential to examine how, if at all, the effects of audit committees differ geographically and across different corporate environments. Through such investigation, researchers can elicit the implications of recommendations for audit committees made at the international level. In undertaking such research attention should be paid to the economic and corporate characteristics of each country as well as the nature of the corporate entities themselves. It may be possible that audit committees as a significant accountability and governance structure are only appropriate in certain economic environments or for companies with particular characteristics.'

# The international context B26.3

The Cadbury Committee was set up in the early part of the Thatcher years, in the first half of 1991, and reported towards the end of 1992. It had rather similar roots to the US equivalent Treadway Commission which had reported five years earlier (1987) and which had been born out of concerns about fraudulent financial reporting. Although the UK came behind the US in enquiring formally into corporate governance, the UK took the matter further in one very significant way in that the Cadbury Report contained what was possibly the world's first code of best practice for corporate governance. It was grounded on what the Cadbury Committee found to be the best practices actually being followed in listed companies.

We should also not overlook the COSO report on internal control from the US, the King Report from South Africa (1994), the work of the Toronto Stock Exchange's Committee on Corporate Governance (also 1994) and the still ongoing work of the Canadian Institute of Chartered Accountants' Criteria of

Control Committee (CoCo), not to mention the Viénot Report from France and now the work in India, and so on. More recently we have also seen the development and publication of both the Commonwealth and the OECD Corporate Governance Codes and Principles. The OECD publication is:

> 'intended to assist Member and non-Member governments in their efforts to evaluate and improve the legal, institutional and regulatory framework for corporate governance in their countries, and to provide guidance and suggestions for stock exchanges, investors, corporations, and other parties that have a role in the process of developing good corporate governance.'

## OECD                                                                      B26.4

OECD has this to say:

> 'Of particular relevance is the relation between corporate governance practices and the increasingly international character of investment. International flows of capital enable companies to access financing from a much larger pool of investors. If countries are to reap the full benefits of the global capital market, and if they are to attract long-term "patient" capital, corporate governance arrangements must be credible and well understood across borders. Even if corporations do not rely primarily on foreign sources of capital, adherence to good corporate governance practices will help improve the confidence of domestic investors, may reduce the cost of capital, and ultimately induce more stable sources of financing.'

While the stimulus for Treadway had been fraudulent financial reporting of Wall Street listed companies and the specific stimulus for setting up the Cadbury Committee had been the conspicuous corporate collapses of the late 1980's (BCCI, The Maxwell Corporation, British and Commonwealth) in both cases it was the lack of trustworthiness of directors and senior management.

## Further information                                                       B26.5

1.  eg: American Law Institute, (1994), 'Principles of Corporate Governance: Analysis and Recommendations', (American Law Institute, St Paul, Minnesota). The Australian Stock Exchange, (1994), 'Disclosure of Corporate Governance Practices by Listed Companies' (Melbourne). International Capital Markets Group (June 1995), 'Who Holds the Reins? – An Overview of Corporate Governance Practice in Japan, Germany, France, United States of America and the United Kingdom', a co-operative venture of the International Federation of Accountants, the section on Business Law of the International Bar Association and the Fédération Internationale des Bourses de Valeurs; 105pps. c/o International Bar Association, 2 Harewood Place, Hanover Square, London, W1R 9HB.

2.  CACG Guidelines – 'Principles for Corporate Governance in the Commonwealth – Towards Global Competitiveness and Economic Accountability', (1999), following the 1997 resolution that 'Capacity should be established in all Commonwealth countries to create or reinforce

institutions to promote best practice in corporate governance; in particular, codes of good practice establishing standards of behaviour in the public and private sector should be agreed to secure greater transparency, and to reduce corruption.' [Commonwealth Business Forum Resolution, October 1997, endorsed by the Edinburgh Commonwealth Economic Declaration]. (www.cbc.to/Governance/FinalVer/fin1vndx.htm).

3.   Late in June 1999, having received inputs from both member and non-member countries as well as from the World Bank and the International Monetary Fund, the Organisation for Economic Co-operation and Development published their Principles of Corporate Governance, having gone through an exposure draft process. The publication can be downloaded in HTML or PDF format from their website: www.oecd.org/daf/governance/principles.htm or /principles.pdf.

# A case for global corporate governance rules: an auditor's perspective   B26.6

*Robert Roussey's article reflects on the premise that there is a need for global corporate governance rules. In coming to this premise, the views of various authors regarding the need for harmonisation of financial reporting systems are considered. If, in the view of these authors, there is a need for a uniform set of international accounting standards and international auditing standards, then it is reasoned that there is also a need for global corporate governance standards.*

*The article considers the importance of corporate governance and, particularly, the auditor's involvement in the governance process, including new rules issued by the International Auditing Practices Committee on communicating mattes of governance interest to those in an entity charged with governance. The article also considers the new initiative of the Organisation for Economic Cooperate Development and the World Bank, and the use of Global Shares by global business enterprises as further compelling reasons to start a movement for global governance rules.*

*The paper concludes with a recommendation for the international securities regulators to seriously consider the formation and implementation of such rules.*

*Robert S Roussey is a Professor of Accounting in the Leventhal School of Accounting at the University of Southern California, is the immediate past-chairman of the International Auditing Practices Committee, and is a retired partner of Arthur Andersen. He can be contacted at University of Southern California, Leventhal School of Accounting, Los Angeles, CA 90089–1421, USA. E-mail: robert.roussey@marshall.usc.edu.*

## Summary

Corporate governance is an important part of the capital markets and is becoming more important with the growth of the global capital markets and the significant frauds perpetrated in these markets. There have been great accomplishments in the development of transparent national and international accounting standards and in the development of national and international auditing standards that provide a high level of assurance on the viability of financial reporting. The incredible growth of global business and the growth of the global capital markets indicates that corporate governance can play an increasing role in these markets to counter financial statement fraud, corruption and money laundering.

Research shows that top management was identified as being involved with a high percentage of the financial statement frauds and that the governance in the companies involved in such frauds was weak. On the other side, research also shows that entities using outside directors in governance roles provide protection to entity stakeholders.

Corporate governance has been developed and implemented on a national basis. This was appropriate when investing and financing by public companies was also on a national basis. With the increase of global investing and financing outside of national boundaries, it appears that there is a good case for these public companies to be subject to global corporate governance rules. Thus, to participate in the global capital markets these companies would have to follow global rules v national rules, which differ significantly from nation to nation. The global rules would add another degree of protection to the global investors and other stakeholders.

Auditors are an important part of the governance process, and can provide useful information to be considered by those charged with governance responsibilities. In this regard, the International Auditing Practices Committee issued a new International Standard on Auditing (ISA) that requires auditors, in all audits, to communicate audit matters of governance interest to those charged with these responsibilities. If an entity has not identified people responsible for governance, the ISA requires the auditor to work with the entity in identifying appropriate parties to receive and act on the audit communications. This opens a significant portal for the advancement of governance in all entities, including public sector entities, having their financial statements audited in accordance with the International Standards on Auditing.

The Organisation for Economic Cooperation and Development and the World Bank are also actively involved in the promotion of improved corporate governance through a range of new initiatives. While the initiatives, at present, do not focus on global corporate governance, they do increase the debate and the focus on the need for corporate governance to be applied in a more vigorous manner in regions and nations around the world. The use of global shares by global business enterprises provides further impetus for considering global corporate governance rules.

This paper provides a setting for the further discussion of corporate governance. It also encourages the international securities commissions to consider the development and implementation of a set of global corporate governance rules applicable, at a minimum, to business entities listing shares or obtaining financing in the public capital markets outside of their national borders.

# Introduction

*Once a business entity lists its shares outside of its national borders, it should be subject to a set of global corporate governance rules.*

Corporate governance initiatives have been around for many years, if not centuries, if we consider the stewardship applied over the vast holdings of the Roman Empire. Modern day governance has evolved with virtually all of the studies, committees and commissions discussing implementation of governance on a nation by nation basis. While the nation basis is still the basis for governance implementation, there are some new developments that may have more of a global impact than any governance initiatives to this point in time, except for perhaps the initiatives of the Romans. Before discussing these developments, however, it is important to focus briefly on some of the fundamental changes in our global environment over the last several decades that create some imperatives regarding the need for global corporate governance rules.

The literature is replete with discussions giving general views toward the need for harmonisation of financial reporting systems (Schweikart). Also, papers have been prepared discussing various aspects on the harmonisation of international accounting standards (ICMG, 1992), and articles have been written describing the reasons for the need for global accounting and auditing standards (Roussey, 1992).

In general, this literature describes the importance of the global capital markets and the globalisation of business as two of the key reasons why there is a need for a uniform set of international accounting standards to provide for transparency and consistency in financial reporting. They also describe why there is a need for a uniform set of international auditing standards to provide for greater reliability in such financial reporting.

There are other articles, for example, indicating that credible accounting and high quality financial reporting provides the transparency that enables investors to make informed evaluations of investment opportunities (Sutton). There are others exhorting US investors to invest overseas and providing them with investment imperatives for global investing (Hexner). These exhortations must be working. As an example, the College Retirement Equities Fund Stock Account, a retirement fund for academics in the United States, has been slowly increasing its investments in foreign entities. As of June 30, 1999 these foreign investments were $23.4 billion, or 18.45 per cent of the total portfolio, with investments in 32 countries (CREF).

All of this information has to be considered in light of the quadrupling of the market value of all publicly traded companies from $8 trillion in 1987 to $33.5

trillion, as of April 28, 2000 (NYSE, June 22, 2000). It also has to be considered in light of significant frauds perpetrated in the capital markets in countries all over the world, rampant corruption, and expanding money laundering activities.

Corporate governance can play an increasing role in protecting the global capital markets and can play an increasing role in helping the war against financial statement fraud, corruption and money laundering.

## Governance – what is it and why is it important?

The current concept of governance has been around for many decades. The growth of public companies (shareholder-owned enterprises), and the problems mentioned above, have been the prime causes for the increasing importance of governance in the modern business entity. Governance in the private sector is generally referred to as 'Corporate Governance'. In this relationship, we can simply refer to corporate governance as the ethical corporate behavior by directors or others charged with governance in the creation of wealth for all stakeholders. More specifically, it is how these persons provide stewardship over the business of an entity to achieve the corporate objectives, balance the corporate objectives with the expectations of society, and provide appropriate accountability to stakeholders.

For the last 50 plus years, the increase in size and global reach of public companies, together with the increasing shareholder base, has moved the shareholders further and further away from the management and control of the enterprises they own. Because of this change, large shareholder-owned companies are required to employ professional managers to run the day-to-day operations of the companies. In some cases, however, the professional management has caused serious losses to the shareholders through mismanagement or though financial statement fraud. While there are many ways to exercise greater control over professional operating management, probably the most important way relates to the use of directors who accept stewardship/fiduciary responsibilities and who oversee the actions of the professional operating managers.

In the current day public company environment, the boards of directors are providing stewardship over the resources entrusted to them. In addition, a recent focus is to place the corporate governance stewardship responsibilities more and more on the non-executive members of the board. The reasoning is that these members are or should be more independent from the day-to-day operations of the entities; and that they are or should be more independent from the actions of the professional operating managers.

Why is it then that corporate governance is important and why should the corporate governance responsibilities be placed on the shoulders of the non-executive directors? It is because these persons are the true representatives of the stakeholders. The non-executive directors have or should have the interests of the stakeholders in developing the business strategies, supervising the business to achieve the entity objectives, balancing the entity objectives with the expectations of society, and providing appropriate accountability to its all of the entity stakeholders.

There have been a number of studies focusing on corporate governance and the non-executive, or outside, directors. The empirical results of one such study confirms the prediction that the proportion of outside members of the board of director is lower for firms experiencing financial statement fraud compared to no-fraud firms (Beasley). This leads a reader to believe that the presence of outside directors helps in preventing or reducing financial statement fraud for entities that have a greater proportion of outside directors.

Another study, sponsored by the Committee of Sponsoring Organizations of the Treadway Commission (COSO), focused on fraudulent financial reporting. As related to governance, the study found:

- top management was usually involved:
  - the CEO was named in 72 per cent of the cases, the CFO in 43 per cent. In 83 per cent of cases, either the CEO or the CFO was identified as being associated with the fraud,
- boards and audit committees were weak:
  - 25 per cent of companies had no audit committee; but where audit committees did exist, the median number of meetings each year was just one and 65 per cent of audit committee members had no accounting or finance expertise;
  - 60 per cent of directors were insiders or 'grey' directors (outsiders with ties to the company or management);
  - 39 per cent of the boards had no director that had served as an outside or grey director on another company's board, suggesting they had little board experience.

These studies provide some empirical evidence that corporate governance, particularly when outside directors are present seem to provide protection to the entity stakeholders.

In this regard, it is important to focus on the concept of stakeholders. The use of the word 'stakeholders' does not mean just the shareholders of an entity, but it does mean a broad array of society that has an interest in the various activities of an entity. Some of the stakeholders of a typical business entity are:

- shareholders – who make an equity investment in an enterprise and who expect share investment growth and dividend distributions;
- banks – who provide loans and who expect to be repaid;
- executive management and employees – who provide services to an entity and who expect to be paid for the services and to receive various employee benefits;

- suppliers – who provide goods and services and who expect to be paid for them;

- other companies – who have cross-holding interests, who have a vested interest in the entity and who can significantly influence the corporate behavior of the entity; and

- national and local governments – who provide services to the entity and to society and who need to receive revenue through taxation.

If all entities had the most outstanding business managers as the executive management, and who truly had the stakeholders' interest foremost, or if we did not have fraud and corruption in the world, we might not have a need for corporate governance. Since, unfortunately, entities always do not have the best executive management, and since we have experienced fraud and corruption in our business entities; there is a need not only for representatives to assist in the overall strategy and development of the business enterprises but also to eliminate these illegal acts.

This is when those people charged with corporate governance responsibilities start to play a very important role in the national and global economic environment. In general, governance responsibilities involve a number of oversight activities, including those matters relating to:

- entity strategy development and implementation;

- economic development, including mergers and acquisitions;

- appointment of professional operating management executives;

- compensation of these executives;

- formation of adequate accounting systems and related internal controls over financial reporting, operations and compliance with laws and regulations; and

- engaging independent auditors.

In some countries, these activities are all included in a single, unitary board of directors, although there may be an audit committee that assists that board in its governance responsibilities with respect to financial reporting and in the dealings with the independent auditors. In other countries, these activities may be separated into different boards, such a supervisory board wholly or mainly made up of non-executive members, and an executive or management board.

To be effective, however, corporate governance principles have to be applied by those with governance responsibilities in good faith, consistently, ethically, and with skills needed to apply the principles. This is when the auditor can play an important role in the governance process.

# The auditor's involvement in the governance process

Since an auditor focuses primarily on an entity's financial reporting process, an involvement with those who have governance responsibilities can only help to improve the governance process. The auditor can encourage executive management to adopt appropriate accounting systems and internal controls, but it is the governance people who can direct executive management to do so. Governance people, in effect, have the power to provide these directions, whereas the auditor does not. The auditor, however, because of experience, knowledge and skills can assist the governance people in the establishment of sound practices, and can provide valuable information and counsel to them.

If governance responsibilities are taken seriously and performed with intelligence, competence and due regard for the stakeholders, society stands a better chance of being protected from financial statement fraud, money-laundering, and other ills imbedded in some entities. At the same time, society stands a better chance that public company personnel will have an early focus on going concern issues, appropriate business strategies, and the implementation of the strategies. These responsibilities are of benefit not only to the stakeholders, but they are of benefit to auditors, as auditors will be able to perform their audits within an expanded system of governance scrutiny that focuses on the entire financial reporting process, and within a more ethical business environment.

# Global corporate governance rules – why?

For the last several decades, the accountancy profession has been at the forefront in fostering the development of corporate governance. This clearly indicates that the accountancy profession supports the development and implementation of governance principles in the market place. To date, however, all of the development of corporate governance has been at a national level and the implementation of the governance principles has been at that level. When a task force of the International Capital Markets Group studied international corporate governance in 1994 to 1995 (ICMG, 1995), it concluded 'that it was not appropriate, given the need to respect diverse cultures and legal structures, to prescribe an international standard for corporate governance. Instead, it favored a natural process of convergence, which is likely to flow from an informed global debate.' But during the intervening period from 1995 to 2000, the global market capitalisation has increased by about another $18 trillion, and the global debate has not created global governance rules as yet!

Considering the issues raised earlier in this commentary, I believe it is time to further debate the premise that:

> 'Once a business entity lists its shares outside of its national borders, it should be subject to a set of global corporate governance rules (Roussey, 1997).'

There is no doubt in my mind that corporate governance has to be implemented at the national level. There is also no doubt in my mind that global investors and other stakeholders would be better protected if all countries required, at least initially, a prescribed set of corporate governance principles for an entity desiring to list its shares in a country outside of its national securities jurisdiction. While this goal may not be attainable in the short term, it should be at least a near term goal of the national securities commissions and the accountancy profession.

In the meantime, there are several new initiatives that may further the development of governance rules on a global basis. These include a new initiative of the International Auditing Practices Committee of the International Federation of Accountants, and a new initiative of the Organisation for Economic Cooperation and Development and the World Bank.

## The initiative of the International Auditing Practices Committee

The International Auditing Practices Committee (IAPC) considered the role of the auditor with respect to governance several years ago. The members of the IAPC determined that the auditor needed to have a more defined part in the communication between the audit team and the people who accepted the governance responsibilities for economic entities being audited. The IAPC then developed an Exposure Draft of an International Standard on Auditing (ISA) on the subject, received comments from the public exposure process, and then finalised and approved the new ISA (IFAC, 1999) at a meeting held in Toronto, Canada in June 1999. The new ISA will be effective for financial statement audits ending on or after December 31, 2000.

The basic principle of the new ISA is that the auditor should communicate audit matters of governance interest arising from the audit of financial statements with those charged with governance of an entity. Under the ISA, an auditor has to communicate these audit matters with those charged with governance of an entity in all audit situations, and not just in audits of publicly traded entities.

Because of the different governance structures around the world, one of the tasks the IAPC had to consider was how to determine who was responsible for governance. For purposes of the ISA, the IAPC defined governance as the term used to describe the role of persons entrusted with the supervision, control and direction of an entity.

In some countries and in some entities, it is clear who has the governance responsibilities. In other situations, it is not so clear. Thus, the IAPC had to establish another principle that the auditor should determine the relevant persons who are charged with the governance responsibilities and with whom audit matters should be communicated.

The diversity around the world made it difficult for the IAPC to establish a universal identification of the persons who are charged with governance. Thus, the auditor has to use judgment in making this determination, taking into account such matters as:

- the governance structure of an entity, for example, in entities with supervisory boards or with audit committees, the relevant persons may be those bodies;

- the circumstances of the audit engagement, for example, owner-managed entities;

- relevant legislation, for example, that defines certain aspects of governance communications; and

- the legal responsibilities of those persons.

In some engagements, the auditor may have to come to an agreement with the entity as to whom audit matters of governance interest are to be communicated. These engagements may include those where the governance structure is not well defined, or those charged with governance are not clearly identified within the entity or by legislation. Examples of these situations may include not for profit organisations and some government agencies.

Thus, this audit requirement will initiate governance discussions with entities that do not have people charged with governance responsibilities. Further, it will expand the communication of audit matters of governance interest with those entities that have established a governance system.

The new ISA also describes the matters ordinarily communicated as including:

- The general approach and overall scope of the audit, including any expected limitations thereon, or any additional requirements.

- The selection of, or changes in, significant accounting policies and practices that have or could have a material effect on the entity's financial statements.

- The potential effect on the financial statements of any significant risks and exposures, such as pending litigation, that are required to be disclosed in the financial statements.

- Audit adjustments, whether or not recorded by the entity, that have or could have a significant effect on the entity's financial statements.

- Material uncertainties related to events and conditions that may cast significant doubt on the entity's ability to continue as a going concern.

- Disagreements with management about matters that, individually or in aggregate, could be significant to the entity's financial statements or the auditor's report. These communications include consideration of whether the matter has or has not been resolved, and the significant of the matter.

- Expected modifications to the auditor's report.

- Other matters warranting attention by those charged with governance, such as material weaknesses in internal control, questions regarding management integrity, and fraud involving management.

- Any other matters agreed upon in the terms of the audit engagement.

There are a number of other matters covered in the new ISA such as timing and forms of communication. The new ISA also mentions that there may be confidentiality requirements of various national professional accountancy bodies and other bodies that restrict the auditor's communications of audit matters of governance interest. It also mentions that the requirements of the various national bodies may impose obligations on the auditor to make communications on governance related matters. Both of these situations need to be considered on a country-by-country basis.

With the issuance of this new standard, the IAPC believes that it is raising to a higher level the issue of good communications between the auditor and those charged with the responsibilities for governance, and that it will continue the movement toward better financial management and reporting.

Since, at present, 57 countries around the world have either adopted the ISAs as the national standards, or use the ISAs in developing the national standards (IFAC, 2000), the IAPC believes that the new ISA on communications with those having governance responsibilities will have a very significant in these countries. While the implementation will still be on a nation-by-nation basis, there will be more auditors involved with governance communications globally than ever before.

## The initiative of the Organisation for Economic Cooperation and Development and the World Bank

An important agreement was reached recently between the Organisation for Economic Cooperation and Development (OECD) and the World Bank (OECD, 21 June 1999). The agreement provides for these two organisations to co-operate on the promotion of improved corporate governance through a range of new initiatives. The initiatives include holding an annual Global Corporate Governance Forum and a series of Policy Dialogue and Development Round Tables.

The objectives of the Global Corporate Governance Forum will be 'to provide a framework for international cooperation and create synergies for the design and implementation of joint or individual projects by participating countries and institutions.' The Forums will be designed to develop consensus in the area of policy and reform, coordinate activities, provide support for the activities, disseminate information, and provide training.

The Policy Dialogue and Development Round Tables will be run on a regional and, where appropriate, on a national basis to 'provide the framework for continuing policy dialogue and a multilateral process of exchange of experience.' The purpose here is to allow for an exchange of ideas and implementation more on the region or specific country basis.

In addition, the agreement includes the establishment of a senior Private Sector Advisory Group (PSAG). Since improvements in corporate governance require the involvement of both public and private sector, the PSAG will be part of obtaining support and input from the private sector.

The agreement intends to build upon a new set of Corporate Governance Principles that has recently been issued by the OECD (OECD, 22 June 1999). While the Principles are non-binding, they do reflect the views of the OECD member countries. The Principles focus primarily on publicly traded entities, but may be of use to improve governance in other entities and government-owned enterprises.

The Principles draw heavily on governance concepts currently in the literature as previously discussed; however, the Principles are organised in a logical and understandable manner. The OECD document covers five areas, with each area headed by a single Principle, followed by supporting recommendations. The five areas are:

1.  the rights of shareholders;

2.  the equitable treatment of shareholders;

3.  the role of stakeholders;

4.  disclosure and transparency; and

5.  the responsibilities of the board.

The OECD Principles document is another step in the direction of working towards better financial management and reporting, and the Principles should further the corporate governance debate.

## Global Shares

The development of global business organisations is another compelling case for the development and implementation of Global Corporate Governance rules. Organisations following a global business model are starting to use Global Shares, i.e., using the same form of shares for listing in a home country and in non-home country capital markets. In November 1999, for example, Daimler-Chrysler listed on the New York Stock Exchange the same shares listed in its home market.

According to the New York Stock Exchange (NYSE, July 2, 2000):

'Global Shares enable virtually seamless cross-border trading, allowing non-U.S. companies to increase liquidity and pricing efficiency in the U.S. market while permitting U.S. investors access to the home market shares on the same terms as local investors.

In essence, NYSE-listed Global Shares:

□ Are actual shares of a company that trade and transfer freely across borders;

□ May be used to raise capital or as currency for U.S. acquisitions. The same shares may be listed and traded on stock exchanges around the world;

□ Are quoted, traded and settled in U.S. dollars.'

As more and more global business organizations use Global Shares, there is a greater and greater need for them to use high-quality global accounting, auditing and corporate governance standards for reporting to their global stakeholders.

## Concluding comments

In 1999, Stephen Byers, the Secretary of State for Trade and Industry in the United Kingdom, expressed his sentiments, when he said:

'Good corporate governance matters. It matters to business because it contributes to sustainable long-term success. It matters to shareholders – and others interested in the company – because it ensures them a transparent and productive relationship with the enterprise concerned (Byers).'

While this sentiment is expressed in terms of national corporate governance, it can easily be applied to global shareholders. Simply stated:

A set of global corporate governance rules matters!

I encourage securities regulators around the world, primarily through the International Organisation of Securities Commissions, to consider the development and implementation of a set of global corporate governance rules, applicable, at a minimum, to business entities listing shares or obtaining financing in the public capital markets outside of their national borders.

# OECD Principles of Corporate Governance    B26.7

Late in June 1999, having received inputs from both member and non-member countries as well as from the World Bank and the International Monetary Fund, the Organisation for Economic Co-operation and Development published their Principles of Corporate Governance, having gone through an exposure draft process. The publication can be downloaded in HTML or PDF format from their website: www.oecd.org/daf/governance/principles.htm or /principles.pdf.

As with the UK Combined Code and the Cadbury and Greenbury Codes before it, the focus is on publicly listed companies but it is anticipated that the guidance will often be applicable to private and state-owned enterprises.

It is clear that a key driver behind this publication is to encourage quality corporate governance in OECD's client developing nations, in view of OECD's mission.

Although the whole document is much longer than the UK's Combined Code this should not be interpreted as indicating that the OECD guidance is more demanding than the corporate governance rules which apply in the UK or in other developed countries. To get a meaningful comparison, the Hampel Report together with the Combined Code should be weighed against the OECD guidance. Indeed, because the OECD guidance covers broader issues such as share registration and share transfer it could be argued that much of the contents of the UK Listing Rules (ie the FSA Purple Book, previously the Stock Exchange Yellow Book) covers for the UK what the OECD guidance attempts to embrace.

While the whole publication is titled 'OECD Principles of Corporate Governance', it contains just five OECD Principles which, unlike the UK Combined Code's Principles, are intended as non-binding reference points and not as detailed prescriptions for national legislation. OECD regards these Principles as evolutionary in nature, pointing out that to remain competitive in a changing world, corporations must innovate and adapt their corporate governance practices. Each of the five OECD Principles heads up a section, and is followed by a number of supporting recommendations, totalling 22 in all.

Compared in a crude numerical way, the UK Combined Code has 17 Principles and 53 Provisions, the latter corresponding quite closely to the OECD 'supporting recommendations'. It is not surprising that there is on the whole less detail in the OECD guidance. First, it is their initial attempt at anything like this: in the UK the Cadbury Code was less detailed than the more recent Combined Code. Secondly, the OECD could really only go to print with a lowest common denominator consensus position or, as they put it, what:

> 'represents a common basis that OECD Member countries consider essential for the development of good governance practice … not intended to substitute for private sector initiatives to develop more detailed 'best practice' in governance.'

Individual countries clearly have scope to be more detailed and prescriptive depending upon their macroeconomic policies, legal, regulatory and institutional environment and other factors such a business ethics and environmental and societal interests.

The OECD has not been in a position to advocate a particular board structure, and indeed even the term 'board' was a bit of a challenge to them in view of existence of both unitary and two-tier board structures in different countries. OECD resolved this challenge by applying the term 'board' to the 'supervisory board' in a typical two-tier system, and the phrase 'key executives' to the 'management board' in a two-tier system. They add:

> 'In systems where a unitary board is overseen by an internal auditor's board, the term "board" [as used in this OECD publication] includes both.'

As with so much other corporate governance guidance, this publication avoids being very prescriptive on the criteria for assessing the independence of directors.

OECD sees the need to stress the equitable treatment of shareholders and the role of other stakeholders. On the other hand, since the Greenbury Code, there is more preoccupation in the UK on the vexed issue of directors' remuneration.

The OECD publication has a useful supplement of annotations that contain commentary on the Principles and are intended to help readers understand their rationale.

The five sections, each with its own Principle, contrast to some extent with the four sections of the UK's Combined Code, which are as follows:

1. directors;

2. directors' remuneration;

3. relationships with shareholders; and

4. accountability and audit.

Here we reproduce just the five section titles and the Principle contained within each.

---

**1.   The rights of shareholders**

The corporate governance framework should protect shareholders' rights.

**2.   The equitable treatment of shareholders**

The corporate governance framework should ensure the equitable treatment of all shareholders, including minority and foreign shareholders. All shareholders should have the opportunity to obtain redress for violation of their rights.

**3.   The role of stakeholders in corporate governance**

The corporate governance framework should recognise the rights of stakeholders as established by law and encourage active co-operation between corporations and stakeholders in creating wealth, jobs, and the sustainability of financially sound enterprises.

**4.   Disclosure and transparency**

The corporate governance framework should ensure that timely and accurate disclosure is made on all material matters regarding the corporation, including the financial situation, performance, ownership, and governance of the company.

**5.   The responsibilities of the board**

The corporate governance framework should ensure the strategic guidance of the company, the effective monitoring of management by the board, and the board's accountability to the company and the shareholders.

---

# Hermes International Corporate Governance Principles

Hermes Investment Management is a fund manager wholly owned by the largest British pension fund. Hermes believes that in the long term good governance adds value to its clients' equity investments. The following principles will be used to guide Hermes' voting decisions and will apply to all publicly quoted companies in which Hermes' clients invest outside the United Kingdom. Hermes will be pragmatic in applying these principles, which are goals for strong corporate governance, and which may, at times, have to be adapted for local laws.

Further corporate governance guidance can be obtained from the Hermes website (www.hermes.co.uk/corporate-governance). This handbook carries certain Hermes guidance and discussion as follows:

- 'The Value of Corporate Governance' (**B1.44**)

- 'Hermes on Auditor Independence' (**B6.6**)

- 'Hermes: Statement on UK Corporate Governance and Voting Policy (2001)' (**B7.7**)

- 'Hermes' Guide for Shareholders and Independent Outside Directors' (**B10.79**)

- 'Not Badly Paid, But Paid Badly?' (**B15.15**)

- 'Value Drivers: Paying a Fair Price for Non-executive Directors' (Michelle Edkins) (**B15.16**)

## Hermes' code of conduct in support of companies

1. Hermes acknowledges, on behalf of its clients, that shareholders have responsibilities as owners to participate in the stewardship of companies and that, in companies outside their home market, the primary way of achieving this is through proxy voting. Accordingly, Hermes will endeavour to lodge proxies at company general meetings, subject to excessive costs or administrative difficulties, in accordance with the principles outlined in this document. Companies, for their part, can promote good practice and system development in their own market, thus minimising the obstacles to shareholder voting. We recommend following the International Corporate Governance Network's Global Share Voting Principles to achieve this end.

2. Management of companies run in the long term interests of shareholders can be confident of Hermes' continuing support. Hermes is committed to applying its corporate governance and voting policies with thought, giving due consideration to the specific circumstances of individual companies, and will adopt a pragmatic approach where appropriate. Hermes will reconsider, at the request of a company, any company-specific circumstances that may make it inappropriate to apply Hermes' standard policies.

3. Hermes will contact companies to explain its reasons for voting against or abstaining on resolutions. Hermes prefers these discussions to be kept private. Hermes welcomes correspondence from companies in which its clients invest and where a Corporations should disclose upon appointment to the board and thereafter in each annual report or proxy statement information on the identities, core competencies, professional or other backgrounds, factors affecting independence, and overall qualifications of board members and nominees so as to enable investors to weigh the value they add to the company. Information on the appointment procedure should also be disclosed annually.

# Corporate Governance Principles

Note: These Principles are based on those adopted at the 9 July 1999 meeting of the International Corporate Governance Network, a group representing the interests of major institutional investors, corporates, financial intermediaries and other parties interested in the development of global corporate governance practices. These Principles are the investors' interpretation of the OECD's Principles of Corporate Governance published in May 1999.

## 1. Corporate objective

The overriding objective of the corporation should be to optimise over time the returns to its shareholders. Where other considerations affect this objective, they should be clearly stated and disclosed. To achieve this objective, the corporation should endeavour to ensure the long-term viability of its business, and to manage effectively its relationships with stakeholders.

## 2. Communications and reporting

Corporations should disclose accurate, adequate and timely information, in particular meeting market guidelines where they exist, so as to allow investors to make informed decisions about the acquisition, ownership obligations and rights, and sale of shares.

## 3. Voting rights

Corporations' ordinary shares should feature one vote for each share. Corporations should act to ensure the owners' rights to vote. Fiduciary investors have a responsibility to vote. Regulators and law should facilitate voting rights and timely disclosure of the levels of voting.

## 4. Corporate boards

The board of directors, or supervisory board, as an entity, and each of its members, as an individual, is a fiduciary for all shareholders, and should be accountable to the shareholder body as a whole. Each member should stand for election on a regular basis.

Boards should include a sufficient number of independent non-executive members with appropriate competencies. Responsibilities should include monitoring and contributing effectively to the strategy and performance of management, staff key committees of the board, and influence the conduct of the board as a whole. Accordingly, independent non-executives should comprise no fewer than three members and as much as a substantial majority. Audit, remuneration and nomination board committees should be composed wholly or predominantly of independent non-executives.

## 5. Corporate remuneration policies

Remuneration of corporate directors or supervisory board members and key executives should be aligned with the interests of shareholders. Corporations should disclose in each annual report or proxy statement the board's policies on remuneration and, preferably, the remuneration break up of individual board members and top executives so that investors can judge whether corporate pay policies and practices meet that standard. Broad-based employee share ownership plans or other profit-sharing programs are effective market mechanisms that promote employee participation.

## 6. Strategic focus

Major strategic modifications to the core business(es) of a corporation should not be made without prior shareholder approval of the proposed modification. Equally, major corporate changes which in substance or effect materially dilute the equity or erode the economic interests or share ownership rights of existing shareholders should not be made without prior shareholder approval of the proposed change. Shareholders should be given sufficient information about any such proposal, sufficiently early, to allow them to make an informed judgement and exercise their voting rights.

## 7. Operating performance

Corporate governance practices should focus board attention on optimising over time the company's operating performance. In particular, the company should strive to excel in specific sector peer group comparisons.

## 8. Shareholder returns

Corporate governance practices should also focus board attention on optimising over time the returns to shareholders. In particular, the company should strive to excel in comparison with the specific equity sector peer group benchmark.

## 9. Corporate citizenship

Corporations should adhere to all applicable laws of the jurisdictions in which they operate. Boards that strive for active co-operation between corporations and stakeholders will be most likely to create wealth, employment and sustainable economies. They should disclose their policies on issues involving stakeholders, for example workplace and environmental matters.

## 10. Corporate governance implementation

Where codes of best corporate governance practice exist, they should be applied pragmatically. Where they do not yet exist, investors and others should endeavour to develop them. Corporate governance issues between shareholders, the board and management should be pursued by dialogue and, where appropriate, with government and regulatory representatives as well as other concerned bodies, so as to resolve disputes, if possible, through negotiation, mediation or arbitration. Where those means fail, more forceful actions should be possible. For instance, investors should have the right to sponsor resolutions or convene extraordinary meetings.

### Further information

1. Hermes believes that in principle fiduciary investors have a responsibility to vote but also recognises that there are situations where it is in the interests of the beneficial owners not to vote.

2. Hermes' definition of independence and our views on the appropriate number of non-executive directors are available on our website (www.hermes.co.uk).

3. For instance, through share ownership schemes or performance-linked pay. Hermes does not believe that simple share options adequately align the interests of shareholders and directors. Our recommendations on remuneration are available on our website (www.hermes.co.uk).

For further information please contact: Corporate Governance Director. Tel: + 44 (0)20 7702 0888. Website: www.hermes.co.uk.

# Commonwealth Corporate Governance Principles

**B26.9**

The Commonwealth Business Council has published corporate governance principles in association with the Commonwealth Association for Corporate Governance in the publication 'Principles for Corporate Governance in the Commonwealth: Towards Global Competitiveness and Economic Accountability'. The Commonwealth corporate governance principles are given below.

## Commonwealth Corporate Governance Principles

The board should:

| | |
|---|---|
| **Principle 1** | Exercise leadership, enterprise, integrity and judgement in directing the corporation so as to achieve continuing prosperity for the corporation and to act in the best interest of the business enterprise in a manner based on transparency, accountability and responsibility. |
| **Principle 2** | Ensure that through a managed and effective process board appointments are made that provide a mix of proficient directors, each of whom is able to add value and to bring independent judgement to bear on the decision-making process. |

| Principle 3 | Determine the corporation's purpose and values, determine the strategy to achieve its purpose and to implement its values in order to ensure that it survives and thrives, and ensure that procedures and practices are in place that protect the corporation's assets and reputation. |
| --- | --- |
| Principle 4 | Monitor and evaluate the implementation of strategies, policies, management performance criteria and business plans. |
| Principle 5 | Ensure that the corporation complies with all relevant laws, regulations and codes of best business practice. |
| Principle 6 | Ensure that the corporation communicates with shareholders and other stakeholders effectively. |
| Principle 7 | Serve the legitimate interests of the shareholders of the corporation and account to them fully. |
| Principle 8 | Identify the corporation's internal and external stakeholders and agree a policy, or policies, determining how the corporation should relate to them. |
| Principle 9 | Ensure that no one person or block of persons has unfettered power and that there is an appropriate balance of power and authority on the board which is, inter alia, usually reflected by separating the roles of chief executive officer and chairman, and by having a balance between executive and non-executive directors. |
| Principle 10 | Regularly review processes and procedures to ensure the effectiveness of its internal systems of control, so that its decision-making capability and the accuracy of its reporting and financial results are maintained at a high level at all times. |
| Principle 11 | Regularly assess its performance and effectiveness as a whole, and that of the individual directors, including the chief executive officer. |
| Principle 12 | Appoint the chief executive officer and at least participate in the appointment of senior management, ensure the motivation and protection of intellectual capital intrinsic to the corporation, ensure that there is adequate training in the corporation for management and employees, and a succession plan for senior management. |
| Principle 13 | Ensure that all technology and systems used in the corporation are adequate to properly run the business and for it to remain a meaningful competitor. |
| Principle 14 | Identify key risk areas and key performance indicators of the business enterprise and monitor these factors. |
| Principle 15 | Ensure annually that the corporation will continue as a going concern for its next fiscal year. |

# NYSE Corporate Governance rule proposals to SEC

**B26.10**

The recent US corporate governance debacles have generated with some alacrity, though possibly with too much haste, two principal responses. First there is the *Sarbanes-Oxley Act 2002* which became law at end July 2002 with the requirement to be implemented by the Securities and Exchange Commission no later than 29 August 2002. Secondly, on 16 August 2002 the New York Stock Exchange submitted a rule filing to the SEC which includes new, proposed corporate governance Standards intended to be codified in a new section 303A of the Exchange's Listed Company Manual. The draft Standards follow closely the recommendations of the Corporate Accountability and Listing Standards Committee which NYSE appointed early in 2002. We should stress they are not yet mandatory for companies listed in the US and will only become so if they are, and in the form they may be, implemented by the SEC.

Because of the likely global influence of US developments, it is important to take note of them.

For ease of reference, in addition to referring to these new proposed Standards in the text, we reproduce them in one place at the end of this text (see below).

The Cadbury Code of 1992 was a response to spectacular corporate collapses of UK-listed companies. In effect it was the Mark I version of a UK Code of Best Practice for Corporate Governance. The Mark II version (The Combined Code) came along in 1998 and now, post-Higgs, we have the Mark III version.. With the proposed Section 303A we have the Mark I version of a US Code – a response to similar challenges as had rocked the UK corporate world in the late 1980's – early 1990's.

It would be complacent in the extreme to claim that the UK had put its corporate governance in order ten years ago so that an Enron or a WorldCom could not happen to a UK-listed company. Nevertheless, we would attribute to three things the success of corporate UK to emerge relatively unscathed from the inevitable 'skeletons in cupboards' which tend to reveal themselves when economies experience a downturn. The first is that the UK is ten years in front of the US in developing its corporate governance codes. The second is the 'principles-driven' approach of the UK. The third is the apparent greater willingness, to the extent of keenness, of UK listed companies to observe even discretionary 'provisions' rather than to invest in finding ways around them.

## Certification requirement to extend to overseas companies with secondary US listings

In echoes of the *Sarbanes-Oxley Act 2002*, overseas companies with secondary listings in the US are caught by the requirements of these proposed new corporate governance Standards, and CEOs of *all* US listed companies will be required to certify their companies' compliance with them. There are sanctions which may be applied viz:

> 'Listed foreign private issuers must disclose any significant ways in which their corporate governance practices differ from those followed by domestic companies under NYSE listing standards.

> Each listed company CEO must certify to the NYSE each year that he or she is not aware of any violation by the company of NYSE corporate governance listing standards.

> The NYSE may issue a public reprimand letter to any listed company that violates an NYSE listing standard.'[1]

**Style and scope of the proposed new US corporate governance Standards**

While length should not be the main criterion to judge these proposed new Standards, it is not without some significance that they total just 1,146 words. While this is twice as long as the old 1992 UK Cadbury Code, the 1998 UK Combined Code weighs in at 2,394 words of which 532 are the 17 mandatory 'Principles' and the rest are the 48 more discretionary 'Provisions' which, although discretionary, are complied with very widely.

As with the now superseded Cadbury Code, these proposed US corporate governance Standards do not distinguish between 'Principles' and 'Provisions': unlike the old Cadbury Code it is intended that *all* of the US proposed Standards will be mandatory. Much of the content of these proposed new US Standards is couched more at the level of prescriptive rules than overarching 'Principles'. For instance, a glance at the lead clauses in each of the 13 sections does not allow one to conclude that each section starts with the enunciation of a fundamental 'Principle': some of them are very much at the lower level which, in the UK, would be dealt with as 'Provisions' or, on occasion, even lower level 'Guidance' on 'Provisions'. The scope of these new, proposed US Standards is thus much narrower than the scope of the UK's Combined Code which gives much more comprehensive coverage of essential elements of corporate governance. These proposed US Standards appear to be a focussed 'fix' designed to address almost exclusively the corporate governance weaknesses revealed by the recent US corporate debacles.

**US 'rules-based' approach manifest**

Nevertheless the new proposed US Standards are all intended to become mandatory. This reinforces the recently often-stated contention that US standards (whether for accounting, auditing or now for corporate governance) are 'rules-based'. The snag is that detailed compliance with these rules might nevertheless mean that fundamental principles are not achieved or can be deliberately circumvented – as for instance appears to have been the case in Enron:

> 'Legalistic interpretation of detailed rules can lead to their intentions being circumvented. If something is not prohibited, how can you then argue that it is not permitted.'[2]

The risk of this is even greater when the fundamental principles are not clearly set out. Different cultures work in different ways. The suggestion implicit in the US approach is that their corporate culture cannot be trusted to observe mandatory principles, but can presumably be forced, on pain of penalties, to comply with prescriptive rules.

### Independence of the US board

The NYSE proposes that there will be a 24 month transition period before full compliance with these new Standards will be required. For instance, the proposed new section 303A requires that listed US companies must have a majority of independent directors and this clearly may take time to effect. This goes much further than in the UK where the intention is that boards should be approximately balanced with no less than one-third of the board being 'non-executive' and the majority of the non-executive directors being independent. Even so, it may not be difficult for US companies to comply since there are many US listed company boards which, with the exception of the CEO, are entirely or almost entirely non-executive. However the new proposed US requirement is that the majority of the board should be 'independent' not merely 'non-executive'. One fifth of the proposed new US Standards elaborate upon the criteria to assess 'independence' whereas in the UK independence is expressed simply as:

> ' ... independent of management and free from any business or other relationship which could materially interfere with the exercise of their independent judgement. Non-executive directors considered by the board to be independent in this sense should be identified in the annual report.'[3]

Beyond that, in the UK it is for the board to decide whether a director is independent, and indeed the guidance to the US proposed standard also states that the concern is 'independence from management' and a proposed standard reads:

> 'No director qualifies as "independent" unless the board of directors affirmatively determines that the director has no material relationship with the listed company (either directly or as a partner, shareholder or officer of an organization that has a relationship with the company). Companies must disclose these determinations.'[4]

Guidance to this proposed Standard allows immaterial relationships but states that:

> 'The basis for a board determination that a relationship is not material must be disclosed in the company's annual proxy statement.'[5]

which goes further than is required in the UK.

While we have said that in the UK it is for the board to decide whether a particular director is independent, the Combined Code does require that this determination (though not the basis for it, as is proposed in the US) is disclosed in the annual report. And it needs to be added that institutional investors in the UK and their representative bodies have developed their own detailed criteria to assess director independence.

Detailed specific independence criteria are set out as binding in the proposed new US standards as follows:[6]

'No director who is a former employee of the listed company can be "independent" until five years after the employment has ended.

No director who is, or in the past five years has been, affiliated with or employed by a (present or former) auditor of the company (or of an affiliate) can be "independent" until five years after the end of either the affiliation or the auditing relationship.

No director can be "independent" if he or she is, or in the past five years has been, part of an interlocking directorate in which an executive officer of the listed company serves on the compensation committee of another company that concurrently employs the director.

Directors with immediate family members in the foregoing categories are likewise subject to the five-year "cooling-off" provisions for purposes of determining "independence".'

In practice there are many other possible impediments to independence and it would be worrying if US boards ignored them. Guidance below the level of the proposed standards does however state:

' ... it is best that boards making "independence" determinations broadly consider all relevant facts and circumstances.'[7]

It is also a concern that the above 'interlocking' test is limited to membership of compensation committees rather than to interlocking board directorships generally.

Notable amongst the above four given criteria is the introduction of a past audit relationship as an impediment to independence. While one can understand that recent crises have suggested this, it is ironic that an independent auditor cannot be regarded subsequently as an independent director. If auditors regarded their clients as being the shareholders (and not either the board nor management) this problem might not exist.

It is also notable that, in the third of these independence tests, interlocking directorships are seen as an impediment to independence – as indeed they should be. But it is disappointing that the criterion only applies if one of the directors serves on the compensation (i.e. remuneration) committee of one of the listed companies concerned. If the two directors serve on each others' boards it should be enough to imperil effective independence. Clearly this is a reflection that these draft Standards have been developed as a specific and limited response to recent problems.

## Non-management directors to meet regularly on their own

In the UK, the Combined Code requires there to be a designated and disclosed senior non-executive director. The non-executive directors on the board can rally round this director. Although it is being discussed in the UK, there is as yet no requirement for the non-executive directors to meet regularly on their own, as this emerging US Standard will require:

> 'To empower non-management directors to serve as a more effective check on management, the non-management directors of each company must meet at regularly scheduled executive sessions without management.'[8]

## Board committees

As with the UK, the proposed US standards will mean that compliant companies will have at least three board committees. In the UK, the nomination committee is not 'required' if the board is small.[9] They are the same committees on both sides of the Atlantic but with significant differences set out in this table:

## UK and US board committees

| | U.K. | | | U.S. | | |
|---|---|---|---|---|---|---|
| | **Title** | **Member-ship** | **Purpose** | **Title** | **Member-ship** | **Purpose** |
| 1. | Nomination committee | A majority of the members should be non-executive directors and the chairman should be either the chairman of the board or a non-executive director. The chairman and members of the nomination committee should be identified in the annual report.[10] | To make recom-mendations to the board on all new board appoint-ment.[11] | Nominating/ corporate governance committee | Entirely of independent directors.[12] | At minimum to: identify individuals qualified to become board members; select, or recommend that the board select, the director nominees for the next annual meeting of share-holders; develop and |

|  | U.K. | | | U.S. | | |
|---|---|---|---|---|---|---|
|  | **Title** | **Member-ship** | **Purpose** | **Title** | **Member-ship** | **Purpose** |
|  |  |  |  |  |  | recommend to the board a set of corporate governance principles applicable to the corpora-tion.[13] |
| 2. | Remunera-tion committee | Entirely independent directors [14] | To make recom-mendations to the board, on the company's framework of executive remuneration and its cost: and to determine on their behalf specific remunera-tion packages for each of the executive directors, including pension rights and any com-pensation payments. | Compensa-tion committee | Entirely of independent directors.[15] | At minimum to: discharge the board's responsi-bilities relating to compensa-tion of the company's executives; produce an annual report on executive compensa-tion for inclusion in the company's proxy statement, in accord-ance with applicable rules and regula-tions.[16] |
| 3. | Audit committee | Entirely non-executive directors, the majority being independent | Keeping under review the scope and results of the audit and its cost | Audit committee | Entirely of independent directors. | Assist board oversight of: the integrity of the |

| U.K. | | | U.S. | | |
|------|------|------|------|------|------|
| Title | Member-ship | Purpose | Title | Member-ship | Purpose |
| | | effectiveness and the independence and objectivity of the auditors. Where the auditors also supply a substantial volume of non-audit services to the company, the committee should keep the nature and extent of such services under review, seeking to balance the maintenance of objectivity and value for money.' | | | the company's financial statements; the company's compliance with legal and regulatory requirements; the independent auditor's qualifications and inde- the performance of the company's internal audit function and independent auditors; prepare the report that SEC rules require be included in the company's annual proxy statement.[17] ('Duties and responsibilities' are separate from 'Purpose' and are set out in 7. (b) (ii)) |

## A nominating committee with governance responsibilities too

There is no Provision in the UK Combined Code that the nominations committee should have written terms of reference. The US requires this and also goes much further than the UK by requiring that the written charter addresses:

'(i) the committee's purpose – which, at minimum, must be to: identify individuals qualified to become board members, and to select, or to recommend that the board select, the director nominees for the next annual meeting of shareholders; and develop and recommend to the board a set of corporate governance principles applicable to the corporation.

(ii) the committee's goals and responsibilities – which must reflect, at minimum, the board's criteria for selecting new directors, and oversight of the evaluation of the board and management.

(iii) an annual performance evaluation of the committee.'[18]

## Directors' remuneration and the 'compensation committee'

In the UK the Combined Code requires at the level of a Provision[19] that the remuneration committee has terms of reference. The US plans to be more prescriptive: their compensation committees will need a written charter that addresses:

'(i) the committee's purpose – which, at minimum, must be to discharge the board's responsibilities relating to compensation of the company's executives, and to produce an annual report on executive compensation for inclusion in the company's proxy statement, in accordance with applicable rules and regulations.

(ii) the committee's duties and responsibilities – which, at minimum, must be to:

(A) review and approve corporate goals and objectives relevant to CEO compensation, evaluate the CEO's performance in light of those goals and objectives, and set the CEO's compensation level based on this evaluation.

(B) make recommendations to the board with respect to incentive-compensation plans and equity-based plans.

(iii) an annual performance evaluation of the compensation committee.'[20]

The UK has always held that the only component of a non-executive director's remuneration should be the fee he or she receives which should be proportionate to his/her time commitment and contribution as a non-executive director. However there is nothing in the UK against a proportion of the fee being paid in shares: it is generally regarded that this could justify a higher total compensation package than would otherwise be the case – without incurring the wrath of institutional investors. An arrangement to award part of the fee in the form of shares would also have the advantage that it could, indeed should, continue during closed periods when directors are otherwise precluded from dealing in their company's shares. While in the US (though not in the UK) it has, controversially, been widely held as permissible for non-executive directors to benefit from share *options*, a new proposed US corporate governance Standard would now debar members of the audit committee from this potential benefit viz:

'Add to the "independence" requirement for audit committee member-ship the requirement that director's fees are the only compensation an audit committee member may receive from the company.'[21]

There are important exclusions to the new proposed requirements for share-holders to approve directors' remuneration viz:

'To increase shareholder control over equity-compensation plans, share-holders must be given the opportunity to vote on all equity-compensation plans, except inducement options, plans relating to mergers or acquisi-tions, and tax qualified and excess benefit plans.'[22]

### The audit committee and the appointment of auditors

As this proposed Standard infers, in the US all members of the audit committee should be independent directors whereas in the UK it is required that all should be non-executive and that the *majority* should be independent.

New proposed US Standard 7 is striking in that it cedes responsibility from the board to the audit committee for the hiring and firing of the independent auditors, thus breaking the convention that the audit committee, as a sub-committee of the board, is no more than a means by which the board ensures it discharges certain of its responsibilities well. The audit committee is given:

'sole authority to hire and fire independent auditors, and to approve any significant non-audit relationship with the independent auditors.'[23]

and it must:

'set clear hiring policies for employees or former employees of the independent auditors.'[24]

A new proposed US Standard also prescribes that the audit committee must receive at least annually a report on the independent auditor's quality control and information about certain inquiries and investigations of the independent auditor within the last five years. As far as published financial information is concerned, the US audit committee's brief runs to quarterly releases (which must be discussed by the committee with both management and the inde-pendent auditor) and the release of information to the media, analysts, ratings agencies – each of which must be 'discussed' by the committee. It is not clear whether the information itself must be discussed in advance by the committee, or whether it is regarded as sufficient to discuss the 'process' the company follows to manage the generation and release of such information. It could be difficult for an audit committee to approve in advance the release of all information at many different briefings of analysts and investors, for instance. Likewise the word 'discuss' is used in the context of the audit committees remit with respect to 'risk assessment and risk management' with the let out that the discussion may relate to 'policies' only. There is no suggestion that the audit committee is required to communicate to the board their opinion of the effectiveness of risk assessment and risk management; there is also no suggestion in these proposed new Standards that the audit committee's purview extends in any way to internal control – unless one can assume that this is subsumed within the phrase 'risk management'. We would take issue with the separation of 'risk assessment' from 'risk management' as we consider the latter includes the former.

It is common ground between the new proposed US corporate governance Standards and the UK Combined Code that audit committees should have charters, but additional features further to those referred to above, while generally being regarded as good practice in the UK, are referred to only in the proposed US Standards. These are that the audit committee should:

- meet separately, periodically, with management, with internal auditors (or other personnel responsible for the internal audit function) and with independent auditors;

- review with the independent auditor any audit problems or difficulties and management's response;

- report regularly to the board of directors; and

- its charter should address the need for an annual performance evaluation of the audit committee.

The UK wording is limited to:

**Audit Committee and Auditors**

| | |
|---|---|
| **Principle** | The board should establish formal and transparent arrangements for considering how they should apply the financial reporting and internal control principles and for maintaining an appropriate relationship with the company's auditors. |

**Code Provisions**

The board should establish an audit committee of at least three directors, all non-executive, with written terms of reference which deal clearly with its authority and duties. The members of the committee, a majority of whom should be independent non-executive directors, should be named in the report and accounts.

The duties of the audit committee should include keeping under review the scope and results of the audit and its cost effectiveness and the independence and objectivity of the auditors. Where the auditors also supply a substantial volume of non-audit services to the company, the committee should keep the nature and extent of such services under review, seeking to balance the maintenance of objectivity and value for money.'[25]

## Requirement for internal audit

The new US proposal that US listed companies should have an internal audit ('Each listed company must have an internal audit function.'[26]) goes further than in the UK where, although the relevant Provision was strengthened in the subsequent Turnbull guidance, the wording is merely:

'Companies which do not have an internal audit function should from time to time review the need for one.'[27]

However, it is not clear that in practise there is much distinction between the present UK and the intended US positions with respect to internal audit. The UK Turnbull guidance requires that the review of risk management and internal control be embedded within the business. The NYSE commentary to their proposed new Standard on internal audit states that:

'this requirement [to have internal audit] does not necessarily mean that a company must establish a separate internal audit department or dedicate employees to the task on a full-time basis; it is enough for a company to have in place an appropriate control process for reviewing internal transactions and accounting. a company may outsource this function to a firm other than its independent auditor.' [28]

## The section on audit committees

The full wording of this section of the proposed US corporate governance Standards reads:

7.(a) Increase the authority and responsibilities of the audit committee, including granting it the sole authority to hire and fire independent auditors, and to approve any significant non-audit relationship with the independent auditors.

(b) The audit committee must have a written charter that addresses:

(i) the committee's purpose – which, at minimum, must be to:

(A) assist board oversight of (1) the integrity of the company's financial statements, (2) the company's compliance with legal and regulatory requirements, (3) the independent auditor's qualifications and independence, and (4) the performance of the company's internal audit function and independent auditors; and

(B) prepare the report that SEC rules require be included in the company's annual proxy statement.

(ii) the duties and responsibilities of the audit committee – which, at minimum, must be to:

(A) retain and terminate the company's independent auditors (subject, if applicable to shareholder ratification).

(B) at least annually, obtain and review a report by the independent auditor describing: the firm's internal quality-control procedures; any material issues raised by the most recent internal quality-control review, or peer review, of the firm, or by any inquiry or investigation by governmental or professional authorities, within the preceding five years, respecting one or more independent audits carried out by the firm, and any steps taken to deal with any such issues; and (to assess the auditor's independence) all relationships between the independent auditor and the company.

(C) discuss the annual audited financial statements and quarterly financial statements with management and the independent auditor, including the company's disclosures under "Management's Discussion and Analysis of Financial Condition and Results of Operations."

(D) discuss earnings press releases, as well as financial information and earnings guidance provided to analysts and rating agencies.

(E) as appropriate, obtain advice and assistance from outside legal, accounting or other advisors.

(F) discuss policies with respect to risk assessment and risk management.

(G) meet separately, periodically, with management, with internal auditors (or other personnel responsible for the internal audit function) and with independent auditors.

(H) review with the independent auditor any audit problems or difficulties and management's response.

(I) set clear hiring policies for employees or former employees of the independent auditors.

(J) report regularly to the board of directors.

(iii) an annual performance evaluation of the audit committee.

(c) Each listed company must have an internal audit function.'

**Adoption and disclosure of corporate governance guidelines**

The proposed requirements to adopt and disclose (a) corporate governance guidelines, and (b) a code of business conduct, have little or no counterparts in UK requirements viz:

'Listed companies must adopt and disclose corporate governance guidelines.

- Director qualification standards
- Director responsibilities

- Director access to management and, as necessary and appropriate, independent advisors
- Director compensation
- Director orientation and continuing education
- Management succession
- Annual performance evaluation of the board

Listed companies must adopt and disclose a code of business conduct and ethics for directors, officers and employees, and promptly disclose any waivers of the code for directors or executive officers.

Including:

- Conflicts of interest
- Corporate opportunities
- Confidentiality
- Fair dealing
- Protection and proper use of company assets
- Compliance with laws, rules and regulations (including inside trading laws).
- Encouraging the reporting of any illegal or unethical behavior.' [29]

## The New York Stock Exchange's proposed new Standards for corporate governance

(to become Section 303A, if adopted)

1. Listed companies must have a majority of independent directors.

2. In order to tighten the definition of "independent director" for purposes of these standards:

    (a) No director qualifies as "independent" unless the board of directors affirmatively determines that the director has no material relationship with the listed company (either directly or as a partner, shareholder or officer of an organization that has a relationship with the company). Companies must disclose these determinations.

    (b) In addition:

        (i) No director who is a former employee of the listed company can be "independent" until five years after the employment has ended.

        (ii) No director who is, or in the past five years has been, affiliated with or employed by a (present or former) auditor of the company (or of an affiliate) can be "independent" until five years after the end of either the affiliation or the auditing relationship.

      (iii) No director can be "independent" if her or she is, or in the past five years has been, part of an interlocking directorate in which an executive officer of the listed company serves on the compensation committee of another company that concurrently employs the director.

      (iv) Directors with immediate family members in the foregoing categories are likewise subject to the five-year "cooling-off" provisions for purposes of determining "independence".

3. To empower non-management directors to serve as a more effective check on management, the non-management directors of each company must meet at regularly scheduled executive sessions without management.

4. (a) Listed companies must have a nominating/corporate governance committee composed entirely of independent directors.

    (b) The nominating/corporate governance committee must have a written charter that addresses:

      (i) the committee's purpose – which, at minimum, must be to: identify individuals qualified to become board members, and to select, or to recommend that the board select, the director nominees for the next annual meeting of shareholders; and develop and recommend to the board a set of corporate governance principles applicable to the corporation.

      (ii) the committee's goals and responsibilities – which must reflect, at minimum, the board's criteria for selecting new directors, and oversight of the evaluation of the board and management.

      (iii) an annual performance evaluation of the committee.

5. (a) Listed companies must have a compensation committee composed entirely of independent directors.

    (b) The compensation committee must have a written charter that addresses:

      (i) the committee's purpose – which, at minimum, must be to discharge the board's responsibilities relating to compensation of the company's executives, and to produce an annual report on executive compensation for inclusion in the company's proxy statement, in accordance with applicable rules and regulations.

      (ii) the committee's duties and responsibilities – which, at minimum, must be to:

        (A) review and approve corporate goals and objectives relevant to CEO compensation, evaluate the CEO's performance in light of those goals and objectives, and set the CEO's compensation level based on this evaluation.

        (B) make recommendations to the board with respect to incentive-compensation plans and equity-based plans.

(iii) an annual performance evaluation of the compensation committee.

6. Add to the "independence" requirement for audit committee membership the requirement that director's fees are the only compensation an audit committee member may receive from the company.

7. (a) Increase the authority and responsibilities of the audit committee, including granting it the sole authority to hire and fire independent auditors, and to approve any significant non-audit relationship with the independent auditors.

   (b) The audit committee must have a written charter that addresses:

   (i) the committee's purpose – which, at minimum, must be to:

      (A) assist board oversight of (1) the integrity of the company's financial statements, (2) the company's compliance with legal and regulatory requirements, (3) the independent auditor's qualifications and independence, and (4) the performance of the company's internal audit function and independent auditors; and

      (B) prepare the report that SEC rules require be included in the company's annual proxy statement.

   (ii) the duties and responsibilities of the audit committee – which, at minimum, must be to:

      (A) retain and terminate the company's independent auditors (subject, if applicable to shareholder ratification).

      (B) at least annually, obtain and review a report by the independent auditor describing: the firm's internal quality-control procedures; any material issues raised by the most recent internal quality-control review, or peer review, of the firm, or by any inquiry or investigation by governmental or professional authorities, within the preceding five years, respecting one or more independent audits carried out by the firm, and any steps taken to deal with any such issues; and (to assess the auditor's independence) all relationships between the independent auditor and the company.

      (C) discuss the annual audited financial statements and quarterly financial statements with management and the independent auditor, including the company's disclosures under "Management's Discussion and Analysis of Financial Condition and Results of Operations."

      (D) discuss earnings press releases, as well as financial information and earnings guidance provided to analysts and rating agencies.

      (E) as appropriate, obtain advice and assistance from outside legal, accounting or other advisors.

          (F)  discuss policies with respect to risk assessment and risk management.

          (G)  meet separately, periodically, with management, with internal auditors (or other personnel responsible for the internal audit function) and with independent auditors.

          (H)  review with the independent auditor any audit problems or difficulties and management's response.

          (I) set clear hiring policies for employees or former employees of the independent auditors.

          (J) report regularly to the board of directors.

        (iii) an annual performance evaluation of the audit committee.

    (c)  Each listed company must have an internal audit function.

8.    To increase shareholder control over equity-compensation plans, shareholders must be given the opportunity to vote on all equity-compensation plans, except inducement options, plans relating to mergers or acquisitions, and tax qualified and excess benefit plans.

9.    Listed companies must adopt and disclose corporate governance guidelines.

- Director qualification standards

- Director responsibilities

- Director access to management and, as necessary and appropriate, independent advisors

- Director compensation

- Director orientation and continuing education

- Management succession

- Annual performance evaluation of the board

10. Listed companies must adopt and disclose a code of business conduct and ethics for directors, officers and employees, and promptly disclose any waivers of the code for directors or executive officers.

Including:

- Conflicts of interest

- Corporate opportunities

- Confidentiality

- Fair dealing

- Protection and proper use of company assets

- Compliance with laws, rules and regulations (including inside trading laws).

- Encouraging the reporting of any illegal or unethical behaviour.

11. Listed foreign private issuers must disclose any significant ways in which their corporate governance practices differ from those followed by domestic companies under NYSE listing standards.

12. Each listed company CEO must certify to the NYSE each year that he or she is not aware of any violation by the company of NYSE corporate governance listing standards.

13. The NYSE may issue a public reprimand letter to any listed company that violates an NYSE listing standard.

# The US Sarbanes-Oxley Act 2002     B26.11

## Short summary of the US Sarbanes-Oxley Act     B26.12

This became law at end July 2002 and had to be implemented by the SEC by August 29. It was the hasty product of work by Democratic Senator Sarbenes from Maryland with input from Michael Oxley (Republican Chairman of the House Committee on Financial Services). It sets out a new system of audit regulation and tougher penalties for corporate wrongdoing. Here is a summary of the main features and issues.

1. Outright ban on nine kinds of non-audit service which must not be provided by the independent auditor of the company. These banned services include building financial information systems, legal services, actuarial services and investment banking.

2. Any non-audit work at all must be approved first by the company's audit committee.

3. But, still no requirement to rotate clients every few years, as is being considered in the UK.

4. A ban on corporate loans to officers. This raises a question about the permissibility of travel expense advances and use of company credit cards.

5. There is now a new board, funded and staffed independently, to oversee audits of public companies, with the power to investigate and fine auditors, and with the power to set auditing standards. Investigations could even be of auditors outside the US who could find themselves inspected by the new US accounting regulator if their clients include companies with secondary listings on US stock exchanges (unless exemption provisions of the Act are applied).[30]

6. Lawyers who represent public companies will be subject to similar scrutiny as accountants. The rationalise for this is that they are hired to protect shareholders, not executives; and their relationship should not remain confidential since they are not representing an individual.[31]

7. Wilful violation of a new obligation to certify the accuracy ('true in all respects', 'beyond reasonable doubt') of their annual and quarterly accounts will carry a prison sentence of up to 20 years. While this is intended to give

more confidence in the financial statements of US companies, it initially had the opposite effect as speculation ran rife as to which companies would not apply.

8.   The new obligation to certify accounts is broadly worded so that it deepens the potential liability of CEOs and CFOs.

9.   The new obligation to certify accounts is likely to enforced upon non-US companies with secondary stock exchange listings in US. There are 1,344 non-US companies with secondary listings in the US.

10.  Initially the SEC selected 947 from the Fortune 1000 list to certify their accounts. The rest of the 13,000 – 14,000 U.S. public companies had until the end of August to follow suit.

11.  CEO and CFO must certify, within 45 days of their year end (for most this meant August 14) their companies' financial reports under oath. In essence this means they must personally certify their companies' integrity – or watch their share price plunge still further. In turn, to give them valuable assurance, CEOs and CFOs are extracting written statements from executives further down the line (e.g. divisional presidents and divisional CFOs). It is said there is now more dialogue between CEOs and CFOs and (a) the audit committee, (b) outside directors (c) their auditors.

12.  A relevant question is how the Act applies in the event of the acquisition of a business to which the certification requirement did not apply (perhaps because it was not listed) by one to which it did. The CEO and CFO would not have designed or evaluated the internal controls of the company being taken over, so it might be impossible for them to vouch for them.

13.  Certifying statements (or declining to do so) will give new executive teams the opportunity to move their starting line.

14.  There is a risk of developing and following bureaucratic approaches to certifying the truth of financial statements in order to 'cover the back' of those making the certifications.

## Sarbanes-Oxley is more of a challenge for some UK listed companies than has been reported     B26.13

In some important respects the *Sarbanes-Oxley Act 2002* means that the US has leapfrogged over and beyond UK reporting practice on internal control – to an extent which is likely to need modifications of practice within UK companies with secondary listings in the US, and which may influence the development of corporate governance practices more generally in the UK.

The 1987 Report of the Treadway Commission on Fraudulent Financial Reporting had proposed that directors of US listed companies should report publicly on internal control. A similar proposal had been made in the late 1970's by the Securities and Exchange Commission (SEC) following the unambiguous statement in the 1977 Foreign Corrupt Practices Act that directors are responsible for internal control. The argument went that where there is responsibility there should also be accountability. In the late 1970's the SEC backed off making internal control reporting mandatory in view of strong opposition to it. Similar opposition greeted Treadway's proposal a decade later. One of the key objectives of the COSO study 'Internal Control – Integrated Framework' (1992) had been to address the concerns of those who were opposed to internal control reporting, as well as the concerns of those who were merely confused as to how to approach it. In 1992 'Internal Control – Integrated Framework' was published as four different volumes (sections) – with a later addendum to follow a year later.

One of the four volumes (sections) explained the COSO recommended approach to internal control reporting. That section is no longer provided when 'Internal Control – Integrated Framework' is purchased. The reasons are simple. First, the recommended approach failed to win general support. Secondly, internal control reporting did not become a mandatory requirement for US listed companies – the SEC backed off again as it had done in the late 1970's. The US was left behind compared, for instance, with the UK. Even so, the majority of large US-listed companies have voluntarily been reporting, annually and publicly, on internal control – though in a variety of non-standard ways.

Now, post-Enron and WorldCom, things have changed dramatically. The new *Sarbanes-Oxley Act 2002* requires that the CEO and the CFO must certify in 'each annual or quarterly report' that they are responsible for establishing and maintaining internal controls, that they have evaluated the effectiveness of the company's internal controls and that they have presented in the report their conclusions about the effectiveness of their internal controls based on their evaluation 'as of that date'.

In some respects this goes much further than the UK listed company position. UK listed companies with secondary listings in the US, all of whom are caught by the requirements of the *Sarbanes-Oxley Act 2002*, should not be too relaxed about their position. In the UK, while there is a 'requirement' for directors to 'review the effectiveness' of their systems of internal control, strictly there is no requirement for their review to lead to a specific conclusion as to whether internal control has been, and is, effective; and certainly no requirement that the directors' conclusion about effectiveness, if arrived at, need be published. Now, in the US, the CEO and CFO must report their conclusions on internal control effectiveness. Furthermore, in the US this is now a legal requirement with dire penalties for violation, whereas in the UK the whole matter of internal control review and effectiveness is at the level of a discretionary Combined Code 'Provision' (and the Turnbull guidance thereto); in the UK it is not even at the level of a mandatory 'Principle' and is certainly not enshrined in law.

It is probable that most, if not all, UK listed companies with secondary listings in the US *do* reach a conclusion about internal control effectiveness for internal use. It is however the case that most do not publish this conclusion – an 'opt out' not intended by the Cadbury Committee, but permitted first by the

Rutteman working party and then endorsed (as an 'opt out') by the Hampel and Turnbull committees. So there is a very significant change of practice which will be required in this respect. It poses the question as to whether the conclusion about internal control effectiveness, which must now be published, will be made only in the US filings of UK companies with secondary listings in the US, or whether these companies will also make the same disclosure on control effectiveness in their annual report and accounts prepared under UK listing rules. It also raises the question as to whether other UK listed companies (not having secondary listings in the US) as well as other UK entities will now move towards disclosing their opinions about internal control effectiveness – as the Cadbury committee had originally intended.

A key question is what are the US criteria of 'effectiveness' in this context? As we will see below, it does seem that it is effectiveness of internal *financial* control alone which is being addressed, but this is not entirely clear from the Act. The *Sarbanes-Oxley Act 2002 (section 404* – see box below) states it to be management's responsibility to establish and maintain an adequate internal control structure and procedures for financial reporting. So 'effectiveness' is presumably to be a matter of whether there has been 'an adequate internal control structure and procedures for financial reporting'.

*Section 404* reads as follows.

---

**Section 404: Management assessment of internal controls**

(a) RULES REQUIRED. – The Commission shall prescribe rules requiring each annual report required by section 13(a) or 15(d) of the Securities Exchange Act of 1934 (15 U.S.C. 78m, 78o(d)) to contain an internal control report, which shall –

   (1) state the responsibility of management for establishing and maintaining an adequate internal control structure and procedures for financial reporting; and

   (2) contain an assessment as of the end of the most recent fiscal year of the issuer, of the effectiveness of the internal control structure and procedures of the issuer for financial reporting.

(b) INTERNAL CONTROL EVALUATION AND REPORTING. – With respect to the internal control assessment required by subsection (a), each registered public accounting firm that prepares or issues the audit report for the issuer shall attest to, and report on, the assessment made by the management of the issuer. An attestation made under this subsection shall be made in accordance with standards for attestation engagements issued or adopted by the Board. Any such attestation shall not be the subject of a separate engagement.

---

There is also a distinct difference between the US and the UK in that in the former it is the CEO and CFO who make these assertions whereas in the UK the report on internal control (albeit with no disclosure on effectiveness) is in the name of all the directors. Again, this poses a significant new demand for UK listed companies with secondary US listings – in that there must now be in train processes which will allow UK CEOs and CFOs to personally be able to make these assertions. It is true that if each director in the UK lends his or her support to a report, then the CEO and the CFO are included in this. But a report specifically in the name of the CEO and CFO will be likely to focus the minds of those two directors rather more than would a report in the name of the board as a whole – indeed that is the intention. While, in the past, possibly some UK CEOs and CFOs might have been sheltering behind the collective sentiment of the board with respect to their confidence in the company's systems of internal control, this will not longer be adequate in the future for those with secondary US listings.

There is also the question as to what is the UK equivalent of the 'CEO' who is often an altogether more dominant figure in the US than is the chief executive in the UK. Except where the roles of chairman and chief executive are combined, UK companies with a secondary US listing may find that both their chairmen and their chief executives (as well as their finance directors) must sign off to these matters in the US,

The *Sarbanes-Oxley Act 2002* is clear that the scope of the internal control report covers all of the operations consolidated into the results of the group which is listed in the US – wherever across the world those operations are located. UK best practice is similar.

In the UK the guidance is that directors should consider the effectiveness of internal control over the whole of the period being reported (usually a financial year) and also over the period of time between the year-end and the date of the annual report. The *Sarbanes-Oxley Act 2002* requires that the evaluation of the effectiveness of a US e issuer's internal controls must be made within 90 days prior to the report and that the company must publish an assessment as of the end of the most recent fiscal year of the issuer. For UK companies caught by these requirements, this may require a revision of the timing of the directors' consideration of the effectiveness of internal control. Both the US and the UK are at one in that the period between (a) the consideration of internal control effectiveness and (b) the date of the report must be taken into account, including the period after the year-end up to the date of publication [see box].

If this were all, a pragmatic interpretation would indicate that affected companies will need at least two audit committee meetings within 90 days of the annual report – one to evaluate internal control and the other to scrutinise the year-end financial statements: it would be too much to properly cover both in one meeting. But this is not all! Section 302 (see box below) of the Act indicates that the year-end requirement also applies for the reports of the quarter-ends: the same assurances are stated as being required of the CEO and the CFO and the same '90 day' provision applies. On the other hand Section 404 refers only to an *annual* reporting requirement. We will have to wait and see how the new Public Company Accounting Oversight Board and the SEC interpret this. If one adds to this the US audit committee's other duties with respect to quarterly published results, then it is apparent that audit committee meetings are going to be much more frequent in the future.

*Section 302* of the *Sarbanes-Oxley Act 2002* reads as follows.

---

**Section 302: Corporate responsibility for financial reports**

(a) REGULATIONS REQUIRED. – The Commission shall, by rule, require for each company filing periodic reports under section 13(a) or 15(d) of the Securities Exchange Act of 1934 (15 U.S.C. 78m, 78o(d)), that the principal executive officer or officers and the principal financial officer or officers, or persons performing similar functions, certify in each annual or quarterly report filed or submitted under either such section of such Act that –

(1) the signing officer has reviewed the report;

(2) based on the officer's knowledge, the report does not contain any untrue statement of a material fact or omit to state a material fact necessary in order to make the statements made, in light of the circumstances under which such statements were made, not misleading;

(3) based on such officer's knowledge, the financial statements, and other financial information included in the report, fairly present in all material respects the financial condition and results of operations of the issuer as of, and for, the period presented in the report;

(4) The signing officers –

   (A) are responsible for establishing and maintaining internal controls;

   (B) have designed such internal controls to ensure that material information relating to the issuer and its consolidated subsidiaries is made known to such officers by others within those entities, particularly during the period in which the periodic reports are being prepared;

   (C) have evaluated the effectiveness of the issuer's internal controls as of a date within 90 days prior to the report; and

   (D) have presented in the report their conclusions about the effectiveness of their internal controls based on their evaluation as of that date;

(5) the signing officers have disclosed to the issuer's auditors and the audit committee of the board of directors (or persons fulfilling the equivalent function) –

   (A) all significant deficiencies in the design or operation of internal controls which could adversely affect the issuer's

---

> ability to record, process, summarize, and report financial data and have identified for the issuer's auditors any material weaknesses in internal controls; and
>
> (B) any fraud, whether or not material, that involves management or other employees who have a significant role in the issuer's internal controls; and
>
> (6) the signing officers have indicated in the report whether or not there are any significant changes in internal controls or in other factors that could significantly affect internal controls subsequent to the date of their evaluation, including any corrective actions with regard to significant deficiencies and material weaknesses.

The US position now specifically requires the CEO and the CFO to notify the independent auditors and the audit committee of anything which, following the evaluation of internal control, may impact the effectiveness of internal control. Some UK audit committees and independent auditors can therefore now expect specific reports on this to be addressed to them by the CEO and CFO.

Under the *Sarbanes-Oxley Act 2002* independent auditors in the US will be required to attest to the CEOs' and CFOs' internal control assertions. So far the Act does not make the fine distinction which is made in the UK between the level of external auditor scrutiny which constitutes an 'audit' and the lesser level which constitutes a 'review'. However the Act does require the new US Public Company Accounting Oversight Board to adopt an audit standard for implementing the internal control review required of the independent auditors per Section 404(b) [see Box]; and the Act does indicate that it is not the legislators' intention that this new requirement will be a separate engagement from the audit engagement itself. When the Act was a Bill it also indicated that this new requirement should not be a basis for increased audit charges or fees.

Corporate governance matters are now being swept into the US independent audit in a way that external auditors in the UK have been adamantly opposed to.

There is however an apparent partial 'let out' in the US. While much of the wording of the *Sarbanes-Oxley Act 2002* refers to 'internal control' rather than 'internal financial control', some wording would seem to imply that the CEO's and CFO's assertions about internal control effectiveness may be limited to internal *financial* control (see box) viz:

'such internal controls [designed] to ensure that material information relating to the issuer and its consolidated subsidiaries is made known to such officers by others within those entities, particularly during the period in which the periodic reports are being prepared.

all significant deficiencies in the design or operation of internal controls which could adversely affect the issuer's ability to record, process, summarize, and report financial data and have identified for the issuer's auditors any material weaknesses in internal controls;

any fraud, whether or not material, that involves management or other employees who have a significant role in the issuer's internal controls;'

This apparent narrowing of the scope of internal control reporting under the *Sarbanes-Oxley Act 2002* is clearly a consequence of the impetus behind the drafting of this Act which has been the significant concern about fraudulent financial reporting of some US companies. The wording of the *Sarbanes-Oxley Act 2002* does however give scope for interpreting the Act as requiring the CEO and CFO to report on operational and compliance (legal and regulatory etc) control as well as internal financial control – not least because the phrase 'internal control' rather than 'internal *financial* control' is used throughout. If a narrower scope (just internal *financial* control) becomes the US requirement when this has been clarified by the Public Company Accounting Oversight Board and the SEC, then in this respect the UK is in advance of the US. In the UK the scope of the directors' review, per the Combined Code, covers 'financial, operational and compliance control and risk management'

To reinforce the role of the CFO and his or her colleagues with respect to their assertions on the reliability of the published financial statements and the effectiveness of internal control, the *Sarbanes-Oxley Act 2002* requires a US listed company to disclose whether or not (and, if not, the reason therefore) it has adopted a code of ethics for its senior financial officers. Changes or waiver of the Code must be published, and the implication must surely be that the Code itself should also be published.[32]

## US Securities and Exchange Commission's Final Rule on 'Management's Reports on Internal Control Over Financial Reporting and Certification of Disclosure in Exchange Act Periodic Reports'   B26.14

On 11 June 2003 the US Securities and Exchange Commission issued its final rule interpreting Section 404 (and also 302) of the *Sarbanes-Oxley Act 2002*, having made modifications from an earlier exposure draft. It can be downloaded from http://www.sec.gov/rules/final/33–8238.htm. In this final rule, the SEC also adopted amendments to the SEC rules and forms under the *Securities Exchange Act 1934* and the *Investment Company Act 1940* to revise the section 302 certification requirements and to require issuers to provide the certifications required by *sections 302* and *906* of the *Sarbanes-Oxley Act 2002* as exhibits to certain periodic reports.

*Section 404* applies to companies listed in the US including overseas companies with secondary listings in the US. In this critique the transitional arrangements contained within this final rule are not covered; also not covered are the requirement relating to certifying internal control over *disclosures* (re. *section 302* of the *Sarbanes-Oxley Act 2002*) which also are to be made in quarterly, half-yearly and annual reports, and which the SEC addresses as well. This critique focuses on approaching the challenge and reporting on the effectiveness of internal control over financial reporting.

SEC defines 'internal control over financial reporting' as given in the following box.

---

**SEC definition of 'internal control over financial reporting'**

'A process designed by, or under the supervision of, the registrant's principal executive and principal financial officers, or persons performing similar functions, and effected by the registrant's board of directors, management and other personnel, to provide reasonable assurance regarding the reliability of financial reporting and the preparation of financial statements for external purposes in accordance with generally accepted accounting principles and includes those policies and procedures that:

(1) Pertain to the maintenance of records that in reasonable detail accurately and fairly reflect the transactions and dispositions of the assets of the registrant;

(2) Provide reasonable assurance that transactions are recorded as necessary to permit preparation of financial statements in accordance with generally accepted accounting principles[1], and that receipts and expenditures of the registrant are being made only in accordance with authorizations of management and directors of the registrant; and

(3) Providing reasonable assurance regarding prevention or timely detection of unauthorized acquisition, use or disposition of the registrant's assets which could have a material effect on the financial statements.'

[1] Meaning financial statements prepared for regulatory reporting purposes [SEC, page 83 of 93: endnote 51.

---

**Internal audit**                                                         **B26.15**

There is much in this SEC Rule to delight that small band of internal control cognoscenti! But we could see no mention of internal audit in this long (93 pages) SEC Rule Notice. Under the *Sarbanes-Oxley Act 2002* a listed company must now have an internal audit of internal financial control. We assume that the SEC permits management to enlist the services of their internal audit function to undertake much of the background work required for their assessment of the effectiveness of internal control over financial reporting, and we expect many more managements to require their internal audit functions to provide formal reports with opinions about the effectiveness of internal financial control over financial reporting. Clearly this may reorientate the focus of internal audit – away from the provision of consulting services and towards the more effective provision of assurance services – assurance services in the highly focused area of internal control over financial reporting.

Another interpretation would be that management's assessment should be additional to whatever internal audit is routinely undertaking for management to provide assurance on internal control over financial reporting. The rationale for this interpretation would be that internal audit in a broad sense is part of the system of internal control: internal audit fits into the COSO/Rutteman/ Turnbull 'monitoring' component of internal control. The definition of internal auditing of The Institute of Internal Auditors points out that internal audit has a mission to 'improve' things. Material weaknesses of controls over financial reporting may be uncovered and rectified as a result of routine internal auditing: should these be regarded as weaknesses which require management to conclude that there are reportable material weaknesses in internal control over financial reporting? Or, on the contrary, is it evidence that internal control is working?

There is also another point of principle here. Internal audit should be independent of management. The guidance of The Institute of Internal Auditors is that internal audit should report *directly* to the audit committee of the board. So, the question has to be posed whether, from this standpoint, management should be permitted to rely on internal audit's assessment of the effectiveness of internal control, when the SEC requirement is that *management* does this assessment.

**The scope of internal control covered by section 404 of Sarbanes-Oxley**                                                                **B26.16**

Companies subject to the reporting requirements of the SEC Act (1934) must now include within their annual report a report of management on the company's internal control over financial reporting which was the scope expressed in *section 404* of the *Sarbanes-Oxley Act 2002*. The SEC mention a number of reasons for not extending the scope of internal control to be covered beyond the boundary of internal control over financial reporting, one of which is that ...

> 'Independent accountants traditionally have not been responsible for reviewing and testing, or attesting to an assessment by management of, internal controls that are outside the boundary of financial reporting.' [33]

We note that the addendum to the 1992 COSO report had principally classified under *operational control* the internal controls which safeguard assets from unauthorized acquisition, use or disposition. In this SEC rule these controls are classified as part of internal financial control which is consistent with the UK Rutteman committee's guidance, now superceded by the Turnbull Report. (The Turnbull Report is silent on this issue). Both the SEC and Rutteman are being pragmatic: it is convenient to regard the control over assets as belonging to internal financial control (even to internal financial *reporting* control) as it is an aspect of internal control which impinges upon the reliability of published financial statements and has thus always been a concern of external auditors (whereas other aspects of operational control rarely are such a concern). SEC concede that whether or not controls for safeguarding of assets fall within this subset of internal control 'could be subject to varying interpretation'.[34] The SEC also points out that COSO had said that although controls for safeguarding resources are primarily operational controls they can also be regarded as financial controls to the extent that the financial statements depend upon them.[35]

We observe that, conceptually, internal control over financial reporting is rather less than all of internal financial control as it omits those internal controls which contribute to the reliability of financial information used within the business but which have no impact upon financial information which is reported publicly. However, SEC believes that their definition of internal control over financial reporting encompasses the subset of internal controls addressed in the COSO report that pertains to financial reporting objectives.[36]

**The published report on internal control – contrasts with the UK**   **B26.17**

Note that it is a report of management in contrast to the UK where, under the Combined Code, it is a report of the directors. Secondly, it is a report on just internal control over financial reporting whereas in the UK it the report embraces operational and compliance control as well (that is, all of internal control) and risk management.

The US's more modest scope is perhaps more than counterbalanced first by the requirement to disclose an opinion on the effectiveness of internal control over financial reporting (whereas in the nearest the UK gets to this that under Combined Code Provision D.2.1, directors must report only that they have *reviewed* the effectiveness of internal control, not what opinion about effectiveness they have drawn that review, if indeed they drew any opinion. Secondly there are potentially severe criminal sanctions under *section 906* of the *Sarbanes-Oxley Act 2002* which are associated with false or negligent reporting by management on internal financial control effectiveness. We reproduce *section 906* in the following box:

---

**Section 906: Corporate responsibility for financial reports**

(a)  IN GENERAL. – Chapter 63 of title 18, United States Code, is amended by inserting after section 1349, as created by this Act, the following:

'§ 1350. Failure of corporate officers to certify financial reports

(a)  CERTIFICATION OF PERIODIC FIANCAIL REPORTS. – Each periodic report containing financial statements filed by an issuer with the |Securities Exchange Commission pursuant to section 13(a) or 15(d) of the Securities Exchange Act of 1934 (15 U.S.C. 78m(a) or 78o(d) shall be accompanied by a written statement by the chief executive officer and chief financial officer (or equivalent thereof) of the issuer.

---

(b) CONTENT. – The statement required under subsection (a) shall certify that the periodic report containing the financial statements fully complies with the requirements of section 13(a) or 15(d) of the Securities Exchange Act of 1934 (15 U.S.C. 78m or 78o(d) and that information contained in the periodic report fairly presents, in all material respects, the financial condition and results of operations of the issuer.

(c) CRIMINAL PENALTIES. – Whoever –

  (1) certifies any statement as set forth in subsections (a) and (b) of this section knowing that the periodic report accompanying the statement does not comport with all the requirements set forth in this section shall be fined not more that $1,000,000 or imprisoned not more than 10 years, or both; or

  (2) Willfully certifies any statement as set forth in subsections (a) and (b) of this section knowing that the periodic report accompanying the statement does not comport with all the requirements set forth in this section shall be fined not more than $5,000,000, or imprisoned not more than 20 years, or both.'

In the UK the relevant Code Provision D.2.1 is (as with all Provisions) is discretionary on a 'comply or explain' basis.

Despite the above, it should however be noted that 'effectiveness' is reported in the UK to the extent that the Turnbull guidance on Code Provision D.2.1 requires that the directors' internal control report must address the *process* the board has followed in the event that a significant control failure is known to have occurred, unless the board were to choose to opt out of complying with this Provision:

'In relation to Code provision D.2.1, the board should summarise the process it (where applicable, through its committees) has applied in reviewing the effectiveness of the system of internal control. It should also disclose the process it has applied to deal with material internal control aspects of any significant problems disclosed in the annual report and accounts.' [37]

**The US requirements**                                    **B26.18**

In the US, management must now include in their annual report a report on the company's internal control over financial reporting which must address each of the first four of the following, with the fifth to be included in quarterly filings, if necessary:

1. A statement of management's responsibility for establishing and maintaining adequate internal control over financial reporting for the company.

2. Management's assessment of the effectiveness of the company's internal control over financial reporting as of the end of the company's most recent fiscal year, including a statement as to whether or not the company's internal control over financial reporting is effective.

3. A statement identifying the framework used by management to conduct the required evaluation of the effectiveness of the company's internal control over financial reporting

4. A statement that the registered public accounting firm that audited the company's reported financial statements included in the annual report has issued an attestation report on management's assessment of the company's internal control over financial reporting.

5. The result of management's evaluation of any change during a fiscal quarter that has materially affected, or is reasonably likely to affect, the company's internal control over financial reporting.

### Material weakness and 'significant deficiency'; management's assessment of effectiveness · B26.19

The final SEC rule precludes management concluding that internal control over financial reporting is effective if management has identified one or more 'material weakness'; and any material weakness identified by management must be disclosed.[38]

We give the SEC's definitions of 'material weakness' and 'significant deficiency' in the following box. Note that an aggregation of 'significant deficiencies' could constitute a material weakness. Note that a 'significant weakness' has the same meaning as the already established meaning of a 'reportable condition' under GAAS and attestation standards (AU §325 and AT §501).

---

**Material weakness' and 'significant deficiency'**

These terms both represent deficiencies in the design or operation of internal control that could adversely affect the company's ability to record, process, summarize and report financial data consistent with the assertions of management in the company's financial statements, with a material weakness constituting a great deficiency than a significant deficiency. Because of this relationship an aggregation of and significant deficiencies could constitute a material weakness.

---

Although this phraseology used to define 'material weakness' and 'significant deficiency' is tortuous, it seems to refer to the existence of a condition which would have the *potential* to impact the reliability of the financial statement, even if it has not done so. If, perhaps but not necessarily as a result of their assessment of internal control required by this Rule, management uncovered a control weakness which was resulting in a major management fraud, we assume that this would constitute a 'material weakness' to be reported. Yet such an event would not result in unreliable financial statements if management then made sure that the fraud was accounted for properly in those financial statements. Furthermore, it could be argued that management's discovery of the fraud was an example of internal control over financial reporting working, not failing.

This Rule does however preclude management from regarding their assessment of internal control as required by this Rule as being part of their system of internal control itself: this is clear from the statement:

> 'The final rules therefore preclude management from determining that a company's internal control over financial reporting is effective if it identifies one or more material weakness in the company's internal; control over financial reporting.' [39]

But, logically, if management has succeeded in uncovering a material weakness then it ceases to be a material weakness if management does not allow it to result in a material misstatement in the financial results – especially if management has corrected the material weakness. Such could be expected to be the outcome – not least because management's assessment is attested to by the external auditors.

In instances when management's assessment *fails* to uncover a material weakness, clearly management will be unable to report a material weakness of which they were unaware. This leads us to the conclusion that we can expect section 906 (which relates to criminal sanctions – see earlier box) to be applied in such circumstances when subsequent events show that management had been negligent or deceitful.

We also conclude that we are unlikely to see a rash of candid disclosures about control failures and inadequacies – not least because of the impracticality of disregarding management's assessment of internal financial reporting control as being part of the system of control itself. We think that errors etc identified in the assessment will be corrected, the financial statements will end up being reliable and no disclosure of control weakness usually will be made. It is likely only to be when prior period adjustments are required (because a concealed, material control weakness has been long-running) that management will be unable to avoid disclosing the material weakness. In so doing they are being required to incriminate themselves because they have finally been successful in uncovering a material weakness in internal financial reporting control. It is all very unfair!

**Method of conducting the evaluation of the effectiveness of internal control over financial reporting**                                    **B26.20**

The SEC points out that even though the external auditor may assist management in documenting internal controls (and there will be a need for coordination), management must be actively involved in the process; and that management cannot delegate its responsibility for assessing internal control over financial reporting to the external auditor.[40]

A negative assurance statement indicating that nothing has come to management's attention to suggest that the company's internal control over financial reporting is not effective will not be acceptable.[41]

The SEC does not specify the method to be followed to conduct the evaluation of the effectiveness of internal control over financial reporting. The SEC prudently considers this will vary from company to company. The SEC does however set out the general approach, which we reproduce in the box below:

---

' ... a company must obtain evidential matter, including documentation, to provide reasonable support for management's assessment of the effectiveness of the company's internal control over financial reporting ...

... the assessment ... must be based on procedures sufficient both to evaluate its design and to test its operating effectiveness. Controls subject to such assessment include, but are not limited to:

- Controls over initiating, recording, processing and reconciling account balances, classes of transactions and disclosure and related assertions included in the financial statements;

- Controls relating to the initiation and processing on non-routine and non-systematic transactions;

- Controls related to the selection and application of appropriate accounting policies; and

- Controls relating to the identification and detection of fraud.

The nature of a company's testing activities will largely depend on the circumstances of the company and the significance of the control. However, inquiry alone will generally not provide an adequate basis for management's assessment.

An assessment of the effectiveness of internal control over financial reporting must be supported by evidential matter, including documentation, regarding both the design of internal controls and the testing processes. This evidential matter should provided reasonable support:

- For the evaluation of whether the control is designed to prevent or detect material misstatements or omissions;

- For the conclusion that the tests were appropriately planned and performed; and

- That the results of the tests were appropriately considered.

---

> The public accounting firm that is required to attest to, and report on, management's assessment of the effectiveness of the company's internal control over financial reporting also will require that the company develop and maintain such evidential matter to support management's assessment.'

### Using an acceptable framework as the basis for the evaluation     B26.21

The SEC requires that management bases its evaluation:

> 'on a suitable, recognized control framework that is established by a body or group that has followed due-process procedures, including the broad distribution of the framework for public comment.[42]

> The Guidance on Assessing Control published by the Canadian Institute of Chartered Accountants and the Turnbull Report published by The Institute of Chartered Accountants in England & Wales are examples of other suitable frameworks.'[43]

The frameworks mentioned by the SEC as being satisfactory to use are not intended to be a complete list, nor for all time. The SEC recognizes that further suitable frameworks are likely to be developed – even in the US. We would expect one of these to be COSO's Enterprise Risk Management framework, the development of which is currently entailing 10,000 professional hours of time from PricewaterhouseCoopers New York office. If this new framework is found to be acceptable for this purpose it will be interesting to see whether, in the fullness of time 'enterprise risk management' comes to replace 'internal control' as the terminology used. We do know that COSO intends that their 1992 internal control framework should not be superceded by the new one since the former has been built into laws and regulations across the world – of which this new SEC rule is an example. Even the *Sarbanes-Oxley Act 2002* would require amendment before 'enterprise risk management' could replace 'internal control' since it is the latter wording which appears in the Act.

The SEC does set out the criteria to judge whether a framework is suitable to use:

> 'Specifically, a suitable framework must: be free of bias; permit reasonably consistent qualitative and quantitative measurements of a company's internal control; be sufficiently complete so that those relevant factors that would alter a conclusion about the effectiveness of a company's internal controls are not omitted; and be relevant to an evaluation of internal control over financial reporting.'[44]

On the basis of 'being]sufficiently complete so that those relevant factors that would alter a conclusion about the effectiveness of a company's internal controls are not omitted' we consider the Turnbull Report to have been fortunate to have been included as acceptable by the SEC, admirable though its brevity is in other respects.

The SEC covers the point that while some evaluation frameworks, for instance the Turnbull Report, do not require a conclusion to be reported about effectiveness, nevertheless for the purposes of complying with Sarbanes-Oxley/SEC such a conclusion must be drawn even if a framework is being applied which requires no such conclusion to be made.[45]

**Quarterly assessments and reporting**                                **B26.22**

The SEC has considered the implications of *section 404* of the *Sarbanes-Oxley Act 2002* with respect to the quarterly reporting requirement of US listed companies (with the exception of foreign private issuers who do not report quarterly) and has decided that, while quarterly certifications are required, the quarterly evaluations of internal control over financial reporting need not be so extensive. There should be an evaluation of the entire system of internal control over financial reporting over a period of time so as to adequately determine whether, as at the end of the company's fiscal year, the design and operation of the company's internal control over financial reporting are effective.

A company must disclose any change in its internal control over financial reporting that have occurred during the fiscal quarter covered by the quarterly report, or in the last fiscal quarter in the case of the annual report, that has materially affected, or is likely to materially affect, the company's internal control over financial reporting. The reasons for the change may have to be disclosed if failure to do so would make the information about the change misleading.[46] The SEC says that the evaluation of changes, quarter by quarter, should be made by 'a company's management, with the participation of the principal executive and financial officers'.[47]

**External audit involvement**                                         **B26.23**

The external auditor's attestation must be part of the published annual report. Guidance for auditors on their approach to attesting management's assessment[48] was adopted on 16 April 2003 by PCAOB and almost immediately approved by SEC for the purpose of attestations required under *section 404* of the *Sarbanes-Oxley Act 2002*.

There is no doubt that this attestation is a more rigorous matter than the review which external auditors of UK companies undertake with respect to directors' assertions with regard to Code Provision D.2.1. In the UK it is a negative assurance review and the results of this review are normally not published. It is only if the external auditors of a UK company consider there is evidence to deny the contentions that the directors are making in their internal control statement that the external auditors will refer to this in their audit report. We know of no example where this has occurred.

The *Sarbanes-Oxley Act 2002* requires the external audit attestation to be undertaken as part of the audit engagement – not as a separate engagement. The original intention of this requirement might have been to endeavour to contain the extra fees that companies might have to pay to their external auditors; but there is the additional affect that the conduct and results of this external audit work could be regarded in court as evidence of the quality of the annual audit itself.

**Code of ethics for senior financial officers**                                   **B26.24**

The rules are being extended to include a new code of ethics for senior financial officers, as trailed in *section 406* of the *Sarbanes-Oxley Act 2002* (see box below).

---

**Section 406: Code of ethics for senior financial officers**

(a) CODE OF ETHICS DISCLOSURE. – The Commission shall issue rules to require each issuer, together with periodic reports required pursuant to section 13(a) or 15(d) of the Securities Exchange Act of 1934, to disclose whether or not, and if not, the reason therefor, such issuer has adopted a code of ethics for senior financial officers, applicable to its principal financial officer and comptroller or principal financial officer, or persons performing similar functions.

(b) CHANGES IN CODES OF ETHICS. – The Commission shall revise its regulations concerning matters requiring prompt disclosure on Form 8-K (or any successor thereto) to require the immediate disclosure, by means of the filing of such form, dissemination by the Internet or by other electronic means, by any issuer of any change in or waiver of the code of ethics for senior financial officer.

[The Act then provides a definition of what must be contained within this code of ethics.]

---

**Notes**
1. New proposed US Standards 11, 12 and 13.
2. Michael Groom, president of The Institute of Chartered Accountants in England Wales, to a conference in Beijing on 26 August 2002, speaking mainly about accounting and auditing standards, reported in The Times, (26 August 2002): 'Accountants want UK ethics to be adopted worldwide', p2.
3. Combined Code 'Provision' A.3.2.
4. New proposed US Standard 2. (a).
5. See 'Corporate Governance Rule Proposals reflecting Recommendations from the NYSE Corporate Accountability and Listing Standards Committee, As Approved by the NYSE Board of Directors August 1, 2002' which can be found on the NYSE website: www.nyse.com, p9/10.
6. New proposed US Standard 2. (a), (i) to (iv).
7. See 'Corporate Governance Rule Proposals reflecting Recommendations from the NYSE Corporate Accountability and Listing Standards Committee, As Approved by the NYSE Board of Directors August 1, 2002' which can be found on the NYSE website: !!!!!!!!!`÷"http://www.nyse.com" ˜˜≠www.nyse.com˜§, p9.
8. New proposed US Standard 3.
9. Under UK Combined Code Provision A.5.1.
10. UK Combined Code Provision A.5.1
11. UK Combined Code Provision A.5.1

12. New proposed US Standard 4. (a).
13. New proposed US Standard 4. (b) (i)
14. UK Combined Code Provisions B.2.1 and B.2.2
15. New proposed US Standard 5.(a).
16. New proposed US Standard 5.(b) (i)
17. New proposed US Standard 7.(b) (i) (A) and (B)
18. New proposed US Standard 4.(b)
19. Code Provision B.2.1
20. New proposed US Standard 5.(b)
21. New proposed US Standard 6.
22. New proposed US Standard 8.
23. New proposed US Standard 7. (a).
24. New proposed US Standard 7. (b) (ii) (I).
25. The Combined Code, Principle D.3 and Provisions D.3.1 and D.3.2
26. The Combined Code, Principle D.3 and Provisions D.3.1 and D.3.2
27. New proposed US Standard 7. (b) (i) (C).
28. The Combined Code, Provision D.2.2.
29. See 'Corporate Governance Rule Proposals reflecting Recommendations from the NYSE Corporate Accountability and Listing Standards Committee, As Approved by the NYSE Board of Directors August 1, 2002' which can be found on the NYSE website: www.nyse.com, p9/18.
30. New proposed US Standard 9 and 10.
31. Andrew Parker, (13 August 2002): 'British companies may be hit by US fraud law', Financial Times, p2.
32. Peter Spiegel, (13 August 2002): 'SEC chief warns lawyers on scrutiny', Financial Times, p6.
33. We could not find any statement in the Act which specifically requires publication of the Code itself.
34. p9 of 93.
35. Page 10 of 93.
36. Page 86 of 93Ú‰endnote 57.
37. p10 of 93
38. Para 38 of The Turnbull Report.
39. Pages 14–15 of 93.
40. Page 14 of 93.
41. Page 14 of 93.
42. Page 84 of 93: endnote 62.
43. Page 13 of 93.
44. Page 85 of 93: endnote 67.
45. Page 14 of 93.
46. Page 85 of 93: endnote 68.
47. Page 21 of 93.
48. Page 17 of 93.
49. Statements on Standards for Attestation Engagements, SSAE No. 10.

# Bibliography

## Introduction APP1.1

Inevitably, this collection of hard copy resources is to some extent the subjective judgement of the complier. For ease of reference it has been divided into the following sections:

- Key UK reports and pronouncements of an official/regulatory character (see **APP1.2**).

- International and overseas reports and pronouncements (see **APP1.3**).

- Other UK reports and pronouncements (see **APP1.4**).

- Books and guides (see **APP1.5**).

- Research reports (see **APP1.6**).

- Articles (see **APP1.7**).

- Journals and newsletters (see **APP1.8**).

In addition, APPENDIX 5 provides details on websites not included in this section.

## Key UK reports and pronouncements of an official/regulatory character APP1.2

- Cadbury report: 'Report of the Committee on the Financial Aspects of Corporate Governance' (1 December 1992), chaired by Sir Adrian Cadbury; Gee Publishing Ltd, 100 Avenue Road, Swiss Cottage, London, NW3 3PG, Freephone: +44 (0)345 573113; Fax.: +44 (0)171 393 7463, ISBN 0 85258 913 1 (Report); ISBN 0 85258 915 8 (Report with Code of Best Practice), 91 A5 pages. Available from http://www.ecgi.org/codes/country_pages/codes_uk.htm. This Code is reproduced at PARAGRAPH 3.4 to 3.9 of this handbook.

- Combined Code, (July 1998): originally an appendix to The Stock Exchange Listing Rules ('the Yellow Book') and available from Gee Publishing Limited, 100 Avenue Road, Swiss Cottage, London, NW3 3PG, England [Tel.: +44 (0)171 393 7400; fax.: +44 (0)171 722 4762]. Now an appendix to the SFA's 'Purple Book'. UK Listing Authority, a division of the Financial Services Authority, 25 The North Colonnade, Canary Wharf, London, E14 5HS, [Tel.: +44 (0)20 7676 1000; http://www.fsa.gov.uk. Available from http://www.ecgi.org/codes/country_pages/codes_uk.htm.

The Combined Code is reproduced at PARAGRAPHS 3.14 to 3.32 of this handbook.

● Combined Code, (July 2003), reproduced in Part 1 of this Handbook. Available on line from the Financial reporting Council: http://www.frc.org.uk; Hard copies can be obtained from:

● Financial Reporting Council, Holborn Hall, 100 Gray 's Inn Road, London WC1X 8AL, Tel:+44 (0)20 7611 9700, Fax:+44 (0)20 7404 4497, 82 pages.

● Greenbury Report: 'Directors' Remuneration – Report of a Study Group, chaired by Sir Richard Greenbury', (July 1995),.Confederation of British Industry – the Greenbury committee (Report with Code of Best Practice). Available from http://www.ecgi.org/codes/country_pages/codes_uk.htmThe Code of Best Practice is reproduced at PARAGRAPHS 3.10 to 3.13 of this handbook.

● Hampel Preliminary Report, (August 1997): 'Committee on corporate governance – preliminary report', chaired by Sir Ronald Hampel.

● Hampel report: 'Final Report of the Committee on Corporate Governance', (January 1998), chaired by Sir Ronald Hampel; Gee Publishing Ltd, 100 Avenue Road, Swiss Cottage, London, NW3 3PG, Freephone: +44 (0)345 573113; Fax.: +44 (0)171 393 7463. ISBN 1 86089 034 2. 66 A5 pages; Available from http://www.ecgi.org/codes/country_pages/codes_uk.htm

● Higgs Report, (January 2003): 'Review of the role and effectiveness of non-executive directors ', a report to the Chancellor of the Exchequer and the Secretary of State for Trade and Industry by Derek Higgs. On-line copies of the report and background research which underpinned the report (including a MORI survey) are available at http://www.dti.gov.uk/cld/non_exec_review. Hard copies from The Department of Trade and Industry, Room 507, 1 Victoria Street, London, SW1H 0ET (Tel.: 020 7215 0409). 120 pages.

● Myners Report (March 2001): 'Institutional Investment in the United Kindgom – A Review', 199 pages. [obtain from http://www.hm-treasury.gov.uk/Documents/Financial_Services/Securities_and_Investments/fin_sec_mynfinal.cfm]

● Rutteman report: 'Internal control and financial reporting: guidance for directors of listed companies registered in the UK', (December 1994), 'The Rutteman Report', ICAEW, London.

● Smith Report, (January 2003): 'AUDIT COMMITTEES – COMBINED CODE GUIDANCE', A report and proposed guidance by an FRC-appointed group chaired by Sir Robert Smith. Electronic copies of this report are available on line at: http://www.frc.org.uk/publications. Hard copies can be obtained from:

● Financial Reporting Council, Holborn Hall, 100 Gray 's Inn Road, London WC1X 8AL, Tel:+44 (0)20 7611 9700, Fax:+44 (0)20 7404 4497, 52 pages.

- Standards in Public Life, First Report of the Committee on Standards in Public Life (Chairman: Lord Nolan), Volume 1: Report, May 1995, Cm 2850–1, 109 pps, price: £11.80. (The second volume was evidence submitted to the Committee). Available from HMSO Publications Centre, PO Box 276, London, SW8 5DT (tel.: +44 (0)171 873 9090; fax.: +44 (0)171 873 8200). The Nolan Principles and Code of Best Practice for Non-departmental Public Bodies are reproduced at **B9.1–B9.3**.

- Turnbull Report: 'Internal Control – Guidance to Directors on the Combined Code', published by The Institute of Chartered Accountants in England & Wales, ISBN 1 84152 010 1. It is available from Accountancy Books, PO Box 21375, London, WC1N 1QP. Tel: +44 (0)20 7920 8991. Fax: +44 (0)20 7920 8992. Website: www.accountancybooks.co.uk. Currently the guidance can be downloaded from ICAEW's website: www.icaew.co.uk/internal control. The Turnbull Report is reproduced in **PART A**.

# International and overseas reports and pronouncements APP1.3

- American Stock Exchange, Enhance Corporate Governance – Text of Proposed Rule Changes (5/16/03). New York: AMEX, 2003. Available at www.amex.com Look for Spotlight, Click on item noted

- Australian Stock Exchange, (1994), 'Disclosure of Corporate Governance Practices by Listed Companies' (Melbourne).

- CACG Guidelines – 'Principles for Corporate Governance in the Common-wealth – towards global competitiveness and economic accountability', (1999), following the 1997 resolution that 'Capacity should be established in all Commonwealth countries to create or reinforce institutions to promote best practice in corporate governance; in particular, codes of good practice establishing standards of behaviour in the public and private sector should be agreed to secure greater transparency, and to reduce corruption.' [Commonwealth Business Forum Resolution, October 1997, endorsed by the Edinburgh Commonwealth Economic Declaration] (http://www.cbc.to/Governance/FinalVer/fin1vndx.htm)

- California Pension and Retirement System, U.S. Corporate Governance Principles. Sacramento CA: CALPERS, April 13, 1998. Available at www.calpers-governance.org/principles/domestic/us/page01.asp

- California Pension and Retirement System, International Corporate Governance Principles. Sacramento, CA: CALPERS. Available at www.calpers-governance.org/principles/international/global/page07.asp

- CoCo (Criteria of Control Board) : 'Control & Governance' series of the CoCo Board, (Canadian Institute of Chartered Accountants, 277 Wellington Street West, Toronto, Ontario, M5V 3H2 (tel.: (001) 416 977 0748; fax.: (001) 416 204 3416; www.cica.ca).

- CoCo (Criteria of Control Board), Guidance for Directors – Dealing With Risk in the Boardroom. Toronto: CICA, 2000 Available online at http://www.cica.ca/cica/cicawebsite.nsf/public/SGCRGe_risk

- Conference Board, The Conference Board Commission on Public Trust and Private Enterprise: Findings and Recommendations, New York: Conference Board, 2003. Available at www.conference-board.org/pdf_free/758.pdf

- COSO: 'Internal Control – Integrated Framework', known as 'The COSO Report' (September 1992), Framework volume (published by The Committee of Sponsoring Organizations of the Treadway Commission, obtainable from American Institute of Certified Public Accountants, Harborside Financial Center, 201 Plaza III, Jersey City, NJ 07311–3881, and also available from The Institute of Internal Auditors – UK for about £35. Note the new (1999) website: www.coso.org; and Addendum to 'Reporting to External Parties', New York: COSO, 1994

- COSO: 'Enterprise Risk Management' (July 2003), Exposure Draft 'Executive Summary' and 'Framework, (published by The Committee of Sponsoring Organizations of the Treadway Commission, obtainable on-line at
  www.erm.coso.org/Coso/coserm.nsf/vwWebResources/PDF_Manuscript/ $file/COSO_ERM_Framework.pdf

- Global Reporting Initiative, (June 2000): 'Sustainability Reporting Guidelines on Economic, Environmental and Social Performance', www.globalreporting.org

- Institute of Directors in Southern Africa, The (1994), 'The King Report on Corporate Governance', (chairman: Mervyn King),, (29 November ; ISBN 0–620–18908–8; from IOD in SA, 2nd Floor, Van Leer house, 15 Wellington road, Parktown 2193, Johannesburg, Republic of South Africa, PO Box 908, Parklands 212,

- Republic of South Africa; Tel.: 27–011–643–8086; Fax.: 29–011–484–1416). The second King Report from S. Africa (2001), while not formally adopted as a corporate governance Code, does not have the same defect of neglecting the social and environmental 'triple bottom line' issues. Described at www.iodsa.co.za/~§ Click on Corporate Governance

- Institute of Internal Auditors, The, (2001), 'Standards for the Professional Practice of Internal Auditing', Altamonte Springs, FL.

- International Federation of Accountants (1999). 'Communications of Audit Matters with Those Charged with Governance,' International Standard on Auditing issued by the International Auditing Practices Committee, New York, June.

- Joint Committee on Corporate Governance, Beyond Compliance: Building a Governance Culture, Toronto: Chartered Accountants of Canada and Toronto Stock Exchange, November 2002. Available at
  www.cica.ca/multimedia/Download_Library/Research_Guidance/Risk_ Management_Governance/Governance_Eng_Nov26.pdf

- Joint Standards Australia/Standards New Zealand Committee, (1999): 'Risk Management', (AS/NZS 4360:1999).

- National Association of Corporate Directors, Risk Oversight: Board Lessons for Turbulent Times, Washington, DC: NACD, 2003. Ordering information available at www.nacdonline.org/publications/PubDetails.asp?user=32E84FEFD7 BD4B85B61C12020E023598&pubID=204

- National Association of Corporate Directors, The Governance Committee, Washington, DC: NACD, 2003. Described at www.nacdonline.org/publications/PubDetails.asp?user=11ED3586E2CE4 537847274A2337A2552&pubID=212

- National Association of Securities Dealers, Summary of NASDAQ Corporate Governance Proposals as of February 26, 2003. New York: NASD, 2003. Available at www.nasdaq.com/about/Web_Corp_Gov_Summary%20Feb-revised.pdf

- New York Stock Exchange, Amendment No. 1 to the NYSE's Corporate Governance Rule Proposal. New York: NYSE, 2003. Available at www.nyse.com/pdfs/amend1–04–09–03.pd

- Organisation for Economic Co-operation and Development (22 June 1999). 'OECD Principles of Corporate Governance,' Paris, France., www.oecd.org

- Organisation for Economic Co-operation and Development, (June 2000): 'Guidelines for Multinational Enterprises', www.oecd.org

- Organisation for Economic Co-operation and Development, (10 May 2001): 'The Well-Being of Nations: the Role of Human and Social Capital', Paris, France., www.oecd.org

- SEC, Final Rule: Certification of Disclosure in Companies' Quarterly and Annual Reports, Release No. 33–8124. Washington, DC: SEC, August 2002. Available at www.sec.gov/rules/final/33–8124.htm

- SEC, Final Rule: Disclosure Required by Sections 406 and 407 of the Sarbanes-Oxley Act of 2002, Release No. 33–8177, Washington, DC: SEC, January 2003

- SEC, Final Rule: Management's Reports on Internal Control Over Financial Reporting and Certification of Disclosure in Exchange Act Periodic Reports, Release 33–8238. Washington, DC: SEC, June 2003. Available at www.sec.gov/rules/final/33–8238.htm

- SEC, Standards Relating to Listed Company Audit Committees, Release 33–8220. Washington, DC: SEC, April 2003. Available at www.sec.gov/rules/final/33–8220.htm

- Treadway report: 'Report of the Committee on Fraudulent Financial Reporting', (1987), Committee Of Sponsoring Organizations Of The Treadway Commission, (COSO). This 200 page report can be downloaded even today from the new COSO website: www.coso.org

- Viénot, report (Rapport Viénot), Le Conseil d'Administration des Sociétés Cotées, (July 1995), Paris. Equivalent of the UK's Cadbury Committee set up at request of Patronat and AFEP.

## Other UK reports and pronouncements APP1.4

- Amos, N., Sillanpää, M. and Wheeler, D., (1996): The Body Shop Approach to Ethical Auditing, 32 pages.

- Audit Commission, (1995): 'Taken on Board – Corporate Governance in the NHS: Developing the Role of Non-Executive Directors', (HMSO, ISBN 011 886 403 3), 27 pps.

- Auditing Practices Board, (July 1998), 'Auditors' responsibility statements and auditors' reports on corporate governance', APB, 117 Houndsditch, London, EC3A 7BT [obtainable from ABG Professional Information, PO Box 21375. London, WC1N 1QP (tel.: +44 (0)20 7920 8991; fax.: +44 (0)20 7920 8992); e-mail: info@abgpublications.co.uk].

- Auditing Practices Board, (July 2001), 'Providing assurance on the effectiveness of internal control', APB, 117 Houndsditch, London, EC3A 7BT [obtainable for £5.50 each, post-free from ABG Professional Information, PO Box 21375. London, WC1N 1QP (tel.: +44 (0)20 7920 8991; fax.: +44 (0)20 7920 8992); e-mail: info@abgpublications.co.uk].

- Auditing Practices Board, (November 1999), 'The Combined Code: requirements of auditors under the listing rules of the London Stock Exchange', Bulletin 1999/5 of, ISBN 1–85355–055–8, APB, 117 Houndsditch, London, EC3A 7BT [obtainable from ABG Professional Information, PO Box 21375. London, WC1N 1QP (tel.: +44 (0)20 7920 8991; fax.: +44 (0)20 7920 8992); e-mail: info@abgpublications.co.uk].

- Institute of Chartered Accountants of Scotland, (2003): 'Appraising your auditors: a guide to the assessment and appointment of auditors', ICAS, 21 Haymarket Yards, Edinburgh EH12 5BH (tel: +44 (0)131 347 0233; fax: +44 (0)131 347 0105; contact David Wood Deputy Director, Accounting and Auditing at ICAS: e-mail: accountingandauditing@icas.org.uk. The booklet can be downloaded without charge from the Institute's website at http://www.icas.org.uk/CMS/articleView.asp?article=2274. This publication is reproduced in full at PARAGRAPHS ?? to ?? of this handbook.

- International Capital Markets Group (1992). 'Harmonization of International Accounting Standards,' London, England, July.

## Books and guides APP1.5

- AICPA and CICA, Managing Risk in the New Economy, New York and Toronto: AICPA and CICA, 2001. Available online at http://www.aicpa.org/surveys/2001/advisory.htm

- Audit Faculty, ICAEW, Risk Management and the Value Added by Internal Audit, London: ICAEW, 2000. Available online at http://libcat.icaew.co.uk/uhtbin/cgisirsi/ Click on Login Then Catlog and enter title of item

- Baker, Matthew, (2002), 'Tolley's Company Secretary's Checklists', (Reed Elsevier (UK) Ltd., ISBN 0 7545 1897 3), 217 pages. (See also entry under Lai for Tolley's Company Secretary's Handbook 2003–2004. and entry under Morris for Tolley's Non-Executive Director's Handbook).

- Barton, Thomas L., Shenkir, William G., Walker, Paul L., Making Enterprise Risk Management Pay Off, Morristown, NJ: Financial Executives International, 2001. Ordering information available at www.fei.org/rfbookstore/PubDetail.cfm?Pub=58

- Bingham, Kit, (ed), (2001): 'Corporate Governance Handbook', (Gee, London), loose leaf. ISBN: 1 86089 060 1.

- Brancato, Carolyn and Plath, Christopher, Corporate Governance Best Practices, New York: Conference Board, 2003. Described at www.conference-board.org/publications/describe.cfm?id=674

- Burke, Tom and Julie Hill, (1990): 'Ethics, Environment and the Company – a Guide to Effective Action', (The Institute of Business Ethics, 12 Palace Street, London, SW1E 5JA, tel.: 0171 931 0495, ISBN 0 951 3671 5 3).

- Business Council for Sustainable Development, 1999: 'Corporate Social Responsibility', (World Business Council for Sustainable Development, 160, route de Florissant, CG-1231 Conches-Geneva, Switzerland, tel.: +41 (22)839 31 00; fax.: +41 (22)839 31 31, e-mail: info@wbcsd.ch)

- Business Round Table, Principles of Corporate Governance, Washington, DC: BRT, 2002. Available at www.brtable.org/pdf/704.pdf

- Cadbury, Sir Adrian, (2002): 'Corporate Governance and Chairmanship – A Personal View', [Oxford University Press, England].

- Cadbury, Sir Adrian, (1990): 'The Company Chairman', (Director Books, Cambridge, England), ISBN 1–870555–26–0, 226 pages.

- Chambers, Andrew and Graham Rand, (1997 reprinted 1999): 'The Operational Auditing Handbook – Auditing Business Processes', (John Wiley & Sons, Chichester, England), ISBN 0 471 97060 3, £75, 532 pages and diskette of checklists in Word format.

- Cairncross, Frances, (2002), 'The company of the future', (Harvard Business school Press, ISBN, 1 86197 405 1), 229 pages.

- 'Corporate governance and directors' duties handbook 2003', a Global Counsel handbook [Practical law Company Ltd., 1 Bargehouse Crescent, 34 Upper Ground, London, SE1 9PD, tel.: +44 (0)20 7202 1200; www.practicalaw.com/global], ISBN 1477–7972. This handbook focussed on differing corporate governance practices in countries across the world.

- Council on Economic Priorities, 'The Better World Investment Guide', [Council on Economic Priorities, 30 Irving Place, New York, NY 10003].

- Economist Intelligence Unit, Corporate governance: The new strategic imperative, London: EIU, 2002. Available at www.us.kpmg.com/microsite/Attachments/corp_govern_newstrat.pdf

- European Foundation for Quality Management, (1999): 'The EFQM Excellence Model', [Belgium], www.efqm.org

- Financial Times: (June 1999): 'Responsible Business in the Global Economy', (a Financial Times Guide, 30 pages).

- Garratt, R., (1996): 'The Fish Rots from the Head: the Crisis in Our Boardrooms', (Paperback 1997: ISBN 0 00 638670 9, HarperCollins Business), 225 pages

- Garratt, R., (2000): 'The Learning Organisation: Developing Democracy at Work', (Harper Collins, London), ISBN 0 00 653053 2, 137 pages.

- Garratt, R., (ed.), (1994): 'Developing Strategic Thought'

- Garratt, R.: (2000): 'Twelve Organisational Capabilities: Valuing People at Work', (Harper Collins, London), ISBN 0 00 638896 5, 188 pages.

- Garratt, R., (2003): 'Thin on top – Why corporate governance matters and how to measure and improve board performance', (Nicholas Brealey Publishing, London, ISBN1–85788–319–5), 246 pages.

- Hanson Green (non-executive search consultants) and Ashurst Morris Crisp (solicitors), (2000): 'The Guide for Non-Executive Directors', 20 pages.

- Henley Management College and The Institute of Directors, (March 1995): 'Good Practice for Directors – Standards for the Board', (Institute of Directors, ISBN 0–901–23045–6), 58 pps.

- Hitachi Foundation: 'Global corporate citizenship – rationale and strategies', (The Hitachi Foundation, 1509 22nd St. NW, Washington, DC, USA 20037–1073).

- Humble, John, (1973): 'Social responsibility audit', Foundation for Business Responsibilities, London], out of print.

- Institute of Directors, (1999): 'Reputation Management', 12 contributors, (Institute of Directors, 116 Pall Mall, London, SW1 5ED, ISBN 0 7494 3030 3, 80 pages).

- Interfaith Centre on Corporate Responsibility: 'Principles for global corporate responsibility', (Interfaith Centre on Corporate Responsibility, 475 Riverside Drive, room 550, New York, NY, USA 10115–0050).

- Kaplan, Jim, (2000): 'The auditor's guide to internet resources', 2nd edition, The Institute of Internal Auditors Inc., USA, www.theiia.org

- Lai, Jerry, (2002), 'Company Secretary's Handbook, 2003–2004', ISBN 0 7545 1789–6., 627 pages (see also entry under Morris for 'Tolley's Non-executive Director's Handbook', and entry under Baker for Tolley's Company Secretary's Checklist).

- Management of Business Risk, (2000), (Croner, CCH Group, Kingston upon Thames, England), ISBN 1 85524 555 9. A loose leaf manual, with occasional updates.

- Mitroff, Ian: 'We're so big and powerful nothing bad can happen to us', (Carol Publishing, 600 Madison Avenue, New York, NY, USA 10022).

- Morris, Glynis D. and Patrick Dunne, (2003): 'Tolley's Non-executive Director's Handbook', ISBN 0–754 50239 2, 461 pages. (See also entry under Baker for Tolley's Company Secretary's Checklist; and entry under Lai for Tolley's Company Secretary's Handbook, 2003–2004').

- Peters, Glen, (1999): 'Waltzing with the raptors', (John Wiley & Sons, Bognor Regis, England), ISBN 0471 327 32 8.

- Rayner, Jenny (executive editor) and Mark Stock (consultant editor), (2000): 'Business Risk Management', (Gee Publishing Ltd), ISBN 1 86089 853 X, A loose leaf manual and CD, with occasional updates.

- Rayner, Jenny, (2003): 'Managing reputational risk', Wiley and The Institute of Internal Auditors (UK), ISBN 0–471–49951-X, 323 pages.

- Schwartz, Peter and Blair Gibb, (1999): 'When good companies do bad things – responsibility and risk in an age of globalization', (John Wiley & Sons Inc., New York), ISBN 0–471–32332–2, 194 pages.

- Spira, Laura F., (2002): 'The Audit Committee: Performing Corporate Governance', [Kluwer Academic Publishers, 101 Philip Drive, Assinippi Park, Norwell, Massachusetts 02061 (no given ISBN number)], 191 pages.

- Steinberg, Richard M. and Bromilow, Catherine L., Audit Committee Effectiveness – What Works Best, 2nd Edition. Altamonte Springs, FL: The Institute of Internal Auditors Research Foundation, 2000.

- Styles, P. and Taylor, B. (2002): Boards at work – how directors view their roles and responsibilities, [Oxford, Oxford University Press].

- Toffler, A.. (1970): 'Future Shock', (New York, Random House), out of print.

- Tricker, Robert I., (1976): 'The independent director – A study of the non-executive director and of the audit committee, (Croydon, UK, Tolley Publishing, ISBN 0 510 49378–5), 104 pages, out of print.

- Tricker, Robert I., (1984): 'Corporate governance – practices, procedures and powers in British companies and their boards of directors', (UK, Gower, ISBN 0–566–00749–5), 319 pages, out of print.

- Tricker, Robert I., (1994): 'International Corporate Governance', (Singapore: Prentice Hall , Simon & Schuster (Asia) Pte. Ltd.) ISBN 0–13–475070–5; 0–13–475054–3 (pbk)), 587 pages.

- Tricker, Robert I., editor, (2000), 'Corporate Governance' (Ashgate, Dartmouth, England), ISBN 1 84014 016 X, 471 pages. A collection of previously published papers on corporate governance.

- World Wide Fund for Nature, (1997): 'The Better Business Pack – Increasing Profits by Reducing Environmental Impact', (World Wide Fund for Nature/NatWest Group, Better Business Programme, World Wide Fund for Nature, Panda House, Wayside Park, Godalming, Surrey, GU7 1XR, ISBN 1 85850 133 2)

# Research reports APP1.6

- American Law Institute, (1994), 'Principles of Corporate Governance: Analysis and Recommendations', (American Law Institute, St Paul, Minnesota).

- Adams, Carol and George Harte, (1999): 'Towards Corporate Accountability for Equal Opportunities Performance, (ACCA Occasional Research Paper No. 26, The Association of Chartered Certified Accountants, 29 Lincoln's Inn Fields, London, WC2A 3EE, ISBN 1 85908 184 30), 76 pages.

- Albrecht, W. Steve, (1992): ' Common Body of Knowledge for the Practice of Internal Auditing', (The Institute of Internal Auditors Inc, USA).

- Barca, Fabrizio and Marco Becht, (2001): 'The Control of Corporate Europe' (Oxford University Press) based on research undertaken in the context of the old European Corporate Governance Network, now superseded by the European Corporate Governance Institute (www.ecgi.org). This book reports the research undertaken in the context of the old ECGN which provided the first comprehensive picture of large corporate governance holdings in the European Union and concluded that current practice is not up to standard. (ecgi.org). Becht is ECGI's executive director and also associate professor of finance at the Université Libre de Bruxelles.

- Beattie, Vivien and Ken Pratt, (2001), 'Business reporting: Harnessing the Power of the Internet for Users', [The Institute of Chartered Accountants of Scotland, ISBN 1 871250 90 0], 80 pages.

- Birkett, William et al, (1999): 'Competency Framework for Internal Auditing (CFIA)', (The Institute of Internal Auditors Inc, USA).

- Blumberg, Jerald, Georges Blum and Age Korsvold: 'Environmental Performance and Shareholder Value', (World Business Council for Sustainable Development)

- Cadbury Committee: 'Compliance with the code of best practice', (24 May 1995), Report of the committee on the financial aspects of corporate governance – the 'Cadbury Committee', (Gee Publishing, London], ISBN 1 86089 006 7).

- Dulewicz, Victor and Peter Herbert, (2003), Does the composition and practice of UK boards bear any relationship to the performance of listed companies?, [Henley Management College (Greenlands, Henley-on-Thames, Oxon, RG9 3AU), Working Paper Series, HWP 0304; ISBN 1 86181 158 6].

- Frazer, Ian, William Henry and Philip Wallace, (2000): 'The Future of Corporate Governance: Insights from the Netherlands', (The Institute of Chartered Accountants of Scotland, Edinburgh), ISBN 1 871250 76 5), 228 pages.

- Gonella, Claudia, Alison Pilling and Simon Zadek, (1998): 'Making Values Count: Contemporary Experience in Social and Ethical Accounting, Auditing, and Reporting', Research Report 57, (The Association of Chartered Certified Accountants, 29 Lincoln's Inn Fields, London, WC2A 3EE, ISBN 1 85908 195 9), 106 pages.

- Henley Management College (authors Victor Dulewicz and Peter Herbert) (2003 working paper no.: HWP 0304): 'Does the composition and opractice of UK boards bear any relationship to the performance of UK listed companies?', ISBN 1 86181 158 6, obtainable from Henley Management College, Greenlands, Henley on Thames, Oxon, RG9 3AU, England, (Tel.: +44 (0)1491 571454; fax.: +44 (0)1491 418867.

- Higgs: on-line copies of the Higgs Report and background research which underpinned the report (including a MORI survey) are available at http://www.dti.gov.uk/cld/non_exec_review Hard copies from The Department of Trade and Industry, Room 507, 1 Victoria Street, London, SW1H 0ET (Tel.: 020 7215 0409). 120 pages.

- ICAS (The Institute of Chartered Accountants of Scotland), (1993): 'Auditing into the twenty-first century', ISBN 1 871250 27 7], 63 pps.

- Institute of Internal Auditors Inc., (2001): 'Audit Committee Effectiveness – What Works Best', 2nd Edition (an international research paper), http://www.theiia.org/ecm/bookstore.cfm?doc_id=1257) Institute of Internal Auditors Inc., (2001): 'Corporate Governance and the Board – What Works Best' (an international research paper), http://www.theiia.org/ecm/bookstore.cfm?doc_id=1011)

- International Capital Markets Group (June 1995), 'Who Holds the Reins?' An Overview of Corporate Governance Practice in Japan, Germany, France, United States of America and the United Kingdom, a co-operative venture of the International Federation of Accountants, the section on Business Law of the International Bar Association and the Fédération Internationale des Bourses de Valeurs; 105pps. c/o International Bar Association, 2 Harewood Place, Hanover Square, London, W1R 9HB)

- 'International Handbook of Corporate Governance,', (1996), (International Thomson Business Press, UK, ISBN 0–412–63920–3, 278 pages. A tabulation of corporate governance rules and practices in 32 countries.

- McKinsey & Company, in cooperation with the Global Corporate Governance Forum: 'Global Investor Opinion Survey', undertaken between April and May 2002. Obtainable from http://www.mckinsey.com/governance, or from Paul coombes (+44 (0)20 7961 5493).

- International Confederation of Trade Unions: 'Worlds apart – women and the global economy', (International Confederation of Free Trade Unions, Blvd Emile Jacmain 155, B-1210 Brussels, Belgium.)

- PIRC (Pensions and Investment Research Consultants) (December 1999), Survey. PIRC, 4th Floor, Cityside, 40 Adler Street, London, E1 1EE (tel.: +44 (0)207 247 2323; fax: +44 (0)207 247 2457; e-mail: Info@pirc.co.uk; website:www.pirc.co.uk

- Vagneur, Kathryn and Sheila Evers, (1998): 'Beyond Compliance: Evolution and Opportunity in Non-Mandatory Governance', (a discussion paper published by the London Society of Chartered Accountants, 15 Basinghall Street, London, EC2V 5BR).

- World Bank Group, (1999): Magdi R. Iskander and Nadereh Chamlou's Corporate Governance: A Framework for Implementation, foreword by Sir Adrian Cadbury

# Articles APP1.7

- Beasley, Mark S., (October 1996). 'An Empirical Analysis of the Relation Between the Board of Director Composition and Financial Statement Fraud,' The Accounting Review, Volume 71, No. 4.

- Berardino, Joseph F; Jonas, Gregory J, "Power to the Audit Committee People," Financial Executive, November/December 1999, p. 36–38

- Birchmore, Ian (1st quarter 2000): 'The contribution of internal audit to stakeholder engagement', AccountAbility Quarterly, [The Institute for Social and Ethical Accountability (ISEA).

- Gay, K. (2002): 'Board theories and governance practices: agents, stewards and the evolving relationship with stakeholders', Journal of General management, (Volume 27, number 3).

- 'Harnessing Knowledge', Auditwire, May 2001, newsletter of The Institute of Internal Auditors Inc.

- Hexner, Thomas S. (September 1998). 'The Eight Imperatives of Global Investing,' The CPA Journal..

- Hodge, Neil, (February 2001), 'Knowledge and power', Internal Auditing & Business Risk, journal of The Institute of Internal Auditors, UK, pp. 14–18.

- Julien, Rick and Rieger, Larry, "The missing link in corporate governance," Risk Management, April 2003, Volume 50, No. 4

- Korac-Kakabadse, N, Kakabadse, A.K. and Kouzmin, A. (2001), 'Board governance and company performance: an correlations?, Corporate Governance.

- Muth, M. and Donaldson, L. (1998): 'Stewardship theory and board structure – a contingency approach', Corporate Governance, [Blackwells, volume 6, number 1, pp 5– 28].

- O'Regan, David, (2001): 'Genesis of a profession: towards professional status for internal auditing', Managerial Auditing Journal, 16/4, pp. 215–226.

- Roussey, Robert S. (1992). 'International Accounting and Auditing Standards for World Markets,' Journal of International Accounting Auditing & Taxation, JAI Press Inc. Volume 1, Number 1.

- Sonnenfeld, Jeffrey A., (September 2002): 'What makes great boards GREAT – it's not rules and regulations. It's the way people work together', Harvard Business Review.

# Journals and newsletters APP1.8

(Refer also to the journals and newsletters in which the listed articles (above) have appeared).

- The British Accounting Review, ISSN 0890–8389, the quarterly research journal of the British Accounting Association. BAR is also accessible on-line. While annual, institutional subscription is £250 worldwide, it is free of charge to BAA members. Members also receive a copy of The British Accounting Review Register – an invaluable authoritative reference work on UK accounting and finance departments and the lecturing/research interests and contact details of 1,500 academic staff members across over 100 UK institutions.

- CG Watch – Corporate Governance in Emerging Markets, from www.cisa.com, or contact amar.gill@cisa.com.

- Corporate governance – an international review, ISSN 0964 8410, editor: Professor Christine Mallin, Director, Centre for Corporate Governance Research, Birmingham Business School, Ashley Building, The University of Birmingham, Edgbaston, Birmingham, B15 2TT, UK (tel.: + 44 (0)121 414 2273; fax.: +44 (0)121 414 6238; e-mail: c.a.mallin@bham.ac.uk. Corporate Governance – an International Review is a serious research journal which also carries a news section; it is published quarterly by Blackwell Publishers,. PO Box 805, 108 Cowley Road, Oxford, OX4 1FH, UK (tel.: +44 (0)1865 244084; fax.: +44 (0)1865 381381; e-mail: jnlinfo@blackwellpublishers.co.uk.

- Corporate Governance, ISSN 0219–1040, a bi-monthly newsletter, published six times a year. Editor Andrew Chambers, Director, Management Audit Limited, 6 Market Street, Sleaford, Lincolnshire, NG34 7SF, (tel.: +44 (0) 1529 413344, fax: +44 (0) 1529 413355. e-mail: e-mail@management-audit.com, website: http://www.management-audit.com)). Subscription enquiries to the publisher in Singapore: FTMS Consultants (S) Pte. Ltd, 391B Orchard Road Tower B, #15–09 Ngee Ann City, Singapore 238874 (tel.: (65) 735 0003, fax.: (65) 735 1911, e-mail: colleen@ftms.com.sg, www.ftmsglobal.com.

- European Business Forum (EBF), ISSN 1469 6460, c/o PriceWaterhouseCoopers, Plumtree Court, London, EC4A 4HT, London, UK (subscription service: tel.: + 44 (0)20 8597 0181; e-mail: subscription@ebfonline.com, www.ebfonline.com

- Governance, ISSN 1358–5142, a monthly newsletter, twelve issues a year. Editor: Kit Bingham: e-mail kbingham@governance.co.uk. Subscription enquiries to info@governance.co.uk.ICGNews (International Corporate Governance News) is published three times a year, and is available for free. It can be downloaded from the ICGN website at www.icgn.org. It is published only in electronic form.

- Internal control, ISSN 1367–2517, editor Andrew Chambers, Director, Management Audit Limited, 6 Market Street, Sleaford, Lincolnshire, NG34 7SF, e-mail: e-mail@management-audit.com, website: http://www.management-audit.com, tel.: +44 (0) 1529 413344, fax: +44 (0) 1529 413355. A monthly newsletter, appearing ten times a year, of ABG Professional Information, the publishing arm of The Institute of Chartered Accountants in England & Wales, PO Box 21375, London, WC1N 1QP (tel.: +44 (0)20 7920 8991; fax.: +44 (0)20 7920 8992; website: www.abgweb.com)

- International Journal of Auditing, ISSN 1090–6738, general editor Andrew Chambers. Now in its seventh year of publication, each of the three issues of IJA which appear annually comprises refereed research papers on all aspects of auditing, with most having international relevance. Volume 4, Number 1 (March 2000) was a particularly notable issue dedicated to 'the audit society' and guest edited by Professor Mike Power of LSE with significant input from members of the Auditing Special Interest Group. Volume 5, No. 1 (March 2002) is a themes issue on audit fees. Copies are available from the publisher. International Journal of Auditing has an individual subscription price of £140 with institutional subscriptions being £190. It is now available on-line. Enquiries to the publisher – Management Audit Ltd, 6 Market Street, Sleaford, Lincolnshire, NG34 7SF, England (tel.: +44 (0) 1529 413344; fax.: +44 (0) 1529 413355; e-mail: email@management-audit.com; website: www.management-audit.com.

# Contact Details

- Association of Chartered Certified Accountants, 29 Lincoln's Inn Fields, London, WC2A 3EE. ACCA offers a Diploma in Corporate Governance.

- Auditing Practices Board, 117 Houndsditch, London, EC3A 7BT

- Bell Pottinger Communications (part of The Chime Group), 14 Curzon Street, London, W1J 5HN – main contact on reputational risk is Kate Watts, director (e-mail: kwatts@bell-pottinger.co.uk). Their on-line relationship audit can undertaken by logging on to website www.bell-pottinger.yougov.com/

- Centre for Responsibility and Business, 30 Irving Place, 9th Floor, New York, NY 10024, tel.: 001 212 420 1133

- CoCo Board, Canadian Institute of Chartered Accountants, 277 Wellington Street West, Toronto, Ontario, M5V 3H2 (tel.: (001) 416 977 0748; fax.: (001) 416 204 3416, www.cica.ca)

- Financial Services Authority, 25 The North Colonnade, Canary Wharf, London, E14 5HS,

- FSA Publications: (tel.: (direct): 020 7943 0770

- Paul Geradine, Director of Listing (tel.: (direct): 020 7943 0770);

- Iain Wright, Head of Company Monitoring and Enquiries (tel.: (direct): 020 7943 0866; e-mail: iain.wright@fsa.gov.uk)

- Independent Remuneration Solutions, 9 Savoy Street, London WC2R 0BA Phone 020 7836 5831 or cliffweight@msn.com. IRS provide advice on executive directors' remuneration packages, annual and long term incentives and non-executive directors' Fees. Cliff Weight contributed extensively to remuneration packages in this handbook..

- Institute of Business Ethics, 24 Greencoat Palace Street, London, SW1P IBE, tel.: 020 7798 6040

- Institute of Chartered Accountants of Scotland, Haymarket Yards, Edinburgh EH12 5BH (tel: +44 (0)131 347 0233; fax: +44 (0)131 347 0105; www.accounting.auditing@icas.org.uk

- Institute of Directors in South Africa, 2nd Floor, Van Leer house, 15 Wellington road, Parktown 2193, Johannesburg, Republic of South Africa, PO Box 908, Parklands 212, Republic of South Africa (tel.: 27–011–643–8086; fax.: 29–011–484–1416).

- Institute of Directors, 116 Pall Mall, London, SW1 5ED. The IOD offers the 'Chartered Director' training and qualification programme, as well as a range of short courses on aspects of directorship.

- Institute of Internal Auditors Inc., 249 Maitland Avenue, Altamonte Springs, 32701, Florida, US (tel.: 407 830 76004; fax.: 407 831 5171).

- Interbrand Newall & Sorrell Consultancy (the international branding consultancy) 85 Strand, London, WC2R ODW [Tel.: 020 7240 4040; Fax.: 020 7836 0516; http://www.interbrand.com]. Interbrand is owned by

- Omnicom (the US advertising group).

- Interfaith Center on Corporate Responsibility, 475 Riverside Drive, Room 550, New York, NY, USA 10115–0050 tel.: 001 212 870 2295

- Management Audit Limited, 6 Market Street, Sleaford, Lincolnshire, NG34 7SF, e-mail: e-mail@management-audit.com; Website: http://www.management-audit.com, tel. +44 (0) 1529 413344; fax.: +44 (0) 1529 413355. Specialises in advice to audit committees and boards on corporate governance matters. Responsible for this Handbook.

- Pensions and Investments Research Consultants, 4th Floor, Cityside, 40 Adler Street, London, E11EE

- World Business Council for Sustainable Development, 4 Cheminde, 1231 Conches-Geneva, Switzerland, tel.: +41 (22) 839 31 00; fax.: +41 (22)839 31 31, e-mail: info@wbcsd.ch

# Corporate Governance Special Interest Groups

## Auditing special interest group of the British Accounting Association APP3.1

A special interest group of the British Accounting Association (BAA). For details of membership of the Auditing Special Interest Group of the British Accounting Association (which is available only to members of BAA itself (see **APP3.2**), contact Iain Gray, 7 George Street, Cellardyke Anstruther, KY10 3AS, Fyfe, Scotland (Tel: (01333) 313 277. E-mail: grayiain@aol.com), or Kathryn Hewitt, BAA Administrator, British Accounting Association, c/o Sheffield University Management School, 9 Mappin Street, Sheffield, S1 4DT.

## The British Accounting Association APP3.2

The BAA is the body of academic specialists (teachers and researchers) in all aspects of accounting in rather a similar way to the American Accounting Association. Membership, which costs only £27 a year, is also open to practitioners, standards setters and others with an interest in the academic side of the profession. BAA has about 800 members. Details of membership are available from Kathryn Hewitt (see **APP3.1**). The BAA has its own annual conference which each year takes place shortly after the National Auditing Conference, this time at the University of Nottingham (26–28 March).

Special interest groups of BAA are:

● auditing (see **APP3.1**);

● corporate governance (see **APP3.3**);

● education;

● interdisciplinary perspectives;

● international accounting/finance; and

● public services.

The BAA also has Regional Groups.

# Corporate governance special interest group of the British Accounting Association
APP3.3

Newer than the Auditing Special Interest Group, the Corporate Governance Special Interest Group held their first annual conference at Sheffield University in December 1999. Their website is www.baacgsig.qub.ac.uk and they also run 'The Corporate Governance Research Bulletin Board' and a twice yearly newsletter. The Group's chairman is Professor Istemi Demirag, formerly at Sheffield University and now at Queen's University, Belfast where he is professor of accounting in the School of Management and Economics (tel: (028) 9027 3486; e-mail: i.demirag@qub.ac.uk (Istemi Demirag)). The secretary is Kathryn Hewitt, BAA Administrator, British Accounting Association, c/o Sheffield University Management School, 9 Mappin Street, Sheffield, S1 4DT.

From their website: addition to our website, www.baacgsig.qub.ac.uk/, we are developing a web page of research information to which we will refer as 'The Corporate Governance Research Bulletin Board'. This will be edited by the chair of the group, Professor Istemi Demirag at Queen's University, Belfast. The editor will disseminate the information among the group members who indicate their willingness to receive such information on a regular basis. The information collected may, for instance, involve some of the research papers or books the group members read over the last few months and would recommend others to read or avoid; special requests for a particular information for research; or to share other ideas with the rest of the group members. The e-mail address of this 'Research Bulletin Board' is corp.gov@qub.ac.uk. The editor will reserve the right to decide whether or not to disseminate the information received. The 'Research Bulletin Board' will be posted initially once every month, issue number one is scheduled for the beginning of March 1998.

> 'We also plan to publish a **Newsletter** twice a year, on 15 September and 15 March. The launch issue is scheduled for the BAA Conference in April 1998. The first issue is scheduled for 15 September 1998. The **Newsletter** will provide a focus for supplying and receiving information on research and teaching in the corporate governance area, in the hope that new networks involving active contact and collaboration will arise. We particularly hope that some of these networks will involve a multi-disciplinary approach. In the longer term, we would hope that a number of other activities will develop out of the Newsletter. For example workshops may be organised in which small sub-groups will meet, so that researchers can present their ideas and receive some feedback in an informal and friendly environment. Experienced members of such groups might provide advice, support and help in formulating ideas into sound research questions. Members might exchange their data with each other, thus reducing duplication of research and saving time and money. Contacts may be facilitated with researchers in other countries, with a view to setting up joint comparative international research projects in this area. Co-operation on teaching may also develop.'

# European Auditing Network Symposium   APP3.4

At a European level, and organisation broadly equivalent to the Auditing Special Interest Group of the BAA has been formed. Further information on the Network, on membership and on the Symposium are available on the website: www.earnet.uni-essen.de.

# Management Control Association   APP3.5

The Association, which is not affiliated to the British Accounting Association, is a body of about seventy members from about fifty different institutions. Most members are university academics with a few practitioners also amongst the membership.

The Association holds doctoral colloquia and also research conferences.

The secretary of the Association is Dr Derek Purdy of the Department of Economics, University of Reading. Website: www.ms.rhbnc.ac.uk/mca2001. The contact person for prospective new members is the Association's treasurer, Paul A Collier, Finance and Accounting Group, Aston Business School, Aston University, Birmingham, B4 7ET. Tel: (0121) 359 3011, ext 5025. E-mail: P M Collier@aston.ac.uk.

# Research Centres in Corporate Governance

We recognise that this section of the handbook is far from complete. Please also refer to the section on Corporate Governance Special Interest Groups in APPENDIX 3.

## Bournemouth University                                    APP4.1

The person in charge of corporate governance is Professor David Marshall (e-mail: dmarshal@bournemouth.ac.uk; Bournemouth University, Poole House, Talbot Campus, Fern Barrow, Poole, Dorset, England (Tel: +44 (0)1203 595065).

## European Corporate Governance Institute                  APP4.2

This Institute, based in Brussels, was established in January 2002. Its roots are in the now discontinued European Corporate Governance Network, set up with the support of the Bank of Italy in 1997 to foster comparative research on corporate governance. ECGI has a governing body of six academics and five non-academics to preserve its autonomy and the independence of its research, and is funded by subscriptions. ECGI's executive director is Marco Becht, who is also associate professor of finance at the Université Libre de Bruxelles. Becht is co-author of 'The Control of Corporate Europe' (Oxford University Press, 2001) based on research undertaken in the context of the old ECGN which provided the first comprehensive picture of large corporate governance holdings in the European Union and concluded that current practice is not up to standard (www.ecgi.org).

## Henley Management College                                 APP4.3

Henley continues to be active, under the guidance of Professor Bernard Taylor. One of the notable aspects of their corporate governance programme is their short courses for company directors.

## Imperial College, University of London                    APP4.4

The Management School is beginning to integrate corporate governance into its MBA programmes and is encouraging research into this field.

The most exciting development is of the Imperial College Entrepreneurs' Programme – a series of seminars, workshops and master classes for members of Imperial College. This is part of a strategy for Imperial faculty and students to be able to spin-off their intellectual property and build sound companies with College backing (and its minority shareholding).

Led by the Entrepreneurship Centre under Professor Sue Birley, and a special company to encourage spin-off companies from members (IC Innovations Ltd led by Dr Jon Taylor) the College is working with the Management School to create hundreds of companies over the next few years. 50 are already up and running. A rigorous selection process is run by the College to decide three key questions.

- Is this good science and technology?

- Is this a good business proposition?

- Are these the right people to run a company?

The College then helps with the development of the intellectual property, with the creation of a business plan, and the selection of appropriate funding methods.

The College recognises that none of this will help create long-lived companies unless they have properly trained directors. From the corporate governance point of view special induction and development courses are run by visiting Professor Bob Garratt. The College funds and encourages strongly attendance at the Roles and Responsibilities of Directors Workshop which has already had some 120 executive, and non-executive, directors pass through it. This programme is being expended by the addition of three new workshops:

- developing strategic thought;

- effective decision-making; and

- effective board working.

In the medium-term it is hoped to be able to offer an accredited programme for directors of the spin-off companies, which may, subject to negotiation, include the Institute of Directors' Chartered Director qualification.

# Nottingham Business School                                    APP4.5

International Centre of Corporate Governance, Nottingham Business School, The Nottingham Trent University, Burton Street, Nottingham, NG1 4BU. Tel: +44 (0) (1115) 948 6099. Fax (0115) 948 6512.

# Queen's University, Belfast                              APP4.6

Professor Istemi Demirag, professor of accounting in the School of Management and Economics, is also chairman of the Corporate Governance Special Interest Group of The British Accounting Association (Tel: (028) 9027 3486. E-mail: i.demirag@qub.ac.uk (Istemi Demirag)). See the section of this handbook on Corporate Governance Special Interest Groups at APPENDIX 3.

# University of Birmingham                                 APP4.7

Professor Christine Mallin is Director of the Centre for Corporate Governance Research, Birmingham Business School, Ashley Building, The University of Birmingham, Edgbaston, Birmingham, B15 2TT, UK. Tel: + 44 (0)121 414 2273. Fax: +44 (0)121 414 6238. E-mail: c.a.mallin@bham.ac.uk.

# Websites on Corporate Governance

## Introduction APP5.1

In this section we list sites of interest to corporate governance specialists. While some sites are shown in more than one category of this listing, users are advised refer across sections as some entries are applicable to other categories within which they may not appear. The categories in this listing are:

- Accounting (**APP5.2**).

- Professional bodies/institutions (**APP5.3**).

- Journals, books and on-line magazines (**APP5.4**).

- Market information (**APP5.5**).

- Internal auditing (**APP5.6**).

- IT governance (**APP5.7**).

- Audit products/services (**APP5.8**).

- External auditing (**APP5.9**).

- Internal control (**APP5.10**).

- Corporate governance (**APP5.11**).

- Risk, reputation, corporate responsibility and sustainability (**APP5.12**).

- Fraud, whistleblowing etc (**APP5.13**).

- Stock exchanges (**APP5.14**).

Users of this listing will realise that websites change rapidly, so success will not always be achieved. We would like to learn of any changes or additions we should make for the next edition of this handbook. Please e-mail us at achambers@management-audit.com.

# Accounting

| Organisation/Title | URL/Country of Location | Comments/Further Links |
|---|---|---|
| Accountancy Network | http://www.csu. edu.au/anet<br><br>Australia | ANet is a co-operative venture involving individuals and academic institutions from around the world.<br><br>Provides a digital forum for the discussion of Accounting, Auditing and related disciplines.<br><br>Site hosted by the School of Financial Studies at Charles Stuart University in New South Wales, Australia. |
| Accounting & Finance Abstracts The<br><br>Maintained by ANBAR Electronic Intelligence. | http://www.anbar. co.uk/products/afa.<br><br>htm<br><br>UK | This site affords access to the latest practice and solutions.<br><br>library contains article summaries of more than 16,000 articles dating back to 1989. |
| Accounting and Audit Resources | http://www. disastercenter. com/audit.html<br><br>USA | Comprehensive set of links to accounting and audit organisations. |
| Accounting Research Network<br><br>Maintained by Professor Ross Watts of the William Simon School of Business at the University of Rochester, NY, USA. | http://www.ssrn. com/update/arn/ arn_about.html<br><br>USA | The Accounting Research Network (ARN) was founded to increase communication among scholars and practitioners of accounting worldwide. The site features abstracts of research papers taken from three journals under the following headings:<br><br>Auditing, Litigation and Tax Abstracts, Financial Accounting Abstracts and Managerial Accounting Abstracts. |
| Accounting Web | http://www. accountingweb. co.uk/<br><br>UK | Features link listings, databases and a connection to the Company Information Zone which can be used to access the statutory information held at Companies House. |

| Organisation/Title | URL/Country of Location | Comments/Further Links |
|---|---|---|
| AccountingNet | http://www. accting.net<br><br>USA | Accounting related information, products and services. Serves as a communication network between CPAs.<br><br>60 Orland Square Drive Suite 101, Orland Park, Illinois 60462. Tel: 708/403–8333. Fax: 708/403–8770. |
| American Accounting Association<br><br>5717 Bessie Drive, Sarasota, FL 34233–2399, USA.<br><br>Telephone: (941) 921 7747<br><br>Fax: (941) 923 4093<br><br>Email: aaahq@packet.net | http://www. rutgers.edu/ Accounting/ raw/aaa<br><br>USA<br><br>Formerly: http://www. aaa-edu.org | The AAA promotes worldwide excellence in accounting education, research and practice.<br><br>Access to document search facility and on-line marketplace.<br><br>The AAA Auditing Section can be found at:<br><br>http://raw.rutgers. edu/raw/aaa/audit/ |
| Australian Accounting Research Foundation | http://www.aarf. asn.au/<br><br>Australia | The AARF focuses on improving the operation of capital markets, improving accountability, improving professional services and improving Australian commercial law.<br><br>This site reflects the co-operation between the AARF and the AASB (Australian Accounting Standards Board) and contains guidelines and other relevant resources. |
| Australian Centre for Management Accounting Development. | http://www.ace. unsw.edu.au/ acmad/welcome. html<br><br>Australia | ACMAD's mission is to promote innovation in resource management within organisations within Australia. |

| Organisation/Title | URL/Country of Location | Comments/Further Links |
|---|---|---|
| British Accounting Association | http://www.bham. ac.uk/BAA <br><br> UK | The British Accounting Association (BAA) is the UK body of those interested in accounting research, broadly equivalent to the American Accounting Association (AAA) in the USA. <br><br> Details of the BAA Corporate Governance Special Interest Group can be found on: <br><br> http://www.shef.ac. uk/~baacgsig <br><br> Details of the Auditing Special Interest Group (ASIG) can be found on: <br><br> http://www.bham.ac. uk/BAA/sigs/audit/index.html |
| Centre for Accounting and Auditing Research | http://caarnet.ntu. edu.sg/ <br><br> Singapore | CAARNet is a member of the International Accounting Network and is jointly hosted by the Nanyang Business School and Nanyang Technological University in Singapore. <br><br> Email caarnet@ntu.edu.sg |
| Electronic Accountant | http://www. electronic accountant.com/ <br><br> USA | This site hosts a comprehensive source listing of resource materials of interest to accountants. <br><br> Separate listings for available by topic, for example Accounting and Auditing, Taxation and Technology. |
| European Accounting Association | http://www.bham. ac.uk/EAA/home page.htm <br><br> UK | Hosted by the Department of Accounting and Finance, The Birmingham Business School, University of Birmingham, UK. <br><br> The site includes archives covering the abstracts of papers presented at all the EAA Congresses since 1995. |

| Organisation/Title | URL/Country of Location | Comments/Further Links |
|---|---|---|
| International Federation of Accountants | http://www.ifac.org<br><br>http://www.ifac.org/Standards AndGuidance/ FMAC/Study9-Enhancing Shareholder/ Study9.html (Keynote Report – an IFAC 1999 Study of 'Risk Management':<br><br>'Enhancing Shareholder Wealth by Better Managing Business Risk')<br><br>USA | World-wide organisation for the accountancy profession with 142 member body organisations in 103 countries, representing over 2 million accountants.<br><br>The IFAC strives to develop the profession and harmonise its standards world-wide. |
| Irish Accounting & Finance Association | http://www.ucd.ie/~account/iafa/home.html<br><br>Ireland | Details of programmes, courses and links to other sites. |
| Rutgers Accounting Web (RAW) | http://www.rutgers.edu/Accounting/ raw/main1.htm<br><br>USA | Extensive source of material on accounting and related matters. Includes a Search facility with the ability to download those documents found.<br><br>Maintained by the Accounting Research Center at Rutgers University, USA and supported by the National Center for Automated Information Research (NCAIR). |
| Summa Project<br><br>The European Accounting Research Website sponsored by the Research Board of the ICAEW. | http://www.summa.org.uk<br><br>UK | Information and Search facilities on accounting related materials. |

| Organisation/Title | URL/Country of Location | Comments/Further Links |
|---|---|---|
| The Canadian Academic Accounting Association. (L'Association Canadienne des Professeurs de Comptabilite) | http://www. stmarys.ca/ partners/caaa/ caaa.html Canada | Site available in both English and French. Links to accounting research documents and organisations. |
| The Confederation of Asian and Pacific Accountants. | http://www.capa. com.my/ Malaysia | CAPA represents national accountancy organisation in the Asia Pacific region on behalf of 30 accountancy organisations in 21 countries. Individual members within member organisation exceeds 700,000. Some links to documents describing current projects. |
| The Nordic Accounting Network | http://www. nan.shh.fi/ Finland | Site available in English, Swedish and Finnish. The site, which is a member of the International Accounting Network, provides hypertext archives, databases and indexes of accounting and auditing knowledge. In addition to data of general world-wide interest there is also a specific resource covering the interests of Nordic and Baltic countries (The NAN Regional Archives). |

# Professional and official bodies/institutions APP5.3

| Organisation/Title | URL/Country of Location | Comments/Further Links |
|---|---|---|
| American Institute of Certified Public Accountants | http://www. aicpa.org USA | With in excess of 330,000 members, the AICPA is the premier national professional association for CPAs in the United States. |

| Organisation/Title | URL/Country of Location | Comments/Further Links |
|---|---|---|
| | | Link listings for Accounting & Audit, Accounting Associations, Technology and Year 2000 issues. |
| Association des Tresoriers d'Enterprise en Belgique | http://www.ac.ucl. ac.be/ateb/Ateb-Index.html<br><br>Belgium | |
| Association of Accounting Technicians | http://www.aat. co.uk<br><br>UK | Accounting Technicians work alongside chartered accountants. The AAT is the professional body for Accounting Technicians, with more than 80,000 members and students world-wide.<br><br>Information about the qualification and membership benefits, together with details of training and resource links. |
| Association of Certified Fraud Examiners | http://www.cfenet. com<br><br>USA | The Association of Certified Fraud Examiners is a 20,000 member professional organisation dedicated to educating qualified individuals. There are 90 local chapters in over 50 countries.<br><br>The Association publishes a bimonthly magazine The White Paper. See the entry under the Journals section of this listing.<br><br>The site includes information, publications and products of interest to those with fraud detection and prevention responsibilities. There are also links to Courses, Conferences and world-wide contacts. |
| Association of Chartered Accountants in the US | http://www.acaus. org/info/index.html<br><br>USA | The ACAUS is a professional, non-profit, organisation representing the interests of some 4,000 US-based chartered |

| Organisation/Title | URL/Country of Location | Comments/Further Links |
|---|---|---|
| | | accountants from the home institutes of chartered accountants in Australia, Canada, England & Wales, Ireland, New Zealand, Scotland and South Africa. The site contains an on-line library and a bookstore. |
| Association of College and University Auditors | http://www. acua.org USA | ACUA is an international professional organisation dedicated to the practice of internal auditing in higher education. ACUA has over 500 institutional members. Membership for both Regular (voting) and Associate (non-voting) members costs US$150. The site features contacts and lists of relevant links. |
| Association of Corporate Treasurers | http://www. corporate-treasurers.co.uk UK | The Association of Corporate Treasurers,Ocean House10/12 Little Trinity LaneLondonEC4V 2DJUnited Kingdom Tel: 020 7213 9728 Fax: 020 7248 2591 Email: enquiries@treasurers.co.uk |
| Association of Information Technology Professionals | http://aitp.org USA | The mission of the AITP is to provide superior leadership and education in Information Technology. |
| Australian Institute of Company Directors | http://www. companydirectors. com.au | |
| Australian Society of Certified Practising Accountants | http://www. cpaonline.com.au Australia | Range of sections covering Tax Reform, study programmes and technology issues. Access to the majority of the site contents requires a |

| Organisation/Title | URL/Country of Location | Comments/Further Links |
|---|---|---|
| | | personalised username and a password, however the Links page is open to general access. |
| Bain & Company, USA, | http://www.bain.com<br><br>USA | Management Tools 2001 – An Executive's Guide |
| Bank for International Settlements | http://www.bis.org | |
| Bank of England | http://www.bankofengland.co.uk<br><br>UK | |
| British Computer Society | http://www.bcs.org.uk<br><br>UK | As the only chartered professional Institution for the field of information systems engineering, the BCS exists to provide service and support to the IS community.<br><br>This site features information on the BCS, membership, publications and topical IT matters.<br><br>Also see the BCS practical guide to the year 2000 on<br><br>http://www.bcs.org.uk/millen.htm<br><br>Listing of BCS Special Interest Groups available on:<br><br>http://www.bcs.org.uk/siggroup/siglist/htm<br><br>Information on the BCS Computer Audit Specialist Group can be found at:<br><br>http://www.bcs.org.uk/siggroup/sg07.htm |

| Organisation/Title | URL/Country of Location | Comments/Further Links |
|---|---|---|
| Canadian Institute of Chartered Accountants | http://www.cica.ca<br><br>Canada<br><br>Joint Committee on Corporate Governance (TSE/CICA): | The CICA, together with the provincial and territorial institutes of chartered accountants, represents a membership of 60,000 professional accountants on Canada and Bermuda. |
| | http://www.cica.ca/ cica/cicawebsite. nsf/public/JCCG<br><br>http://www.cica.ca/ cica/cicawebsite. nsf/public/JCCG/ $file/Governance_ Eng_Nov | The web site is available in either English or French, and features extensive links to other international accounting sites.<br><br>An index search facility is provided with the download of identified documents in Adobe Acrobat format. |
| | http://www.cica.ca/ cica/cicawebsite. nsf/public/JCCG/ $file/Governance_ Eng_Nov26.pdf> | Separate listing of links for the year 2000 are provided.<br><br>Discussion groups on control and related topics. These groups are intended to enable people experimenting with CoCo concepts to interact with both the CICA and others outside the CICA. This site also carries an overview of CoCo, as well as CoCo No. 3: Guidance on Assessing Control – the CoCo Principles.<br><br>The CICA journal The Canadian Accountant is published quarterly to provide current information on CICA activities. Details can be requested via Email on canadian.account@cica.ca |
| Canadian Centre for Management Development | http://www. ccmd-ccg.gc.ca/ main_e.html<br><br>Canada | CCMD do excellent research; all their research reports are now available for download at their web site, e.g.<br><br>'Governance in the 21st century – revitalizing the public |

| Organisation/Title | URL/Country of Location | Comments/Further Links |
|---|---|---|
| | | sector'edited by Guy Peters and Donald Savoie – around 450 pages released in 2000; and 'Governance in a changing environment' (by the same two people) released in 1995. |
| Certified Management Accountant – The Society of Management Accountants. | http://www.cma-maritimes.com/ USA | Site geared to the interests of Management Accountants (CMAs). |
| Certified Management Accountants Canada | http://www.cma-canada.org/ Canada | CMA Canada represents more than 30,000 Certified Management Accountants and 9,000 CMA candidates in Canada. The site features the usual member contact and provincial association details. In addition there is a Resources section featuring articles taken from CMA Management magazine, the CMA Canada's business management publication. |
| Chartered Institute of Bankers | http://www.cib.org.uk UK | Email: institute@cib.org.uk |
| Chartered Institute of Public Finance and Accountancy. | http://www.cipfa.org.uk UK | Although founded on service to local government in the UK, more than half of CIPFA members now work in organisations outside of local government. In addition to details of the CIPFA qualification and membership, this site has numerous links to public sector and service organisations. The CIPFA journal Public Finance also has a area, where subscriptions can be requested. |

| Organisation/Title | URL/Country of Location | Comments/Further Links |
|---|---|---|
| CISCO (The City Group for Smaller Companies) | UK | Now called the Quoted Companies Alliance – see separate entry in this section under that title. |
| City of London | http://www. cityoflondon.co.uk<br><br>UK | |
| Conseil Supérieur de l'Ordre des Experts Comptables | http://www.experts-comptables.com/<br><br>France | In French only.<br><br>Features the normal membership, publications and archive facilities of interest to accountants operating in France. |
| Consiglio Nazionale Dei Regionieri Commercialisti Ed Economisti D'Impresa | http://www.consrag<br><br>Italy | In Italian only<br><br>In addition to relevant links, there is a section dedicated to the Euro. |
| Council for Excellence in Government | http://www. excelgov.org | |
| Department of Trade and Industry | http://www.dti. gov.uk/ | |
| European Commission | http://www.europa. eu.int/comm/ | The European Commission launched a consultation on auditor independence in December 2000; it, and other documents on the topic, can be found at www.europa.eu.int/ comm/internal_market/en/ company/audit/news/ index.htm).<br><br>The Report of the EU High Level Group of Company Law Experts (the 'Winter Group') can be accessed at http://europa.eu.int/comm/ internal_market/en/company/ modern/index.htm |

| Organisation/Title | URL/Country of Location | Comments/Further Links |
|---|---|---|
| European Corporate Governance Institute | http://www. ecgi.org | Established late 2001. Cabdury, Greenbury, Hampel and 1998 Combined Code, and codes of other countries can be found at this site. |
| European Foundation for Quality Management | http://www. efqm.org<br><br>Belgium | The EFQM Excellence Model |
| Federal Trade Commission | http://www.ftc.gov<br><br>USA | |
| Financial Executives Institute | http://www.fei.org/<br><br>USA | The FEI, which has its headquarters in Morristown, New Jersey, represents 14,000 senior financial executives from over 8,000 corporations throughout Canada and the United States. |
| Financial Executives Institute<br><br>Canadian branches | http://www. feicanada.org/<br><br>http://www. feicanada.org/ winnipeg.asp | |
| Financial Reporting Council | http://www. frc.org.uk | Smith Report on audit committees and the 2003 Combined Code publication on this site. |
| Financial Services Authority | http://www.fsa. gov.uk<br><br>UK | The Combined Code can be downloaded in pdf format from http://www.fsa.gov.uk/ pubs/ukla/lr_comcode.pdf<br><br>The 2002 Listing Rules are at http://www.fsa.gov.uk/ pubs/ukla |
| Föreningen Auktoriserade Revisorer<br><br>(The Swedish Institute of Authorised Public | http://www.far.se<br><br>Sweden | Site available in both Swedish and English.<br><br>FAR is the professional institute for Sweden's 2,300 authorised public accountants. FAR plays a leading role in the |

| Organisation/Title | URL/Country of Location | Comments/Further Links |
|---|---|---|
| Accountants) | | development of professional standards, education and information for the audit profession. |
| Futures & Options Association | http://www.foa. co.uk<br><br>UK | |
| Hermes Pensions Management Limited | http://www. hermes.co. uk/corporate-governance | Hermes is a stand-alone investment manager, wholly owned by the largest UK pension fund, BT Pension Scheme. As the principal investment manager for both the BT and Post Office pension funds, Hermes has c£45 billion under management. Its clients hold over 1% of the value of nearly all of the largest 900 quoted companies on the London Stock Exchange. Through its long-term holdings in index stocks, Hermes is necessarily exposed to underperforming assets. It has therefore been a leader on issues of corporate governance and shareholder involvement.<br><br>Colin Melvin is their director of corporate governance. |
| Hong Kong Society of Accountants | http://www.hksa. org.hk<br><br>Hong Kong | Incorporated in 1973, the HKSA is the statutory licensing for accountants operating in the Hong Kong territory. The HKSA has around 15,200 members.<br><br>The site contains Guidelines for Professional Accountants, information on Y2K issues and a 'Members Only' section which is subject to access control. |

| Organisation/Title | URL/Country of Location | Comments/Further Links |
|---|---|---|
| HM Treasury | http://www.hm-treasury.gov.uk | Site for the Myners report and for Government Internal Auditing Standards etc. |
| IIA Inc.<br><br>The website of the Institute of Internal Auditors Inc. | http://www.theiia.org<br><br>USA | Established in 1941, the IIA is the only international professional association dedicated to the promotion and development of internal auditing.<br><br>Full range of on-line documents, auditor's discussion groups, training, publication details and qualifications. |
| IIA UK<br><br>The website of the Institute of Internal Auditors (UK) | http://www.iia.org.uk<br><br>UK | The IIA UK is the primary body in the UK and Ireland representing, promoting and developing the professional practice of internal auditing.<br><br>This site features sections covering membership, publications, training, events, district societies, recruitment and links to sites of interest. |
| Ikatan Akuntan Indonesia<br><br>(The Indonesian Institute of Accountants) | http://www.akuntan-iai.or.id/<br><br>Indonesia | In local languages only. |
| Information Systems Security Association, Inc. | http://www.issa-intl.org/<br><br>USA | ISSA is a non-profit organisation of information security professionals. Links are provided to IT security sites. |
| Institut der Wirtschaftsprüfer in Deutschland e.V.<br><br>Institut des Experts-Comptables (Institute of Public Accountants) | http://www.idw.de/text1.stm<br><br>Germany<br><br>http://www.ibr-ire.be/eng/home/intro/asp<br><br>Belgium | Currently only in German, but an English version is being developed.<br><br>Joint Website with the Institut des Reviseurs D'Entreprises (Institute of Auditors). |

| Organisation/Title | URL/Country of Location | Comments/Further Links |
|---|---|---|
| | | English pages available, but some key documents are only available in either French or Dutch. |
| Institute of Certified Management Accountants  Institute of Management Accountants | http://www.rutgers.edu/Accounting/raw/ima/  USA | Sections include qualifications, information resources and member details. |
| Institute of Certified Public Accountants of Singapore | http://www.accountants.org.sg  Singapore | Bulletin Board, FAQ's and overseas links. |
| Institute of Chartered Accountants in New Zealand | http://www.icanz.co.nz/homepage4.asp  New Zealand | With 26,000 members, the ICANZ is New Zealand's only professional accountancy body.  Links to the library and Y2K resources. |
| Institute of Corporate Directors | http://www.icd.ca  Canada | |
| Institute of Directors (UK) | http://www.iod.com | |
| Institute of Directors in New Zealand | http://www.iod.org.nz | |
| Institute of Directors of South Africa | http://www.iodsa.co.za | Site includes the 2001 King Report (241 pages) |
| Interbrand | http://www.Interbrand.com | The consultancy who has developed the well respected method for valuing brands – which shows that for some companies the majority of their market capitalisation is attributed to the value of the brand. |

| Organisation/Title | URL/Country of Location | Comments/Further Links |
|---|---|---|
| International Association of Facilitators | http://www. iaf.com | An international professional body of facilitators, with their own certification programme etc. |
| International Finance & Commodities Institute | http://risk.ifci. ch/about.htm | IFCI Risk Management web site |
| Koninklijk Nederlands Instituut van Registeraccountants  The Royal Netherlands Institute of Registered Accountants | http://www. accountnet.nl/  Netherlands | Membership details and links to resources. An English version of the site is under development. |
| L'Association Française de Comptabilité | http://www.univ-valenciennes.fr/ AFC/SOMMAIRE. html  France | In French only.  Includes an archive facility and news of forthcoming events of interest to accountants operating in France. |
| Malaysian Institute of Accountants | http://www. mia.org.my/  Malaysia | The MIA is involved in the registration of accountants and the provision of professional support activities within Malaysia. |
| National Partnership for Reinventing Government | http://govinfo. library.unt.edu/ npr/default.html | |
| Project Management Institute | http://www. pmi.org | |
| Quoted Companies Alliance | http://www. qcanet.co.uk | QCA (previously CISCO) exists to serve the needs of all quoted companies, particularly those outside the top UK 350 (FTSE100 and FTSE250) companies) |

| Organisation/Title | URL/Country of Location | Comments/Further Links |
|---|---|---|
| Securities & Exchange Commission | http://www.sec.gov USA | For instance, after much debate, the SEC published its revised rules on auditor independence in November 2000 (see www.sec.gov/rules/ final/33–7919.htm). |
| Society for Information Management | http://www. simnet.org USA | The Society for Information Management comprises of 2,700 senior executives who are corporate and divisional heads of IT organisations and their management staff, leading academicians, consultants and other leaders who shape and influence the management and use of IT. Features sections on SIM membership, events, contacts and Year 2000 Working Group. |
| Swiss Institute of Certified Accountants and Tax Consultants Treuhand-Kammer | http://www. treuhand- kammer.ch/ Switzerland | Site available in French and German. |
| The Accounting Association of Australia and New Zealand | http://www. commerce.uq.edu. au:8000/AAANZ/ home.html Australia | AAANZ represents the interests of accounting academics and other persons interested in accounting education and research in Australia and New Zealand. Publications, conferences and links are featured on the site. |
| The Association of Chartered Certified Accountants | http://www. acca.co.uk UK | The Association of Chartered Certified Accountants is the professional body for Chartered Certified Accounts, Certified Accounting Technicians and holders of the Certified Diploma in Accounting and Finance (CDipAF) and the Diploma in Corporate Governance. It is the |

| Organisation/Title | URL/Country of Location | Comments/Further Links |
|---|---|---|
| | | largest professional accountancy body operating on an international basis, with 200,000 members and students. The site features sections on qualifications, membership and training courses. There are details of primary global contacts in Australia, Canada, Hong Kong, Malaysia, Singapore and the USA. |
| The Association of Chartered Certified Accountants | http://www. ACCAdemy.com | Site to register for the 'Diploma in Corporate Governance' qualification: http://www.accaglobal. com/students/dicg |
| The Certified General Accountants' Association of Canada | http://www. cga-canada.org/ index.html Canada | The Certified General Accountants' Association of Canada is a national body with some 60,500 accountants and students. This site is available in both English and French. Access to the member's area is controlled by User ID and password. Public access is afforded to the article archive of the CGA Magazine. |
| The Chartered Institute of Management Accountants | http://www. cima.org.uk UK | Founded in 1919, the Institute now has more than 49,000 members in 130 countries and over 67,000 registered students. Beyond the membership and publication details, this site provides research details and links to many other sites. A range of Master Courses are described which cover a wide range of relevant subject areas. |

| Organisation/Title | URL/Country of Location | Comments/Further Links |
|---|---|---|
| The Finance and Treasury Association Limited | http://www. fra.asn.au<br><br>Australia | Email: info@fra.asn.au |
| The Institute of Chartered Accountants in Australia | http://www. icaa.org.au<br><br>Australia | and ethical standards for members and provides leadership for the profession<br><br>Information on accounting and Y2K issues as well as details of the Institute. |
| The Institute of Chartered Accountants in England & Wales | http://www. icaew.co.uk<br><br>UK | The ICAEW is the largest professional body in Europe. Established in 1880, the Institute now has a worldwide membership of over 115,000.<br><br>In addition to professional qualification and membership information, this site has many useful links, including those to:<br><br>The Audit Faculty contains papers on internal audit topics. Annual membership costs £63. Details on http://www.icaew.co.uk/depts/ td/tdaf/content/front.html<br><br>The Information Technology Faculty charges an annual subscription of £64. Details on:<br><br>http://www.icaew.co.uk/ depts/td/tditf/7td001.htm<br><br>The Faculty of Finance and Management costs £57 per year to join. Further details provided on:<br><br>http://www.icae.co.uk/depts/ td/tdfmf/5td001.htm<br><br>The Faculty of Taxation has an annual subscription of £61. Details on: http://www.icaew.co.uk/depts/ td/tdtf/10td000.htm |

| Organisation/Title | URL/Country of Location | Comments/Further Links |
|---|---|---|
| | | The Corporate Finance Faculty more details available on: http://www.icaew.co.uk/depts/td/tdcff/tdcff001.htm |
| The Institute of Chartered Accountants in India | http://www.icai.org/index1.html India | Sections addressing research, publications and regulations. |
| The Institute of Chartered Accountants in Ireland | http://www.icai.ie/ Ireland | News, press releases and other links. Details of the ICAI journal Accountancy Ireland can be found at: http://www.icai.ie/Accountancy-Ireland/Welcome.html |
| The Institute of Chartered Accountants in Pakistan | http://www.icap.org.pk Pakistan | The site includes links to available publications and guidelines for Y2K issues. |
| The Institute of Chartered Accountants in Scotland | http://www.icas.org.uk Scotland | Numerous links to other sites of interest to the accounting profession. A series of documents and reports are available for download in Adobe Acrobat format, including the report Appraising Your Auditors – a Framework for the Review and Appointment by Listed Companies. Link provided to details of CA Magazine, the ICAS journal. http://www.icas.org.uk/members/camagazine.html |
| The Institute of Commercial and Financial Accountants of Southern Africa | http://www.cfa-sa.co.za/intro.html South Africa | From this site it is possible to download (in ZIP format) the Institute's Technical Bulletins going back to 1991. In addition there is a useful Links page. |

| Organisation/Title | URL/Country of Location | Comments/Further Links |
|---|---|---|
| The International Group of Treasury Associations | http://www. intltreasury.org UK | The International Group of Treasury Associations |
| The Japanese Institute of Certified Public Accountants. | http://www. jicpa.or.jp/ Japan | In both Japanese and English The JICPA was formed in 1949 as a self-disciplinary association, and reorganised under the Certified Public Accountants Law in 1966 and is now the sole organisation for the CPA profession in Japan. There are a number of key documents available in English, such as Corporate Disclosure requirements in Japan. |
| The Law Commission | http://www.open. gov.uk/lawcomm/ UK | |
| The Risk and Insurance Management Society, Inc. | http://www. rims.org/ | |
| The Risk Institute – Risk Management Resource Center | http://www. riskinstitute.org/ | |
| The South African Institute of Chartered Accountants. | http://www. saica.co.za/ South Africa | The SAICA has over 18,000 members and associates. Resources, publications, guidelines and related sites are available. Accountancy SA is the journal of the SAICA. Details and an archive of past articles can be found at: http://www.accountancysa. org.za |

| Organisation/Title | URL/Country of Location | Comments/Further Links |
|---|---|---|
| Treasury Management Association of Canada | http://www. tmac.ca<br><br>Canada | Email: treasury@baldhead.com |
| UK Government – The Treasury | http://www.hm-treasury.gov.uk<br><br>UK | |
| Union of Chambers of Certified Public Accountants of Turkey<br><br>TÜRMOB | http://www. turmob.org.tr<br><br>Turkey | In Turkish only. |
| Wirtschaftsprüfer-kammer | http://www.wpk.de<br><br>Germany | In German with a limited English version.<br><br>Wirtschaftsprüfer are best known as auditors of the annual financial statements of businesses and other organisations subject to statutory audit.<br><br>The work of the WPK is described and a number of general documents are obtainable in English, French, etc. |
| World Bank | http://www. worldbank. org/html/fpd/ privatesector/cg/ index.htm | The World Bank's corporate governance website – which is massive.)<br><br>For corporate governance codes: http://www.worldbank. org/html/fpd/privatesector/ cg/codes.htm<br><br>For worldwide links to other Corporate Governance websites: http://www.worldbank.org/html |

# Journals, books and online magazines    APP5.4

| Organisation/Title | URL/Country of Location | Comments/Further Links |
|---|---|---|
| Accountancy<br><br>The journal of the Institute of Chartered Accountants in England & Wales. | http://www.<br>accountancymag.<br>co.uk<br><br>UK | Published monthly,<br>Accountancy is available on subscription as follows:<br><br>Student/retired: UK £35, Europe £44, rest of world £52<br><br>1 year: UK: £50, Europe £60, rest of world £68<br><br>Site also has links to the International edition of the journal. Extracts from both the UK and international editions are available on-line.<br><br>A total of 73 issues (covering the period 1993 to 1998) are available to purchase on CD-ROM. |
| Accountancy Age<br>Published by VNU. | http://webserv.<br>vnunet.com/<br>www_user/plsql/<br>pkg_vnu_aa.<br>homepage<br><br>UK | On line news, reviews and features.<br><br>Those holding membership of a recognised accountancy body are eligible for a free subscription to Accountancy Age. Applications can be made on-line from this site. |
| Accountancy Books<br><br>The publishing arm of the Institute of Chartered Accountants in England and Wales. | http:/www.icaew.<br>co.uk/books.htm<br><br>UK | Site contains details of some 300 ICAEW and other publications. |
| Accountancy Ireland<br><br>Published by the Institute of Chartered Accountants in Ireland (ICAI) | http://www.icai.<br>ie/Accountancy-<br>Ireland/Welcome.<br>html<br><br>Ireland | Subscription:<br><br>Ireland & UK- IR & GB £25<br><br>Rest of the World – US$60 |

| Organisation/Title | URL/Country of Location | Comments/Further Links |
|---|---|---|
| Accountancy SA<br><br>Published by the SAICA<br><br>(South African Institute of Chartered Accountants). | http://www.accountancysa.org.za<br><br>South Africa | Previous article archive and subscription details. |
| Accountant's Ledger<br><br>On line magazine for accountants. | http://www.accountantsledger.com<br><br>USA | Includes feature articles, reviews, and online resources for such areas as Auditing and Y2K issues. |
| Accounting, Auditing & Accountability Journal<br><br>Published by MCB University Press.<br><br>Orders and subscription enquiries via Email: kgott@mcb.co.uk | http://www.mcb.co.uk/cgi-bin/journal1/aaaj<br><br>UK | On-line access to current and previous issues.<br><br>Subscriptions:<br><br>USA, Canada & South America: US$1,139<br><br>Australasia: A$1,139<br><br>All other regions: Sterling £829 +VAT (or Euro 1,249 + VAT). |
| Audit Vision<br><br>Published by Audit Serve Inc. | http://www.auditserve.com/magazine/subscription.html<br><br>USA | Audit Vision is an annually published magazine containing technical articles relating to Y2K conversion, EDP Audit and Security professions.<br><br>Application for a free subscription can be made on-line. |
| Auditing, A Journal of Practice & Theory<br><br>Published by the Audit Section of the American Accounting Association.<br><br>Editor: William L. Felix, Jr. | http://raw.rutger.edu/raw/aaa/audit/newjc.html<br><br>USA | Site contains abstracts of current and previous issues.<br><br>Published twice a year.<br><br>Subscriptions: Free to members of the Auditing Section; US$15 p.a. to members of the AAA who are not members of the Auditing Section; and US$25 to non-members of the AAA. |

| Organisation/Title | URL/Country of Location | Comments/Further Links |
|---|---|---|
| McClelland Hall 301University of ArizonaPO Box 210108 Tucson AZ 85721–0108 USA | | Subscription enquiries to the AAA via Email: AAAhq@packet.net |
| Australian Investor | http://www. australianinvestor. com.au | A free of charge on-line finance and investment magazine featuring articles from the Australian Stock Exchange, the Australian Department of Trade, the Australian Treasury and about a dozen other organisations. |
| Best Practices in Risk Management | http://www.tbs-sct. gc.ca/pubs_pol/ dcgpubs/Risk Management/ rm-ccpmn_e.html <http://www.tbs- | Four excellent risk management reports (from a 1999 Cdn Federal Gov't Study)Summary Report-Best Practices in Risk Management |
| Co-ordinated Conclusions from PMV and KPMG | http://www.tbs-sct. gc.ca/pubs_pol/ dcgpubs/Risk Management/ rm-pps_e.html | |
| Private and Public Sectors Internationally. | http://www.tbs-sct. gc.ca/pubs_pol/ dcgpubs/Risk Management/ rm-rcbp_e.html | |
| Review of Canadian Best Practices in Risk Management Risk, Innovation and Values | http://www.tbs-sct. gc.ca/pubs_pol/ dcgpubs/Risk Management/ rm-riv_e.html | |
| Boardroom Journal with review, analysis and guidance for corporate directors | http://www. boardroomnews. com Canada | Site contain abstracts of current and previous issues. Selective index of book reviews, editorials and articles. |

| Organisation/Title | URL/Country of Location | Comments/Further Links |
|---|---|---|
| | | Also available are a series of audio tapes covering a range of corporate board related issues. |
| Business Finance<br><br>Published by<br><br>Duke Communications International<br>221 East 29th Street<br>Loveland<br>CO 80538 USA<br><br>Tel: (877) 217 1827<br><br>Subscription applications can also be made via the www site. | http://www.businessfinancemag.com/Homepage/main.cfm<br><br>USA | This journal, which is published 12 time a year, is a resource for financial and accounting executives.<br><br>The www site features an article archive facility.<br><br>Subscriptions:<br><br>USA – US$59<br><br>Canada – US$89 + GST<br><br>Mexico/Central America – US$89<br><br>All other countries – US$115 |
| Canadian Institute of Chartered Accountants Magazine,<br>CA Magazine<br><br>Published by<br><br>Canadian Institute of Chartered Accountants<br>CA magazine 227 Wellington Street West Toronto<br>ON M5V 3H Canada<br><br>Tel: (416) 204–3369<br>Fax: (416) 204–3416 | http://www.cica.ca/new/camag/e_subs.htm<br><br>Canada | Published 10 times per year.<br><br>Archive copies are available on-line.<br><br>Subscriptions:<br><br>CICA Members – $28<br>CICA Students – $25<br>Non-members – $47<br>Other students & faculty – $37<br>Outside Canada – $72<br>(GST added to all Canadian domestic subscriptions) |
| Corporate Governance<br><br>Available from Blackwell Publishers. | http://www.blackwellpublishers.co.uk/asp/journal.asp?ref=0964–8410<br><br>UK | Corporate Governance acts as a forum for the exchange of information, insight and knowledge based on both theoretical development and practical experience.<br><br>Previous issue contents available on line. |

| Organisation/Title | URL/Country of Location | Comments/Further Links |
|---|---|---|
| | | Annual subscription: Europe: £195 North America: US$273 (plus GST for Canadian customers) Rest of the World: £195 |
| European Accounting Review Published by Routledge. Subscriptions Dept. Cheriton House North Way Andover SP10 SBE United Kingdom Tel: +44 (0) 1264 342062 Fax: +44 (0) 1264 343005 Edited by: Anne Loft, Copenhagen Business School (Email al.aa@cbs.dk) and Peter Walton, University of Geneva (Email: walton@uni2a. unige.ch) | http://www.bham. ac.uk/EAA/ear/ UK | This is European Accounting Association journal and it is provided free to Association members. It is published quarterly. The www site features issue archives. Subscriptions: Institute rate (print & electronic) £200 for EU locations, US$330 for the rest of the world. Institute rate (print only) £165 for EU and US$275 for the rest of the world. |
| Financial Director | http://www. financial-director. co.uk UK | |
| Financial Times | http://www.FT.com UK | |
| FT Television | http://www. ft-television.com | |

| Organisation/Title | URL/Country of Location | Comments/Further Links |
|---|---|---|
| Institute of Chartered Accountants in England & Wales – library site | http://www.icaew.co.uk/library/ | Site holds some excellent, detailed reading lists (with abstracts) on a number of different topics. |
| International Journal of Intelligent Systems in Accounting, Finance and Management. Formerly: Expert Systems Review for Business and Accounting 1987–1990 Published by John Wiley & Sons and the University of Southern California. Subscriptions enquiries to: Subscriptions Department John Wiley & Sons Ltd. Baffins Lane Chichester West Sussex PO19 1UD United Kingdom Fax: +44 (0) 1243 775878 | http://www.usc.edu/dept/sba/atisp/AI/IJISAFM/forthcom.htm USA | Subscriptions: Institutional US$175 Personal US$80 AAA AI/ES Section Members US$50 |
| IS Audit & Control Journal | http://www.isaca.org/jrnlhome.htm USA | The IS Audit & Control Journal is a bi-monthly publication of the ISACA. IT provides information on professional development to those involved with information systems audit, control and security. On-line article index. Free to members of the ISACA. |

| Organisation/Title | URL/Country of Location | Comments/Further Links |
|---|---|---|
| | | Other US subscribers: US$75 p.a. |
| | | Non-US subscribers: US$90 p.a. |
| | | Discounts for 2 and 3 year subscriptions. |
| | | On-line subscription request form. |
| Journal of Accountancy<br><br>Subscriptions can be sent either via Email on journal@aicpa.org or telephone on (888) 777 7077. | http://www.aicpa.org/pubs/jofa/index.htm<br><br>USA | The Journal of Accountancy is a monthly publication of the AICPA that focuses on the latest news and developments related to the field of accountancy.<br><br>Selected issues/articles are available on-line.<br><br>Subscriptions:<br><br>Free to AICPA members<br><br>United States – US$56<br><br>Outside the USA – US$81 |
| Journal of Internet Security, JISec<br><br>On line Journal of Internet Security<br><br>Free of charge on-line journal produced by CSCI (Computer Security Canada Inc.), based in Ottawa. | http://www.csci.ca/jisec<br><br>Canada | JISec informs security professionals and executives on principal developments, benchmark practices and future trends in the Internet-based security practices of governments and industry.<br><br>CSCI provides computer security audit services to Canadian corporations, financial institutions and government agencies. |
| Management Accounting<br><br>Published by the Institute of Management Accountants (IMA) | http://www.rutgers.edu/Accounting/raw/ima/inforesource.htm<br><br>USA | Monthly magazine free to IMA members. |

| Organisation/Title | URL/Country of Location | Comments/Further Links |
|---|---|---|
| Management Accounting Research<br><br>Published by the Academic Press on behalf of The Chartered Institute of Management Accountants.<br><br>Subscriptions can be processed on-line from the www site. | http://www.academicpress.com/mar<br><br>UK | This publication features original research in the field of management accounting.<br><br>Annual subscription for all countries is £149. |
| Managerial Auditing Journal<br><br>Published by MCB University Press 60/62 Toller Lane Bradford West Yorkshire BD8 9BY United Kingdom<br><br>Tel: +44 (0) 1274 777700<br><br>Fax: +44 (0) 1274 785200<br><br>Subscriptions can be processed on-line via the www site. | http://www.mcb.co.uk/cgi-bin/journal1/maj<br><br>UK | This journal aims to explore the changing role of the auditor and to examine current and innovative approaches to auditing.<br><br>Subscriptions:<br><br>North & South America and Canada – US$2,499<br><br>Australasia – A$3,249<br><br>Other Regions: £1,679 + VAT |
| National Association of Security Dealers | http://www.nasd.com/corpinfo/co_pub.html | This site has the information put together by the Blue Ribbon Committee in the US on the financial abilities of audit committee members (see www.nasd.com/docs/textapp.pdf). |
| Public Finance<br><br>Published by the Chartered Institute of Public Finance and Accountancy (CIPFA). | http://www.cipfa.org.uk/PFO/Media_Pack.html<br><br>UK | Example subscriptions for 12 months:<br><br>UK – £90<br><br>Overseas (surface mail) – £120<br><br>Overseas (air mail) – £190 |

| Organisation/Title | URL/Country of Location | Comments/Further Links |
|---|---|---|
| | | Subscription requests can be logged on-line at this site. |
| Secure Computing<br><br>Monthly magazine from West Coast Publishing. | http://www. westcoast.com<br><br>UK | Secure Computing magazine is free to qualifying individuals in the UK. For others in the UK, it can be purchased for £3.50 per month. Applications for free subscriptions can be submitted on-line from this site.<br><br>On line articles |
| The Auditor's Report<br><br>Published on-line by the Audit Section of the American Accounting Association.<br><br>Editor:<br>Gary P. Braun.<br><br>Email: gbruan@mail. utep.edu | http://raw.rutger. edu/raw/aaa/audit/ newjc.html<br><br>USA | Recent copies of this on-line report are available for downloading in both HTML and Adobe Acrobat formats. Copies prior to Summer 1998 are only available in HTML format. |
| The Australian Financial Review | http://www.afr. com.au/<br><br>Australia | Current issue and an archive of previous issues. |
| The Board Seat | http://www. boardseat.com/ Articles.asp | |
| The British Accounting Review<br><br>Published by Academic Press for the British Accounting Association.<br><br>On-line subscription details at:<br><br>http://customerservice. apnet.com/journals/ | http://www. academicpress. com/bar<br><br>UK | On-line access to current and previous issues in the form of a searchable database.<br><br>Subscription (all countries) £235 |

| Organisation/Title | URL/Country of Location | Comments/Further Links |
|---|---|---|
| The Certified General Accountants' Association of Canada Magazine | http://www.cga-canada.org/eng/magazine/default.htm<br><br>Canada | The CGA Magazine is published 11 times per year and is available on subscription, which costs Cnd$32<br><br>Subscription requests can be Emailed to Ann Saxe at<br><br>asaxe@cga-canada.org |
| The Economist | http://www.economist.com | |
| The European Business Forum | http://www.ebfonline.com | |
| The Institute of Chartered Accountants in Scotland Magazine, CA Magazine<br><br>Published by the Institute of Chartered Accountants in Scotland | http://www.icas.org.uk/members/camagazine.html<br><br>Scotland | CA Magazine is published 12 times a year.<br><br>Subscriptions for one year:<br><br>UK – £30<br><br>Overseas (air mail) £65<br><br>Discounted rates are available for students and 2 and 3 year subscriptions. |
| The Institute of Internal Auditors bookstore catalogue | http://www.theiia.org/ecm/bookstore | |
| The White Paper<br><br>Published by the Association of Certified Fraud Examiners. | http://www.cfenet.com/whtpaper.html<br><br>USA | The White Paper features articles of interest to those involved in fraud prevention and detection.<br><br>Free to members of the ACFE. Non-member subscriptions are available. US only – US$36 or Other Countries – US$56 |
| Wall Street Journal | http://www.wsj.com<br><br>USA | |

1227

# Market information

| Organisation/Title | URL/Country of Location | Comments/Further Links |
|---|---|---|
| Bloomberg | http://www. bloomberg.com | |
| Central European Business Daily | http://www. cebd.com | |
| Chicago Board of Trade | http://www.cbot. com/dow <br> USA | |
| Company Annual Reports (UK) | http://www.carol. co.uk <br> UK | |
| ESI (Electronic Share Information) | http://www.esi. co.uk <br> UK | |
| Hemmington Scott | http://www. hemscott.com | |
| Interactive Investor (UK) | http://www.iii. co.uk <br> UK | |
| London International Financial Futures and Options Exchange | http://www.liffe. com <br> UK | |
| Micropal | http://www. micropal.com | |
| Philadelphia Stock Exchange | http://www. phix.com | |
| Reuters | http://www. reuters.com | |
| Telerate/Bridge | http://www. telerate.co.uk <br> or <br> http://www.bridge. com <br> UK | |

| Organisation/Title | URL/Country of Location | Comments/Further Links |
|---|---|---|
| Tullett & Tokyo | http://www.tullett. co.uk  UK | |

# Internal auditing

| Organisation/Title | URL/Country of Location | Comments/Further Links |
|---|---|---|
| Audit Force  Audit Force is a consulting organisation that provides internal audit and compliance expertise. | http://www. auditforce.com/  USA | This site provides an on-line magazine with articles of interest to auditors. |
| Auditing the Human Resource Function | http://www. auxillium.com/ audit.htm  USA | This is an example of an audit programme provided by Auxillium West, a human resources consulting firm, which outlines the basic approach as well as information that should be included to cover a regulatory compliance review (for the USA). |
| AuditNet | http://www. auditnet.org  USA | AuditNet is an information and resources site developed for the benefit of the audit profession by Jim Kaplan. It now incorporates the IIA Inc. AuditBahn, the information superhighway for auditors, accountants and financial professionals.  There are a number of discrete areas on AuditNet, and some of these are listed below in alphabetical sequence.  A useful glossary of Internet terms can be found at: http://www.auditnet.org/tag.htm |

| Organisation/Title | URL/Country of Location | Comments/Further Links |
|---|---|---|
| | | The IIA Inc. is now the host of this site which has links to and from www.theiia.org and www.itaudit.org |
| AuditNet – Audit Best | http://www. auditnet.org/ best.htm<br><br>USA | The Audit Best Practices section of AuditNet is designed to encourage internal auditors to share with others their best practices.<br><br>An Index of available documents is provided and items can be downloaded. |
| AuditNet – Audit Surveys | http://www. auditnet.org/ audsurvy.htm<br><br>USA | A listing of audit customer surveys submitted by the world-wide network of auditors that form AuditNet. |
| AuditNet – Auditors Sharing Audit Programs | http://www. auditnet.org/ asapind.htm<br><br>USA | This site features a collection of audit programmes used by auditors from around the world. The audit programmes listed cover Management, Financial and IT subjects.<br><br>The listed programmes can be downloaded.<br><br>In addition, there are further links to sources of audit programme and audit tool materials, such as the two following examples:<br><br>Standardised Audit Workplans can be accessed on:<br><br>http://www.aetna.com/audit/ ST-WPLNS.htm<br><br>Gallaudet University (Washington DC), Audit Programs and Review Kits on:<br><br>http://www.gallaudet. edu/~auditweb/index.html |

| Organisation/Title | URL/Country of Location | Comments/Further Links |
|---|---|---|
| AuditNet – Clearinghouse for Audit Research on Internet Topics | http://www.auditnet.org/carit.htm<br><br>USA | Listing of student research papers on the joint topics of auditing and the Internet. |
| AuditNet – FraudNet | http://www.auditnet.org/fruadnet.htm<br><br>USA | This section of AuditNet is devoted to the sharing of fraud policies, procedures, code of ethics and resources. |
| AuditNet – Audit Books | http://www.auditnet.org/booklist.htm<br><br>USA | Listing of books relating to auditing and technology issues. |
| AuditNet – AuditZine | http://www.auditnet.org/aud_zine.htm<br><br>USA | A compendium of articles about the Internet for auditors and accountants. |
| AuditNet – KARL (Kaplan's AuditNet Resources List). Maintained by James Kaplan. | http://www.auditnet.org/karl.htm<br><br>Previously http://users.aol.com/auditnet/karl.htm<br><br>USA | Launched by Kaplan in the early 1990s, a very comprehensive listing (now over 105 pages) of sites of interest to the auditing community.<br><br>Most of the listed items have active links to the relevant WWW sites.<br><br>Updates to the KARL site can be automatically notified by Email using the Subscription Form at: http://www.itaudit.org/auditnet_area/subscribe.htm<br><br>Jim Kaplan is the author of The Auditor's Guide to Internet Resources (published by IIA Inc.). |
| AuditNet – PolicyNet | http://www.auditnet.org/iupaudit.htm<br><br>USA | Provides links to various Internet Use Policies (IUPs) that can be used as models for internal auditors in their own situations. |

| Organisation/Title | URL/Country of Location | Comments/Further Links |
|---|---|---|
| AuditNet Audit Training | http://www.auditnet.org/train.htm<br><br>USA | Listing of conferences, seminars and training courses relevant to internal auditors. |
| Australian & New Zealand University Internal Audit Group | http://www.curtin.edu.au/curtin/audit/anzuiag1.htm<br><br>Australia | ANZUIAG is a discussion group of Internal Audit Staff from Australian and New Zealand universities. Full contact details for the group and the minutes of previous meetings are accessible on the site. |
| Canadian Environmental Auditing Association.<br><br>(Association Canadienne de Verification Environnementale) | http://www.mgmt14k.com.ceaa/<br><br>Canada | The CEAA/ACVE is a non-profit organisation dedicated to furthering the development and professional practice of environmental auditing.<br><br>A useful Guidelines area is available together with details of environmental auditing qualifications. |
| Compliance Desk | http://www.compliancedesk.com/<br><br>USA | This site provides news and resources for the compliance professional. There are links to Y2K resources and articles. |
| Data Protection Registrar | http://www.open.gov.uk/dpr/dprhome.htm<br><br>UK | General information on the Data Protection Act 1998 and the work of the DPR.<br><br>On line search of the public register.<br><br>Ability to download texts of the Data Protection Guidelines in Adobe Acrobat .PDF format. Included in this listing are items related to the work of the European Commission Working Party on the Protection of Individuals with Regard to the Processing of Personal Data. |

| Organisation/Title | URL/Country of Location | Comments/Further Links |
|---|---|---|
| Institute of Internal Auditors Inc.<br><br>The website of the Institute of Internal Auditors Inc. | http://www.theiia.org<br><br>USA | Full range of on-line documents, auditor's discussion groups, publication details and qualifications. |
| Institute of Internal Auditors Singapore | http://www.iia.org.sg<br><br>Singapore | A site representing the 622 members of the IIA Singapore.<br><br>Membership details, standards, examinations, and links to other sites. |
| Institute of Internal Auditors Spain<br><br>Instituto de Auditores Internos de España | http://www.arrakis.es/~iai<br><br>Spain | In Spanish only<br>Membership details, etc. |
| Institute of Internal Auditors UK<br><br>The website of the Institute of Internal Auditors (UK) | http://www.iia.org.uk<br><br>UK | Sections covering membership, publications, training and links to sites of interest. |
| Institute of Internal Auditors Uruguay | http://www.uruguaytrade.com/congresso<br><br>Uruguay | In Spanish only |
| Internal Auditing World Wide Web | http://www.bitwise.net/iawww<br><br>USA | Conceived by John K. Peterson, this site is a warehouse of information and knowledge pertaining to the internal auditing profession and functions across all associations, industries and countries.<br><br>Comprehensive international contacts section. |
| Quality Auditor | http://www.earthlink.net/~rj143/qa-home.htm<br><br>USA | Reference point for those engaged in Quality Auditing. Links listing. |

| Organisation/Title | URL/Country of Location | Comments/Further Links |
|---|---|---|
| Risk Assessment & Risk Management | http://www. mc2consulting. com/riskpage.htm | Details of tools and articles on he subject of Risk. Useful tinternal audit risk bibliography. Some articles available in French |
| The Information Systems Audit and Control Association | http://www. isaca.org USA | A world-wide not-for-profit association of more than 19,000 members. Administrators of the Certified Information Systems Auditor (CISA®) certification. The ISACA's Information Systems Audit & Control Foundation also features on the site with the Control Objectives for Information Technology (COBIT). Year 2000 resources list can be found at: http://www.isaca.org/ yr2000.htm |

# IT governance

| Organisation/Title | URL/Country of Location | Comments/Further Links |
|---|---|---|
| Canaudit Inc. Canaudit Inc. performs technical audits of a range of IT platforms. | http://www. canaudit.com/ Canada | This site contains information on training courses addressing IT audit and security review methods. |
| Center for Education and Research on Information assurance and Security CERIAS has subsumed a former project at Purdue | http://www.cerias. purdue.edu/ about.html USA | The mission of CERIAS is to provide innovation and leadership in technology for the protection of information and information resources, and in the development and enhancement of expertise in formation assurance and |

| Organisation/Title | URL/Country of Location | Comments/Further Links |
|---|---|---|
| University called COAST (Computer Operations, Audit, and Security Technology). | | security. |
| Centre for Internet Security | http://www. cisecurity.org | |
| CERT Co-ordination Center | http://www.cert. org/security-improvement/ | |
| Computer Audit BCS Specialist Group<br><br>Membership enquiries can be directed to Jean Brown. Telephone: +44 (0)1803 872775 or Email: 100125.66@ compuserve.com | http://www.bcs. org.uk/siggroup/ sg07.htm | This British Computer Society group exists to support practitioners in the areas of computer audit and security and to promote the awareness and use of computer auditing and control techniques.<br><br>The following membership fees apply:<br><br>BCS: £15<br><br>Non-BCS: £25<br><br>Student: £10<br><br>Corporate: £75 |
| Computer Security Institute | http://www. gocsi.com/<br><br>USA | Established in 1974, the CSI is an international membership organisation offering training specifically targeted to information security professionals.<br><br>Useful features and an article archive are available, as well as listings of links to relevant sites. |
| Computer Security Resource Clearinghouse<br><br>This site is part of the NIST (National Institute of Standards and Technology), | http://www.csrc. ncsl.nist.gov/<br><br>USA | The CSRC is designed to collect and disseminate computer security information and<br><br>resources to help users, systems administrators, managers and security professionals better protect their data and systems. |

| Organisation/Title | URL/Country of Location | Comments/Further Links |
|---|---|---|
| which is part of the U.S. Department of Commerce's Technology Administration. | | |
| Information Systems – Best Practice Guidelines Developed by the Queensland Audit Office in Australia. | http://www.qao.qld.gov.au/bestprac.html Australia | This document, provides a comprehensive guide to the key areas of control over IS security. |
| IT Governance Institute | http://www.itgovernance.org | Linking Business objectives and information technology. Resource Section: http://www.itgovernance.org/itgi/resources.htm IT Governance Institute, 3701 Algonquin Road, Suite 1010, Rolling Meadows, IL 60008 USA Tel: +1.847.590.7491. Fax: +1.847.253.1443. E-mail: info@itgi.org |
| IT security cookbook | http://www.boran.com/security | |
| ITAudit Forum Supported by sponsorship and advertising. ACL is an active sponsor. Built and managed by Online Networks Inc., Portland, Oregon, USA. Contact John Yu via Email on editor@itaudit.org or telephone 1–503–644–1001 | http://www.itaudit.org | Launched in September 1998, a new web site geared specifically to the information technology needs of audit professionals. The site's most visible feature is 'The Forum' – which contains a number of articles on timely topics that address the special interests, needs and concerns of auditors. Readers can initiate or participate in threaded discussions in response to the issues raised in the articles. 'The Forum' is published twice a month. The 'Conference Center' is a threaded discussion area |

| Organisation/Title | URL/Country of Location | Comments/Further Links |
|---|---|---|
| | | which allows visitors to post questions on topics of interest, respond to the entries of other professionals and obtain views and opinions on modern technology issues. In addition there is an online chat area for the exchange of information and ideas in real time, and 'Yellow Pages' on available products, services and resources. |
| Software Engineering Institute | http://www.sei. cmu.edu/arm/ | Software acquisition management improvement |
| Software Engineering Institute | http://www. sei.cmu.edu | Software Risk Evaluation Method – Version 1.0 |
| System Administration, Networking and Security Institute | http://www. sans.org | |
| United States General Accounting Office – Accounting and Information Management Division | http://www.gao. gov/special.pubs/ pdf_sing.pdf | Information security management |
| United States General Accounting Office – Information Security Risk Assessment | http://www.gao. gov./special.pubs/ ai00033.pdf | Information Security Risk Assessment – Practices of Leading Organizations |

# Audit products/services                    APP5.8

| Organisation/Title | URL/Country of Location | Comments/Further Links |
|---|---|---|
| Audit Command Language | http://www.acl.com<br><br>USA | ACL is software, which provides data analysis, presentation and management facilities. The site offers product information, training schedules, |

| Organisation/Title | URL/Country of Location | Comments/Further Links |
|---|---|---|
| | | and details of consultancy services. Site contents available in English, German, Spanish, French and Portuguese. |
| Audit Department Manager Plus (ADM Plus) Pleier & Associates | http://www. admplus.com USA | ADM (Audit Department Manager) Plus is a software package to automate the management of the internal auditing function. The site gives an overview of system facilities together with price and ordering details. Site visitors can also view, print or download copies of the quarterly newsletter Audit Productivity Trends. |
| auditMASTERPLAN J.E. Boritz Consultants Ltd. | http://www. jebcl.com Canada | auditMASTERPLAN is a computer-based risk assessment, planning and work tracking system for internal auditors. Full product overview, licensing and ordering details are provided. |
| Auditor Assistant Auditor Assistant is a registered trade mark of First Chicago NBD. | http://audit. wordlink.com/ aahome/ USA | A risk-based audit management system created in Lotus Notes. A demonstration presentation is available for download in PowerPoint format. |
| IDEA | http://www. caseware-idea.com | IDEA for Windows is a productivity tool that allows the display, analysis, manipulation, sampling and extraction of data from a wide variety of file formats. |
| Management Audit Limited | http://www. management-audit. com UK | Provider of software, training and consultancy specifically for the internal audit and corporate governance communities. |

| Organisation/Title | URL/Country of Location | Comments/Further Links |
|---|---|---|
| MIS Training Institute | http://www. misti.com<br><br>USA | Founded in 1978, MIS Training Institute offers audit and information security education courses, details of which can be interrogated on the site.<br><br>The security and consulting division of MIS training Institute, Information Security Institute (ISI) focuses exclusively on providing high-quality infosecurity training and consulting services. Details can be found on: http://www.misti.com/ISI.asp |
| Risk Alert<br><br>J.E. Boritz Consultants Ltd. | http://www. jebcl.com/risk/ risk2.htm<br><br>Canada | Risk Alert, the business condition analyst is a tool designed to support the evaluation of the business condition of an enterprise, including the validity of going concern assumption that underlies the preparation of most general purpose financial statements. |

# External auditing

**APP5.9**

| Organisation/Title | URL/Country of Location | Comments/Further Links |
|---|---|---|
| American Accounting Association – Auditing Section<br><br>The Auditing Section Secretary, Jean C. Bedard can be contacted on Email via: bedard@neu.edu | http://raw.rutgers. edu/raw/aaa/audit/<br><br>USA | The purpose of this site is to promote advances in the auditing area. This is being addressed in three key areas namely Education, Research and closer Professional association.<br><br>The AAA Auditing Section has a related journal, Auditing, A Journal of Practice and Theory (See the Journals section of this listing for further details). |

| Organisation/Title | URL/Country of Location | Comments/Further Links |
|---|---|---|
| | | An on-line journal The Auditor's Report is also accessible in Adobe Acrobat format.<br><br>These pages are also accessible via the main AAA site (see earlier listing under Accounting) |
| Audit Report Writing Guide | http://www.psc-cfp. ge.ca/aduit/ metod1-e.html<br><br>Canada | The Public Service Commission (PSC) of Canada has provided on this site some guidelines for the design, style and content of audit reports.<br><br>In addition, a Client Satisfaction Measurement Questionnaire can also be accessed at:<br><br>http://www.psc-cfp.ge.ca/ aduit/metod2-e.html |
| Auditing Practices Board | http://www. apb.org.uk<br><br>UK | Website launched September 1999 |
| Auditing Special Interest Group of the British Accounting Association. | http://www.bham. ac.uk/BAA/sigs/ audit/index.html<br><br>UK | This site describes the work of ASIG and provides links to details of both past and forthcoming activities. |
| European Audit Research Network | http://www.earnet. uni-essen.de | At a European level, an organisation broadly equivalent to the Auditing Special Interest Group of the British Accounting Association. |
| Institut des Reviseurs D'Entreprises (Institute of Auditors) | http://www.ibr-ire. be/eng/home/ intro/asp<br><br>Belgium | Joint Website with the Institut des Experts-Comptables (Institute of Public Accountants)<br><br>English pages available, but some key documents are only available in either French or Dutch. |

| Organisation/Title | URL/Country of Location | Comments/Further Links |
|---|---|---|
| Instituto de Auditores-Censores Jurados de Cuentas de España | http://www.iacjce.es/main.htm<br><br>Spain | In Spanish only. |
| International Auditing Practices Committee (of the International Federation of Accountants). | http://www.ifac.org/Committees/IPAC/index.html<br><br>USA | The IAPC works to improve the degree of uniformity of auditing practices and related services throughout the world. |

# Internal control

**APP5.10**

| Organisation/Title | URL/Country of Location | Comments/Further Links |
|---|---|---|
| Control Self Assessment Tool | http://www.vpf-web.harvard.edu/audit/home/CSA_frame.bot.html<br><br>USA | This site features an example CSA Questionnaire designed by the internal audit department (in co-operation with the financial deans) at Harvard University, to assist in the performance of reviews of controls over financial systems and activities.<br><br>In addition to the questionnaire, guidance on its' completion is also provided. |
| Control Self Assessment Resource Center<br><br>Site maintained by John Wyckoff, Internal Audit Manager for Portland Teachers Credit Union. | http://www.teleport.com/~jhw/csa<br><br>USA | Website provides links to CSA resources, consultants, facilitators and trainers available via the Internet.<br><br>Links to CSA software and tools are listed at:<br>http://www.jhw.com/csa/tools.htm |
| Fraud & Investigation Links<br><br>Originally developed for a presentation to the Alabama Chapter | http://www.bham.net/users/jwrhymes/fraud/fraud.html<br><br>USA | A page of links to federal agencies, information sources on security, auditing, investigations, etc. |

| Organisation/Title | URL/Country of Location | Comments/Further Links |
|---|---|---|
| of the Association of Certified Fraud Examiners. | | |
| Fraud Report | http://www.hm-treasury.gov.uk/ pub/html/docs/ fraud/9596fr/ main.html<br><br>UK | The text of a report that analyses reported fraud in UK government departments. Includes a section of guidance on the management of the risk of fraud. |
| Internal Control Resources | http://pw1.netcom. com/~jstorres/ internalaudit/ content.html<br><br>USA | Listing of links to organisations, resources, books and articles. |
| Management Control Association | http://www.ms. rhbnc.ac.uk/ mca2001 | The Association holds doctoral colloquia and also research conferences. The secretary of the Association is Dr. Derek Purdy of the Department of Economics, University of Reading |
| MIS Training Institute | http://www. misti.com<br><br>USA | Offers a wide range of training courses, many related closely to internal control issues. |

# Corporate governance                                    APP5.11

| Organisation/Title | URL/Country of Location | Comments/Further Links |
|---|---|---|
| Audit Committee Institute | http://www.us. kpmg.com/ microsite/ auditcommittee) | KPMG |
| California Public Employees' Retirement System | http://www. calpers.ca.gov | |
| Canadian Deposit Insurance Corporation | http://www. cdic.ca | Their 'Standards of Sound Business and Financial Practices' covering governance, |

| Organisation/Title | URL/Country of Location | Comments/Further Links |
|---|---|---|
| | | risk management, and many other important management practices is available at http://www.cdic.ca/bin/ ENG_Stand_report.pdf |
| Canadian Institute of Chartered Accountants | http://www.cica.ca<br>Canada<br><br>Joint Committee on Corporate Governance (TSE/CICA): | The CICA, together with the provincial and territorial institutes of chartered accountants, represents a membership of 60,000 professional accountants on Canada and Bermuda. |
| | http://www.cica. ca/cica/cicawebsite. nsf/public/JCCG http://www.cica. ca/cica/cicawebsite. nsf/public/JCCG/ $file/Governance_ Eng_Novhttp:// www.cica.ca/cica/ cicawebsite.nsf/ public/JCCG/$file/ Governance_Eng_ Nov26.pdf> | The web site is available in either English or French, and features extensive links to other international accounting sites.<br><br>An index search facility is provided with the download of identified documents in Adobe Acrobat format.<br><br>Discussion groups on control and related topics. These groups are intended to enable people experimenting with CoCo concepts to interact with both the CICA and others outside the CICA. This site also carries an overview of CoCo, as well as CoCo No. 3: Guidance on Assessing Control – the CoCo Principles.<br><br>The CICA journal The Canadian Accountant is published quarterly to provide current information on CICA activities. Details can be requested via Email on canadian.account@cica.ca |
| Committee of Sponsoring Organisations of the Treadway | http://www. coso.org<br>USA | Website commenced January 2000. COSO started in 1985 to sponsor the National Commission on Fraudulent |

| Organisation/Title | URL/Country of Location | Comments/Further Links |
|---|---|---|
| Commission (IIA, AICPA, AAA etc). | | Financial Reporting (Treadway Commission). 1992: Internal Control – Integrated Framework; 1999: Fraudulent Financial reporting: 1987–1997 – an analysis of 204 financial statement/reporting fraud cases investigated by SEC. The Treadway Report can be downloaded from this site (197 pages). |
| Commonwealth Business Council | http://www.cbc.to/ | Commonwealth Corporate Governance principles. |
| Corporate Governance | http://www. corpgov.net http://www. corpgov.net/links/ links.html | A leading corporate governance portal |
| Corporate Governance Site | http://www. corpgov.net USA | Regarded as a leading portal. Site designed to be a springboard for explorations and discussions concerning the movement to enhance wealth by creating more democratic forms of corporate governance. Listing of links provided, including those to the Governance Disclosures of a number of well known corporations. |
| Corporate Governance Special Interest group of the British Accounting Association | http://www. baacgsig.qub.ac.uk/ | |
| Department of Trade and Industry | http://www.dti. gov.uk | Higgs Report and background research at http://www.dti. gov.uk/cld/non_exec_review Information on the Company Law Review and the Company Law White Paper can be accessed on this site |

| Organisation/Title | URL/Country of Location | Comments/Further Links |
|---|---|---|
| Directorship Search Group | http://www. directorship.com | |
| European Corporate Governance Institute | http://www. ecgi.org<br><br>Belgium | Established in January 2002, with its roots in the now discontinued European Corporate Governance Network (see entry below). ECGI's executive director is Marco Becht. See section on 'Research Centres in Corporate Governance' for more information. |
| European Corporate Governance Network<br><br>*Superseded in January 2002 by the European Corporate Governance Institute (see entry above).* | http://www.ecgn. ulb.ac.be/ecgn<br><br>Belgium | Links to Corporate Governance documents produced in Australia, Belgium, Canada, Europe, France, Germany, Hong Kong, India, Italy, Japan, Netherlands, OECD, South Africa, Spain, UK and USA.<br><br>The European Corporate Governance Network was set up with the support of the Bank of Italy in 1997 to foster comparative research on corporate governance. Inter alia, it resulted in Barca, Fabrizio and Marco Becht (2001): 'The Control of Corporate Europe' (Oxford University Press) – see Bibliography. |
| European Commission | http://www.europa. eu.int/comm/ | The European Commission launched a consultation on auditor independence in December 2000; it, and other documents on the topic, can be found at http://europa.eu.int/comm/ internal_market/en/company/ audit/news/index.htm).<br><br>The report of the EU High Level Company Law Experts (the 'Winter Group') can be accessed at http://europa.eu. int/comm/internal_market/en/ company/modern/index.htm |

| Organisation/Title | URL/Country of Location | Comments/Further Links |
|---|---|---|
| E-Vote | http://www. e-vote.net | |
| Financial Executives International – Canada | http://www. feicanada.org | |
| Financial Reporting Council | http://www. frc.org.uk | Smith Report on Audit Committees and the 2003 Combined Code publication on this site at http://www.frc. org.uk/publications/content/ ACReport.pdf |
| Financial Services Authority | http://www. fsa.gov.uk<br><br>UK | The Combined Code can be downloaded in pdf format from http://www.fsa.gov.uk/ pubs/ukla/lr_comcode.pdf<br><br>The 2002 Listing Rules are at http://www.fsa.gov.uk/ pubs/ukla |
| Governance Newsletter | http://www. governance.co.uk | International monthly newsletter |
| Handbook for Audit Committee Members<br><br>Text provided and site hosted by Grant Thornton. | http://www.gt. com/gtonline/ assuranc/ handtoc.html<br><br>USA | Reference material for those advising on the structure and operation of audit committees. |
| HM Treasury | http://www. hm-treasury. gov.uk | Site for the Myners report and for Government Internal Auditing Standards etc. |
| Institutional Shareholder Service | http://www. isstf.com | |
| Joint Committee on Corporate Governance (TSE/CICA) | http://www.cica. ca/cica/cicawebsite. nsf/public/JCCG | Toronto Stock Exchange and Canadian Institute of Chartered Accountants |
| Lens | http://www. lens-inc.com | |

| Organisation/Title | URL/Country of Location | Comments/Further Links |
|---|---|---|
| National Association of Corporate Directors | http:// www. nacdonline.org<br><br>A list of NACD publications is available at:<br><br>http://www. nacdonline.org/ publications/ | |
| National Association of Pension Funds | http://www. napf.co.uk | |
| Organisation for Economic Co-operation and Development | http://www.oecd. org/daf/governance/ principles.htm | OECD principles of corporate governance: since April 1998 an ad-hoc OECD Task Force on Corporate Governance has been developing these principles which it submitted to OECD Ministers at their annual meeting on 26–27 May 1999. The document, which is 18 or so pages, can be downloaded from this website in .pdf format. |
| Organisation for Economic Co-operation and Development – Public Management and Governance (PUMA) | http://www.oecd. org/puma/pubs/ index.htm | |
| Pensions & Investments | http://www. pionline.com | |
| Pensions Investment Research Consultant | http://www. pirc.co.uk | |
| Proxinvest | http://www. proxinvest.com | |
| Quoted Companies Alliance | http://www. qcanet.co.uk<br><br>UK | Previously CISCO (The City Group for Smaller Companies). Established at the time of the proposed Cadbury Code of Best Practice for Corporate Governance to represent the |

| Organisation/Title | URL/Country of Location | Comments/Further Links |
|---|---|---|
|  |  | interests of the FTSE 250 companies below the level of the top FTSE 100 companies. |
| The Board Seat | http://www. boardseat.com/ Articles.asp |  |
| The Conference Board | http://www. conference-board. org<br><br>http://www. conferenceboard. ca/cgov.htm<br><br>Canada |  |
| The Council of Institutional Investors (USA) | http://www.cii.org |  |
| The European Business Forum | http://www. ebfonline.com |  |
| The Global Corporate Governance Forum (World Bank and OECD) | http://www. gcgf.org |  |
| The Library | http://www. thecorporatelibrary. com |  |
| The World Bank Group | http://www. worldbank.org |  |

# Risk, reputation, corporate responsibility and sustainability
APP5.12

| Organisation/Title | URL/Country of Location | Comments/Further Links |
|---|---|---|
| Amnesty International in the UK. | http://www. amnesty.org.uk<br><br>UK |  |

| Organisation/Title | URL/Country of Location | Comments/Further Links |
|---|---|---|
| Best Practices in Risk Management | http://www.tbs-sct. gc.ca/pubs_pol/ dcgpubs/Risk Management/ rm-ccpmn_e.html | 4 excellent risk management reports (from a 1999 Cdn Federal Gov't Study) Summary Report-Best Practices in Risk Management |
| Co-ordinated Conclusions from PMV and KPMG | <http://www.tbs- http://www.tbs-sct. gc.ca/pubs_pol/ dcgpubs/Risk Management/ rm-pps_e.html | |
| Private and Public Sectors Internationally. | http://www.tbs-sct. gc.ca/pubs_pol/ dcgpubs/Risk Management/ rm-rcbp_e.html | |
| Review of Canadian Best Practices in Risk Management | http://www.tbs-sct. gc.ca/pubs_pol/ dcgpubs/Risk Management/ rm-riv_e.html | |
| Risk, Innovation and Values | | |
| Centre for the Analysis of Risk and Regulation (CARR) | http://www.lse.ac. uk/Depts/carr/ UK | A London School of Economics research centre well endowed by industry and financial institutions, headed by Professor Mike Power who previously was head of the department of accounting at LSE. |
| Global Reporting Initiative | http://www. globalreporting.org | Sustainability Reporting Guidelines on Economic, Environmental and Social Performance |
| Institute of Social and Ethical AccountAbility (ISEA) | http://www. AccountAbility. org.uk | |
| International Federation of Accountants | http://www. ifac.org/ | Keynote Report – an IFAC 1999 Study of 'Risk Management': |

| Organisation/Title | URL/Country of Location | Comments/Further Links |
|---|---|---|
| | http://www.ifac. org/Standards AndGuidance/ FMAC/Study9- Enhancing Shareholder/ Study9.html | 'Enhancing Shareholder Wealth by Better Managing Business Risk' |
| Other risk management sites | http://www. asisonline.org/ http://cfonet.com/ html/rcntt&rm. htmlhttp://www. sra.org/ http://opim.wharton. upenn.edu/risk/ http://www.riskweb. comhttp://www. osbie.on.ca:80 http://www. businessinsurance. com:808/> | |
| Prompt reputation protection system | http://www. promptrps.com | The website of the '360° approach to vulnerability assessment' devised by Hill & Knowlton (communications), Clifford Chance (law), Kroll (security), Dames & Moore (health, safety and environment) and Deloitte & Touche (finance) |
| The Body Shop | http://www.think-act-change.com UK | |
| World Business Council for Sustainable Development | http://www. wbcsd.ch | |

# Fraud, whistleblowing etc APP5.13

| Organisation/Title | URL/Country of Location | Comments/Further Links |
|---|---|---|
| A collaborative site of fraud information | http://www. fraud.org.uk UK | The site is supported by The Association of British Insurers, The Arson Prevention Bureau, The Institute of Chartered Accountants in England & Wales, The British Bankers' Association, the Confederation of British Industry, Crimestoppers, The Department of Trade and Industry, the Department of Social Security, the Financial Services Association, the Credit Industry Avoidance System and the Home Office. |
| Centre for Fraud Management Studies | http://www. fraudstudies.com | Liverpool Business School, Liverpool John Moores University, Liverpool, L3 5UZ (tel: +44 (0)151 231 3440; fax: +44 (0)151 709 3156) |
| Fraudwatch (US) | http://www. fraudnewsletter. com USA | |
| Internet Scambusters | http://www. scambusters.org | |
| National Fraud Information Center (US) | http://www. fraud.org USA | |
| Whistleblowers' website | http://www. fraudhotline.net and http://www. forensicaccounting. co.uk UK | In July 2001, Forensic Accounting, a breakaway from PwC, launched this website to allow employees to send in anonymous tip-offs which are then relayed to top management if the company in question has signed up. Contact Raj Bairoliya at Forensic Accounting. |

# Stock exchanges APP5.14

| STOCK EXCHANGES | | |
|---|---|---|
| Amsterdam Stock Exchange | http://www.aex.nl/ | Available in Dutch or English |
| Athens Stock Exchange | http://www.ase.gr/ | Available in Greek and English |
| Australian Stock Exchange | http://www.asx.com.au | |
| Chicago Stock Exchange | http://www.chicagostockex.com | |
| German Stock Exchange Deutsche Börse AG | http://www.exchange.de/dbag/dbag_d.html | Available in German or English |
| Helsinki Stock Exchange Helsingen Pörssi | http://www.hex.fi/ | Available in Finnish or English |
| Hong Kong Stock Exchange | http://www.sehk.com.hk | Choice of an English language site |
| Italian Stock Exchange Borsa Italia | http://www.borsaitalia.it | Available in Italian or English |
| Johannesburg Stock Exchange | http://ww.jse.co.za | |
| Kuala Lumpur Stock Exchange | http://www.klse.com.my | English language site |
| London Stock Exchange | http://www.londonstockuser.co.uk | The London Stock Exchange website which carries consultation documents. Site also features a Year 2000 section, which describes the business and technical aspects of the Exchange's Year 2000 preparations. |
| Madrid Stock Exchange Bolsa de Madrid | http://www.bolsamadrid.es | Available in Spanish or English |

| | | |
|---|---|---|
| Mexican Stock Exchange<br><br>Bolsa Mexicana de Valores | http://www.bmv.com.mx/ | Available in Spanish or English |
| Montreal Stock Exchange | http://www.me.org/ | Available in French or English |
| New York Stock Exchange | http://www.nyse.com | |
| New Zealand Stock Exchange | http://www.nzse.co.nz | |
| Oslo Stock Exchange<br>Oslo BØRS | http://www.ose.no/ | Available in Norwegian or English |
| Paris Stock Exchange<br>La SBF – Bourse de Paris | http://www.bourse-de-paris.fr/ | Available in French or English |
| Rio de Janeiro Stock Exchange | http://www.bvrj.com.br/pagina.`htm | |
| Singapore Stock Exchange | http://www.ses.com.sg | English language site |
| Stockholm Stock Exchange<br>Stockholms Fondbörs | http://www.xsse.se/www/welcome.nsf/ | Available in Swedish and English |
| Swiss Stock Exchange | http://www.bourse.ch/ | Available in English, French and German |
| Taiwan Stock Exchange | http://www.tse.com.tw/ | Available in English and Chinese |
| Tel-Aviv Stock Exchange<br><br>TASE | http://www.tase.co.il/ | |
| Thailand Stock Exchange | http://www.set.or.th/ | In English |
| Tokyo Stock Exchange | http://www.tse.or.jp | Available in Japanese or English |
| Vancouver Stock Exchange | http://www.vse.ca/ | |

**BAPP5.14** *Stock exchanges*

| | | |
|---|---|---|
| Vienna Stock Exchange<br><br>Wiener Borse | http://www. wbag.at/ | Available in German or English |

# Table of Cases

# Table of Statutes

# Table of Statutory Instruments

# Table of International Legislation

# Index

*Index*

*Index*

**Internal control**

**Shareholders**—*contd*
value—*contd*
   corporate governance, delivery by     B11.36
   graphical representations     B11.20–B11.22
   information on     B11.23, B11.24
   tracking     B11.17
  voting
   ABI Institutional Voting Information Services     B15.2, B15.3
   Hermes guidance     B7.7
   IVIS monitoring checklist     B7.3
   NAPF issues service     B7.5
   NAPF policy     B7.4
   NAPF Voting Issues Service     B15.6
   responsible, ABI/NAPF statement on     B7.1
**Shares**
  directors owning     B17.43
**Singapore**
  audit committee requirements     B10.64
**Smaller companies**
  comparison of 2003 and 1998 Combined Codes     A2.14
**Smith Report**
  audit committees, guidance on     A1.3
  Combined Code, in     A2.5
  status of     A2.5
**Social responsibility**
  ABI guidelines
   complying with     B25.1
   text of     B25.2
  audit     B25.12
  challenge of     B25.12
  corporate governance, and     B25.12
  environmental issues checklist     B25.4, B25.5
  large US firms, financial performance of     B25.11
  management of     B25.12
**Social, environmental and ethical matters**
  issues     B10.79
  investment institutions, policies of     B7.8
**Stakeholders**
  audit     B22.1
   approach     B22.6
  management of relationship with     B22.1
  risk     B22.5
**Standard Life**
  remuneration, best practice guidance     B15.10
**Stewardship**
  theory     B1.12
  trustees     B1.19
**Summary financial statements**
  directors' remuneration report, disclosure of     B14.33